A CONCORDANCE OF *THE HYMNAL 1982*

According to the Use of The Episcopal Church

compiled by

ROBERT F. KLEPPER

The Scarecrow Press, Inc.
Metuchen, N.J., & London
1989

British Library Cataloguing-in-Publication data available

Library of Congress Cataloging-in-Publication Data

Klepper, Robert F.
A concordance of The Hymnal 1982.

"Covers the verbal text of hymns in The Hymnal 1982"
--Pref.
Includes index.
1. Hymnal 1982--Concordances. 2. Episcopal Church--
Hymns--Concordances. 3. Hymns, English--Concordances.
I. Hymnal 1982. II. Title.
M2125.H974 (1982) 1985 Suppl. 782.27'03 89-10479
ISBN 0-8108-2250-4

PREFACE

This concordance covers the verbal text of hymns in *The Hymnal 1982*, according to the use of The Episcopal Church. It functions for the words of the hymns as a Bible concordance functions for the text of the Bible. It will help to find quotations or to complete partially remembered phrases. A survey of phrases under any word can enlarge concepts, suggest thematic outlines, and stimulate idea associations.

There is a vast amount of inspiration to be found in the poetry of the hymns. A simple perusal of the phrases listed under a word may be satisfying in itself. Checking phrases under synonyms of the word may enlarge concepts. Reading around the phrases from the poetry of the hymn once it is located is instructive.

The format of the listings includes three elements in this order: the hymn number, the phrase, and the verse in which the phrase appears. Verse locations are in parentheses following the phrase. Parentheses may also include R for Refrain; RC for Rounds and Canons; A for Antiphon; or D for Descant. When there is more than one set of verses a lower case letter will indicate which set (as: 2c in hymn No. 18).

To illustrate the usage of this volume, the phrase, "Cure thy children's warring madness," is found under four words: *cure, children's, warring,* and *madness.* Looking under any of these words will locate the phrase. Choosing the word considered to have the fewest entries may speed the process. Compounds like Christ-like or Father-like are listed under the second part of the word.

To facilitate the coordination of hymn numbers with first lines, a numerical index is included.

For his expertise in typography and proofreading, I am indebted to a friend, Bernhard Zinkgraf of Atlanta. Thanks also to my son, Timothy Klepper, for loaning me his computer so that this task could be done in reasonable time, and to my wife, Dorothy E. Schemske, for the help and encouragement to complete this volume.

Robert F. Klepper
Bella Vista, Arkansas
October, 1988

abandonment
160   O mysterious condescending! O abandonment sublime! (3)

abased
443   the King abased to honor all, praised be your glory (5)

abate
411   his wrath is ever slow to rise and ready to abate (3)

abhors
83   lo! he abhors not the Virgin's womb (2)

abide
78, 79   O come to us, abide with us, our Lord Emmanuel (5)
142   yea, evermore, in life and death, Jesus, with us abide (4)
142   Abide with us, that so, this life of suffering overpast (5)
151   could we abide thy presence? (1)
175   life that in all dost abide (7)
193   O Lord of all, with us abide (4)
194, 195   alone to Jesus living, pure in heart may we abide (2)
216   life that in all dost abide (5)
223, 224   with their children still abide (4)
225   life that in all dost abide (4)
290   there, forever purified, in thy presence to abide (4)
343   Savior, abide with us, and spread thy table in our heart (3)
350   Eternal love, with them abide (3)
351   Thus may they abide in union with each other and the Lord (2)
436   here, Lord, abide! Let me thy inner presence feel (4)
441, 442   joys that through all time abide (4)
475   Come, abide within me (4)
486   O Savior, with protecting care abide in this thy house (3)
495   Jesus, hail, enthroned in glory, there for ever to abide (3)
609   among these restless throngs abide (4)
662   Abide with me, fast falls the eventide (1)
662   the darkness deepens, Lord, with me abide (1)
662   help of the helpless, O abide with me (1)
662   Through cloud and sunshine, Lord, abide with me (2)
662   I triumph still if thou abide with me (3)
662   in life, in death, O Lord, abide with me (4)

abideth
360, 361   Hallowed this dwelling where the Lord abideth (4)
687, 688   That word above all earthly powers ... abideth (4)
687, 688   no thanks to them, abideth (4)
687, 688   the body they may kill, God's truth abideth still (4)

abiding
93   Shepherds in the field abiding (2)
122, 123   in the house of God abiding thus they sing eternally (1)
343   in strength of which we travel on to our abiding place (2)
385   thou star-abiding one (2)
498   I take, O cross, thy shadow for my abiding place (3)
667   God the same abiding, his praise shall tune my voice (4)

ablaze
9   So let the love of Jesus come and set thy soul ablaze (5)

able
97   all creation to redeem I alone am able (2)

abode
522, 523   formed thee for his own abode (1)
524   I love thy kingdom, Lord, the house of thine abode (1)
621, 622   Light's abode, celestial Salem (1)
656   their soul is Christ's abode (1)
664   may thy house be mine abode and all my work be praise (3)
702   in death's abode? Lo, thou art there (3)
709   at our Father's loved abode our souls arrive in peace (4)

abound
125, 126   peace abound below (5)
209   may our faith abound (3)
292   thine the wealth that in our halls abound (1)
344   may the fruits of thy salvation ... abound (2)
344   in our hearts and lives abound (2)
392   Then let our song abound and let our tears be dry (4)
484, 485   hymns on every tongue abound (1)
544   Blessings abound wheree'er he reigns (4)
588, 589   let the dew of heaven descend and righteous fruits abound (1)
625   as in his sight with sweet delight ye do abound (2)
699   let the healing streams abound (3)

aboundeth
360, 361   Here in our sickness healing grace aboundeth (3)

abounding
65   for grace and joy abounding (2)
413   peal out the praise of grace abounding (2)

above
5   pour down thy radiance from above (2)
10   fit us for perfect rest above (6)
11   praise him above, ye heavenly host (4)
42   their white wings above me, watching round my bed (5)
43   praise him above, ye heavenly host (4)
63, 64   pour light upon us from above (2)
65   He brings God's rule, O Zion, he comes from heaven above (2)
68   arise, thou Sun so longed for, above this darkened sphere (3
77   angels in the sky sang praise above the silent field (4)
78, 79   Above thy deep and dreamless sleep the silent stars go by (1)
78, 79   gathered all above, while mortals sleep (2)
80   From heaven above to earth I come (1)
83   sing, all ye citizens of heaven above (3)
89, 90   above its sad and lowly plains they bend on hovering wing (2)
96   See him in a manger laid whom the angels praise above (4)
98   lead us all with hearts aflame unto the joys above us (4)
99   when lo! above the earth rang out the angel chorus (2)

422	saints on earth and saints above we join in full accord (2)
423	thy justice like mountains high soaring above (2)
426	learning here, by faith and love ... to sing above (5)
426	songs of praise to sing above (5)
432	praise him who hath brought you his grace from above (2)
455, 456	we read thee in the sky above (2)
467	from yon bright throne above ... extends his grace (1)
471	he brings us mercy from above (2)
471	the angel's theme in heaven above (5)
481	when he had purged our stains, he took his seat above (2)
483	the joy of all who dwell above, the joy of all below (3)
483	they reign with him above (5)
486	above, beneath us, and around, both dead and living (2)
493	saints below and saints above (6)
494	Crown him the Lord of heaven, enthroned in worlds above (5)
503, 504	Thy blessed unction from above is comfort, life and fire (3)
505	his dear Son, who reigns above (5)
509	let thy Church on earth become blest as the Church above (4)
512	Come ... with light and comfort from above (1)
519, 520	living stones art builded in the height of heaven above (1)
526	One family we dwell in him, one Church, above, beneath (2)
530	how his never-failing love guides us on to heaven above (4)
531	give power and unction from above (2)
535	honor and blessing, with angels above (4)
538	let all be, below, above, one in joy, and light and love (2)
539	died on earth that all might live above (2)
543	till sovereign love in worlds above the glory raise (3)
545	now he reigns above (4)
566	O pour them from above (1)
590	as you once wept above Jerusalem (3)
603, 604	his arms stretched out above through every culture (1)
609	above the noise of selfish strife (1)
609	till glorious from thy heaven above shall come the city (5)
613	When shall all hatred cease, as in the realms above (2)
625	My soul, bear thou thy part, triumph in God above (4)
629	O Father, Son, and Spirit, send us increase from above (3)
633	Word that sends us from above God the Spirit (4)
634	hold by thy word evermore, above all things (1)
652, 653	O Sabbath rest by Galilee, O calm of hills above (3)
655	above the storms of passion, the murmurs of self-will (2)
657	serve thee as thy hosts above (2)
665	high above all praises praising for ... Christ, his son (5)
668	My help is from the Lord above (1)
669	him whose faithful mercy the skies above declare (1)
681	whose stars serenely burn above this earth's confusion (1)
681	inspire us from above with joy and strength for duty (5)
686	sung by flaming tongues above (1)
686	seal it for thy courts above (3)
687, 688	That word above all earthly powers ... abideth (4)
693	here for a season, then above (6)
704	thou who camest from above the fire celestial to impart (1)
706	Now my heart sets none above you (3)
716	For her our prayers shall rise to God, above the skies (2)
717	my heart with rapture thrills like that above (2)

719   for purple mountain majesties above the fruited plain (1)

Abraham
401   The God of Abraham praise, who reigns enthroned above (1)

Abraham's
401   hail, Abraham's Lord divine (5)

abroad
67   For the glory of the Lord now o'er earth is shed abroad (3)
210   The day of resurrection, Earth tell it out abroad (1)
235   through whom the living Gospels came sounding all abroad (1)
375   his mighty wonders tell abroad (1)
389   Let us blaze his Name abroad (2)
392   children of the heavenly King may speak their joys abroad (2)
398   spread the flowing seas abroad and built the lofty skies (1)
434   spread her Maker's praise abroad (1)
493   spread through all the earth abroad the honors of thy Name (2)
510   come, shed abroad a Savior's love (4)
530   word for which the nations long, spread abroad (5)
532, 533   thy truth and thy judgments shall spread all abroad (2)
535   publish abroad his wonderful Name (1)
543   while rays divine stream all abroad (1)
579   Spirit ... the Father sent to spread abroad the firmament (3)
615   knowledge ... shall walk the earth abroad (5)

absolving
511   quickening, strengthening and absolving (2)

abstain
150   from worldly joys abstain (2)

abstinence
152   Give us the discipline that springs from abstinence (4)
152   abstinence in outward things with inward fasting (4)

abundance
191   will all its full abundance at his second coming yield (3)
308, 309   of thine abundance give us, and all we need provide (2)
503, 504   the abundance of thy grace (5)

abundant
250   His love abundant far exceeds ... a whole year's needs (3)
528   life abundant meant for each (2)
610   your abundant iife to share (3)
675   it guides you to abundant life (4)

accents
210   listening to his accents, may hear ... (2)
655   O let me hear thee speaking in accents clear and still (2)

accept
154, 155   Thou didst accept their praises (5)

154, 155   accept the prayers we bring (5)
348   all that it means to accept you as Lord (3)
603, 604   may I in Christ be free to welcome and accept his own (4)
644   accept the praise I bring (4)
697   My God, accept my heart this day (1)
697   accept my heart this day, and make it always thine (1)

acceptance
159   a purer love attaining, may with thee acceptance find (5)

accepted
603, 604   as Christ accepted me (4)
675   the Lord for you accepted death upon a cross (3)

acclaim
144   we shall acclaim your majesty, eternal Three in One (5)
170   In mock acclaim ... they snatched a purple cloak (2)
299   earth, kindling, blazed her loud acclaim (1)
399   Your heavenly Father praise, acclaim his only Son (3)
413   honor the Lord with wild acclaim (3)
478   the God of peace acclaim as Lord and Savior (3)

acclaims
364   holy Church in faith acclaims thy Son who for us died (5)

acclamation
159   mocked with cruel acclamation, scourged and crowned (3)

accord
60   all things on earth with one accord ... call you Lord (4)
60   with one accord, like those in heaven (4)
103   in one accord adoring Christ the Lord (R)
109   Then let us all with one accord sing praises (6)
146, 147   Now let us all with one accord ... keep vigil (1)
205   sing today with one accord the life laid down (4)
217, 218   all praise to you let earth accord (3)
220, 221   let earth accord, who art, while endless ages run (4)
298   With one accord, O God, we pray, grant us the Holy Spirit (2)
345   with one accord our parting hymn of praise (1)
366   fill the heavens with sweet accord (2)
392   join in a song with sweet accord (1)
393   raising hymns in glad accord (1)
422   saints on earth and saints above we join in full accord (2)
432   in tuneful accord (2)
477   Let every tongue confess with one accord (5)
477   with one accord in heaven and earth (5)
506, 507   Trinity in deep accord (6)
537   with one accord (3)
597   all creatures find their true accord (2)

achieved
386, 387   now the matchless deed's achieved (4)

achievements
232   know not his achievements but know that he was true (2/8-24)

achieves
452   faith achieves what reason planned (3)

aching
33-35   strength for our weak hearts, rest for aching bodies (4)
246   aching hearts in every land cry out (3)
379   find that self-same aching deep within the heart of God (2)
585   God, whose arms of love aching, spent, the world sustain (6)

across
42   shadows of the evening steal across the sky (1)
255   God's light ... broke across the path (1)
431   writes in fire across the skies God's majesty and praise (2)
460, 461   songs of all the sinless sweep across the crystal sea (3)

act
18   when we must act in day's hard light (2b)
322   When Jesus died to save us, a word, an act he gave us (1)

acted
157   On this day the Lord has acted (R)
170   acted out their grim charade to its apointed end (3)

action
592   makes that and the action fine (3)

actions
19, 20   God's mighty actions tell at length (2)
271, 272   prophetic utterance told his actions great and manifold (2)
448, 449   by words and signs and actions, thus still seeking ... us (3)

active
1, 2   active and watchful, stand we all before thee (1)

acts
393   all his mighty acts proclaim (1)
404   your mighty acts with joy and fear relate (2)
414   speak of thy dread acts the story (3)
602   Master who acts as a slave to them (1)
704   my acts of faith and love repeat (4)

Adam
176, 177   so from the empty tomb the Second Adam issued triumphant (1)
445, 446   When all was sin and shame, a second Adam ... came (2)
445, 446   second Adam to the fight and to the rescue came (2)
445, 446   flesh and blood, which did in Adam fail (3)

Adam's
88   he on Adam's fallen race sheds the fullness of his grace (3)
270   Adam's chains shall be unbound (3)
295   Sing praise to our Creator, O you of Adam's race (1)

addressed

94, 95	angels praising God, who thus addressed their joyful song (5)
135	anthems be to thee addressed, God in man made manifest (1-3)
143	to thee be every prayer addressed (5)

addressing

329-331	honor, thanks, and praise addressing (6)
414	day by day thy throne addressing (1)

adds

441, 442	from the cross the radiance streaming adds more luster (3)
441, 442	adds more luster to the day (3)

adoption

295	God's children by adoption, baptized into his grace (1)

adoration

117, 118	richer by far is the heart's adoration (4)
219	His rising, his ascension sing with grateful adoration (2)
344	Thanks we give and adoration for thy Gospel's joyful sound (2)
360, 361	thine be the glory, praise and adoration, now and forever (6)
390	sounding in glad adoration (1)
420	adoration leaves no room for pride (1)

adore

1, 2	singing we offer prayer and meditation: thus we adore (1)
14, 15	whom with the Spirit we adore for ever and forevermore (3)
19, 20	whom with the Spirit we adore for ever and for evermore (3)
21, 22	whom with theSpirit we adore for ever and for evermore (3)
27, 28	Trinity whom we adore be with us now and evermore (5)
44, 45	whom with the Spirit we adore for ever and for evermore (4)
52	whom with the Spirit, we adore for ever and for evermore (4)
55	the birth which ages all adore (1)
57, 58	Yea, amen, let all adore thee (4)
61, 62	Lamb of God, the heavens adore you (3)
63, 64	behold thee, love thee, and adore (4)
65	their voices will adore him (3)
76	whom with the Father we adore and Holy Spirit evermore (5)
82	Let the heights of heaven adore him (3)
83	O come, let us adore him, Christ, the Lord (R)
85, 86	whom with the Father we adore and Holy Spirit evermore (6)
92	lay their gifts before him, praise him and adore him (3)
96	come, adore on bended knee Christ, the Lord (3)
106	rise to adore the mystery of love (1)
117, 118	angels adore him in slumber reclining (2)
119	to bend the knee before him whom heaven and earth adore (2)
129, 130	let creation now adore him (4)
131, 132	whom with the Father we adore and Holy Ghost for evermore (5)
158	I do adore thee, and will ever pray thee (5)
168, 169	O countenance whose splendor the hosts of heaven adore (1)
179	Him their true Creator, all his works adore (1)
198	Christ rose from death ... adore for ever ... evermore (1)
198	whom as true God and our hymns adore for ... evermore (2)
219	O earth, adore thy glorious King (2)
226, 227	To thy people who adore and confess thee evermore (5)

125, 126   His name shall be the Prince of Peace for evermore adored (4)
143   who art in three-fold Name adored (5)
212   O Dead arise! O Friendless stand by seraphim adored (5)
215   Jesus reigns, adored by angels (3)
219   by saints, by angel hosts adored (2)
254   For ever be adored that Name in earth and sky (1)
257   with speechless praise adored (4)
279   followed thee, obeyed, adored, our grateful hymn receive (1)
284   all adored your rising Lord with joy unknown (6)
326   thy Name with the Father and Spirit be ever adored (1)
364   everlasting Father art, by all the earth adored (1)
365   Come, thou incarnate Word, by heaven and earth adored (2)
404   your holy Name for ever be adored (1)
425   He only is to be adored for he alone can strength bestow (3)
435   ever to be worshiped, trusted, and adored (4)
454   Jesus came, adored by angels (1)
496, 497   by highest seraphim adored (2)
538   be by all that live adored (2)
643   by prostrate spirits day and night incessantly adored (2)

adoremus
110   Venite adoremus Dominum (1,3,R)

adoring
36   thee, his incarnate Son, and Holy Spirit adoring (2)
103   in one accord adoring Christ the Lord (R)
103   We praise you, Holy Trinity ... adoring you eternally (4)
133, 134   now all faithful hearts adoring bow (3)
171   there, adoring at his feet, mark the miracle of time (3)
248, 249   we, in love adoring, this most blessed Name revere (4)
360   humbly adoring, take thy Body broken (2)

adorn
85,86   let songs of praise your Name adorn (6)

adorned
175   adorned with the glory of blossom (3)
216   adorned with the glory of blossom (2)
436   adorned with prayer and love and joy (3)

adorning
91   our Lord a crib adorning (1)
117, 118   star of the east, the horizon adorning (1,5)
145   your way through life adorning (5)

adornment
33-35   to the night give glittering adornment (1)

adorns
483   a royal diadem adorns the mighty victor's brow (1)

advance
161   The flaming banners of our King advance (1)
161   advance through his self-offering (1)

advancing
68   The evening is advancing, and darker night is near (1)
326   From glory to glory advancing, we praise thee, O Lord (1)

advent
76   whose advent doth thy people free (5)
598   New advent of the love of Christ (3)

adventures
463, 464   you will see rare beasts and have unique adventures (1)

adversity
228   Grant enabling energy, courage in adversity (5)

advise
491   Prophets, shepherds, kings, advise (1)

advocate
364   also the Holy Comforter, our advocate and guide (5)

afar
93   brighter visions beam afar (3)
111   glories stream from heaven afar (2)
124   True spake the prophet from afar who told the rise (2)
128   bearing gifts we traverse afar (1)
135   manifested by the star to the sages from afar (1)
346   beheld afar that life which soon shall be (2)
419   Lord of all being, throned afar (1)
496, 497   with mercy beaming from afar (1)

affection
199, 200   with true affection welcomes ... Jesus' resurrection (3)

affection's
238, 239   with affection's recollections greet we your return again (1)

afflicted
158   By foes derided, by thine own rejected, O most afflicted (1)
347   help the afflicted (2)

affliction
159   Deep the woe of her affliction (2)

affliction's
545   Behold a Witness nobler still who trod affliction's path (3)

afflicts
379   God is Love, and though with blindness sin afflicts (3)
379   sin afflicts all human life (3)

afford
97   purer praise than ours on earth, angels' songs afford (3)
201   new life to all he doth afford (4)
231   a steadfast faith afford (2/12-21)
351   possess, in sweet communion, joys ... earth cannot afford (2)

447   no power earth can afford will separate us (4)

affords
483   highest place that heaven affords is his ... by right (2)

affright
105   Fear not then, said the angel, Let nothing you affright (3)

aflame
98   lead us all with hearts aflame unto the joys above us (4)
478   all who confess his Name, come then with hearts aflame (3)
591   in ire and exultation aflame with faith, and free (3)

afoot
472   afoot on dusty highways (3)

afraid
600, 601   Bring to our troubled minds, uncertain and afraid (2)
668   sun by day nor moon by night need make thy soul afraid (3)
669   Hope on, then, broken spirit; hope on, be not afraid (4)

afresh
318   here taste afresh the calm of sin forgiven (2)
445, 446   should strive afresh against the foe (3)

after
248, 249   that hereafter, heavenward soaring, we may sing (4)
316, 317   Feast after feast thus comes and passes by (3)
357   Rest eternal grant them, after weary fight (4)
518   hereafter in thy glory evermore with thee to reign (4)
560   Blessed ... who hunger and thirst after righteousness (4)
621, 622   hereafter these thy labors may with endless gifts be paid (5)
667   to cheer it after rain (1)
675   humbly follow after me (1)
701   heart ... longeth after thee (1)

again
9   give and give, and give again what God hath given thee (6)
49   rise again to fall no more (2)
52   in might victorious rose again (2)
88   Christ is born for us that we born again in him may be (4)
104   God's blood upon the spear-head, God's love refused again (3)
106   till our first heavenly state again takes place (5)
128   gold I bring to crown him again (2)
179   all that now is fallen raise to life again (6)
179   bring again our daylight: day returns with thee (6)
184   Christ the Lord is risen again (1)
188, 189   Lives again our glorious King (2)
193   who, dead, again dost live (5)
204   love lives again, that with the dead has been (1)
204   Love is come again like wheat that springeth green (R)
204   thinking that never he would wake again (2)
204   thy touch can call us back to life again (4)
212   again rejoice and on his praises dwell (1)
212   O Solitude again command your host from heaven restored (5)

213	Now created again that our lives may remain ... thine (3)
213	to the Lamb that was slain, hallelujah again (5)
238, 239	with affection's recollections greet we your return again (1)
276	slain by Herod's flashing blade, he saw thy face again (4)
278	Sing again the joys of Mary when she saw the risen Lord (3)
280	When Christ comes again in glory (4)
287	hearts are brave again, and arms are strong (5)
292	kindly earth with timely birth may yield her fruits again (2)
299	O Holy Spirit, come again (2)
345	Savior, again to thy dear Name we raise ... praise (1)
345	thy peace in death, the hope to rise again (4)
349	once again in love draw near (1)
390	Let the amen sound from his people again (4)
435	Christians, this Lord Jesus shall return again (6)
447	Christ who died but rose again triumphant from the grave (1)
448, 449	For us he rose from death again (5)
454	again in mercy, when our hearts are bowed with care (2)
454	again in answer to our earnest heart-felt prayer (2)
454	again in glory; let us then our homage pay (4)
481	Rejoice, again I say rejoice (R)
486	thy flock, redeemed from sinful stain ... praise again (5)
486	shall swell the sound of praise again (5)
492	praises of your Savior let his house resound again (1)
539	He comes again, O Zion, ere thou meet him (4)
544	angels descend with songs again (5)
578	give peace, O God, give peace again (1-3)
582, 583	tears are wiped from eyes that shall not weep again (1)
598	shall we again refuse thee (3)
600, 601	let there be light again (5)
609	O tread the city's streets again (4)
614	seek again the Way disciples followed then (2)
619	with glad songs resounding wake again (3)
667	he grants the soul again a season of clear shining (1)
676	but then the Holy Spirit revives my soul again (1)
695, 696	Yet when again in this new world you give us the joy (4)

against

74	For him let doors be opened, no hearts against him barred (1)
113	Oh sleep now, holy baby, with your head against my breast (1)
243	When Stephen preached against the laws (2)
382	Thou my sins against me cried, thou didst clear me (2)
420	when utmost evil strove against the Light (4)
445, 446	should strive afresh against the foe (3)
458	at these themselves displease, and 'gainst him rise (4)
540	contending from the walls of Zion against the foe (1)
560	utters all manner of evil against you falsely for my sake (9)
561	ye that are his now serve him against unnumbered foes (2)
562	Christ, the royal Master, leads against the foe (1)
562	gates of hell can never 'gainst that Church prevail (4)
564, 565	He who would valiant be 'gainst all disaster (1)

age

60	praise, honor, might, and glory be from age to age (6)
60	age to age eternally (6)
63, 64	from age to age eternally (5)

age

60	praise, honor, might, and glory be from age to age (6)
60	age to age eternally (6)
63, 64	from age to age eternally (5)
143	from age to age, the only Lord (5)
179	"Welcome, happy morning!" age to age shall say (1,R)
182	His Spirit burns through this and every future age (5)
229	still from age to age convey the wonders of this... day (1)
271	praise, honor, might, and glory ... age to age eternally (5)
272	praise, honor, might, and glory ... age to age eternally (5)
285	pours on the Church from age to age the healing unction (2)
359	each age for thine own solemn task prepares (1)
377, 378	shall from age to age endure (4)
404	Age shall to age pass on the endless song (2)
414	Age to age his works transmitteth (2)
414	age to age his power shall teach (2)
437, 438	his mercy sure, from age to age the same (2)
511	Holy Spirit, ever binding age to age and soul to soul (2)
521	what apostles learned of thee be ours from age to age (3)
522, 523	Grace ... never fails from age to age (2)
556	youth to age, by night and day, in gladness and in woe (4)
557	youth to age, by night and day, in gladness and in woe (4)
616	age to age more glorious, all blessing and all blest (5)
630	record of the revelation showing God to every age (3)
632	a lantern to our footsteps, shines on from age to age (1)
687, 688	Lord Sabaoth his Name, from age to age the same (2)

aged

257	The aged Simeon sees at last his Lord, so long desired (3)
610	go to the child, the youth, the aged (4)

agents

541	by feeblest agents may our God fulfill his righteous will (3

ages

48	this day the high and lowly, through ages joined in tune (1)
55	the birth which ages all adore (1)
59	with the everlasting Spirit while unending ages run (4)
74	All things are in his hand, all ages and all peoples (3)
146, 147	in company with ages past (1)
160	Here the King of all the ages (2)
165, 166	one in might and one in glory while eternal ages run (6)
217, 218	while endless ages run, with Father and with Spirit, One (3)
220, 221	let earth accord, who art, while endless ages run (4)
246	But down the ages rings the cry of those who saw (2)
257	all glory, Holy Ghost, to thee, while endless ages run (5)
268, 269	all the ages call be blessed (4)
289	our harvest may be garnered by ages yet unknown (3)
293	They lived not only in ages past (3)
329-331	while eternal ages run (6)
346	to whom be praise while endless ages run (3)
363	O holy Father, who hast led thy children in all the ages (2)
372	his love shall be our strength and stay while ages roll (4)
432	Thanksgiving and song to him be outpoured all ages along (4)

605   Still down the ages ring the prophet's stern commands (3)
614   Christ through all ages is the same (2)
615   Thy kingdom come, on bended knee the passing ages pray (1)
629   the nations, tongues and climes and all the ages given (2)
640   Traveler, ages are its own (2)
680   O God, our help in ages past, our hope for years to come (1,5)
680   A thousand ages in thy sight are like an evening gone (4)
685   Rock of ages, cleft for me, let me hide myself in thee (1,3)

ago
98   Now may Mary's son, who came so long ago to love us (4)
112   in the bleak midwinter long ago (1)

agony
18   dark midday could not conceal your cry of awful agony (3c)
284   ye saw his agony, ye heard the plaint he cried (4)
585   hidden is love's agony, love's endeavor, love's expense (2)
682   griefs and torments numberless, and sweat of agony (3)

agree
612   joining hand in hand, agree (4)

aid
18   athirst and spent, you asked for aid (4a)
96   Mary, Joseph, lend your aid (4)
117, 118   dawn on our darkness, and lend us thine aid (1,5)
226, 227   In our labor, be our aid (2)
228   On our journey grant us aid (2)
310, 311   thine aid supply, thy strength bestow (1)
377, 378   without our aid he did us make (2)
391   His sovereign power without our aid formed us of clay (2)
505   in every need thou bringest aid (1)
573   light to our blindness, O be thou our aid (1)
610   counsel, aid, and peace we give (4)
636, 637   For I am thy God, and will still give thee aid (2)
663   I will not fear, for thou art here to comfort and to aid (3)
668   from whence shall come my aid (1)

aiding
282, 283   health-bringer blessed, aiding every sufferer (4)

aim
237   vain the tyrant's sharpest aim, vain each fierce endeavor (2)
626   thy glory be my aim, thy holy will my choice (1)

aims
472   by our own false hopes and aims are spent (1)

air
81   O Flower, whose fragrance tender ... fills the air (3)
81   with sweetness fills the air (3)
112   cherubim and seraphim thronged the air (3)
388   It breathes in the air, it shines in the light (4)
394, 395   let water's fragile blend with air, enabling life (2)
406, 407   Let wind and air and cloud and calm and weathers all (3)

579	keep them by thy watchful care from every peril in the air (3)
579	glad praise from space, air, land, and sea (4)
621, 622	cloud nor passing vapor dims the brightness of the air (3)
720	the rockets' red glare, the bombs bursting in air (1)

alarm

386, 387	glorious the trumpet and alarm (3)
675	let not its weight fill your weak spirit with alarm (2)

alas

158	Alas, my treason, Jesus, hath undone thee (2)

alert

334	Sins forgiven, wrong forgiving, we go forth alert (3)
334	alert and living in your Spirit, strong and free (3)

alight

506, 507	till ... we, too, set the world alight (5)

alike

281	alike the symbol ... tool of foreign master's hated rule (1)
345	for dark and light are both alike to thee (2)
490	The night and the day are both alike (R)

alive

182	Christ is alive (1,2,5)
406, 407	from whom no one alive can flee (7)
611	Christ the worker, Love alive for us (7)

Alleluia

57, 58	Alleluia, Christ the Lord returns to reign (1)
57, 58	Alleluia, Thou shalt reign, and thou alone (4)
61, 62	Alleluia (1,2,3)
86	Alleluia (6)
103, 129, 130, 185, 186, 201, 203, 207, 214, 224	Alleluia (1-4)
111	heavenly hosts sing alleluia (2)
122, 123	Alleluia, song of gladness, voice of joy that cannot die (1)
122, 123	alleluia is the anthem ever raised by choirs on high (1)
122, 123	Alleluia thou resoundest, true Jerusalem and free (2)
122, 123	alleluia, joyful mother, all thy children sing with thee (2)
122, 123	Alleluia though we cherish and would chant for evermore (3)
122, 123	alleluia in our singing, let us for a while give o'er (3)
122, 123	there to thee for ever singing alleluia joyfully (4)
128	heaven sings alleluia: alleluia the earth replies (5)
178	Alleluia, alleluia, Give thanks to the risen Lord (R)
178	Alleluia, alleluia, Give praise to his Name (R)
183	have mercy, victor King, ever reigning. Amen. Alleluia (8)
184	alleluia, Christ, our Paschal lamb indeed (R)
184	Christ, today your people feed. Alleluia (R)
185, 186	sing to God right thankfully loud songs of alleluia (1)
187	Alleluia (1-3)
191	alleluia! Hearts and voices heavenward raise (1)
191	alleluia! Glory be to God on high (5)
191	Alleluia! to the Savior who has won the victory (5)
191	Alleluia! to the Spirit, fount of love and sanctity (5)

426	heaven with alleluias rang when creation was begun (1)
556, 557	Your clear hosannas raise, and alleluias loud (3)

alloy

119	so may we with holy joy, pure and free from sin's alloy (3)

alluring

480	Safe from the world's alluring harms (2)

Almighty

14, 15	Almighty Father, hear our cry through Jesus Christ (3)
19, 20	Almighty Father, hear our cry through Jesus Christ (3)
21, 22	Almighty Father, hear our cry (3)
43	keep me, King of kings, beneath thine own almighty wings (1)
44, 45	Almighty Father, hear our cry (4)
106	eternal praise to heaven's almighty King (6)
231	hold them when they waver with your almighty arm (2/1-18)
282, 283	Father Almighty, Son and Holy Spirit, God ever blessed (6)
291	but it is fed and watered by God's almighty hand (1)
362	Lord God Almighty (1,4)
365	Come, thou almighty King, help us thy Name to sing (1)
365	thou, who almighty art, now rule in every heart (3)
369	long to see the blessed Three in the Almighty One (2)
371	Thou, whose almighty word chaos and darkness heard (1)
386, 387	glorious the almighty stretched-out arm (3)
388	Almighty, thy power hath founded of old (3)
390	the Almighty, the King of creation (1)
390	ponder anew what the Almighty can do (3)
391	almighty Maker (3)
401	"Holy, holy, holy," cry, "Almighty King" (4)
405	lips that we might tell how great is God Almighty (4)
405	God Almighty, who has made all things well (5)
408	What God's almighty power hath made ... mercy keepeth (2)
409	publishes to every land the work of an almighty hand (1)
421	We bless, we worship you ... O God, Almighty Father (1)
423	almighty, victorious, thy great Name we praise (1)
430	O come, our voices raise, sounding God Almighty praise (1,6)
495	by almighty love anointed, thou hast full atonement made (2)
527	the one almighty Father reigns in love for evermore (4)
535	God ruleth on high, almighty to save (2)
567	now, O Lord, be near to bless, almighty as of yore (2)
567	soothe and bless with thine almighty breath (3)
579	Almighty Father, strong to save (1)
588, 589	Almighty God, your word is cast like seed upon the ground (1)
607	redeem the whole creation with your almighty hand (1)
619	Almighty Christ, to thee our voices sing (7)
633	Word almighty, we revere you (1)
643	Yet I may love thee too, O Lord, almighty as thou art (5)
657	Come, almighty to deliver, let us all thy life receive (2)
665	Daily ... almighty Giver boundless gifts on us bestow (4)
670	Israel, now and evermore in the Lord Almighty trust (4)
718	God of our fathers, whose almighty hand leads forth (1)

aloft

400	you clouds that ride the heavens aloft, O praise him (2)

alone

18	betrayed, forsaken, all alone (3a)
27, 28	for you alone can make us strong (4)
47	God, the blessed Three in One dwell within my heart alone (6)
57, 58	Alleluia, Thou shalt reign, and thou alone (4)
66	By thine own eternal Spirit rule in all our hearts alone (4)
85, 86	salvation comes from you alone (4)
97	all creation to redeem I alone am able (2)
129, 130	Christ upon the mountain peak stands alone in glory (1)
138	those refreshing streams which you alone can give (3)
143	Alone and fasting Moses saw the loving God (2)
151	thy grace alone availeth (2)
164	Alone thou goest forth, O Lord, in sacrifice to die (1)
174	Easter triumph, Easter joy, these alone do sin destroy (4)
185, 186	an empty form alone remains; his sting is lost for ever (2)
185, 186	Christ alone our souls will feed (4)
194, 195	alone to Jesus living, pure in heart may we abide (2)
212	lest dead and friendless and alone he ... deceive (4)
231, 232	ascribe all power and glory and praise to God alone (3)
242	teach us in that Word alone to find the truth (5)
300	Christ alone calls for all our praises (2)
307	Thou alone ... liftest up thy people's head (1)
307	Thou alone, our strong defender (1)
318	my strength is in thy might, thy might alone (3)
329, 331	faith alone the true heart waketh to behold the mystery (4)
343	would not live by bread alone, but by thy word of grace (2)
357	Jesus, Son of Mary, fount of life alone (1)
382	alone, when they replied, thou didst hear me (2)
391	know that the Lord is God alone (1)
406, 407	From thee alone all creatures came (1)
408	the Lord is God, and he alone (3)
421	with the Spirit, you alone share in the Father's glory (3)
425	He only is to be adored for he alone can strength bestow (3)
440	thou alone to God canst win us (2)
457	to thee alone from sin and death we flee (1)
457	thy word alone true wisdom can impart (2)
460, 461	his the triumph, his the victory alone (1,5)
462	thou in thy everlasting seat remainest God alone (5)
475	thou alone shalt be known Lord of all our being (2)
518	holy Zion's help forever, and her confidence alone (1)
548	ye may o'ercome, through Christ alone (5)
561	stand in his strength alone (3)
586	where the solitary labor, thou art there with them alone (2)
598	thy peace by which alone we choose thee (3)
610	we, your servants, bring the worship not of voice alone (1)
610	not of voice alone, but heart (1)
638, 639	my company before is gone, and I am left alone with thee (1)
640	Watchman, will its beams alone gild the spot (2)
665	God unknown, he alone calls my heart to be his own (1)
670	teach me thou alone art Lord (2)
674	you alone can grant us grace to live the words we say (1)
680	sufficient is thine arm alone, and our defense is sure (2)
685	thou must save and thou alone (2)
693	now to be thine, yea, thine alone (5)
695, 696	our whole life shall then be yours alone (4)

699	leave, ah, leave me not alone (2)
701	only where thou art is pleasure, thee alone I treasure (1)
703	blindly we stumble when we walk alone (2)
706	for your grace alone I thirst (3)

along

170	set you with taunts along that road (1)
205	Sing songs of praise along his way (2)
289	for thine unfailing mercies far-strewn along our way (1)
432	Thanksgiving and song to him be outpoured all ages along (4)
444	He guides the feet of pilgrims along the paths of peace (3)
503, 504	through the ages all along this may be our endless song (8)

aloud

129, 130	Nations cry aloud in wonder (3)
248, 249	but with holy exultation we may sing aloud today (1)
256	cried aloud, "Who are you, Lord?" (1)
284	for such a birth ye sang aloud (2)
364	To thee all angels cry aloud (2)
535	Let all cry aloud, and honor the Son (3)
596	the city's crowded clangor cries aloud for sin to cease (2)
716	to thee aloud we cry, God save the state (2)
408	all who know his power proclaim aloud the wondrous story (3)

Alpha

82	he is Alpha and Omega, he the source, the ending he (1)

already

546	forget the steps already trod, and onward urge thy way (2)
582, 583	Already in the mind of God that city riseth fair (4)
615	And lo, already on the hills the flags of dawn appear (3)
671	I have already come (4)

also

153	The Lord be with you. And also with you (2)
261, 262	grant that we also may like him be faithful (3)
364	also the Holy Comforter, our advocate and guide (5)
400	flowers and fruits that in you grow ... glory also show (4)
400	let them his glory also show (4)
687, 688	let goods and kindred go, this mortal life also (4)

altar

93	Saints before the altar bending (4)
157	up to the horns of the altar (R)
332	thus inspired with holy fear, before thine altar kneel (1)
336	leaving now thine altar let us nevermore leave thee (1)
357	now we hail thee present on thine altar throne (1)
450, 451	Crown him ye martyrs of our God who from his altar call (2)
459	an altar candle sheds its light as surely as a star (2)
591	O God of earth and altar, bow down and hear our cry (1)
704	kindle a flame of sacred love upon the altar of my heart (1)

altars

419	till all thy living altars claim one holy light (4)
517	Beside thine altars ... the swallows find a nest (2)

alter
607 with faith that none can alter, your servants undergird (3)

alternate
367 repeated each to each the alternate hymn (1)

although
40, 41 Although our eyes in sleep be closed (3)
476 Although his being is too bright for human eyes to scan (2)

alway
230 for God the Holy Spirit dwells with the Church alway (3)
518 thy fullest benediction shed within its walls alway (3)
657 Thee we would be alway blessing (2)

always
18 let us cling always to your love (2c)
138 in you always to live and drink of those ... streams (3)
205 To God the Father ... Son ... Spirit, always One (5)
304 His presence, always near (4)
363 still imploring thy love and favor, kept to us always (5)
377, 378 praise, laud, and bless his Name always (3)
411 He will not always chide; he will with patience wait (3)
420 may God give us faith to sing always Alleluia, Amen.
576, 577 Christ, our God, be always present here among us (2)
603, 604 always, near or far, he calls and claims us (2)
606 let us rejoice and be glad now and always (1)
689 always thou lovedst me (3)
697 accept my heart this day, and make it always thine (1)
707 Take my voice, and let me sing always, only, for my King (2)

AM

387 Tell them I AM, the Lord God said (2)
401 the Lord, the great I AM, by earth and heaven confessed (1)
401 eternal Father, great I AM, we worship thee (4)
439 to the Lamb who is the great I AM (2)

AM's
245 Your great I AM's Saint John records (2)

amain
579 traffic runs amain by mountain pass or valley low (2)

amaze
124 eastern sages with amaze upon the wondrous token gaze (2)

amazed
106 amazed, the wondrous story they proclaim (4)

amazing
159 pierced by anguish so amazing (4)
229 God's amazing glory sung (2)
474 love so amazing, so divine, demands my soul ... all (4)

| 474 | love so amazing ... demands my soul, my life, my all (4) |
| 671 | Amazing grace (1) |

amber

235	as, in the prophet's vision from out the amber flame (2)
360, 361	This is the temple; here thy presence-chamber (2)
719	O beautiful for spacious skies, for amber waves of grain (1)

ambitious

| 574, 575 | for pride ambitious to succeed (3) |

amen

57, 58	Yea, amen, let all adore thee (4)
153	It is right to give him thanks and praise ever. Amen (2)
153	Let us go forth in peace. In the name of Christ. Amen (3)
390	Let the amen sound from his people again (4)
417, 418	might be to God and the Lamb for ever. Amen (4)
420	may God give us faith to sing always Alleluia, Amen (5)
496, 497	Amen, amen! Alleluia, alleluia (3)
544	earth repeat the loud amen (5)
555	holiness shall whisper the sweet amen of peace (2)

amid

12, 13	Amid our customary round, we offer ... prayer and praise (1)
81	amid the cold of winter, when half spent was the night (1)
409	amid their radiant orbs be found (3)
430	amid the mortal throng, be you masters of the song (3)
528	amid the cares that claim us, hold in mind eternity (5)
608	calm amid its rage didst sleep (2)
687, 688	our helper he amid the flood of mortal ills prevailing (1)

amidst

199, 200	but today amidst thine own thou didst stand (4)
203, 206	amidst them came their Lord most dear (4)
369	dwells amidst the dazzling light of vast eternity (1)
426	amidst eternal joy songs of praise their powers employ (6)

among

104	By whose descent among us The worlds are reconciled (4)
106	Then may we hope, the angelic throngs among, to sing (6)
165, 166	Thirty years among us dwelling (2)
298	stand among the glorious heavenly band (1)
329, 331	once on earth among us dwelling (1)
444	a Savior comes among us to raise us up to heaven (2)
492	sinless one, among the sinful (3)
492	Prince of life, among the dead (3)
576, 577	Christ, our God, be always present here among us (2)
581	Let strife among us be unknown (4)
586	Where the many toil together ... art thou among thine own (2)
609	among these restless throngs abide (4)

ample

| 117, 118 | Vainly we offer each ample oblation (4) |
| 146, 118 | Christ by his own example sealed (2) |

anchor
627   our anchor and our stay (3)

ancient
38, 39   Lord, free us from our ancient foe (3)

56   who to thy tribes on Sinai's height in ancient times (3)
60   In sorrow that the ancient curse should doom to death (2)
89, 90   its ancient splendors fling (4)
165, 166 awhile the ancient rigor that thy birth bestowed, suspend (5)
363   Ancient of Days, who sittest throned in glory (1)
365   build in our hearts thy throne, Ancient of Days (1)
388   Our shield and defender, the Ancient of Days (1)
401   Ancient of everlasting days, and God of love (1)
423   most blessed, most glorious, the Ancient of Days (1)
542   In Christ all races meet, their ancient feuds forgetting (2)
542   heal its ancient wrong, come, Prince of Peace, and reign (3)
594, 595 crown thine ancient Church's story (1)
614   praise for his brave saints of ancient days (1)
687, 688 for still our ancient foe doth seek to work us woe (1)

Andrew
231   praise, O Lord, for Andrew, the first to follow (2/11-30)
549, 550 as, of old, Saint Andrew heard it by the Galilean lake (2)

anew
163   for God doth make his world anew (1)
232   from all unrighteous mammon, O raise our eyes anew (2/9-21)
232   walking in their footsteps we give you praise anew (2/11-1)
390   ponder anew what the Almighty can do (3)
508   fill me with life anew (1)
580   As each far horizon beckons, may it challenge us anew (4)

angel
82   angel hosts, his praises sing (3)
94, 95   the angel of the Lord came down, and glory shone around (1)
99   when lo! above the earth rang out the angel chorus (2)
103   Come, join the angel throng in songs of joy (R)
105   From God our heavenly Father a blessed angel came (2)
105   Fear not then, said the angel, Let nothing you affright (3)
109   The first Nowell the angel did say was to ... shepherds (1)
114   O children of the forest free, the angel song is true (4)
156   the angel armies of the sky look down (3)
174   death's dark angel sheathes his sword (2)
191   by angel hands be gathered, and be ever, Lord, with thee (4)
201   "Whom seek ye here?" the angel said (3)
203   An angel clad in white they see (3)
215   Hark, the choirs of angel voices joyful alleluias sing (1)
219   by saints, by angel hosts adored (3)
252   kneeling in her lowly cell, by the angel Gabriel (2)
259   not with his angel host, not in his kingly state (1)
265   The angel Gabriel from heaven came (1)
266   Said the angel, "Have no fear ... " (4)
284   E'en angel eyes slow tears did shed (5)
366   Hark, the loud celestial hymn angel choirs ... raising (2)

366	angel choirs above are raising (2)
367	with thine angel hosts we cry, " Holy, holy, holy " (3)
377, 378	from men and... angel host be praise and glory evermore (5)
479	angel hosts, rejoicing, make their glad reply (4)
489	He sent no angel of his host to bear this mighty word (2)
519, 520	angel hosts encircled, as a bride dost earthward move (1)
556, 557	With all the angel choirs, with all the saints of earth (2)
624	bright with many an angel, and all the martyr throng (2)

angel's

202	Protected ... from the destroying angel's might (2)
232	youthful and unready, she heard the angel's word (2/8-15)
278	blessed Mother who received the angel's word (1)
292	gathering round thy throne ... in the holy angel's sight (3)
471	the angel's theme in heaven above (5)

angelic

87	with the angelic host proclaim Christ is born (1)
106	who heard the angelic herald's voice (2)
106	Then may we hope, the angelic throngs among, to sing (6)
336	Come with us, O King of glory, by angelic voices praised (3)
368	Holy Jesus, Lord of glory, whom angelic hosts proclaim (2)
495	Help, ye bright angelic spirits (4)

angels

42	Through the long night watches may thine angels spread (5)
61, 62	let saints and angels sing before you (3)
77	angels in the sky sang praise above the silent field (4)
78	angels keep their watch of wondering love (2)
78	We hear the Christmas angels the great glad tidings tell (5)
79	angels keep their watch of wondering love (2)
79	We hear the Christmas angels the great glad tidings tell (5)
83	come, and behold him born the King of angels (1)
83	Sing, choirs of angels, sing in exultation (3)
84	star and angels gave the sign (1)
87	Hark! the herald angels sing glory to the new-born King (1,R)
89	from angels bending near the earth (1)
89	The world in solemn stillness lay to hear the angels sing (1)
89	ever o'er its Babel-sounds the blessed angels sing (2)
89	hear the angels sing (3)
89	world give back the song which now the angels sing (4)
90	from angels bending near the earth (1)
90	The world in solemn stillness lay to hear the angels sing (1)
90	ever o'er its Babel-sounds the blessed angels sing (2)
90	hear the angels sing (3)
90	world give back the song which now the angels sing (4)
92	On this day angels sing (4)
93	Angels, from the realms of glory (1)
94, 95	forthwith appeared a shining throng of angels (5)
94, 95	angels praising God, who thus addressed their joyful song (5
96	Angels we have heard on high (1)
96	Come to Bethlehem and see him whose birth the angels sing (3
96	See him in a manger laid whom the angels praise above (4)
106	mystery ... which hosts of angels chanted from above (1)
110	the angels hovered round, and sang this song (3)

anger
404   slow to anger, merciful and kind (3)
414   Full of kindness and compassion, slow to anger (5)
576, 577   Banished now be anger, strife and every quarrel (2)

angry
608   bid its angry tumult cease (3)

anguish
158   For me ... thy death of anguish (4)
159   there she waited in her anguish (1)
159   pierced by anguish so amazing (4)
238, 239   by contempt of every anguish, by unyielding battle done (2)
246   love that cannot cease to bear our human anguish (4)
246   human anguish everywhere (4)
286   whose hearts were riven, sore with woe and anguish tried (4)
375   his comfort all my anguish stills (1)
669   the needs of all thy children, their anguish or delight (3)

anguished
27, 28   anguished and in mind distressed be crushed by guilt (3)

anima
268   Magnificat anima mea Dominum. Magnificat, magnificat (4-D)

animating
546   God's all-animating voice that calls thee from on high (3)

Anna
257   Anna welcomes Israel's hope, with holy rapture fired (3)

Anne
110   'Twas Mary, daughter pure of holy Anne (2)

announces
76   Baptist's cry announces that the Lord is nigh (1)

announcing
127   to the world its God announcing (2)

annoy
441, 442   hopes deceive and fears annoy (2)

anoint
51   that he might anoint us a royal priesthood (1)
201   all to anoint fair Mary's Son (2)
232   with true balm of Gilead anoint us evermore (2/10-18)
359   Anoint them prophets. Teach them thine intent (2)
359   Anoint them priests (3)
359   Anoint them kings. Yea, kingly kings, O Lord (4)
359   Anoint them with the Spirit of thy Son (4)
503, 504   Anoint and cheer our soiled face with ... thy grace (5)
697   Anoint me with thy heavenly grace (3)

anointed

50	Hosanna to the anointed King, to David's holy Son (3)
120	now by the Holy spirit shed upon the Son's anointed head (3)
156	Father ... expects his own anointed Son (4)
337	Look Father, look on his anointed face (2)
495	by almighty love anointed, thou hast full atonement made (2)
616	Hail to the Lord's Anointed, great David's greater Son (1)

anointing

503, 504	Thou the anointing Spirit art (2)

another

24	dawn leads on another day (3)
102	brought us love for one another (3)
250	rejoice, with thanks embrace another year of grace (1-3,5)
251	Another year its course has run (2)
318	nor do I need another arm save thine to lean upon (3)
576, 577	Loving him, let each love Christ in one another (1)

answer

18	he knew you, Lord, would answer him (2b)
454	again in answer to our earnest heart-felt prayer (2)
669	God ever sends his blessing in answer to thy prayer (2)
689	the whole of love is but my answer, Lord, to thee (3)

answered

157	for you answered me and have become my salvation (R)
630	Word is answered by the Spirit's voice within (5)

answering

556, 557	while answering echoes upward float (3)
603, 604	through ... every birth, to draw an answering love (1)

answers

164	through our pity and our shame love answers love's appeal (2)

anthem

106	God's highest glory was their anthem still (3)
122, 123	alleluia is the anthem ever raised by choirs on high (1)
240, 241	Hearken to the anthem glorious of the martyrs (1)
367	bid we thus our anthem flow (2)
494	Hark, how the heavenly anthem drowns all music but its own (1)
625	onward as ye go some joyful anthem sing (3)

anthems

115	Whom angels greet with anthems sweet (1)
135	anthems be to thee addressed, God in man made manifest (1-3)
154, 155	praise and prayers and anthems before thee we present (3)
284	The joyous notes pursue and louder anthems raise (8)
336	in our hearts as in thy heaven ... anthems raised (3)
336	be enraptured anthems raised (3)
495	all your noblest anthems raise (4)
562	Christians, lift your voices, loud your anthems raise (2)
614	O friends upraise anthems of joy and holy praise (1)
618	supernal anthems echoing (4)

623   we the sweet anthems of Zion shall sing (3)
681   hymns thy people raise, the psalms and anthems strong (3)

antiphon
427   No lovelier antiphon in all high heaven is known (3)

anxiety
146, 147   lest in anxiety (4)
463, 464   He is the Truth. Seek him in the Kingdom of Anxiety (2)
670   When I come before thy Word, quiet my anxiety (2)

anxious
145   Now quit your care and anxious fear and worry (1)
690   bid my anxious fears subside (3)

any
293   there's not any reason ... why I shouldn't be one too (2)
293   not any reason -- no, not the least (2)
339   Joy, the best that any knoweth (2)
431   more rich than any prize (3)
682   not for the sake of winning heaven, nor any fear of hell (4)

anything
592   what I do in anything, to do it as for thee (1)

apart
436   make it a temple set apart from earthly use (3)
436   a temple set apart from earthly use for heaven's employ (3)
567   leper set apart and shunned, the sick with fevered frame (1)
702   Where can I go apart from thee (3)

appointed
165, 166   his appointed time fulfilled (2)
170   acted out their grim charade to its appointed end (3)
261, 262   By the Creator, Joseph was appointed (1)
261, 262   appointed spouse of the Virgin (1)
492   till the appointed work be done (4)
495   Paschal Lamb, by God appointed (2)
579   ocean deep its own appointed limits keep (1)
608   its own appointed limits keep (1)
616   Hail, in the time appointed, his reign on earth begun (1)

apostate
531   descend on our apostate race (1)

apostle
230   each Apostle spoke the word beneath the Spirit's thunder (1)
232   Praise for your blest apostle surnamed Bartholomew (2/8-24)
232   for he at the ascension was an apostle still (2/8-24)
245   Your brightness, O eternal Word, Apostle John unfurled (1)
275   king, apostle, saint, confessor, martyr and evangelist (2)

apostle's
285   great apostle's chosen friend (3)

apostles

23	Apostles made a lame man walk (2)
193	the apostles saw their risen Lord (1)
203	That night the apostles met in fear (4)
206	That night the apostles met in fear (2)
225	his chosen apostles, preach to the ends of the earth (3)
231	the apostles sought God's choice (2/2-24)
231	May we like true apostles your holy Church defend (2/2-24)
232	O God, your two apostles won life through martyrdom (2/6-29)
232	Praise, Lord, for your apostles (2/10-28)
232	Apostles, prophets, martyrs ... the noble throng (2/11-1)
278	in prayer with Christ's apostles, waited on his ... word (3)
280	In the roll of your apostles stands the name Bartholemew (2)
359	Make them apostles, heralds of thy cross (5)
364	apostles glorious company ... thy constant praise recite (4)
521	what apostles learned of thee be ours from age to age (3)

apostles'

233, 234	the apostles' glorious deeds we sing (1)
370	confessors' faith, apostles' word (3)

apostolic

366	Lo, the apostolic train join, thy sacred Name to hallow (3)

appall

174	now no more can death appall (3)
194, 195	thy terrors now can no longer, death, appall us (1)
344	fear of death shall not appall us (3)
703	doubts appall, and sorrows still increase (1)

apparel

275	clothed in white apparel (1)

appeal

164	through our pity and our shame love answers love's appeal (2)
337	then for those, our dearest and our best ... we appeal (3)
337	by this prevailing presence we appeal (3)

appear

6, 7	Day-star, in my heart appear (1)
56	mourns in lonely exile here until the Son of God appear (1,8)
65	Let every hill and valley a level way appear (1)
68	Rejoice, rejoice, believers, and let your lights appear (1)
68	Our hope and expectation, O Jesus, now appear (3)
93	suddenly the Lord, descending, in his temple shall appear (4)
145	make clear, make clear where truth and light appear (2)
150	that with thee we may appear at the Eternal Eastertide (5)
163	the cross on Calvary's height gleams of eternity appear (2)
246	King Herod's troops would soon appear (1)
290	then the full corn shall appear (2)
326	to appear before God in the city of infinite day (1)
366	As our judge thou wilt appear (7)
386, 387	glorious the assembled fires appear (3)
475	with awe appear before him (1)
495	ever for us interceding, till in glory we appear (3)

516	O Comforter, draw near, within my heart appear (1)
522, 523	the cloud and fire appear for a glory and a covering (3)
615	And lo, already on the hills the flags of dawn appear (3)
671	how precious ... grace appear the hour I first believed (2)

appearance
| 242 | when thou didst thine appearance make, he saw and hailed (3) |

appeared
| 94, 95 | forthwith appeared a shining throng of angels (5) |

appearing
33, 34	in the heavens choirs of stars appearing (2)
33, 34	stars appearing hallow the night-fall (2)
35	in the heavens choirs of stars appearing (2)
35	stars appearing hallow the night-fall (2)
36	our Savior Jesus Christ, joyful in thine appearing (1)
83	Word of the Father, now in flesh appearing (6)
131, 132	When Christ's appearing was made known (1)
225	on those who await his appearing (1)
286	Who are these like stars appearing (1)

appears
54	Thus on earth the Word appears (3)
372	the one eternal God ere aught that now appears (1)
434	Here his whole Name appears complete (3)
496, 497	How bright appears the Morning Star (1)
555	gladness breaks like morning where'er thy face appears (3)

appointed
165, 166	his appointed time fulfilled (2)
170	acted out their grim charade to its appointed end (3)
261, 262	By the Creator, Joseph was appointed (1)
261, 262	appointed spouse of the Virgin (1)
492	till the appointed work be done (4)
495	Paschal Lamb, by God appointed (2)
579	ocean deep its own appointed limits keep (1)
608	its own appointed limits keep (1)
616	Hail, in the time appointed, his reign on earth begun (1)

approach
49	with solemn prayer approach the throne (3)
327, 328	Approach ye then with faithful hearts sincere (5)
377, 378	approach with joy his courts unto (3)

approaching
| 156 | sad and wondering eyes to see the approaching sacrifice (3) |

approve
| 213 | We with thanks do approve the design of that love (4) |

approved
| 285 | beloved on earth, approved of thee (4) |

archangel

263, 264 To Mary the Archangel came (2)
282, 283 Send thine archangel Michael to our succor (2)
282, 283 Send thine archangel Gabriel the mighty herald of heaven (3)
282, 283 Send from the heavens Raphael thine archangel (4)

archangels

112 Angels and archangels may have gathered there (3)
401 the God who reigns on high the great archangels sing (4)
618 cry out ... virtues, archangels, angels' choirs (1)

arched

31, 32 who in the high arched sky has placed the sun (1)
658 longs the deer ... in parched and barren ways (1)
702 Lord, thou hast searched me (1)

arches

71, 72 heaven's eternal arches ring with thy beloved Name (4)

architect

38, 39 The whole creation's architect (2)
519, 520 in their places now compacted by the heavenly Architect (4)

Architect's

260 The Architect's high miracles he saw, and what was done (2)

ardent

63, 64 fire our hearts with ardent love (2)

ardor

159 my heart fresh ardor gaining (5)
516 visit it with thine own ardor glowing (1)

aright

21, 22 you order time and change aright (1)
81 To show God's love aright, she bore to us a Savior (2)
133, 134 May all who seek to praise aright ... show ... your light (3)
210 Our hearts be pure from evil, that we may see aright (2)
271, 272 John, still unborn, yet gave aright his witness (3)
292 that we may feed the poor aright (3)
627 Lord, grant us all aright to learn the wisdom it imparts (5)
669 Thy lasting truth and mercy, O Father, see aright (3)

arise

6, 7 Sun of Righteousness, arise (1)
47 by love inflamed, arise unto thee a sacrifice (4)
49 Come, let us with our Lord arise (1)
61, 62 Awake, Jerusalem, arise (1)
68 arise, thou Sun so longed for, above this darkened sphere (3)
128 Glorious now behold him arise (5)
145 arise, arise, and make a paradise (5)
149 If dead in you, so in you we arise (3)
212 Awake, arise, lift up your voice (1)
212 O Dead arise! O Friendless stand by seraphim adored (5)
213 arise and rejoice in the day thou wast born (1)
380 From all that dwell below the skies let ... praise arise (1)

380   let the Creator's praise arise (1)
398   clouds arise, and tempests blow by order from thy throne (3)
543   Cheerful in God, arise and shine (1)
547   Awake, arise, go forth in faith (5)
548   Soldiers of Christ, arise, and put your armor on (1)
613   We pray thee, Lord, arise, and come in thy great might (4)
613   arise, O Morning Star, arise, and never set (5)
681   May thy fresh light arise within each clouded heart (5)
718   our grateful songs before thy throne arise (1)

arisen
183   Yes, Christ my hope is arisen (7)
192   but now is Christ arisen (R)

arising
68   The Bridegroom is arising, and soon he will draw nigh (1)
175   from the death of the winter arising (1)

arm
75   the arm of the Lord is strong (3)
231   hold them when they waver with your almighty arm (2/1-18)
318   nor do I need another arm save thine to lean upon (3)
386, 387   from whose right arm, beneath whose eyes (1)
386, 387   glorious the almighty stretched-out arm (3)
437, 438   Make known his might, the deeds his arm has done (2)
457   the rending tomb proclaims thy conquering arm (3)
457   who put their trust in thee nor death nor hell ... harm (3)
471   nerves the feeble arm for fight (4)
474   all the vain things that charm me most, I sacrifice (2)
484, 485   his holy arm hath wrought salvation (1)
505   that charity may warm each heart (3)
541   No arm so weak but may do service here (3)
548   take to arm you for the fight, the panoply of God (3)
561   arm of flesh will fail you, ye dare not trust your own (3)
567   Thine arm, O Lord, in days of old was strong to heal (1)
579, 608   whose arm hath bound the restless wave (1)
626   thine arm my strong support; thyself my great reward (2)
675   let not its weight fill your weak spirit with alarm (2)
675   brace your spirit, and nerve your arm (2)
680   sufficient is thine arm alone, and our defense is sure (2)
691   may my love to thee pure, warm, and changeless be (2)
705   farm and market, shop and home (1)
718   be thy strong arm our ever sure defense (3)

armed
347   be of good courage, armed with heavenly grace (1)
506, 507   Tell of how the ascended Jesus armed a people for his own (4)
687, 688   armed with cruel hate, on earth is not his equal (1)

armies
156   the angel armies of the sky look down (3)

armor
548   Soldiers of Christ, arise, and put your armor on (1)
561   put on the Gospel armor, and watching unto prayer (3)

| 563 | till Christ himself ... call thee to lay thine armor by (3) |
| 617 | Oh, clothe us with thy heavenly armor, Lord (3) |

arms

113	so rest in the arms of your mother who sings you a la ru (2)
165, 166	the King of heavenly beauty gently on thine arms extend (5)
168	see in my last strife to me thine arms extended (5)
168	thine arms extended upon the cross of life (5)
169	see in my last strife to me thine arms extended (5)
169	thine arms extended upon the cross of life (5)
259	watched by her duteous love, in her fond arms at rest (2)
287	hearts are brave again, and arms are strong (5)
333	Now the keeling Now the plea ... Father's arms in welcome (1)
394, 395	your arms embrace all now despised for creed or race (3)
396, 397	who from our mother's arms hath blessed us on our way (1)
480	infants in his arms he took and on his bosom blessed (2)
480	in the circle of his arms may we forever lie (2)
482	your hands swift to welcome, your arms to embrace (3)
552, 553	Faint not nor fear, his arms are near (4)
585	God, whose arms of love aching, spent, the world sustain (6)
603, 604	his arms stretched out above through every culture (1)
663	filled my cup, and borne me up in everlasting arms (4)

army

412	O victory, loud shouting army (1)
526	One army of the living God, to his command we bow (3)
561	from victory unto victory his army shall he lead (1)
562	Like a mighty army moves the Church of God (3)

arose

175	day whereon Christ arose, breaking the kingdom of death (R)
215	he who from the grave arose (91)
426	songs of praise arose when he captive led captivity (2)
452	Glorious the day when Christ arose (2)

around

10	New mercies, each returning day around us hover (2)
10	new mercies ... around us hover while we pray (2)
94, 95	the angel of the Lord came down, and glory shone around (1)
106	around us all his glory shall display (6)
170	mercy throw around our naked shame (2)
256	A light from heaven shone around (1)
284	Around his sacred tomb a willing watch ye kept (6)
284	waved around your golden wings and struck your strings (7)
291	All good gifts around us are sent from heaven above (R)
362	casting down their golden crowns around the glassy sea (2)
370	the deep salt sea, around the old eternal rocks (4)
376	stars and angels sing around thee (2)
386, 387	at once, above, beneath, around, all nature ... replied (2)
416	for the love ... from our birth over and around us lies (1)
427	Let all the earth around ring joyous with the sound (4)
432	each jubilant chord reecho around (3)
480	When Jesus into Zion rode, the children sang around ((3)
486	above, beneath us, and around, both dead and living (2)
528	asking ... world around us share your children's liberty (3)

541	while all around us waves the golden grain (1)
543	his all-resplendent grace he pours around thy head (2)
545	Lo, what a cloud of witnesses encompass us around (1)
546	A cloud of witnesses around hold thee in full survey (2)
691	griefs around me spread (3)
709	O spread thy sheltering wings around (4)
715	a trembling fear seized all the guilty world around (RC)

arraigned

171	view the Lord of life arraigned (2)

array

136, 137	With shining face and bright array (3)
287	the saints triumphant rise in bright array (7)
320	today the new oblation ... bids us feast in glad array (4)
556, 557	Still lift your standard high, still march in firm array (5)

arrayed

202	arrayed in garments white and fair (1)
284	Ye saw the heaven-born child in human flesh arrayed (2)
284	When all arrayed in light the shining conqueror rode (7)
286	these in God's own truth arrayed (2)
432	worship before him, in brightness arrayed (1)
448, 449	in purple robe arrayed (4)
621, 622	in everlasting glory thou with brightness be arrayed (5)

arrive

453	when we arrive at the haven of rest, we shall hear (4)
686	I hope, by thy good pleasure, safely to arrive at home (2)
709	at our Father's loved abode our souls arrive in peace (4)

art

270	Art by art shall be assailed (4)
284	With equal flame and equal art ... extol his Name (8)
382	Wherefore with my utmost art, I will sing thee (2)

ascend

219	O may our hearts to him ascend (3)
310, 311	All praise and thanks to thee ascend for evermore (2)
364	thou didst ascend to God's right hand in glory evermore (7)
401	we shall, on eagle-wings upborne, to heaven ascend (2)
484, 485	let praise from all to thee ascend (2)
524	For her my tears shall fall, for her my prayers ascend (2)
616	to him shall prayer unceasing and daily vows ascend (4)

ascended

24	to thee our morning hymns ascended (1)
217, 218	O risen Christ, ascended Lord (3)
220, 221	O risen Christ, ascended Lord, all praise to thee (4)
223, 224	morn when our ascended Lord ... his Spirit poured (1)
307	Risen, ascended, glorified (5)
468	he's risen from darkness ... he's 'scended into glory (4)
506, 507	Tell of how the ascended Jesus armed a people for his own (4)

ascendeth
219   The Lord ascendeth up on high (1)
282, 283 thine is the glory which from all creation ever ascendeth (6)

Ascending
220, 221 Ascending to the Father's throne (2)

ascends
54   then the heavenly throne ascends (3)
215   he upon the clouds ascends (2)
216   day when the Christ ascends, high in the heavens to reign (R)
222   Rejoice, the Lord of life ascends in triumph (1)
277   from all saints the song ascends (3)
640   higher yet that star ascends (2)

ascension
215   mighty Lord, in thine ascension, we ... behold our own (3)
215   in thine ascension, we by faith behold our own (3)
219   His rising, his ascension sing with grateful adoration (2)
232   for he at the ascension was an apostle still (2/8-24)

ascribe
231, 232 ascribe all power and glory and praise to God alone (3)
253   with united breath, ascribe their conquest to the Lamb (2)
450, 451 to him all majesty ascribe (6)

ascribing
535   ascribing salvation to Jesus our King (2)

ashamed
53   Thus, if thou canst name him, not ashamed to claim him (3)
554   to bow and to bend we shan't be ashamed (1)

ashes
145   To bow the head in sackcloth and in ashes (2)
516   turn to dust and ashes in its heat consuming (2)

aside
318   here would I lay aside each earthly load (2)
439   that caused the Lord of bliss to lay aside his crown (1)
439   lay aside his crown for my soul (1)
552, 553 Cast care aside, lean on thy Guide (3)
691   nor let me ever stray from thee aside (3)

ask
10   all we ought to ask: room to deny ourselves (5)
44, 45   A healthy life we ask of you (3)
101   I ask thee to stay close by me for ever (3)
243   no shield I ask, no faithful friend (4)
253   We ask them whence their victory came (2)
267   Ask not how this should be, but worship and adore (3)
307   Thou art here, we ask not how (2)
419   before thy ever-blazing throne we ask no luster (3)
419   we ask no luster of our own (3)
433   We gather together to ask the Lord's blessing (1)

498	I ask no other sunshine than the sunshine of his face (3)
518	Here vouchsafe to all thy servants what they ask of thee (4)
518	what they ask of thee to gain (4)
617	we ask no victories that are not thine (3)
638, 639	I ask thee, who art thou? Tell me thy name (2)
643	thou hast stooped to ask of me the love of my poor heart (5)
687, 688	dost ask who that may be? Christ Jesus, it is he (2)
698	I know not how to ask or what to say (1)
711	Ask, and it shall be given you (RC)

asked

18	athirst and spent, you asked for aid (4a)
284	unmasked in every dress, in every combat foiled (3)

asking

528	asking ... world around us share your children's liberty (3)

asleep

101	the little Lord Jesus asleep on the hay (1)

aspiring

228	Enter each aspiring heart (3)
546	his own hand presents the prize to thine aspiring eye (3)

ass

92	ox and ass beside him from the cold would hide him (2)
107	ox and ass before him bow, and he is in the manger now (1)
110	the ass and oxen shared the roof with them (2)
115	mean estate where ox and ass are feeding (2)

assail

594, 595	assail his ways (2)

assailed

270	Art by art shall be assailed (4)

assaults

60	defend us while we dwell below from all assaults (5)
60	assaults of our dread foe (5)

assembled

201	the women three assembled there (2)
386, 387	glorious the assembled fires appear (3)
486	house of prayer, where we assembled in thy Name (3)
513	to the Church in faith assembled (2)

assembly

282, 283	may the assembly of the saints in heaven ... help us (5)

asses

98	Cradled in a stall was he with sleepy cows and asses (2)

assign

226, 227	thy blest seven-fold gift assign (5)

assigned
348   So, in the world where each duty assigned us (4)

assist
18   assist us to endure that light (1)
493   My gracious Master and my God, assist me to proclaim (2)
625   assist our song, for else the theme too high doth seem (1)

assisted
106   treading his steps, assisted by his grace (5)

assuage
522, 523   Who can faint when such a river ever ... thirst assuage (2)

assumed
496, 497   whole creation's Head and Lord ... assumed our very nature (2)

assure
273, 274   The words of Paul assure us of Christ's redeeming word (3)

assuring
528   Lord, you bless with words assuring (5)

astound
424   For the wonders that astound us (3)

astounds
61, 62   "Sleepers, wake" A voice astounds us (1)

astray
38, 39   let him never lead astray those you have ransomed (3)
105   save us all from Satan's power when we were gone astray (1)
563   heed not the treacherous voices that lure thy soul astray (2)
641   nor let me go astray (3)
703   without thy guiding hand we go astray (1)

asunder
525   by schisms rent asunder, by heresies distressed (3)

athirst
18   athirst and spent, you asked for aid (4a)

athlete
412   Athlete and band, loud cheering people (5)

atom
580   probed the secrets of the atom, yielding unimagined power (3)

atonement
74   Christ, who is the Promise, who has atonement made (2)
158   for our atonement ... God interceded (3)
495   by almighty love anointed, thou hast full atonement made (2)

attain
142   an Easter of unending joy we may attain at last (5)

584   that as to knowledge we attain we may in wisdom grow (2)

attained
14, 15 by a holy death attained, eternal glory may be gained (2)

attaining
48   at length our rest attaining, our endless Sabbath day (4)
159   a purer love attaining, may with thee acceptance find (5)

attend
365   our prayer attend (2)
390   surely his goodness and mercy shall ever attend thee (3)
509   Spirit divine, attend our prayers (1,5)
664   The sure provisions of my God attend me all my days (3)
665   splendor, light, and life attend him (3)

attending
58   thousand saints attending swell the triumph of his train (1)

attentive
334   one voice hearing, ears attentive to your word (2)

attest
135   cross and Easter Day attest God in man made manifest (4)

attesting
183   bright angels attesting, the shroud and napkin resting (6)

aught
151   For none may boast themselves of aught (2)
372   the one eternal God ere aught that now appears (1)
640   aught of joy or hope foretell (1)
682   with the hope of gaining aught, not seeking a reward (5)

author
146, 147 author of mercy, turn your face (3)
175   Rise from the grave now ... author of life and creation (4)
175   Thou Love who art author of concord (8)
179   Thou, of life the author, death didst undergo (5)
216   Thou Love who art author of concord (6)
515   Author of the new creation, come with unction (2)
545   Jesus, the author, finisher, rewarder of our faith (3)
717   Our father's God, to thee, author of liberty (4)

autumn
9   royal robes of autumn moors the golden gates of spring (2)
585   scholar's truth, flight of swallows, autumn leaves (1)

autumn's
288   autumn's rich o'erflowing stores (2)

avail
162   Still may thy power with us avail to save us sinners (5)

availeth
151   thy grace alone availeth (2)

ave
266   Nova, nova. Ave fit ex Eva (R)

avowed
564, 565   his first avowed intent to be a pilgrim (1)

await
225   on those who await his appearing (1)
624   I know not, O, I know not, what joys await us there (1)

awaited
97   stretching infant hands on high, Savior, long awaited (1)

awaits
555   the crown awaits the conquest (3)

awake
9   Awake, awake to love and work (4)
9   worlds awake to cry their blessings on the Lord of life (4)
11   Awake, my soul ... with the sun thy daily stage of duty run (1)
43   vigorous make to serve my God when I awake (3)
61, 62   Awake, Jerusalem, arise (1)
69   Lord, give us grace to awake us (3)
76   awake and hearken, for he brings glad tidings (1)
77   let every heart awake and sing the holy child
106   Christians awake, salute the happy morn (1)
181   Awake and sing the song of Moses and the Lamb (1)
212   Awake, arise, lift up your voice (1)
359   to human need their quickened hearts awake (2)
494   awake, my soul, and sing of him who died for thee (1)
540   Awake, thou Spirit of the watchmen (1)
546   Awake, my soul, stretch every nerve (1)
547   Awake, O sleeper, rise from death (1)
547   Awake, arise, go forth in faith (5)
717   let mortal tongues awake, let all that breathes partake (3)

awaken
569   bid not thy wrath in its terrors awaken (2)

awakes
73   life to joy awakes (1)
101   The cattle are lowing, the baby awakes (2)
530   until from night all the world awakes to light (5)
542   new life, new hope awakes, for all who own his sway (1)

awaking
427   When morning gilds the skies, my heart, awaking, cries (1)

aware
257   Aware of hidden deity (1)

away

24	nor dies the strain of praise away (3)
24	thy throne shall never ... pass away (4)
40, 41	you drive away the shadowed night (1)
59	Cast away the works of darkness, O ye children of the day (1)
63, 64	all wrong desires may burn away (2)
75	power and pomp of nations shall pass away like a dream away (2)
76	without thy grace we waste away like flowers (3)
101	Away in a manger, no crib for his bed (1)
112	heaven and earth shall flee away when he comes to reign (2)
167	There is a green hill far away, outside a city wall (1)
171	turn not from his griefs away (1)
184	take our sin and guilt away that with angels we may say (2)
185, 186	word of grace hath purged away the old and wicked leaven (4)
192	This joyful Eastertide, away with sin and sorrow (1)
213	Come away to the skies, my beloved (1)
213	on this festival day, come exulting away (1)
235	drove away the shadows, and filled the world with light (1)
270	Gabriel's message does away Satan's curse and ... sway (1)
290	from his field shall in that day all offenses purge away (3)
324	powers of hell may vanish as the darkness clears away (3)
344	call us, Savior, from the world away (3)
357	Every taint of evil, frailty and decay ... purge away (3)
357	good and gracious Savior, cleanse and purge away (3)
376	drive the dark of doubt away (1)
426	Heaven and earth must pass away (3)
454	on clouds triumphant, when the heavens shall pass away (4)
458	They rise, and needs will have my dear Lord made away (5)
471	The cross, it takes our guilt away (3)
472	lure us away from thee to endless night (3)
486	dreadful day when earth and heaven shall melt away (5)
517	One day within thy courts excels a thousand spent away (4)
541	to sow the tares, to snatch the seed away (2)
541	Away with gloomy doubts and faithless fear (3)
564, 565	Then fancies flee away; I'll fear not what men say (3)
591	take not thy thunder from us, but take away our pride (1)
602	neighbors are near-by and far away (2)
612	Prophecy will fade away, melting in the light of day (3)
616	to take away transgression, and rule in equity (1)
641	purge away my sin (1)
644	drives away our fear (1)
649, 650	chase the night of sin away (4)
664	one word of thy supporting breath drives ... fears away (2)
680	Time ... bears all our years away (5)
691	Now hear me while I pray, take all my guilt away (1)
691	bid darkness turn to day, wipe sorrows tears away (2)
702	far away my dwelling make (4)

awe

56	didst give the law, in cloud, and majesty, and awe (3)
83	we would embrace thee, with love and awe (5)
135	disciples filled with awe thy transfigured glory saw (4)
231	Praise for the light from heaven ... voice of awe (2/1-25)
232	whose heart with awe was stirred (2/8-15)
304	in awe and wonder to recall his life laid down for me (1)

| 435 | name with awe and wonder and with bated breath (4) |
| 475 | with awe appear before him (1) |

awed
| 413 | awed by his love his foes surrender (1) |

aweful
284	sad desire that aweful sight to see (5)
598	O aweful Love, which found no room in life (2)
643	thine endless wisdom, boundless power, and aweful purity (3)

awesome
| 337 | by this food, so awesome and so sweet, deliver us (4) |

awful
18	dark midday could not conceal your cry of awful agony (3c)
278	looked upon her Son ... reigning from the awful tree (2)
702	wondrous knowledge, awful might (2)

awhile
| 165, 166 | awhile the ancient rigor that thy birth bestowed, suspend (5) |
| 214 | Christ, awhile to mortals given (1) |

awoke
| 426 | Songs of praise awoke the morn (2) |
| 426 | awoke the morn when the Prince of Peace was born (2) |

Baal
| 18 | Elijah taunted Baal at noon (2b) |

babe
82	Babe ... world's Redeemer first revealed his sacred face (2)
94, 95	The heavenly Babe you there shall find (4)
103	The babe within a manger poor (2)
106	trace we the Babe, who hath retrieved our loss (5)
114	Within a lodge of broken bark the tender babe was found (2)
115	haste to bring him laud, the babe, the son of Mary (R)
257	lowly Virgin brings her new-born babe (2)

Babel
| 230 | by the triumph of the Son the curse of Babel was undone (2) |
| 230 | curse of Babel was undone when God did send the Spirit (2) |

baby
101	The cattle are lowing, the baby awakes (2)
102	where a mother laid her baby in a manger for his bed (1)
113	Oh sleep now, holy baby, with your head against my breast (1)

Babylon's
| 122, 123 | by Babylon's sad waters mourning exiles now are we (2) |
| 623 | through our long exile on Babylon's strand (4) |

back
| 89, 90 | world give back the song which now the angels sing (4) |
| 204 | thy touch can call us back to life again (4) |

400	You lead back home the child of God (6)
435	brought it back victorious, when from death he passed (2)
472	we render back the love thy mercy gave us (4)
664	brings my wandering spirit back when I forsake his ways (1)

bade
443	bade the fallen to come in, praised be his mercy (3)
572	your dying bade us sheathe the foolish sword (2)
572	bade us cease denying (2)

ball
| 409 | all move round the dark terrestrial ball (3) |
| 450, 451 | Let every kindred, every tribe on this terrestrial ball (6) |

balm
48	O balm of care and sadness, most beautiful, most bright (1)
175	pour out thy balm on our souls (8)
216	pour out thy balm on our souls (6)
232	with true balm of Gilead anoint us evermore (2/10-18)
345	thy peace in life, the balm of every pain (4)
357	heal them, Good Physician, with the balm of life (3)
375	With balm my inmost heart he fills (1)
408	with healing balm my soul he fills (1)
471	The balm of life, the cure of woe (5)
482	whose voice is contentment, whose presence is balm (4)
652, 653	thy coolness and thy balm (5)
676	There is a balm in Gilead to make the wounded whole (R)
676	there is a balm in Gilead to heal the sinsick soul (R)

band
12, 13	the third hour your faithful band was clothed with power (3)
233, 234	in heaven's hall a victor band (2)
236	King of the martyrs' noble band (1)
286	who are all this glorious band (1)
286	Whence comes all this glorious band (2)
298	stand among the glorious heavenly band (1)
298	heavenly band of every tribe and nation (1)
329, 330	mid the twelve, his chosen band (3)
353	join every husband, every wife in mutual love (3)
412	Athlete and band, loud cheering people (5)
527	Singing songs of expectation ... goes the pilgrim band (1)
527	onward goes the pilgrim band (1)
718	in beauty all the starry band of shining worlds (1)

bands
94, 95	all meanly wrapped in swathing bands (4)
145	of wickedness the grievous bands to loosen (3)
185, 186	Christ Jesus lay in death's strong bands (1)
526	greet the ever-living bands on the eternal shore (4)

Bane
| 441, 442 | Bane and blessing, pain and pleasure ... sanctified (4) |

banish
| 1, 2 | banish our weakness, health and wholeness sending (2) |

| 282, 283 | may he banish from us striving and hatred (2) |
| 312 | from light do thou not banish (3) |

banished

85, 86	his banished children to reclaim (5)
492	thence his banished ones to save (2)
576, 577	Banished now be anger, strife and every quarrel (2)

bank

| 76 | On Jordan's bank the Baptist's cry (1) |

banner

275	Marching with thy cross, their banner (3)
522, 523	Thus deriving from their banner, light ... and shade (3)
534	with the banner of Christ unfurled that the light (3)
556, 557	Your glorious banner wave on high (1,7)
561	lift high his royal banner, it must not suffer loss (1)
563	beneath his banner true (1)
720	O say does that star-spangled banner yet wave (1)
720	the star-spangled banner in triumph shall wave (2)

banners

161	The flaming banners of our King advance (1)
162	The royal banners forward go (1)
562	forward into battle, see, his banners go (1)

banquet

51	day of the Spirit, sign of heaven's banquet (3)
61, 62	call to come into the banquet hall (2)
202	The Lamb's high banquet called to share (1)
316, 317	This is the hour of banquet and of song (1)
339	whose grace unbounded hath this wondrous banquet founded (1)
339	from this banquet let me measure, Lord ... its treasure (3)
360, 361	here may thy servants, at the mystic banquet (2)

baptism

| 370 | his baptism in the Jordan river (2) |
| 547 | one Lord, one Faith ... Baptism, one Father of us all (3) |

baptismal

| 299 | revive in us baptismal grace (3) |
| 349 | from their bright baptismal day you have led them (1) |

Baptist

| 232 | All praise for John the Baptist (2/6-24) |

Baptist's

| 76 | On Jordan's bank the Baptist's cry (1) |
| 76 | Baptist's cry announces that the Lord is nigh (1) |

baptize

121	Baptize us with your Spirit, Lord (4)
139	trust in Christ who will baptize with water and the Spirit (3)
297	baptize all nations with your Word (2)
528	In my name baptize and teach (2)

baptized

120	O Christ, may we baptized from sin, go forth with you (5)
121	Christ, when for us you were baptized (1)
139	baptized by John, there came a voice from heaven saying (1)
149	knowing ourselves baptized into your death (2)
187	In that cloud and in that sea ... baptized were we (3)
187	buried and baptized were we (3)
294	Baptized in water, sealed by the Spirit (1-3)
295	God's children by adoption, baptized into his grace (1)
296	Baptized we live with God the Three in One (3)
298	All who believe and are baptized shall see (1)
298	baptized shall see the Lord's salvation (1)
298	baptized into the death of Christ (1)
443	the Pure baptized, the Life who died (5)
448, 449	For us baptized (2)

bare

119	offered gifts most rare at that manger rude and bare (3)
204	fields of our hearts that dead and bare have been (4)

bark

114	Within a lodge of broken bark the tender babe was found (2)
627	when waves would whelm our tossing bark (3)

barn

104	A barn shall harbor heaven (1)

Barnabas

231	For Barnabas we praise you (2/6-11)

barred

74	For him let doors be opened, no hearts against him barred (1)

barren

226, 227	what is barren bring to flower (4)
658	longs the deer ... in parched and barren ways (1)
690	pilgrim through this barren land (1)

bars

175	heaven her gates unbars, flinging her increase of light (3)
191	Now the iron bars are broken (2)
208	the bars from heaven's high portals fell (4)
216	heaven her gates unbars, flinging her increase of light (2)

Bartholomew

232	Praise for your blest apostle surnamed Bartholomew (2/8-24)

bated

435	name with awe and wonder and with bated breath (4)

bathes

85, 86	Today, as year by year its light bathes all the world (4)
85, 86	bathes all the world in radiance bright (4)

battle

165, 166	Sing, my tongue, the glorious battle (1)
188, 189	fought the fight, the battle won (1)
208	The strife is o'er, the battle done (1)
238, 239	by contempt of every anguish, by unyielding battle done (2)
555	now, O King eternal, we lift our battle song (1)
561	this day the noise of battle, the next the victor's song (4)
562	forward into battle, see, his banners go (1)
655	I shall not fear the battle, if thou art by my side (1)
687, 688	he must win the battle (2)

battlefield

222	triumph from earth's battlefield (1)

beacon

236	beacon by night and cloud by day (1)

beam

5	Spirit's sanctifying beam upon our earthly senses stream (2)
93	brighter visions beam afar (3)
180	a brighter Easter beam on our longing eyes shall stream (4)

beaming

119	leading onward, beaming bright (1)
441, 442	When the sun of bliss is beaming light and love (3)
496, 497	with mercy beaming from afar (1)
640	see that glory-beaming star (1)

beams

6, 7	joyless is the day's return till thy mercy's beams I see (2)
55	Our faith reflects those radiant beams (5)
111	Son of God, love's pure light radiant beams (3)
111	radiant beams from thy holy face (3)
124	What star is this, with beams so bright (1)
400	Bright burning sun with golden beams (1)
412	Limestone and beams, loud building workers (4)
440	till thy Spirit breaks our night with the beams of truth (2)
440	beams of truth unclouded (2)
543	He gilds thy morning face with beams that cannot fade (2)
640	Watchman, will its beams alone gild the spot (2)

bear

5	to give us grace our wrongs to bear (4)
12, 13	Now help us bear our daily load (2)
73	child, to bear, and fight, and die (2)
74	he would have us bear it so he can make us free (4)
125, 126	joyous as when the reapers bear their ... treasures home (2)
142	As thou didst hunger bear and thirst (3)
162	ordained those holy limbs to bear (3)
167	We may not know, we cannot tell what pains he had to bear (2)
171	learn of him to bear the cross (2)
245	the faith to bear your Name (3)
246	love that cannot cease to bear our human anguish (4)
263, 264	Hail, Mary, you shall bear a son (2)
266	the Savior Jesus shall you bear (4)

267	virgin born of David's line shall bear the promised seed (2)
305, 306	one Name we bear, one Bread of life we break (3)
336	glory veiling so that we may bear the sight (2)
350	in power to do and grace to bear (2)
365	thy sacred witness bear in this glad hour (3)
400	All you that pain and sorrow bear (5)
402, 403	above all, the heart must bear the longest part (2)
411	His mercies bear in mind (2)
447	troubles that are ours to bear are trials we cannot flee (3)
455, 456	read thee best in him who came to bear for us the cross (3)
484, 485	The cross meanwhile we bear (2)
489	He sent no angel of his host to bear this mighty word (2)
537	with us the cross to bear, for Christ our Lord (3)
539	Send heralds forth to bear the message glorious (3)
541	to young and old the Gospel gladness bear (4)
570, 571	all who bear its daily stress (1)
573	his saving cross no nation yet will bear (2)
610	burdens your compassion bids us bear (4)
621, 622	Now with gladness, now with courage, bear the burden (5)
621, 622	bear the burden laid on thee (5)
625	My soul, bear thou thy part, triumph in God above (4)
632	to bear before the nations thy true light as of old (3)
635	bear thee through the evil days (1)
659, 660	help me bear the strain of toil, the fret of care (1)
667	It can bring with it nothing but he will bear us through (3)
675	his strength shall bear your spirit up (2)
675	only those who bear the cross may hope to wear ... crown (5)
682	for us didst bear the nails and spear (2)
682	for us didst bear ... manifold disgrace (2)
695, 696	still evil days bring burdens hard to bear (2)

bearer

495	Hail, thou universal Savior, bearer of our sin and shame (1)
618	Thou bearer of the eternal Word (2)

bearers

586	workers, burden bearers of the earth (1)

bearest

164	Our sins, not thine, thou bearest, Lord (2)

bearing

128	bearing gifts we traverse afar (1)
160	Very God himself is bearing all the sufferings of time (3)
371	Move on the waters' face bearing the gifts of grace (3)

bears

57, 58	dear tokens of his passion still his dazzling body bears (3
136, 137	from the cloud, the Holy One bears record to the only Son (2)
223, 224	Thou who did our forebears guide (4)
245	Our thanks we raise that all John wrote bears witness (3)
410	in his hand he gently bears us (3)
471	he bears our sins upon the tree (2)
473	Each new-born servant of the Crucified bears ... seal (2)
473	bears on the brow the seal of him who died (2)

| 494 | takes and bears them for his own, that all in him may rest (2) |
| 680 | Time ... bears all our years away (5) |

beast

| 156 | thy humble beast pursues his road with palms ... strowed (1) |
| 293 | one was slain by a fierce wild beast (2) |

beasts

98	but the very beasts could see that he all men surpasses (2)
117, 118	low lies his head with the beasts of the stall (2)
463, 464	you will see rare beasts and have unique adventures (1)
568	sharing a stable with beasts at thy birth (2)
597	as beasts and cattle calmly graze (2)

beat

542	to ploughshare beat the sword, to pruning hook the spear (2)
558	O how our hearts beat high with joy whene'er we hear (1)
599	yet, with a steady beat (2)

beatific

| 275 | all truth and knowledge see in the beatific vision (4) |
| 275 | beatific vision of the blessed Trinity (4) |

beauteous

91	Break forth, O beauteous light, and usher in the morning (1)
124	more beauteous than the noonday light (1)
284	his beauteous face in heaven ye view (1)
640	Watchman, does its beauteous ray ... hope foretell (1)

beautiful

48	O balm of care and sadness, most beautiful, most bright (1)
405	All things bright and beautiful (R)
643	how beautiful thy mercy seat in depths of burning light (1)
643	How wonderful, how beautiful, the sight of thee must be (3)
719	O beautiful for spacious skies, for amber waves of grain (1)
719	O beautiful for heroes proved in liberating strife (2)
719	O beautiful for patriot dream that sees beyond the years (3)

beauty

46	for joy of beauty not our own (2)
73	beauty gilds the eastern hills (1)
73	light and beauty brings (5)
114	a ragged robe of rabbit skin enwrapped his beauty round (2)
114	boy, who brings you beauty, peace, and joy (4)
128	star with royal beauty bright (R)
145	God brings new beauty nigh (1)
145	his beauty to come near (2)
162	O tree of beauty, tree most fair (3)
165, 166	the King of heavenly beauty gently on thine arms extend (5)
168, 169	Thy beauty, long desired, hath vanished from our sight (2)
175	Lo the fair beauty of earth (1)
292	thine the beauty ... joy with which the years are crowned (1)
416	For the beauty of the earth, for the beauty of the skies (1)
416	For the beauty of each hour of the day and of the night (2)
475	let thy radiant beauty light mine eyes to see my duty (3)

600, 601	O day of God, draw nigh in beauty and in power (1)
621, 622	endued with heavenly beauty (4)
628	to teach the beauty of your ways (3)
652, 653	let our ordered lives confess the beauty of thy peace (4)
665	beauty springeth out of nought (3)
681	All beauty speaks of thee: the mountains and the rivers (3)
681	Thou hidden fount of love, of peace ... truth ... beauty (5)
718	in beauty all the starry band of shining worlds (1)

beaver
114	gifts of fox and beaver-pelt (3)

became
77	A maid in lowly human place became ... the chosen (3)
110	thus that manger poor became a throne (4)
143	John, the Bridegroom's friend, became the herald (3)
232	as once for our salvation your mother she became (2/8-15)
277	Son most holy, who became her little child (1)

beckons
31, 32	beckons us to worship you (2)
580	As each far horizon beckons, may it challenge us anew (4)

become
104	A stall become a shrine (1)
157	for you answered me and have become my salvation (R)
157	has become the chief cornerstone (R)
509	let thy Church on earth become blest as the Church above (4)

becomes
116	Thus it becomes us to fulfill all righteousness, he said (2)
231	his witness in his gospel becomes victorious song (2/4-25)

bed
42	their white wings above me, watching round my bed (5)
92	Wise Men three to him led, kneel they low by his bed (3)
101	Away in a manger, no crib for his bed (1)
102	where a mother laid her baby in a manger for his bed (1)
119	As with joyful steps they sped to that lowly manger bed (2)
471	gilds the bed of death with light (4)

befall
488	Heart of my heart, whatever befall (3)

befits
67	as befits his holy reign (3)

befitteth
414	Honor great our God befitteth, who his majesty can reach (2)

befitting
55	a wondrous birth, befitting God (1)

befriend
320	Jesus, of thy love befriend us (5)

390   who with his love doth befriend thee (3)

befriended
168, 169   that I may fight befriended (5)

befriending
329-331   faith, our outward sense befriending, makes ... clear (5)

began
82   Of the Father's love begotten, ere the worlds began to be (1)
345   with thee began, with thee shall end the day (2)
494   Crown him the Son of God before the worlds began (2)
681   the world began, endures, and shall endure (1)

begin
63, 64   bid the saints their reign begin (3)
73   let the endless bliss begin, by weary saints foretold (4)
94, 95   good will ... begin and never cease (6)
148   in us the work of grace begin (4)
156   O Christ, thy triumphs now begin o'er captive death (2)
201   see where he lay; let joy begin (3)
210   Now let the heavens be joyful, let earth her song begin (3)
237   who will first begin it (3)
290   all is safely gathered in, ere the winter storms begin (1)
436   Let new and nobler life begin (5)
506, 507 life in whom all lives begin (1)
613   Thy kingdom come, O God ! Thy rule, O Christ, begin (1)

beginning
433   so from the beginning the fight we were winning (2)
435   who from the beginning was the mighty Word (1)

begins
69   to see the branch that begins to bloom (3)
444   On prisoners of darkness the sun begins to rise (3)

begotten
55   All praise, O unbegotten God (6)
63, 64   begotten of the Father's might (1)
82   Of the Father's love begotten, ere the worlds began to be (1)
83   only begotten Son of the Father (2)
159   when she saw the crucifixion of the sole-begotten one (2)
175   Redeemer, Son of the Father supreme, only begotten of God (6)
216   Son of the Father supreme, only begotten of God (4)
307   first-begotten from the dead (1)
360, 361 Only begotten, Word of God eternal (1)
381   to ... Light of Light begotten, praise be sung eternally (4)
581   Let us recall that in our midst dwells God's begotten Son (5)

begun
106   with them the joyful tidings first begun (1)
120   How blest that mission then begun (4)
140, 141 Wilt thou forgive that sin, where I begun (1)
205   we sing for life in us begun (5)
208   the song of triumph has begun (1)

392	The heirs of grace have found glory begun below (3)
417, 418	the Lamb who was slain has begun his reign. Alleluia (5)
426	heaven with alleluias rang when creation was begun (1)
452	all is ended, all begun (4)
527	one the march in God begun (3)
580	each endeavor well begun (4)
599	facing the rising sun of our new day begun (1)
614	new lamps be lit, new tasks begun (3)
616	Hail, in the time appointed, his reign on earth begun (1)
671	no less days ... than when we'd first begun (5)

beheld

18	At noontime Paul beheld your light (4b)
284	Ye in the wilderness beheld the Tempter spoiled (3)
346	beheld afar that life which soon shall be (2)

behest

| 24 | the darkness falls at thy behest (1) |

behind

187	Egypt's chains behind we cast (1)
370	Christ be with me, Christ within me, Christ behind me (6)
506, 507	his the truth behind the wisdoms (3)
545	forgetting things behind (5)
677	behind a frowning providence he hides a smiling face (4)

behold

57, 58	Every eye shall now behold him robed in dreadful majesty (2)
63	with thy saints for evermore behold thee (4)
63	behold thee, love thee, and adore (4)
64	with thy saints for evermore behold thee (4)
64	behold thee, love thee, and adore (4)
77	Behold, the world's creator wears the form and fashion (2)
81	with Mary we behold it, the Virgin Mother kind (2)
83	come, and behold him born the King of angels (1)
87	late in time behold him come (2)
99	behold, throughout the heavens there shone a holy light (1)
106	Behold, I bring good tidings of a Savior's birth (2)
116	At Jordan's stream, behold (1)
119	As with gladness men of old did the guiding star behold (1)
128	Glorious now behold him arise (5)
149	Eternal Lord of love, behold your Church (1)
209	in realms of clearer light we may behold you as you are (4)
215	while their eager eyes behold him (2)
215	mighty Lord, in thine ascension, we ... behold our own (3)
215	in thine ascension, we by faith behold our own (3)
231	Instill in us his longing, your glory to behold (2/12-27)
270	so, behold, all the gates of heaven unfold (R)
308, 309	Grant when the veil is riven, we may behold, in heaven (3)
308, 309	we may behold, in heaven, thy countenance divine (3)
314	Jesus, whom now hidden, I by faith behold (4)
329, 331	faith alone the true heart waketh to behold the mystery (4)
347	till in his kingdom we behold his face (1)
401	we shall behold his face, we shall his power adore (2)
410	Angels, help us to adore him, ye behold him face to face (4)

436	behold the King of glory waits (1)
493	ye blind, behold, your Savior comes (5)
545	Behold a Witness nobler still who trod affliction's path (3)
587	that they may all behold thy face (2)
625	now, from sin released, behold the Savior's face (2)
658	O when shall I behold thy face, thou Majesty divine (2)
685	rise to worlds unknown and behold thee on thy throne (3)
692	Behold, I freely give the living water (2)
697	Before the cross of him who died, behold, I prostrate fall (2)

beholding
179	thou from heaven beholding human nature's fall (4)

beholds
278	beholds her Son and Savior reigning as the Lord of love (4)
314	tranced as it beholds thee, shrined within the cloud (1)

being
46	we, this marvel seeing, forget our selfish being (2)
175	fount of our being, light that dost lighten all (7)
216	now flow in us, fount of our being (5)
225	all praise to the fount of our being (4)
278	heavenly breath of God's own being (3)
339	Fount, whence all my being floweth (2)
419	Lord of all being, throned afar (1)
429	praise ... while life and thought and being last (1,4)
475	thou alone shalt be known Lord of all our being (2)
476	Although his being is too bright for human eyes to scan (2)
494	died eternal life to bring and lives that death may die (3)
573	How shall we love thee, holy hidden Being (5)

belief
6	scatter all my unbelief (3)
209	Help then, O Lord, our unbelief (3)
284	When hope was dim, and pain and grief beyond belief (4)
677	Blind unbelief is sure to err and scan his work in vain (6)

belief's
242	at once he rose to full belief's unclouded height (4)

believe
40, 41	with your right hand you will protect those who believe (3)
40, 41	those who believe and trust in you (3)
167	but we believe it was for us he hung and suffered there (2)
209	but we believe him near (1)
228	As your promise we believe (5)
298	All who believe and are baptized shall see (1)
314	I believe whate'er the Son of God hath told (2)
322	what that Word did make it, I do believe and take it (2)
335	they who believe in me shall not thirst (1)
335	who believe in me, even if they die ... live for ever (4)
335	Yes, Lord, we believe that you are the Christ (5)
493	mournful broken hearts rejoice, the humble poor believe (4)
500	practice all that we believe (3)
505	unless thy grace the power should give, none can believe (2)

505	none can believe in Christ and live (2)
552, 553	only believe ... see that Christ is all in all to thee (4)
670	my doubts I sorely feel, thy sure promise I believe (3)
693	because thy promise I believe (4)

believed

108	who truly have believed that on this blessed morn (1)
386, 387	seers that stupendous truth believed (4)
671	how precious ... grace appear the hour I first believed (2)

believer's

644	How sweet the Name of Jesus sounds in a believer's ear (1)

believers

68	Rejoice, rejoice, believers, and let your lights appear (1)
327, 328	to all believers life eternal yields (6)

believes

460, 461	he is near us, faith believes, nor questions how (2)
673	blessed is she who believes in the Lord (1)

believing

48	We journey on, believing, renewed with heavenly might (3)
206	not faithless, but believing be (4)
334	in your Body, firm believing (2)

belong

36	To thee of right belong all praise of holy songs (3)
148	to whom the words of life belong (1)
404	telling the wonders which to you belong (2)
425	All praise and thanks to him belong who came to ... free (2)
484, 485	wisdom and might to thee belong (2)
537	inspired with hope and praise, to Christ belong (4)
615	But the slow watches of the night not less to God belong (2)

beloved

71, 72	heaven's eternal arches ring with thy beloved Name (4)
112	worshiped the beloved with a kiss (3)
116	This is my Son, my well-beloved in whom I take delight (3)
116	The Savior Jesus, well-beloved (4)
121	God called you his beloved Son ... his servant true (2)
129, 130	This is God's beloved Son (4)
139	This is my dear beloved Son upon whom rests my favor (1)
168, 169	mourn thee, well beloved, yet thank thee for thy death (3)
213	Come away to the skies, my beloved (1)
232	For Luke, beloved physician, all praise (2/10-18)
285	beloved on earth, approved of thee (4)
338	bring before thee Christ thy well-beloved (1)
695, 696	we take it ... out of so good and so beloved a hand (3)

below

11, 43	praise him, all creatures here below (4)
60	defend us while we dwell below from all assaults (5)
125, 126	peace abound below (5)
214	blessings on his Church below (3)

252	when the cup of human woe first he tasted here below (4)
310, 311	opening wide the gate of heaven to us below (1)
329, 330	Given for us, and condescending to be born for us below (2)
349	gifts of blessing to bestow on your waiting Church below (1)
367	with his holy Church below (2)
372	everywhere above, below, his will obeys (2)
380	From all that dwell below the skies let ... praise arise (1)
380	praise him, all creatures here below (3)
392	The heirs of grace have found glory begun below (3)
398	not a plant or flower below but makes thy glories known (3)
419	Lord of all life, below, above (3)
426	Saints below, with heart and voice ... rejoice (5)
455, 456	we read thee in the earth below (2)
462	justice, from her heavenly bower, look down on us below (2)
467	what are we that he should show so much love to us below (2)
471	the sinner's refuge here below (5)
475	Where I go here below, let me bow before thee (4)
480	Like him may we be found below in wisdom's path of peace (1)
483	the joy of all who dwell above, the joy of all below (3)
483	They suffer with their Lord below (5)
493	saints below and saints above (6)
510	See how we trifle here below, fond of these earthly toys (2)
538	let all be, below, above, one in joy, and light and love (2)
580	windows ... stare on canyoned streets below (2)
625	Ye saints, who toil below, adore your heavenly King (3)

bench

| 611 | praising God by labor at his bench (3) |

bend

60	At your great Name, O Jesus, now all knees must bend (4)
83	we too will thither bend our joyful footsteps (4)
89, 90	above its sad and lowly plains they bend on hovering wing (2)
104	The stars shall bend their voices (1,4)
119	to bend the knee before him whom heaven and earth adore (2)
139	till God's will is fully done he will not bend or waver (1)
151	Bend down thy gracious ear to me (1)
165	Bend thy boughs, O tree of glory (5)
165	Thy relaxing sinews bend (5)
166	Bend thy boughs, O tree of glory (5)
166	Thy relaxing sinews bend (5)
223, 224	Lord, to you your people bend (3)
226, 227	Bend the stubborn heart and will (4)
366	adoring, bend the knee and confess the mystery (4)
554	to bow and to bend we shan't be ashamed (1)
594, 595	bend our pride to thy control (3)

bended

| 96 | come, adore on bended knee Christ, the Lord (3) |
| 615 | Thy kingdom come, on bended knee the passing ages pray (1) |

bending

89, 90	from angels bending near the earth (1)
93	Saints before the altar bending (4)
329-331	Therefore we, before him bending (5)

beneath

12, 13	you stumbled, Lord, beneath its weight (2)
43	keep me, King of kings, beneath thine own almighty wings (1)
67	mourning 'neath their sorrows' load (1)
89, 90	beneath the heavenly hymn have rolled two thousand years (3)
168, 169	Ah, keep my heart thus moved to stand thy cross beneath (3)
174	hell's fierce powers beneath thee lie (3)
202	all sufficient Sacrifice, beneath thee hell defeated lies (4)
211	Then shout beneath the racing skies (2)
230	each Apostle spoke the word beneath the Spirit's thunder (1)
243	crushed beneath the stones (3)
276	he knelt beneath the olive shade (4)
278	beneath the cross of Jesus ... weight of suffering knew (2)
314	who thy glory hidest 'neath these shadows mean (1)
369	still how far beneath thy feet our ... knowledge lies (3)
370	Christ beneath me, Christ above me (6)
375	beneath thy shadowing pinions (2)
386, 387	from whose right arm, beneath whose eyes (1)
386, 387	at once, above, beneath, around, all nature ... replied (2)
480	beneath his watchful eye (2)
486	above, beneath us, and around, both dead and living (2)
498	Beneath the cross of Jesus I fain would take my stand (1)
526	One family we dwell in him, one Church, above, beneath (2)
563	beneath his banner true (1)
599	shadowed beneath thy hand may we for ever stand (3)
624	beneath thy contemplation sink heart and voice oppressed (1)
667	beneath the spreading heavens no creature but is fed (3)

benediction

518	thy fullest benediction shed within its walls alway (3)

benefits

228	all the benefits the earth, you bring to maturity (3)
411	forget not all his benefits ! The Lord to thee is kind (2)

benign

124	leads them on with power benign to seek the Giver (3)
514	for all thy grace and power benign (1)

bent

149	moved by your love and toward your presence bent (1)
363	to thee all knees are bent, all voices pray (1)

bereft

574, 575	for lives bereft of purpose high, forgive (3)

beseech

360, 361	Lord, we beseech thee, as we throng thy temple (5)

beseecheth

248, 249	who in prayer this Name beseecheth ... comfort findeth (3)

beset

27, 28	Lest we, beset by doubt and strife forget (3)

564, 565   Who so beset him round with dismal stories (2)

beside
92   ox and ass beside him from the cold would hide him (2)
260   beside his spouse ... he joins the heavenly song (4)
276   he stood with thee beside the dead (3)
362   only thou art holy, there is none beside thee (3)
370   Christ before me, Christ beside me, Christ to win me (6)
433   Beside us to guide us, our God with us joining (2)
472   walk thou beside us lest the tempting byways lure us (3)
476   earthly values stand beside the manger and the cross (3)
517   Beside thine altars ... the swallows find a nest (2)
569   falsehood and wrong shall not tarry beside thee (3)
598   pride, overthrown, went down to dust beside thee (2)
645, 646   I fear no ill with thee, dear Lord, beside me (4)
652, 653   simple trust like theirs who heard beside the Syrian sea (2)
664   pastures fresh he makes me feed beside the living stream (1)

bespeaks
381   Thy strong word bespeaks us righteous (3)

best
47   best of gifts, thyself bestow (5)
117, 118   Brightest and best of the stars of the morning (1,5)
151   yea, e'en the best life faileth (2)
161   The best are shamed before that wood (5)
198   best and greatest shinest (1)
198   of seasons, best, divinest (1)
226, 227   Thou, of comforters the best (2)
258   love thee most and serve thee best (2)
288   may we give thee of our best (3)
337   then for those, our dearest and our best ... we appeal (3)
339   Joy, the best that any knoweth (2)
434   which ... best is writ ... power ... wisdom, or the love (3)
455, 456   read thee best in him who came to bear for us the cross (3)
488   thou my best thought, by day or by night (1)
549, 550   serve and love thee best of all (5)
586   Jesus ... divine Companion, help us all to work our best (3)
612   but the greatest of the three, and the best, is love (4)
631   all the best we have we owe thee (1)
703   through joy or sorrow, as thou deemest best (3)
705   With gratitude and humble trust we bring our best to thee (3)

bestow
12, 13   Bestow your Spirit on us now (3)
40, 41   bestow on us who rest in you ... a quiet night (2)
47   best of gifts, thyself bestow (5)
214   Hark, his gracious lips bestow (3)
310, 311   thine aid supply, thy strength bestow (1)
349   gifts of blessing to bestow on your waiting Church below (1)
425   He only is to be adored for he alone can strength bestow (3)
458   He came from his blest throne salvation to bestow (2)
584   yet greater far this gift, O God, bestow (2)
665   Daily ... almighty Giver boundless gifts on us bestow (4)

bestowed
131, 132	in streams that nature ne'er bestowed (4)
165, 166	awhile the ancient rigor that thy birth bestowed, suspend (5)
213	days, by our heavenly Father bestowed (2)
300	Glory ... for our food now bestowed render we the Donor (1)

bestowest
175	treading the pathway of death, life ... bestowest on all (4)
320	who on earth such food bestowest (6)

bestowing
199, 200	bestowing that thy peace (4)
516	kindle it, thy holy flame bestowing (1)

Bethlehem
78, 79	O little town of Bethlehem, how still we see thee lie (1)
78, 79	O holy Child of Bethlehem, descend to us, we pray (5)
83	come ye, O come ye to Bethlehem (1)
87	born in Bethlehem (1)
92	Bethlehem saw his birth (2)
96	Come to Bethlehem and see him whose birth the angels sing (3)
98	All the little boys he killed at Bethlehem in his fury (3)
103	A child is born in Bethlehem (1)
105	how that in Bethlehem was born the Son of God by name (2)
106	In Bethlehem the happy shepherds sought to see (4)
109	o'er Bethlehem it took its rest (4)
110	She laid him in a stall at Bethlehem (2)
127	Bethlehem thou dost all excel (1)
135	branch of royal David's stem in thy birth at Bethlehem (1)
246	In Bethlehem a new-born boy was hailed with songs (1)
265	in Bethlehem, all on a Christmas morn (4)
307	as of old in Bethlehem (3)
611	Christ the worker, born in Bethlehem (1)

Bethlehem's
128	Born a King on Bethlehem's plain (2)
492	bowed himself to Bethlehem's cave (2)

betide
635	he'll give thee strength whate'er betide thee (1)

betray
231	not betray our calling but serve you to the end (2/2-24)
665	sword and crown betray our trust (2)

betrayed
18	betrayed, forsaken, all alone (3a)
146, 147	help us, lest ... we cause your Name to be betrayed (4)
448, 449	For us to wicked hands betrayed, scourged, mocked (4)

better
97	Better witness to thy worth (3)
244	the better Eden planted by our Lord most dear (2)
304	His presence ... is in such friendship better known (4)

573   Bind us in thine own love for better seeing thy Word (5)
629   let a new and better hope within our hearts be stirred (1)

between
337   between our sins and their reward, we set the passion (2)
720   between their loved homes and the war's desolation (2)

bewildering
363   through seas dry-shod, through weary wastes bewildering (2)

beyond
77   in ways beyond all thought (3)
109   shining in the east beyond them far (2)
214   Lord beyond our mortal sight (4)
248, 249   Name beyond what words can tell (2)
256   he saw the love of God ... beyond the law (3)
284   When hope was dim, and pain and grief beyond belief (4)
289   days of old have dowered us with gifts beyond all praise (3)
321   Bread that lives beyond the tomb (3)
372   first, the last, beyond all thought his timeless years (1)
422   Not far beyond the sea, nor high above the heavens (1)
455, 456   beyond all knowledge and all thought (1)
491   Far beyond the seraph's thought (2)
513   with the peace beyond compare (3)
524   Beyond my highest joy I prize her heavenly ways (3)
624   what radiancy of glory, what bliss beyond compare (1)
627   guide and chart wherein we read of realms beyond the sky (2)
633   one with him beyond all telling (4)
715   the falling tear in mercy flowed beyond all bound (RC)
719   O beautiful for patriot dream that sees beyond the years (3)

Bible's
630   word was written in the Bible's sacred page (3)

bid
56   bid thou our sad divisions cease (7)
63, 64   bid the saints their reign begin (3)
76   bid the fallen sinner stand (4)
179   show thy face in brightness, bid the nations see (6)
286   painful conflict o'er, God has bid them weep no more (4)
345   Then, when thy voice shall bid our conflict cease (4)
357   there, the warfare ended, bid them rest in peace (2)
367   bid we thus our anthem flow (2)
486   Eternal, bid thy Spirit rest (4)
521   bid thy Church increase, in breadth and length (1)
526   when the word is given bid Jordan's narrow stream divide (5)
531   bid mercy triumph over wrath (3)
569   bid not thy wrath in its terrors awaken (2)
605   What sacrifice desire, or tribute bid you bring (1)
608   bid its angry tumult cease (3)
616   to help the poor and needy, and bid the weak be strong (2)
674   bid resentment cease (4)
690   bid my anxious fears subside (3)
691   bid darkness turn to day, wipe sorrows tears away (2)

bidd'st

579   who bidd'st the mighty ocean deep its ... limits keep (1)
693   that thou bidd'st me come to thee (1)

bidden

308, 309   O Jesus, by thee bidden, we here adore thee (3)

bids

304   As Christ breaks bread and bids us share (3)
320   today the new oblation ... bids us feast in glad array (4)
493   Name that ... bids our sorrows cease (3)
582, 583   yea, bids us seize the whole of life and build its glory (4)
610   burdens your compassion bids us bear (4)

billion

394, 395   your gospel claims one family with a billion names (4)

billows

187   through the billows Israel led (2)

bind

56   bind in one the hearts of all mankind (7)
71, 72   He comes, the broken heart to bind (3)
228   remove our stains; bind up all our injuries (4)
251   neither time nor space can limit, hold, or bind (1)
255   grace, by ways mysterious, our sinful wrath can bind (3)
319   No greater love than this to you could bind us (2)
319   Bind our hearts as one we implore you (2)
348   help us to make those decisions that bind us (4)
348   bind us, Lord, to yourself, in obedience and joy (4)
370   I bind unto myself today the strong Name of the Trinity (1)
370   I bind this day to me for ever ... Christ's incarnation (2)
370   I bind unto myself today (2)
370   I bind unto myself the power of the great love (3)
370   bind unto myself today the virtues of the starlit heaven (4)
370   I bind unto myself today the power of God (5)
370   bind unto myself the Name ... strong Name of the Trinity (7)
568   bind in thy love every nation and race (4)
573   Bind us in thine own love for better seeing thy Word (5)
587   O Spirit, who dost bind our hearts in unity (3)
591   bind all our lives together, smite us and save us all (3)
629   dares to bind to one's own sense the oracles of heaven (2)
681   tried with thoughts uncouth, in feeble words to bind thee (2)
686   Let thy goodness ... bind my wandering heart to thee (3)

binding

511   Holy Spirit, ever binding age to age and soul to soul (2)
511   binding ... in a fellowship unending (2)
518   binding all the Church in one (1)

bird

8   black-bird has spoken like the first bird (1)
376   flashing sea, chanting bird and flowing fountain (2)
405   each little bird that sings (1)

birds

114	when all the birds had fled (1)
211	The birds do sing on every bough (1)
291	the winds and waves obey him, by him the birds are fed (2)

birth

27, 28	you brought all things to glorious birth (1)
48	This day at the creation, the light first had its birth (2)
54	Marvel ... that the Lord chose such a birth (1)
54	Wondrous birth ... wondrous child of the Virgin undefiled (2)
55	reveal yourself in virgin birth (1)
55	the birth which ages all adore (1)
55	a wondrous birth, befitting God (1)
78, 79	O morning stars, together proclaim the holy birth (2)
80	this new-born child of lowly birth shall be the joy (2)
82	O that birth for ever blessed (2)
87	born to give us second birth (3)
88	one with us in human birth (2)
92	Bethlehem saw his birth (2)
93	who sang creation's story now proclaim Messiah's birth (1)
96	Come to Bethlehem and see him whose birth the angels sing (3)
97	By this lowly birth of mine, sinner, riches ... thine (2)
99	chorus that hailed our Savior's birth (1)
106	Behold, I bring good tidings of a Savior's birth (2)
111	Jesus, Lord, at thy birth (3)
127	the star that told his birth (2)
131, 132	he who offers heavenly birth sought not the kingdoms (1)
133, 134	O Light of Light, Love given birth (1)
135	branch of royal David's stem in thy birth at Bethlehem (1)
165, 166	awhile the ancient rigor that thy birth bestowed, suspend (5)
263, 264	most blest to bring to human birth the long-desired (3)
267	the incarnate Savior's birth (5)
271, 272	Christ ... fulfilled that witness at his birth (3)
277	our very brother, takes our nature by his birth (1)
284	for such a birth ye sang aloud (2)
292	kindly earth with timely birth may yield her fruits again (2)
297	Forbid us not this second birth (2)
399	he made the sea and land, he brought the world to birth (2)
409	repeats the story of her birth (2)
416	for the love ... from our birth over and around us lies (1)
426	songs of praise shall hail their birth (3)
432	Praise him upon earth ... all ye of new birth (2)
476	makes birth and death his own (4)
480	he chose an humble birth (1)
525	her charter of salvation, one Lord, one faith, one birth (2)
568	sharing a stable with beasts at thy birth (2)
573	rulers ... still fail to bring us to the blissful birth (4)
586	by thy lowly human birth ... come to join the workers (1)
600, 601	O day of God, draw nigh as at creation's birth (5)
603, 604	through ... every birth, to draw an answering love (1)
616	love, joy, hope, like flowers spring in his path to birth (3)
633	touch our hearts and bring to birth faith and hope (1)
640	gild the spot that gave them birth (2)
673	first one ... to know of the birth of Jesus was the Maid (1)

biting
519, 520   Many a blow and biting sculpture polished ... stones (4)

bitter
80   who hears your sad and bitter cry (3)
106   from his poor manger to his bitter cross (5)
128   Myrrh is mine; its bitter perfume ... gathering gloom (4)
158   thy bitter passion, for my salvation (4)
168, 169   In thy most bitter passion my heart to share doth cry (3)
171   watch with him one bitter hour (1)
199, 200   loosed from Pharaoh's bitter yoke (1)
226, 227   Every bitter tear refine (2)
471   sweetens every bitter cup (3)
472   to heal earth's wounds and end her bitter strife (2)
479   Glory be to Jesus, who in bitter pains poured for me (1)
582, 583   bitter lips in blind despair cry (2)
596   purge this land of bitter things (1)
599   Stony the road we trod, bitter the chastening rod (2)
607   hate and fear divide us and bitter threats are hurled (1)
677   bud may have a bitter taste ... sweet will be the flower (5)
695, 696   bitter suffering, hard to understand (3)

black
602   neighbors are black and white (2)

blade
204   Now the green blade riseth from the buried grain (1)
276   slain by Herod's flashing blade, he saw thy face again (4)
290   first the blade, and then the ear (2)

blame
3, 4   with conscience free from sin and blame (4)
170   though we merit blame you will your robe of mercy throw (2)
701   Be it blame or scorn or shame, thou art with me (3)

blameless
60   the child of Mary, blameless mother mild (3)

blank
580   yet their windows, blank, unfeeling, stare (2)

blaze
9   So let the love of Jesus come and set thy soul ablaze (5)
389   Let us blaze his Name abroad (2)
431   The dawn returns in splendor, the heavens burn and blaze (2)
704   burn with ever bright, undying blaze (2)

blazed
299   earth, kindling, blazed her loud acclaim (1)

blazing
129, 130   Christ ... in glory blazing (1)
278   blazing glory of the Spirit's presence (3)
296   our despair he turned to blazing joy (1)

419	before thy ever-blazing throne we ask no luster (3)
674	In blazing light your cross reveals the truth (3)

bleak

112	In the bleak midwinter, frosty wind made moan (1)
112	in the bleak midwinter long ago (1)
112	in the bleak midwinter a stable-place sufficed (2)

bled

160	perfect God on thee has bled (1,4)
191	for the world's salvation bled (1)

bleed

212	those feet still free to move and bleed for millions (3)

bleeding

71, 72	the bleeding soul to cure (3)
128	sorrowing, sighing, bleeding, dying (4)
434	his dear wounds and bleeding side (4)

blend

210	let all things seen and unseen their notes together blend (3)
394, 395	let water's fragile blend with air, enabling life (2)
562	blend with ours your voices in the triumph song (5)

blending

329, 331	he with us in converse blending dwelt (2)
559	love with every passion blending (3)

bless

3, 4	may praise and bless his holy Name (4)
12, 13	we praise and bless you every hour (4)
18	we praise and bless you every hour (5)
23	we praise and bless you every hour (4)
51	that Christ may take them, bless them, break and give (4)
53	let us here confess thee till in heaven we bless thee (4)
101	Bless all the dear children in thy tender care (3)
103	Upon this joyful holy night ... we bless your name (3)
157	we bless you from the house of the Lord (R)
205	Your Name we bless, O risen Lord (4)
231	Lord, for Paul's conversion we bless your Name today (2/1-25)
279	Jesus, thy Name we bless (4)
300	God, who thus blessest us, right it is to bless thee (1)
343	Shepherd of souls, refresh and bless thy chosen (1)
343	bless thy chosen pilgrim flock with manna (1)
352	their marriage bless with gladness from above (1)
353	Bless those who in your presence wait (2)
359	God of the prophets, bless the prophets' heirs (1)
365	come, and thy people bless; come, give thy word success (2)
368	heavenly Father, through the Savior hear and bless (1)
374	The whole creation joins in one to bless the sacred Name (4)
377, 378	praise, laud, and bless his Name always (3)
385	bless us with life that has no end (2)
399	To God with gladness sing, your Rock and Savior bless (1)

400	Let all things their creator bless (7)
401	we bow and bless the sacred Name for ever blest (1)
410	slow to chide and swift to bless (2)
411	O bless the Lord, my soul (1-2,6)
411	all that is within me join to bless his holy Name (1)
411	bless his holy Name, whose grace hath made thee whole (6)
414	ever will I bless thy Name (1)
414	All thy works, O Lord, shall bless thee (6)
421	We bless, we worship you ... O God, Almighty Father (1)
428	O angels, sing and bless the Lord (1)
428	bless the Lord and praise him evermore (1-5)
428	O changing seasons bless the Lord (2)
428	heat and cold, O night and day ... bless the Lord (3)
428	O storms and thunder's roar, O fields and forests bless (3)
428	O men and women, bless the Lord (4)
428	people bless the Lord like righteous souls of yore (5)
440	hear, and bless our prayers and praises (3)
444	O bless our God and Savior with songs that never cease (3)
455, 456	We read thy power to bless and save (4)
455, 456	bless and save e'en in the darkness of the grave (4)
517	thou shalt surely bless ... who live the words they pray (4)
528	Lord, you bless with words assuring (5)
567	now, O Lord, be near to bless, almighty as of yore (2)
567	soothe and bless with thine almighty breath (3)
570, 571	all who curse and all who bless (1)
586	bless us in our daily labor (3)
587	bless thou all parents, guarding well (1)
587	our children bless, in every place (2)
636, 637	for I will be with thee, thy troubles to bless (3)
662	I fear no foe, with thee at hand to bless (3)
663	doth in mercy bless (2)
674	How can your pardon reach and bless the unforgiving heart (2)
716	God bless our native land (1)

blessed

1, 2	All holy Father, Son, and equal Spirit, Trinity blessed (3)
27, 28	forget your blessed gift of life (3)
29, 30	O Trinity of blessed light (1)
47	God, the blessed Three in One dwell within my heart alone (6)
77	All glory for this blessed morn to God the Father ever be (5)
78, 79	Where children pure and happy pray to the blessed Child (4)
82	O that birth for ever blessed (2)
88	Sing, O sing, this blessed morn, unto us a child is born (1)
88	O sing, this blessed morn, Jesus Christ today is born (R)
89, 90	ever o'er its Babel-sounds the blessed angels sing (2)
99	God sent us salvation that blessed Christmas morn (3)
105	From God our heavenly Father a blessed angel came (2)
106	found, with Joseph and the blessed maid, her Son (4)
108	who truly have believed that on this blessed morn (1)
122, 123	grant us, blessed Trinity ... to keep thine Easter (4)
152	Grant, O thou blessed Trinity ... O unchanging Unity (5)
153	Blessed is the King who comes in the name of the Lord (1)
153	Blessed is he who comes in the name of the Lord (2)
154, 155	who in the Lord's Name comest, the King and Blessed One (1)
157	Blessed is he who comes in the name of the Lord (1)

161	grant, most blessed Trinity ... all may share the victory (5)
190	love has brought the blessed morrow (3)
230	to the blessed Three in One be honor, praise and merit (2)
231	your holy Name, O Jesus, for evermore be blessed (1)
231	Like you, our suffering Savior ... he blessed (2/12-26)
231	his enemies he blessed (2/12-26)
232	your holy Name, O Jesus for evermore be blessed (1)
238, 239	Blessed feasts of blessed martyrs, holy women, holy men (1)
244	blessed tidings of salvation (1)
248, 249	we, in love adoring, this most blessed Name revere (4)
256	It was the blessed Son come down to save him (2)
258	blessed was the womb that bore thee (1,2)
258	blessed was she in her Child (1,2)
258	Blessed was the breast that fed thee (1)
258	blessed was the hand that led thee (1)
258	blessed was the parent's eye that watched (1)
258	Blessed she by all creation (2)
258	blessed they, for ever blest, who love thee most (2)
265	For know a blessed Mother thou shalt be (2)
268, 269	Blessed were the chosen people (2)
268, 269	blessed ... land of promise fashioned for his ... home (2)
268, 269	more blessed far the mother, she who bore him in her womb (2)
268, 269	all the ages call be blessed (4)
275	beatific vision of the blessed Trinity (4)
277	from the heart of blessed Mary (3)
278	Sing we of the blessed Mother (1)
278	blessed Mother who received the angel's word (1)
280	There are named the blessed faithful of the new Jerusalem (4)
282, 283	peace maker blessed (2)
282, 283	health-bringer blessed, aiding every sufferer (4)
282, 283	Father Almighty, Son and Holy Spirit, God ever blessed (6)
287	thy Name, O Jesus, be forever blessed (1)
288	As thy prospering hand hath blessed, may we give (3)
312	thy blessed hope perceiving (2)
313	Blessed Lord, thou cam'st to save me(2)
314	in the glorious vision, blessed Lord, of thee (4)
315	more blessed still, in peace and love to be (3)
315	more blessed ... to be one with the Trinity in Unity (3)
321	till with this bread shall all be blessed (4)
283	Father Almighty, Son and Holy Spirit, God ever blessed (6)
336	Come with us, O blessed Jesus, with us evermore to be (1)
339	let me be a fit partaker of ... blessed food from heaven (2)
340, 341	our blessed ones adore you, seated at our Father's board (3)
360, 361	Son coeternal, ever-blessed Spirit (6)
362	God in three Persons, blessed Trinity (1,4)
363	thy love has blessed the wide world's wondrous story (1)
366	wast of a virgin born humbly on that blessed morn (5)
369	long to see the blessed Three in the Almighty One (2)
371	Holy and blessed Three, glorious Trinity (4)
396, 397	who from our mother's arms hath blessed us on our way (1)
396, 397	blessed us on our way with countless gifts of love (1)
396, 397	with ever joyful hearts and blessed peace to cheer us (2)
404	We will extoll you, ever-blessed Lord (1)
406, 407	By sister water be thou blessed (4)
423	most blessed, most glorious, the Ancient of Days (1)

440	Blessed Jesus, at thy word we are gathered all to hear (1)
444	Blessed be the God of Israel, who comes to set us free (1)
480	infants in his arms he took and on his bosom blessed (2)
503, 504	Thy blessed unction from above is comfort, life and fire (3)
515	hear our supplication, blessed Spirit, God of peace (2)
518	with the blessed to retain (4)
519, 520	Blessed city, heavenly Salem (1)
525	till with the vision glorious her longing eyes are blessed (4)
560	Blessed are the poor in spirit (1)
560	Blessed are those who mourn, for they shall be comforted (2)
560	Blessed are the meek, for they shall inherit the earth (3)
560	Blessed ... who hunger and thirst after righteousness (4)
560	Blessed are the merciful, for they shall obtain mercy (5)
560	Blessed are the pure in heart, for they shall see God (6)
560	Blessed are the peace-makers (7)
560	Blessed ... who are persecuted for righteousness sake (8)
560	Blessed are you when the world reviles ... persecutes (9)
568	Blessed Lord Jesus, who camest in poverty (2)
576, 577	Grant us love's fulfillment, joy with all the blessed (3)
606	Now we pray that with the blessed you grant us grace (3)
611	Blessed manchild, boy of Nazareth (2)
611	Skillful craftsman, blessed carpenter (3)
620	blessed martyrs' harmony doth ring in every street (4)
623	those endless Sabbaths the blessed ones see (1)
623	voices of praise thy blessed people eternally raise (3)
624	the pastures of the blessed are decked in glorious sheen (2)
624	Oh, sweet and blessed country, the home of God's elect (4)
624	Oh, sweet and blessed country that eager hearts expect (4)
625	Ye blessed souls at rest, who ran this earthly race (2)
673	blessed is she who believes in the Lord (1)
673	blessed is she who perceives the Lord (2)
673	blessed are they who see the Lord (3)
708	Blessed Jesus! Thou has bought us, thine we are (1)
708	Blessed Jesus! Thou hast loved us, love us still (2)

blessedness

254	Oh, Peter was most blest with blessedness unpriced (2)
640	Treaveler, blessedness and light ... portends (2)
683, 684	Where is the blessedness I knew when first I saw the Lord (2)

blesses

525	one holy Name she blesses, partakes one holy food (2)
534	All we can do is nothing worth unless God blesses the deed (4)

blessest

300	God, who thus blessest us, right it is to bless thee (1)

blessing

40, 41	the blessing of a quiet night (2)
42	with thy tenderest blessing may our eyelids close (2)
53	Once he came in blessing, all our ills redressing (1)
59	Honor, glory, might, and blessing to the Father ... Son (4)
63, 64	who in these latter days wast born for blessing (1)
63, 64	born for blessing to a world forlorn (1)
80	The blessing which the Father planned (4)

215	While he lifts his hands in blessing (2)
282, 283	healing and blessing (4)
300	Thankful for our every blessing, let us sing (2)
305, 306	thou at the table, blessing, yet dost stand (2)
324	for with blessing in his hand (1)
326	Thanksgiving and glory and worship ... blessing and love (2)
329-331	Glory let us give and blessing to the Father and the Son (6)
333	Now the Father's blessing Now Now Now (1)
344	Lord, dismiss us with thy blessing (1)
349	gifts of blessing to bestow on your waiting Church below (1)
367	blessing thee, the Lord of hosts Most High (3)
375	Give praise and glory unto God ... Father of all blessing (1)
376	Thou art giving and forgiving, ever blessing, ever blest (3)
417, 418	honor, blessing, and glory are his (2)
417, 418	Blessing, honor, glory, and might be to God and the Lamb (4)
433	We gather together to ask the Lord's blessing (1)
441, 442	Bane and blessing, pain and pleasure ... sanctified (4)
495	Worship, honor, power, and blessing thou art worthy (4)
535	honor and blessing, with angels above (4)
559	yet possessing every blessing, if our God our Father be (1)
616	age to age more glorious, all blessing and all blest (5)
656	may ours this blessing be (4)
657	Thee we would be alway blessing (2)
669	God ever sends his blessing in answer to thy prayer (2)
686	Come, thou fount of every blessing (1)

blessings

9	worlds awake to cry their blessings on the Lord of life (4)
11	Praise God, from whom all blessings flow (4)
43	for all the blessings of the light (1)
43	Praise God, from whom all blessings flow (4)
78, 79	God imparts to human hearts the blessings of his heaven (3)
100	he comes to make his blessings flow far as the curse (3)
214	blessings on his Church below (3)
223, 224	blessings of this sacred day grant us ... we pray (3)
226, 227	come, thou source of blessings sure (1)
288	source whence all our blessings flow (1)
289	hand hath crowned her children with blessings manifold (1)
332	the blessings of thy love (2)
360, 361	by thy past blessings, by thy present bounty, favor (5)
374	may blessings ... be, Lord for ever thine (3)
374	blessings, more than we can give (3)
380	Praise God, from whom all blessings flow (3)
400	Dear mother earth, you day by day unfold your blessings (4)
400	unfold your blessings on our way (4)
404	in your compassion we your blessings find (3)
406, 407	blessings without measure (1,8)
437, 438	Unnumbered blessings give my spirit voice (1)
544	infant voices shall proclaim their early blessings (3)
544	their early blessings on his Name (3)
544	Blessings abound wheree'er he reigns (4)
638, 639	speak to my heart, in blessings speak (3)
664	my cup with blessings overflows (2)
677	clouds ... shall break in blessings on your head (3)
709	Such blessings from thy gracious hand (5)

709   Such blessings ... our humble prayers implore (5)

blest

25, 26	Immortal, holy, blest is he (1)
25, 26	blest are you, his holy Son (1)
27, 28	O blest Creator, source of light (1)
36	eternal splendor wearing; celestial, holy, blest (1)
37	most holy, heavenly, blest, Lord Jesus Christ (1)
47	shine, blest Spirit in my heart (5)
48	grace more grace receiving on this blest day of light (3)
48	Church her voice upraises to thee, blest Three in One (4)
50	Blest be the Lord who comes to us with messages of grace (4)
65	Oh, blest is Christ that came in God's most holy name (R)
74	Blest be the King whose coming is in the name of God (1-4)
107	we are blest for evermore (2)
120	How blest that mission then begun (4)
143	O Father, Son, and Spirit blest (5)
144	The universe your glory shows, blest Father, Spirit, Son (5)
162	Blest tree, whose chosen branches bore the wealth (4)
173	Blest shall they be eternally who ponder in their weeping (3)
173	O Jesus blest, my help and rest (4)
175	Hail thee, festival day! blest day ... hallowed for ever (R)
206	How blest are they who have not seen (6)
216, 225	Hail thee, festival day! blest day ... hallowed for ever (R)
226, 227	thy blest seven-fold gift assign (5)
231	blest guide to Greek and Jew (2/5-1)
232	Praise for your blest apostle surnamed Bartholomew (2/8-24)
235	How blest this habitation of gospel liberty (3)
254	Oh, Peter was most blest with blessedness unpriced (2)
257	But silent knelt the mother blest of the yet silent word (4)
258	blessed they, for ever blest, who love thee most (2)
263, 264	Blest in the message Gabriel brought (3)
263, 264	blest in the work the Spirit wrought (3)
263, 264	most blest to bring to human birth the long-desired (3)
267	Most blest shall be her name in all the Church on earth (5)
273, 274	who with the Holy Spirit, now reign, blest Three in One (4)
276	For thy blest saints ... we praise thy Name, O Lord (1)
282, 283	May the blest mother of our God and Savior ... help us (5)
286	Now in God's most holy place, blest they stand (5)
286	blest they stand before his face (5)
287	O blest communion, fellowship divine (4)
287	sweet is the calm of paradise the blest (6)
305, 306	one Church united in communion blest (3)
310, 311	blest One in Three (2)
315	through this blest sacrament of unity (1-2)
323	Vine of heaven, thy Blood supplies this blest cup (2)
323	this blest cup of sacrifice (2)
346	blest by the Spirit, breath and flame of life (3)
376	Thou art giving and forgiving, ever blessing, ever blest (3)
401	we bow and bless the sacred Name for ever blest (1)
406, 407	blest be they who do thy will and follow thy commandments (7)
436	O blest the land, the city blest (2)
436	the city blest where Christ the ruler is confessed (2)
453	hear the glad words, "Come to me all the blest" (4)

458	He came from his blest throne salvation to bestow (2)
479	blest be his compassion infinitely kind (2)
479	Blest through endless ages be the precious stream (3)
509	let thy Church on earth become blest as the Church above (4)
512	to be with him for ever blest (4)
522, 523	Blest inhabitants of Zion, washed in the Redeemer's blood (4)
524	the Church our blest Redeemer saved (1)
544	all those who suffer want are blest (4)
556, 557	pilgrims find their Father's house, Jerusalem the blest (6)
590	grant the glad surprising that your blest Spirit rouses (1)
616	age to age more glorious, all blessing and all blest (5)
618	ye patriarchs and prophets blest (3)
620	ten thousand times would one be blest who might ... hear (3)
620	blest who might this music hear (3)
623	God shall be all, and in all ever blest (1)
624	Jerusalem the golden, with milk and honey blest (1)
624	who art, with God the Father, and Spirit, ever blest (4)
649, 650	blest, when our faith can hold you fast (3)
656	Blest are the pure in heart, for they shall see our God (1)
720	Blest with victory and peace (2)

blind

371	heal to the sick in mind, sight to the inly blind (2)
429	The Lord pours eyesight on the blind (3)
458	He made the lame to run, he gave the blind their sight (4)
493	ye blind, behold, your Savior comes (5)
567	To thee they went, the blind ... deaf ... palsied ... lame (1)
582, 583	bitter lips in blind despair cry (4)
633	Word that caused blind eyes to see (3)
671	was blind but now I see (1)
677	Blind unbelief is sure to err and scan his work in vain (6)
693	poor, wretched, blind ... all I need, in thee to find (3)
706	to glory kept me blind (1)

blinded

18	you blinded and converted him (4b)
255	His presence pierced and blinded the zealot in his wrath (1)
256	Then Saul fell blinded to the ground (1)
503, 504	Enable with perpetual light ... our blinded sight (4)
503, 504	the dullness of our blinded sight (4)

blinding

| 31, 32 | Free us from bonds of blinding sin (5) |

blindness

46	long our mortal blindness has missed God's lovingkindness (3)
360, 361	light in our blindness, in our toil refreshment (3)
379	God is Love, and though with blindness sin afflicts (3)
573	light to our blindness, O be thou our aid (1)
607	from pride of race and nation and blindness to your way (2)
633	speak and heal our mortal blindness (3)

bliss

| 73 | let the endless bliss begin, by weary saints foretold (4) |
| 107 | now ye hear of endless bliss (2) |

112	but his mother only, in her maiden bliss, worshiped (3)
238, 239	by his grace we may be worthy of eternal bliss at last (3)
275	now they drink, as from a river, holy bliss and infinite (4)
316, 317	the Lamb's great marriage fest of bliss and love (3)
439	that caused the Lord of bliss to lay aside his crown (1)
441, 442	When the sun of bliss is beaming light and love (3)
453	here are regions of light, here are mansions of bliss (4)
482	your bliss in our hearts, Lord, at the break of the day (1)
524	brighter bliss of heaven (5)
556, 557	pour out the strains of joy and bliss (2)
576, 577	be our bliss while endless ages sing your praises (3)
624	what radiancy of glory, what bliss beyond compare (1)

blissful

573	rulers ... still fail to bring us to the blissful birth (4)

blood

38, 39	those you have ransomed by your blood (3)
40, 41	whom you have purchased with your blood (4)
104	God's blood upon the spear-head, God's love refused again (3)
109	with his blood our life hath bought (6)
139	in his great endeavor to save us, his own blood was shed (2)
139	He came by water and by blood to heal our lost condition (3)
160	where the blood of Christ was shed (1,4)
161	A Roman soldier drew a spear to mix his blood with water (2)
161	mix his blood with water clear (2)
161	That blood retains its living power (2)
165, 166	where his precious blood is spilled (2)
165, 166	from that holy body broken blood and water forth proceed (3)
165, 166	by that blood from stain are freed (3)
167	saved by his precious blood (3)
167	we must love him too, and trust in his redeeming blood (5)
173	in blood was offered for us (2)
174	praise we him, whose love divine gives his sacred Blood (1)
174	give his sacred Blood for wine (1)
174	Where the Paschal blood is poured (2)
174	Praise we Christ, whose blood was shed (2)
196, 197	let the blood flow from his flesh to fill ... hope (2)
294	cleansed by the blood of Christ our King (1)
296	as Christ's new body takes on flesh and blood (4)
298	help us in our infirmity through Jesus blood and merit (2)
313	Let thy Blood in mercy poured (1)
318	mine is the guilt, but thine the cleansing Blood (4)
318	thy Blood, thy righteousness, O Lord, my God (4)
323	Vine of heaven, thy Blood supplies this blest cup (2)
324	the Body and the Blood he will give to all the faithful (2)
327, 328	drink the holy Blood for you outpoured (1)
327, 328	Saved by that Body and that holy Blood (2)
327, 328	by his dear cross and blood the victory won (3)
329, 330	the Blood, all price excelling (1)
329, 330	Blood ... which the Gentiles' Lord and King ... shed (1)
329, 330	wine his sacred Blood he maketh (4)
332	meat the Body of the Lord, our drink his precious Blood (3)
333	Now the Body Now the Blood ... the joyful celebration (1)
334	By your Blood new life receiving (2)

335	Unless you ... drink of his Blood (3)
336	in our life thy love divine ... flesh and blood has taken (1)
336	flesh and blood ... and to us thou givest thine (1)
343	Lord, sup with us in love divine, thy Body and thy Blood (4)
417, 418	whose blood set us free to be people of God (1)
434	here, on the cross, 'tis fairest drawn in precious blood (2)
434	precious blood and crimson lines (2)
445, 446	O wisest love, that flesh and blood, which ... did fail (3)
445, 446	flesh and blood, which did in Adam fail (3)
445, 446	highest gift of grace should flesh and blood refine (4)
460, 461	Jesus out of every nation hath redeemed us by his blood (1,5)
467	bought us with the Savior's blood (3)
469, 470	there is healing in his blood (1)
469, 470	plentiful redemption in the blood that has been shed (2)
474	I sacrifice them to his blood (2)
479	poured for me the life-blood from his sacred veins (1)
479	Grace and life eternal in that blood I find (2)
479	louder still and louder praise the precious blood (5)
495	thy people are forgiven through the virtue of by blood (2)
522, 523	Blest inhabitants of Zion, washed in the Redeemer's blood (4)
524	saved with his own precious blood (1)
525	with his own blood he bought her ... for her life he died (1)
528	This my body, this my blood (3)
599	treading our path through the blood of the slaughtered (2)
681	the blood of friend as sign of love for comrade spilt (4)
685	let the water and the blood ... be of sin the double cure (2)
685	water and the blood from thy wounded side that flowed (1)
686	to rescue me from danger, interposed his precious blood (2)
693	without one plea, but that thy blood was shed for me (1)

bloom

69	to see the branch that begins to bloom (3)
144	nearer draws the day of days when paradise shall bloom (4)
168, 169	Can death thy bloom deflower (1)
179	bloom in every meadow, leaves on every bough (2)

blooming

81	Lo, how a Rose e'er blooming from tender stem hath sprung (1)
376	field and forest, vale and mountain, blooming meadow (2)
383, 384	woodlands robed in the blooming garb of spring (2)

blossom

81	It came, a blossom bright (1)
165, 166	None in foliage ... blossom ... fruit thy peer may be (4)
175	adorned with the glory of blossom (3)
216	adorned with the glory of blossom (2)
423	we blossom and flourish, like leaves on the tree (3)
462	truth ... like a flower shall bud and blossom show (2)

blow

398	clouds arise, and tempests blow by order from thy throne (3)
519, 520	Many a blow and biting sculpture polished ... stones (4)
519, 520	Many a blow ... polished well those stones elect (4)

blowing
412 Hail, wind, and rain, loud blowing snow-storms (2)

blown
506, 507 dark and furthest corners by the wind of heaven blown (4)

blue
42 guard the sailors tossing on the deep, blue sea (3)
409 with all the blue ethereal sky (1)
566 when ever-blue the sky shall gleam (2)

board
305, 306 thyself at thine own board make manifest (1)
321 gather from their Father's board the Bread that lives (3)
340, 341 our blessed ones adore you, seated at our Father's board (3)

boast
151 For none may boast themselves of aught (2)
211 Our God most high, our joy and boast (4)
383, 384 Jesus shines purer than all the angels heaven can boast (3)
474 Forbid it, Lord, that I should boast (2)
474 boast, save in the cross of Christ, my God (2)
543 tell all the earth thy joys, and boast salvation nigh (1)

boastfulness
476 Our boastfulness is turned to shame (3)

bodies
33-35 strength for our weak hearts, rest for aching bodies (4)
33-35 Though bodies slumber, hearts shall keep their vigil (5)
38, 39 give to our wearied bodies rest (2)
44, 45 rested bodies wake in peace (2)
312 bodies by thy Body fed with thy new life replenish (3)

body
21, 22 while you keep our body whole (2)
57, 58 dear tokens of his passion still his dazzling body bears (3)
165, 166 from that holy body broken blood and water forth proceed (3)
174 gives his Body for the feast (1)
176, 177 regenerated into the body of our risen Savior (2)
230 whole in body, mind, and spirit (3)
263, 264 in Mary's body deigned to dwell (1)
286 soul and body consecrated (5)
295 as members of his Body we live in him as one (2)
296 as Christ's new body takes on flesh and blood (4)
305, 306 "This is my Body"; so thou givest yet (2)
305, 306 One body we, one Body who partake (3)
312 bodies by thy Body fed with thy new life replenish (3)
313 let thy gracious Body broken (1)
315 may we all one bread, one body be (1-2)
324 the Body and the Blood he will give to all the faithful (2)
327, 328 Draw nigh and take the Body of the Lord (1)
327, 328 Saved by that Body and that holy Blood (2)
329, 331 the mystery of the glorious Body sing (1)
332 meat the Body of the Lord, our drink his precious Blood (3)
333 Now the Body Now the Blood ... the joyful celebration (1)
334 in your Body, firm believing (2)

343	Lord, sup with us in love divine, thy Body and thy Blood (4)
360, 361	humbly adoring, take thy Body broken (2)
501, 502	that as one body we may sing (5)
513	To the members of Christ's Body (2)
528	This my body, this my blood (3)
547	There is one Body and one hope, one Spirit and one call (3)
562	we are not divided, all one body we (3)
576, 577	When we Christians gather, members of one Body (2)
581	as members of his Body joined we are in him made one (5)
596	cleanse the body of this nation (3)
606	Since the love of Christ has joined us in one body (1)
606	As we are all of one body (2)
621, 622	glorious and resplendent, fragile body, shalt thou be (4)
687, 688	the body they may kill, God's truth abideth still (4)

boiling
| 412 | Classrooms and labs loud boiling test tubes (5) |

bold
97	Christ we praise with voices bold (3)
231	so eager and so bold, thrice failing, yet repentant (2/1-18)
287	O may thy soldiers, faithful, true, and bold (3)
394, 395	your fingers trace the bold designs of farthest space (1)

boldly
| 53 | but wilt trust him boldly nor dost love him coldly (3) |

bombs
| 607 | trust in bombs that shower destruction through the night (2) |
| 720 | the rockets' red glare, the bombs bursting in air (1) |

bond
| 40, 41 | O Spirit, bond of peace and love (5) |
| 547 | to give the Spirit's unity, the very bond of peace (2) |

bondage
59	from earth's bondage let us rise (2)
71, 72	in Satan's bondage held (2)
187	deep and wide flows the tide severing us from bondage past (1)
542	freedom her bondage breaks, and night is turned to day (1)
648	Oh, let us all from bondage flee (4)

bonds
31, 32	Free us from bonds of blinding sin (5)
116	his in bonds of love (5)
116	may such bonds for ever draw our souls to things above (5)
220, 221	The bonds of death are burst by thee (1)
256	free him from the bonds of sin (2)

bones
| 243 | no curse nor vengeful cry for those who broke his bones (3) |

book
| 280 | veiled ... but written in the Lamb's great book of life (3) |
| 631 | Book of books, our people's strength (1) |

books

631   Book of books, our people's strength (1)

bore

18   shield frail human eyes from all the woe you bore for us (3b)
53   bore the cross to save us, hope and freedom gave us (1)
77   child whom Mary bore, the Christ, the everlasting King (1)
81   To show God's love aright, she bore to us a Savior (2)
82   bore the Savior of our race (2)
110   for he whom Mary bore was God the Son (4)
162   Blest tree, whose chosen branches bore the wealth (4)
180   the passion that he bore -- sin and pain can vex no more (2)
181   sing how he interecedes above for ... whose sins he bore (2)
184   He who bore all pain and loss comfortless upon the cross (3)
190   see the wounds for you he bore (2)
238, 239   wonders, worthy of the Name they bore (1)
238, 239   glorious and victorious, bravely bore the martyr's part (2)
243   he bore no shield before his face (1)
245   John ... who bore the Spirit's sword (1)
250   this Name of names for us he bore (2)
258   blessed was the womb that bore thee (1,2)
268, 269   more blessed far the mother ... who bore him in her womb (2)
278   obedient to the summons bore in love the infant Lord (1)
435   faithfully he bore it spotless to the last (2)
435   bore it up triumphant, with its human light (3)
448, 449   for us he bore his holy fast and hungered sore (2)
448, 449   he bore the shameful cross and death (4)
483   The cross he bore is life and health (6)
489   as one with us he dwelt with us, and bore a human name (4)
492   bore the pain, the cross, the grave (2)
519, 520   for Christ's dear Name ... pain and tribulation bore (3)
519, 520   in this world pain and tribulation bore (3)
610   Lord, whose love through humble service bore the weight (1)

born

8   born of the one light Eden saw play (3)
63, 64   who in these latter days wast born for blessing (1)
63, 64   born for blessing to a world forlorn (1)
66   Come thou long-expected Jesus, born to set thy people free (1)
66   Born thy people to deliver (3)
66   born a child, and yet a king (3)
66   born to reign in us forever (3)
69   in joy and terror the Word is born (4)
77   all praise to thee, O Virgin-born (5)
78, 79   For Christ is born of Mary (2)
78, 79   cast out our sin and enter in, be born in us today (5)
80   to you this night is born a child of Mary (2)
80   this new-born child of lowly birth shall be the joy (2)
83   come, and behold him born the King of angels (1)
83   Yea, Lord, we greet thee, born this happy morning (6)
84   love was born at Christmas (1)
85, 86   O Christ, Redeemer virgin-born (6)
87   Hark! the herald angels sing glory to the new-born King (1,R)
87   with the angelic host proclaim Christ is born (1)

87	born in Bethlehem (1)
87	Mild he lays his glory by, born that we no more may die (3)
87	born to raise us from the earth (3)
87	born to give us second birth (3)
87	hail, the heaven-born Prince of Peace (3)
88	Sing, O sing, this blessed morn, unto us a child is born (1)
88	O sing, this blessed morn, Jesus Christ today is born (R)
88	Christ is born for us that we born again in him may be (4)
92	born on earth to save us; him the Father gave us (1)
92	born on earth to save us; peace and love he gave us (4)
93	come and worship, worship Christ, the new-born King (R)
94, 95	To you, in David's town, this day is born of David's line (3)
96	Christ, the Lord, the new-born King (3)
98	Unto us a boy is born, the King of all creation (1,5)
99	go tell it on the mountain, that Jesus Christ is born (R)
99	Down in a lowly manger the humble Christ was born (3)
103	A child is born in Bethlehem (1)
105	remember Christ our Savior was born on Christmas Day (1)
105	how that in Bethlehem was born the Son of God by name (2)
105	this day is born a Savior of a pure virgin bright (3)
106	morn whereon the Savior of the world was born (1)
106	this day is born a Savior, Christ the Lord (2)
106	he that was born upon this joyful day (6)
107	give ye heed to what we say: Jesus Christ is born today (1)
107	Christ is born today (1)
107	Jesus Christ was born for this (2)
107	Christ was born for this (2)
107	Jesus Christ was born to save (3)
107	Christ was born to save (3)
108	in holiness conceived, the Son of God was born (1)
109	Nowell, Nowell ... born is the King of Israel (R)
110	when Christ our Lord was born on Christmas night (1)
111	Christ, the Savior, is born (2)
114	Jesus your King is born, Jesus is born (R)
114	the holy child of earth and heaven is born today for you (4)
125, 126	To us the promised Child is born, to us the Son is given (3)
128	Born a King on Bethlehem's plain (2)
149	you, the first-born of all the faithful dead (3)
159	born of woman (4)
165, 166	born for this, he meets his passion (2)
174	From sin's power do thou set free soul's new-born (4)
174	set free soul's new-born, O Lord, in thee (4)
191	Christ from death to life is born (2)
213	arise and rejoice in the day thou wast born (1)
226, 227	Bend the stubborn heart and will (4)
246	In Bethlehem a new-born boy was hailed with songs (1)
257	lowly Virgin brings her new-born babe (2)
258	Virgin-born, we bow before thee (1,2)
263, 264	Lord Jesus, Virgin-born ... eternal praise and glory be (4)
265	Of her, Emmanuel, the Christ, was born (4)
267	virgin born of David's line shall bear the promised seed (2)
271, 272	the herald of the Word, is born (1)
271, 272	woman born shall never be a greater prophet than was he (4)
275	by death to life immortal they were born and glorified (3)
284	Ye saw the heaven-born child in human flesh arrayed (2)

294	born of one Father, we are his children (3)
299	You came in power; the Church was born (2)
324	King of kings, yet born of Mary (2)
329, 331	Given for us, and condescending to be born for us below (2)
359	priesthood born of grace (3)
366	wast of a virgin born humbly on that blessed morn (5)
426	awoke the morn when the Prince of Peace was born (2)
452	Glorious the day when Christ was born to wear the crown (1)
452	born to wear the crown that Ceasars scorn (1)
460, 461	born of Mary, earth thy footstool, heaven thy throne (4)
468	he was born on Christmas ... and laid in a manger (1)
473	Each new-born servant of the Crucified bears ... seal (2)
537	new-born souls, whose days, reclaimed from error's ways (4)
574, 575	a new-born people may we rise (4)
611	Christ the worker, born in Bethlehem (1)
611	born to work and die for every one (1)
665	Evermore from his store new-born worlds rise and adore (3)

borne

259	but, borne upon the throne of Mary's gentle breast (2)
390	borne as on eagle-wings, safely his saints he sustaineth (2)
420	through centuries of wrong, borne witness to the truth (3)
426	Borne upon their latest breath ... conquer death (6)
537	the faint and over-borne (1)
663	filled my cup, and borne me up in everlasting arms (4)

borrow

168, 169	What language ... borrow to thank thee, dearest friend (4)

borrows

398	all that borrows life from thee is ever in thy care (3)

bosom

480	infants in his arms he took and on his bosom blessed (2)
699	Jesus, Lover of my soul, let me to thy bosom fly (1)

bough

162	each crimsoned bough proclaims the King of glory now (3)
179	bloom in every meadow, leaves on every bough (2)
211	The birds do sing on every bough (1)

boughs

165, 166	Bend thy boughs, O tree of glory (5)

bought

109	with his blood our life hath bought (6)
337	And now, O Father, mindful of the love that bought us (1)
364	bring us whom thou hast bought to dwell on high (8)
455, 456	uncomprehended and unbought (1)
467	God, the merciful and good, bought us (3)
467	bought us with the Savior's blood (3)
525	with his own blood he bought her ...for her life he died (1)
708	Blessed Jesus! Thou has bought us, thine we are (1)

bound

38, 39	as mortals clothed in earth-bound frame (4)
179	Loose the souls long prisoned, bound with Satan's chain (6)
182	No longer bound to distant years in Palestine (2)
232	be bound in love together, and life eternal gain (2/10-28)
284	join with our earth-bound song to make the Savior known (1)
304	Together met, together bound, we'll go our different ways (5)
530	to earth's remotest bound all may heed the joyful sound (1)
579	whose arm hath bound the restless wave (1)
581	by love are we thus bound (1)
585	bound in setting others free (4)
594, 589	From the fears that long have bound us free our hearts (2)
598	upon a cross they bound thee (1)
608	whose arm hath bound the restless wave (1)
715	the falling tear in mercy flowed beyond all bound (RC)

boundaries

31, 32	you in the primal world once set the boundaries (4)
31, 32	boundaries of the day and night (4)

boundless

54	Boundless shall your kingdom be (4)
226, 227	boundless mercy our reward (5)
313	be to me ... Lord, of thy boundless love the token (1)
351	Father's boundless love, with the Holy Spirit's favor (1)
371	wisdom, love, might; boundless to ocean's tide (4)
406, 407	signifies thy boundless sway (2)
552, 553	his boundless mercy will provide (3)
606	our boundless source of joy and truth, of peace and love (3)
643	thine endless wisdom, boundless power, and aweful purity (3)
644	filled with boundless stores of grace (3)
665	Daily ... almighty Giver boundless gifts on us bestow (4)

bounds

38, 39	you set the bounds of night and day (2)
287	From earth's wide bounds, from ocean's farthest coast (8)
430	song shall over-climb all the bounds of space and time (6)
666	Let Israel trust in God, no bounds his mercy knows (4)

bounteous

288	bounteous source of every joy (1)
292	breathe from the bounteous heaven (2)
300	Bounteous God, we now confess thee (1)
396, 397	O may this bounteous God through all our life be near us (2)
491	God all-bounteous, all-creative (4)
705	God the giver of all good, the source of bounteous yield (1)
718	thy bounteous goodness nourish us in peace (3)

bountiful

388	Thy bountiful care, what tongue can recite (4)

bounty

213	while his grace we receive from his bounty (2)
360, 361	by thy past blessings, by thy present bounty, favor (5)

bow

60	all hearts must bow (4)
65	All lands will bow before him (3)
67	the hills bow down to greet him (2)
82	powers, dominions bow before him (3)
107	ox and ass before him bow, and he is in the manger now (1)
133, 134	To you, the King of glory ... faithful hearts ... bow (3)
133, 134	now all faithful hearts adoring bow (3)
145	To bow the head in sackcloth and in ashes (2)
156	bow thy meek head to mortal pain (5)
252	Unto which must every knee bow in deep humility (1)
258	Virgin-born, we bow before thee (1,2)
307	here in loving reverence bow (2)
327, 328	Alpha-Omega, unto whom shall bow all nations at the doom (8)
350	O God of love, to thee we bow (1)
366	Lord of all, we bow before thee (1)
391	Before the Lord's eternal throne ... bow with sacred joy (1)
391	ye nations bow with sacred joy (1)
401	we bow and bless the sacred Name for ever blest (1)
410	sun and moon bow down before him (4)
435	At the Name of Jesus every knee shall bow (1)
462	all shall frame to bow them low before thee, Lord (4)
475	Where I go here below, let me bow before thee (4)
475	bow before thee, know thee, and adore thee (4)
477	given the Name to which all knees shall bow (4)
484, 485	we bow the knee, we fall before thee (2)
526	One army of the living God, to his command we bow (3)
554	to bow and to bend we shan't be ashamed (1)
591	O God of earth and altar, bow down and hear our cry (1)
616	Kings shall bow down before him (4)

bowed

265	Then gentle Mary meekly bowed her head (3)
267	She meekly bowed her head to hear the gracious word (4)
314	lo, to thee surrendered, my whole heart is bowed (1)
363	to thee in reverent love our hearts are bowed (2)
454	again in mercy, when our hearts are bowed with care (2)
492	bowed himself to Bethlehem's cave (2)

bower

462	justice, from her heavenly bower, look down on us below (2)

boy

91	This child, this little helpless boy ... our confidence (1)
91	boy, shall be our confidence and joy (1)
98	Unto us a boy is born, the King of all creation (1,5)
114	Come kneel before the radiant boy (4)
114	boy, who brings you beauty, peace, and joy (4)
246	In Bethlehem a new-born boy was hailed with songs (1)
611	Blessed manchild, boy of Nazareth (2)

boys

98	All the little boys he killed at Bethlehem in his fury (3)

brake
322   he took the bread and brake it (2)

branch
56   O come, thou Branch of Jesse's tree (4)
69   to see the branch that begins to bloom (3)
135   branch of royal David's stem in thy birth at Bethlehem (1)
307   branch and flower of Jesse's stem (3)
496, 497   O righteous branch, O Jesse's Rod (1)

branches
104   The palm shall strew its branches (2)
157   form a procession with branches (R)
162   Blest tree, whose chosen branches bore the wealth (4)
198   today the branches with the root in resurrection sharing (2)
231   as faithful branches grow strong in you, the Vine (2/4-25)
513   to the branches of the Vine (2)

brand
297   brand us this day with Jesus' Name (1)

brass
71, 72   gates of brass before him burst, the iron fetters yield (2)

brave
96   the mountains in reply echoing their brave delight (1)
287   hearts are brave again, and arms are strong (5)
293   saints of God, patient and brave and true (1)
471   It makes the coward spirit brave (4)
614   praise for his brave saints of ancient days (1)
614   round him drew thousands of servants brave and true (1)
675   in his strength, and calmly every danger brave (4)
720   o'er the land of the free and the home of the brave (1-2)

bravely
238, 239   glorious and victorious, bravely bore the martyr's part (2)

braves
114   but as the hunter braves drew nigh, the angel-song rang (2)

bread
48   living presence greeting, through Bread and Wine made near (3)
51   In the Lord's service bread and wine are offered (4)
120   know you are the Bread indeed (6)
174   Paschal victim, Paschal bread (2)
185, 186   let us feast this holy day on the true bread of heaven (4)
202   his flesh, the true unleavened bread (3)
245   the light, the living vine, your soul's true bread (2)
278   Son of God eternal and the everlasting Bread (1)
291   much more to us, his children, he gives our daily bread (2)
301   Bread of the world, in mercy broken (1)
302, 303   giving in Christ the Bread eternal (1)
302, 303   As grain ... was in this broken bread made one (2)
304   new community of love in Christ's communion bread (2)
304   As Christ breaks bread and bids us share (3)

305	make manifest in thine own Sacrament of Bread and Wine (1)
305, 306	one Name we bear, one Bread of life we break (3)
305, 306	be known to us in breaking of the Bread (4)
307	Jesus true and living Bread (1)
308, 309	O Food to pilgrims given, O Bread of life from heaven (1)
308, 309	hidden in forms of bread and wine (3)
314	living Bread that givest all thy creatures breath (3)
315	may we all one bread, one body be (1-2)
316, 317	the Bread and Wine consumed (2)
318	Here would I feed upon the Bread of God (2)
306	make manifest in thine own Sacrament of Bread and Wine (1)
320	Let the Bread, life giving, living, be our theme (2)
320	Let the Bread ... be our theme of thanksgiving (2)
320	Bread ... now in truth before thee set (2)
320	command for guidance taking, bread and wine we hallow (3)
320	Very Bread, good Shepherd, tend us (5)
321	gather from their Father's board the Bread that lives (3)
321	Bread that lives beyond the tomb (3)
321	till with this bread shall all be blessed (4)
322	still that word is spoken, and still the bread is broken (1)
322	he took the bread and brake it (2)
323	Bread of heaven, on thee we feed (1)
323	ever may our souls be fed with this true and living Bread (1)
325	Let us break bread together on our knees (1)
327, 328	with heavenly bread he makes the hungry whole (7)
329, 330	Word made flesh, the bread he taketh (4)
335	I am the bread of life (1)
335	The Bread that I will give is my Flesh (2)
335	they who eat of this bread ... shall live forever (2)
339	Jesus, Bread of life, I pray thee (3)
340, 341	For the bread which you have broken (1)
342	O Bread of life, for sinners broken (1)
343	would not live by bread alone, but by thy word of grace (2)
343	Be known to us in breaking bread, and do not then depart (3)
343	living bread, that heavenly wine, be our immortal food (4)
460, 461	Bread of Heaven, thou on earth our food, our stay (3)
472	bringing to hungry souls the bread of life (2)
563	he can with bread of heaven thy fainting spirit feed (1)
586	Bread of heaven, art broken in the sacrament of life (2)
610	still the hungry cry for bread (2)
627	bread of our souls, whereon we feed (2)
633	Word of life, with one Bread feed us (4)
649, 650	we taste in you our living bread (2)
667	he who feeds the ravens will give his children bread (3)
690	bread of heaven, feed me now and evermore (1)
709	give us each day our daily bread ... raiment fit provide (3)

breadth

422	to know the breadth, length, depth, and height (2)
521	bid thy Church increase, in breadth and length (1)
547	so learn his love -- its length and breadth (1)
693	love, the breadth, length, depth, and height to prove (6)

break

51	that Christ may take them, bless them, break and give (4)

51	break and give them to all his people (4)
91	Break forth, O beauteous light, and usher in the morning (1)
145	Then shall your light break forth as doth the morning (5)
149	as through stony ground the green shoots break (3)
203	That Easter morn, at break of day (2)
228	With your soft, refreshing rains break our drought (4)
305, 306	one Name we bear, one Bread of life we break (3)
325	Let us break bread together on our knees (1)
359	eloquent for righteousness that shall all evil break (2)
422	more truth and light to break forth from thy Holy Word (1)
482	your bliss in our hearts, Lord, at the break of the day (1)
506, 507	let your flame break out within us (5)
540	break down the realm of Satan, death, and sin (3)
606	when we gather let no discord or enmity break our oneness (2)
613	Break with thine iron rod the tyrannies of sin (1)
616	He comes to break oppression, to set the captive free (1)
629	more light and truth to break forth from his word (1-3)
638, 639	wrestle till the break of day (1)
677	clouds ... shall break in blessings on your head (3)
717	let rocks their silence break, the sound prolong (3)

breaketh

| 617 | one with the joy that breaketh into song (2) |

breaking

91	the power of Satan breaking, our peace eternal making (1)
175	day whereon Christ arose, breaking the kingdom of death (R)
180	breaking o'er the purple east (3)
305, 306	be known to us in breaking of the Bread (4)
343	Be known to us in breaking bread, and do not then depart (3)
379	when human hearts are breaking under sorrow's iron rod (2)

breaks

46	Now all the heavenly splendor breaks forth (2)
73	light triumphant breaks (1)
78, 79	dark night wakes, the glory breaks (4)
287	But lo, there breaks a yet more glorious day (7)
304	As Christ breaks bread and bids us share (3)
440	till thy Spirit breaks our night with the beams of truth (2)
476	There God breaks in upon our search (4)
542	freedom her bondage breaks, and night is turned to day (1)
555	gladness breaks like morning where'er thy face appears (3)
638, 639	the morning breaks, the shadows flee (4)
662	heaven's morning breaks, and earth's vain shadows flee (4)

breast

76	Then cleansed be every breast from sin (2)
113	Oh sleep now, holy baby, with your head against my breast (1)
258	Blessed was the breast that fed thee (1)
259	but, borne upon the throne of Mary's gentle breast (2)
278	Mary at whose breast the child was fed who is Son of God (1)
337	O fold them closer to thy mercy's breast (3)
382	thou didst note my working breast, thou hast spared me (1)
435	to the throne of Godhead, to the Father's breast (3)
486	But chiefest, in our cleansed breast ... rest (4)

494	who every grief hath known that wrings the human breast (2)
642	thought of thee with sweetness fills the breast (1)
644	calms the troubled breast (2)
683, 684	drove thee from my breast (3)
692	in your weariness lay down your head upon my breast (1)

breath

9	what time there comes the breath of dawn (3)
23	Inspire us by your dying breath to live for you (3)
240, 241	Christ ... triumphed in his parting breath (3)
253	with united breath, ascribe their conquest to the Lamb (2)
278	heavenly breath of God's own being (3)
279	learned from thy Holy Spirit's breath to suffer and to do (2)
314	living Bread that givest all thy creatures breath (3)
346	blest by the Spirit, breath and flame of life (3)
366	on the cross thy dying breath opened ... heaven (6)
381	breathed thine own life-giving breath (2)
390	All that hath life and breath come now with praises (4)
391	formed us of clay and gave us breath (2)
400	most gentle death, waiting to hush our final breath (6)
411	He pardons all thy sins, prolongs thy feeble breath (4)
426	Borne upon their latest breath ... conquer death (6)
429	I'll praise my Maker while I've breath (1)
429	I'll praise him while he lends me breath (4)
435	name with awe and wonder and with bated breath (4)
448, 449	for us gave up his dying breath (4)
458	Then " Crucify !" is all their breath (3)
465, 466	eternal Spirit, give me breath (2)
487	such a way as gives us breath (1)
501, 502	O Holy Spirit, by whose breath life rises vibrant (1)
506, 507	Praise the Spirit in creation, breath of God (1)
506, 507	breath of God, life's origin (1)
506, 507	source of breath to all things breathing (1)
508	Breathe on me, Breath of God (1-4)
567	soothe and bless with thine almighty breath (3)
572	Trumpet with your Spirit's breath (2)
572	with your Spirit's breath through each height and hollow (2)
664	one word of thy supporting breath drives ... fears away (2)
685	While I draw this fleeting breath (3)

breathe

292	all fostering power, all influence sweet breathe (2)
292	breathe from the bounteous heaven (2)
508	Breathe on me, Breath of God (1-4)
515	breathe thy life and spread thy light (1)
559	Savior, breathe forgiveness o'er us (2)
652, 653	Breathe through the heats of our desire thy coolness (5)
717	let mortal tongues awake, let all that breathe partake (3)

breathed

| 381 | breathed thine own life-giving breath (2) |

breathes

| 128 | perfume breathes a life of gathering gloom (4) |
| 379 | God who breathes through all creation (1) |

388   It breathes in the air, it shines in the light (4)

breathing
506, 507   source of breath to all things breathing (1)

breeze
228   freshening breeze and cooling shade (2)
717   Let music swell the breeze (3)

breezes
291   the breezes and the sunshine, and soft refreshing rain (1)
400   Great rushing winds and breezes soft (2)

brethren's
242   His brethren's word he would not take (3)

bridal
519, 520   bridal glory round thee shed (2)

bride
519, 520   angel hosts encircled, as a bride dost earthward move (1)
525   from heaven he came and sought her to be his holy bride (1)

Bridegroom
61, 62   Forth he comes, her Bridegroom glorious (2)
61, 62   the Bridegroom is in sight (1)
68   The Bridegroom is arising, and soon he will draw nigh (1)
68   rise up, ye heirs of glory, the Bridegroom is at hand (2)

Bridegroom's
143   John, the Bridegroom's friend, became the herald (3)

brief
316, 317   prolong the brief, bright hour of fellowhip with thee (1)

bright
5   O splendor of God's glory bright (1)
18   so bright it cancelled out the sun (4b)
18   By noon's bright light, destruction stalks (2c)
27, 28   you gave the day with splendor bright (1)
27, 28   with your Son, and Spirit bright (5)
42   Grant to little children visions bright of thee (3)
48   O balm of care and sadness, most beautiful, most bright (1)
53   One who thus endureth bright reward secureth (4)
60   but not in splendor bright (3)
61, 62   her star is risen, her light grows bright (2)
80   that in his kingdom bright and fair ... his glory share (4)
81   It came, a blossom bright (1)
85, 86   bathes all the world in radiance bright (4)
92   God's bright star, o'er his head (3)
101   The stars in the bright sky looked down where he lay (1)
105   this day is born a Savior of a pure virgin bright (3)
108   Let every house be bright; let praises never cease (2)
110   The snow lay on the ground, the stars shone bright (1)
111   all is calm ... bright round yon virgin mother and child (1)

brighten

339   Sun, who all my life dost brighten (2)

brightening

527   brightening all the path we tread (2)
672   even now, though dull and gray, the east is brightening (3)
672   the east is brightening fast (3)

brightens

287   The golden evening brightens in the west (6)
405   the sunset and the morning that brightens up the sky (2)

brighter

93   brighter visions beam afar (3)
136, 137   where brighter than the sun he glows (1)
180   a brighter Easter beam on our longing eyes shall stream (4)
226, 227   Brighter than the noonday sun (3)
383, 384   Jesus shines brighter (3)
524   brighter bliss of heaven (5)
543   There on his holy hill a brighter sun shall rise (4)
621, 622   brighter than the heart can fancy (1)

brightest

117, 118   Brightest and best of the stars of the morning (1,5)
434   his brightest form of glory shines (2)
524   to Zion shall be given the brightest glories (5)
524   brightest glories earth can yield (5)

brightness

37   O brightness of the immortal Father's face (1)
85, 86   O Brightness of the Father's face (1)
96   What great brightness did you see (2)
168, 169   show me, O Love most highest, the brightness of thy face (2)
179   Brightness of the morning, sky and fields and sea (3)
179   show thy face in brightness, bid the nations see (6)
191   glory from the brightness of thy face (4)
245   Your brightness, O eternal Word, Apostle John unfurled (1)
286   Who are these of dazzling brightness (2)
406, 407   with brightness he doth fill the day (2)
432   worship before him, in brightness arrayed (1)
465, 466   eternal brightness, help me see (2)
490   I want to see the brightness of God (2)
538   God of mercy ... grace, show the brightness of thy face (1)
621, 622   cloud nor passing vapor dims the brightness of the air (3)
621, 622   in everlasting glory thou with brightness be arrayed (5)
641   when the flood is passed, I may the eternal brightness see (4)
695, 696   joy we had, the brightness of your Sun (4)

brilliant

231   Lord, grant us crowns as brilliant (2/12-28)
406, 407   shines in brilliant splendor (2)

brimmed

333   Now the hearing ... power ... vessel brimmed for pouring (1)

bring

1, 2	bring us to heaven where thy saints united joy (2)
10	a road to bring us daily nearer God (5)
31, 32	moon with cool reflected glow will bring the silences (3)
44, 45	when the dawn new light will bring (3)
47	did the world from darkness bring (1)
50	bring salvation from thy throne (3)
66	now thy gracious kingdom bring (3)
75	bring them safe to his fold (3)
80	to bring good news to everyone (1)
80	Glad tidings of great joy I bring to all the world (1)
89, 90	warring human-kind hears not the tidings which they bring (3)
94, 95	Glad tidings of great joy I bring to you and all mankind (2)
105	this holy tide of Christmas doth bring redeeming grace (4)
106	Behold, I bring good tidings of a Savior's birth (2)
112	If I were a shepherd, I would bring a lamb (4)
113	he will bring no harm to you (2)
115	haste to bring him laud, the babe, the son of Mary (R)
115	So bring him incense, gold and myrrh (3)
119	all our costliest treasures bring (3)
119	bring our ransomed souls at last where they need no star (4)
124	Gentiles to his crib to bring (1)
128	gold I bring to crown him again (2)
136, 137	vouchsafe to bring us by thy grace to see thy glory (5)
145	the friends you make shall bring God's glory bright (5)
154, 155	accept the prayers we bring (5)
161	he died eternal life to bring (1)
164	as we share this hour, thy cross may bring us to thy joy (4)
165, 166	to his cross thy tribute bring (1)
179	Vanquisher of darkness, bring their praise to thee (3)
179	bring again our daylight: day returns with thee (6)
205	To all the world glad news we bring (1)
226, 227	what is barren bring to flower (4)
228	all the benefits the earth, you bring to maturity (3)
228	bring to light our perjuries (4)
263, 264	most blest to bring to human birth the long-desired (3)
313	Wilt thou own the gift I bring (4)
338	Wherefore, O Father, we thy humble servants here bring (1)
338	bring before thee Christ thy well-beloved (1)
354	bring you into the holy city Jerusalem (1)
364	bring us whom thou hast bought to dwell on high (8)
366	but deliverence to bring thou all honors didst surrender (5)
371	come to bring on thy redeeming wing healing and sight (2)
382	the cream of all my heart, I will bring thee (2)
399	into his temple bring your songs of thankfulness (1)
410	to his feet thy tribute bring (1)
430	hither bring in one consent heart ... voice ... instrument (1)
444	God shall fulfill his promise and bring his people peace (1)
450, 451	bring forth the royal diadem
489	grace and peace to bring (3)
494	died, eternal life to bring (3)
495	thou didst free salvation bring (1)
500	come, and thy sacred unction bring to sanctify us (2)
501, 502	To fuller life your people bring (5)
524	thy hand from every snare and foe ... deliverance bring (4)

524	thy hand ... shall great deliverance bring (4)
526	bring us safe to heaven (5)
537	The world to Christ we bring (1-4)
539	till God shall bring his kingdom's joyful day (3)
544	Let every creature rise and bring peculiar honors (5)
547	To us on earth he came to bring from sin and fear release (2)
551	Lord, bring the day of truth and love (2)
573	rulers ... still fail to bring us to the blissful birth (4)
574, 575	whate'er the pain and shame maybe, bring us ... nearer (1)
574, 575	bring us, O Father, nearer thee (1)
588, 589	give it root in every heart to bring forth fruits of love (2)
594, 595	bring her bud to glorious flower (1)
598	must bring to doom the powers which crucified thee (2)
598	we bring our hearts before thy cross (4)
600, 601	Bring to our troubled minds, uncertain and afraid (2)
600, 601	Bring justice to our land, that all may dwell secure (3)
600, 601	Bring to our world of strife thy sovereign word of peace (4)
605	What sacrifice desire, or tribute bid you bring (1)
610	we, your servants, bring the worship not of voice alone (1)
616	gold and incense bring (4)
619	glory for evermore; to thee we bring ... alleluia (7)
623	There, where no troubles distraction can bring (3)
624	Jesus, in mercy bring us to that dear land of rest (4)
633	touch our hearts and bring to birth faith and hope (1)
644	accept the praise I bring (4)
656	Lord, who left the heavens our life and peace to bring (2)
667	let the unknown tomorrow bring with it what it may (2)
667	It can bring with it nothing but he will bear us through (3)
669	what profit doth it bring thee to pine in grief and care (2)
669	bring to sure fulfillment thy counsel good and true (3)
685	in my hand no price I bring, simply to thy cross I cling (2)
695, 696	still evil days bring burdens hard to bear (2)
699	all my help from thee I bring (2)
705	so we today our frist fruits bring (1)
705	With gratitude and humble trust we bring our best to thee (3)

bringer

282, 283	health-bringer blessed, aiding every sufferer (4)

bringest

5	O thou that bringest light from light (1)
75	O Zion, that bringest good tidings (2)
505	in every need thou bringest aid (1)

bringeth

406, 407	Sustained by thee, through every hour, she bringeth forth (5)
406, 407	bringeth forth fruit, herb, and flower (5)

bringing

18	O Spirit bringing truth and love (5)
23	O Spirit, bringing power and health (4)
70	bringing God's own love and power (4)
135	manifest in gracious will, ever bringing good from ill (3)
176, 177	bringing forth creation (1)
289	new comrades ever bringing in comrades' steps to tread (2)

454	to hearts rejoicing, bringing news of sins forgiven (3)
472	bringing to hungry souls the bread of life (2)
515	bringing down the richest treasure we can wish (1)
530	word of how the Spirit came bringing peace in Jesus' name (4)
540	bringing peoples to thy holy will (1)
631	bringing freedom, spreading truth (1)

brings

31, 32	brings the splendors of the dawn (1)
65	He brings God's rule, O Zion, he comes from heaven above (2)
70	pathway ... for the one who brings God near (2)
73	light and beauty brings (5)
76	awake and hearken, for he brings glad tidings (1)
87	light and life to all he brings (3)
114	boy, who brings you beauty, peace, and joy (4)
115	the King of kings salvation brings (3)
145	for schemes are vain and fretting brings no gain (1)
145	God brings new beauty nigh (1)
163	sin is slain, and death brings life (3)
185, 186	brings us life from heaven (1)
196, 197	what he brings in his hurt hands is life (1,4)
257	lowly Virgin brings her new-born babe (2)
270	out of darkness brings our Day (1)
471	he brings us mercy from above (2)
522, 523	as priests, his solemn praises ... a thankoffering brings (4)
596	pining for the hour that brings release (2)
605	To merchant, worker, king he brings God's high demands (3)
621, 622	there no night brings rest from labor (3)
623	city of peace that brings joy evermore (2)
640	Traveler, yes, it brings the day, promised day of Israel (1)
664	brings my wandering spirit back when I forsake his ways (1)

broad

448, 449	O love, how deep, how broad, how high (1)
448, 449	glory ... for love so deep, so high, so broad (6)
720	whose broad stripes and bright stars (1)

broader

469, 470	For the love of God is broader than the ... mind (3)
469, 470	broader than the measure of the mind (3)

broke

38, 39	You broke the chains of death and hell (3)
125, 126	on them broke forth the heavenly dawn (1)
243	no curse nor vengeful cry for those who broke his bones (3)
255	God's light ... broke across the path (1)
296	Embraced by death he broke its fearful hold (1)
381	broke the light of thy salvation (2)
661	peace ... filled their hearts brimful and broke them, too (2)

broken

8	Morning has broken like the first morning (1)
61, 62	Midnight's peace their cry has broken (1)
67	token that the word is never broken (3)
71, 72	He comes, the broken heart to bind (3)

114	Within a lodge of broken bark the tender babe was found (2)
165, 166	from that holy body broken blood and water forth proceed (3)
184	Christ has broken every chain (1)
190	the strength of death is broken (3)
191	Now the iron bars are broken (2)
301	Bread of the world, in mercy broken (1)
301	look on the heart by sorrow broken (1)
302, 303	As grain ... was in this broken bread made one (2)
313	let thy gracious Body broken (1)
322	still that word is spoken, and still the bread is broken (1)
340, 341	For the bread which you have broken (1)
342	O Bread of life, for sinners broken (1)
360, 361	humbly adoring, take thy Body broken (2)
373	laws which never shall be broken (1)
493	mournful broken hearts rejoice, the humble poor believe (4)
522, 523	he whose word cannot be broken formed thee (1)
586	Bread of heaven, art broken in the sacrament of life (2)
633	heal the world, by our sin broken (3)
669	Hope on, then, broken spirit; hope on, be not afraid (4)
693	thy love unknown has broken every barrier down (5)

brood
| 608 | Most Holy Spirit, who didst brood upon the chaos (3) |

broodeth
| 613 | wherever near or far thick darkness broodeth yet (5) |

brooding
| 590 | Show us your Spirit, brooding o'er each city (3) |

brook
| 627 | brook by the traveler's way (1) |

brother
102	yet this child, our Lord and brother, brought us love (3)
196, 197	Look there! the Christ, our Brother, comes resplendent (1,4)
196, 197	Good Jesus Christ, our Brother, died in darkest hurt (3)
231	witnessed to his brother, "This is Messiah true ... (2/11-30)
232	Praise ... Lord's own brother, James of Jerusalem (2/10-23)
277	our very brother, takes our nature by his birth (1)
376	Thou our Father, Christ our Brother (3)
406, 407	My Lord be praised by brother sun (2)
406, 407	be praised by brother fire (4)
416	joy of human love, brother, sister, parent, child (4)

brought
10	through sleep and darkness safely brought (1)
27, 28	you brought all things to glorious birth (1)
75	valleys shall be exalted, the lofty hills brought low (1)
97	For the world a love supreme brought me to this stable (2)
102	yet this child, our Lord and brother, brought us love (3)
102	brought us love for one another (3)
105	unto certain shepherds brought tidings of the same (2)
108	with mercies infinite our Christ hath brought us peace (2)
110	that brought into this world the God made man (2)

158	Who was the guilty? Who brought this upon thee? (2)
174	thou hast brought us life and light (3)
187	Through the Red Sea brought at last (1)
187	Earthly night brought us light which is ours eternally (3)
190	love has brought the blessed morrow (3)
199, 200	God hath brought his Israel into joy from sadness (1)
210	our Christ hath brought us over with hymns of victory (1)
258	who brought forth the world's salvation (2)
263, 264	Blest in the message Gabriel brought (3)
278	Lord of all creation brought her to his heavenly home (4)
356	at your coming thither may you be brought by them (2)
356	brought by them into the holy city (2)
386, 387	him that brought salvation down by meekness, Mary's son (4)
399	he made the sea and land, he brought the world to birth (2)
432	praise him who hath brought you his grace from above (2)
435	brought it back victorious, when from death he passed (2)
567	lo, thy touch brought life and health (2)
581	brought here together by Christ's love (1)
599	sing a song full of the hope ... the present has brought (1)
599	thou who hast brought us thus far on the way (3)
633	Word that brought to life creation (2)
645, 646	home, rejoicing, brought me (3)
671	'tis grace that brought me safe thus far (4)
705	As those of old their first fruits brought (1)
705	first fruits brought of vineyard, flock, and field (1)

brow

163	on the Redeemer's thorn-crowned brow the wonders ... view (1)
170	that thorns would flower upon your brow (1)
180	Come ... with glad smile and radiant brow (2)
313	By the thorns that crowned thy brow (3)
435	for all wreaths of empire meet upon his brow (6)
473	bears on the brow the seal of him who died (2)
483	a royal diadem adorns the mighty victor's brow (1)
598	new thorns to pierce that steady brow (1)

bud

462	truth ... like a flower shall bud and blossom show (2)
594, 595	bring her bud to glorious flower (1)
677	bud may have a bitter taste ... sweet will be the flower (5)

build

145	who build the old waste places and in the darkness shine (4)
246	till, pledged to build and not destroy (5)
365	build in our hearts thy throne, Ancient of Days (1)
582, 583	Give us, O God, the strength to build the city (3)
582, 583	yea, bids us seize the whole of life and build its glory (4)
598	O wounded hands of Jesus, build in us thy new creation (4)
600, 601	finely build for days to come foundations that endure (3)
644	Dear Name, the rock on which I build (3)
665	though with care and toil we build them (2)

builded

519, 520	living stones art builded in the height of heaven above (1)

builder
231   He taught the trade of builder (2/3-19)

builder
157   the same stone which the builders rejected (R)

building
412   Limestone and beams, loud building workers (4)
573   building proud towers which shall not reach to heaven (3)

buildings
580   stately buildings row on row (2)

builds
635   Who trusts in God's unchanging love builds on a rock (1)

built
289   Our Father, by whose servants our house was built of old (1)
323   Jesus, may we ever be grafted, rooted, built in thee (2)
398   spread the flowing seas abroad and built the lofty skies (1)
666   hopes are on thy promise built, thy never-failing word (2)
681   reflects the vast design by which thy house is built (4)

bulwarks
519, 520   all thy streets and all thy bulwarks of pure gold (2)

burden
498   the burden of the day (1)
530   word of how the Savior's love ... burden doth remove (3)
530   earth's sore burden doth remove (3)
586   workers, burden bearers of the earth (1)
611   he will make that heavy burden light (5)
621, 622   Now with gladness, now with courage, bear the burden (5)
621, 622   bear the burden laid on thee (5)

burdened
74   He offers to the burdened the rest and grace they need (4)
236   sinners who are burdened by the wrong we do (2)

burdening
350   share of quickening joy or burdening care (2)

burdens
610   making known the needs and burdens (3)
610   burdens your compassion bids us bear (4)
695, 696   still evil days bring burdens hard to bear (2)

buried
47   Holy Jesus, may I be dead and buried here with thee (4)
179   'tis thine own third morning! rise, O buried Lord! (5)
187   buried and baptized were we (3)
204   Now the green blade riseth from the buried grain (1)

burn
47   make me burn thy love to know (5)

63, 64	all wrong desires may burn away (2)
223, 224	fire, that love may burn in all (2)
409	whilst all the stars that round her burn (2)
419	kindling hearts that burn for thee (4)
431	The dawn returns in splendor, the heavens burn and blaze (2)
516	O let it freely burn, till earthly passions turn to dust (2)
574, 575	Let the fierce fires which burn and try ... purify (4)
681	whose stars serenely burn above this earth's confusion (1)
704	There let it for thy glory burn (2)
704	burn with ever bright, undying blaze (2)

burning

68	See that your lamps are burning, replenish them with oil (2)
299	With burning words of victory won inspire our hearts (3)
369	soaring spirits upward rise to reach the burning throne (2)
400	Bright burning sun with golden beams (1)
498	from the burning of the noon-tide heat (1)
501, 502	of burning love the living source (2)
580	flung the suns in burning radiance through ... space (1)
631	Light of knowledge, ever burning (3)
643	how beautiful thy mercy seat in depths of burning light (1)

burns

18	your light, O Lord, burns in our hearts (1)
182	His Spirit burns through this and every future age (5)
527	gleams and burns the guiding light (1)

burst

71, 72	gates of brass before him burst, the iron fetters yield (2)
180	he has burst his three days' prison (1)
192	Had Christ ... ne'er burst his three-day prison (R)
199, 200	Christ hath burst his prison (2)
208	let shout of holy joy outburst (2)
220, 221	The bonds of death are burst by thee (1)
252	whereby those to sin enslaved, burst their fetters (5)
252	burst their fetters and are saved (5)

bursting

370	his bursting from the spiced tomb (2)
720	the rockets' red glare, the bombs bursting in air (1)

bursts

640	see, it bursts o'er all the earth (2)

bye

247	bye-bye, Lully lullay (R)
247	for thy parting nor say nor sing bye-bye, lully lullay (3)

byways

472	walk thou beside us lest the tempting byways lure us (3)

call

60	we pray you hear us when we call (1)
60	all things on earth with one accord ... call you Lord (4)
61, 62	We follow all and heed your call (2)

61, 62	call to come into the banquet hall (2)
75	a call from the ways untrod (1)
121	you then obeyed his call (3)
150	Then if Satan on us press, Jesus, Savior, hear our call (3)
204	thy touch can call us back to life again (4)
209	to call on you when you are near (3)
223, 224	tongues, that earth may hear their call (2)
237	turn from fear, and heed the call to a glorious morrow (3)
268, 269	all the ages call be blessed (4)
281	he rose, responsive to the call, and left his task (3)
340, 341	by your call to heaven above us (2)
344	so that when thy love shall call us (3)
344	call us, Savior, from the world away (3)
345	call us, O Lord, to thine eternal peace (4)
376	call us to rejoice in thee (2)
393	call upon his holy Name (1)
404	close to your children when on you they call (3)
427	When evening shadows fall, this rings my curfew call (1)
435	'tis the Father's pleasure we should call him Lord (1)
450, 451	Crown him ye martyrs of our God who from his altar call (2)
450, 451	whom David Lord did call (3)
506, 507	we, your creatures, call you Lord (6)
518	To this temple, where we call thee, come, O Lord (3)
528	Lord, you call us to your service (2)
531	Name of Jesus glorify till every people call him Lord (4)
547	There is one Body and one hope, one Spirit and one call (3)
549, 550	By thy mercies, Savior, may we hear thy call (5)
561	the trumpet call obey (2)
563	till Christ himself ... call thee to lay thine armor by (3)
570, 571	call to mind the word of Jesus (3)
572	into your self-giving death call us all to follow (2)
600, 601	quiet of a steadfast faith, calm of a call obeyed (2)
611	All who labor, listen to his call (5)
634	I call on thee, Lord Jesus Christ (1)
636, 637	When through the deep waters I call thee to go (3)
665	Christ doth call one and all (5)
666	Out of the depths I call, to God I send my cry (1)
686	Streams of mercy ... call for songs of loudest praise (1)

called

27, 28	you found it good and called it 'day' (2)
51	praise him who called us out of sin and darkness (1)
121	God called you his beloved Son ... his servant true (2)
176, 177	By the same Spirit we are called to worship God (3)
202	The Lamb's high banquet called to share (1)
231	You called him from his fishing upon Lake Galilee (2/11-30)
231	whom your mysterious love called early (2/12-28)
231	called early from life's conflicts (2/12-28)
263, 264	who shall be called the Holy One (2)
345	that in this house have called upon thy Name (1)
353	Your love, O God, has called us here (1)
560	for they shall be called the children of God (7)
578	None ever called on thee in vain (3)
610	Called by worship to your service (4)
630	His the voice that called a nation (1)

638, 639	thyself hast called me by my name (2)
706	In your mercy, Lord, you called me (1)

calling

46	on God our Maker calling ... the Giver good (1)
67	calling us to new repentance (2)
231	not betray our calling but serve you to the end (2/2-24)
363	calling the least, the last, the lost to thee (3)
413	calling the whole world to rejoice (2)
541	Claim the high calling angels cannot share (4)
576, 577	Here in Christ we gather, love of Christ our calling (1)
652, 653	gracious calling of the Lord (2)
705	Church of Christ is calling us to make the dream come true (2)

calls

16, 17	each day the sun at zenith calls the faithful (1)
16, 17	calls the faithful to their noon-day prayers (1)
50	he calls the hours his own (1)
107	Calls you one and calls you all to gain his ... hall (3)
145	Lent calls to prayer, to trust and dedication (1)
300	Christ alone calls for all our praises (2)
467	praise him till he calls thee home (4)
546	God's all-animating voice that calls thee from on high (3)
549, 550	Jesus calls us o'er the tumult (1)
549, 550	Jesus calls us from the worship of the vain world's (3)
549, 550	still he calls, in cares and pleasures (4)
549, 550	Jesus calls us (5)
561	when duty calls, or danger, be never wanting there (3)
603, 604	always, near or far, he calls and claims us (2)
665	God unknown, he alone calls my heart to be his own (1)

calm

27, 28	we pray you, Father, calm our fears (2)
42	Jesus, give the weary calm and sweet repose (2)
44, 45	so calm our minds that fears may cease (2)
111	all is calm ... bright round yon virgin mother and child (1)
210	may hear so calm and plain his own "All hail" (2)
287	sweet is the calm of paradise the blest (6)
318	here taste afresh the calm of sin forgiven (2)
406, 407	Let wind and air and cloud and calm and weathers all (3)
482	Lord of all gentleness, Lord of all calm (4)
566	From thee ... all calm and courage, faith and hope (1)
600, 601	quiet of a steadfast faith, calm of a call obeyed (2)
608	calm amid its rage didst sleep (2)
649, 650	make all our moments calm and bright (4)
652, 653	O Sabbath rest by Galilee, O calm of hills above (3)
652, 653	O still, small voice of calm (5)
683, 684	O for a closer walk with God, a calm and heavenly frame (1)
683, 684	calm and serene my frame (5)

calmed

567	youth renewed and frenzy calmed owned thee, the Lord (2)

calmly

475	to the sunlight calmly hold them (3)

597   as beasts and cattle calmly graze (2)
675   in his strength, and calmly every danger brave (4)

calms
644   calms the troubled breast (2)

Calvary
277   till on Calvary he died (2)
284   Ye thronged to Calvary and pressed with sad desire (5)
477   humbling thyself to death on Calvary (3)
691   My faith looks up to thee, thou Lamb of Calvary (1)

Calvary's
163   the cross on Calvary's height gleams of eternity appear (2)
171   Calvary's mournful mountain climb (3)
337   once for all, on Calvary's tree (1)
570, 571   offering peace from Calvary's hill (4)
675   on Calvary's hill (3)

cam'st
313   Blessed Lord, thou cam'st to save me(2)
364   humbly thou cam'st to set us free (6)
477   Thou cam'st to us in lowliness of thought (2)
598   Lord Christ, when first thou cam'st to earth (1)

came
16, 17   For at this hour to all the world ... salvation came (2)
16, 17   grace of true salvation came (2)
18   At noon you came to Jacob's well (4a)
47   this day the Spirit came with his gifts of living flame (2)
52   This day the Holy Spirit came (3)
53   Once he came in blessing, all our ills redressing (1)
53   came in likeness lowly, Son of God most holy (1)
55   You came forth from the eternal God (3)
60   you came, O Savior, to set free your own (2)
60   When this old world drew on toward night you came (3)
65   Oh, blest is Christ that came in God's most holy name (R)
81   It came, a blossom bright (1)
84   Love came down at Christmas, love all lovely, love divine (1)
85, 86   and came to us as Mary's son (3)
85, 86   For from the Father's throne you came (5)
89, 90   It came upon the midnight clear (1)
92   His the doom, ours the mirth when he came down to earth (2)
94, 95   the angel of the Lord came down, and glory shone around (1)
98   came he to a world forlorn, the Lord of every nation (1,5)
98   Now may Mary's son, who came so long ago to love us (4)
102   He came down to earth from heaven ... God and Lord of all (2)
105   From God our heavenly Father a blessed angel came (2)
108   What tribute shall we pay to him who came in weakness (2)
109   by the light of that same star three wise men came (3)
109   three wise men came from country far (3)
120   The sinless one to Jordan came (1)
121   God's Spirit on you came (1)
127   out of thee the Lord from heaven came to rule his Israel (1)
129, 130   Swift the cloud of glory came (3)

139	baptized by John, there came a voice from heaven saying (1)
139	He came by water and by blood to heal our lost condition (3)
143	to Elijah fasting, came the steeds and chariots of flame (2)
203	amidst them came their Lord most dear (4)
204	Forth he came at Easter, like the risen grain (3)
206	amidst them came their Lord most dear (2)
223, 224	Like to cloven tongues of flame on the twelve ... came (2)
223, 224	on the twelve the Spirit came (2)
230	A mighty sound from heaven at Pentecost there came (1)
231	when they to Nazareth came (2/3-19)
235	through whom the living Gospels came sounding all abroad (1)
235	in mystic form and image four living creatures came (2)
246	Then warning came of danger near (1)
250	For Jesus came to wage sins's war (2)
253	We ask them whence their victory came (2)
255	Saul, the church's spoiler came spreading fear and hate (1)
263, 264	To Mary the Archangel came (2)
265	The angel Gabriel from heaven came (1)
267	like her whom heaven's Majesty came down to shadow o'er (3)
267	through whom that wondrous mercy came (5)
271, 272	With heavenly message Gabriel came (2)
277	God the Lord who came to earth (1)
278	from on high ... glory of the Spirit's presence came (3)
281	it came, true Lord of souls, from thee (2)
299	You came in power; the Church was born (2)
358	You came from dust and to dust shall return (3)
406, 407	From thee alone all creatures came (1)
421	who came for our salvation (3)
425	All praise and thanks to him belong who came to ... free (2)
425	came to set his people free (2)
435	Name from the lips of sinners, unto whom he came (2)
443	From God Christ's deity came forth (1)
445, 446	When all was sin and shame, a second Adam ... came (2)
445, 446	second Adam to the fight and to the rescue came (2)
454	Jesus came, adored by angels (1)
454	came with peace from realms on high (1)
454	Jesus came for our redemption (1)
454	lowly came on earth to die (1)
454	came in deep humility (1)
455, 456	read thee best in him who came to bear for us the cross (3)
458	He came from his blest throne salvation to bestow (2)
480	like us, unhonored and unknown, he came to dwell on earth (1)
489	He sent him down as sending God, in flesh to us he came (4)
489	He came as Savior to his own, the way of love he trod (5)
489	he came to win us by good will, for force is not of God (5)
492	Sing how he came forth from heaven (2)
494	rose victorious in the strife for those he came to save (3)
525	from heaven he came and sought her to be his holy bride (1)
530	word of how the Spirit came bringing peace in Jesus' name (4)
547	To us on earth he came to bring from sin and fear release (2)
631	till they came, who told the story of the Word (2)
633	Word that came from heaven to die (2)
648	came at length to Canaan's land (3)
661	such happy, simple fisher-folk before the Lord came down (1)

| 692 | I came to Jesus as I was, so weary, worn, and sad (1) |
| 692 | I came to Jesus, and I drank of that life-giving stream (2) |

camest

| 568 | Blessed Lord Jesus, who camest in poverty (2) |
| 704 | thou who camest from above the fire celestial to impart (1) |

can

27, 28	for you alone can make us strong (4)
50	Hosanna in the highest strains the Church ... can raise (5)
50	the highest strains the Church on earth can raise (5)
74	he would have us bear it so he can make us free (4)
112	What can I give him, poor as I am (4)
112	yet what I can I give him give my heart (3)
138	those refreshing streams which you alone can give (3)
168, 169	Can death thy bloom deflower (1)
174	now no more can death appall (3)
180	the passion that he bore -- sin and pain can vex no more (2)
193	from every weapon death can wield ... shield (4)
194, 195	thy terrors now can no longer, death, appall us (1)
204	thy touch can call us back to life again (4)
248, 249	Name beyond what words can tell (2)
251	O God, whom neither time nor space can limit (1)
251	neither time nor space can limit, hold, or bind (1)
255	grace, by ways mysterious, our sinful wrath can bind (3)
255	in those least expected true servants you can find (3)
275	Multitude which none can number ... in glory stands (1)
293	You can meet them in school, or in lanes, or at sea (3)
335	No one can come to me unless the Father draw them (1)
356	dwell the white-robed martyrs who now no more can die (1)
357	Here mid stress and conflict toils can never cease (2)
372	holy, no holiness of earth can his express (2)
374	blessings, more than we can give (3)
382	in my heart, though not in heaven, I can raise thee (3)
383, 384	Jesus shines purer than all the angels heaven can boast (3)
388	Thy bountiful care, what tongue can recite (4)
390	ponder anew what the Almighty can do (3)
391	he can create, and he destroy (1)
402, 403	Church with psalms must shout, no door can keep them out (2)
406, 407	from whom no one alive can flee (7)
414	Honor great our God befitteth, who his majesty can reach (2)
425	He only is the mighty Lord. He only can destroy the foe (3)
425	He only is to be adored for he alone can strength bestow (3)
427	God's holy house of prayer hath none that can compare (2)
434	nor wit can guess, nor reason prove which of the letters (3)
447	What now can separate us from the love of Christ our Lord (2)
447	Can persecution, nakedness, or peril, or the sword (2)
447	no power earth can afford will separate us (4)
450, 451	Sinners, whose love can ne'er forget the wormwood (5)
457	thy word alone true wisdom can impart (2)
476	Can we by searching find out God or formulate his ways (1)
476	Can numbers measure what he is (1)
476	can ... words contain his praise (1)
476	Although his being is too bright for human eyes to scan (2)
487	such a joy as none can move (3)

487	such a love as none can part (3)
498	Upon the cross of Jesus mine eyes at times can see (2)
503, 504	where thou art guide, no ill can come (6)
505	unless thy grace the power should give, none can believe (2)
505	none can believe in Christ and live (2)
515	bringing down the richest treasure we can wish (1)
515	richest treasure we can wish or God can send (1)
516	for none can guess its grace, till Love create a place (3)
522, 523	what can shake thy sure repose (1)
522, 523	Who can faint when such a river ever ... thirst assuage (2)
524	brightest glories earth can yield (5)
534	All we can do is nothing worth unless God blesses the deed (4)
559	pleasure that can never cloy (3)
559	nothing can our peace destroy (3)
562	gates of hell can never 'gainst that Church prevail (4)
563	he can with bread of heaven thy fainting spirit feed (1)
563	far more o'er thee are watching than human eyes can know (2)
573	sharing not our griefs, no joy can share (2)
581	Love can exclude no race or creed if honored be God's Name (6)
592	All may of thee partake, nothing can be so mean (2)
607	with faith that none can alter, your servants undergird (3)
621, 622	brighter than the heart can fancy (1)
623	There, where no troubles distraction can bring (3)
631	shedding light that none can measure (1)
635	a rock which nought can move (1)
636, 637	What more can he say than to you he hath said (1)
642	No voice can sing, no heart can frame (2)
642	nor can the memory find a sweeter sound than Jesus' Name (2)
642	this nor tongue nor pen can show (4)
647	I know not if the way is long, and no one else can say (1)
649, 650	blest, when our faith can hold you fast (3)
662	what but thy grace can foil the tempter's power (2)
662	Who, like thyself, my guide and stay can be (2)
663	surely I can trust thy love for all the days to come (5)
667	set free from present sorrow, we cheerfully can say (2)
667	It can bring with it nothing but he will bear us through (3)
674	you alone can grant us grace to live the words we say (1)
674	How can your pardon reach and bless the unforgiving heart (2)
676	you can tell the love of Jesus (2)
681	our hearts can find no rest (2)
687, 688	his rage we can endure (3)
698	only you can teach me how to pray (1)
702	Where can I go apart from thee (3)
720	O say can you see by the dawn's early light (1)

Cana

| 135 | at Cana, wedding guest, in thy God-head manifest (2) |

Cana's

| 138 | did manifest your glory forth in Cana's marriage hour (1) |

Canaan's

393	how he leads his chosen unto Canaan's promised land (1)
648	came at length to Canaan's land (3)
690	land me safe on Canaan's side (3)

cancelled

18   so bright it cancelled out the sun (4b)

candle

459   an altar candle sheds its light as surely as a star (2)

cannot

112   Our God, heaven cannot hold him, nor earth sustain (2)
122, 123   Alleluia, song of gladness, voice of joy that cannot die (1)
158   Therefore, kind Jesus, since I cannot pay thee (5)
167   We may not know, we cannot tell what pains he had to bear (2)
205   that life which cannot die (3)
246   cry out, "We cannot understand" (3)
246   love that cannot cease to bear our human anguish (4)
270   he that cannot die, be slain (2)
277   toil and labor cannot weary love enduring unto death (2)
351   possess, in sweet communion, joys ... earth cannot afford (2)
447   troubles that are ours to bear are trials we cannot flee (3)
462   his footsteps cannot err (1)
481   His kingdom cannot fail, he rules o'er earth and heaven (3)
522, 523   he whose word cannot be broken formed thee (1)
541   Claim the high calling angels cannot share (4)
543   He gilds thy morning face with beams that cannot fade (2)
562   we have Christ's own promise, and that cannot fail (4)
592   which God doth touch and own cannot for less be told (4)
638, 639   whom still I hold, but cannot see (1)
667   while in him confiding, I cannot but rejoice (4)
676   If you cannot preach like Peter (2)
676   if you cannot pray like Paul (2)
702   My words from thee I cannot hide (2)

canopy

388   whose robe is the light, whose canopy space (2)

canst

53   Thus, if thou canst name him, not ashamed to claim him (3)
194, 195   by this we know thou, O grave, canst not enthrall us (1)
320   never canst thou reach his due (1)
320   thou, who all things canst and knowest (6)
337   most patient Savior, who canst love us still (4)
415   But thou canst read it there (2)
440   thou alone to God canst win us (2)
457   thou only canst inform the mind and purify the heart (2)
659, 660   in peace that only thou canst give (4)

canyoned

580   windows ... stare on canyoned streets below (2)

captain

275   Captain of salvation, thee, their Savior and their King (3)
287   thou, Lord, their Captain in the well-fought fight (2)
435   crown him as your Captain in temptation's hour (5)
484, 485   Jesus, Lord, our Captain glorious (2)
542   Christ is the world's true Light ... captain of salvation (1)
563   trust only Christ, thy Captain (2)

572   Captain Christ, O lowly Lord, Servant King (2)

captive
56   O come, O come, Emmanuel and ransom captive Israel (1,8)
156   O Christ, thy triumphs now begin o'er captive death (2)
156   captive death and conquered sin (2)
202   thy captive people are set free (4)
219   the grave and hell are captive led (1)
426   songs of praise arose when he captive led captivity (2)
492   the captor captive led (3)
511   setting captive sinners free (2)
616   He comes to break oppression, to set the captive free (1)

captives
534   to set their captives free (3)
610   still the captives long for freedom (2)

captivity
426   songs of praise arose when he captive led captivity (2)

captor
492   the captor captive led (3)

care
10   love ... shall dawn on every cross and care (4)
48   O balm of care and sadness, most beautiful, most bright (1)
101   Bless all the dear children in thy tender care (3)
144   restore us by your loving care to peace and joy within (2)
145   Now quit your care and anxious fear and worry (1)
251   thy loving care renew (2)
350   share of quickening joy or burdening care (2)
388   Thy bountiful care, what tongue can recite (4)
391   We are his people, we his care (3)
394, 395   proclaim your care (2)
398   all that borrows life from thee is ever in thy care (3)
400   praise God, and cast on him your care (5)
454   again in mercy, when our hearts are bowed with care (2)
486   O Savior, with protecting care abide in this thy house (3)
528   May your care and mercy lead us to a just society (4)
552, 553   Cast care aside, lean on thy Guide (3)
566   From thee ... all pity, care, and love (1)
568   truly to care for the poor of the earth (2)
579   keep them by thy watchful care from every peril in the air (3)
590   hymns be rising in every city for your love and care (1)
621, 622   for unknown are toil and care (3)
624   there from care released, the shout of them that triumph (3)
641   with care and woe oppressed (2)
659, 660   help me bear the strain of toil, the fret of care (1)
665   though with care and toil we build them (2)
669   fills thy heart with care (1)
669   what profit doth it bring thee to pine in grief and care (2)
701   Hence, for pomps I care not (2)
708   much we need thy tender care (1)

cared
170   for all they cared (2)

career
386, 387   Glorious the sun in mid career (3)

cares
222   he takes upon his heart the cares, the pain, and shame (3)
231   they're free from pain and cares (2/12-28)
482   whose trust, ever child-like, no cares could destroy (1)
524   to her my cares and toils be given till toils ... end (2)
524   till toils and cares shall end (2)
528   amid the cares that claim us, hold in mind eternity (5)
549, 550   still he calls, in cares and pleasures (4)
588, 589   Let not the world's deceitful cares ... destroy (3)

caring
261, 262   he by his caring ministered to Jesus (1)
424   world-wide task of caring for the hungry and despairing (2)
580   scarcely caring where they go (2)

carpenter
260   carpenter whose life fulfilled our gracious God's design (1)
586   carpenter of Nazareth, toiling for thy daily food (1)
611   Skillful craftsman, blessed carpenter (3)

cast
59   Cast away the works of darkness, O ye children of the day (1
78, 79   cast out our sin and enter in, be born in us today (5)
187   Egypt's chains behind we cast (1)
268, 269   he has cast down all the mighty ... lowly are his choice (4)
290   in the fire the tares to cast (3)
359   Elijah's mantle o'er Elisha cast (1)
388   and round it hath cast, like a mantle, the sea (3)
400   praise God, and cast on him your care (5)
408   Cast each false idol from its throne (3)
425   horse ... rider ... sword he cast into the raging sea (1)
496, 497   deigned to cast a pitying eye upon his helpless creature (2)
542   cast out our pride and shame that hinder to enthrone thee (3)
552, 553   Cast care aside, lean on thy Guide (3)
588, 589   Almighty God, your word is cast like seed upon the ground (1)
599   where the white gleam of our bright star is cast (2)
649, 650   where'er our changing lot is cast (3)
657   till we cast our crowns before thee (3)
658   Why restless, why cast down, my soul (3)
661   They cast their nets in Galilee (1)
718   in this free land by thee our lot is cast (2)

casting
362   casting down their golden crowns around the glassy sea (2)

casts
353   the perfect love that casts out fear (1)
700   O love that casts out fear, O love that casts out sin (1)

catch

574, 575	for crafty trade and subtle snare to catch the simple (3)
574, 575	to catch the simple unaware (3)
609	we catch the vision of thy tears (2)

cattle

101	The cattle are lowing, the baby awakes (2)
102	Once in royal David's city stood a lowly cattle shed (1)
597	as beasts and cattle calmly graze (2)

cause

57, 58	cause of endless exultation to his ransomed worshipers (3)
146, 147	help us, lest ... we cause your Name to be betrayed (4)
243	he had no friend to plead his cause (2)
243	Let me, O Lord, thy cause defend (4)
447	now pleads our cause at God's right hand (1)
636, 637	I'll strengthen thee, help thee, and cause thee to stand (2)
705	serve thy cause and share thy love with all humanity (3)
720	Then conquer we must, when our cause it is just (2)

caused

389	He the golden-tressed sun caused all day his course to run (4)
439	that caused the Lord of bliss to lay aside his crown (1)
633	Word that caused blind eyes to see (3)

causes

172	Oh! Sometimes it causes me to tremble, tremble (1-4)

causing

3, 4	keep us from causing others pain (2)

cave

492	bowed himself to Bethlehem's cave (2)

Ceasars

452	born to wear the crown that Ceasars scorn (1)

cease

27, 28	to turn from sin and cease from wrong (4)
44, 45	so calm our minds that fears may cease (2)
56	bid thou our sad divisions cease (7)
89, 90	O hush the noise and cease your strife (3)
94, 95	good will ... begin and never cease (6)
108	Let every house be bright; let praises never cease (2)
146, 147	so when our wanderings here shall cease (5)
170	though empires rise and fall ... Kingdom shall not cease (3)
170	Kingdom shall not cease to grow till love embraces all (3)
223, 224	till our earthly wanderings cease (4)
231	O Rachel, cease your weeping (2/12-28)
246	love that cannot cease to bear our human anguish (4)
315	make thou our sad divisions soon to cease (2)
315	So, Lord, at length when sacraments shall cease (3)
320	ordained to be repeated, his memorial ne'er to cease (3)
345	Then, when thy voice shall bid our conflict cease (4)
357	Here mid stress and conflict toils can never cease (2)

226, 227	come with thy celestial light (1)
282, 283	may the celestial company of angels ... help us (5)
366	Hark, the loud celestial hymn angel choirs ... raising (2)
392	celestial fruits on earthly ground (3)
392	celestial fruits ... from faith and hope may grow (3)
503, 504	lighten with celestial fire (1)
519, 520	from celestial realms descending (2)
621, 622	Light's abode, celestial Salem (1)
645, 646	with food celestial feedeth (2)
704	thou who camest from above the fire celestial to impart (1)

cell

252	kneeling in her lowly cell, by the angel Gabriel (2)

cellos

412	Harp, lute, and lyre, loud humming cellos (3)

center

376	center of unbroken praise (2)
419	center and soul of every sphere (1)

central

435	through all ranks of creatures, to the central height (3)

centuries

420	through centuries of wrong, borne witness to the truth (3)

certain

105	unto certain shepherds brought tidings of the same (2)
109	certain poor shepherds in fields as they lay (1)

chain

179	Loose the souls long prisoned, bound with Satan's chain (6)
184	Christ has broken every chain (1)

chains

38, 39	You broke the chains of death and hell (3)
187	Egypt's chains behind we cast (1)
270	Adam's chains shall be unbound (3)
544	the prisoners leap to lose their chains (4)

chalice

360, 361	drink of thy chalice (2)
645, 646	what transport of delight from thy pure chalice floweth (5)

challenge

231	he rose to meet your challenge (2/11-30)
513	like the challenge of her flight (1)
580	As each far horizon beckons, may it challenge us anew (4)

challenges

582, 583	how its splendor challenges the souls that greatly dare (4)

chamber

360, 361	This is the temple; here thy presence-chamber (2)

chance

348	each duty ... give us the chance to create or destroy (4)
350	through change and chance be thou their guide (3)
665	me through change and chance he guideth (1)

change

21, 22	you order time and change aright (1)
292	Lord, in their change, let frost and heat ... be given (2)
350	through change and chance be thou their guide (3)
630	See its glory undiminished by the change of time or place (4)
665	me through change and chance he guideth (1)

changed

220, 221	angels wonder when they see how changed is our humanity (2)
256	Saint Paul was changed by God's free love (3)
657	changed from glory into glory (3)

changeful

| 289 | changeful years unresting their silent course have sped (2) |

changeless

372	Established is his law, and changeless it shall stand (3)
388	hath stablished it fast by a changeless decree (3)
393	how the word we have heard firm and changeless ... stand (1)
393	changeless still shall stand (1)
616	Name shall stand for ever, his changeless Name of Love (5)
691	may my love to thee pure, warm, and changeless be (2)

changes

| 14, 15 | through all its changes guide the day (1) |
| 163 | Sunset to sunrise changes now (1) |

changest

| 289 | who changest not with years (2) |

changeth

| 423 | then wither and perish, but nought changeth thee (3) |
| 552, 553 | he changeth not, and thou art dear (4) |

changing

135	manifest in power divine, changing water into wine (2)
250	Now greet the swiftly changing year with joy (1)
428	O changing seasons bless the Lord (2)
649, 650	where'er our changing lot is cast (3)
686	mount of God's unchanging love (1)

chant

82	hymn and chant and high thanksgiving (4)
122, 123	Alleluia though we cherish and would chant for evermore (3)
495	help to chant Emmanuel's praise (4)

chanted

| 106 | mystery ... which hosts of angels chanted from above (1) |

chanting

33-35	joyfully chanting holy hymns to praise you (3)
275	Hark, the sound of holy voices, chanting (1)
275	chanting at the crystal sea ... alleluia, Lord, to thee (1)
376	flashing sea, chanting bird and flowing fountain (2)
556, 557	Yes, on through life's long path ... chanting as ye go (4)

chaos

176, 177	Over the chaos of the empty waters hovered the Spirit (1)
371	Thou, whose almighty word chaos and darkness heard (1)
371	chaos and darkness ... took their flight (1)
608	Most Holy Spirit, who didst brood upon the chaos (3)
608	chaos dark and rude (3)

charade

170	acted out their grim charade to its appointed end (3)

charge

290	give his angels charge at last (3)

charged

231	thrice charged to feed your fold (2/1-18)
247	Herod the King, in his raging charged he hath this day (2)
247	charged ... his men of might, in his own sight (2)

chariot

215	clouds, his chariot (1)

chariots

143	to Elijah fasting, came the steeds and chariots of flame (2)
388	His chariots of wrath the deep thunderclouds form (2)

charity

78, 79	charity stands watching and faith holds wide the door (4)
97	Father, glory be to thee for the wondrous charity (3)
97	wondrous charity of thy Son, our Lord (3)
105	with true love and charity each other now embrace (4)
505	that charity may warm each heart (3)
562	one in hope and doctrine, one in charity (3)
568	stir us to work for thy justice and charity (2)
581	Where charity and love prevail there God is ever found (1)
581	With grateful joy and holy fear his charity we learn (2)
606	Where true charity and love dwell, God himself is there (A)

charm

474	all the vain things that charm me most, I sacrifice (2)

charms

493	Jesus, the Name that charms our fears (3)

chart

627	guide and chart wherein we read of realms beyond the sky (2)
632	It is the chart and compass that o'er life's surging sea (2)

charter
525   her charter of salvation, one Lord, one faith, one birth (2)

chasing
527   chasing far the gloom and terror (2)

chaste
406, 407   water ... most humble, useful, precious, chaste (4)

chastening
569   earth by thy chastening yet shall ... be restored (4)
574, 575   a ready mind to understand the meaning of thy chastening (1)
574, 575   thy chastening hand (1)
599   Stony the road we trod, bitter the chastening rod (2)

chastens
433   he chastens and hastens his will to make known (1)

cheer
56   cheer us by thy drawing nigh (6)
96   why these songs of happy cheer (2)
368   Source of comfort, cheer us with the Savior's love (3)
396, 397   with ever joyful hearts and blessed peace to cheer us (2)
448, 449   Spirit here to guide, to strengthen, and to cheer (5)
503, 504   Anoint and cheer our soiled face with ... thy grace (5)
667   to cheer it after rain (1)

cheerful
374   Come, let us join our cheerful songs with angels (1)
377, 378   sing to the Lord with cheerful voice (1)
415   nor is the least a cheerful heart (3)
415   cheerful heart that tastes those gifts with joy (3)
543   Cheerful in God, arise and shine (1)

cheering
267   promise shone with cheering ray on waiting saints of old (1)
412   Athlete and band, loud cheering people (5)

cheerless
6, 7   Dark and cheerless is the morn unaccompanied by thee (2)

cheers
300   cheers our hearts, fills with food and gladness (3)
419   star of our hope, thy softened light cheers the ... night (2)
419   cheers the long watches of the night (2)
471   cheers with hope the gloomy day (3)

cherish
122, 123   Alleluia though we cherish and would chant for evermore (3)
348   intention ever to cherish the gifts you provide (2)
383, 384   thee will I cherish, thee will I honor (1)

cherubim
112   cherubim and seraphim thronged the air (3)

115	What child is this, who, laid to rest, on Mary's lap (1)
125, 126	To us the promised Child is born, to us the Son is given (3)
246	The soldiers sought the child in vain (2)
247	Lully, Lullay, thou little tiny child (R)
247	That woe is me, poor child for thee (3)
252	Jesus, Name of mercy mild, given to the holy child (4)
258	blessed was she in her Child (1,2)
259	in his hands takes up the promised child (3)
259	child, the glory of all lands (3)
277	Son most holy, who became her little child (1)
277	Fairest child of fairest mother (1)
278	Mary at whose breast the child was fed who is Son of God (1)
284	Ye saw the heaven-born child in human flesh arrayed (2)
379	every child of every race (2)
400	You lead back home the child of God (6)
416	joy of human love, brother, sister, parent, child (4)
444	He from the house of David a child of grace has given (2)
468	child of Mary ... didn't have a cradle (2)
490	I want to walk as a child of the light (1)
529	Who serves my Father as his child is surely kin to me (2)
587	O Christ, thyself a child within an earthly home (2)
597	a little child shall lead them all (2)
610	go to the child, the youth, the aged (4)
611	Blessed manchild, boy of Nazareth (2)
664	no more a stranger or a guest, but like a child at home (3)

childhood

| 580 | since the childhood of our race (3) |

childlike

| 627 | to its heavenly teaching turn, with ... childlike hearts (5) |

children

42	Grant to little children visions bright of thee (3)
44, 45	from all ill dreams your children keep (2)
59	Cast away the works of darkness, O ye children of the day (1)
70	God receives his wayward children (3)
78, 79	Where children pure and happy pray to the blessed Child (4)
85, 86	his banished children to reclaim (5)
92	song children sing to the Lord, Christ our King (1)
101	Bless all the dear children in thy tender care (3)
102	he leads his children on to the place where he is gone (5)
114	O children of the forest free, the angel song is true (4)
122, 123	alleluia, joyful mother, all thy children sing with thee (2)
154, 155	to whom the lips of children made sweet hosannas ring (R)
223, 224	with their children still abide (4)
246	those who saw their children die (2)
247	all young children to slay (2)
259	O Light of all the earth, thy children wait for thee (4)
289	hand hath crowned her children with blessings manifold (1)
291	much more to us, his children, he gives our daily bread (2)
294	born of one Father, we are his children (3)
295	God's children by adoption, baptized into his grace (1)
321	be all thy children thither led (1)

338	See now thy children, making intercession (2)
345	from harm and danger keep thy children free (2)
358	We are your creatures and children of earth (2)
360, 361	favor thy children (5)
363	O holy Father, who hast led thy children in all the ages (2)
363	led thy children ... with the fire and cloud (2)
388	Frail children of dust, and feeble as frail (5)
392	children of the heavenly King may speak their joys abroad (2)
404	close to your children when on you they call (3)
437, 438	to children's children and for evermore (4)
478	in love your children keep to life unending (2)
480	When Jesus into Zion rode, the children sang around (3)
560	for they shall be called the children of God (7)
580	your children in your likeness, share inventive powers (1)
580	children of creative purpose (4)
587	our children bless, in every place (2)
608	thy children shield in danger's hour (4)
610	Still your children wander homeless (2)
617	one in the power that makes thy children free (2)
648	to lead the children of Israel through (2)
667	he who feeds the ravens will give his children bread (3)
669	the needs of all thy children, their anguish or delight (3)

children's

437, 438	to children's children and for evermore (4)
528	asking ... world around us share your children's liberty (3)
594, 595	Cure thy children's warring madness (3)

chill

192	Death's flood hath lost its chill (2)
226, 227	melt the frozen, warm the chill (4)
228	melt with fire our icy chill (4)

choice

231	the apostles sought God's choice (2/2-24)
268, 269	he has cast down all the mighty ... lowly are his choice (4)
626	thy glory be my aim, thy holy will my choice (1)

choir

106	He spoke ... straightway the celestial choir ... conspire (3)
430	this huge wide orb we see shall one choir, one temple be (4)
620	David stands with harp in hand as master of the choir (3)

choirs

33-35	in the heavens choirs of stars appearing (2)
83	Sing, choirs of angels, sing in exultation (3)
114	God the Lord of all the earth sent angel-choirs instead (1)
122, 123	alleluia is the anthem ever raised by choirs on high (1)
215	Hark, the choirs of angel voices joyful alleluias sing (1)
235	Come sing, ye choirs exultant, those messengers of God (1)
354	May the choirs of angels welcome you (2)
356	May choirs of angels lead you to Paradise on high (1)
366	Hark, the loud celestial hymn angel choirs ... raising (2)
366	angel choirs above are raising (2)

556, 557	With all the angel choirs, with all the saints of earth (2)
618	cry out ... virtues, archangels, angels' choirs (1)
619	let all your choirs reecho to the height (2)

choose

512	make us know and choose thy way (2)
598	thy peace by which alone we choose thee (3)
656	for his dwelling ... throne will choose the pure in heart (3)
706	Lord, I did not freely choose you (2)
706	did not freely choose you till by grace you set me free (2)
707	take my intellect ... use every power as thou ... choose (2)

chord

| 432 | each jubilant chord reecho around (3) |

chorus

99	when lo! above the earth rang out the angel chorus (2)
99	chorus that hailed our Savior's birth (2)
336	Let the mighty chorus ever sing its glad exultant songs (3)
366	cherubim and seraphim, in unceasing chorus praising (2)
430	in this chorus take your place (3)

chose

54	Marvel ... that the Lord chose such a birth (1)
120	chose the path his Father willed (1)
480	he chose an humble birth (1)

chosen

77	A maid in lowly human place became ... the chosen (3)
77	chosen vessel of his grace (3)
80	Mary, chosen virgin mild (2)
145	For is not this the fast that I have chosen (3)
162	Blest tree, whose chosen branches bore the wealth (4)
198	Thou hallowed chosen morn of praise (1)
225	his chosen apostles, preach to the ends of the earth (3)
235	In one harmonious witness the chosen four combine (2)
268, 269	Blessed were the chosen people (2)
268, 269	chosen people out of whom the Lord did come (2)
276	saw the glory round thy head, one of the chosen three (3)
285	great apostle's chosen friend (3)
329, 331	mid the twelve, his chosen band (3)
343	Shepherd of souls, refresh and bless thy chosen (1)
343	bless thy chosen pilgrim flock with manna (1)
348	chosen by you, to be counted as friends (1)
393	how he leads his chosen unto Canaan's promised land (1)
450, 451	heirs of Israel's chosen race, ye ransomed from the fall (4)
518	chosen of the Lord, and precious (1)
706	had your love not chosen me (2)
718	thy word our law, thy paths our chosen way (2)

Christ

3, 4	to Christ, revealed in earthly night (5)
6, 7	Christ, whose glory fills the skies (1)
6, 7	Christ, the true, the only Light (1)

14, 15	Almighty Father, hear our cry through Jesus Christ (3)
14, 15	Jesus Christ, our Lord Most High (3)
16, 17	All glory be to you, Lord Christ (4)
19, 20	Almighty Father, hear our cry through Jesus Christ (3)
19, 20	Christ, our Lord Most High (3)
21, 22	through Jesus Christ, our Lord Most High (3)
25, 26	O gracious Light, Lord Jesus Christ (1)
29, 30	to Christ revealed in earthly night (3)
33-35	Christ, mighty Savior, Light of all creation (1)
36	our Savior Jesus Christ, joyful in thine appearing (1)
37	most holy, heavenly, blest, Lord Jesus Christ (1)
38, 39	All glory be to you, Lord Christ (5)
40, 41	O Christ, you are both light and day (1)
40, 41	O Christ, Redeemer of the world (5)
44, 45	through Jesus Christ, our Lord Most High (4)
48	day for our salvation Christ rose from depths of earth (2)
51	that Christ may take them, bless them, break and give (4)
57, 58	Alleluia, Christ the Lord returns to reign (1)
59	"Christ is nigh," it seems to say (1)
59	Christ our sun, all sloth dispelling (2)
60	O Christ, Redeemer of us all (1)
65	Prepare the way, O Zion, your Christ is drawing near (1)
65	Oh, blest is Christ that came in God's most holy name (R)
70	tell the news that Christ is here (2)
70	Christ has come to share our life (4)
70	Christ, the Savior King, has come (R)
73	Hail, Christ the Lord (5)
74	have not learned to heed the Christ (2)
74	Christ, who is the Promise, who has atonement made (2)
77	child whom Mary bore, the Christ, the everlasting King (1)
78, 79	For Christ is born of Mary (2)
78, 79	still the dear Christ enters in (3)
80	This is the Christ, God's Son most high (3)
82	Christ, to thee with God the Father (4)
83	O come, let us adore him, Christ, the Lord (R)
85, 86	O Christ, Redeemer virgin-born (6)
87	with the angelic host proclaim Christ is born (1)
87	Christ, by highest heaven adored (2)
87	Christ, the everlasting Lord (2)
88	O sing, this blessed morn, Jesus Christ today is born (R)
88	Christ is born for us that we born again in him may be (4)
92	song children sing to the Lord, Christ our King (1)
92	praising Christ, heaven's King (4)
93	come and worship, worship Christ, the new-born King (R)
94, 95	Savior who is Christ the Lord ... this shall be the sign (3)
96	come, adore on bended knee Christ, the Lord (3)
96	Christ, the Lord, the new-born King (3)
97	Christ we praise with voices bold (3)
99	go tell it on the mountain, that Jesus Christ is born (R)
99	Down in a lowly manger the humble Christ was born (3)
102	Mary was that mother mild, Jesus Christ her little child (1)
102	Christ ... set at God's right hand on high (6)
103	in one accord adoring Christ the Lord (R)

105	remember Christ our Savior was born on Christmas Day (1)
106	this day is born a Savior, Christ the Lord (2)
107	give ye heed to what we say: Jesus Christ is born today (1)
107	Christ is born today (1)
107	Jesus Christ was born for this (2)
107	Christ was born for this (2)
107	Jesus Christ was born to save (3)
107	Christ was born to save (3)
108	Now yield we thanks and praise to Christ (1)
108	to Christ enthroned in glory (1)
108	with mercies infinite our Christ hath brought us peace (2)
110	when Christ our Lord was born on Christmas night (1)
111	Christ, the Savior, is born (2)
112	stable ... sufficed the Lord God incarnate, Jesus Christ (2)
115	This, this is Christ the King who shepherds guard (R)
119	Christ, to thee, our heavenly King (3)
120	Christ, the Son of God, had come to lead his ... people (2)
120	O Christ, may we baptized from sin, go forth with you (5)
121	Christ, when for us you were baptized (1)
124	to Christ, revealed in earthly night (5)
129, 130	Christ upon the mountain peak stands alone in glory (1)
129, 130	Christ ... in glory blazing (1)
136	which Christ upon the mountain shows (1)
136	Christ deigns to manifest today what glory shall be (3)
137	which Christ upon the mountain shows (1)
137	Christ deigns to manifest today what glory shall be (3)
139	for he is Christ the Savior (1)
139	Triune God is thus made known in Christ as love unending (2)
139	trust in Christ who will baptize with water and the Spirit (3)
143	Christ, through whom all things were made (1)
143	Christ ... himself has fasted and has prayed (1)
146, 147	Christ by his own example sealed (2)
156	O Christ, thy triumphs now begin o'er captive death (2)
159	seeing Christ in torment languish (1)
160	where the blood of Christ was shed (1,4)
165, 166	Jesus Christ, the world's Redeemer ... reigns as King (1)
171	learn of Jesus Christ to pray (1)
171	learn of Jesus Christ to die (3)
174	Christ the victim, Christ the priest (1)
174	Praise we Christ, whose blood was shed (2)
175	day whereon Christ arose, breaking the kingdom of death (R)
178	We have been crucified with Christ (3)
180	Christ has won the victory (1)
181	rejoicing in the Lamb of God, to Christ the eternal King (3)
182	Christ is alive (1,2,5)
183	Christ, who only is sinless, reconcileth sinners (2)
183	Christ ... reconcileth sinners to the Father (2)
183	The tomb of Christ, who is living (5)
183	Yes, Christ my hope is arisen (7)
183	Christ indeed from death is risen (8)
184	Christ the Lord is risen again (1)
184	Christ has broken every chain (1)
184	alleluia, Christ, our Paschal lamb indeed (R)

184	Christ, today your people feed. Alleluia (R)
185, 186	Christ Jesus lay in death's strong bands (1)
185, 186	Christ is himself the joy of all (3)
185, 186	Christ ... the sun that warms and lights us (3)
185, 186	Christ alone our souls will feed (4)
187	by his tomb Christ makes room (2)
188, 189	Christ has opened paradise (1)
188, 189	Soar we now where Christ has led (3)
190	Christ has risen from the tomb (1)
191	Jesus Christ, the King of glory (1)
191	Christ from death to life is born (2)
191	Christ has triumphed (1)
191	Christ is risen (3,4)
191	Christ, the first-fruits of the holy harvest-field (3)
192	Had Christ, that once was slain (R)
192	Had Christ ... ne'er burst his three-day prison (R)
192	but now is Christ arisen (R)
193	Christ was risen from the grave (2)
196, 197	Look there! the Christ, our Brother, comes resplendent (1,4)
196, 197	Good Jesus Christ inside his pain looked down (2)
196, 197	Good Jesus Christ, our Brother, died in darkest hurt (3)
198	Christ rose from death ... adore for ever ... evermore (1)
199, 200	Christ hath burst his prison (2)
201	For Christ is risen from the tomb (1)
201	in praise of Christ, our risen Lord (4)
202	Now Christ our Passover is slain (3)
207	Jesus Christ is risen today ... our triumphant holy day (1)
207	praise ... unto Christ our heavenly King (2)
208	but Christ their legions hath dispersed (2)
210	our Christ hath brought us over with hymns of victory (1)
210	for Christ the Lord is risen, our joy that hath no end (3)
212	rejoice in Christ (1)
214	Christ, awhile to mortals given (1)
216	day when the Christ ascends, high in the heavens to reign (R)
217, 218	by a new way none ever trod Christ takes his place (1)
217, 218	Christ takes his place -- the throne of God (1)
217, 218	O risen Christ, ascended Lord (3)
220, 221	O risen Christ, ascended Lord, all praise to thee (4)
225	Christ and his wonderful works (3)
230	what Christ had promised now occurred (1)
231	to be, for Christ, God's Name (2/3-19)
231	O Christ, our Lord and Savior (2/6-11)
232	taught both Jew and Gentile ... Christ is all in all (2/6-29)
232	her Lord, the risen Christ (2/7-22)
232	the faith of Christ maintain (2/10-28)
233, 234	The eternal gifts of Christ the King ... we sing (1)
233, 234	the perfect love of Christ they know (3)
235	Four-square ... foundation the Church of Christ remains (3)
236	glory to Christ, who set us free (4)
238, 239	loving Christ with single heart (2)
238, 239	fellow-heirs with Christ on high (3)
240	they, like Christ, in death victorious (1)
240	Christ, for cruel traitors pleading (3)
240	Christ ... triumphed in his parting breath (3)

547	Christ shall give you light (1)
547	Then walk in love as Christ has loved (4)
547	forgive as God in Christ forgave (4)
547	For us Christ lived, for us he died (5)
547	Christ shall give you life (5)
548	Soldiers of Christ, arise, and put your armor on (1)
548	ye may o'ercome, through Christ alone (5)
551	Lift high the cross of Christ (3)
552, 553	Christ is thy strength and Christ thy right (1)
552, 553	Christ is the path and Christ the prize (2)
552, 553	trust, and thy trusting soul shall prove Christ ... life (3)
552, 553	Christ is its life and Christ its love (3)
552, 553	only believe ... see that Christ is all in all to thee (4)
556, 557	the cross of Christ your King (1,7)
561	till every foe is vanquished and Christ is Lord indeed (1)
562	Christ, the royal Master, leads against the foe (1)
562	glory, laud, and honor, unto Christ the King (5)
563	trust only Christ, thy Captain (2)
563	till Christ himself ... call thee to lay thine armor by (3)
572	we would raise, O Christ, one song (1)
572	Captain Christ, O lowly Lord, Servant King (2)
576, 577	Here in Christ we gather, love of Christ our calling (1)
576, 577	Christ, our love, is with us, gladness be his greeting (1)
576, 577	Loving him, let each love Christ in one another (1)
576, 577	Christ, our God, be always present here among us (2)
579	O Christ, the Lord of hill and plain (2)
582, 583	O holy city ... where Christ, the Lamb, doth reign (1)
582, 583	Christ hath died in vain (2)
587	O Christ, thyself a child within an earthly home (2)
590	O Jesus Christ, may grateful hymns be rising (1)
594, 595	Lo, the hosts of evil round us scorn thy Christ (2)
598	Lord Christ, when first thou cam'st to earth (1)
598	New advent of the love of Christ (3)
603, 604	When Christ was lifted from the earth (1)
603, 604	may I in Christ be free to welcome and accept his own (4)
603, 604	as Christ accepted me (4)
605	Let Christ endue our will with grace to fortify (4)
606	Since the love of Christ has joined us in one body (1)
606	that Christ the Lord may be with us through all our days (2)
606	grace to see your exalted glory, O Christ our God (3)
607	Christ shall rule victorious o'er all the world's domain (4)
608	O Christ, whose voice the waters heard (2)
611	Christ the worker, born in Bethlehem (1)
611	Christ the worker, Love alive for us (7)
613	Thy kingdom come, O God! Thy rule, O Christ, begin (1)
614	Christ is the King (1)
614	Christ through all ages is the same (2)
619	Almighty Christ, to thee our voices sing (7)
628	that yearning souls may find the Christ (3)
632	O Christ, the Word Incarnate, O Wisdom from on high (1)
632	guides, O Christ, to thee (2)
634	I call on thee, Lord Jesus Christ (1)
648	let us all in Christ be free (4)
665	high above all praises praising for ... Christ, his son (5)
665	gift of Christ, his son (5)

665	Christ doth call one and all (5)
675	follow Christ, nor think till death to lay it down (5)
682	most loving Jesus Christ (4)
687, 688	dost ask who that may be? Christ Jesus, it is he (2)
697	let every sin be crucified, and Christ be all in all (2)
698	Eternal Spirit of thy living Christ (1)
698	my life in you, O Christ, your love in me (3)
703	lead us through Christ, the true and living Way (1)
705	Church of Christ is calling us to make the dream come true (2)
705	all life in Christ made new (2)
705	O thou who gavest us thyself in Jesus Christ thy Son (3)
713	Christ is arisen. Alleluia (RC)

Christ's

131, 132	When Christ's appearing was made known (1)
159	Who, on Christ's dear mother gazing ... would not weep (4)
159	Who, on Christ's dear mother thinking (4)
225	Hark, for in myriad tongues Christ's own ... preach (3)
268, 269	what Christ's mother sang in gladness ... people sing (3)
268, 269	let Christ's people sing the same (3)
273, 274	The words of Paul assure us of Christ's redeeming word ((3)
278	in prayer with Christ's apostles, waited on his ... word (3)
296	as Christ's new body takes on flesh and blood (4)
297	sign us as Christ's, within, without (1)
298	Through Christ's redemption we shall stand (1)
304	new community of love in Christ's communion bread (2)
359	in word and deed Christ's one true sacrifice (3)
370	I bind this day to me for ever ... Christ's incarnation (2)
408	Let all who name Christ's holy Name give God all praise (3)
443	From God Christ's deity came forth (1)
513	To the members of Christ's Body (2)
519, 520	for Christ's dear Name ... pain and tribulation bore (3)
562	we have Christ's own promise, and that cannot fail (4)
581	brought here together by Christ's love (1)
597	Christ's promised reign of peace (1)
656	their soul is Christ's abode (1)

Christian

107	Good Christian friends, rejoice (1-3)
115	Good Christian, fear (2)
230	Then come, all Christian people, keep festival today (3)
230	grieve him not, O Christian soul (3)
242	flows to Christian souls (4)
265	Christian folk throughout the world will ever say (4)
484, 485	Praise your King, ye Christian legions (1)
545	strive in the Christian race (2)
549, 550	saying "Christian, follow me" (1)
549, 550	saying "Christian, love me more" (3)
549, 550	Christian, love me more than these (4)
562	Onward, Christian soldiers, marching as to war (1,R)
562	on, then, Christian soldiers, on to victory (2)
563	Go forward, Christian soldier (1-4)
581	let us love each other well in Christian holiness (3)
614	O Christian women, Christian men, all the world over (2)
667	Sometimes a light surprises the Christian while he sings (1)

Christians

106	Christians awake, salute the happy morn (1)
182	Let Christians sing (1)
183	Christians, to the Paschal victim offer your ... praises (1)
205	Good Christians all, rejoice and sing (1)
237	Up and follow, Christians all (3)
237	Christians, up and win it (3)
304	I come with Christians far and near (2)
426	shall Christians fail to sing till on earth Christ come (4)
435	Name him, Christians ... with love strong as death (4)
435	Christians, this Lord Jesus shall return again (6)
562	Christians, lift your voices, loud your anthems raise (2)
562	Christians, we are treading where the saints have trod (3)
576, 577	When we Christians gather, members of one Body (2)

Christly

529	all Christly souls are one in him (3)

Christmas

78, 79	Christmas comes once more (4)
78, 79	We hear the Christmas angels the great glad tidings tell (5)
84	Love came down at Christmas, love all lovely, love divine (1)
84	love was born at Christmas (1)
99	God sent us salvation that blessed Christmas morn (3)
102	the world's creator, cradled there on Christmas Day (3)
105	remember Christ our Savior was born on Christmas Day (1)
105	this holy tide of Christmas doth bring redeeming grace (4)
110	when Christ our Lord was born on Christmas night (1)
265	in Bethlehem, all on a Christmas morn (4)
468	he was born on Christmas ... and laid in a manger (1)

Church

24	We thank thee that thy Church, unsleeping (2)
48	Church her voice upraises to thee, blest Three in One (4)
50	Hosanna in the highest strains the Church ... can raise (5)
50	the highest strains the Church on earth can raise (5)
136, 137	O vision fair of glory that the Church may share (1)
149	Eternal Lord of love, behold your Church (1)
214	blessings on his Church below (3)
219	upon his Church his grace to pour (3)
223, 224	on his Church his Spirit poured (1)
229	still o'er thy holy Church preside (3)
230	for God the Holy Spirit dwells with the Church alway (3)
231	May we like true apostles your holy Church defend (2/2-24)
233, 234	The princes of the Church are they (2)
235	Four-square ... foundation the Church of Christ remains (3)
254	For of your Church, Lord, you made known this saint (2)
267	Most blest shall be her name in all the Church on earth (5)
268, 269	let the Church ... part in her thanksgiving claim (3)
268, 269	Church, in her foreshadowed (3)
277	Church the strain re-echoes unto earth's remotest ends (3)
285	pours on the Church from age to age the healing unction (2)
293	in church, or in trains, or in shops, or at tea (3)
296	The Spirit's power shakes the Church of God (3)
299	You came in power; the Church was born (2)

302	Watch o'er thy Church, O Lord (2)
302	so, from all lands thy Church be gathered ... by thy Son (2)
302	thy Church be gathered into thy kingdom (2)
303	Watch o'er thy Church, O Lord (3)
303	so from all lands thy Church be gathered ... by thy Son (4)
303	thy Church be gathered into thy kingdom by thy Son (4)
305,306	one Church united in communion blest (3)
315	pray that all thy Church might be for ever one (1)
315	For all thy Church, O Lord, we intercede (2)
315	may we be one with all thy Church above (3)
340, 341	may the Church still waiting for you keep love's tie (3)
345	peace to thy Church from error and from strife (3)
349	gifts of blessing to bestow on your waiting Church below (1)
359	through them thy Church presents ... true sacrifice (3)
364	holy Church in faith acclaims thy Son who for us died (5)
366	through the Church the song goes on (3)
367	with his holy Church below (2)
402, 403	Church with psalms must shout, no door can keep them out (2)
416	For the Church which evermore lifteth holy hands above (5)
420	the Church, in liturgy and song, in faith and love (3)
426	No, the Church delights to raise psalms and hymns (4)
440	Hear the cry thy Church upraises (3)
493	the Church in earth and heaven (6)
509	let thy Church on earth become blest as the Church above (4)
511	Spirit, ever forming in the Church the mind of Christ (1)
513	to the Church in faith assembled (2)
518	binding all the Church in one (1)
521	bid thy Church increase, in breadth and length (1)
524	the Church our blest Redeemer saved (1)
525	the great Church victorious shall be the Church at rest (4)
526	One family we dwell in him, one Church, above, beneath (2)
528	Lest the Church neglect its mission (1)
538	fill thy Church with light divine (1)
562	Like a mighty army moves the Church of God (3)
562	but the Church of Jesus constant will remain (4)
562	gates of hell can never 'gainst that Church prevail (4)
568	flood the whole Church with thy glorious light (3)
614	the whole Church at last be one (3)
632	The Church from our dear Master received the word divine (2)
632	O make thy Church, dear Savior, a lamp of purest gold (3)
705	Church of Christ is calling us to make the dream come true (2)

church's

255	Saul, the church's spoiler came spreading fear and hate (1)
511	Holy Spirit, ever living as the Church's very life (1)
511	Holy Spirit, ever working through the Church's ministry (2)
525	The Church's one foundation is Jesus Christ her Lord (1)
594, 595	crown thine ancient Church's story (1)

circle

480	in the circle of his arms may we forever lie (2)
540	the circle of the earth shall then proclaim thy kingdom (3)

circled

496, 497	Though circled by the hosts on high (2)

519, 520   angel hosts encircled, as a bride dost earthward move (1)

circling
617   Eternal Ruler of the ceaseless round of circling planets (1)

cities
580   Proudly rise our modern cities (2)
719   thine alabaster cities gleam, undimmed by human tears (3)

citizens
83   sing, all ye citizens of heaven above (3)
619   ye citizens of heaven, O sweetly raise (1)

city
102   Once in royal David's city stood a lowly cattle shed (1)
104   This child through David's city Shall ride in triumph by (2)
127   Earth has many a noble city (1)
167   There is a green hill far away, outside a city wall (1)
181   You pilgrims on the road to Zion's city, sing (3)
326   to appear before God in the city of infinite day (1)
354   bring you into the holy city Jerusalem (1)
356   brought by them into the holy city (2)
436   O blest the land, the city blest (2)
436   the city blest where Christ the ruler is confessed (2)
463, 464   you will come to a great city (2)
463, 464   great city that has expected your return for years (2)
490   The Lamb is the light of the city of God (R)
518   All that dedicated city, dearly loved of God on high (2)
519, 520   Blessed city, heavenly Salem (1)
522, 523   Glorious things of thee are spoken, Zion city of our God (1)
570, 571   All who love and serve your city (1)
570, 571   Risen Lord, shall yet the city be the city of despair (5)
582, 583   O holy city, seen of John (1)
582, 583   O holy city ... where Christ, the Lamb, doth reign (1)
582, 583   Give us, O God, the strength to build the city (3)
582, 583   city that hath stood too long a dream (3)
582, 583   city ... whose laws are love, whose crown is servanthood (3)
582, 583   Already in the mind of God that city riseth fair (4)
590   hymns be rising in every city for your love and care (1)
590   Show us your Spirit, brooding o'er each city (3)
609   till glorious from thy heaven above shall come the city (5)
609   shall come the city of our God (5)
619   Then let the holy city raise the strain (3)
623   city of peace that brings joy evermore (2)

city's
61, 62   Twelve great pearls, the city's portals (3)
580   the lonely drift unnoticed in the city's ebb and flow (2)
596   the city's crowded clangor cries aloud for sin to cease (2)
609   O tread the city's streets again (4)

clad
74   clad as are the poorest, such his humility (1)
203   An angel clad in white they see (3)
286   clad in robes of purest whiteness (2)

624   for ever and for ever are clad in robes of white (3)

claim
53   Thus, if thou canst name him, not ashamed to claim him (3)
57, 58   claim the kingdom for thine own (4)
182   he comes to claim the here and now (2)
268, 269   Ye who claim the faith of Jesus (1)
268, 269   let the Church ... part in her thanksgiving claim (3)
313   by the pain and death, I now claim ... love unfailing (3)
313   I now claim, O Christ, thy love unfailing (3)
366   all on earth thy scepter claim (1)
366   while in essence only One, undivided God we claim thee (4)
419   till all thy living altars claim one holy light (4)
486   in faith thy parting promise claim (3)
528   amid the cares that claim us, hold in mind eternity (5)
541   Claim the high calling angels cannot share (4)

claim'st
220, 221   thou claim'st the kingdom as thine own (2)

claims
253   Our glorious Leader claims our praise (4)
394, 395   your gospel claims one family with a billion names (4)
603, 604   always, near or far, he calls and claims us (2)
603, 604   claims us as his friends and loves us as we are (2)

clamor
312   to clamor never waken (1)

clan
609   where sound the cries of race and clan (1)

clangor
596   the city's crowded clangor cries aloud for sin to cease (2)

clarion
569   King who ordainest thunder thy clarion (1)

clashing
412   Trumpet and pipes, loud clashing cymbals (3)
555   for not with swords loud clashing (2)

class
603, 604   Where generation, class, or race divide us to our shame (3)

classrooms
412   Classrooms and labs loud boiling test tubes (5)

clause
592   A servant with this clause makes drudgery divine (3)

clay
391   His sovereign power without our aid formed us of clay (2)
391   formed us of clay and gave us breath (2)

clean

18	all you made was pure and clean (4c)
592	nothing ... will not grow bright and clean (2)
651	He trust us with his world, to keep it clean and fair (2)

cleanse

131, 132	he, to whom no sin was known, might cleanse his people (3)
131, 132	cleanse his people from their own (3)
175	guard us from harm without, cleanse from the evil within (5)
216	guard us from harm without, cleanse us from evil within (3)
226, 227	Cleanse us with thy healing power (4)
357	good and gracious Savior, cleanse and purge away (3)
596	cleanse the body of this nation (3)
596	cleanse ... through the glory of the Lord (3)
674	Lord, cleanse the depths within our souls (4)
685	cleanse me from its guilt and power (1)
693	wilt receive, wilt welcome, pardon, cleanse, relieve (4)
699	grace to cleanse from every sin (3)

cleansed

76	Then cleansed be every breast from sin (2)
294	cleansed by the blood of Christ our King (1)
302	cleansed and conformed unto thy will (2)
303	cleansed and conformed unto thy will (3)
486	But chiefest, in our cleansed breast ... rest (4)

cleanses

139	he cleanses, reconciles to God (3)
161	the water cleanses to this hour (2)

cleansing

307	Cleansing us from every stain (4)
318	Mine is the guilt, but thine the cleansing blood (4)

clear

9	that clear voice that saith (3)
89, 90	It came upon the midnight clear (1)
145	make clear, make clear where truth and light appear (2)
161	mix his blood with water clear (2)
222	he makes his glorious presence clear (2)
320	Full and clear sing out thy praising (4)
329-331	faith, our outward sense befriending, makes ... clear (5)
329-331	makes our inward vision clear (5)
337	From tainting mischief keep them pure and clear (3)
382	Thou my sins against me cried, thou didst clear me (2)
400	Swift flowing water, pure and clear, make music (3)
490	Clear sun of righteousness, shine on my path (2)
506, 507	fire our hearts and clear our sight (5)
527	Clear before us through the darkness gleams ... light (1)
542	the Day-star clear and bright of every race and nation (1)
549, 550	day by day his clear voice soundeth (1)
556, 557	Your clear hosannas raise, and alleluias loud (3)
615	day by whose clear shining light all wrong ... revealed (4)
655	O let me hear thee speaking in accents clear and still (2)
659, 660	move by some clear, winning word of love (2)

667   he grants the soul again a season of clear shining (1)

clearer
124   within them shines a clearer light (3)
209   in realms of clearer light we may behold you as you are (4)

clearly
61, 62   their urgent summons clearly spoken (1)
654   to see thee more clearly, love thee more dearly (1)

clears
324   powers of hell may vanish as the darkness clears away (3)

cleave
381   Thy strong word did cleave the darkness (1)
596   cleave our darkness with thy sword (3)

clemency
44, 45   we pray that in your constant clemency (1)

climb
171   Calvary's mournful mountain climb (3)
430   song shall over-climb all the bounds of space and time (6)
453   Come, let us ascend. All may climb it who will (3)
453   Who would not want to climb such a ladder as this (4)
517   climb from height to height till Zion's temple rings (3)

climbed
276   he climbed the mount with thee (3)
453   many millions have climbed it and reached Zion's hill (2)

climbing
453   many millions by faith now are climbing it still (2)

climbs
369   Our reason ... climbs above the skies (3)

clime
229   In every clime, by every tongue, be God's ... glory sung (2)

climes
629   the nations, tongues and climes and all the ages given (2)

cling
18   let us cling always to your love (2c)
685   in my hand no price I bring, simply to thy cross I cling (2)

cloak
170   In mock acclaim ... they snatched a purple cloak (2)

close
42   with thy tenderest blessing may our eyelids close (2)
43   with sweet sleep mine eyelids close (3)
44, 45   To you before the close of day, Creator of all things (1)
56   close the path to misery (5)

101	I ask thee to stay close by me for ever (3)
142	close by thee to stay (1)
404	close to your children when on you they call (3)
506, 507	Spirit, close companion of our inmost thoughts and ways (2)
683, 684	So shall my walk be close with God (5)
685	when mine eyelids close in death (3)

closed

40, 41	Although our eyes in sleep be closed (3)
208	He closed the yawning gates of hell (4)
329, 331	he closed with wondrous ending his most patient life (2)
661	no peace, but strife closed in the sod (4)

closely

| 350 | that closely knit in holy vow, they may in thee be one (1) |

closer

337	O fold them closer to thy mercy's breast (3)
528	give us all new fervor, draw us closer in community (2)
659, 660	still with thee in closer, dearer company (3)
683, 684	O for a closer walk with God, a calm and heavenly frame (1)

closeth

| 46 | The duteous day now closeth (1) |

clothe

368	look upon the Mediator, clothe us with his righteousness (1)
516	clothe me round, the while my path illuming (2)
617	Oh, clothe us with thy heavenly armor, Lord (3)
667	who gives the lilies clothing will clothe his people too (3)
670	clothe me with humility (1)

clothed

12, 13	the third hour your faithful band was clothed with power (3)
12, 13	clothed with power on Pentecost (3)
38, 39	as mortals clothed in earth-bound frame (4)
275	clothed in white apparel (1)

clothes

270	by the hands, in grave clothes wound (3)
296	The Father's splendor clothes the Son with life (3)
411	clothes thee with his love, upholds thee with his truth (5)

clothing

| 179 | Earth her joy confesses, clothing her for spring (2) |
| 667 | who gives the lilies clothing will clothe his people too (3) |

cloud

56	didst give the law, in cloud, and majesty, and awe (3)
129, 130	Swift the cloud of glory came (3)
136, 137	from the cloud, the Holy One bears record to the only Son (2)
149	led by your cloud by day, by night your fire (1)
180	not one darksome cloud is dimming ... morning ray (3)
187	Like the cloud that overhead ... Isreal led (2)

187	In that cloud and in that sea ... baptized were we (3)
236	beacon by night and cloud by day (1)
253	long cloud of witnesses show the same path to heaven (4)
314	tranced as it beholds thee, shrined within the cloud (1)
363	led thy children ... with the fire and cloud (2)
393	God has given the cloud by day (2)
406, 407	Let wind and air and cloud and calm and weathers all (3)
460, 461	though the cloud from sight received him (2)
522, 523	Round each habitation hovering, see the cloud and fire (3)
522, 523	the cloud and fire appear for a glory and a covering (3)
545	Lo, what a cloud of witnesses encompass us around (1)
546	A cloud of witnesses around hold thee in full survey (2)
556, 557	echoes upward float like wreaths of incense cloud (3)
621, 622	cloud nor passing vapor dims the brightness of the air (3)
627	radiant cloud by day (3)
662	Through cloud and sunshine, Lord, abide with me (2)

clouds

56	disperse the gloomy clouds of night (6)
57, 58	Lo, he comes, with clouds descending (1)
119	no star to guide, where no clouds thy glory hide (4)
215	riding on the clouds ... to his heavenly palace gate (1)
215	clouds, his chariot (1)
215	he upon the clouds ascends (2)
215	on the clouds to God's right hand (3)
376	Melt the clouds of sin and sadness (1)
388	His chariots of wrath the deep thunderclouds form (2)
398	clouds arise, and tempests blow by order from thy throne (3)
400	you clouds that ride the heavens aloft, O praise him (2)
423	thy clouds, which are fountains of goodness and love (2)
454	on clouds triumphant, when the heavens shall pass away (4)
515	pierce the clouds of nature's night (1)
632	clouds and darkness ended, they see thee face to face (3)
669	who points the clouds their way (1)
677	the clouds ye so much dread are big with mercy (3)
677	clouds ... shall break in blessings on your head (3)
701	Flee, dark clouds that lower (3)

cloven

52	with fiery tongues of cloven flame (3)
89, 90	Still through the cloven skies they come (2)
223, 224	Like to cloven tongues of flame on the twelve ... came (2)

cloy

559	pleasure that can never cloy (3)

coast

287	From earth's wide bounds, from ocean's farthest coast (8)

coeternal

295	To Jesus Christ give glory, God's coeternal Son (2)
360, 361	Son coeternal, ever-blessed Spirit (6)
519, 520	consubstantial, coeternal, while unending ages run (5)

cold

81	amid the cold of winter, when half spent was the night (1)
92	ox and ass beside him from the cold would hide him (2)
109	lay keeping their sheep on a cold winter's night (1)
109	cold winter's night that was so deep (1)
117, 118	Cold on his cradle the dewdrops are shining (2)
128	sealed in the stone-cold tomb (4)
299	hearts grown cold with fear (3)
405	the cold wind in the winter, the pleasant summer sun (3)
428	heat and cold, O night and day ... bless the Lord (3)
510	kindle a flame of sacred love in ... cold hearts of ours (1)
574, 575	from sins which make the heart grow cold, wean us (2)
644	cold my warmest thought (5)
672	cold is the night (2)

coldly

53	but wilt trust him boldly nor dost love him coldly (3)

color

182	where color, scorn or wealth divide, he suffers still (4)

colors

405	he made their glowing colors (1)

combat

183	Death and life have contended in that combat stupendous (3)
284	unmasked in every dress, in every combat foiled (3)

combine

145	divine, divine it is when all combine (4)
235	In one harmonious witness the chosen four combine (2)
368	In the song of thy salvation every tongue ... combine (4)
368	every tongue and race combine (4)
473	the hosts of God in conquering ranks combine (1)

come

9	Come, let thy voice be one with theirs (5)
9	So let the love of Jesus come and set thy soul ablaze (5)
33-35	Therefore we come now evening rites to offer (3)
40, 41	the Herald of the light to come (1)
49	Come, let us with our Lord arise (1)
53	Come, then, O Lord Jesus, from our sins release us (4)
54	Savior of the nations, come (1)
54	Come, O Father's saving Son, who o'er sin the victory won (4)
55	Redeemer of the nations come (1)
55	O Word of God, come (2)
56	O come, O come, Emmanuel and ransom captive Israel (1,8)
56	O come, thou Wisdom from on high (2)
56	O come, O come, thou Lord of might (3)
56	O come, thou Branch of Jesse's tree (4)
56	O come, thou Key of David, come (5)
56	O come, Thou Day-spring from on high (6)
56	O come, Desire of nations (7)
56	Rejoice, rejoice, Emmanuel shall come to thee, O Israel (R)
60	Come in your holy might, we pray (5)

61, 62	The time has come, O maidens wise (1)
61, 62	now come, most worthy Lord, God's Son, Incarnate Word (2)
61, 62	call to come into the banquet hall (2)
66	Come ... long-expected Jesus, born to set thy people free (1)
70	Christ has come to share our life (4)
70	Christ, the Savior King, has come (R)
73	The King shall come when morning dawns (1,3,5)
73	Thy people pray, come quickly, King of kings (5)
76	a home where such a mighty guest may come (2)
78, 79	O come to us, abide with us, our Lord Emmanuel (5)
80	From heaven above to earth I come (1)
83	O come, all ye faithful, joyful and triumphant (1)
83	come ye, O come ye to Bethlehem (1)
83	come, and behold him born the King of angels (1)
83	O come, let us adore him, Christ, the Lord (R)
87	late in time behold him come (2)
89, 90	Still through the cloven skies they come (2)
89, 90	with the everlasting years shall come the time foretold (4)
93	come and worship, worship Christ, the new-born King (R)
96	Come to Bethlehem and see him whose birth the angels sing (3)
96	come, adore on bended knee Christ, the Lord (3)
100	Joy to the world! the Lord is come (1)
103	Come, join the angel throng in songs of joy (R)
104	lie within the roadway To pave his kingdom come (2)
110	O come, then, let us join the heavenly host (4)
114	Come kneel before the radiant boy (4)
115	come, peasant, king, to own him (3)
116	I come, the great Redeemer cries, to do thy will, O Lord (1)
120	Christ, the Son of God, had come to lead his ... people (2)
125, 126	To hail thy rising, Sun of life, the ... nations come (2)
125, 126	the gathering nations come (2)
145	his beauty to come near (2)
148	For this ... we come to you in penitence (4)
178	Come, let us praise the living God (4)
179	come then, true and faithful, now fulfill thy word (5)
180	Come, ye sad and fearful hearted (2)
180	Come ... with glad smile and radiant brow (2)
180	Come ... hail our Lord's triumphant day (3)
190	now as victor he is come (1)
190	for your light is come once more (3)
198	Come, let us taste the vine's new fruit (2)
199, 200	Come, ye faithful, raise the strain of triumphant gladness (1)
204	Love is come again like wheat that springeth green (R)
213	Come away to the skies, my beloved (1)
213	on this festival day, come exulting away (1)
222	He reigns in heaven until the hour when he ... shall come (4)
222	he, who once was crucified, shall come (4)
222	shall come in all love's glorious power to rule (4)
226, 227	Come, thou Holy Spirit bright (1)
226, 227	come with thy celestial light (1)
226, 227	Come, protector of the poor (1)
226, 227	come, thou source of blessings sure (1)
226, 227	come within our hearts to shine (1)
228	come and touch our hearts today (1)
230	Then come, all Christian people, keep festival today (3)

430	Come ye all before his face (3)
436	Redeemer come, I open wide my heart to thee (4)
436	So come, my Sovereign, enter in (5)
443	bade the fallen to come in, praised be his mercy (3)
453	Come, let us ascend. All may climb it who will (3)
453	hear the glad words, "Come to me all the blest" (4)
462	The Lord will come and not be slow (1)
462	The nations all whom thou hast made shall come (4)
463, 464	you will come to a great city (2)
465, 466	eternal Savior, come to me (2)
465, 466	until by your most costly grace ... I come (3)
465, 466	at last I come before your face to know you (3)
467	trust his love for all to come (4)
475	Come, abide within me (4)
475	Come, indwelling Spirit, with transfiguring splendor (4)
478	all who confess his Name, come then with hearts aflame (3)
481	Rejoice in glorious hope. Our Lord the Judge shall come (4)
487	Come, my Way, my Truth, my Life (1)
487	Come, my Light, my Feast, my Strength (2)
487	Come, my Joy, my Love, my Heart (3)
496, 497	great Emmanuel, come and hear us (1)
500	Creator Spirit ... come visit every humble mind (1)
500	come, pour thy joys on humankind (1)
500	come, and thy sacred unction bring to sanctify us (2)
500	Plenteous of grace, come from on high (3)
501, 502	come to create, renew, inspire (1)
501, 502	come, kindle in our hearts your fire (1)
503, 504	Come, Holy Ghost, our souls inspire (1)
503, 504	where thou art guide, no ill can come (6)
509	O come, great Spirit, come (1,5)
509	Come as the light, to us reveal our emptiness and woe (2)
509	Come as the fire, and purge our hearts (3)
509	Come as the dove, and spread thy wings (4)
509	let thy Church on earth become blest as the Church above (4)
510	Come, Holy Spirit, heavenly Dove (1,4)
510	come, shed abroad a Savior's love (4)
512	Come, Gracious Spirit, heavenly Dove (1)
513	come, Holy Spirit, come (1-3)
515	come, thou source of joy and gladness (1)
515	Author of the new creation, come with unction (2)
516	Come down, O love divine, seek thou this soul of mine (1)
518	To this temple, where we call thee, come, O Lord (3)
518	come, O Lord of hosts, today (3)
532, 533	their worship and vows shall come to thy throne (2)
536	God has come to you (1,4)
541	Come, labor on (1-5)
542	heal its ancient wrong, come, Prince of Peace, and reign (3)
554	'tis the gift to come down where we ought to be (1)
554	till by turning, turning we come round right (1)
555	the day of march has come (1)
560	Remember your servants, Lord, when you come in ... power (A)
560	when you come in your kingly power (A)
568	Come, Holy Spirit, create in us holiness (3)
570, 571	Come today, our Judge, our Glory (5)
573	thy kingdom come, O Lord, thy will be done (R)

582, 583	within whose four-square walls shall come no night (1)
586	by thy lowly human birth ... come to join the workers (1)
587	with heart still undefiled, thou didst to manhood come (2)
599	have not our wearied feet come to the place (2)
599	We have come over a way that with tears has been watered (2)
599	we have come (2)
600, 601	come with thy timeless judgment now (1)
600, 601	finely build for days to come foundations that endure (3)
609	till glorious from thy heaven above shall come the city (5)
609	shall come the city of our God (5)
611	Heavy laden, gladly come to him (6)
613	Thy kingdom come, O God! Thy rule, O Christ, begin (1)
613	We pray thee, Lord, arise, and come in thy great might (4)
615	Thy kingdom come, on bended knee the passing ages pray (1)
616	He shall come down like showers upon the fruitful earth (3)
620	Jerusalem, my happy home, when shall I come to thee (1)
623	nor do things prayed for come short of the prayer (2)
633	Word of God, come down on earth (1)
638, 639	Come, O thou Traveler unknown (1)
640	Traveler, lo, the Prince of Peace ... Son of God is come (3)
657	joy of heaven, to earth come down (1)
657	Come, almighty to deliver, let us all thy life receive (2)
663	surely I can trust thy love for all the days to come (5)
664	There ... I find a settled rest while others go and come (3)
668	from whence shall come my aid (1)
670	When I come before thy Word, quiet my anxiety (2)
671	I have already come (4)
672	till thou shalt come our gloom to chase (5)
678, 679	with you has come to dwell ... Holy One of Israel (2)
680	O God, our help in ages past, our hope for years to come (1,5)
686	Come, thou fount of every blessing (1)
686	hither by thy help, I've come (2)
692	Come unto me and rest (1)
693	Just as I am ... O Lamb of God, I come (1-6)
693	that thou bidd'st me come to thee (1)
695, 696	confidently waiting come what may (1)
698	Come, pray in me the prayer I need this day (2)
698	Come with the vision and the strength I need to serve (3)
700	tarry no more without, but come and dwell within (1)
700	Great love of God, come in (3)
700	Well-spring of heavenly peace, thou Living Water, come (2)
705	Church of Christ is calling us to make the dream come true (2)

comes

9	what time there comes the breath of dawn (3)
25, 26	Now sunset comes, but light shines forth (2)
33-35	Now comes the day's end as the sun is setting (2)
50	Blest be the Lord who comes to us with messages of grace (4)
50	comes, in God his Father's name, to save our sinful race (4)
53	Still he comes within us, still his voice would win us (2)
57, 58	Lo, he comes, with clouds descending (1)
59	comes with pardon down from heaven (3)
59	so when next he comes with glory (4)
61, 62	Forth he comes, her Bridegroom glorious (2)
65	Greet One who comes in glory, foretold in sacred story (1)

65	He brings God's rule, O Zion, he comes from heaven above (2)
68	up, watch in expectation, at midnight comes the cry (1)
69	Now comes the day of salvation (4)
71, 72	Hark! the glad sound! the Savior comes (1)
71, 72	He comes, the prisoners to release (2)
71, 72	He comes, the broken heart to bind (3)
74	Not robed in royal splendor, in power and pomp comes he (1)
78, 79	Christmas comes once more (4)
85, 86	salvation comes from you alone (4)
88	God himself comes down from heaven (1)
88	God from God, and Light from Light, comes with mercies (2)
88	comes with mercies infinite (2)
88	from high heaven he comes to earth (2)
88	God comes down that we may rise (4)
100	he comes to make his blessings flow far as the curse (3)
112	heaven and earth shall flee away when he comes to reign (2)
116	Thus it becomes us to fulfill all righteousness, he said (2)
153	Blessed is the King who comes in the name of the Lord (1)
153	Blessed is he who comes in the name of the Lord (2)
157	Blessed is he who comes in the name of the Lord (1)
182	he comes to claim the here and now (2)
196, 197	Look there! the Christ, our Brother, comes resplendent (1,4)
199, 200	with the royal feast of feasts, comes its joy to render (3)
199, 200	comes to glad Jerusalem (3)
225	Forth from the Father he comes with ... mystical offering (2)
259	Hail to the Lord who comes, comes to his temple gate (1)
259	thus to his Father's house he comes, the heavenly guest (2)
270	He that comes despised shall reign (2)
280	When Christ comes again in glory (4)
286	Whence comes all this glorious band (2)
296	A new creation comes to life and grows (4)
314	faith, that comes by hearing, pierces through the veil (2)
316, 317	Feast after feast thus comes and passes by (3)
350	Whatever comes to be their share of quickening joy (2)
436	happy hearts and happy homes to whom this King ... comes (2)
436	happy homes to whom this King of triumph comes (2)
444	Blessed be the God of Israel, who comes to set us free (1)
444	a Savior comes among us to raise us up to heaven (2)
454	Jesus comes (2-4)
454	comes to save us from despair (2)
493	ye blind, behold, your Savior comes (5)
536	israel comes to greet the Savior (3)
539	He comes again, O Zion, ere thou meet him (4)
541	a glad sound comes with the setting sun (5)
555	the heavenly kingdom comes (2)
558	through the truth that comes from God (2)
613	When comes the promised time that war shall be no more (3)
616	He comes to break oppression, to set the captive free (1)
616	He comes with succor speedy to those who suffer wrong (2)
631	wisdom comes to those who know thee (1)
681	Where goodness comes to light we glimpse thy plan (4)

comest

| 154, 155 | who in the Lord's Name comest, the King and Blessed One (1) |
| 505 | thou comest forth from God's great throne (1) |

comet's
386, 387   glorious the comet's train (3)

cometh
287   soon, soon to faithful warriors cometh rest (6)

comfort
42   Comfort every sufferer watching late in pain (4)
67   Comfort, comfort ye my people (1)
67   comfort those who sit in darkness (1)
105   O tidings of comfort and joy (R)
151   he is merciful and just, here is my comfort and my trust (3)
229   Unfailing Comfort, heavenly Guide ... preside (3)
248, 249   who in prayer this Name beseecheth ... comfort findeth (3)
248, 249   sweetest comfort findeth near (3)
368   Source of comfort, cheer us with the Savior's love (3)
370   Christ to comfort and restore me (6)
375   his comfort all my anguish stills (1)
503, 504   Thy blessed unction from above is comfort, life and fire (3)
512   Come ... with light and comfort from above (1)
591   from all the easy speeches that comfort cruel men (2)
610   hope and health, good will and comfort ... give (4)
645, 646   thy rod and staff my comfort still (4)
663   I will not fear, for thou art here to comfort and to aid (3)
699   still support and comfort me (2)

comforted
560   Blessed are those who mourn, for they shall be comforted (2)
634   till thy sweet word have comforted me (1)

Comforter
16, 17   Creator of all things and with the Spirit, Comforter (4)
38, 39   with the Spirit, Comforter (5)
228   comforter in time of grief, enter in and be our guest (2)
364   also the Holy Comforter, our advocate and guide (5)
365   Come, holy Comforter (3)
514   To thee, O Comforter divine ... sing we alleluia (1)
516   O Comforter, draw near, within my heart appear (1)

comforters
226, 227   Thou, of comforters the best (2)

comfortless
184   He who bore all pain and loss comfortless upon the cross (3)

coming
74   Blest be the King whose coming is in the name of God (1-4)
75   Proclaim to a desolate people the coming of their King (2)
78, 79   No ear may hear his coming (3)
81   Of Jesse's lineage coming as seers of old have sung (1)
191   will all its full abundance at his second coming yield (3)
259   no shouts proclaim him nigh, no crowds his coming wait (1)
271, 272   his witness to the coming light (3)
289   our Father, make us faithful to serve the coming days (3)
354   At your coming may the martyrs receive you (1)

356   at your coming thither may you be brought by them (2)
370   his coming at the day of doom (2)
443   his work done, went up to heaven, praised be his coming (4)
490   I'm looking for the coming of Christ (3)
531   Be darkness, at thy coming, light (3)

command
212   O Solitude again command your host from heaven restored (5)
320   command for guidance taking, bread and wine we hallow (3)
391   Wide as the world is thy command (5)
398   moon shines full at his command and all the stars obey (1)
526   One army of the living God, to his command we bow (3)
625   through the realms of light fly at your Lord's command (1)
648   They journeyed on at his command (3)
665   joy doth wait on his command (4)

commanding
389   He with all-commanding might filled the new-made world (3)
413   Righteous, commanding, ever glorious (3)

commandments
406, 407   blest be they who do thy will and follow thy commandments (7)
431   So shine the Lord's commandments to make the simple wise (3)

commands
116   faithful to the Lord's commands (2)
605   Still down the ages ring the prophet's stern commands (3)

commences
386, 387   period, power, and enterprise commences, reigns and ends (1)

commission
139   gives the Great Commission (3)
235   while each his own commission fulfills in every line (2)
528   Lord, you give the great commission (1)

commitment
348   ours a commitment we know never ends (1)

common
9   but for the common things of earth (1)
10   The trivial round, the common task, will furnish all (5)
528   Lord, you make the common holy (3)
581   our common life embraces all whose Father is the same (6)

communion
279   in one communion ever knit, one fellowship of love (3)
287   O blest communion, fellowship divine (4)
304   new community of love in Christ's communion bread (2)
305, 306   one Church united in communion blest (3)
351   possess, in sweet communion, joys ... earth cannot afford (2)
385   Grant unto us communion with thee (2)
524   her sweet communion, solemn vows (3)

525   mystic sweet communion with those whose rest is won (5)

community
304   new community of love in Christ's communion bread (2)
528   give us all new fervor, draw us closer in community (2)

compacted
519, 520   in their places now compacted by the heavenly Architect (4)

companies
614   scattered companies unite in service to the Lord of light (3)

companion
506, 507   Spirit, close companion of our inmost thoughts and ways (2)
586   Jesus, thou divine Companion (1)
586   Jesus ... divine Companion, help us all to work our best (3)

company
133, 134   with your elect found company (2)
146, 147   in company with ages past (1)
154, 155   The company of angels is praising thee on high (2)
282, 283   may the celestial company of angels ... help us (5)
364   apostles glorious company ... thy constant praise recite (4)
638, 639   my company before is gone, and I am left alone with thee (1)
659, 660   still with thee in closer, dearer company (3)

compare
266   by conception without compare the Savior ... bear (4)
427   God's holy house of prayer hath none that can compare (2)
513   with the peace beyond compare (3)
624   what radiancy of glory, what bliss beyond compare (1)

compares
443   Who then, my Lord, compares to you (5)

compass
632   It is the chart and compass that o'er life's surging sea (2)

compassion
404   in your compassion we your blessings find (3)
414   Full of kindness and compassion, slow to anger (5)
472   Christ of great compassion, speak to our fearful hearts (1)
479   blest be his compassion infinitely kind (2)
609   yet long these multitudes to see the true compassion (3)
609   the true compassion of thy face (3)
610   As, O Lord, your deep compassion healed the sick (2)
610   burdens your compassion bids us bear (4)
657   Jesus, thou art all compassion (1)

complete
171   God's own sacrifice complete (3)
434   Here his whole Name appears complete (3)
542   whole round world complete, from sunrise to its setting (2)

548   stand complete at last (5)
704   make the sacrifice complete (4)

completed
238, 239 praying that, this life completed (3)
346   Completed, Lord, the Holy Mysteries (1)

completeness
8   sprung in completeness where his feet pass (2)

completing
631   many diverse scrolls completing (2)

complying
329, 331 Jesus, with the Law complying, keeps the feast (3)

compose
474   or thorns compose so rich a crown (3)

comprehend
629   enlarge, expand all living souls to comprehend your love (3)

comrades
289   new comrades ever bringing in comrades' steps to tread (2)

conceal
18   dark midday could not conceal your cry of awful agony (3c)

conceived
108   in holiness conceived, the Son of God was born (1)
266   six months gone since Elizabeth conceived John (5)

conceiving
82   Virgin, full of grace, by the Holy Ghost conceiving (2)

conception
266   by conception without compare the Savior ... bear." (4)

concert
82   every voice in concert ring (3)
275   joined in holy concert, singing to the Lord of all (2)
526   Let saints on earth in concert sing (1)
526   in concert sing with those whose work is done (1)

concord
175   Thou Love who art author of concord (8)
216   Thou Love who art author of concord (6)
427   Ye nations of mankind, in this your concord find (4)

condemn
489   in love God sent his Son to save not to condemn mankind (6)

condemneth
568   judgment is thine, and condemneth our pride (1)

condemned

616   souls, condemned and dying were precious in his sight (2)

condescending

160   O mysterious condescending! O abandonment sublime! (3)
329, 331   Given for us, and condescending to be born for us below (2)

condition

139   He came by water and by blood to heal our lost condition (3)

conferred

629   make us all go on to know with nobler powers conferred (3)

confess

53   let us here confess thee till in heaven we bless thee (4)
151   must confess thy grace (2)
152   Spare us, O Lord, who now confess our sins (3)
152   confess our sins and all our wickedness (3)
226, 227   To thy people who adore and confess thee evermore (5)
300   Bounteous God, we now confess thee (1)
319   who adore you and confess your Name (2)
364   O God, we praise thee, and confess ... thou the only Lord (1)
366   adoring, bend the knee and confess the mystery (4)
381   our lives our hopes confess (3)
413   salvation which all his friends with joy confess (1)
414   King supreme shall they confess thee (6)
435   every tongue confess him King of glory now (1)
435   our hearts confess him King of glory now (6)
477   Let every tongue confess with one accord (5)
477   confess ... that Jesus Christ is Lord (5)
478   all who confess his Name, come then with hearts aflame (3)
484, 485   we confess, proclaim, adore thee (2)
498   from my smitten heart with tears two wonders I confess (2)
532, 533   till earth's every people confess thee their God (2)
581   Forgive we now each other's faults ... our faults confess (3)
652, 653   let our ordered lives confess the beauty of thy peace (4)

confessed

131, 132   by their gifts confessed their God (2)
231   his faith, in death, confessed (2/12-26)
254   who, taught of God, confessed the God-head in the Christ (2)
287   Who thee by faith before the world confessed (1)
401   the Lord, the great I AM, by earth and heaven confessed (1)
436   the city blest where Christ the ruler is confessed (2)

confesses

179   Earth her joy confesses, clothing her for spring (2)

confessing

244   O that we, thy truth confessing (3)
329-331   ever too his love confessing (6)
367   Thus thy glorious Name confessing (3)
375   his graciousness confessing (1)
414   God, my King, thy might confessing (1)

confession
242   still through his confession flows .. thy life and light (4)

confessor
275   king, apostle, saint, confessor, martyr and evangelist (2)

confessors'
370   confessors' faith, apostles' word (3)

confidence
91   This child, this little helpless boy ... our confidence (1)
91   boy, shall be our confidence and joy (1)
148   our foolish confidence, our pride of knowledge ... sin (4)
518   holy Zion's help forever, and her confidence alone (1)

confident
638, 639   I am weak but confident in self-despair (3)

confiding
540   confiding in thy might (1)
667   while in him confiding, I cannot but rejoice (4)

confined
629   crude, partial, and confined (1)

confirm
297   Confirm our faith, consume our doubt (1)
348   Here, at your table, confirm our intention (2)
409   confirm the tidings as they roll (2)
501, 502   confirm our weak, uncertain wills (4)
704   Jesus, confirm my heart's desire to work ... for thee (3)
719   confirm thy soul in self control, thy liberty in law (2)

conflict
165, 166   of the mighty conflict sing (1)
171   your Redeemer's conflict see (1)
286   painful conflict o'er, God has bid them weep no more (4)
345   Then, when thy voice shall bid our conflict cease (4)
357   Here mid stress and conflict toils can never cease (2)
472   speak to our fearful hearts by conflict rent (1)
527   one the conflict, one the peril (3)
561   forth to the mighty conflict in this his glorious day (2)
693   though tossed about with many a conflict, many a doubt (2)

conflicts
231   called early from life's conflicts (2/12-28)
548   having all things done, and all your conflicts past (5)

conformed
302, 303   cleansed and conformed unto thy will ((2)

confound
270   Weakness shall the strong confound (3)
424   for the truths that still confound us (3)
564, 565   do but themselves confound, his strength the more is (2)

confounded

102	We, like Mary, rest confounded (3)
102	confounded that a stable should display heaven's Word (3)
573	Envious of heart, blind-eyed, with tongues confounded (3)

confront

| 255 | in all that may confront us (2) |

confusion

266	she was filled with confusion strong (3)
531	confusion, order in thy path (3)
608	give, for wild confusion, peace (3)
681	whose stars serenely burn above this earth's confusion (1)

congregation

433	Let thy congregation escape tribulation (3)
515	Rest upon this congregation ... fullness of thy grace (2)
535	the great congregation his triumph shall sing (2)

conquer

5	we plead with thee for grace and power to conquer (3)
5	conquer in temptation's hour (3)
142	O give us strength in thee to fight ... to conquer sin (2)
182	conquer every place and time (2)
191	we conquer by his mighty enterprise (2)
246	May that great love our lives control and conquer hate (5)
246	conquer hate in every soul (5)
349	daily power to conquer sin (2)
426	Borne upon their latest breath ... conquer death (6)
426	songs of praise shall conquer death (6)
472	who by this sign didst conquer grief and pain (5)
720	Then conquer we must, when our cause it is just (2)

conquered

156	captive death and conquered sin (2)
174	thou hast conquered in the fight (3)
180	death is conquered, we are free (1)
201	light and joy have conquered doom (1)
547	for us ... conquered in the strife (5)
624	they who with their Leader have conquered in the fight (3)
638, 639	be conquered by my instant prayer (3)

conquering

16, 17	who, conquering death, reign gloriously with God (4)
38, 39	who, conquering death, reign gloriously with God (5)
457	the rending tomb proclaims thy conquering arm (3)
473	the hosts of God in conquering ranks combine (1)
478	the Father's conquering Word, true source of gladness (1)
521	works of darkness disappear before thy conquering light (2)

conqueror

215	See the Conqueror mounts in triumph (1)
284	When all arrayed in light the shining conqueror rode (7)
459	Lord of interstellar space and Conqueror of time (1)

| 496, 497 | ride on, great Conqueror, till all know thy salvation (3) |
| 548 | who in the strength of Jesus trusts is more than conqueror (2) |

conquest
253	with united breath, ascribe their conquest to the Lamb (2)
255	We sing the glorious conquest before Damascus' gate (1)
555	henceforth in fields of conquest thy tents ... our home (1)
555	the crown awaits the conquest (3)

conquests
| 222 | as sin and death their conquests yield (1) |

conscience
3, 4	with conscience free from sin and blame (4)
429	sends the laboring conscience peace (3)
574, 575	give us a conscience quick to feel (1)

consecrate
| 353 | O gracious God, you consecrate all that is lovely (2) |
| 353 | you consecrate all that is lovely, good, and true (2) |

consecrated
| 286 | soul and body consecrated (5) |
| 707 | Take my life, and let it be consecrated, Lord, to thee (1) |

consecrating
| 610 | consecrating to your purpose every gift that you impart (1) |

consent
| 430 | hither bring in one consent heart .. voice .. instrument (1) |

consign
| 226, 227 | to thy love our sins consign (4) |

consolation
| 66 | Israel's strength and consolation (2) |
| 231 | your true consolation may through the world extend (2/6-11) |

console
| 593 | may we not seek to be consoled, but to console (3) |

consoled
| 593 | may we not seek to be consoled, but to console (3) |

conspire
| 106 | He spoke ... straightway the celestial choir .. conspire (3) |
| 369 | all the heavenly powers conspire eternal praise to sing (4) |

constancy
| 564, 565 | let him in constancy follow the Master (1) |

constant
| 40, 41 | let hearts in constant vigil watch (3) |
| 44, 45 | we pray that in your constant clemency (1) |

85, 86	our constant star in sin's deep night (2)
150	O keep us, Savior dear, ever constant by thy side (5)
206	yet whose faith has constant been (6)
277	Constant was the love he gave her (2)
364	apostles glorious company ...thy constant praise recite (4)
526	Jesus, be thou our constant Guide (5)
562	but the Church of Jesus constant will remain (4)
587	with constant love as sentinel (1)
617	our inspiration be thy constant word (3)

consubstantial
| 519, 520 | consubstantial, coeternal, while unending ages run (5) |

consume
297	Confirm our faith, consume our doubt (1)
574, 575	consume the ill, purge out the shame (4)
636, 637	I only design thy dross to consume and thy gold to refine (4)

consumed
| 316, 317 | the Bread and Wine consumed (2) |

consuming
| 472 | Save us, thy people, from consuming passion (1) |
| 516 | turn to dust and ashes in its heat consuming (2) |

consummation
| 525 | she waits the consummation of peace for evermore (4) |

contain
| 476 | can ... words contain his praise (1) |

contemplation
| 624 | beneath thy contemplation sink heart and voice oppressed (1) |
| 667 | In holy contemplation we sweetly then pursue the theme (2) |

contemplations
| 93 | Sages, leave your contemplations (3) |

contempt
| 238, 239 | by contempt of every anguish, by unyielding battle done (2) |
| 474 | pour contempt on all my pride (1) |

contend
| 142 | As thou with Satan didst contend and ... the victory win (2) |

contended
18	while he contended, Lord, for you (2a)
183	Death and life have contended in that combat stupendous (3)
185, 186	when life and death contended (2)
286	they who have contended for their Savior's honor long (3)

contending
| 540 | contending from the walls of Zion against the foe (1) |

content

498   content to let my pride go by, to know no gain nor loss (3)

582, 583   O shame to us who rest content while lust and greed (2)

contention

581   let all contention cease (4)

contentment

482   whose voice is contentment, whose presence is balm (4)

continent

24   As o'er each continent and island the dawn leads on (3)

continents

534   give ear to me, ye continents, ye isles give ear to me (2)

continually

364   to thee the powers on high ... continually do cry (2)

continued

109   so it continued both day and night (2)

contrite

151   I rest upon his faithful word to them of contrite spirit (3)

642   O hope of every contrite heart, O joy of all the meek (3)

control

11   Direct, control, suggest, this day, all I design (3)

246   May that great love our lives control and conquer hate (5)

594, 595   bend our pride to thy control (3)

655   O speak to reassure me, to hasten or control (2)

719   confirm thy soul in self control, thy liberty in law (2)

converged

18   all shadows of the morn and eve converged (3b)

converse

136, 137   the incarnate Lord holds converse high (2)

329, 331   he with us in converse blending dwelt (2)

conversion

231   Lord, for Paul's conversion we bless your Name today (2/1-25)

convert

53   from the sins that hurt us, would to Truth convert us (2)

531   Convert the nations (4)

converted

18   you blinded and converted him (4b)

convey

229   still from age to age convey the wonders of this... day (1)

conveys

506, 507   God's will ... by a still small voice conveys (2)

cool
  31, 32   moon with cool reflected glow will bring the silences (3)

cooling
  226, 227   in our summer, cooling shade (2)
  228   freshening breeze and cooling shade (2)
  658   As longs the deer for cooling streams (1)

corn
  290   then the full corn shall appear (2)

corner
  402, 403   Let all the world in every corner sing, my God and King (R)

corners
  506, 507   dark and furthest corners by the wind of heaven blown (4)

cornerstone
  157   has become the chief cornerstone (R)
  518   Christ the head and cornerstone (1)

corridors
  459   suns his footsteps trace through corridors sublime (1)

cosmos
  256   the cosmos move in time with grace (3)

cost
  9   to spend thyself nor count the cost (6)
  537   redeemed at countless cost from dark despair (2)

costliest
  119   all our costliest treasures bring (3)

costly
  117, 118   Shall we then yield him, in costly devotion, odors (3)
  465, 466   until by your most costly grace ... I come (3)

couch
  567   crowded street, by restless couch ... Gennesaret's shore (2)

could
  18   dark midday could not conceal your cry of awful agony (3c)
  98   but the very beasts could see that he all men surpasses (2)
  139   death could hold him never. He rose and lives forever (2)
  151   could we abide thy presence? (1)
  151   Our works could ne'er our guilt remove (2)
  160   throned in light ere worlds could be (2)
  162   the price which none but he could pay (4)
  167   he only could unlock the gate of heaven and let us in (4)
  276   he heard what could not be denied, thy summons (2)
  313   all that love of God could give Jesus by his sorrows gave (2)
  319   No greater love than this to you could bind us (2)
  398   everywhere that I could be, thou, God, art present there (3)

458   in whose sweet praise I all my days could gladly spend (7)
482   whose trust, ever child-like, no cares could destroy (1)
627   without thee how could earth be trod (4)
648   oppressed so hard they could not stand (1)
663   how could I want or need (1)
685   all for sin could not atone (2)

council
232   presiding at the council that set the Gentiles free (2/10-23)

counsel
610   counsel, aid, and peace we give (4)
669   bring to sure fulfillment thy counsel good and true (3)

Counsellor
125, 126   the Wonderful, the Counsellor, the mighty God and Lord (4)

count
9   to spend thyself nor count the cost (6)
116   No more we'll count ourselves our own but his (5)
346   oh, count us worthy, Christ, thy joys to share (2)
359   inspired of thee, may they count all but loss (5)
471   for this we count the world but loss (1)
474   my richest gain I count but loss (1)

counted
348   chosen by you, to be counted as friends (1)

countenance
168, 169   O countenance whose splendor the hosts of heaven adore (1)
190   see his countenance, how gracious (2)
308, 309   we may behold, in heaven, thy countenance divine (3)

countless
10   new treasures still, of countless price, God will provide (3)
287   through gates of pearl streams in the countless host (8)
321   in countless numbers let them come (3)
396, 397   blessed us on our way with countless gifts of love (1)
537   redeemed at countless cost from dark despair (2)
562   this through countless ages we with angels sing (5)
647   The countless hosts lead on before (3)

country
109   three wise men came from country far (3)
119   In the heavenly country bright need they no created light (5)
623   we for that country must yearn and must sigh (4)
624   Oh, sweet and blessed country, the home of God's elect! (4)
624   Oh, sweet and blessed country that eager hearts expect (4)
716   do thou our country save by thy great might (1)
717   My country, 'tis of thee, sweet land of liberty (1)
717   My native country, thee, land of the noble free (2)
719   who more than self their country loved (2)

counts
476   our profit counts as loss (3)

courage

228	Grant enabling energy, courage in adversity (5)
347	be of good courage, armed with heavenly grace (1)
347	strengthen the faint, give courage to the weak (2)
348	vows are renewed, and our courage restored (3)
561	let courage rise with danger (2)
566	From thee ... all calm and courage, faith and hope (1)
586	by thy patience ... courage ... taught us toil is good (1)
590	Grant us new courage, sacrificial, humble (2)
594, 595	Grant us wisdom, grant us courage (1-4)
607	when hope and courage falter (3)
621, 622	Now with gladness, now with courage, bear the burden (5)
677	Ye fearful saints, fresh courage take (3)

course

10	If on our daily course our mind be set (3)
251	Another year its course has run (2)
289	changeful years unresting their silent course have sped (2)
389	He the golden-tressed sun caused all day his course to run (4)
406, 407	sun who through the skies his course doth run (2)
640	peace and truth its course portends (2)

court

97	Where thy court on thee to wait (1)

courts

49	fill his courts with songs of praise (3)
312	feet that tread thy hallowed courts (3)
377, 378	approach with joy his courts unto (3)
391	earth, with her ten thousand tongues ... fill thy courts (4)
391	fill thy courts with sounding praise (4)
517	thirsty soul desires and longs within thy courts to be (1)
517	One day within thy courts excels a thousand spent away (4)
686	seal it for thy courts above (3)

covenant

146, 147	The covenant, so long revealed to those of faith (2)
514	God's great covenant of grace (2)
616	the tide of time shall never his covenant remove (5)
709	thou shalt be our covenant God and portion evermore (5)

cover

67	tell her that her sins I cover (1)
534	filled ... as the waters cover the sea (1-4)
699	cover my defenseless head with the shadow of thy wing (2)
702	If deepest darkness cover me (5)

covering

522, 523	the cloud and fire appear for a glory and a covering (3)
573	through the thick darkness covering every nation (1)

covet

612	taught by thee we covet most ... holy, heavenly, love (1)

coward
471   It makes the coward spirit brave (4)

cows
98   Cradled in a stall was he with sleepy cows and asses (2)

cradle
55   Your cradle shines with glory's light (5)
83   See how the shepherds, summoned to his cradle (4)
102   his shelter was a stable, and his cradle was a stall (2)
117, 118   Cold on his cradle the dewdrops are shining (2)
127   Eastern sages at his cradle make oblations rich and rare (3)
468   child of Mary ... didn't have a cradle (2)

cradled
97   nought but need and penury; why thus cradled here (1)
98   Cradled in a stall was he with sleepy cows and asses (2)
102   the world's creator, cradled there on Christmas Day (3)

cradles
399   He cradles in his hand the heights and depths of earth (2)

craftsman
611   Skillful craftsman, blessed carpenter (3)

crafty
574, 575   for crafty trade and subtle snare to catch the simple (3)

craved
242   but craved to touch those hands of thine (3)

cream
382   the cream of all my heart, I will bring thee (2)

create
348   each duty ... give us the chance to create or destroy (4)
391   he can create, and he destroy (1)
501, 502   come to create, renew, inspire (1)
516   for none can guess its grace, till Love create a place (3)
568   Come, Holy Spirit, create in us holiness (3)

created
54   gracing his created spheres (3)
97   Dost thou in a manger lie, who hast all created (1)
119   In the heavenly country bright need they no created light (5)
175   all things created on earth sing to the glory of God (2)
213   For the glory we were first created to share (3)
213   Now created again that our lives may remain ... thine (3)
216   all things created on earth sing to the glory of God (1)
355   For so did you ordain when you created me (1)
365   Father whose love unknown all things created own (1)
381   for created light we thank thee (1)
431   mute witness of the Master's hand in all created things (1)

creating

52	This day at thy creating word (1)
394, 395	Creating God (1)
580	Great Creator, still creating, show us what we yet may do (1)

creation

1, 2	glory, gleaming and resounding through all creation (3)
33-35	Christ, mighty Savior, Light of all creation (1)
33-35	creation joining hearts and voices singing your glory (3)
48	This day at the creation, the light first had its birth (2)
51	day of creation, day of resurrection (3)
97	all creation to redeem I alone am able (2)
98	Unto us a boy is born, the King of all creation (1,5)
129, 130	let creation now adore him (4)
154, 155	we with all creation in chorus make reply (2)
175	Rise from the grave now ... author of life and creation (4)
176, 177	bringing forth creation (1)
176, 177	seek through the power of the new creation (2)
178	He is the King of creation (1)
182	till all creation lives and learns his joy (5)
256	Your new creation let us be (4)
258	Blessed she by all creation (2)
278	Lord of all creation brought her to his heavenly home (4)
282, 283	thine is the glory which from all creation ever ascendeth (6)
296	A new creation comes to life and grows (4)
298	each is a new creation (1)
319	all creation knows the love of God (1)
334	Partners in your new creation (3)
336	peace for which creation longs (3)
358	God-spoken prophecy, word at creation (3)
360, 361	Lord of creation, merciful and mighty (1)
363	summoning all to share thy new creation (3)
370	Of whom all nature hath creation (7)
372	Lo, he is Lord of all. Creation speaks his praise (2)
373	heaven and earth, and all creation, Laud ... his Name (2)
373	all creation, laud and magnify his Name (2)
374	The whole creation joins in one to bless the sacred Name (4)
379	let creation sing before him ... exalt him with one voice (1)
379	God who breathes through all creation (1)
390	the Almighty, the King of creation (1)
408	the God of all creation, the God of power (1)
414	vast in love, God is good to all creation (5)
417, 418	join in the hymn of all creation (3)
420	it is as though the whole creation cried (1)
421	only you are God's true Son, who was before creation (3)
424	For the fruit of all creation (1)
426	heaven with alleluias rang when creation was begun (1)
427	God's whole creation o'er both now and evermore (5)
432	For love in creation, for heaven restored (4)
501, 502	Your power the whole creation fills (4)
506, 507	Praise the Spirit in creation, breath of God (1)
515	Author of the new creation, come with unction (2)
525	she is his new creation by water and the word (1)
539	tell how he stooped to save his lost creation (2)
573	Father eternal, Ruler of creation (1)

576, 577	Shine on us, O purest Light of all creation (3)
598	O wounded hands of Jesus, build in us thy new creation (4)
607	redeem the whole creation with your almighty hand (1)
633	Word that brought to life creation (2)
657	Finish then thy new creation (3)

creation's

12, 13	O God, creation's ruling force (4)
14, 15	O God, creation's secret force (1)
18	O God, creation's ruling force (5)
23	O God, creation's ruling force (4)
38, 39	The whole creation's architect (2)
47	creation's Lord and spring (1)
93	who sang creation's story now proclaim Messiah's birth (1)
496, 497	whole creation's Head and Lord ... assumed our very nature (2)
600, 601	O day of God, draw nigh as at creation's birth (5)

creative

375	exult in thy creative might (2)
375	thy creative might that doeth all things well and right (2)
491	God all-bounteous, all-creative (4)
580	children of creative purpose (4)

Creator

16, 17	Creator of all things and with the Spirit, Comforter (4)
27, 28	O blest Creator, source of light (1)
31, 32	You, Holy One, Creator, Lord (4)
38, 39	God, Creator of all things (5)
44, 45	To you before the close of day, Creator of all things (1)
60	Creator of the stars of night (1)
77	Behold, the world's creator wears the form and fashion (2)
102	the world's creator, cradled there on Christmas Day (3)
148	Creator of the earth and skies (1)
175	God the Creator ... who rulest the earth and the heavens (5)
175	God the Creator, the Lord (5)
176, 177	God our Creator, Savior, Sanctifier (3)
179	Him their true Creator, all his works adore (1)
216	God the Creator, the Lord (3)
261, 262	By the Creator, Joseph was appointed (1)
295	Sing praise to our Creator, O you of Adam's race (1)
355	the creator and maker of mankind (1)
358	Only Immortal One, Mighty Creator (2)
368	Holy Father, great Creator (1)
369	How wondrous great, how glorious bright ... our Creator (1)
369	how glorious bright must our Creator be (1)
381	God the Father, Light-Creator, to thee laud and honor be (4)
400	Let all things their creator bless (7)
486	To Christ, Creator Savior, King ... hosanna sing (1)
489	The great Creator of the worlds (1)
500	Creator Spirit ... come visit every humble mind (1)
580	Great Creator, still creating, show us what we yet may do (1)
580	Great Creator, give us guidance (4)

Creator's

380   let the Creator's praise arise (1)
409   does his Creator's power display (1)

creature

430   nor a voiceless creature found (2)
430   nor ... creature found that hath neither note nor sound (2)
496, 497   deigned to cast a pitying eye upon his helpless creature (2)
544   Let every creature rise and bring peculiar honors (5)
667   beneath the spreading heavens no creature but is fed (3)

creatures

11   praise him, all creatures here below (4)
24   till all thy creatures own thy sway (4)
43   praise him, all creatures here below (4)
77   his fallen creatures all to save (2)
235   in mystic form and image four living creatures came (2)
314   living Bread that givest all thy creatures breath (3)
358   We are your creatures and children of earth (2)
380   praise him, all creatures here below (3)
398   he formed the creatures with his Word (2)
398   formed the creatures ... then pronounced them good (2)
400   All creatures of our God and King, lift up your voices (1)
405   all creatures great and small (R)
406, 407   From thee alone all creatures came (1)
406, 407   Let creatures all give thanks to thee (8)
435   through all ranks of creatures, to the central height (3)
477   thou art high exalted o'er all creatures now (4)
506, 507   we, your creatures, call you Lord (6)
597   all creatures find their true accord (2)
651   all creatures everywhere (2)

creed

394, 395   your arms embrace all now despised for creed or race (3)
581   Love can exclude no race or creed if honored be God's Name (6)

creeps

46   shade creeps o'er wild and wood (1)

crib

91   our Lord a crib adorning (1)
101   Away in a manger, no crib for his bed (1)
124   Gentiles to his crib to bring (1)

cried

206   "Thou art my Lord and God," he cried (5)
256   cried aloud, "Who are you, Lord?" (1)
284   ye saw his agony, ye heard the plaint he cried (4)
382   Thou my sins against me cried, thou didst clear me (2)
420   it is as though the whole creation cried (1)
568   sorrow for sins that for vengeance have cried (1)

cries

78, 79   where misery cries out to thee, Son of the mother mild (4)
116   I come, the great Redeemer cries, to do thy will, O Lord (1)
427   When morning gilds the skies, my heart, awaking, cries (1)

596 the city's crowded clangor cries aloud for sin to cease (2)
609 where sound the cries of race and clan (1)

crieth
67 Hark, the voice of one that crieth in the desert (2)

crime
605 Will God your pleading hear, while crime and cruelty grow (2)
613 oppression, lust, and crime shall flee thy face before (3)

crimson
434 precious blood and crimson lines (2)

crimsoned
162 each crimsoned bough proclaims the King of glory now (3)

crooked
67 Make ye straight what long was crooked (3)
75 make straight all the crooked places (1)

cross
10 love ... shall dawn on every cross and care (4)
12, 13 At the third hour you took your cross (2)
16, 17 by virtue of his saving cross (2)
18 At noon you hung upon the cross (3a)
53 bore the cross to save us, hope and freedom gave us (1)
106 from his poor manger to his bitter cross (5)
121 your cross on us be signed (4)
135 cross and Easter Day attest God in man made manifest (4)
159 At the cross her vigil keeping stood the mournful mother (1)
160 Cross of Jesus, cross of sorrow (1,4)
162 the cross shines forth in mystic glow (1)
162 O cross, our one reliance, hail (5)
162 as by the cross thou dost restore (6)
163 the cross on Calvary's height gleams of eternity appear (2)
164 as we share this hour, thy cross may bring us to thy joy (4)
164 thy cross may bring us to thy joy and resurrection power (4)
165, 166 to his cross thy tribute bring (1)
165, 166 from that cross now reigns as King (1)
165, 166 on the cross the Lamb is lifted (2)
165, 166 Faithful cross, above all other, one and only noble tree (4)
168, 169 with thee for my salvation upon the cross to die (3)
168, 169 Ah, keep my heart thus moved to stand thy cross beneath (3)
168, 169 thine arms extended upon the cross of life (5)
171 learn of him to bear the cross (2)
175 He who was nailed to the cross is Lord (2)
182 His cross stands empty to the sky (1)
184 He who bore all pain and loss comfortless upon the cross (3)
188, 189 ours the cross, the grave, the skies (3)
190 on the cross a suffering victim (1)
191 He, who on the cross a victim (1)
207 did once upon the cross ... suffer to redeem our loss (1)
207 who endured the cross and grave (2)
215 He who on the cross did suffer (2)
216 He who was nailed to the cross is Lord (1)

609	Where cross the crowded ways of life (1)
610	upon the cross, forsaken, offered mercy's perfect deed (1)
645, 646	thy cross before to guide me (4)
662	Hold thou thy cross before my closing eyes (4)
674	In blazing light your cross reveals the truth (3)
675	Take up your cross (1-5)
675	Take up your cross, the Savior said (1)
675	take up your cross with willing heart (1)
675	the Lord for you accepted death upon a cross (3)
675	only those who bear the cross may hope to wear ... crown (5)
682	for that thou didst all the world upon the cross embrace (2)
685	in my hand no price I bring, simply to thy cross I cling (2)
697	Before the cross of him who died, behold, I prostrate fall (2)
701	Want and gloom, cross, death and tomb (2)

crossed

192	since Jesus crossed the river (2)
526	part of the host have crossed the flood (3)

crossing

526	part are crossing now (3)

crowd

161	The crowd would have been satisfied to see ... crucified (3)
230	In Salem's street was gathered a crowd from many a land (2)
391	We'll crowd thy gates with thankful songs (4)

crowded

567	crowded street, by restless couch ... Gennesaret's shore (2)
596	the city's crowded clangor cries aloud for sin to cease (2)
609	Where cross the crowded ways of life (1)

crowds

259	no shouts proclaim him nigh, no crowds his coming wait (1)

crown

97	Scepter, crown, and sphere (1)
119	thou its light, its joy, its crown (5)
128	gold I bring to crown him again (2)
168, 169	O kingly head, surrounded with mocking crown of thorn (1)
170	To mock your reign ... they made a crown of thorns (1)
170	that glorious is your crown (1)
231	that we might wear the crown and ever shine in splendor (1)
231	we with all your servants may wear the crown of life (2/5-1)
232	You rose ... that they might wear the crown (1)
236	crown of the true of every land (1)
237	joy that martyrs won their crown opened heaven's portal (1)
243	the stones of earthly shame a jeweled crown may seem (4)
255	In us you seek disciples to share your cross and crown (3)
260	For him ... no glory here, no crown or martyr's fame (3)
286	Each a golden crown is wearing (1)
287	win, with them, the victor's crown of gold (3)
337	crown thy gifts with strength to persevere (3)
349	patient faith, the crown to win (2)
359	theirs not a monarch's crown or tyrant's sword (4)

363	praise we the goodness that doth crown our days (5)
383, 384	thou my soul's glory, joy, and crown (1)
386, 387	Glorious, most glorious, is the crown of him (4)
426	songs of praise shall crown that day (3)
435	crown him as your Captain in temptation's hour (5)
436	Holy Spirit guide us on until the glorious crown be won (5)
439	that caused the Lord of bliss to lay aside his crown (1)
439	lay aside his crown for my soul (1)
450, 451	and crown him lord of all (1-6)
450, 451	Crown him ye martyrs of our God who from his altar call (2)
452	Glorious the day when Christ was born to wear the crown (1)
452	born to wear the crown that Ceasars scorn (1)
474	or thorns compose so rich a crown (3)
484, 485	the crown ere-long to wear: Alleluia (2)
494	Crown him with many crowns, the Lamb upon his throne (1)
494	Crown him the Son of God before the worlds began (2)
494	who tread where he hath trod, crown him the Son of man (2)
494	Crown him the Lord of life, who triumphed o'er the grave (3)
494	Crown him of lords the Lord, who over all doth reign (4)
494	Crown him the Lord of heaven, enthroned in worlds above (5)
494	crown him the King, to whom is given the wondrous name (5)
494	Crown him with many crowns, as thrones before him fall (5)
494	crown him, ye kings, with many crowns ... King of all (5)
514	of all his gifts the sum and crown (4)
544	praises throng to crown his head (2)
546	and an immortal crown (1,4)
552, 553	lay hold on life ... thy joy and crown eternally (1)
555	the crown awaits the conquest (3)
561	To valiant hearts triumphant a crown of life shall be (4)
563	wear in endless glory the crown of victory (3)
582, 583	city ... whose laws are love, whose crown is servanthood (3)
585	nails and crown of thorns tell of what God's love must be (5)
594, 595	crown thine ancient Church's story (1)
596	Crown, O God, thine own endeavor (3)
623	crown for the valiant, to weary ones rest (1)
657	all thy faithful mercies crown (1)
665	sword and crown betray our trust (2)
675	only those who bear the cross may hope to wear ... crown (5)
675	wear the glorious crown (5)
719	crown thy good with brotherhood from sea to shining sea (1,3)

crowned

73	crowned with glory like the sun ... lights the morning sky (2)
159	mocked with cruel acclamation, scourged and crowned (3)
159	crowned with thorns entwined (3)
163	on the Redeemer's thorn-crowned brow the wonders ... view (1)
276	up where thine elect are crowned (5)
284	With great delight ye crowned his head (3)
289	hand hath crowned her children with blessings manifold (1)
292	O Jesus, crowned with all renown (1)
292	thine the beauty ... joy with which the years are crowned (1)
313	By the thorns that crowned thy brow (3)
364	prophets crowned with light (4)
483	The head that once was crowned with thorns (1)
483	once ... with thorns, is crowned with glory now (1)

543	with luster new divinely crowned (2)
545	now with glory crowned (1)
598	mocked ... by thorns with which they crowned thee (1)
620	Thy saints are crowned with glory great (2)

crowns
231	Lord, grant us crowns as brilliant (2/12-28)
288	Praise to God ... for the love that crowns our days (1)
362	casting down their golden crowns around the glassy sea (2)
411	whose loving-kindness crowns thy days (6)
494	Crown him with many crowns, the Lamb upon his throne (1)
494	Crown him with many crowns, as thrones before him fall (5)
494	crown him, ye kings, with many crowns ... King of all (5)
562	Crowns and thrones may perish, kingdoms rise and wane (4)
657	till we cast our crowns before thee (3)

crucified
12, 13	O Jesus, crucified for us (4)
18	O Jesus, crucified for us (5)
23	O Jesus, crucified for us (4)
158	I crucified thee (1)
160	robed in mortal flesh is dying, crucified by sin for me (2)
161	The crowd would have been satisfied to see ... crucified (3)
161	to see a prophet crucified (3)
167	where our dear Lord was crucified who died to save us all (1)
172	Were you there when they crucified my Lord (1)
178	We have been crucified with Christ (3)
182	lives, though ever crucified (4)
192	My Love, the Crucified, hath sprung to life this morrow (1)
222	he, who once was crucified, shall come (4)
422	crucified and risen might of Christ, the incarnate Word (2)
473	Each new-born servant of the Crucified bears ... seal (2)
473	praise to the Crucified for victory (4)
598	must bring to doom the powers which crucified thee (2)
633	crucified for our salvation (2)
661	Peter ... hauled the teeming net, head-down was crucified (3)
697	let every sin be crucified, and Christ be all in all (2)

crucifixion
| 159 | when she saw the crucifixion of the sole-begotten one (2) |

crucify
| 458 | Then "Crucify!" is all their breath (3) |

crude
| 629 | crude, partial, and confined (1) |

cruel
159	mocked with cruel acclamation, scourged and crowned (3)
202	free from Pharaoh's cruel tyranny (2)
236	faith undeterred by cruel hate (2)
240, 241	Christ, for cruel traitors pleading (3)
591	from all the easy speeches that comfort cruel men (2)
687, 688	armed with cruel hate, on earth is not his equal (1)

cruelty

605   Will God your pleading hear, while crime and cruelty grow (2)

crushed

27, 28   anguished and in mind distressed be crushed by guilt (3)
243   When Stephen, young and doomed to die, fell crushed (3)
243   crushed beneath the stones (3)

cry

9   worlds awake to cry their blessings on the Lord of life (4)
14, 15   Almighty Father, hear our cry through Jesus Christ (3)
18   dark midday could not conceal your cry of awful agony (3c)
19, 20   Almighty Father, hear our cry through Jesus Christ (3)
21, 22   Almighty Father, hear our cry (3)
44, 45   Almighty Father, hear our cry (4)
61, 62   Midnight's peace their cry has broken (1)
67   Oh, that warning cry obey (2)
68   up, watch in expectation, at midnight comes the cry (1)
76   On Jordan's bank the Baptist's cry (1)
76   Baptist's cry announces that the Lord is nigh (1)
80   who hears your sad and bitter cry (3)
104   And every stone shall cry (1-4)
129, 130 Nations cry aloud in wonder (3)
151   From deepest woe I cry to thee (1)
156   Hark, all the tribes hosanana cry (1)
168, 169 In thy most bitter passion my heart to share doth cry (3)
171   "It is finished!" hear him cry (3)
209   cry, "My Lord and God!" (2)
243   no curse nor vengeful cry for those who broke his bones (3)
246   But down the ages rings the cry of those who saw (2)
246   aching hearts in every land cry out (3)
246   cry out, "We cannot understand" (3)
250   "... peace on earth," the angels cry (5)
324   as with ceaseless voice they cry, "Alleluia ..." (4)
339   at thy feet I cry, my Maker (2)
364   To thee all angels cry aloud (2)
364   to thee the powers on high ... continually do cry (2)
367   earth takes up the angels'cry (2)
367   with thine angel hosts we cry, "Holy, holy, holy" (3)
374   Worthy the Lamb that died, they cry, to be exalted thus (2)
401   "Holy, holy, holy," cry, "Almighty King" (4)
401   "Hail, Father, Son, and Holy Ghost" they ever cry (5)
440   Hear the cry thy Church upraises (3)
458   for his death they thirst and cry (3)
486   Hosanna Lord, thine angels cry ... thy saints reply (2)
517   my very heart and flesh cry out, O living God, for thee (1)
525   their cry goes up, "How long?" (3)
535   Let all cry aloud, and honor the Son (3)
540   Throughout the world their cry is ringing still (1)
570, 571 all who cry for peace and justice (1)
574, 575 forgive, O Lord, we cry (3)
579   hear us when we cry to thee for those in peril on the sea (1)
582, 583 bitter lips in blind despair cry (2)
591   O God of earth and altar, bow down and hear our cry (1)
608   O hear us when we cry to thee (1-3)

608	cry to thee for those in peril on the sea (1-3)
610	still the hungry cry for bread (2)
618	Cry out, dominions, princedoms, powers (1)
618	cry out ... virtues, archangels, angels' choirs (1)
666	Out of the depths I call, to God I send my cry (1)
716	to thee aloud we cry, God save the state (2)

crying

69	What is the crying at Jordan (1)
75	There's a voice in the wilderness crying (1)
101	but little Lord Jesus no crying he makes (2)

crystal

275	chanting at the crystal sea ... alleluia, Lord, to thee (1)
460, 461	songs of all the sinless sweep across the crystal sea (3)
690	Open now the crystal fountain (2)

culture

| 603, 604 | his arms stretched out above through every culture (1) |

cup

159	such a cup of sorrow drinking (4)
232	He drank the cup of suffering (2/7-25)
252	when the cup of human woe first he tasted here below (4)
276	he drank thy cup of pain (4)
276	Lord, may we learn to drink thy cup (5)
305, 306	faith still receives the cup as from thy hand (2)
321	thy cup with love doth overflow (1)
323	Vine of heaven, thy Blood supplies this blest cup (2)
323	this blest cup of sacrifice (2)
471	sweetens every bitter cup (3)
609	The cup of water given for thee (3)
663	filled my cup, and borne me up in everlasting arms (4)
664	my cup with blessings overflows (2)
695, 696	when this cup you give is filled to brimming (3)

curb

| 232 | Lord, curb our vain impatience for glory ... fame (2/7-25) |

cure

71, 72	the bleeding soul to cure (3)
471	The balm of life, the cure of woe (5)
594, 595	Cure thy children's warring madness (3)
685	let the water and the blood ... be of sin the double cure (2)

curfew

| 427 | When evening shadows fall, this rings my curfew call (1) |

curse

60	In sorrow that the ancient curse should doom to death (2)
100	he comes to make his blessings flow far as the curse (3)
100	far as the curse is found (3)
230	by the triumph of the Son the curse of Babel was undone (2)
230	curse of Babel was undone when God did send the Spirit (2)
243	no curse nor vengeful cry for those who broke his bones (3)

270   Gabriel's message does away Satan's curse and ... sway (1)
570, 571   all who curse and all who bless (1)

customary
12, 13   Amid our customary round, we offer ... prayer and praise (1)

customs
281   He sat to watch o'er customs paid (1)

cymbals
61, 62   as harps and cymbals swell the sound (3)
412   Trumpet and pipes, loud clashing cymbals (3)

daily
10   If on our daily course our mind be set (3)
10   a road to bring us daily nearer God (5)
11   Awake, my soul ... with the sun thy daily stage of duty run (1)
12, 13   Now help us bear our daily load (2)
102   daily, when on earth he grew, he was tempted (4)
149   So daily dying to the way of self (2)
149   so daily living to your way of love (2)
175   Daily the loveliness grows (3)
182   but daily, in the midst of life (3)
216   Daily the loveliness grows (2)
291   much more to us, his children, he gives our daily bread (2)
319   daily still your mercies find us (2)
347   in God's good Spirit daily to increase (1)
349   daily power to conquer sin (2)
415   Ten thousand ... precious gifts my daily thanks employ (3)
448, 449   for us his daily works he wrought (3)
528   Let your priests, for earth's true glory, daily lift (3)
528   daily lift life heavenward (3)
570, 571   all who bear its daily stress (1)
586   carpenter of Nazareth, toiling for thy daily food (1)
586   thou ... dwellest in the daily strife (2)
586   bless us in our daily labor (3)
616   to him shall prayer unceasing and daily vows ascend (4)
665   Daily ... almighty Giver boundless gifts on us bestow (4)
686   to grace how great a debtor daily I'm constrained to be (3)
709   give us each day our daily bread ... raiment fit provide (3)

Damascus'
255   We sing the glorious conquest before Damascus' gate (1)

damnation
591   from sleep and from damnation, deliver us, good Lord (2)

dance
463, 464   at your marriage all its occasions shall dance for joy (3)

danger
246   Then warning came of danger near (1)
251   In doubt or danger, all our days (3)
251   In doubt or danger ... be near to guard us still (3)
345   from harm and danger keep thy children free (2)

370	Christ in quiet, Christ in danger (6)
561	let courage rise with danger (2)
561	when duty calls, or danger, be never wanting there (3)
675	in his strength, and calmly every danger brave (4)
686	to rescue me from danger, interposed his precious blood (2)

danger's

| 579 | our people shield in danger's hour (4) |
| 608 | thy children shield in danger's hour (4) |

dangers

| 563 | When morn his face revealeth thy dangers all are past (4) |
| 671 | Through many dangers, toils, and snares (4) |

Daniel

| 143 | So Daniel trained his mystic sight (3) |

dare

129, 130	let us, if we dare to speak ... praise him (1)
537	with us the work to share, with us reproach to dare (3)
561	arm of flesh will fail you, ye dare not trust your own (3)
579	save all who dare the eagle's flight (3)
582, 583	how its splendor challenges the souls that greatly dare (4)
590	strong in your strength to venture and to dare (2)

dared

| 386, 387 | determined, dared, and done (4) |

dares

| 541 | Who dares stand idle on the harvest plain (1) |
| 629 | dares to bind to one's own sense the oracles of heaven (2) |

dark

6, 7	Dark and cheerless is the morn unaccompanied by thee (2)
18	On Golgatha the sky turned dark (3b)
18	dark midday could not conceal your cry of awful agony (3c)
56	death's dark shadow put to flight (6)
69	Dark is the season, dark our hearts and shut to mystery (1)
73	earth's dark night is past (3)
78, 79	yet in thy dark streets shineth the everlasting Light (1)
78, 79	dark night wakes, the glory breaks (4)
171	Go to dark Gethsemane, ye that feel the tempter's power (1)
174	death's dark angel sheathes his sword (2)
180	we are free from sin's dark prison (4)
199, 200	all the winter of our sins, long and dark (2)
199, 200	Neither might the gates of death ... tomb's dark portal (4)
204	wheat that in dark earth many days has lain (1)
284	In dark Gethsemane the night before he died (4)
345	for dark and light are both alike to thee (2)
376	drive the dark of doubt away (1)
381	dark as night and deep as death (2)
388	dark is his path on the wings of the storm (2)
409	all move round the dark terrestrial ball (3)
422	though our vision now is dark, to live by what we see (3)
472	by thy cross didst save us from death and dark despair (4)

David

56	O come, thou Key of David, come (5)
162	Fulfilled is all that David told (2)
444	He from the house of David a child of grace has given (2)
450, 451	whom David Lord did call (3)
620	David stands with harp in hand as master of the choir (3)
624	There is the throne of David (3)

David's

50	Hosanna to the anointed King, to David's holy Son (3)
94, 95	To you, in David's town, this day is born of David's line (3)
102	Once in royal David's city stood a lowly cattle shed (1)
104	This child through David's city Shall ride in triumph by (2)
135	branch of royal David's stem in thy birth at Bethlehem (1)
154, 155	Thou art the King of Israel, thou David's royal Son (1)
260	Come now, and praise the humble saint of David's house (1)
260	David's house and line (1)
260	Virgin's spouse ... guardian of great David's greater Son (2)
267	virgin born of David's line shall bear the promised seed (2)
443	his royalty from David's tree, praised be his Oneness (1)
450, 451	Hail him, the Heir of David's line (3)
616	Hail to the Lord's Anointed, great David's greater Son (1)

dawn

9	what time there comes the breath of dawn (3)
9	dawn that rustles through the trees (3)
10	some softening gleam of love and prayer shall dawn (4)
10	love ... shall dawn on every cross and care (4)
24	As o'er each continent and island the dawn leads on (3)
24	dawn leads on another day (3)
31, 32	brings the splendors of the dawn (1)
40, 41	as Day-star you precede the dawn (1)
44, 45	when the dawn new light will bring (3)
69	O let salvation dawn (4)
111	with the dawn of redeeming grace (3)
117, 118	dawn on our darkness, and lend us thine aid (1,5)
125, 126	on them broke forth the heavenly dawn (1)
163	the wonders of that dawn we view (1)
393	light of dawn leads us on (2)
431	The dawn returns in splendor, the heavens burn and blaze (2)
454	till the dawn of endless day (4)
615	And lo, already on the hills the flags of dawn appear (3)
640	for the morning seems to dawn (3)

dawned

201	On earth has dawned this day of days (1)

dawning

9	purple pageantry of dawning and of dying days (1)
196, 197	joy to the heart and all in this good day's dawning (R)
232	last and greatest prophet, he saw the dawning ray (2/6-24)
363	with light and life since Eden's dawning day (1)
444	the dawning of forgiveness upon the sinner's eyes (3)
666	more duly than the morning watch to spy the dawning day (3)

dawns

73	The King shall come when morning dawns (1,3,5)
556, 557	till dawns the golden day (5)
607	dawns the morning glorious when truth and justice reign (4)
610	till your love's revealing light ... dawns (3)
610	light ... dawns upon our quickened sight (3)
647	till dawns the endless day (3)

day

3, 4	that he ... would keep us free from harm this day (1)
3, 4	that we, when this new day is gone (4)
5	O Day, all days illumining (1)
6, 7	more and more thyself display, shining to the perfect day (3)
8	praise every morning, God's recreation of the new day (3)
10	New mercies, each returning day around us hover (2)
10	help us ... every day, to live more nearly as we pray (6)
11	Direct, control, suggest, this day, all I design (3)
12, 13	sun ... imparting vigor to the day (1)
14, 15	through all its changes guide the day (1)
16, 17	each day the sun at zenith calls the faithful (1)
21, 22	light the glow of perfect day (1)
23	The fleeting day is nearly gone (1)
24	The day thou gavest, Lord, is ended (1)
24	and rests not now by day or night (2)
24	dawn leads on another day (3)
27, 28	you gave the day with splendor bright (1)
27, 28	you found it good and called it 'day' (2)
31, 32	The day departs (3)
31, 32	boundaries of the day and night (4)
31, 32	Like sun and day, shine in our hearts (5)
36	Now, ere day fadeth quite, we see the evening light (2)
38, 39	you set the bounds of night and day (2)
40, 41	O Christ, you are both light and day (1)
42	Now the day is over, night is drawing nigh (1)
43	the ill that I this day have done (2)
44, 45	To you before the close of day, Creator of all things (1)
46	The duteous day now closeth (1)
46	yet when life's day is over (3)
47	On this day, the first of days, God ... we praise (1)
47	On this day the eternal Son over death his triumph won (2)
47	this day the Spirit came with his gifts of living flame (2)
48	O day of radiant gladness, O day of joy and light (1)
48	this day the high and lowly, through ages joined in tune (1)
48	This day at the creation, the light first had its birth (2)
48	day for our salvation Christ rose from depths of earth (2)
48	this day our Lord victorious the Spirit sent from heaven (2)
48	thus this day most glorious a triple light was given (2)
48	This day, God's people meeting, his Holy Scripture hear (3)
48	grace more grace receiving on this blest day of light (3)
48	at length our rest attaining, our endless Sabbath day (4)
49	stamped the day for ever his (1)
49, 50	This is the day the Lord hath made (2)
51	This is the Lord's day, day of God's own making (3)
51	day of creation, day of resurrection (3)

51	day of the Spirit ... day for rejoicing (3)
52	This day at thy creating word (1)
52	O Lord, this day upon us shine (1)
52	This day the Lord for sinners slain (2)
52	This day the Holy Spirit came (3)
52	O Spirit, fill our hearts this day with grace to hear (4)
59	Cast away the works of darkness, O ye children of the day (1)
60	redeem us for eternal day (5)
68	see the day of earth's redemption, and ever be with thee (3)
69	Now comes the day of salvation (4)
73	the day that e'er shall last (3)
85, 86	before the world knew day or night (1)
85, 86	throughout the world this holy day (2)
88	O renew us, Lord, we pray, with thy Spirit day by day (5)
92	On this day earth shall ring with the song (1)
92	On this day angels sing (4)
94, 95	To you, in David's town, this day is born of David's line (3
102	the world's creator, cradled there on Christmas Day (3)
105	remember Christ our Savior was born on Christmas Day (1)
105	this day is born a Savior of a pure virgin bright (3)
106	this day hath God fulfilled his promised word (2)
106	this day is born a Savior, Christ the Lord (2)
106	he that was born upon this joyful day (6)
108	on this day of days tell out redemption's story (1)
109	so it continued both day and night (2)
119	Holy Jesus, every day keep us in the narrow way (4)
133, 134	more bright than day your face did show (1)
135	cross and Easter Day attest God in man made manifest (4)
144	be to us as day (1)
144	nearer draws the day of days when paradise shall bloom (4)
148	turn our darkness into day (5)
149	led by your cloud by day, by night your fire (1)
157	On this day the Lord has acted (R)
175	Hail thee, festival day! (R)
175	blest day that art hallowed forever (R)
175	day whereon Christ arose, breaking the kingdom of death (R)
179	bring again our daylight: day returns with thee (6)
180	Come ... hail our Lord's triumphant day (3)
185, 186	let us feast this holy day on the true bread of heaven (4)
192	Had Christ ... ne'er burst his three-day prison (R)
193	That Easter day with joy was bright (1)
199, 200	Now the queen of seasons, bright with the day of splendor (3)
201	On earth has dawned this day of days (1)
201	day ... whereon the faithful give God praise (1)
203	That Easter morn, at break of day (2)
203	On this most holy day of days (5)
210	The day of resurrection, Earth tell it out abroad (1)
213	arise and rejoice in the day thou wast born (1)
213	on this festival day, come exulting away (1)
214	Hail the day that sees him rise (1)
216	Hail thee, festival day (R)
216	blest day that art hallowed for ever (R)
216	day when the Christ ascends, high in the heavens to reign (R)
219	O day of exultation (2)
223, 224	blessings of this sacred day grant us ... we pray (3)

225	Hail thee, festival day! blest day ... hallowed for ever (R)
225	day ... Holy Ghost shone in the world with God's grace (R)
229	still from age to age convey the wonders of this ... day (1)
229	wonders of this sacred day (1)
232	light that grows in splendor until the perfect day (2/6-24)
236	beacon by night and cloud by day (1)
237	Let us now our voices raise, wake the day with gladness (1)
247	O sisters, too, how may we do for to preserve this day (1)
247	Herod the King, in his raging charged he hath this day (2)
247	And every morn and day (3)
267	Praise we the Lord this day, this day so long foretold (1)
270	out of darkness brings our Day (1)
286	day and night they serve him still (5)
287	But lo, there breaks a yet more glorious day (7)
290	from his field shall in that day all offenses purge away (3)
297	brand us this day with Jesus' Name (1)
298	Grant us to grow in grace each day (2)
323	day by day with strength supplied (1)
324	Light of Life descendeth from the realms of endless day (3)
326	to appear before God in the city of infinite day (1)
335	And I will raise them up on the last day (R)
342	I am with you, this day and ever (3)
344	May we ever reign with thee in endless day (3)
345	with thee began, with thee shall end the day (2)
347	to serve God's people every day and hour (4)
349	from their bright baptismal day you have led them (1)
353	every day their love renew (2)
363	with light and life since Eden's dawning day (1)
366	Grant that ... we may dwell in everlasting day (7)
370	I bind this day to me for ever ... Christ's incarnation (2)
371	where the Gospel day sheds not its glorious ray (1)
376	giver of immortal gladness, fill us with the light of day (1)
389	He the golden-tressed sun caused all day his course to run (4)
393	God has given the cloud by day (2)
398	I sing the wisdom that ordained the sun to rule the day (1)
400	Dear mother earth, you day by day unfold your blessings (4)
404	each day we live our psalm to you we raise (1)
406, 407	with brightness he doth fill the day (2)
409	The unwearied sun from day to day ... power display (1)
414	day by day thy throne addressing (1)
415	day and night divide thy works no more (4)
416	For the beauty of each hour of the day and of the night (2)
419	sheds on our path the glow of day (2)
426	songs of praise shall crown that day (3)
428	heat and cold, O night and day ... bless the Lord (3)
441, 442	adds more luster to the day (3)
444	the prophet of salvation, the harbinger of Day (2)
452	Glorious the day when Christ was born to wear the crown (1)
452	Glorious the day when Christ arose (2)
452	Glorious the day when Christ fulfills what self rejects (4)
453	As Jacob with travel was weary one day (1)
454	till the dawn of endless day (4)
458	resounding all the day hosannas to their King (3)
460, 461	here the sinful flee to thee from day to day (3)
471	cheers with hope the gloomy day (3)

478	lead us then day by day in your own steps, we pray (2)
482	your bliss in our hearts, Lord, at the break of the day (1)
482	strength in our hearts, Lord, at the noon of the day (2)
482	your love in our hearts, Lord, at the eve of the day (3)
482	your peace in our hearts, Lord, at the end of the day (4)
486	So in the last and dreadful day (5)
486	dreadful day when earth and heaven shall melt away (5)
488	thou my best thought, by day or by night (1)
490	The night and the day are both alike (R)
494	sing ... before him day and night (4)
498	the burden of the day (1)
517	One day within thy courts excels a thousand spent away (4)
522, 523	light by night and shade by day (3)
536	Judah is glad to see his day (3)
539	till God shall bring his kingdom's joyful day (3)
540	watchmen who never held their peace by day or night (1)
541	The enemy is watching night and day (2)
542	freedom her bondage breaks, and night is turned to day (1)
548	win the well-fought day (4)
549, 550	day by day his clear voice soundeth (1)
551	Lord, bring the day of truth and love (2)
555	the day of march has come (1)
556, 557	youth to age, by night and day, in gladness and in woe (4)
556, 557	till dawns the golden day (5)
561	forth to the mighty conflict in this his glorious day (2)
561	this day the noise of battle, the next the victor's song (4)
564, 565	I'll labor night and day to be a pilgrim (3)
566	hasten, Lord, that perfect day (2)
566	perfect day when pain and death shall cease (2)
570, 571	in your day of loss and sorrow (2)
570, 571	in your day of helpless strife (2)
570, 571	In your day of wealth and plenty (3)
570, 571	I must work while it is day (3)
593	reborn through death's dark night to endless day (5)
597	O day of peace that dimly shines through all our hopes (1)
599	facing the rising sun of our new day begun (1)
600, 601	O day of God, draw nigh in beauty and in power (1)
600, 601	O day of God, draw nigh as at creation's birth (5)
612	Prophecy will fade away, melting in the light of day (3)
615	faithful souls have yearned to see ... that kingdom's day (1)
615	see on earth that kingdom's day (1)
615	proclaim the day is near (3)
615	day by whose clear shining light all wrong ... revealed (4)
615	day of perfect righteousness, the promised day of God (5)
617	from ... night profound into the glory of the perfect day (1)
627	radiant cloud by day (3)
629	notions of our day and place (1)
638, 639	wrestle till the break of day (1)
640	Traveler, yes, it brings the day, promised day of Israel (1)
643	by prostrate spirits day and night incessantly adored (2)
647	I know not where the road will lead I follow day by day (1)
647	till dawns the endless day (3)
654	Day by day, dear Lord, of thee three things I pray (1)
654	follow thee more nearly, day by day (1)
666	more duly than the morning watch to spy the dawning day (3)

203	On this most holy day of days (5)
204	wheat that in dark earth many days has lain (1)
204	he that for three days in the grave had lain (3)
208	The three sad days are quickly sped (3)
213	Now with singing and praise, let us spend all the days (2)
213	days, by our heavenly Father bestowed (2)
251	In doubt or danger, all our days (3)
288	Praise to God ... for the love that crowns our days (1)
288	singing thus through all our days praise to God (3)
289	days of old have dowered us with gifts beyond all praise (3)
289	our Father, make us faithful to serve the coming days (3)
292	That we may praise thee all our days (3)
302, 303	didst give us food for all our days (1)
316, 317	yet all our days thou still art here with us (2)
363	Ancient of Days, who sittest throned in glory (1)
363	praise we the goodness that doth crown our days (5)
365	build in our hearts thy throne, Ancient of Days (1)
382	Seven whole days, not one in seven, I will praise thee (3)
388	Our shield and defender, the Ancient of Days (1)
401	Ancient of everlasting days, and God of love (1)
411	whose loving-kindness crowns thy days (6)
423	most blessed, most glorious, the Ancient of Days (1)
429	My days of praise shall ne'er be past (1,4)
431	rising sun renews the race that measures all our days (2)
431	So order too this life of mine, direct it all my days (4)
452	Glorious the days of gospel grace (3)
458	in whose sweet praise I all my days could gladly spend (7)
460, 461	when the forty days were o'er (2)
537	new-born souls, whose days, reclaimed from error's ways (4)
549, 550	days of toil and hours of ease (4)
555	through days of preparation thy grace has made us strong (1)
567	Thine arm, O Lord, in days of old was strong to heal (1)
570, 571	For all days are days of judgment (4)
594, 595	for the living of these days (2)
599	felt in the days when hope unborn had died (2)
600, 601	finely build for days to come foundations that endure (3)
606	that Christ the Lord may be with us through all our days (2)
607	Keep bright in us the vision of days when war shall cease (4)
614	praise for his brave saints of ancient days (1)
625	Let all thy days till life shall end ... praise (4)
625	days ... whate'er he send, be filled with praise (4)
635	bear thee through the evil days (1)
645, 646	through all the length of days thy goodness faileth never (6)
663	surely I can trust thy love for all the days to come (5)
664	The sure provisions of my God attend me all my days (3)
671	we've no less days to sing God's praise (5)
671	no less days ... than when we'd first begun (5)
692	in that light of life I'll walk till pilgrim days are done (3)
695, 696	still evil days bring burdens hard to bear (2)
695, 696	we shall remember all the days we lived through (4)
707	take my moments and my days (1)

days'

| 180 | he has burst his three days' prison (1) |
| 199, 200 | from three days' sleep in death as a sun hath risen (2) |

daytime

33-35	you make the daytime radiant with the sunlight (1)

dazzling

16, 17	So dazzling is its holy light (3)
31, 32	for you the dazzling star shines forth (2)
57, 57	dear tokens of his passion still his dazzling body bears (3)
228	occupy its inmost part with your dazzling purity (3)
286	Who are these of dazzling brightness (2)
369	dwells amidst the dazzling light of vast eternity (1)

dead

47	Holy Jesus, may I be dead and buried here with thee (4)
49	rose triumphant from the dead (1)
50	Today he rose and left the dead, and Satan's empire fell (2)
139	He taught, he healed, he raised the dead (2)
149	so we are dead and live with you in God (2)
149	If dead in you, so in you we arise (3)
149	you, the first-born of all the faithful dead (3)
179	Lo! the dead is living, God for evermore (1)
187	souls restoring from the dead (2)
191	Jesus ... now is risen from the dead (1)
192	trump from east to west shall wake the dead in number (3)
193	who, dead, again dost live (5)
201	The Lord is risen from the dead (3)
204	love lives again, that with the dead has been (1)
204	quick from the dead my risen Lord is seen (3)
204	fields of our hearts that dead and bare have been (4)
208	he rises glorious from the dead (3)
212	lest dead and friendless and alone he ... deceive (4)
212	O Dead arise! O Friendless stand by seraphim adored (5)
276	he stood with thee beside the dead (3)
284	ye mourned the dead in sad surprise (5)
294	dead in the tomb with Christ our King (2)
301	in whose death our sins are dead (1)
307	first-begotten from the dead (1)
486	above, beneath us, and around, both dead and living (2)
486	both dead and living swell the sound (2)
492	Prince of life, among the dead (3)
493	new life the dead receive (4)
610	still in grief we mourn our dead (2)

deadly

357	Often were they wounded in the deadly strife (3)
718	From war's alarms, from deadly pestilence (3)

deaf

493	Hear him, ye deaf (5)
567	To thee they went, the blind ... deaf ... palsied ... lame (1)
633	deaf we are, our healer be (3)

dear

10	Only, O Lord, in thy dear love, fit us for perfect rest (6)
43	Forgive me, Lord, for thy dear Son (2)
57, 58	dear tokens of his passion still his dazzling body bears (3)

66	dear desire of every nation, joy of every longing heart (2)
78, 79	still the dear Christ enters in (3)
101	Bless all the dear children in thy tender care (3)
139	This is my dear beloved Son upon whom rests my favor (1)
150	O keep us, Savior dear, ever constant by thy side (5)
159	Who, on Christ's dear mother gazing ... would not weep (4)
159	Who, on Christ's dear mother thinking (4)
167	where our dear Lord was crucified who died to save us all (1)
203	amidst them came their Lord most dear (4)
206	amidst them came their Lord most dear (2)
244	the better Eden planted by our Lord most dear (2)
279	For thy dear saints, O Lord, who strove in thee to live (1)
293	They loved their Lord so dear (2)
327, 328	by his dear cross and blood the victory won (3)
345	Savior, again to thy dear Name we raise ... praise (1)
368	dear Redeemer, in our hearts thy peace proclaim (2)
400	Dear mother earth, you day by day unfold your blessings (4)
434	Her noblest life my spirit draws from his dear wounds (4)
434	his dear wounds and bleeding side (4)
458	They rise, and needs will have my dear Lord made away (5)
458	never was love, dear King, never was grief like thine (7)
493	O for a thousand tongues to sing my dear Redeemer's praise (1)
505	increase our faith in our dear Lord (2)
505	his dear Son, who reigns above (5)
519, 520	vision dear of peace and love (1)
519, 520	for Christ's dear Name ... pain and tribulation bore (3)
549, 550	leaving all for his dear sake (2)
552, 553	he changeth not, and thou art dear (4)
610	forth in your dear name we go (4)
623	seeking Jerusalem, dear native land (4)
624	Jesus, in mercy bring us to that dear land of rest (4)
632	The Church from our dear Master received the word divine (2)
632	O make thy Church, dear Savior, a lamp of purest gold (3)
644	Dear Name, the rock on which I build (3)
645, 646	I fear no ill with thee, dear Lord, beside me (4)
652, 653	Dear Lord and Father of mankind forgive our foolish ways (1)
654	Day by day, dear Lord, of thee three things I pray (1)
689	not so much that I ... as thou, dear Lord, on me (2)

dearer

| 117, 118 | dearer to God are the prayers of the poor (4) |
| 659, 660 | still with thee in closer, dearer company (3) |

dearest

168, 169	What language ... borrow to thank thee, dearest friend (4)
170	O dearest Lord (1)
173	now, and even unto death, dearest Lord, be near me (4)
223, 224	grant us, dearest Lord, we pray (3)
337	then for those, our dearest and our best ... we appeal (3)
342	of God's own love his dearest token (1)
683, 684	The dearest idol I have know, whate'er that idol be (4)

dearly

| 83 | who would not love thee, loving us so dearly (5) |
| 167 | O dearly, dearly has he loved (5) |

| 518 | All that dedicated city, dearly loved of God on high (2) |
| 654 | to see thee more clearly, love thee more dearly (1) |

death

9	undying still through death (3)
14, 15	by a holy death attained, eternal glory may be gained (2)
16, 17	who, conquering death, reign gloriously with God (4)
38, 39	You broke the chains of death and hell (3)
38, 39	who, conquering death, reign gloriously with God (5)
47	On this day the eternal Son over death his triumph won (2)
52	Jesus, may we lifted be from death of sin to life in thee (2)
54	hence to death and hell descends (3)
55	You suffered death and harrowed hell (3)
60	In sorrow that the ancient curse should doom to death (2)
60	doom to death a universe (2)
81	from sin and death now save us, and share our every load (3)
121	Straightway and steadfast until death (2)
125, 126	who dwelt in death and night (1)
139	death could hold him never. He rose and lives forever (2)
140, 141	swear by thyself, that at my death thy Son shall shine (3)
142	yea, evermore, in life and death, Jesus, with us abide (4)
149	knowing ourselves baptized into your death (2)
156	O Christ, thy triumphs now begin o'er captive death (2)
156	captive death and conquered sin (2)
158	For me ... thy death of anguish (4)
159	in death by all forsaken, till his spirit he resigned (3)
161	He lived to rob death of its sting (1)
163	sin is slain, and death brings life (3)
168, 169	Can death thy bloom deflower (1)
168, 169	mourn thee, well beloved, yet thank thee for thy death (3)
173	the glorious Prince of Life should in death be sleeping (3)
173	now, and even unto death, dearest Lord, be near me (4)
174	now no more can death appall (3)
175	day whereon Christ arose, breaking the kingdom of death (R)
175	from the death of the winter arising (1)
175	treading the pathway of death, life ... bestowest on all (4)
179	Thou, of life the author, death didst undergo (5)
180	death is conquered, we are free (1)
182	His love in death shall never die (1)
183	Death and life have contended in that combat stupendous (3)
183	Christ indeed from death is risen (8)
185, 186	when life and death contended (2)
185, 186	the reign of death was ended (2)
188, 189	Death in vain forbids him rise (1)
188, 189	where, O death, is now thy sting (2)
190	Whom your tears in death were mourning, welcome (1)
190	the strength of death is broken (3)
191	Christ from death to life is born (2)
193	from every weapon death can wield ... shield (4)
194, 195	thy terrors now can no longer, death, appall us (1)
194, 195	life, nor death, nor powers of hell tear us (3)
198	Christ rose from death ... adore for ever ... evermore (1)
199, 200	from three days' sleep in death as a sun hath risen (2)
199, 200	Neither might the gates of death ... tomb's dark portal (4)
201	who over death had victory won (2)

202	from death to endless life restored (5)
203, 206	King of heaven ... o'er death and hell rose triumphing (1)
208	The powers of death have done their worst (2)
210	From death to life eternal, from earth unto the sky (1)
215	he by death has spoiled his foes (2)
220, 221	The bonds of death are burst by thee (1)
222	as sin and death their conquests yield (1)
231	his faith, in death, confessing (2/12-26)
240, 241	they, like Christ, in death victorious (1)
240, 241	o'er all miracles preceding his inestimable death (3)
253	their triumph to his death (2)
270	death by death its death shall gain (2)
275	by death to life immortal they were born and glorified (3)
277	toil and labor cannot weary love enduring unto death (2)
279	They all in life and death, with thee their Lord in view (2)
296	Embraced by death he broke its fearful hold (1)
296	We share by water in his saving death (2)
298	baptized into the death of Christ (1)
301	in whose death our sins are dead (1)
313	by the pain and death, I now claim ... love unfailing (3)
314	O memorial wondrous of the Lord's own death (3)
342	Thus by your death our life obtaining (2)
344	fear of death shall not appall us (3)
345	thy peace in death, the hope to rise again (4)
346	Thy death remembered, feeding thus on thee (1)
352	nor life nor death may part those ... one in heart (2)
357	Think, O Lord, in mercy on the souls ... in death repose (2)
357	in faith gone from us, now in death repose (2)
363	thou, Lord, by death hast won life's victory (3)
366	Thou didst take the sting from death (6)
370	his death on cross for my salvation (1)
373	sin and death shall not prevail (2)
379	Sin and death and hell shall never ... triumph (3)
381	dark as night and deep as death (2)
391	he saved us from the power of death (2)
400	even you, most gentle death (6)
400	most gentle death, waiting to hush our final breath (6)
406, 407	For death our sister, praised be (7)
411	he healeth thine infirmities and ransoms thee from death (4)
426	Borne upon their latest breath ... conquer death (6)
426	songs of praise shall conquer death (6)
429	when my voice is lost in death praise shall employ (1,4)
435	brought it back victorious, when from death he passed (2)
435	Name him, Christians ... with love strong as death (4)
439	when from death I'm free, I'll sing on (3)
448, 449	he bore the shameful cross and death (4)
448, 449	For us he rose from death again (5)
452	whose life and death that love reveal which mortals need (1)
454	now the gate of death is riven (3)
455, 456	our life to live, our death to die (3)
457	to thee alone from sin and death we flee (1)
457	who put their trust in thee nor death nor hell ... harm (3)
458	for his death they thirst and cry (3)
458	in death no friendly tomb but what a stranger gave (6)
465, 466	Eternal life, raise me from death (2)

471	gilds the bed of death with light (4)
472	by thy cross didst save us from death and dark despair (4)
472	O Christ, o'er death victorious (5)
476	makes birth and death his own (4)
477	by thy death was God's salvation wrought (2)
477	humbling thyself to death on Calvary (3)
481	the keys of death and hell to Christ the Lord are given (3)
483	though shame and death to him (6)
484, 485	o'er sin, and death, and hell victorious (2)
487	such a life as killeth death (1)
492	So, he tasted death for mortals (3)
494	died eternal life to bring and lives that death may die (3)
501, 502	life rises vibrant out of death (1)
526	though now divided by the ... narrow stream of death (2)
530	earth from sin and death to save (2)
530	through his death the world is freed (3)
540	break down the realm of Satan, death, and sin (3)
547	Awake, O sleeper, rise from death (1)
558	holy faith! We will be true to thee till death (R)
566	perfect day when pain and death shal! cease (2)
567	it triumphed o'er disease and death (1)
567	thou our great deliverer still ... Lord of life and death (3)
572	into your self-giving death call us all to follow (2)
598	doomed to death (2)
612	love than death itself more strong (2)
630	Deeds and words and death and rising (2)
630	life redeemed from death and sin (5)
662	in life, in death, O Lord, abide with me (4)
664	When I walk through the shades of death (2)
675	the Lord for you accepted death upon a cross (3)
675	follow Christ, nor think till death to lay it down (5)
682	e'en death itself, and all for one who was thine enemy (3)
685	when mine eyelids close in death (3)
690	death of death, and hell's destruction (3)
697	death the gate of heaven (4)
701	Want and gloom, cross, death and tomb (2)
704	till death thy endless mercies seal (4)

death's

46	death's fair night discover ... everlasting life (3)
56	death's dark shadow put to flight (6)
168, 169	hold me that I quail not in death's most fearful hour (5)
174	death's dark angel sheathes his sword (2)
180	Death's long shadows have departed (2)
185, 186	Christ Jesus lay in death's strong bands (1)
192	Death's flood hath lost its chill (2)
208	from death's dread sting thy servants free (5)
284	out from death's vast room, up from the grave, he leapt (6)
364	hadst overcome death's sting and opened heaven's door (7)
593	reborn through death's dark night to endless day (5)
645, 646	In death's dark vale I fear no ill (4)
662	Where is death's sting? where, grave, thy victory? (3)
663	valley of death's shade (3)
702	in death's abode? Lo, thou art there (3)

deathless

631   Light of knowledge ... shed on us thy deathless learning (3)

decay

75   like grass our works decay (2)
76   flowers that wither and decay (3)
357   Every taint of evil, frailty and decay ... purge away (3)

decayed

453   has stood hundreds of years and is not yet decayed (2)

deceitful

475   Help us to surrender earth's deceitful treasures (2)
588, 589   Let not the world's deceitful cares ... destroy (3)

deceive

212   lest dead and friendless and alone he ... deceive (4)
212   he should their skill deceive (4)
441, 442   hopes deceive and fears annoy (2)

deceiving

312   keep free from all deceiving (2)

decisions

348   help us to make those decisions that bind us (4)

Deck

339   Deck thyself, my soul, with gladness (1)

decked

237   for by faith they saw the land decked in all its glory (2)
519, 520   therewith hath willed for ever ... palace ... be decked (4)
624   the pastures of the blessed are decked in glorious sheen (2)

declare

120   the Father's voice did then declare (2)
232   whose gospel words declare ... your path (2/9-21)
372   Formless, all lovely forms declare his loveliness (2)
415   how shall words with equal warmth the gratitude declare (2)
431   The stars declare his glory (1)
630   grace in human form declare (2)
638, 639   my misery or sin declare (2)
669   him whose faithful mercy the skies above declare (1)

declares

31, 32   its gleaming path declares the wonders of your ... power (2)

declaring

183   Speak, Mary, declaring what thou sawest, wayfaring (4)
334   by this Eucharist declaring yours the final victory (1)

decree

388   hath stablished it fast by a changeless decree (3)

decreed

252   Jesus, Name decreed of old, to the maiden mother told (2)

decreeing

475   life's true way decreeing (2)

dedicated

518   All that dedicated city, dearly loved of God on high (2)

dedication

145   Lent calls to prayer, to trust and dedication (1)

deed

226, 227   word and deed and thought twisted from thy true design (3)
359   in word and deed Christ's one true sacrifice (3)
534   All we can do is nothing worth unless God blesses the deed (4)
566   rise, like incense ... in noble thought and deed (1)
574, 575   For sins of heedless word and deed (3)
586   every deed of human kindness done in love is done to thee (3)
610   upon the cross, forsaken, offered mercy's perfect deed (1)
630   Word was spoken in the deed that made the earth (1)

deed's

386, 387   now the matchless deed's achieved (4)

deeds

229   let all the listening earth be taught the deeds (2)
229   the deeds our great Redeemer wrought (2)
233, 234   the apostles' glorious deeds we sing (1)
238, 239   Worthy deeds they wrought (1)
245   O Word made flesh, your deeds and words refresh (3)
245   your deeds and words refresh our hearts like dew (3)
271, 272   His mighty deeds exalt his fame (4)
288   by deeds of kindly love for thy mercies grateful prove (3)
370   all good deeds done unto the Lord (3)
414   thy deeds of wonder tell (3)
437, 438   Make known his might, the deeds his arm has done (2)
555   nor roll of stirring drums, but deeds of love and mercy (2)
558   preach thee, too, as love knows how, by kindly deeds (3)
558   by kindly deeds and virtuous life (3)
610   love in living deeds to show (4)
628   our thoughts and words and deeds may glorify your Name (2)
630   Deeds and words and death and rising (2)
678, 679   Make his deeds known to the peoples (2)

deep

42   guard the sailors tossing on the deep, blue sea (3)
78, 79   Above thy deep and dreamless sleep the silent stars go by (1)
85, 86   our constant star in sin's deep night (2)
109   cold winter's night that was so deep (1)
127   see them give, in deep devotion (3)
159   Deep the woe of her affliction (2)
159   who ... would not share her sorrows deep (4)
159   Jesus, may her deep devotion stir in me the same emotion (5)
173   O sorrow deep! Who would not weep (1)

187	deep and wide flows the tide severing us from bondage past (1)
252	Unto which must every knee bow in deep humility (1)
339	how vast and deep its treasure (3)
370	the deep salt sea, around the old eternal rocks (4)
372	deep writ upon the human heart, on sea and land (3)
379	find that self-same aching deep within the heart of God (2)
381	dark as night and deep as death (2)
385	deep seas obey thy voice (1)
388	His chariots of wrath the deep thunderclouds form (2)
432	loud organs, his glory forth tell in deep tone (3)
448, 449	O love, how deep, how broad, how high (1)
448, 449	glory ... for love so deep, so high, so broad (6)
454	came in deep humility (1)
506, 507	Trinity in deep accord (6)
579, 608	who bidd'st the mighty ocean deep its ... limits keep (1)
579, 608	ocean deep its own appointed limits keep (1)
608	who walkedst on the foaming deep (2)
610	As, O Lord, your deep compassion healed the sick (2)
619	Such song is rest and food and deep delight (6)
636, 637	When through the deep waters I call thee to go (3)
665	deep his wisdom passing thought (3)
677	Deep in unfathomable mines, with never-failing skill (2)
698	I only know my need, as deep as life (1)

deepest

151	From deepest woe I cry to thee (1)
440	our knowledge, sense, and sight lie in deepest darkness (2)
440	in deepest darkness shrouded (2)
636, 637	and sanctify to thee thy deepest distress (3)
643	fear ... with deepest, tenderest fears (4)
702	If deepest darkness cover me (5)
702	the deepest darkness hideth not from thee (5)

deeply

| 57, 58 | deeply wailing, shall the true Messiah see (2) |

deface

| 566 | our rude work deface no more the handiwork of God (2) |

defeated

| 202 | all sufficient Sacrifice, beneath thee hell defeated lies (4) |

defend

27, 28	Defend us, Father, through the night (5)
60	defend us while we dwell below from all assaults (5)
231	May we like true apostles your holy Church defend (2/2-24)
243	Let me, O Lord, thy cause defend (4)
320	Lord, refresh us and defend us (5)
340, 341	In your service, Lord, defend us (4)
352	Spirit of God, whom we adore: preserve, protect, defend (3)
390	who doth prosper thy way and defend thee (3)
564, 565	Since, Lord, thou dost defend us with thy Spirit (3)

defender

| 40, 41 | Defender of us all, look down (4) |

307	Thou alone, our strong defender (1)
348	led by your Spirit, defender and guide (2)
388	Our shield and defender, the Ancient of Days (1)
388	Our Maker, Defender, Redeemer, and Friend (5)
433	pray that thou still our defender wilt be (3)

defending
478	Good Shepherd of your sheep, your own defending (2)

defied
569	God the All-righteous One, earth hath defied thee (3)

defiled
168, 169	O sacred head, sore wounded, defiled and put to scorn (1)

deflower
168, 169	Can death thy bloom deflower (1)

degree
212	those hands of liberal love indeed in infinite degree (3)
266	Gabriel of high degree (1)

deign
305, 306	Come, risen Lord, and deign to be our guest (1)

deigned
263, 264	in Mary's body deigned to dwell (1)
496, 497	deigned to cast a pitying eye upon his helpless creature (2)

deigneth
339	yet to dwell with thee he deigneth (1)

deigns
88	God with us, Emmanuel, deigns for ever now to dwell (3)
136, 137	Christ deigns to manifest today what glory shall be (3)

deity
87	hail the incarnate Deity (2)
128	incense owns a Deity nigh (3)
257	Aware of hidden deity (1)
443	From God Christ's deity came forth (1)

delight
61, 62	No eye has known the sight, no ear heard such delight (3)
96	the mountains in reply echoing their brave delight (1)
116	This is my Son, my well-beloved in whom I take delight (3)
284	With great delight ye crowned his head (3)
416	for the heart and mind's delight (3)
554	'twill be in the valley of love and delight (1)
554	to turn, turn, will be our delight
619	Such song is rest and food and deep delight (6)
625	as in his sight with sweet delight ye do abound (2)
645, 646	what transport of delight from thy pure chalice floweth (5)
669	the needs of all thy children, their anguish or delight (3)

delightest
154, 155   who in all good delightest, thou good and gracious King (5)

delighting
248, 249   ear and heart delighting well (2)

delights
308, 309   nor thy delights deny us, whose hearts to thee draw nigh (1)
346   Here we have tasted infinite delights (2)
426   No, the Church delights to raise psalms and hymns (4)

deliver
66   Born thy people to deliver (3)
179   mankind to deliver, manhood didst put on (4)
192   Lord of all life, from ill my passing life deliver (2)
337   by this food, so awesome and so sweet, deliver us (4)
337   deliver us from every touch of ill (4)
591   from sleep and from damnation, deliver us, good Lord (2)
607   deliver every nation, eternal God, we pray (2)
657   Come, almighty to deliver, let us all thy life receive (2)

deliverance
366   but deliverance to bring thou all honors didst surrender (5)
524   thy hand from every snare and foe ... deliverance bring (4)
524   thy hand ... shall great deliverance bring (4)
678, 679   in the day of your deliverance thank the Lord (1)

delivered
143   delivered from the lions' might (3)
597   delivered from our selfish schemes (1)

deliverer
567   thou our great deliverer still ... Lord of life and death (3)
690   strong deliverer, be thou still my strength and shield (2)

demand
324   Christ ... descendeth our full homage to demand (1)
329, 331   its rites demand (3)

demands
474   love so amazing, so divine, demands my soul ... all (4)
474   love so amazing ... demands my soul, my life, my all (4)
546   a heavenly race demands thy zeal (1,4)
605   To merchant, worker, king he brings God's high demands (3)

denied
158   'Twas I, Lord Jesus, I it was denied thee (2)
206   No longer Thomas then denied (5)
276   he heard what could not be denied, thy summons (2)
598   found no room in life where sin denied thee (2)

deny
10   all we ought to ask: room to deny ourselves (5)
308, 309   nor thy delights deny us, whose hearts to thee draw nigh (1)

denying
572   bade us cease denying (2)

Deo
92   Ideo, Ideo, Ideo gloria in excelsis Deo (R)
96   Gloria in excelsis Deo (R)

depart
343   Be known to us in breaking bread, and do not then depart (3)
365   ne'er from us depart, Spirit of power (3)
512   that we from thee may ne'er depart (2)
674   broods on wrongs and will not let old bitterness depart (2)

departed
180   Death's long shadows have departed (2)
338   intercession ... for all thy people, living and departed (2)

departs
31, 32   The day departs (3)

depend
401   He by himself hath sworn: we on his oath depend (2)

depends
386, 387   the stupendous force on which all strength depends (1)

deplore
140, 141   do run still, though still I do deplore (1)
594, 595   Save us from weak resignation to the evils we deplore (4)

depth
231   the depth of your true love (2/12-21)
376   ocean-depth of happy rest (3)
422   to know the breadth, length, depth, and height (2)
445, 446   in the depth be praise (1,5)
521   increase ... in depth and height, her unity and peace (1)
547   his love ... its fullness, depth, and height (1)
610   light, in its height and depth and greatness (3)
693   love, the breadth, length, depth, and height to prove (6)
702   unfathomed depth, unmeasured height (2)

depths
48   day for our salvation Christ rose from depths of earth (2)
399   He cradles in his hand the heights and depths of earth (2)
447   Thus nothing in the heights or depths (4)
584   God, you have given us power to sound depths ... unknown (1)
584   depths hitherto unknown (1)
630   Word Incarnate heights and depths of life did share (2)
643   how beautiful thy mercy seat in depths of burning light (1)
666   Out of the depths I call, to God I send my cry (1)
674   Lord, cleanse the depths within our souls (4)

deride
471   the sinner's hope let sin deride (1)

derided
158	By foes derided, by thine own rejected, O most afflicted (1)
573	by wars and tumults love is mocked, derided (2)

deriving
522, 523	Thus deriving from their banner, light ... and shade (3)

descend
78, 79	O holy Child of Bethlehem, descend to us, we pray (5)
231	let gifts of grace descend (2/6-11)
297	Descend, O Spirit, purging flame (1)
399	O Dove of peace, on us descend (3)
506, 507	Pray we then, O Lord the Spirit, on our lives descend (5)
506, 507	on our lives descend in might (5)
509	descend with all thy gracious powers (1,5)
515	as a gracious shower descend (1)
531	descend on our apostate race (1)
544	angels descend with songs again (5)
588, 589	let the dew of heaven descend and righteous fruits abound (1)

descended
319	You, Lord, in our stead to the grave descended (2)
349	Holy Spirit, Lord of love, who descended from above (1)
443	he descended to the earth (4)

descendeth
324	Christ our God to earth descendeth (1)
324	Christ ... descendeth our full homage to demand (1)
324	Light of Life descendeth from the realms of endless day (3)

descending
57, 58	Lo, he comes, with clouds descending (1)
93	suddenly the Lord, descending, in his temple shall appear (4)
139	The Holy Spirit then was shown, a dove on him descending (2)
342	Now may your life to us descending enter our lives (3)
394, 395	let peace, descending like a dove, make known ... love (3)
519, 520	from celestial realms descending (2)
559	Spirit of our God, descending, fill our hearts (3)
633	living rain from heaven descending (1)

descends
54	hence to death and hell descends (3)
225	he whom the Lord foretold suddenly, swiftly descends (1)
388	it streams from the hills, it descends to the plain (4)

descent
104	By whose descent among us The worlds are reconciled (4)

desert
67	Hark, the voice of one that crieth in the desert (2)
67	in the desert far and near (2)
70	make a pathway through the desert (2)
75	Prepare in the desert a highway, a highway for our God (1)
332	the streams that through the desert flow (2)
517	They who go through the desert vale will find it filled (3)

| 517 | desert vale ... filled with springs (3) |
| 636, 637 | I will not, I will not desert to its foes (5) |

deserving

| 158 | think on thy pity ... love unswerving, not my deserving (5) |
| 635 | trust his word, though undeserving (2) |

design

11	Direct, control, suggest, this day, all I design (3)
11	all I design, or do, or say (3)
213	We with thanks do approve the design of that love (4)
226, 227	word and deed and thought twisted from thy true design (3)
260	carpenter whose life fulfilled our gracious God's design (1)
636, 637	I only design thy dross to consume and thy gold to refine (4)
681	reflects the vast design by which thy house is built (4)

designs

| 394, 395 | your fingers trace the bold designs of farthest space (1) |
| 677 | he treasures up his bright designs (2) |

desire

56	O come, Desire of nations (7)
93	seek the great Desire of nations (3)
149	far off yet here -- the goal of all desire (1)
284	Ye thronged to Calvary and pressed with sad desire (5)
284	sad desire that aweful sight to see (5)
605	What sacrifice desire, or tribute bid you bring (1)
652, 653	Breathe through the heats of our desire thy coolness (5)
665	his desire our soul delighteth (4)
701	thou art all my pleasure, Jesus, my desire (2)
704	Jesus, confirm my heart's desire to work ... for thee (3)

desired

168, 169	Thy beauty, long desired, hath vanished from our sight (2)
257	The aged Simeon sees at last his Lord, so long desired (3)
263, 264	most blest to bring to human birth the long-desired (3)
263, 264	the long-desired of all the earth (3)

desires

| 63, 64 | all wrong desires may burn away (2) |
| 517 | thirsty soul desires and longs within thy courts to be (1) |

desirest

| 291 | but chiefly thou desirest our humble thankful hearts (3) |

desirous

| 116 | like him desirous to fulfill God's will in righteousness (4) |

desolate

| 75 | Proclaim to a desolate people the coming of their King (2) |

desolation

| 159 | With what pain and desolation (2) |
| 600, 601 | war may haunt the earth no more and desolation cease (4) |

701   Joy from tribulation, hope from desolation (3)
720   between their loved homes and the war's desolation (2)

desolations
573   Lust of possession worketh desolations (4)

despair
296   our despair he turned to blazing joy (1)
454   comes to save us from despair (2)
472   by thy cross didst save us from death and dark despair (4)
537   redeemed at countless cost from dark despair (2)
570, 571   Risen Lord, shall yet the city be the city of despair (5)
582, 583   bitter lips in blind despair cry (2)
638, 639   I am weak but confident in self-despair (3)

despairing
424   world-wide task of caring for the hungry and despairing (2)

despised
270   He that comes despised shall reign (2)
394, 395   your arms embrace all now despised for creed or race (3)
495   Hail, thou once despised Jesus, Hail, thou Galilean King (1)
545   He ... endured the cross, despised the shame (4)

destroy
174   Easter triumph, Easter joy, these alone do sin destroy (4)
246   till, pledged to build and not destroy (5)
348   each duty ... give us the chance to create or destroy (4)
391   he can create, and he destroy (1)
425   He only is the mighty Lord. He only can destroy the foe (3)
482   whose trust, ever child-like, no cares could destroy (1)
559   nothing can our peace destroy (3)
584   lest, maddened by the lust for power .. ourselves destroy (4)
588, 589   Let not the world's deceitful cares ... destroy (3)
588, 589   the rising plant destroy (3)

destroying
202   Protected ... from the destroying angel's might (2)

destruction
18   By noon's bright light, destruction stalks (2c)
580   facing us with life's destruction (3)
580   life's destruction or our most triumphant hour (3)
607   trust in bombs that shower destruction through the night (2)
690   death of death, and hell's destruction (3)

determined
386, 387   determined, dared, and done (4)

devil's
135   manifest in valiant fight, quelling all the devil's might (3)

devotion
117, 118   Shall we then yield him, in costly devotion, odors (3)
127   see them give, in deep devotion (3)

159   Jesus, may her deep devotion stir in me the same emotion (5)
334   worship, thanks, devotion voicing (1)
510   hosannas languish on our tongues and our devotion dies (3)

devour
597   nor shall the fierce devour the small (2)

dew
9   the fields are wet with diamond dew (4)
11   disperse my sins as morning dew (2)
191   rain and dew and gleams of glory from ... thy face (4)
245   your deeds and words refresh our hearts like dew (3)
388   sweetly distills in the dew and the rain (4)
588, 589   let the dew of heaven descend and righteous fruits abound (1)

dewdrops
117, 118   Cold on his cradle the dewdrops are shining (2)

dewfall
8   like the first dewfall on the first grass (2)

dews
292   let frost and heat, and winds and dews be given (2)
652, 653   Drop thy still dews of quietness (4)

diadem
450, 451   bring forth the royal diadem
483   a royal diadem adorns the mighty victor's brow (1)

diamond
9   the fields are wet with diamond dew (4)

die
73   child, to bear, and fight, and die (2)
87   Mild he lays his glory by, born that we no more may die (3)
104   Yet he shall be forsaken, and yielded up to die (3)
122, 123   Alleluia, song of gladness, voice of joy that cannot die (1)
142   so teach us, gracious Lord, to die to self (3)
156   In lowly pomp ride on to die (2,5)
164   Alone thou goest forth, O Lord, in sacrifice to die (1)
168, 169   with thee for my salvation upon the cross to die (3)
171   learn of Jesus Christ to die (3)
182   His love in death shall never die (1)
205   that life which cannot die (3)
242   Come, let us go and die with him (2)
243   When Stephen, young and doomed to die, fell crushed (3)
246   those who saw their children die (2)
270   he that cannot die, be slain (2)
313   Thou didst die that I might live (2)
335   who believe in me, even if they die ... live for ever (4)
356   dwell the white-robed martyrs who now no more can die (1)
443   his people saw him die at last, praised be his teaching (2)
454   lowly came on earth to die (1)
455, 456   our life to live, our death to die (3)

458	O who am I that for my sake my Lord should ... die (1)
458	Lord should take frail flesh and die (1)
478	you gave yourself to die for our salvation (1)
494	died eternal life to bring and lives that death may die (3)
508	so shall I never die (4)
591	our earthly rulers falter, our people drift and die (1)
611	born to work and die for every one (1)
633	Word that came from heaven to die (2)
682	nor yet for fear that loving not I might for ever die (1)

died

23	at that ninth hour you died for us (3)
49	Who died to save the world he made (1)
120	who gives eternal life to those that with you died (6)
161	he died eternal life to bring (1)
167	where our dear Lord was crucified who died to save us all (1)
167	He died that we might be forgiven (3)
167	he died to make us good (3)
178	Jesus has died and has risen (2)
183	the Prince of life, who died, reigns immortal (3)
188, 189	Once he died our souls to save (2)
194, 195	for us he died (2)
196, 197	Good Jesus Christ, our Brother, died in darkest hurt (3)
222	to rule the world for which he died (4)
240, 241	they died in imitation of their Savior's final hour (2)
275	gladly, Lord, with thee they died (3)
276	fell by fire and sword, or early died or flourished long (1)
277	till on Calvary he died (2)
279	follow them ... who live and died for thee (4)
284	In dark Gethsemane the night before he died (4)
293	who toiled and fought and lived and died for the Lord (1)
293	lived and died for the Lord they loved and knew (1)
307	worship thee, the Lamb who died (5)
322	When Jesus died to save us, a word, an act he gave us (1)
323	strength supplied through the life of him who died (1)
364	holy Church in faith acclaims thy Son who for us died (5)
366	Savior, who hast died to win us (7)
374	Worthy the Lamb that died, they cry, to be exalted thus (2)
434	cross where Christ my Savior loved and died (4)
443	the Pure baptized, the Life who died (5)
447	Christ who died but rose again triumphant from the grave (1)
453	Alleluia to Jesus, who died on the tree (R)
471	We sing the praise of him who died (1)
471	of him who died upon the cross (1)
473	bears on the brow the seal of him who died (2)
474	When I survey the wondrous cross where ... died (1)
474	cross where the young Prince of Glory died (1)
494	awake, my soul, and sing of him who died for thee (1)
494	his glories now we sing who died, and rose on high (3)
494	died eternal life to bring and lives that death may die (3)
525	with his own blood he bought her ... for her life he died (1)
539	died on earth that all might live above (2)
547	who died that he might save (4)
547	For us Christ lived, for us he died (5)

582, 583	Christ hath died in vain (2)
599	felt in the days when hope unborn had died (2)
661	Young John who trimmed the flapping sail ... died (3)
661	homeless, in Patmos died (3)
676	say "He died for all" (2)
691	as thou hast died for me (2)
697	Before the cross of him who died, behold, I prostrate fall (2)
717	land where my fathers died, land of the pilgrim's pride (1)

diedst
| 638, 639 | 'Tis Love, 'tis Love! Thou diedst for me! (4) |

dies
24	nor dies the strain of praise away (3)
296	We know that Christ is raised and dies no more (1)
510	hosannas languish on our tongues and our devotion dies (3)
680	they fly, forgotten, as a dream dies at the opening day (5)

diest
| 168, 169 | Ah me! for whom thou diest, hide not so far thy grace (2) |

different
| 304 | Together met, together bound, we'll go our different ways (5) |

dim
114	before their light the stars grew dim (1)
242	mid all its light his faith was dim (2)
284	When hope was dim, and pain and grief beyond belief (4)
337	our prayer so languid, and our faith so dim (2)

dimension
| 420 | How often, making music, we have found a new dimension (2) |
| 420 | a new dimension in the world of sound (2) |

dimly
| 597 | O day of peace that dimly shines through all our hopes (1) |
| 674 | the truth we dimly knew (3) |

dimming
| 180 | not one darksome cloud is dimming ... morning ray (3) |
| 180 | dimming yonder glorious morning ray (3) |

dims
| 621, 622 | cloud nor passing vapor dims the brightness of the air (3) |

direct
11	Direct, control, suggest, this day, all I design (3)
40, 41	direct our faithful household Lord (4)
431	So order too this life of mine, direct it all my days (4)

directs
| 631 | inspired those whose wisdom still directs us (3) |

disappear
| 257 | let symbols disappear (1) |

521   works of darkness disappear before thy conquering light (2)

disaster
564, 565 He who would valiant be 'gainst all disaster (1)

discern
232   May we discern your presence (2/8-24)
314   Taste and touch and vision to discern thee fail (2)
649, 650 glad, when your presence we discern (3)

discernment
307   here for faith's discernment pray we (2)

disciple
231   John, your loved disciple, exiled to Patmos' shore (2/12-27)
675   if you would my disciple be (1)

disciples
135   disciples filled with awe thy transfigured glory saw (4)
255   In us you seek disciples to share your cross and crown (3)
529   Join hands, disciples of the faith (2)
614   seek again the Way disciples followed then (2)

disciples'
206   he doubted the disciples' word (3)

discipline
152   Give us the discipline that springs from abstinence (4)

disclose
127   incense doth their God disclose (4)

discord
576, 577 let there be in us no discord but one spirit (2)
606   when we gather let no discord or enmity break our oneness (2)

discouraged
676   Sometimes I feel discouraged and think my work's in vain (1)

discouragement
564, 565 There's no discouragement shall make him once relent (1)

discover
46   death's fair night discover ... everlasting life (3)

disease
567   it triumphed o'er disease and death (1)

dismal
564, 565 Who so beset him round with dismal stories (2)

dismay
105   God rest you merry, gentlemen, let nothing you dismay (1)

dismayed
636, 637 Fear not, I am with thee, O be not dismayed (2)
669 griefs that ... keep thy heart dismayed (4)

dismiss
344 Lord, dismiss us with thy blessing (1)

dispel
81 dispel in glorious splendor the darkness everywhere (3)
144 dispel the gloom that shades our minds (1)
515 Holy Ghost, dispel our sadness (1)
584 Let wisdom's godly fear dispel the fears ... hate impart (3)

dispelling
59 Christ our sun, all sloth dispelling (2)

dispels
300 He dispels our sin and sadness, life imparts (3)

disperse
11 disperse my sins as morning dew (2)
56 disperse the gloomy clouds of night (6)

dispersed
208 but Christ their legions hath dispersed (2)

display
6, 7 more and more thyself display, shining to the perfect day (3)
102 confounded that a stable should display heaven's Word (3)
106 around us all his glory shall display (6)
409 The unwearied sun from day to day ... power display (1)
409 does his Creator's power display (1)
512 The light of truth to us display (2)

displayed
49 that all may see his love displayed (2)
94, 95 to human view displayed (4)
398 Lord, how thy wonders are displayed (2)
398 thy wonders are displayed where'er I turn my eye (2)

displease
458 at these themselves displease, and 'gainst him rise (4)

disregard
443 He did not disregard the sick (4)

dissolute
443 The dissolute he did not scorn (3)

dissuade
491 whom no ills from good dissuade (4)

dist
56 dist give the law, in cloud, and majesty, and awe (3)

distraction
623   There, where no troubles distraction can bring (3)

distant
182   No longer bound to distant years in Palestine (2)
287   steals on the ear the distant triumph song (5)

distills
388   sweetly distills in the dew and the rain (4)

distress
410   grace and favor to his people in distress (2)
429   He helps the stranger in distress (3)
636, 637   and sanctify to thee thy deepest distress (3)

distressed
27, 28   anguished and in mind distressed be crushed by guilt (3)
525   by schisms rent asunder, by heresies distressed (3)

distressing
433   the wicked oppressing now cease from distressing (1)

diverse
631   many diverse scrolls completing (2)

divide
182   where color, scorn or wealth divide, he suffers still (4)
350   let nothing in this life divide ... whom thou makest one (3)
415   day and night divide thy works no more (4)
526   when the word is given bid Jordan's narrow stream divide (5)
591   the walls of gold entomb us, the swords of scorn divide (1)
603, 604   Where generation, class, or race divide us to our shame (3)
607   hate and fear divide us and bitter threats are hurled (1)

divided
366   while in essence only One, undivided God we claim thee (4)
526   though now divided by the ... narrow stream of death (2)
562   we are not divided, all one body we (3)
573   Races and peoples, lo, we stand divided (2)

divine
6   Fill me, radiancy divine (3)
37   we hymn the eternal Father ... Son ... Holy Ghost divine (2)
47   fill me with thy love divine (3)
52   fill our souls with light divine (1)
84   Love came down at Christmas, love all lovely, love divine (1)
84   Worship we the Godhead, love incarnate, love divine (2)
117, 118   odors of Edom, and offerings divine (3)
131, 132   Oh, what a miracle divine, when water ... into wine (4)
135   manifest in power divine, changing water into wine (2)
145   divine, divine it is when all combine (4)
150   So shall we have peace divine (4)
174   praise we him, whose love divine gives his sacred Blood (1)
213   share both the nature and kingdom divine (3)
226, 227   pour on us thy love divine (1)

231	May we, in... weakness, receive your power divine (2/4-25)
242	saw and hailed his Lord Divine (3)
245	signs of your grace divine (2)
285	eternal God and Word divine (1)
287	O blest communion, fellowship divine (4)
308, 309	we may behold, in heaven, thy countenance divine (3)
332	go rejoicing on our way, renewed with strength divine (4)
336	in our life thy love divine ... flesh and blood has taken (1)
343	Lord, sup with us in love divine, thy Body and thy Blood (4)
374	Jesus is worthy to receive honor and power divine (3)
376	lift us to the joy divine (3)
401	hail, Abraham's Lord divine (5)
409	The hand that made us is divine (3)
416	faith and hope and love divine (6)
433	ordaining, maintaining his kingdom divine (2)
445, 446	God's presence and his very self, and essence all divine (4)
450, 451	the God incarnate, Man divine (3)
458	Here might I stay and sing, no story so divine (7)
459	where his loving people meet to share the gift divine (2)
474	love so amazing, so divine, demands my soul ... all (4)
477	All praise to thee, for thou, O King divine, didst yield (1)
508	glows with thy fire divine (3)
509	Spirit divine, attend our prayers (1,5)
514	To thee, O Comforter divine ... sing we alleluia (1)
516	Come down, O love divine, seek thou this soul of mine (1)
521	O Judge divine of human strife (4)
524	Jesus, thou friend divine, our Savior and our King (4)
538	fill thy Church with light divine (1)
543	while rays divine stream all abroad (1)
586	Jesus, thou divine Companion (1)
586	Jesus ... divine Companion, help us all to work our best (3)
592	A servant with this clause makes drudgery divine (3)
617	thy trusty shield, thy sword of love divine (3)
632	The Church from our dear Master received the word divine (2)
657	Love divine, all loves excelling (1)
658	O when shall I behold thy face, thou Majesty divine (2)
691	Savior divine (1)
702	my support thy power divine (4)
718	Thy love divine hath led us in the past (2)
718	fill all our lives with love and grace divine (4)

divinely

320	when the twelve, divinely guided, at the holy table met (2)
543	with luster new divinely crowned (2)

divinest

198	of seasons, best, divinest (1)

division

304	each proud division ends (3)
513	With the healing of division (3)
607	when hatred and division give way to love and peace (4)

divisions

56	bid thou our sad divisions cease (7)

315   make thou our sad divisions soon to cease (2)

doctor
293   one was a doctor, and one was a queen (1)

doctrine
562   one in hope and doctrine, one in charity (3)

domain
366   infinite thy vast domain, everlasting is thy reign (1)
375   Through all his kingdom's wide domain ... justice reign (3)
607   Christ shall rule victorious o'er all the world's domain (4)

dominion
82   honor, glory and dominion, and eternal victory (4)
596   solace all its wide dominion with the healing of thy wings (1)

dominions
82   powers, dominions bow before him (3)
375   host of heaven praiseth thee, O Lord of all dominions (2)
437, 438   Powers and dominions lay their glory by (3)
618   Cry out, dominions, princedoms, powers (1)

Dominum
110   Venite adoremus Dominum (1,3,R)

Donor
300   Glory ... for our food now bestowed render we the Donor (1)

doom
60   In sorrow that the ancient curse should doom to death (2)
60   doom to death a universe (2)
92   His the doom, ours the mirth when he came down to earth (2)
201   light and joy have conquered doom (1)
327, 328   Alpha-Omega, unto whom shall bow all nations at the doom (8)
370   his coming at the day of doom (2)
598   must bring to doom the powers which crucified thee (2)
687, 638   lo, his doom is sure, one little word shall fell him (3)

doomed
243   When Stephen, young and doomed to die, fell crushed (3)
598   doomed to death (2)

door
78, 79   charity stands watching and faith holds wide the door (4)
107   He hath opened heaven's door (2)
140, 141   made my sin their door (2)
245   faithful shepherd of the flock ... sheep-fold's only door (2)
364   hadst overcome death's sting and opened heaven's door (7)
402, 403   Church with psalms must shout, no door can keep them out (2)
711   knock, and the door shall be opened unto you (RC)

doors
74   For him let doors be opened, no hearts against him barred (1)

doubt

27, 28	Lest we, beset by doubt and strife forget (3)
242	O Savior, make thy presence known to all who doubt (5)
242	to all who doubt thy Word and thee (5)
251	In doubt or danger, all our days (3)
251	In doubt or danger ... be near to guard us still (3)
297	Confirm our faith, consume our doubt (1)
376	drive the dark of doubt away (1)
527	through the night of doubt and sorrow (1)
593	Where all is doubt, may we sow faith (2)
640	doubt and terror are withdrawn (3)
693	though tossed about with many a conflict, many a doubt (2)

doubted

206	how they had seen the risen Lord, he doubted (3)
206	he doubted the disciples' word (3)

doubters

452	when doubters kneel and waverers stand (3)

doubting

242	How oft, O Lord, thy face hath shone on doubting souls (1)
242	doubting souls whose wills were true (1)

doubtings

231	whose short-lived doubtings prove (2/12-21)

doubts

541	Away with gloomy doubts and faithless fear (3)
670	my doubts I sorely feel, thy sure promise I believe (3)
703	doubts appall, and sorrows still increase (1)

dove

120	Above him see the heavenly Dove (3)
121	as peaceful as a dove and yet as urgent as a flame (1)
139	The Holy Spirit then was shown, a dove on him descending (2)
371	Spirit of truth and love, life-giving, holy Dove (3)
394, 395	let peace, descending like a dove, make known ... love (3)
399	O Dove of peace, on us descend (3)
509	Come as the dove, and spread thy wings (4)
510	Come, Holy Spirit, heavenly Dove (1,4)
512	Come, Gracious Spirit, heavenly Dove (1)
683, 684	Return, O holy Dove, return, sweet messenger of rest (3)

dove's

513	Like the murmur of the dove's song (1)

doves

257	two young doves, her humble offerings (2)

dowered

289	days of old have dowered us with gifts beyond all praise (3)

down

5	pour down thy radiance from above (2)

18	As now the sun shines down at noon (1)
40, 41	Defender of us all, look down (4)
59	comes with pardon down from heaven (3)
67	the hills bow down to greet him (2)
69	Mortal in darkness we lie down (2)
84	Love came down at Christmas, love all lovely, love divine (1)
88	God himself comes down from heaven (1)
88	God comes down that we may rise (4)
92	His the doom, ours the mirth when he came down to earth (2)
94, 95	the angel of the Lord came down, and glory shone around (1)
99	Down in a lowly manger the humble Christ was born (3)
101	the little Lord Jesus laid down his sweet head (1)
101	The stars in the bright sky looked down where he lay (1)
101	I love thee, Lord Jesus! Look down from the sky (2)
102	He came down to earth from heaven ... God and Lord of all (2)
119	thou its sun which goes not down (5)
151	Bend down thy gracious ear to me (1)
156	the angel armies of the sky look down (3)
196, 197	Good Jesus Christ inside his pain looked down (2)
196, 197	Jesus ... looked down Golgatha's stony slope (2)
205	sing today with one accord the life laid down (4)
237	when they laid the mortal down for the life immortal (1)
246	But down the ages rings the cry of those who saw (2)
251	look down from heaven, thy dwelling place (1)
251	look down ... with love for human-kind (1)
255	God's light shone down from heaven (1)
256	It was the blessed Son come down to save him (2)
266	there he knelt down before her face (2)
267	like her whom heaven's Majesty came down to shadow o'er (3)
268, 269	he has cast down all the mighty ... lowly are his choice (4)
292	by thee come down henceforth the gifts of God (1)
304	in awe and wonder to recall his life laid down for me (1)
355	All of us go down to the dust (1)
362	casting down their golden crowns around the glassy sea (2)
362	cherubim and seraphim falling down before thee (2)
386, 387	him that brought salvation down by meekness, Mary's son (4)
410	sun and moon bow down before him (4)
462	justice, from her heavenly bower, look down on us below (2)
474	sorrow and love flow mingled down (3)
489	He sent him down as sending God, in flesh to us he came (4)
506, 507	hundred men and women turned the known world upside down (4)
514	to thee, by Jesus Christ send down (4)
515	bringing down the richest treasure we can wish (1)
516	Come down, O love divine, seek thou this soul of mine (1)
535	fall down on their faces, and worship the Lamb (3)
540	look down on us and view how white the fields (2)
540	break down the realm of Satan, death, and sin (3)
548	tread all the powers of darkness down (4)
554	'tis the gift to come down where we ought to be (1)
591	O God of earth and altar, bow down and hear our cry (1)
598	pride, overthrown, went down to dust beside thee (2)
605	Still down the ages ring the prophet's stern commands (3)
616	He shall come down like showers upon the fruitful earth (3)
616	Kings shall bow down before him (4)
633	Word of God, come down on earth (1)

647	but rough or smooth, up hill or down (1)
648	Go down, Moses, way down in Egypt's land (R)
657	joy of heaven, to earth come down (1)
658	Why restless, why cast down, my soul (3)
659, 660	in hope that sends a shining ray far down the ... way (4)
661	such happy, simple fisher-folk before the Lord came down (1)
661	Peter ... hauled the teeming net, head-down was crucified (3)
675	follow Christ, nor think till death to lay it down (5)
692	in your weariness lay down your head upon my breast (1)
692	thirsty one, stoop down and drink, and live (2)
693	thy love unknown has broken every barrier down (5)

drained

| 585 | Drained is love in making full (4) |

drank

232	He drank the cup of suffering (2/7-25)
276	he drank thy cup of pain (4)
692	I came to Jesus, and I drank of that life-giving stream (2)

draw

59	with words of love draw near (4)
68	The Bridegroom is arising, and soon he will draw nigh (1)
83	leaving their flocks, draw nigh to gaze (4)
116	may such bonds for ever draw our souls to things above (5)
238, 239	when before him we draw nigh (3)
308, 309	nor thy delights deny us, whose hearts to thee draw nigh (1)
315	draw us the nearer each to each, we plead (2)
327, 328	Draw nigh and take the Body of the Lord (1)
335	No one can come to me unless the Father draw them (1)
337	so we come, O draw us to thy feet (4)
349	once again in love draw near (1)
349	draw near to your servants gathered here (1)
473	as thou hast promised, draw the world to thee (3)
475	humbly, fervently draw near him (1)
496, 497	Jesus, Holy, holy, yet most lowly draw thou near us (1)
516	O Comforter, draw near, within my heart appear (1)
528	give us all new fervor, draw us closer in community (2)
600, 601	O day of God, draw nigh in beauty and in power (1)
600, 601	O day of God, draw nigh as at creation's birth (5)
603, 604	through ... every birth, to draw an answering love (1)
678, 679	rejoice as you draw water from salvation's living spring (1)
685	While I draw this fleeting breath (3)

drawest

| 63, 64 | when as judge, thou drawest nigh (3) |

drawing

3, 4	night in turn is drawing on (4)
42	Now the day is over, night is drawing nigh (1)
56	cheer us by thy drawing nigh (6)
65	Prepare the way, O Zion, your Christ is drawing near (1)
315	by drawing all to thee, O Prince of Peace (2)
366	help thy servants, drawing near (7)
436	The King of kings is drawing near (1)

| 534 | God is working his purpose out ... time is drawing near (1) |
| 570, 571 | drawing near a world that spurns him (4) |

drawn

321	Drawn by thy quickening grace, O Lord (3)
434	here, on the cross, 'tis fairest drawn in precious blood (2)
440	drawn from earth to love thee solely (1)

draws

144	nearer draws the day of days when paradise shall bloom (4)
434	Her noblest life my spirit draws from his dear wounds (4)
534	nearer draws the time, the time that shall surely be (1,4)
541	The night draws nigh (4)

dread

40, 41	repel our dread, malicious foe (4)
60	assaults of our dread foe (5)
94, 95	for mighty dread has seized their troubled mind (2)
208	from death's dread sting thy servants free (5)
386, 387	Moses while on earth in dread and smitten to the heart (2)
414	speak of thy dread acts the story (3)
607	fear of rattling saber, from dread of war's increase (3)
643	How dread are thine eternal years, O everlasting Lord (2)
677	the clouds ye so much dread are big with mercy (3)

dreadful

57, 58	Every eye shall now behold him robed in dreadful majesty (2)
185, 186	It was a strange and dreadful strife (2)
486	So in the last and dreadful day (5)
486	dreadful day when earth and heaven shall melt away (5)

dream

75	power and pomp of nations shall pass like a dream away (2)
243	only in my heart a flame and in my soul a dream (4)
563	nor dream of peaceful rest (3)
582, 583	city that hath stood too long a dream (3)
680	they fly, forgotten, as a dream dies at the opening day (5)
705	Church of Christ is calling us to make the dream come true (2)
719	O beautiful for patriot dream that sees beyond the years (3)

dreamless

| 78, 79 | Above thy deep and dreamless sleep the silent stars go by (1) |

dreams

44, 45	from all ill dreams your children keep (2)
580	May our dreams prove rich with promise (4)
597	through all our hopes and prayers and dreams (1)

drear

| 287 | thou, in the darkness drear, the one true Light (2) |

dress

| 149 | glorious in springtime dress of leaf and flower (3) |
| 284 | unmasked in every dress, in every combat foiled (3) |

drew

60	When this old world drew on toward night you came (3)
109	This star drew night to the northwest (4)
114	but as the hunter braves drew nigh, the angel-song rang (2)
161	A Roman soldier drew a spear to mix his blood with water (2)
614	round him drew thousands of servants brave and true (1)
673	first one ... the Samaritan woman who drew from the well (2)

drift

580	the lonely drift unnoticed in the city's ebb and flow (2)
591	our earthly rulers falter, our people drift and die (1)

drifted

265	his wings as drifted snow, his eyes as flame (1)

drink

18	your living water give to drink (4a)
138	in you always to live and drink of those ... streams (3)
185, 186	he is our meat and drink indeed (4)
244	drink, O Zion's son and daughters (2)
244	drink, and find salvation here (2)
275	now they drink, as from a river, holy bliss and infinite (4)
276	Lord, may we learn to drink thy cup (5)
318	here drink with thee the royal Wine of heaven (2)
325	Let us drink wine together on our knees (2)
327, 328	drink the holy Blood for you outpoured (1)
332	meat the Body of the Lord, our drink his precious Blood (3)
335	Unless you ... drink of his Blood (3)
360, 361	drink of thy chalice (2)
630	Here we drink of joy unmeasured (5)
649, 650	we drink of you, the fountain-head (2)
692	thirsty one, stoop down and drink, and live (2)

drinking

159	such a cup of sorrow drinking (4)

drive

40, 41	you drive away the shadowed night (1)
282, 283	may he, from us mortals, drive every evil (3)
376	drive the dark of doubt away (1)

driven

63, 64	let us not, for evil past be driven from thy face at last (4)
681	it is because thou art we're driven to the quest (2)

drives

644	drives away our fear (1)
664	one word of thy supporting breath drives ... fears away (2)

dross

636, 637	I only design thy dross to consume and thy gold to refine (4)

drought

228	With your soft, refreshing rains break our drought (4)

drove
235   drove away the shadows, and filled the world with light (1)
683, 684   drove thee from my breast (3)

drowns
174   through the wave that drowns the foe (2)
494   Hark, how the heavenly anthem drowns all music but its own (1)

drudgery
592   A servant with this clause makes drudgery divine (3)

drums
555   nor roll of stirring drums, but deeds of love and mercy (2)

drunk
599   our hearts drunk with the wine of the world (3)

dry
392   Then let our song abound and let our tears be dry (4)
412   Flowers and trees, loud rustling dry leaves (2)

due
179   Months in due succession, days of lengthening light (3)
233, 234   with hearts of gladness raise due hymns (1)
320   never canst thou reach his due (1)
574, 575   help us to give to all their due (2)

dull
11   shake off dull sloth (1)
104   Though heavy, dull and dumb (2)
501, 502   Flood our dull senses with your light (4)
672   even now, though dull and gray, the east is brightening (3)

dullness
503, 504   the dullness of our blinded sight (4)

dumb
104   Though heavy, dull and dumb (2)
652, 653   let sense be dumb, let flesh retire (5)

dungeon
558   living still in spite of dungeon, fire, and sword (1)

dust
355   saying, "You are dust, and to dust you shall return" (1)
355   All of us go down to the dust (1)
358   You came from dust and to dust shall return (3)
388   Frail children of dust, and feeble as frail (5)
516   O let it freely burn, till earthly passions turn to dust (2)
516   turn to dust and ashes in its heat consuming (2)
598   pride, overthrown, went down to dust beside thee (2)
598   our pride is dust, our vaunt is stilled (4)
665   tower and temple fall to dust (2)

dusty

472   afoot on dusty highways (3)

duteous

46   The duteous day now closeth (1)

259   watched by her duteous love, in her fond arms at rest (2)

619   Sing alleluia forth in duteous praise (1)

duty

11   Awake, my soul ... with the sun thy daily stage of duty run (1)

348   So, in the world where each duty assigned us (4)

348   each duty ... give us the chance to create or destroy (4)

475   let thy radiant beauty light mine eyes to see my duty (3)

541   while we in sleep our duty have forgot, he slumbered not (2)

561   when duty calls, or danger, be never wanting there (3)

681   inspire us from above with joy and strength for duty (5)

dwell

47   God, the blessed Three in One dwell within my heart alone (6)

60   defend us while we dwell below from all assaults (5)

87   Pleased as man with us to dwell; Jesus, our Emmanuel (2)

88   God with us, Emmanuel, deigns for ever now to dwell (3)

152   so that we in heart and soul may dwell with thee (4)

212   again rejoice and on his praises dwell (1)

240, 241   dwell forever in the light (1)

263, 264   in Mary's body deigned to dwell (1)

339   yet to dwell with thee he deigneth (1)

356   dwell the white-robed martyrs who now no more can die (1)

364   bring us whom thou hast bought to dwell on high (8)

364   dwell ... with all thy saints in joy surpassing thought (8)

366   Grant that with thy saints we may dwell (7)

366   Grant that ... we may dwell in everlasting day (7)

377, 378   All people that on earth do dwell, sing to the Lord (1)

380   From all that dwell below the skies let ... praise arise (1)

385   come unto us and dwell with us (2)

414   on thy might and greatness dwell (3)

480   like us, unhonored and unknown, he came to dwell on earth (1)

483   the joy of all who dwell above, the joy of all below (3)

512   holiness, the road that we must take to dwell with God (3)

517   how happy they who dwell with thee (2)

525   the meek and lowly, on high may dwell with thee (5)

526   One family we dwell in him, one Church, above, beneath (2)

544   People and realms of evry tongue dwell on his love (3)

544   dwell on his love with sweetest song (3)

587   guarding ... the homes in which thy people dwell (1)

597   Then shall the wolf dwell with the lamb (2)

600, 601   Bring justice to our land, that all may dwell secure (3)

606   Where true charity and love dwell, God himself is there (A)

656   to dwell in lowliness with us, our pattern and our King (2)

663   I may tell thy praise, and dwell for ever in thy home (5)

678, 679   with you has come to dwell ... Holy One of Israel (2)

700   tarry no more without, but come and dwell within (1)

dwellers

410   dwellers all in time and space (4)

dwellest

586   thou ... dwellest in the daily strife (2)

dwelling

165, 166   Thirty years among us dwelling (2)
191   hearts in heaven dwelling, we on earth may fruitful be (4)
219   Lo, he returns ... to his eternal dwelling (1)
251   look down from heaven, thy dwelling place (1)
329, 331   once on earth among us dwelling (1)
360, 361   Hallowed this dwelling where the Lord abideth (4)
422   thy truth and light our dwelling place for evermore (3)
488   thou in me dwelling, and I one with thee (2)
516   a place wherein the Holy Spirit makes a dwelling (3)
587   every home ... may be the dwelling place of peace (3)
633   with us dwelling (4)
656   for his dwelling ... throne will choose the pure in heart (3)
657   fix in us thy humble dwelling (1)
702   In heaven? It is thy dwelling fair (3)
702   far away my dwelling make (4)

dwells

25, 26   God who dwells in the eternal light (2)
230   for God the Holy Spirit dwells with the Church alway (3)
235   where with a holy people God dwells in Unity (3)
369   dwells amidst the dazzling light of vast eternity (1)
401   There dwells the Lord, our King ... our Righteousness (3)
581   Let us recall that in our midst dwells God's begotten Son (5)

dwelt

125, 126   who dwelt in death and night (1)
329, 331   he with us in converse blending dwelt (2)
381   Lo, on those who dwelt in darkness (2)
489   as one with us he dwelt with us, and bore a human name (4)
680   thy saints have dwelt secure (2)

dying

9   purple pageantry of dawning and of dying days (1)
23   Inspire us by your dying breath to live for you (3)
49   with thanks his dying love record (3)
55   Oh, fill our weak and dying frame with godly strength (4)
128   sorrowing, sighing, bleeding, dying (4)
149   So daily dying to the way of self (2)
159   mother weeping, where he hung, the dying Lord (1)
159   with ... grief and resignation Mary watched her dying son (2)
160   robed in mortal flesh is dying, crucified by sin for me (2)
168, 169   for this thy dying sorrow, thy pity without end (4)
181   Sing of his dying love, his resurrection power (2)
236   Dying, through thee they overcame (3)
273, 274   both triumph in their dying ... glorious sainthood gain (2)
366   on the cross thy dying breath opened ... heaven (6)
448, 449   for us gave up his dying breath (4)
498   see the very dying form of one who suffered there for me (2)
572   your dying bade us sheathe the foolish sword (2)

593   Dying, we live, and are reborn (5)
616   souls, condemned and dying were precious in his sight (2)

eager
54   Mighty God and Mary's son, eager now his race to run (2)
215   while their eager eyes behold him (2)
231   so eager and so bold, thrice failing, yet repentant (2/1-18)
513   like the new flame's eager might (1)
585   gives with zeal, with eager hands (3)
624   Oh, sweet and blessed country that eager hearts expect (4)

eagerly
475   As the tender flowers eagerly unfold them (3)

eagerness
482   Lord of all eagerness, Lord of all faith (2)

eagle
411   like the eagle he renews the vigor of thy youth (5)

eagle's
579   save all who dare the eagle's flight (3)

eagles'
245   words reflect, like eagles' wings, the glory of our Lord (1)

ear
61, 62   No eye has known the sight, no ear heard such delight (3)
79   No ear may hear his coming (3)
151   Bend down thy gracious ear to me (1)
248, 249   ear and heart delighting well (2)
248, 249   speaks like music to the ear (3)
287   steals on the ear the distant triumph song (5)
290   first the blade, and then the ear (2)
370   his ear to hearken to my need (5)
409   In reason's ear they all rejoice (3)
416   For the joy of ear and eye (3)
501, 502   yours is the tongue and yours the ear (3)
534   give ear to me, ye continents, ye isles give ear to me (2)
644   How sweet the Name of Jesus sounds in a believer's ear (1)

earliest
106   the earliest heralds of the Savior's name (4)
114   The earliest moon of winter-time is not so round and fair (3)

early
21, 22   you send the early morning ray (1)
201   At early morn, with spices rare (2)
231   whom your mysterious love called early (2/12-28)
231   called early from life's conflicts (2/12-28)
232   On Easter morning early, a word from you sufficed (2/7-22)
276   fell by fire and sword, or early died or flourished long (1)
362   Early in the morning our song shall rise to thee (1)
544   infant voices shall proclaim their early blessings (3)

544	their early blessings on his Name (3)
708	Early let us seek thy favor, early let us learn thy will (2)
720	O say can you see by the dawn's early light (1)

earnest

232	May we with zeal as earnest (2/10-28)
454	again in answer to our earnest heart-felt prayer (2)
527	one the earnest looking forward (2)

ears

3, 4	guard ... our ears from empty praise and lies (3)
191	golden ears of harvest will their heads before him wave (3)
212	nor will they trust their ears and eyes (2)
230	the ears of all who heard proclaimed salvation's wonder (1)
290	but the fruitful ears to store in his garner evermore (3)
312	let ears that now have heard thy songs ... never waken (1)
334	one voice hearing, ears attentive to your word (2)
434	speak his Name in sounds to mortal ears unknown (5)
440	open thou our ears and heart (3)
493	'tis music in the sinner's ears (3)
536	Open your ears, O faithful people (1,4)
536	Open your ears and hear God's word (1,4)
536	They who have ears to hear the message (2)
536	they who have ears, then let them hear (2)
651	to my listening ears all nature sings (1)

earth

9	but for the common things of earth (1)
21,22	Quench now on earth the flames of strife (2)
24	while earth rolls onward into light (2)
25, 26	through all the earth and in the highest heaven adored (3)
27, 28	when on the new and living earth (1)
48	day for our salvation Christ rose from depths of earth (2)
49	our Lord who made both earth and skies (1)
50	let heaven rejoice, let earth be glad (1)
50	the highest strains the Church on earth can raise (5)
52	first o'er the earth the light was poured (1)
54	Marvel now, both heaven and earth (1)
54	Thus on earth the Word appears (3)
60	all things on earth with one accord ... call you Lord (4)
66	hope of all the earth thou art (2)
67	For the glory of the Lord now o'er earth is shed abroad (3)
78, 79	praises sing to God the King, and peace to men on earth (2)
80	From heaven above to earth I come (1)
80	joy of all the earth (2)
82	let no tongue on earth be silent (3)
85, 86	earth and sea and sky revere the love of him (5)
87	Peace on earth and mercy mild (1)
87	born to raise us from the earth (3)
88	from high heaven he comes to earth (2)
89, 90	from angels bending near the earth (1)
89, 90	Peace on earth, good will to men (1)
89, 90	when peace shall over all the earth its ... splendors (4)

92	On this day earth shall ring with the song (1)
92	born on earth to save us; him the Father gave us (1)
92	His the doom, ours the mirth when he came down to earth (2)
92	with their song earth shall ring (4)
92	born on earth to save us; peace and love he gave us (4)
93	wing your flight o'er all the earth (1)
94, 95	All glory be to God on high and on the earth be peace (6)
97	purer praise than ours on earth, angels' songs afford (3)
99	when lo! above the earth rang out the angel chorus (2)
100	let earth receive her King (1)
102	He came down to earth from heaven ... God and Lord of all (2)
102	lived on earth our Savior holy (2)
102	daily, when on earth he grew, he was tempted (4)
106	to you and all the nations on the earth (2)
106	peace on the earth, and unto men good will (3)
109	to the earth it gave great light (2)
109	that hath made heaven and earth of nought (6)
112	earth stood hard as iron, water like a stone (1)
112	Our God, heaven cannot hold him, nor earth sustain (2)
112	heaven and earth shall flee away when he comes to reign (2)
114	God the Lord of all the earth sent angel-choirs instead (1)
114	the holy child of earth and heaven is born today for you (4)
119	to bend the knee before him whom heaven and earth adore (2)
125, 126	him shall the tribes of earth obey (3)
127	Earth has many a noble city (1)
127	seen in fleshly form on earth (2)
128	heaven sings alleluia: alleluia the earth replies (5)
131, 132	sought not the kingdoms of this earth (1)
133, 134	Jesus, Redeemer of the earth (1)
148	Creator of the earth and skies (1)
163	earth inherits heaven's key (3)
165, 166	earth, and stars, and sky, and ocean (3)
175	Lo the fair beauty of earth (1)
175	all things created on earth sing to the glory of God (2)
175	God the Creator ... who rulest the earth and the heavens (5)
176, 177	of whom the glory in both earth and heaven is manifested (3)
178	Jesus is Lord of all the earth (1)
178	Spread the good news o'er all the earth (2)
179	Earth her joy confesses, clothing her for spring (2)
180	let the whole wide earth rejoice (1)
191	hearts in heaven dwelling, we on earth may fruitful be (4)
201	On earth has dawned this day of days (1)
204	wheat that in dark earth many days has lain (1)
204	laid in the earth like grain that sleeps unseen (2)
205	let all the earth rejoice and say (2)
210	The day of resurrection, Earth tell it out abroad (1)
210	From death to life eternal, from earth unto the sky (1)
210	Now let the heavens be joyful, let earth her song begin (3)
216	all things created on earth sing to the glory of God (1)
216	God ... who rulest the earth and the heavens (2)
217, 218	all praise to you let earth accord (3)
219	O earth, adore thy glorious King (2)
220, 221	let earth accord, who art, while endless ages run (4)
223, 224	tongues, that earth may hear their call (2)

225	his chosen apostles, preach to the ends of the earth (3)
226, 227	joys which earth and heaven entwine (5)
228	all the benefits the earth, you bring to maturity (3)
229	let all the listening earth be taught the deeds (2)
244	peace on earth their proclamation (1)
250	what need we fear in earth or space in this new year (4)
250	All glory be to God on high and peace on earth (5)
250	"... peace on earth," the angels cry (5)
251	help us here on earth to live from selfish passions free (4)
252	Jesus, Name of priceless worth to the fallen of the earth (3)
254	For ever be adored that Name in earth and sky (1)
259	O Light of all the earth, thy children wait for thee (4)
261, 262	Ruler of all things, Lord of earth and heaven (2)
263, 264	The Word whom earth and sea and sky adore (1)
263, 264	the long-desired of all the earth (3)
267	Most blest shall be her name in all the Church on earth (5)
271, 272	Christ, the Sun of all the earth fulfilled that witness (3)
277	God the Lord who came to earth (1)
278	joy of Mary when on earth her work was done (4)
280	many saints by earth forgotten live for ever (1)
284	On earth ye knew his wondrous grace (1)
284	Glory to God and peace on earth (2)
285	beloved on earth, approved of thee (4)
292	since thou the earth hast trod (1)
292	kindly earth with timely birth may yield her fruits again (2)
295	praise the Holy Spirit poured forth upon the earth (3)
299	Spirit of God, unleashed on earth with rush of wind (1)
299	earth, kindling, blazed her loud acclaim (1)
305, 306	with all thy saints on earth and saints at rest (3)
307	heaven and earth with loud hosanna worship thee (5)
320	who on earth such food bestowest (6)
324	Christ our God to earth descendeth (1)
324	as of old on earth he stood (2)
326	one heart ... song have the saints upon earth and above (2)
326	ever fit us by service on earth for thy service on high (2)
329, 331	once on earth among us dwelling (1)
351	possess, in sweet communion, joys ... earth cannot afford (2)
355	formed of the earth, and to earth shall we return (1)
358	We are your creatures and children of earth (2)
358	From earth you formed us, both glorious and mortal (2)
358	to the earth shall we all return (2)
362	praise thy Name in earth, and sky, and sea (4)
364	everlasting Father art, by all the earth adored (1)
365	Come, thou incarnate Word, by heaven and earth adored (2)
366	all on earth thy scepter claim (1)
367	earth is with thy fullness stored (1,3)
367	earth takes up the angels'cry (2)
370	the stable earth (4)
372	holy, no holiness of earth can his express (2)
373	heaven and earth, and all creation, Laud ... his Name (2)
376	earth and heaven reflect thy rays (2)
377, 378	All people that on earth do dwell, sing to the Lord (1)
377, 378	the God whom heaven and earth adore (5)
379	God is love, let earth rejoice (1)

385	maker of earth and sky (1)
386, 387	Moses while on earth in dread and smitten to the heart (2)
388	The earth, with its store of wonders untold (3)
391	earth, with her ten thousand tongues ... fill thy courts (4)
394, 395	let peace ... make known on earth your healing love (3)
396, 397	eternal, Triune God, whom earth and heaven adore (3)
398	goodness of the Lord that filled the earth with food (2)
399	He cradles in his hand the heights and depths of earth (2)
400	Dear mother earth, you day by day unfold your blessings (4)
401	the Lord, the great I AM, by earth and heaven confessed (1)
402, 403	earth is not too low, his praises there may grow (1)
406, 407	By mother earth my Lord be praised (5)
409	nightly to the listening earth repeats the story (2)
412	Earth and all stars, loud rushing planets (1)
413	all things that live in earth and ocean make music (2)
416	For the beauty of the earth, for the beauty of the skies (1)
416	friends on earth and friends above (4)
416	peace on earth and joy in heaven (6)
421	peace on earth from heaven (1)
422	saints on earth and saints above we join in full accord (2)
426	Heaven and earth must pass away (3)
426	God will make new heavens and earth (3)
426	shall Christians fail to sing till on earth Christ come (4)
427	Let all the earth around ring joyous with the sound (4)
428	earth and sea, O all that live in water or on shore (4)
429	made the sky and earth and seas with all their train (2)
432	Praise him upon earth ... all ye of new birth (2)
435	with his Father's glory o'er the earth to reign (6)
440	drawn from earth to love thee solely (1)
443	he descended to the earth (4)
447	no power earth can afford will separate us (4)
453	its foot was on earth and its top in the sky (1)
454	lowly came on earth to die (1)
455, 456	we read thee in the earth below (2)
458	In life no house, no home my Lord on earth might have (6)
460, 461	Bread of Heaven, thou on earth our food, our stay (3)
460, 461	born of Mary, earth thy footstool, heaven thy throne (4)
460, 461	thou on earth both Priest and Victim (4)
462	Truth from the earth (2)
462	Rise, God, judge thou the earth in might (3)
462	this wicked earth redress (3)
467	Heaven and earth by him were made (2)
477	with one accord in heaven and earth (5)
479	Oft as earth exulting wafts its praise on high (4)
480	like us, unhonored and unknown, he came to dwell on earth (1)
481	His kingdom cannot fail, he rules o'er earth and heaven (3)
486	let earth, let heaven, hosanna sing (1)
486	dreadful day when earth and heaven shall melt away (5)
489	his holy and immortal truth to all on earth hath given (1)
493	spread through all the earth abroad the honors of thy Name (2)
493	the Church in earth and heaven (6)
494	once on earth the incarnate Word (4)
496, 497	Rejoice, ye heavens; thou earth, reply (3)
496, 497	Praise be given evermore, by earth and heaven (3)

509	let thy Church on earth become blest as the Church above (4)
524	brightest glories earth can yield (5)
525	Elect from every nation, yet one o'er all the earth (2)
525	Yet she on earth hath union with God, the Three in One (5)
526	Let saints on earth in concert sing (1)
526	all the servants of our King in heaven and earth are one (1)
529	fellowship of love throughout the whole wide earth (1)
529	one in him throughout the whole wide earth (3)
530	earth from sin and death to save (2)
532, 533	To nations of earth thy light shall be shown (2)
534	earth shall be filled with the glory of God (1-4)
539	died on earth that all might live above (2)
540	the circle of the earth shall then proclaim thy kingdom (3)
543	tell all the earth thy joys, and boast salvation nigh (1)
544	earth repeat the loud amen (5)
547	To us on earth he came to bring from sin and fear release (2)
556, 557	With all the angel choirs, with all the saints of earth (2)
556, 557	with all the saints of earth pour out the strains of joy (2)
559	thou didst tread this earth before us (2)
560	Blessed are the meek, for they shall inherit the earth (3)
566	thy just rule shall fill the earth (2)
566	fill the earth with health and light and peace (2)
568	truly to care for the poor of the earth (2)
569	earth hath forsaken thy ways all holy (2)
569	God the All-righteous One, earth hath defied thee (3)
569	earth by thy chastening yet shall ... be restored (4)
569	earth ... shall to freedom and truth be restored (4)
573	there is no meekness in the powers of earth (4)
586	workers, burden bearers of the earth (1)
591	O God of earth and altar, bow down and hear our cry (1)
597	for all the earth shall know the Lord (2)
598	Lord Christ, when first thou cam'st to earth (1)
599	Lift every voice and sing till earth and heaven ring (1)
600, 601	war may haunt the earth no more and desolation cease (4)
600, 601	set thy judgments in the earth (5)
603, 604	When Christ was lifted from the earth (1)
605	Rulers of earth, give ear. Should you not justice show (2)
614	so shall God's will on earth be done (3)
615	see on earth that kingdom's day (1)
615	knowledge ... shall walk the earth abroad (5)
616	Hail, in the time appointed, his reign on earth begun (1)
616	He shall come down like showers upon the fruitful earth (3)
627	without thee how could earth be trod (4)
630	Word was spoken in the deed that made the earth (1)
632	still that light is lifted o'er all the earth to shine (2)
633	Word of God, come down on earth (1)
640	see, it bursts o'er all the earth (2)
651	all earth and trees, all skies and seas (2)
657	joy of heaven, to earth come down (1)
665	from earth to God eternal sacrifice of praise be done (5)
668	who heaven and earth hath made (1)
680	Before ... earth received her frame (3)
687, 688	armed with cruel hate, on earth is not his equal (1)

earth's

24	never, like earth's proud empires, pass away (4)
59	from earth's bondage let us rise (2)
68	see the day of earth's redemption, and ever be with thee (3)
73	earth's dark night is past (3)
76	restore earth's own true loveliness once more ((4)
164	This is earth's darkest hour (3)
222	triumph from earth's battlefield (1)
277	Church the strain re-echoes unto earth's remotest ends (3)
287	From earth's wide bounds, from ocean's farthest coast (8)
371	in earth's darkest place, let there be light (3)
379	God who laid the earth's foundation (1)
394, 395	your hands uphold earth's mysteries known or yet untold (2)
424	future needs in earth's safe-keeping (1)
460, 461	earth's Redeemer, plead for me (3)
469, 470	There is no place where earth's sorrows are more felt (2)
469, 470	no place ... earth's failures have such kindly judgment (2)
472	to heal earth's wounds and end her bitter strife (2)
475	Help us to surrender earth's deceitful treasures (2)
528	Let your priests, for earth's true glory, daily lift (3)
530	to earth's remotest bound all may heed the joyful sound (1)
530	earth's sore burden doth remove (3)
532, 533	till earth's every people confess thee their God (2)
538	thy saving health extend unto earth's remotest end (1)
584	to probe earth's hidden mysteries (1)
662	heaven's morning breaks, and earth's vain shadows flee (4)
672	whose feet this earth's dark valley trod (1)
681	whose stars serenely burn above this earth's confusion (1)
701	with me in earth's sadness, Jesus, all my gladness (3)

earthly

3, 4	to Christ, revealed in earthly night (5)
5	Spirit's sanctifying beam upon our earthly senses stream (2)
29, 30	to Christ revealed in earthly night (3)
119	when earthly things are past (4)
124	to Christ, revealed in earthly night (5)
187	Earthly night brought us light which is ours eternally (3)
222	troubles of our earthly life (3)
223, 224	till our earthly wanderings cease (4)
231	leaving earthly treasures, sought riches from above (2/6-11)
243	the stones of earthly shame a jeweled crown may seem (4)
261, 262	to his earthly father freely was subject (2)
268, 269	fashioned for his earthly home (2)
279	Thine earthly members fit to join thy saints above (3)
318	here would I lay aside each earthly load (2)
324	ponder nothing earthly minded (1)
345	Grant us thy peace throughout our earthly life (3)
357	in the mystic symbols veiled from earthly sight (1)
379	guides us through our earthly strife (3)
392	celestial fruits on earthly ground (3)
436	make it a temple set apart from earthly use (3)
436	a temple set apart from earthly use for heaven's employ (3)
475	let my soul, like Mary, be thine earthly sanctuary (4)

476	earthly values stand beside the manger and the cross (3)
508	till all this earthly part of me glows (3)
510	See how we trifle here below, fond of these earthly toys (2)
516	O let it freely burn, till earthly passions turn to dust (2)
587	O Christ, thyself a child within an earthly home (2)
591	our earthly rulers falter, our people drift and die (1)
625	Ye blessed souls at rest, who ran this earthly race (2)
665	Mortal pride and earthly glory (2)
687, 688	That word above all earthly powers ... abideth (4)
701	Hence with earthly treasure (2)
709	through this earthly pilgrimage ... all thine Israel led (1)

earthward
| 519, 520 | angel hosts encircled, as a bride dost earthward move (1) |

ease
| 549, 550 | days of toil and hours of ease (4) |
| 611 | he will ease your load and give you rest (6) |

east
31, 32	the sun that flames up from the east (1)
77	From east to west, from shore to shore (1)
109	They looked up and saw a star shining in the east (2)
109	shining in the east beyond them far (2)
117, 118	star of the east, the horizon adorning (1,5)
180	breaking o'er the purple east (3)
192	trump from east to west shall wake the dead in number (3)
529	In Christ there is no East or West (1)
529	In Christ now meet both East and West (3)
534	From utmost east to utmost west, wherever foot hath trod (2)
536	From east and west the peoples travel (3)
603, 604	Still east and west his love extends (2)
672	even now, though dull and gray, the east is brightening (3)
672	the east is brightening fast (3)

Easter
122, 123	grant us, blessed Trinity ... to keep thine Easter (4)
122, 123	at the last to keep thine Easter with thy faithful saints (4)
135	cross and Easter Day attest God in man made manifest (4)
142	an Easter of unending joy we may attain at last (5)
174	Easter triumph, Easter joy, these alone do sin destroy (4)
180	symbol of our Easter feast (3)
180	a brighter Easter beam on our longing eyes shall stream (4)
193	That Easter day with joy was bright (1)
198	fair Easter, queen of all the days (1)
203	That Easter morn, at break of day (2)
204	Forth he came at Easter, like the risen grain (3)
212	let Easter music swell (1)
232	On Easter morning early, a word from you sufficed (2/7-22)
296	Reborn we share with him an Easter life (2)

eastern
| 73 | beauty gilds the eastern hills (1) |

124   eastern sages with amaze upon the wondrous token gaze (2)
127   Eastern sages at his cradle make oblations rich and rare (3)
131, 132   The eastern sages saw from far (2)

Eastertide
150   that with thee we may appear at the Eternal Eastertide (5)
192   This joyful Eastertide, away with sin and sorrow (1)
193   in this our joyful Eastertide (4)

easy
585   throned in easy state to reign (6)
591   from all the easy speeches that comfort cruel men (2)
611   easy yokes that made the labor less (4)

eat
174   with sincerity and love eat we manna from above (2)
335   they who eat of this bread ... shall live forever (2)
335   Unless you eat of the Flesh of the Son of Man (3)

ebb
580   the lonely drift unnoticed in the city's ebb and flow (2)

echoes
18   teach us to hear its echoes still in every human misery (3c)
277   Church the strain re-echoes unto earth's remotest ends (3)
556, 557   while answering echoes upward float (3)
556, 557   echoes upward float like wreaths of incense cloud (3)

echoing
96   the mountains in reply echoing their brave delight (1)
618   supernal anthems echoing (4)

ecstasy
580   known the ecstasy of winging through untraveled realms (3)

Eden
8   born of the one light Eden saw play (3)
244   the better Eden planted by our Lord most dear (2)

Eden's
363   with light and life since Eden's dawning day (1)

Edom
117, 118   odors of Edom, and offerings divine (3)

Egypt's
187   Egypt's chains behind we cast (1)
648   When Israel was in Egypt's land (1)
648   Go down, Moses, way down in Egypt's land (R)

elation
8   Praise with elation (3)

elect
133, 134   with your elect found company (2)

276	up where thine elect are crowned (5)
519, 520	Many a blow ... polished well those stones elect (4)
525	Elect from every nation, yet one o'er all the earth (2)
624	Oh, sweet and blessed country, the home of God's elect (4)

eleison
| 319 | Kyrie eleison (1-2) |

Elijah
18	Elijah taunted Baal at noon (2b)
129, 130	Trembling at his feet we saw Moses and Elijah speaking (2)
136, 137	With Moses and Elijah nigh (2)
143	to Elijah fasting, came the steeds and chariots of flame (2)
232	our true Elijah, making a highway for the Lord (2/6-24)

Elijah's
| 359 | Elijah's mantle o'er Elisha cast (1) |

Elisha
| 359 | Elijah's mantle o'er Elisha cast (1) |

Elizabeth
| 266 | six months gone since Elizabeth conceived John (5) |

eloquent
| 359 | fill them with power, their lips make eloquent (2) |
| 359 | eloquent for righteousness that shall all evil break (2) |

else
488	all else be nought to me, save that thou art (1)
625	assist our song, for else the theme too high doth seem (1)
647	I know not if the way is long, and no one else can say (1)
706	else this world had still enthralled me (1)

embrace
16, 17	Then let us all with joy embrace the flaming splendor (3)
65	Fling wide your gates, O Zion, your Savior's rule embrace (3)
83	we would embrace thee, with love and awe (5)
105	with true love and charity each other now embrace (4)
250	rejoice, with thanks embrace another year of grace (1-3,5)
379	God is Love ... enfolds us, all the world in one embrace (2)
394, 395	your arms embrace all now despised for creed or race (3)
482	your hands swift to welcome, your arms to embrace (3)
682	for that thou didst all the world upon the cross embrace (2)

embraced
| 296 | Embraced by death he broke its fearful hold (1) |

embraces
| 170 | Kingdom shall not cease to grow till love embraces all (3) |
| 581 | our common life embraces all whose Father is the same (6) |

embracing
| 455, 456 | O wide-embracing, wondrous Love (2) |

Emmanuel

56	O come, O come, Emmanuel and ransom captive Israel (1,8)
56	Rejoice, rejoice, Emmanuel shall come to thee, O Israel (R)
78, 79	O come to us, abide with us, our Lord Emmanuel (5)
87	Pleased as man with us to dwell; Jesus, our Emmanuel (2)
88	God with us, Emmanuel, deigns for ever now to dwell (3)
265	thy Son shall be Emmanuel, by seers foretold (2)
265	Of her, Emmanuel, the Christ, was born (4)
342	all veils thus rending, Emmanuel, our joy unending (3)
496, 497	great Emmanuel, come and hear us (1)

Emmanuel's

392	we're marching through Emmanuel's ground to fairer worlds (4)
495	help to chant Emmanuel's praise (4)

emotion

159	Jesus, may her deep devotion stir in me the same emotion (5)

empire

50	Today he rose and left the dead, and Satan's empire fell (2)
435	for all wreaths of empire meet upon his brow (6)

empires

24	never, like earth's proud empires, pass away (4)
170	though empires rise and fall ... Kingdom shall not cease (3)

employ

100	let us our songs employ (2)
106	Let us, like these good shepherds, then employ (5)
106	employ our grateful voices to proclaim the joy (5)
288	let thy praise our tongues employ (1)
347	serving Christ, our every gift employ (4)
415	Ten thousand ... precious gifts my daily thanks employ (3)
426	amidst eternal joy songs of praise their powers employ (6)
429	when my voice is lost in death praise shall employ (1,4)
429	praise shall employ my nobler powers (1,4)
436	a temple set apart from earthly use for heaven's employ (3)
493	ye voiceless ones, your loosened tongues employ (5)
584	So for your glory and our good may we your gifts employ (4)

empower

528	the Spirit's gifts empower us for the work of ministry (R)

emptiness

509	Come as the light, to us reveal our emptiness and woe (2)

empty

3, 4	guard ... our ears from empty praise and lies (3)
176, 177	Over the chaos of the empty waters hovered the Spirit (1)
176, 177	so from the empty tomb the Second Adam issued triumphant (1)
182	His cross stands empty to the sky (1)
185, 186	an empty form alone remains; his sting is lost for ever (2)
201	the tomb is empty: enter in (3)
333	Now the silence Now the peace ... empty hands uplifted (1)

enable
503, 504   Enable with perpetual light ... our blinded sight (4)

enabling
228   Grant enabling energy, courage in adversity (5)
394, 395   let water's fragile blend with air, enabling life (2)

encircled
519, 520   angel hosts encircled, as a bride dost earthward move (1)

encompass
545   Lo, what a cloud of witnesses encompass us around (1)

end
33-35   Now comes the day's end as the sun is setting (2)
40, 41   O God, our Maker and our end (5)
68   Look now for your salvation, the end of sin and toil (2)
74   till time itself shall end (3)
125, 126   his reign no end shall know (5)
168, 169   for this thy dying sorrow, thy pity without end (4)
170   acted out their grim charade to its appointed end (3)
210   for Christ the Lord is risen, our joy that hath no end (3)
231   not betray our calling but serve you to the end (2/2-24)
285   still found faithful to the end (3)
310, 311   O grant us life that shall not end (2)
345   with thee began, with thee shall end the day (2)
352   restore their love till life shall end (3)
381   Alleluia, alleluia, Alleluia without end (1-3)
385   bless us with life that has no end (2)
388   thy mercies, now tender, how firm to the end (5)
399   that strife may end and joy increase (3)
472   to heal earth's wounds and end her bitter strife (2)
482   your peace in our hearts, Lord, at the end of the day (4)
484, 485   Thy reign extend world without end (2)
524   to her my cares and toils be given till toils ... end (2)
524   till toils and cares shall end (2)
528   I am with you to the end (5)
538   thy saving health extend unto earth's remotest end (1)
556, 557   At last the march shall end (6)
564, 565   we know we at the end shall life inherit (3)
606   for ever and for evermore, world without end (3)
616   his kingdom still increasing, a kingdom without end (4)
620   When shall my sorrows have an end (1)
625   Let all thy days till life shall end ... praise (4)
644   my Lord, my Life, my Way, my End (4)
647   some I love have reached the end (2)
655   O Jesus, I have promised to serve thee to the end (1)
655   Jesus, I have promised to serve thee to the end (3)

endeavor
139   in his great endeavor to save us, his own blood was shed (2)
237   vain the tyrant's sharpest aim, vain each fierce endeavor (2)
475   soul and life and each endeavor (2)

580	each endeavor well begun (4)
585	hidden is love's agony, love's endeavor, love's expense (2)
596	Crown, O God, thine own endeavor (3)
636, 637	that soul, though all hell shall endeavor to shake (5)

ended

24	The day thou gavest, Lord, is ended (1)
179	speak his sorrow ended, hail his triumph now (2)
185, 186	the reign of death was ended (2)
185, 186	the night of sin is ended (3)
190	Ended now the night of sorrow (3)
286	wrestling on till life was ended (3)
319	when by sin our life was ended (2)
357	there, the warfare ended, bid them rest in peace (2)
358	Grief and pain ended, and sighing no longer (1,4)
452	that strong Light puts out the sun and all is ended (4)
452	all is ended, all begun (4)
632	clouds and darkness ended, they see thee face to face (3)

ending

1, 2	joy without ending (2)
82	he is Alpha and Omega, he the source, the ending he (1)
104	But now, as at the ending, The low is lifted high (4)
329, 331	he closed with wondrous ending his most patient life (2)
329-331	types and shadows have their ending (5)
430	Let in praise of God, the sound run a never-ending round (4)
718	lead us from night to never-ending day (4)

endless

25, 26	Worthy are you of endless praise, O Son of God (3)
40, 41	to you be thanks and endless praise (5)
48	at length our rest attaining, our endless Sabbath day (4)
57, 58	cause of endless exultation to his ransomed worshipers (3)
73	let the endless bliss begin, by weary saints foretold (4)
107	now ye hear of endless bliss (2)
181	Soon ... each raptured tongue his endless praise proclaim (4)
202	endless life restored in thee (4)
202	from death to endless life restored (5)
209	with full and endless sight (4)
217, 218	while endless ages run, with Father and with Spirit, One (3)
220, 221	let earth accord, who art, while endless ages run (4)
257	all glory, Holy Ghost, to thee, while endless ages run (5)
324	Light of Life descendeth from the realms of endless day (3)
344	May we ever reign with thee in endless day (3)
346	to whom be praise while endless ages run (3)
357	Humbly we adore thee, Lord of endless might (1)
401	all might and majesty are thine, and endless praise (5)
404	Age shall to age pass on the endless song (2)
428	sun ... moon ... stars ... your endless praise outpour (2)
454	till the dawn of endless day (4)
472	lure us away from thee to endless night (3)
479	Blest through endless ages be the precious stream (3)
503, 504	through the ages all along this may be our endless song (8)

511	thee we praise with endless worship (1)
544	To him shall endless prayer be made (2)
563	wear in endless glory the crown of victory (3)
576, 577	be our bliss while endless ages sing your praises (3)
593	reborn through death's dark night to endless day (5)
618	Respond, ye souls in endless rest (3)
619	an endless alleluia (1-7)
620	Jerusalem, God grant that I may see thine endless joy (5)
621, 622	endless noon-day ... from the Sun of suns is there (3)
621, 622	hereafter these thy labors may with endless gifts be paid (5)
623	those endless Sabbaths the blessed ones see (1)
643	thine endless wisdom, boundless power, and aweful purity (3)
647	till dawns the endless day (3)
680	from everlasting thou art God, to endless years the same (3)
704	till death thy endless mercies seal (4)

endowed

240, 241	heaven-endowed with grace and power (2)

ends

222	his strife with human hatred ends (1)
225	his chosen apostles, preach to the ends of the earth (3)
277	Church the strain re-echoes unto earth's remotest ends (3)
304	each proud division ends (3)
348	ours a commitment we know never ends (1)
386, 387	period, power, and enterprise commences, reigns and ends (1)
487	such a truth as ends all strife (1)
647	or where it ends, I only know (1)
680	short as the watch that ends the night (4)

endue

605	Let Christ endue our will with grace to fortify (4)

endued

525	to one hope she presses, with every grace endued (2)
548	with all his strength endued (3)
621, 622	endued with heavenly beauty (4)

endure

18	assist us to endure that light (1)
377, 378	shall from age to age endure (4)
389	for his mercies ay endure, ever faithful, ever sure (R)
406, 407	Happy, who peaceably endure (6)
508	until with thee I will one will, to do or to endure (2)
600, 601	finely build for days to come foundations that endure (3)
669	his work must thou consider for thy work to endure (2)
681	the world began, endures, and shall endure (1)
687, 688	his rage we can endure (3)

endured

184	He who gave for us his life ... for us endured the strife (2)
207	who endured the cross and grave (2)
207	pains which he endured ... our salvation have procured (3)
545	He ... endured the cross, despised the shame (4)

endures

157	his mercy endures for ever (R)
165, 166	He endures the nails, the spitting (3)
429	immortality endures (1,4)
671	he will my shield and portion be as long as life endures (3)
681	the world began, endures, and shall endure (1)

endureth

53	One who thus endureth bright reward secureth (4)
75	but the word of our God endureth (3)
665	God's great goodness e'er endureth (3)

enduring

277	toil and labor cannot weary love enduring unto death (2)

enemies

212	His enemies had sealed the stone (4)
231	his enemies he blessed (2/12-26)
597	Then enemies shall learn to love (2)

enemy

425	he saved us from our enemy (2)
541	The enemy is watching night and day (2)
682	e'en death itself, and all for one who was thine enemy (3)

energy

228	Grant enabling energy, courage in adversity (5)
500	rich in thy sevenfold energy (3)
501, 502	In you God's energy is shown (3)

enfold

53	not in torment hold us, but in love enfold us (2)
435	let his will enfold you in its light and power (5)
689	Thou didst reach forth thy hand and mine enfold (2)

enfolding

38, 39	rest in night's enfolding quietness (2)

enfolds

379	God is Love ... enfolds us, all the world in one embrace (2)

engines

412	Engines and steel, loud pounding hammers (4)

enjoying

352	enjoying your sweet grace (2)

enkindle

540	O Lord, now let thy fire enkindle our hearts (2)

enlarge

629	enlarge, expand all living souls to comprehend your love (3)

enlighten

175	Jesus the health of the world, enlighten our minds (6)
216	enlighten our minds, thou Redeemer (4)
339	Light, who dost my soul enlighten (2)
505	O Spirit of Life, O Spirit orf God, enlighten us (4)
505	enlighten us by that same word (4)
514	enlighten, sanctify, and seal (3)

enlightened

506, 507	who enlightened priests and prophets with the word (3)

enlist

297	Enlist us in your service, Lord (2)

enmity

606	when we gather let no discord or enmity break our oneness (2)

enough

167	There was no other good enough to pay the price of sin (4)
281	Enough, when thou wast passing by (3)
281	Enough ... to hear thy voice, to meet thine eye (3)
318	it is enough, my Lord, enough indeed (3)
617	enough to know that we are serving thee (3)

enraptured

336	be enraptured anthems raised (3)
386, 387	glorious the enraptured main (3)

enrich

71, 72	treasures of his grace to enrich the humble poor (3)

enroll

382	Small it is in this poor sort to enroll thee (3)

enslaved

252	whereby those to sin enslaved, burst their fetters (5)

ensures

447	yet he who loved us from the first ensures our victory (3)

enter

78, 79	cast out our sin and enter in, be born in us today (5)
157	Open for me the gates of righteousness; I will enter them (1)
157	I will enter them; I will offer thanks to the Lord (1)
157	he who is righteous may enter (R)
201	the tomb is empty: enter in (3)
228	comforter in time of grief, enter in and be our guest (2)
228	Enter each aspiring heart (3)
342	Now may your life to us descending enter our lives (3)
377, 378	O enter then his gates with praise (3)
436	So come, my Sovereign, enter in! (5)
436	enter in! Let new and nobler life begin (5)
657	visit us with thy salvation, enter every trembling heart (1)

entered
109   Then entered in those wise men three (5)
460, 461 thou within the veil hast entered, robed in flesh (4)

enterprise
191   we conquer by his mighty enterprise (2)
386, 387 period, power, and enterprise commences, reigns and ends (1)

enters
78, 79   still the dear Christ enters in (3)
214   enters now the highest heaven (1)
701   for my joy bestower, Jesus, enters in (3)

enthrall
174   now no more the grave enthrall (3)
194, 195 by this we know thou, O grave, canst not enthrall us (1)

enthrone
115   let loving hearts enthrone him (3)
435   In your hearts enthrone him (5)
542   cast out our pride and shame that hinder to enthrone thee (3)

enthroned
108   to Christ enthroned in glory (1)
307   Lord, enthroned in heavenly splendor (1)
366   Son of God enthroned in splendor (5)
399   enthroned as King on heaven's height (1)
401   The God of Abraham praise, who reigns enthroned above (1)
494   Crown him the Lord of heaven, enthroned in worlds above (5)
495   Jesus, hail, enthroned in glory, there for ever to abide (3)

entomb
591   the walls of gold entomb us, the swords of scorn divide (1)

entwine
226, 227 joys which earth and heaven entwine (5)

entwined
159   crowned with thorns entwined (3)

envious
573   Envious of heart, blind-eyed, with tongues confounded (3)

envy
5   with love all envy to subdue (4)
597   our hearts from envy find release (1)

enwrapped
114   a ragged robe of rabbit skin enwrapped his beauty round (2)

epiphany
127   Jesus, whom the Gentiles worshiped at thy glad epiphany (5)
131, 132 All glory, Jesus, be to thee for this thy glad epiphany (5)

| 138 | the great epiphany (4) |
| 333 | Now the Spirit's visitation Now the Son's epiphany (1) |

equal
1, 2	All holy Father, Son, and equal Spirit, Trinity blessed (3)
3, 4	our equal and unceasing praise (5)
5	in equal and unending praise (5)
29, 30	our equal and unceasing praise (3)
124	to ... Holy Ghost we raise our equal and unceasing praise (5)
193	to God the Father equal praise (5)
232	he welcomed them as kindred on equal terms to be (2/10-23)
284	With equal flame and equal art ... extol his Name (8)
415	how shall words with equal warmth the gratitude declare (2)
687, 688	armed with cruel hate, on earth is not his equal (1)

equip
| 232 | equip us for such sufferings as glorify your Name (2/7-25) |

equity
| 616 | to take away transgression, and rule in equity (1) |

err
| 462 | his footsteps cannot err (1) |
| 677 | Blind unbelief is sure to err and scan his work in vain (6) |

error
| 345 | peace to thy Church from error and from strife (3) |

error's
| 537 | new-born souls, whose days, reclaimed from error's ways (4) |

escape
| 433 | Let thy congregation escape tribulation (3) |

espoused
| 519, 520 | meet for him whose love espoused thee (2) |

essence
| 366 | while in essence only One, undivided God we claim thee (4) |
| 445, 446 | God's presence and his very self, and essence all divine (4) |

established
| 372 | Established is his law, and changeless it shall stand (3) |

establishes
| 413 | whose truth victorious establishes the world in peace (3) |

estate
| 115 | Why lies he in such mean estate (2) |
| 115 | mean estate where ox and ass are feeding (2) |

eternal
| 5 | all praise, eternal Son, to thee (5) |

14, 15	by a holy death attained, eternal glory may be gained (2)
25, 26	God who dwells in the eternal light (2)
27, 28	Eternal Father, help us rise (4)
36	eternal splendor wearing; celestial, holy, blest (1)
37	we hymn the eternal Father ... Son ... Holy Ghost divine (2)
47	On this day the eternal Son over death his triumph won (2)
52	all praise, eternal Son, to thee (4)
55	You came forth from the eternal God (3)
55	all praise to you, eternal Word (6)
57, 58	high on thine eternal throne (4)
60	redeem us for eternal day (5)
63, 64	O heavenly Word, eternal Light (1)
66	By thine own eternal Spirit rule in all our hearts alone (4)
71, 72	heaven's eternal arches ring with thy beloved Name (4)
76	All praise, eternal Son, to thee (5)
82	honor, glory and dominion, and eternal victory (4)
83	God from God, Light from Light eternal (2)
91	the power of Satan breaking, our peace eternal making (1)
106	eternal praise to heaven's almighty King (6)
120	who gives eternal life to those that with you died (6)
136, 137	O Father, with the eternal Son ... Holy Spirit, ever One (5)
144	we shall acclaim your majesty, eternal Three in One (5)
149	Eternal Lord of love, behold your Church (1)
150	that with thee we may appear at the Eternal Eastertide (5)
161	he died eternal life to bring (1)
162	To thee, eternal Three in One (6)
165, 166	one in might and one in glory while eternal ages run (6)
181	rejoicing in the Lamb of God, to Christ the eternal King (3)
185, 186	by his grace he doth impart eternal sunshine to the heart (3)
191	we with him to life eternal by his resurrection rise (2)
206	for they eternal life shall win (6)
207	Sing we to our God above ... praise eternal as his love (4)
210	From death to life eternal, from earth unto the sky (1)
210	the Lord in rays eternal of resurrection light (2)
214	lift your heads, eternal gates (2)
219	Lo, he returns ... to his eternal dwelling (1)
220, 221	O Lord Most High, eternal King (1)
231	sing to God the Spirit, eternal Three in One (3)
232	be bound in love together, and life eternal gain (2/10-28)
232	sing to God the Spirit, eternal Three in One (3)
233, 234	The eternal gifts of Christ the King ... we sing (1)
238, 239	by his grace we may be worthy of eternal bliss at last (3)
245	Your brightness, O eternal Word, Apostle John unfurled (1)
251	to us at last in mercy give eternal life with thee (4)
261, 262	To God eternal be all praise and glory (3)
263, 264	Lord Jesus, Virgin-born ... eternal praise and glory be (4)
278	Son of God eternal and the everlasting Bread (1)
285	eternal God and Word divine (1)
298	that as is promised here we may eternal life inherit (2)
302, 303	giving in Christ the Bread eternal (1)
318	here grasp with firmer hand eternal grace (1)
320	eternal goodness send us in the land of life to see (5)
327, 328	to all believers life eternal yields (6)

329-331	while eternal ages run (6)
345	call us, O Lord, to thine eternal peace (4)
350	Eternal love, with them abide (3)
357	Rest eternal grant them, after weary fight (4)
360, 361	Only begotten, Word of God eternal (1)
360, 361	strangers and pilgrims, seeking homes eternal (4)
369	all the heavenly powers conspire eternal praise to sing (4)
370	the deep salt sea, around the old eternal rocks (4)
370	eternal Father, Spirit, Word (7)
372	the one eternal God ere aught that now appears (1)
372	Eternal life hath he implanted in the soul (4)
379	God is Love, eternal Love (1)
379	God's eternal lovingkindness guides us through (3)
380	Eternal are thy mercies, Lord (2)
380	truth eternal is thy word (2)
385	eternal life with thee (2)
391	Before the Lord's eternal throne ... bow with sacred joy (1)
396, 397	eternal, Triune God, whom earth and heaven adore (3)
401	eternal Father, great I AM, we worship thee (4)
426	amidst eternal joy songs of praise their powers employ (6)
427	There to the eternal Word the eternal psalm is heard (3)
455, 456	eternal and yet ever new (1)
457	that life to win, whose joys eternal flow (4)
460, 461	King eternal, thee the Lord of lords we own (4)
465, 466	Eternal light, shine in my heart (1)
465, 466	eternal hope, lift up my eyes (1)
465, 466	eternal power, be my support (1)
465, 466	eternal wisdom, make me wise (1)
465, 466	Eternal life, raise me from death (2)
465, 466	eternal brightness, help me see (2)
465, 466	eternal Spirit, give me breath (2)
465, 466	eternal Savior, come to me (2)
465, 466	to know you, my eternal God (3)
469, 470	the heart of the Eternal is most wonderfully kind (3)
477	Wherefore, by God's eternal purpose, thou ... exalted (4)
479	Grace and life eternal in that blood I find (2)
481	take his servants up to their eternal home (4)
483	heaven's eternal Light (2)
486	Eternal, bid thy Spirit rest (4)
491	strength of infant weakness, if eternal is so young (3)
494	died eternal life to bring and lives that death may die (3)
500	make us eternal truth receive (3)
503, 504	praise to thy eternal merit, Father, Son and Holy Spirit (9)
510	our souls, how heavily they go to reach eternal joys (2)
521	To know thee is eternal life (4)
522, 523	living waters, springing from eternal love (2)
526	greet the ever-living bands on the eternal shore (4)
527	one the gladness of rejoicing on the far eternal shore (3)
544	the weary find eternal rest (4)
548	God supplies through his eternal Son (1)
555	Lead on, O King eternal (1-3)
555	now, O King eternal, we lift our battle song (1)
573	Father eternal, Ruler of creation (1)

576, 577	Let us fear and love him, holy God eternal (1)
596	Judge eternal, throned in splendor (1)
607	deliver every nation, eternal God, we pray (2)
608	Eternal Father, strong to save (1)
617	Eternal Ruler of the ceaseless round of circling planets (1)
618	Thou bearer of the eternal Word (2)
619	Ye powers who stand before the eternal Light (2)
619	ye victors, now take up the eternal song (4)
633	Word eternal, throned on high (2)
641	when the flood is passed, I may the eternal brightness see (4)
643	How dread are thine eternal years, O everlasting Lord (2)
658	thy health's eternal spring (3)
665	from earth to God eternal sacrifice of praise be done (5)
680	our shelter from the stormy blast, and our eternal home (1)
680	our eternal home (6)
681	hint at the glorious praise of thy eternal song (3)
682	my eternal King (6)
698	Eternal Spirit of thy living Christ (1)

eternally

60	age to age eternally (6)
63, 64	from age to age eternally (5)
103	We praise you, Holy Trinity ... adoring you eternally (4)
122, 123	in the house of God abiding thus they sing eternally (1)
173	Blest shall they be eternally who ponder in their weeping (3)
187	Earthly night brought us light which is ours eternally (3)
202	all praise to God the Father be and Holy Ghost eternally (5)
271, 272	praise, honor, might, and glory ... age to age eternally (5)
381	to ... Light of Light begotten, praise be sung eternally (4)
518	God the One in Three adoring in glad hymns eternally (2)
552, 553	lay hold on life ... thy joy and crown eternally (1)
561	they with the King of glory shall reign eternally (4)
621, 622	full of vigor ... of pleasure that shall last eternally (4)
623	voices of praise thy blessed people eternally raise (3)

eternity

29, 30	praise thee through eternity (2)
163	the cross on Calvary's height gleams of eternity appear (2)
213	lives may remain, throughout time and eternity thine (3)
217, 218	great the light in you we see to guide us to eternity (2)
220, 221	let all our glory be in thee both now and ... eternity (3)
346	for ever in eternity with thee (2)
365	to eternity love and adore (4)
369	dwells amidst the dazzling light of vast eternity (1)
391	vast as eternity thy love (5)
415	Through all eternity, to thee a joyful song I'll raise (5)
439	sing and joyful be, and through eternity, I'll sing on (3)
494	hail him as thy matchless King through all eternity (1)
501, 502	to whom all honor, glory be both now and for eternity (6)
508	but live with thee the perfect life of thine eternity (4)
528	amid the cares that claim us, hold in mind eternity (5)
568	may we adore thee for time and eternity (4)
569	yet to eternity standeth thy word (3)

642	in thee be all our glory now, and through eternity (5)
652, 653	Jesus knelt to share with thee the silence of eternity (3)
652, 653	silence of eternity interpreted by love (3)
699	spring thou up within my heart, rise to all eternity (3)

eternity's

| 382 | e'en eternity's too short to extol thee (3) |
| 415 | eternity's too short to utter all thy praise (5) |

ethereal

| 409 | with all the blue ethereal sky (1) |

Eucharist

315	Thou, who at thy first Eucharist didst pray (1)
315	grant us at every Eucharist to say ... Thy will be done (1)
334	by this Eucharist declaring yours the final victory (1)

eucharistic

| 460, 461 | Priest and Victim in the eucharistic feast (4) |

Eva

| 266 | Nova, nova. Ave fit ex Eva (R) |

Evangel

| 540 | Send forth, O Lord, thy strong Evangel (3) |

evangelist

| 245 | Praise God for John, the evangelist (1) |
| 275 | king, apostle, saint, confessor, martyr and evangelist (2) |

eve

| 18 | all shadows of the morn and eve converged (3b) |
| 482 | your love in our hearts, Lord, at the eve of the day (3) |

even

173	now, and even unto death, dearest Lord, be near me (4)
290	Even so, Lord, quickly come to thy final harvest-home (4)
335	who believe in me, even if they die ... live for ever (4)
355	yet even at the grave we make our song: Alleluia (1)
370	the whiteness of the moon at even (4)
400	even you, most gentle death (6)
663	Yea, even when I must pass through the valley (3)
672	even now, though dull and gray, the east is brightening (3)

evening (see also even)

14, 15	the glorious evening that shall last (2)
27, 28	You joined the morn and evening ray (2)
30	to thee our evening prayer we raise (2)
31, 32	evening stars serenely light the darkening sky (3)
33-35	Therefore we come now evening rites to offer (3)
36	Now, ere day fadeth quite, we see the evening light (2)
37	one by one the lamps of evening shine (2)
42	shadows of the evening steal across the sky (1)

68	The evening is advancing, and darker night is near (1)
287	The golden evening brightens in the west (6)
291	he paints the wayside flower, he lights the evening star (2)
408	by morning glow or evening shade ... ne'er sleepeth (2)
409	Soon as the evening shades prevail (2)
427	When evening shadows fall, this rings my curfew call (1)
680	A thousand ages in thy sight are like an evening gone (4)

evening's
| 14, 15 | you, from the morn till evening's ray (1) |

ever
19, 20	Now Holy Spirit, ever One with God the Father and the Son (1)
21, 22	Spirit we adore for ever and for evermore (3)
24	thy kingdom stands, and grows for ever (4)
33-35	for ever resting in the peace of Jesus (5)
33-35	worshiping our Savior now and for ever (5)
36	thee ... shall exalt for ever (3)
44, 45	whom with the Spirit we adore for ever and for evermore (4)
49	stamped the day for ever his (1)
52	with the Spirit, we adore for ever and for evermore (4)
61, 62	for ever let our praises ring (3)
63, 64	To God the Father ... Son ... Spirit, ever One (5)
68	see the day of earth's redemption, and ever be with thee (3)
77	All glory for this blessed morn to God the Father ever be (5)
82	O that birth for ever blessed (2)
88	God with us, Emmanuel, deigns for ever now to dwell (3)
88	that we ever one may be with the Father and with thee (5)
89, 90	ever o'er its Babel-sounds the blessed angels sing (2)
101	I ask thee to stay close by me for ever (3)
116	may such bonds for ever draw our souls to things above (5)
119	so may we with willing feet ever seek thy mercy seat (2)
119	there for ever may we sing alleluias to our King (5)
122, 123	alleluia is the anthem ever raised by choirs on high (1)
122, 123	there to thee for ever singing alleluia joyfully (4)
128	King for ever, ceasing never over us all to reign (2)
135	manifest in gracious will, ever bringing good from ill (3)
136, 137	O Father, with the eternal Son ... Holy Spirit, ever One (5)
146, 147	may with you for ever live in love and unity and peace (5)
150	O keep us, Savior dear, ever constant by thy side (5)
157	his mercy endures for ever (R)
158	I do adore thee, and will ever pray thee (5)
165, 166	praise and honor to the Spirit, ever Three and ever One (6)
168, 169	Oh, make me thine for ever (4)
174	risen Lord, all praise to thee with the Spirit ever be (4)
178	Now we shall live for ever (3)
182	lives, though ever crucified (4)
183	have mercy, victor King, ever reigning. Amen. Alleluia (8)
185, 186	an empty form alone remains; his sting is lost for ever (2)
190	Life is yours for ever, Mary (3)
191	by angel hands be gathered, and be ever, Lord, with thee (4)
193	thine own redeemed for ever shield (4)
194, 195	tear us from his keeping ever (3)

198	Christ rose from death ... adore for ever ... evermore (1)
207	where the angels ever sing (3)
216	blest day that art hallowed for ever (R)
217, 218	by a new way none ever trod Christ takes his place (1)
217, 218	you will be ever our reward (2)
219	may all within us upward tend to him who ever liveth (3)
225	Hail thee, festival day! blest day ... hallowed ever (R)
231	that we might wear the crown and ever shine in splendor (1)
232	ever shine in splendor reflected from your throne (1)
244	thee with all thy ransomed praising ever ... evermore (3)
254	For ever be adored that Name in earth and sky (1)
256	redeemed for ever and restored (4)
258	blessed they, for ever blest, who love thee most (2)
265	Christian folk throughout the world will ever say (4)
275	love and peace they taste for ever (4)
279	in one communion ever knit, one fellowship of love (3)
280	many saints by earth forgotten live for ever (1)
280	live for ever round your throne (1)
282, 283	Father Almighty, Son and Holy Spirit, God ever blessed (6)
282, 283	thine is the glory which from all creation ever ascendeth (6)
289	new comrades ever bringing in comrades' steps to tread (2)
314	grant my spirit ever by thy life may live (3)
315	pray that all thy Church might be for ever one (1)
319	Thus may we ever be yours in peace and unity (2)
323	ever may our souls be fed with this true and living Bread (1)
323	Jesus, may we ever be grafted, rooted, built in thee (2)
326	thy Name with the Father and Spirit be ever adored (1)
326	ever fit us by service on earth for thy service on high (2)
329-331	ever too his love confessing (6)
332	O God, unseen yet ever near, thy presence may we feel (1)
335	who believe in me, even if they die ... live for ever (4)
336	Let the mighty chorus ever sing its glad exultant songs (3)
336	let its hymn be heard for ever -- peace (3)
342	I am with you, this day and ever (3)
344	ever faithful to thy truth may we be found (2)
344	May we ever reign with thee in endless day (3)
346	for ever in eternity with thee (2)
348	intention ever to cherish the gifts you provide (2)
353	the love that Christ makes ever new (1)
370	I bind this day to me for ever ... Christ's incarnation (2)
374	may blessings ... be, Lord for ever thine (3)
376	Thou art giving and forgiving, ever blessing, ever blest (3)
379	Love for ever o'er the universe must reign (3)
381	mortals, angels, now and ever praise the Holy Trinity (4)
389	for his mercies ay endure, ever faithful, ever sure (R)
390	surely his goodness and mercy shall ever attend thee (3)
390	gladly for ever adore him (4)
396, 397	with ever joyful hearts and blessed peace to cheer us (2)
398	all that borrows life from thee is ever in thy care (3)
401	we bow and bless the sacred Name for ever blest (1)
401	"Hail, Father, Son, and Holy Ghost" they ever cry (5)
401	glorious with his saints in light, for ever reigns (3)
404	your holy Name for ever be adored (1)

409	for ever singing as they shine (3)
410	praise him still the same as ever (2)
411	his wrath is ever slow to rise and ready to abate (3)
413	Righteous, commanding, ever glorious (3)
414	ever will I bless thy Name (1)
415	my ever grateful heart, O Lord, thy mercy shall adore (4)
429	whose truth for ever stands secure (2)
433	thy Name be ever praised! O Lord, make us free (3)
434	I would for ever speak his Name (5)
435	ever to be worshiped, trusted, and adored (4)
448, 449	Trinity whom we adore for ever and for evermore (6)
452	transcends the world he never leaves (2)
455, 456	eternal and yet ever new (1)
467	ever watchful o'er our race (1)
472	thou art our Lord, Thou dost for ever reign (5)
473	So shall our song of triumph ever be (4)
482	whose trust, ever child-like, no cares could destroy (1)
488	I ever with thee and thou with me, Lord (2)
492	Now on high, yet ever with us (4)
493	Glory to God and praise and love be now and ever given (6)
495	Jesus, hail, enthroned in glory, there for ever to abide (3)
495	ever for us interceding, till in glory we appear (3)
511	Holy Spirit, ever living as the Church's very life (1)
511	Spirit, ever striving through her in a ceaseless strife (1)
511	Spirit, ever forming in the Church the mind of Christ (1)
511	Holy Spirit, ever working through the Church's ministry (2)
511	Holy Spirit, ever binding age to age and soul to soul (2)
512	fullness of joy for ever there (4)
512	to be with him for ever blest (4)
516	let thy glorious light shine ever on my sight (2)
519, 520	therewith hath willed for ever ... palace ... be decked (4)
519, 520	laud and honor to the Spirit, ever Three, and ever One (5)
522, 523	Who can faint when such a river ever ... thirst assuage (2)
578	None ever called on thee in vain (3)
581	Where charity and love prevail there God is ever found (1)
599	shadowed beneath thy hand may we for ever stand (3)
606	for ever and for evermore, world without end (3)
612	love will ever with us stay (3)
614	who with a faith for ever new followed the King (1)
616	Name shall stand for ever, his changeless Name of Love (5)
617	rule in our hearts that we may ever be ... upheld (1)
619	Your songs of triumph shall for ever ring (5)
620	joy, and of the same partaker ever be (5)
621, 622	There for ever and for ever alleluia is outpoured (2)
623	God shall be all, and in all ever blest (1)
623	through whom, the Spirit, with them ever One (5)
624	the Prince is ever in them, the daylight is serene (2)
624	for ever and for ever are clad in robes of white (3)
624	who art, with God the Father, and Spirit, ever blest (4)
625	praise him still, through good or ill, who ever lives (3)
631	Light of knowledge, ever burning (3)
645, 646	I nothing lack if I am his, and he is mine for ever (1)
645, 646	sing thy praise within thy house for ever (6)

649, 650	O Jesus, ever with us stay (4)
655	be thou for ever near me, my Master and my friend (1)
661	before they ever knew the peace of God (2)
663	I may tell thy praise, and dwell for ever in thy home (5)
666	source and spring from whence redemption ever flows (4)
667	theme of God's salvation, and find it ever new (2)
669	God ever sends his blessing in answer to thy prayer (2)
670	Lord, for ever at thy side let my place and portion be (1)
673	The first one ever, oh, ever to know (1-3)
682	nor yet for fear that loving not I might for ever die (1)
682	but as thyself hast loved me, O ever loving Lord (5)
685	Should my tears for ever flow (2)
687, 688	his kingdom is for ever (4)
690	songs of praises, I will ever give to thee (3)
691	nor let me ever stray from thee aside (3)
697	every thought and work and word, to thee be ever given (4)
701	nought that I may suffer ever shall from Jesus sever (2)
704	burn with ever bright, undying blaze (2)
707	Take myself, and I will be ever, only, all for thee (2)
716	firm may she ever stand through storm and night (1)
716	thou who art ever nigh, guarding with watchful eye (2)
718	be thy strong arm our ever sure defense (3)
718	glory, laud, and praise be ever thine (4)
720	O thus be it ever when free men shall stand (2)

everlasting

46	death's fair night discover ... everlasting life (3)
46	the fields of everlasting life (3)
51	his own life imparting, food everlasting (4)
59	with the everlasting Spirit while unending ages run (4)
60	your people's everlasting light (1)
77	child whom Mary bore, the Christ, the everlasting King (1)
78, 79	yet in thy dark streets shineth the everlasting Light (1)
87	Christ, the everlasting Lord (2)
89, 90	with the everlasting years shall come the time foretold (4)
107	to gain his everlasting hall (3)
176, 177	seek ... life everlasting (2)
278	Son of God eternal and the everlasting Bread (1)
346	ordained by thee, the everlasting Son (3)
354	may you have peace everlasting (2)
355	neither sighing, but life everlasting (1)
356	so may they give you welcome to everlasting peace (3)
358	there may they find everlasting life (1,4)
360, 361	God in three Persons, Father everlasting (6)
364	everlasting Father art, by all the earth adored (1)
364	Thou art the King of glory, Christ, the everlasting Son (6)
366	infinite thy vast domain, everlasting is thy reign (1)
366	Grant that ... we may dwell in everlasting day (7)
401	Ancient of everlasting days, and God of love (1)
410	Praise the everlasting King (1)
413	revealed to every nation his everlasting righteousness (1)
430	that our songs of praise may be everlasting, as is he (4)
462	thou in thy everlasting seat remainest God alone (5)

483	their name, an everlasting name (4)
483	his people's hope ... wealth, their everlasting theme (6)
489	the everlasting Lord (2)
615	for the everlasting right the silent stars are strong (2)
621, 622	in everlasting glory thou with brightness be arrayed (5)
643	How dread are thine eternal years, O everlasting Lord (2)
663	filled my cup, and borne me up in everlasting arms (4)
672	where thou, our everlasting Sun, art shining evermore (4)
680	from everlasting thou art God, to endless years the same (3)

evermore

5	O Father, glorious evermore, we plead with thee (3)
19, 20	whom with the Spirit we adore forever and for evermore (3)
21, 22	Spirit we adore for ever and for evermore (3)
27, 27	Trinity whom we adore be with us now and evermore (5)
44, 45	whom with the Spirit we adore for ever and for evermore (4)
52	with the Spirit, we adore for ever and for evermore (4)
63, 64	with thy saints for evermore behold thee (4)
76	whom with the Father we adore and Holy Spirit evermore (5)
82	evermore and evermore (1-4)
85, 86	whom with the Father we adore and Holy Spirit evermore (6)
103	will rule the world for evermore (2)
107	we are blest for evermore (2)
119	so, most gracious Lord, may we evermore be led to thee (1)
122, 123	Alleluia though we cherish and would chant for evermore (3)
125, 126	His name shall be the Prince of Peace for evermore adored (4)
131, 132	whom with the Father we adore and Holy Ghost for evermore (5)
142	yea, evermore, in life and death, Jesus, with us abide (4)
162	so rule and guide us evermore (6)
164	let all praise be given thee who livest evermore (3)
179	Lo! the dead is living, God for evermore (1)
190	see him living evermore (2)
198	Christ rose from death ... adore for ever ... evermore (1)
198	whom as true God and our hymns adore for ... evermore (2)
199, 200	peace which evermore passeth human knowing (4)
226, 227	To thy people who adore and confess thee evermore (5)
228	joys that last for evermore (5)
231, 232	your holy Name, O Jesus, for evermore be blessed (1)
231	for his faithful record we praise you evermore (2/12-27)
232	with true balm of Gilead anoint us evermore (2/10-18)
238, 239	with meetest praise and sweetest, honor them for evermore (1)
244	thee with all thy ransomed praising ever ... evermore (3)
263, 264	whom with the Father we adore and Holy Spirit evermore (4)
290	but the fruitful ears to store in his garner evermore (3)
307	in its fullness undiminished shall for evermore remain (4)
310, 311	All praise and thanks to thee ascend for evermore (2)
326	O Lord, evermore to thy servants thy presence be nigh (2)
336	Come with us, O blessed Jesus, with us evermore to be (1)
362	which wert, and art, and evermore shalt be (2)
364	thou didst ascend to God's right hand in glory evermore (7)
365	highest praises be, hence evermore (4)
375	what God hath wrought ... he evermore sustaineth (3)
377, 378	from men and ... angel host be praise and glory evermore (5)

396, 397	for thus it was, is now, and shall be, evermore (3)
401	Who was, and is, the same, and evermore shall be (4)
401	sing the wonders of his grace for evermore (2)
410	evermore his praises sing (1)
416	For the Church which evermore lifteth holy hands above (5)
422	thy truth and light our dwelling place for evermore (3)
427	God's whole creation o'er both now and evermore (5)
428	bless the Lord and praise him evermore (1-5)
428	let those of holy, humble heart come praise him evermore (5)
437, 438	to children's children and for evermore (4)
448, 449	Trinity whom we adore for ever and for evermore (6)
460, 461	I am with you evermore (2)
481	Mortals, give thanks and sing, and triumph evermore (1)
496, 497	Praise be given evermore, by earth and heaven (3)
518	hereafter in thy glory evermore with thee to reign (4)
519, 520	thy gates ... they are open evermore (3)
525	she waits the consummation of peace for evermore (4)
527	the one almighty Father reigns in love for evermore (4)
567	praise thee evermore (3)
579	thus evermore shall rise to thee glad praise (4)
585	Love that gives, gives evermore (3)
594, 595	let the gift of thy salvation be our glory evermore (4)
606	for ever and for evermore, world without end (3)
608	thus evermore shall rise to thee glad hymns of praise (4)
619	glory for evermore; to thee we bring ... alleluia (7)
623	city of peace that brings joy evermore (2)
634	hold by thy word evermore, above all things (1)
658	be glory, as it was, is now, and shall be evermore (4)
665	Evermore from his store new-born worlds rise and adore (3)
668	guard thy going out and in, both now and evermore (4)
670	Israel, now and evermore in the Lord Almighty trust (4)
672	where thou, our everlasting Sun, art shining evermore (4)
690	bread of heaven, feed me now and evermore (1)
709	thou shalt be our covenant God and portion evermore (5)
710	give him glory evermore (RC)

every

8	praise every morning, God's recreation of the new day (3)
10	New every morning is the love (1)
10	love ... shall dawn on every cross and care (4)
10	help us ... every day, to live more nearly as we pray (6)
12, 13	we praise and bless you every hour (4)
18	teach us to hear its echoes still in every human misery (3c)
18	we praise and bless you every hour (5)
23	we praise and bless you every hour (4)
42	Comfort every sufferer watching late in pain (4)
47	let my every thought be thine (3)
57, 58	Every eye shall now behold him robed in dreadful majesty (2)
65	Let every hill and valley a level way appear (1)
65	His tidings of salvation proclaim in every place (3)
66	dear desire of every nation, joy of every longing heart (2)
71, 72	let every heart prepare a throne, and every voice a song (1)
76	Then cleansed be every breast from sin (2)

77	let every heart awake and sing the holy child (1)
81	from sin and death now save us, and share our every load (3)
82	every voice in concert ring (3)
98	came he to a world forlorn, the Lord of every nation (1,5)
100	let every heart prepare him room (1)
104	And every stone shall cry (1-4)
108	Let every house be bright; let praises never cease (2)
119	Holy Jesus, every day keep us in the narrow way (4)
143	to thee be every prayer addressed (5)
145	To shatter every yoke (3)
145	to fight, to fight till every wrong's set right (3)
151	If thou rememberest every sin (1)
175	every good gift of the year now with its Master returns (1)
179	bloom in every meadow, leaves on every bough (2)
181	wake every heart and every tongue (1)
182	conquer every place and time (2)
182	In every insult, rift, and war (4)
182	His Spirit burns through this and every future age (5)
182	conquer every place and time (2)
184	Christ has broken every chain (1)
193	from every weapon death can wield ... shield (4)
211	The birds do sing on every bough (1)
226, 227	Every bitter tear refine (2)
229	In every clime, by every tongue, be God's ... glory sung (2)
233, 234	true lights that lighten every land (2)
235	while each his own commission fulfills in every line (2)
236	crown of the true of every land (1)
238, 239	by contempt of every anguish, by unyielding battle done (2)
246	aching hearts in every land cry out (3)
246	conquer hate in every soul (5)
247	And every morn and day (3)
252	Unto which must every knee bow in deep humility (1)
255	that we, in every hour ... will trust your hidden power (2)
282, 283	may he, from us mortals, drive every evil (3)
282, 283	health-bringer blessed, aiding every sufferer (4)
284	unmasked in every dress, in every combat foiled (3)
288	bounteous source of every joy (1)
298	heavenly band of every tribe and nation (1)
300	Thankful for our every blessing, let us sing (2)
307	Cleansing us from every stain (4)
310, 311	our foes press on from every side (1)
315	grant us at every Eucharist to say ... Thy will be done (1)
319	Here at your table every life you nourish (1)
334	seeking peace in every nation (3)
337	deliver us from every touch of ill (4)
345	thy peace in life, the balm of every pain (4)
347	to serve God's people every day and hour (4)
347	serving Christ, our every gift employ (4)
353	every day their love renew (2)
353	join every husband, every wife in mutual love (3)
357	Every taint of evil, frailty and decay ... purge away (3)
365	thou, who almighty art, now rule in every heart (3)
368	God the Lord, through every nation ... shine (4)

368	In the song of thy salvation every tongue ... combine (4)
375	he watches o'er us every hour (3)
379	every child of every race (2)
380	Let the Redeemer's Name be sung through every land (1)
380	sung ... by every tongue (1)
394, 395	let every life be touched by grace (4)
402, 403	Let all the world in every corner sing, my God and King (R)
405	the ripe fruits in the garden, he made them every one (3)
406, 407	Sustained by thee through every hour, she bringeth forth (5)
408	every faithless murmur stills (1)
409	publishes to every land the work of an almighty hand (1)
413	revealed to every nation his everlasting righteousness (1)
413	let every instrument and voice peal out the praise (2)
416	offering up on every shore thy pure sacrifice of love (5)
419	center and soul of every sphere (1)
420	witness to the truth in every tongue (3)
420	Let every instrument be tuned for praise (5)
424	For his gifts to every nation (1)
434	every labor of his hands shows something worthy of a God (1)
435	At the Name of Jesus every knee shall bow (1)
435	every tongue confess him King of glory now (1)
450, 451	Let every kindred, every tribe on this terrestrial ball (6)
460, 461	Jesus out of every nation hath redeemed us by his blood (1,5)
471	sweetens every bitter cup (3)
477	Let every tongue confess with one accord (5)
484, 485	Praise the Lord through every nation (1)
484, 485	hymns on every tongue abound (1)
494	who every grief hath known that wrings the human breast (2)
500	Creator Spirit ... come visit every humble mind (1)
505	in every need thou bringest aid (1)
512	o'er every thought and step preside (1)
512	plant holy fear in every heart (2)
524	thy hand from every snare and foe ... deliverance bring (4)
525	Elect from every nation, yet one o'er all the earth (2)
525	to one hope she presses, with every grace endued (2)
531	Name of Jesus glorify till every people call him Lord (4)
532, 533	till earth's every people confess thee their God (2)
539	Proclaim to every people, tongue and nation (2)
539	make known to every heart his saving grace (4)
542	the Day-star clear and bright of every race and nation (1)
544	rise with every morning sacrifice (2)
544	Let every creature rise and bring peculiar honors (5)
545	freed from every weight of sin ... holy footsteps trace (2)
546	Awake, my soul, stretch every nerve (1)
546	Then wake, my soul, stretch every nerve (4)
559	yet possessing every blessing, if our God our Father be (1)
559	love with every passion blending (3)
561	till every foe is vanquished and Christ is Lord indeed (1)
568	stir every will to new ventures of faithfulness (3)
568	bind in thy love every nation and race (4)
573	through the thick darkness covering every nation (1)
576, 577	Banished now be anger, strife and every quarrel (2)
579	protect them ... from every peril on the land (2)
579	keep them by thy watchful care from every peril in the air (3)

210	Our hearts be pure from evil, that we may see aright (2)
216	guard us from harm without, cleanse us from evil within (3)
282, 283	may he, from us mortals, drive every evil (3)
302, 303	in mercy, save it from evil, guard it still (2)
347	render to no one evil (3)
357	Every taint of evil, frailty and decay ... purge away (3)
359	eloquent for righteousness that shall all evil break (2)
420	when utmost evil strove against the Light (4)
560	utters all manner of evil against you falsely for my sake (9)
594, 595	Lo, the hosts of evil round us scorn thy Christ (2)
635	bear thee through the evil days (1)
668	From evil he shall keep thee safe (4)
695, 696	still evil days bring burdens hard to bear (2)

evils
| 148 | evils wrought by human pride recoil on unrepentant heads (3) |
| 594, 595 | Save us from weak resignation to the evils we deplore (4) |

exalt
36	thee ... shall exalt for ever (3)
157	you are my God, and I will exalt you (R)
271, 272	His mighty deeds exalt his fame (4)
379	let creation sing before him... exalt him with one voice (1)
484, 485	exalt him on his Father's throne (1)
492	your songs exalt his reign (1)

exalted
75	valleys shall be exalted, the lofty hills brought low (1)
116	The Father speaks from heaven's exalted height (3)
154, 155	to thee, now high exalted, our melody we raise (4)
184	exalted now to save, wresting victory from the grave (3)
188, 189	following our exalted Head (3)
313	thou art my exalted King (4)
374	Worthy the Lamb that died, they cry, to be exalted thus (2)
477	Wherefore, by God's eternal purpose, thou ... exalted (4)
477	thou art high exalted o'er all creatures now (4)
606	grace to see your exalted glory, O Christ our God (3)
678, 679	tell out his exalted Name (2)

example
| 146, 147 | Christ by his own example sealed (2) |

exceeding
| 560 | Rejoice and be exceeding glad (9) |

exceeds
| 250 | His love abundant far exceeds ... a whole year's needs (3) |

excel
| 127 | Bethlehem thou dost all excel (1) |

excellent
| 636, 637 | is laid for your faith in his excellent word (1) |

excelling
219   in power and might excelling (1)
329, 331   the Blood, all price excelling (1)
657   Love divine, all loves excelling (1)

excels
517   One day within thy courts excels a thousand spent away (4)

excelsis
92   Ideo, Ideo, Ideo gloria in excelsis Deo (R)
96   Gloria in excelsis Deo (R)
114   in excelsis gloria (R)

exchange
281   O wise exchange, with these to part (4)

exclude
581   Love can exclude no race or creed if honored be God's Name (6)

exile
56   mourns in lonely exile here until the Son of God appear (1,8)
623   through our long exile on Babylon's strand (4)

exiled
231   John, your loved disciple, exiled to Patmos' shore (2/12-27)

exiles
122, 123   by Babylon's sad waters mourning exiles now are we (2)

expand
629   enlarge, expand all living souls to comprehend your love (3)

expect
624   Oh, sweet and blessed country that eager hearts expect (4)

expectation
68   up, watch in expectation, at midnight comes the cry (1)
68   Our hope and expectation, O Jesus, now appear (3)
527   Singing songs of expectation ... goes the pilgrim band (1)

expected
59   Lo, the Lamb, so long expected (3)
66   Come ... long-expected Jesus, born to set thy people free (1)
255   in those least expected true servants you can find (3)
463, 464   great city that has expected your return for years (2)

expects
156   Father ... expects his own anointed Son (4)

expends
585   ventures all, its all expends (3)

expense
585   hidden is love's agony, love's endeavor, love's expense (2)

expire
284   the Lord of life expire (5)

expired
168, 169   thy power is all expired ... quenched the light of light (2)

express
372   holy, no holiness of earth can his express (2)

expressed
37   in whom his truth and grace are visibly expressed (1)

extend
165, 166   the King of heavenly beauty gently on thine arms extend (5)
231   your true consolation may through the world extend (2/6-11)
484, 485   Thy reign extend world without end (2)
538   thy saving health extend unto earth's remotest end (1)

extended
168, 169   see in my last strife to me thine arms extended (5)
168, 169   thine arms extended upon the cross of life (5)

extends
467   from yon bright throne above ... extends his grace (1)
467   still to us extends his grace (1)
603, 604   Still east and west his love extends (2)

extol
82   extol our God and King (3)
284   With equal flame and equal art ... extol his Name (8)
284   do thou my heart extol his Name (8)
382   e'en eternity's too short to extol thee (3)
433   We all do extol thee, thou leader triumphant (3)
484, 485   with voice and minstrelsy extol his majesty: Alleluia (1)
511   thee we worship and extol (2)
535   the Name all-victorious of Jesus extol (1)

extolled
73   truth shall be extolled (4)

exult
375   mortals then, on land and sea ... exult (2)
375   exult in thy creative might (2)

exultant
235   Come sing, ye choirs exultant, those messengers of God (1)
336   Let the mighty chorus ever sing its glad exultant songs (3)
518   in exultant jubilation pours perpetual melody (2)

exultation
57, 58   cause of endless exultation to his ransomed worshipers (3)
83   Sing, choirs of angels, sing in exultation (3)
219   O day of exultation (2)
248, 249   but with holy exultation we may sing aloud today (1)
320   Zion, praise thy Savior, singing hymns with exultation (1)

320	hymns with exultation ringing (1)
591	in ire and exultation aflame with faith, and free (3)

exulting

213	on this festival day, come exulting away (1)
479	Oft as earth exulting wafts its praise on high (4)

exults

233, 234	the Son himself exults in them (4)

eye

57, 58	Every eye shall now behold him robed in dreadful majesty (2)
61, 62	No eye has known the sight, no ear heard such delight (3)
102	revealed to faithful eye (6)
258	blessed was the parent's eye that watched (1)
281	Enough ... to hear thy voice, to meet thine eye (3)
324	cherubim with sleepless eye (4)
362	though the sinful human eye thy glory may not see (3)
370	his eye to watch, his might to stay (5)
398	thy wonders are displayed where'er I turn my eye (2)
399	on us you keep your shepherd's eye (2)
408	his watchful eye ne'er sleepeth (2)
416	For the joy of ear and eye (3)
480	beneath his watchful eye (2)
496, 497	deigned to cast a pitying eye upon his helpless creature (2)
546	his own hand presents the prize to thine aspiring eye (3)
668	watchful and untiring eye he slumbers not, nor sleeps (2)
716	thou who art ever nigh, guarding with watchful eye (2)

eyed

573	Envious of heart, blind-eyed, with tongues confounded (3)

eyelids

42	with thy tenderest blessing may our eyelids close (2)
43	with sweet sleep mine eyelids close (3)
190	Raise your weary eyelids, Mary (2)
685	when mine eyelids close in death (3)

eyes

3, 4	From evil may he guard our eyes (3)
6, 7	glad my eyes, and warm my heart (2)
18	shield frail human eyes from all the woe you bore for us (3b)
40, 41	Although our eyes in sleep be closed (3)
102	And our eyes at last shall see him (5)
156	sad and wondering eyes to see the approaching sacrifice (3)
157	This is the Lord's doing, and it is marvelous in our eyes (R)
180	a brighter Easter beam on our longing eyes shall stream (4)
193	to their longing eyes restored (1)
212	nor will they trust their ears and eyes (2)
215	while their eager eyes behold him (2)
232	from all unrighteous mammon, O raise our eyes anew (2/9-21)
243	on his eyes a light wherewith God's daybreak to proclaim (2)
256	the scales fell from his eyes (3)
265	his wings as drifted snow, his eyes as flame (1)
284	E'en angel eyes slow tears did shed (5)

266	there he knelt down before her face (2)
276	slain by Herod's flashing blade, he saw thy face again (4)
284	his beauteous face in heaven ye view (1)
285	we, with him, thy face shall see (4)
286	blest they stand before his face (5)
314	face to face thy splendor, I at last shall see (4)
318	Here, O my Lord, I see the face to face (1)
325	when I fall on my knees, with my face to the rising sun (R)
337	Look Father, look on his anointed face (2)
347	till in his kingdom we behold his face (1)
357	where thy saints made perfect gaze upon thy face (4)
359	stand at last with joy before thy face (5)
371	Move on the waters' face bearing the gifts of grace (3)
394, 395	until we praise you face to face (4)
401	we shall behold his face, we shall his power adore (2)
410	Angels, help us to adore him, ye behold him face to face (4)
422	when we see thee face to face (3)
427	Sing, suns and stars of space ... ye that see his face (5)
430	Come ye all before his face (3)
465, 466	at last I come before your face to know you (3)
498	I ask no other sunshine than the sunshine of his face (3)
503, 504	Anoint and cheer our soiled face with ... thy grace (5)
538	God of mercy ... grace, show the brightness of thy face (1)
539	through thy neglect, unfit to see his face (4)
543	He gilds thy morning face with beams that cannot fade (2)
552, 553	lift up thine eyes and seek his face (2)
555	gladness breaks like morning where'er thy face appears (3)
563	When morn his face revealeth thy dangers all are past (4)
576, 577	when we see your face, O Savior, in its glory (3)
587	that they may all behold thy face (2)
603, 604	he sees not labels but a face, a person, and a name (3)
609	the true compassion of thy face (3)
613	oppression, lust, and crime shall flee thy face before (3)
620	they see God face to face (2)
625	now, from sin released, behold the Savior's face (2)
632	clouds and darkness ended, they see thee face to face (3)
642	sweeter far thy face to see and in thy presence rest (1)
658	O when shall I behold thy face, thou Majesty divine (2)
672	turn our face to where the daylight springs (5)
677	behind a frowning providence he hides a smiling face (4)
697	that I may see thy glorious face (3)

faces

145	For righteousness and peace will show their faces (4)
324	cherubim ... veil their faces to the Presence (4)
535	fall down on their faces, and worship the Lamb (3)

facing

580	facing us with life's destruction (3)
594, 595	for the facing of this hour (1)
599	facing the rising sun of our new day begun (1)

fade

129, 130	Law and prophets fade before him (4)

286	robes whose luster ne'er shall fade (2)
543	He gilds thy morning face with beams that cannot fade (2)
612	Prophecy will fade away, melting in the light of day (3)

fadeth

| 36 | Now, ere day fadeth quite, we see the evening light (2) |

fail

168, 169	My days are few, O fail not, with thine immortal power (5)
254	though mortal strength may fail (1)
271, 272	faithful hearts shall never fail ... his light to hail (1)
307	lest we fail to know thee now (2)
314	Taste and touch and vision to discern thee fail (2)
329, 331	though the senses fail to see (4)
373	never shall his promise fail (2)
388	in thee do we trust, nor find thee to fail (5)
414	Nor shall fail from memory's treasure works ... wrought (4)
426	shall Christians fail to sing till on earth Christ come (4)
445, 446	O wisest love, that flesh and blood, which ... did fail (3)
445, 446	flesh and blood, which did in Adam fail (3)
481	His kingdom cannot fail, he rules o'er earth and heaven (3)
539	he who made all nations is not willing one soul ... fail (1)
539	one soul should fail to know his love and might (1)
539	let none whom he hath ransomed fail to greet him (4)
561	arm of flesh will fail you, ye dare not trust your own (3)
562	we have Christ's own promise, and that cannot fail (4)
573	led by no star, the rulers of the nations still fail (4)
573	rulers ... still fail to bring us to the blissful birth (4)
662	when other helpers fail and comforts flee (1)

failed

| 251 | forgive ... the good we failed to do (2) |
| 698 | where I have failed, what I have done amiss (2) |

faileth

151	yea, e'en the best life faileth (2)
645, 646	whose goodness faileth never (1)
645, 646	through all the length of days thy goodness faileth never (6)

failing

231	so eager and so bold, thrice failing, yet repentant (2/1-18)
314	to my taste thy sweetness never failing give (3)
530	how his never-failing love guides us on to heaven above (4)
644	my never-failing treasury (3)
666	hopes are on thy promise built, thy never-failing word (2)
677	Deep in unfathomable mines, with never-failing skill (2)
687, 688	A mighty fortress is our God, a bulwark never failing (1)

fails

55	strength which never fails (4)
415	When nature fails (4)
522, 523	Grace which like the Lord, the giver, never fails (2)
522, 523	Grace ... never fails from age to age (2)
695, 696	never fails to greet us each new day (1)

failures
469, 470   no place ... earth's failures have such kindly judgment (2)

fain
498   Beneath the cross of Jesus I fain would take my stand (1)

faint
150   Victor in the wilderness, grant we may not faint nor fall (3)
308, 309   We faint with thirst, revive us (2)
347   strengthen the faint, give courage to the weak (2)
522, 523   Who can faint when such a river ever ... thirst assuage (2)
537   the faint and over-borne (1)
552, 553   Faint not nor fear, his arms are near (4)

fainting
135   Manifest in making whole palsied limbs and fainting soul (3)
168, 169   should I fainting be (4)
429   the Lord supports the fainting mind (3)
471   holds the fainting spirit up (3)
563   he can with bread of heaven thy fainting spirit feed (1)
691   May thy rich grace impart strength to my fainting heart (2)

faints
233, 234   the hope that never yields or faints (3)

fair
5   to make ill fortune turn to fair (4)
46   death's fair night discover ... everlasting life (3)
80   that in his kingdom bright and fair ... his glory share (4)
114   The earliest moon of winter-time is not so round and fair (3)
136, 137   O vision fair of glory that the Church may share (1)
162   O tree of beauty, tree most fair (3)
175   Lo the fair beauty of earth (1)
198   fair Easter, queen of all the days (1)
201   all to anoint fair Mary's Son (2)
202   arrayed in garments white and fair (1)
282, 283   Christ, the fair glory of the holy angels (1)
292   At temper fair with gentle air the sunshine and the rain (2)
383, 384   Fair are the meadows, fairer still the woodlands (2)
383, 384   Fair is the sunshine, fairer still the moonlight (3)
400   Fair rising morn, with praise rejoice (2)
582, 583   Already in the mind of God that city riseth fair (4)
617   one in the love of all things sweet and fair (2)
651   He trust us with his world, to keep it clean and fair (2)
702   In heaven? It is thy dwelling fair (3)

fairer
127   Fairer than the sun at morning was the star (2)
193   the sun shone out with fairer light (1)
383, 384   Fair are the meadows, fairer still the woodlands (2)
383, 384   Jesus is fairer, Jesus is purer (2)
383, 384   Fair is the sunshine, fairer still the moonlight (3)
392   we're marching through Emmanuel's ground to fairer worlds (4)
392   fairer worlds on high (4)
543   with his radiance fill those fairer purer skies (4)

fairest

277	Fairest child of fairest mother (1)
383, 384	Fairest Lord Jesus, Ruler of all nature (1)
434	here, on the cross, 'tis fairest drawn in precious blood (2)

faith

9	of faith and hope and love undimmed (3)
55	Our faith reflects those radiant beams (5)
78, 79	charity stands watching and faith holds wide the door (4)
133, 134	Two prophets, who had faith to see (2)
146, 147	The covenant, so long revealed to those of faith (2)
146, 147	those of faith in former time (2)
185, 186	faith lives upon no other (4)
192	our faith had been in vain (R)
206	yet whose faith has constant been (6)
209	We walk by faith, and not by sight (1)
209	may our faith abound (3)
209	that, when our life of faith is done (4)
215	in thine ascension, we by faith behold our own (3)
231	a steadfast faith afford (2/12-21)
231	his faith, in death, confessed (2/12-26)
232	her faith was first to see you, her Lord (2/7-22)
232	saw the risen Savior and placed his faith in him (2/10-23)
232	the faith of Christ maintain (2/10-28)
233, 234	Theirs is the steadfast faith of saints (3)
236	hear us as now we celebrate faith undeterrred (2)
236	faith undeterred by cruel hate (2)
237	for by faith they saw the land decked in all its glory (2)
238, 239	Faith prevailing, hope unfailing (2)
242	mid all its light his faith was dim (2)
245	the faith to bear your Name (3)
253	Give us wings of faith to rise within the veil (1)
260	for him ... was the patient life of faith and humble name (3)
268, 269	Ye who claim the faith of Jesus (1)
273, 274	Two stalwart trees both rooted in faith and holy love (1)
280	All his faith and prayer and patience (3)
287	Who thee by faith before the world confessed (1)
297	Confirm our faith, consume our doubt (1)
302, 303	Knowledge and faith and life immortal Jesus ... imparts (1)
305, 306	faith still receives the cup as from thy hand (2)
314	faith, that comes by hearing, pierces through the veil (2)
314	Jesus, whom now hidden, I by faith behold (4)
329, 331	faith alone the true heart waketh to behold the mystery (4)
329-331	faith, our outward sense befriending, makes ... clear (5)
337	our prayer so languid, and our faith so dim (2)
349	patient faith, the crown to win (2)
357	in faith gone from us, now in death repose (2)
363	from thee have flowed, as from a mighty river, our faith (4)
363	our faith and hope, our fellowship and peace (4)
364	holy Church in faith acclaims thy Son who for us died (5)
369	let faith in humble notes adore the great mysterious King (4)
370	by power of faith (2)
370	confessors' faith, apostles' word (3)
392	celestial fruits ... from faith and hope may grow (3)
416	faith and hope and love divine (6)

420	the Church, in liturgy and song, in faith and love (3)
420	may God give us faith to sing always Alleluia, Amen. (5)
422	For each new step of faith we take thou hast more truth (1)
426	learning here, by faith and love ... to sing above (5)
452	faith achieves what reason planned (3)
453	many millions by faith now are climbing it still (2)
453	remember, each step that by faith we pass o'er (3)
460, 461	he is near us, faith believes, nor questions how (2)
482	Lord of all eagerness, Lord of all faith (2)
486	in faith thy parting promise claim (3)
505	increase our faith in our dear Lord (2)
513	to the Church in faith assembled (2)
521	steadfast faith our unity, their peace our heritage (3)
525	her charter of salvation, one Lord, one faith, one birth (2)
526	by faith we join our hands with those that went before (4)
527	one the faith which never tires (2)
528	faith and hope and love restoring (5)
529	Join hands, disciples of the faith (2)
545	Jesus, the author, finisher, rewarder of our faith (3)
547	one Lord, one Faith ... Baptism, one Father of us all (3)
547	Awake, arise, go forth in faith (5)
558	Faith of our fathers (1-3,R)
558	holy faith! We will be true to thee till death (R)
558	faith and prayer shall win all nations unto thee (2)
563	O pray that faith and virtue may keep thee to the last (4)
566	From thee ... all calm and courage, faith and hope (1)
591	in ire and exultation aflame with faith, and free (3)
593	Where all is doubt, may we sow faith (2)
594, 595	free our hearts to faith and praise (2)
599	Sing a song full of the faith (1)
599	faith that the dark past has taught us (1)
600, 601	quiet of a steadfast faith, calm of a call obeyed (2)
607	with faith that none can alter, your servants undergird (3)
612	Faith and hope and love we see (4)
614	who with a faith for ever new followed the King (1)
614	with the same faith his word proclaim (2)
628	to live the faith which we proclaim (2)
633	touch our hearts and bring to birth faith and hope (1)
634	steadfast faith grant me therefore (1)
634	never resisting but to increase in faith more and more (1)
636, 637	is laid for your faith in his excellent word (1)
647	their faith and hope still guiding me (2)
647	with them, the pilgrims of the faith (3)
649, 650	blest, when our faith can hold you fast (3)
659, 660	in work that keeps faith sweet and strong (3)
670	What thy Spirit doth reveal, that may I in faith receive (3)
672	We wait in faith (5)
691	My faith looks up to thee, thou Lamb of Calvary (1)
704	my acts of faith and love repeat (4)

faith's

| 307 | here for faith's discernment pray we (2) |

faithful

| 12, 13 | the third hour your faithful band was clothed with power (3) |

faithful

16, 17	each day the sun at zenith calls the faithful (1)
16, 17	calls the faithful to their noon-day prayers (1)
40, 41	direct our faithful household Lord (4)
51	school for the faithful, refuge for the sinner (2)
83	O come, all ye faithful, joyful and triumphant (1)
102	revealed to faithful eye (6)
116	faithful to the Lord's commands (2)
122, 123	at the last to keep thine Easter with thy faithful saints (4)
122, 123	with thy faithful saints on high (4)
133, 134	To you, the King of glory ... faithful hearts ... bow (3)
133, 134	now all faithful hearts adoring bow (3)
136, 137	faithful hearts are raised on high by this ... mystery (4)
149	you, the first-born of all the faithful dead (3)
151	I rest upon his faithful word to them of contrite spirit (3)
165, 166	Faithful cross, above all other, one and only noble tree (4)
179	come then, true and faithful, now fulfill thy word (5)
199, 200	Come, ye faithful, raise the strain of triumphant gladness (1)
201	day ... whereon the faithful give God praise (1)
203	the faithful women went their way to seek the tomb (2)
231	for his faithful record we praise you evermore (2/12-27)
231	Lord, make your pastors faithful (2/1-18)
231	as faithful branches grow strong in you, the Vine (2/4-25)
231	young James the faithful, who heard and followed you (2/5-1)
232	wholeness was restored by you, her faithful Master (2/7-22)
236	living, were faithful to thy Name (3)
243	no shield I ask, no faithful friend (4)
245	faithful shepherd of the flock ... sheep-fold's only door (2)
261, 262	grant that we also may like him be faithful (3)
261, 262	faithful in our obedience (3)
267	The prophet gave the sign for faithful folk to read (2)
268, 269	let all faithful people sing the honor of her name (3)
271, 272	faithful hearts shall never fail ... his light to hail (1)
280	for this faithful saint we offer ... our thanks to you (2)
280	There are named the blessed faithful of the new Jerusalem (4)
285	through weary years of toil and strife ... faithful (3)
285	still found faithful to the end (3)
287	O may thy soldiers, faithful, true, and bold (3)
287	soon, soon to faithful warriors cometh rest (6)
289	our Father, make us faithful to serve the coming days (3)
324	the Body and the Blood he will give to all the faithful (2)
327, 328	Approach ye then with faithful hearts sincere (5)
332	Here may thy faithful people know ... thy love (2)
334	may we faithful followers be (3)
344	ever faithful to thy truth may we be found (2)
389	for his mercies ay endure, ever faithful, ever sure (R)
469, 470	If our love were but more faithful (3)
472	we would be faithful to thy gospel glorious (4)
492	Sing, ye faithful, sing with gladness (1)
514	To thee, whose faithful love had place in ... grace (2)
514	To thee, whose faithful power doth heal (3)
519, 520	by virtue of his merits thither faithful souls do soar (3)
536	Open your ears, O faithful people (1,4)
578	Where rest but on thy faithful word (3)

615	faithful souls have yearned to see ... that kingdom's day (1)
657	all thy faithful mercies crown (1)
668	Thy faithful guardian is the Lord (3)
669	him whose faithful mercy the skies above declare (1)

faithfully

18	so may we struggle faithfully (2a)
294	faithfully now God's praises we sing (1)
435	faithfully he bore it spotless to the last (2)
635	so do thine own part faithfully (2)

faithfulness

410	Glorious in his faithfulness (2)
568	stir every will to new ventures of faithfulness (3)

faithless

206	not faithless, but believing be (4)
408	every faithless murmur stills (1)
541	Away with gloomy doubts and faithless fear (3)

fall

8	Sweet the rain's new fall sunlit from heaven (2)
33-35	stars appearing hallow the night-fall (2)
49	rise again to fall no more (2)
150	Victor in the wilderness, grant we may not faint nor fall (3)
170	though empires rise and fall ... Kingdom shall not cease (3)
179	thou from heaven beholding human nature's fall (4)
213	sing, all heaven, and fall at his feet (5)
325	when I fall on my knees, with my face to the rising sun (R)
413	fall before the Mighty One (1)
427	When evening shadows fall, this rings my curfew call (1)
450, 451	Let angels prostrate fall (1)
450, 451	heirs of Israel's chosen race, ye ransomed from the fall (4)
484, 485	we bow the knee, we fall before thee (2)
494	Crown him with many crowns, as thrones before him fall (5)
524	For her my tears shall fall, for her my prayers ascend (2)
535	fall down on their faces, and worship the Lamb (3)
597	May swords of hate fall from our hands (1)
623	Low before him with our praises we fall (5)
642	to those who fall, how kind thou art (3)
665	tower and temple fall to dust (2)
665	ye who follow shall not fall (5)
697	Before the cross of him who died, behold, I prostrate fall (2)

fallen

76	bid the fallen sinner stand (4)
77	his fallen creatures all to save (2)
85, 86	O Savior of our fallen race (1)
85, 86	how once, to save our fallen race (3)
88	he on Adam's fallen race sheds the fullness of his grace (3)
112	snow had fallen snow on snow (1)
179	all that now is fallen raise to life again (6)
252	Jesus, Name of priceless worth to the fallen of the earth (3)
443	bade the fallen to come in, praised be his mercy (3)

far

67	in the desert far and near (2)
100	he comes to make his blessings flow far as the curse (3)
100	far as the curse is found (3)
109	shining in the east beyond them far (2)
109	three wise men came from country far (3)
114	The chiefs from far before him knelt with gifts of fox (3)
117, 118	richer by far is the heart's adoration (4)
131, 132	The eastern sages saw from far (2)
148	far and wide the wreckage of our hatred spreads (3)
149	far off yet here -- the goal of all desire (1)
167	There is a green hill far away, outside a city wall (1)
168, 169	Ah me! for whom thou diest, hide not so far thy grace (2)
250	His love abundant far exceeds ... a whole year's needs (3)
268, 269	more blessed far the mother ... who bore him in her womb (2)
291	He only is the Maker of all things near and far (2)
304	I come with Christians far and near (2)
346	as far as lies within our mortal power (1)
369	still how far beneath thy feet our ... knowledge lies (3)
371	rolling in fullest pride, through the world far and wide (4)
422	Not far beyond the sea, nor high above the heavens (1)
459	heaven ... knows neither near nor far (2)
474	that were an offering far too small (4)
491	Far beyond the seraph's thought (2)
503, 504	Keep far our foes, give peace at home (6)
516	yearning ... shall far outpass the power of human telling (3)
527	chasing far the gloom and terror (2)
527	one the gladness of rejoicing on the far eternal shore (3)
531	far and nigh the triumphs of the cross record (4)
563	far more o'er thee are watching than human eyes can know (2)
580	As each far horizon beckons, may it challenge us anew (4)
584	yet greater far this gift, O God, bestow (2)
599	thou who hast brought us thus far on the way (3)
602	neighbors are near-by and far away (2)
603, 604	always, near or far, he calls and claims us (2)
613	wherever near or far thick darkness broodeth yet (5)
642	sweeter far thy face to see and in thy presence rest (1)
659, 660	in hope that sends a shining ray far down the ... way (4)
671	'tis grace that brought me safe thus far (4)
702	far away my dwelling make (4)

farthest

287	From earth's wide bounds, from ocean's farthest coast (8)
394, 395	your fingers trace the bold designs of farthest space (1)

fashion

47	Maker, who didst fashion me image of thyself to be (3)
77	Behold, the world's creator wears the form and fashion (2)
77	form and fashion of a slave (2)

fashioned

268, 269	blessed ... land of promise fashioned for his ... home (2)
268, 269	fashioned for his earthly home (2)
519, 520	of pure gold are fashioned (2)
611	Yoke maker, fashioned by his hands (4)

fast

142	Lord, who throughout these forty days for us didst fast (1)
142	for us didst fast and pray (1)
143	Then grant us, Lord, like them to be full oft in fast (4)
143	full oft in fast and prayer with thee (4)
145	For is not this the fast that I have chosen (3)
146, 147	keep vigil ... in his temptation and his fast (1)
152	the penitent who keep this holy fast of Lent (1)
152	fast of forty days may work our profit and thy praise (5)
347	hold fast the good, be urgent for the right (3)
388	hath stablished it fast by a changeless decree (3)
443	yet in the wilderness did fast (2)
448, 449	for us he bore his holy fast and hungered sore (2)
649, 650	blest, when our faith can hold you fast (3)
662	Abide with me, fast falls the eventide (1)
669	God, in his great mercy, will save thee, hold thee fast (4)
672	the east is brightening fast (3)
677	He purposes will ripen fast, unfolding every hour (5)

fasted

143	Christ ... himself has fasted and has prayed (1)

fasting

122, 123	our Savior in his fasting pleasures of the world forebore (3)
143	Alone and fasting Moses saw the loving God (2)
143	to Elijah fasting, came the steeds and chariots of flame (2)
150	Forty days and forty nights thou wast fasting in the wild (1)
150	fasting with unceasing prayer (2)
152	abstinence in outward things with inward fasting (4)

Father

1, 2	Father, we praise thee, now the night is over (1)
1, 2	All holy Father, Son, and equal Spirit, Trinity blessed (3)
3, 4	To God the Father, heavenly Light (5)
5	With prayer the Father we implore (3)
5	O Father, glorious evermore, we plead with thee (3)
5	All laud to God the Father be (5)
11	praise Father, Son and Holy Ghost (4)
14, 15	Almighty Father, hear our cry through Jesus Christ (3)
19, 20	Now Holy Spirit, ever One with God the Father and the Son (1)
19, 20	Almighty Father, hear our cry through Jesus Christ (3)
21, 22	Almighty Father, hear our cry (3)
25, 26	Praise Father, Son, and Spirit (2)
27, 28	we pray you, Father, calm our fears (2)
27, 28	Eternal Father, help us rise (4)
27, 28	Defend us, Father, through the night (5)
29, 30	To God the Father, heavenly Light (3)
36	Father of might unknown (2)
37	we hymn the eternal Father ... Son ... Holy Ghost divine (2)
38, 39	Word of the Father throned on high (1)
43	praise Father, Son, and Holy Ghost (4)
44, 45	Almighty Father, hear our cry (4)
48	We sing to thee our praises, O Father, Spirit, Son (4)
52	All praise to God the Father be (4)
55	With God the Father you are one (4)

59	Honor, glory, might, and blessing to the Father ... Son (4)
60	To God the Father ... Son, ... Spirit, Three in One (6)
63, 63	To God the Father ... Son ... Spirit, ever One (5)
76	whom with the Father we adore and Holy Spirit evermore (5)
77	All glory for this blessed morn to God the Father ever be (5)
80	The blessing which the Father planned (4)
82	Christ, to thee with God the Father (4)
83	only begotten Son of the Father (2)
83	Word of the Father, now in flesh appearing (6)
85, 86	whom with the Father we adore and Holy Spirit evermore (6)
88	that we ever one may be with the Father and with thee (5)
92	born on earth to save us; him the Father gave us (1)
97	Father, glory be to thee for the wondrous charity (3)
105	From God our heavenly Father a blessed angel came (2)
110	to praise the Father, Son, and Holy Ghost (4)
116	The Father speaks from heaven's exalted height (3)
120	chose the path his Father willed (1)
124	To God the Father, heavenly Light (5)
127	unto thee, with God the Father and the Spirit, glory be (5)
131, 132	whom with the Father we adore and Holy Ghost for evermore (5)
136, 137	O Father, with the eternal Son ... Holy Spirit, ever One (5)
143	O Father, Son, and Spirit blest (5)
144	The universe your glory shows, blest Father, Spirit, Son (5)
156	Father on his sapphire throne (4)
156	Father ... expects his own anointed Son (4)
165, 166	Praise and honor to the Father (6)
174	Hymns of glory, songs of praise, Father ... we raise (4)
175	Redeemer, Son of the Father supreme, only begotten of God (6)
182	our Savior with the Father reigns (3)
183	Christ ... reconcileth sinners to the Father (2)
193	to God the Father equal praise (5)
202	all praise to God the Father be and Holy Ghost eternally (5)
205	To God the Father ... Son ... Spirit, always One (5)
207	Father, Son, and Holy Ghost (4)
211	To Father, Son, and Holy Ghost (4)
213	days, by our heavenly Father bestowed (2)
213	Hallelujah we sing, to our Father and King (5)
216	Son of the Father supreme, only begotten of God (4)
217, 218	while endless ages run, with Father and with Spirit, One (3)
220	with Father and with Spirit, One (4)
221	with Father and with Spirit, One. Alleluia (4)
225	Forth from the Father he comes with ... mystical offering (2)
228	Father of the fatherless, giver of gifts limitless (1)
231	Joseph's love made "Father" to be ... God's Name (2/3-19)
231, 232	Then let us praise the Father and worship God the Son (3)
236	Glory to God the Father be (4)
257	All glory to the Father be, all glory to the Son (5)
261, 262	to his earthly father freely was subject (2)
263, 264	whom with the Father we adore and Holy Spirit evermore (4)
268, 269	when the love of God the Father over sin the victory won (1)
271, 272	To God the Father, God the Son ... Spirit, Three in One (5)
273, 274	All glory to the Father, all glory to the Son (4)
277	Glory be to God the Father ... Son ... the Spirit (3)
282, 283	Father Almighty, Son and Holy Spirit, God ever blessed (6)
287	singing to Father, Son, and Holy Ghost, Alleluia (8)

289	Our Father, by whose servants our house was built of old (1)
289	our Father, make us faithful to serve the coming days (3)
291	We thank thee ... O Father, for all things bright and good (3)
294	born of one Father, we are his children (3)
302, 303	Father, we thank thee who hast planted thy holy Name (1)
326	thy Name with the Father and Spirit be ever adored (1)
329-331	Glory let us give and blessing to the Father and the Son (6)
335	No one can come to me unless the Father draw them (1)
337	And now, O Father, mindful of the love that bought us (1)
337	Look Father, look on his anointed face (2)
338	Wherefore, O Father, we thy humble servants here bring (1)
360, 361	God in three Persons, Father everlasting (6)
363	O holy Father, who hast led thy children in all the ages (2)
364	everlasting Father art, by all the earth adored (1)
365	Father whose love unknown all things created own (1)
366	Holy Father, holy Son, Holy Spirit, three we name thee (4)
368	Holy Father, great Creator (1)
368	heavenly Father, through the Savior hear and bless (1)
370	eternal Father, Spirit, Word (7)
375	Give praise and glory unto God ... Father of all blessing (1)
376	Thou our Father, Christ our Brother (3)
377, 378	To Father, Son, and Holy Ghost (5)
380	praise Father, Son, and Holy Ghost (3)
381	God the Father, Light-Creator, to thee laud and honor be (4)
396, 397	All praise and thanks to God the Father now be given (3)
399	Your heavenly Father praise, acclaim his only Son (3)
400	Praise God the Father, praise the Son (7)
401	"Hail, Father, Son, and Holy Ghost" they ever cry (5)
401	eternal Father, great I AM, we worship thee (4)
421	We bless, we worship you ... O God, Almighty Father (1)
421	Lamb of God ... whom God the Father gave us (2)
455, 456	sent by the Father from on high, our life to live (3)
457	who would the Father seek, must seek him, Lord, by thee (1)
477	God the Father be by all adored. Alleluia, Amen. (5)
488	thou my great Father, thine own may I be (2)
490	show me the way to the Father (2)
500	give us thyself, that we may see the Father and the Son (3)
501, 502	Praise to the Father, Christ, his Word (6)
503, 504	Teach us to know the Father, Son, and thee (7)
503, 504	praise to thy eternal merit, Father, Son and Holy Spirit (9)
505	from God, the Father and the Son (1)
506, 507	Praise, O praise the Holy Spirit, praise the Father (6)
519, 520	Laud and honor to the Father (5)
527	the one almighty Father reigns in love for evermore (4)
528	Father, what they do, forgive (4)
529	Who serves my Father as his child is surely kin to me (2)
547	one Lord, one Faith ... Baptism, one Father of us all (3)
559	Lead us, heavenly Father (1)
559	yet possessing every blessing, if our God our Father be (1)
568	Father all loving, who rulest in majesty (1)
568	Father, Redeemer, and Spirit of grace (4)
573	Father eternal, Ruler of creation (1)
574, 575	bring us, O Father, nearer thee (1)
579	Almighty Father, strong to save (1)
579	Spirit ... the Father sent to spread abroad the firmament (3)

581	our common life embraces all whose Father is the same (6)
587	Our Father, by whose Name all fatherhood is known (1)
608	Eternal Father, strong to save (1)
618	To God the Father ... Son ... Spirit, Three in One (4)
623	of whom, the Father, and in whom the Son (5)
624	who art, with God the Father, and Spirit, ever blest (4)
629	O Father, Son, and Spirit, send us increase from above (3)
651	God is our Father yet (2)
652, 653	Dear Lord and Father of mankind forgive our foolish ways (1)
658	To Father, Son, and Holy Ghost, the God whom we adore (4)
669	Thy lasting truth and mercy, O Father, see aright (3)
700	Love of the living God, of Father and of Son (4)
703	Lead us, O Father, in the paths of peace (1)
703	Lead us, O Father, in the paths of right (2)
703	Lead us, O Father, to the heavenly rest (3)

Father's

25, 26	in you the Father's glory shone (1)
36	O gladsome Light, O grace of God the Father's face (1)
37	O brightness of the immortal Father's face (1)
47	God the Father's Name we praise (1)
50	comes, in God his Father's name, to save our sinful race (4)
54	Come, O Father's saving Son, who o'er sin the victory won (4)
63, 64	begotten of the Father's might (1)
82	Of the Father's love begotten, ere the worlds began to be (1)
85, 86	O Brightness of the Father's face (1)
85, 86	O Son who shared the Father's might (1)
85, 86	For from the Father's throne you came (5)
120	the Father's voice did then declare (2)
120	the sign of God the Father's love (3)
133, 134	your Father's voice his Son proclaimed (2)
139	Jesus went to Jordan's stream his Father's will obeying (1)
149	so in the Father's glory shall we wake (3)
173	God the Father's only Son in the tomb is lying (1)
179	of the Father's God-head true and only Son (4)
220, 221	Ascending to the Father's throne (2)
233, 234	In them the Father's glory shone (4)
259	thus to his Father's house he comes, the heavenly guest (2)
259	before thy Father's face may all presented be (4)
260	now within the Father's grace (4)
276	For James who left his father's side (2)
292	with the Father's Name ... Savior's love proclaim (3)
292	with the Father's Name, and with the Holy Spirit's gifts (3)
296	The Father's splendor clothes the Son with life (3)
321	gather from their Father's board the Bread that lives (3)
333	Now the keeling Now the plea ... Father's arms in welcome (1)
333	Now the Father's blessing Now Now Now (1)
340, 341	our blessed ones adore you, seated at our Father's board (3)
351	Father's boundless love, with the Holy Spirit's favor (1)
421	with the Spirit, you alone share in the Father's glory (3)
434	worship at his Father's throne (5)
435	'tis the Father's pleasure we should call him Lord (1)
435	to the throne of Godhead, to the Father's breast (3)
435	with his Father's glory o'er the earth to reign (6)
478	the Father's conquering Word, true source of gladness (1)

480	When Jesus left his Father's throne (1)
484, 485	exalt him on his Father's throne (1)
492	from his Father's throne the Son rules and guides (4)
495	seated at the Father's side (3)
500	the Father's promised Paraclete (2)
505	teach us to know the Father's love (4)
530	word of how the Father's will made the world (2)
556, 557	pilgrims find their Father's house, Jerusalem the blest (6)
633	Word that speaks your Father's love (4)
651	This is my Father's world (1,2)
709	at our Father's loved abode our souls arrive in peace (4)
717	Our father's God, to thee, author of liberty (4)

fatherhood
587	Our Father, by whose Name all fatherhood is known (1)

fatherless
228	Father of the fatherless, giver of gifts limitless (1)
429	the widowed and the fatherless (3)

fathers
558	Faith of our fathers (1-3,R)
717	land where my fathers died, land of the pilgrim's pride (1)
718	God of our fathers, whose almighty hand leads forth (1)

faults
574, 575	teach us to know our faults, O God (2)
581	Forgive we now each other's faults ... our faults confess (3)

favor
117, 118	vainly with gifts would his favor secure (4)
139	This is my dear beloved Son upon whom rests my favor (1)
351	Father's boundless love, with the Holy Spirit's favor (1)
360, 361	by thy past blessings, by thy present bounty, favor (5)
360, 361	favor thy children (5)
363	still imploring thy love and favor, kept to us always (5)
410	Praise him for his grace and favor to his people (2)
410	grace and favor to his people in distress (2)
495	By thy merit we find favor (1)
708	Early let us seek thy favor, early let us learn thy will (2)

favored
265	most highly favored lady, "Gloria!" (1-4)
267	Mary, the pure and lowly maid, the favored of the Lord (4)

fear
59	the world is wrapped in fear (4)
93	watching long in hope and fear (4)
94, 95	"Fear not" said he (2)
98	Herod then with fear was filled (3)
105	Fear not then, said the angel, Let nothing you affright (3)
107	now ye need not fear the grave (3)
113	You need not fear King Herod (2)
115	Good Christian, fear (2)
140, 141	I have a sin of fear that when I've spun my last thread (3)

140, 141	fear ... I shall perish on the shore (3)
140, 141	having done that, thou hast done, I fear no more (3)
145	Now quit your care and anxious fear and worry (1)
203	That night the apostles met in fear (4)
206	That night the apostles met in fear (2)
237	turn from fear, and heed the call to a glorious morrow (3)
250	what need we fear in earth or space in this new year (4)
255	Saul, the church's spoiler came spreading fear and hate (1)
266	Said the angel, "Have no fear ..." (4)
299	hearts grown cold with fear (3)
324	and with fear and trembling stand (1)
332	thus inspired with holy fear, before thine altar kneel (1)
344	fear of death shall not appall us (3)
353	the perfect love that casts out fear (1)
360, 361	sin is forgiven, hope o'er fear prevaileth (3)
404	your mighty acts with joy and fear relate (2)
440	to seek and love and fear thee (1)
475	souls in silence fear him (1)
512	plant holy fear in every heart (2)
521	hatred and tormenting fear pass with the passing night (2)
522, 523	all fear of want remove (2)
532, 533	O who shall not fear thee, and honor thy Name (1)
541	Away with gloomy doubts and faithless fear (3)
542	when Christ is throned as Lord all ... forsake their fear (2)
547	To us on earth he came to bring from sin and fear release (2)
552, 553	Faint not nor fear, his arms are near (4)
563	fear not the secret foe (2)
563	fear not the gathering night (4)
564, 565	Then fancies flee away; I'll fear not what men say (3)
573	in wrath and fear, by jealousies surrounded (3)
576, 577	Let us fear and love him, holy God eternal (1)
581	With grateful joy and holy fear his charity we learn (2)
584	Let wisdom's godly fear dispel the fears ... hate impart (3)
607	hate and fear divide us and bitter threats are hurled (1)
607	fear of rattling saber, from dread of war's increase (3)
636, 637	Fear not, I am with thee, O be not dismayed (2)
643	O how I fear thee, living God (4)
643	fear ... with deepest, tenderest fears (4)
644	drives away our fear (1)
645, 646	In death's dark vale I fear no ill (4)
645, 646	I fear no ill with thee, dear Lord, beside me (4)
647	I must not fear nor stray (3)
655	I shall not fear the battle, if thou art by my side (1)
662	I fear no foe, with thee at hand to bless (3)
663	I will not fear, for thou art here to comfort and to aid (3)
669	fear not the griefs that plague thee (4)
671	'Twas grace that taught my heart to fear (2)
678, 679	trusting him, I shall not fear (1)
682	nor yet for fear that loving not I might for ever die (1)
682	not for the sake of winning heaven, nor any fear of hell (4)
687, 688	we will not fear (3)
700	O love that casts out fear, O love that casts out sin (1)
715	a trembling fear seized all the guilty world around (RC)

feared

99	The shepherds feared and trembled (2)
266	feared that she had done a wrong (3)

fearful

168, 169	hold me that I quail not in death's most fearful hour (5)
180	Come, ye sad and fearful hearted (2)
256	to save him from his fearful ways and free him (2)
296	Embraced by death he broke its fearful hold (1)
472	Christ of great compassion, speak to our fearful hearts (1)
472	speak to our fearful hearts by conflict rent (1)
677	Ye fearful saints, fresh courage take (3)

fearless

527	stepping fearless through the night (1)

fears

27, 28	we pray you, Father, calm our fears (2)
44, 45	so calm our minds that fears may cease (2)
66	from our fears and sins release us (1)
78, 79	hopes and fears of all the years are met in thee tonight (1)
289	long spent their hopes and fears (2)
441, 442	hopes deceive and fears annoy (2)
493	Jesus, the Name that charms our fears (3)
555	we follow, not with fears (3)
584	Let wisdom's godly fear dispel the fears ... hate impart (3)
594, 595	From the fears that long have bound us free our hearts (2)
609	on shadowed thresholds dark with fears (2)
643	fear ... with deepest, tenderest fears (4)
664	one word of thy supporting breath drives ... fears away (2)
671	grace my fears relieved (2)
672	Our hopes are weak, our fears are strong (2)
690	bid my anxious fears subside (3)
693	fightings and fears within, without (2)

feast

61, 62	that you the wedding feast may share (1)
68	The marriage-feast is waiting, the gates wide open stand (2)
174	At the Lamb's high feast we sing praise (1)
174	gives his Body for the feast (1)
180	symbol of our Easter feast (3)
185, 185	let us feast this holy day on the true bread of heaven (4)
199, 200	with the royal feast of feasts, comes its joy to render (3)
213	till we meet at the feast of the Lamb (4)
300	us he leads to a feast in heaven (3)
301	be thy feast to us the token that ... our souls are fed (1)
305, 306	nay, let us be thy guests, the feast is thine (1)
316, 317	here let me feast, and feasting still prolong (1)
316, 317	the feast, though not the love, is past and gone (2)
316, 317	Feast after feast thus comes and passes by (3)
316, 317	yet, passing, points to the glad feast above (3)
319	for this feast of our salvation (1)
320	today the new oblation ... bids us feast in glad array (4)
320	where the heavenly feast thou showest (6)
329, 331	Jesus, with the Law complying, keeps the feast (3)

332	We come, obedient to thy word, to feast on heavenly food (3)
417, 418	This is the feast of victory for our God. Alleluia (R)
443	He joined with guests at wedding feast (2)
460, 461	Priest and Victim in the eucharistic feast (4)
487	Come, my Light, my Feast, my Strength (2)
487	such a light as shows a feast (2)
487	such a feast as mends in length (2)
624	the song of them that feast (3)
649, 650	long to feast upon you still (2)

feasting

316, 317	here let me feast, and feasting still prolong (1)

feasts

199, 200	with the royal feast of feasts, comes its joy to render (3)
238, 239	Blessed feasts of blessed martyrs, holy women, holy men (1)

fed

258	Blessed was the breast that fed thee (1)
278	Mary at whose breast the child was fed who is Son of God (1)
291	but it is fed and watered by God's almighty hand (1)
291	the winds and waves obey him, by him the birds are fed (2)
301	be thy feast to us the token that ... our souls are fed (1)
301	by thy grace our souls are fed (1)
304	to find, as all are fed (2)
312	bodies by thy Body fed with thy new life replenish (3)
323	ever may our souls be fed with this true and living Bread (1)
437, 438	the hungry fed, the humble lifted high (3)
667	beneath the spreading heavens no creature but is fed (3)
709	O God of Bethel, by whose hand thy people still are fed (1)

feeble

388	Frail children of dust, and feeble as frail (5)
410	well our feeble frame he knows (3)
411	He pardons all thy sins, prolongs thy feeble breath (4)
471	nerves the feeble arm for fight (4)
677	Judge not the Lord by feeble sense (4)
681	tried with thoughts uncouth, in feeble words to bind thee (2)

feeblest

541	by feeblest agents may our God fulfill his righteous will (3)

feebly

287	We feebly struggle, they in glory shine (4)
452	what self rejects yet feebly wills (4)

feed

75	He shall feed his flock like a shepherd (3)
120	On you may all your people feed (6)
145	who feed the hungry in their need, and wrongs redress (4)
185, 186	Christ alone our souls will feed (4)
231	thrice charged to feed your fold (2/1-18)
292	that we may feed the poor aright (3)
318	Here would I feed upon the Bread of God (2)
323	Bread of heaven, on thee we feed (1)

377, 378	we are his folk, he doth us feed (2)
389	All things living he doth feed (6)
522, 523	safe they feed upon the manna which he gives them (3)
559	guard us, guide us, keep us, feed us (1)
563	he can with bread of heaven thy fainting spirit feed (1)
596	feed all those who do not know thee (3)
596	feed ... with the richness of thy word (3)
627	bread of our souls, whereon we feed (2)
633	Word of life, with one Bread feed us (4)
664	pastures fresh he makes me feed beside the living stream (1)
690	bread of heaven, feed me now and evermore (1)
708	in thy pleasant pastures feed us (1)

feeding

115	mean estate where ox and ass are feeding (2)
346	Thy death remembered, feeding thus on thee (1)

feeds

300	Who himself for all hath given, us he feeds ((3)
429	saves the oppressed, and feeds the poor (2)
667	he who feeds the ravens will give his children bread (3)

feel

49	may feel his resurrection's power (2)
171	Go to dark Gethsemane, ye that feel the tempter's power (1)
321	who see the light or feel the sun (4)
332	O God, unseen yet ever near, thy presence may we feel (1)
436	here, Lord, abide! Let me thy inner presence feel (4)
452	mortals need and need to feel (1)
559	thou didst feel its keenest woe (2)
574, 575	give us a conscience quick to feel (1)
670	my doubts I sorely feel, thy sure promise I believe (3)
676	Sometimes I feel discouraged and think my work's in vain (1)
686	prone to wander, Lord, I feel it (3)
702	I feel thy power on every side (2)

feels

102	Thus he feels for all our sadness (4)

feet

8	sprung in completeness where his feet pass (2)
119	so may we with willing feet ever seek thy mercy seat (2)
129, 130	Trembling at his feet we saw Moses and Elijah speaking (2)
171	there, adoring at his feet, mark the miracle of time (3)
193	his wounded hands and feet he showed (2)
206	my hands, my feet, I show to thee (4)
206	he saw the feet, the hands, the side (5)
212	but by his hands and feet (2)
212	those feet still free to move and bleed for millions (3)
213	sing, all heaven, and fall at his feet (5)
312	feet that tread thy hallowed courts (3)
324	At his feet the six-winged seraph (4)
337	so we come, O draw us to thy feet (4)
339	at thy feet I cry, my Maker (2)
369	still how far beneath thy feet our ... knowledge lies (3)

410	to his feet thy tribute bring (1)
444	He guides the feet of pilgrims along the paths of peace (3)
450, 451	go, spread your trophies at his feet (5)
459	there stands he with unhurrying feet (2)
474	See, from his head, his hands, his feet (3)
551	Tread where his feet have trod (3)
590	to lift the fallen, guide the feet that stumble (2)
599	have not our wearied feet come to the place (2)
599	Lest our feet stray from the places ... we met thee (3)
602	Kneels at the feet of his friends (1)
602	silently washes their feet (1)
609	and follow where thy feet have trod (5)
627	Lamp of our feet, whereby we trace our path (1)
659, 660	teach me the wayward feet to stay (2)
672	whose feet this earth's dark valley trod (1)
700	so shall our way be safe, our feet no straying know (2)

fell

50	Today he rose and left the dead, and Satan's empire fell (2)
208	the bars from heaven's high portals fell (4)
231	the lot fell to Matthias for whom we now rejoice (2/2-24)
232	who fell to Herod's sword (2/7-25)
243	When Stephen, young and doomed to die, fell crushed (3)
256	Then Saul fell blinded to the ground (1)
256	the scales fell from his eyes (3)
276	fell by fire and sword, or early died or flourished long (1)
687, 688	lo, his doom is sure, one little word shall fell him (3)

fellowship

279	in one communion ever knit, one fellowship of love (3)
287	O blest communion, fellowship divine (4)
363	our faith and hope, our fellowship and peace (4)
511	binding ... in a fellowship unending (2)
529	but one great fellowship of love (1)
529	fellowship of love throughout the whole wide earth (1)

felt

469, 470	There is no place where earth's sorrows are more felt (2)
469, 470	no place ... sorrows are more felt than up in heaven (2)
599	felt in the days when hope unborn had died (2)

fervent

16, 17	with fervent heart and ready mind (1)
152	Kind Maker of the world, O hear the fervent prayer (1)
415	gratitude ... that glows within my fervent heart (2)
537	with fervent prayer (2)
704	return in humble prayer and fervent praise (2)

fervently

| 475 | humbly, fervently draw near him (1) |

fervor

| 528 | give us all new fervor, draw us closer in community (2) |

fest
316, 317   the Lamb's great marriage fest of bliss and love (3)

festal
316, 317   giving us foretaste of the festal joy (3)

festival
175   Hail thee, festival day! blest day ... hallowed for ever (R)
185, 186   So let us keep the festival to which the Lord invites us (3)
213   on this festival day, come exulting away (1)
216   Hail thee, festival day! blest day ... hallowed for ever (R)
225   Hail thee, festival day! blest day ... hallowed for ever (R)
230   Then come, all Christian people, keep festival today (3)

fetters
71, 72   gates of brass before him burst, the iron fetters yield (2)
252   whereby those to sin enslaved, burst their fetters (5)
252   burst their fetters and are saved (5)

feuds
542   In Christ all races meet, their ancient feuds forgetting (2)

fevered
567   leper set apart and shunned, the sick with fevered frame (1)

few
168, 169   My days are few, O fail not, with thine immortal power (5)
540   O harvest Lord ... the laborers how few (2)

field
75   Like the flowers of the field they perish (2)
77   angels in the sky sang praise above the silent field (4)
93   Shepherds in the field abiding (2)
128   field and fountain, moor and mountain (1)
191   Christ, the first-fruits of the holy harvest-field (3)
290   All the world is God's own field (2)
290   from his field shall in that day all offenses purge away (3)
376   field and forest, vale and mountain, blooming meadow (2)
705   first fruits brought of vineyard, flock, and field (1)

fields
9   the fields are wet with diamond dew (4)
46   the fields of everlasting life (3)
100   while fields and floods, rocks, hills and plains repeat (2)
109   certain poor shepherds in fields as they lay (1)
179   Brightness of the morning, sky and fields and sea (3)
204   fields of our hearts that dead and bare have been (4)
291   We plow the fields and scatter the good seed on the land (1)
428   O storms and thunder's roar, O fields and forests bless (3)
540   look down on us and view how white the fields (2)
555   henceforth in fields of conquest thy tents ... our home (1)
580   through the silent fields of space (1)
667   though all the fields should wither (4)

fierce

174	hell's fierce powers beneath thee lie (3)
237	vain the tyrant's sharpest aim, vain each fierce endeavor (2)
287	when the strife is fierce, the warfare long (5)
293	one was slain by a fierce wild beast (2)
555	till sin's fierce war shall cease (2)
574, 575	Let the fierce fires which burn and try ... purify (4)
597	nor shall the fierce devour the small (2)

fiercely

400	Fire, so intense and fiercely bright (3)

fiercest

156	Thy last and fiercest strife is nigh (4)

fiery

29, 30	the fiery sun now goes his way (1)
52	with fiery tongues of cloven flame (3)
636, 637	When through fiery trials thy pathway shall lie (4)

fight

73	child, to bear, and fight, and die (2)
135	manifest in valiant fight, quelling all the devil's might (3)
142	O give us strength in thee to fight ... to conquer sin (2)
145	to fight, to fight till every wrong's set right (3)
168, 169	that I may fight befriended (5)
174	thou hast conquered in the fight (3)
188, 189	fought the fight, the battle won (1)
286	these, who well the fight sustained (3)
287	thou, Lord, their Captain in the well-fought fight (2)
287	fight as the saints who nobly fought of old (3)
357	Rest eternal grant them, after weary fight (4)
420	Then let us sing, for whom he won the fight (4)
433	so from the beginning the fight we were winning (2)
445, 446	second Adam to the fight and to the rescue came (2)
471	nerves the feeble arm for fight (4)
534	fight we the fight with sorrow and sin (3)
548	take to arm you for the fight, the panoply of God (3)
548	wrestle, and fight, and pray (4)
552, 553	Fight the good fight with all thy might (1)
564, 565	No foes shall stay his might, though he with giants fight (2)
624	they who with their Leader have conquered in the fight (3)
681	where justice wins its fight thou art the Kingdom molding (4)
720	through the perilous fight (1)

filled

49	filled with all the life of God (2)
98	Herod then with fear was filled (3)
135	disciples filled with awe thy transfigured glory saw (4)
230	filled the place of meeting with rushing wind and flame (1)
235	drove away the shadows, and filled the world with light (1)
259	filled with holy joy, old Simeon (3)
266	she was filled with confusion strong (3)
364	the world is with the glory filled of thy majestic sway (3)
367	cherubim and seraphim filled his temple (1)

389	He with all-commanding might filled the new-made world (3)
389	filled the new-made world with light (3)
398	goodness of the Lord that filled the earth with food (2)
435	filled it with the glory of that perfect rest (3)
517	They who go through the desert vale will find it filled (3)
517	desert vale ... filled with springs (3)
534	earth shall be filled with the glory of God (1-4)
534	filled ... as the waters cover the sea (1-4)
625	days ... whate'er he send, be filled with praise (4)
644	filled with boundless stores of grace (3)
661	peace ... filled their hearts brimful and broke them, too (2)
663	filled my cup, and borne me up in everlasting arms (4)
687, 688	though this world, with devils filled should threaten (3)
695, 696	when this cup you give is filled to brimming (3)
706	taught my sin-filled heart and mind (1)

fills

3, 4	Now that the daylight fills the sky, we lift our hearts (1)
6, 7	Christ, whose glory fills the skies (1)
81	O Flower, whose fragrance tender ... fills the air (3)
81	with sweetness fills the air (3)
233, 234	joy fills the new Jerusalem (4)
300	cheers our hearts, fills with food and gladness (3)
367	Lord, thy glory fills the heaven (1,3)
375	With balm my inmost heart he fills (1)
408	with healing balm my soul he fills (1)
501, 502	Your power the whole creation fills (4)
642	thought of thee with sweetness fills the breast (1)
669	fills thy heart with care (1)

final

163	Here in o'erwhelming final strife (3)
240, 241	they died in imitation of their Savior's final hour (2)
255	give you final service in glory at your throne (3)
290	Even so, Lord, quickly come to thy final harvest-home (4)
334	by this Eucharist declaring yours the final victory (1)
379	never o'er us final triumph gain (3)
400	most gentle death, waiting to hush our final breath (6)
512	lead us to God, our final rest (4)

find

10	mind be set to hallow all we find (3)
18	through your judgment find your grace (1)
51	all find a welcome (2)
66	let us find our rest in thee (1)
94, 95	The heavenly Babe you there shall find (4)
121	likewise in God's service we may perfect freedom find (4)
159	a purer love attaining, may with thee acceptance find (5)
214	find our heaven of heavens in thee (4)
240, 241	till you find him face to face (4)
242	teach us in that Word alone to find the truth (5)
244	drink, and find salvation here (2)
246	we share your pain and find your joy (5)
255	in those least expected true servants you can find (3)
304	to find, as all are fed (2)

319	daily still your mercies find us (2)
358	there may they find everlasting life (1,4)
379	find that self-same aching deep within the heart of God (2)
388	in thee do we trust, nor find thee to fail (5)
400	stars nightly shining, find a voice (2)
404	in your compassion we your blessings find (3)
413	find a voice to praise his Name (3)
427	Ye nations of mankind, in this your concord find (4)
429	none shall find his promise vain (2)
476	Can we by searching find out God or formulate his ways (1)
479	Grace and life eternal in that blood I find (2)
489	Not to oppress, but summon all their truest life to find (6)
495	By thy merit we find favor (1)
517	Beside thine altars ... the swallows find a nest (2)
517	They who go through the desert vale will find it filled (3)
544	the weary find eternal rest (4)
554	when we find ourselves in the place just right (1)
556, 557	pilgrims find their Father's house, Jerusalem the blest (6)
587	who teachest us to find the love from self set free (3)
597	our hearts from envy find release (1)
597	all creatures find their true accord (2)
607	Lord, strengthen all who labor that we may find release (3)
628	that yearning souls may find the Christ (3)
635	thou yet shall find it true for thee (2)
642	nor can the memory find a sweeter sound than Jesus' Name (2)
642	But what to those who find (4)
652, 653	in purer lives thy service find (1)
664	There ... I find a settled rest while others go and come (3)
667	theme of God's salvation, and find it ever new (2)
670	let my heart find rest in thee (2)
681	though we who seek to find thee have tried (2)
681	till truth from falsehood part ...find no rest (2)
681	our hearts can find no rest (2)
686	Here I find my greatest treasure (2)
689	I find, I walk, I love (3)
693	poor, wretched, blind ... all I need, in thee to find (3)
693	sight, riches, healing of the mind ... in thee to find (3)
711	seek, and he shall find (RC)

findeth
| 248, 249 | who in prayer this Name beseecheth ... comfort findeth (3) |
| 248, 249 | sweetest comfort findeth near (3) |

finds
| 319 | in you finds release that we all might live in peace (1) |
| 353 | for all love finds its source in you (1) |

fine
| 592 | who sweeps a room, as for thy laws, makes that ... fine (3) |
| 592 | makes that and the action fine (3) |

finely
| 600, 601 | finely build for days to come foundations that endure (3) |

fingers

385	thy fingers spread the mountains and plains (1)
394, 395	your fingers trace the bold designs of farthest space (1)

finish

598	to finish thy salvation (4)
657	Finish then thy new creation (3)

finished

23	With "It is finished" on your lips (3)
171	"It is finished!" hear him cry (3)
307	Paschal Lamb, thine offering, finished once for all (4)
307	finished once for all when thou was slain (4)

finisher

545	Jesus, the author, finisher, rewarder of our faith (3)

fire

19, 20	let love in flames of living fire the hearts ... inspire (2)
44, 45	the fire of love in us renew (3)
63, 64	fire our hearts with ardent love (2)
149	led by your cloud by day, by night your fire (1)
223, 224	fire, that love may burn in all (2)
225	Lo, in the likeness of fire (1)
228	melt with fire our icy chill (4)
276	fell by fire and sword, or early died or flourished long (1)
290	in the fire the tares to cast (3)
299	With tongues of fire saints spread good news (1)
363	led thy children ... with the fire and cloud (2)
368	touch our hearts with sacred fire (3)
393	given the moving fire by night (2)
400	Fire, so intense and fiercely bright (3)
400	fire ... you give to us both warmth and light (3)
406, 407	be praised by brother fire (4)
431	writes in fire across the skies God's majesty and praise (2)
500	thrice holy Fount, thrice holy Fire (2)
501, 502	come, kindle in our hearts your fire (1)
503, 504	lighten with celestial fire (1)
503, 504	Thy blessed unction from above is comfort, life and fire (3)
503, 504	comfort, life, and fire of love (3)
506, 507	fire our hearts and clear our sight (5)
508	glows with thy fire divine (3)
509	Come as the fire, and purge our hearts (3)
522, 523	Round each habitation hovering, see the cloud and fire (3)
522, 523	the cloud and fire appear for a glory and a covering (3)
531	Give tongues of fire and hearts of love to preach (2)
540	O Lord, now let thy fire enkindle our hearts (2)
558	living still in spite of dungeon, fire, and sword (1)
579, 608	from rock and tempest, fire and foe, protect them (4)
596	with thy living fire of judgment purge this land (1)
627	pillar of fire, through watches dark (3)
652, 653	speak through the earthquake, wind, and fire (5)
690	let the fire and cloudy pillar lead me all my journey (2)
691	a living fire (2)

704 thou who camest from above the fire celestial to impart (1)
704 still let me guard the holy fire (3)

fired
257 Anna welcomes Israel's hope, with holy rapture fired (3)

fires
246 Still rage the fires of hate today (3)
386, 387 glorious the assembled fires appear (3)
574, 575 Let the fierce fires which burn and try ... purify (4)
630 his the fires that tried her worth (1)

firm
276 meek and firm be found (5)
334 in your Body, firm believing (2)
388 thy mercies, how tender, how firm to the end (5)
391 firm as a rock thy truth must stand (5)
393 how the word we have heard firm and changeless ... stand (1)
437, 438 Firm is his promise, and his mercy sure (4)
556, 557 Still lift your standard high, still march in firm array (5)
636, 637 How firm a foundation, ye saints of the Lord (1)
716 firm may she ever stand through storm and night (1)

firmament
409 The spacious firmament on high (1)
579 Spirit ... the Father sent to spread abroad the firmament (3)

firmer
318 here grasp with firmer hand eternal grace (1)

firmly
242 He loved thee well, and firmly said, "Come, let us go ..." (2)
377, 378 his truth at all times firmly stood (4)

first
8 Morning has broken like the first morning (1)
8 black-bird has spoken like the first bird (1)
8 like the first dewfall on the first grass (2)
11 guard my first springs of thought and will (2)
47 On this day, the first of days, God ... we praise (1)
48 This day at the creation, the light first had its birth (2)
52 first o'er the earth the light was poured (1)
82 Babe ... world's Redeemer first revealed his sacred face (2)
106 with them the joyful tidings first begun (1)
106 till our first heavenly state again takes place (5)
109 The first Nowell the angel did say was to ... shepherds (1)
129, 130 first and last and only One (4)
206 When Thomas first the tidings heard (3)
213 For the glory we were first created to share (3)
231 praise, O Lord, for Andrew, the first to follow (2/11-30)
232 her faith was first to see you, her Lord (2/7-22)
237 who will first begin it (3)
252 when the cup of human woe first he tasted here below (4)
290 first the blade, and then the ear (2)

315	Thou, who at thy first Eucharist didst pray (1)
372	first, the last, beyond all thought his timeless years (1)
447	yet he who loved us from the first ensures our victory (3)
500	by whose aid the world's foundations first were laid (1)
564, 565	his first avowed intent to be a pilgrim (1)
598	Lord Christ, when first thou cam'st to earth (1)
671	how precious ... grace appear the hour I first believed (2)
671	no less days ... than when we'd first begun (5)
673	The first one ever, oh, ever to know (1-3)
673	first one ... to know of the birth of Jesus was the Maid (1)
673	first one ... to know of Messiah, Jesus (2)
673	first one ... the Samaritan woman who drew from the well (2)
673	first ones ... to know of the rising of Jesus (3)
673	first ones ... were Mary, Joanna, and Magdalene (3)
683, 684	Where is the blessedness I knew when first I saw the Lord (2)
705	As those of old their first fruits brought (1)
705	first fruits brought of vineyard, flock, and field (1)
706	knowing well, that if I love you, you ... loved me first (3)
706	you, O Lord, have loved me first (3)
711	Seek ye first the kingdom of God and its righteousness (RC)

fishing
| 231 | You called him from his fishing upon Lake Galilee (2/11-30) |

fit
1, 2	Monarch of all things, fit us for thy mansions (2)
10	Only, O Lord, in thy dear love, fit us for perfect rest (6)
10	fit us for perfect rest above (6)
101	fit us for heaven to live with thee there (3)
279	Thine earthly members fit to join thy saints above (3)
326	ever fit us by service on earth for thy service on high (2)
339	let me be a fit partaker of ... blessed food from heaven (2)
656	give us a pure and lowly heart, a temple fit for thee (4)
709	give us each day our daily bread ... raiment fit provide (3)

fit (Latin)
| 266 | Nova, nova. Ave fit ex Eva (R) |

flags
| 615 | And lo, already on the hills the flags of dawn appear (3) |

flame
47	this day the Spirit came with his gifts of living flame (2)
52	with fiery tongues of cloven flame (3)
121	as peaceful as a dove and yet as urgent as a flame (1)
143	to Elijah fasting, came the steeds and chariots of flame (2)
223, 224	Like to cloven tongues of flame on the twelve ... came (2)
230	filled the place of meeting with rushing wind and flame (1)
235	as, in the prophet's vision from out the amber flame (2)
236	and to the Spirit, living flame (4)
237	Never flinched they from the flame ... the torment never (2)
243	but only in his heart a flame (1-3)
243	only in my heart a flame and in my soul a dream (4)
265	his wings as drifted snow, his eyes as flame (1)

278	manifest in wind and flame (3)
284	With equal flame and equal art ... extol his Name (8)
297	Descend, O Spirit, purging flame (1)
299	rush of wind and roar of flame (1)
299	fan our smoldering lives to flame (3)
346	blest by the Spirit, breath and flame of life (3)
419	one heavenly flame (4)
505	the holy flame of love impart (3)
506, 507	let your flame break out within us (5)
509	purge our hearts like sacrificial flame (3)
510	kindle a flame of sacred love in ... cold hearts of ours (1)
516	kindle it, thy holy flame bestowing (1)
540	that everywhere its flame may go (2)
574, 575	O God, be with us in the flame (4)
636, 637	the flame shall not hurt thee (4)
704	kindle a flame of sacred love upon the altar of my heart (1)

flame's

| 513 | like the new flame's eager might (1) |

flames

19, 20	let love in flames of living fire the hearts ... inspire (2)
21, 22	Quench now on earth the flames of strife (2)
31, 32	the sun that flames up from the east (1)
419	thy glory flames from sun and star (1)

flaming

16, 17	Then let us all with joy embrace the flaming splendor (3)
161	The flaming banners of our King advance (1)
459	Do flaming suns his footsteps trace (1)
686	sung by flaming tongues above (1)

flashes

| 145 | to be led to where God's glory flashes (2) |

flashing

276	slain by Herod's flashing blade, he saw thy face again (4)
370	the flashing of the lightning free (4)
376	flashing sea, chanting bird and flowing fountain (2)

fled

114	when all the birds had fled (1)
284	when Satan fled the Savior's might (3)
636, 637	to you that for refuge to Jesus have fled (1)
636, 637	The soul that to Jesus hath fled for repose (5)

flee

112	heaven and earth shall flee away when he comes to reign (2)
252	pleading only this we flee, helpless, O our God, to thee (6)
406, 407	from whom no one alive can flee (7)
447	troubles that are ours to bear are trials we cannot flee (3)
457	to thee alone from sin and death we flee (1)
460, 451	here the sinful flee to thee from day to day (3)
562	At the sign of triumph Satan's host doth flee (2)

564, 565	Then fancies flee away; I'll fear not what men say (3)
613	oppression, lust, and crime shall flee thy face before (3)
638, 639	the morning breaks, the shadows flee (4)
648	Oh, let us all from bondage flee (4)
662	when other helpers fail and comforts flee (1)
662	heaven's morning breaks, and earth's vain shadows flee (4)
701	Flee, dark clouds that lower (3)
702	wither from thy presence flee (3)

fleeting

23	The fleeting day is nearly gone (1)
238, 239	all its fleeting moments past (3)
685	While I draw this fleeting breath (3)

flesh

55	take our flesh and grow as child in Mary's womb (2)
55	one with us in human flesh (4)
67	all flesh shall see the token (3)
77	our very flesh our Maker shares (2)
83	Word of the Father, now in flesh appearing (6)
87	Veiled in flesh the God-head see (2)
160	robed in mortal flesh is dying, crucified by sin for me (2)
162	where he through whom our flesh was made (1)
162	in that same flesh our ransom paid (1)
192	My flesh in hope shall rest, and for a season slumber (3)
193	His risen flesh with radiance glowed (2)
196, 197	let the blood flow from his flesh to fill ... hope (2)
202	his flesh, the true unleavened bread (3)
202	his flesh ... is freely offered in our stead (3)
231	grant us grace to know you, made flesh (2/12-21)
231	made flesh, yet God and Lord (2/12-21)
245	O Word made flesh, your deeds and words refresh (3)
277	Word made flesh (1)
284	Ye saw the heaven-born child in human flesh arrayed (2)
296	as Christ's new body takes on flesh and blood (4)
323	for thy Flesh is meat indeed (1)
324	Let all mortal flesh keep silence (1)
329, 331	Word made flesh, the bread he taketh (4)
329, 331	by his word his Flesh to be (4)
335	The Bread that I will give is my Flesh (2)
335	my Flesh for the life of the world (2)
335	Unless you eat of the Flesh of the Son of Man (3)
336	in our life thy love divine ... flesh and blood has taken (1)
336	flesh and blood ... and to us thou givest thine (1)
445, 446	O wisest love, that flesh and blood, which ... did fail (3)
445, 446	flesh and blood, which did in Adam fail (3)
445, 446	highest gift of grace should flesh and blood refine (4)
458	Lord should take frail flesh and die (1)
460, 461	thou within the veil hast entered, robed in flesh (4)
463, 464	He is the Life. Love him in the World of the Flesh (3)
489	He sent him down as sending God, in flesh to us he came (4)
517	my very heart and flesh cry out, O living God, for thee (1)
561	arm of flesh will fail you, ye dare not trust your own (3)
573	thy Word made flesh, and in a manger laid (5)
631	praise him for the Word made flesh (3)

| 633 | Word made flesh, we long to hear you (1) |
| 652, 653 | let sense be dumb, let flesh retire (5) |

fleshly

| 127 | seen in fleshly form on earth (2) |

flight

56	death's dark shadow put to flight (6)
93	wing your flight o'er all the earth (1)
145	oppression put to flight (3)
179	hours and passing moments praise thee in their flight (3)
284	ye hailed his wondrous flight up to the throne of God (7)
371	chaos and darkness ... took their flight (1)
371	speed forth thy flight (3)
437, 438	Proud hearts and stubborn wills are put to flight (3)
513	like the challenge of her flight (1)
579	save all who dare the eagle's flight (3)
585	scholar's truth, flight of swallows, autumn leaves (1)
640	Traveler, darkness takes its flight (3)

flinched

| 237 | Never flinched they from the flame ... the torment never (2) |

fling

65	Fling wide your gates, O Zion, your Savior's rule embrace (3
89, 90	its ancient splendors fling (4)
436	Fling wide the portals of your heart (3)

flinging

| 175 | heaven her gates unbars, flinging her increase of light (3) |
| 216 | heaven her gates unbars, flinging her increase of light (2) |

float

| 556, 557 | while answering echoes upward float (3) |
| 556, 557 | echoes upward float like wreaths of incense cloud (3) |

floats

| 89, 90 | still ... heavenly music floats o'er all the weary world (2) |

flock

75	He shall feed his flock like a shepherd (3)
231	to guard your flock from harm (2/1-18)
245	faithful shepherd of the flock ... sheep-fold's only door (2)
334	Scattered flock, one shepherd sharing, lost and lonely (2)
343	bless thy chosen pilgrim flock with manna (1)
486	thy flock, redeemed from sinful stain ... praise again (5)
705	first fruits brought of vineyard, flock, and field (1)

flocks

83	leaving their flocks, draw nigh to gaze (4)
93	watching o'er your flocks by night (2)
94, 95	While shepherds watched their flocks by night (1)
99	o'er silent flocks by night (1)
288	flocks that whiten all the plain (2)
667	nor flocks nor herds be there (4)

flood

116	through Jordan's flood was led (2)
131, 132	Within the Jordan's sacred flood the ... Lamb ... stood (3)
192	Death's flood hath lost its chill (2)
460, 461	thunder like a mighty flood (1,5)
479	Lift ye then your voices, swell the mighty flood (5)
501, 502	Flood our dull senses with your light (4)
526	part of the host have crossed the flood (3)
568	flood the whole Church with thy glorious light (3)
641	when the flood is passed, I may the eternal brightness see (4)
687, 688	our helper he amid the flood of mortal ills prevailing (1)

floods

100	while fields and floods, rocks, hills and plains repeat (2)
235	a house to stand unshaken by floods or winds or rains (3)

flourish

319	by your grace we all may flourish (1)
423	we blossom and flourish, like leaves on the tree (3)

flourished

276	fell by fire and sword, or early died or flourished long (1)

flow

11, 43	Praise God, from whom all blessings flow (4)
100	he comes to make his blessings flow far as the curse (3)
175	Spirit of life and of power, now flow in us (7)
196, 197	let the blood flow from his flesh to fill ... hope (2)
216	now flow in us, fount of our being (5)
288	source whence all our blessings flow (1)
332	the streams that through the desert flow (2)
367	bid we thus our anthem flow (2)
380	Praise God, from whom all blessings flow (3)
455, 456	read thee ... in seas that swell and streams that flow (2)
457	that life to win, whose joys eternal flow (4)
474	sorrow and love flow mingled down (3)
566	From thee all skill and science flow (1)
580	the lonely drift unnoticed in the city's ebb and flow (2)
616	righteousness in fountains from hill to valley flow (3)
636, 637	the rivers of woe shall not thee overflow (3)
645, 646	Where streams of living water flow ... he leadeth (2)
685	Should my tears for ever flow (2)
690	fountain, whence the healing stream doth flow (2)
707	let them flow in ceaseless praise (1)

flowed

131, 132	He spoke the word, and forth it flowed (4)
363	from thee have flowed, as from a mighty river, our faith (4)
685	water and the blood from thy wounded side that flowed (1)
715	the falling tear in mercy flowed beyond all bound (RC)

flower

46	each flower and tree reposeth (1)
81	O Flower, whose fragrance tender ... fills the air (3)
149	glorious in springtime dress of leaf and flower (3)

170	that thorns would flower upon your brow (1)
226, 227	what is barren bring to flower (4)
291	he paints the wayside flower, he lights the evening star (2)
307	branch and flower of Jesse's stem (3)
398	not a plant or flower below but makes thy glories known (3)
405	Each little flower that opens (1)
406, 407	bringeth forth fruit, herb, and flower (5)
416	hill and vale, and tree and flower (2)
462	truth ... like a flower shall bud and blossom show (2)
594, 595	bring her bud to glorious flower (1)
677	bud may have a bitter taste ... sweet will be the flower (5)

flowers

75	Like the flowers of the field they perish (2)
76	without thy grace we waste away like flowers (3)
76	flowers that wither and decay (3)
376	hearts unfold like flowers before thee (1)
400	flowers and fruits that in you grow ... glory also show (4)
412	Flowers and trees, loud rustling dry leaves (2)
475	As the tender flowers eagerly unfold them (3)
616	love, joy, hope, like flowers spring in his path to birth (3)

floweth

339	Fount, whence all my being floweth (2)
372	His Spirit floweth free, high surging where it will (3)
645, 646	what transport of delight from thy pure chalice floweth (5)

flowing

174	washed us with the tide flowing from his pierced side (1)
376	flashing sea, chanting bird and flowing fountain (2)
398	spread the flowing seas abroad and built the lofty skies (1)
400	Swift flowing water, pure and clear, make music (3)

flows

187	deep and wide flows the tide severing us from bondage past (1)
242	still through his confession flows ... thy life and light (4)
242	flows to Christian souls (4)
410	Widely yet his mercy flows (3)
666	source and spring from whence redemption ever flows (4)

flung

| 580 | flung the suns in burning radiance through ... space (1) |

fly

402, 403	The heavens are not too high, his praise may thither fly (1)
541	redeem the time, its hours too swiftly fly (4)
625	through the realms of light fly at your Lord's command (1)
680	they fly, forgotten, as a dream dies at the opening day (5)
699	Jesus, Lover of my soul, let me to thy bosom fly (1)

flying

| 199, 200 | is flying from his light (2) |

foaming

| 608 | who walkedst on the foaming deep (2) |

focus

228	Holy Spirit, font of light, focus of God's glory bright (1)

foe

38, 39	Lord, free us from our ancient foe (3)
40, 41	repel our dread, malicious foe (4)
60	assaults of our dread foe (5)
174	through the wave that drowns the foe (2)
425	He only is the mighty Lord. He only can destroy the foe (3)
445, 446	should strive afresh against the foe (3)
524	thy hand from every snare and foe ... deliverance bring (4)
540	contending from the walls of Zion against the foe (1)
558	we will love both friend and foe in all our strife (3)
561	till every foe is vanquished and Christ is Lord indeed (1)
562	Christ, the royal Master, leads against the foe (1)
563	fear not the secret foe (2)
579, 608	from rock and tempest, fire and foe, protect them (4)
616	O'er every foe victorious, he on his throne shall rest (5)
662	I fear no foe, with thee at hand to bless (3)
687, 688	for still our ancient foe doth seek to work us woe (1)
695, 696	Yet is this heart by its old foe tormented (2)

foemen

243	overcame the foemen of the Lord (1)

foes

120	wrestle with his people's foes (4)
158	By foes derided, by thine own rejected, O most afflicted (1)
215	he by death has spoiled his foes (2)
310, 311	our foes press on from every side (1)
410	rescues us from all our foes (3)
413	awed by his love his foes surrender (1)
452	the surest friend of all his foes (2)
458	that he his foes from thence might free (5)
503, 504	Keep far our foes, give peace at home (6)
522, 523	thou may'st smile at all thy foes (1)
561	ye that are his now serve him against unnumbered foes (2)
563	the Lord himself, thy Leader, shall all thy foes subdue (1)
564, 565	No foes shall stay his might, though he with giants fight (2)
636, 637	I will not, I will not desert to its foes (5)
664	in sight of all my foes (2)

foiled

284	unmasked in every dress, in every combat foiled (3)

fold

75	bring them safe to his fold (3)
231	thrice charged to feed your fold (2/1-18)
337	O fold them closer to thy mercy's breast (3)
686	wandering from the fold of God (2)

fold's

245	faithful shepherd of the flock ... sheep-fold's only door (2)

foliage

165, 166   None in foliage ... blossom ... fruit thy peer may be (4)

folk

265   Christian folk throughout the world will ever say (4)
267   The prophet gave the sign for faithful folk to read (2)
293   for the saints of God are just folk like me (3)
377, 378   we are his folk, he doth us feed (2)
596   Still the weary folk are pining (2)
661   such happy, simple fisher-folk before the Lord came down (1)

follow

12, 13   strive to follow where you lead (2)
61, 62   We follow all and heed your call (2)
109   to follow the star wherever it went (3)
148   humbly follow in your way (5)
171   Follow to the judgment hall (2)
209   nor follow where he trod (2)
231   praise, O Lord, for Andrew, the first to follow (2/11-30)
231   "Leave all and follow me" (2/11-30)
232   we, whate'er our station may rise and follow you (2/9-21)
237   Up and follow, Christians all (3)
276   thy summons, "Follow me" (2)
279   humbly pray that we may follow them in holiness (4)
279   follow them ... who live and died for thee (4)
281   that royal summons, "Follow me" (2)
366   the white robed martyrs follow (3)
406, 407   blest be they who do thy will and follow thy commandments (7)
463, 464   He is the Way. Follow him through the Land of Unlikeness (1)
490   I want to follow Jesus (1)
549, 550   saying "Christian, follow me" (1)
555   we follow, not with fears (3)
564, 565   let him in constancy follow the Master (1)
572   into your self-giving death call us all to follow (2)
609   and follow where thy feet have trod (5)
617   free to follow truth, and thus to follow thee (2)
647   I know not where the road will lead I follow day by day (1)
652, 653   let us, like them, without a word, rise up and follow (2)
654   follow thee more nearly, day by day (1)
655   O Jesus, thou hast promised to all who follow thee (3)
655   O give me grace to follow, my Master and my friend (3)
665   ye who follow shall not fall (5)
675   humbly follow after me (1)
675   follow Christ, nor think till death to lay it down (5)

followed

131, 132   followed on his guiding star (2)
231   young James the faithful, who heard and followed you (2/5-1)
279   followed thee, obeyed, adored, our grateful hymn receive (1)
293   they followed the right, for Jesus' sake (2)
293   followed the right ... whole of their good lives long (2)
614   who with a faith for ever new followed the King (1)
614   seek again the Way disciples followed then (2)

followers
334   may we faithful followers be (3)

following
128   following yonder star (1)
188, 189   following our exalted Head (3)
253   following their incarnate God (3)
275   they have triumphed following thee (3)
286   following not the sinful throng (3)

folly
148   to the skies our monuments of folly soar (2)

fond
259   watched by her duteous love, in her fond arms at rest (2)
510   See how we trifle here below, fond of these earthly toys (2)

font
228   Holy Spirit, font of light, focus of God's glory bright (1)

food
51   his own life imparting, food everlasting (4)
291   seed-time and the harvest, our life ... health ... food (3)
300   Glory, love, and praise, and honor for our food (1)
300   Glory ... for our food now bestowed render we the Donor (1)
300   cheers our hearts, fills with food and gladness (3)
302, 303   didst give us food for all our days (1)
308, 309   O Food to pilgrims given, O Bread of life from heaven (1)
320   who on earth such food bestowest (6)
324   he will give ... his own self for heavenly food (2)
329, 331   then, more precious food supplying, gives himself (3)
332   We come, obedient to thy word, to feast on heavenly food (3)
337   by this food, so awesome and so sweet, deliver us (4)
339   let me be a fit partaker of ... blessed food from heaven (2)
339   food ... for our good, thy glory, given (2)
343   living bread, that heavenly wine, be our immortal food (4)
398   goodness of the Lord that filled the earth with food (2)
460, 461   Bread of Heaven, thou on earth our food, our stay (3)
525   one holy Name she blesses, partakes one holy food (2)
586   carpenter of Nazareth, toiling for thy daily food (1)
619   Such song is rest and food and deep delight (6)
645, 646   with food celestial feedeth (2)

foolish
148   our foolish confidence, our pride of knowledge ... sin (4)
572   your dying bade us sheathe the foolish sword (2)
645, 646   Perverse and foolish oft I strayed (3)
652. 653   Dear Lord and Father of mankind forgive our foolish ways (1)
675   heed not the shame, and let your foolish heart be still (3)

foot
199, 200   led them with unmoistened foot through the Red Sea waters (1)
453   its foot was on earth and its top in the sky (1)
472   afoot on dusty highways (3)
531   where'er the foot of man hath trod (1)

| 534 | From utmost east to utmost west, wherever foot hath trod (2) |
| 668 | He will not let thy foot be moved (2) |

footsteps

83	we too will thither bend our joyful footsteps (4)
232	walking in their footsteps we give you praise anew (2/11-1)
253	They marked the footsteps that he trod (3)
459	Do flaming suns his footsteps trace (1)
459	suns his footsteps trace through corridors sublime (1)
462	his footsteps cannot err (1)
545	freed from every weight of sin ... holy footsteps trace (2)
632	a lantern to our footsteps, shines on from age to age (1)
669	he will guide thy footsteps and be thy staff and stay (1)
677	plants his footsteps in the sea ... rides upon the storm (1)
709	our wandering footsteps guide (3)

footstool

| 460, 461 | born of Mary, earth thy footstool, heaven thy throne (4) |

forbid

| 297 | Forbid us not this second birth (2) |
| 474 | Forbid it, Lord, that I should boast (2) |

forbids

| 188, 189 | Death in vain forbids him rise (1) |

force

12, 13	O God, creation's ruling force (4)
14, 15	O God, creation's secret force (1)
18	O God, creation's ruling force (5)
23	O God, creation's ruling force (4)
386, 387	the stupendous force on which all strength depends (1)
489	he came to win us by good will, for force is not of God (5)

forebears

| 223, 224 | Thou who did our forebears guide (4) |

forebore

| 122, 123 | our Savior in his fasting pleasures of the world forebore (3) |

foreign

| 281 | alike the symbol ... tool of foreign master's hated rule (1) |

forerunner

232	forerunner of the Word (2/6-24)
271, 272	The great forerunner of the morn (1)
444	Before him goes his herald, forerunner in the way (2)

foreshadowed

| 268, 269 | Church, in her foreshadowed (3) |

foreshows

| 127 | myrrh his sepulcher foreshows (4) |

forest

114	O children of the forest free, the angel song is true (4)
117, 118	myrrh from the forest, and gold from the mine (3)
376	field and forest, vale and mountain, blooming meadow (2)

forests

428	O storms and thunder's roar, O fields and forests bless (3)

foretaste

316, 317	giving us foretaste of the festal joy (3)

foretell

640	Watchman, does its beauteous ray ... hope foretell (1)
640	aught of joy or hope foretell (1)

foretold

65	Greet One who comes in glory, foretold in sacred story (1)
73	let the endless bliss begin, by weary saints foretold (4)
81	Isaiah 'twas foretold it, the Rose I have in mind (2)
89, 90	with the everlasting years shall come the time foretold (4)
225	he whom the Lord foretold suddenly, swiftly descends (1)
265	thy Son shall be Emmanuel, by seers foretold (2)
267	Praise we the Lord this day, this day so long foretold (1)
314	what my soul doth long for, that thy word foretold (4)

forever (also see ever)

14, 15	whom with the Spirit we adore forever and for evermore (3)
19, 20	whom with the Spirit we adore forever and for evermore (3)
66	born to reign in us forever (3)
139	death could hold him never. He rose and lives forever (2)
175	Hail thee, festival day! blest day ... hallowed for ever (R)
240, 241	dwell forever in the light (1)
287	thy Name, O Jesus, be forever blessed (1)
290	there, forever purified, in thy presence to abide (4)
335	they who eat of this bread ... shall live forever (2)
336	Be thou one with us forever (1)
360, 361	thine be the glory, praise and adoration, now and forever (6)
377, 378	his mercy is forever sure (4)
475	Gladly, Lord, we offer thine to be forever (2)
480	in the circle of his arms may we forever lie (2)
518	holy Zion's help forever, and her confidence alone (1)
518	what they gain from thee, forever ... to retain (4)
530	how forever, in its need ... the world is freed (3)
599	keep us forever in the path, we pray (3)

forevermore

14, 15	whom with the Spirit we adore forever and forevermore (3)

forgave

547	forgive as God in Christ forgave (4)

forget

27, 28	Lest we, beset by doubt and strife forget (3)
27, 28	forget your blessed gift of life (3)
46	we, this marvel seeing, forget our selfish being (2)

411	forget not all his benefits! The Lord to thee is kind (2)
450, 451	Sinners, whose love can ne'er forget the wormwood (5)
450, 451	ne'er forget the wormwood and the gall (5)
460, 461	shall our hearts forget his promise (2)
480	Should we forget our Savior's praise, the stones ... sing (3)
546	forget the steps already trod, and onward urge thy way (2)
599	lest ... we forget thee (3)
651	let us not forget that though the wrong is great (2)

forgets
| 433 | sing praises to his Name, he forgets not his own (1) |

forgetting
| 542 | In Christ all races meet, their ancient feuds forgetting (2) |
| 545 | forgetting things behind (5) |

forgive
43	Forgive me, Lord, for thy dear Son (2)
53	he will then receive thee, heal thee, and forgive thee (3)
140, 141	Wilt thou forgive that sin, where I begun (1)
140, 141	Wilt thou forgive those sins through which I run (1)
140, 141	Wilt thou forgive that sin, by which I won others to sin (2)
140, 141	Wilt thou forgive that sin which I did shun a year or two (2)
144	forgive us, Lord, our sin (2)
146, 147	Therefore, we pray you, Lord, forgive (5)
141	Wilt thou forgive those sins through which I run (1)
236	hear and forgive us (2)
251	forgive the ill that we have done (2)
251	forgive ... the good we failed to do (2)
313	of thy matchless love forgive me (4)
528	Father, what they do, forgive (4)
547	with kind and gentle hearts forgive (4)
547	forgive as God in Christ forgave (4)
574, 575	for lives bereft of purpose high, forgive (3)
574, 575	forgive, O Lord, we cry (3)
581	Forgive we now each other's faults ... our faults confess (3)
593	where there is hurt, may we forgive (1)
652, 653	Dear Lord and Father of mankind forgive our foolish ways (1)
674	Forgive our sins as we forgive (1)

forgiven
10	new perils past, new sins forgiven (2)
59	haste ... one and all to be forgiven (3)
70	those repenting are forgiven (3)
167	He died that we might be forgiven (3)
294	one with his rising, freed and forgiven (2)
304	I come with joy to meet my Lord, forgiven, loved and free (1)
318	here taste afresh the calm of sin forgiven (2)
333	Now the wedding Now the songs ... heart forgiven leaping (1)
334	Sins forgiven, wrong forgiving, we go forth alert (3)
360, 361	sin is forgiven, hope o'er fear prevaileth (3)
410	ransomed, healed, restored, forgiven (1)
454	to hearts rejoicing, bringing news of sins forgiven (3)
495	thy people are forgiven through the virtue of by blood (2)

593   in forgiving are forgiven (4)
619   to saints forgiven, let them all unite (6)

forgiveness
444   the dawning of forgiveness upon the sinner's eyes (3)
559   Savior, breathe forgiveness o'er us (2)

forgiveness'
243   in sweet forgiveness' name, should understand and spare (3)

forgiving
334   Sins forgiven, wrong forgiving, we go forth alert (3)
376   Thou art giving and forgiving, ever blessing, ever blest (3)
400   forgiving others, take your part (5)
593   in forgiving are forgiven (4)
674   How can your pardon reach and bless the unforgiving heart (2)
698   held in forgiving love, let me be still (2)

forgivingness
406, 407 prove in free forgivingness their love (6)

forgot
541   while we in sleep our duty have forgot, he slumbered not (2)

forgotten
280   many saints by earth forgotten live for ever (1)
289   some are long forgotten (2)
680   they fly, forgotten, as a dream dies at the opening day (5)

forlorn
63, 64 born for blessing to a world forlorn (1)
98   came he to a world forlorn, the Lord of every nation (1,5)

form
77   Behold, the world's creator wears the form and fashion (2)
77   form and fashion of a slave (2)
127   seen in fleshly form on earth (2)
157   form a procession with branches (R)
185, 186 an empty form alone remains; his sting is lost for ever (2)
222   No more his mortal form we see (2)
235   in mystic form and image four living creatures came (2)
307   Though the lowliest form doth veil thee as of old (3)
368   Great Jehovah, form our hearts and make them thine (4)
388   His chariots of wrath the deep thunderclouds form (2)
434   his brightest form of glory shines (2)
448, 449 God, the Son of God, should take our mortal form (1)
448, 449 God ... should take our mortal form for mortal's sake (1)
498   see the very dying form of one who suffered there for me (2)
543   the nations round thy form shall view (2)
573   Spirit of life which moved ere form was made (1)
630   grace in human form declare (2)

formal
510   In vain we tune our formal songs (3)

formed

355	formed of the earth, and to earth shall we return (1)
358	From earth you formed us, both glorious and mortal (2)
385	Lo, at thy word the waters were formed (1)
391	His sovereign power without our aid formed us of clay (2)
391	formed us of clay and gave us breath (2)
398	he formed the creatures with his Word (2)
398	formed the creatures ... then pronounced them good (2)
522, 523	he whose word cannot be broken formed thee (1)
522, 523	formed thee for his own abode (1)

former

146, 147	those of faith in former time (2)

forming

511	Spirit, ever forming in the Church the mind of Christ (1)

formless

372	Formless, all lovely forms declare his loveliness (2)

forms

308, 309	hidden in forms of bread and wine (3)
372	Formless, all lovely forms declare his loveliness (2)

formulate

476	Can we by searching find out God or formulate his ways (1)

forsake

441, 442	never shall the cross forsake me (2)
542	when Christ is throned as Lord all ... forsake their fear (2)
636, 637	I'll never, no, never, no, never forsake (5)
664	brings my wandering spirit back when I forsake his ways (1)

forsaken

18	betrayed, forsaken, all alone (3a)
104	Yet he shall be forsaken, and yielded up to die (3)
159	in death by all forsaken, till his spirit he resigned (3)
569	earth hath forsaken thy ways all holy (2)
610	upon the cross, forsaken, offered mercy's perfect deed (1)

forsaking

232	worldly gain forsaking, your path of life we share (2/9-21)

forsook

635	God never yet forsook in need the soul that trusted him (2)

fortells

563	His love fortells thy trials (1)

forth

19, 20	pour forth into our hearts, we pray, the fullness (1)
25, 26	Now sunset comes, but light shines forth (2)
31, 32	for you the dazzling star shines forth (2)
46	Now all the heavenly splendor breaks forth (2)
46	forth in starlight tender from myriad world's unknown (2)

55	You came forth from the eternal God (3)
61, 62	Forth he comes, her Bridegroom glorious (2)
76	shine forth, and let thy light restore (4)
91	Break forth, O beauteous light, and usher in the morning (1)
94, 95	good will henceforth from heaven to men (6)
120	O Christ, may we baptized from sin, go forth with you (5)
120	go forth with you a world to win (5)
124	It shines to herald forth the King (1)
125, 126	on them broke forth the heavenly dawn (1)
131, 132	He spoke the word, and forth it flowed (4)
133, 134	through purer lives show forth your light (3)
138	did manifest your glory forth in Cana's marriage hour (1)
145	Then shall your light break forth as doth the morning (5)
152	with many a tear poured forth by all (1)
153	Let us go forth in peace. In the name of Christ. Amen (3)
162	the cross shines forth in mystic glow (1)
164	Alone thou goest forth, O Lord, in sacrifice to die (1)
165, 166	from that holy body broken blood and water forth proceed (3)
176, 177	bringing forth creation (1)
204	Forth he came at Easter, like the risen grain (3)
225	Forth from the Father he comes with ... mystical offering (2)
243	When Stephen, full of power and grace, went forth (1)
243	went forth throughout the land (1)
258	who brought forth the world's salvation (2)
277	though he went forth from her side (2)
277	forth to preach, and heal, and suffer (2)
292	by thee come down henceforth the gifts of God (1)
295	praise the Holy Spirit poured forth upon the earth (3)
334	Sins forgiven, wrong forgiving, we go forth alert (3)
337	we here spread forth to thee that only offering perfect (1)
347	Go forth for God (1-4)
359	forth may they go to tell all realms thy grace (5)
371	speed forth thy flight (3)
377, 378	him serve with mirth, his praise forth tell (1)
406, 407	Sustained by thee through every hour, she bringeth forth (5)
406, 407	bringeth forth fruit, herb, and flower (5)
409	utter forth a glorious voice (3)
422	more truth and light to break forth from thy Holy Word (1)
432	loud organs, his glory forth tell in deep tone (3)
443	From God Christ's deity came forth (1)
450, 451	bring forth the royal diadem (1)
484, 485	thy love henceforth shall be our song (2)
492	Sing how he came forth from heaven (2)
496, 497	Incarnate God, put forth thy power (3)
505	thou comest forth from God's great throne (1)
521	Put forth, O God, thy Spirit's might (1)
534	by ... mouth of many messengers goes forth the voice of God (2)
534	March we forth in the strength of God (3)
539	Send heralds forth to bear the message glorious (3)
540	Send forth, O Lord, thy strong Evangel (3)
547	Awake, arise, go forth in faith (5)
555	henceforth in fields of conquest thy tents ... our home (1)
561	forth to the mighty conflict in this his glorious day (2)
569	show forth thy pity on high where thou reignest (1)
588, 589	give it root in every heart to bring forth fruits of love (2)

308, 309	O purest fountain, welling from out the Savior's side (2)
376	flashing sea, chanting bird and flowing fountain (2)
690	Open now the crystal fountain (2)
690	fountain, whence the healing stream doth flow (2)
699	Thou of life the fountain art (3)

fountains

423	thy clouds, which are fountains of goodness and love (2)
616	righteousness in fountains from hill to valley flow (3)

four

235	In one harmonious witness the chosen four combine (2)
235	in mystic form and image four living creatures came (2)
244	See the rivers four that gladden, with their streams (2)

fox

114	The chiefs from far before him knelt with gifts of fox (3)
114	gifts of fox and beaver-pelt (3)

fragile

394, 395	let water's fragile blend with air, enabling life (2)
621, 622	glorious and resplendent, fragile body, shalt thou be (4)

fragrance

81	O Flower, whose fragrance tender ... fills the air (3)

frail

18	shield frail human eyes from all the woe you bore for us (3b)
146, 147	though frail we be (4)
388	Frail children of dust, and feeble as frail (5)
458	Lord should take frail flesh and die (1)

frailty

357	Every taint of evil, frailty and decay ... purge away (3)

frame

38, 39	as mortals clothed in earth-bound frame (4)
55	Oh, fill our weak and dying frame with godly strength (4)
391	our souls and all our mortal frame (3)
409	spangled heavens, a shining frame (1)
410	well our feeble frame he knows (3)
459	light-years frame the Pleiades and point Orion's sword (1)
462	all shall frame to bow them low before thee, Lord (4)
567	leper set apart and shunned, the sick with fevered frame (1)
642	No voice can sing, no heart can frame (2)
680	Before ... earth received her frame (3)
683, 684	O for a closer walk with God, a calm and heavenly frame (1)
683, 684	calm and serene my frame (5)

frankincense

109	gold, and myrrh, and frankincense (5)
127	see them give ... gold and frankincense and myrrh (3)
128	Frankincense to offer have I (3)

fray
233, 234   triumphant leaders in the fray (2)

free
3   he, in all we do or say, would keep us free from harm (1)
3   that he ... would keep us free from harm this day (1)
3   with conscience free from sin and blame (4)
4   that he, in all we do or say, would keep us free (1)
4   keep us free from harm this day (1)
4   with conscience free from sin and blame (4)
31, 32   Free us from bonds of blinding sin (5)
38, 39   Lord, free us from our ancient foe (3)
56   free them from Satan's tyranny (4)
60   you came, O Savior, to set free your own (2)
60   set free your own in glorious liberty (2)
66   Come ... long-expected Jesus, born to set thy people free (1)
74   he would have us bear it so he can make us free (4)
76   whose advent doth thy people free (5)
80   from all sin will set you free (3)
97   matchless gifts and free (2)
105   free all those who trust in him ... (3)
105   free all ... from Satan's power and might (3)
114   O children of the forest free, the angel song is true (4)
119   so may we with holy joy, pure and free from sin's alloy (3)
122, 123   Alleluia thou resoundest, true Jerusalem and free (2)
161   the ransom of a world set free (4)
174   From sin's power do thou set free soul's new-born (4)
174   set free soul's new-born, O Lord, in thee (4)
180   death is conquered, we are free (1)
180   we are free from sin's dark prison (4)
202   free from Pharaoh's cruel tyranny (2)
202   thy captive people are set free (4)
208   from death's dread sting thy servants free (5)
212   those feet still free to move and bleed for millions (3)
231   they're free from pain and cares (2/12-28)
232   presiding at the council that set the Gentiles free (2/10-23)
236   glory to Christ, who set us free (4)
242   the truth that sets us free (5)
251   help us here on earth to live from selfish passions free (4)
256   to save him from his fearful ways and free him (2)
256   free him from the bonds of sin (2)
256   Saint Paul was changed by God's free love (3)
259   Come to thy temples here, that we, from sin set free (4)
278   paid to set the sinner free (2)
290   gather thou thy people in, free from sorrow ... from sin (4)
304   I come with joy to meet my Lord, forgiven, loved and free (1)
312   Lord, may the tongues which "Holy" sang keep free (2)
312   keep free from all deceiving (2)
334   alert and living in your Spirit, strong and free (3)
337   in thine own service make us glad and free (4)
345   from harm and danger keep thy children free (2)
364   humbly thou cam'st to set us free (6)
370   the flashing of the lightning free (4)
372   His Spirit floweth free, high surging where it will (3)
396, 397   free us from all ills in this world and the next (2)

406, 407	prove in free forgivingness their love (6)
417, 418	whose blood set us free to be people of God (1)
419	Grant us thy truth to make us free (4)
425	All praise and thanks to him belong who came to ... free (2)
425	came to set his people free (2)
433	thy Name be ever praised! O Lord, make us free (3)
439	when from death I'm free, I'll sing on (3)
444	Blessed be the God of Israel, who comes to set us free (1)
458	that he his foes from thence might free (5)
477	who wast a servant that we might be free (3)
495	thou didst free salvation bring (1)
499	Lord God, you have set your servant free to go in peace (1)
500	from sin and sorrow set us free (1)
511	setting captive sinners free (2)
534	to set their captives free (3)
554	'Tis the gift to be simple, 'tis the gift to be free (1)
558	mankind shall then indeed be free (2)
585	bound in setting others free (4)
586	Every task, however simple, sets the soul ... free (3)
586	every task ... sets the soul that does it free (3)
587	who teachest us to find the love from self set free (3)
591	in ire and exultation aflame with faith, and free (3)
594, 595	From the fears that long have bound us free our hearts (2)
594, 595	free our hearts to faith and praise (2)
603, 604	may I in Christ be free to welcome and accept his own (4)
616	He comes to break oppression, to set the captive free (1)
617	one in the power that makes thy children free (2)
617	free to follow truth, and thus to follow thee (2)
621, 622	full of health, and strong, and free (4)
641	from harmful passions set me free (1)
648	let us all in Christ be free (4)
659, 660	in lowly paths of service free (1)
667	set free from present sorrow, we cheerfully can say (2)
706	did not freely choose you till by grace you set me free (2)
717	My native country, thee, land of the noble free (2)
718	in this free land by thee our lot is cast (2)
720	o'er the land of the free and the home of the brave (1-2)
720	O thus be it ever when free men shall stand (2)

freed

165, 166	by that blood from stain are freed (3)
294	one with his rising, freed and forgiven (2)
530	how forever, in its need ... the world is freed (3)
530	through his death the world is freed (3)
545	freed from every weight of sin ... holy footsteps trace (2)
610	healed the sick and freed the soul (2)

freedom

53	bore the cross to save us, hope and freedom gave us (1)
65	His rule is peace and freedom ... justice, truth and love (2)
121	likewise in God's service we may perfect freedom find (4)
444	The prophets spoke of mercy, of freedom and release (1)
542	freedom her bondage breaks, and night is turned to day (1)
569	earth ... shall to freedom and truth be restored (4)
610	still the captives long for freedom (2)

610	that your servants, Lord, in freedom may your mercy know (4)
631	bringing freedom, spreading truth (1)
717	from every mountain-side let freedom ring (1)

freely

121	freely as Son of Man to serve and give your life for all (3)
165, 166	this the Savior freely willed (2)
202	his flesh ... is freely offered in our stead (3)
261, 262	to his earthly father freely was subject (2)
416	each perfect gift of thine to the world so freely given (6)
516	O let it freely burn, till earthly passions turn to dust (2)
528	all that you so freely give (4)
603, 604	Thus freely loved, though fully known (4)
692	Behold, I freely give the living water (2)
699	freely let me take of thee (3)
706	Lord, I did not freely choose you (2)
706	did not freely choose you till by grace you set me free (2)

frenzy

| 567 | youth renewed and frenzy calmed owned thee, the Lord (2) |

fresh

8	Praise for them, springing fresh from the Word (1)
159	my heart fresh ardor gaining (5)
179	all fresh gifts returned with her returning King (2)
245	O Word made flesh, your deeds and words refresh (3)
664	pastures fresh he makes me feed beside the living stream (1)
677	Ye fearful saints, fresh courage take (3)
681	May thy fresh light arise within each clouded heart (5)

freshening

| 228 | freshening breeze and cooling shade (2) |

freshness

| 609 | still holds the freshness of thy grace (3) |

fretting

| 145 | for schemes are vain and fretting brings no gain (1) |

friend

143	John, the Bridegroom's friend, became the herald (3)
168, 169	What language ... borrow to thank thee, dearest friend (4)
243	he had no friend to plead his cause (2)
243	no shield I ask, no faithful friend (4)
285	great apostle's chosen friend (3)
365	stablish thy righteousness, Savior and friend (2)
370	Christ in mouth of friend and stranger (6)
388	Our Maker, Defender, Redeemer, and Friend (5)
452	the surest friend of all his foes (2)
458	my friend, indeed, who at my need his life did spend (2)
458	But O my friend, my friend indeed (2)
458	This is my friend (7)
460, 461	Intercessor, friend of sinners (3)
524	Jesus, thou friend divine, our Savior and our King (4)

558	we will love both friend and foe in all our strife (3)
644	O Jesus, Shepherd, Guardian, Friend (4)
655	be thou for ever near me, my Master and my friend (1)
655	O give me grace to follow, my Master and my friend (3)
681	the blood of friend as sign of love for comrade spilt (4)

friendless

| 212 | lest dead and friendless and alone he ... deceive (4) |
| 212 | O Dead arise! O Friendless stand by seraphim adored (5) |

friendly

| 458 | in death no friendly tomb but what a stranger gave (6) |

friends

10	Old friends, old scenes, will lovelier be (4)
107	Good Christian friends, rejoice (1-3)
145	the friends you make shall bring God's glory bright (5)
215	he is parted from his friends (2)
304	and strangers now are friends (3)
348	chosen by you, to be counted as friends (1)
413	salvation which all his friends with joy confess (1)
416	friends on earth and friends above (4)
602	Kneels at the feet of his friends (1)
603, 604	claims us as his friends and loves us as we are (2)
614	O friends upraise anthems of joy and holy praise (1)
618	O friends, in gladness let us sing (4)
714	Shalom, my friends (RC)

friendship

| 304 | His presence ... is in such friendship better known (4) |

frost

| 292 | Lord, in their change, let frost and heat ... be given (2) |
| 292 | let frost and heat, and winds and dews be given (2) |

frosty

| 112 | In the bleak midwinter, frosty wind made moan (1) |

frozen

| 226, 227 | melt the frozen, warm the chill (4) |

fruit

165, 166	None in foliage ... blossom ... fruit thy peer may be (4)
198	Come, let us taste the vine's new fruit (2)
290	fruit unto his praise to yield (2)
345	peace to our land, the fruit of truth and love (3)
406, 407	bringeth forth fruit, herb, and flower (5)
424	For the fruit of all creation (1)
667	Though vine nor fig tree neither ... wonted fruit should (4)

fruitful

191	hearts in heaven dwelling, we on earth may fruitful be (4)
290	but the fruitful ears to store in his garner evermore (3)
616	He shall come down like showers upon the fruitful earth (3)

fruits

191	Christ, the first-fruits of the holy harvest-field (3)
292	kindly earth with timely birth may yield her fruits again (2)
344	may the fruits of thy salvation ... abound (2)
392	celestial fruits on earthly ground (3)
392	celestial fruits ... from faith and hope may grow (3)
400	flowers and fruits that in you grow ... glory also show (4)
405	the ripe fruits in the garden, he made them every one (3)
511	praise ... for thy fruits and gifts unpriced (1)
588, 589	let the dew of heaven descend and righteous fruits abound (1)
588, 589	give it root in every heart to bring forth fruits of love (2)
588, 589	let it yield a hundred-fold the fruits of peace and joy (3)
705	As those of old their first fruits brought (1)
705	first fruits brought of vineyard, flock, and field (1)
705	so we today our frist fruits bring (1)

fulfill

116	Thus it becomes us to fulfill all righteousness, he said (2)
116	like him desirous to fulfill God's will in righteousness (4)
179	come then, true and faithful, now fulfill thy word (5)
444	God shall fulfill his promise and bring his people peace (1)
541	by feeblest agents may our God fulfill his righteous will (3)
605	How shall my soul fulfill God's law so hard and high (4)

fulfilled

106	this day hath God fulfilled his promised word (2)
120	God's righteousness he thus fulfilled (1)
162	Fulfilled is all that David told (2)
165, 166	his appointed time fulfilled (2)
232	thus fulfilled your word (2/7-25)
260	carpenter whose life fulfilled our gracious God's design (1)
271, 272	Christ, the Sun of all the earth fulfilled that witness (3)
271, 272	Christ ... fulfilled that witness at his birth (3)
597	the hope of peace shall be fulfilled (2)

fulfilling

539	O Zion, haste, thy mission high fulfilling (1)

fulfillment

576, 577	Grant us love's fulfillment, joy with all the blessed (3)
623	wish and fulfillment are not severed there (2)
669	bring to sure fulfillment thy counsel good and true (3)
698	fulfillment of my life in love outpoured (3)

fulfills

235	while each his own commission fulfills in every line (2)
452	Glorious the day when Christ fulfills what self rejects (4)

full

82	Virgin, full of grace, by the Holy Ghost conceiving (2)
109	full reverently upon their knee (5)
143	Then grant us, Lord, like them to be full oft in fast (4)
143	full oft in fast and prayer with thee (4)
191	will all its full abundance at his second coming yield (3)
209	with full and endless sight (4)

242	at once he rose to full belief's unclouded height (4)
243	When Stephen, full of power and grace, went forth (1)
266	said, "Hail Mary, full of grace." (2)
286	in prayer full oft have striven (4)
290	then the full corn shall appear (2)
269	Hail Mary, Full of grace (1-4)
320	Full and clear sing out thy praising (4)
324	Christ ... descendeth our full homage to demand (1)
389	his full hand supplies their need (6)
398	moon shines full at his command and all the stars obey (1)
414	Full of kindness and compassion, slow to anger (5)
422	saints on earth and saints above we join in full accord (2)
492	thus he wrought the full redemption (3)
495	by almighty love anointed, thou hast full atonement made (2)
546	A cloud of witnesses around hold thee in full survey (2)
585	Drained is love in making full (4)
599	Sing a song full of the faith (1)
599	sing a song full of the hope ... the present has brought (1)
621, 622	full of health, and strong, and free (4)
621, 622	full of vigor ... of pleasure that shall last eternally (4)

fuller
| 501, 502 | To fuller life your people bring (5) |

fullest
| 371 | rolling in fullest pride, through the world far and wide (4) |
| 518 | thy fullest benediction shed within its walls alway (3) |

fullness
19, 20	pour forth into our hearts, we pray, the fullness (1)
19, 20	fullness of your grace today (1)
88	he on Adam's fallen race sheds the fullness of his grace (3)
240, 241	of his fullness grace for grace (4)
245	fullness of your grace and truth for us and all the world (1)
307	in its fullness undiminished shall for evermore remain (4)
367	earth is with thy fullness stored (1,3)
455, 456	still more in resurrection light we read the fullness (4)
455, 456	in resurrection light we read the fullness of thy might (4)
512	Lead us to heaven, that we may share the fullness of joy (4)
512	fullness of joy for ever there (4)
515	Rest upon this congregation ... fullness of thy grace (2)
547	his love ... its fullness, depth, and height (1)

fully
| 139 | till God's will is fully done he will not bend or waver (1) |
| 603, 604 | Thus freely loved, though fully known (4) |

furnish
| 10 | The trivial round, the common task, will furnish all (5) |

furnished
| 321 | furnished well with joyful guests (2) |

furrows
| 191 | ripened ... from the furrows of the grave (3) |

furthest
506, 507   dark and furthest corners by the wind of heaven blown (4)

fury
98   All the little boys he killed at Bethlehem in his fury (3)

future
82   of the things that are, that have been and that future (1)
82   that future years shall see (1)
182   His Spirit burns through this and every future age (5)
424   future needs in earth's safe-keeping (1)

Gabriel
252   kneeling in her lowly cell, by the angel Gabriel (2)
263, 264   Blest in the message Gabriel brought (3)
265   The angel Gabriel from heaven came (1)
266   Gabriel of high degree (1)
271, 272   With heavenly message Gabriel came (2)
282, 283   Send thine archangel Gabriel the mighty herald of heaven (3)

Gabriel's
270   Gabriel's message does away Satan's curse and ... sway (1)

gain
27, 28   strive to gain the heavenly prize (4)
107   Calls you one and calls you all to gain his ... hall (3)
107   to gain his everlasting hall (3)
145   for schemes are vain and fretting brings no gain (1)
161   the worst gain power to be good (5)
232   worldly gain forsaking, your path of life we share (2/9-21)
232   be bound in love together, and life eternal gain (2/10-28)
270   death by death its death shall gain (2)
273, 274   both triumph in their dying ... glorious sainthood gain (2)
379   never o'er us final triumph gain (3)
474   my richest gain I count but loss (1)
498   content to let my pride go by, to know no gain nor loss (3)
518   what they ask of thee to gain (4)
518   what they gain from thee, forever ... to retain (4)
582, 583   greed for gain in street and shop and tenement (2)

gained
14, 15   by a holy death attained, eternal glory may be gained (2)
286   triumph by the Lamb have gained (3)
554   When true simplicity is gained (1)

gaining
159   my heart fresh ardor gaining (5)
572   summon us to love by loss, gaining all by giving (3)
682   with the hope of gaining aught, not seeking a reward (5)

gains
281   left his task, his gains, his all (3)

Galilean
495   Hail, thou once despised Jesus, Hail, thou Galilean King (1)

549, 550   as, of old, Saint Andrew heard it by the Galilean lake (2)

Galilee
183   to Galilee he will go before you (7)
203   Your Lord doth go to Galilee (3)
231   You called him from his fishing upon Lake Galilee (2/11-30)
266   he was sent from the Trinity, to Nazareth in Galilee (1)
652, 653   O Sabbath rest by Galilee, O calm of hills above (3)
661   They cast their nets in Galilee (1)
673   Mary the Maid of Galilee (1)

gall
171   O the wormwood and the gall (2)
450, 451   ne'er forget the wormwood and the gall (5)

gallows
196, 197   resplendent from the gallows tree (1,4)

garb
383, 384   woodlands robed in the blooming garb of spring (2)

garden
8   Praise for the sweetness of the wet garden (2)
405   the ripe fruits in the garden, he made them every one (3)

garment's
590   healing those who touch your garment's hem (3)

garments
156   with palms and scattered garments strowed (1)
202   arrayed in garments white and fair (1)
480   strowed their garments on the ground (3)

garner
290   but the fruitful ears to store in his garner evermore (3)

garnered
289   our harvest may be garnered by ages yet unknown (3)

gate
23   At prayer time, near the Temple gate (2)
157   This is the gate of the Lord (R)
167   he only could unlock the gate of heaven and let us in (4)
180   He is risen ... He hath opened heaven's gate (4)
215   riding on the clouds ... to his heavenly palace gate (1)
255   We sing the glorious conquest before Damascus' gate (1)
259   Hail to the Lord who comes, comes to his temple gate (1)
310, 311   opening wide the gate of heaven to us below (1)
360, 361   this is none other than the gate of heaven (4)
454   now the gate of death is riven (3)
495   opened is the gate of heaven, reconciled are we with God (2)
697   death the gate of heaven (4)

gates
9   royal robes of autumn moors the golden gates of spring (2)

65	Fling wide your gates, O Zion, your Savior's rule embrace (3)
68	The marriage-feast is waiting, the gates wide open stand (2)
71, 72	gates of brass before him burst, the iron fetters yield (2)
157	Open for me the gates of righeousness (1)
175	heaven her gates unbars, flinging her increase of light (3)
199, 200	Neither might the gates of death ... tomb's dark portal (4)
208	He closed the yawning gates of hell (4)
214	lift your heads, eternal gates (2)
216	heaven her gates unbars, flinging her increase of light (2)
257	O Zion, open wide thy gates (1)
270	so, behold, all the gates of heaven unfold (R)
287	through gates of pearl streams in the countless host (8)
377, 378	O enter then his gates with praise (3)
391	We'll crowd thy gates with thankful songs (4)
436	Lift up your heads, ye mighty gates (1)
443	he taught within the temple's gates (2)
492	passed within the gates of darkness (2)
519, 520	Bright thy gates of pearl are shining (3)
519, 520	thy gates ... they are open evermore (3)
562	gates of hell can never 'gainst that Church prevail (4)

gather

290	gather thou thy people in, free from sorrow ... from sin (4)
321	gather from their Father's board the Bread that lives (3)
433	We gather together to ask the Lord's blessing (1)
576	Here in Christ we gather, love of Christ our calling (1)
576	When we Christians gather, members of one Body (2)
577	Here in Christ we gather, love of Christ our calling (1)
577	When we Christians gather, members of one Body (2)
590	seeking to gather all in love and pity (3)
606	when we gather let no discord or enmity break our oneness (2)

gathered

78, 79	gathered all above, while mortals sleep (2)
112	Angels and archangels may have gathered there (3)
191	by angel hands be gathered, and be ever, Lord, with thee (4)
230	In Salem's street was gathered a crowd from many a land (2)
290	all is safely gathered in, ere the winter storms begin (1)
302	so, from all lands thy Church be gathered ... by thy Son (2)
302	thy Church be gathered into thy kingdom (2)
303	so from all lands thy Church be gathered ... by thy Son (4)
303	thy Church be gathered into thy kingdom by thy Son (4)
349	draw near to your servants gathered here (1)
440	Blessed Jesus, at thy word we are gathered all to hear (1)
492	till he see ... all things gathered into one (4)

gathering

125, 126	the gathering nations come (2)
128	Myrrh is mine; its bitter perfume ... gathering gloom (4)
128	perfume breathes a life of gathering gloom (4)
292	gathering round thy throne ... in the holy angel's sight (3)
563	fear not the gathering night (4)

gathers

441, 442	all the light of sacred story gathers round its head (1,5)

441, 442   gathers round its head sublime (1,5)

gave
   9   God who gave all worlds that are, and all that are to be (6)
  23   They gave him healing in your Name (2)
 27, 28 you gave the day with splendor bright (1)
 53   bore the cross to save us, hope and freedom gave us (1)
 84   star and angels gave the sign (1)
 92   born on earth to save us; him the Father gave us (1)
 92   born on earth to save us; peace and love he gave us (4)
 109   to the earth it gave great light (2)
 143   loving God who gave the law (2)
 184   He who gave for us his life ... for us endured the strife (2)
 193   those scars their solemn witness gave (2)
 212   as Pilate gave them leave (4)
 252   promise that it gave, "Jesus shall his people save" (3)
261, 262 to Saint Joseph gave supernal honor (3)
 267   The prophet gave the sign for faithful folk to read (2)
271, 272 John, still unborn, yet gave aright his witness (3)
 277   Constant was the love he gave her (2)
 313   all that love of God could give Jesus by his sorrows gave (2)
 322   When Jesus died to save us, a word, an act he gave us (1)
 356   As angels gave poor Lazarus from all his ills release (3)
 391   formed us of clay and gave us breath (2)
 405   He gave us eyes to see them (4)
 421   Lamb of God ... whom God the Father gave us (2)
448, 449 for us gave up his dying breath (4)
 458   He made the lame to run, he gave the blind their sight (4)
 458   in death no friendly tomb but what a stranger gave (6)
 472   we render back the love thy mercy gave us (4)
 478   you gave yourself to die for our salvation (1)
 530   how his only Son he gave (2)
 567   thy touch ... gave hearing, strength, and sight (2)
 640   gild the spot that gave them birth (2)
 720   gave proof through the night ... our flag was still there (1)

gavest
 24   The day thou gavest, Lord, is ended (1)
 705   O thou who gavest us thyself in Jesus Christ thy Son (3)

gaze
 57, 58 with what rapture gaze we on those glorious scars (3)
 83   leaving their flocks, draw nigh to gaze (4)
 124   eastern sages with amaze upon the wondrous token gaze (2)
 357   where thy saints made perfect gaze upon thy face (4)
 398   if I survey the ground I tread, or gaze upon the sky (2)
506, 507 showing us God's wonders, is himself the power to gaze (2)

gazing
 159   Who, on Christ's dear mother gazing ... would not weep (4)

gems
117, 118 gems of the mountain, and pearls of the ocean (3)

generation

| 248, 249 | for many a generation hid in God's fore-knowledge lay (1) |
| 603, 604 | Where generation, class, or race divide us to our shame (3) |

generations

| 265 | all generations laud and honor thee (2) |

Gennesaret's

| 567 | crowded street, by restless couch ... Gennesaret's shore (2) |

Gentile

| 232 | taught both Jew and Gentile ... Christ is all in all (2/6-29) |

Gentiles

124	Gentiles to his crib to bring (1)
127	Jesus, whom the Gentiles worshiped at thy glad epiphany (5)
232	presiding at the council that set the Gentiles free (2/10-23)

Gentiles'

| 329, 331 | Blood ... which the Gentiles' Lord and King ... shed (1) |

gentle

74	Gentle is he and humble, And light his yoke shall be (4)
259	but, borne upon the throne of Mary's gentle breast (2)
265	Then gentle Mary meekly bowed her head (3)
292	At temper fair with gentle air the sunshine and the rain (2)
400	even you, most gentle death (6)
400	most gentle death, waiting to hush our final breath (6)
416	for all gentle thoughts and mild (4)
547	with kind and gentle hearts forgive (4)

gentlemen

| 105 | God rest you merry, gentlemen, let nothing you dismay (1) |

gentleness

| 193 | O Jesus, King of gentleness (3) |
| 482 | Lord of all gentleness, Lord of all calm (4) |

gently

75	the lambs he'll gently hold (3)
165, 166	the King of heavenly beauty gently on thine arms extend (5)
342	we hear the words so gently spoken (1)
400	pale silver moon that gently gleams (1)
410	in his hand he gently bears us (3)
645, 646	on his shoulder gently laid (3)

get

| 75 | get thee up to the heights and sing (2) |

Gethsemane

| 171 | Go to dark Gethsemane, ye that feel the tempter's power (1) |
| 284 | In dark Gethsemane the night before he died (4) |

Ghost

| 3, 4 | to God the Holy Ghost we raise our ... praise (5) |

11	praise Father, Son and Holy Ghost (4)
29, 30	to God the Holy Ghost we raise our … praise (3)
37	we hymn the eternal Father … Son … Holy Ghost divine (2)
43	praise Father, Son, and Holy Ghost (4)
77	all praise, O Holy Ghost, to thee (5)
82	Virgin, full of grace, by the Holy Ghost conceiving (2)
82	O Holy Ghost, to thee … unwearied praises be (4)
110	to praise the Father, Son, and Holy Ghost (4)
124	to … Holy Ghost we raise our equal and unceasing praise (5)
131, 132	whom with the Father we adore and Holy Ghost for evermore (5
193	God the Holy Ghost, we raise (5)
202	all praise to God the Father be and Holy Ghost eternally (5)
207	Father, Son, and Holy Ghost (4)
211	To Father, Son, and Holy Ghost (4)
225	day … Holy Ghost shone in the world with God's grace (R)
257	all glory, Holy Ghost, to thee, while endless ages run (5)
287	singing to Father, Son, and Holy Ghost, Alleluia (8)
363	O Holy Ghost, the Lord and the Life-giver (4)
377, 378	To Father, Son, and Holy Ghost (5)
380	praise Father, Son, and Holy Ghost (3)
401	"Hail, Father, Son, and Holy Ghost" they ever cry (5)
503, 504	Come, Holy Ghost, our souls inspire (1)
515	Holy Ghost, dispel our sadness (1)
612	Gracious Spirit, Holy Ghost (1)
658	To Father, Son, and Holy Ghost, the God whom we adore (4)
700	love of the Holy Ghost, fill thou each needy one (4)

giant

| 9 | see how the giant sun soars up (5) |

giants

| 564, 565 | No foes shall stay his might, though he with giants fight (2) |

gift

27, 28	forget your blessed gift of life (3)
78, 79	How silently, how silently, the wondrous gift is given (3)
84	love for plea and gift and sign (3)
144	through your saving sacrifice receive your gift of grace (3)
175	every good gift of the year now with its Master returns (1)
226, 227	thy blest seven-fold gift assign (5)
313	Wilt thou own the gift I bring (4)
340, 341	by your gift of peace restored (2)
347	serving Christ, our every gift employ (4)
349	come … with your strengthening gift of power (2)
416	each perfect gift of thine to the world so freely given (6)
445, 446	highest gift of grace should flesh and blood refine (4)
459	where his loving people meet to share the gift divine (2)
472	God's gift from highest heaven (2)
513	to her midst as gift and sign (2)
554	'Tis the gift to be simple, 'tis the gift to be free (1)
554	'tis the gift to come down where we ought to be (1)
584	yet greater far this gift, O God, bestow (2)
594, 595	let the gift of thy salvation be our glory evermore (4)
610	consecrating to your purpose every gift that you impart (1)

665   gift of Christ, his son (5)
704   still stir up the gift in me (3)

gifts
47   this day the Spirit came with his gifts of living flame (2)
47   Thou, who didst all gifts impart (4)
47   best of gifts, thyself bestow (5)
92   lay their gifts before him, praise him and adore him (3)
97   matchless gifts and free (2)
114   The chiefs from far before him knelt with gifts of fox (3)
114   gifts of fox and beaver-pelt (3)
117, 118 vainly with gifts would his favor secure (4)
119   offered gifts most rare at that manger rude and bare (3)
127   Sacred gifts of mystic meaning (4)
128   bearing gifts we traverse afar (1)
131, 132 by their gifts confessed their God (2)
179   all fresh gifts returned with her returning King (2)
228   Father of the fatherless, giver of gifts limitless (1)
228   make us ready to receive gifts from your unbounded store (5)
231   let gifts of grace descend (2/6-11)
233, 234 The eternal gifts of Christ the King ... we sing (1)
289   days of old have dowered us with gifts beyond all praise (3)
291   All good gifts around us are sent from heaven above (R)
291   the gifts we have to offer are what thy love imparts (3)
292   by thee come down henceforth the gifts of God (1)
292   with the Father's Name, and with the Holy Spirit's gifts (3)
300   Source of all our gifts and graces, Christ we own (2)
337   crown thy gifts with strength to persevere (3)
339   through the gifts thou here dost give me ... receive me (3)
348   intention ever to cherish the gifts you provide (2)
349   gifts of blessing to bestow on your waiting Church below (1)
371   Move on the waters' face bearing the gifts of grace (3)
385   with thee are found the gifts of life (2)
396, 397 blessed us on our way with countless gifts of love (1)
415   Ten thousand ... precious gifts my daily thanks employ (3)
415   cheerful heart that tastes those gifts with joy (3)
424   For his gifts to every nation (1)
501, 502 to us your varied gifts make known (3)
503, 504 who dost thy sevenfold gifts impart (2)
511   praise ... for thy fruits and gifts unpriced (1)
514   of all his gifts the sum and crown (4)
528   the Spirit's gifts empower us for the work of ministry (R)
584   Great are your gifts (2)
584   So for your glory and our good may we your gifts employ (4)
585   Open are the gifts of God (2)
585   gifts of love to mind and sense (2)
612   of thy gifts at Pentecost (1)
621, 622 hereafter these thy labors may with endless gifts be paid (5)
665   Daily ... almighty Giver boundless gifts on us bestow (4)
687, 688 the Spirit and the gifts are ours through him (4)

gild
640   Watchman, will its beams alone gild the spot (2)
640   gild the spot that gave them birth (2)

gilds

73	beauty gilds the eastern hills (1)
427	When morning gilds the skies, my heart, awaking, cries (1)
471	gilds the bed of death with light (4)
543	He gilds thy morning face with beams that cannot fade (2)

Gilead

232	with true balm of Gilead anoint us evermore (2/10-18)
676	There is a balm in Gilead to make the wounded whole (R)
676	there is a balm in Gilead to heal the sinsick soul (R)

gird

615	gird up your loins, ye prophet souls (3)

girded

388	pavilioned in splendor, and girded with praise (1)

give

5	to give us grace our wrongs to bear (4)
9	give and give, and give again what God hath given thee (6)
12, 13	give us strength to do your will (3)
18	your living water give to drink (4a)
23	now give us grace to walk your way (2)
31, 32	like moon and night, give loving peace (5)
33, 33	to the night give glittering adornment (1)
33, 33	Give heed, we pray you, to our supplication (4)
35	to the night give glittering adornment (1)
35	Give heed, we pray you, to our supplication (4)
38, 39	give to our wearied bodies rest (2)
42	Jesus, give the weary calm and sweet repose (2)
46	let us, as night is falling ... give thanks to him (1)
47	thou dost give thyself to me, help me give myself to thee (6)
50	highest heavens in which he reigns shall give ... praise (5)
50	shall give him nobler praise (5)
51	that Christ may take them, bless them, break and give (4)
51	break and give them to all his people (4)
56	didst give the law, in cloud, and majesty, and awe (3)
56	give them victory o'er the grave (4)
61, 62	Rise up, and give us light (1)
69	Lord, give us grace to awake us (3)
87	born to give us second birth (3)
89, 90	world give back the song which now the angels sing (4)
107	give ye heed to what we say: Jesus Christ is born today (1)
112	What can I give him, poor as I am (4)
112	yet what I can I give him give my heart (3)
121	freely as Son of Man to serve and give your life for all (3)
122, 123	alleluia in our singing, let us for a while give o'er (3)
127	see them give, in deep devotion (3)
127	see them give ... gold and frankincense and myrrh (3)
138	those refreshing streams which you alone can give (3)
142	O give us strength in thee to fight ... to conquer sin (2)
143	give us joy to see thy face (4)
144	Give guidance to our wandering ways (2)
152	Give us the discipline that springs from abstinence (4)
153	Let us give thanks to the Lord our God (2)

153	It is right to give him thanks and praise ever. Amen (2)
157	I will give thanks to you (R)
157	Give thanks to the Lord, for he is good (R)
178	Alleluia, alleluia, Give thanks to the risen Lord (R)
178	Alleluia, alleluia, Give praise to his Name (R)
193	that we may give thee all our days ... praise (3)
193	All praise, O risen Lord, we give to thee (5)
199, 200	to whom we give laud and praise undying (2)
201	day ... whereon the faithful give God praise (1)
232	walking in their footsteps we give you praise anew (2/11-1)
240, 241	Take from him what ye will give him (4)
245	your glory to proclaim whereby your Spirit give us life (3)
251	to us at last in mercy give eternal life with thee (4)
253	Give us wings of faith to rise within the veil (1)
255	give you final service in glory at your throne (3)
285	till thou at last the summons give (4)
288	As thy prospering hand hath blessed, may we give (3)
288	may we give thee of our best (3)
290	give his angels charge at last (3)
295	To Jesus Christ give glory, God's coeternal Son (2)
302, 303	didst give us food for all our days (1)
308, 309	of thine abundance give us, and all we need provide (2)
313	Thou didst give thyself for me, now I give myself to thee (R)
313	all that love of God could give Jesus by his sorrows gave (2)
313	All my penitence I give thee (4)
314	to my taste thy sweetness never failing give (3)
323	Lord, thy wounds our healing give (2)
324	the Body and the Blood he will give to all the faithful (2)
324	he will give ... his own self for heavenly food (2)
329-331	Glory let us give and blessing to the Father and the Son (6)
335	The Bread that I will give is my Flesh (2)
339	through the gifts thou here dost give me ... receive me (3)
340, 341	now we give you thanks, O Lord (1)
344	Thanks we give and adoration for thy Gospel's joyful sound (2)
347	strengthen the faint, give courage to the weak (2)
348	each duty ... give us the chance to create or destroy (4)
349	Give them light, your truth to see (2)
349	give them life, your own to be (2)
355	Give rest, O Christ, to your servant with your saints (1)
356	so may they give you welcome to everlasting peace (3)
358	Christ the Victorious, give to your servants rest (1,4)
365	come, and thy people bless; come, give thy word success (2)
370	the word of God to give me speech (5)
374	blessings, more than we can give (3)
375	Give praise and glory unto God ... Father of all blessing (1)
392	Hosanna, hosanna! Rejoice, give thanks and sing (R)
400	fire ... you give to us both warmth and light (3)
401	The whole triumphant host give thanks to God on high (5)
406, 407	Let creatures all give thanks to thee (8)
408	Let all who name Christ's holy Name give God all praise (3)
408	give God all praise and glory (3)
420	may God give us faith to sing always Alleluia! Amen (5)
424	In the help we give our neighbor (2)
432	All things that give sound (3)

437, 438	Unnumbered blessings give my spirit voice (1)
465, 466	eternal Spirit, give me breath (2)
481	Mortals, give thanks and sing, and triumph evermore (1)
482	and give us, we pray (1-4)
490	God set the stars to give light to the world (1)
495	highest praises, without ceasing ... give (4)
495	highest praises ... right it is for us to give (4)
500	give us thyself, that we may see the Father and the Son (3)
503, 504	Keep far our foes, give peace at home (6)
505	unless thy grace the power should give, none can believe (2)
525	Lord, give us grace that we like them, the meek (5)
528	Lord, you give the great commission (1)
528	give us all new fervor, draw us closer in community (2)
528	Father, what they do, forgive (4)
528	Yet we hoard as private treasure all that you ... give (4)
528	all that you so freely give (4)
531	Give tongues of fire and hearts of love to preach (2)
531	give power and unction from above (2)
534	give ear to me, ye continents, ye isles give ear to me (2)
535	Then let us adore, and give him his right (4)
539	give of thy wealth to speed them on their way (3)
547	Christ shall give you light (1)
547	to give the Spirit's unity, the very bond of peace (2)
547	with kind and gentle hearts forgive (4)
547	forgive as God in Christ forgave (4)
547	Christ shall give you life (5)
549, 550	give our hearts to thine obedience (5)
551	give heart and soul and mind and strength (1)
556, 557	Rejoice, ye pure in heart! Rejoice, give thanks and sing (1)
556, 557	Rejoice, rejoice, rejoice, give thanks, and sing (R)
556, 557	on, ye pure in heart! Rejoice, give thanks and sing (7)
567	give wisdom's heavenly lore (3)
569	give to us peace in our time, O Lord (1-3)
569	thou wilt give peace in thy time, O Lord (4)
574, 575	give us a conscience quick to feel (1)
574, 575	help us to give to all their due (2)
578	give peace, O God, give peace again (1-3)
580	Great Creator, give us guidance (4)
580	give us guidance till our goals and yours are one (4)
582, 583	Give us, O God, the strength to build the city (3)
584	give understanding to the mind (3)
588, 589	give it root in every heart to bring forth fruits of love (2)
593	where there is hurt, may we forgive (1)
605	Rulers of earth, give ear. Should you not justice show (2)
607	when hatred and division give way to love and peace (4)
608	give, for wild confusion, peace (3)
610	hope and health, good will and comfort ... give (4)
610	counsel, aid, and peace we give (4)
611	he will ease your load and give you rest (6)
612	therefore, give us love (2-3)
616	give them songs for sighing ... darkness turn to light (2)
617	give or withhold, let pain or pleasure be (3)
635	he'll give thee strength whate'er betide thee (1)
636, 637	For I am thy God, and will still give thee aid (2)
655	O give me grace to follow, my Master and my friend (3)

656	give us a pure and lowly heart, a temple fit for thee (4)
659, 660	in peace that only thou canst give (4)
667	he who feeds the ravens will give his children bread (3)
681	give us open eyes to see thee as thou art (5)
690	songs of praises, I will ever give to thee (3)
692	Behold, I freely give the living water (2)
695, 696	O give our frightened souls the sure salvation (2)
695, 696	when this cup you give is filled to brimming (3)
695, 696	Yet when again in this new world you give us the joy (4)
705	A world in need now summons us to labor, love and give (2)
705	help us to give ourselves each day (3)
709	give us each day our daily bread ... raiment fit provide (3)
710	give him glory evermore (RC)

given

9	give and give, and give again what God hath given thee (6)
48	thus this day most glorious a triple light was given (2)
70	to them new life is given (3)
78, 79	How silently, how silently, the wondrous gift is given (3)
83	Jesus, to thee be glory given (6)
88	unto us a son is given (1)
125, 126	To us the promised Child is born, to us the Son is given (3)
133, 134	O Light of Light, Love given birth (1)
164	let all praise be given thee who livest evermore (3)
185, 186	for our offenses given (1)
194, 195	to him the throne over all the world is given (4)
214	Christ, awhile to mortals given (1)
252	Jesus, Name of mercy mild, given to the holy child (4)
252	Jesus, only Name that's given under all the mighty heaven (5)
253	our praise for his own pattern given (4)
292	Lord, in their change, let frost and heat ... be given (2)
292	let frost and heat, and winds and dews be given (2)
300	Who himself for all hath given, us he feeds (3)
308, 309	O Food to pilgrims given, O Bread of life from heaven (1)
329, 331	Given for us, and condescending to be born for us below (2)
339	food ... for our good, thy glory, given (2)
366	Son of God, as Savior given (6)
367	unto thee be glory given, holy, holy, holy Lord (1,3)
393	God has given the cloud by day (2)
393	given the moving fire by night (2)
396, 397	All praise and thanks to God the Father now be given (3)
416	each perfect gift of thine to the world so freely given (6)
421	God's good will unfailingly be to all people given (1)
443	to simple ones his word was given (4)
444	He from the house of David a child of grace has given (2)
469, 470	such kindly judgment given (2)
472	still let thy Spirit unto us be given (2)
477	given the Name to which all knees shall bow (4)
481	the keys of death and hell to Christ the Lord are given (3)
483	To them the cross with all its shame ... grace is given (4)
489	his holy and immortal truth to all on earth hath given (1)
493	Glory to God and praise and love be now and ever given (6)
494	crown him the King, to whom is given the wondrous name (5)
495	life is given through thy Name (1)
496, 497	Praise be given evermore, by earth and heaven (3)

524	to her my cares and toils be given till toils ... end (2)
524	to Zion shall be given the brightest glories (5)
526	when the word is given bid Jordan's narrow stream divide (5)
584	God, you have given us power to sound depths ... unknown (1)
609	The cup of water given for thee (3)
629	the nations, tongues and climes and all the ages given (2)
697	every thought and work and word, to thee be ever given (4)
711	Ask, and it shall be given unto you (RC)

giver

36	O Son of God, Life-giver (3)
46	on God our Maker calling ... the Giver good (1)
124	leads them on with power benign to seek the Giver (3)
124	to seek the Giver of the sign (3)
175	Praise to the Giver of good (8)
216	Praise to the Giver of good (6)
228	Father of the fatherless, giver of gifts limitless (1)
327, 328	Salvation's giver, Christ, the only Son (3)
363	O Holy Ghost, the Lord and the Life-giver (4)
376	giver of immortal gladness, fill us with the light of day (1)
501, 502	the giver and the Lord of life (2)
522, 523	Grace which like the Lord, the giver, never fails (2)
665	Daily ... almighty Giver boundless gifts on us bestow (4)
705	God the giver of all good, the source of bounteous yield (1)

gives

69	God gives himself into our lives (4)
120	who gives eternal life to those that with you died (6)
139	gives the Great Commission (3)
174	praise we him, whose love divine gives his sacred Blood (1)
174	gives his sacred Blood for wine (1)
174	gives his Body for the feast (1)
228	All that gives to us our worth (3)
291	much more to us, his children, he gives our daily bread (2)
327, 328	gives living waters to the thirsting soul (7)
329, 331	then, more precious food supplying, gives himself (3)
329, 331	gives himself with his own hand (3)
363	thine is the quickening power that gives increase (4)
487	such a way as gives us breath (1)
522, 523	safe they feed upon the manna which he gives them (3)
522, 523	manna which he gives them when they pray (3)
534	vainly we hope for the harvest-tide till God gives life (4)
534	till God gives life to the seed (4)
585	Love that gives, gives evermore (3)
585	gives with zeal, with eager hands (3)
625	take what he gives and praise him still (3)
667	who gives the lilies clothing will clothe his people too (3)
669	who gives the winds their courses (1)

givest

305, 306	"This is my Body", so thou givest yet (2)
314	living Bread that givest all thy creatures breath (3)
336	flesh and blood ... and to us thou givest thine (1)
423	To all life thou givest, to both great and small (3)

giveth

219   still his love be giveth (3)

giving

12, 13 O Spirit, love's life-giving ray (4)
25, 26 Life-giving Lord (3)
55   all praise, life-giving Spirit, praise (6)
194, 195 glory to our Savior giving (2)
302, 303 giving in Christ the Bread eternal (1)
316, 317 giving us foretaste of the festal joy (3)
320   Let the Bread, life giving, living, be our theme (2)
370   glorious sun's life-giving ray (4)
371   Spirit of truth and love, life-giving, holy Dove (3)
381   breathed thine own life-giving breath (2)
572   into your self-giving death call us all to follow (2)
572   summon us to love by loss, gaining all by giving (3)
585   weak in giving power to be (4)
593   for in our giving we receive (4)
593   in forgiving are forgiven (4)
692   I came to Jesus, and I drank of that life-giving stream (2)

glad

6, 7   glad my eyes, and warm my heart (2)
50   let heaven rejoice, let earth be glad (1)
71, 72 Hark! the glad sound! the Savior comes (1)
71, 72 glad hosannas, Prince of Peace, thy welcome ... proclaim (4)
76   awake and hearken, for he brings glad tidings (1)
76   glad tidings of the King of kings (1)
78, 79 We hear the Christmas angels the great glad tidings tell (5)
80   Glad tidings of great joy I bring to all the world (1)
94, 95 Glad tidings of great joy I bring to you and all mankind (2)
96   What glad tidings did you hear (2)
106   sing, redeemed, a glad triumphal song (6)
116   Hark, a glad voice (3)
127   Jesus, whom the Gentiles worshiped at thy glad epiphany (5)
131, 132 All glory, Jesus, be to thee for this thy glad epiphany (5)
157   we will rejoice and be glad in it (R)
180   Come ... with glad smile and radiant brow (2)
199, 200 comes to glad Jerusalem (3)
205   To all the world glad news we bring (1)
316, 317 yet, passing, points to the glad feast above (3)
320   today the new oblation ... bids us feast in glad array (4)
336   Let the mighty chorus ever sing its glad exultant songs (3)
337   in thine own service make us glad and free (4)
344   glad thy summons to obey (3)
358   Yet at the grave shall we raise up our glad song (3)
365   thy sacred witness bear in this glad hour (3)
390   sounding in glad adoration (1)
393   raising hymns in glad accord (1)
404   glad in the knowledge of your love so great (2)
453   hear the glad words, "Come to me all the blest" (4)
478   Glorious their life who sing, with glad thanksgiving (3)
479   angel hosts, rejoicing, make their glad reply (4)
480   Hosanna our glad voices raise, hosanna to our King (3)
518   God the One in Three adoring in glad hymns eternally (2)

536	Judah is glad to see his day (3)
539	Publish glad tidings: tidings of peace (R)
541	a glad sound comes with the setting sun (5)
560	Rejoice and be exceeding glad (9)
579	thus evermore shall rise to thee glad praise (4)
579	glad praise from space, air, land, and sea (4)
590	grant the glad surprising that your blest Spirit rouses (1)
606	let us rejoice and be glad now and always (1)
608	thus evermore shall rise to thee glad hymns of praise (4)
618	raise the glad strain (1)
619	with glad songs resounding wake again (3)
649, 650	glad, when your presence we discern (3)
692	I found in him a resting place, and he has made me glad (1)

gladden

244	See the rivers four that gladden, with their streams (2)

gladly

80	gladly sing (1)
128	prayer and praising, gladly raising (3)
275	Gladly, Lord, with thee they suffered (3)
275	gladly, Lord, with thee they died (3)
339	let me gladly here obey thee (3)
390	gladly for ever adore him (4)
458	in whose sweet praise I all my days could gladly spend (7)
475	Gladly, Lord, we offer thine to be forever (2)
611	Heavy laden, gladly come to him (6)

gladness

48	O day of radiant gladness, O day of joy and light (1)
70	Herald, sound the note of gladness (2)
102	he shares in all our gladness (4)
119	As with gladness men of old did the guiding star behold (1)
122, 123	Alleluia, song of gladness, voice of joy that cannot die (1)
150	holier gladness ours shall be (4)
191	sing to God a hymn of gladness (1)
199, 200	Come, ye faithful, raise the strain of triumphant gladness (1)
210	the Passover of gladness, the Passover of God (1)
212	Oh, with what gladness and surprise the saints ... greet (2)
233, 234	with hearts of gladness raise due hymns (1)
237	Let us now our voices raise, wake the day with gladness (1)
248, 249	Name of gladness, Name of pleasure (2)
268, 269	what Christ's mother sang in gladness ... people sing (3)
300	cheers our hearts, fills with food and gladness (3)
339	Deck thyself, my soul, with gladness (1)
352	their marriage bless with gladness from above (1)
376	giver of immortal gladness, fill us with the light of day (1)
399	To God with gladness sing, your Rock and Savior bless (1)
454	in sounds of gladness, leading souls redeemed to heaven (3)
478	the Father's conquering Word, true source of gladness (1)
492	Sing, ye faithful, sing with gladness (1)
515	come, thou source of joy and gladness (1)
527	one the gladness of rejoicing on the far eternal shore (3)
541	to young and old the Gospel gladness bear (4)
555	gladness breaks like morning where'er thy face appears (3)

556, 557	youth to age, by night and day, in gladness and in woe (4)
576, 577	Christ, our love, is with us, gladness be his greeting (1)
594, 595	shame our wanton, selfish gladness (3)
618	O friends, in gladness let us sing (4)
621, 622	Now with gladness, now with courage, bear the burden (5)
701	Jesus, all my gladness, my repose in sadness (1)
701	with me in earth's sadness, Jesus, all my gladness (3)

gladsome

| 36 | O gladsome Light, O grace of God the Father's face (1) |
| 389 | Let us, with a gladsome mind, praise the Lord (1,7) |

glassy

| 362 | casting down their golden crowns around the glassy sea (2) |

gleam

10	some softening gleam of love and prayer shall dawn (4)
566	when ever-blue the sky shall gleam (2)
599	where the white gleam of our bright star is cast (2)
719	thine alabaster cities gleam, undimmed by human tears (3)

gleaming

1, 2	thine is the glory, gleaming and resounding (3)
1, 2	glory, gleaming and resounding through all creation (3)
31, 32	its gleaming path declares the wonders of your ... power (2)
720	what so proudly we hailed at the twilight's last gleaming (1)

gleams

163	the cross on Calvary's height gleams of eternity appear (2)
191	rain and dew and gleams of glory from ... thy face (4)
400	pale silver moon that gently gleams (1)
527	Clear before us through the darkness gleams ... light (1)
527	gleams and burns the guiding light (1)

glistering

| 9 | silver glistering of all the million million stars (2) |

glittering

| 33-35 | to the night give glittering adornment (1) |
| 406, 407 | stars that ... soon will point the glittering heavens (3) |

gloom

6, 7	Pierce the gloom of sin and grief (3)
55	its splendor pierces all our gloom (5)
128	Myrrh is mine; its bitter perfume ... gathering gloom (4)
128	perfume breathes a life of gathering gloom (4)
144	dispel the gloom that shades our minds (1)
527	chasing far the gloom and terror (2)
593	where all is gloom, may we sow hope (2)
662	shine through the gloom, and point me to the skies (4)
672	till thou shalt come our gloom to chase (5)
701	Want and gloom, cross, death and tomb (2)

gloomy

| 56 | disperse the gloomy clouds of night (6) |

339	leave the gloomy haunts of sadness (1)
471	cheers with hope the gloomy day (3)
541	Away with gloomy doubts and faithless fear (3)
599	out from the gloomy past (2)

gloria

92	Ideo, Ideo, Ideo gloria in excelsis Deo (R)
96	Gloria in excelsis Deo (R)
114	in excelsis gloria (R)
265	"... most highly favored lady," Gloria! (1-4)

glories

54	grant that we its glories see (4)
100	makes the nations prove the glories of his righteousness (4)
111	glories stream from heaven afar (2)
253	how bright their glories be (1)
398	not a plant or flower below but makes thy glories known (3)
437, 438	Tell out, my soul, the glories of his word (4)
493	glories of my God and King, the triumphs of his grace (1)
494	his glories now we sing who died, and rose on high (3)
524	to Zion shall be given the brightest glories (5)
524	brightest glories earth can yield (5)

glorified

275	by death to life immortal they were born and glorified (3)
286	striven with the God they glorified (4)
307	Risen, ascended, glorified (5)
420	When in our music God is glorified (1)

glorify

36	thee, therefore, O Most High, the world doth glorify (3)
232	equip us for such sufferings as glorify your Name (2/7-25)
462	glorify thy Name (4)
478	your Name we glorify, O Jesus, throned on high (1)
531	Name of Jesus glorify till every people call him Lord (4)
628	our thoughts and words and deeds may glorify your Name (2)

glorious

5	O Father, glorious evermore, we plead with thee (3)
14, 15	Grant us, when this short life is past, the glorious (2)
14, 15	the glorious evening that shall last (2)
27, 28	you brought all things to glorious birth (1)
31, 32	wonders of your glorious power (2)
48	thus this day most glorious a triple light was given (2)
57, 58	with what rapture gaze we on those glorious scars (3)
60	set free your own in glorious liberty (2)
61, 62	Forth he comes, her Bridegroom glorious (2)
61, 62	glorious in strength of grace, in truth victorious (2)
66	raise us to thy glorious throne (4)
81	dispel in glorious splendor the darkness everywhere (3)
89, 90	that glorious song of old (1)
91	O shepherds, greet that glorious sight (1)
125, 126	people who in darkness walked have seen a glorious light (1)
128	Glorious now behold him arise (5)

149	glorious in springtime dress of leaf and flower (3)
165, 166	Sing, my tongue, the glorious battle (1)
170	that glorious is your crown (1)
173	the glorious Prince of Life should in death be sleeping (3)
180	dimming yonder glorious morning ray (3)
188, 189	Lives again our glorious King (2)
191	glorious life ... immortal, on his resurrection morn (2)
191	ripened by his glorious sunshine (3)
203, 206	the glorious King (1)
208	he rises glorious from the dead (3)
214	glorious to his native skies (1)
214	There the glorious triumph waits (2)
219	our glorious Head (1)
219	O earth, adore thy glorious King (2)
222	he makes his glorious presence clear (2)
222	shall come in all love's glorious power to rule (4)
231	praise for the glorious vision the persecutor saw (2/1-25)
233, 2234	the apostles' glorious deeds we sing (1)
237	turn from fear, and heed the call to a glorious morrow (3)
238, 239	glorious and victorious, bravely bore the martyr's part (2)
240, 241	Hearken to the anthem glorious of the martyrs (1)
253	Our glorious Leader claims our praise (4)
255	We sing the glorious conquest before Damascus' gate (1)
273, 274	both triumph in their dying ... glorious sainthood gain (2)
286	who are all this glorious band (1)
286	Whence comes all this glorious band (2)
287	But lo, there breaks a yet more glorious day (7)
290	raise the glorious harvest-home (4)
298	stand among the glorious heavenly band (1)
314	in the glorious vision, blessed Lord, of thee (4)
329, 331	the mystery of the glorious Body sing (1)
358	From earth you formed us, both glorious and mortal (2)
364	apostles glorious company ... thy constant praise recite (4)
366	Christ, thou art our glorious King (5)
367	Thus thy glorious Name confessing (3)
369	How wondrous great, how glorious bright ... our Creator (1)
369	how glorious bright must our Creator be (1)
370	glorious sun's life-giving ray (4)
371	where the Gospel day sheds not its glorious ray (1)
371	Holy and blessed Three, glorious Trinity (4)
373	Praise the Lord, for he is glorious (2)
381	glorious now, we press toward glory (3)
386, 387	Glorious the sun in mid career (3)
386, 387	glorious the assembled fires appear (3)
386, 387	glorious the comet's train (3)
386, 387	glorious the trumpet and alarm (3)
386, 387	glorious the almighty stretched-out arm (3)
386, 387	glorious the enraptured main (3)
386, 387	Glorious, most glorious, is the crown of him (4)
388	O worship the King, all glorious above (1)
401	glorious with his saints in light, for ever reigns (3)
409	utter forth a glorious voice (3)
410	Glorious in his faithfulness (2)
413	Righteous, commanding, ever glorious (3)
423	most blessed, most glorious, the Ancient of Days (1)

436	Holy Spirit guide us on until the glorious crown be won (5)
452	Glorious the day when Christ was born to wear the crown (1)
452	Glorious the day when Christ arose (2)
452	Glorious the days of gospel grace (3)
452	Glorious the day when Christ fulfills what self rejects (4)
472	we would be faithful to thy gospel glorious (4)
473	O Lord, once lifted on the glorious tree (3)
478	Glorious their life who sing, with glad thanksgiving (3)
481	Rejoice in glorious hope. Our Lord the Judge shall come (4)
484, 485	Jesus, Lord, our Captain glorious (2)
516	let thy glorious light shine ever on my sight (2)
522, 523	Glorious things of thee are spoken, Zion city of our God (1)
525	till with the vision glorious her longing eyes are blessed (4)
534	glorious gospel of truth may shine throughout the world (3)
535	his kingdom is glorious, he rules over all (1)
539	Send heralds forth to bear the message glorious (3)
556, 557	Your glorious banner wave on high (1,7)
558	whene'er we hear that glorious word (1)
561	forth to the mighty conflict in this his glorious day (2)
568	flood the whole Church with thy glorious light (3)
594, 595	bring her bud to glorious flower (1)
607	dawns the morning glorious when truth and justice reign (4)
609	till glorious from thy heaven above shall come the city (5)
616	age to age more glorious, all blessing and all blest (5)
618	more glorious than the seraphim, lead their praises (2)
621, 622	glorious are the praises which of thee the prophets sing (1)
621, 622	glorious noon-day (3)
621, 622	glorious and resplendent, fragile body, shalt thou be (4)
624	the pastures of the blessed are decked in glorious sheen (2)
627	word of the ever-living God, will of his glorious Son (4)
675	wear the glorious crown (5)
681	hint at the glorious praise of thy eternal song (3)
697	that I may see thy glorious face (3)

gloriously

9	to serve right gloriously the God (6)
16, 17	who, conquering death, reign gloriously with God (4)
38, 39	who, conquering death, reign gloriously with God (5)
219	the Lord hath triumphed gloriously (1)
390	over all things he gloriously reigneth (2)
425	for he has triumphed gloriously (1)

glory

1	thine is the glory, gleaming and resounding (3)
1	glory, gleaming and resounding through all creation (3)
2	thine is the glory gleaming and resounding (3)
2	glory, gleaming and resounding through all creation
5	O splendor of God's glory bright (1)
5	all glory to the Spirit raise (5)
6, 7	Christ, whose glory fills the skies (1)
11	all my powers ... in thy sole glory may unite (3)
14, 15	by a holy death attained, eternal glory may be gained (2)
16, 17	All glory be to you, Lord Christ (4)
25, 26	in you the Father's glory shone (1)
33-35	creation joining hearts and voices singing your glory (3)

38, 39	All glory be to you, Lord Christ (5)
44, 45	your praise and glory we shall sing (3)
55	all glory to our God Triune (6)
57, 58	Savior, take the power and glory (4)
59	so when next he comes with glory (4)
59	Honor, glory, might, and blessing to the Father ... Son (4)
60	praise, honor, might, and glory be from age to age (6)
63, 64	praise, honor, might and glory be (5)
65	Greet One who comes in glory, foretold in sacred story (1)
67	For the glory of the Lord now o'er earth is shed abroad (3)
68	rise up, ye heirs of glory, the Bridegroom is at hand (2)
73	crowned with glory like the sun ... lights the morning sky (2)
74	All power is his, all glory (3)
77	All glory for this blessed morn to God the Father ever be (5
78, 79	dark night wakes, the glory breaks (4)
80	that in his kingdom bright and fair ... his glory share (4)
80	you may with us his glory share (4)
82	honor, glory and dominion, and eternal victory (4)
83	glory to God, glory in the highest (3)
83	Jesus, to thee be glory given (6)
87	Hark! the herald angels sing glory to the new-born King (1,R)
87	Mild he lays his glory by, born that we no more may die (3)
93	Angels, from the realms of glory (1)
94, 95	the angel of the Lord came down, and glory shone around (1)
94, 95	All glory be to God on high and on the earth be peace (6)
97	Father, glory to thee for the wondrous charity (3)
106	God's highest glory was their anthem still (3)
106	around us all his glory shall display (6)
108	to Christ enthroned in glory (1)
114	as was the ring of glory on the helpless infant there (3)
119	no star to guide, where no clouds thy glory hide (4)
127	unto thee, with God the Father and the Spirit, glory be (5)
129, 130	Christ upon the mountain peak stands alone in glory (1)
129, 130	Christ ... in glory blazing (1)
129, 130	Swift the cloud of glory came (3)
131, 132	All glory, Jesus, be to thee for this thy glad epiphany (5)
133, 134	the heavens above your glory named (2)
133, 134	To you, the King of glory ... faithful hearts ... bow (3)
135	disciples filled with awe thy transfigured glory saw (4)
136, 137	O vision fair of glory that the Church may share (1)
136, 137	Christ deigns to manifest today what glory shall be (3)
136, 137	vouchsafe to bring us by thy grace to see thy glory (5)
136, 137	to see thy glory face to face (5)
138	did manifest your glory forth in Cana's marriage hour (1)
143	The glory of these forty days we celebrate with songs (1)
144	The universe your glory shows, blest Father, Spirit, Son (5)
145	to be led to where God's glory flashes (2)
145	the friends you make shall bring God's glory bright (5)
149	so in the Father's glory shall we wake (3)
152	for the glory of thy Name (3)
153	Peace in heaven and glory in the highest (1)
154, 155	All glory, laud, and honor to thee, Redeemer, King (R)
162	each crimsoned bough proclaims the King of glory now (3)
165, 166	Bend thy boughs, O tree of glory (5)
165, 166	one in might and one in glory while eternal ages run (6)

174	Hymns of glory, songs of praise, Father ... we raise (4)
175	all things created on earth sing to the glory of God (2)
175	adorned with the glory of blossom (3)
176, 177	of whom the glory in both earth and heaven is manifested (3)
183	the glory of Jesus' resurrection (5)
190	All the glory of the morning pales before those wounds (2)
191	Jesus Christ, the King of glory (1)
191	rain and dew and gleams of glory from ... thy face (4)
191	glory from the brightness of thy face (4)
191	alleluia! Glory be to God on high (5)
194, 195	glory to our Savior giving (2)
208	all glory to our risen Head (3)
213	live to the honor and glory of God (2)
213	For the glory we were first created to share (3)
214	take the King of glory in (2)
215	there with thee in glory stand (3)
216	all things created on earth sing to the glory of God (1)
216	adorned with the glory of blossom (2)
217, 218	A hymn of glory let us sing (1)
220, 221	let all our glory be in thee both now and ... eternity (3)
228	Holy Spirit, font of light, focus of God's glory bright (1)
229	In every clime, by every tongue, be God's ... glory sung (2)
229	God's amazing glory sung (2)
231	Instill in us his longing, your glory to behold (2/12-27)
231, 232	ascribe all power and glory and praise to God alone (3)
232	Lord, curb our vain impatience for glory ... fame (2/7-25)
232	yet she her voice upraises God's glory to proclaim (2/8-15)
233, 234	In them the Father's glory shone (4)
236	Glory to God the Father be (4)
236	glory to Christ, who set us free (4)
236	glory unceasing we proclaim (4)
237	for by faith they saw the land decked in all its glory (2)
238, 239	Therefore, ye that reign in glory (1)
245	words reflect, like eagles' wings, the glory of our Lord (1)
245	your glory to proclaim whereby your Spirit give us life (3)
250	All glory be to God on high and peace on earth (5)
255	give you final service in glory at your throne (3)
257	All glory to the Father be, all glory to the Son (5)
257	all glory, Holy Ghost, to thee, while endless ages run (5)
259	child, the glory of all lands (3)
260	For him ... no glory here, no crown or martyr's fame (3)
261, 262	To God eternal be all praise and glory (3)
263	Lord Jesus, Virgin-born ... eternal praise and glory be (4)
264	Lord Jesus, Virgin-born ... eternal praise and glory be (4)
271, 272	praise, honor, might, and glory ... age to age eternally (5)
273, 274	All glory to the Father, all glory to the Son (4)
275	Multitude which none can number ... in glory stands (1)
275	Now they reign in heavenly glory (4)
276	saw the glory round thy head, one of the chosen three (3)
277	Glory be to God the Father ... Son ... the Spirit (3)
277	glory to the Three in One (3)
278	from on high ... glory of the Spirit's presence came (3)
278	blazing glory of the Spirit's presence (3)
280	When Christ comes again in glory (4)
282, 283	Christ, the fair glory of the holy angels (1)

282, 283	thine is the glory which from all creation ever ascendeth (6)
284	Glory to God and peace on earth (2)
287	We feebly struggle, they in glory shine (4)
287	the King of glory passes on his way (7)
295	To Jesus Christ give glory, God's coeternal Son (2)
300	Glory, love, and praise, and honor for our food (1)
300	Glory ... for our food now bestowed render we the Donor (1)
314	who thy glory hidest 'neath these shadows mean (1)
326	From glory to glory advancing, we praise thee, O Lord (1)
326	Thanksgiving and glory and worship ... blessing and love (2)
329-331	Glory let us give and blessing to the Father and the Son (6)
334	glory be to God on high (1)
336	thou art God, thy glory veiling
336	glory veiling so that we may bear the sight (2)
336	Come with us, O King of glory, by angelic voices praised (3)
339	food ... for our good, thy glory, given (2)
348	may we increasingly glory in learning all that it means (3)
360, 361	thine be the glory, praise and adoration, now and forever (6)
362	though the sinful human eye thy glory may not see (3)
363	Ancient of Days, who sittest throned in glory (1)
364	the world is with the glory filled of thy majestic sway (3)
364	Thou art the King of glory, Christ, the everlasting Son (6)
364	thou didst ascend to God's right hand in glory evermore (7)
365	thy sovereign majesty may we in glory see (4)
366	In the glory of that land ... set at God's right hand (6)
367	Round the Lord in glory seated cherubim and seraphim (1)
367	Lord, thy glory fills the heaven (1,3)
367	unto thee be glory given, holy, holy, holy Lord (1,3)
367	Heaven is still with glory ringing (2)
368	Holy Jesus, Lord of glory, whom angelic hosts proclaim (2)
375	Give praise and glory unto God ... Father of all blessing (1)
375	To God be praise and glory (1-3)
376	Joyful, joyful, we adore thee, God of glory, Lord of love (1)
377, 378	from men and... angel host be praise and glory evermore (5)
381	glorious now, we press toward glory (3)
381	Holy Spirit, Light-Revealer, glory, glory be to thee (4)
382	King of glory, King of peace, I will love thee (1)
383, 384	thou my soul's glory, joy, and crown (1)
392	The heirs of grace have found glory begun below (3)
400	flowers and fruits that in you grow ... glory also show (4)
400	let them his glory also show (4)
404	praise we your glory while on you we wait (2)
408	to God all praise and glory (1-3)
408	give God all praise and glory (3)
414	They shall talk of all thy glory (3)
417, 418	honor, blessing, and glory are his (2)
417, 418	Blessing, honor, glory, and might be to God and the Lamb (4)
419	thy glory flames from sun and star (1)
421	All glory be to God on high (1)
421	we raise for your great glory thanks and praise (1)
421	with the Spirit, you alone share in the Father's glory (3)
423	Thou reignest in glory, thou rulest in light (4)
431	The stars declare his glory (1)
432	loud organs, his glory forth tell in deep tone (3)
433	thou, Lord, wast at our side: all glory be thine (2)

434	But in the grace that rescued man his ... glory shines (2)
434	his brightest form of glory shines (2)
435	every tongue confess him King of glory now (1)
435	filled it with the glory of that perfect rest (3)
435	with his Father's glory o'er the earth to reign (6)
435	our hearts confess him King of glory now (6)
436	behold the King of glory waits (1)
437, 438	Powers and dominions lay their glory by (3)
441, 442	In the cross of Christ I glory (1,5)
443	the King abased to honor all, praised be your glory (5)
448, 449	All glory to our Lord and God (6)
448, 449	glory ... for love so deep, so high, so broad (6)
454	again in glory; let us then our homage pay (4)
467	Let his glory be thy theme (4)
468	he's risen from darkness ... he's 'scended into glory (4)
474	cross where the young Prince of Glory died (1)
476	he speaks to us in human terms to make his glory known (4)
477	yield the glory that of right was thine (1)
479	Glory be to Jesus, who in bitter pains poured for me (1)
483	once ... with thorns, is crowned with glory now (1)
493	Glory to God and praise and love be now and ever given (6)
495	Jesus, hail, enthroned in glory, there for ever to abide (3)
495	ever for us interceding, till in glory we appear (3)
498	my sinful self my only shame, my glory all the cross (3)
499	the glory of your people, and their light (1)
501, 502	to whom all honor, glory be both now and for eternity (6)
517	in glory throned, Lord God, great King of kings (3)
518	hereafter in thy glory evermore with thee to reign (4)
519, 520	bridal glory round thee shed (2)
522, 523	the cloud and fire appear for a glory and a covering (3)
528	Let your priests, for earth's true glory, daily lift (3)
534	earth shall be filled with the glory of God (1-4)
535	All glory and power, all wisdom and might (4)
538	Let the nations shout and sing glory to their Savior King (2)
540	spread the glory of redemption (2)
540	proclaim ... the glory of thy Name (3)
543	till sovereign love in worlds above the glory raise (3)
545	now with glory crowned (1)
561	they with the King of glory shall reign eternally (4)
562	glory, laud, and honor, unto Christ the King (5)
563	wear in endless glory the crown of victory (3)
570, 571	Come today, our Judge, our Glory (5)
576, 577	when we see your face, O Savior, in its glory (3)
581	be his the glory that we seek, be ours his holy peace (4)
582, 583	yea, bids us seize the whole of life and build its glory (4)
584	So for your glory and our good may we your gifts employ (4)
585	Morning glory, starlit sky, soaring music (1)
594, 595	God of grace and God of glory (1)
594, 595	let the gift of thy salvation be our glory evermore (4)
596	cleanse ... through the glory of the Lord (3)
606	grace to see your exalted glory, O Christ our God (3)
617	from ... night profound into the glory of the perfect day (1)
619	glory for evermore; to thee we bring ... alleluia (7)
620	Thy saints are crowned with glory great (2)
621, 622	in everlasting glory thou with brightness be arrayed (5)

623	O what their joy and their glory must be (1)
624	what radiancy of glory, what bliss beyond compare (1)
626	thy glory be my aim, thy holy will my choice (1)
630	See its glory undiminished by the change of time or place (4)
631	showed his glory (2)
642	in thee be all our glory now, and through eternity (5)
655	that where thou art in glory there shall thy servant be (3)
657	glory in thy perfect love (2)
657	changed from glory into glory (3)
658	be glory, as it was, is now, and shall be evermore (4)
665	Mortal pride and earthly glory (2)
673	his glory to be (3)
704	There let it for thy glory burn (2)
706	to glory kept me blind (1)
710	give him glory evermore (RC)
718	glory, laud, and praise be ever thine (4)

glory's

| 55 | Your cradle shines with glory's light (5) |

glow

21, 22	light the glow of perfect day (1)
31, 32	moon with cool reflected glow will bring the silences (3)
104	A stable lamp is lighted Whose glow shall wake the sky (1)
162	the cross shines forth in mystic glow (1)
408	by morning glow or evening shade ... ne'er sleepeth (2)
419	Sun of our life, thy quickening ray sheds ... the glow (2)
419	sheds on our path the glow of day (2)

glowed

| 193 | His risen flesh with radiance glowed (2) |

glowing

| 405 | he made their glowing colors (1) |
| 516 | visit it with thine own ardor glowing (1) |

glows

136, 137	where brighter than the sun he glows (1)
415	gratitude ... that glows within my fervent heart (2)
441, 442	lo, it glows with peace and joy (2)
508	till all this earthly part of me glows (3)
508	glows with thy fire divine (3)
541	No time for rest, till glows the western sky (5)

go

56	teach us in her ways to go (2)
75	where the Lord our God may go (1)
78, 79	Above thy deep and dreamless sleep the silent stars go by (1)
99	Go tell it on the mountain, over the hills and everywhere (R)
99	go tell it on the mountain, that Jesus Christ is born (R)
120	O Christ, may we baptized from sin, go forth with you (5)
120	go forth with you a world to win (5)
162	The royal banners forward go (1)
167	that we might go at last to heaven (3)

171	Go to dark Gethsemane, ye that feel the tempter's power (1)
174	Israel's hosts triumphant go through the wave (2)
183	to Galilee he will go before you (7)
194, 195	may we go where he has gone (4)
203	Your Lord doth go to Galilee (3)
242	He loved thee well, and firmly said, "Come, let us go" (2)
242	Come, let us go and die with him (2)
304	Together met, together bound, we'll go our different ways (5)
316, 317	Too soon we rise; we go our several ways (2)
326	strength unto strength we go forward on Zion's highway (1)
332	go rejoicing on our way, renewed with strength divine (4)
334	Sins forgiven, wrong forgiving, we go forth alert (3)
336	Now we go to seek and serve thee (2)
347	Go forth for God (1-4)
347	go to the world in peace (1)
347	go to the world in love (2)
347	go to the world in strength (3)
347	go to the world in joy (4)
355	All of us go down to the dust (1)
359	forth may they go to tell all realms thy grace (5)
450, 451	go, spread your trophies at his feet (5)
462	before him righteousness shall go, his royal harbinger (1)
475	Where I go here below, let me bow before thee (4)
498	content to let my pride go by, to know no gain nor loss (3)
499	Lord God, you have set your servant free to go in peace (1)
499	go in peace as promised in your word (1)
509	lead us in those paths of life whereon the righteous go (2)
510	our souls, how heavily they go to reach eternal joys (2)
517	They who go through the desert vale will find it filled (3)
528	Lest ... the Gospel go unheard (1)
540	that everywhere its flame may go (2)
541	to each servant does the Master say, "Go work today" (1)
547	Awake, arise, go forth in faith (5)
548	From strength to strength go on (4)
556, 557	Yes, on through life's long path ... chanting as ye go (4)
559	yet unfearing, persevering, to thy passion thou didst go (2)
562	forward into battle, see, his banners go (1)
563	Go forward, Christian soldier (1-4)
579	wherever, Lord, thy people go, protect them (2)
579, 608	protect them wheresoe'er they go (4)
580	scarcely caring where they go (2)
610	forth in your dear name we go (4)
610	go to the child, the youth, the aged (4)
616	before him on the mountains shall peace, the herald, go (3)
625	onward as ye go some joyful anthem sing (3)
629	make us all go on to know with nobler powers conferred (3)
636, 637	When through the deep waters I call thee to go (3)
641	nor let me go astray (3)
648	let my people go (1-4)
648	Go down, Moses, way down in Egypt's land (R)
648	tell old Pharoah to let my people go (R)
664	There ... I find a settled rest while others go and come (3)
665	pleasure leads us where we go (4)
687, 688	let goods and kindred go, this mortal life also (4)
700	True sunlight of the soul, surround us as we go (2)

702	Lord thou ... dost know where'er I rest, where'er I go (1)
702	Where can I go apart from thee (3)
703	without thy guiding hand we go astray (1)

goal

145	or rend the soul, such grief is not Lent's goal (2)
149	far off yet here -- the goal of all desire (1)
230	until you reach the promised goal, a kingdom to inherit (3)
594, 595	lest we miss thy kingdom's goal (3)

goals

| 580 | give us guidance till our goals and yours are one (4) |

God

3, 4	we lift our hearts to God on high (1)
3, 4	To God the Father, heavenly Light (5)
3, 4	to God the Holy Ghost we raise our ... praise (5)
5	All laud to God the Father be (5)
9	give and give, and give again what God hath given thee (6)
9	to serve right gloriously the God (6)
9	God who gave all worlds that are, and all that are to be (6)
10	new thoughts of God, new hopes of heaven (2)
10	new treasures still, of countless price, God will provide (3)
10	God will provide for sacrifice (3)
10	a road to bring us daily nearer God (5)
11	Praise God, from whom all blessings flow (4)
12, 13	O God, creation's ruling force (4)
14, 15	O God, creation's secret force (1)
16, 17	Now let us sing our praise to God (1)
16, 17	Lamb of God restored our peace (2)
16, 17	who, conquering death, reign gloriously with God (4)
18	O God, creation's ruling force (5)
19, 20	Now Holy Spirit, ever One with God the Father and the Son (1)
21, 22	O God of truth, O Lord of might (1)
23	O God, creation's ruling force (4)
25, 26	God who dwells in the eternal light (2)
25, 26	Worthy are you of endless praise, O Son of God (3)
29, 30	To God the Father, heavenly Light (3)
29, 30	to God the Holy Ghost we raise our ... praise (3)
31, 32	Most Holy God, the Lord of heaven (1)
36	O gladsome Light, O grace of God the Father's face (1)
36	O Son of God, Life-giver (3)
37	O Son of God, be thou ... through all the world adored (3)
38, 39	who, conquering death, reign gloriously with God (5)
38, 39	God, Creator of all things (5)
40, 41	O God, our Maker and our end (5)
43	All praise to thee, my God this night (1)
43	vigorous make to serve my God when I awake (3)
43	Praise God, from whom all blessings flow (4)
46	on God our Maker calling ... the Giver good (1)
47	On this day, the first of days, God ... we praise (1)
47	God the Father's Name we praise (1)
47	God, the blessed Three in One dwell within my heart alone (6)
48	sing, "Holy, holy, holy," to the great God Triune (1)
49	filled with all the life of God (2)

50	comes, in God his Father's name, to save our sinful race (4)
52	All praise to God the Father be (4)
53	came in likeness lowly, Son of God most holy (1)
54	Mighty God and Mary's son, eager now his race to run (2)
55	a wondrous birth, befitting God (1)
55	but from the Spirit of our God (2)
55	O Word of God, come (2)
55	You came forth from the eternal God (3)
55	With God the Father you are one (4)
55	All praise, O unbegotten God (6)
55	all glory to our God Triune (6)
56	mourns in lonely exile here until the Son of God appear (1,8)
60	To God the Father ... Son, ... Spirit, Three in One (6)
61, 62	Lamb of God, the heavens adore you (3)
63, 64	To God the Father ... Son ... Spirit, ever One (5)
67	speak ye peace, thus saith our God (1)
67	Now prepare for God a way (2)
69	Who hears, O God, the prophecy (1)
69	God gives himself into our lives (4)
70	pathway ... for the one who brings God near (2)
70	God receives his wayward children (3)
74	Blest be the King whose coming is in the name of God (1-4)
74	He only to the humble reveals the face of God (3)
75	Prepare in the desert a highway, a highway for our God (1)
75	where the Lord our God may go (1)
75	but the word of our God endureth (3)
76	make straight the way for God within (2)
77	All glory for this blessed morn to God the Father ever be (5)
78, 79	praises sing to God the King, and peace to men on earth (2)
78, 79	God imparts to human hearts the blessings of his heaven (3)
81	true man, yet very God (3)
82	extol our God and King (3)
82	Christ, to thee with God the Father (4)
83	God from God, Light from Light eternal (2)
83	glory to God, glory in the highest (3)
84	love to God and neighbor (3)
87	God and sinners reconciled (1)
88	God himself comes down from heaven (1)
88	God from God, and Light from Light, comes with mercies (2)
88	God with us, Emmanuel, deigns for ever now to dwell (3)
88	God comes down that we may rise (4)
93	God with you is now residing (2)
94, 95	angels praising God, who thus addressed their joyful song (5)
94, 95	All glory be to God on high and on the earth be peace (6)
99	God sent us salvation that blessed Christmas morn (3)
102	He came down to earth from heaven ... God and Lord of all (2)
105	God rest you merry, gentlemen, let nothing you dismay (1)
105	From God our heavenly Father a blessed angel came (2)
105	how that in Bethlehem was born the Son of God by name (2)
106	tidings ... of God incarnate and the Virgin's Son (1)
106	this day hath God fulfilled his promised word (2)
106	see the wonder God for us had wrought (4)
108	in holiness conceived, the Son of God was born (1)
110	that brought into this world the God made man (2)
110	for he whom Mary bore was God the Son (4)

111	Son of God, love's pure light radiant beams (3)
112	Our God, heaven cannot hold him, nor earth sustain (2)
112	stable ... sufficed the Lord God incarnate, Jesus Christ (2)
114	God the Lord of all the earth sent angel-choirs instead (1)
117, 118	dearer to God are the prayers of the poor (4)
120	Christ, the Son of God, had come to lead his ... people (2)
120	the sign of God the Father's love (3)
121	God called you his beloved Son ... his servant true (2)
122, 123	in the house of God abiding thus they sing eternally (1)
124	To God the Father, heavenly Light (5)
125, 126	the Wonderful, the Counsellor, the mighty God and Lord (4)
127	to the world its God announcing (2)
127	incense doth their God disclose (4)
127	unto thee, with God the Father and the Spirit, glory be (5)
128	worship him, God Most High (3)
128	King and God and Sacrifice (5)
129, 130	God proclaiming in its thunder Jesus as his Son by name (3)
131, 132	by their gifts confessed their God (2)
135	anthems be to thee addressed, God in man made manifest (1-3)
135	cross and Easter Day attest God in man made manifest (4)
136, 137	shall be theirs above who joy in God with perfect love (3)
139	Triune God is thus made known in Christ as love unending (2)
139	he cleanses, reconciles to God (3)
143	Alone and fasting Moses saw the loving God (2)
143	loving God who gave the law (2)
145	God brings new beauty nigh (1)
149	so we are dead and live with you in God (2)
153	Let us give thanks to the Lord our God (2)
156	then take, O God, thy power and reign (5)
157	God is the Lord; he has shined upon us (R)
157	You are my God, and I will thank you (R)
157	you are my God, and I will exalt you (R)
158	for our atonement ... God interceded (3)
160	perfect God on thee has bled (1,4)
160	Very God himself is bearing all the sufferings of time (3)
162	how God the nations' King should be (2)
162	for God is reigning from the tree (2)
163	for God doth make his world anew (1)
173	God the Father's only Son in the tomb is lying (1)
175	all things created on earth sing to the glory of God (2)
175	God the Creator ... who rulest the earth and the heavens (5)
175	God the Creator, the Lord (5)
175	Redeemer, Son of the Father supreme, only begotten of God (6)
176, 177	By the same Spirit we are called to worship God (3)
176, 177	God our Creator, Savior, Sanctifier (3)
178	Come, let us praise the living God (4)
179	Lo! the dead is living, God for evermore (1)
181	rejoicing in the Lamb of God, to Christ the eternal King (3)
185, 186	sing to God right thankfully loud songs of alleluia (1)
191	sing to God a hymn of gladness (1)
191	sing to God a hmn of praise (1)
191	alleluia! Glory be to God on high (5)
193	to God the Father equal praise (5)
193	God the Holy Ghost, we raise (5)
198	whom as true God and our hymns adore for ... evermore (2)

199, 200	God hath brought his Israel into joy from sadness (1)
201	day ... whereon the faithful give God praise (1)
202	the Lamb of God without a stain (3)
202	all praise to God the Father be and Holy Ghost eternally (5)
203	to God your hears and voices raise (5)
205	To God the Father ... Son ... Spirit, always One (5)
206	"Thou art my Lord and God," he cried (5)
207	Sing we to our God above ... praise eternal as his love (4)
209	cry, "My Lord and God!" (2)
210	the Passover of gladness, the Passover of God (1)
211	Our God most high, our joy and boast (4)
213	live to the honor and glory of God (2)
215	Man with God is on the throne (3)
216	all things created on earth sing to the glory of God (1)
216	God the Creator, the Lord (3)
216	God ... who rulest the earth and the heavens (2)
216	Son of the Father supreme, only begotten of God (4)
217, 218	Christ takes his place -- the throne of God (1)
225	pouring on all human souls infinite riches of God (2)
230	curse of Babel was undone when God did send the Spirit (2)
230	for God the Holy Spirit dwells with the Church alway (3)
231	made flesh, yet God and Lord (2/12-21)
231	All praise, O God, for Joseph (2/3-19)
231, 232	Then let us praise the Father and worship God the Son (3)
231, 232	sing to God the Spirit, eternal Three in One (3)
231, 232	ascribe all power and glory and praise to God alone (3)
232	O God, your two apostles won life through martyrdom (2/6-29)
235	Come sing, ye choirs exultant, those messengers of God (1)
235	where with a holy people God dwells in Unity (3)
236	Glory to God the Father be (4)
237	God himself to joy and praise turns our human sadness (1)
243	on his lips a prayer that God ... spare (3)
244	love from God to lost mankind (1)
245	Praise God for John, the evangelist (1)
250	All glory be to God on high and peace on earth (5)
251	O God, whom neither time nor space can limit (1)
252	Human Name of God above (6)
252	pleading only this we flee, helpless, O our God, to thee (6)
253	following their incarnate God (3)
254	You are the Christ, O Lord, the Son of God most high (1)
254	the saints of God at last prevail (1)
254	who, taught of God, confessed the God-head in the Christ (2)
256	he saw the love of God ... beyond the law (3)
261, 262	To God eternal be all praise and glory (3)
265	To me be as it pleaseth God (3)
268, 269	when the love of God the Father over sin the victory won (1)
271, 272	To God the Father, God the Son ... Spirit, Three in One (5)
273, 274	by hope of God united they reach to heaven above (1)
277	God the Lord who came to earth (1)
277	Glory be to God the Father ... Son ... the Spirit (3)
278	Mary at whose breast the child was fed who is Son of God (1)
278	Son of God eternal and the everlasting Bread (1)
280	God of the saints (1)
280	God ... to whom the number of the starry host is known (1)
282, 283	May the blest mother of our God and Savior ... help us (5)

366	Holy God, we praise thy Name (1)
366	while in essence only One, undivided God we claim thee (4)
366	Son of God enthroned in splendor (5)
366	Son of God, as Savior given (6)
368	God the Lord ... let thy wondrous mercies shine (4)
368	God the Lord, through every nation ... shine (4)
370	I bind unto myself today the power of God (5)
370	the power of God to hold and lead (5)
370	the wisdom of my God to teach (5)
370	the word of God to give me speech (5)
372	Praise to the living God! All praised be his Name (1,4)
372	the one eternal God ere aught that now appears (1)
373	God hath made his saints victorious (2)
373	Praise the God of our salvation (2)
375	Give praise and glory unto God ... Father of all blessing (1)
375	To God be praise and glory (1-3)
375	What God hath wrought to show his power he ... sustaineth (3)
375	What God hath wrought ... he evermore sustaineth (3)
376	Joyful, joyful, we adore thee, God of glory, Lord of love (1)
377, 378	Know that the Lord is God indeed (2)
377, 378	For why? the Lord our God is good (4)
377, 378	the God whom heaven and earth adore (5)
379	God is love, let heaven adore him (1)
379	God is love, let earth rejoice (1)
379	God who laid the earth's foundation (1)
379	God who spread the heavens above (1)
379	God who breathes through all creation (1)
379	God is Love, eternal Love (1)
379	God is Love ... enfolds us, all the world in one embrace (2)
379	with unfailing grasp God holds us (2)
379	find that self-same aching deep within the heart of God (2)
379	God is Love, and though with blindness sin afflicts (3)
380	Praise God, from whom all blessings flow (3)
381	God the Father, Light-Creator, to thee laud and honor be (4)
383, 384	O thou of God and man the Son (1)
385	Many and great, O God, are thy works (1)
386, 387	We sing of God, the mighty source of all things (1)
386, 387	Tell them I AM, the Lord God said (2)
389	for of gods he is the God (2)
391	know that the Lord is God alone (1)
392	Let those refuse to sing that never knew our God (2)
393	God has given the cloud by day (2)
393	God it is who grants us sure retreat and refuge nigh (2)
394, 395	Creating God (1)
394, 395	Sustaining God (2)
394, 395	Redeeming God (3)
394, 395	Indwelling God (4)
396, 397	Now thank we all our God with heart and hands and voices (1)
396, 397	O may this bounteous God through all our life be near us (2)
396, 397	All praise and thanks to God the Father now be given (3)
396, 397	eternal, Triune God, whom earth and heaven adore (3)
398	I sing the mighty power of God (1)
398	power of God that made the mountains rise (1)
398	everywhere that I could be, thou, God, art present there (3)
399	To God with gladness sing, your Rock and Savior bless (1)

399	O God of might, to you we sing (1)
399	O God Most High, we are your sheep (2)
400	All creatures of our God and King, lift up your voices (1)
400	praise God, and cast on him your care (5)
400	You lead back home the child of God (6)
400	Praise God the Father, praise the Son (7)
401	The God of Abraham praise, who reigns enthroned above (1)
401	Ancient of everlasting days, and God of love (1)
401	the God who reigns on high the great archangels sing (4)
401	The whole triumphant host give thanks to God on high (5)
402, 403	Let all the world in every corner sing, my God and King (R)
404	you, God and King, are worthy of all praise (1)
405	all things wise and wonderful ... Lord God made them all (R)
405	lips that we might tell how great is God Almighty (4)
405	God Almighty, who has made all things well (5)
408	Sing praise to God who reigns above (1)
408	the God of all creation, the God of power (1)
408	the God of love, the God of our salvation (1)
408	to God all praise and glory (1-3)
408	Let all who name Christ's holy Name give God all praise (3)
408	give God all praise and glory (3)
408	the Lord is God, and he alone (3)
410	Praise with us the God of grace (4)
413	just is our God (3)
414	God, my King, thy might confessing (1)
414	Honor great our God befitteth, who his majesty can reach (2)
414	vast in love, God is good to all creation (5)
415	When all thy mercies, O my God, my rising soul surveys (1)
416	Christ our God, to thee we raise this our hymn (R)
417, 418	whose blood set us free to be people of God (1)
417, 418	Sing with all the people of God (3)
417, 418	Blessing, honor, glory, and might be to God and the Lamb (4)
417, 418	might be to God and the Lamb for ever. Amen (4)
420	When in our music God is glorified (1)
420	may God give us faith to sing always Alleluia, Amen (5)
421	All glory be to God on high (1)
421	We bless, we worship you ... O God, Almighty Father (1)
421	O Lamb of God, Lord Jesus Christ (2)
421	Lamb of God ... whom God the Father gave us (2)
422	very high thy voice, O God, is heard (1)
423	Immortal, invisible, God only wise (1)
424	thanks be to God (1,3)
425	God is our strength, he is our song (2)
426	when God spake and it was done (1)
426	God will make new heavens and earth (3)
428	O all ye works of God, now come to thank him and adore (1)
429	How happy they whose hopes rely on Israel's God (2)
430	O come, our voices raise, sounding God Almighty praise (1,6)
430	Let in praise of God, the sound run a never-ending round (4)
433	Beside us to guide us, our God with us joining (2)
434	every labor of his hands shows something worthy of a God (1)
435	he is God the Savior, he is Christ the Lord (4)
437, 438	in God my Savior shall my heart rejoice (1)
439	To God and to the Lamb, I will sing (2)
440	thou alone to God canst win us (2)

574, 575	Before thy throne, O God, we kneel (1)
574, 575	teach us to know our faults, O God (2)
574, 575	O God, be with us in the flame (4)
576, 577	God is love ... where true love is, God himself is there (R)
576, 577	Let us fear and love him, holy God eternal (1)
576, 577	Christ, our God, be always present here among us (2)
578	O God of love, O King of peace (1)
578	give peace, O God, give peace again (1-3)
580	God, who stretched the spangled heavens (1)
581	Where charity and love prevail there God is ever found (1)
582, 583	Give us, O God, the strength to build the city (3)
582, 583	Already in the mind of God that city riseth fair (4)
584	God, you have given us power to sound depths ... unknown (1)
584	yet greater far this gift, O God, bestow (2)
585	Open are the gifts of God (2)
585	he who shows us God helpless hangs upon the tree (5)
585	Here is God, no monarch he (6)
585	God, whose arms of love aching, spent, the world sustain (6)
588, 589	Almighty God, your word is cast like seed upon the ground (1)
591	O God of earth and altar, bow down and hear our cry (1)
592	Teach me, my God and King, in all things thee to see (1)
592	which God doth touch and own cannot for less be told (4)
594, 595	God of grace and God of glory (1)
596	Crown, O God, thine own endeavor (3)
599	God of our weary years, God of our silent tears (3)
599	places our God, where we met thee (3)
599	true to our God, true to our native land (3)
600, 601	O day of God, draw nigh in beauty and in power (1)
600, 601	O day of God, draw nigh as at creation's birth (5)
605	Do justly, love mercy, walk humbly with your God (1-3)
605	Will God your pleading hear, while crime and cruelty grow (2)
605	Then justly, in mercy we'll humbly walk with God (4)
606	Where true charity and love dwell, God himself is there (A)
606	as we hear and love our Lord, the living God (1)
606	grace to see your exalted glory, O Christ our God (3)
607	O God of every nation, of every race and land (1)
607	deliver every nation, eternal God, we pray (2)
609	shall come the city of our God (5)
611	praising God by labor at his bench (3)
611	teach us how to do all work for God (7)
613	Thy kingdom come, O God! Thy rule, O Christ, begin (1)
615	But the slow watches of the night not less to God belong (2)
615	day of perfect righteousness, the promised day of God (5)
618	To God the Father ... Son ... Spirit, Three in One (4)
620	they see God face to face (2)
620	Jerusalem, God grant that I may see thine endless joy (5)
623	God shall be all, and in all ever blest (1)
624	who art, with God the Father, and Spirit, ever blest (4)
625	My soul, bear thou thy part, triumph in God above (4)
627	word of the ever-living God, will of his glorious Son (4)
629	We limit not the truth of God to our poor reach of mind (1)
630	Thanks to God (1-5)
630	God has spoken: praise God for his open word (1-4)
630	record of the revelation showing God to every age (3)
630	God is speaking; praise God for his open word (5)

698	serve my God and all humanity (3)
700	Great love of God, come in (3)
700	Love of the living God, of Father and of Son (4)
701	they who love God win (3)
705	God the giver of all good, the source of bounteous yield (1)
705	to make our life an offering to God that all may live (2)
709	O God of Bethel, by whose hand thy people still are fed (1)
709	O God of Israel, be the God of this succeeding race (2)
709	thou shalt be our covenant God and portion evermore (5)
711	Seek ye first the kingdom of God and its righteousness (RC)
716	God bless our native land (1)
716	For her our prayers shall rise to God, above the skies (2)
716	to thee aloud we cry, God save the state (2)
717	Our father's God, to thee, author of liberty (4)
717	protect us by thy might, great God, our King (4)
718	God of our fathers, whose almighty hand leads forth (1)
719	God shed his grace on thee (1,3)
719	God mend thine every flaw (2)
720	this be our motto, "In God is our trust" (2)

God's

5	O splendor of God's glory bright (1)
8	praise every morning, God's recreation of the new day (3)
19, 20	God's mighty actions tell at length (2)
46	long our mortal blindness has missed God's lovingkindness (3)
48	This day, God's people meeting, his Holy Scripture hear (3)
51	This is the Lord's day, day of God's own making (3)
55	reigned once more from God's high throne (3)
61, 62	now come, most worthy Lord, God's Son, Incarnate Word (2)
65	He brings God's rule, O Zion, he comes from heaven above (2)
65	Oh, blest is Christ that came in God's most holy name (R)
70	bringing God's own love and power (4)
80	This is the Christ, God's Son most high (3)
81	To show God's love aright, she bore to us a Savior (2)
92	God's bright star, o'er his head (3)
102	Christ ... set at God's right hand on high (6)
104	God's blood upon the spear-head, God's love refused again (3)
106	God's highest glory was their anthem still (3)
116	like him desirous to fulfill God's will in righteousness (4)
120	God's righteousness he thus fulfilled (1)
121	God's Spirit on you came (1)
121	likewise in God's service we may perfect freedom find (4)
129, 130	This is God's beloved Son (4)
139	till God's will is fully done he will not bend or waver (1)
145	to be led to where God's glory flashes (2)
145	the friends you make shall bring God's glory bright (5)
162	save ... from our sin, God's righteousness for all to win (5)
171	God's own sacrifice complete (3)
185, 186	but now at God's right hand he stands (1)
215	Thou hast raised our human nature ... to God's right hand (3)
215	on the clouds to God's right hand (3)
225	day ... Holy Ghost shone in the world with God's grace (R)
228	Holy Spirit, font of light, focus of God's glory bright (1)
229	In every clime, by every tongue, be God's ... glory sung (2)
229	God's amazing glory sung (2)

536	Open your ears and hear God's word (1,4)
536	who would learn the way of wisdom ... hear God's word (2)
545	Thither ... press we to God's right hand (5)
546	God's all-animating voice that calls thee from on high (3)
552, 553	Run the straight race through God's good grace (2)
581	Let us recall that in our midst dwells God's begotten Son (5)
581	Love can exclude no race or creed if honored be God's Name (6)
582, 583	where the sun that shineth is God's grace for human good (3)
585	nails and crown of thorns tell of what God's love must be (5)
590	seek out the lonely and God's mercy share (2)
597	till by God's grace our warring world shall see ... peace (1)
605	How shall my soul fulfill God's law so hard and high (4)
605	To merchant, worker, king he brings God's high demands (3)
614	so shall God's will on earth be done (3)
624	Oh, sweet and blessed country, the home of God's elect (4)
625	Ye holy angels bright, who wait at God's right hand (1)
625	God's praises sound (2)
635	Who trusts in God's unchanging love builds on a rock (1)
665	But God's power, hour by hour, is my temple and my tower (2)
665	God's great goodness e'er endureth (3)
667	theme of God's salvation, and find it ever new (2)
671	we've no less days to sing God's praise (5)
686	mount of God's unchanging love (1)
687, 688	the man of God's own choosing (2)
687, 688	the body they may kill, God's truth abideth still (4)

Godhead

84	Worship we the Godhead, love incarnate, love divine (2)
435	to the throne of Godhead, to the Father's breast (3)

godly

55	Oh, fill our weak and dying frame with godly strength (4)
275	saintly maiden, godly matron, widows who have watched (2)
584	Let wisdom's godly fear dispel the fears ... hate impart (3)

gods

389	for of gods he is the God (2)

goes

9	Lord of life, as he goes meekly by (4)
29, 30	the fiery sun now goes his way (1)
119	thou its sun which goes not down (5)
120	Straight to the wilderness he goes to wrestle (4)
366	from morn till set of sun ... the song goes on (3)
366	through the Church the song goes on (3)
444	Before him goes his herald, forerunner in the way (2)
458	Yet steadfast he to suffering goes (5)
525	their cry goes up, "How long?" (3)
527	Singing songs of expectation ... goes the pilgrim band (1)
527	onward goes the pilgrim band (1)
534	by ... mouth of many messengers goes forth the voice of God (2)
573	nation by nation still goes unforgiven (3)

goest

164	Alone thou goest forth, O Lord, in sacrifice to die (1)

going

562	with the cross of Jesus going on before (1,R)
668	guard thy going out and in, both now and evermore (4)

gold

89, 90	to touch their harps of gold (1)
104	And straw like gold shall shine (1)
109	offered there in his presence their gold (5)
109	gold, and myrrh, and frankincense (5)
115	So bring him incense, gold and myrrh (3)
117, 118	myrrh from the forest, and gold from the mine (3)
127	see them give ... gold and frankincense and myrrh (3)
127	gold the King of kings proclaimeth (4)
128	gold I bring to crown him again (2)
287	win, with them, the victor's crown of gold (3)
519, 520	all thy streets and all thy bulwarks of pure gold (2)
519, 520	of pure gold are fashioned (2)
574, 575	From love of pleasure, lust of gold ... wean us (2)
582, 583	wring gold from human pain (2)
591	the walls of gold entomb us, the swords of scorn divide (1)
592	This is the famous stone that turneth all to gold (4)
616	gold and incense bring (4)
632	O make thy Church, dear Savior, a lamp of purest gold (3)
636, 637	I only design thy dross to consume and thy gold to refine (4)

golden

9	royal robes of autumn moors the golden gates of spring (2)
12, 13	The golden sun lights up the sky (1)
191	golden ears of harvest will their heads before him wave (3)
275	now they walk in golden light (4)
284	waved around your golden wings and struck your strings (7)
286	Each a golden crown is wearing (1)
287	The golden evening brightens in the west (6)
362	casting down their golden crowns around the glassy sea (2)
400	Bright burning sun with golden beams (1)
541	while all around us waves the golden grain (1)
549, 550	worship of the vain world's golden store (3)
556, 557	till dawns the golden day (5)
624	Jerusalem the golden, with milk and honey blest (1)

Golgatha

18	On Golgatha the sky turned dark (3b)

Golgatha's

196, 197	Jesus ... looked down Golgatha's stony slope (2)

gone

3, 4	that we, when this new day is gone (4)
23	The fleeting day is nearly gone (1)
102	he leads his children on to the place where he is gone (5)
105	save us all from Satan's power when we were gone astray (1)
162	gone is thy shame (2)
194, 195	may we go where he has gone (4)
219	Our great High Priest hath gone before (3)
266	There are yet but six months gone (5)

266	six months gone since Elizabeth conceived John (5)
316, 317	the feast, though not the love, is past and gone (2)
357	in faith gone from us, now in death repose (2)
638, 639	my company before is gone, and I am left alone with thee (1)
680	A thousand ages in thy sight are like an evening gone (4)

good

18	that we may see your world is good (4c)
27, 28	you found it good and called it 'day' (2)
46	on God our Maker calling ... the Giver good (1)
75	O Zion, that bringest good tidings (2)
80	to bring good news to everyone (1)
89, 90	Peace on the earth, good will to men (1)
94, 95	good will henceforth from heaven to men (6)
94, 95	good will ... begin and never cease (6)
106	Behold, I bring good tidings of a Savior's birth (2)
106	peace on the earth, and unto men good will (3)
106	Let us, like these good shepherds, then employ (5)
107	Good Christian friends, rejoice (1-3)
115	Good Christian, fear (2)
135	manifest in gracious will, ever bringing good from ill (3)
154, 155	who in all good delightest, thou good and gracious King (5)
157	Give thanks to the Lord, for he is good (R)
158	Lo, the Good Shepherd for the sheep is offered (3)
161	the worst gain power to be good (5)
167	he died to make us good (3)
167	There was no other good enough to pay the price of sin (4)
175	every good gift of the year now with its Master returns (1)
175	Praise to the Giver of good (8)
178	Spread the good news o'er all the earth (2)
196, 197	joy to the heart and all in this good day's dawning (R)
196, 197	Good Jesus Christ inside his pain looked down (2)
196, 197	Good Jesus Christ, our Brother, died in darkest hurt (3)
205	Good Christians all, rejoice and sing (1)
216	Praise to the Giver of good (6)
251	forgive ... the good we failed to do (2)
291	We plow the fields and scatter the good seed on the land (1)
291	All good gifts around us are sent from heaven above (R)
291	We thank thee ... O Father, for all things bright and good (3)
293	followed the right ... whole of their good lives long (2)
299	With tongues of fire saints spread good news (1)
320	Very Bread, good Shepherd, tend us (5)
339	food ... for our good, thy glory, given (2)
346	Through God's good grace these Mysteries are ours (3)
347	be of good courage, armed with heavenly grace (1)
347	in God's good Spirit daily to increase (1)
347	hold fast the good, be urgent for the right (3)
353	you consecrate all that is lovely, good, and true (2)
357	heal them, Good Physician, with the balm of life (3)
357	good and gracious Savior, cleanse and purge away (3)
370	all good deeds done unto the Lord (3)
377, 378	For why? the Lord our God is good (4)
398	formed the creatures ... then pronounced them good (2)
406, 407	Most High, omnipotent, good Lord (1,8)
414	vast in love, God is good to all creation (5)

good / 321

421	God's good will unfailingly be to all people given (1)
424	For the good we all inherit (3)
440	thou must work all good within us (2)
467	God, the merciful and good, bought us (3)
469, 470	welcome for the sinner, and more graces for the good (1)
478	Good Shepherd of your sheep, your own defending (2)
489	he came to win us by good will, for force is not of God (5)
491	whom no ills from good dissuade (4)
552, 553	Fight the good fight with all thy might (1)
552, 553	Run the straight race through God's good grace (2)
564, 565	he will make good his right to be a pilgrim (2)
582, 583	where the sun that shineth is God's grace for human good (3)
584	So for your glory and our good may we your gifts employ (4)
586	by thy patience ... courage ... taught us toil is good (1)
591	from sleep and from damnation, deliver us, good Lord (2)
610	hope and health, good will and comfort ... give (4)
625	praise him still, through good or ill, who ever lives (3)
642	how good to those who seek (3)
645, 646	Good Shepherd, may I sing thy praise (6)
665	only good and only true (1)
669	bring to sure fulfillment thy counsel good and true (3)
671	The Lord has promised good to me (3)
686	I hope, by thy good pleasure, safely to arrive at home (2)
695, 696	we take it ... out of so good and so beloved a hand (3)
705	God the giver of all good, the source of bounteous yield (1)
705	the wealth of this good land (1)
719	crown thy good with brotherhood from sea to shining sea (1,3)

goodness

320	eternal goodness send us in the land of life to see (5)
363	praise we the goodness that doth crown our days (5)
390	surely his goodness and mercy shall ever attend thee (3)
398	I sing the goodness of the Lord (2)
398	goodness of the Lord that filled the earth with food (2)
414	all his works his goodness prove (5)
423	thy clouds, which are fountains of goodness and love (2)
469, 470	life would be thanksgiving for the goodness of the Lord (3)
645, 646	whose goodness faileth never (1)
645, 646	through all the length of days thy goodness faileth never (6)
665	God's great goodness e'er endureth (3)
681	Where goodness comes to light we glimpse thy plan (4)
686	Let thy goodness ... bind my wandering heart to thee (3)
718	thy bounteous goodness nourish us in peace (3)

gospel

49	with meekness hear the gospel word (3)
230	all in their own tongues did the Gospel understand (2)
231	his witness in his gospel becomes victorious song (2/4-25)
232	whose gospel words declare ... your path (2/9-21)
232	whose Gospel shows the healer of the nations (2/10-18)
235	How blest this habitation of gospel liberty (3)
321	Nor let thy spreading Gospel rest (4)
371	where the Gospel day sheds not its glorious ray (1)
394, 395	your gospel claims one family with a billion names (4)
452	Glorious the days of gospel grace (3)

472	we would be faithful to thy gospel glorious (4)
528	Lest ... the Gospel go unheard (1)
534	glorious gospel of truth may shine throughout the world (3)
541	to young and old the Gospel gladness bear (4)
561	put on the Gospel armor, and watching unto prayer (3)

Gospel's
| 344 | Thanks we give and adoration for thy Gospel's joyful sound (2) |

Gospels
235	through whom the living Gospels came sounding all abroad (1)
244	sing of those who spread the treasure in the holy Gospels (1)
244	in the holy Gospels shrined (1)

governed
| 406, 407 | governed by thee she hath upraised what ... is needful (5) |

grace
5	we plead with thee for grace and power to conquer (3)
5	to give us grace our wrongs to bear (4)
16, 17	grace of true salvation came (2)
16, 17	splendor of such grace (3)
18	through your judgment find your grace (1)
18	held by your unrelenting grace (2c)
19, 20	fullness of your grace today (1)
23	now give us grace to walk your way (2)
36	O gladsome Light, O grace of God the Father's face (1)
37	in whom his truth and grace are visibly expressed (1)
48	grace more grace receiving on this blest day of light (3)
50	Blest be the Lord who comes to us with messages of grace (4)
52	O Spirit, fill our hearts this day with grace to hear (4)
52	grace to pray (4)
61, 62	glorious in strength of grace, in truth victorious (2)
65	for grace and joy abounding (2)
69	Lord, give us grace to awake us (3)
71, 72	treasures of his grace to enrich the humble poor (3)
74	He offers to the burdened the rest and grace they need (4)
76	without thy grace we waste away like flowers (3)
77	chosen vessel of his grace (3)
82	Virgin, full of grace, by the Holy Ghost conceiving (2)
85, 86	Remember, Lord of life and grace (3)
88	he on Adam's fallen race sheds the fullness of his grace (3)
100	He rules the world with truth and grace (4)
105	this holy tide of Christmas doth bring redeeming grace (4)
106	treading his steps, assisted by his grace (5)
111	with the dawn of redeeming grace (3)
124	O Jesus, while the star of grace impels us on (4)
124	grace impels us on to seek thy face (4)
136, 137	vouchsafe to bring us by thy grace to see thy glory (5)
138	Oh, may this grace be ours (3)
143	our spirits strengthen with thy grace (4)
144	through your saving sacrifice receive your gift of grace (3)
148	in us the work of grace begin (4)
151	thy grace alone availeth (2)
151	must confess thy grace (2)

151	grace hath wrought whate'er in them is worthy (2)
152	grant unto us thy pardoning grace (2)
168, 169	Ah me! for whom thou diest, hide not so far thy grace (2)
185, 186	by his grace he doth impart eternal sunshine to the heart (3)
185, 186	word of grace hath purged away the old and wicked leaven (4)
191	we are risen! Shed upon us heavenly grace (4)
213	while his grace we receive from his bounty (2)
219	upon his Church his grace to pour (3)
220, 221	grace has won the victory (1)
225	day ... Holy Ghost shone in the world with God's grace (R)
230	his grace within shall make you whole (3)
231	grant us grace to know you, made flesh (2/12-21)
231	the weak by grace made strong (2/4-25)
231	grant us grace to know you, the victor in the strife (2/5-1)
231	let gifts of grace descend (2/6-11)
238, 239	by his grace we may be worthy of eternal bliss at last (3)
240, 241	heaven-endowed with grace and power (2)
240, 241	of his fullness grace for grace (4)
243	When Stephen, full of power and grace, went forth (1)
245	fullness of your grace and truth for us and all the world (1)
245	signs of your grace divine (2)
250	rejoice, with thanks embrace another year of grace (1-3,5)
250	in this new year of grace (4)
255	grace, by ways mysterious, our sinful wrath can bind (3)
256	a sinner saved by Jesus' grace (2)
256	the cosmos move in time with grace (3)
260	now within the Father's grace (4)
281	But grace within his heart had stirred (2)
284	On earth ye knew his wondrous grace (1)
295	God's children by adoption, baptized into his grace (1)
298	Grant us to grow in grace each day (2)
299	revive in us baptismal grace (3)
301	by thy grace our souls are fed (1)
318	here grasp with firmer hand eternal grace (1)
319	by your grace we all may flourish (1)
269	Hail Mary, Full of grace (1-4)
321	Drawn by thy quickening grace, O Lord (3)
337	look not on our misusings of thy grace (2)
339	whose grace unbounded hath this wondrous banquet founded (1)
342	For all we seek your grace sustaining (2)
343	would not live by bread alone, but by thy word of grace (2)
344	triumph in redeeming grace (1)
346	Through God's good grace these Mysteries are ours (3)
347	be of good courage, armed with heavenly grace (1)
347	richly from above his love supplies the grace and power (2)
347	the grace and power we seek (2)
350	in power to do and grace to bear (2)
351	May the grace of Christ our Savior (1)
352	enjoying your sweet grace (2)
359	priesthood born of grace (3)
359	forth may they go to tell all realms thy grace (5)
360, 361	Here in our sickness healing grace aboundeth (3)
371	Move on the waters' face bearing the gifts of grace (3)
388	O tell of his might, O sing of his grace (2)
392	The heirs of grace have found glory begun below (3)

394, 395	let every life be touched by grace (4)
396, 397	keep us in his grace, and guide us when perplexed (2)
401	sing the wonders of his grace for evermore (2)
410	Praise him for his grace and favor to his people (2)
410	grace and favor to his people in distress (2)
410	Praise with us the God of grace (4)
411	His grace to thee proclaim (1)
411	bless his holy Name, whose grace hath made thee whole (6)
413	peal out the praise of grace abounding (2)
432	praise him who hath brought you his grace from above (2)
432	for grace of salvation, O praise ye the Lord (4)
434	But in the grace that rescued man his ... glory shines (2)
436	thy grace and love in me reveal (4)
444	He from the house of David a child of grace has given (2)
445, 446	highest gift of grace should flesh and blood refine (4)
450, 451	hail him who saves you by his grace (4)
452	Glorious the days of gospel grace (3)
452	grace when Christ restores the fallen race (3)
465, 466	until by your most costly grace ... I come (3)
467	from yon bright throne above ... extends his grace (1)
467	still to us extends his grace (1)
477	that in our darkened hearts thy grace might shine (1)
479	Grace and life eternal in that blood I find (2)
480	like him in grace and knowledge grow as years (1)
480	grace and knowledge grow as years and strength increase (1)
482	Lord of all kindliness, Lord of all grace (3)
483	To them the cross with all its shame ... grace is given (4)
489	grace and peace to bring (3)
493	glories of my God and King, the triumphs of his grace (1)
500	Plenteous of grace, come from on high (3)
503, 504	Anoint and cheer our soiled face with ... thy grace (5)
503, 504	the abundance of thy grace (5)
505	unless thy grace the power should give, none can believe (2)
514	for all thy grace and power benign (1)
514	To thee, whose faithful love had place in ... grace (2)
514	God's great covenant of grace (2)
515	with thy grace our spirits shower (2)
515	Rest upon this congregation ... fullness of thy grace (2)
516	for none can guess its grace, till Love create a place (3)
522, 523	Grace which like the Lord, the giver, never fails (2)
522, 523	Grace ... never fails from age to age (2)
525	to one hope she presses, with every grace endued (2)
525	Lord, give us grace that we like them, the meek (5)
531	in all thy plenitude of grace (1)
538	God of mercy ... grace, show the brightness of thy face (1)
539	make known to every heart his saving grace (4)
540	till all the world thy saving grace shall know (2)
543	his all-resplendent grace he pours around thy head (2)
543	loud that grace proclaim, which makes thy darkness bright (3)
552, 553	Run the straight race through God's good grace (2)
555	through days of preparation thy grace has made us strong (1)
568	Father, Redeemer, and Spirit of grace (4)
582, 583	where the sun that shineth is God's grace for human good (3)
585	memory's treasure, grace of youth (1)
587	knowing thee may grow in grace (2)

594, 595	God of grace and God of glory (1)
597	till by God's grace our warring world shall see ... peace (1)
605	Let Christ endue our will with grace to fortify (4)
606	Now we pray that with the blessed you grant us grace (3)
606	grace to see your exalted glory, O Christ our God (3)
609	still holds the freshness of thy grace (3)
623	while for thy grace, Lord ... voices of praise ... raise (3)
627	stream from the fount of heavenly grace (1)
630	grace in human form declare (2)
636	my grace, all sufficient, shall be thy supply (4)
644	filled with boundless stores of grace (3)
645, 646	thy unction grace bestoweth (5)
655	O give me grace to follow, my Master and my friend (3)
658	longs my soul, O God, for thee and thy refreshing grace (1)
662	what but thy grace can foil the tempter's power (2)
663	Thou hast in grace my table spread (4)
664	leads me ... in paths of truth and grace (1)
671	Amazing grace (1)
671	'Twas grace that taught my heart to fear (2)
671	grace my fears relieved (2)
671	how precious ... grace appear the hour I first believed (2)
671	'tis grace that brought me safe thus far (4)
671	grace will lead me home (4)
674	you alone can grant us grace to live the words we say (1)
677	trust him for his grace (4)
686	tune my heart to sing thy grace (1)
686	to grace how great a debtor daily I'm constrained to be (3)
691	May thy rich grace impart strength to my fainting heart (2)
697	Anoint me with thy heavenly grace (3)
699	Plenteous grace with thee is found (3)
699	grace to cleanse from every sin (3)
706	did not freely choose you till by grace you set me free (2)
706	for your grace alone I thirst (3)
709	present before thy throne of grace (2)
718	fill all our lives with love and grace divine (4)
719	God shed his grace on thee (1,3)

graces

300	Source of all our gifts and graces, Christ we own (2)
469, 470	welcome for the sinner, and more graces for the good (1)

gracing

54	gracing his created spheres (3)

gracious

25, 26	O gracious Light, Lord Jesus Christ (1)
66	now thy gracious kingdom bring (3)
89, 90	from heaven's all-gracious King (1)
119	so, most gracious Lord, may we evermore be led to thee (1)
135	manifest in gracious will, ever bringing good from ill (3)
142	so teach us, gracious Lord, to die to self (3)
151	Bend down thy gracious ear to me (1)
154, 155	who in all good delightest, thou good and gracious King (5)
170	O gracious Lord (2)
190	see his countenance, how gracious (2)

209	no gracious words we hear from him (1)
214	Hark, his gracious lips bestow (3)
260	carpenter whose life fulfilled our gracious God's design (1)
267	She meekly bowed her head to hear the gracious word (4)
285	through whom we know so many gracious words of thine (1)
313	let thy gracious Body broken (1)
313	O gracious Lord (1)
320	gracious hymns of joy upraising in thy heart and soul (4)
353	O gracious God, you consecrate all that is lovely (2)
357	good and gracious Savior, cleanse and purge away (3)
393	Praise our great and gracious Lord (1)
404	You, Lord, are gracious, merciful to all (3)
408	his gracious mercy keepeth (2)
440	Gracious Lord, thyself impart (3)
493	My gracious Master and my God, assist me to proclaim (2)
509	descend with all thy gracious powers (1,5)
512	Come, Gracious Spirit, heavenly Dove (1)
515	as a gracious shower descend (1)
517	gracious Lord (2)
612	Gracious Spirit, Holy Ghost (1)
618	most gracious, magnify the Lord (2)
652, 653	gracious calling of the Lord (2)
695, 696	By gracious powers so wonderfully sheltered (1)
709	Such blessings from thy gracious hand (5)

graciousness
| 375 | his graciousness confessing (1) |

grafted
| 323 | Jesus, may we ever be grafted, rooted, built in thee (2) |

grain
204	Now the green blade riseth from the buried grain (1)
204	laid in the earth like grain that sleeps unseen (2)
204	Forth he came at Easter, like the risen grain (3)
288	yellow sheaves of ripened grain (2)
290	grant, ... Lord, that we wholesome grain and pure may be (2)
291	sends the snow in winter, the warmth to swell the grain (1)
302	As grain ... was in this broken bread made one (2)
302	grain, once scattered on the hillsides (2)
303	As grain, once scattered on the hillsides (4)
303	As grain ... was in this broken bread made one (4)
541	while all around us waves the golden grain (1)
719	O beautiful for spacious skies, for amber waves of grain (1)

grandeur
| 168, 169 | what sorrow mars thy grandeur (1) |

grant
14, 15	Grant us, when this short life is past, the glorious (2)
18	grant us that same revealing light (4c)
23	Now grant us undiminished strength to stand (1)
29, 30	O grant us with thy saints on high to praise thee (2)
33-35	that you may grant us pardon for offenses (4)
42	Grant to little children visions bright of thee (3)

54	grant that we its glories see (4)
120	grant us the Holy Spirit's power to shield us (5)
122, 123	grant us, blessed Trinity ... to keep thine Easter (4)
138	So, led from strength to strength, grant us ... to see (4)
138	grant us, O Lord, to see the marriage supper of the Lamb (4)
143	Then grant us, Lord, like them to be full oft in fast (4)
144	Lord, grant that we in penitence may offer you our praise (3)
146, 147	grant repentance for our pride (3)
148	grant us your truth to make us wise (1)
148	grant us your power to make us strong (1)
150	Victor in the wilderness, grant we may not faint nor fall (3)
152	grant unto us thy pardoning grace (2)
152	Grant, O thou blessed Trinity ... O unchanging Unity (5)
161	grant, most blessed Trinity ... all may share the victory (5)
164	Grant us with thee to suffer pain (4)
223, 224	blessings of this sacred day grant us ... we pray (3)
223, 224	grant us, dearest Lord, we pray (3)
223, 224	grant us pardon, grant us peace (4)
226, 227	Grant us thy salvation, Lord (5)
228	On our journey grant us aid (2)
228	Grant enabling energy, courage in adversity (5)
231	grant us grace to know you, made flesh (2/12-21)
231	Lord, grant us crowns as brilliant (2/12-28)
231	grant us grace to know you, the victor in the strife (2/5-1)
261, 262	grant that we also may like him be faithful (3)
282, 283	grant of thy mercy ... us thy servants steps up to heaven (1)
285	So grant us, Lord, like him to live (4)
290	grant, ... Lord, that we wholesome grain and pure may be (2)
297	grant unto us the greater worth (2)
298	With one accord, O God, we pray, grant us the Holy Spirit (2)
298	Grant us to grow in grace each day (2)
308, 309	Grant when the veil is riven, we may behold, in heaven (3)
310, 311	O grant us life that shall not end (2)
314	grant my spirit ever by thy life may live (3)
315	grant us at every Eucharist to say ... Thy will be done (1)
320	grant us ... fellow-heirs and guests to be (6)
320	grant us, with thy saints, though lowest (6)
336	grant us light to see and know thee (2)
337	grant us nevermore to part from thee (4)
345	Grant us thy peace upon our homeward way (2)
345	Grant us thy peace throughout our earthly life (3)
352	grant joy and peace (1)
352	Christ, grant that neither grief nor place ... may part (2)
357	Rest eternal grant them, after weary fight (4)
366	Grant that with thy saints we may dwell (7)
366	Grant that ... we may dwell in everlasting day (7)
385	Grant unto us communion with thee (2)
419	Grant us thy truth to make us free (4)
457	grant us that way to know, that truth to keep (4)
496, 497	Jesus, grant us ... to inherit thy salvation (2)
501, 502	From inner strife grant us release (5)
576, 577	Grant us love's fulfillment, joy with all the blessed (3)
590	grant the glad surprising that your blest Spirit rouses (1)
590	Grant us new courage, sacrificial, humble (2)
594, 595	Grant us wisdom, grant us courage (1-4)

606	Now we pray that with the blessed you grant us grace (3)
610	As we worship, grant us vision (3)
620	Jerusalem, God grant that I may see thine endless joy (5)
627	Lord, grant us all aright to learn the wisdom it imparts (5)
634	steadfast faith grant me therefore (1)
669	in his own time grant thee the sun of joy at last (4)
674	you alone can grant us grace to live the words we say (1)

granted

382	Thou hast granted my request, thou hast heard me (1)
390	Hast thou not seen how all thou needest hath been granted (2)
390	granted in what he ordaineth (2)

grantest

| 151 | Thou grantest pardon through thy love (2) |

granting

| 70 | granting victory in our strife (4) |

grants

393	God it is who grants us sure retreat and refuge nigh (2)
429	grants the prisoner sweet release (3)
444	he visits and redeems us, he grants us liberty (1)
483	to whom he manifests his love and grants his Name to know (3)
667	he grants the soul again a season of clear shining (1)

grasp

237	Who will grasp the land of Life (3)
318	here grasp with firmer hand eternal grace (1)
379	with unfailing grasp God holds us (2)

grass

| 8 | like the first dewfall on the first grass (2) |
| 75 | like grass our works decay (2) |

grateful

106	employ our grateful voices to proclaim the joy (5)
219	His rising, his ascension sing with grateful adoration (2)
279	followed thee, obeyed, adored, our grateful hymn receive (1)
288	grateful vows and solemn praise (2)
288	by deeds of kindly love for thy mercies grateful prove (3)
415	my ever grateful heart, O Lord, thy mercy shall adore (4)
416	this our hymn of grateful praise (R)
581	With grateful joy and holy fear his charity we learn (2)
590	O Jesus Christ, may grateful hymns be rising (1)
718	our grateful songs before thy throne arise (1)

gratefully

| 388 | O gratefully sing his power and his love (1) |

gratitude

415	how shall words with equal warmth the gratitude declare (2)
415	gratitude ... that glows within my fervent heart (2)
705	With gratitude and humble trust we bring our best to thee (3)

grave

56	give them victory o'er the grave (4)
107	now ye need not fear the grave (3)
174	now no more the grave enthrall (3)
175	Rise from the grave now ... author of life and creation (4)
184	exalted now to save, wresting victory from the grave (3)
188, 189	where thy victory, O grave (2)
188, 189	ours the cross, the grave, the skies (3)
191	ripened ... from the furrows of the grave (3)
193	Christ was risen from the grave (2)
194, 195	by this we know thou, O grave, canst not enthrall us (1)
204	In the grave they laid him, Love whom hate had slain (2)
204	he that for three days in the grave had lain (3)
207	who endured the cross and grave (2)
215	he who from the grave arose (1)
219	the grave and hell are captive led (1)
270	by the hands, in grave clothes wound (3)
270	from the grave shall hope be hailed (4)
284	out from death's vast room, up from the grave, he leapt (6)
319	You, Lord, in our stead to the grave descended (2)
355	yet even at the grave we make our song: Alleluia (1)
358	Yet at the grave shall we raise up our glad song (3)
447	Christ who died but rose again triumphant from the grave (1)
455, 456	bless and save e'en in the darkness of the grave (4)
471	it takes its terror from the grave (4)
492	bore the pain, the cross, the grave (2)
494	Crown him the Lord of life, who triumphed o'er the grave (3)
567	it triumphed ... o'er darkness and the grave (1)
662	Where is death's sting? where, grave, thy victory? (3)
675	leads you to victory o'er the grave (4)

graze

597	as beasts and cattle calmly graze (2)

great

9	sun ... great lord of years and days (5)
48	sing, "Holy, holy, holy," to the great God Triune (1)
60	At your great Name, O Jesus, now all knees must bend (4)
61, 62	Twelve great pearls, the city's portals (3)
69	in great humility is hid all heaven in a little room (3)
76	our refuge, and our great reward (3)
77	Lord Most High, the one great Shepherd (4)
78, 79	We hear the Christmas angels the great glad tidings tell (5)
80	Glad tidings of great joy I bring to all the world (1)
93	seek the great Desire of nations (3)
94, 95	Glad tidings of great joy I bring to you and all mankind (2)
96	What great brightness did you see (2)
109	to the earth it gave great light (2)
116	I come, the great Redeemer cries, to do thy will, O Lord (1)
136, 137	this great vision's mystery (4)
138	the great epiphany (4)
139	in his great endeavor to save us, his own blood was shed (2)
139	gives the Great Commission (3)
217, 218	great the light in you we see to guide us to eternity (2)
219	Our great High Priest hath gone before (3)

220, 221	as thou wilt be our great reward (3)
229	the deeds our great Redeemer wrought (2)
245	Your great I AM's Saint John records (2)
246	May that great love our lives control and conquer hate (5)
253	see the saints above, how great their joys (1)
260	Virgin's spouse ... guardian of great David's greater Son (2)
271, 272	The great forerunner of the morn (1)
271, 272	prophetic utterance told his actions great and manifold (2)
280	veiled ... but written in the Lamb's great book of life (3)
284	With great delight ye crowned his head (3)
285	great apostle's chosen friend (3)
316, 317	the Lamb's great marriage fest of bliss and love (3)
329-331	this great Sacrament revere (5)
365	To Thee, great One in Three, the highest praises be (4)
368	Holy Father, great Creator (1)
368	Great Jehovah, form our hearts and make them thine (4)
369	How wondrous great, how glorious bright ... our Creator (1)
369	let faith in humble notes adore the great mysterious King (4)
370	I bind unto myself the power of the great love (3)
370	the great love of cherubim (3)
385	Many and great, O God, are thy works (1)
390	join the great throng, psaltery, organ, and song (1)
393	Praise our great and gracious Lord (1)
400	Great rushing winds and breezes soft (2)
401	the Lord, the great I AM, by earth and heaven confessed (1)
401	the God who reigns on high the great archangels sing (4)
401	eternal Father, great I AM, we worship thee (4)
404	great and unsearchable in all your ways (1)
404	glad in the knowledge of your love so great (2)
405	all creatures great and small (R)
405	lips that we might tell how great is God Almighty (4)
406, 407	serve in great humility (8)
409	their great Original proclaim (1)
413	new songs ... render to him who has great wonders done (1)
413	He has made known his great salvation (1)
414	Honor great our God befitteth, who his majesty can reach (2)
421	we raise for your great glory thanks and praise (1)
423	almighty, victorious, thy great Name we praise (1)
423	To all life thou givest, to both great and small (3)
439	to the Lamb who is the great I AM (2)
443	The Watcher slept, the Great was small (5)
460, 461	our great High Priest (4)
462	For great thou art (5)
462	wonders great by thy strong hand are done (5)
463, 464	you will come to a great city (2)
463, 464	great city that has expected your return for years (2)
472	Christ of great compassion, speak to our fearful hearts (1)
488	thou my great Father, thine own may I be (2)
489	The great Creator of the worlds (1)
496, 497	great Emmanuel, come and hear us (1)
496, 497	ride on, great Conqueror, till all know thy salvation (3)
505	thou comest forth from God's great throne (1)
509	O come, great Spirit, come (1,5)
514	God's great covenant of grace (2)
517	in glory throned, Lord God, great King of kings (3)

524	thy hand ... shall great deliverance bring (4)
525	the great Church victorious shall be the Church at rest (4)
528	Lord, you give the great commission (1)
529	but one great fellowship of love (1)
532, 533	How wondrous and great thy works, God of praise (1)
535	the great congregation his triumph shall sing (2)
542	One Lord, in one great Name unite us all who own thee (3)
548	Stand then in his great might (3)
560	for great is your reward in heaven (9)
567	thou our great deliverer still ... Lord of life and death (3)
572	we ... join in singing that great music pure and strong (1)
580	Great Creator, still creating, show us what we yet may do (1)
580	Great Creator, give us guidance (4)
584	Great are your gifts (2)
613	We pray thee, Lord, arise, and come in thy great might (4)
614	place the same hope in this great Name (2)
616	Hail to the Lord's Anointed, great David's greater Son (1)
620	Thy saints are crowned with glory great (2)
626	thine arm my strong support; thyself my great reward (2)
651	let us not forget that though the wrong is great (2)
651	though the wrong is great and strong (2)
657	see thy great salvation perfectly restored in thee (3)
665	God's great goodness e'er endureth (3)
669	God, in his great mercy, will save thee, hold thee fast (4)
674	how great our debt to you (3)
678, 679	Praise the Lord, who has done great things (2)
678, 679	in your very midst, the great and Holy One (2)
686	to grace how great a debtor daily I'm constrained to be (3)
687, 688	his craft and power are great (1)
690	Guide me, O thou great Jehovah (1)
693	of thy great love ... to prove (6)
700	Great love of God, come in (3)
716	do thou our country save by thy great might (1)
717	protect us by thy might, great God, our King (4)

greater

260	Virgin's spouse ... guardian of great David's greater Son (2)
271, 272	greater than a prophet's name (4)
271, 272	woman born shall never be a greater prophet than was he (4)
297	grant unto us the greater worth (2)
319	No greater love than this to you could bind us (2)
584	yet greater far this gift, O God, bestow (2)
616	Hail to the Lord's Anointed, great David's greater Son (1)

greatest

198	best and greatest shinest (1)
232	last and greatest prophet, he saw the dawning ray (2/6-24)
327, 328	Offered was he for greatest and for least (4)
612	but the greatest of the three, and the best, is love (4)
686	Here I find my greatest treasure (2)

greatly

| 582, 503 | how its splendor challenges the souls that greatly dare (4) |

greatness

268, 269	Magnify, my soul, God's greatness (4)
414	on thy might and greatness dwell (3)
437, 438	Tell out, my soul, the greatness of the Lord (1,4)
437, 438	Tell out, my soul, the greatness of his Name (2)
437, 438	Tell out, my soul, the greatness of his might (3)
610	light, in its height and depth and greatness (3)

greed

582, 583	O shame to us who rest content while lust and greed (2)
582, 583	greed for gain in street and shop and tenement (2)
609	from paths where hide the lures of greed (2)

Greek

231	blest guide to Greek and Jew (2/5-1)

green

149	as through stony ground the green shoots break (3)
167	There is a green hill far away, outside a city wall (1)
204	Now the green blade riseth from the buried grain (1)
204	Love is come again like wheat that springeth green (R)
293	one was a shepherd on the green (1)
566	ever-green the sod (2)
663	In pastures green (1)

greet

61, 62	therefore we sing to greet our King (3)
65	Greet One who comes in glory, foretold in sacred story (1)
67	the hills bow down to greet him (2)
83	Yea, Lord, we greet thee, born this happy morning (6)
91	O shepherds, greet that glorious sight (1)
115	Whom angels greet with anthems sweet (1)
212	Oh, with what gladness and surprise the saints ... greet (2)
212	saints their Savior greet (2)
238, 239	with affection's recollections greet we your return again (1)
250	Now greet the swiftly changing year with joy (1)
526	greet the ever-living bands on the eternal shore (4)
536	Israel comes to greet the Savior (3)
539	let none whom he hath ransomed fail to greet him (4)
695, 696	never fails to greet us each new day (1)

greeting

48	living presence greeting, through Bread and Wine made near (3)
129, 130	shout through them their joyful greeting (2)
576, 577	Christ, our love, is with us, gladness be his greeting (1)

grew

102	daily, when on earth he grew, he was tempted (4)
114	before their light the stars grew dim (1)
611	grew in wisdom as he grew in skill (2)

grief

6, 7	Pierce the gloom of sin and grief (3)
18	help us to share your pain and grief (3a)
145	or rend the soul, such grief is not Lent's goal (2)

159	with ... grief and resignation Mary watched her dying son (2)
228	comforter in time of grief, enter in and be our guest (2)
284	When hope was dim, and pain and grief beyond belief (4)
352	Christ, grant that neither grief nor place ... may part (2)
358	Grief and pain ended, and sighing no longer (1,4)
458	never was love, dear King, never was grief like thine (7)
472	who by this sign didst conquer grief and pain (5)
494	who every grief hath known that wrings the human breast (2)
610	still in grief we mourn our dead (2)
617	one with the grief that trembleth into prayer (2)
669	what profit doth it bring thee to pine in grief and care (2)

griefs

171	turn not from his griefs away (1)
573	sharing not our griefs, no joy can share (2)
669	fear not the griefs that plague thee (4)
669	griefs that ... keep thy heart dismayed (4)
682	griefs and torments numberless, and sweat of agony (3)
691	griefs around me spread (3)

grieve

| 230 | grieve him not, O Christian soul (3) |

grieves

| 452 | for the sake of those he grieves transcends the world (2) |
| 669 | Commit thou all that grieves thee ... to him (1) |

grieving

| 204 | when our hearts are wintry, grieving, or in pain (4) |

grievous

| 145 | of wickedness the grievous bands to loosen (3) |

grim

| 170 | acted out their grim charade to its appointed end (3) |
| 687, 688 | the prince of darkness grim, we tremble not for him (3) |

groan

| 104 | The sky shall groan and darken (3) |

ground

94, 95	all seated on the ground (1)
100	nor thorns infest the ground (3)
110	The snow lay on the ground, the stars shone bright (1)
149	as through stony ground the green shoots break (3)
256	Then Saul fell blinded to the ground (1)
392	celestial fruits on earthly ground (3)
392	we're marching through Emmanuel's ground to fairer worlds (4)
398	if I survey the ground I tread, or gaze upon the sky (2)
480	strowed their garments on the ground (3)
588, 589	Almighty God, your word is cast like seed upon the ground (1)

grounded

| 422 | Rooted and grounded in thy love (2) |

groundling
369   our groundling knowledge lies (3)

grow
3, 4   grow in love for every-one (2)
55   take our flesh and grow as child in Mary's womb (2)
100   No more let sins and sorrows grow (3)
170   Kingdom shall not cease to grow till love embraces all (3)
231   as faithful branches grow strong in you, the Vine (2/4-25)
298   Grant us to grow in grace each day (2)
392   celestial fruits ... from faith and hope may grow (3)
400   flowers and fruits that in you grow ... glory also show (4)
402, 403 earth is not too low, his praises there may grow (1)
480   like him in grace and knowledge grow as years (1)
480   grace and knowledge grow as years and strength increase (1)
574, 575 from sins which make the heart grow cold, wean us (2)
584   that as to knowledge we attain we may in wisdom grow (2)
587   knowing thee may grow in grace (2)
592   nothing ... will not grow bright and clean (2)
605   Will God your pleading hear, while crime and cruelty grow (2)
645, 646 where the verdant pastures grow (2)

grown
290   wheat and tares together sown, unto joy or sorrow grown (2)
299   hearts grown cold with fear (3)

grows
24   thy kingdom stands, and grows for ever (4)
61, 62   her star is risen, her light grows bright (2)
175   Daily the loveliness grows (3)
216   Daily the loveliness grows (2)
232   light that grows in splendor until the perfect day (2/6-24)
296   A new creation comes to life and grows (4)

growth
424   silent growth while we are sleeping (1)

guard
3, 4   From evil may he guard our eyes (3)
3, 4   guard ... our ears from empty praise and lies (3)
11   guard my first springs of thought and will (2)
42   guard the sailors tossing on the deep, blue sea (3)
44, 45   we pray ... our guard and keeper you would be (1)
110   to guard him, and protect his mother mild (3)
115   This, this is Christ the King who shepherds guard (R)
115   whom shepherds guard and angels sing (R)
125, 126 justice shall guard his throne above (5)
175, 216 guard us from harm without, cleanse us from evil within (5)
231   to guard your flock from harm (2/1-18)
251   In doubt or danger ... be near to guard us still (3)
302, 303 in mercy, save it from evil, guard it still (2)
345   guard thou the lips from sin, the hearts from shame (1)
370   his heavenly host to be my guard (5)
559   guard us, guide us, keep us, feed us (1)

626	thy promises my hope; thy providence my guard (2)
668	guard thy going out and in, both now and evermore (4)
704	still let me guard the holy fire (3)

guardian

38, 39	watchful guardian over all (1)
40, 41	We pray you, O most holy Lord, to be our guardian (2)
40, 41	be our guardian while we sleep (2)
231	the guardian of your Son (2/3-19)
260	Virgin's spouse ... guardian of great David's greater Son (2)
261, 262	guardian of the Incarnate (1)
512	be thou our guardian, thou our guide (1)
644	O Jesus, Shepherd, Guardian, Friend (4)
655	O speak, and make me listen, thou guardian of my soul (2)
668	Thy faithful guardian is the Lord (3)
718	be thou our ruler, guardian, guide, and stay (2)

guarding

453	the angels of Jacob are guarding it still (3)
579	protect them by thy guarding hand (2)
587	bless thou all parents, guarding well (1)
587	guarding ... the homes in which thy people dwell (1)
716	thou who art ever nigh, guarding with watchful eye (2)

guards

| 61, 62 | shout of rampart-guards surrounds us (1) |

guess

| 434 | nor wit can guess, nor reason prove which of the letters (3) |
| 516 | for none can guess its grace, till Love create a place (3) |

guest

76	a home where such a mighty guest may come (2)
135	at Cana, wedding guest, in thy God-head manifest (2)
226, 227	thou, the soul's most welcome guest (2)
228	comforter in time of grief, enter in and be our guest (2)
259	thus to his Father's house he comes, the heavenly guest (2)
305, 306	Come, risen Lord, and deign to be our guest (1)
339	as thy guest in heaven receive me (3)
487	such a strength as makes his guest (2)
664	no more a stranger or a guest, but like a child at home (3)

guests

305, 305	nay, let us be thy guests, the feast is thine (1)
320	grant us ... fellow-heirs and guests to be (6)
321	furnished well with joyful guests (2)
443	He joined with guests at wedding feast (2)

guidance

124	let not our slothful hearts refuse the guidance (4)
124	the guidance of thy light to use (4)
144	Give guidance to our wandering ways (2)
320	command for guidance taking, bread and wine we hallow (3)
373	laws ... for their guidance he hath made (1)
580	Great Creator, give us guidance (4)

580   give us guidance till our goals and yours are one (4)

guide

5   to guide whate'er we nobly do (4)
14, 15   through all its changes guide the day (1)
31, 32   guide us on our path to you (5)
117, 118   guide where our infant Redeemer is laid (1,5)
119   no star to guide, where no clouds thy glory hide (4)
128   guide us to thy perfect light (R)
162   so rule and guide us evermore (6)
217, 218   great the light in you we see to guide us to eternity (2)
223, 224   Thou who did our forebears guide (4)
229   Unfailing Comfort, heavenly Guide ... preside (3)
231   guide us in the Way (2/1-25)
231   blest guide to Greek and Jew (2/5-1)
282, 283   in thy service, he may wisely guide us (4)
348   led by your Spirit, defender and guide (2)
350   through change and chance be thou their guide (3)
364   also the Holy Comforter, our advocate and guide (5)
370   his hand to guide, his shield to ward (5)
396, 397   keep us in his grace, and guide us when perplexed (2)
433   Beside us to guide us, our God with us joining (2)
436   Holy Spirit guide us on until the glorious crown be won (5)
448, 449   Spirit here to guide, to strengthen, and to cheer (5)
503, 504   where thou art guide, no ill can come (6)
512   be thou our guardian, thou our guide (1)
526   Jesus, be thou our constant Guide (5)
552, 553   Cast care aside, lean on thy Guide (3)
559   guard us, guide us, keep us, feed us (1)
590   to lift the fallen, guide the feet that stumble (2)
597   guide us to justice, truth, and love (1)
607   in love and mercy guide us and heal our strife-torn world (1)
617   guide of the nations (1)
627   guide and chart wherein we read of realms beyond the sky (2)
635   If thou but trust in God to guide thee (1)
645, 646   thy cross before to guide me (4)
655   nor wander from the pathway if thou wilt be my guide (1)
659, 660   guide them in the homeward way (2)
662   Who, like thyself, my guide and stay can be (2)
669   he will guide thy footsteps and be thy staff and stay (1)
672   O guide us till our path is done (4)
680   be thou our guide while life shall last (6)
690   Guide me, O thou great Jehovah (1)
691   be thou my guide (3)
699   safe into the haven guide (1)
709   our wandering footsteps guide (3)
718   be thou our ruler, guardian, guide, and stay (2)

guided
320   when the twelve, divinely guided, at the holy table met (2)
559   thus provided, pardoned, guided (3)
617   guided and strengthened and upheld by thee (1)

guides
295   who sanctifies and guides us, made strong in our rebirth (3)

379   God's eternal lovingkindness guides us through (3)
379   guides us through our earthly strife (3)
393   guides his Israel on their way ... darkness into light (2)
444   He guides the feet of pilgrims along the paths of peace (3)
467   to make salvation sure, guides us by his Spirit pure (3)
492   from his Father's throne the Son rules and guides (4)
492   rules and guides the world he ransomed (4)
530   how his never-failing love guides us on to heaven above (4)
632   mid mists and rocks and quicksands still guides (2)
632   guides, O Christ, to thee (2)
675   it guides you to abundant life (4)

guideth
211   He guideth you on all your ways (3)
665   me through change and chance he guideth (1)

guiding
119   As with gladness men of old did the guiding star behold (1)
124   The guiding star above is bright (3)
131   followed on his guiding star (2)
132   followed on his guiding star (2)
527   gleams and burns the guiding light (1)
647   their faith and hope still guiding me (2)
703   without thy guiding hand we go astray (1)

guilt
27, 28   anguished and in mind distressed be crushed by guilt (3)
151   Our works could ne'er our guilt remove (2)
184   take our sin and guilt away that with angels we may say (2)
318   mine is the guilt, but thine the cleansing Blood (4)
471   The cross, it takes our guilt away (3)
472   save us ... from sin and guilt (4)
685   cleanse me from its guilt and power (1)
691   Now hear me while I pray, take all my guilt away (1)

guilty
158   Who was the guilty? Who brought this upon thee? (2)
715   a trembling fear seized all the guilty world around (RC)

habitation
235   How blest this habitation of gospel liberty (3)
515   Make our hearts thy habitation (2)
522, 523   Round each habitation hovering, see the cloud and fire (3)

hail
73   Hail, Christ the Lord (5)
87   hail the incarnate Deity (2)
87   hail, the Sun of Righteousness (3)
87   hail, the heaven-born Prince of Peace (3)
125, 126   To hail thy rising, Sun of life, the ... nations come (2)
162   O cross, our one reliance, hail (5)
175   Hail thee, festival day! blest day ... hallowed for ever (R)
179   speak his sorrow ended, hail his triumph now (2)
180   Come ... hail our Lord's triumphant day (3)
210   listening to his accents, may hear ... "All hail" (2)

210	may hear so calm and plain his own "All hail" (2)
214	Hail the day that sees him rise (1)
216	Hail thee, festival day! blest day ... hallowed for ever (R)
223, 224	Hail this joyful day's return (1)
223, 224	hail the Pentecostal morn (1)
225	Hail thee, festival day! blest day ... hallowed for ever (R)
259	Hail to the Lord who comes, comes to his temple gate (1)
263, 264	Hail, Mary, you shall bear a son (2)
265	"All hail ... thou lowly maiden Mary" (1)
266	said, "Hail Mary, full of grace." (2)
271, 272	faithful hearts shall never fail ... his light to hail (1)
271, 272	with thanks and praise his light to hail (1)
299	let new tongues hail the risen Lord (2)
307	here as there thine angels hail thee (3)
269	Hail Mary, Full of grace (1-4)
357	now we hail thee present on thine altar throne (1)
401	"Hail, Father, Son, and Holy Ghost" they ever cry (5)
401	hail, Abraham's Lord divine (5)
412	Hail, wind, and rain, loud blowing snow-storms (2)
426	songs of praise shall hail their birth (3)
450, 451	All hail the power of Jesus' Name (1)
450, 451	Hail him, the Heir of David's line (3)
450, 451	hail him who saves you by his grace (4)
494	hail him as thy matchless King through all eternity (1)
495	Hail, thou once despised Jesus, Hail, thou Galilean King (1)
495	Hail, thou universal Savior, bearer of our sin and shame (1)
495	Jesus, hail, enthroned in glory, there for ever to abide (3)
616	Hail to the Lord's Anointed, great David's greater Son (1)
616	Hail, in the time appointed, his reign on earth begun (1)

hailed

99	chorus that hailed our Savior's birth (2)
119	as with joy they hailed its light (1)
242	when thou didst thine appearance make, he saw and hailed (3)
242	saw and hailed his Lord Divine (3)
246	In Bethlehem a new-born boy was hailed with songs (1)
270	from the grave shall hope be hailed (4)
284	ye hailed his wondrous flight up to the throne of God (7)
720	what so proudly we hailed at the twilight's last gleaming (1)

half

81	amid the cold of winter, when half spent was the night (1)
81	when half spent was the night (1,2)

hall

61, 62	call to come into the banquet hall (2)
107	Calls you one and calls you all to gain his ... hall (3)
107	to gain his everlasting hall (3)
171	Follow to the judgment hall (2)
233, 234	in heaven's hall a victor band (2)

Hallelujah

213	Hallelujah we sing, to our Father and King (5)
213	to the Lamb that was slain, hallelujah again (5)
536	God has spoken to his people, Hallelujah (R)

hallow

10	mind be set to hallow all we find (3)
33-35	stars appearing hallow the night-fall (2)
320	command for guidance taking, bread and wine we hallow (3)
340, 341	hallow all our lives, O Lord (2)
366	Lo, the apostolic train join, thy sacred Name to hallow (3)

hallowed

37	Worthy are thou ... to receive our hallowed praises, Lord (3)
175	blest day that art hallowed forever (R)
198	Thou hallowed chosen morn of praise (1)
216	blest day that art hallowed for ever (R)
225	Hail thee, festival day! blest day ... hallowed ever (R)
312	feet that tread thy hallowed courts (3)
360, 361	Hallowed this dwelling where the Lord abideth (4)

halls

292	thine the wealth that in our halls abound (1)
624	They stand, those halls of Zion, all jubilant with song (2)

hammers

412	Engines and steel, loud pounding hammers (4)

hand

40, 41	with your right hand you will protect those who believe (3)
68	rise up, ye heirs of glory, the Bridegroom is at hand (2)
74	All things are in his hand, all ages and all peoples (3)
76	To heal the sick stretch out thine hand (4)
80	the Son holds in his infant hand (4)
102	Christ ... set at God's right hand on high (6)
170	A sceptered reed ... they thrust into your hand (3)
185, 186	but now at God's right hand he stands (1)
215	Thou hast raised our human nature ... to God's right hand (3)
215	on the clouds to God's right hand (3)
231	to plead at God's right hand (2/12-26)
243	no weapon in his hand (1)
258	blessed was the hand that led thee (1)
286	ne'er be touched by time's rude hand (2)
288	As thy prospering hand hath blessed, may we give (3)
289	hand hath crowned her children with blessings manifold (1)
291	but it is fed and watered by God's almighty hand (1)
305, 306	faith still receives the cup as from thy hand (2)
318	here grasp with firmer hand eternal grace (1)
324	for with blessing in his hand (1)
329, 331	gives himself with his own hand (3)
364	thou didst ascend to God's right hand in glory evermore (7)
366	In the glory of that land ... set at God's right hand (6)
370	his hand to guide, his shield to ward (5)
389	his full hand supplies their need (6)
399	He cradles in his hand the heights and depths of earth (2)
409	publishes to every land the work of an almighty hand (1)
409	The hand that made us is divine (3)
410	in his hand he gently bears us (3)
421	as you sit at God's right hand ... mercy, Lord, upon us (2)
431	mute witness of the Master's hand in all created things (1)

447	now pleads our cause at God's right hand (1)
462	wonders great by thy strong hand are done (5)
524	thy hand from every snare and foe ... deliverance bring (4)
524	thy hand ... shall great deliverance bring (4)
545	Thither ... press we to God's right hand (5)
546	his own hand presents the prize to thine aspiring eye (3)
574, 575	thy chastening hand (1)
579	protect them by thy guarding hand (2)
599	shadowed beneath thy hand may we for ever stand (3)
607	redeem the whole creation with your almighty hand (1)
612	joining hand in hand, agree (4)
615	when knowledge, hand in hand with peace (5)
620	David stands with harp in hand as master of the choir (3)
625	Ye holy angels bright, who wait at God's right hand (1)
636, 637	upheld by my righteous, omnipotent hand (2)
651	of skies and seas, his hand the wonders wrought (1)
662	I fear no foe, with thee at hand to bless (3)
664	Thy hand ... doth still my table spread (2)
665	Love doth stand at his hand (4)
685	in my hand no price I bring, simply to thy cross I cling (2)
689	Thou didst reach forth thy hand and mine enfold (2)
689	for thou wert long beforehand with my soul (3)
690	hold me with thy powerful hand (1)
695, 696	we take it ... out of so good and so beloved a hand (3)
702	all my ways are in thy hand (1)
702	the hand that leadeth me is thine (4)
703	without thy guiding hand we go astray (1)
705	mind, and heart, and hand (1)
709	O God of Bethel, by whose hand thy people still are fed (1)
709	Such blessings from thy gracious hand (5)
718	God of our fathers, whose almighty hand leads forth (1)

handiwork

566	our rude work deface no more the handiwork of God (2)

handle

318	here would I touch and handle things unseen (1)

hands

68	With hearts and hands uplifted, we plead, O Lord, to see (3)
97	stretching infant hands on high, Savior, long awaited (1)
191	by angel hands be gathered, and be ever, Lord, with thee (4)
193	his wounded hands and feet he showed (2)
196, 197	what he brings in his hurt hands is life (1,4)
206	my hands, my feet, I show to thee (4)
206	he saw the feet, the hands, the side (5)
209	We may not touch his hands and side (2)
212	but by his hands and feet (2)
212	those hands of liberal love indeed in infinite degree (3)
214	See! he lifts his hands above (3)
215	While he lifts his hands in blessing (2)
242	but craved to touch those hands of thine (3)
259	in his hands takes up the promised child (3)
270	by the hands, in grave clothes wound (3)
275	holding palms of victory in their hands (1)

harbor

104	A barn shall harbor heaven (1)

hard

18	when we must act in day's hard light (2b)
112	earth stood hard as iron, water like a stone (1)
605	How shall my soul fulfill God's law so hard and high (4)
648	oppressed so hard they could not stand (1)
695, 696	still evil days bring burdens hard to bear (2)
695, 696	bitter suffering, hard to understand (3)

hardening

281	a man of scorned and hardening trade (1)

hark

59	Hark, a thrilling voice is sounding (1)
67	Hark, the voice of one that crieth in the desert (2)
71, 72	Hark! the glad sound! the Savior comes (1)
87	Hark! the herald angels sing glory to the new-born King (1,R)
116	Hark, a glad voice (3)
156	Hark, all the tribes hosanana cry (1)
214	Hark, his gracious lips bestow (3)
215	Hark, the choirs of angel voices joyful alleluias sing (1)
225	Hark, for in myriad tongues Christ's own ... preach (3)
275	Hark, the sound of holy voices, chanting (1)
286	Alleluia, hark, they sing (1)
366	Hark, the loud celestial hymn angel choirs ... raising (2)
460, 461	Hark, the songs of peaceful Zion thunder (1,5)
494	Hark, how the heavenly anthem drowns all music but its own (1)

harm

3	he, in all we do or say, would keep us free from harm (1)
3	that he ... would keep us free from harm this day (1)
4	keep us free from harm this day (1)
113	he will bring no harm to you (2)
175	guard us from harm without, cleanse us from evil within (5)
216	guard us from harm without, cleanse us from evil within (3)
231	to guard your flock from harm (2/1-18)
345	from harm and danger keep thy children free (2)
457	who put their trust in thee nor death nor hell ... harm (3)

harmful

641	from harmful passions set me free (1)

harmonies

599	ring with the harmonies of liberty (1)

harmonious

235	In one harmonious witness the chosen four combine (2)

harmony

416	for the mystic harmony linking sense to sound and sight (3)
620	blessed martyrs' harmony doth ring in every street (4)

harms
| 480 | Safe from the world's alluring harms (2) |
| 493 | Jesus, the Name that charms our fears (3) |

harp
412	Harp, lute, and lyre, loud humming cellos (3)
432	tell ... sweet harp, the story of what he hath done (3)
448, 449	for us temptations sharp he knew (2)
620	David stands with harp in hand as master of the choir (3)

harps
| 61, 62 | as harps and cymbals swell the sound (3) |
| 89, 90 | to touch their harps of gold (1) |

harrowed
| 55 | You suffered death and harrowed hell (3) |

harvest
23	we harvest what the morning sowed (1)
125, 126	their harvest treasures home (2)
191	golden ears of harvest will their heads before him wave (3)
289	our harvest may be garnered by ages yet unknown (3)
290	O harvest Lord (2)
290	For the Lord our God shall come ... take his harvest home (3)
291	seed-time and the harvest, our life ... health ... food (3)
540	O harvest Lord ... the laborers how few (2)
541	Who dares stand idle on the harvest plain (1)

harvests
| 424 | in the harvests we are sharing (2) |
| 424 | For the harvests of the Spirit (3) |

haste
50	Make haste to help us, Lord (3)
59	let us haste, with tears of sorrow (3)
59	haste ... one and all to be forgiven (3)
73	O haste the rising of the morn (3)
115	haste to bring him laud, the babe, the son of Mary (R)
539	O Zion, haste, thy mission high fulfilling (1)
540	make haste to help us in our weakness (3)
609	make haste to heal these hearts of pain (4)

hasten
61, 62	Your lamps prepare and hasten there (1)
566	hasten, Lord, that perfect day (2)
655	O speak to reassure me, to hasten or control (2)

hastening
| 89, 90 | For lo! the days are hastening on (4) |
| 569 | through the thick darkness thy kingdom is hastening (4) |

hastens
| 433 | he chastens and hastens his will to make known (1) |

hate

158	man to judge thee hath in hate pretended (1)
204	In the grave they laid him, Love whom hate had slain (2)
236	faith undeterred by cruel hate (2)
246	Still rage the fires of hate today (3)
246	May that great love our lives control and conquer hate (5)
246	conquer hate in every soul (5)
255	Saul, the church's spoiler came spreading fear and hate (1)
584	Let wisdom's godly fear dispel the fears ... hate impart (3)
588, 589	Let not our selfishness and hate this holy seed remove (2)
593	where there is hate, may we sow love (1)
597	May swords of hate fall from our hands (1)
598	in the night of hate and war we perish as we lose thee (3)
607	hate and fear divide us and bitter threats are hurled (1)
683, 684	I hate the sins that made thee mourn (3)
687, 688	armed with cruel hate, on earth is not his equal (1)

hated

281	alike the symbol ... tool of foreign master's hated rule (1)

hatred

148	far and wide the wreckage of our hatred spreads (3)
222	his strife with human hatred ends (1)
282, 283	may he banish from us striving and hatred (2)
521	hatred and tormenting fear pass with the passing night (2)
606	May all our petty jealousies and hatred cease (2)
607	when hatred and division give way to love and peace (4)
613	When shall all hatred cease, as in the realms above (2)
617	We would be one in hatred of all wrong (2)

haughty

74	pity the proud and haughty (2)

haunt

600, 601	war may haunt the earth no more and desolation cease (4)

haunts

339	leave the gloomy haunts of sadness (1)
609	In haunts of wretchedness and need (2)

haven

51	rest for the pilgrim, haven for the weary (2)
453	when we arrive at the haven of rest, we shall hear (4)
699	safe into the haven guide (1)

having

140, 141	having done that, thou hast done, I fear no more (3)
337	having with us him that pleads above, we here present (1)
548	having all things done, and all your conflicts past (5)

hay

101	the little Lord Jesus asleep on the hay (1)

hazard

250	such a Lord to lead our way in hazard and prosperity (4)

head

84	Worship we the Godhead, love incarnate, love divine (2)
87	Veiled in flesh the God-head see (2)
92	God's bright star, o'er his head (3)
101	the little Lord Jesus laid down his sweet head (1)
113	Oh sleep now, holy baby, with your head against my breast (1)
117, 118	low lies his head with the beasts of the stall (2)
120	now by the Holy spirit shed upon the Son's anointed head (3)
135	at Cana, wedding guest, in thy God-head manifest (2)
145	To bow the head in sackcloth and in ashes (2)
156	bow thy meek head to mortal pain (5)
168, 169	O sacred head, sore wounded, defiled and put to scorn (1)
168, 169	O kingly head, surrounded with mocking crown of thorn (1)
179	of the Father's God-head true and only Son (4)
187	Like the cloud that overhead ... Isreal led (2)
188, 189	following our exalted Head (3)
208	all glory to our risen Head (3)
219	our glorious Head (1)
254	who, taught of God, confessed the God-head in the Christ (2)
265	Then gentle Mary meekly bowed her head (3)
267	She meekly bowed her head to hear the gracious word (4)
276	saw the glory round thy head, one of the chosen three (3)
284	With great delight ye crowned his head (3)
305, 306	who art one Savior and one living Head (4)
307	Thou alone ... liftest up thy people's head (1)
435	to the throne of Godhead, to the Father's breast (3)
441, 442	all the light of sacred story gathers round its head (1,5)
441, 442	gathers round its head sublime (1,5)
469, 470	joy for all the members in the sorrows of the Head (2)
474	See, from his head, his hands, his feet (3)
483	The head that once was crowned with thorns (1)
492	he, of humankind the head (3)
496, 497	whole creation's Head and Lord ... assumed our very nature (2)
518	Christ the head and cornerstone (1)
543	his all-resplendent grace he pours around thy head (2)
544	praises throng to crown his head (2)
649, 650	we drink of you, the fountain-head (2)
664	thy oil anounts my head (2)
677	clouds ... shall break in blessings on your head (3)
692	in your weariness lay down your head upon my breast (1)
694	God be in my head, and in my understanding (1)
699	cover my defenseless head with the shadow of thy wing (2)

headed

405	The purple-headed mountain, the river running by (2)

heads

148	evils wrought by human pride recoil on unrepentant heads (3)
191	golden ears of harvest will their heads before him wave (3)
214	lift your heads, eternal gates (2)
436	Lift up your heads, ye mighty gates (1)

heal

53	he will then receive thee, heal thee, and forgive thee (3)
76	To heal the sick stretch out thine hand (4)

120	to heal and save a race undone (4)
139	He came by water and by blood to heal our lost condition (3)
170	your sorrow heal our own (1)
277	forth to preach, and heal, and suffer (2)
357	heal them, Good Physician, with the balm of life (3)
371	heal to the sick in mind, sight to the inly blind (2)
472	to heal earth's wounds and end her bitter strife (2)
514	To thee, whose faithful power doth heal (3)
528	Heal the sick and preach the word (1)
537	sin-sick and sorrow-worn, whom Christ doth heal (1)
542	heal its ancient wrong, come, Prince of Peace, and reign (3)
567	Thine arm, O Lord, in days of old was strong to heal (1)
567	strong to heal and save (1)
607	in love and mercy guide us and heal our strife-torn world (1)
609	make haste to heal these hearts of pain (4)
633	speak and heal our mortal blindness (3)
633	heal the world, by our sin broken (3)
676	there is a balm in Gilead to heal the sinsick soul (R)

healed

139	He taught, he healed, he raised the dead (2)
410	ransomed, healed, restored, forgiven (1)
610	As, O Lord, your deep compassion healed the sick (2)
610	healed the sick and freed the soul (2)
615	every hurt be healed (4)

healer

232	whose Gospel shows the healer of the nations (2/10-18)
633	deaf we are, our healer be (3)

healeth

411	he healeth thine infirmities and ransoms thee from death (4)

healing

21, 22	pouring healing peace upon our soul (2)
23	They gave him healing in your Name (2)
87	Risen with healing in his wings (3)
226, 227	Cleanse us with thy healing power (4)
282, 283	healing and blessing (4)
285	pours on the Church from age to age the healing unction (2)
285	healing unction from above (2)
323	Lord, thy wounds our healing give (2)
360, 361	Here in our sickness healing grace aboundeth (3)
371	come to bring on thy redeeming wing healing and sight (2)
394, 395	let peace ... make known on earth your healing love (3)
408	with healing balm my soul he fills (1)
469, 470	there is healing in his blood (1)
513	With the healing of division (3)
590	healing those who touch your garment's hem (3)
596	solace all its wide dominion with the healing of thy wings (1)
667	it is the Lord who rises with healing in his wings (1)
672	with healing in thy wings (5)
690	fountain, whence the healing stream doth flow (2)
693	sight, riches, healing of the mind ... in thee to find (3)
699	let the healing streams abound (3)

heals
644   It soothes our sorrows, heals our wounds (1)

health
1, 2   banish our weakness, health and wholeness sending (2)
23   O Spirit, bringing power and health (4)
145   your health shall spring (5)
152   our weakened souls to health reclaim (3)
175   Jesus the health of the world, enlighten our minds (6)
179   Maker and Redeemer, life and health of all (4)
216   Jesus the health of the world (4)
291   seed-time and the harvest, our life ... health ... food (3)
292   Thine is the health and thine the wealth (1)
390   O my soul, praise him for he is thy health and salvation (1)
483   The cross he bore is life and health (6)
493   'tis life and health and peace (3)
538   thy saving health extend unto earth's remotest end (1)
566   fill the earth with health and light and peace (2)
567   lo, thy touch brought life and health (2)
610   hope and health, good will and comfort ... give (4)
621, 622   full of health, and strong, and free (4)

healthy
44, 45   A healthy life we ask of you (3)

heaping
97   heaping joys for thee (2)

hear
14, 15   Almighty Father, hear our cry through Jesus Christ (3)
18   teach us to hear its echoes still in every human misery (3c)
19, 20   Almighty Father, hear our cry through Jesus Christ (3)
21, 22   Almighty Father, hear our cry (3)
44, 45   Almighty Father, hear our cry (4)
48   This day, God's people meeting, his Holy Scripture hear (3)
49   with meekness hear the gospel word (3)
52   O Spirit, fill our hearts this day with grace to hear (4)
60   we pray you hear us when we call (1)
63, 64   as we hear thy truth today (2)
78, 79   No ear may hear his coming (3)
78, 79   We hear the Christmas angels the great glad tidings tell (5)
85, 86   now hear the prayers your people pray (2)
89, 90   The world in solemn stillness lay to hear the angels sing (1)
89, 90   hear the angels sing (3)
96   What glad tidings did you hear (2)
107   now ye hear of endless bliss (2)
150   Then if Satan on us press, Jesus, Savior, hear our call (3)
151   Lord, hear me, I implore thee (1)
152   Kind Maker of the world, O hear the fervent prayer (1)
171   "It is finished!" hear him cry (3)
173   with tears I pray thee, hear me (4)
209   no gracious words we hear from him (1)
210   listening to his accents, may hear ... "All hail" (2)
210   may hear so calm and plain his own "All hail" (2)
223, 224   tongues, that earth may hear their call (2)

236	hear us as now we celebrate faith undeterrred (2)
236	hear and forgive us (2)
267	She meekly bowed her head to hear the gracious word (4)
281	Enough ... to hear thy voice, to meet thine eye (3)
282, 283	hear our thankful praises (6)
342	we hear the words so gently spoken (1)
360, 361	hear now thy servants when their joyful voices rise (1)
360, 361	with tender mercy hear our petitions (5)
363	pray we that thou wilt hear us (5)
368	heavenly Father, through the Savior hear and bless (1)
368	while we hear thy wondrous story (2)
371	hear us, we humbly pray (1)
382	alone, when they replied, thou didst hear me (2)
400	make music for your Lord to hear (3)
440	Blessed Jesus, at thy word we are gathered all to hear (1)
440	Hear the cry thy Church upraises (3)
440	hear, and bless our prayers and praises (3)
453	when we arrive at the haven of rest, we shall hear (4)
453	hear the glad words, "Come to me all the blest" (4)
493	Hear him, ye deaf (5)
496, 497	great Emmanuel, come and hear us (1)
496, 497	hear, O hear our supplication (2)
501, 502	Teach us to speak, teach us to hear (3)
515	hear our supplication, blessed Spirit, God of peace (2)
518	with thy wonted lovingkindness hear thy servants (3)
518	hear thy servants as they pray (3)
536	Open your ears and hear God's word (1,4)
536	They who have ears to hear the message (2)
536	they who have ears, then let them hear (2)
536	who would learn the way of wisdom ... hear God's word (2)
549. 550	By thy mercies, Savior, may we hear thy call (5)
558	O how our hearts beat high with joy whene'er we hear (1)
558	whene'er we hear that glorious word (1)
579	hear us when we cry to thee for those in peril on the sea (1)
591	O God of earth and altar, bow down and hear our cry (1)
605	Will God your pleading hear, while crime and cruelty grow (2)
606	as we hear and love our Lord, the living God (1)
608	O hear us when we cry to thee (1-3)
609	we hear thy voice, O Son of Man (1)
620	ten thousand times would one be blest who might ... hear (3)
620	blest who might this music hear (3)
633	Word made flesh, we long to hear you (1)
638, 639	I hear thy whisper in my heart (4)
655	O let me hear thee speaking in accents clear and still (2)
666	Lord, hear my supplicating voice and graciously reply (1)
691	Now hear me while I pray, take all my guilt away (1)

heard

61, 62	No eye has known the sight, no ear heard such delight (3)
74	By those who truly listen his voice is truly heard (2)
96	Angels we have heard on high (1)
106	who heard the angelic herald's voice (2)
114	wondering hunters heard the hymn (1)
206	When Thomas first the tidings heard (3)
230	the ears of all who heard proclaimed salvation's wonder (1)

231	young James the faithful, who heard and followed you (2/5-1)
232	youthful and unready, she heard the angel's word (2/8-15)
256	in that light a voice was heard (1)
266	When the maiden heard his song (3)
276	he heard what could not be denied, thy summons (2)
284	ye saw his agony, ye heard the plaint he cried (4)
312	let ears that now have heard thy songs ... never waken (1)
336	let its hymn be heard for ever -- peace (3)
371	Thou, whose almighty word chaos and darkness heard (1)
382	Thou hast granted my request, thou hast heard me (1)
393	how the word we have heard firm and changeless ... stand (1)
422	very high thy voice, O God, is heard (1)
427	There to the eternal Word the eternal psalm is heard (3)
506, 507	in Jesus God himself was seen and heard (3)
528	Lest ... the Gospel go unheard (1)
531	whene'er the joyful sound is heard (2)
549, 550	as, of old, Saint Andrew heard it by the Galilean lake (2)
607	your still small voice be heard (3)
608	O Christ, whose voice the waters heard (2)
652, 653	simple trust like theirs who heard beside the Syrian sea (2)
692	I heard the voice of Jesus say (1-3)

hearing

210	hearing, may raise the victor strain (2)
314	faith, that comes by hearing, pierces through the veil (2)
333	Now the hearing ... power ... vessel brimmed for pouring (1)
334	one voice hearing, ears attentive to your word (2)
567	thy touch ... gave hearing, strength, and sight (2)

hearken

76	awake and hearken, for he brings glad tidings (1)
240, 241	Hearken to the anthem glorious of the martyrs (1)
370	his ear to hearken to my need (5)

hears

61, 62	Zion hears the watchman singing (2)
69	Who hears, O God, the prophecy (1)
80	who hears your sad and bitter cry (3)
89, 90	warring human-kind hears not the tidings which they bring (3)
203	to God your hears and voices raise (5)

heart

6, 7	Day-star, in my heart appear (1)
6, 7	glad my eyes, and warm my heart (2)
16, 17	with fervent heart and ready mind (1)
47	shine, blest Spirit in my heart (5)
47	God, the blessed Three in One dwell within my heart alone (6)
51	We the Lord's people, heart and voice uniting (1)
61, 62	her heart with joyful hope is springing (2)
66	dear desire of every nation, joy of every longing heart (2)
71, 72	let every heart prepare a throne, and every voice a song (1)
71, 72	He comes, the broken heart to bind (3)
76	let each heart prepare a home (2)
77	let every heart awake and sing the holy child (1)
100	let every heart prepare him room (1)

107		rejoice with heart and soul and voice (1-3)
112		yet what I can I give him give my heart (3)
152		Each heart is manifest to thee (2)
152		so that we in heart and soul may dwell with thee (4)
159		in her heart the piercing sword (1)
159		my heart fresh ardor gaining (5)
168, 169		In thy most bitter passion my heart to share doth cry (3)
168, 169		Ah, keep my heart thus moved to stand thy cross beneath (3)
181		wake every heart and every tongue (1)
185, 186		by his grace he doth impart eternal sunshine to the heart (3)
194, 195		alone to Jesus living, pure in heart may we abide (2)
196, 197		joy to the heart and all in this good day's dawning (R)
213		so united in heart, let us nevermore part (4)
222		he takes upon his heart the cares, the pain, and shame (3)
226, 227		Bend the stubborn heart and will (4)
228		Enter each aspiring heart (3)
232		whose heart with awe was stirred (2/8-15)
238, 239		loving Christ with single heart (2)
243		but only in his heart a flame (1-3)
243		only in my heart a flame and in my soul a dream (4)
248, 249		ear and heart delighting well (2)
257		pondering all things in her heart (4)
277		from the heart of blessed Mary (3)
281		But grace within his heart had stirred (2)
281		lay up treasures in the heart (4)
284		do thou my heart extol his Name (8)
301		look on the heart by sorrow broken (1)
314		lo, to thee surrendered, my whole heart is bowed (1)
315		with longing heart and soul (1)
320		gracious hymns of joy upraising in thy heart and soul (4)
320		hymns ... in thy heart and soul today (4)
326		one heart ... song have the saints upon earth and above (2)
329, 331		faith alone the true heart waketh to behold the mystery (4)
333		Now the wedding Now the songs ... heart forgiven leaping (1)
343		Savior, abide with us, and spread thy table in our heart (3)
345		peace in each heart, thy Spirit from above (3)
352		nor life nor death may part those ... one in heart (2)
363		O Triune God, with heart and voice adoring, praise we (5)
365		thou, who almighty art, now rule in every heart (3)
372		deep writ upon the human heart, on sea and land (3)
375		With balm my inmost heart he fills (1)
379		find that self-same aching deep within the heart of God (2)
382		the cream of all my heart, I will bring thee (2)
382		in my heart, though not in heaven, I can raise thee (3)
383, 384		who makes the woeful heart to sing (2)
386, 387		Moses while on earth in dread and smitten to the heart (2)
396, 397		Now thank we all our God with heart and hands and voices (1)
400		All you with mercy in your heart (5)
402, 403		above all, the heart must bear the longest part (2)
404		We love you with our heart and strength and mind (3)
415		gratitude ... that glows within my fervent heart (2)
415		nor is the least a cheerful heart (3)
415		cheerful heart that tastes those gifts with joy (3)
415		my ever grateful heart, O Lord, thy mercy shall adore (4)
416		for the heart and mind's delight (3)

419	yet to each loving heart how near (1)
426	Saints below, with heart and voice ... rejoice (5)
427	When morning gilds the skies, my heart, awaking, cries (1)
428	let those of holy, humble heart come praise him evermore (5)
430	hither bring in one consent heart ... voice ... instrument (1)
431	meditations of my heart be innocence and praise (4)
436	Fling wide the portals of your heart (3)
436	Redeemer come, I open wide my heart to thee (4)
437, 438	in God my Savior shall my heart rejoice (1)
440	open thou our ears and heart (3)
457	thou only canst inform the mind and purify the heart (2)
465, 466	Eternal light, shine in my heart (1)
469, 470	the heart of the Eternal is most wonderfully kind (3)
481	Lift up your heart, lift up your voice (R)
487	Come, my Joy, my Love, my Heart (3)
487	such a heart as joys in love (3)
488	Be thou my vision, O Lord of my heart (1)
488	Heart of my heart, whatever befall (3)
490	Shine in my heart, Lord Jesus (R)
498	from my smitten heart with tears two wonders I confess (2)
505	that charity may warm each heart (3)
508	until my heart is pure (2)
512	plant holy fear in every heart (2)
516	O Comforter, draw near, within my heart appear (1)
517	my very heart and flesh cry out, O living God, for thee (1)
527	lift as from the heart of one (3)
539	make known to every heart his saving grace (4)
551	give heart and soul and mind and strength (1)
556, 557	Rejoice, ye pure in heart! Rejoice, give thanks and sing (1)
556, 557	on, ye pure in heart! Rejoice, give thanks and sing (7)
560	Blessed are the pure in heart, for they shall see God (6)
573	Envious of heart, blind-eyed, with tongues confounded (3)
574, 575	from sins which make the heart grow cold, wean us (2)
581	with heart and mind and strength now love him in return (2)
584	with new mind, new heart (3)
587	with heart still undefiled, thou didst to manhood come (2)
588, 589	give it root in every heart to bring forth fruits of love (2)
610	not of voice alone, but heart (1)
621, 622	brighter than the heart can fancy (1)
624	beneath thy contemplation sink heart and voice oppressed (1)
625	with a well-tuned heart sing thou the songs of love (4)
634	My heart is never set at rest till thy sweet word (1)
638, 639	speak to my heart, in blessings speak (3)
638, 639	I hear thy whisper in my heart (4)
642	No voice can sing, no heart can frame (2)
642	O hope of every contrite heart, O joy of all the meek (3)
643	thou hast stooped to ask of me the love of my poor heart (5)
644	Weak is the effort of my heart (5)
656	Blest are the pure in heart, for they shall see our God (1)
656	for his dwelling ... throne will choose the pure in heart (3)
656	give us a pure and lowly heart, a temple fit for thee (4)
657	visit us with thy salvation, enter every trembling heart (1)
659, 660	Help me the slow of heart to move (2)
665	God unknown, he alone calls my heart to be his own (1)
669	fills thy heart with care (1)

669	griefs that ... keep thy heart dismayed (4)
670	let my heart find rest in thee (2)
671	'Twas grace that taught my heart to fear (2)
674	How can your pardon reach and bless the unforgiving heart (2)
675	take up your cross with willing heart (1)
675	heed not the shame, and let your foolish heart be still (3)
681	May thy fresh light arise within each clouded heart (5)
686	tune my heart to sing thy grace (1)
686	Let thy goodness ... bind my wandering heart to thee (3)
686	here's my heart, oh, take and seal it (3)
691	May thy rich grace impart strength to my fainting heart (2)
694	God be in my heart, and in my thinking (1)
695, 696	Yet is this heart by its old foe tormented (2)
697	My God, accept my heart this day (1)
697	accept my heart this day, and make it always thine (1)
699	spring thou up within my heart, rise to all eternity (3)
701	my heart long paineth, ah, my spirit straineth (1)
701	heart ... longeth after thee (1)
704	kindle a flame of sacred love upon the altar of my heart (1)
705	mind, and heart, and hand (1)
706	taught my sin-filled heart and mind (1)
706	for my heart would still refuse you (2)
706	Now my heart sets none above you (3)
707	take my heart, it is thine own (1)
717	my heart with rapture thrills like that above (2)

heart's

117, 118	richer by far is the heart's adoration (4)
704	Jesus, confirm my heart's desire to work ... for thee (3)

hearted

69	blind-hearted seeing no light (2)
180	Come, ye sad and fearful hearted (2)

heartfelt

173	Who would not weep with heartfelt pain and sighing (1)
454	again in answer to our earnest heartfelt prayer (2)

heartily

413	Joyfully, heartily resounding (2)

hearts

3, 4	Now that the daylight fills the sky, we lift our hearts (1)
3, 4	lift our hearts to God on high (1)
3, 4	Our hearts and lips may he restrain (2)
3, 4	from selfishness our hearts release (3)
18	your light, O Lord, burns in our hearts (1)
19, 20	pour forth into our hearts, we pray, the fullness (1)
19, 20	let love in flames of living fire the hearts ... inspire (2)
19, 20	hearts of all the world inspire (2)
29, 30	shed thou within our hearts thy ray (1)
31, 32	Like sun and day, shine in our hearts (5)
33-35	creation joining hearts and voices singing your glory (3)
33-35	strength for our weak hearts, rest for aching bodies (4)
33-35	Though bodies slumber, hearts shall keep their vigil (5)

40, 41	let hearts in constant vigil watch (3)
49	our joyful hearts and voices raise (3)
52	O Spirit, fill our hearts this day with grace to hear (4)
56	bind in one the hearts of all mankind (7)
60	all hearts must bow (4)
63, 64	fire our hearts with ardent love (2)
63, 64	the secrets of our hearts to try (3)
66	By thine own eternal Spirit rule in all our hearts alone (4)
67	let your hearts be true and humble (3)
68	With hearts and hands uplifted, we plead, O Lord, to see (3)
69	Dark is the season, dark our hearts and shut to mystery (1)
74	For him let doors be opened, no hearts against him barred (1)
78, 79	God imparts to human hearts the blessings of his heaven (3)
96	while we raise our hearts in love (4)
98	lead us all with hearts aflame unto the joys above us (4)
104	for stony-hearts of men (3)
115	let loving hearts enthrone him (3)
124	let not our slothful hearts refuse the guidance (4)
133, 134	To you, the King of glory ... faithful hearts ... bow (3)
133, 134	now all faithful hearts adoring bow (3)
136, 137	faithful hearts are raised on high by this ... mystery (4)
144	Lord Jesus, Sun of Righteousness, shine in our hearts (1)
144	shine in our hearts, we pray (1)
191	alleluia! Hearts and voices heavenward raise (1)
191	hearts in heaven dwelling, we on earth may fruitful be (4)
193	do thou thyself our hearts possess (3)
194, 195	our hearts know well nought from us his love shall sever (3)
204	when our hearts are wintry, grieving, or in pain (4)
204	fields of our hearts that dead and bare have been (4)
205	sing with hearts uplifted high (3)
210	Our hearts be pure from evil, that we may see aright (2)
214	raise our hearts to reach thy height (4)
219	O may our hearts to him ascend (3)
226, 227	come within our hearts to shine (1)
226, 227	fill our hearts and make them thine (3)
228	come and touch our hearts today (1)
233, 234	with hearts of gladness raise due hymns (1)
236	Turn our rebellious hearts (3)
244	Come, pure hearts, in joyful measure sing (1)
245	your deeds and words refresh our hearts like dew (3)
246	aching hearts in every land cry out (3)
271, 272	faithful hearts shall never fail ... his light to hail (1)
286	whose hearts were riven, sore with woe and anguish tried (4)
287	hearts are brave again, and arms are strong (5)
291	but chiefly thou desirest our humble thankful hearts (3)
299	With burning words of victory won inspire our hearts (3)
299	hearts grown cold with fear (3)
300	cheers our hearts, fills with food and gladness (3)
302, 303	planted thy holy Name within our hearts (1)
308, 309	nor thy delights deny us, whose hearts to thee draw nigh (1)
319	Bind our hearts as one we implore you (2)
327, 328	Approach ye then with faithful hearts sincere (5)
336	in our hearts as in thy heaven ... anthems raised (3)
340, 341	in our hearts keep watch and ward (4)
344	fill our hearts with joy and peace (1)

344	in our hearts and lives abound (2)
345	guard thou the lips from sin, the hearts from shame (1)
359	to human need their quickened hearts awake (2)
363	to thee in reverent love our hearts are bowed (2)
365	build in our hearts thy throne, Ancient of Days (1)
366	Lord, renew our hearts within us (7)
368	dear Redeemer, in our hearts thy peace proclaim (2)
368	touch our hearts with sacred fire (3)
368	Great Jehovah, form our hearts and make them thine (4)
370	Christ in hearts of all that love me (6)
376	hearts unfold like flowers before thee (1)
379	when human hearts are breaking under sorrow's iron rod (2)
396, 397	with ever joyful hearts and blessed peace to cheer us (2)
419	kindling hearts that burn for thee (4)
431	a law of love within our hearts (3)
435	In your hearts enthrone him (5)
435	our hearts confess him King of glory now (6)
436	happy hearts and happy homes to whom this King ... comes (2)
437, 438	Proud hearts and stubborn wills are put to flight (3)
440	let our hearts and souls be stirred now to seek and love (1)
454	again in mercy, when our hearts are bowed with care (2)
454	to hearts rejoicing, bringing news of sins forgiven (3)
460, 461	shall our hearts forget his promise (2)
472	Christ of great compassion, speak to our fearful hearts (1)
472	speak to our fearful hearts by conflict rent (1)
477	that in our darkened hearts thy grace might shine (1)
478	all who confess his Name, come then with hearts aflame (3)
482	your bliss in our hearts, Lord, at the break of the day (1)
482	strength in our hearts, Lord, at the noon of the day (2)
482	your love in our hearts, Lord, at the eve of the day (3)
482	your peace in our hearts, Lord, at the end of the day (4)
493	mournful broken hearts rejoice, the humble poor believe (4)
500	our hearts with heavenly love inspire (2)
501, 502	come, kindle in our hearts your fire (1)
501, 502	in mutual love our hearts unite (4)
506, 507	fire our hearts and clear our sight (5)
509	Come as the fire, and purge our hearts (3)
509	purge our hearts like sacrificial flame (3)
510	kindle a flame of sacred love in ... cold hearts of ours (1)
515	Make our hearts thy habitation (2)
517	happy they whose hearts are set upon the pilgrim's quest (2)
531	Give tongues of fire and hearts of love to preach (2)
536	Open your hearts, O royal priesthood (1,4)
540	O Lord, now let thy fire enkindle our hearts (2)
540	by many messengers, all hearts to win (3)
547	with kind and gentle hearts forgive (4)
549, 550	give our hearts to thine obedience (5)
558	O how our hearts beat high with joy whene'er we hear (1)
559	Spirit of our God, descending, fill our hearts (3)
559	fill our hearts with heavenly joy (3)
561	To valiant hearts triumphant a crown of life shall be (4)
574, 575	Search out our hearts and make us true (2)
587	O Spirit, who dost bind our hearts in unity (3)
587	in all our hearts such love increase (3)
593	nor look to understanding hearts (3)

593	but look for hearts to understand (3)
594, 595	From the fears that long have bound us free our hearts (2)
594, 595	free our hearts to faith and praise (2)
597	our hearts from envy find release (1)
598	we bring our hearts before thy cross (4)
599	our hearts drunk with the wine of the world (3)
609	make haste to heal these hearts of pain (4)
617	rule in our hearts that we may ever be ... upheld (1)
623	Now, in the meanwhile, with hearts raised on high (4)
624	Oh, sweet and blessed country that eager hearts expect (4)
627	to its heavenly teaching turn, with ... childlike hearts (5)
627	simple, child-like hearts (5)
628	study, that your laws may be inscribed upon our hearts (1)
629	let a new and better hope within our hearts be stirred (1)
633	touch our hearts and bring to birth faith and hope (1)
649, 650	O Jesus, joy of loving hearts (1)
661	peace ... filled their hearts brimful and broke them, too (2)
681	our hearts can find no rest (2)
718	thy true religion in our hearts increase (3)

heat

21, 22	from passion's heat preserve our life (2)
292	Lord, in their change, let frost and heat ... be given (2)
292	let frost and heat, and winds and dews be given (2)
428	heat and cold, O night and day ... bless the Lord (3)
498	from the burning of the noon-tide heat (1)
516	turn to dust and ashes in its heat consuming (2)

heaven

1, 2	bring us to heaven where thy saints united joy (2)
8	Sweet the rain's new fall sunlit from heaven (2)
10	new thoughts of God, new hopes of heaven (2)
10	as more of heaven in each we see (4)
25, 26	through all the earth and in the highest heaven adored (3)
31, 32	Most Holy God, the Lord of heaven (1)
48	this day our Lord victorious the Spirit sent from heaven (2)
50	let heaven rejoice, let earth be glad (1)
53	let us here confess thee till in heaven we bless thee (4)
54	Marvel now, both heaven and earth (1)
59	comes with pardon down from heaven (3)
60	with one accord, like those in heaven (4)
65	He brings God's rule, O Zion, he comes from heaven above (2)
69	in great humility is hid all heaven in a little room (3)
78, 79	God imparts to human hearts the blessings of his heaven (3)
80	From heaven above to earth I come (1)
82	Let the heights of heaven adore him (3)
83	sing, all ye citizens of heaven above (3)
87	Christ, by highest heaven adored (2)
88	God himself comes down from heaven (1)
88	from high heaven he comes to earth (2)
94, 95	good will henceforth from heaven to men (6)
100	heaven and nature sing (1)
101	fit us for heaven to live with thee there (3)
102	He came down to earth from heaven ... God and Lord of all (2)
102	child who seemed so helpless is our Lord in heaven above (5)

102	but in heaven, where his saints his throne surround (6)
104	A barn shall harbor heaven (1)
109	that hath made heaven and earth of nought (6)
111	glories stream from heaven afar (2)
112	Our God, heaven cannot hold him, nor earth sustain (2)
112	heaven and earth shall flee away when he comes to reign (2)
114	the holy child of earth and heaven is born today for you (4)
119	to bend the knee before him whom heaven and earth adore (2)
125, 126	all the hosts of heaven (3)
127	out of thee the Lord from heaven came to rule his Israel (1)
128	heaven sings alleluia: alleluia the earth replies (5)
139	baptized by John, there came a voice from heaven saying (1)
153	Peace in heaven and glory in the highest (1)
167	that we might go at last to heaven (3)
167	he only could unlock the gate of heaven and let us in (4)
168, 169	O countenance whose splendor the hosts of heaven adore (1)
175	heaven her gates unbars, flinging her increase of light (3)
176, 177	of whom the glory in both earth and heaven is manifested (3)
179	hell today is vanquished, heaven is won today (1)
179	thou from heaven beholding human nature's fall (4)
185, 186	brings us life from heaven (1)
185, 186	let us feast this holy day on the true bread of heaven (4)
191	hearts in heaven dwelling, we on earth may fruitful be (4)
194, 195	rest and reign with him in heaven (4)
201	So let our songs to heaven wing (4)
203, 206	King of heaven ... o'er death and hell rose triumphing (1)
212	O Solitude again command your host from heaven restored (5)
213	sing, all heaven, and fall at his feet (5)
214	enters now the highest heaven (1)
214	find our heaven of heavens in thee (4)
216	heaven her gates unbars, flinging her increase of light (2)
222	He reigns in heaven until the hour when he ... shall come (4)
226, 227	joys which earth and heaven entwine (5)
230	A mighty sound from heaven at Pentecost there came (1)
231	Praise for the light from heaven ... voice of awe (2/1-25)
251	look down from heaven, thy dwelling place (1)
252	Jesus, only Name that's given under all the mighty heaven (5)
253	long cloud of witnesses show the same path to heaven (4)
255	God's light shone down from heaven (1)
256	A light from heaven shone around (1)
261, 262	Ruler of all things, Lord of earth and heaven (2)
265	The angel Gabriel from heaven came (1)
270	so, behold, all the gates of heaven unfold (R)
273, 274	by hope of God united they reach to heaven above (1)
282, 283	grant of thy mercy ... us thy servants steps up to heaven (1)
282, 283	Send thine archangel Gabriel the mighty herald of heaven (3)
282, 283	may the assembly of the saints in heaven ... help us (5)
284	his beauteous face in heaven ye view (1)
291	All good gifts around us are sent from heaven above (R)
292	breathe from the bounteous heaven (2)
300	us he leads to a feast in heaven (3)
307	heaven and earth with loud hosanna worship thee (5)
308, 309	O Food to pilgrims given, O Bread of life from heaven (1)
308, 309	Grant when the veil is riven, we may behold, in heaven (3)
308, 309	we may behold, in heaven, thy countenance divine (3)

310, 311	opening wide the gate of heaven to us below (1)
318	here drink with thee the royal Wine of heaven (2)
323	Bread of heaven, on thee we feed (1)
323	Vine of heaven, thy Blood supplies this blest cup (2)
324	Rank on rank the host of heaven spreads its vanguard (3)
336	in our hearts as in thy heaven ... anthems raised (3)
339	let me be a fit partaker of ... blessed food from heaven (2)
339	as thy guest in heaven receive me (3)
340, 341	by your call to heaven above us (2)
360, 361	this is none other than the gate of heaven (4)
365	Come, thou incarnate Word, by heaven and earth adored (2)
366	all in heaven above adore thee (1)
366	on the cross thy dying breath opened ... heaven (6)
366	opened wide the realm of heaven (6)
367	Lord, thy glory fills the heaven (1,3)
367	Heaven is still with glory ringing (2)
370	bind unto myself today the virtues of the starlit heaven (4)
373	heaven and earth, and all creation, Laud ... his Name (2)
375	host of heaven praiseth thee, O Lord of all dominions (2)
376	earth and heaven reflect thy rays (2)
377, 378	the God whom heaven and earth adore (5)
379	God is love, let heaven adore him (1)
382	in my heart, though not in heaven, I can raise thee (3)
383, 384	Jesus shines purer than all the angels heaven can boast (3)
391	high as the heaven our voices raise (4)
396, 397	the Son, and him who reigns with them in highest heaven (3)
396, 397	eternal, Triune God, whom earth and heaven adore (3)
401	the Lord, the great I AM, by earth and heaven confessed (1)
401	we shall, on eagle-wings upborne, to heaven ascend (2)
401	With heaven our songs we raise (5)
410	Praise, my soul, the King of heaven (1)
416	peace on earth and joy in heaven (6)
421	peace on earth from heaven (1)
426	heaven with alleluias rang when creation was begun (1)
426	Heaven and earth must pass away (3)
427	No lovelier antiphon in all high heaven is known (3)
428	O sun and moon and stars of heaven (2)
431	vault of heaven springs mute witness (1)
432	For love in creation, for heaven restored (4)
443	his work done, went up to heaven, praised be his coming (4)
444	a Savior comes among us to raise us up to heaven (2)
454	in sounds of gladness, leading souls redeemed to heaven (3)
458	What may I say? Heaven was his home (6)
458	Heaven was his home, but mine the tomb wherein he lay (6)
459	The heaven that hides him from our sight (2)
459	heaven ... knows neither near nor far (2)
460, 461	Bread of Heaven, thou on earth our food, our stay (3)
460, 461	born of Mary, earth thy footstool, heaven thy throne (4)
467	Heaven and earth by him were made (2)
469, 470	no place ... sorrows are more felt than up in heaven (2)
471	the angel's theme in heaven above (5)
472	God's gift from highest heaven (2)
477	with one accord in heaven and earth (5)
481	His kingdom cannot fail, he rules o'er earth and heaven (3)

483	highest place that heaven affords is his ... by right (2)
483	their joy, the joy of heaven (4)
486	let earth, let heaven, hosanna sing (1)
486	dreadful day when earth and heaven shall melt away (5)
488	High King of heaven, when victory is won (3)
489	the sovereign God of heaven (1)
492	Sing how he came forth from heaven (2)
493	the Church in earth and heaven (6)
494	Crown him the Lord of heaven, enthroned in worlds above (5)
495	opened is the gate of heaven, reconciled are we with God (2)
496, 497	the host of heaven rejoices (1)
496, 497	Praise be given evermore, by earth and heaven (3)
506, 507	dark and furthest corners by the wind of heaven blown (4)
512	Lead us to heaven, that we may share the fullness of joy (4)
519, 520	living stones art builded in the height of heaven above (1)
524	brighter bliss of heaven (5)
525	from heaven he came and sought her to be his holy bride (1)
526	all the servants of our King in heaven and earth are one (1)
526	bring us safe to heaven (5)
530	how his never-failing love guides us on to heaven above (4)
560	for theirs is the kingdom of heaven (1,8)
560	for great is your reward in heaven (9)
563	he can with bread of heaven thy fainting spirit feed (1)
563	Satan's host is vanquished and heaven is all possessed (3)
572	music ... wherewith heaven is ringing (1)
573	building proud towers which shall not reach to heaven (3)
579	O Wind of heaven, by thy might save all (3)
586	Bread of heaven, art broken in the sacrament of life (2)
588, 589	let the dew of heaven descend and righteous fruits abound (1)
599	Lift every voice and sing till earth and heaven ring (1)
609	till glorious from thy heaven above shall come the city (5)
619	ye citizens of heaven, O sweetly raise (1)
627	or heaven itself be won (4)
629	dares to bind to one's own sense the oracles of heaven (2)
633	living rain from heaven descending (1)
633	Word that came from heaven to die (2)
657	joy of heaven, to earth come down (1)
657	till in heaven we take our place (3)
668	who heaven and earth hath made (1)
682	I love thee Lord ... not because I hope for heaven thereby (1)
682	not for the sake of winning heaven, nor any fear of hell (4)
690	bread of heaven, feed me now and evermore (1)
697	death the gate of heaven (4)
701	Jesus, heaven to me (1)
702	In heaven? It is thy dwelling fair (3)

heaven's

51	day of the Spirit, sign of heaven's banquet (3)
71, 72	heaven's eternal arches ring with thy beloved Name (4)
89, 90	from heaven's all-gracious King (1)
92	praising Christ, heaven's King (4)
102	confounded that a stable should display heaven's Word (3)
106	heaven's whole orb with alleluias rang (3)
106	eternal praise to heaven's almighty King (6)
107	He hath opened heaven's door (2)

229	Unfailing Comfort, heavenly Guide ... preside (3)
248, 249	heavenly joy posesseth here (3)
259	thus to his Father's house he comes, the heavenly guest (2)
260	beside his spouse ... he joins the heavenly song (4)
271, 272	With heavenly message Gabriel came (2)
275	Now they reign in heavenly glory (4)
278	heavenly breath of God's own being (3)
278	Lord of all creation brought her to his heavenly home (4)
286	praising loud their heavenly King (1)
298	stand among the glorious heavenly band (1)
298	heavenly band of every tribe and nation (1)
307	Lord, enthroned in heavenly splendor (1)
307	Life-imparting heavenly Manna (5)
316, 317	this is the heavenly table spread for me (1)
320	where the heavenly feast thou showest (6)
324	he will give ... his own self for heavenly food (2)
327, 328	with heavenly bread he makes the hungry whole (7)
332	We come, obedient to thy word, to feast on heavenly food (3)
343	living bread, that heavenly wine, be our immortal food (4)
347	be of good courage, armed with heavenly grace (1)
357	shed on them the radiance of thy heavenly light (4)
364	O holy, holy, holy Lord, whom heavenly hosts obey (3)
368	heavenly Father, through the Savior hear and bless (1)
369	all the heavenly powers conspire eternal praise to sing (4)
370	his riding up the heavenly way (2)
370	his heavenly host to be my guard (5)
380	praise him above, ye heavenly host (3)
392	children of the heavenly King may speak their joys abroad (2)
399	Your heavenly Father praise, acclaim his only Son (3)
419	one heavenly flame (4)
459	there heavenly splendors shine (2)
462	justice, from her heavenly bower, look down on us below (2)
484, 485	now prepares in heavenly regions unfailing mansions (1)
494	Hark, how the heavenly anthem drowns all music but its own (1)
495	all the heavenly hosts adore thee (3)
500	our hearts with heavenly love inspire (2)
510	Come, Holy Spirit, heavenly Dove (1,4)
512	Come, Gracious Spirit, heavenly Dove (1)
519, 520	Blessed city, heavenly Salem (1)
519, 520	in their places now compacted by the heavenly Architect (4)
524	Beyond my highest joy I prize her heavenly ways (3)
546	a heavenly race demands thy zeal (1,4)
555	the heavenly kingdom comes (2)
559	Lead us, heavenly Father (1)
559	fill our hearts with heavenly joy (3)
567	give wisdom's heavenly lore (3)
612	taught by thee we covet most ... holy, heavenly, love (1)
617	Oh, clothe us with thy heavenly armor, Lord (3)
621, 622	endued with heavenly beauty (4)
625	Ye saints, who toil below, adore your heavenly King (3)
627	stream from the fount of heavenly grace (1)
627	to its heavenly teaching turn, with ... childlike hearts (5)
641	through darkness and perplexity point ... heavenly way (3)
683, 684	O for a closer walk with God, a calm and heavenly frame (1)
697	Anoint me with thy heavenly grace (3)

| 700 | Well-spring of heavenly peace, thou Living Water, come (2) |
| 703 | Lead us, O Father, to the heavenly rest (3) |

heavens

33-35	stars in the heavens (1)
33-35	in the heavens choirs of stars appearing (2)
50	highest heavens in which he reigns shall give ... praise (5)
61, 62	Lamb of God, the heavens adore you (3)
99	behold, throughout the heavens there shone a holy light (1)
133, 134	the heavens above your glory named (2)
175	God the Creator ... who rulest the earth and the heavens (5)
210	Now let the heavens be joyful, let earth her song begin (3)
214	find our heaven of heavens in thee (4)
216	day when the Christ ascends, high in the heavens to reign (R)
216	God ... who rulest the earth and the heavens (2)
219	The heavens with joy receive their Lord (2)
282, 283	Send from the heavens Raphael thine archangel (4)
339	high o'er all the heavens he reigneth (1)
366	fill the heavens with sweet accord (2)
373	Praise the Lord, ye heavens adore him (1)
379	God who spread the heavens above (1)
385	thy hands have set the heavens with stars (1)
400	you clouds that ride the heavens aloft, O praise him (2)
402, 403	The heavens are not too high, his praise may thither fly (1)
406, 407	stars that ... soon will point the glittering heavens (3)
409	spangled heavens, a shining frame (1)
413	such sounds as make the heavens ring (2)
422	Not far beyond the sea, nor high above the heavens (1)
426	God will make new heavens and earth (3)
431	The dawn returns in splendor, the heavens burn and blaze (2)
432	ye heavens, adore him by whom ye were made (1)
454	on clouds triumphant, when the heavens shall pass away (4)
496, 497	Rejoice, ye heavens; thou earth, reply (3)
580	God, who stretched the spangled heavens (1)
580	heavens infinite in time and place (1)
656	Lord, who left the heavens our life and peace to bring (2)
667	beneath the spreading heavens no creature but is fed (3)

heavenward

191	alleluia! Hearts and voices heavenward raise (1)
248, 249	that hereafter, heavenward soaring, we may sing (4)
528	daily lift life heavenward (3)

heavily

| 510 | our souls, how heavily they go to reach eternal joys (2) |

heavy

104	Though heavy, dull and dumb (2)
342	Come unto me, you heavy laden (2)
611	he will make that heavy burden light (5)
611	Heavy laden, gladly come to him (6)

Hebrews

| 154, 155 | The people of the Hebrews with palms before thee went (3) |

heed

33-35	Give heed, we pray you, to our supplication (4)
61, 62	We follow all and heed your call (2)
74	have not learned to heed the Christ (2)
107	give ye heed to what we say: Jesus Christ is born today (1)
139	let us not heed worldly lies nor rest upon our merit (3)
237	turn from fear, and heed the call to a glorious morrow (3)
530	to earth's remotest bound all may heed the joyful sound (1)
563	heed not the treacherous voices that lure thy soul astray (2)
675	heed not the shame, and let your foolish heart be still (3)

heeded

158	while we nothing heeded (3)

heedless

574, 575	For sins of heedless word and deed (3)

height

56	who to thy tribes on Sinai's height in ancient times (3)
116	The Father speaks from heaven's exalted height (3)
135	Manifest on mountain height, shining in resplendent light (4)
163	the cross on Calvary's height gleams of eternity appear (2)
214	raise our hearts to reach thy height (4)
242	at once he rose to full belief's unclouded height (4)
373	praise him angels in the height (1)
399	enthroned as King on heaven's height (1)
401	On Zion's sacred height his kingdom he maintains (3)
422	to know the breadth, length, depth, and height (2)
432	Praise him in the height (1)
435	through all ranks of creatures, to the central height (3)
445, 446	Praise to the Holiest in the height (1,5)
515	From the height which knows no measure (1)
517	climb from height to height till Zion's temple rings (3)
519, 520	living stones art builded in the height of heaven above (1)
521	increase ... in depth and height, her unity and peace (1)
547	his love ... its fullness, depth, and height (1)
572	with your Spirit's breath through each height and hollow (2)
610	light, in its height and depth and greatness (3)
619	let all your choirs reecho to the height (2)
640	Traveler, o'er yon mountain's height see ... star (1)
693	love, the breadth, length, depth, and height to prove (6)
702	unfathomed depth, unmeasured height (2)

heights

75	get thee up to the heights and sing (2)
82	Let the heights of heaven adore him (3)
399	He cradles in his hand the heights and depths of earth (2)
447	Thus nothing in the heights or depths (4)
630	Word Incarnate heights and depths of life did share (2)

heir

450, 451	Hail him, the Heir of David's line (3)

heirs

68	rise up, ye heirs of glory, the Bridegroom is at hand (2)

238, 239	fellow-heirs with Christ on high (3)
294	heirs of salvation, trusting his promise (1)
320	grant us ... fellow-heirs and guests to be (6)
359	God of the prophets, bless the prophets' heirs (1)
392	The heirs of grace have found glory begun below (3)
450, 451	heirs of Israel's chosen race, ye ransomed from the fall (4)

held
18	held by your unrelenting grace (2c)
71, 72	in Satan's bondage held (2)
255	O Love that sought and held him a prisoner of his Lord (2)
540	watchmen who never held their peace by day or night (1)
698	held in forgiving love, let me be still (2)

hell
38, 39	You broke the chains of death and hell (3)
54	hence to death and hell descends (3)
55	You suffered death and harrowed hell (3)
179	hell today is vanquished, heaven is won today (1)
194, 195	life, nor death, nor powers of hell tear us (3)
202	all sufficient Sacrifice, beneath thee hell defeated lies (4)
203, 206	King of heaven ... o'er death and hell rose triumphing (1)
208	He closed the yawning gates of hell (4)
219	the grave and hell are captive led (1)
248, 249	saving us from sin and hell (2)
261, 262	Christ in whose presence hosts of hell must tremble (2)
324	powers of hell may vanish as the darkness clears away (3)
379	Sin and death and hell shall never ... triumph (3)
457	who put their trust in thee nor death nor hell ... harm (3)
481	the keys of death and hell to Christ the Lord are given (3)
484, 485	o'er sin, and death, and hell victorious (2)
562	gates of hell can never 'gainst that Church prevail (4)
636, 637	that soul, though all hell shall endeavor to shake (5)
682	not for the sake of winning heaven, nor any fear of hell (4)

hell's
174	hell's fierce powers beneath thee lie (3)
562	Hell's foundations quiver at the shout of praise (2)
690	death of death, and hell's destruction (3)

help
10	help us ... every day, to live more nearly as we pray (6)
12, 13	Now help us bear our daily load (2)
18	help us to share your pain and grief (3a)
27, 28	Eternal Father, help us rise (4)
47	thou dost give thyself to me, help me give myself to thee (6)
50	Make haste to help us, Lord (3)
146, 147	help us, lest ... we cause your Name to be betrayed (4)
151	his help I wait with patience (3)
173	O Jesus blest, my help and rest (4)
209	Help then, O Lord, our unbelief (3)
231	who, martyred, saw you stand to help (2/12-26)
231	to help in time of torment (2/12-26)
251	help us here on earth to live from selfish passions free (4)
255	help us to know your kingship (2)

282, 283	May the blest mother of our God and Savior ... help us (5)
282, 283	may the celestial company of angels ... help us (5)
282, 283	may the assembly of the saints in heaven ... help us (5)
282, 283	help us to praise thee (5)
298	help us in our infirmity through Jesus blood and merit (2)
318	I have no help but thine (3)
347	help the afflicted (2)
348	help us to make those decisions that bind us (4)
359	help them intercede with all the royal priesthood (3)
365	Come, thou almighty King, help us thy Name to sing (1)
365	help us to praise (1)
366	help thy servants, drawing near (7)
410	Angels, help us to adore him, ye behold him face to face (4)
422	Help us to press on toward that mark (3)
423	help us to see 'tis only the splendor of light hideth thee (4)
424	In the help we give our neighbor (2)
440	help us by thy Spirit's pleading (3)
465, 466	eternal brightness, help me see (2)
475	Help us to surrender earth's deceitful treasures (2)
495	Help, ye bright angelic spirits (4)
495	help to sing our Savior's merits (4)
495	help to chant Emmanuel's praise (4)
518	holy Zion's help forever, and her confidence alone (1)
528	help us witness to your purpose with renewed integrity (1)
540	make haste to help us in our weakness (3)
559	for we have no help but thee (1)
574, 575	help us to give to all their due (2)
586	Jesus ... divine Companion, help us all to work our best (3)
616	to help the poor and needy, and bid the weak be strong (2)
628	Help us, O Lord (1-3)
634	I have none other help but thee (1)
636, 637	I'll strengthen thee, help thee, and cause thee to stand (2)
659, 660	help me bear the strain of toil, the fret of care (1)
659, 660	Help me the slow of heart to move (2)
662	help of the helpless, O abide with me (1)
668	My help is from the Lord above (1)
678, 679	his saving help is near (1)
680	O God, our help in ages past, our hope for years to come (1,5)
683, 684	help me to tear it from thy throne and worship only thee (4)
686	hither by thy help, I've come (2)
698	help me to see your purpose and your will (2)
699	all my help from thee I bring (2)
705	help us to give ourselves each day (3)

helping

| 293 | I mean, God helping, to be one too (1) |

helpless

91	This child, this little helpless boy ... our confidence (1)
102	child who seemed so helpless is our Lord in heaven above (5)
114	as was the ring of glory on the helpless infant there (3)
252	pleading only this we flee, helpless, O our God, to thee (6)
496, 497	deigned to cast a pitying eye upon his helpless creature (2)
570, 571	in your day of helpless strife (2)
585	he who shows us God helpless hangs upon the tree (5)

| 662 | help of the helpless, O abide with me (1) |
| 699 | hangs my helpless soul on thee (2) |

helps
| 429 | He helps the stranger in distress (3) |
| 663 | helps me take ... the paths of righteousness (2) |

hem
| 590 | healing those who touch your garment's hem (3) |

hence
365	highest praises be, hence evermore (4)
638, 639	Speak, or thou never hence shalt move (3)
701	Hence with earthly treasure (2)
701	Hence, for pomps I care not (2)

henceforth
94, 95	good will henceforth from heaven to men (6)
292	by thee come down henceforth the gifts of God (1)
484, 485	thy love henceforth shall be our song (2)
555	henceforth in fields of conquest thy tents ... our home (1)

herald
40, 41	the Herald of the light to come (1)
70	Herald, sound the note of judgment (1)
70	Herald, sound the note of gladness (2)
70	Herald, sound the note of pardon (3)
70	Herald, sound the note of triumph (4)
87	Hark! the herald angels sing glory to the new-born King (1,R)
124	It shines to herald forth the King (1)
143	John, the Bridegroom's friend, became the herald (3)
143	herald of Messiah's name (3)
266	to be the herald of God's Son (5)
271, 272	the herald of the Word, is born (1)
282, 283	Send thine archangel Gabriel the mighty herald of heaven (3)
444	Before him goes his herald, forerunner in the way (2)
616	before him on the mountains shall peace, the herald, go (3)

herald's
| 106 | who heard the angelic herald's voice (2) |
| 271, 272 | that John should be that herald's name (2) |

heralds
106	the earliest heralds of the Savior's name (4)
359	Make them apostles, heralds of thy cross (5)
539	Send heralds forth to bear the message glorious (3)

herb
| 406, 407 | bringeth forth fruit, herb, and flower (5) |

hereafter
248, 249	that hereafter, heavenward soaring, we may sing (4)
518	hereafter in thy glory evermore with thee to reign (4)
621, 622	hereafter these thy labors may with endless gifts be paid (5)

heresies
525   by schisms rent asunder, by heresies distressed (3)

heretofore
140, 141 thy Son shall shine as he shines now, and heretofore (3)

heritage
521   steadfast faith our unity, their peace our heritage (3)

hero's
631   statesman's, teacher's, hero's treasure (1)

Herod
98   Herod then with fear was filled (3)
113   You need not fear King Herod (2)
131, 132 King Herod trembled for his throne (1)
231   saved him from King Herod when safety there was none (2/3-19)
247   Herod the King, in his raging charged he hath this day (2)

Herod's
232   who fell to Herod's sword (2/7-25)
246   King Herod's troops would soon appear (1)
276   slain by Herod's flashing blade, he saw thy face again (4)

hid
69   in great humility is hid all heaven in a little room (3)
248, 249 for many a generation hid in God's fore-knowledge lay (1)
423   in light inaccessible hid from our eyes (1)

hidden
63, 64   to recompense each hidden sin (3)
255   that we, in every hour ... will trust your hidden power (2)
257   Aware of hidden deity (1)
308, 309 hidden in forms of bread and wine (3)
314   Jesus, whom now hidden, I by faith behold (4)
394, 395 what lies hidden praise your might (1)
573   How shall we love thee, holy hidden Being (5)
584   to probe earth's hidden mysteries (1)
585   hidden is love's agony, love's endeavor, love's expense (2)
681   Thou hidden fount of love, of peace ... truth ... beauty (5)

hide
92   ox and ass beside him from the cold would hide him (2)
119   no star to guide, where no clouds thy glory hide (4)
168, 169 Ah me! for whom thou diest, hide not so far thy grace (2)
362   Though the darkness hide thee (3)
609   from paths where hide the lures of greed (2)
685   Rock of ages, cleft for me, let me hide myself in thee (1,3)
699   hide me, O my Savior ... till the storm of life is past (1)
702   My words from thee I cannot hide (2)

hides
459   The heaven that hides him from our sight (2)
677   behind a frowning providence he hides a smiling face (4)

hidest

314   who thy glory hidest 'neath these shadows mean (1)

hideth

423   help us to see 'tis only the splendor of light hideth thee (4)
702   the deepest darkness hideth not from thee (5)

hiding

644   my shield and hiding place (3)

hie

640   hie thee to thy quiet home (3)

high

3, 4   we lift our hearts to God on high (1)
6, 7   Day-spring from on high, be near (1)
9   Not here for high and holy things we render thanks (1)
14, 15   Jesus Christ, our Lord Most High (3)
19, 20   Christ, our Lord Most High (3)
21, 22   through Jesus Christ, our Lord Most High (3)
29, 30   O grant us with thy saints on high to praise thee (2)
31, 32   who in the high arched sky has placed the sun (1)
36   thee, therefore, O Most High, the world doth glorify (3)
38, 39   Word of the Father throned on high (1)
44, 45   through Jesus Christ, our Lord Most High (4)
48   this day the high and lowly, through ages joined in tune (1)
55   reigned once more from God's high throne (3)
56   O come, thou Wisdom from on high (2)
56   make safe the way that leads on high (5)
56   O come, Thou Day-spring from on high (6)
57, 58   high on thine eternal throne (4)
65   Lift high your praise resounding (2)
77   to shepherds poor the Lord Most High ... was revealed (4)
77   Lord Most High, the one great Shepherd (4)
80   This is the Christ, God's Son most high (3)
82   hymn and chant and high thanksgiving (4)
88   from high heaven he comes to earth (2)
94, 95   All glory be to God on high and on the earth be peace (6)
96   Angels we have heard on high (1)
97   stretching infant hands on high, Savior, long awaited (1)
102   Christ ... set at God's right hand on high (6)
104   But now, as at the ending, The low is lifted high (4)
114   angel-song rang loud and high (2)
122, 123   alleluia is the anthem ever raised by choirs on high (1)
122, 123   with thy faithful saints on high (4)
128   worship him, God Most High (3)
136, 137   the incarnate Lord holds converse high (2)
136, 137   faithful hearts are raised on high by this ... mystery (4)
145   reply, reply with love to love most high (1)
154, 155   The company of angels is praising thee on high (2)
154, 155   to thee, now high exalted, our melody we raise (4)
174   At the Lamb's high feast we sing praise (1)
174   Mighty victim from on high (3)
180   with high and holy hymning (3)
182   Not throned above, remotely high (3)

191	alleluia! Glory be to God on high (5)
202	The Lamb's high banquet called to share (1)
205	sing with hearts uplifted high (3)
208	the bars from heaven's high portals fell (4)
210	round world keep high triumph, and all that is therein (3)
211	Our God most high, our joy and boast (4)
215	portals high are lifted to receive their heavenly King (1)
216	day when the Christ ascends, high in the heavens to reign (R)
219	The Lord ascendeth up on high (1)
219	Our great High Priest hath gone before (3)
220, 221	O Lord Most High, eternal King (1)
238, 239	fellow-heirs with Christ on high (3)
250	All glory be to God on high and peace on earth (5)
254	You are the Christ, O Lord, the Son of God most high (1)
260	The Architect's high miracles he saw, and what was done (2)
266	Gabriel of high degree (1)
278	from on high ... glory of the Spirit's presence came (3)
278	raised high with saints and angels, in Jerusalem above (4)
308, 309	O Manna from on high (1)
324	Alleluia, Lord Most High (4)
326	ever fit us by service on earth for thy service on high (2)
334	glory be to God on high (1)
339	high o'er all the heavens he reigneth (1)
356	May choirs of angels lead you to Paradise on high (1)
364	to thee the powers on high ... continually do cry (2)
364	bring us whom thou hast bought to dwell on high (8)
367	Holy, holy ... singing, Lord of hosts ... Lord Most High (2)
367	blessing thee, the Lord of hosts Most High (3)
372	His Spirit floweth free, high surging where it will (3)
373	Hosts on high, his power proclaim (2)
391	high as the heaven our voices raise (4)
392	fairer worlds on high (4)
393	'tis the Day-spring from on high (2)
399	O God Most High, we are your sheep (2)
401	the God who reigns on high the great archangels sing (4)
401	The whole triumphant host give thanks to God on high (5)
402, 403	The heavens are not too high, his praise may thither fly (1)
406, 407	Most High, omnipotent, good Lord (1,8)
409	The spacious firmament on high (1)
421	All glory be to God on high (1)
422	Not far beyond the sea, nor high above the heavens (1)
422	very high thy voice, O God, is heard (1)
423	thy justice like mountains high soaring above (2)
427	No lovelier antiphon in all high heaven is known (3)
437, 438	the hungry fed, the humble lifted high (3)
448	O love, how deep, how broad, how high (1)
448	for us he went on high to reign (5)
448	glory ... for love so deep, so high, so broad (6)
449	O love, how deep, how broad, how high (1)
449	for us he went on high to reign (5)
449	glory ... for love so deep, so high, so broad (6)
453	he saw in a vision a ladder so high (1)
454	came with peace from realms on high (1)
455, 456	sent by the Father from on high, our life to live (3)
460, 461	our great High Priest (4)

473	Lift high the cross, the love of Christ proclaim (R)
477	thou art high exalted o'er all creatures now (4)
478	your Name we glorify, O Jesus, throned on high (1)
479	Oft as earth exulting wafts its praise on high (4)
488	High King of heaven, when victory is won (3)
492	Now on high, yet ever with us (4)
494	his glories now we sing who died, and rose on high (3)
496, 497	Though circled by the hosts on high (2)
500	Plenteous of grace, come from on high (3)
518	All that dedicated city, dearly loved of God on high (2)
525	the meek and lowly, on high may dwell with thee (5)
535	God ruleth on high, almighty to save (2)
539	O Zion, haste, thy mission high fulfilling (1)
541	Claim the high calling angels cannot share (4)
543	O Zion, tune thy voice, and raise thy hands on high (1)
546	God's all-animating voice that calls thee from on high (3)
551	Lift high the cross of Christ (3)
556, 557	Your glorious banner wave on high (1,7)
556, 557	Still lift your standard high, still march in firm array (5)
558	O how our hearts beat high with joy whene'er we hear (1)
561	lift high his royal banner, it must not suffer loss (1)
569	show forth thy pity on high where thou reignest (1)
574, 575	for lives bereft of purpose high, forgive (3)
599	Let our rejoicing rise high as the listening skies (1)
605	How shall my soul fulfill God's law so hard and high (4)
605	To merchant, worker, king he brings God's high demands (3)
623	Now, in the meanwhile, with hearts raised on high (4)
625	assist our song, for else the theme too high doth seem (1)
625	too high doth seem for mortal tongue (1)
627	true manna from on high (2)
632	O Christ, the Word Incarnate, O Wisdom from on high (1)
633	Word eternal, throned on high (2)
665	high above all praises praising for ... Christ, his son (5)
699	while the tempest still is high (1)

higher

| 618 | O higher than the cherubim (2) |
| 640 | higher yet that star ascends (2) |

highest

25, 26	through all the earth and in the highest heaven adored (3)
50	Hosanna in the highest strains the Church ... can raise (5)
50	the highest strains the Church on earth can raise (5)
50	highest heavens in which he reigns shall give ... praise (5)
83	glory to God, glory in the highest (3)
87	Christ, by highest heaven adored (2)
106	God's highest glory was their anthem still (3)
153	Peace in heaven and glory in the highest (1)
153	Hosanana in the highest (2)
157	Hosanna in the highest (1)
168, 169	show me, O Love most highest, the brightness of thy face (2)
214	enters now the highest heaven (1)
365	To Thee, great One in Three, the highest praises be (4)
365	highest praises be, hence evermore (4)
396, 397	the Son, and him who reigns with them in highest heaven (3)

445, 446	highest gift of grace should flesh and blood refine (4)
472	God's gift from highest heaven (2)
483	highest place that heaven affords is his ... by right (2)
486	Hosanna Lord, Hosanna in the highest (R)
495	highest praises, without ceasing ... give (4)
495	highest praises ... right it is for us to give (4)
496, 497	by highest seraphim adored (2)
524	Beyond my highest joy I prize her heavenly ways (3)
621, 622	mansion of the highest King (1)

highly
265	most highly favored lady, "Gloria!" (1-4)

highway
75	Prepare in the desert a highway, a highway for our God (1)
232	our true Elijah, making a highway for the Lord (2/6-24)
326	strength unto strength we go forward on Zion's highway (1)
647	I walk the King's highway (1-3)

highways
472	afoot on dusty highways (3)

hilariter
211	Hilariter, hilariter ... Alleluia, alleluia (1-4)

hill
65	Let every hill and valley a level way appear (1)
167	There is a green hill far away, outside a city wall (1)
416	hill and vale, and tree and flower (2)
453	many millions have climbed it and reached Zion's hill (2)
543	There on his holy hill a brighter sun shall rise (4)
570, 571	offering peace from Calvary's hill (4)
579	O Christ, the Lord of hill and plain (2)
616	righteousness in fountains from hill to valley flow (3)
647	but rough or smooth, up hill or down (1)
675	on Calvary's hill (3)

hills
67	the hills bow down to greet him (2)
73	beauty gilds the eastern hills (1)
75	valleys shall be exalted, the lofty hills brought low (1)
99	Go tell it on the mountain, over the hills and everywhere (R)
100	while fields and floods, rocks, hills and plains repeat (2)
388	it streams from the hills, it descends to the plain (4)
615	And lo, already on the hills the flags of dawn appear (3)
652, 653	O Sabbath rest by Galilee, O calm of hills above (3)
661	just off the hills of brown (1)
668	I to the hills will lift mine eyes (1)
680	Before the hills in order stood (3)
717	I love thy rocks and rills, thy woods and templed hills (2)

hillsides
302	grain, once scattered on the hillsides (2)
303	As grain, once scattered on the hillsides (4)

hinder
542   cast out our pride and shame that hinder to enthrone thee (3)

historian
285   Historian of the Savior's life (3)

hither
430   hither bring in one consent heart ... voice ... instrument (1)
686   hither by thy help, I've come (2)

hitherto
584   depths hitherto unknown (1)

hoard
528   Yet we hoard as private treasure all that you ... give (4)

hold
53   not in torment hold us, but in love enfold us (2)
75   the lambs he'll gently hold (3)
112   Our God, heaven cannot hold him, nor earth sustain (2)
139   death could hold him never. He rose and lives forever (2)
168, 169   hold me that I quail not in death's most fearful hour (5)
199, 200   nor the watchers, nor the seal hold thee as a mortal (4)
231   hold them when they waver with your almighty arm (2/1-18)
251   neither time nor space can limit, hold, or bind (1)
296   Embraced by death he broke its fearful hold (1)
314   what the Truth hath spoken, that for truth I hold (2)
347   hold fast the good, be urgent for the right (3)
370   the power of God to hold and lead (5)
475   to the sunlight calmly hold them (3)
528   amid the cares that claim us, hold in mind eternity (5)
546   A cloud of witnesses around hold thee in full survey (2)
552, 553   lay hold on life ... thy joy and crown eternally (1)
634   hold by thy word evermore, above all things (1)
638, 639   whom still I hold, but cannot see (1)
649, 650   blest, when our faith can hold you fast (3)
662   Hold thou thy cross before my closing eyes (4)
669   God, in his great mercy, will save thee, hold thee fast (4)
689   'twas not so much that I on thee took hold (2)
690   hold me with thy powerful hand (1)

holding
275   holding palms of victory in their hands (1)

holds
78, 79   charity stands watching and faith holds wide the door (4)
80   the Son holds in his infant hand (4)
136, 137   the incarnate Lord holds converse high (2)
379   with unfailing grasp God holds us (2)
471   holds the fainting spirit up (3)
609   still holds the freshness of thy grace (3)

holier
150   holier gladness ours shall be (4)
180   risen to a holier state (4)

holiest

445, 446	Praise to the Holiest in the height (1,5)
568	Holiest Trinity, perfect in unity (4)

holiness

108	in holiness conceived, the Son of God was born (1)
279	humbly pray that we may follow them in holiness (4)
372	holy, no holiness of earth can his express (2)
381	bright with thine own holiness (3)
512	lead us to holiness (3)
512	holiness, the road that we must take to dwell with God (3)
555	holiness shall whisper the sweet amen of peace (2)
568	Come, Holy Spirit, create in us holiness (3)
581	let us love each other well in Christian holiness (3)

hollow

572	with your Spirit's breath through each heights and hollow (2)

holy

1, 2	All holy Father, Son, and equal Spirit, Trinity blessed (3)
3, 4	may praise and bless his holy Name (4)
3, 4	to God the Holy Ghost we raise our ... praise (5)
9	Not here for high and holy things we render thanks (1)
11	praise Father, Son and Holy Ghost (4)
14, 15	by a holy death attained, eternal glory may be gained (2)
16, 17	So dazzling is its holy light (3)
19, 20	Now Holy Spirit, ever One with God the Father and the Son (1)
25, 26	Immortal, holy, blest is he (1)
25, 26	blest are you, his holy Son (1)
29, 30	to God the Holy Ghost we raise our ... praise (3)
31, 32	Most Holy God, the Lord of heaven (1)
31, 32	You, Holy One, Creator, Lord (4)
33-35	joyfully chanting holy hymns to praise you (3)
36	eternal splendor wearing; celestial, holy, blest (1)
36	thee, his incarnate Son, and Holy Spirit adoring (2)
36	To thee of right belong all praise of holy songs (3)
37	most holy, heavenly, blest, Lord Jesus Christ (1)
37	we hymn the eternal Father ... Son ... Holy Ghost divine (2)
40, 41	We pray you, O most holy Lord, to be our guardian (2)
43	praise Father, Son, and Holy Ghost (4)
47	Holy Jesus, may I be dead and buried here with thee (4)
48	sing, "Holy, holy, holy," to the great God Triune (1)
48	This day, God's people meeting, his Holy Scripture hear (3)
50	Hosanna to the anointed King, to David's holy Son (3)
52	This day the Holy Spirit came (3)
53	came in likeness lowly, Son of God most holy (1)
60	Come in your holy might, we pray (5)
65	Oh, blest is Christ that came in God's most holy name (R)
67	as befits his holy reign (3)
76	whom with the Father we adore and Holy Spirit evermore (5)
77	let every heart awake and sing the holy child (1)
77	all praise, O Holy Ghost, to thee (5)
78, 79	O morning stars, together proclaim the holy birth (2)
78, 79	O holy Child of Bethlehem, descend to us, we pray (5)
82	Virgin, full of grace, by the Holy Ghost conceiving (2)

82	O Holy Ghost, to thee ... unwearied praises be (4)
85	throughout the world this holy day (2)
85	whom with the Father we adore and Holy Spirit evermore (6)
86	throughout the world this holy day (2)
86	whom with the Father we adore and Holy Spirit evermore (6)
99	behold, throughout the heavens there shone a holy light (1)
102	lived on earth our Savior holy (2)
103	Upon this joyful holy night ... we bless your name (3)
103	We praise you, Holy Trinity ... adoring you eternally (4)
105	this holy tide of Christmas doth bring redeeming grace (4)
110	'Twas Mary, daughter pure of holy Anne (2)
110	to praise the Father, Son, and Holy Ghost (4)
111	Silent night, holy night (1-3)
111	Holy infant, so tender and mild, sleep in heavenly peace (1)
111	radiant beams from thy holy face (3)
113	Oh sleep now, holy baby, with your head against my breast (1)
114	the holy child of earth and heaven is born today for you (4)
119	so may we with holy joy, pure and free from sin's alloy (3)
119	Holy Jesus, every day keep us in the narrow way (4)
120	now by the Holy spirit shed upon the Son's anointed head (3)
120	grant us the Holy Spirit's power to shield us (5)
121	sent you his kingdom to proclaim, his holy will to do (2)
124	to... Holy Ghost we raise our equal and unceasing praise (5)
131, 132	whom with the Father we adore and Holy Ghost for evermore (5)
136, 137	from the cloud, the Holy One bears record to the only Son (2)
136, 137	O Father, with the eternal Son ... Holy Spirit, ever One (5)
139	The Holy Spirit then was shown, a dove on him descending (2)
142	chiefly live by thy most holy word (3)
152	the penitent who keep this holy fast of Lent (1)
158	Ah, holy Jesus, how hast thou offended (1)
162	ordained those holy limbs to bear (3)
165, 166	from that holy body broken blood and water forth proceed (3)
180	with high and holy hymning (3)
185, 186	let us feast this holy day on the true bread of heaven (4)
191	Christ, the first-fruits of the holy harvest-field (3)
193	God the Holy Ghost, we raise (5)
202	all praise to God the Father be and Holy Ghost eternally (5)
203	On this most holy day of days (5)
207	Jesus Christ is risen today ... our triumphant holy day (1)
207	Father, Son, and Holy Ghost (4)
208	let shout of holy joy outburst (2)
211	To Father, Son, and Holy Ghost (4)
225	day ... Holy Ghost shone in the world with God's grace (R)
226, 227	Come, thou Holy Spirit bright (1)
228	Holy Spirit, font of light, focus of God's glory bright (1)
229	still o'er thy holy Church preside (3)
230	for God the Holy Spirit dwells with the Church alway (3)
231, 232	your holy Name, O Jesus, for evermore be blessed (1)
231	May we like true apostles your holy Church defend (2/2-24)
235	where with a holy people God dwells in Unity (3)
238, 239	Blessed feasts of blessed martyrs, holy women, holy men (1)
244	sing of those who spread the treasure in the holy Gospels (1)
244	in the holy Gospels shrined (1)
244	thy holy word possessing, Jesus may thy love adore (3)
248, 249	but with holy exultation we may sing aloud today (1)

248, 249	holy Jesus, thee imploring so to write it in us here (4)
252	Jesus, Name of mercy mild, given to the holy child (4)
257	Anna welcomes Israel's hope, with holy rapture fired (3)
257	all glory, Holy Ghost, to thee, while endless ages run (5)
259	filled with holy joy, old Simeon (3)
263	who shall be called the Holy One (2)
263	whom with the Father we adore and Holy Spirit evermore (4)
264	who shall be called the Holy One (2)
264	whom with the Father we adore and Holy Spirit evermore (4)
265	my soul shall laud and magnify his holy Name (3)
273, 274	Two stalwart trees both rooted in faith and holy love (1)
273, 274	who with the Holy Spirit, now reign, blest Three in One (4)
275	Hark, the sound of holy voices, chanting (1)
275	Patriarch, and holy prophet, who prepared the way (2)
275	joined in holy concert, singing to the Lord of all (2)
275	now they drink, as from a river, holy bliss and infinite (4)
277	sing of God's own Son most holy (1)
277	Son most holy, who became her little child (1)
279	learned from thy Holy Spirit's breath to suffer and to do (2)
282, 283	Christ, the fair glory of the holy angels (1)
282, 283	Father Almighty, Son and Holy Spirit, God ever blessed (6)
286	Now in God's most holy place, blest they stand (5)
287	singing to Father, Son, and Holy Ghost, Alleluia (8)
292	gathering round thy throne ... in the holy angel's sight (3)
292	with the Father's Name, and with the Holy Spirit's gifts (3)
295	praise the Holy Spirit poured forth upon the earth (3)
298	With one accord, O God, we pray, grant us the Holy Spirit (2)
299	O Holy Spirit, come again (2)
302, 303	Father, we thank thee who hast planted thy holy Name (1)
302, 303	planted thy holy Name within our hearts (1)
312	hands that holy things have taken (1)
312	Lord, may the tongues which "Holy" sang keep free (2)
320	when the twelve, divinely guided, at the holy table met (2)
327, 328	drink the holy Blood for you outpoured (1)
327, 328	Saved by that Body and that holy Blood (2)
332	thus inspired with holy fear, before thine altar kneel (1)
346	Completed, Lord, the Holy Mysteries (1)
347	rejoicing in the Holy Spirit's power (4)
349	Holy Spirit, Lord of love, who descended from above (1)
350	that closely knit in holy vow, they may in thee be one (1)
351	Father's boundless love, with the Holy Spirit's favor (1)
354	bring you into the holy city Jerusalem (1)
356	brought by them into the holy city (2)
357	Lead them onward, upward, to the holy place (4)
362	Holy, holy, holy (1-4)
362	only thou art holy, there is none beside thee (3)
363	O holy Father, who hast led thy children in all the ages (2)
363	O holy Jesus, Lord of our salvation (3)
363	O Holy Ghost, the Lord and the Life-giver (4)
364	O holy, holy, holy Lord, whom heavenly hosts obey (3)
364	holy Church in faith acclaims thy Son who for us died (5)
364	also the Holy Comforter, our advocate and guide (5)
365	Come, holy Comforter (3)
366	Holy God, we praise thy Name (1)
366	holy, holy, holy Lord (2)

366	Holy Father, holy Son, Holy Spirit, three we name thee (4)
367	unto thee be glory given, holy, holy, holy Lord (1,3)
367	Holy, holy ... singing, Lord of hosts ... Lord Most High (2)
367	with his holy Church below (2)
367	with thine angel hosts we cry, "Holy, holy, holy" (3)
368	Holy Father, great Creator (1)
368	Holy Jesus, Lord of glory, whom angelic hosts proclaim (2)
368	Holy Spirit, Sanctifier, come with unction from above (3)
371	Spirit of truth and love, life-giving, holy Dove (3)
371	Holy and blessed Three, glorious Trinity (4)
372	holy, no holiness of earth can his express (2)
377, 378	To Father, Son, and Holy Ghost (5)
380	praise Father, Son, and Holy Ghost (3)
381	Holy Spirit, Light-Revealer, glory, glory be to thee (4)
381	mortals, angels, now and ever praise the Holy Trinity (4)
393	call upon his holy Name (1)
401	"Holy, holy, holy," cry, "Almighty King" (4)
401	"Hail, Father, Son, and Holy Ghost" they ever cry (5)
404	your holy Name for ever be adored (1)
408	Let all who name Christ's holy Name give God all praise (3)
411	all that is within me join to bless his holy Name (1)
411	bless his holy Name, whose grace hath made thee whole (6)
416	For the Church which evermore lifteth holy hands above (5)
419	till all thy living altars claim one holy light (4)
421	You only are the Holy One (3)
422	more truth and light to break forth from thy Holy Word (1)
427	God's holy house of prayer hath none that can compare (2)
428	let those of holy, humble heart come praise him evermore (5)
435	there let him subdue all that is not holy ... not true (5)
436	Holy Spirit guide us on until the glorious crown be won (5)
437, 438	his holy Name -- The Lord, the Mighty One (2)
440	by thy teachings pure and holy (1)
448, 449	for us he bore his holy fast and hungered sore (2)
465, 466	invited by your holy word (3)
478	O Lord most holy (2)
484, 485	his holy arm hath wrought salvation (1)
489	his holy and immortal truth to all on earth hath given (1)
491	O Most Mighty, O Most Holy (2)
496, 497	Jesus, Holy, holy, yet most lowly draw thou near us (1)
500	thrice holy Fount, thrice holy Fire (2)
501, 502	O Holy Spirit, by whose breath life rises vibrant (1)
503, 504	Come, Holy Ghost, our souls inspire (1)
503, 504	praise to thy eternal merit, Father, Son and Holy Spirit (9)
505	the holy flame of love impart (3)
506, 507	Praise, O praise the Holy Spirit, praise the Father (6)
510	Come, Holy Spirit, heavenly Dove (1,4)
511	Holy Spirit, ever living as the Church's very life (1)
511	Holy Spirit, ever working through the Church's ministry (2)
511	Holy Spirit, ever binding age to age and soul to soul (2)
512	plant holy fear in every heart (2)
513	come, Holy Spirit, come (1-3)
515	Holy Ghost, dispel our sadness (1)
516	kindle it, thy holy flame bestowing (1)
516	a place wherein the Holy Spirit makes a dwelling (3)
518	holy Zion's help forever, and her confidence alone (1)

525	from heaven he came and sought her to be his holy bride (1)
525	one holy Name she blesses, partakes one holy food (2)
525	O happy ones and holy (5)
528	Lord, you make the common holy (3)
532, 533	Thou only art holy, thou only supreme (1)
540	bringing peoples to thy holy will (1)
543	There on his holy hill a brighter sun shall rise (4)
545	freed from every weight of sin ... holy footsteps trace (2)
558	holy faith! We will be true to thee till death (R)
568	Come, Holy Spirit, create in us holiness (3)
569	earth hath forsaken thy ways all holy (2)
573	How shall we love thee, holy hidden Being (5)
576, 577	Let us fear and love him, holy God eternal (1)
581	With grateful joy and holy fear his charity we learn (2)
581	be his the glory that we seek, be ours his holy peace (4)
582, 583	O holy city, seen of John (1)
582, 583	O holy city ... where Christ, the Lamb, doth reign (1)
588, 589	Let not our selfishness and hate this holy seed remove (2)
608	Most Holy Spirit, who didst brood upon the chaos (3)
612	Gracious Spirit, Holy Ghost (1)
612	taught by thee we covet most ... holy, heavenly, love (1)
614	O friends upraise anthems of joy and holy praise (1)
618	Ye watchers and ye holy ones (1)
618	Ye holy twelve, ye martyrs strong (3)
619	Then let the holy city raise the strain (3)
621, 622	all is pure ... holy that within thy walls is stored (2)
625	Ye holy angels bright, who wait at God's right hand (1)
626	thy glory be my aim, thy holy will my choice (1)
649, 650	shed o'er the world your holy light (4)
658	To Father, Son, and Holy Ghost, the God whom we adore (4)
667	In holy contemplation we sweetly then pursue the theme (2)
676	but then the Holy Spirit revives my soul again (1)
678, 679	with you has come to dwell ... Holy One of Israel (2)
678, 679	in your very midst, the great and Holy One (2)
683, 684	Return, O holy Dove, return, sweet messenger of rest (3)
700	love of the Holy Ghost, fill thou each needy one (4)
701	Thine I am, O holy Lamb (1)
704	still let me guard the holy fire (3)
710	O sing the honor of his holy Name (RC)
717	long may our land be bright with freedom's holy light (4)

homage

162	let homage meet by all be done (6)
307	Here our humblest homage pay we (2)
324	Christ ... descendeth our full homage to demand (1)
399	your voice in homage raise to him who makes all one (3)
454	again in glory; let us then our homage pay (4)

home

51	This is the Lord's house, home of all his people (2)
54	Virgin's Son, make here your home (1)
56	open wide our heavenly home (5)
76	let each heart prepare a home (2)
76	a home where such a mighty guest may come (2)
120	lead his scattered people home (2)

125, 126	joyous as when the reapers bear their ... treasures home (2)
125, 126	their harvest treasures home (2)
268, 269	blessed ... land of promise fashioned for his ... home (2)
268, 269	fashioned for his earthly home (2)
278	Lord of all creation brought her to his heavenly home (4)
290	raise the song of harvest-home (1)
290	For the Lord our God shall come ... take his harvest home (3)
290	Even so, Lord, quickly come to thy final harvest-home (4)
290	raise the glorious harvest-home (4)
400	You lead back home the child of God (6)
458	In life no house, no home my Lord on earth might have (6)
458	What may I say? Heaven was his home (6)
458	Heaven was his home, but mine the tomb wherein he lay (6)
467	praise him till he calls thee home (4)
481	take his servants up to their eternal home (4)
498	a home within the wilderness, a rest upon the way (1)
503, 504	Keep far our foes, give peace at home (6)
509	make this house thy home (1)
509	make a lost world thy home (5)
549, 550	turned from home and toil and kindred (2)
555	henceforth in fields of conquest thy tents ... our home (1)
587	O Christ, thyself a child within an earthly home (2)
587	every home ... may be the dwelling place of peace (3)
620	Jerusalem, my happy home, when shall I come to thee (1)
624	Oh, sweet and blessed country, the home of God's elect (4)
640	hie thee to thy quiet home (3)
645, 646	home, rejoicing, brought me (3)
663	I may tell thy praise, and dwell for ever in thy home (5)
664	no more a stranger or a guest, but like a child at home (3)
671	grace will lead me home (4)
680	our shelter from the stormy blast, and our eternal home (1)
680	our eternal home (6)
686	I hope, by thy good pleasure, safely to arrive at home (2)
705	farm and market, shop and home (1)
720	o'er the land of the free and the home of the brave (1-2)

homeless

610	Still your children wander homeless (2)
661	homeless, in Patmos died (3)

homes

182	Let streets and homes with praises ring (1)
360, 361	strangers and pilgrims, seeking homes eternal (4)
436	happy hearts and happy homes to whom this King ... comes (2)
436	happy homes to whom this King of triumph comes (2)
587	guarding ... the homes in which thy people dwell (1)
720	between their loved homes and the war's desolation (2)

homesteads

596	homesteads and the woodlands plead in silence (2)

homeward

345	Grant us thy peace upon our homeward way (2)
659, 660	guide them in the homeward way (2)

homesteads
596   homesteads and the woodlands plead in silence (2)

homeward
345   Grant us thy peace upon our homeward way (2)
659, 660   guide them in the homeward way (2)

homing
482   be there at our homing (3)

honey
431   more sweet than honey to the taste (3)
624   Jerusalem the golden, with milk and honey blest (1)

honor
59   Honor, glory, might, and blessing to the Father ... Son (4)
60   praise, honor, might, and glory be from age to age (6)
63, 64   praise, honor, might and glory be (5)
82   honor, glory and dominion, and eternal victory (4)
97   laud and honor raising (3)
154, 155 All glory, laud, and honor to thee, Redeemer, King (R)
165, 166 Praise and honor to the Father (6)
165, 166 praise and honor to the Son (6)
165, 166 praise and honor to the Spirit, ever Three and ever One (6)
213   live to the honor and glory of God (2)
230   to the blessed Three in One be honor, praise and merit (2)
238, 239 with meetest praise and sweetest, honor them for evermore (1)
248, 249 To the Name of our salvation laud and honor let us pay (1)
261, 262 to Saint Joseph gave supernal honor (3)
265   all generations laud and honor thee (2)
268, 269 let all faithful people sing the honor of her name (3)
271, 272 praise, honor, might, and glory ... age to age eternally (5)
286   they who have contended for their Savior's honor long (3)
300   Glory, love, and praise, and honor for our food (1)
320   Honor Christ, thy voice upraising (1)
329-331   honor, thanks, and praise addressing (6)
374   Jesus is worthy to receive honor and power divine (3)
381   God the Father, Light-Creator, to thee laud and honor be (4)
383, 384 thee will I cherish, thee will I honor (1)
413   Rivers and seas and torrents roaring, honor the Lord (3)
413   honor the Lord with wild acclaim (3)
414   Honor great our God befitteth, who his majesty can reach (2)
417, 418 honor, blessing, and glory are his (2)
417, 418 Blessing, honor, glory, and might be to God and the Lamb (4)
443   the King abased to honor all, praised be your glory (5)
475   love and honor will I render (4)
492   him let all your music honor (1)
495   Worship, honor, power, and blessing thou art worthy (4)
501, 502 to whom all honor, glory be both now and for eternity (6)
519, 520 Laud and honor to the Father (5)
519, 520 Laud and honor to the Son (5)
519, 520 laud and honor to the Spirit, ever Three, and ever One (5)
532, 533 O who shall not fear thee, and honor thy Name (1)
535   Let all cry aloud, and honor the Son (3)
535   honor and blessing, with angels above (4)

472	Hope of the world (1-5)
483	his people's hope ... wealth, their everlasting theme (6)
525	to one hope she presses, with every grace endued (2)
527	one the hope our God inspires (2)
528	faith and hope and love restoring (5)
534	vainly we hope for the harvest-tide till God gives life (4)
537	inspired with hope and praise, to Christ belong (4)
542	new life, new hope awakes, for all who own his sway (1)
547	There is one Body and one hope, one Spirit and one call (3)
562	one in hope and doctrine, one in charity (3)
566	From thee ... all calm and courage, faith and hope (1)
593	where all is gloom, may we sow hope (2)
597	the hope of peace shall be fulfilled (2)
599	sing a song full of the hope ... the present has brought (1)
599	felt in the days when hope unborn had died (2)
607	when hope and courage falter (3)
610	hope and health, good will and comfort ... give (4)
612	Faith and hope and love we see (4)
614	place the same hope in this great Name (2)
616	love, joy, hope, like flowers spring in his path to birth (3)
626	thy promises my hope; thy providence my guard (2)
629	let a new and better hope within our hearts be stirred (1)
633	touch our hearts and bring to birth faith and hope (1)
635	hope in him through all thy ways (1)
640	Watchman, does its beauteous ray ... hope foretell (1)
640	aught of joy or hope foretell (1)
642	O hope of every contrite heart, O joy of all the meek (3)
643	worship thee with trembling hope and penitential tears (4)
647	their faith and hope still guiding me (2)
658	Hope still ... sing the praise of him who is thy God (3)
659, 660	in hope that sends a shining ray far down the ... way (4)
665	All my hope on God is founded (1)
669	Hope on, then, broken spirit; hope on, be not afraid (4)
671	his word my hope secures (3)
675	only those who bear the cross may hope to wear ... crown (5)
680	O God, our help in ages past, our hope for years to come (1,5)
682	I love thee Lord ... not because I hope for heaven thereby (1)
682	with the hope of gaining aught, not seeking a reward (5)
686	I hope, by thy good pleasure, safely to arrive at home (2)
701	Joy from tribulation, hope from desolation (3)

hopefulness

482	Lord of all hopefulness, Lord of all joy (1)

hopes

10	new thoughts of God, new hopes of heaven (2)
78, 79	hopes and fears of all the years are met in thee tonight (1)
289	long spent their hopes and fears (2)
381	our lives our hopes confess (3)
429	How happy they whose hopes rely on Israel's God (2)
441, 442	hopes deceive and fears annoy (2)
472	by our own false hopes and aims are spent (1)
597	O day of peace that dimly shines through all our hopes (1)
597	through all our hopes and prayers and dreams (1)
666	hopes are on thy promise built, thy never-failing word (2)

672   Our hopes are weak, our fears are strong (2)

horizon
117, 118   star of the east, the horizon adorning (1,5)
580   As each far horizon beckons, may it challenge us anew (4)

horned
389   The horned moon to shine by night (5)

horns
157   up to the horns of the altar (R)

horse
425   horse ... rider ... sword he cast into the raging sea (1)

hosanna
50   Hosanna to the anointed King, to David's holy Son (3)
50   Hosanna in the highest strains the Church ... can raise (5)
157   Hosanna in the highest (1)
157   Hosanna, Lord, hosanna. Lord, send us now success (R)
307   heaven and earth with loud hosanna worship thee (5)
392   Hosanna, hosanna! Rejoice, give thanks and sing (R)
480   Hosanna our glad voices raise, hosanna to our King (3)
486   Hosanna to the living Lord ... to the incarnate Word (1)
486   To Christ, Creator Savior, King ... hosanna sing (1)
486   let earth, let heaven, hosanna sing (1)
486   Hosanna Lord, Hosanna in the highest (R)
486   Hosanna Lord, thine angels cry ... thy saints reply (2)
557   Hosanna, hosanna, rejoice, give thanks, and sing (R)

hosannas
71, 72   glad hosannas, Prince of Peace, thy welcome ... proclaim (4)
154, 155 to whom the lips of children made sweet hosannas ring (R)
458   resounding all the day hosannas to their King (3)
510   hosannas languish on our tongues and our devotion dies (3)
556, 557 Your clear hosannas raise, and alleluias loud (3)

host
11, 43   praise him above, ye heavenly host (4)
87   with the angelic host proclaim Christ is born (1)
110   O come, then, let us join the heavenly host (4)
207   praise him, all ye heavenly host (4)
212   O Solitude again command your host from heaven restored (5)
238, 239 with the host of angels one (2)
259   not with his angel host, not in his kingly state (1)
280   God ... to whom the number of the starry host is known (1)
287   through gates of pearl streams in the countless host (8)
324   Rank on rank the host of heaven spreads its vanguard (3)
364   with all the martyrs' noble host (4)
370   his heavenly host to be my guard (5)
375   host of heaven praiseth thee, O Lord of all dominions (2)
377, 378 from men and ... angel host be praise and glory evermore (5)
380   praise him above, ye heavenly host (3)
383, 384 all the twinkling, starry host (3)
401   The whole triumphant host give thanks to God on high (5)

489	He sent no angel of his host to bear this mighty word (2)
496, 497	the host of heaven rejoices (1)
526	part of the host have crossed the flood (3)
562	At the sign of triumph Satan's host doth flee (2)
563	Satan's host is vanquished and heaven is all possessed (3)

hosts

82	angel hosts, his praises sing (3)
97	for these mercies manifold join the hosts in praising (3)
106	mystery ... which hosts of angels chanted from above (1)
111	heavenly hosts sing alleluia (2)
125, 126	all the hosts of heaven (3)
168, 169	O countenance whose splendor the hosts of heaven adore (1)
174	Israel's hosts triumphant go through the wave (2)
219	by saints, by angel hosts adored (2)
261, 262	Christ in whose presence hosts of hell must tremble (2)
364	O holy, holy, holy Lord, whom heavenly hosts obey (3)
367	Holy, holy ... singing, Lord of hosts ... Lord Most High (2)
367	with thine angel hosts we cry, "Holy, holy, holy" (3)
367	blessing thee, the Lord of hosts Most High (3)
368	Holy Jesus, Lord of glory, whom angelic hosts proclaim (2)
373	Hosts on high, his power proclaim (2)
473	the hosts of God in conquering ranks combine (1)
479	angel hosts, rejoicing, make their glad reply (4)
495	all the heavenly hosts adore thee (3)
496, 497	Though circled by the hosts on high (2)
517	How lovely is thy dwelling-place, O Lord of hosts, to me (1)
518	come, O Lord of hosts, today (3)
519, 520	angel hosts encircled, as a bride dost earthward move (1)
548	strong in the Lord of hosts, and in his mighty power (2)
594, 595	Lo, the hosts of evil round us scorn thy Christ (2)
647	The countless hosts lead on before (3)
657	serve thee as thy hosts above (2)

hot

| 506, 507 | white-hot in your possession (5) |

hour

5	conquer in temptation's hour (3)
12, 13	At the third hour you took your cross (2)
12, 13	the third hour your faithful band was clothed with power (3)
12, 13	we praise and bless you every hour (4)
16, 17	For at this hour to all the world ... salvation came (2)
18	we praise and bless you every hour (5)
23	at that ninth hour you died for us (3)
23	we praise and bless you every hour (4)
120	shield us in temptation's hour (5)
138	did manifest your glory forth in Cana's marriage hour (1)
161	the water cleanses to this hour (2)
164	This is earth's darkest hour (3)
164	as we share this hour, thy cross may bring us to thy joy (4)
168, 169	hold me that I quail not in death's most fearful hour (5)
171	watch with him one bitter hour (1)
222	He reigns in heaven until the hour when he ... shall come (4)
240, 241	they died in imitation of their Savior's final hour (2)

255	that we, in every hour ... will trust your hidden power (2)
316, 317	This is the hour of banquet and of song (1)
316, 317	prolong the brief, bright hour of fellowhip with thee (1)
346	we here have known the resurrection hour (1)
347	to serve God's people every day and hour (4)
349	come in this most solemn hour (2)
365	thy sacred witness bear in this glad hour (3)
370	the sweet "Well done" in judgment hour (3)
375	he watches o'er us every hour (3)
406, 407	Sustained by thee through every hour, she bringeth forth (5)
416	For the beauty of each hour of the day and of the night (2)
435	crown him as your Captain in temptation's hour (5)
579	our people shield in danger's hour (4)
580	life's destruction or our most triumphant hour (3)
594, 595	for the facing of this hour (1)
596	pining for the hour that brings release (2)
600, 601	to match our present hour (1)
608	thy children shield in danger's hour (4)
662	I need thy presence every passing hour (2)
665	But God's power, hour by hour, is my temple and my tower (2)
671	how precious ... grace appear the hour I first believed (2)
677	He purposes will ripen fast, unfolding every hour (5)

hourly

563	he knows thine hourly need (1)

hours

50	he calls the hours his own (1)
179	hours and passing moments praise thee in their flight (3)
541	redeem the time, its hours too swiftly fly (4)
549, 550	days of toil and hours of ease (4)

house

51	This is the Lord's house, home of all his people (2)
108	Let every house be bright; let praises never cease (2)
122, 123	in the house of God abiding thus they sing eternally (1)
157	we bless you from the house of the Lord (R)
235	a house to stand unshaken by floods or winds or rains (3)
259	thus to his Father's house he comes, the heavenly guest (2)
260	Come now, and praise the humble saint of David's house (1)
260	David's house and line (1)
277	Sing of Jesus, son of Mary, in the house at Nazareth (2)
289	Our Father, by whose servants our house was built of old (1)
345	that in this house have called upon thy Name (1)
427	God's holy house of prayer hath none that can compare (2)
444	He from the house of David a child of grace has given (2)
458	In life no house, no home my Lord on earth might have (6)
486	O Savior, with protecting care abide in this thy house (3)
486	house of prayer, where we assembled in thy Name (3)
492	praises of your Savior let his house resound again (1)
509	make this house thy home (1)
524	I love thy kingdom, Lord, the house of thine abode (1)
556, 557	pilgrims find their Father's house, Jerusalem the blest (6)
645, 646	sing thy praise within thy house for ever (6)
664	may thy house be mine abode and all my work be praise (3)

681   reflects the vast design by which thy house is built (4)

household
40, 41   direct our faithful household Lord (4)

hover
10   New mercies, each returning day around us hover (2)
10   new mercies ... around us hover while we pray (2)

hovered
110   the angels hovered round, and sang this song (3)
176, 177   Over the chaos of the empty waters hovered the Spirit (1)

hovering
89, 90   above its sad and lowly plains they bend on hovering wing (2)
522, 523   Round each habitation hovering, see the cloud and fire (3)

however
586   Every task, however simple, sets the soul ... free (3)
703   however rough and steep the path may be (3)

huge
430   this huge wide orb we see shall one choir, one temple be (4)

human
18   shield frail human eyes from all the woe you bore for us (3b)
18   teach us to hear its echoes still in every human misery (3c)
55   From human will you do not spring (2)
55   one with us in human flesh (4)
77   A maid in lowly human place became ... the chosen (3)
78, 79   God imparts to human hearts the blessings of his heaven (3)
85, 86   you put our human vesture on (3)
88   one with us in human birth (2)
94, 95   to human view displayed (4)
148   evils wrought by human pride recoil on unrepentant heads (3)
179   thou from heaven beholding human nature's fall (4)
182   not ... untouched, unmoved by human pains (3)
199, 200   peace which evermore passeth human knowing (4)
215   Thou hast raised our human nature ... to God's right hand (3)
222   his strife with human hatred ends (1)
222   shame of human strife (3)
225   pouring on all human souls infinite riches of God (2)
237   God himself to joy and praise turns our human sadness (1)
246   love that cannot cease to bear our human anguish (4)
246   human anguish everywhere (4)
252   when the cup of human woe first he tasted here below (4)
252   Human Name of God above (6)
263, 264   most blest to bring to human birth the long-desired (3)
284   Ye saw the heaven-born child in human flesh arrayed (2)
324   Lord of lords in human vesture (2)
359   to human need their quickened hearts awake (2)
362   though the sinful human eye thy glory may not see (3)
372   deep writ upon the human heart, on sea and land (3)
379   when human hearts are breaking under sorrow's iron rod (2)
379   sin afflicts all human life (3)

416	joy of human love, brother, sister, parent, child (4)
435	bore it up triumphant, with its human light (3)
476	Although his being is too bright for human eyes to scan (2)
476	he speaks to us in human terms to make his glory known (4)
489	as one with us he dwelt with us, and bore a human name (4)
494	who every grief hath known that wrings the human breast (2)
516	yearning ... shall far outpass the power of human telling (3)
521	O Judge divine of human strife (4)
563	far more o'er thee are watching than human eyes can know (2)
582, 583	wring gold from human pain (2)
582, 583	where the sun that shineth is God's grace for human good (3)
586	by thy lowly human birth ... come to join the workers (1)
586	every deed of human kindness done in love is done to thee (3)
610	the weight of human need (1)
630	grace in human form declare (2)
719	thine alabaster cities gleam, undimmed by human tears (3)

humanity
220, 221	angels wonder when they see how changed is our humanity (2)
443	his manhood from humanity (1)
698	serve my God and all humanity (3)
705	serve thy cause and share thy love with all humanity (3)

humankind
89, 90	warring humankind hears not the tidings which they ring (3)
251	look down ... with love for humankind (1)
371	now to all humankind, let there be light (2)
492	he, of humankind the head (3)
500	come, pour thy joys on humankind (1)

humble
67	let your hearts be true and humble (3)
71, 72	treasures of his grace to enrich the humble poor (3)
74	He only to the humble reveals the face of God (3)
74	Gentle is he and humble, And light his yoke shall be (4)
99	Down in a lowly manger the humble Christ was born (3)
156	thy humble beast pursues his road with palms ... strowed (1)
257	two young doves, her humble offerings (2)
260	Come now, and praise the humble saint of David's house (1)
260	for him ... was the patient life of faith and humble name (3)
291	but chiefly thou desirest our humble thankful hearts (3)
338	Wherefore, O Father, we thy humble servants here bring (1)
369	let faith in humble notes adore the great mysterious King (4)
406, 407	water ... most humble, useful, precious, chaste (4)
428	let those of holy, humble heart come praise him evermore (5)
437, 438	the hungry fed, the humble lifted high (3)
480	he chose an humble birth (1)
493	mournful broken hearts rejoice, the humble poor believe (4)
500	Creator Spirit ... come visit every humble mind (1)
590	Grant us new courage, sacrificial, humble (2)
610	Lord, whose love through humble service bore the weight (1)
657	fix in us thy humble dwelling (1)
704	return in humble prayer and fervent praise (2)
705	With gratitude and humble trust we bring our best to thee (3)
709	Such blessings ... our humble prayers implore (5)

humbled
435   Humbled for a season, to receive a Name (2)

humbleness
400   worship him in humbleness (7)

humblest
307   Here our humblest homage pay we (2)

humbling
477   humbling thyself to death on Calvary (3)

humbly
148   humbly follow in your way (5)
279   humbly pray that we may follow them in holiness (4)
314   Humbly I adore thee, Verity unseen (1)
357   Humbly we adore thee, Lord of endless might (1)
360, 361   humbly adoring, take thy Body broken (2)
364   humbly thou cam'st to set us free (6)
366   wast of a virgin born humbly on that blessed morn (5)
371   hear us, we humbly pray (1)
475   humbly, fervently draw near him (1)
605   Do justly, love mercy, walk humbly with your God (1-3)
605   Then justly, in mercy we'll humbly walk with God (4)
675   humbly follow after me (1)

humility
69   in great humility is hid all heaven in a little room (3)
74   clad as are the poorest, such his humility (1)
252   Unto which must every knee bow in deep humility (1)
406, 407 serve in great humility (8)
454   came in deep humility (1)
670   clothe me with humility (1)

humming
412   Harp, lute, and lyre, loud humming cellos (3)

hundred
506, 507 hundred men and women turned the known world upside down (4)

hundreds
293   there are hundreds of thousands still (3)
453   has stood hundreds of years and is not yet decayed (2)

hung
18   At noon you hung upon the cross (3a)
159   mother weeping, where he hung, the dying Lord (1)
165, 166 sweetest weight is hung on thee (4)
167   but we believe it was for us he hung and suffered there (2)
468   nailed him to the cross, Lord ... hung him with a robber (3)

hunger
142   As thou didst hunger bear and thirst (3)
308, 309 We hunger; Lord, supply us (1)

| 335 | they who come to me shall not hunger (1) |
| 560 | Blessed ... who hunger and thirst after righteousness (4) |

hungered

| 448, 449 | for us he bore his holy fast and hungered sore (2) |

hungry

145	who feed the hungry in their need, and wrongs redress (4)
327, 328	with heavenly bread he makes the hungry whole (7)
424	world-wide task of caring for the hungry and despairing (2)
437, 438	the hungry fed, the humble lifted high (3)
472	bringing to hungry souls the bread of life (2)
610	still the hungry cry for bread (2)
644	'tis manna to the hungry soul, and to the weary, rest (2)

hunter

| 114 | but as the hunter braves drew nigh, the angel-song rang (2) |

hunters

| 114 | wondering hunters heard the hymn (1) |

hurled

| 607 | hate and fear divide us and bitter threats are hurled (1) |

hurries

| 61, 62 | she wakes and hurries through the night (2) |

hurt

53	from the sins that hurt us, would to Truth convert us (2)
196, 197	what he brings in his hurt hands is life (1,4)
196, 197	Good Jesus Christ, our Brother, died in darkest hurt (3)
196, 197	in darkest hurt upon the tree (3)
339	never to my hurt invited (3)
593	where there is hurt, may we forgive (1)
615	every hurt be healed (4)
636, 637	the flame shall not hurt thee (4)

husband

| 353 | join every husband, every wife in mutual love (3) |

hush

| 89, 90 | O hush the noise and cease your strife (3) |
| 400 | most gentle death, waiting to hush our final breath (6) |

hushed

| 608 | hushed their raging at thy word (2) |

hymn

36	our wonted hymn out-pouring (2)
37	we hymn the eternal Father ... Son ... Holy Ghost divine (2)
82	hymn and chant and high thanksgiving (4)
89, 90	beneath the heavenly hymn have rolled two thousand years (3)
114	wondering hunters heard the hymn (1)
136, 137	the voice of prayer, the hymn of praise (4)
191	sing to God a hymn of gladness (1)

191	sing to God a hymn of praise (1)
217, 218	A hymn of glory let us sing (1)
279	followed thee, obeyed, adored, our grateful hymn receive (1)
336	let its hymn be heard for ever -- peace (3)
345	with one accord our parting hymn of praise (1)
366	Hark, the loud celestial hymn angel choirs ... raising (2)
367	repeated each to each the alternate hymn (1)
416	Christ our God, to thee we raise this our hymn (R)
416	this our hymn of grateful praise (R)
417, 418	join in the hymn of all creation (3)

hymning

180	with high and holy hymning (3)

hymns

24	to thee our morning hymns ascended (1)
33-35	joyfully chanting holy hymns to praise you (3)
106	in hymns of joy, unknown before (3)
122, 123	Therefore in our hymns we pray thee (4)
154, 155	To thee before thy passion they sang ... hymns of praise (4)
174	Hymns of glory, songs of praise, Father ... we raise (4)
198	whom as true God and our hymns adore for ... evermore (2)
207	Hymns of praise then let us sing (2)
208	let hymns of praise his triumphs tell (4)
210	our Christ hath brought us over with hymns of victory (1)
217, 218	new hymns throughout the world shall ring (1)
233, 234	with hearts of gladness raise due hymns (1)
233, 234	hymns of thankful love and praise (1)
320	Zion, praise thy Savior, singing hymns with exultation (1)
320	hymns with exultation ringing (1)
320	gracious hymns of joy upraising in thy heart and soul (4)
320	hymns ... in thy heart and soul today (4)
393	raising hymns in glad accord (1)
426	No, the Church delights to raise psalms and hymns (4)
426	psalms and hymns and songs of praise (4)
478	true hymns to Christ the King in all their living (3)
484, 485	hymns on every tongue abound (1)
518	God the One in Three adoring in glad hymns eternally (2)
524	her hymns of love and praise (3)
590	O Jesus Christ, may grateful hymns be rising (1)
590	hymns be rising in every city for your love and care (1)
608	thus evermore shall rise to thee glad hymns of praise (4)
608	hymns of praise from land and sea (4)
619	the hymns which tell the honor of your King (5)
681	hymns thy people raise, the psalms and anthems strong (3)

icy

228	melt with fire our icy chill (4)

Ideo

92	Ideo, Ideo, Ideo gloria in excelsis Deo (R)

idle

541	Who dares stand idle on the harvest plain (1)

idol

408	Cast each false idol from its throne (3)
549, 550	from each idol that would keep us (3)
683, 684	The dearest idol I have know, whate'er that idol be (4)

ill

5	to make ill fortune turn to fair (4)
43	the ill that I this day have done (2)
44, 45	from all ill dreams your children keep (2)
192	Lord of all life, from ill my passing life deliver (2)
251	forgive the ill that we have done (2)
337	deliver us from every touch of ill (4)
503, 504	where thou art guide, no ill can come (6)
574, 575	consume the ill, purge out the shame (4)
625	praise him still, through good or ill, who ever lives (3)
645, 646	In death's dark vale I fear no ill (4)
645, 646	I fear no ill with thee, dear Lord, beside me (4)

ills

53	Once he came in blessing, all our ills redressing (1)
356	As angels gave poor Lazarus from all his ills release (3)
396, 397	free us from all ills in this world and the next (2)
491	whom no ills from good dissuade (4)
662	ills have no weight, and tears no bitterness (3)
687, 688	our helper he amid the flood of mortal ills prevailing (1)

illuming

516	clothe me round, the while my path illuming (2)

illumining

5	O Day, all days illumining (1)

image

47	Maker, who didst fashion me image of thyself to be (3)
146, 147	Remember, Lord ... in your own image were we made (4)
235	in mystic form and image four living creatures came (2)
709	through this earthly pilgrimage ... all thine Israel led (1)

imbue

475	so let me quietly in thy rays imbue me (3)

imitation

240, 241	they died in imitation of their Savior's final hour (2)

immensities

459	And have the bright immensities received our risen Lord (1)

immortal

25, 26	Immortal, holy, blest is he (1)
37	O brightness of the immortal Father's face (1)
168, 169	My days are few, O fail not, with thine immortal power (5)
183	the Prince of life, who died, reigns immortal (3)
191	glorious life ... immortal, on his resurrection morn (2)

237	when they laid the mortal down for the life immortal (1)
275	by death to life immortal they were born and glorified (3)
284	O ye immortal throng of angels round the throne (1)
288	Praise to God, immortal praise (1,3)
302, 303	Knowledge and faith and life immortal Jesus ... imparts (1)
337	the one true, pure, immortal sacrifice (1)
338	All-perfect Offering, sacrifice immortal (1)
343	living bread, that heavenly wine, be our immortal food (4)
355	You only are immortal (1)
358	Only Immortal One, Mighty Creator (2)
376	giver of immortal gladness, fill us with the light of day (1)
423	Immortal, invisible, God only wise (1)
489	his holy and immortal truth to all on earth hath given (1)
491	Worth from worth immortal sprung (3)
546	and an immortal crown (1,4)

immortality

| 429 | immortality endures (1,4) |

immortals

| 61, 62 | through them we stream to join the immortals (3) |

impart

6, 7	till they inward light impart (2)
47	Thou, who didst all gifts impart (4)
185, 186	by his grace he doth impart eternal sunshine to the heart (3)
440	Gracious Lord, thyself impart (3)
457	thy word alone true wisdom can impart (2)
503, 504	who dost thy sevenfold gifts impart (2)
505	the holy flame of love impart (3)
566	Impart them, Lord, to each and all, as each and ... need (1)
584	Let wisdom's godly fear dispel the fears ... hate impart (3)
610	consecrating to your purpose every gift that you impart (1)
656	he to the lowly soul will still himself impart (3)
691	May thy rich grace impart strength to my fainting heart (2)
704	thou who camest from above the fire celestial to impart (1)

imparting

12, 13	sun ... imparting vigor to the day (1)
51	his own life imparting, food everlasting (4)
307	Life-imparting heavenly Manna (5)

imparts

78, 79	God imparts to human hearts the blessings of his heaven (3)
291	the gifts we have to offer are what thy love imparts (3)
300	He dispels our sin and sadness, life imparts (3)
302, 303	Knowledge and faith and life immortal Jesus ... imparts (1)
302, 303	Jesus thy Son to us imparts (1)
627	Lord, grant us all aright to learn the wisdom it imparts (5)
628	to learn the truths your word imparts (1)
649, 650	we seek the peace your love imparts (1)

impatience

| 232 | Lord, curb our vain impatience for glory ... fame (2/7-25) |

impelled
232   one love, one hope, impelled them (2/10-28)

impels
124   O Jesus, while the star of grace impels us on (4)
124   grace impels us on to seek thy face (4)

implanted
372   Eternal life hath he implanted in the soul (4)

implore
5   With prayer the Father we implore (3)
151   Lord, hear me, I implore thee (1)
319   Bind our hearts as one we implore you (2)
709   Such blessings ... our humble prayers implore (5)

imploring
248, 249   holy Jesus, thee imploring so to write it in us here (4)
363   still imploring thy love and favor, kept to us always (5)

inaccessible
423   in light inaccessible hid from our eyes (1)

incarnate
36   thee, his incarnate Son, and Holy Spirit adoring (2)
61, 62   now come, most worthy Lord, God's Son, Incarnate Word (2)
84   Worship we the Godhead, love incarnate, love divine (2)
87   hail the incarnate Deity (2)
106   tidings ... of God incarnate and the Virgin's Son (1)
112   stable ... sufficed the Lord God incarnate, Jesus Christ (2)
136, 137   the incarnate Lord holds converse high (2)
253   following their incarnate God (3)
261, 262   guardian of the Incarnate (1)
267   the incarnate Savior's birth (5)
338   intercession through him our Savior, Son of God incarnate (2)
365   Come, thou incarnate Word, by heaven and earth adored (2)
422   crucified and risen might of Christ, the incarnate Word (2)
450 , 451   the God incarnate, Man divine (3)
486   Hosanna to the living Lord ... to the incarnate Word (1)
491   incarnate, and a native of the very world he made (4)
494   once on earth the incarnate Word (4)
496, 497   Incarnate God, put forth thy power (3)
630   Word Incarnate heights and depths of life did share (2)
632   O Christ, the Word Incarnate, O Wisdom from on high (1)

incarnation
158   For me, kind Jesus, was thy incarnation (4)
370   I bind this day to me for ever ... Christ's incarnation (2)
496, 497   praise ... for this his Incarnation (3)

incense
115   So bring him incense, gold and myrrh (3)
127   incense doth their God disclose (4)
128   incense owns a Deity nigh (3)
556, 557   echoes upward float like wreaths of incense cloud (3)

566	to rise, like incense, each to thee (1)
566	rise, like incense ... in noble thought and deed (1)
616	gold and incense bring (4)

incessant
| 106 | saved by his love, incessant we shall sing (6) |

incessantly
| 643 | by prostrate spirits day and night incessantly adored (2) |

increase
175	heaven her gates unbars, flinging her increase of light (3)
216	heaven her gates unbars, flinging her increase of light (2)
347	in God's good Spirit daily to increase (1)
352	increase, rekindle, and restore their love (3)
363	thine is the quickening power that gives increase (4)
399	that strife may end and joy increase (3)
480	grace and knowledge grow as years and strength increase (1)
505	increase our faith in our dear Lord (2)
521	bid thy Church increase, in breadth and length (1)
521	increase ... in depth and height, her unity and peace (1)
587	in all our hearts such love increase (3)
607	fear of rattling saber, from dread of war's increase (3)
629	O Father, Son, and Spirit, send us increase from above (3)
634	never resisting but to increase in faith more and more (1)
703	doubts appall, and sorrows still increase (1)
718	thy true religion in our hearts increase (3)

increasing
| 125, 126 | His power increasing still shall spread (5) |
| 616 | his kingdom still increasing, a kingdom without end (4) |

increasingly
| 348 | may we increasingly glory in learning all that it means (3) |

indeed
120	know you are the Bread indeed (6)
183	Christ indeed from death is risen (8)
184	alleluia, Christ, our Paschal lamb indeed (R)
185, 186	he is our meat and drink indeed (4)
212	those hands of liberal love indeed in infinite degree (3)
318	it is enough, my Lord, enough indeed (3)
323	for thy Flesh is meat indeed (1)
377, 378	Know that the Lord is God indeed (2)
458	my friend, indeed, who at my need his life did spend (2)
458	But O my friend, my friend indeed (2)
558	mankind shall then indeed be free (2)
561	till every foe is vanquished and Christ is Lord indeed (1)
635	soul that trusted him indeed (2)

indwelling
| 394, 395 | Indwelling God (4) |
| 475 | Come, indwelling Spirit, with transfiguring splendor (4) |

inestimable
240, 241   o'er all miracles preceding his inestimable death (3)

infancy
258   that watched thy slumbering infancy (1)

infant
80   the Son holds in his infant hand (4)
93   yonder shines the infant Light (2)
97   stretching infant hands on high, Savior, long awaited (1)
111   Holy infant, so tender and mild, sleep in heavenly peace (1)
114   as was the ring of glory on the helpless infant there (3)
117, 118   guide where our infant Redeemer is laid (1,5)
231   Praise for your infant martyrs (2/12-28)
278   obedient to the summons bore in love the infant Lord (1)
491   strength of infant weakness, if eternal is so young (3)
544   infant voices shall proclaim their early blessings (3)

infants
480   infants in his arms he took and on his bosom blessed (2)

infest
100   nor thorns infest the ground (3)

infinite
88   comes with mercies infinite (2)
108   with mercies infinite our Christ hath brought us peace (2)
212   those hands of liberal love indeed in infinite degree (3)
225   pouring on all human souls infinite riches of God (2)
275   now they drink, as from a river, holy bliss and infinite (4)
326   to appear before God in the city of infinite day (1)
346   Here we have tasted infinite delights (2)
366   infinite thy vast domain, everlasting is thy reign (1)
535   thanks never ceasing and infinite love (4)
580   heavens infinite in time and place (1)

infinitely
479   blest be his compassion infinitely kind (2)

infirmities
411   he healeth thine infirmities and ransoms thee from death (4)

infirmity
152   thou knowest our infirmity (2)
298   help us in our infirmity through Jesus blood and merit (2)

inflamed
47   by love inflamed, arise unto thee a sacrifice (4)

influence
229   O shed thine influence from above (1,3)
292   all fostering power, all influence sweet breathe (2)
543   ten thousand stars in nobler spheres his influence own (4)

inform
457   thou only canst inform the mind and purify the heart (2)

inhabitants
522, 523   Blest inhabitants of Zion, washed in the Redeemer's blood (4)

inherit
139   that we may life inherit (3)
230   until you reach the promised goal, a kingdom to inherit (3)
298   that as is promised here we may eternal life inherit (2)
424   For the good we all inherit (3)
496, 497   Jesus, grant us ... to inherit thy salvation (2)
560   Blessed are the meek, for they shall inherit the earth (3)
564, 565   we know we at the end shall life inherit (3)

inherits
163   earth inherits heaven's key (3)

injuries
228   remove our stains; bind up all our injuries (4)
458   Sweet injuries! (4)

inly
371   heal to the sick in mind, sight to the inly blind (2)

inmost
228   occupy its inmost part with your dazzling purity (3)
375   With balm my inmost heart he fills (1)
506, 507   Spirit, close companion of our inmost thoughts and ways (2)
574, 575   our inmost spirits purify (4)

inner
436   here, Lord, abide! Let me thy inner presence feel (4)
501, 502   From inner strife grant us release (5)

innocence
431   meditations of my heart be innocence and praise (4)

innocent
284   so innocent and mild while in the manger laid (2)

innocents
246   innocents the price must pay (2)

inscribed
471   Inscribed upon the cross we see in shining letters (2)
628   study, that your laws may be inscribed upon our hearts (1)

inside
196, 197   Good Jesus Christ inside his pain looked down (2)
196, 197   offer us the worlds of light that live inside the Trinity (3)

inspiration
506, 507   praise the Word, Source, and Truth, and Inspiration (6)
617   our inspiration be thy constant word (3)

inspire

19, 20	let love in flames of living fire the hearts ... inspire (2)
19, 20	hearts of all the world inspire (2)
23	Inspire us by your dying breath to live for you (3)
299	With burning words of victory won inspire our hearts (3)
353	O God of love, inspire our life (3)
500	our hearts with heavenly love inspire (2)
501, 502	come to create, renew, inspire (1)
503, 504	Come. Holy Ghost, our souls inspire (1)
531	souls without strength inspire with might (3)
590	inspire our worship (1)
681	inspire us from above with joy and strength for duty (5)
691	my zeal inspire (2)

inspired

253	his zeal inspired their quest (3)
332	thus inspired with holy fear, before thine altar kneel (1)
359	inspired of thee, may they count all but loss (5)
537	inspired with hope and praise, to Christ belong (4)
545	Let us, with zeal like theirs inspired, strive (2)
631	inspired those whose wisdom still directs us (3)

inspires

527	one the hope our God inspires (2)

instant

638, 639	be conquered by my instant prayer (3)

instead

114	God the Lord of all the earth sent angel-choirs instead (1)

instill

231	Instill in us his longing, your glory to behold (2/12-27)

instrument

413	let every instrument and voice peal out the praise (2)
420	Let every instrument be tuned for praise (5)
430	hither bring in one consent heart ... voice ... instrument (1)

insult

182	In every insult, rift, and war (4)

integrity

528	help us witness to your purpose with renewed integrity (1)

intend

528	may we serve as you intend (5)

intense

400	Fire, so intense and fiercely bright (3)

intent

109	to seek for a king was their intent (3)
359	Anoint them prophets. Teach them thine intent (2)
564, 565	his first avowed intent to be a pilgrim (1)

intention
348   Here, at your table, confirm our intention (2)
348   intention ever to cherish the gifts you provide (2)

intercede
315   For all thy Church, O Lord, we intercede (2)
359   help them intercede with all the royal priesthood (3)

interceded
158   for our atonement ... God interceded (3)

intercedes
181   sing how he intercedes above for those whose sins he bore (2)

interceding
495   ever for us interceding, till in glory we appear (3)

intercession
338   See now thy children, making intercession (2)
338   intercession through him our Savior, Son of God incarnate (2)
338   intercession ... for all thy people, living and departed (2)

intercessor
460, 461   Intercessor, friend of sinners (3)

interstellar
459   Lord of interstellar space and Conqueror of time (1)

inventive
580   your children in your likeness, share inventive powers (1)
580   we ... share inventive powers with you (1)

invisible
38, 39   light from the light invisible (1)
222   he reigns invisible but near (2)
423   Immortal, invisible, God only wise (1)

invitation
348   Lord, we have come at your own invitation (1)

invited
339   never to my hurt invited (3)
465, 466   invited by your holy word (3)

invites
185, 186   So let us keep the festival to which the Lord invites us (3)

invocation
370   invocation of the same ... Three in One ... One in Three (1,7)

inward
6, 7   till they inward light impart (2)
152   abstinence in outward things with inward fasting (4)
228   in our labor inward rest (2)
329-331   makes our inward vision clear (5)

ire

591   in ire and exultation aflame with faith, and free (3)

iron

71, 72   gates of brass before him burst, the iron fetters yield (2)
112   earth stood hard as iron, water like a stone (1)
165, 166 sweetest wood and sweetest iron (4)
191   Now the iron bars are broken (2)
379   when human hearts are breaking under sorrow's iron rod (2)
613   Break with thine iron rod the tyrannies of sin (1)

Isaac's

173   The Paschal Lamb, like Isaac's ram (2)

Isaiah

81   Isaiah 'twas foretold it, the Rose I have in mind (2)

island

24   As o'er each continent and island the dawn leads on (3)

isles

534   give ear to me, ye continents, ye isles give ear to me (2)

Israel

56   O come, O come, Emmanuel and ransom captive Israel (1,8)
56   Rejoice, rejoice, Emmanuel shall come to thee, O Israel (R)
109   Nowell, Nowell ... born is the King of Israel (R)
127   out of thee the Lord from heaven came to rule his Israel (1)
154, 155 Thou art the King of Israel, thou David's royal Son (1)
187   through the billows Israel led (2)
199, 200 God hath brought his Israel into joy from sadness (1)
393   guides his Israel on their way ... darkness into light (2)
444   Blessed be the God of Israel, who comes to set us free (1)
536   Israel comes to greet the Savior (3)
640   Traveler, yes, it brings the day, promised day of Israel (1)
648   When Israel was in Egypt's land (1)
648   to lead the children of Israel through (2)
666   Let Israel trust in God, no bounds his mercy knows (4)
670   Israel, now and evermore in the Lord Almighty trust (4)
678, 679 with you has come to dwell ... Holy One of Israel (2)
709   through this earthly pilgrimage ... all thine Israel led (1)
709   O God of Israel, be the God of this succeeding race (2)

Israel's

66   Israel's strength and consolation (2)
174   Israel's hosts triumphant go through the wave (2)
257   Anna welcomes Israel's hope, with holy rapture fired (3)
429   How happy they whose hopes rely on Israel's God (2)
450, 451 heirs of Israel's chosen race, ye ransomed from the fall (4)

issued

176, 177 so from the empty tomb the Second Adam issued triumphant (1)

itself

74   till time itself shall end (3)

itself
612   love than death itself more strong (2)
627   or heaven itself be won (4)
682   e'en death itself, and all for one who was thine enemy (3)

Jacob
453   As Jacob with travel was weary one day (1)
453   the angels of Jacob are guarding it still (3)

Jacob's
18   At noon you came to Jacob's well (4a)
124   who told the rise of Jacob's star (2)
199, 200   Jacob's sons and daughters (1)

James
231   young James the faithful, who heard and followed you (2/5-1)
232   O Lord, for James, we praise you (2/7-25)
232   Praise ... Lord's own brother, James of Jerusalem (2/10-23)
276   For James who left his father's side (2)

jealousies
573   in wrath and fear, by jealousies surrounded (3)
606   May all our petty jealousies and hatred cease (2)

Jehovah
368   Great Jehovah, form our hearts and make them thine (4)
664   My Shepherd will supply my need, Jehovah is his Name (1)
690   Guide me, O thou great Jehovah (1)

Jerusalem
61, 62   Awake, Jerusalem, arise (1)
67   Speak ye to Jerusalem of the peace that waits for them (1)
103   therefore rejoice Jerusalem (1)
122, 123   Alleluia thou resoundest, true Jerusalem and free (2)
135   from there thou leddest them steadfast to Jerusalem (4)
199, 200   comes to glad Jerusalem (3)
232   Praise ... Lord's own brother, James of Jerusalem (2/10-23)
233, 234   joy fills the new Jerusalem (4)
278   raised high with saints and angels, in Jerusalem above (4)
280   There are named the blessed faithful of the new Jerusalem (4)
354   bring you into the holy city Jerusalem (1)
356   God's true Jerusalem (2)
556, 557   pilgrims find their Father's house, Jerusalem the blest (6)
590   as you once wept above Jerusalem (3)
620   Jerusalem, my happy home, when shall I come to thee (1)
620   Jerusalem, God grant that I may see thine endless joy (5)
623   Truly, "Jerusalem," name we that shore (2)
623   seeking Jerusalem, dear native land (4)
624   Jerusalem the golden, with milk and honey blest (1)

Jesse's
56   O come, thou Branch of Jesse's tree (4)
81   Of Jesse's lineage coming as seers of old have sung (1)
307   branch and flower of Jesse's stem (3)
496, 497   O righteous branch, O Jesse's Rod (1)

Jesu

602	Jesu, Jesu, fill us with your love (R)

Jesus

9	So let the love of Jesus come and set thy soul ablaze (5)
12, 13	O Jesus, crucified for us (4)
14, 15	Almighty Father, hear our cry through Jesus Christ (3)
14, 15	Jesus Christ, our Lord Most High (3)
18	O Jesus, crucified for us (5)
19, 20	Almighty Father, hear our cry through Jesus Christ (3)
21, 22	through Jesus Christ, our Lord Most High (3)
23	O Jesus, crucified for us (4)
25, 26	O gracious Light, Lord Jesus Christ (1)
33-35	for ever resting in the peace of Jesus (5)
36	our Savior Jesus Christ, joyful in thine appearing (1)
37	most holy, heavenly, blest, Lord Jesus Christ (1)
38, 39	Jesus, Redeemer of the world (1)
42	Jesus, give the weary calm and sweet repose (2)
44, 45	through Jesus Christ, our Lord Most High (4)
47	Holy Jesus, may I be dead and buried here with thee (4)
52	Jesus, may we lifted be from death of sin to life in thee (2)
53	Come, then, O Lord Jesus, from our sins release us (4)
60	At your great Name, O Jesus, now all knees must bend (4)
66	Come ... long-expected Jesus, born to set thy people free (1)
68	Our hope and expectation, O Jesus, now appear (3)
83	Jesus, to thee be glory given (6)
84	worship we our Jesus, but wherewith for sacred sign (2)
85, 86	O Jesus, very Light of Light (2)
87	Pleased as man with us to dwell; Jesus, our Emmanuel (2)
88	O sing, this blessed morn, Jesus Christ today is born (R)
99	go tell it on the mountain, that Jesus Christ is born (R)
101	the little Lord Jesus laid down his sweet head (1)
101	the little Lord Jesus asleep on the hay (1)
101	but little Lord Jesus no crying he makes (2)
101	I love thee, Lord Jesus! Look down from the sky (2)
101	Be near me, Lord Jesus (3)
102	Mary was that mother mild, Jesus Christ her little child (1)
107	give ye heed to what we say: Jesus Christ is born today (1)
107	Jesus Christ was born for this (2)
107	Jesus Christ was born to save (3)
109	right over the place where Jesus lay (4)
111	Jesus, Lord, at thy birth (3)
112	stable ... sufficed the Lord God incarnate, Jesus Christ (2)
114	Jesus your King is born, Jesus is born (R)
116	The Savior Jesus, well-beloved (4)
119	Holy Jesus, every day keep us in the narrow way (4)
124	O Jesus, while the star of grace impels us on (4)
127	Jesus, whom the Gentiles worshiped at thy glad epiphany (5)
129, 130	God proclaiming in its thunder Jesus as his Son by name (3)
131, 132	All glory, Jesus, be to thee for this thy glad epiphany (5)
133, 134	Jesus, Redeemer of the earth (1)
135	praise ... Jesus, Lord, to thee we raise (1)
139	Jesus went to Jordan's stream his Father's will obeying (1)
142	yea, evermore, in life and death, Jesus, with us abide (4)
144	Lord Jesus, Sun of Righteousness, shine in our hearts (1)

506, 507	by whose love and power, in Jesus God himself was seen (3)
506, 507	in Jesus God himself was seen and heard (3)
506, 507	Tell of how the ascended Jesus armed a people for his own (4)
514	to thee, by Jesus Christ send down (4)
522, 523	Jesus, whom their souls rely on (4)
522, 523	Jesus ... makes them kings and priests to God (4)
524	Jesus, thou friend divine, our Savior and our King (4)
525	The Church's one foundation is Jesus Christ her Lord (1)
526	Jesus, be thou our constant Guide (5)
531	Name of Jesus glorify till every people call him Lord (4)
535	the Name all-victorious of Jesus extol (1)
535	ascribing salvation to Jesus our King (2)
535	The praises of Jesus the angels proclaim (3)
539	tidings of Jesus, redemption and release (R)
544	Jesus shall reign where'er the sun (1)
545	Jesus, the author, finisher, rewarder of our faith (3)
548	who in the strength of Jesus trusts is more than conqueror (2)
549, 550	Jesus calls us o'er the tumult (1)
549, 550	Jesus calls us from the worship of the vain world's (3)
549, 550	Jesus calls us (5)
561	Stand up, stand up for Jesus (1-4)
562	with the cross of Jesus going on before (1,R)
562	but the Church of Jesus constant will remain (4)
568	Blessed Lord Jesus, who camest in poverty (2)
570, 571	call to mind the word of Jesus (3)
586	Jesus, thou divine Companion (1)
586	Jesus ... divine Companion, help us all to work our best (3)
590	O Jesus Christ, may grateful hymns be rising (1)
593	Jesus, our lord (3)
598	O wounded hands of Jesus, build in us thy new creation (4)
624	Jesus, in mercy bring us to that dear land of rest (4)
634	I call on thee, Lord Jesus Christ (1)
636, 637	to you that for refuge to Jesus have fled (1)
636, 637	The soul that to Jesus hath fled for repose (5)
641	Lord Jesus, think on me (1-4)
642	Jesus, the very thought of thee (1)
642	love of Jesus, what it is, none but who love him know (4)
642	Jesus, our only joy be thou, as thou our prize wilt be (5)
644	How sweet the Name of Jesus sounds in a believer's ear (1)
644	O Jesus, Shepherd, Guardian, Friend (4)
649, 650	O Jesus, joy of loving hearts (1)
649, 650	O Jesus, ever with us stay (4)
652, 653	Jesus knelt to share with thee the silence of eternity (3)
655	Jesus, I have promised to serve thee to the end (1,3)
655	O Jesus, thou hast promised to all who follow thee (3)
657	Jesus, thou art all compassion (1)
673	first one ... to know of the birth of Jesus was the Maid (1)
673	first one ... to know of Messiah, Jesus (2)
673	Jesus, when he said, "I am he" (2)
673	first ones ... to know of the rising of Jesus (3)
676	you can tell the love of Jesus (2)
682	most loving Jesus Christ (4)
683, 684	Where is the soul-refreshing view of Jesus and his word (2)
686	Jesus sought me when a stranger (2)
687, 688	dost ask who that may be? Christ Jesus, it is he (2)

245	Your great I AM's Saint John records (2)
245	Our thanks we raise that all John wrote bears witness (3)
266	six months gone since Elizabeth conceived John (5)
271, 272	that John should be that herald's name (2)
271, 272	John, still unborn, yet gave aright his witness (3)
582, 583	O holy city, seen of John (1)
661	Young John who trimmed the flapping sail ... died (3)

John's

| 245 | We praise you that John's voice still lives (3) |

join

61, 62	through them we stream to join the immortals (3)
87	join the triumph of the skies (1)
97	for these mercies manifold join the hosts in praising (3)
103	Come, join the angel throng in songs of joy (R)
110	O come, then, let us join the heavenly host (4)
238, 239	join to ours your supplication (3)
279	Thine earthly members fit to join thy saints above (3)
284	join with our earth-bound song to make the Savior known (1)
307	We in worship join with them (3)
353	join every husband, every wife in mutual love (3)
366	Lo, the apostolic train join, thy sacred Name to hallow (3)
374	Come, let us join our cheerful songs with angels (1)
390	join the great throng, psaltery, organ, and song (1)
392	join in a song with sweet accord (1)
411	all that is within me join to bless his holy Name (1)
417, 418	join in the hymn of all creation (3)
422	saints on earth and saints above we join in full accord (2)
434	with angels join to praise the Lamb (5)
439	while millions join the theme, I will sing (2)
526	by faith we join our hands with those that went before (4)
529	Join hands, disciples of the faith (2)
529	Join hands ... whate'er your race may be (2)
562	Onward, then, ye people, join our happy throng (5)
572	we ... join in singing that great music pure and strong (1)
586	by thy lowly human birth ... come to join the workers (1)

joined

27, 28	You joined the morn and evening ray (2)
48	this day the high and lowly, through ages joined in tune (1)
213	love which hath joined us to Jesus' Name (4)
275	joined in holy concert, singing to the Lord of all (2)
443	He joined with guests at wedding feast (2)
581	as members of his Body joined we are in him made one (5)
606	Since the love of Christ has joined us in one body (1)
619	Ye who have fought and joined the starry throng (4)

joining

33-35	creation joining hearts and voices singing your glory (3)
433	Beside us to guide us, our God with us joining (2)
612	joining hand in hand, agree (4)

joins

| 260 | beside his spouse ... he joins the heavenly song (4) |

374   The whole creation joins in one to bless the sacred Name (4)

joke
170   your passion turned ... into a soldier's joke (2)

Jordan
69   What is the crying at Jordan (1)
120   The sinless one to Jordan came (1)
370   his baptism in the Jordan river (2)
690   When I tread the verge of Jordan (3)

Jordan's
76   On Jordan's bank the Baptist's cry (1)
116   At Jordan's stream, behold (1)
116   through Jordan's flood was led (2)
131, 132   Within the Jordan's sacred flood the ... Lamb ... stood (3)
135   Manifest at Jordan's stream (2)
139   Jesus went to Jordan's stream his Father's will obeying (1)
526   when the word is given bid Jordan's narrow stream divide (5)

Joseph
96   Mary, Joseph, lend your aid (4)
106   found, with Joseph and the blessed maid, her Son (4)
110   Saint Joseph, too, was by to tend the child (3)
231   All praise, O God, for Joseph (2/3-19)
259   There Joseph at her side in reverent wonder stands (3)
261, 262   By the Creator, Joseph was appointed (1)
261, 262   to Saint Joseph gave supernal honor (3)

Joseph's
231   Joseph's love made "Father" to be ... God's Name (2/3-19)

Joshua
18   The sun stood still for Joshua (2a)

journey
48   We journey on, believing, renewed with heavenly might (3)
228   On our journey grant us aid (2)
527   one the object of our journey (2)
555   Thy cross is lifted o'er us; we journey in its light (3)
690   let the fire and cloudy pillar lead me all my journey (2)
703   only with thee we journey safely on (2)

journeys
544   where'er the sun doth his successive journeys run (1)

joy
1, 2   bring us to heaven where thy saints united joy (2)
1, 2   joy without ending (2)
16, 17   Then let us all with joy embrace the flaming splendor (3)
46   for joy of beauty not our own (2)
48   O day of radiant gladness, O day of joy and light (1)
61, 62   as we with joy your throne surround (3)
65   for grace and joy abounding (2)
66   dear desire of every nation, joy of every longing heart (2)

69	prepare for joy in the winter night (2)
69	in joy and terror the Word is born (4)
73	life to joy awakes (1)
80	Glad tidings of great joy I bring to all the world (1)
80	this new-born child of lowly birth shall be the joy (2)
80	joy of all the earth (2)
91	boy, shall be our confidence and joy (1)
94, 95	Glad tidings of great joy I bring to you and all mankind (2)
100	Joy to the world! the Lord is come (1)
100	Joy to the world! the Savior reigns (2)
100	repeat the sounding joy (2)
103	Come, join the angel throng in songs of joy (R)
105	O tidings of comfort and joy (R)
106	in hymns of joy, unknown before (3)
106	employ our grateful voices to proclaim the joy (5)
114	boy, who brings you beauty, peace, and joy (4)
119	as with joy they hailed its light (1)
119	so may we with holy joy, pure and free from sin's alloy (3)
119	thou its light, its joy, its crown (5)
122, 123	Alleluia, song of gladness, voice of joy that cannot die (1)
136, 137	shall be theirs above who joy in God with perfect love (3)
142	an Easter of unending joy we may attain at last (5)
143	give us joy to see thy face (4)
144	restore us by your loving care to peace and joy within (2)
164	as we share this hour, thy cross may bring us to thy joy (4)
164	thy cross may bring us to thy joy and resurrection power (4)
174	Easter triumph, Easter joy, these alone do sin destroy (4)
179	Earth her joy confesses, clothing her for spring (2)
182	till all creation lives and learns his joy (5)
182	learns his joy, his justice, love, and praise (5)
185, 186	Christ is himself the joy of all (3)
190	now your songs of joy outpour (3)
193	That Easter day with joy was bright (1)
196, 197	joy to the heart and all in this good day's dawning (R)
198	for heavenly joy preparing (2)
199, 200	God hath brought his Israel into joy from sadness (1)
199, 200	with the royal feast of feasts, comes its joy to render (3)
201	light and joy have conquered doom (1)
201	see where he lay; let joy begin (3)
208	let shout of holy joy outburst (2)
210	for Christ the Lord is risen, our joy that hath no end (3)
211	Our God most high, our joy and boast (4)
217, 218	You are a present joy, O Lord (2)
219	The heavens with joy receive their Lord (2)
220, 221	Be thou our joy, O Mighty Lord (3)
232	We sing with joy of Mary (2/8-15)
233, 234	joy fills the new Jerusalem (4)
237	God himself to joy and praise turns our human sadness (1)
237	joy that martyrs won their crown opened heaven's portal (1)
246	songs of praise and joy (1)
246	we share your pain and find your joy (5)
248, 249	who its perfect wisdom reacheth ... joy posesseth (3)
248, 249	heavenly joy posesseth here (3)
250	Now greet the swiftly changing year with joy (1)
250	with joy and penitence sincere (1)

512	fullness of joy for ever there (4)
515	come, thou source of joy and gladness (1)
524	Beyond my highest joy I prize her heavenly ways (3)
538	let all be, below, above, one in joy, and light and love (2)
545	for the joy before him set, and moved by pitying love (4)
552, 553	lay hold on life ... thy joy and crown eternally (1)
556, 557	pour out the strains of joy and bliss (2)
558	O how our hearts beat high with joy whene'er we hear (1)
559	fill our hearts with heavenly joy (3)
573	sharing not our griefs, no joy can share (2)
576, 577	Grant us love's fulfillment, joy with all the blessed (3)
581	With grateful joy and holy fear his charity we learn (2)
588, 589	let it yield a hundred-fold the fruits of peace and joy (3)
593	where all is tears, may we sow joy (2)
606	our boundless source of joy and truth, of peace and love (3)
614	O friends upraise anthems of joy and holy praise (1)
616	love, joy, hope, like flowers spring in his path to birth (3
617	one with the joy that breaketh into song (2)
620	Jerusalem, God grant that I may see thine endless joy (5)
620	joy, and of the same partaker ever be (5)
623	O what their joy and their glory must be (1)
623	city of peace that brings joy evermore (2)
630	Here we drink of joy unmeasured (5)
640	aught of joy or hope foretell (1)
641	share thy joy at last (4)
642	O hope of every contrite heart, O joy of all the meek (3)
642	Jesus, our only joy be thou, as thou our prize wilt be (5)
649, 650	O Jesus, joy of loving hearts (1)
657	joy of heaven, to earth come down (1)
665	joy doth wait on his command (4)
669	in his own time grant thee the sun of joy at last (4)
681	inspire us from above with joy and strength for duty (5)
695, 696	Yet when again in this new world you give us the joy (4)
695, 696	joy we had, the brightness of your Sun (4)
701	for my joy bestower, Jesus, enters in (3)
701	Joy from tribulation, hope from desolation (3)
703	through joy or sorrow, as thou deemest best (3)

joyful

11	joyful rise to pay thy morning sacrifice (1)
36	our Savior Jesus Christ, joyful in thine appearing (1)
49	our joyful hearts and voices raise (3)
61, 62	her heart with joyful hope is springing (2)
83	O come, all ye faithful, joyful and triumphant (1)
83	we too will thither bend our joyful footsteps (4)
87	Joyful, all ye nations, rise (1)
94, 95	angels praising God, who thus addressed their joyful song (5)
103	Upon this joyful holy night ... we bless your name (3)
106	with them the joyful tidings first begun (1)
106	he that was born upon this joyful day (6)
119	As with joyful steps they sped to that lowly manger bed (2)
122, 123	alleluia, joyful mother, all thy children sing with thee (2)
129, 130	shout through them their joyful greeting (2)
136, 137	for which in joyful strains we raise the voice of prayer (4)
180	He is risen, he is risen! Tell it out with joyful voice (1)

185, 186	therefore let us joyful be (1)
192	This joyful Eastertide, away with sin and sorrow (1)
193	in this our joyful Eastertide (4)
210	Now let the heavens be joyful, let earth her song begin (3)
215	Hark, the choirs of angel voices joyful alleluias sing (1)
223, 224	Hail this joyful day's return (1)
244	Come, pure hearts, in joyful measure sing (1)
321	furnished well with joyful guests (2)
333	Now the Body Now the Blood ... the joyful celebration (1)
344	Thanks we give and adoration for thy Gospel's joyful sound (2)
360, 361	hear now thy servants when their joyful voices rise (1)
376	Joyful, joyful, we adore thee, God of glory, Lord of love (1)
396, 397	with ever joyful hearts and blessed peace to cheer us (2)
415	Through all eternity, to thee a joyful song I'll raise (5)
439	sing and joyful be, and through eternity, I'll sing on (3)
530	to earth's remotest bound all may heed the joyful sound (1)
531	whene'er the joyful sound is heard (2)
537	with joyful song (4)
539	till God shall bring his kingdom's joyful day (3)
625	onward as ye go some joyful anthem sing (3)
710	Make a joyful noise unto the Lord (RC)

joyfully

33-35	joyfully chanting holy hymns to praise you (3)
122, 123	there to thee for ever singing alleluia joyfully (4)
178	joyfully sing to our Savior (4)
294	joyfully now God's praises we sing (3)
413	Joyfully, heartily resounding (2)

joyless

6, 7	joyless is the day's return till thy mercy's beams I see (2)

joyous

125, 126	joyous as when the reapers bear their ... treasures home (2)
284	The joyous notes pursue and louder anthems raise (8)
293	the world is bright with the joyous saints (3)
427	Let all the earth around ring joyous with the sound (4)

joys

97	heaping joys for thee (2)
98	lead us all with hearts aflame unto the joys above us (4)
150	from worldly joys abstain (2)
226, 227	joys which earth and heaven entwine (5)
228	joys that last for evermore (5)
253	see the saints above, how great their joys (1)
278	sing we of the joys of Mary (1)
278	Sing again the joys of Mary when she saw the risen Lord (3)
346	oh, count us worthy, Christ, thy joys to share (2)
351	possess, in sweet communion, joys ... earth cannot afford (2)
374	but all their joys are one (1)
392	Come, we who love the Lord, and let our joys be known (1)
392	children of the heavenly King may speak their joys abroad (2)
441, 442	joys that through all time abide (4)
457	that life to win, whose joys eternal flow (4)
487	such a heart as joys in love (3)

488	may I reach heaven's joys, bright heaven's Sun (3)
500	come, pour thy joys on humankind (1)
510	our souls, how heavily they go to reach eternal joys (2)
543	tell all the earth thy joys, and boast salvation nigh (1)
549, 550	In our joys and in our sorrows (4)
620	Thy joys when shall I see (1)
624	I know not, O, I know not, what joys await us there (1)

jubilant

432	each jubilant chord reecho around (3)
624	They stand, those halls of Zion, all jubilant with song (2)

jubilation

518	in exultant jubilation pours perpetual melody (2)

jubilee

96	Shepherds, why this jubilee (2)
203	in laud and jubilee and praise (5)

Judah

536	Judah is glad to see his day (3)

Judas

231	For one in place of Judas (2/2-24)

Jude

232	Saint Simon and Saint Jude (2/10-28)

judge

63, 64	when as judge, thou drawest nigh (3)
158	man to judge thee hath in hate pretended (1)
364	When you shalt come to be our judge (8)
366	As our judge thou wilt appear (7)
462	Rise, God, judge thou the earth in might (3)
481	Rejoice in glorious hope. Our Lord the Judge shall come (4)
521	O Judge divine of human strife (4)
570, 571	Come today, our Judge, our Glory (5)
596	Judge eternal, throned in splendor (1)
677	Judge not the Lord by feeble sense (4)

judgment

18	through your judgment find your grace (1)
70	Herald, sound the note of judgment (1)
159	saw him then from judgment taken (3)
171	Follow to the judgment hall (2)
370	the sweet "Well done" in judgment hour (3)
421	we for judgment there must stand (2)
469, 470	no place ... earth's failures have such kindly judgment (2)
469, 470	such kindly judgment given (2)
568	judgment is thine, and condemneth our pride (1)
570, 571	For all days are days of judgment (4)
596	with thy living fire of judgment purge this land (1)
600, 601	come with thy timeless judgment now (1)

judgment's
226, 227   rule us by thy judgment's line (4)

judgments
532, 533   thy truth and thy judgments shall spread all abroad (2)
600, 601   set thy judgments in the earth (5)

just
151   if nought but just reward we win (1)
151   he is merciful and just, here is my comfort and my trust (3)
293   for the saints of God are just folk like me (3)
408   Within the kingdom of his might, Lo, all is just (2)
408   all is just and all is right (2)
413   just is our God (3)
424   In the just reward of labor (2)
528   May your care and mercy lead us to a just society (4)
532, 533   How just, King of saints, and true are thy ways (1)
554   when we find ourselves in the place just right (1)
566   thy just rule shall fill the earth (2)
661   just off the hills of brown (1)
670   him, in all his ways, adore, wise ... wonderful ... just (4)
693   Just as I am ... O Lamb of God, I come (1-6)
720   Then conquer we must, when our cause it is just (2)

justice
65   His rule is peace and freedom ... justice, truth and love (2)
125, 126   justice shall guard his throne above (5)
182   learns his joy, his justice, love, and praise (5)
375   Through all his kingdom's wide domain ... justice reign (3)
375   his righteousness and justice reign (3)
423   thy justice like mountains high soaring above (2)
462   justice, from her heavenly bower, look down on us below (2)
469, 470   there's a kindness in his justice ... more than liberty (1)
568   stir us to work for thy justice and charity (2)
570, 571   all who cry for peace and justice (1)
597   guide us to justice, truth, and love (1)
600, 601   Bring justice to our land, that all may dwell secure (3)
605   Rulers of earth, give ear. Should you not justice show (2)
607   dawns the morning glorious when truth and justice reign (4)
615   when justice shall be throned in might (4)
681   where justice wins its fight thou art the Kingdom molding (4)

justly
605   Do justly, love mercy, walk humbly with your God (1-3)
605   Then justly, in mercy we'll humbly walk with God (4)

keenest
559   thou didst feel its keenest woe (2)

keep
3, 4   he, in all we do or say, would keep us free from harm (1)
3, 4   that he ... would keep us free from harm this day (1)
3, 4   keep us from causing others pain (2)
21, 22   while you keep our body whole (2)
33-35   Though bodies slumber, hearts shall keep their vigil (5)

43	keep me, O keep me, King of kings (1)
43	keep me, King of kings, beneath thine own almighty wings (1)
44, 45	from all ill dreams your children keep (2)
78, 79	angels keep their watch of wondering love (2)
119	Holy Jesus, every day keep us in the narrow way (4)
122, 123	grant us, blessed Trinity ... to keep thine Easter (4)
122, 123	at the last to keep thine Easter with thy faithful saints (4)
146, 147	Now let us all with one accord ... keep vigil (1)
146, 147	keep vigil with our heavenly Lord in his temptation (1)
146, 147	keep vigil ... in his temptation and his fast (1)
150	O keep us, Savior dear, ever constant by thy side (5)
152	the penitent who keep this holy fast of Lent (1)
168, 169	Ah, keep my heart thus moved to stand thy cross beneath (3)
185, 186	So let us keep the festival to which the Lord invites us (3)
210	round world keep high triumph, and all that is therein (3)
230	Then come, all Christian people, keep festival today (3)
312	Lord, may the tongues which "Holy" sang keep free (2)
312	keep free from all deceiving (2)
324	Let all mortal flesh keep silence (1)
337	From tainting mischief keep them pure and clear (3)
340, 341	may the Church still waiting for you keep love's tie (3)
340, 341	keep love's tie unbroken, Lord (3)
340, 341	in our hearts keep watch and ward (4)
345	from harm and danger keep thy children free (2)
396, 397	keep us in his grace, and guide us when perplexed (2)
399	on us you keep your shepherd's eye (2)
402, 403	Church with psalms must shout, no door can keep them out (2)
457	grant us that way to know, that truth to keep (4)
478	in love your children keep to life unending (2)
503, 504	Keep far our foes, give peace at home (6)
517	happy they who keep thy laws nor from thy precepts stray (4)
549, 550	from each idol that would keep us (3)
559	guard us, guide us, keep us, feed us (1)
563	O pray that faith and virtue may keep thee to the last (4)
579	who bidd'st the mighty ocean deep its ... limits keep (1)
579	ocean deep its own appointed limits keep (1)
579	keep them by thy watchful care from every peril in the air (3)
599	keep us forever in the path, we pray (3)
607	Keep bright in us the vision of days when war shall cease (4)
608	who bidds't the mighty ocean deep its ... limits keep (1)
608	its own appointed limits keep (1)
635	Sing, pray, and keep his ways unswerving (2)
651	He trust us with his world, to keep it clean and fair (2)
668	From evil he shall keep thee safe (4)
669	griefs that ... keep thy heart dismayed (4)
699	make and keep me pure within (3)

keeper

44, 45	we pray ... our guard and keeper you would be (1)

keepeth

408	What God's almighty power hath made ... mercy keepeth (2)
408	his gracious mercy keepeth (2)

keeping
- 24 through all the world her watch is keeping (2)
- 109 lay keeping their sheep on a cold winter's night (1)
- 115 while shepherds watch are keeping (1)
- 159 At the cross her vigil keeping stood the mournful mother (1)
- 194, 195 tear us from his keeping ever (3)
- 289 safe rest they in thy keeping (2)
- 424 future needs in earth's safe-keeping (1)
- 525 yet saints their watch are keeping (3)

keeps
- 329, 331 Jesus, with the Law complying, keeps the feast (3)
- 530 made the world and keeps it still (2)
- 585 spares not, keeps not, all outpours (3)
- 659, 660 in work that keeps faith sweet and strong (3)
- 668 his own he safely keeps (2)

kept
- 99 While shepherds kept their watching (1)
- 231 who kept your law of love (2/6-11)
- 284 Around his sacred tomb a willing watch ye kept (6)
- 363 still imploring thy love and favor, kept to us always (5)
- 706 to glory kept me blind (1)

key
- 56 O come, thou Key of David, come (5)
- 163 earth inherits heaven's key (3)

keys
- 481 the keys of death and hell to Christ the Lord are given (3)

killed
- 98 All the little boys he killed at Bethlehem in his fury (3)

killeth
- 487 such a life as killeth death (1)

killing
- 572 Weary of all trumpeting, weary of all killing (1)

kin
- 529 Who serves my Father as his child is surely kin to me (2)

kind
- 81 with Mary we behold it, the Virgin Mother kind (2)
- 152 Kind Maker of the world, O hear the fervent prayer (1)
- 158 For me, kind Jesus, was thy incarnation (4)
- 158 Therefore, kind Jesus, since I cannot pay thee (5)
- 159 Fount of love, Redeemeer kind (5)
- 389 for he is kind (1,7)
- 404 slow to anger, merciful and kind (3)
- 411 forget not all his benefits! The Lord to thee is kind (2)
- 469, 470 the heart of the Eternal is most wonderfully kind (3)
- 479 blest be his compassion infinitely kind (2)
- 480 Sweet were his words and kind his look (2)

547	with kind and gentle hearts forgive (4)
612	Love is kind, and suffers long (2)
642	to those who fall, how kind thou art (3)

kindle
501, 502	come, kindle in our hearts your fire (1)
510	kindle a flame of sacred love in ... cold hearts of ours (1)
510	love, and that shall kindle ours (4)
516	kindle it, thy holy flame bestowing (1)
704	kindle a flame of sacred love upon the altar of my heart (1)

kindles
610	use the love your Spirit kindles still to save (2)

kindliness
482	Lord of all kindliness, Lord of all grace (3)

kindling
299	earth, kindling, blazed her loud acclaim (1)
419	kindling hearts that burn for thee (4)
672	kindling to the perfect day that never shall be past (3)

kindly
288	by deeds of kindly love for thy mercies grateful prove (3)
292	kindly earth with timely birth may yield her fruits again (2)
469, 470	no place ... earth's failures have such kindly judgment (2)
469, 470	such kindly judgment given (2)
558	preach thee, too, as love knows how, by kindly deeds (3)
558	by kindly deeds and virtuous life (3)

kindness
414	Full of kindness and compassion, slow to anger (5)
469, 470	there's a kindness in his justice ... more than liberty (1)
489	in kindness, as a king might send his son, himself a king (3)
586	every deed of human kindness done in love is done to thee (3)
633	loose our tongues to tell your kindness (3)

kindred
232	he welcomed them as kindred on equal terms to be (2/10-23)
450, 451	Let every kindred, every tribe on this terrestrial ball (6)
549, 550	turned from home and toil and kindred (2)
687, 688	let goods and kindred go, this mortal life also (4)

king
43	keep me, O keep me, King of kings (1)
43	keep me, King of kings, beneath thine own almighty wings (1)
50	Hosanna to the anointed King, to David's holy Son (3)
56	be thyself our King of Peace (7)
61, 62	therefore we sing to greet our King (3)
66	born a child, and yet a king (3)
70	Christ, the Savior King, has come (R)
73	The King shall come when morning dawns (1,3,5)
73	Thy people pray, come quickly, King of kings (5)
74	Blest be the King whose coming is in the name of God (1-4)
75	Proclaim to a desolate people the coming of their King (2)

76	glad tidings of the King of kings (1)
77	child whom Mary bore, the Christ, the everlasting King (1)
78, 79	praises sing to God the King, and peace to men on earth (2)
82	extol our God and King (3)
83	come, and behold him born the King of angels (1)
87	Hark! the herald angels sing glory to the new-born King (1,R)
89, 90	from heaven's all-gracious King (1)
92	song children sing to the Lord, Christ our King (1)
92	praising Christ, heaven's King (4)
93	come and worship, worship Christ, the new-born King (R)
96	Christ, the Lord, the new-born King (3)
98	Unto us a boy is born, the King of all creation (1,5)
100	let earth receive her King (1)
106	eternal praise to heaven's almighty King (6)
109	Nowell, Nowell ... born is the King of Israel (R)
109	to seek for a king was their intent (3)
113	You need not fear King Herod (2)
114	Jesus your King is born, Jesus is born (R)
115	This, this is Christ the King whom shepherds guard (R)
115	come, peasant, king, to own him (3)
115	the King of kings salvation brings (3)
119	Christ, to thee, our heavenly King (3)
119	there for ever may we sing alleluias to our King (5)
124	It shines to herald forth the King (1)
127	gold the King of kings proclaimeth (4)
128	Born a King on Bethlehem's plain (2)
128	King for ever, ceasing never over us all to reign (2)
128	King and God and Sacrifice (5)
131, 132	King Herod trembled for his throne (1)
133, 134	To you, the King of glory ... faithful hearts ... bow (3)
135	Prophet, Priest, and King supreme (2)
153	Blessed is the King who comes in the name of the Lord (1)
154, 155	All glory, laud, and honor to thee, Redeemer, King (R)
154, 155	Thou art the King of Israel, thou David's royal Son (1)
154, 155	who in the Lord's Name comest, the King and Blessed One (1)
154, 155	who in all good delightest, thou good and gracious King (5)
160	Here the King of all the ages (2)
161	The flaming banners of our King advance (1)
162	how God the nations' King should be (2)
162	each crimsoned bough proclaims the King of glory now (3)
165	Jesus Christ, the world's Redeemer ... reigns as King (1)
165	from that cross now reigns as King (1)
165	the King of heavenly beauty gently on thine arms extend (5)
166	Jesus Christ, the world's Redeemer ... reigns as King (1)
166	from that cross now reigns as King (1)
166	the King of heavenly beauty gently on thine arms extend (5)
174	praise to our victorious King (1)
178	He is the King of creation (1)
179	all fresh gifts returned with her returning King (2)
181	rejoicing in the Lamb of God, to Christ the eternal King (3)
183	have mercy, victor King, ever reigning. Amen. Alleluia (8)
184	that the Lamb is King of kings (1)
188, 189	Lives again our glorious King (2)
191	Jesus Christ, the King of glory (1)
193	O Jesus, King of gentleness (3)

King's

647   I walk the King's highway (1-3)

kingdom

24	thy kingdom stands, and grows for ever (4)
54	Boundless shall your kingdom be (4)
57, 58	claim the kingdom for thine own (4)
66	now thy gracious kingdom bring (3)
67	since the kingdom now is here (2)
80	that in his kingdom bright and fair ... his glory share (4)
104	lie within the roadway To pave his kingdom come (2)
121	sent you his kingdom to proclaim, his holy will to do (2)
170	though empires rise and fall ... Kingdom shall not cease (3)
170	Kingdom shall not cease to grow till love embraces all (3)
175	day whereon Christ arose, breaking the kingdom of death (R)
213	share both the nature and kingdom divine (3)
220, 221	thou claim'st the kingdom as thine own (2)
230	until you reach the promised goal, a kingdom to inherit (3)
232	saw the kingdom come (2/6-29)
302	thy Church be gathered into thy kingdom (2)
303	thy Church be gathered into thy kingdom by thy Son (4)
340, 341	in the world to which you send us, let your kingdom come (4)
340, 341	let your kingdom come, O Lord (4)
347	till in his kingdom we behold his face (1)
359	theirs by the love of Christ a kingdom won (4)
401	On Zion's sacred height his kingdom he maintains (3)
408	Within the kingdom of his might, Lo, all is just (2)
433	ordaining, maintaining his kingdom divine (2)
463, 464	He is the Truth. Seek him in the Kingdom of Anxiety (2)
481	His kingdom cannot fail, he rules o'er earth and heaven (3)
524	I love thy kingdom, Lord, the house of thine abode (1)
530	spread, thou mighty word, spread the kingdom of the Lord (1)
535	his kingdom is glorious, he rules over all (1)
540	the circle of the earth shall then proclaim thy kingdom (3)
544	his kingdom stretch from shore to shore (1)
551	His kingdom tarries long (2)
555	the heavenly kingdom comes (2)
560	for theirs is the kingdom of heaven (1,8)
569	through the thick darkness thy kingdom is hastening (4)
573	thy kingdom come, O Lord, thy will be done (R)
598	seek the kingdom of thy peace (3)
613	Thy kingdom come, O God! Thy rule, O Christ, begin (1)
615	Thy kingdom come, on bended knee the passing ages pray (1)
616	his kingdom still increasing, a kingdom without end (4)
681	where justice wins its fight thou art the Kingdom molding (4)
687, 688	his kingdom is for ever (4)
711	Seek ye first the kingdom of God and its righteousness (RC)

kingdom's

375	Through all his kingdom's wide domain ... justice reign (3)
539	till God shall bring his kingdom's joyful day (3)
594, 595	lest we miss thy kingdom's goal (3)
615	faithful souls have yearned to see ... that kingdom's day (1)
615	see on earth that kingdom's day (1)

kingdoms

131, 132	he who offers heavenly birth sought not the kingdoms (1)
131, 132	sought not the kingdoms of this earth (1)
562	Crowns and thrones may perish, kingdoms rise and wane (4)

kingly

168, 169	O kingly head, surrounded with mocking crown of thorn (1)
259	not with his angel host, not in his kingly state (1)
359	Anoint them kings. Yea, kingly kings, O Lord (4)
560	when you come in your kingly power (A)

kings

43	keep me, O keep me, King of kings (1)
43	keep me, King of kings, beneath thine own almighty wings (1)
73	Thy people pray, come quickly, King of kings (5)
76	glad tidings of the King of kings (1)
115	the King of kings salvation brings (3)
127	gold the King of kings proclaimeth (4)
128	We three kings of Orient are (1)
184	that the Lamb is King of kings (1)
324	King of kings, yet born of Mary (2)
359	Anoint them kings. Yea, kingly kings, O Lord (4)
436	The King of kings is drawing near (1)
483	King of kings, and Lord of lords (2)
491	Prophets, shepherds, kings, advise (1)
494	crown him, ye kings, with many crowns ... King of all (5)
517	in glory throned, Lord God, great King of kings (3)
522, 523	Jesus ... makes them kings and priests to God (4)
522, 523	his love his people raises over self to reign as kings (4)
551	to serve the King of kings (1)
596	Lord of lords and King of kings (1)
616	Kings shall bow down before him (4)

kingship

255	help us to know your kingship (2)
598	mocked thy saving kingship (1)

kiss

112	worshiped the beloved with a kiss (3)

knee

96	come, adore on bended knee Christ, the Lord (3)
109	full reverently upon their knee (5)
119	to bend the knee before him whom heaven and earth adore (2)
252	Unto which must every knee bow in deep humility (1)
366	adoring, bend the knee and confess the mystery (4)
435	At the Name of Jesus every knee shall bow (1)
484, 485	we bow the knee, we fall before thee (2)
615	Thy kingdom come, on bended knee the passing ages pray (1)

kneel

92	Wise Men three to him led, kneel they low by his bed (3)
114	Come kneel before the radiant boy (4)
332	thus inspired with holy fear, before thine altar kneel (1)
452	when doubters kneel and waverers stand (3)

574, 575   Before thy throne, O God, we kneel (1)

kneeling
252   kneeling in her lowly cell, by the angel Gabriel (2)
333   Now the kneeling, now the plea ... Father's arms in welcome (1)

kneels
602   Kneels at the feet of his friends (1)

knees
60   At your great Name, O Jesus, now all knees must bend (4)
325   Let us break bread together on our knees (1)
325   when I fall on my knees, with my face to the rising sun (R)
325   Let us drink wine together on our knees (2)
325   Let us praise God together on our knees (3)
363   to thee all knees are bent, all voices pray (1)
477   given the Name to which all knees shall bow (4)
602   Loving puts us on our knees (4)

knelt
114   The chiefs from far before him knelt with gifts of fox (3)
257   But silent knelt the mother blest of the yet silent word (4)
266   there he knelt down before her face (2)
276   he knelt beneath the olive shade (4)
652, 653   Jesus knelt to share with thee the silence of eternity (3)

knew
18   he knew you, Lord, would answer him (2b)
85, 86   before the world knew day or night (1)
102   scorned, rejected, tears and smiles like us he knew (4)
278   beneath the cross of Jesus ... weight of suffering knew (2)
284   On earth ye knew his wondrous grace (1)
293   lived and died for the Lord they loved and knew (1)
392   Let those refuse to sing that never knew our God (2)
448, 449   for us temptations sharp he knew (2)
661   before they ever knew the peace of God (2)
674   the truth we dimly knew (3)
683, 684   Where is the blessedness I knew when first I saw the Lord (2)
689   afterward I knew he moved my soul to seek him, seeking me (1)

knight
243   a knight without a sword (4)

knit
279   in one communion ever knit, one fellowship of love (3)
350   that closely knit in holy vow, they may in thee be one (1)

know
3, 4   that we may serve, and know his peace (3)
18   sharing, know life's victory won (3a)
47   make me burn thy love to know (5)
120   know you are the Bread indeed (6)
125, 126   his reign no end shall know (5)
148   Teach us to know and love you, Lord (5)
167   We may not know, we cannot tell what pains he had to bear (2)

170	They did not know, as we do now (1-3)
194, 195	by this we know thou, O grave, canst not enthrall us (1)
194, 195	our hearts know well nought from us his love shall sever (3)
231	grant us grace to know you, made flesh (2/12-21)
231	grant us grace to know you, the victor in the strife (2/5-1)
232	know not his achievements but know that he was true (2/8-24)
233, 234	the perfect love of Christ they know (3)
255	help us to know your kingship (2)
265	For know a blessed Mother thou shalt be (2)
285	Luke, thy saint, through whom we know so many ... words (1)
285	through whom we know so many gracious words of thine (1)
296	We know that Christ is raised and dies no more (1)
307	lest we fail to know thee now (2)
321	let them thy sweet mercies know (1)
332	Here may thy faithful people know ... thy love (2)
336	grant us light to see and know thee (2)
348	ours a commitment we know never ends (1)
377, 378	Know that the Lord is God indeed (2)
391	know that the Lord is God alone (1)
422	to know the breadth, length, depth, and height (2)
457	grant us that way to know, that truth to keep (4)
458	none the longed-for Christ would know (2)
465, 466	at last I come before your face to know you (3)
465, 466	to know you, my eternal God (3)
475	bow before thee, know thee, and adore thee (4)
483	to whom he manifests his love and grants his Name to know (3)
483	profit and their joy to know the mystery of his love (5)
490	When we have run with patience the race ... know the joy (3)
490	we shall know the joy of Jesus (3)
496, 497	ride on, great Conqueror, till all know thy salvation (3)
498	content to let my pride go by, to know no gain nor loss (3)
503, 504	Teach us to know the Father, Son, and thee (7)
505	teach us to know the Father's love (4)
506, 507	wisdoms which as yet know not the Lord (3)
512	make us know and choose thy way (2)
521	To know thee is eternal life (4)
539	one soul should fail to know his love and might (1)
540	till all the world thy saving grace shall know (2)
559	all our weakness thou dost know (2)
563	far more o'er thee are watching than human eyes can know (2)
564, 565	we know we at the end shall life inherit (3)
574, 575	teach us to know our faults, O God (2)
596	feed all those who do not know thee (3)
597	for all the earth shall know the Lord (2)
610	that your servants, Lord, in freedom may your mercy know (4)
610	may your mercy know and live (4)
617	enough to know that we are serving thee (3)
624	I know not, O, I know not, what joys await us there (1)
629	make us all go on to know with nobler powers conferred (3)
631	wisdom comes to those who know thee (1)
642	love of Jesus, what it is, none but who love him know (4)
647	I know not where the road will lead I follow day by day (1)
647	or where it ends, I only know (1)
647	I know not if the way is long, and no one else can say (1)
647	when I shall know why in this life I walk (3)

673	The first one ever, oh, ever to know (1-3)
673	first one ... to know of the birth of Jesus was the Maid (1)
673	first one ... to know of Messiah, Jesus (2)
673	first ones ... to know of the rising of Jesus (3)
683, 684	The dearest idol I have known, whate'er that idol be (4)
685	should my zeal no languor know (2)
695, 696	we know that God is with us night and morning (1)
698	I know not how to ask or what to say (1)
698	I only know my need, as deep as life (1)
700	so shall our way be safe, our feet no straying know (2)
702	Lord thou ... dost know where'er I rest, where'er I go (1)
408	all who know his power proclaim aloud the wondrous story (3)

knowest
152	thou knowest our infirmity (2)
320	thou, who all things canst and knowest (6)
702	thou knowest all that I have planned (1)

knoweth
339	Joy, the best that any knoweth (2)

knowing
149	knowing ourselves baptized into your death (2)
199, 200	peace which evermore passeth human knowing (4)
587	knowing thee may grow in grace (2)
706	knowing well, that if I love you, you ... loved me first (3)

knowledge
56	to us the path of knowledge show (2)
148	our foolish confidence, our pride of knowledge ... sin (4)
248, 249	for many a generation hid in God's fore-knowledge lay (1)
275	all truth and knowledge see in the beatific vision (4)
302, 303	Knowledge and faith and life immortal Jesus ... imparts (1)
369	still how far beneath thy feet our ... knowledge lies (3)
369	our groundling knowledge lies (3)
404	glad in the knowledge of your love so great (2)
412	Knowledge and truth, loud sounding wisdom (6)
440	our knowledge, sense, and sight lie in deepest darkness (2)
455, 456	beyond all knowledge and all thought (1)
480	like him in grace and knowledge grow as years (1)
480	grace and knowledge grow as years and strength increase (1)
584	that as to knowledge we attain we may in wisdom grow (2)
586	thou, the peace that passeth knowledge (2)
615	when knowledge, hand in hand with peace (5)
615	knowledge ... shall walk the earth abroad (5)
631	Light of knowledge, ever burning (3)
631	Light of knowledge ... shed on us thy deathless learning (3)
702	wondrous knowledge, awful might (2)

known
61, 62	No eye has known the sight, no ear heard such delight (3)
131, 132	When Christ's appearing was made known (1)
131, 132	he, to whom no sin was known, might cleanse his people (3)
139	Triune God is thus made known in Christ as love unending (2)
148	We have not known you (2)

232	for ... those whose witness is only known to you (2/11-1)
242	O Savior, make thy presence known to all who doubt (5)
254	For of your Church, Lord, you made known this saint (2)
280	God ... to whom the number of the starry host is known (1)
284	join with our earth-bound song to make the Savior known (1)
304	His presence ... is in such friendship better known (4)
305, 306	be known to us in breaking of the Bread (4)
343	Be known to us in breaking bread, and do not then depart (3)
346	we here have known the resurrection hour (1)
392	Come, we who love the Lord, and let our joys be known (1)
394, 395	your hands uphold earth's mysteries known or yet untold (2)
394, 395	let peace, descending like a dove, make known ... love (3)
394, 395	let peace ... make known on earth your healing love (3)
398	not a plant or flower below but makes thy glories known (3)
413	He has made known his great salvation (1)
427	No lovelier antiphon in all high heaven is known (3)
433	he chastens and hastens his will to make known (1)
437, 438	Make known his might, the deeds his arm has done (2)
475	Now his own who have known God (1)
475	thou alone shalt be known Lord of all our being (2)
476	he speaks to us in human terms to make his glory known (4)
494	who every grief hath known that wrings the human breast (2)
501, 502	to us your varied gifts make known (3)
506, 507	hundred men and women turned the known world upside down (4)
539	make known to every heart his saving grace (4)
580	known the ecstasy of winging through untraveled realms (3)
587	Our Father, by whose Name all fatherhood is known (1)
603, 604	Thus freely loved, though fully known (4)
610	making known the needs and burdens (3)
678, 679	Make his deeds known to the peoples (2)
683, 684	the dearest idol I have known, whate'er that idol be (4)

knows

319	all creation knows the love of God (1)
410	well our feeble frame he knows (3)
441, 442	peace is there that knows no measure (4)
459	heaven ... knows neither near nor far (2)
515	From the height which knows no measure (1)
558	preach thee, too, as love knows how, by kindly deeds (3)
563	he knows thine hourly need (1)
666	Let Israel trust in God, no bounds his mercy knows (4)

Kyrie

319	Kyrie eleison (1-2)

labels

603, 604	he sees not labels but a face, a person, and a name (3)

labor

226, 227	In our labor, be our aid (2)
228	in our labor inward rest (2)
277	toil and labor cannot weary love enduring unto death (2)
424	In the just reward of labor (2)
434	every labor of his hands shows something worthy of a God (1)
541	Come, labor on (1-5)

564, 565	I'll labor night and day to be a pilgrim (3)
586	where the solitary labor, thou art there with them alone (2)
586	bless us in our daily labor (3)
607	Lord, strengthen all who labor that we may find release (3)
611	praising God by labor at his bench (3)
611	easy yokes that made the labor less (4)
611	All who labor, listen to his call (5)
621, 622	there no night brings rest from labor (3)
705	A world in need now summons us to labor, love and give (2)

labored

289	They reap not where they labored (3)

laborers

540	O harvest Lord ... the laborers how few (2)

laboring

429	sends the laboring conscience peace (3)

labors

287	For all the saints, who from their labors rest (1)
482	be there at our labors (2)
621, 622	hereafter these thy labors may with endless gifts be paid (5)

labs

412	Classrooms and labs loud boiling test tubes (5)

ladder

453	he saw in a vision a ladder so high (1)
453	has raised up a ladder of mercy for me (R)
453	The ladder is long, it is strong and well made (2)
453	Who would not want to climb such a ladder as this (4)

laden

342	Come unto me, you heavy laden (2)
611	Heavy laden, gladly come to him (6)

lady

265	most highly favored lady, "Gloria!" (1-4)
620	Our Lady sings Magnificat with tune surpassing sweet (4)

laid

94, 95	in a manger laid (4)
96	See him in a manger laid whom the angels praise above (4)
101	the little Lord Jesus laid down his sweet head (1)
102	where a mother laid her baby in a manger for his bed (1)
106	her Son, the Savior, in a manger laid (4)
110	She laid him in a stall at Bethlehem (2)
115	What child is this, who, laid to rest, on Mary's lap (1)
117, 118	guide where our infant Redeemer is laid (1,5)
172	Were you there when they laid him in the tomb (4)
204	In the grave they laid him, Love whom hate had slain (2)
204	laid in the earth like grain that sleeps unseen (2)
205	sing today with one accord the life laid down (4)
237	when they laid the mortal down for the life immortal (1)

284	so innocent and mild while in the manger laid (2)
304	in awe and wonder to recall his life laid down for me (1)
349	when the hands are on them laid (2)
379	God who laid the earth's foundation (1)
468	he was born on Christmas ... and laid in a manger (1)
495	all our sins on thee were laid (2)
500	by whose aid the world's foundations first were laid (1)
573	thy Word made flesh, and in a manger laid (5)
621, 622	bear the burden laid on thee (5)
636, 637	is laid for your faith in his excellent word (1)
645, 646	on his shoulder gently laid (3)

lain

204	wheat that in dark earth many days has lain (1)
204	he that for three days in the grave had lain (3)

lake

231	You called him from his fishing upon Lake Galilee (2/11-30)
549, 550	as, of old, Saint Andrew heard it by the Galilean lake (2)

Lamb

16, 17	Lamb of God restored our peace (2)
59	Lo, the Lamb, so long expected (3)
61, 62	Lamb of God, the heavens adore you (3)
112	If I were a shepherd, I would bring a lamb (4)
131, 132	Within the Jordan's sacred flood the ... Lamb ... stood (3)
131, 132	heavenly Lamb in meekness stood (3)
138	grant us, O Lord, to see the marriage supper of the Lamb (4)
165, 166	on the cross the Lamb is lifted (2)
173	The Paschal Lamb, like Isaac's ram (2)
181	Awake and sing the song of Moses and the Lamb (1)
181	rejoicing in the Lamb of God, to Christ the eternal King (3)
181	sing in sweeter notes the song of Moses and the Lamb (4)
183	A lamb the sheep redeemeth (2)
184	that the Lamb is King of kings (1)
184	alleluia, Christ, our Paschal lamb indeed (R)
202	the Lamb of God without a stain (3)
213	till we meet at the feast of the Lamb (4)
213	to the Lamb that was slain, hallelujah again (5)
253	with united breath, ascribe their conquest to the Lamb (2)
286	triumph by the Lamb have gained (3)
307	Paschal Lamb, thine offering, finished once for all (4)
307	worship thee, the Lamb who died (5)
374	Worthy the Lamb that died, they cry, to be exalted thus (2)
374	Worthy the Lamb, our lips reply, for he was slain for us (2)
374	to adore the Lamb (4)
417, 418	Worthy is Christ, the Lamb who was slain (1)
417, 418	Blessing, honor, glory, and might be to God and the Lamb (4)
417, 418	might be to God and the Lamb for ever. Amen (4)
417, 418	the Lamb who was slain has begun his reign. Alleluia (5)
421	O Lamb of God, Lord Jesus Christ (2)
421	Lamb of God ... whom God the Father gave us (2)
434	with angels join to praise the Lamb (5)
439	To God and to the Lamb, I will sing (2)
439	to the Lamb who is the great I AM (2)

490	The Lamb is the light of the city of God (R)
494	Crown him with many crowns, the Lamb upon his throne (1)
495	Paschal Lamb, by God appointed (2)
535	fall down on their faces, and worship the Lamb (3)
582, 583	O holy city ... where Christ, the Lamb, doth reign (1)
597	Then shall the wolf dwell with the lamb (2)
683, 684	a light to shine upon the road that leads me to the Lamb (1)
683, 684	purer light ... mark the road that leads me to the Lamb (5)
691	My faith looks up to thee, thou Lamb of Calvary (1)
693	Just as I am ... O Lamb of God, I come (1-6)
701	Thine I am, O holy Lamb (1)

Lamb's

174	At the Lamb's high feast we sing praise (1)
202	The Lamb's high banquet called to share (1)
280	veiled ... but written in the Lamb's great book of life (3)
316, 317	the Lamb's great marriage fest of bliss and love (3)

lambs

| 75 | the lambs he'll gently hold (3) |

lame

23	Apostles made a lame man walk (2)
458	He made the lame to run, he gave the blind their sight (4)
493	leap, ye lame, for joy (5)
567	To thee they went, the blind ... deaf ... palsied ... lame (1)

lamp

104	A stable lamp is lighted Whose glow shall wake the sky (1)
163	lo, a more heavenly lamp shines here (2)
627	Lamp of our feet, whereby we trace our path (1)
632	O make thy Church, dear Savior, a lamp of purest gold (3)

lamps

25, 26	the lamps are lit to pierce the night (2)
37	one by one the lamps of evening shine (2)
61, 62	Your lamps prepare and hasten there (1)
68	See that your lamps are burning, replenish them with oil (2)
614	new lamps be lit, new tasks begun (3)

land

230	In Salem's street was gathered a crowd from many a land (2)
233, 234	true lights that lighten every land (2)
236	crown of the true of every land (1)
237	for by faith they saw the land decked in all its glory (2)
237	Who will grasp the land of Life (3)
243	went forth throughout the land (1)
246	aching hearts in every land cry out (3)
268, 269	blessed ... land of promise fashioned for his ... home (2)
291	We plow the fields and scatter the good seed on the land (1)
310, 311	life ... in our true native land with thee (2)
320	eternal goodness send us in the land of life to see (5)
345	peace to our land, the fruit of truth and love (3)
366	In the glory of that land ... set at God's right hand (6)
372	deep writ upon the human heart, on sea and land (3)

375	mortals then, on land and sea ... exult (2)
380	Let the Redeemer's Name be sung through every land (1)
393	how he leads his chosen unto Canaan's promised land (1)
399	he made the sea and land, he brought the world to birth (2)
409	publishes to every land the work of an almighty hand (1)
436	O blest the land, the city blest (2)
463, 464	He is the Way. Follow him through the Land of Unlikeness (1)
498	the shadow of a mighty rock within a weary land (1)
527	marching to the promised land (1)
579	protect them ... from every peril on the land (2)
579	glad praise from space, air, land, and sea (4)
596	with thy living fire of judgment purge this land (1)
596	purge this land of bitter things (1)
599	true to our God, true to our native land (3)
600, 601	Bring justice to our land, that all may dwell secure (3)
607	O God of every nation, of every race and land (1)
608	hymns of praise from land and sea (4)
623	seeking Jerusalem, dear native land (4)
624	Jesus, in mercy bring us to that dear land of rest (4)
648	When Israel was in Egypt's land (1)
648	Go down, Moses, way down in Egypt's land (R)
648	came at length to Canaan's land (3)
690	pilgrim through this barren land (1)
690	land me safe on Canaan's side (3)
705	the wealth of this good land (1)
716	God bless our native land (1)
717	My country, 'tis of thee, sweet land of liberty (1)
717	land where my fathers died, land of the pilgrim's pride (1)
717	My native country, thee, land of the noble free (2)
717	long may our land be bright with freedom's holy light (4)
718	in this free land by thee our lot is cast (2)
720	o'er the land of the free and the home of the brave (1-2)
720	may the heaven-rescued land praise the Power (2)

lands

65	All lands will bow before him (3)
259	child, the glory of all lands (3)
302	so, from all lands thy Church be gathered ... by thy Son (2)
303	so from all lands thy Church be gathered ... by thy Son (4)
383, 384	Fair are the meadows, fairer still the woodlands (2)
383, 384	woodlands robed in the blooming garb of spring (2)
596	homesteads and the woodlands plead in silence (2)

lanes

293	You can meet them in school, or in lanes, or at sea (3)

language

168, 169	What language ... borrow to thank thee, dearest friend (4)

languid

337	our prayer so languid, and our faith so dim (2)

languish

159	seeing Christ in torment languish (1)
510	hosannas languish on our tongues and our devotion dies (3)

613   revive our longing eyes, which languish for thy sight (4)

lantern
632   a lantern to our footsteps, shines on from age to age (1)

lap
115   What child is this, who, laid to rest, on Mary's lap (1)
115   on Mary's lap is sleeping (1)

lark
9   The lark is in the sky (4)

last
14, 15	the glorious evening that shall last (2)
63, 64	let us not, for evil past be driven from thy face at last (4)
73	the day that e'er shall last (3)
102	And our eyes at last shall see him (5)
119	bring our ransomed souls at last where they need no star (4)
122, 123	at the last to keep thine Easter with thy faithful saints (4)
129, 130	first and last and only One (4)
140, 141	I have a sin of fear that when I've spun my last thread (3)
142	an Easter of unending joy we may attain at last (5)
156	Thy last and fiercest strife is nigh (4)
167	that we might go at last to heaven (3)
168, 169	see in my last strife to me thine arms extended (5)
187	Through the Red Sea brought at last (1)
228	joys that last for evermore (4)
232	last and greatest prophet, he saw the dawning ray (2/6-24)
238, 239	victors at the last, they triumph (2)
238, 239	by his grace we may be worthy of eternal bliss at last (3)
251	to us at last in mercy give eternal life with thee (4)
254	the saints of God at last prevail (1)
257	The aged Simeon sees at last his Lord, so long desired (3)
285	till thou at last the summons give (4)
290	give his angels charge at last (3)
314	face to face thy splendor, I at last shall see (4)
329, 331	That last night at supper lying (3)
335	And I will raise them up on the last day (R)
359	make each one stronger, nobler than the last (1)
359	stand at last with joy before thy face (5)
363	calling the least, the last, the lost to thee (3)
372	first, the last, beyond all thought his timeless years (1)
429	praise ... while life and thought and being last (1,4)
435	faithfully he bore it spotless to the last (2)
443	his people saw him die at last, praised be his teaching (2)
465, 466	at last I come before your face to know you (3)
486	So in the last and dreadful day (5)
524	Sure as thy truth shall last (5)
548	stand complete at last (5)
556, 557	At last the march shall end (6)
563	O pray that faith and virtue may keep thee to the last (4)
593	to wake at last in heaven's light (5)
599	till now we stand at last (2)
614	the whole Church at last be one (3)
621, 622	full of vigor ... of pleasure that shall last eternally (4)

641	share thy joy at last (4)
669	in his own time grant thee the sun of joy at last (4)
680	be thou our guide while life shall last (6)
699	O receive my soul at last (1)
720	what so proudly we hailed at the twilight's last gleaming (1)

lasting
391	what lasting honors shall we rear ... to thy Name (3)
669	Thy lasting truth and mercy, O Father, see aright (3)

late
42	Comfort every sufferer watching late in pain (4)
87	late in time behold him come (2)

latest
426	Borne upon their latest breath ... conquer death (6)

lathe
482	strong hands were skilled at the plane and the lathe (2)

latter
63, 64	who in these latter days wast born for blessing (1)

laud
5	All laud to God the Father be (5)
97	laud and honor raising (3)
115	haste to bring him laud, the babe, the son of Mary (R)
154, 155	All glory, laud, and honor to thee, Redeemer, King (R)
199, 200	to whom we give laud and praise undying (2)
203	in laud and jubilee and praise (5)
248, 249	To the Name of our salvation laud and honor let us pay (1)
263, 264	adore and laud and magnify (1)
265	all generations laud and honor thee (2)
265	my soul shall laud and magnify his holy Name (3)
373	heaven and earth, and all creation, Laud ... his Name (2)
373	all creation, laud and magnify his Name (2)
377, 378	praise, laud, and bless his Name always (3)
381	God the Father, Light-Creator, to thee laud and honor be (4)
423	all laud we would render (4)
519, 520	Laud and honor to the Father (5)
519, 520	Laud and honor to the Son (5)
519, 520	laud and honor to the Spirit, ever Three, and ever One (5)
562	glory, laud, and honor, unto Christ the King (5)
718	glory, laud, and praise be ever thine (4)

law
56	didst give the law, in cloud, and majesty, and awe (3)
129, 130	All the prophets and the Law shout through them (2)
129, 130	Law and prophets fade before him (4)
143	loving God who gave the law (2)
231	who kept your law of love (2/6-11)
256	he saw the love of God ... beyond the law (3)
329, 331	Jesus, with the Law complying, keeps the feast (3)
372	Established is his law, and changeless it shall stand (3)
431	a law of love within our hearts (3)

605	How shall my soul fulfill God's law so hard and high (4)
718	thy word our law, thy paths our chosen way (2)
719	confirm thy soul in self control, thy liberty in law (2)

laws
243	When Stephen preached against the laws (2)
243	by those laws was tried (2)
373	laws which never shall be broken (1)
373	laws ... for their guidance he hath made (1)
517	happy they who keep thy laws nor from thy precepts stray (4)
582, 583	city ... whose laws are love, whose crown is servanthood (3)
592	who sweeps a room, as for thy laws, makes that ... fine (3)
628	study, that your laws may be inscribed upon our hearts (1)

lay
89, 90	The world in solemn stillness lay to hear the angels sing (1)
92	lay their gifts before him, praise him and adore him (3)
101	The stars in the bright sky looked down where he lay (1)
108	in a manger lay to teach his people meekness (2)
109	certain poor shepherds in fields as they lay (1)
109	lay keeping their sheep on a cold winter's night (1)
109	right over the place where Jesus lay (4)
110	The snow lay on the ground, the stars shone bright (1)
151	I lay my sins before thee (1)
185, 186	Christ Jesus lay in death's strong bands (1)
201	see where he lay; let joy begin (3)
203	seek the tomb where Jesus lay (2)
233, 234	these lay the prince of this world low (3)
248, 249	for many a generation hid in God's fore-knowledge lay (1)
281	lay up treasures in the heart (4)
318	here would I lay aside each earthly load (2)
437, 438	Powers and dominions lay their glory by (3)
439	that caused the Lord of bliss to lay aside his crown (1)
439	lay aside his crown for my soul (1)
453	at night on a stone for a pillow he lay (1)
458	Heaven was his home, but mine the tomb wherein he lay (6)
552, 553	lay hold on life ... thy joy and crown eternally (1)
563	till Christ himself ... call thee to lay thine armor by (3)
675	follow Christ, nor think till death to lay it down (5)
692	in your weariness lay down your head upon my breast (1)

lays
| 87 | Mild he lays his glory by, born that we no more may die (3) |

Lazarus
| 354 | with Lazarus who once was poor may you have peace (2) |
| 356 | As angels gave poor Lazarus from all his ills release (3) |

lead
12, 13	strive to follow where you lead (2)
38, 39	let him never lead astray those you have ransomed (3)
75	to pastures of peace he'll lead them (3)
98	lead us all with hearts aflame unto the joys above us (4)
120	Christ, the Son of God, had come to lead his ... people (2)
120	lead his scattered people home (2)

250	such a Lord to lead our way in hazard and prosperity (4)
354	Into paradise may the angels lead you (1)
356	May choirs of angels lead you to Paradise on high (1)
357	Lead them onward, upward, to the holy place (4)
370	the power of God to hold and lead (5)
400	You lead back home the child of God (6)
478	lead us then day by day in your own steps, we pray (2)
491	Lead me to my Master's manger (1)
509	lead us in those paths of life whereon the righteous go (2)
512	Lead us to Christ, the living way (3)
512	lead us to holiness (3)
512	Lead us to heaven, that we may share the fullness of joy (4)
512	lead us to God, our final rest (4)
528	May your care and mercy lead us to a just society (4)
555	Lead on, O King eternal (1-3)
555	lead on, O God of might (3)
559	Lead us, heavenly Father (1)
559	lead us o'er the world's tempestuous sea (1)
561	from victory unto victory his army shall he lead (1)
586	lead us to our Sabbath rest (3)
597	a little child shall lead them all (2)
618	more glorious than the seraphim, lead their praises (2)
633	Word of truth, to all truth lead us (4)
647	I know not where the road will lead I follow day by day (1)
647	The countless hosts lead on before (3)
648	to lead the children of Israel through (2)
663	by streams serene, he safely doth me lead (1)
671	grace will lead me home (4)
690	let the fire and cloudy pillar lead me all my journey (2)
703	Lead us, O Father, in the paths of peace (1)
703	lead us through Christ, the true and living Way (1)
703	Lead us, O Father, in the paths of right (2)
703	Lead us, O Father, to the heavenly rest (3)
708	Savior, like a shepherd lead us (1)
718	lead us from night to never-ending day (4)

leader

253	Our glorious Leader claims our praise (4)
433	We all do extol thee, thou leader triumphant (3)
563	the Lord himself, thy Leader, shall all thy foes subdue (1)
624	they who with their Leader have conquered in the fight (3)

leaders

233, 234	triumphant leaders in the fray (2)
568	stir up our leaders and peoples to penitence (1)

leading

119	leading onward, beaming bright (1)
128	westward leading, still proceeding (R)
454	in sounds of gladness, leading souls redeemed to heaven (3)

leads

24	As o'er each continent and island the dawn leads on (3)
24	dawn leads on another day (3)
56	make safe the way that leads on high (5)

102	he leads his children on to the place where he is gone (5)
124	leads them on with power benign to seek the Giver (3)
300	us he leads to a feast in heaven (3)
393	how he leads his chosen unto Canaan's promised land (1)
393	light of dawn leads us on (2)
562	Christ, the royal Master, leads against the foe (1)
647	Through light and dark the road leads on (3)
664	leads me ... in paths of truth and grace (1)
665	pleasure leads us where we go (4)
675	leads you to victory o'er the grave (4)
683, 684	a light to shine upon the road that leads me to the Lamb (1)
683, 684	purer light ... mark the road that leads me to the Lamb (5)
718	God of our fathers, whose almighty hand leads forth (1)

leaf
| 149 | glorious in springtime dress of leaf and flower (3) |

lean
318	all my weariness upon thee lean (1)
318	nor do I need another arm save thine to lean upon (3)
552, 553	Cast care aside, lean on thy Guide (3)

leap
| 493 | leap, ye lame, for joy (5) |
| 544 | the prisoners leap to lose their chains (4) |

leaping
| 333 | Now the wedding Now the songs ... heart forgiven leaping (1) |

leapt
| 284 | out from death's vast room, up from the grave, he leapt (6) |

learn
171	learn of Jesus Christ to pray (1)
171	learn of him to bear the cross (2)
171	learn of Jesus Christ to die (3)
276	Lord, may we learn to drink thy cup (5)
536	who would learn the way of wisdom ... hear God's word (2)
547	so learn his love -- its length and breadth (1)
581	With grateful joy and holy fear his charity we learn (2)
597	Then enemies shall learn to love (2)
609	till all the world shall learn thy love (5)
627	Lord, grant us all aright to learn the wisdom it imparts (5)
628	to learn the truths your word imparts (1)
708	Early let us seek thy favor, early let us learn thy will (2)

learned
74	have not learned to heed the Christ (2)
279	learned from thy Holy Spirit's breath to suffer and to do (2)
521	what apostles learned of thee be ours from age to age (3)

learning
348	may we increasingly glory in learning all that it means (3)
426	learning here, by faith and love ... to sing above (5)
631	Light of knowledge ... shed on us thy deathless learning (3)

learns
  182   till all creation lives and learns his joy (5)
  182   learns his joy, his justice, love, and praise (5)

least
  255   in those least expected true servants you can find (3)
  293   not any reason -- no, not the least (2)
  327, 328 Offered was he for greatest and for least (4)
  363   calling the least, the last, the lost to thee (3)
  415   nor is the least a cheerful heart (3)

leave
  93   Sages, leave your contemplations (3)
  212   as Pilate gave them leave (4)
  231   "Leave all and follow me" (2/11-30)
  336   leaving now thine altar let us nevermore leave thee (1)
  339   leave the gloomy haunts of sadness (1)
  657   suddenly return, and never, nevermore thy temples leave (2)
  686   prone to leave the God I love (3)
  699   leave, ah, leave me not alone (2)

leaven
  185, 186 word of grace hath purged away the old and wicked leaven (4)

leaves
  179   bloom in every meadow, leaves on every bough (2)
  412   Flowers and trees, loud rustling dry leaves (2)
  420   adoration leaves no room for pride (1)
  423   we blossom and flourish, like leaves on the tree (3)
  452   transcends the world he never leaves (2)
  585   scholar's truth, flight of swallows, autumn leaves (1)

leaving
  83   leaving their flocks, draw nigh to gaze (4)
  231   leaving earthly treasures, sought riches from above (2/6-11)
  336   leaving now thine altar let us nevermore leave thee (1)
  549, 550 leaving all for his dear sake (2)
  572   leaving all, that we may be partners in your splendor (3)

led
  92   Wise Men three to him led, kneel they low by his bed (3)
  116   through Jordan's flood was led (2)
  119   so, most gracious Lord, may we evermore be led to thee (1)
  138   So, led from strength to strength, grant us ... to see (4)
  145   to be led to where God's glory flashes (2)
  149   led by your cloud by day, by night your fire (1)
  187   Like the cloud that overhead ... Isreal led (2)
  187   through the billows Israel led (2)
  188, 189 Soar we now where Christ has led (3)
  199, 200 led them with unmoistened foot through the Red Sea waters (1)
  219   the grave and hell are captive led (1)
  258   blessed was the hand that led thee (1)
  321   be all thy children thither led (1)
  348   led by your Spirit, defender and guide (2)
  349   from their bright baptismal day you have led them (1)

349	you have led them on their way (1)
363	O holy Father, who hast led thy children in all the ages (2)
363	led thy children ... with the fire and cloud (2)
426	songs of praise arose when he captive led captivity (2)
473	Led on their way by this triumphant sign (1)
492	the captor captive led (3)
519, 520	to thy Lord shalt thou be led (2)
573	led by no star, the rulers of the nations still fail (4)
599	thou who hast by thy might led us into the light (3)
709	through this earthly pilgrimage ... all thine Israel led (1)
718	Thy love divine hath led us in the past (2)

leddest

135	from there thou leddest them steadfast to Jerusalem (4)

left

50	Today he rose and left the dead, and Satan's empire fell (2)
276	For James who left his father's side (2)
281	he rose, responsive to the call, and left his task (3)
281	left his task, his gains, his all (3)
460, 461	not as orphans are we left in sorrow now (2)
480	When Jesus left his Father's throne (1)
598	till not a stone was left on stone (2)
638, 639	my company before is gone, and I am left alone with thee (1)
656	Lord, who left the heavens our life and peace to bring (2)

legions

208	but Christ their legions hath dispersed (2)
484, 485	Praise your King, ye Christian legions (1)

lend

96	Mary, Joseph, lend your aid (4)
117, 118	dawn on our darkness, and lend us thine aid (1,5)

lends

429	I'll praise him while he lends me breath (4)

length

19, 20	God's mighty actions tell at length (2)
48	at length our rest attaining, our endless Sabbath day (4)
315	So, Lord, at length when sacraments shall cease (3)
347	Christ at length ... overcome all darkness with his light (3)
422	to know the breadth, length, depth, and height (2)
487	such a feast as mends in length (2)
521	bid thy Church increase, in breadth and length (1)
547	so learn his love -- its length and breadth (1)
645, 646	through all the length of days thy goodness faileth never (6)
648	came at length to Canaan's land (3)
693	love, the breadth, length, depth, and height to prove (6)

lengthening

179	Months in due succession, days of lengthening light (3)

Lent

145	Lent calls to prayer, to trust and dedication (1)

149   walking once more the pilgrim way of Lent (1)
152   the penitent who keep this holy fast of Lent (1)

Lent's
145   or rend the soul, such grief is not Lent's goal (2)

leper
567   leper set apart and shunned, the sick with fevered frame (1)

less
592   which God doth touch and own cannot for less be told (4)
611   easy yokes that made the labor less (4)
615   But the slow watches of the night not less to God belong (2)
671   we've no less days to sing God's praise (5)
671   no less days ... than when we'd first begun (5)

lesser
551   have done with lesser things (1)

lest
146, 147   help us, lest ... we cause your Name to be betrayed (4)
146, 147   lest in anxiety (4)
212   lest dead and friendless and alone he ... deceive (4)
307   lest we fail to know thee now (2)
472   walk thou beside us lest the tempting byways lure us (3)
528   Lest the Church neglect its mission (1)
528   Lest ... the Gospel go unheard (1)
584   lest, maddened by the lust for power ... ourselves destroy (4)
594, 595   lest we miss thy kingdom's goal (3)
599   Lest our feet stray from the places ... we met thee (3)
599   lest ... we forget thee (3)

letters
434   nor wit can guess, nor reason prove which of the letters (3)
471   Inscribed upon the cross we see in shining letters (2)
471   we see in shining letters, God is love (2)

level
65   Let every hill and valley a level way appear (1)

liberal
212   those hands of liberal love indeed in infinite degree (3)

liberty
60   set free your own in glorious liberty (2)
235   How blest this habitation of gospel liberty (3)
444   he visits and redeems us, he grants us liberty (1)
469, 470   there's a kindness in his justice ... more than liberty (1)
528   asking ... world around us share your children's liberty (3)
599   ring with the harmonies of liberty (1)
717   My country, 'tis of thee, sweet land of liberty (1)
717   Our father's God, to thee, author of liberty (4)
719   confirm thy soul in self control, thy liberty in law (2)

lie

69	Mortal in darkness we lie down (2)
78, 79	O little town of Bethlehem, how still we see thee lie (1)
97	Dost thou in a manger lie, who hast all created (1)
104	lie within the roadway To pave his kingdom come (2)
174	hell's fierce powers beneath thee lie (3)
440	our knowledge, sense, and sight lie in deepest darkness (2)
480	in the circle of his arms may we forever lie (2)
541	till the long shadows o'er our pathway lie (5)
636, 637	When through fiery trials thy pathway shall lie (4)

lies

3, 4	guard ... our ears from empty praise and lies (3)
115	Why lies he in such mean estate (2)
117, 118	low lies his head with the beasts of the stall (2)
139	let us not heed worldly lies nor rest upon our merit (3)
202	all sufficient Sacrifice, beneath thee hell defeated lies (4)
346	as far as lies within our mortal power (1)
369	still how far beneath thy feet our ... knowledge lies (3)
369	our groundling knowledge lies (3)
394, 395	what lies hidden praise your might (1)
416	for the love ... from our birth over and around us lies (1)
491	show me where my Savior lies (1)
552, 553	life with its way before us lies (2)
591	From all that terror teaches ... lies of tongue and pen (2)

life

9	worlds awake to cry their blessings on the Lord of life (4)
9	Lord of life, as he goes meekly by (4)
10	restored to life and power and thought (1)
14, 15	Grant us, when this short life is past, the glorious ... (2)
21, 22	from passion's heat preserve our life (2)
27, 28	forget your blessed gift of life (3)
44, 45	A healthy life we ask of you (3)
46	death's fair night discover ... everlasting life (3)
46	the fields of everlasting life (3)
49	he rose, the prince of life and peace (1)
49	filled with all the life of God (2)
51	his own life imparting, food everlasting (4)
52	Jesus, may we lifted be from death of sin to life in thee (2)
70	to them new life is given (3)
70	Christ has come to share our life (4)
73	life to joy awakes (1)
85, 86	Remember, Lord of life and grace (3)
87	light and life to all he brings (3)
109	with his blood our life hath bought (6)
120	who gives eternal life to those that with you died (6)
121	freely as Son of Man to serve and give your life for all (3)
125, 126	To hail thy rising, Sun of life, the ... nations come (2)
128	perfume breathes a life of gathering gloom (4)
139	that we may life inherit (3)
142	yea, evermore, in life and death, Jesus, with us abide (4)
142	Abide with us, that so, this life of suffering overpast (5)
145	your way through life adorning (5)
148	to whom the words of life belong (1)

151	yea, e'en the best life faileth (2)
161	he died eternal life to bring (1)
163	the Lord of life hath victory (3)
163	sin is slain, and death brings life (3)
164	thou dost light and life restore (3)
168, 169	thine arms extended upon the cross of life (5)
171	view the Lord of life arraigned (2)
173	pouring out his life that he might to life restore us (2)
173	the glorious Prince of Life should in death be sleeping (3)
174	thou hast brought us life and light (3)
175	Rise from the grave now ... author of life and creation (4)
175	treading the pathway of death, life ... bestowest on all (4)
175	Spirit of life and of power, now flow in us (7)
175	life that in all dost abide (7)
176, 177	seek ... life everlasting (2)
179	Maker and Redeemer, life and health of all (4)
179	Thou, of life the author, death didst undergo (5)
179	all that now is fallen raise to life again (6)
182	but daily, in the midst of life (3)
183	Death and life have contended in that combat stupendous (3)
183	the Prince of life, who died, reigns immortal (3)
183	our new life obtaining (8)
184	He who gave for us his life ... for us endured the strife (2)
185, 186	brings us life from heaven (1)
185, 186	when life and death contended (2)
185, 186	the victory remained with life (2)
190	Life is yours for ever, Mary (3)
191	Christ from death to life is born (2)
191	glorious life ... immortal, on his resurrection morn (2)
191	we with him to life eternal by his resurrection rise (2)
192	My Love, the Crucified, hath sprung to life this morrow (1)
192	Lord of all life, from ill my passing life deliver (2)
194, 195	life, nor death, nor powers of hell tear us (3)
196, 197	what he brings in his hurt hands is life (1,4)
196, 197	life on life for you and me (1,4)
201	new life to all he doth afford (4)
202	endless life restored in thee (4)
202	from death to endless life restored (5)
204	thy touch can call us back to life again (4)
205	The Lord of life is risen today (2)
205	that life which cannot die (3)
205	sing today with one accord the life laid down (4)
205	the life restored (4)
205	we sing for life in us begun (5)
206	for they eternal life shall win (6)
208	the victory of life is won (1)
209	that, when our life of faith is done (4)
210	From death to life eternal, from earth unto the sky (1)
216	Spirit of life and of power (5)
216	life that in all dost abide (5)
222	Rejoice, the Lord of life ascends in triumph (1)
222	troubles of our earthly life (3)
225	Praise to the Spirit of Life (4)
225	life that in all dost abide (4)

231	we with all your servants may wear the crown of life (2/5-1)
232	O God, your two apostles won life through martyrdom `/6-29)
232	worldly gain forsaking, your path of life we share (2/9-21)
232	be bound in love together, and life eternal gain (2/10-28)
237	when they laid the mortal down for the life immortal (1)
237	Who will grasp the land of Life (3)
238, 239	praying that, this life completed (3)
242	still through his confession flows ... thy life and light (4)
245	I am the way, the truth, the life (2)
245	your glory to proclaim whereby your Spirit give us life (3)
251	to us at last in mercy give eternal life with thee (4)
260	carpenter whose life fulfilled our gracious God's design (1)
260	for him ... was the patient life of faith and humble name (3)
270	to the cross shall Life be nailed (4)
275	by death to life immortal they were born and glorified (3)
279	They all in life and death, with thee their Lord in view (2)
280	veiled ... but written in the Lamb's great book of life (3)
284	the Lord of life expire (5)
285	Historian of the Savior's life (3)
286	wrestling on till life was ended (3)
291	seed-time and the harvest, our life ... health ... food (3)
296	Reborn we share with him an Easter life (2)
296	The Father's splendor clothes the Son with life (3)
296	A new creation comes to life and grows (4)
298	that as is promised here we may eternal life inherit (2)
300	He dispels our sin and sadness, life imparts (3)
301	by whom the words of life were spoken (1)
302, 303	Knowledge and faith and life immortal Jesus ... imparts (1)
304	in awe and wonder to recall his life laid down for me (1)
305, 306	one Name we bear, one Bread of life we break (3)
308, 309	O Food to pilgrims given, O Bread of life from heaven (1)
310, 311	O grant us life that shall not end (2)
310, 311	life ... in our true native land with thee (2)
312	bodies by thy Body fed with thy new life replenish (3)
314	grant my spirit ever by thy life may live (3)
319	Here at your table every life you nourish (1)
319	when by sin our life was ended (2)
320	Let the Bread, life giving, living, be our theme (2)
320	eternal goodness send us in the land of life to see (5)
323	strength supplied through the life of him who died (1)
324	Light of Life descendeth from the realms of endless day (3)
327, 328	to all believers life eternal yields (6)
329, 331	he closed with wondrous ending his most patient life (2)
334	By your Blood new life receiving (2)
335	I am the bread of life (1)
335	my Flesh for the life of the world (2)
335	Unless ... you shall not have life within you (3)
335	I am the resurrection, I am the life (4)
336	in our life thy love divine ... flesh and blood has taken (1)
339	Sun, who all my life dost brighten (2)
339	Jesus, Bread of life, I pray thee (3)
342	O Bread of life, for sinners broken (1)
342	Thus by your death our life obtaining (2)
342	Now may your life to us descending enter our lives (3)
345	Grant us thy peace throughout our earthly life (3)

345	thy peace in life, the balm of every pain (4)
346	beheld afar that life which soon shall be (2)
346	blest by the Spirit, breath and flame of life (3)
349	give them life, your own to be (2)
350	let nothing in this life divide ... whom thou makest one (3)
352	nor life nor death may part those ... one in heart (2)
352	restore their love till life shall end (3)
353	O God of love, inspire our life (3)
355	neither sighing, but life everlasting (1)
357	Jesus, Son of Mary, fount of life alone (1)
357	heal them, Good Physician, with the balm of life (3)
358	there may they find everlasting life (1,4)
363	with light and life since Eden's dawning day (1)
372	Eternal life hath he implanted in the soul (4)
379	sin afflicts all human life (3)
385	with thee are found the gifts of life (2)
385	bless us with life that has no end (2)
385	eternal life with thee (2)
390	All that hath life and breath come now with praises (4)
394, 395	let water's fragile blend with air, enabling life (2)
394, 395	let every life be touched by grace (4)
396, 397	O may this bounteous God through all our life be near us (2)
398	all that borrows life from thee is ever in thy care (3)
406, 407	what for our life is needful (5)
419	Sun of our life, thy quickening ray sheds ... the glow (2)
419	Lord of all life, below, above (3)
423	To all life thou givest, to both great and small (3)
423	in all life thou livest, the true life of all (3)
429	praise ... while life and thought and being last (1,4)
431	So order too this life of mine, direct it all my days (4)
434	Her noblest life my spirit draws from his dear wounds (4)
436	Let new and nobler life begin (5)
441, 442	When the woes of life o'ertake me (2)
443	the Pure baptized, the Life who died (5)
452	whose life and death that love reveal which mortals need (1)
455, 456	sent by the Father from on high, our life to live (3)
455, 456	our life to live, our death to die (3)
457	Thou art the Life (3)
457	Thou art the Way, the Truth, the Life (4)
457	that life to win, whose joys eternal flow (4)
458	my friend, indeed, who at my need his life did spend (2)
458	a murderer they save, the Prince of Life they slay (5)
458	In life no house, no home my Lord on earth might have (6)
465, 466	Eternal life, raise me from death (2)
469, 470	life would be thanksgiving for the goodness of the Lord (3)
471	The balm of life, the cure of woe (5)
472	bringing to hungry souls the bread of life (2)
474	love so amazing ... demands my soul, my life, my all (4)
475	soul and life and each endeavor (2)
475	pride of life and sinful pleasures (2)
478	in love your children keep to life unending (2)
478	Glorious their life who sing, with glad thanksgiving (3)
479	Grace and life eternal in that blood I find (2)
483	The cross he bore is life and health (6)
487	Come, my Way, my Truth, my Life (1)

487	such a life as killeth death (1)
489	Not to oppress, but summon all their truest life to find (6)
490	The star of my life is Jesus (1)
492	Prince of life, among the dead (3)
493	'tis life and health and peace (3)
493	new life the dead receive (4)
494	Crown him the Lord of life, who triumphed o'er the grave (3)
494	died eternal life to bring and lives that death may die (3)
495	life is given through thy Name (1)
501, 502	O Holy Spirit, by whose breath life rises vibrant (1)
501, 502	life rises vibrant out of death (1)
501, 502	the giver and the Lord of life (2)
501, 502	To fuller life your people bring (5)
503, 504	Thy blessed unction from above is comfort, life and fire (3)
503, 504	comfort, life, and fire of love (3)
505	O Spirit of Life, O Spirit of God (1-4)
506, 507	Spirit, moving on the waters quickening worlds to life (1)
506, 507	quickening worlds to life within (1)
506, 507	life in whom all lives begin (1)
508	fill me with life anew (1)
508	but live with thee the perfect life of thine eternity (4)
509	lead us in those paths of life whereon the righteous go (2)
511	Holy Spirit, ever living as the Church's very life (1)
515	breathe thy life and spread thy light (1)
521	To know thee is eternal life (4)
525	with his own blood he bought her ... for her life he died (1)
528	life abundant meant for each (2)
528	daily lift life heavenward (3)
530	Word of life, most pure and strong (5)
534	vainly we hope for the harvest-tide till God gives life (4)
534	till God gives life to the seed (4)
542	new life, new hope awakes, for all who own his sway (1)
547	Christ shall give you life (5)
552, 553	lay hold on life ... thy joy and crown eternally (1)
552, 553	life with its way before us lies (2)
552, 553	trust, and thy trusting soul shall prove Christ ... life (3)
552, 553	Christ is its life and Christ its love (3)
558	by kindly deeds and virtuous life (3)
561	To valiant hearts triumphant a crown of life shall be (4)
564, 565	we know we at the end shall life inherit (3)
567	lo, thy touch brought life and health (2)
567	thou our great deliverer still ... Lord of life and death (3)
570, 571	seek the Lord, who is your life (2)
573	Spirit of life which moved ere form was made (1)
581	our common life embraces all whose Father is the same (6)
582, 583	yea, bids us seize the whole of life and build its glory (4)
586	Bread of heaven, art broken in the sacrament of life (2)
598	O aweful Love, which found no room in life (2)
598	found no room in life where sin denied thee (2)
609	Where cross the crowded ways of life (1)
610	your abundant life to share (3)
625	Let all thy days till life shall end ... praise (4)
628	live a life of praise (3)
630	Word Incarnate heights and depths of life did share (2)
630	life redeemed from death and sin (5)

633	Word that brought to life creation (2)
633	Word of life, with one Bread feed us (4)
644	my Lord, my Life, my Way, my End (4)
647	through the years of life, to God I walk (2)
647	when I shall know why in this life I walk (3)
649, 650	the fount of life and our true light (1)
656	Lord, who left the heavens our life and peace to bring (2)
657	Come, almighty to deliver, let us all thy life receive (2)
662	in life, in death, O Lord, abide with me (4)
665	splendor, light, and life attend him (3)
671	he will my shield and portion be as long as life endures (3)
675	it guides you to abundant life (4)
680	be thou our guide while life shall last (6)
687, 688	let goods and kindred go, this mortal life also (4)
692	in that light of life I'll walk till pilgrim days are done (3)
695, 696	our whole life shall then be yours alone (4)
697	life shall be thy service, Lord (4)
698	I only know my need, as deep as life (1)
698	fulfillment of my life in love outpoured (3)
698	my life in you, O Christ, your love in me (3)
699	hide me, O my Savior ... till the storm of life is past (1)
699	Thou of life the fountain art (3)
705	to make our life an offering to God that all may live (2)
705	all life in Christ made new (2)
707	Take my life, and let it be consecrated, Lord, to thee (1)
709	Through each perplexing path of life (3)
719	mercy more than life (2)

life's

18	sharing, know life's victory won (3a)
46	yet when life's day is over (3)
158	for me ... thy mortal sorrow, and thy life's oblation (4)
231	called early from life's conflicts (2/12-28)
363	thou, Lord, by death hast won life's victory (3)
475	life's true way decreeing (2)
506, 506	breath of God, life's origin (1)
549, 550	tumult of our life's wild, restless sea (1)
556, 557	Yes, on through life's long path ... chanting as ye go (4)
580	facing us with life's destruction (3)
580	life's destruction or our most triumphant hour (3)
632	It is the chart and compass that o'er life's surging sea (2)
691	While life's dark maze I tread (3)
705	until life's work is done (3)

lift

3	Now that the daylight fills the sky, we lift our hearts (1)
3	lift our hearts to God on high (1)
4	we lift our hearts to God on high (1)
65	Lift high your praise resounding (2)
190	Lift your voice rejoicing, Mary (1)
212	Awake, arise, lift up your voice (1)
214	lift your heads, eternal gates (2)
268, 269	in his praise I lift my voice (4)
376	lift us to the joy divine (3)
400	All creatures of our God and King, lift up your voices (1)

436	Lift up your heads, ye mighty gates (1)
465, 466	eternal hope, lift up my eyes (1)
473	Lift high the cross, the love of Christ proclaim (R)
479	Lift ye then your voices, swell the mighty flood (5)
481	Lift up your heart, lift up your voice (R)
496, 497	We, too, will lift our voices (1)
527	One the strain the lips of thousands lift (3)
527	lift as from the heart of one (3)
528	Let your priests, for earth's true glory, daily lift (3)
528	daily lift life heavenward (3)
551	Lift high the cross of Christ (3)
552, 553	lift up thine eyes and seek his face (2)
555	now, O King eternal, we lift our battle song (1)
556, 557	Still lift your standard high, still march in firm array (5)
561	lift high his royal banner, it must not suffer loss (1)
562	Christians, lift your voices, loud your anthems raise (2)
568	lift up our lives to thy standard of right (3)
590	to lift the fallen, guide the feet that stumble (2)
591	lift up a living nation, a single sword to thee (3)
599	Lift every voice and sing till earth and heaven ring (1)
668	I to the hills will lift mine eyes (1)
678, 679	Zion, lift your voice in singing (2)

lifted

52	Jesus, may we lifted be from death of sin to life in thee (2)
68	With hearts and hands uplifted, we plead, O Lord, to see (3)
88	lifted by him to the skies (4)
104	But now, as at the ending, The low is lifted high (4)
165, 166	on the cross the Lamb is lifted (2)
205	sing with hearts uplifted high (3)
215	portals high are lifted to receive their heavenly King (1)
333	Now the silence Now the peace ... empty hands uplifted (1)
437, 438	the hungry fed, the humble lifted high (3)
473	O Lord, once lifted on the glorious tree (3)
555	Thy cross is lifted o'er us; we journey in its light (3)
603, 604	When Christ was lifted from the earth (1)
632	still that light is lifted o'er all the earth to shine (2)
681	line of lifted sea, where spreading moonlight quivers (3)

liftest

| 307 | Thou alone ... liftest up thy people's head (1) |

lifteth

| 416 | For the Church which evermore lifteth holy hands above (5) |

lifts

| 214 | See! he lifts his hands above (3) |
| 215 | While he lifts his hands in blessing (2) |

light

3, 4	To God the Father, heavenly Light (5)
5	O thou that bringest light from light (1)
5	O Light of Light, light's living spring (1)
6, 7	Christ, the true, the only Light (1)

6, 7	till they inward light impart (2)
8	born of the one light Eden saw play (3)
16, 17	So dazzling is its holy light (3)
18	your light, O Lord, burns in our hearts (1)
18	assist us to endure that light (1)
18	when we must act in day's hard light (2b)
18	At noontime Paul beheld your light (4b)
18	By noon's bright light, destruction stalks (2c)
18	grant us that same revealing light (4c)
21, 22	light the glow of perfect day (1)
24	while earth rolls onward into light (2)
25, 26	O gracious Light, Lord Jesus Christ (1)
25, 26	Now sunset comes, but light shines forth (2)
25, 26	God who dwells in the eternal light (2)
27, 28	O blest Creator, source of light (1)
29, 30	O Trinity of blessed light (1)
29, 30	To God the Father, heavenly Light (3)
31, 32	evening stars serenely light the darkening sky (3)
33-35	Christ, mighty Savior, Light of all creation (1)
33-35	in light or darkness worshiping our Savior (5)
36	O gladsome Light, O grace of God the Father's face (1)
36	Now, ere day fadeth quite, we see the evening light (2)
38, 39	light from the light invisible (1)
40, 41	O Christ, you are both light and day (1)
40, 41	the Herald of the light to come (1)
43	for all the blessings of the light (1)
44, 45	when the dawn new light will bring (3)
48	O day of radiant gladness, O day of joy and light (1)
48	This day at the creation, the light first had its birth (2)
48	thus this day most glorious a triple light was given (2)
48	grace more grace receiving on this blest day of light (3)
48	That light our hope sustaining, we walk the pilgrim way (4)
51	into his own light (1)
52	first o'er the earth the light was poured (1)
52	fill our souls with light divine (1)
55	Your cradle shines with glory's light (5)
60	your people's everlasting light (1)
61, 62	Rise up, and give us light (1)
61, 62	her star is risen, her light grows bright (2)
63, 64	O heavenly Word, eternal Light (1)
63, 64	pour light upon us from above (2)
69	blind-hearted seeing no light (2)
73	light triumphant breaks (1)
73	light and beauty brings (5)
74	Gentle is he and humble, And light his yoke shall be (4)
76	shine forth, and let thy light restore (4)
78, 79	yet in thy dark streets shineth the everlasting Light (1)
83	God from God, Light from Light eternal (2)
85, 86	O Jesus, very Light of Light (2)
85, 86	Today, as year by year its light bathes all the world (4)
87	light and life to all he brings (3)
88	God from God, and Light from Light, comes with mercies (2)
91	Break forth, O beauteous light, and usher in the morning (1)
93	yonder shines the infant Light (2)
99	behold, throughout the heavens there shone a holy light (1)

103	O Lord of Light (3)
109	to the earth it gave great light (2)
109	by the light of that same star three wise men came (3)
111	Son of God, love's pure light radiant beams (3)
114	before their light the stars grew dim (1)
119	as with joy they hailed its light (1)
119	In the heavenly country bright need they no created light (5)
119	thou its light, its joy, its crown (5)
124	more beauteous than the noonday light (1)
124	within them shines a clearer light (3)
124	the guidance of thy light to use (4)
124	To God the Father, heavenly Light (5)
125, 126	people who in darkness walked have seen a glorious light (1)
128	guide us to thy perfect light (R)
131, 132	by light their way to Light they trod (2)
133, 134	O Light of Light, Love given birth (1)
133, 134	May all who seek to praise aright ... show ... your light (3)
133, 134	through purer lives show forth your light (3)
135	Manifest on mountain height, shining in resplendent light (4)
145	make clear, make clear where truth and light appear (2)
145	Then shall your light break forth as doth the morning (5)
160	throned in light ere worlds could be (2)
161	With what strange light the rough trunk shone (4)
163	E'en though the sun withholds its light (2)
164	thou dost light and life restore (3)
168, 169	thy power is all expired ... quenched the light of light (2)
174	thou hast brought us life and light (3)
175	heaven her gates unbars, flinging her increase of light (3)
175	fount of our being, light that dost lighten all (7)
179	Months in due succession, days of lengthening light (3)
187	Earthly night brought us light which is ours eternally (3)
190	for your light is come once more (3)
193	the sun shone out with fairer light (1)
196, 197	offer us the worlds of light that live inside the Trinity (3)
199, 200	is flying from his light (2)
201	light and joy have conquered doom (1)
209	in realms of clearer light we may behold you as you are (4)
210	the Lord in rays eternal of resurrection light (2)
216	heaven her gates unbars, flinging her increase of light (2)
216	light that dost lighten all (5)
217, 218	great the light in you we see to guide us to eternity (2)
225	light that dost lighten all (4)
226, 227	come with thy celestial light (1)
228	Holy Spirit, font of light, focus of God's glory bright (1)
228	bring to light our perjuries (4)
231	Praise for the light from heaven ... voice of awe (2/1-25)
232	light that grows in splendor until the perfect day (2/6-24)
235	drove away the shadows, and filled the world with light (1)
240, 241	dwell forever in the light (1)
242	mid all its light his faith was dim (2)
242	still through his confession flows ... thy life and light (4)
243	on his eyes a light wherewith God's daybreak to proclaim (2)
245	the light, the living vine, your soul's true bread (2)
255	God's light shone down from heaven (1)
255	God's light ... broke across the path (1)

256	A light from heaven shone around (1)
256	in that light a voice was heard (1)
259	O Light of all the earth, thy children wait for thee (4)
271, 272	faithful hearts shall never fail ... his light to hail (1)
271, 272	with thanks and praise his light to hail (1)
271, 272	his witness to the coming light (3)
275	now they walk in golden light (4)
284	When all arrayed in light the shining conqueror rode (7)
287	thou, in the darkness drear, the one true Light (2)
312	from light do thou not banish (3)
319	in the light of your Incarnantion (1)
321	who see the light or feel the sun (4)
324	Light of Life descendeth from the realms of endless day (3)
336	God from God and Light from Light (2)
336	grant us light to see and know thee (2)
336	light ... in thy people everywhere (2)
339	Light, who dost my soul enlighten (2)
345	for dark and light are both alike to thee (2)
347	Christ at length ... overcome all darkness with his light (3)
349	Give them light, your truth to see (2)
357	shed on them the radiance of thy heavenly light (4)
358	rest with your saints in the regions of light (1,4)
360, 361	light in our blindness, in our toil refreshment (3)
363	with light and life since Eden's dawning day (1)
364	prophets crowned with light (4)
369	dwells amidst the dazzling light of vast eternity (1)
371	let there be light (1-4)
371	now to all human-kind, let there be light (2)
371	in earth's darkest place, let there be light (3)
373	praise him, all ye stars of light (1)
376	giver of immortal gladness, fill us with the light of day (1)
381	for created light we thank thee (1)
381	Alleluia, alleluia, Praise to thee who light dost send (1-3)
381	broke the light of thy salvation (2)
381	to ... Light of Light begotten, praise be sung eternally (4)
388	whose robe is the light, whose canopy space (2)
388	It breathes in the air, it shines in the light (4)
389	filled the new-made world with light (3)
393	guides his Israel on their way ... darkness into light (2)
393	light of dawn leads us on (2)
394, 395	let sun and moon and stars and light ... praise (1)
400	fire ... you give to us both warmth and light (3)
401	glorious with his saints in light, for ever reigns (3)
416	sun and moon, and stars of light (2)
419	star of our hope, thy softened light cheers the ... night (2)
419	whose light is truth, whose warmth is love (3)
419	till all thy living altars claim one holy light (4)
420	when utmost evil strove against the Light (4)
422	more truth and light to break forth from thy Holy Word (1)
422	thy truth and light our dwelling place for evermore (3)
423	in light inaccessible hid from our eyes (1)
423	Unresting, unhasting, and silent as light (2)
423	Thou reignest in glory, thou rulest in light (4)
423	help us to see 'tis only the splendor of light hideth thee (4)
431	a light before our eyes (3)

432	rejoice in his word, ye angels of light (1)
435	bore it up triumphant, with its human light (3)
435	let his will enfold you in its light and power (5)
440	Light of Light, from God proceeding (3)
441, 442	all the light of sacred story gathers round its head (1,5)
441, 442	When the sun of bliss is beaming light and love (3)
441, 442	light and love upon my way (3)
452	that strong Light puts out the sun and all is ended (4)
453	here are regions of light, here are mansions of bliss (4)
455, 456	still more in resurrection light we read the fullness (4)
455, 456	in resurrection light we read the fullness of thy might (4)
459	an altar candle sheds its light as surely as a star (2)
465, 466	Eternal light, shine in my heart (1)
471	gilds the bed of death with light (4)
472	showing to wandering souls the path of light (3)
475	let thy radiant beauty light mine eyes to see my duty (3)
475	let thy light shine through me (3)
483	heaven's eternal Light (2)
487	Come, my Light, my Feast, my Strength (2)
487	such a light as shows a feast (2)
488	waking or sleeping, thy presence my light (1)
490	I want to walk as a child of the light (1)
490	God set the stars to give light to the world (1)
490	The Lamb is the light of the city of God (R)
494	now lives in realms of light (4)
499	the glory of your people, and their light (1)
500	O Source of uncreated light (2)
501, 503	Flood our dull senses with your light (4)
503, 504	Enable with perpetual light ... our blinded sight (4)
509	Come as the light, to us reveal our emptiness and woe (2)
512	Come ... with light and comfort from above (1)
512	The light of truth to us display (2)
515	breathe thy life and spread thy light (1)
516	let thy glorious light shine ever on my sight (2)
521	works of darkness disappear before thy conquering light (2)
522, 523	Thus deriving from their banner, light ... and shade (3)
522, 523	light by night and shade by day (3)
527	Clear before us through the darkness gleams ... light (1)
527	gleams and burns the guiding light (1)
527	One the light of God's own presence (2)
527	light ... o'er his ransomed people shed (2)
530	until from night all the world awakes to light (5)
531	Be darkness, at thy coming, light (3)
532, 533	To nations of earth thy light shall be shown (2)
534	with the banner of Christ unfurled that the light (3)
538	fill thy Church with light divine (1)
538	let all be, below, above, one in joy, and light and love (2)
539	mission ... to tell to all the world that God is Light (1)
542	Christ is the world's true Light ... captain of salvation (1)
543	In honor to his Name reflect that sacred light (3)
547	Christ shall give you light (1)
555	Thy cross is lifted o'er us; we journey in its light (3)
563	Lord has been thy shelter, the Lord will be thy light (4)
566	fill the earth with health and light and peace (2)

216	light that dost lighten all (5)
225	light that dost lighten all (4)
233, 234	true lights that lighten every land (2)
406, 407	strong to lighten all the night (4)
503, 504	lighten with celestial fire (1)

lightening

569	the lightening thy sword (1)

lightning

370	the flashing of the lightning free (4)

lights

12, 13	The golden sun lights up the sky (1)
68	Rejoice, rejoice, believers, and let your lights appear (1)
73	crowned with glory like the sun ... lights the morning sky (2)
185, 186	Christ ... the sun that warms and lights us (3)
233, 234	true lights that lighten every land (2)
291	he paints the wayside flower, he lights the evening star (2)
476	his meaning lights our shadowed world through Christ (2)

like

8	Morning has broken like the first morning (1)
8	black-bird has spoken like the first bird (1)
8	like the first dewfall on the first grass (2)
18	to us, like her who saw your need (4a)
24	never, like earth's proud empires, pass away (4)
31, 32	Like sun and day, shine in our hearts (5)
31, 32	like moon and night, give loving peace (5)
60	with one accord, like those in heaven (4)
73	crowned with glory like the sun ... lights the morning sky (2)
75	Like the flowers of the field they perish (2)
75	like grass our works decay (2)
75	power and pomp of nations shall pass like a dream away (2)
75	He shall feed his flock like a shepherd (3)
76	without thy grace we waste away like flowers (3)
102	We, like Mary, rest confounded (3)
102	scorned, rejected, tears and smiles like us he knew (4)
104	And straw like gold shall shine (1)
106	Let us, like these good shepherds, then employ (5)
112	earth stood hard as iron, water like a stone (1)
116	like him desirous to fulfill God's will in righteousness (4)
143	Then grant us, Lord, like them to be full oft in fast (4)
173	The Paschal Lamb, like Isaac's ram (2)
187	Like the cloud that overhead ... Israel led (2)
188, 189	made like him, like him we rise (3)
204	Love is come again like wheat that springeth green (R)
204	laid in the earth like grain that sleeps unseen (2)
204	Forth he came at Easter, like the risen grain (3)
223, 224	Like to cloven tongues of flame on the twelve ... came (2)
231	Like you, our suffering Savior ... he blessed (2/12-26)
231	May we like true apostles your holy Church defend (2/2-24)
232	seek, like him, your will (2/8-24)
236	thus win a like victory in us (3)
240, 241	they, like Christ, in death victorious (1)

245	words reflect, like eagles' wings, the glory of our Lord (1)
245	your deeds and words refresh our hearts like dew (3)
248, 249	'Tis the Name that whoso preachest speaks like music (3)
248, 249	speaks like music to the ear (1)
261, 262	grant that we also may like him be faithful (3)
267	like her whom heaven's Majesty came down to shadow o'er (3)
275	Multitude ... like the stars (1)
285	So grant us, Lord, like him to live (4)
286	Who are these like stars appearing (1)
286	These, like priests, have watched and waited (5)
293	for the saints of God are just folk like me (3)
376	hearts unfold like flowers before thee (1)
388	and round it hath cast, like a mantle, the sea (3)
391	when like wandering sheep we strayed, he saved us (2)
394, 395	let peace, descending like a dove, make known ... love (3)
410	Father-like he tends and spares us (3)
411	like the eagle he renews the vigor of thy youth (5)
423	thy justice like mountains high soaring above (2)
423	we blossom and flourish, like leaves on the tree (3)
428	people bless the Lord like righteous souls of yore (5)
458	never was love, dear King, never was grief like thine (7)
460, 461	thunder like a mighty flood (1,5)
462	truth ... like a flower shall bud and blossom show (2)
469, 470	There's a wideness in God's mercy like the ... sea (1)
469, 470	like the wideness of the sea (1)
475	let my soul, like Mary, be thine earthly sanctuary (4)
480	like us, unhonored and unknown, he came to dwell on earth (1)
480	Like him may we be found below in wisdom's path of peace (1)
480	like him in grace and knowledge grow as years (1)
482	whose trust, ever child-like, no cares could destroy (1)
509	purge our hearts like sacrificial flame (3)
513	Like the murmur of the dove's song (1)
513	like the challenge of her flight (1)
513	like the vigor of the wind's rush (1)
513	like the new flame's eager might (1)
522, 523	Grace which like the Lord, the giver, never fails (2)
525	Lord, give us grace that we like them, the meek (5)
544	his Name like sweet perfume shall rise (2)
545	They, once like us with suffering tried (1)
545	Let us, with zeal like theirs inspired, strive (2)
555	gladness breaks like morning where'er thy face appears (3)
556, 557	echoes upward float like wreaths of incense cloud (3)
562	Like a mighty army moves the Church of God (3)
566	to rise, like incense, each to thee (1)
566	rise, like incense ... in noble thought and deed (1)
588, 589	Almighty God, your word is cast like seed upon the ground (1)
616	He shall come down like showers upon the fruitful earth (3)
616	love, joy, hope, like flowers spring in his path to birth (3)
652, 653	simple trust like theirs who heard beside the Syrian sea (2)
652, 653	let us, like them, without a word, rise up and follow (2)
662	Who, like thyself, my guide and stay can be (2)
664	no more a stranger or a guest, but like a child at home (3)
671	how sweet the sound that saved a wretch like me (1)
676	If you cannot preach like Peter (2)
676	if you cannot pray like Paul (2)

680	A thousand ages in thy sight are like an evening gone (4)
680	Time, like an ever-rolling stream (5)
686	like a fetter (3)
705	a world redeemed by Christ-like love (2)
708	Savior, like a shepherd lead us (1)
717	my heart with rapture thrills like that above (2)

likeness
53	came in likeness lowly, Son of God most holy (1)
225	Lo, in the likeness of fire (1)
580	your children in your likeness, share inventive powers (1)

likewise
| 121 | likewise in God's service we may perfect freedom find (4) |

limbs
135	Manifest in making whole palsied limbs and fainting soul (3)
161	its purple limbs a royal throne (4)
162	ordained those holy limbs to bear (3)
369	Our reason ... climbs above the skies (3)

limestone
| 412 | Limestone and beams, loud building workers (4) |

limit
251	O God, whom neither time nor space can limit (1)
251	neither time nor space can limit, hold, or bind (1)
629	We limit not the truth of God to our poor reach of mind (1)

limitless
| 228 | Father of the fatherless, giver of gifts limitless (1) |

limits
| 579, 608 | who bidd'st the mighty ocean deep its ... limits keep (1) |
| 579, 608 | ocean deep its own appointed limits keep (1) |

line
94, 95	To you, in David's town, this day is born of David's line (3)
226, 227	rule us by thy judgment's line (4)
235	while each his own commission fulfills in every line (2)
260	David's house and line (1)
267	virgin born of David's line shall bear the promised seed (2)
450, 451	Hail him, the Heir of David's line (3)
681	line of lifted sea, where spreading moonlight quivers (3)

lineage
| 81 | Of Jesse's lineage coming as seers of old have sung (1) |

lines
| 434 | precious blood and crimson lines (2) |

lingering
| 276 | not lingering by the sea (2) |

linking

416	for the mystic harmony linking sense to sound and sight (3)

lions'

143	delivered from the lions' might (3)

lips

3, 4	Our hearts and lips may he restrain (2)
23	With "It is finished" on your lips (3)
154, 155	to whom the lips of children made sweet hosannas ring (R)
214	Hark, his gracious lips bestow (3)
243	on his lips a sword wherewith he smote and overcame (1)
243	on his lips a prayer that God ... spare (3)
345	guard thou the lips from sin, the hearts from shame (1)
359	fill them with power, their lips make eloquent (2)
374	Worthy the Lamb, our lips reply, for he was slain for us (2)
405	lips that we might tell how great is God Almighty (4)
435	Name from the lips of sinners, unto whom he came (2)
527	One the strain the lips of thousands lift (3)
582, 583	bitter lips in blind despair cry (2)

listen

74	By those who truly listen his voice is truly heard (2)
506, 507	to those who listen (2)
611	All who labor, listen to his call (5)
655	O speak, and make me listen, thou guardian of my soul (2)

listening

210	listening to his accents, may hear ... All hail (2)
229	let all the listening earth be taught the deeds (2)
409	nightly to the listening earth repeats the story (2)
493	He speaks, and listening to his voice ... receive (4)
599	Let our rejoicing rise high as the listening skies (1)
651	to my listening ears all nature sings (1)

lit

25, 26	the lamps are lit to pierce the night (2)
614	new lamps be lit, new tasks begun (3)

little

42	Grant to little children visions bright of thee (3)
69	in great humility is hid all heaven in a little room (3)
73	Not, as of old, a little child (2)
78, 79	O little town of Bethlehem, how still we see thee lie (1)
91	This child, this little helpless boy ... our confidence (1)
98	All the little boys he killed at Bethlehem in his fury (3)
101	the little Lord Jesus laid down his sweet head (1)
101	the little Lord Jesus asleep on the hay (1)
101	but little Lord Jesus no crying he makes (2)
102	Mary was that mother mild, Jesus Christ her little child (1)
247	Lully, Lullay, thou little tiny child (R)
277	Son most holy, who became her little child (1)
405	Each little flower that opens (1)
405	each little bird that sings (1)
468	It was poor little Jesus, yes, yes (1-4)

597   a little child shall lead them all (2)
687, 688   lo, his doom is sure, one little word shall fell him (3)

liturgy
420   the Church, in liturgy and song, in faith and love (3)

live
10   help us ... every day, to live more nearly as we pray (6)
23   Inspire us by your dying breath to live for you (3)
37   be thou, in whom we live (3)
38, 39   Lord, while we live for this short time (4)
101   fit us for heaven to live with thee there (3)
138   in you always to live and drink of those ... streams (3)
142   chiefly live by thy most holy word (3)
146, 147   may with you for ever live in love and unity and peace (5)
149   so we are dead and live with you in God (2)
178   Now we shall live for ever (3)
193   who, dead, again dost live (5)
196, 197   offer us the worlds of light that live inside the Trinity (3)
208   that we may live and sing to thee (5)
213   live to the honor and glory of God (2)
231   To all who live with questions (2/12-21)
240, 241   strive to think him, speak him, live him (4)
251   help us here on earth to live from selfish passions free (4)
279   For thy dear saints, O Lord, who strove in thee to live (1)
279   follow them ... who live and died for thee (4)
280   many saints by earth forgotten live for ever (1)
280   live for ever round your throne (1)
285   So grant us, Lord, like him to live (4)
295   as members of his Body we live in him as one (2)
296   Baptized we live with God the Three in One (3)
304   as his people in the world we'll live (5)
304   we'll live and speak his praise (5)
313   Thou didst die that I might live (2)
314   grant my spirit ever by thy life may live (3)
319   in you finds release that we all might live in peace (1)
323   to thy cross we look and live (2)
335   they who eat of this bread ... shall live forever (2)
335   who believe in me, even if they die ... live for ever (4)
343   would not live by bread alone, but by thy word of grace (2)
376   all who live in love are thine (3)
404   each day we live our psalm to you we raise (1)
413   all things that live in earth and ocean make music (2)
422   though our vision now is dark, to live by what we see (3)
428   earth and sea, O all that live in water or on shore (4)
455, 456   sent by the Father from on high, our life to live (3)
455, 456   our life to live, our death to die (3)
505   none can believe in Christ and live (2)
508   but live with thee the perfect life of thine eternity (4)
517   thou shalt surely bless ... who live the words they pray (4)
538   be by all that live adored (2)
539   God, in whom they live and move, is Love (2)
539   died on earth that all might live above (2)
593   Dying, we live, and are reborn (5)

602	this is the way we should live with you (4)
610	may your mercy know and live (4)
628	to live the faith which we proclaim (2)
628	live a life of praise (3)
659, 660	with thee, O Master, let me live (4)
674	you alone can grant us grace to live the words we say (1)
692	thirsty one, stoop down and drink, and live (2)
692	now I live in him (2)
705	to make our life an offering to God that all may live (2)

lived

102	with the poor, the scorned, the lowly lived ... Savior (2)
102	lived on earth our Savior holy (2)
161	He lived to rob death of its sting (1)
231	whose short-lived doubtings prove (2/12-21)
293	who toiled and fought and lived and died for the Lord (1)
293	lived and died for the Lord they loved and knew (1)
293	They lived not only in ages past (3)
547	For us Christ lived, for us he died (5)
695, 696	we shall remember all the days we lived through (4)

lives

69	God gives himself into our lives (4)
133, 134	through purer lives show forth your light (3)
139	death could hold him never. He rose and lives forever (2)
182	lives, though ever crucified (4)
182	till all creation lives and learns his joy (5)
185, 186	faith lives upon no other (4)
188, 189	Lives again our glorious King (2)
194, 195	Jesus lives ... Alleluia! (1-4)
204	love lives again, that with the dead has been (1)
213	Now created again that our lives may remain ... thine (3)
213	lives may remain, throughout time and eternity thine (3)
231	lives as pure as theirs (2/12-28)
245	We praise you that John's voice still lives (3)
246	May that great love our lives control and conquer hate (5)
227	fill our lives which Christ has won (3)
293	followed the right ... whole of their good lives long (2)
299	fan our smoldering lives to flame (3)
321	gather from their Father's board the Bread that lives (3)
321	Bread that lives beyond the tomb (3)
340, 341	hallow all our lives, O Lord (2)
342	Now may your life to us descending enter our lives (3)
344	in our hearts and lives abound (2)
381	our lives our hopes confess (3)
472	take thou our lives, and use them as thou wilt (4)
494	died eternal life to bring and lives that death may die (3)
494	now lives in realms of light (4)
506, 507	life in whom all lives begin (1)
506, 507	Pray we then, O Lord the Spirit, on our lives descend (5)
506, 507	on our lives descend in might (5)
568	lift up our lives to thy standard of right (3)
574, 585	for lives bereft of purpose high, forgive (3)
591	bind all our lives together, smite us and save us all (3)
625	praise him still, through good or ill, who ever lives (3)

511	Holy Spirit, ever living as the Church's very life (1)
512	Lead us to Christ, the living way (3)
517	my very heart and flesh cry out, O living God, for thee (1)
519, 520	living stones art builded in the height of heaven above (1)
522, 523	See, the streams of living waters (2)
522, 523	living waters, springing from eternal love (2)
526	One army of the living God, to his command we bow (3)
526	greet the ever-living bands on the eternal shore (4)
531	O Spirit of the living God (1)
558	living still in spite of dungeon, fire, and sword (1)
572	To the triumph of your cross summon all the living (3)
591	Tie in a living tether the prince and priest and thrall (3)
591	lift up a living nation, a single sword to thee (3)
594, 595	for the living of these days (2)
596	with thy living fire of judgment purge this land (1)
606	as we hear and love our Lord, the living God (1)
610	love in living deeds to show (4)
627	word of the ever-living God, will of his glorious Son (4)
629	enlarge, expand all living souls to comprehend your love (3)
633	living rain from heaven descending (1)
643	O how I fear thee, living God (4)
645, 646	Where streams of living water flow ... he leadeth (2)
649, 650	we taste in you our living bread (2)
658	For thee ... the living God, my thirsty soul doth pine (2)
664	pastures fresh he makes me feed beside the living stream (1)
666	My soul with patience waits for thee, the living Lord (2)
678, 679	rejoice as you draw water from salvation's living spring (1)
691	a living fire (2)
692	Behold, I freely give the living water (2)
698	Eternal Spirit of thy living Christ (1)
700	Well-spring of heavenly peace, thou Living Water, come (2)
700	Love of the living God, of Father and of Son (4)
703	lead us through Christ, the true and living Way (1)

load
12, 13	Now help us bear our daily load (2)
67	mourning 'neath their sorrows' load (1)
81	from sin and death now save us, and share our every load (3)
161	its load a royal treasury (4)
318	here would I lay aside each earthly load (2)
611	he will ease your load and give you rest (6)

lodge
114	Within a lodge of broken bark the tender babe was found (2)

lofty
75	valleys shall be exalted, the lofty hills brought low' (1)
398	spread the flowing seas abroad and built the lofty skies (1)

loins
615	gird up your loins, ye prophet souls (3)

lonely
56	mourns in lonely exile here until the Son of God appear (1,8)
334	Scattered flock, one shepherd sharing, lost and lonely (2)

| 580 | the lonely drift unnoticed in the city's ebb and flow (2) |
| 590 | seek out the lonely and God's mercy share (2) |

long

42	Through the long night watches may thine angels spread (5)
46	long our mortal blindness has missed God's lovingkindness (3)
59	Lo, the Lamb, so long expected (3)
67	Make ye straight what long was crooked (3)
71, 72	the Savior promised long (1)
89, 90	the world has suffered long (3)
93	watching long in hope and fear (4)
97	stretching infant hands on high, Savior, long awaited (1)
98	Now may Mary's son, who came so long ago to love us (4)
102	For he is our life-long pattern (4)
112	in the bleak midwinter long ago (1)
146, 147	The covenant, so long revealed to those of faith (2)
168, 169	Thy beauty, long desired, hath vanished from our sight (2)
179	Loose the souls long prisoned, bound with Satan's chain (6)
180	Death's long shadows have departed (2)
199, 200	all the winter of our sins, long and dark (2)
253	long cloud of witnesses show the same path to heaven (4)
257	The aged Simeon sees at last his Lord, so long desired (3)
267	Praise we the Lord this day, this day so long foretold (1)
276	fell by fire and sword, or early died or flourished long (1)
286	they who have contended for their Savior's honor long (3)
287	when the strife is fierce, the warfare long (5)
289	some are long forgotten (2)
289	long spent their hopes and fears (2)
293	followed the right ... whole of their good lives long (2)
314	what my soul doth long for, that thy word foretold (4)
352	their vows of life-long love (1)
369	long to see the blessed Three in the Almighty One (2)
419	cheers the long watches of the night (2)
453	The ladder is long, it is strong and well made (2)
484, 485	the crown ere-long to wear: Alleluia (2)
516	so the yearning strong, with which the soul will long (3)
525	their cry goes up, "How long?" (3)
530	word for which the nations long, spread abroad (5)
541	till the long shadows o'er our pathway lie (5)
542	the world has waited long, has travailed long in pain (3)
551	His kingdom tarries long (2)
556, 557	Yes, on through life's long path ... chanting as ye go (4)
561	the strife will not be long (4)
582, 583	city that hath stood too long a dream (3)
594, 595	From the fears that long have bound us free our hearts (2)
609	yet long these multitudes to see the true compassion (3)
610	still the captives long for freedom (2)
612	Love is kind, and suffers long (2)
623	through our long exile on Babylon's strand (4)
633	Word made flesh, we long to hear you (1)
647	I know not if the way is long, and no one else can say (1)
649, 650	long to feast upon you still (2)
671	he will my shield and portion be as long as life endures (3)

672	thy people long that thou, their Sun, wouldst rise (2)
689	for thou wert long beforehand with my soul (3)
701	my heart long paineth, ah, my spirit straineth (1)
717	long may our land be bright with freedom's holy light (4)

longed

| 68 | arise, thou Sun so longed for, above this darkened sphere (3) |

longer

182	No longer bound to distant years in Palestine (2)
194, 195	thy terrors now can no longer, death, appall us (1)
206	No longer Thomas then denied (5)
358	Grief and pain ended, and sighing no longer (1,4)
707	Take my will, and make it thine ... no longer mine (2)

longest

| 402, 403 | above all, the heart must bear the longest part (2) |

longing

66	dear desire of every nation, joy of every longing heart (2)
180	a brighter Easter beam on our longing eyes shall stream (4)
193	to their longing eyes restored (1)
231	Instill in us his longing, your glory to behold (2/12-27)
315	with longing heart and soul (1)
525	till with the vision glorious her longing eyes are blessed (4)
613	revive our longing eyes, which languish for thy sight (4)
666	My longing eyes look out for thy enlivening ray (3)

longs

336	peace for which creation longs (3)
427	When mirth for music longs, this is my song of songs (2)
517	thirsty soul desires and longs within thy courts to be (1)
658	As longs the deer for cooling streams (1)
658	longs the deer ... in parched and barren ways (1)
658	longs my soul, O God, for thee and thy refreshing grace (1)

look

40, 41	Defender of us all, look down (4)
68	look now for your salvation, the end of sin and toil (2)
101	I love thee, Lord Jesus! Look down from the sky (2)
156	the angel armies of the sky look down (3)
196, 197	Look there! the Christ, our Brother, comes resplendent (1,4)
251	look down from heaven, thy dwelling place (1)
251	look down ... with love for human-kind (1)
301	look on the heart by sorrow broken (1)
301	look on the tears by sinners shed (1)
323	to thy cross we look and live (2)
337	Look Father, look on his anointed face (2)
337	only look on us as found in him (2)
337	look not on our misusings of thy grace (2)
368	look upon the Mediator, clothe us with his righteousness (1)
413	mountains and stones look up adoring (3)
462	justice, from her heavenly bower, look down on us below (2)
480	Sweet were his words and kind his look (2)

490	I want to look at Jesus (2)
540	look down on us and view how white the fields (2)
593	nor look to understanding hearts (3)
593	but look for hearts to understand (3)
593	May we not look for love's return (4)
638, 639	look on thy hands, and read it there (2)
666	My longing eyes look out for thy enlivening ray (3)
692	look unto me, your morn shall rise (3)

looked

101	The stars in the bright sky looked down where he lay (1)
109	They looked up and saw a star shining in the east (2)
196, 197	Good Jesus Christ inside his pain looked down (2)
196, 197	Jesus ... looked down Golgatha's stony slope (2)
278	looked upon her Son ... reigning from the awful tree (2)
278	looked upon her Son and Savior (2)
692	I looked to Jesus, and I found in him my Star, my Sun (3)

looking

490	I'm looking for the coming of Christ (3)
527	one the earnest looking forward (2)
694	God be in mine eyes, and in my looking (1)

loose

| 179 | Loose the souls long prisoned, bound with Satan's chain (6) |
| 633 | loose our tongues to tell your kindness (3) |

loosed

| 199, 200 | loosed from Pharaoh's bitter yoke (1) |

loosen

| 145 | of wickedness the grievous bands to loosen (3) |

loosened

| 493 | ye voiceless ones, your loosened tongues employ (5) |

Lord

9	worlds awake to cry their blessings on the Lord of life (4)
9	Lord of life, as he goes meekly by (4)
9	sun ... great lord of years and days (5)
10	Only, O Lord, in thy dear love, fit us for perfect rest (6)
11	Lord, I my vows to thee renew (2)
12, 13	you stumbled, Lord, beneath its weight (2)
14, 15	Jesus Christ, our Lord Most High (3)
16, 17	All glory be to you, Lord Christ (4)
18	your light, O Lord, burns in our hearts (1)
18	while he contended, Lord, for you (2a)
18	he knew you, Lord, would answer him (2b)
19, 20	Christ, our Lord Most High (3)
21, 22	O God of truth, O Lord of might (1)
21, 22	through Jesus Christ, our Lord Most High (3)
24	The day thou gavest, Lord, is ended (1)
24	So be it, Lord (4)
25, 26	O gracious Light, Lord Jesus Christ (1)
25, 26	Life-giving Lord (3)

101	I love thee, Lord Jesus! Look down from the sky (2)
101	Be near me, Lord Jesus (3)
102	He came down to earth from heaven ... God and Lord of all (2)
102	yet this child, our Lord and brother, brought us love (3)
102	child who seemed so helpless is our Lord in heaven above (5)
103	in one accord adoring Christ the Lord (R)
103	O Lord of Light (3)
105	Now to the Lord sing praises, all you within this place (4)
106	this day is born a Savior, Christ the Lord (2)
109	sing praises to our heavenly Lord (6)
110	when Christ our Lord was born on Christmas night (1)
111	Jesus, Lord, at thy birth (3)
112	stable ... sufficed the Lord God incarnate, Jesus Christ (2)
114	God the Lord of all the earth sent angel-choirs instead (1)
116	I come, the great Redeemer cries, to do thy will, O Lord (1)
119	so, most gracious Lord, may we evermore be led to thee (1)
121	Baptize us with your Spirit, Lord (4)
125, 126	the Wonderful, the Counsellor, the mighty God and Lord (4)
127	out of thee the Lord from heaven came to rule his Israel (1)
135	praise ... Jesus, Lord, to thee we raise (1)
136, 137	the incarnate Lord holds converse high (2)
138	All praise to you, O Lord, who by your mighty power (1)
138	water reddening into wine proclaims the present Lord (2)
138	grant us, O Lord, to see the marriage supper of the Lamb (4)
142	Lord, who throughout these forty days for us didst fast (1)
142	so teach us, gracious Lord, to die to self (3)
143	Then grant us, Lord, like them to be full oft in fast (4)
143	from age to age, the only Lord (5)
144	Lord Jesus, Sun of Righteousness, shine in our hearts (1)
144	forgive us, Lord, our sin (2)
144	Lord, grant that we in penitence may offer you our praise (3)
144	we shall be at one with you, Lord, risen from the tomb (4)
146, 147	keep vigil with our heavenly Lord in his temptation (1)
146, 147	the Lord of love, in love sublime (2)
146, 147	Your love, O Lord, our sinful race has not returned (3)
146, 147	Remember, Lord ... in your own image were we made (4)
146, 147	Therefore, we pray you, Lord, forgive (5)
148	Teach us to know and love you, Lord (5)
149	Eternal Lord of love, behold your Church (1)
149	we walk the road, Lord Jesus, that you trod (2)
151	Lord, hear me, I implore thee (1)
151	thus my hope is in the Lord and not in my own merit (3)
152	Spare us, O Lord, who now confess our sins (3)
153	Blessed is the King who comes in the name of the Lord (1)
153	The Lord be with you. And also with you (2)
153	Let us give thanks to the Lord our God (2)
153	Blessed is he who comes in the name of the Lord (2)
157	Blessed is he who comes in the name of the Lord (1)
157	I will enter them; I will offer thanks to the Lord (1)
157	This is the gate of the Lord (R)
157	On this day the Lord has acted (R)
157	Hosanna, Lord, hosanna. Lord, send us now success (R)
157	we bless you from the house of the Lord (R)
157	God is the Lord; he has shined upon us (R)
157	Give thanks to the Lord, for he is good (R)

276	For thy blest saints ... we praise thy Name, O Lord (1)
276	Lord, may we learn to drink thy cup (5)
277	God the Lord who came to earth (1)
278	obedient to the summons bore in love the infant Lord (1)
278	Sing again the joys of Mary when she saw the risen Lord (3)
278	Lord of all creation brought her to his heavenly home (4)
278	beholds her Son and Savior reigning as the Lord of love (4)
279	For thy dear saints, O Lord, who strove in thee to live (1)
279	They all in life and death, with thee their Lord in view (2)
281	it came, true Lord of souls, from thee (2)
284	the Lord of life expire (5)
284	all adored your rising Lord with joy unknown (6)
285	So grant us, Lord, like him to live (4)
287	thou, Lord, their Captain in the well-fought fight (2)
288	Lord, for these our souls shall raise ... praise (2)
290	grant, ... Lord, that we wholesome grain and pure may be (2)
290	O harvest Lord (2)
290	For the Lord our God shall come ... take his harvest home (3)
290	Even so, Lord, quickly come to thy final harvest-home (4)
291	then thank the Lord, O thank the Lord for all his love (R)
292	Lord, in their change, let frost and heat ... be given (2)
293	who toiled and fought and lived and died for the Lord (1)
293	lived and died for the Lord they loved and knew (1)
293	They loved their Lord so dear (2)
297	Enlist us in your service, Lord (2)
299	let new tongues hail the risen Lord (2)
302, 303	Thou, Lord, didst make all for thy pleasure (1)
302, 303	Watch o'er thy Church, O Lord (2)
304	I come with joy to meet my Lord, forgiven, loved and free (1)
304	thus with joy we meet our Lord (4)
305, 306	Come, risen Lord, and deign to be our guest (1)
305, 306	One with each other, Lord, for one in thee (4)
307	Lord, enthroned in heavenly splendor (1)
308, 309	We hunger; Lord, supply us (1)
312	Strengthen for service, Lord, the hands (1)
312	Lord, may the tongues which "Holy" sang keep free (2)
313	be to me ... Lord, of thy boundless love the token (1)
313	O gracious Lord (1)
313	Blessed Lord, thou cam'st to save me(2)
314	in the glorious vision, blessed Lord, of thee (4)
315	For all thy Church, O Lord, we intercede (2)
315	So, Lord, at length when sacraments shall cease (3)
318	Here, O my Lord, I see the face to face (1)
318	it is enough, my Lord, enough indeed (3)
318	thy Blood, thy righteousness, O Lord, my God (4)
319	You, Lord, we praise in songs of celebration (1)
319	You, Lord, in our stead to the grave descended (2)
320	as of old the Lord provided (2)
320	Lord, refresh us and defend us (5)
321	Drawn by thy quickening grace, O Lord (3)
323	Lord, thy wounds our healing give (2)
324	Lord of lords in human vesture (2)
324	Alleluia, Lord Most High (4)
325	O Lord, have mercy on me (R)
326	From glory to glory advancing, we praise thee, O Lord (1)

375	host of heaven praiseth thee, O Lord of all dominions (2)
376	Joyful, joyful, we adore thee, God of glory, Lord of love (1)
377, 378	All people that on earth do dwell, sing to the Lord (1)
377, 378	sing to the Lord with cheerful voice (1)
377, 378	Know that the Lord is God indeed (2)
377, 378	For why? the Lord our God is good (4)
380	Eternal are thy mercies, Lord (2)
383, 384	Fairest Lord Jesus, Ruler of all nature (1)
386. 387	Tell them I AM, the Lord God said (2)
386, 387	nature without voice or sound replied, O Lord, thou art (2)
389	Let us, with a gladsome mind, praise the Lord (1,7)
390	Praise to the Lord (1-4)
391	know that the Lord is God alone (1)
392	Come, we who love the Lord, and let our joys be known (1)
393	Praise our great and gracious Lord (1)
398	I sing the goodness of the Lord (2)
398	goodness of the Lord that filled the earth with food (2)
398	Lord, how thy wonders are displayed (2)
400	make music for your Lord to hear (3)
400	for Christ our Lord that way has trod (6)
401	the Lord, the great I AM, by earth and heaven confessed (1)
401	There dwells the Lord, our King ... our Righteousness (3)
401	hail, Abraham's Lord divine (5)
404	We will extoll you, ever-blessed Lord (1)
404	You, Lord, are gracious, merciful to all (3)
405	all things wise and wonderful ... Lord God made them all (R)
406, 407	Most High, omnipotent, good Lord (1,8)
406, 407	My Lord be praised by brother sun (2)
406, 407	My Lord be praised by sister moon and all the stars (3)
406, 407	By mother earth my Lord be praised (5)
406, 407	My Lord be praised by those who prove ... their love (6)
406, 407	with thee, Lord, their reward is sure (6)
408	the Lord is God, and he alone (3)
411	O bless the Lord, my soul (1-2,6)
411	forget not all his benefits! The Lord to thee is kind (2)
412	sing to the Lord a new song (1-6)
413	Rivers and seas and torrents roaring, honor the Lord (3)
413	honor the Lord with wild acclaim (3)
414	All thy works, O Lord, shall bless thee (6)
415	my ever grateful heart, O Lord, thy mercy shall adore (4)
419	Lord of all being, throned afar (1)
419	Lord of all life, below, above (3)
421	O Lamb of God, Lord Jesus Christ (2)
421	as you sit at God's right hand ... mercy, Lord, upon us (2)
421	You, only, Christ, as Lord we own (3)
425	Sing now with joy unto the Lord (1)
428	O angels, sing and bless the Lord (1)
428	bless the Lord and praise him evermore (1-5)
428	O changing seasons bless the Lord (2)
428	heat and cold, O night and day ... bless the Lord (3)
428	O men and women, bless the Lord (4)
428	people bless the Lord like righteous souls of yore (5)
429	The Lord pours eyesight on the blind (3)
429	the Lord supports the fainting mind (3)
431	my rock, and my redeeming Lord, in all my words and ways (4)

484	Praise the Lord through every nation (1)
484	Jesus, Lord, our Captain glorious (2)
485	Praise the Lord through every nation (1)
485	Jesus, Lord, our Captain glorious (2)
486	Hosanna to the living Lord ... to the incarnate Word (1)
486	Hosanna Lord, Hosanna in the highest (R)
486	Hosanna Lord, thine angels cry ... thy saints reply (2)
488	Be thou my vision, O Lord of my heart (1)
488	I ever with thee and thou with me, Lord (2)
489	the everlasting Lord (2)
490	Shine in my heart, Lord Jesus (R)
494	Crown him the Lord of life, who triumphed o'er the grave (3)
494	Crown him of lords the Lord, who over all doth reign (4)
494	Crown him the Lord of heaven, enthroned in worlds above (5)
496, 497	whole creation's Head and Lord ... assumed our very nature (2)
499	Lord God, you have set your servant free to go in peace (1)
499	my eyes have seen the Savior, Christ the Lord (1)
501, 502	the giver and the Lord of life (2)
501, 502	and to the Spirit: God the Lord (6)
505	increase our faith in our dear Lord (2)
506, 507	wisdoms which as yet know not the Lord (3)
506, 507	Pray we then, O Lord the Spirit, on our lives descend (5)
506, 507	we, your creatures, call you Lord (6)
517	How lovely is thy dwelling-place, O Lord of hosts, to me (1)
517	gracious Lord (2)
517	in glory throned, Lord God, great King of kings (3)
518	chosen of the Lord, and precious (1)
518	To this temple, where we call thee, come, O Lord (3)
518	come, O Lord of hosts, today (3)
519, 520	to thy Lord shalt thou be led (2)
522, 523	Grace which like the Lord, the giver, never fails (2)
522, 523	showing that the Lord is near (3)
524	I love thy kingdom, Lord, the house of thine abode (1)
525	The Church's one foundation is Jesus Christ her Lord (1)
525	her charter of salvation, one Lord, one faith, one birth (2)
525	Lord, give us grace that we like them, the meek (5)
528	Lord, you give the great commission (1)
528	Lord, you call us to your service (2)
528	Lord, you make the common holy (3)
528	Lord, you show us love's true measure (4)
528	Lord, you bless with words assuring (5)
530	spread, thou mighty word, spread the kingdom of the Lord (1)
531	Name of Jesus glorify till every people call him Lord (4)
537	with us the cross to bear, for Christ our Lord (3)
538	Let thy people praise thee, Lord (2)
540	O Lord, now let thy fire enkindle our hearts (2)
540	O harvest Lord ... the laborers how few (2)
540	Send forth, O Lord, thy strong Evangel (3)
542	when Christ is throned as Lord all ... forsake their fear (2)
542	One Lord, in one great Name unite us all who own thee (3)
547	one Lord, one Faith ... Baptism, one Father of us all (3)
548	strong in the Lord of hosts, and in his mighty power (2)
551	Lord, bring the day of truth and love (2)
560	Remember your servants, Lord, when you come in ... power (A)
561	till every foe is vanquished and Christ is Lord indeed (1)

563	the Lord himself, thy Leader, shall all thy foes subdue (1)
563	Lord has been thy shelter, the Lord will be thy light (4)
564, 565	Since, Lord, thou dost defend us with thy Spirit (3)
566	Impart them, Lord, to each and all, as each and ... need (1)
566	hasten, Lord, that perfect day (2)
567	Thine arm, O Lord, in days of old was strong to heal (1)
567	youth renewed and frenzy calmed owned thee, the Lord (2)
567	the Lord of light (2)
567	now, O Lord, be near to bless, almighty as of yore (2)
567	thou our great deliverer still ... Lord of life and death (3)
568	Blessed Lord Jesus, who camest in poverty (2)
569	give to us peace in our time, O Lord (1-3)
569	thou wilt give peace in thy time, O Lord (4)
570, 571	seek the Lord, who is your life (2)
570, 571	the Lord is waiting still (4)
570, 571	Risen Lord, shall yet the city be the city of despair (5)
570, 571	be its name, "The Lord is there" (5)
572	Captain Christ, O lowly Lord, Servant King (2)
573	thy kingdom come, O Lord, thy will be done (R)
574, 575	forgive, O Lord, we cry (3)
578	Remember, Lord, thy works of old (2)
578	Whom shall we trust but thee, O Lord (3)
579	O Christ, the Lord of hill and plain (2)
579	wherever, Lord, thy people go, protect them (2)
591	from sleep and from damnation, deliver us, good Lord (2)
593	Lord, make us servants of your peace (1)
593	Jesus, our lord (3)
593	Lord, make us servants of your peace (5)
596	Lord of lords and King of kings (1)
596	cleanse ... through the glory of the Lord (3)
597	for all the earth shall know the Lord (2)
598	Lord Christ, when first thou cam'st to earth (1)
605	What does the Lord require for praise and offering (1)
606	as we hear and love our Lord, the living God (1)
606	that Christ the Lord may be with us through all our days (2)
607	Lord, strengthen all who labor that we may find release (3)
610	Lord, whose love through humble service bore the weight (1)
610	As, O Lord, your deep compassion healed the sick (2)
610	that your servants, Lord, in freedom may your mercy know (4)
613	We pray thee, Lord, arise, and come in thy great might (4)
614	scattered companies unite in service to the Lord of light (3)
617	Oh, clothe us with thy heavenly armor, Lord (3)
618	most gracious, magnify the Lord (2)
621, 622	for unending, for unbroken is the feast-day of the Lord (2)
623	while for thy grace, Lord ... voices of praise ... raise (3)
626	Lord, be thy word my rule; in it may I rejoice (1)
627	Lord, grant us all aright to learn the wisdom it imparts (5)
628	Help us, O Lord (1-3)
629	the Lord has yet more light and truth (1-3)
634	I call on thee, Lord Jesus Christ (1)
636, 637	How firm a foundation, ye saints of the Lord (1)
641	Lord Jesus, think on me (1-4)
643	How dread are thine eternal years, O everlasting Lord (2)
643	Yet I may love thee too, O Lord, almighty as thou art (5)
644	my Lord, my Life, my Way, my End (4)

645, 646	I fear no ill with thee, dear Lord, beside me (4)
648	The Lord told Moses what to do (2)
652, 653	Dear Lord and Father of mankind forgive our foolish ways (1)
652, 653	gracious calling of the Lord (2)
654	Day by day, dear Lord, of thee three things I pray (1)
656	the secret of the Lord is theirs (1)
656	Lord, who left the heavens our life and peace to bring (2)
656	Lord, we thy presence seek (4)
661	such happy, simple fisher-folk before the Lord came down (1)
662	the darkness deepens, Lord, with me abide (1)
662	Through cloud and sunshine, Lord, abide with me (2)
662	in life, in death, O Lord, abide with me (4)
663	The Lord my God my shepherd is (1)
666	Lord, hear my supplicating voice and graciously reply (1)
666	My soul with patience waits for thee, the living Lord (2)
667	it is the Lord who rises with healing in his wings (1)
668	My help is from the Lord above (1)
668	Thy faithful guardian is the Lord (3)
669	O trust the Lord then wholly, if thou wouldst be secure (2)
670	Lord, for ever at thy side let my place and portion be (1)
670	teach me thou alone art Lord (2)
670	Israel, now and evermore in the Lord Almighty trust (4)
671	The Lord has promised good to me (3)
673	blessed is she who believes in the Lord (1)
673	blessed is she who perceives the Lord (2)
673	blessed are they who see the Lord (3)
674	you taught us, Lord, to pray (1)
674	Lord, cleanse the depths within our souls (4)
675	the Lord for you accepted death upon a cross (3)
677	Judge not the Lord by feeble sense (4)
678, 679	For the Lord defends and shields me (1)
678, 679	in the day of your deliverance thank the Lord (1)
678, 679	Praise the Lord, who has done great things (2)
682	I love thee Lord ... not because I hope for heaven thereby (1)
682	but as thyself hast loved me, O ever loving Lord (5)
683, 684	Where is the blessedness I knew when first I saw the Lord (2)
686	prone to wander, Lord, I feel it (3)
687, 688	Lord Sabaoth his Name, from age to age the same (2)
689	I sought the Lord (1)
689	not so much that I ... as thou, dear Lord, on me (2)
689	the whole of love is but my answer, Lord, to thee (3)
695, 696	salvation for which, O Lord, you taught us to prepare (2)
697	life shall be thy service, Lord (4)
702	Lord, thou hast searched me (1)
702	Lord thou ... dost know where'er I rest, where'er I go (1)
706	In your mercy, Lord, you called me (1)
706	Lord, I did not freely choose you (2)
706	you, O Lord, have loved me first (3)
707	Take my life, and let it be consecrated, Lord, to thee (1)
708	do thou, Lord, our only Savior ... our bosoms fill (2)
710	Make a joyful noise unto the Lord (RC)

Lord's

| 51 | We the Lord's people, heart and voice uniting (1) |
| 51 | This is the Lord's house, home of all his people (2) |

lords

lore

lose

loss

lost

509   make a lost world thy home (5)
537   the wayward and the lost, by restless passions tossed (2)
539   tell how he stooped to save his lost creation (2)
580   lost to purpose and to meaning (2)
657   lost in wonder, love, and praise (3)
671   I once was lost but now am found (1)

lot
231   the lot fell to Matthias for whom we now rejoice (2/2-24)
649, 650   where'er our changing lot is cast (3)
718   in this free land by thee our lot is cast (2)

loud
114   angel-song rang loud and high (2)
185, 186   sing to God right thankfully loud songs of alleluia (1)
286   praising loud their heavenly King (1)
299   earth, kindling, blazed her loud acclaim (1)
307   heaven and earth with loud hosanna worship thee (5)
366   Hark, the loud celestial hymn angel choirs ... raising (2)
366   prophets swell the loud refrain (3)
412   Earth and all stars, loud rushing planets (1)
412   O victory, loud shouting army (1)
412   Hail, wind, and rain, loud blowing snow-storms (2)
412   Flowers and trees, loud rustling dry leaves (2)
412   Trumpet and pipes, loud clashing cymbals (3)
412   Harp, lute, and lyre, loud humming cellos (3)
412   Engines and steel, loud pounding hammers (4)
412   Limestone and beams, loud building workers (4)
412   Classrooms and labs loud boiling test tubes (5)
412   Athlete and band, loud cheering people (5)
412   Knowledge and truth, loud sounding wisdom (6)
412   Daughter and son, loud praying members (6)
432   loud organs, his glory forth tell in deep tone (3)
543   loud that grace proclaim, which makes thy darkness bright (3)
544   earth repeat the loud amen (5)
555   for not with swords loud clashing (2)
556, 557   Your clear hosannas raise, and alleluias loud (3)
562   Christians, lift your voices, loud your anthems raise (2)
599   let it resound loud as the rolling sea (1)

louder
284   The joyous notes pursue and louder anthems raise (8)
479   louder still and louder praise the precious blood (5)

love
3, 4   grow in love for every-one (2)
5   O thou true Sun of heavenly love (2)
5   with love all envy to subdue (4)
9   of faith and hope and love undimmed (3)
9   Awake, awake to love and work (4)
9   So let the love of Jesus come and set thy soul ablaze (5)
10   New every morning is the love (1)
10   love our wakening and uprising prove (1)
10   some softening gleam of love and prayer shall dawn (4)
10   love ... shall dawn on every cross and care (4)

10	Only, O Lord, in thy dear love, fit us for perfect rest (6)
18	let us cling always to your love (2c)
18	O Spirit bringing truth and love (5)
19, 20	let love in flames of living fire the hearts ... inspire (2)
40, 41	O Spirit, bond of peace and love (5)
44, 45	the fire of love in us renew (3)
47	fill me with thy love divine (3)
47	by love inflamed, arise unto thee a sacrifice (4)
47	make me burn thy love to know (5)
49	that all may see his love displayed (2)
49	with thanks his dying love record (3)
53	not in torment hold us, but in love enfold us (2)
53	but wilt trust him boldly nor dost love him coldly (3)
59	with words of love draw near (4)
63, 64	fire our hearts with ardent love (2)
63, 64	behold thee, love thee, and adore (4)
65	His rule is peace and freedom ... justice, truth and love (2)
70	bringing God's own love and power (4)
78, 79	angels keep their watch of wondering love (2)
81	To show God's love aright, she bore to us a Savior (2)
82	Of the Father's love begotten, ere the worlds began to be (1)
83	we would embrace thee, with love and awe (5)
83	who would not love thee, loving us so dearly (5)
84	Love came down at Christmas, love all lovely, love divine (1)
84	love was born at Christmas (1)
84	Worship we the Godhead, love incarnate, love divine (2)
84	Love shall be our token; love be yours and love be mine (3)
84	love to God and neighbor (3)
84	love for plea and gift and sign (3)
85, 86	earth and sea and sky revere the love of him (5)
85, 86	love of him who sent you here (5)
92	born on earth to save us; peace and love he gave us (4)
96	while we raise our hearts in love (4)
97	For the world a love supreme brought me to this stable (2)
98	Now may Mary's son, who came so long ago to love us (4)
100	wonders of his love (4)
101	I love thee, Lord Jesus! Look down from the sky (2)
101	love me I pray (3)
102	yet this child, our Lord and brother, brought us love (3)
102	brought us love for one another (3)
102	through his own redeeming love (5)
104	God's blood upon the spear-head, God's love refused again (3)
105	with true love and charity each other now embrace (4)
106	rise to adore the mystery of love (1)
106	praises of redeeming love they sang (3)
106	saved by his love, incessant we shall sing (6)
116	his in bonds of love (5)
120	the sign of God the Father's love (3)
133, 134	O Light of Light, Love given birth (1)
136, 137	shall be theirs above who joy in God with perfect love (3)
139	Triune God is thus made known in Christ as love unending (2)
145	reply, reply with love to love most high (1)
145	love shall be the prize (5)
146, 147	the Lord of love, in love sublime (2)
146, 147	Your love, O Lord, our sinful race has not returned (3)

251	look down ... with love for human-kind (1)
252	Jesus, Name of wondrous love, Name all other names above (1)
252	Jesus, Name of wondrous love (6)
255	O Love that sought and held him a prisoner of his Lord (2)
256	Saint Paul was changed by God's free love (3)
256	he saw the love of God ... beyond the law (3)
256	Renew us with your love, O Lord (4)
258	blessed they, for ever blest, who love thee most (2)
258	love thee most and serve thee best (2)
259	watched by her duteous love, in her fond arms at rest (2)
268, 269	when the love of God the Father over sin the victory won (1)
273, 274	Two stalwart trees both rooted in faith and holy love (1)
275	love and peace they taste for ever (4)
277	toil and labor cannot weary love enduring unto death (2)
277	Constant was the love he gave her (2)
278	obedient to the summons bore in love the infant Lord (1)
278	beholds her Son and Savior reigning as the Lord of love (4)
279	in one communion ever knit, one fellowship of love (3)
285	so rich in words of truth and love (2)
288	Praise to God ... for the love that crowns our days (1)
288	by deeds of kindly love for thy mercies grateful prove (3)
291	then thank the Lord, O thank the Lord for all his love (R)
291	the gifts we have to offer are what thy love imparts (3)
292	with the Father's Name ... Savior's love proclaim (3)
293	their love made them strong (2)
293	saints who love to do Jesus' will (3)
300	Glory, love, and praise, and honor for our food (1)
302, 303	perfect it in thy love, unite it (2)
304	new community of love in Christ's communion bread (2)
304	That love that made us makes us one (3)
308, 309	O stream of love past telling (2)
312	eyes which saw thy love be bright (2)
313	be to me ... Lord, of thy boundless love the token (1)
313	all that love of God could give Jesus by his sorrows gave (2)
313	by the pain and death, I now claim ... love unfailing (3)
313	I now claim, O Christ, thy love unfailing (3)
313	of thy matchless love forgive me (4)
315	one with thy saints in one unbounded love (3)
315	more blessed still, in peace and love to be (3)
316, 317	the feast, though not the love, is past and gone (2)
316, 317	the Lamb's great marriage fest of bliss and love (3)
319	all creation knows the love of God (1)
319	No greater love than this to you could bind us (2)
320	Jesus, of thy love befriend us (5)
321	thy cup with love doth overflow (1)
326	Thanksgiving and glory and worship ... blessing and love (2)
329-331	ever too his love confessing (6)
332	Here may thy faithful people know ... thy love (2)
332	the blessings of thy love (2)
336	in our life thy love divine ... flesh and blood has taken (1)
337	And now, O Father, mindful of the love that bought us (1)
337	most patient Savior, who canst love us still (4)
339	be thy love with love requited (3)
340, 341	By this pledge, Lord, that you love us (2)
342	of God's own love his dearest token (1)

342	your love shines though your strength is waning (2)
343	Lord, sup with us in love divine, thy Body and thy Blood (4)
344	let us each, thy love possessing, triumph (1)
344	so that when thy love shall call us (3)
345	peace to our land, the fruit of truth and love (3)
347	go to the world in love (2)
347	richly from above his love supplies the grace and power (2)
349	Holy Spirit, Lord of love, who descended from above (1)
349	once again in love draw near (1)
350	O God of love, to thee we bow (1)
350	Eternal love, with them abide (3)
351	Father's boundless love, with the Holy Spirit's favor (1)
352	their vows of life-long love (1)
352	increase, rekindle, and restore their love (3)
352	restore their love till life shall end (3)
353	Your love, O God, has called us here (1)
353	for all love finds its source in you (1)
353	the perfect love that casts out fear (1)
353	the love that Christ makes ever new (1)
353	every day their love renew (2)
353	O God of love, inspire our life (3)
353	join every husband, every wife in mutual love (3)
353	mutual love and love for you (3)
359	theirs by the love of Christ a kingdom won (4)
362	perfect in power, in love, and purity (3)
363	thy love has blessed the wide world's wondrous story (1)
363	to thee in reverent love our hearts are bowed (2)
363	still imploring thy love and favor, kept to us always (5)
365	Father whose love unknown all things created own (1)
365	to eternity love and adore (4)
368	source of mercy, love, and peace (1)
368	fill them with the Savior's love (3)
368	Source of comfort, cheer us with the Savior's love (3)
370	I bind unto myself the power of the great love (3)
370	the great love of cherubim (3)
370	Christ in hearts of all that love me (6)
371	Spirit of truth and love, life-giving, holy Dove (3)
371	wisdom, love, might; boundless to ocean's tide (4)
372	his love shall be our strength and stay while ages roll (4)
376	Joyful, joyful, we adore thee, God of glory, Lord of love (1)
376	all who live in love are thine (3)
376	teach us how to love each other (3)
379	God is love, let heaven adore him (1)
379	God is love, let earth rejoice (1)
379	God is Love, eternal Love (1)
379	God is Love ... enfolds us, all the world in one embrace (2)
379	God is Love, and though with blindness sin afflicts (3)
379	Love for ever o'er the universe must reign (3)
382	King of glory, King of peace, I will love thee (1)
382	that love may never cease, I will move thee (1)
388	O gratefully sing his power and his love (1)
390	who with his love doth befriend thee (3)
391	vast as eternity thy love (5)
392	Come, we who love the Lord, and let our joys be known (1)
394, 395	let peace, descending like a dove, make known ... love (3)

394, 395	let peace ... make known on earth your healing love (3)
396, 397	blessed us on our way with countless gifts of love (1)
401	Ancient of everlasting days, and God of love (1)
404	glad in the knowledge of your love so great (2)
404	We love you with our heart and strength and mind (3)
406, 407	My Lord be praised by those who prove ... their love (6)
406, 407	prove in free forgivingness their love (6)
408	the God of love, the God of our salvation (1)
411	clothes thee with his love, upholds thee with his truth (5)
413	awed by his love his foes surrender (1)
414	works by love and mercy wrought (4)
414	works of love surpassing measure (4)
414	vast in love, God is good to all creation (5)
415	I'm lost in wonder, love, and praise (1)
416	for the love ... from our birth over and around us lies (1)
416	joy of human love, brother, sister, parent, child (4)
416	offering up on every shore thy pure sacrifice of love (5)
416	faith and hope and love divine (6)
419	whose light is truth, whose warmth is love (3)
420	the Church, in liturgy and song, in faith and love (3)
422	Rooted and grounded in thy love (2)
423	thy clouds, which are fountains of goodness and love (2)
424	most of all that love has found us (3)
426	learning here, by faith and love ... to sing above (5)
431	a law of love within our hearts (3)
432	praise him who hath taught you to sing of his love (2)
432	For love in creation, for heaven restored (4)
434	which ... best is writ ... power ... wisdom, or the love (3)
435	Name him, Christians ... with love strong as death (4)
436	adorned with prayer and love and joy (3)
436	thy grace and love in me reveal (4)
439	What wondrous love is this, O my soul, O my soul (1)
440	let our hearts and souls be stirred now to seek and love (1)
440	to seek and love and fear thee (1)
440	drawn from earth to love thee solely (1)
441, 442	When the sun of bliss is beaming light and love (3)
441, 442	light and love upon my way (3)
445, 446	O wisest love, that flesh and blood, which ... did fail (3)
447	What now can separate us from the love of Christ our Lord (2)
447	separate us from the love of Jesus Christ our Lord (4)
448, 449	O love, how deep, how broad, how high (1)
448, 449	glory ... for love so deep, so high, so broad (6)
450, 451	Sinners, whose love can ne'er forget the wormwood (5)
452	whose life and death that love reveal which mortals need (1)
455, 456	O Love of God, how strong and true (1)
455, 456	O wide-embracing, wondrous Love (2)
458	My song is love unknown, my Savior's love to me (1)
458	love to the loveless shown that they might lovely be (1)
458	never was love, dear King, never was grief like thine (7)
463, 464	He is the Life. Love him in the World of the Flesh (3)
467	Sing, my soul, his wondrous love (1)
467	what are we that he should show so much love to us below (2)

530	how his never-failing love guides us on to heaven above (4)
531	Give tongues of fire and hearts of love to preach (2)
535	thanks never ceasing and infinite love (4)
538	let all be, below, above, one in joy, and light and love (2)
539	one soul should fail to know his love and might (1)
539	God, in whom they live and move, is Love (2)
543	till sovereign love in worlds above the glory raise (3)
544	People and realms of evry tongue dwell on his love (3)
544	dwell on his love with sweetest song (3)
545	for the joy before him set, and moved by pitying love (4)
547	so learn his love -- its length and breadth (1)
547	his love ... its fullness, depth, and height (1)
547	Then walk in love as Christ has loved (4)
549, 550	saying "Christian, love me more" (3)
549, 550	Christian, love me more than these (4)
549, 550	serve and love thee best of all (5)
551	Lord, bring the day of truth and love (2)
552, 553	Christ is its life and Christ its love (3)
554	'twill be in the valley of love and delight (1)
555	nor roll of stirring drums, but deeds of love and mercy (2)
558	we will love both friend and foe in all our strife (1)
558	preach thee, too, as love knows how, by kindly deeds (3)
559	love with every passion blending (3)
563	His love fortells thy trials (1)
566	From thee ... all pity, care, and love (1)
568	bind in thy love every nation and race (4)
570, 571	All who love and serve your city (1)
570, 571	honor, peace, and love retreating (2)
572	summon us to love by loss, gaining all by giving (3)
573	by wars and tumults love is mocked, derided (2)
573	How shall we love thee, holy hidden Being (5)
573	if we love not the world which thou hast made (5)
573	Bind us in thine own love for better seeing thy Word (5)
574, 575	From love of pleasure, lust of gold ... wean us (2)
576, 577	God is love ... where true love is, God himself is there (R)
576, 577	Here in Christ we gather, love of Christ our calling (1)
576, 577	Christ, our love, is with us, gladness be his greeting (1)
576, 577	Let us fear and love him, holy God eternal (1)
576, 577	Loving him, let each love Christ in one another (1)
578	O God of love, O King of peace (1)
579	O Trinity of love and power (4)
581	Where charity and love prevail there God is ever found (1)
581	brought here together by Christ's love (1)
581	by love are we thus bound (1)
581	with heart and mind and strength now love him in return (2)
581	let us love each other well in Christian holiness (3)
581	Love can exclude no race or creed if honored be God's Name (6)
582, 583	city ... whose laws are love, whose crown is servanthood (3)
585	gifts of love to mind and sense (2)
585	Love that gives, gives evermore (3)
585	Drained is love in making full (4)
585	nails and crown of thorns tell of what God's love must be (5)
585	God, whose arms of love aching, spent, the world sustain (6)
586	every deed of human kindness done in love is done to thee (3)
587	who dost in love proclaim each family thine own (1)

587	with constant love as sentinel (1)
587	who teachest us to find the love from self set free (3)
587	in all our hearts such love increase (3)
588, 589	give it root in every heart to bring forth fruits of love (2)
590	hymns be rising in every city for your love and care (1)
590	seeking to gather all in love and pity (3)
593	where there is hate, may we sow love (1)
593	but seek to love unselfishly (4)
597	guide us to justice, truth, and love (1)
597	Then enemies shall learn to love (2)
598	O aweful Love, which found no room in life (2)
598	New advent of the love of Christ (3)
598	O love that triumphs over loss (4)
602	Jesu, Jesu, fill us with your love (R)
602	these are the ones we should love (3)
603, 604	through ... every birth, to draw an answering love (1)
603, 604	Still east and west his love extends (2)
605	Do justly, love mercy, walk humbly with your God (1-3)
606	Where true charity and love dwell, God himself is there (A)
606	Since the love of Christ has joined us in one body (1)
606	as we hear and love our Lord, the living God (1)
606	so let us in sincerity love all people (1)
606	our boundless source of joy and truth, of peace and love (3)
607	in love and mercy guide us and heal our strife-torn world (1)
607	when hatred and division give way to love and peace (4)
608	O Trinity of love and power (4)
609	till all the world shall learn thy love (5)
610	Lord, whose love through humble service bore the weight (1)
610	use the love your Spirit kindles still to save (2)
610	love in living deeds to show (4)
611	Christ the worker, Love alive for us (7)
612	taught by thee we covet most ... holy, heavenly, love (1)
612	Love is kind, and suffers long (2)
612	love is meek, and thinks no wrong (2)
612	love than death itself more strong (2)
612	therefore, give us love (2-3)
612	love will ever with us stay (3)
612	Faith and hope and love we see (4)
612	but the greatest of the three, and the best, is love (4)
613	Where is thy reign of peace, and purity, and love (2)
616	love, joy, hope, like flowers spring in his path to birth (3)
616	Name shall stand for ever, his changeless Name of Love (5)
617	one in the love of all things sweet and fair (2)
617	thy trusty shield, thy sword of love divine (3)
625	with a well-tuned heart sing thou the songs of love (4)
629	enlarge, expand all living souls to comprehend your love (3)
633	love unending (1)
633	your love outpouring (2)
633	Word that speaks your Father's love (4)
635	Who trusts in God's unchanging love builds on a rock (1)
638, 639	tell me if thy name is Love (3)
638, 639	'Tis Love, 'tis Love! Thou diedst for me! (4)
638, 639	Pure Universal Love thou art (4)
638, 639	thy nature and thy name is Love (4)
642	love of Jesus, what it is, none but who love him know (4)

643	Yet I may love thee too, O Lord, almighty as thou art (5)
643	thou hast stooped to ask of me the love of my poor heart (5)
645, 646	The King of love my shepherd is (1)
645, 646	but yet in love he sought me (3)
647	some I love have reached the end (2)
647	The way is truth, the way is love (2)
649, 650	we seek the peace your love imparts (1)
652, 653	silence of eternity interpreted by love (3)
654	to see thee more clearly, love thee more dearly (1)
657	Love divine, all loves excelling (1)
657	pure, unbounded love thou art (1)
657	glory in thy perfect love (2)
657	lost in wonder, love, and praise (3)
659, 660	move by some clear, winning word of love (2)
663	surely I can trust thy love for all the days to come (5)
665	Love doth stand at his hand (4)
676	you can tell the love of Jesus (2)
681	the blood of friend as sign of love for comrade spilt (4)
681	Thou hidden fount of love, of peace ... truth ... beauty (5)
682	I love thee Lord ... not because I hope for heaven thereby (1)
682	Then why ... should I not love thee well (4)
682	E'en so I love thee, and will love (6)
686	mount of God's unchanging love (1)
686	prone to leave the God I love (3)
689	I find, I walk, I love (3)
689	the whole of love is but my answer, Lord, to thee (3)
691	may my love to thee pure, warm, and changeless be (2)
693	thy love unknown has broken every barrier down (5)
693	of thy great love ... to prove (6)
693	love, the breadth, length, depth, and height to prove (6)
698	held in forgiving love, let me be still (2)
698	fulfillment of my life in love outpoured (3)
698	my life in you, O Christ, your love in me (3)
700	O love that casts out fear, O love that casts out sin (1)
700	Great love of God, come in (3)
700	Love of the living God, of Father and of Son (4)
700	love of the Holy Ghost, fill thou each needy one (4)
701	they who love God win (3)
704	kindle a flame of sacred love upon the altar of my heart (1)
704	my acts of faith and love repeat (4)
705	A world in need now summons us to labor, love and give (2)
705	a world redeemed by Christ-like love (2)
705	serve thy cause and share thy love with all humanity (3)
706	had your love not chosen me (2)
706	knowing well, that if I love you, you ... loved me first (3)
707	Take my hands ... let them move at the impulse of thy love (1)
708	with thy love our bosoms fill (2)
708	Blessed Jesus! Thou hast loved us, love us still (2)
717	thy name I love (2)
717	I love thy rocks and rills, thy woods and templed hills (2)
718	Thy love divine hath led us in the past (2)
718	fill all our lives with love and grace divine (4)

love's

12, 13	O Spirit, love's life-giving ray (4)

111	Son of God, love's pure light radiant beams (3)
164	through our pity and our shame love answers love's appeal (2)
188, 189	Love's redeeming work is done (1)
222	shall come in all love's glorious power to rule (4)
340, 341	may the Church still waiting for you keep love's tie (3)
340, 341	keep love's tie unbroken, Lord (3)
528	Lord, you show us love's true measure (4)
576, 577	Grant us love's fulfillment, joy with all the blessed (3)
585	hidden is love's agony, love's endeavor, love's expense (2)
593	May we not look for love's return (4)
610	till your love's revealing light ... dawns (3)
614	Let Love's unconquerable might ... unite (3)

loved

148	We have not loved you (3)
167	O dearly, dearly has he loved (5)
231	John, your loved disciple, exiled to Patmos' shore (2/12-27)
242	He loved thee well, and firmly said, "Come, let us go ..." (2)
293	lived and died for the Lord they loved and knew (1)
293	They loved their Lord so dear (2)
304	I come with joy to meet my Lord, forgiven, loved and free (1)
434	cross where Christ my Savior loved and died (4)
447	yet he who loved us from the first ensures our victory (3)
518	All that dedicated city, dearly loved of God on high (2)
547	Then walk in love as Christ has loved (4)
603, 604	Thus freely loved, though fully known (4)
682	but as thyself hast loved me, O ever loving Lord (5)
706	knowing well, that if I love you, you ... loved me first (3)
706	you, O Lord, have loved me first (3)
708	Blessed Jesus! Thou hast loved us, love us still (2)
709	at our Father's loved abode our souls arrive in peace (4)
719	who more than self their country loved (2)
720	between their loved homes and the war's desolation (2)

loveless

| 458 | love to the loveless shown that they might lovely be (1) |

lovelier

| 10 | Old friends, old scenes, will lovelier be (4) |
| 427 | No lovelier antiphon in all high heaven is known (3) |

loveliness

76	restore earth's own true loveliness once more ((4)
175	Daily the loveliness grows (3)
216	Daily the loveliness grows (2)
372	Formless, all lovely forms declare his loveliness (2)

lovely

84	Love came down at Christmas, love all lovely, love divine (1)
353	O gracious God, you consecrate all that is lovely (2)
353	you consecrate all that is lovely, good, and true (2)
372	Formless, all lovely forms declare his loveliness (2)
458	love to the loveless shown that they might lovely be (1)
517	How lovely is thy dwelling-place, O Lord of hosts, to me (1)

loves

182	he suffers still, yet loves the more (4)
182	suffers still, yet loves the more (4)
603, 604	claims us as his friends and loves us as we are (2)
657	Love divine, all loves excelling (1)

loving

31, 32	like moon and night, give loving peace (5)
83	who would not love thee, loving us so dearly (5)
115	let loving hearts enthrone him (3)
143	Alone and fasting Moses saw the loving God (2)
143	loving God who gave the law (2)
144	restore us by your loving care to peace and joy within (2)
238, 239	loving Christ with single heart (2)
251	thy loving care renew (2)
307	here in loving reverence bow (2)
419	yet to each loving heart how near (1)
445, 446	O loving wisdom of our God (2)
459	where his loving people meet to share the gift divine (2)
537	with loving zeal (1)
568	Father all loving, who rulest in majesty (1)
576, 577	Loving him, let each love Christ in one another (1)
602	Loving puts us on our knees (4)
641	let me thy loving servant be (2)
649, 650	O Jesus, joy of loving hearts (1)
669	what loving wisdom chooseth, redeeming might will do (3)
682	nor yet for fear that loving not I might for ever die (1)
682	most loving Jesus Christ (4)
682	but as thyself hast loved me, O ever loving Lord (5)

lovingkindness

46	long our mortal blindness has missed God's lovingkindness (3)
379	God's eternal lovingkindness guides us through (3)
518	with thy wonted lovingkindness hear thy servants (3)

low

75	valleys shall be exalted, the lofty hills brought low (1)
92	Wise Men three to him led, kneel they low by his bed (3)
104	But now, as at the ending, The low is lifted high (4)
117, 118	low lies his head with the beasts of the stall (2)
233, 234	these lay the prince of this world low (3)
462	all shall frame to bow them low before thee, Lord (4)
579	traffic runs amain by mountain pass or valley low (2)
623	Low before him with our praises we fall (5)

lowest

320	grant us, with thy saints, though lowest (6)

lowing

101	The cattle are lowing, the baby awakes (2)

lowliest

307	Though the lowliest form doth veil thee as of old (3)

lowliness
477   Thou cam'st to us in lowliness of thought (2)
656   to dwell in lowliness with us, our pattern and our King (2)

lowly
48   this day the high and lowly, through ages joined in tune (1)
53   came in likeness lowly, Son of God most holy (1)
77   A maid in lowly human place became ... the chosen (3)
80   this new-born child of lowly birth shall be the joy (2)
89, 90   above its sad and lowly plains they bend on hovering wing (2)
97   By this lowly birth of mine, sinner, riches ... thine (2)
99   Down in a lowly manger the humble Christ was born (3)
102   Once in royal David's city stood a lowly cattle shed (1)
102   with the poor, the scorned, the lowly lived ... Savior (2)
102   Not in that poor lowly stable ... we shall see him (6)
119   As with joyful steps they sped to that lowly manger bed (2)
156   In lowly pomp ride on to die (2,5)
252   kneeling in her lowly cell, by the angel Gabriel (2)
257   lowly Virgin brings her new-born babe (2)
265   "All hail ... thou lowly maiden Mary" (1)
267   Mary, the pure and lowly maid, the favored of the Lord (4)
268, 269   he has cast down all the mighty ... lowly are his choice (4)
277   Sing of Mary, pure and lowly, virgin mother undefiled (1)
454   lowly came on earth to die (1)
475   his own ... worship lowly, yield their spirits wholly (1)
491   so weak and lowly as unheeded prophets taught (2)
496, 497   Jesus, Holy, holy, yet most lowly draw thou near us (1)
525   the meek and lowly, on high may dwell with thee (5)
572   Captain Christ, O lowly Lord, Servant King (2)
586   by thy lowly human birth ... come to join the workers (1)
656   he to the lowly soul will still himself impart (3)
656   give us a pure and lowly heart, a temple fit for thee (4)
659, 660   in lowly paths of service free (1)

Luke
232   For Luke, beloved physician, all praise (2/10-18)
285   What thanks and praise to thee we owe ... for Luke (1)
285   Luke, thy saint, through whom we know so many ... words (1)

lullay
247   Lully, Lullay, thou little tiny child (R)
247   bye-bye, Lully lullay (R)
247   this poor youngling for whom we sing ... lully lullay (1)
247   for thy parting nor say nor sing bye-bye, lully lullay (3)

lully
247   Lully, Lullay, thou little tiny child (R)
247   bye-bye, Lully lullay (R)
247   this poor youngling for whom we sing ... lully lullay (1)
247   for thy parting nor say nor sing bye-bye, lully lullay (3)

lure
472   walk thou beside us lest the tempting byways lure us (3)
472   lure us away from thee to endless night (3)
563   heed not the treacherous voices that lure thy soul astray (2)

lures
469, 470   no place ... earth's failures have such kindly judgment (2)
609   from paths where hide the lures of greed (2)

lust
573   Lust of possession worketh desolations (4)
574, 575   From love of pleasure, lust of gold ... wean us (2)
582, 583   O shame to us who rest content while lust and greed (2)
584   lest, maddened by the lust for power ... ourselves destroy (4)
613   oppression, lust, and crime shall flee thy face before (3)

luster
286   robes whose luster ne'er shall fade (2)
419   before thy ever-blazing throne we ask no luster (3)
419   we ask no luster of our own (3)
441, 442   from the cross the radiance streaming adds more luster (3)
441, 442   adds more luster to the day (3)
543   with luster new divinely crowned (2)

lute
412   Harp, lute, and lyre, loud humming cellos (3)
430   Sound the trumpet, touch the lute (2)

lying
173   God the Father's only Son in the tomb is lying (1)
329, 331   That last night at supper lying (3)

lyre
412   Harp, lute, and lyre, loud humming cellos (3)

maddened
584   lest, maddened by the lust for power ... ourselves destroy (4)

made
18   all you made was pure and clean (4c)
23   Apostles made a lame man walk (2)
48   living presence greeting, through Bread and Wine made near (3)
49   our Lord who made both earth and skies (1)
49   Who died to save the world he made (1)
49, 50   This is the day the Lord hath made (2)
74   Christ, who is the Promise, who has atonement made (2)
109   that hath made heaven and earth of nought (6)
110   that brought into this world the God made man (2)
112   In the bleak midwinter, frosty wind made moan (1)
131, 132   When Christ's appearing was made known (1)
135   anthems be to thee addressed, God in man made manifest (1-3)
135   cross and Easter Day attest God in man made manifest (4)
139   Triune God is thus made known in Christ as love unending (2)
140, 141   made my sin their door (2)
143   Christ, through whom all things were made (1)
146, 147   Remember, Lord ... in your own image were we made (4)
148   our self-wrought miseries have made us trust ourselves (2)
154, 155   to whom the lips of children made sweet hosannas ring (R)
162   where he through whom our flesh was made (1)

170	To mock your reign ... they made a crown of thorns (1)
188, 189	made like him, like him we rise (3)
231	grant us grace to know you, made flesh (2/12-21)
231	made flesh, yet God and Lord (2/12-21)
231	Joseph's love made "Father" to be ... God's Name (2/3-19)
231	the weak by grace made strong (2/4-25)
245	O Word made flesh, your deeds and words refresh (3)
254	For of your Church, Lord, you made known this saint (2)
268, 269	when he made the Virgin Mary mother of his only Son (1)
277	Word made flesh (1)
293	their love made them strong (2)
295	who sanctifies and guides us, made strong in our rebirth (3)
302, 303	As grain ... was in this broken bread made one (2)
304	That love that made us makes us one (3)
329, 331	Word made flesh, the bread he taketh (4)
349	When the sacred vow is made (2)
357	where thy saints made perfect gaze upon thy face (4)
373	laws ... for their guidance he hath made (1)
373	God hath made his saints victorious (2)
389	He with all-commanding might filled the new-made world (3)
389	filled the new-made world with light (3)
398	power of God that made the mountains rise (1)
399	he made the sea and land, he brought the world to birth (2)
405	all things wise and wonderful ... Lord God made them all (R)
405	he made their glowing colors (1)
405	he made their tiny wings (1)
405	the ripe fruits in the garden, he made them every one (3)
405	God Almighty, who has made all things well (5)
408	What God's almighty power hath made ... mercy keepeth (2)
409	The hand that made us is divine (3)
411	bless his holy Name, whose grace hath made thee whole (6)
413	He has made known his great salvation (1)
429	made the sky and earth and seas with all their train (2)
432	ye heavens, adore him by whom ye were made (1)
453	The ladder is long, it is strong and well made (2)
458	but men made strange (2)
458	He made the lame to run, he gave the blind their sight (4)
458	They rise, and needs will have my dear Lord made away (5)
462	The nations all whom thou hast made shall come (4)
467	Heaven and earth by him were made (2)
489	him through whom the worlds were made (2)
491	incarnate, and a native of the very world he made (4)
495	by almighty love anointed, thou hast full atonement made (2)
518	Christ is made the sure foundation (1)
530	word of how the Father's will made the world (2)
530	made the world and keeps it still (2)
539	he who made all nations is not willing one soul ... fail (1)
544	To him shall endless prayer be made (2)
555	through days of preparation thy grace has made us strong (1)
573	Spirit of life which moved ere form was made (1)
573	if we love not the world which thou hast made (5)
573	thy Word made flesh, and in a manger laid (5)
581	as members of his Body joined we are in him made one (5)
611	easy yokes that made the labor less (4)
630	Word was spoken in the deed that made the earth (1)

631	praise him for the Word made flesh (3)
633	Word made flesh, we long to hear you (1)
668	who heaven and earth hath made (1)
683, 684	I hate the sins that made thee mourn (3)
692	I found in him a resting place, and he has made me glad (1)
705	all life in Christ made new (2)
720	Power that hath made and preserved us a nation (2)

madness
| 594, 595 | Cure thy children's warring madness (3) |

Magdalene
| 232 | All praise for Mary Magdalene (2/7-22) |
| 673 | first ones ... were Mary, Joanna, and Magdalene (3) |

Magnificat
| 268 | Magnificat anima mea Dominum. Magnificat, magnificat (4-D) |
| 620 | Our Lady sings Magnificat with tune surpassing sweet (4) |

magnify
263, 264	adore and laud and magnify (1)
265	my soul shall laud and magnify his holy Name (3)
268, 269	Magnify, my soul, God's greatness (4)
373	all creation, laud and magnify his Name (2)
618	most gracious, magnify the Lord (2)

magnitude
| 491 | O the magnitude of meekness (3) |

maid
77	A maid in lowly human place became ... the chosen (3)
106	found, with Joseph and the blessed maid, her Son (4)
266	the hand-maid of the Lord now see (6)
267	Mary, the pure and lowly maid, the favored of the Lord (4)
673	first one ... to know of the birth of Jesus was the Maid (1)
673	Mary the Maid of Galilee (1)

maiden
112	but his mother only, in her maiden bliss, worshiped (3)
252	Jesus, Name decreed of old, to the maiden mother told (2)
265	"All hail ... thou lowly maiden Mary" (1)
266	He met a maiden in that place (2)
266	When the maiden heard his song (3)
266	Said the maiden, "Verily, I am your servant right truly" (6)
275	saintly maiden, godly matron, widows who have watched (2)

maidens
| 61, 62 | The time has come, O maidens wise (1) |

main
| 386, 387 | glorious the enraptured main (3) |

maintain
| 232 | the faith of Christ maintain (2/10-28) |

maintaining
433   ordaining, maintaining his kingdom divine (2)

maintains
401   On Zion's sacred height his kingdom he maintains (3)

majestic
364   the world is with the glory filled of thy majestic sway (3)

majesty
56   didst give the law, in cloud, and majesty, and awe (3)
57, 58   Every eye shall now behold him robed in dreadful majesty (2)
144   we shall acclaim your majesty, eternal Three in One (5)
156   Ride on! ride on in majesty! (1-5)
191   alleluia! to the Triune Majesty (5)
267   like her whom heaven's Majesty came down to shadow o'er (3)
365   thy sovereign majesty may we in glory see (4)
401   all might and majesty are thine, and endless praise (5)
414   Honor great our God befitteth, who his majesty can reach (2)
431   writes in fire across the skies God's majesty and praise (2)
450, 451   to him all majesty ascribe (6)
484, 485   with voice and minstrelsy extol his majesty: Alleluia (1)
568   Father all loving, who rulest in majesty (1)
643   thy majesty how bright (1)
658   O when shall I behold thy face, thou Majesty divine (2)

make
5   to make ill fortune turn to fair (4)
27, 28   for you alone can make us strong (4)
33-35   you make the daytime radiant with the sunlight (1)
43   sleep that shall me more vigorous make (3)
43   vigorous make to serve my God when I awake (3)
47   make me burn thy love to know (5)
50   Make haste to help us, Lord (3)
54   Virgin's Son, make here your home (1)
56   make safe the way that leads on high (5)
67   Make ye straight what long was crooked (3)
67   make the rougher places plain (3)
70   make a pathway through the desert (2)
74   he would have us bear it so he can make us free (4)
75   make straight all the crooked places (1)
76   make straight the way for God within (2)
97   willingly this yoke I take, and this sacrifice I make (2)
100   he comes to make his blessings flow far as the curse (3)
127   Eastern sages at his cradle make oblations rich and rare (3)
145   make clear, make clear where truth and light appear (2)
145   the friends you make shall bring God's glory bright (5)
145   arise, arise, and make a paradise (5)
148   grant us your truth to make us wise (1)
148   grant us your power to make us strong (1)
154, 155   we with all creation in chorus make reply (2)
163   for God doth make his world anew (1)
164   make us thy sorrow feel(2)
167   he died to make us good (3)
168, 169   Oh, make me thine for ever (4)

211	And all you living things make praise (3)
226, 227	fill our hearts and make them thine (3)
228	make us ready to receive gifts from your unbounded store (5)
230	his grace within shall make you whole (3)
231	Lord, make your pastors faithful (2/1-18)
242	when thou didst thine appearance make, he saw and hailed (3)
242	O Savior, make thy presence known to all who doubt (5)
284	join with our earth-bound song to make the Savior known (1)
289	our Father, make us faithful to serve the coming days (3)
302, 303	Thou, Lord, didst make all for thy pleasure (1)
305, 306	thyself at thine own board make manifest (1)
305, 306	make manifest in thine own Sacrament of Bread and Wine (1)
315	make thou our sad divisions soon to cease (2)
322	what that Word did make it, I do believe and take it (2)
337	in thine own service make us glad and free (4)
348	help us to make those decisions that bind us (4)
355	yet even at the grave we make our song: Alleluia (1)
359	make each one stronger, nobler than the last (1)
359	fill them with power, their lips make eloquent (2)
359	Make them apostles, heralds of thy cross (5)
368	Great Jehovah, form our hearts and make them thine (4)
377, 378	without our aid he did us make (2)
394, 395	let peace, descending like a dove, make known ... love (3)
394, 395	let peace ... make known on earth your healing love (3)
400	Swift flowing water, pure and clear, make music (3)
400	make music for your Lord to hear (3)
413	such sounds as make the heavens ring (2)
413	all things that live in earth and ocean make music (2)
413	make music for your mighty King (2)
419	Grant us thy truth to make us free (4)
426	God will make new heavens and earth (3)
431	So shine the Lord's commandments to make the simple wise (3)
433	he chastens and hastens his will to make known (1)
433	thy Name be ever praised! O Lord, make us free (3)
436	make it a temple set apart from earthly use (3)
437, 438	Make known his might, the deeds his arm has done (2)
465, 466	eternal wisdom, make me wise (1)
467	to make salvation sure, guides us by his Spirit pure (3)
476	he speaks to us in human terms to make his glory known (4)
479	angel hosts, rejoicing, make their glad reply (4)
486	make our secret soul to be a temple pure and worthy thee (4)
500	make thy temples worthy thee (1)
500	make us eternal truth receive (3)
501, 502	to us your varied gifts make known (3)
505	make us to love thy sacred word (3)
509	make this house thy home (1)
509	make a lost world thy home (5)
512	make us know and choose thy way (2)
515	Make our hearts thy habitation (2)
528	Lord, you make the common holy (3)
539	make known to every heart his saving grace (4)
540	make haste to help us in our weakness (3)
564, 565	There's no discouragement shall make him once relent (1)

564, 565	he will make good his right to be a pilgrim (2)
574, 575	Search out our hearts and make us true (2)
574, 575	from sins which make the heart grow cold, wean us (2)
578	make wars throughout the world to cease (1)
584	make their might our own (1)
593	Lord, make us servants of your peace (1,5)
593	where there is strife, may we make one (1)
609	make haste to heal these hearts of pain (4)
610	save and make us whole (2)
611	he will make that heavy burden light (5)
629	make us all go on to know with nobler powers conferred (3)
632	O make thy Church, dear Savior, a lamp of purest gold (3)
641	make me pure within (1)
649, 650	make all our moments calm and bright (4)
655	O speak, and make me listen, thou guardian of my soul (2)
668	sun by day nor moon by night need make thy soul afraid (3)
676	There is a balm in Gilead to make the wounded whole (R)
677	God is his own interpreter, and he will make it plain (6)
678, 679	Make his deeds known to the peoples (2)
697	accept my heart this day, and make it always thine (1)
699	make and keep me pure within (3)
702	far away my dwelling make (4)
704	make the sacrifice complete (4)
705	to make our life an offering to God that all may live (2)
705	Church of Christ is calling us to make the dream come true (2)
707	Take my will, and make it thine ... no longer mine (2)
710	Make a joyful noise unto the Lord (RC)

maker

40, 41	O God, our Maker and our end (5)
46	on God our Maker calling ... the Giver good (1)
47	Maker, who didst fashion me image of thyself to be (3)
77	our very flesh our Maker shares (2)
117, 118	Maker and Monarch and Savior of all (2)
152	Kind Maker of the world, O hear the fervent prayer (1)
179	Maker and Redeemer, life and health of all (4)
282, 283	maker of all things, ruler of all nations (1)
282, 283	peace maker blessed (2)
290	God, our Maker, doth provide for our wants to be supplied (1)
291	He only is the Maker of all things near and far (2)
339	at thy feet I cry, my Maker (2)
355	the creator and maker of mankind (1)
385	maker of earth and sky (1)
388	Our Maker, Defender, Redeemer, and Friend (5)
391	almighty Maker (3)
429	I'll praise my Maker while I've breath (1)
611	Yoke maker, fashioned by his hands (4)

Maker's

434	spread her Maker's praise abroad (1)

makers

560	Blessed are the peace-makers (7)

makes

100	makes the nations prove the glories of his righteousness (4)
101	but little Lord Jesus no crying he makes (2)
187	by his tomb Christ makes room (2)
222	he makes his glorious presence clear (2)
304	That love that made us makes us one (3)
327, 328	with heavenly bread he makes the hungry whole (7)
329-331	faith, our outward sense befriending, makes ... clear (5)
329-331	makes our inward vision clear (5)
353	the love that Christ makes ever new (1)
383, 384	who makes the woeful heart to sing (2)
398	not a plant or flower below but makes thy glories known (3)
399	your voice in homage raise to him who makes all one (3)
458	What makes this rage and spite (4)
471	It makes the coward spirit brave (4)
476	makes birth and death his own (4)
487	such a strength as makes his guest (2)
516	a place wherein the Holy Spirit makes a dwelling (3)
522, 523	Jesus ... makes them kings and priests to God (4)
543	loud that grace proclaim, which makes thy darkness bright (3)
592	A servant with this clause makes drudgery divine (3)
592	who sweeps a room, as for thy laws, makes that ... fine (3)
592	makes that and the action fine (3)
617	one in the power that makes thy children free (2)
644	It makes the wounded spirit whole (2)
664	pastures fresh he makes me feed beside the living stream (1)

makest

350	let nothing in this life divide ... whom thou makest one (3)

maketh

329, 331	wine his sacred Blood he maketh (4)

making

51	This is the Lord's day, day of God's own making (3)
91	the power of Satan breaking, our peace eternal making (1)
135	Manifest in making whole palsied limbs and fainting soul (3)
232	our true Elijah, making a highway for the Lord (2/6-24)
320	making thus our sacrifice of peace (3)
338	See now thy children, making intercession (2)
420	How often, making music, we have found a new dimension (2)
585	Drained is love in making full (4)
585	poor in making many rich (4)
610	making known the needs and burdens (3)

malicious

40, 41	repel our dread, malicious foe (4)

mammon

232	from all unrighteous mammon, O raise our eyes anew (2/9-21)

man

23	Apostles made a lame man walk (2)
81	true man, yet very God (3)
87	Pleased as man with us to dwell; Jesus, our Emmanuel (2)

110	that brought into this world the God made man (2)
121	freely as Son of Man to serve and give your life for all (3)
135	anthems be to thee addressed, God in man made manifest (1-3)
135	cross and Easter Day attest God in man made manifest (4)
158	man to judge thee hath in hate pretended (1)
160	perfect Man on thee did suffer (1,4)
215	Man with God is on the throne (3)
281	a man of scorned and hardening trade (1)
335	Unless you eat of the Flesh of the Son of Man (3)
383, 384	O thou of God and man the Son (1)
434	But in the grace that rescued man his ... glory shines (2)
450, 451	the God incarnate, Man divine (3)
476	Christ, the Son of Man (2)
494	who tread where he hath trod, crown him the Son of man (2)
496, 497	Thou Son of Man and Son of God (1)
531	where'er the foot of man hath trod (1)
609	we hear thy voice, O Son of Man (1)
674	then, reconciled to God and man (4)
687, 688	were not the right man on our side (2)
687, 688	the man of God's own choosing (2)

manchild

| 611 | Blessed manchild, boy of Nazareth (2) |

manger

83	Child for us sinners poor and in the manger (5)
94, 95	in a manger laid (4)
96	See him in a manger laid whom the angels praise above (4)
97	Dost thou in a manger lie, who hast all created (1)
99	Down in a lowly manger the humble Christ was born (3)
101	Away in a manger, no crib for his bed (1)
102	where a mother laid her baby in a manger for his bed (1)
103	The babe within a manger poor (2)
106	her Son, the Savior, in a manger laid (4)
106	from his poor manger to his bitter cross (5)
107	ox and ass before him bow, and he is in the manger now (1)
108	in a manger lay to teach his people meekness (2)
110	thus that manger poor became a throne (4)
119	As with joyful steps they sped to that lowly manger bed (2)
119	offered gifts most rare at that manger rude and bare (3)
284	so innocent and mild while in the manger laid (2)
468	he was born on Christmas ... and laid in a manger (1)
476	earthly values stand beside the manger and the cross (3)
491	Lead me to my Master's manger (1)
573	thy Word made flesh, and in a manger laid (5)

manhood

179	mankind to deliver, manhood didst put on (4)
443	his manhood from humanity (1)
587	with heart still undefiled, thou didst to manhood come (2)

manifest

135	anthems be to thee addressed, God in man made manifest (1-3)
135	Manifest at Jordan's stream (2)
135	at Cana, wedding guest, in thy God-head manifest (2)

135	manifest in power divine, changing water into wine (2)
135	Manifest in making whole palsied limbs and fainting soul (3)
135	manifest in valiant fight, quelling all the devil's might (3)
135	manifest in gracious will, ever bringing good from ill (3)
135	Manifest on mountain height, shining in resplendent light (4)
135	cross and Easter Day attest God in man made manifest (4)
136, 137	Christ deigns to manifest today what glory shall be (3)
138	did manifest your glory forth in Cana's marriage hour (1)
152	Each heart is manifest to thee (2)
278	manifest in wind and flame (3)
305, 306	thyself at thine own board make manifest (1)
305, 306	make manifest in thine own Sacrament of Bread and Wine (1)

manifested
| 135 | manifested by the star to the sages from afar (1) |
| 176, 177 | of whom the glory in both earth and heaven is manifested (3) |

manifests
| 483 | to whom he manifests his love and grants his Name to know (3) |

manifold
97	for these mercies manifold join the hosts in praising (3)
271, 272	prophetic utterance told his actions great and manifold (2)
289	hand hath crowned her children with blessings manifold (1)
682	for us didst bear ... manifold disgrace (2)

mankind
56	bind in one the hearts of all mankind (7)
94, 95	Glad tidings of great joy I bring to you and all mankind (2)
179	mankind to deliver, manhood didst put on (4)
244	love from God to lost mankind (1)
355	the creator and maker of mankind (1)
427	Ye nations of mankind, in this your concord find (4)
489	in love God sent his Son to save not to condemn mankind (6)
558	mankind shall then indeed be free (2)
642	the Savior of mankind (2)
652, 653	Dear Lord and Father of mankind forgive our foolish ways (1)

manna
174	with sincerity and love eat we manna from above (2)
307	Life-imparting heavenly Manna (5)
308, 309	O Manna from on high (1)
332	the manna from above (2)
343	bless thy chosen pilgrim flock with manna (1)
343	manna in the wilderness, with water from the rock (1)
522, 523	safe they feed upon the manna which he gives them (3)
522, 523	manna which he gives them when they pray (3)
627	true manna from on high (2)
644	'tis manna to the hungry soul, and to the weary, rest (2)

manner
| 560 | utters all manner of evil against you falsely for my sake (9) |

mansion
| 621, 622 | mansion of the highest King (1) |

mansions

1, 2	Monarch of all things, fit us for thy mansions (2)
453	here are regions of light, here are mansions of bliss (4)
484, 485	now prepares in heavenly regions unfailing mansions (1)
484, 485	prepares ... mansions for his own (1)

mantle

359	Elijah's mantle o'er Elisha cast (1)
388	and round it hath cast, like a mantle, the sea (3)

many

127	Earth has many a noble city (1)
152	with many a tear poured forth by all (1)
204	wheat that in dark earth many days has lain (1)
230	In Salem's street was gathered a crowd from many a land (2)
248, 249	for many a generation hid in God's fore-knowledge lay (1)
280	many saints by earth forgotten live for ever (1)
285	Luke, thy saint, through whom we know so many ... words (1)
285	through whom we know so many gracious words of thine (1)
385	Many and great, O God, are thy works (1)
453	many millions have climbed it and reached Zion's hill (2)
453	many millions by faith now are climbing it still (2)
453	many prophets and martyrs have trod it before (3)
494	Crown him with many crowns, the Lamb upon his throne (1)
494	Crown him with many crowns, as thrones before him fall (5)
494	crown him, ye kings, with many crowns ... King of all (5)
519, 520	Many a blow and biting sculpture polished ... stones (4)
519, 520	Many a blow ... polished well those stones elect (4)
534	by... mouth of many messengers goes forth the voice of God (2)
540	by many messengers, all hearts to win (3)
585	poor in making many rich (4)
586	Where the many toil together ... art thou among thine own (2)
624	bright with many an angel, and all the martyr throng (2)
631	many diverse scrolls completing (2)
671	Through many dangers, toils, and snares (4)
693	though tossed about with many a conflict, many a doubt (2)

March

527	trusting God we march together (1)
527	one the march in God begun (3)
534	March we forth in the strength of God (3)
555	the day of march has come (1)
556, 557	Still lift your standard high, still march in firm array (5)
556, 557	At last the march shall end (6)
599	let us march on, till victory is won (1)

marching

275	Marching with thy cross, their banner (3)
392	we're marching through Emmanuel's ground to fairer worlds (4)
527	marching to the promised land (1)
562	Onward, Christian soldiers, marching as to war (1,R)

mark

171	there, adoring at his feet, mark the miracle of time (3)

54   Marvel ... that the Lord chose such a birth (1)

marvelous
157   This is the Lord's doing, and it is marvelous in our eyes (R)
412   He has done marvelous things (R)
661   the marvelous peace of God (4)

Mary
12, 13   Amid our customary round, we offer ... prayer and praise (1)
60   the child of Mary, blameless mother mild (3)
77   child whom Mary bore, the Christ, the everlasting King (1)
78, 79   For Christ is born of Mary (2)
80   to you this night is born a child of Mary (2)
80   Mary, chosen virgin mild (2)
81   with Mary we behold it, the Virgin Mother kind (2)
96   Mary, Joseph, lend your aid (4)
102   Mary was that mother mild, Jesus Christ her little child (1)
102   We, like Mary, rest confounded (3)
110   'Twas Mary, daughter pure of holy Anne (2)
110   for he whom Mary bore was God the Son (4)
115   haste to bring him laud, the babe, the son of Mary (R)
159   with ... grief and resignation Mary watched her dying son (2)
183   Speak, Mary, declaring what thou sawest, wayfaring (4)
190   Lift your voice rejoicing, Mary (1)
190   Raise your weary eyelids, Mary (2)
190   Life is yours for ever, Mary (3)
232   All praise for Mary Magdalene (2/7-22)
232   We sing with joy of Mary (2/8-15)
258   Mary, Mother meek and mild (1,2)
263, 264 To Mary the Archangel came (2)
263, 264 Hail, Mary, you shall bear a son (2)
265   "All hail ... thou lowly maiden Mary" (1)
265   Then gentle Mary meekly bowed her head (3)
266   said, "Hail Mary, full of grace." (2)
267   Mary, the pure and lowly maid, the favored of the Lord (4)
268, 269 when he made the Virgin Mary mother of his only Son (1)
277   Sing of Mary, pure and lowly, virgin mother undefiled (1)
277   Sing of Jesus, son of Mary, in the house at Nazareth (2)
277   from the heart of blessed Mary (3)
278   sing we of the joys of Mary (1)
278   Mary at whose breast the child was fed who is Son of God (1)
278   Sing again the joys of Mary when she saw the risen Lord (3)
278   Sing the chiefest joy of Mary (4)
278   joy of Mary when on earth her work was done (4)
269   Hail Mary, Full of grace (1-4)
324   King of kings, yet born of Mary (2)
357   Jesus, Son of Mary, fount of life alone (1)
460, 461 born of Mary, earth thy footstool, heaven thy throne (4)
468   child of Mary ... didn't have a cradle (2)
475   let my soul, like Mary, be thine earthly sanctuary (4)
673   Mary the Maid of Galilee (1)
673   first ones ... were Mary, Joanna, and Magdalene (3)

Mary's
54   Mighty God and Mary's son, eager now his race to run (2)

55	take our flesh and grow as child in Mary's womb (2)
85, 86	and came to us as Mary's son (3)
98	Now may Mary's son, who came so long ago to love us (4)
115	What child is this, who, laid to rest, on Mary's lap (1)
115	on Mary's lap is sleeping (1)
201	all to anoint fair Mary's Son (2)
259	but, borne upon the throne of Mary's gentle breast (2)
263, 264	in Mary's body deigned to dwell (1)
278	Sing we, too, of Mary's sorrows (2)
386, 387	him that brought salvation down by meekness, Mary's son (4)

Master

175	every good gift of the year now with its Master returns (1)
232	wholeness was restored by you, her faithful Master (2/7-22)
493	My gracious Master and my God, assist me to proclaim (2)
535	Ye servants of God, your Master proclaim (1)
541	to each servant does the Master say, "Go work today" (1)
562	Christ, the royal Master, leads against the foe (1)
564, 565	let him in constancy follow the Master (1)
602	Master who acts as a slave to them (1)
609	O Master, from the mountain side (4)
620	David stands with harp in hand as master of the choir (3)
632	The Church from our dear Master received the word divine (2)
655	be thou for ever near me, my Master and my friend (1)
655	O give me grace to follow, my Master and my friend (3)
659, 660	O Master, let me walk with thee (1)
659, 660	with thee, O Master, let me live (4)

Master's

281	alike the symbol ... tool of foreign master's hated rule (1)
431	mute witness of the Master's hand in all created things (1)
491	Lead me to my Master's manger (1)

masters

430	amid the mortal throng, be you masters of the song (3)

match

600, 601	to match our present hour (1)

matchless

97	matchless gifts and free (2)
313	of thy matchless love forgive me (4)
386, 387	now the matchless deed's achieved (4)
494	hail him as thy matchless King through all eternity (1)

matron

275	saintly maiden, godly matron, widows who have watched (2)

Matthew

232	We praise you, Lord, for Matthew (2/9-21)

Matthew's

281	let them of Matthew's wealth partake (4)

maturity
228   all the benefits the earth, you bring to maturity (3)

meadow
179   bloom in every meadow, leaves on every bough (2)
376   field and forest, vale and mountain, blooming meadow (2)

meadows
383, 384 Fair are the meadows, fairer still the woodlands (2)

mean
115   Why lies he in such mean estate (2)
115   mean estate where ox and ass are feeding (2)
293   I mean, God helping, to be one too (1)
293   I mean to be one too (3)
314   who thy glory hidest 'neath these shadows mean (1)
592   All may of thee partake, nothing can be so mean (2)
638, 639 With thee all night I mean to stay (1)

meaning
127   Sacred gifts of mystic meaning (4)
476   his meaning lights our shadowed world through Christ (2)
574, 575 a ready mind to understand the meaning of thy chastening (1)
580   lost to purpose and to meaning (2)

meanly
94, 95   all meanly wrapped in swathing bands (4)

means
348   may we increasingly glory in learning all that it means (3)
348   all that it means to accept you as Lord (3)

meant
528   life abundant meant for each (2)

meanwhile
113   meanwhile the pangs of my sorrow are soothed (1)
484, 485 The cross meanwhile we bear (2)
623   Now, in the meanwhile, with hearts raised on high (4)

measure
244   Come, pure hearts, in joyful measure sing (1)
248, 249 Name of sweetness, passing measure (2)
339   from this banquet let me measure, Lord ... its treasure (3)
406, 407 blessings without measure (1,8)
414   works of love surpassing measure (4)
441, 442 peace is there that knows no measure (4)
469, 470 broader than the measure of the mind (3)
471   the measure and the pledge of love (5)
476   Can numbers measure what he is (1)
515   From the height which knows no measure (1)
528   Lord, you show us love's true measure (4)
631   shedding light that none can measure (1)

meanwhile
113	meanwhile the pangs of my sorrow are soothed (1)
484, 485	The cross meanwhile we bear (2)
623	Now, in the meanwhile, with hearts raised on high (4)

measure
244	Come, pure hearts, in joyful measure sing (1)
248, 249	Name of sweetness, passing measure (2)
339	from this banquet let me measure, Lord ... its treasure (3)
406, 407	blessings without measure (1,8)
414	works of love surpassing measure (4)
441, 442	peace is there that knows no measure (4)
469, 470	broader than the measure of the mind (3)
471	the measure and the pledge of love (5)
476	Can numbers measure what he is (1)
515	From the height which knows no measure (1)
528	Lord, you show us love's true measure (4)
631	shedding light that none can measure (1)

measures
431	rising sun renews the race that measures all our days (2)

meat
185, 186	he is our meat and drink indeed (4)
323	for thy Flesh is meat indeed (1)
332	meat the Body of the Lord, our drink his precious Blood (3)

Mediator
368	look upon the Mediator, clothe us with his righteousness (1)

meditation
1	singing we offer prayer and meditation: thus we adore (1)

meditations
431	meditations of my heart be innocence and praise (4)

meek
78, 79	in this world of sin, where meek souls will receive him (3)
156	bow thy meek head to mortal pain (5)
258	Mary, Mother meek and mild (1,2)
276	meek and firm be found (5)
525	Lord, give us grace that we like them, the meek (5)
525	the meek and lowly, on high may dwell with thee (5)
560	Blessed are the meek, for they shall inherit the earth (3)
612	love is meek, and thinks no wrong (2)
642	O hope of every contrite heart, O joy of all the meek (3)

meekly
9	Lord of life, as he goes meekly by (4)
265	Then gentle Mary meekly bowed her head (3)
267	She meekly bowed her head to hear the gracious word (4)

meekness
49	with meekness hear the gospel word (3)
108	in a manger lay to teach his people meekness (2)

131, 132   heavenly Lamb in meekness stood (3)
386, 387   him that brought salvation down by meekness, Mary's son (4)
491   O the magnitude of meekness (3)
573   there is no meekness in the powers of earth (4)

meet
67   let the valleys rise to meet him (2)
162   let homage meet by all be done (6)
213   till we meet at the feast of the Lamb (4)
231   he rose to meet your challenge (2/11-30)
281   Enough ... to hear thy voice, to meet thine eye (3)
293   You can meet them in school, or in lanes, or at sea (3)
304   I come with joy to meet my Lord, forgiven, loved and free (1)
304   thus with joy we meet our Lord (4)
305, 306   We meet, as in that upper room they met (2)
368   meet and worship in thy Name (2)
435   for all wreaths of empire meet upon his brow (6)
459   where his loving people meet to share the gift divine (2)
474   Did e'er such love and sorrow meet (3)
519, 520   meet for him whose love espoused thee (2)
529   In Christ now meet both East and West (3)
529   in him meet South and North (3)
539   He comes again, O Zion, ere thou meet him (4)
542   In Christ all races meet, their ancient feuds forgetting (2)

meetest
238, 239   with meetest praise and sweetest, honor them for evermore (1)

meeting
48   This day, God's people meeting, his Holy Scripture hear (3)
230   filled the place of meeting with rushing wind and flame (1)

meets
165, 166   born for this, he meets his passion (2)

Melchizedek
443   his priesthood from Melchizedek (1)

melody
154, 155   to thee, now high exalted, our melody we raise (4)
518   in exultant jubilation pours perpetual melody (2)

melt
226, 227   melt the frozen, warm the chill (4)
228   melt with fire our icy chill (4)
376   Melt the clouds of sin and sadness (1)
486   dreadful day when earth and heaven shall melt away (5)

melting
612   Prophecy will fade away, melting in the light of day (3)

members
279   Thine earthly members fit to join thy saints above (3)
295   as members of his Body we live in him as one (2)
296   as living members of a living Christ (2)

412	Daughter and son, loud praying members (6)
469, 470	joy for all the members in the sorrows of the Head (2)
513	To the members of Christ's Body (2)
576, 577	When we Christians gather, members of one Body (2)
581	as members of his Body joined we are in him made one (5)

memorial
| 314 | O memorial wondrous of the Lord's own death (3) |
| 320 | ordained to be repeated, his memorial ne'er to cease (3) |

memory
| 642 | nor can the memory find a sweeter sound than Jesus' Name (2) |

memory's
| 414 | Nor shall fail from memory's treasure works ... wrought (4) |
| 585 | memory's treasure, grace of youth (1) |

men
78, 79	praises sing to God the King, and peace to men on earth (2)
89, 90	Peace on the earth, good will to men (1)
92	Wise Men three to him led, kneel they low by his bed (3)
94, 95	good will henceforth from heaven to men (6)
98	but the very beasts could see that he all men surpasses (2)
104	for stony-hearts of men (3)
106	peace on the earth, and unto men good will (3)
109	by the light of that same star three wise men came (3)
109	three wise men came from country far (3)
109	Then entered in those wise men three (5)
119	As with gladness men of old did the guiding star behold (1)
247	charged ... his men of might, in his own sight (2)
377, 378	from men and ... angel host be praise and glory evermore (5)
458	but men made strange (2)
506, 507	hundred men and women turned the known world upside down (4)
525	Though with a scornful wonder men see her sore oppressed (3)
564, 565	Then fancies flee away; I'll fear not what men say (3)
591	from all the easy speeches that comfort cruel men (2)
614	O Christian women, Christian men, all the world over (2)
674	how small the debts men owe to us (3)
720	O thus be it ever when free men shall stand (2)

mends
| 487 | such a feast as mends in length (2) |

merchant
| 605 | To merchant, worker, king he brings God's high demands (3) |

mercies
10	New mercies, each returning day around us hover (2)
10	new mercies ... around us hover while we pray (2)
88	God from God, and Light from Light, comes with mercies (2)
88	comes with mercies infinite (2)
97	for these mercies manifold join the hosts in praising (3)
108	with mercies infinite our Christ hath brought us peace (2)
288	by deeds of kindly love for thy mercies grateful prove (3)

414	works by love and mercy wrought (4)
414	works of mercy passing thought (4)
415	my ever grateful heart, O Lord, thy mercy shall adore (4)
421	as you sit at God's right hand ... mercy, Lord, upon us (2)
437, 438	his mercy sure, from age to age the same (2)
437, 438	Firm is his promise, and his mercy sure (4)
443	bade the fallen to come in, praised be his mercy (3)
444	The prophets spoke of mercy, of freedom and release (1)
453	has raised up a ladder of mercy for me (R)
454	again in mercy, when our hearts are bowed with care (2)
469, 470	There's a wideness in God's mercy like the ... sea (1)
469, 470	there is mercy with the Savior (1)
471	he brings us mercy from above (2)
472	we render back the love thy mercy gave us (4)
496, 497	with mercy beaming from afar (1)
528	May your care and mercy lead us to a just society (4)
531	bid mercy triumph over wrath (3)
538	God of mercy ... grace, show the brightness of thy face (1)
552, 553	his boundless mercy will provide (3)
555	nor roll of stirring drums, but deeds of love and mercy (2)
560	Blessed are the merciful, for they shall obtain mercy (5)
590	seek out the lonely and God's mercy share (2)
605	Do justly, love mercy, walk humbly with your God (1-3)
605	Then justly, in mercy we'll humbly walk with God (4)
607	in love and mercy guide us and heal our strife-torn world (1)
610	that your servants, Lord, in freedom may your mercy know (4)
610	may your mercy know and live (4)
624	Jesus, in mercy bring us to that dear land of rest (4)
643	how beautiful thy mercy seat in depths of burning light (1)
663	doth in mercy bless (2)
666	Let Israel trust in God, no bounds his mercy knows (4)
669	him whose faithful mercy the skies above declare (1)
669	Thy lasting truth and mercy, O Father, see aright (3)
669	God, in his great mercy, will save thee, hold thee fast (4)
677	the clouds ye so much dread are big with mercy (3)
686	Streams of mercy never ceasing (1)
686	Streams of mercy ... call for songs of loudest praise (1)
706	In your mercy, Lord, you called me (1)
715	the falling tear in mercy flowed beyond all bound (RC)
719	mercy more than life (2)

mercy's

6, 7	joyless is the day's return till thy mercy's beams I see (2)
337	O fold them closer to thy mercy's breast (3)
610	upon the cross, forsaken, offered mercy's perfect deed (1)
664	for his mercy's sake (1)

merit

66	by thine all-sufficient merit raise us (4)
139	let us not heed worldly lies nor rest upon our merit (3)
151	thus my hope is in the Lord and not in my own merit (3)
170	though we merit blame you will your robe of mercy throw (2)
230	to the blessed Three in One be honor, praise and merit (2)
298	help us in our infirmity through Jesus blood and merit (2)
495	By thy merit we find favor (1)

496, 497   through thy merit (2)
503, 504   praise to thy eternal merit, Father, Son and Holy Spirit (9)

merits
495   help to sing our Savior's merits (4)
519, 520   by virtue of his merits thither faithful souls do soar (3)

merry
105   God rest you merry, gentlemen, let nothing you dismay (1)

message
70   Sound the trumpet, Tell the message (R)
263, 264   God's new message did proclaim (2)
263, 264   Blest in the message Gabriel brought (3)
270   Gabriel's message does away Satan's curse and ... sway (1)
271, 272   With heavenly message Gabriel came (2)
536   They who have ears to hear the message (2)
539   Send heralds forth to bear the message glorious (3)

messages
50   Blest be the Lord who comes to us with messages of grace (4)

messengers
235   Come sing, ye choirs exultant, those messengers of God (1)
534   by ... mouth of many messengers goes forth the voice of God (2)
540   by many messengers, all hearts to win (3)

Messiah
57, 58   deeply wailing, shall the true Messiah see (2)
161   They stumbled on a mystery: Messiah reigning from a tree (3)
231   witnessed to his brother, "This is Messiah true" (2/11-30)
673   first one ... to know of Messiah, Jesus (2)

Messiah's
93   who sang creation's story now proclaim Messiah's birth (1)
143   herald of Messiah's name (3)

met
78, 79   hopes and fears of all the years are met in thee tonight (1)
203   That night the apostles met in fear (4)
206   That night the apostles met in fear (2)
266   He met a maiden in that place (2)
304   Together met, together bound, we'll go our different ways (5)
305, 306   We meet, as in that upper room they met (2)
320   when the twelve, divinely guided, at the holy table met (2)
599   Lest our feet stray from the places ... we met thee (3)
599   places our God, where we met thee (3)

Michael
282, 283   Send thine archangel Michael to our succor (2)

mid
242   mid all its light his faith was dim (2)
329, 331   mid the twelve, his chosen band (3)

357   Here mid stress and conflict toils can never cease (2)
386, 387   Glorious the sun in mid career (3)
389   moon ... mid her spangled sisters bright (5)
525   Mid toil and tribulation, and tumult of her war (4)
632   mid mists and rocks and quicksands still guides (2)

midday
18   dark midday could not conceal your cry of awful agony (3c)

midnight
68   up, watch in expectation, at midnight comes the cry (1)
89, 90   It came upon the midnight clear (1)

Midnight's
61, 62   Midnight's peace their cry has broken (1)

midst
75   he stands in the midst of nations (3)
182   but daily, in the midst of life (3)
222   for in the midst of two or three (2)
501, 502   protector in the midst of strife (2)
513   to her midst as gift and sign (2)
581   Let us recall that in our midst dwells God's begotten Son (5)
678, 679   in your very midst, the great and Holy One (2)

midwinter
112   In the bleak midwinter, frosty wind made moan (1)
112   in the bleak midwinter long ago (1)
112   in the bleak midwinter a stable-place sufficed (2)

might
11   that all my powers, with all their might ... may unite (3)
21, 22   O God of truth, O Lord of might (1)
29, 30   O Unity of princely might (1)
36   Father of might unknown (2)
48   We journey on, believing, renewed with heavenly might (3)
51   that he might anoint us a royal priesthood (1)
52   in might victorious rose again (2)
56   O come, O come, thou Lord of might (3)
59   Honor, glory, might, and blessing to the Father ... Son (4)
60   Come in your holy might, we pray (5)
60   praise, honor, might, and glory be from age to age (6)
63, 64   begotten of the Father's might (1)
63, 64   praise, honor, might and glory be (5)
85, 86   O Son who shared the Father's might (1)
105   free all ... from Satan's power and might (3)
131, 132   he, to whom no sin was known, might cleanse his people (3)
135   manifest in valiant fight, quelling all the devil's might (3)
143   delivered from the lions' might (3)
165, 166   one in might and one in glory while eternal ages run (6)
167   He died that we might be forgiven (3)
167   that we might go at last to heaven (3)
173   pouring out his life that he might to life restore us (2)
199, 200   Neither might the gates of death ... tomb's dark portal (4)

552, 553	Fight the good fight with all thy might (1)
555	lead on, O God of might (3)
564, 565	No foes shall stay his might, though he with giants fight (2)
579	O Wind of heaven, by thy might save all (3)
584	make their might our own (1)
599	thou who hast by thy might led us into the light (3)
613	We pray thee, Lord, arise, and come in thy great might (4)
614	Let Love's unconquerable might ... unite (3)
615	when justice shall be throned in might (4)
620	ten thousand times would one be blest who might ... hear (3)
620	blest who might this music hear (3)
669	what loving wisdom chooseth, redeeming might will do (3)
672	that so it might be bright (1)
678, 679	all his works his might proclaim (2)
682	nor yet for fear that loving not I might for ever die (1)
702	wondrous knowledge, awful might (2)
716	do thou our country save by thy great might (1)
717	protect us by thy might, great God, our King (4)

mightily

56	who orderest all things mightily (2)

mighty

19, 20	God's mighty actions tell at length (2)
33-35	Christ, mighty Savior, Light of all creation (1)
54	Mighty God and Mary's son, eager now his race to run (2)
56	trust thy mighty power to save (4)
76	a home where such a mighty guest may come (2)
94, 95	for mighty dread has seized their troubled mind (2)
125, 126	the Wonderful, the Counsellor, the mighty God and Lord (4)
138	All praise to you, O Lord, who by your mighty power (1)
165, 166	of the mighty conflict sing (1)
174	Mighty victim from on high (3)
191	we conquer by his mighty enterprise (2)
215	mighty Lord, in thine ascension, we ... behold our own (3)
220, 221	Be thou our joy, O Mighty Lord (3)
230	A mighty sound from heaven at Pentecost there came (1)
252	Jesus, only Name that's given under all the mighty heaven (5)
268, 269	he has cast down all the mighty ... lowly are his choice (4)
271, 272	His mighty deeds exalt his fame (4)
282, 283	Send thine archangel Gabriel the mighty herald of heaven (3)
336	Come with us, O mighty Savior (1)
336	Let the mighty chorus ever sing its glad exultant songs (3)
358	Only Immortal One, Mighty Creator (2)
360, 361	Lord of creation, merciful and mighty (1)
362	Merciful and mighty (1,4)
363	from thee have flowed, as from a mighty river, our faith (4)
373	worlds his mighty voice obeyed (1)
375	his mighty wonders tell abroad (1)
386, 387	We sing of God, the mighty source of all things (1)
393	all his mighty acts proclaim (1)
398	I sing the mighty power of God (1)
404	your mighty acts with joy and fear relate (2)
413	fall before the Mighty One (1)

413	make music for your mighty King (2)
425	He only is the mighty Lord. He only can destroy the foe (3)
435	who from the beginning was the mighty Word (1)
436	Lift up your heads, ye mighty gates (1)
437, 438	his holy Name -- The Lord, the Mighty One (2)
460, 461	thunder like a mighty flood (1,5)
478	Jesus, our mighty Lord, our strength in sadness (1)
479	Lift ye then your voices, swell the mighty flood (5)
483	a royal diadem adorns the mighty victor's brow (1)
489	He sent no angel of his host to bear this mighty word (2)
491	O Most Mighty, O Most Holy (2)
498	the shadow of a mighty rock within a weary land (1)
530	spread, thou mighty word, spread the kingdom of the Lord (1)
548	strong in the Lord of hosts, and in his mighty power (2)
561	forth to the mighty conflict in this his glorious day (2)
562	Like a mighty army moves the Church of God (3)
579, 608	who bidd'st the mighty ocean deep its ... limits keep (1)
681	thine is the mighty plan, the steadfast order sure (1)
687, 688	A mighty fortress is our God, a bulwark never failing (1)
690	I am weak, but thou art mighty (1)

mild

60	the child of Mary, blameless mother mild (3)
78, 79	where misery cries out to thee, Son of the mother mild (4)
80	Mary, chosen virgin mild (2)
87	Peace on earth and mercy mild (1)
87	Mild he lays his glory by, born that we no more may die (3)
102	Mary was that mother mild, Jesus Christ her little child (1)
110	to guard him, and protect his mother mild (3)
111	Holy infant, so tender and mild, sleep in heavenly peace (1)
252	Jesus, Name of mercy mild, given to the holy child (4)
258	Mary, Mother meek and mild (1,2)
284	so innocent and mild while in the manger laid (2)
416	for all gentle thoughts and mild (4)

milk

624	Jerusalem the golden, with milk and honey blest (1)

million

9	silver glistering of all the million million stars (2)

millions

212	those feet still free to move and bleed for millions (3)
212	for millions and for me (3)
439	while millions join the theme, I will sing (2)
453	many millions have climbed it and reached Zion's hill (2)
453	many millions by faith now are climbing it still (2)

mind

10	If on our daily course our mind be set (3)
10	mind be set to hallow all we find (3)
16, 17	with fervent heart and ready mind (1)
19, 20	Let mouth and tongue, mind, sense, and strength (2)
27, 28	anguished and in mind distressed be crushed by guilt (3)

81	Isaiah 'twas foretold it, the Rose I have in mind (2)
94, 95	for mighty dread has seized their troubled mind (2)
230	whole in body, mind, and spirit (3)
371	heal to the sick in mind, sight to the inly blind (2)
389	Let us, with a gladsome mind, praise the Lord (1,7)
404	We love you with our heart and strength and mind (3)
411	His mercies bear in mind (2)
429	the Lord supports the fainting mind (3)
457	thou only canst inform the mind and purify the heart (2)
469, 470	For the love of God is broader than the ... mind (3)
469, 470	broader than the measure of the mind (3)
477	Let this mind be in us which was in thee (3)
500	Creator Spirit ... come visit every humble mind (1)
511	Spirit, ever forming in the Church the mind of Christ (1)
528	amid the cares that claim us, hold in mind eternity (5)
551	give heart and soul and mind and strength (1)
570, 571	call to mind the word of Jesus (3)
574, 575	a ready mind to understand the meaning of thy chastening (1)
581	with heart and mind and strength now love him in return (2)
582, 583	Already in the mind of God that city riseth fair (4)
584	give understanding to the mind (3)
584	with new mind, new heart (3)
585	gifts of love to mind and sense (2)
629	We limit not the truth of God to our poor reach of mind (1)
652, 653	Reclothe us in our rightful mind (1)
693	sight, riches, healing of the mind ... in thee to find (3)
705	mind, and heart, and hand (1)
706	taught my sin-filled heart and mind (1)

mind's

416	for the heart and mind's delight (3)

minded

324	ponder nothing earthly minded (1)

mindful

337	And now, O Father, mindful of the love that bought us (1)

minds

44, 45	so calm our minds that fears may cease (2)
144	dispel the gloom that shades our minds (1)
175	Jesus the health of the world, enlighten our minds (6)
216	enlighten our minds, thou Redeemer (4)
600, 601	Bring to our troubled minds, uncertain and afraid (2)

mine

6, 7	Visit then this soul of mine (3)
8	Mine is the sunlight, Mine is the morning (3)
43	with sweet sleep mine eyelids close (3)
84	Love shall be our token; love be yours and love be mine (3)
97	By this lowly birth of mine, sinner, riches ... thine (2)
117, 118	myrrh from the forest, and gold from the mine (3)
128	Myrrh is mine; its bitter perfume ... gathering gloom (4)
318	Mine is the sin, but thine the righteousness (4)
318	mine is the guilt, but thine the cleansing Blood (4)

431	So order too this life of mine, direct it all my days (4)
458	Heaven was his home, but mine the tomb wherein he lay (6)
474	Were the whole realm of nature mine (4)
475	let thy radiant beauty light mine eyes to see my duty (3)
498	Upon the cross of Jesus mine eyes at times can see (2)
516	Come down, O love divine, seek thou this soul of mine (1)
645, 646	I nothing lack if I am his, and he is mine for ever (1)
664	may thy house be mine abode and all my work be praise (3)
668	I to the hills will lift mine eyes (1)
685	when mine eyelids close in death (3)
689	Thou didst reach forth thy hand and mine enfold (2)
694	God be in mine eyes, and in my looking (1)
694	God be at mine end, and at my departing (1)
707	Take my will, and make it thine ... no longer mine (2)

mingled

| 474 | sorrow and love flow mingled down (3) |

ministered

| 150 | round us ... angels shine, such as ministered to thee (4) |
| 261, 262 | he by his caring ministered to Jesus (1) |

ministry

| 511 | Holy Spirit, ever working through the Church's ministry (2) |
| 528 | the Spirit's gifts empower us for the work of ministry (R) |

minstrelsy

| 484, 485 | with voice and minstrelsy extol his majesty: Alleluia (1) |

miracle

| 131, 132 | Oh, what a miracle divine, when water ... into wine (4) |
| 171 | there, adoring at his feet, mark the miracle of time (3) |

miracles

| 240, 241 | o'er all miracles preceding his inestimable death (3) |
| 260 | The Architect's high miracles he saw, and what was done (2) |

mirror

| 33-35 | mirror of daybreak, pledge of resurrection (2) |

mirth

92	His the doom, ours the mirth when he came down to earth (2)
377, 378	him serve with mirth, his praise forth tell (1)
427	When mirth for music longs, this is my song of songs (2)
556, 557	true rapture, noblest mirth (2)

mischief

| 337 | From tainting mischief keep them pure and clear (3) |

miseries

| 148 | our self-wrought miseries have made us trust ourselves (2) |

misery

| 18 | teach us to hear its echoes still in every human misery (3c) |
| 56 | close the path to misery (5) |

78, 79   where misery cries out to thee, Son of the mother mild (4)
638, 639   my misery or sin declare (2)

miss
594, 595   lest we miss thy kingdom's goal (3)

missed
46   long our mortal blindness has missed God's lovingkindness (3)

mission
120   How blest that mission then begun (4)
528   Lest the Church neglect its mission (1)
539   O Zion, haste, thy mission high fulfilling (1)
539   mission ... to tell to all the world that God is Light (1)

mists
632   mid mists and rocks and quicksands still guides (2)

misusings
337   look not on our misusings of thy grace (2)

mix
161   A Roman soldier drew a spear to mix his blood with water (2)
161   mix his blood with water clear (2)

moan
112   In the bleak midwinter, frosty wind made moan (1)

mock
170   To mock your reign ... they made a crown of thorns (1)
170   In mock acclaim ... they snatched a purple cloak (2)

mocked
159   Him she saw for our salvation mocked (3)
159   mocked with cruel acclamation, scourged and crowned (3)
448, 449   For us to wicked hands betrayed, scourged, mocked (4)
573   by wars and tumults love is mocked, derided (2)
598   mocked thy saving kingship (1)
598   mocked ... by thorns with which they crowned thee (1)

mocking
168, 169   O kingly head, surrounded with mocking crown of thorn (1)

modern
580   Proudly rise our modern cities (2)

moments
179   hours and passing moments praise thee in their flight (3)
238, 239   all its fleeting moments past (3)
649, 650   make all our moments calm and bright (4)
707   take my moments and my days (1)

monarch
1, 2   Monarch of all things, fit us for thy mansions (2)
60   not as a monarch (3)

97   If a monarch, where thy state (1)
117, 118 Maker and Monarch and Savior of all (2)
261, 262 Monarch of monarchs (2)
585   Here is God, no monarch he (6)

monarch's
359   theirs not a monarch's crown or tyrant's sword (4)

monarchs
261, 262 Monarch of monarchs (2)

months
179   Months in due succession, days of lengthening light (3)
266   There are yet but six months gone (5)
266   six months gone since Elizabeth conceived John (5)

monuments
148   to the skies our monuments of folly soar (2)

moon
31, 32   moon with cool reflected glow will bring the silences (3)
31, 32   like moon and night, give loving peace (5)
114   'Twas in the moon of winter-time (1)
114   The earliest moon of winter-time is not so round and fair (3)
370   the whiteness of the moon at even (4)
373   sun and moon, rejoice before him (1)
389   The horned moon to shine by night (5)
389   moon ... mid her spangled sisters bright (5)
394, 395 let sun and moon and stars and light ... praise (1)
398   moon shines full at his command and all the stars obey (1)
400   pale silver moon that gently gleams (1)
406, 407 My Lord be praised by sister moon and all the stars (3)
409   the moon takes up the wondrous tale (2)
410   sun and moon bow down before him (4)
416   sun and moon, and stars of light (2)
428   O sun and moon and stars of heaven (2)
428   sun ... moon ... stars ... your endless praise outpour (2)
668   sun by day nor moon by night need make thy soul afraid (3)

moonlight
383, 384 Fair is the sunshine, fairer still the moonlight (3)
681   line of lifted sea, where spreading moonlight quivers (3)

moons
544   till moons shall wax and wane no more (1)

moor
128   field and fountain, moor and mountain (1)

moors
9   royal robes of autumn moors the golden gates of spring (2)

more
6, 7   more and more thyself display, shining to the perfect day (3)
10   as more of heaven in each we see (4)

549, 550	saying "Christian, love me more" (3)
549, 550	Christian, love me more than these (4)
563	far more o'er thee are watching than human eyes can know (2)
564, 565	do but themselves confound, his strength the more is (2)
566	our rude work deface no more the handiwork of God (2)
574, 575	more pure, more true, more nobly wise (4)
600, 601	war may haunt the earth no more and desolation cease (4)
612	love than death itself more strong (2)
613	When comes the promised time that war shall be no more (3)
616	age to age more glorious, all blessing and all blest (5)
618	more glorious than the seraphim, lead their praises (2)
629	the Lord has yet more light and truth (1-3)
629	more light and truth to break forth from his word (1-3)
634	never resisting but to increase in faith more and more (1)
636, 637	What more can he say than to you he hath said (1)
654	to see thee more clearly, love thee more dearly (1)
654	follow thee more nearly, day by day (1)
664	no more a stranger or a guest, but like a child at home (3)
666	more duly than the morning watch to spy the dawning day (3)
697	that I from thee no more may stray (1)
697	no more from thee decline (1)
700	tarry no more without, but come and dwell within (1)
719	who more than self their country loved (2)
719	mercy more than life (2)

morn

6, 7	Dark and cheerless is the morn unaccompanied by thee (2)
14, 15	you, from the morn till evening's ray (1)
18	all shadows of the morn and eve converged (3b)
27, 28	You joined the morn and evening ray (2)
73	O haste the rising of the morn (3)
77	All glory for this blessed morn to God the Father ever be (5)
88	Sing, O sing, this blessed morn, unto us a child is born (1)
88	O sing, this blessed morn, Jesus Christ today is born (R)
99	God sent us salvation that blessed Christmas morn (3)
106	Christians awake, salute the happy morn (1)
106	morn whereon the Savior of the world was born (1)
108	who truly have believed that on this blessed morn (1)
191	glorious life ... immortal, on his resurrection morn (2)
198	Thou hallowed chosen morn of praise (1)
201	At early morn, with spices rare (2)
203	That Easter morn, at break of day (2)
223, 224	hail the Pentecostal morn (1)
223, 224	morn when our ascended Lord ... his Spirit poured (1)
247	And every morn and day (3)
265	in Bethlehem, all on a Christmas morn (4)
271, 272	The great forerunner of the morn (1)
366	from morn till set of sun ... the song goes on (3)
366	wast of a virgin born humbly on that blessed morn (5)
400	Fair rising morn, with praise rejoice (2)
426	Songs of praise awoke the morn (2)
426	awoke the morn when the Prince of Peace was born (2)
525	soon the night of weeping shall be the morn of song (3)
563	When morn his face revealeth thy dangers all are past (4)
692	look unto me, your morn shall rise (3)

morning

8	Morning has broken like the first morning (1)
8	Praise for the singing, Praise for the morning (1)
8	Mine is the sunlight, Mine is the morning (3)
8	praise every morning, God's recreation of the new day (3)
10	New every morning is the love (1)
11	joyful rise to pay thy morning sacrifice (1)
11	disperse my sins as morning dew (2)
21, 22	you send the early morning ray (1)
23	we harvest what the morning sowed (1)
24	to thee our morning hymns ascended (1)
29, 30	To thee our morning song of praise (2)
59	shines upon the morning skies (2)
73	The King shall come when morning dawns (1,3,5)
73	crowned with glory like the sun ... lights the morning sky (2)
78, 79	O morning stars, together proclaim the holy birth (2)
83	Yea, Lord, we greet thee, born this happy morning (6)
91	Break forth, O beauteous light, and usher in the morning (1)
101	stay by my side until morning is nigh (2)
117, 118	Brightest and best of the stars of the morning (1,5)
127	Fairer than the sun at morning was the star (2)
145	Then shall your light break forth as doth the morning (5)
179	"Welcome, happy morning!" age to age shall say (1,R)
179	Brightness of the morning, sky and fields and sea (3)
179	'tis thine own third morning! rise, O buried Lord! (5)
180	not one darksome cloud is dimming ... morning ray (3)
180	dimming yonder glorious morning ray (3)
190	All the glory of the morning pales before those wounds (2)
232	On Easter morning early, a word from you sufficed (2/7-22)
362	Early in the morning our song shall rise to thee (1)
405	the sunset and the morning that brightens up the sky (2)
408	by morning glow or evening shade ... ne'er sleepeth (2)
427	When morning gilds the skies, my heart, awaking, cries (1)
496, 497	How bright appears the Morning Star (1)
543	He gilds thy morning face with beams that cannot fade (2)
544	rise with every morning sacrifice (2)
555	gladness breaks like morning where'er thy face appears (3)
585	Morning glory, starlit sky, soaring music (1)
607	dawns the morning glorious when truth and justice reign (4)
613	arise, O Morning Star, arise, and never set (5)
638, 639	the morning breaks, the shadows flee (4)
640	for the morning seems to dawn (3)
662	heaven's morning breaks, and earth's vain shadows flee (4)
666	more duly than the morning watch to spy the dawning day (3)
695, 696	we know that God is with us night and morning (1)
702	If I the wings of morning take (4)

morrow

190	love has brought the blessed morrow (3)
192	My Love, the Crucified, hath sprung to life this morrow (1)
237	turn from fear, and heed the call to a glorious morrow (3)

mortal

46	long our mortal blindness has missed God's lovingkindness (3)
69	Mortal in darkness we lie down (2)

156	bow thy meek head to mortal pain (5)
158	for me ... thy mortal sorrow, and thy life's oblation (4)
160	robed in mortal flesh is dying, crucified by sin for me (2)
199, 200	nor the watchers, nor the seal hold thee as a mortal (4)
214	Lord beyond our mortal sight (4)
222	No more his mortal form we see (2)
237	when they laid the mortal down for the life immortal (1)
254	though mortal strength may fail (1)
324	Let all mortal flesh keep silence (1)
346	as far as lies within our mortal power (1)
355	we are mortal (1)
358	From earth you formed us, both glorious and mortal (2)
391	our souls and all our mortal frame (3)
430	amid the mortal throng, be you masters of the song (3)
434	speak his Name in sounds to mortal ears unknown (5)
448, 449	God, the Son of God, should take our mortal form (1)
448, 449	God ... should take our mortal form for mortal's sake (1)
625	too high doth seem for mortal tongue (1)
633	speak and heal our mortal blindness (3)
665	Mortal pride and earthly glory (2)
687, 688	our helper he amid the flood of mortal ills prevailing (1)
687, 688	let goods and kindred go, this mortal life also (4)
717	let mortal tongues awake, let all that breathe partake (3)

mortal's

448, 449	God ... should take our mortal form for mortal's sake (1)

mortals

38, 39	as mortals clothed in earth-bound frame (4)
78, 79	gathered all above, while mortals sleep (2)
214	Christ, awhile to mortals given (1)
282, 283	may he, from us mortals, drive every evil (3)
284	while mortals sing with you their own Redeemer's praise (8)
375	mortals then, on land and sea ... exult (2)
381	mortals, angels, now and ever praise the Holy Trinity (4)
452	whose life and death that love reveal which mortals need (1)
452	mortals need and need to feel (1)
481	Mortals, give thanks and sing, and triumph evermore (1)
492	So, he tasted death for mortals (3)

Moses

129, 130	Trembling at his feet we saw Moses and Elijah speaking (2)
136, 137	With Moses and Elijah nigh (2)
143	Alone and fasting Moses saw the loving God (2)
181	Awake and sing the song of Moses and the Lamb (1)
181	sing in sweeter notes the song of Moses and the Lamb (4)
386, 387	Moses while on earth in dread and smitten to the heart (2)
648	Go down, Moses, way down in Egypt's land (R)
648	The Lord told Moses what to do (2)

most

14, 15	Jesus Christ, our Lord Most High (3)
19, 20	Christ, our Lord Most High (3)
21, 22	through Jesus Christ, our Lord Most High (3)
31, 32	Most Holy God, the Lord of heaven (1)

36	thee, therefore, O Most High, the world doth glorify (3)
37	most holy, heavenly, blest, Lord Jesus Christ (1)
40, 41	We pray you, O most holy Lord, to be our guardian (2)
44, 45	through Jesus Christ, our Lord Most High (4)
48	O balm of care and sadness, most beautiful, most bright (1)
48	thus this day most glorious a triple light was given (2)
53	came in likeness lowly, Son of God most holy (1)
61, 62	now come, most worthy Lord, God's Son, Incarnate Word (2)
65	Oh, blest is Christ that came in God's most holy name (R)
77	to shepherds poor the Lord Most High ... was revealed (4)
77	Lord Most High, the one great Shepherd (4)
80	This is the Christ, God's Son most high (3)
119	so, most gracious Lord, may we evermore be led to thee (1)
119	offered gifts most rare at that manger rude and bare (3)
128	worship him, God Most High (3)
142	chiefly live by thy most holy word (3)
145	reply, reply with love to love most high (1)
158	By foes derided, by thine own rejected, O most afflicted (1)
161	grant, most blessed Trinity ... all may share the victory (5)
162	O tree of beauty, tree most fair (3)
168, 169	show me, O Love most highest, the brightness of thy face (2)
168, 169	In thy most bitter passion my heart to share doth cry (3)
168, 169	hold me that I quail not in death's most fearful hour (5)
203	amidst them came their Lord most dear (4)
203	On this most holy day of days (5)
206	amidst them came their Lord most dear (2)
211	Our God most high, our joy and boast (4)
220, 221	O Lord Most High, eternal King (1)
226, 227	thou, the soul's most welcome guest (2)
244	the better Eden planted by our Lord most dear (2)
248, 249	we, in love adoring, this most blessed Name revere (4)
254	You are the Christ, O Lord, the Son of God most high (1)
254	Oh, Peter was most blest with blessedness unpriced (2)
258	blessed they, for ever blest, who love thee most (2)
258	love thee most and serve thee best (2)
263, 264	most blest to bring to human birth the long-desired (3)
265	most highly favored lady, "Gloria!" (1-4)
267	Most blest shall be her name in all the Church on earth (5)
277	sing of God's own Son most holy (1)
277	Son most holy, who became her little child (1)
286	Now in God's most holy place, blest they stand (5)
324	Alleluia, Lord Most High (4)
329, 331	he closed with wondrous ending his most patient life (2)
337	most patient Savior, who canst love us still (4)
349	come in this most solemn hour (2)
367	Holy, holy ... singing, Lord of hosts ... Lord Most High (2)
367	blessing thee, the Lord of hosts Most High (3)
386, 387	Glorious, most glorious, is the crown of him (4)
399	O God Most High, we are your sheep (2)
400	even you, most gentle death (6)
400	most gentle death, waiting to hush our final breath (6)
406, 407	Most High, omnipotent, good Lord (1,8)
406, 407	water ... most humble, useful, precious, chaste (4)
423	most blessed, most glorious, the Ancient of Days (1)
424	most of all that love has found us (3)

445, 446   in all his words most wonderful (1,5)
445, 446   most sure in all his ways (1,5)
465, 466   until by your most costly grace ... I come (3)
469, 470   the heart of the Eternal is most wonderfully kind (3)
474   all the vain things that charm me most, I sacrifice (2)
478   O Lord most holy (2)
491   O Most Mighty, O Most Holy (2)
496, 497   Jesus, Holy, holy, yet most lowly draw thou near us (1)
530   Word of life, most pure and strong (5)
580   life's destruction or our most triumphant hour (3)
608   Most Holy Spirit, who didst brood upon the chaos (3)
612   taught by thee we covet most ... holy, heavenly, love (1)
618   most gracious, magnify the Lord (2)
620   they still rejoice in that most happy place (2)
682   most loving Jesus Christ (4)

mother

60   the child of Mary, blameless mother mild (3)
78, 79   where misery cries out to thee, Son of the mother mild (4)
81   with Mary we behold it, the Virgin Mother kind (2)
102   where a mother laid her baby in a manger for his bed (1)
102   Mary was that mother mild, Jesus Christ her little child (1)
110   to guard him, and protect his mother mild (3)
111   all is calm ... bright round yon virgin mother and child (1)
112   but his mother only, in her maiden bliss, worshiped (3)
113   so rest in the arms of your mother who sings you a la ru (2)
122, 123   alleluia, joyful mother, all thy children sing with thee (2)
159   At the cross her vigil keeping stood the mournful mother (1)
159   mother weeping, where he hung, the dying Lord (1)
159   Who, on Christ's dear mother gazing ... would not weep (4)
159   Who, on Christ's dear mother thinking (4)
232   as once for our salvation your mother she became (2/8-15)
252   Jesus, Name decreed of old, to the maiden mother told (2)
257   But silent knelt the mother blest of the yet silent word (4)
258   Mary, Mother meek and mild (1,2)
265   For know a blessed Mother thou shalt be (2)
268, 269   when he made the Virgin Mary mother of his only Son (1)
268, 269   what Christ's mother sang in gladness ... people sing (3)
268, 269   more blessed far the mother ... who bore him in her womb (2)
277   Sing of Mary, pure and lowly, virgin mother undefiled (1)
277   Fairest child of fairest mother (1)
278   Sing we of the blessed Mother (1)
278   blessed Mother who received the angel's word (1)
282, 283   May the blest mother of our God and Savior ... help us (5)
400   Dear mother earth, you day by day unfold your blessings (4)
406, 407   By mother earth my Lord be praised (5)

mother's

396, 397   who from our mother's arms hath blessed us on our way (1)

mothers

480   when mothers round him pressed (2)

motion

159   Jesus, may her deep devotion stir in me the same emotion (5)

413   Trumpets and organs set in motion such sounds (2)

motion's
14, 15   yourself unmoved, all motion's source (1)

mount
276   he climbed the mount with thee (3)
686   Praise the mount, O, fix me on it (1)
686   mount of God's unchanging love (1)

mountain
99   Go tell it on the mountain, over the hills and everywhere (R)
99   go tell it on the mountain, that Jesus Christ is born (R)
117, 118   gems of the mountain, and pearls of the ocean (3)
128   field and fountain, moor and mountain (1)
129, 130   Christ upon the mountain peak stands alone in glory (1)
135   Manifest on mountain height, shining in resplendent light (4)
136, 137   which Christ upon the mountain shows (1)
171   Calvary's mournful mountain climb (3)
376   field and forest, vale and mountain, blooming meadow (2)
405   The purple-headed mountain, the river running by (2)
579   traffic runs amain by mountain pass or valley low (2)
609   O Master, from the mountain side (4)
719   for purple mountain majesties above the fruited plain (1)

mountain's
640   Traveler, o'er yon mountain's height see ... star (1)

mountains
96   the mountains in reply echoing their brave delight (1)
385   thy fingers spread the mountains and plains (1)
398   power of God that made the mountains rise (1)
413   mountains and stones look up adoring (3)
423   thy justice like mountains high soaring above (2)
616   before him on the mountains shall peace, the herald, go (3)
681   All beauty speaks of thee: the mountains and the rivers (3)

mounts
215   See the Conqueror mounts in triumph (1)

mourn
142   teach us with thee to mourn our sins (1)
168, 169   mourn thee, well beloved, yet thank thee for thy death (3)
537   the poor, and them that mourn (1)
560   Blessed are those who mourn, for they shall be comforted (2)
610   still in grief we mourn our dead (2)
683, 684   I hate the sins that made thee mourn (3)

mourned
284   ye mourned the dead in sad surprise (5)

mournful
159   At the cross her vigil keeping stood the mournful mother (1)
171   Calvary's mournful mountain climb (3)
493   mournful broken hearts rejoice, the humble poor believe (4)

mourning
67	mourning 'neath their sorrows' load (1)
122, 123	by Babylon's sad waters mourning exiles now are we (2)
190	Whom your tears in death were mourning, welcome (1)

mourns
56	mourns in lonely exile here until the Son of God appear (1,8)

mouth
19, 20	Let mouth and tongue, mind, sense, and strength (2)
370	Christ in mouth of friend and stranger (6)
534	by ... mouth of many messengers goes forth the voice of God (2)
694	God be in my mouth, and in my speaking (1)

move
212	those feet still free to move and bleed for millions (3)
256	the cosmos move in time with grace (3)
371	Move on the waters' face bearing the gifts of grace (3)
382	that love may never cease, I will move thee (1)
391	when rolling years shall cease to move (5)
409	What though in solemn silence all move round (3)
409	all move round the dark terrestrial ball (3)
487	such a joy as none can move (3)
519, 520	angel hosts encircled, as a bride dost earthward move (1)
539	God, in whom they live and move, is Love (2)
635	a rock which nought can move (1)
638, 639	Speak, or thou never hence shalt move (3)
659, 660	Help me the slow of heart to move (2)
659, 660	move by some clear, winning word of love (2)
707	Take my hands ... let them move at the impulse of thy love (1)

moved
149	moved by your love and toward your presence bent (1)
168, 169	Ah, keep my heart thus moved to stand thy cross beneath (3)
420	as worship moved us to a more profound Alleluia (2)
545	for the joy before him set, and moved by pitying love (4)
573	Spirit of life which moved ere form was made (1)
668	He will not let thy foot be moved (2)
689	afterward I knew he moved my soul to seek him, seeking me (1)

moves
562	Like a mighty army moves the Church of God (3)
677	God moves in a mysterious way his wonders to perform (1)

moving
393	given the moving fire by night (2)
506, 507	Spirit, moving on the waters quickening worlds to life (1)

much
291	much more to us, his children, he gives our daily bread (2)
467	what are we that he should show so much love to us below (2)
629	That universe, how much unknown (2)
677	the clouds ye so much dread are big with mercy (3)
689	'twas not so much that I on thee took hold (2)
689	not so much that I ... as thou, dear Lord, on me (2)

708   much we need thy tender care (1)

multitude
275   Multitude which none can number ... in glory stands (1)
275   Multitude ... like the stars (1)

multitudes
609   yet long these multitudes to see the true compassion (3)

murderer
458   a murderer they save, the Prince of Life they slay (5)

murmur
408   every faithless murmur stills (1)
513   Like the murmur of the dove's song (1)

music
89, 90   still ... heavenly music floats o'er all the weary world (2)
212   let Easter music swell (1)
248, 249   'Tis the Name that whoso preachest speaks like music (3)
248, 249   speaks like music to the ear (3)
400   Swift flowing water, pure and clear, make music (3)
400   make music for your Lord to hear (3)
413   all things that live in earth and ocean make music (2)
413   make music for your mighty King (2)
420   When in our music God is glorified (1)
420   How often, making music, we have found a new dimension (2)
427   When mirth for music longs, this is my song of songs (2)
431   through the silences of space ... soundless music sings (1)
492   him let all your music honor (1)
493   'tis music in the sinner's ears (3)
494   Hark, how the heavenly anthem drowns all music but its own (1)
572   we ... join in singing that great music pure and strong (1)
572   music ... wherewith heaven is ringing (1)
585   Morning glory, starlit sky, soaring music (1)
620   blest who might this music hear (3)
651   round me rings the music of the spheres (1)
717   Let music swell the breeze (3)

must
18   when we must act in day's hard light (2b)
60   At your great Name, O Jesus, now all knees must bend (4)
60   all hearts must bow (4)
151   must confess thy grace (2)
167   we must love him too, and trust in his redeeming blood (5)
246   innocents the price must pay (2)
252   Unto which must every knee bow in deep humility (1)
261, 262   Christ in whose presence hosts of hell must tremble (2)
369   how glorious bright must our Creator be (1)
379   Love for ever o'er the universe must reign (3)
391   firm as a rock thy truth must stand (5)
402, 403   Church with psalms must shout, no door can keep them out (2)
402, 403   above all, the heart must bear the longest part (2)
421   we for judgment there must stand (2)
426   Heaven and earth must pass away (3)

440	thou must work all good within us (2)
457	who would the Father seek, must seek him, Lord, by thee (1)
512	holiness, the road that we must take to dwell with God (3)
561	lift high his royal banner, it must not suffer loss (1)
570, 571	I must work while it is day (3)
585	nails and crown of thorns tell of what God's love must be (5)
598	must bring to doom the powers which crucified thee (2)
623	O what their joy and their glory must be (1)
623	we for that country must yearn and must sigh (4)
643	How wonderful, how beautiful, the sight of thee must be (3)
647	I must not fear nor stray (3)
663	Yea, even when I must pass through the valley (3)
669	his work must thou consider for thy work to endure (2)
685	thou must save and thou alone (2)
687, 688	he must win the battle (2)
720	Then conquer we must, when our cause it is just (2)

mute

430	let no tongue nor string be mute (2)
431	vault of heaven springs mute witness (1)
431	mute witness of the Master's hand in all created things (1)

mutual

353	join every husband, every wife in mutual love (3)
353	mutual love and love for you (3)
501, 502	in mutual love our hearts unite (4)

myriad

46	forth in starlight tender from myriad world's unknown (2)
225	Hark, for in myriad tongues Christ's own ... preach (3)

myrrh

109	gold, and myrrh, and frankincense (5)
115	So bring him incense, gold and myrrh (3)
117, 118	myrrh from the forest, and gold from the mine (3)
127	see them give ... gold and frankincense and myrrh (3)
127	myrrh his sepulcher foreshows (4)
128	Myrrh is mine; its bitter perfume ... gathering gloom (4)

myself

43	with the world, myself, and thee, I ... at peace may be (2)
47	thou dost give thyself to me, help me give myself to thee (6)
313	Thou didst give thyself for me, now I give myself to thee (R)
370	I bind unto myself today the strong Name of the Trinity (1)
370	I bind unto myself today (2)
370	I bind unto myself the power of the great love (3)
370	bind unto myself today the virtues of the starlit heaven (4)
370	I bind unto myself today the power of God (5)
370	bind unto myself the Name ... strong Name of the Trinity (7)
685	Rock of ages, cleft for me, let me hide myself in thee (1,3)
707	Take myself, and I will be ever, only, all for thee (2)

mysteries

346	Completed, Lord, the Holy Mysteries (1)
346	Through God's good grace these Mysteries are ours (3)

394, 395	your hands uphold earth's mysteries known or yet untold (2)
584	to probe earth's hidden mysteries (1)

mysterious

160	O mysterious condescending! O abandonment sublime! (3)
231	whom your mysterious love called early (2/12-28)
255	grace, by ways mysterious, our sinful wrath can bind (3)
369	let faith in humble notes adore the great mysterious King (4)
677	God moves in a mysterious way his wonders to perform (1)

mystery

69	Dark is the season, dark our hearts and shut to mystery (1)
106	rise to adore the mystery of love (1)
106	mystery ... which hosts of angels chanted from above (1)
136, 137	faithful hearts are raised on high by this ... mystery (4)
136, 137	this great vision's mystery (4)
161	They stumbled on a mystery: Messiah reigning from a tree (3)
329, 331	Now, my tongue, the mystery ... sing (1)
329, 331	the mystery of the glorious Body sing (1)
329, 331	faith alone the true heart waketh to behold the mystery (4)
366	adoring, bend the knee and confess the mystery (4)
483	profit and their joy to know the mystery of his love (5)

mystic

127	Sacred gifts of mystic meaning (4)
143	So Daniel trained his mystic sight (3)
162	the cross shines forth in mystic glow (1)
231	praise for his mystic vision (2/12-27)
235	in mystic form and image four living creatures came (2)
357	in the mystic symbols veiled from earthly sight (1)
360, 361	here may thy servants, at the mystic banquet (2)
416	for the mystic harmony linking sense to sound and sight (3)
525	mystic sweet communion with those whose rest is won (5)

mystical

225	Forth from the Father he comes with ... mystical offering (2)
225	sevenfold mystical offering (2)

nailed

57, 58	pierced, and nailed him to the tree (2)
172	Were you there when they nailed him to the tree (2)
175	He who was nailed to the cross is Lord (2)
216	He who was nailed to the cross is Lord (1)
270	to the cross shall Life be nailed (4)
468	nailed him to the cross, Lord ... hung him with a robber (3)

nailing

313	by the spear-wound and the nailing (3)

nails

165, 166	He endures the nails, the spitting (3)
585	nails and crown of thorns tell of what God's love must be (5)
682	for us didst bear the nails and spear (2)

naked

170   mercy throw around our naked shame (2)

nakedness

447   Can persecution, nakedness, or peril, or the sword (2)

name

3, 4	may praise and bless his holy Name (4)
23	They gave him healing in your Name (2)
47	God the Father's Name we praise (1)
50	comes, in God his Father's name, to save our sinful race (4)
53	Thus, if thou canst name him, not ashamed to claim him (3)
60	At your great Name, O Jesus, now all knees must bend (4)
65	Oh, blest is Christ that came in God's most holy name (R)
71, 72	heaven's eternal arches ring with thy beloved Name (4)
74	Blest be the King whose coming is in the name of God (1-4)
85, 86	let songs of praise your Name adorn (6)
103	Upon this joyful holy night ... we bless your name (3)
105	how that in Bethlehem was born the Son of God by name (2)
106	the earliest heralds of the Savior's name (4)
116	His Name we will profess (4)
125, 126	His name shall be the Prince of Peace for evermore adored (4)
129, 130	God proclaiming in its thunder Jesus as his Son by name (3)
143	herald of Messiah's name (3)
143	who art in three-fold Name adored (5)
146, 147	help us, lest ... we cause your Name to be betrayed (4)
152	for the glory of thy Name (3)
154, 155	who in the Lord's Name comest, the King and Blessed One (1)
157	Blessed is he who comes in the name of the Lord (1)
178	Alleluia, alleluia, Give praise to his Name (R)
181	praise the Savior's name (1)
205	Your Name we bless, O risen Lord (4)
213	love which hath joined us to Jesus' Name (4)
231, 232	your holy Name, O Jesus, for evermore be blessed (1)
231	Lord, for Paul's conversion we bless your Name today (2/1-25)
231	Joseph's love made "Father" to be ... God's Name (2/3-19)
231	to be, for Christ, God's Name (2/3-19)
232	equip us for such sufferings as glorify your Name (2/7-25)
236	living, were faithful to thy Name (3)
238, 239	wonders, worthy of the Name they bore (1)
243	in sweet forgiveness' name, should understand and spare (3)
245	the faith to bear your Name (3)
248, 249	To the Name of our salvation laud and honor let us pay (1)
248, 249	Jesus is the Name we treasure (2)
248, 249	Name beyond what words can tell (2)
248, 249	Name of gladness, Name of pleasure (2)
248, 249	Name of sweetness, passing measure (2)
248, 249	'Tis the Name that whoso preachest speaks like music (3)
248, 249	who in prayer this Name beseecheth ... comfort findeth (3)
248, 249	we, in love adoring, this most blessed Name revere (4)
250	this Name of names for us he bore (2)
252	Jesus, Name of wondrous love, Name all other names above (1)
252	Jesus, Name decreed of old, to the maiden mother told (2)

252	Jesus, Name of priceless worth to the fallen of the earth (3)
252	Jesus, Name of mercy mild, given to the holy child (4)
252	Jesus, only Name that's given under all the mighty heaven (5)
252	Jesus, Name of wondrous love (6)
252	Human Name of God above (6)
254	For ever be adored that Name in earth and sky (1)
260	for him ... was the patient life of faith and humble name (3)
265	my soul shall laud and magnify his holy Name (3)
267	Most blest shall be her name in all the Church on earth (5)
268, 269	let all faithful people sing the honor of her name (3)
271, 272	that John should be that herald's name (2)
271, 272	greater than a prophet's name (4)
276	For thy blest saints ... we praise thy Name, O Lord (1)
279	Jesus, thy Name we bless (4)
280	In the roll of your apostles stands the name Bartholemew (2)
284	With equal flame and equal art ... extol his Name (8)
284	do thou my heart extol his Name (8)
287	thy Name, O Jesus, be forever blessed (1)
289	with all who passed before us, we praise thy Name today (1)
292	with the Father's Name ... Savior's love proclaim (3)
292	with the Father's Name, and with the Holy Spirit's gifts (3)
297	brand us this day with Jesus' Name (1)
302, 303	Father, we thank thee who hast planted thy holy Name (1)
302, 303	planted thy holy Name within our hearts (1)
305, 306	one Name we bear, one Bread of life we break (3)
319	who adore you and confess your Name (2)
326	thy Name with the Father and Spirit be ever adored (1)
345	Savior, again to thy dear Name we raise ... praise (1)
345	that in this house have called upon thy Name (1)
362	All thy works shall praise thy Name (4)
362	praise thy Name in earth, and sky, and sea (4)
365	Come, thou almighty King, help us thy Name to sing (1)
366	Holy God, we praise thy Name (1)
366	Lo, the apostolic train join, thy sacred Name to hallow (3)
366	Holy Father, holy Son, Holy Spirit, three we name thee (4)
367	Thus thy glorious Name confessing (3)
368	meet and worship in thy Name (2)
370	I bind unto myself today the strong Name of the Trinity (1)
370	bind unto myself the Name ... strong Name of the Trinity (7)
372	Praise to the living God! All praised be his Name (1,4)
373	heaven and earth, and all creation, Laud ... his Name (2)
373	all creation, laud and magnify his Name (2)
374	The whole creation joins in one to bless the sacred Name (4)
374	Name of him that sits upon the throne (4)
377, 378	praise, laud, and bless his Name always (3)
380	Let the Redeemer's Name be sung through every land (1)
389	Let us blaze his Name abroad (2)
391	what lasting honors shall we rear ... to thy Name (3)
393	call upon his holy Name (1)
401	we bow and bless the sacred Name for ever blest (1)
404	your holy Name for ever be adored (1)
406, 407	no one is worthy thee to name (1)
408	Let all who name Christ's holy Name give God all praise (3)
411	all that is within me join to bless his holy Name (1)

411	bless his holy Name, whose grace hath made thee whole (6)
413	find a voice to praise his Name (3)
414	ever will I bless thy Name (1)
423	almighty, victorious, thy great Name we praise (1)
433	sing praises to his Name, he forgets not his own (1)
433	thy Name be ever praised! O Lord, make us free (3)
434	Here his whole Name appears complete (3)
434	I would for ever speak his Name (5)
434	speak his Name in sounds to mortal ears unknown (5)
435	At the Name of Jesus every knee shall bow (1)
435	Humbled for a season, to receive a Name (2)
435	Name from the lips of sinners, unto whom he came (2)
435	Name him, Christians ... with love strong as death (4)
435	name with awe and wonder and with bated breath (4)
437, 438	Tell out, my soul, the greatness of his Name (2)
437, 438	his holy Name -- The Lord, the Mighty One (2)
450, 451	All hail the power of Jesus' Name (1)
462	glorify thy Name (4)
467	Sing, my soul, adore his Name (4)
473	till all the world adore his sacred Name (R)
477	given the Name to which all knees shall bow (4)
478	your Name we glorify, O Jesus, throned on high (1)
478	all who confess his Name, come then with hearts aflame (3)
483	to whom he manifests his love and grants his Name to know (3)
483	their name, an everlasting name (4)
486	house of prayer, where we assembled in thy Name (3)
489	as one with us he dwelt with us, and bore a human name (4)
493	spread through all the earth abroad the honors of thy Name (2)
493	Jesus, the Name that charms our fears (3)
493	Name that ... bids our sorrows cease (3)
494	crown him the King, to whom is given the wondrous name (5)
494	the wondrous name of Love (5)
495	life is given through thy Name (1)
509	let our whole soul an offering be to our Redeemer's Name (3)
519, 520	for Christ's dear Name ... pain and tribulation bore (3)
525	one holy Name she blesses, partakes one holy food (2)
528	In my name baptize and teach (2)
530	word of how the Spirit came bringing peace in Jesus' name (4)
531	Name of Jesus glorify till every people call him Lord (4)
532, 533	O who shall not fear thee, and honor thy Name (1)
535	publish abroad his wonderful Name (1)
535	the Name all-victorious of Jesus extol (1)
540	proclaim ... the glory of thy Name (3)
542	One Lord, in one great Name unite us all who own thee (3)
543	In honor to his Name reflect that sacred light (3)
544	his Name like sweet perfume shall rise (2)
544	their early blessings on his Name (3)
570, 571	be its name, "The Lord is there" (5)
581	Love can exclude no race or creed if honored be God's Name (6)
587	Our Father, by whose Name all fatherhood is known (1)
603, 604	he sees not labels but a face, a person, and a name (3)
610	forth in your dear name we go (4)
614	place the same hope in this great Name (2)

616	Name shall stand for ever, his changeless Name of Love (5)
623	Truly, "Jerusalem," name we that shore (2)
628	our thoughts and words and deeds may glorify your Name (2)
638, 639	thyself hast called me by my name (2)
638, 639	I ask thee, who art thou? Tell me thy name (2)
638, 639	tell me if thy name is Love (3)
638, 639	thy nature and thy name is Love (4)
642	nor can the memory find a sweeter sound than Jesus' Name (2)
644	How sweet the Name of Jesus sounds in a believer's ear (1)
644	Dear Name, the rock on which I build (3)
664	My Shepherd will supply my need, Jehovah is his Name (1)
678, 679	tell out his exalted Name (2)
687, 688	Lord Sabaoth his Name, from age to age the same (2)
710	O sing the honor of his holy Name (RC)
717	thy name I love (2)

named

133, 134	the heavens above your glory named (2)
232	Praise for your blest apostle surnamed Bartholomew (2/8-24)
280	There are named the blessed faithful of the new Jerusalem (4)

names

250	this Name of names for us he bore (2)
252	Jesus, Name of wondrous love, Name all other names above (1)
394, 395	your gospel claims one family with a billion names (4)

napkin

| 183 | bright angels attesting, the shroud and napkin resting (6) |

narrow

119	Holy Jesus, every day keep us in the narrow way (4)
526	though now divided by the ... narrow stream of death (2)
526	when the word is given bid Jordan's narrow stream divide (5)

natal

| 93 | ye have seen his natal star (3) |

nation

66	dear desire of every nation, joy of every longing heart (2)
98	came he to a world forlorn, the Lord of every nation (1,5)
298	heavenly band of every tribe and nation (1)
334	seeking peace in every nation (3)
368	God the Lord, through every nation ... shine (4)
413	revealed to every nation his everlasting righteousness (1)
424	For his gifts to every nation (1)
460, 461	Jesus out of every nation hath redeemed us by his blood (1,5)
484, 485	Praise the Lord through every nation (1)
525	Elect from every nation, yet one o'er all the earth (2)
539	Proclaim to every people, tongue and nation (2)
542	the Day-star clear and bright of every race and nation (1)
568	bind in thy love every nation and race (4)
573	through the thick darkness covering every nation (1)
573	his saving cross no nation yet will bear (2)
573	nation by nation still goes unforgiven (3)
591	lift up a living nation, a single sword to thee (3)

716   God bless our native land (1)
717   My native country, thee, land of the noble free (2)

nature
100   heaven and nature sing (1)
131, 132   in streams that nature ne'er bestowed (4)
175   Lord and the ruler of nature (2)
213   share both the nature and kingdom divine (3)
215   Thou hast raised our human nature ... to God's right hand (3)
216   Lord and the ruler of nature (1)
231   your perfect two-fold nature (2/12-21)
277   our very brother, takes our nature by his birth (1)
370   Of whom all nature hath creation (7)
383, 384   Fairest Lord Jesus, Ruler of all nature (1)
386, 387   at once, above, beneath, around, all nature ... replied (2)
386, 387   nature without voice or sound replied, O Lord, thou art (2)
415   When nature fails (4)
434   Nature with open volume stands to spread ... praise (1)
474   Were the whole realm of nature mine (4)
484, 485   His praise shall sound all nature round (1)
496, 497   whole creation's Head and Lord ... assumed our very nature (2)
638, 639   thy nature and thy name is Love (4)
651   to my listening ears all nature sings (1)

nature's
179   thou from heaven beholding human nature's fall (4)
515   pierce the clouds of nature's night (1)

nay
305, 306   nay, let us be thy guests, the feast is thine (1)

Nazareth
231   when they to Nazareth came (2/3-19)
266   he was sent from the Trinity, to Nazareth in Galilee (1)
277   Sing of Jesus, son of Mary, in the house at Nazareth (2)
586   carpenter of Nazareth, toiling for thy daily food (1)
611   Blessed manchild, boy of Nazareth (2)

ne'er
131, 132   in streams that nature ne'er bestowed (4)
151   Our works could ne'er our guilt remove (2)
192   Had Christ ... ne'er burst his three-day prison (R)
286   robes whose luster ne'er shall fade (2)
286   ne'er be touched by time's rude hand ((2)
320   ordained to be repeated, his memorial ne'er to cease (3)
365   ne'er from us depart, Spirit of power (3)
408   by morning glow or evening shade ... ne'er sleepeth (2)
408   his watchful eye ne'er sleepeth (2)
429   My days of praise shall ne'er be past (1,4)
450, 451   Sinners, whose love can ne'er forget the wormwood (5)
450, 451   ne'er forget the wormwood and the gall (5)
512   that we from thee may ne'er depart (2)

near
6, 7   Day-spring from on high, be near (1)

23	At prayer time, near the Temple gate (2)
48	living presence greeting, through Bread and Wine made near (3)
59	with words of love draw near (4)
65	Prepare the way, O Zion, your Christ is drawing near (1)
67	in the desert far and near (2)
68	The evening is advancing, and darker night is near (1)
70	pathway ... for the one who brings God near (2)
89, 90	from angels bending near the earth (1)
101	Be near me, Lord Jesus (3)
145	his beauty to come near (2)
173	now, and even unto death, dearest Lord, be near me (4)
209	but we believe him near (1)
209	to call on you when you are near (3)
222	he reigns invisible but near (2)
246	Then warning came of danger near (1)
248, 249	sweetest comfort findeth near (3)
251	In doubt or danger ... be near to guard us still (3)
291	He only is the Maker of all things near and far (2)
304	I come with Christians far and near (2)
304	His presence, always near (4)
332	O God, unseen yet ever near, thy presence may we feel (1)
349	once again in love draw near (1)
349	draw near to your servants gathered here (1)
366	help thy servants, drawing near (7)
396, 397	O may this bounteous God through all our life be near us (2)
419	yet to each loving heart how near (1)
436	The King of kings is drawing near (1)
459	heaven ... knows neither near nor far (2)
460, 461	he is near us, faith believes, nor questions how (2)
475	humbly, fervently draw near him (1)
496, 497	Jesus, Holy, holy, yet most lowly draw thou near us (1)
516	O Comforter, draw near, within my heart appear (1)
522, 523	showing that the Lord is near (3)
534	God is working his purpose out ... time is drawing near (1)
552, 553	Faint not nor fear, his arms are near (4)
567	now, O Lord, be near to bless, almighty as of yore (2)
570, 571	drawing near a world that spurns him (4)
603, 604	always, near or far, he calls and claims us (2)
613	wherever near or far thick darkness broodeth yet (5)
615	proclaim the day is near (3)
655	be thou for ever near me, my Master and my friend (1)
678, 679	his saving help is near (1)
697	worship near thy throne (3)

nearer

10	a road to bring us daily nearer God (5)
144	nearer draws the day of days when paradise shall bloom (4)
315	draw us the nearer each to each, we plead (2)
534	nearer draws the time, the time that shall surely be (1,4)
574, 575	whate'er the pain and shame may be, bring us ... nearer (1)
574, 575	bring us, O Father, nearer thee (1)
699	while the nearer waters roll (1)

nearly

10	help us ... every day, to live more nearly as we pray (6)

| 23 | The fleeting day is nearly gone (1) |
| 654 | follow thee more nearly, day by day (1) |

nears

| 27, 28 | But now the threatening darkness nears (2) |

need

18	to us, like her who saw your need (4a)
74	He offers to the burdened the rest and grace they need (4)
97	nought but need and penury; why thus cradled here (1)
107	now ye need not fear the grave (3)
113	You need not fear King Herod (2)
119	bring our ransomed souls at last where they need no star (4)
119	In the heavenly country bright need they no created light (5)
145	who feed the hungry in their need, and wrongs redress (4)
250	what need we fear in earth or space in this new year (4)
308, 309	of thine abundance give us, and all we need provide (2)
318	nor do I need another arm save thine to lean upon (3)
359	to human need their quickened hearts awake (2)
370	his ear to hearken to my need (5)
389	his full hand supplies their need (6)
452	whose life and death that love reveal which mortals need (1)
452	mortals need and need to feel (1)
458	my friend, indeed, who at my need his life did spend (2)
505	in every need thou bringest aid (1)
530	how forever, in its need ... the world is freed (3)
563	he knows thine hourly need (1)
566	Impart them, Lord, to each and all, as each and ... need (1)
582, 583	no night, no need, nor pain (1)
609	In haunts of wretchedness and need (2)
610	the weight of human need (1)
635	God never yet forsook in need the soul that trusted him (2)
638, 639	I need not tell thee who I am (2)
662	I need thy presence every passing hour (2)
663	how could I want or need (1)
664	My Shepherd will supply my need, Jehovah is his Name (1)
668	sun by day nor moon by night need make thy soul afraid (3)
693	poor, wretched, blind ... all I need, in thee to find (3)
698	I only know my need, as deep as life (1)
698	Come, pray in me the prayer I need this day (2)
698	Come with the vision and the strength I need to serve (3)
705	A world in need now summons us to labor, love and give (2)
708	much we need thy tender care (1)

needed

| 281 | there needed but the timely word (2) |

needest

| 390 | Hast thou not seen how all thou needest hath been granted (2) |

needful

| 406, 407 | governed by thee she hath upraised what ... is needful (5) |
| 406, 407 | what for our life is needful (5) |

needs

250	His love abundant far exceeds ... a whole year's needs (3)
250	the volume of a whole year's needs (3)
424	future needs in earth's safe-keeping (1)
458	They rise, and needs will have my dear Lord made away (5)
610	making known the needs and burdens (3)
669	the needs of all thy children, their anguish or delight (3)

needy

616	to help the poor and needy, and bid the weak be strong (2)
700	love of the Holy Ghost, fill thou each needy one (4)

neglect

528	Lest the Church neglect its mission (1)
539	through thy neglect, unfit to see his face (4)

neighbor

84	love to God and neighbor (3)
424	In the help we give our neighbor (2)

neighbors

602	show us how to serve the neighbors we have from you (R)
602	Neighbors are rich and poor (2)
602	neighbors are black and white (2)
602	neighbors are near-by and far away (2)
602	All are neighbors to us and you (3)

neither

199, 200	Neither might the gates of death ... tomb's dark portal (4)
251	O God, whom neither time nor space can limit (1)
251	neither time nor space can limit, hold, or bind (1)
352	Christ, grant that neither grief nor place ... may part (2)
355	neither sighing, but life everlasting (1)
430	nor ... creature found that hath neither note nor sound (2)
459	heaven ... knows neither near nor far (2)
667	Though vine nor fig tree neither ... wonted fruit should (4)

nerve

546	Awake, my soul, stretch every nerve (1)
546	Then wake, my soul, stretch every nerve (4)
675	brace your spirit, and nerve your arm (2)

nerves

471	nerves the feeble arm for fight (4)

nest

517	Beside thine altars ... the swallows find a nest (2)

never

24	the voice of prayer is never silent (3)
24	thy throne shall never ... pass away (4)
24	never, like earth's proud empires, pass away (4)
38, 39	let him never lead astray those you have ransomed (3)
55	strength which never fails (4)
67	token that the word is never broken (3)

94, 95	good will ... begin and never cease (6)
108	Let every house be bright; let praises never cease (2)
128	King for ever, ceasing never over us all to reign (2)
168, 169	Lord, let me never, never, outlive my love for thee (4)
182	His love in death shall never die (1)
204	thinking that never he would wake again (2)
233, 234	the hope that never yields or faints (3)
237	Never flinched they from the flame ... the torment never (2)
271, 272	faithful hearts shall never fail ... his light to hail (1)
271, 272	woman born shall never be a greater prophet than was he (4)
300	sing Christ the Spring, never, never ceasing (2)
312	let ears that now have heard thy songs ... never waken (1)
312	to clamor never waken (1)
314	to my taste thy sweetness never failing give (3)
320	never canst thou reach his due (1)
339	never to my hurt invited (3)
348	ours a commitment we know never ends (1)
357	Here mid stress and conflict toils can never cease (2)
373	laws which never shall be broken (1)
373	never shall his promise fail (2)
375	his mercy never waneth (3)
379	Sin and death and hell shall never ... triumph (3)
379	never o'er us final triumph gain (3)
382	that love may never cease, I will move thee (1)
392	Let those refuse to sing that never knew our God (2)
413	praises be his that never cease (3)
441, 442	never shall the cross forsake me (2)
444	O bless our God and Savior with songs that never cease (3)
452	transcends the world he never leaves (2)
458	never was love, dear King, never was grief like thine (7)
508	so shall I never die (4)
522, 523	Grace which like the Lord, the giver, never fails (2)
522, 523	Grace ... never fails from age to age (2)
527	one the faith which never tires (2)
535	thanks never ceasing and infinite love (4)
540	watchmen who never held their peace by day or night (1)
559	pleasure that can never cloy (3)
561	when duty calls, or danger, be never wanting there (3)
562	gates of hell can never 'gainst that Church prevail (4)
613	arise, O Morning Star, arise, and never set (5)
616	the tide of time shall never his covenant remove (5)
634	My heart is never set at rest till thy sweet word (1)
634	never resisting but to increase in faith more and more (1)
635	God never yet forsook in need the soul that trusted him (2)
636, 637	I'll never, no, never, no, never forsake (5)
638, 639	Speak, or thou never hence shalt move (3)
638, 639	thy mercies never shall remove (4)
645, 646	whose goodness faileth never (1)
645, 646	through all the length of days thy goodness faileth never (6)
657	suddenly return, and never, nevermore thy temples leave (2)
672	kindling to the perfect day that never shall be past (3)
686	Streams of mercy never ceasing (1)
687, 688	A mighty fortress is our God, a bulwark never failing (1)
695, 696	never fails to greet us each new day (1)
700	Spring up, and never cease (3)

nevermore

213	so united in heart, let us nevermore part (4)
336	leaving now thine altar let us nevermore leave thee (1)
337	grant us nevermore to part from thee (4)
657	suddenly return, and never, nevermore thy temples leave (2)

new

3, 4	that we, when this new day is gone (4)
8	Sweet the rain's new fall sunlit from heaven (2)
8	praise every morning, God's recreation of the new day (3)
10	New every morning is the love (1)
10	New mercies, each returning day around us hover (2)
10	new mercies ... around us hover while we pray (2)
10	new perils past, new sins forgiven (2)
10	new thoughts of God, new hopes of heaven (2)
10	new treasures still, of countless price, God will provide (3)
27, 28	when on the new and living earth (1)
44, 45	when the dawn new light will bring (3)
67	calling us to new repentance (2)
70	to them new life is given (3)
145	God brings new beauty nigh (1)
176, 177	seek through the power of the new creation (2)
183	our new life obtaining (8)
198	Come, let us taste the vine's new fruit (2)
201	new life to all he doth afford (4)
217, 218	new hymns throughout the world shall ring (1)
217, 218	by a new way none ever trod Christ takes his place (1)
233, 234	joy fills the new Jerusalem (4)
250	what need we fear in earth or space in this new year (4)
250	in this new year of grace (4)
256	Your new creation let us be (4)
256	with Paul's new vision, let us see (4)
263, 264	God's new message did proclaim (2)
280	There are named the blessed faithful of the new Jerusalem (4)
289	new comrades ever bringing in comrades' steps to tread (2)
296	A new creation comes to life and grows (4)
296	as Christ's new body takes on flesh and blood (4)
298	each is a new creation (1)
299	From living waters raise new saints (2)
299	let new tongues hail the risen Lord (2)
304	new community of love in Christ's communion bread (2)
312	bodies by thy Body fed with thy new life replenish (3)
320	today the new oblation of the new King's revelation (4)
320	today the new oblation ... bids us feast in glad array (4)
334	By your Blood new life receiving (2)
334	Partners in your new creation (3)
353	the love that Christ makes ever new (1)
363	summoning all to share thy new creation (3)
412	sing to the Lord a new song (1-6)
412	I, too, will praise him with a new song (R)
413	New songs of celebration render to him (1)
413	new songs ... render to him who has great wonders done (1)
420	How often, making music, we have found a new dimension (2)
420	a new dimension in the world of sound (2)
422	For each new step of faith we take thou hast more truth (1)

426	God will make new heavens and earth (3)
432	Praise him upon earth ... all ye of new birth (2)
436	Let new and nobler life begin (5)
455, 456	eternal and yet ever new (1)
493	new life the dead receive (4)
513	like the new flame's eager might (1)
515	Author of the new creation, come with unction (2)
525	she is his new creation by water and the word (1)
528	give us all new fervor, draw us closer in community (2)
542	new life, new hope awakes, for all who own his sway (1)
543	with luster new divinely crowned (2)
568	stir every will to new ventures of faithfulness (3)
584	with new mind, new heart (3)
590	Grant us new courage, sacrificial, humble (2)
598	still our wrongs may weave thee now new thorns (1)
598	new thorns to pierce that steady brow (1)
598	New advent of the love of Christ (3)
598	O wounded hands of Jesus, build in us thy new creation (4)
599	facing the rising sun of our new day begun (1)
614	who with a faith for ever new followed the King (1)
614	new lamps be lit, new tasks begun (3)
629	let a new and better hope within our hearts be stirred (1)
657	Finish then thy new creation (3)
667	theme of God's salvation, and find it ever new (2)
695, 696	never fails to greet us each new day (1)
695, 696	Yet when again in this new world you give us the joy (4)
705	all life in Christ made new (2)

newer

| 329-331 | for the newer rite is here (5) |

news

70	tell the news that Christ is here (2)
80	to bring good news to everyone (1)
178	Spread the good news o'er all the earth (2)
205	To all the world glad news we bring (1)
242	yet when thine Easter-news was spread (2)
299	With tongues of fire saints spread good news (1)
454	to hearts rejoicing, bringing news of sins forgiven (3)

next

59	so when next he comes with glory (4)
396, 397	free us from all ills in this world and the next (2)
561	this day the noise of battle, the next the victor's song (4)

nigh

42	Now the day is over, night is drawing nigh (1)
56	cheer us by thy drawing nigh (6)
59	"Christ is nigh," it seems to say (1)
63, 64	when as judge, thou drawest nigh (3)
68	The Bridegroom is arising, and soon he will draw nigh (1)
76	Baptist's cry announces that the Lord is nigh (1)
83	leaving their flocks, draw nigh to gaze (4)
101	stay by my side until morning is nigh (2)
114	but as the hunter braves drew nigh, the angel-song rang (2)

128	incense owns a Deity nigh (3)
136, 137	With Moses and Elijah nigh (2)
145	God brings new beauty nigh (1)
156	Thy last and fiercest strife is nigh (4)
238, 239	when before him we draw nigh (3)
259	no shouts proclaim him nigh, no crowds his coming wait (1)
308, 309	nor thy delights deny us, whose hearts to thee draw nigh (1)
326	O Lord, evermore to thy servants thy presence be nigh (2)
327, 328	Draw nigh and take the Body of the Lord (1)
393	God it is who grants us sure retreat and refuge nigh (2)
531	far and nigh the triumphs of the cross record (4)
535	still he is nigh, his presence we have (2)
541	The night draws nigh (4)
543	tell all the earth thy joys, and boast salvation nigh (1)
600, 601	O day of God, draw nigh in beauty and in power (1)
600, 601	O day of God, draw nigh as at creation's birth (5)
716	thou who art ever nigh, guarding with watchful eye (2)

night

1, 2	Father, we praise thee, now the night is over (1)
3, 4	night in turn is drawing on (4)
3, 4	to Christ, revealed in earthly night (5)
6, 7	Triumph o'er the shades of night (1)
24	and rests not now by day or night (2)
25, 26	the lamps are lit to pierce the night (2)
27, 28	Defend us, Father, through the night (5)
29, 30	to Christ revealed in earthly night (3)
31, 32	silences of the night (3)
31, 32	boundaries of the day and night (4)
31, 32	like moon and night, give loving peace (5)
33-35	to the night give glittering adornment (1)
38, 39	you set the bounds of night and day (2)
40, 41	you drive away the shadowed night (1)
40, 41	bestow on us who rest in you ... a quiet night (2)
40, 41	the blessing of a quiet night (2)
42	Now the day is over, night is drawing nigh (1)
42	Through the long night watches may thine angels spread (5)
43	All praise to thee, my God this night (1)
46	let us, as night is falling ... give thanks to him (1)
46	death's fair night discover ... everlasting life (3)
55	no night shall overcome it now (5)
56	disperse the gloomy clouds of night (6)
60	Creator of the stars of night (1)
60	When this old world drew on toward night you came (3)
61, 62	she wakes and hurries through the night (2)
68	The evening is advancing, and darker night is near (1)
69	prepare for joy in the winter night (2)
73	earth's dark night is past (3)
78, 79	dark night wakes, the glory breaks (4)
80	to you this night is born a child of Mary (2)
81	amid the cold of winter, when half spent was the night (1)
81	when half spent was the night (1,2)
85, 86	before the world knew day or night (1)
85, 86	our constant star in sin's deep night (2)
93	watching o'er your flocks by night (2)

94, 95	While shepherds watched their flocks by night (1)
96	singing sweetly through the night (1)
99	o'er silent flocks by night (1)
103	Upon this joyful holy night ... we bless your name (3)
109	lay keeping their sheep on a cold winter's night (1)
109	cold winter's night that was so deep (1)
109	so it continued both day and night (2)
110	when Christ our Lord was born on Christmas night (1)
111	Silent night, holy night (1-3)
124	to Christ, revealed in earthly night (5)
125, 126	who dwelt in death and night (1)
128	O star of wonder, star of night (R)
149	led by your cloud by day, by night your fire (1)
185, 186	the night of sin is ended (3)
187	Earthly night brought us light which is ours eternally (3)
190	Ended now the night of sorrow (3)
202	Protected in the Paschal night (2)
203	That night the apostles met in fear (4)
206	That night the apostles met in fear (2)
235	voice proclaimed salvation that poured upon the night (1)
236	beacon by night and cloud by day (1)
243	rend the veils of night (2)
246	Lord Jesus, through our night of loss shines ... the cross (4)
284	In dark Gethsemane the night before he died (4)
286	day and night they serve him still (5)
329, 331	That last night at supper lying (3)
381	dark as night and deep as death (2)
389	The horned moon to shine by night (5)
393	given the moving fire by night (2)
406, 407	strong to lighten all the night (4)
415	day and night divide thy works no more (4)
416	For the beauty of each hour of the day and of the night (2)
419	star of our hope, thy softened light cheers the ... night (2)
419	cheers the long watches of the night (2)
420	did not Jesus sing a psalm that night (4)
428	heat and cold, O night and day ... bless the Lord (3)
440	till thy Spirit breaks our night with the beams of truth (2)
453	at night on a stone for a pillow he lay (1)
472	lure us away from thee to endless night (3)
488	thou my best thought, by day or by night (1)
490	The night and the day are both alike (R)
494	sing ... before him day and night (4)
499	to shine on nations trapped in darkest night (1)
515	pierce the clouds of nature's night (1)
521	hatred and tormenting fear pass with the passing night (2)
522, 523	light by night and shade by day (3)
525	soon the night of weeping shall be the morn of song (3)
527	through the night of doubt and sorrow (1)
527	stepping fearless through the night (1)
530	until from night all the world awakes to light (5)
540	watchmen who never held their peace by day or night (1)
541	The enemy is watching night and day (2)
541	The night draws nigh (4)
542	freedom her bondage breaks, and night is turned to day (1)
551	end the night of wrong (2)

556, 557	youth to age, by night and day, in gladness and in woe (4)
563	fear not the gathering night (4)
564, 565	I'll labor night and day to be a pilgrim (3)
582, 583	within whose four-square walls shall come no night (1)
582, 583	no night, no need, nor pain (1)
593	where all is night, may we sow light (2)
593	reborn through death's dark night to endless day (5)
598	in the night of hate and war we perish as we lose thee (3)
607	trust in bombs that shower destruction through the night (2)
615	But the slow watches of the night not less to God belong (2)
617	from... night profound into the glory of the perfect day (1)
621, 622	there no night brings rest from labor (3)
638, 639	With thee all night I mean to stay (1)
640	Watchman, tell us of the night (1-3)
643	by prostrate spirits day and night incessantly adored (2)
649, 650	chase the night of sin away (4)
668	sun by day nor moon by night need make thy soul afraid (3)
672	cold is the night (2)
680	short as the watch that ends the night (4)
695, 696	we know that God is with us night and morning (1)
702	to thee both night and day are bright (5)
703	involved in shadows of a darksome night (2)
716	firm may she ever stand through storm and night (1)
718	lead us from night to never-ending day (4)
720	gave proof through the night ... our flag was still there (1)

night's

38, 39	rest in night's enfolding quietness (2)
61, 62	Midnight's peace their cry has broken (1)

nightly

400	stars nightly shining, find a voice (2)
409	nightly to the listening earth repeats the story (2)

nights

9	velvet of soft summer nights (2)
150	Forty days and forty nights thou wast fasting in the wild (1)
150	forty days and forty nights tempted, and yet undefiled (1)

ninth

23	at that ninth hour you died for us (3)

noble

127	Earth has many a noble city (1)
165, 166	Faithful cross, above all other, one and only noble tree (4)
232	Apostles, prophets, martyrs ... the noble throng (2/11-1)
236	King of the martyrs' noble band (1)
276	saints, a noble throng (1)
364	with all the martyrs' noble host (4)
566	rise, like incense ... in noble thought and deed (1)
717	My native country, thee, land of the noble free (2)

nobler

50	shall give him nobler praise (5)
359	make each one stronger, nobler than the last (1)

429	praise shall employ my nobler powers (1,4)
436	Let new and nobler life begin (5)
543	ten thousand stars in nobler spheres his influence own (4)
545	Behold a Witness nobler still who trod affliction's path (3)
629	make us all go on to know with nobler powers conferred (3)

noblest
434	Her noblest life my spirit draws from his dear wounds (4)
492	wake your noblest, sweetest strain (1)
495	all your noblest anthems raise (4)
556, 557	true rapture, noblest mirth (2)

nobly
5	to guide whate'er we nobly do (4)
287	fight as the saints who nobly fought of old (3)
574, 575	more pure, more true, more nobly wise (4)

noise
89, 90	O hush the noise and cease your strife (3)
561	this day the noise of battle, the next the victor's song (4)
609	above the noise of selfish strife (1)
710	Make a joyful noise unto the Lord (RC)

none
151	For none may boast themselves of aught (2)
162	the price which none but he could pay (4)
165, 166	None in foliage ... blossom ... fruit thy peer may be (4)
209	him who spoke as none e'er spoke (1)
217, 218	by a new way none ever trod Christ takes his place (1)
231	saved him from King Herod when safety there was none (2/3-19)
275	Multitude which none can number ... in glory stands (1)
360, 361	this is none other than the gate of heaven (4)
362	only thou art holy, there is none beside thee (3)
427	God's holy house of prayer hath none that can compare (2)
429	none shall find his promise vain (2)
458	none the longed-for Christ would know (2)
487	such a joy as none can move (3)
487	such a love as none can part (3)
505	unless thy grace the power should give, none can believe (2)
505	none can believe in Christ and live (2)
516	for none can guess its grace, till Love create a place (3)
539	let none whom he hath ransomed fail to greet him (4)
578	None ever called on thee in vain (1)
607	with faith that none can alter, your servants undergird (3)
631	shedding light that none can measure (1)
634	I have none other help but thee (1)
642	love of Jesus, what it is, none but who love him know (4)
699	Other refuge have I none (2)
706	Now my heart sets none above you (3)

noon
18	As now the sun shines down at noon (1)
18	At noon you hung upon the cross (3a)
18	At noon you came to Jacob's well (4a)
18	Elijah taunted Baal at noon (2b)

482   strength in our hearts, Lord, at the noon of the day (2)

noon's
18   By noon's bright light, destruction stalks (2c)

noonday
18   In noonday vision Peter saw (4c)
124   more beauteous than the noonday light (1)
226, 227   Brighter than the noonday sun (3)

noontime
18   At noontime Paul beheld your light (4b)

North
529   in him no South or North (1)
529   in him meet South and North (3)

northwest
109   This star drew night to the northwest (4)

note
70   Herald, sound the note of judgment (1)
70   Herald, sound the note of gladness (2)
70   Herald, sound the note of pardon (3)
70   Herald, sound the note of triumph (4)
382   thou didst note my working breast, thou hast spared me (1)
430   nor ... creature found that hath neither note nor sound (2)

notes
181   sing in sweeter notes the song of Moses and the Lamb (4)
210   let all things seen and unseen their notes together blend (3)
284   The joyous notes pursue and louder anthems raise (8)
369   let faith in humble notes adore the great mysterious King (4)

nothing
105   God rest you merry, gentlemen, let nothing you dismay (1)
105   Fear not then, said the angel, Let nothing you affright (3)
158   while we nothing heeded (3)
324   ponder nothing earthly minded (1)
350   let nothing in this life divide ... whom thou makest one (3)
447   Thus nothing in the heights or depths (4)
534   All we can do is nothing worth unless God blesses the deed (4)
559   nothing can our peace destroy (3)
592   All may of thee partake, nothing can be so mean (2)
592   nothing ... will not grow bright and clean (2)
645, 646   I nothing lack if I am his, and he is mine for ever (1)
667   It can bring with it nothing but he will bear us through (3)

notions
629   notions of our day and place (1)

nought
57, 58   those who set at nought and sold him (2)
97   nought but need and penury; why thus cradled here (1)
109   that hath made heaven and earth of nought (6)

| 278 | obedient to the summons bore in love the infant Lord (1) |
| 332 | We come, obedient to thy word, to feast on heavenly food (3) |

obey

67	Oh, that warning cry obey (2)
125, 126	him shall the tribes of earth obey (3)
291	the winds and waves obey him, by him the birds are fed (2)
332	Thus may we all thy word obey (4)
339	let me gladly here obey thee (3)
344	glad thy summons to obey (3)
364	O holy, holy, holy Lord, whom heavenly hosts obey (3)
385	deep seas obey thy voice (1)
398	moon shines full at his command and all the stars obey (1)
561	the trumpet call obey (2)

obeyed

121	you then obeyed his call (3)
279	followed thee, obeyed, adored, our grateful hymn receive (1)
373	worlds his mighty voice obeyed (1)
600, 601	quiet of a steadfast faith, calm of a call obeyed (2)

obeying

| 139 | Jesus went to Jordan's stream his Father's will obeying (1) |

obeys

| 372 | everywhere above, below, his will obeys (2) |

object

| 527 | one the object of our journey (2) |

oblation

117, 118	Vainly we offer each ample oblation (4)
158	for me ... thy mortal sorrow, and thy life's oblation (4)
320	today the new oblation of the new King's revelation (4)
320	today the new oblation ... bids us feast in glad array (4)
338	spotless oblation (1)

oblations

| 127 | Eastern sages at his cradle make oblations rich and rare (3) |

obtain

| 560 | Blessed are the merciful, for they shall obtain mercy (5) |

obtaining

| 183 | our new life obtaining (8) |
| 342 | Thus by your death our life obtaining (2) |

occasions

| 463, 464 | at your marriage all its occasions shall dance for joy (3) |

occupy

| 228 | occupy its inmost part with your dazzling purity (3) |

occurred

| 230 | what Christ had promised now occurred (1) |

ocean
117, 118   gems of the mountain, and pearls of the ocean (3)
165, 165   earth, and stars, and sky, and ocean (3)
413   all things that live in earth and ocean make music (2)
579, 608   who bidd'st the mighty ocean deep its ... limits keep (1)
579, 608   ocean deep its own appointed limits keep (1)
629   The ocean unexplored (2)

ocean's
287   From earth's wide bounds, from ocean's farthest coast (8)
371   wisdom, love, might; boundless to ocean's tide (4)

odors
117, 118   Shall we then yield him, in costly devotion, odors (3)
117, 118   odors of Edom, and offerings divine (3)

off
11   shake off dull sloth (1)
149   far off yet here -- the goal of all desire (1)
661   just off the hills of brown (1)

offended
158   Ah, holy Jesus, how hast thou offended (1)

offenses
33-35   that you may grant us pardon for offenses (4)
185, 186   for our offenses given (1)
290   from his field shall in that day all offenses purge away (3)

offer
1, 2   singing we offer prayer and meditation: thus we adore (1)
12, 13   Amid our customary round, we offer ... prayer and praise (1)
33-35   Therefore we come now evening rites to offer (3)
117, 118   Vainly we offer each ample oblation (4)
128   Frankincense to offer have I (3)
144   Lord, grant that we in penitence may offer you our praise (3)
157   I will enter them; I will offer thanks to the Lord (1)
183   Christians, to the Paschal victim offer your ... praises (1)
183   offer your thankful praises (1)
196, 196   offer us the worlds of light that live inside the Trinity (3)
280   for this faithful saint we offer ... our thanks to you (2)
291   the gifts we have to offer are what thy love imparts (3)
475   Gladly, Lord, we offer thine to be forever (2)

offered
51   In the Lord's service bread and wine are offered (4)
109   offered there in his presence their gold (5)
119   offered gifts most rare at that manger rude and bare (3)
158   Lo, the Good Shepherd for the sheep is offered (3)
173   in blood was offered for us (2)
202   his flesh ... is freely offered in our stead (3)
327, 328   Offered was he for greatest and for least (4)
610   upon the cross, forsaken, offered mercy's perfect deed (1)

offering

161	advance through his self-offering (1)
225	Forth from the Father he comes with ... mystical offering (2)
225	sevenfold mystical offering (2)
286	offering up to Christ their will (5)
307	Paschal Lamb, thine offering, finished once for all (4)
337	we here spread forth to thee that only offering perfect (1)
337	only offering perfect in thine eyes (1)
338	All-perfect Offering, sacrifice immortal (1)
416	offering up on every shore thy pure sacrifice of love (5)
474	that were an offering far too small (4)
509	let our whole soul an offering be to our Redeemer's Name (3)
522, 523	as priests, his solemn praises ... a thankoffering brings (4)
570, 571	offering peace from Calvary's hill (4)
605	What does the Lord require for praise and offering (1)
705	to make our life an offering to God that all may live (2)

offerings

117, 118	odors of Edom, and offerings divine (3)
257	two young doves, her humble offerings (2)

offers

74	He offers to the burdened the rest and grace they need (4)
131, 132	he who offers heavenly birth sought not the kingdoms (1)

offspring

87	offspring of the Virgin's womb (2)

oft

143	Then grant us, Lord, like them to be full oft in fast (4)
143	full oft in fast and prayer with thee (4)
242	How oft, O Lord, thy face hath shone on doubting souls (1)
286	in prayer full oft have striven (4)
479	Oft as earth exulting wafts its praise on high (4)
645, 646	Perverse and foolish oft I strayed (3)

often

357	Often were they wounded in the deadly strife (3)
420	How often, making music, we have found a new dimension (2)

oil

68	See that your lamps are burning, replenish them with oil (2)
232	Your wine and oil, O Savior, upon our spirits pour (2/10-18)
664	thy oil anounts my head (2)

old

10	Old friends, old scenes, will lovelier be (4)
60	When this old world drew on toward night you came (3)
73	Not, as of old, a little child (2)
81	Of Jesse's lineage coming as seers of old have sung (1)
89, 90	that glorious song of old (1)
89, 90	by prophets seen of old (4)
119	As with gladness men of old did the guiding star behold (1)
145	who build the old waste places and in the darkness shine (4)
162	in true prophetic song of old (2)

185, 186	word of grace hath purged away the old and wicked leaven (4)
252	Jesus, Name decreed of old, to the maiden mother told (2)
259	filled with holy joy, old Simeon (3)
267	promise shone with cheering ray on waiting saints of old (1)
287	fight as the saints who nobly fought of old (3)
289	Our Father, by whose servants our house was built of old (1)
289	days of old have dowered us with gifts beyond all praise (3)
307	Though the lowliest form doth veil thee as of old (3)
307	as of old in Bethlehem (3)
320	as of old the Lord provided (2)
324	as of old on earth he stood (2)
370	the deep salt sea, around the old eternal rocks (4)
372	in prophet's word he spoke of old, he speaketh still (3)
388	Almighty, thy power hath founded of old (3)
541	to young and old the Gospel gladness bear (4)
549, 550	as, of old, Saint Andrew heard it by the Galilean lake (2)
567	Thine arm, O Lord, in days of old was strong to heal (1)
578	Remember, Lord, thy works of old (2)
598	From old unfaith our souls release (3)
632	to bear before the nations thy true light as of old (3)
648	tell old Pharoah to let my people go (R)
674	broods on wrongs and will not let old bitterness depart (2)
695, 696	Yet is this heart by its old foe tormented (2)
705	As those of old their first fruits brought (1)

olive
| 276 | he knelt beneath the olive shade (4) |

Omega
82	he is Alpha and Omega, he the source, the ending he (1)
327, 328	Alpha-Omega, unto whom shall bow all nations at the doom (8)
327, 328	Alpha-Omega ... is with us now (8)

omnipotent
406, 407	Most High, omnipotent, good Lord (1,8)
569	God the Omnipotent (1)
636, 637	upheld by my righteous, omnipotent hand (2)

one
8	born of the one light Eden saw play (3)
9	Come, let thy voice be one with theirs (5)
19, 20	Now Holy Spirit, ever One with God the Father and the Son (1)
31, 32	You, Holy One, Creator, Lord (4)
37	one by one the lamps of evening shine (2)
47	God, the blessed Three in One dwell within my heart alone (6)
48	Church her voice upraises to thee, blest Three in One (4)
53	One who thus endureth bright reward secureth (4)
55	With God the Father you are one (4)
55	one with us in human flesh (4)
56	bind in one the hearts of all mankind (7)
59	haste ... one and all to be forgiven (3)
60	all things on earth with one accord ... call you Lord (4)
60	with one accord, like those in heaven (4)
60	To God the Father ... Son, ... Spirit, Three in One (6)
63, 64	To God the Father ... Son ... Spirit, ever One (5)

65	Greet One who comes in glory, foretold in sacred story (1)
67	Hark, the voice of one that crieth in the desert (2)
70	pathway ... for the one who brings God near (2)
77	Lord Most High, the one great Shepherd (4)
85, 86	one precious truth outshines the sun (4)
88	one with us in human birth (2)
88	that we ever one may be with the Father and with thee (5)
102	brought us love for one another (3)
103	in one accord adoring Christ the Lord (R)
107	Calls you one and calls you all to gain his ... hall (3)
109	Then let us all with one accord sing praises (6)
120	The sinless one to Jordan came (1)
129, 130	first and last and only One (4)
136, 137	from the cloud, the Holy One bears record to the only Son (2)
136, 137	O Father, with the eternal Son ... Holy Spirit, ever One (5)
144	we shall be at one with you, Lord, risen from the tomb (4)
144	we shall acclaim your majesty, eternal Three in One (5)
146, 147	Now let us all with one accord ... keep vigil (1)
154, 155	who in the Lord's Name comest, the King and Blessed One (1)
159	when she saw the crucifixion of the sole-begotten one (2)
162	O cross, our one reliance, hail (5)
162	To thee, eternal Three in One (6)
165, 166	Faithful cross, above all other, one and only noble tree (4)
165, 166	praise and honor to the Spirit, ever Three and ever One (6)
165, 166	one in might and one in glory while eternal ages run (6)
170	road from which no one returns (1)
171	watch with him one bitter hour (1)
180	not one darksome cloud is dimming ... morning ray (3)
205	sing today with one accord the life laid down (4)
205	To God the Father ... Son ... Spirit, always One (5)
217, 218	while endless ages run, with Father and with Spirit, One (3)
220	with Father and with Spirit, One (4)
230	to the blessed Three in One be honor, praise and merit (2)
231	For one in place of Judas (2/2-24)
231	sing to God the Spirit, eternal Three in One (3)
232	the one who shares our woes (2/10-18)
232	one love, one hope, impelled them (2/10-28)
232	sing to God the Spirit, eternal Three in One (3)
235	In one harmonious witness the chosen four combine (2)
238, 239	with the host of angels one (2)
257	a priest and victim, both in one (1)
263, 264	who shall be called the Holy One (2)
271, 272	To God the Father, God the Son ... Spirit, Three in One (5)
273, 274	One on a cross is martyred, one by the sword is slain (2)
273, 274	who with the Holy Spirit, now reign, blest Three in One (4)
276	saw the glory round thy head, one of the chosen three (3)
277	glory to the Three in One (3)
279	in one communion ever knit, one fellowship of love (3)
287	thou, in the darkness drear, the one true Light (2)
287	yet all are one in thee, for all are thine (4)
293	one was a doctor, and one was a queen (1)
293	one was a shepherd on the green (1)
293	I mean, God helping, to be one too (1)
293	one was a soldier, and one was a priest (2)
293	one was slain by a fierce wild beast (2)

293	there's not any reason ... why I shouldn't be one too (2)
293	I mean to be one too (3)
294	one with his rising, freed and forgiven (2)
294	born of one Father, we are his children (3)
295	as members of his Body we live in him as one (2)
296	Baptized we live with God the Three in One (3)
298	With one accord, O God, we pray, grant us the Holy Spirit (2)
302, 303	As grain ... was in this broken bread made one (2)
304	That love that made us makes us one (3)
305, 306	One body we, one Body who partake (3)
305, 306	one Church united in communion blest (3)
305, 306	one Name we bear, one Bread of life we break (3)
305, 306	One with each other, Lord, for one in thee (4)
305, 306	who art one Savior and one living Head (4)
310, 311	blest One in Three (2)
315	pray that all thy Church might be for ever one (1)
315	may we all one bread, one body be (1-2)
315	may we be one with all thy Church above (3)
315	one with thy saints in one unbroken peace (3)
315	one with thy saints in one unbounded love (3)
315	more blessed ... to be one with the Trinity in Unity (3)
319	Bind our hearts as one we implore you (2)
326	one heart ... song have the saints upon earth and above (2)
329-331	who from both with both is One (6)
334	Scattered flock, one shepherd sharing, lost and lonely (2)
334	one voice hearing, ears attentive to your word (2)
335	No one can come to me unless the Father draw them (1)
336	Be thou one with us forever (1)
337	the one true, pure, immortal scarifice (1)
345	with one accord our parting hymn of praise (1)
347	render to no one evil (3)
350	that closely knit in holy vow, they may in thee be one (1)
350	may they in thee be one (2)
350	let nothing in this life divide ... whom thou makest one (3)
352	nor life nor death may part those ... one in heart (2)
358	Only Immortal One, Mighty Creator (2)
359	make each one stronger, nobler than the last (1)
359	in word and deed Christ's one true sacrifice (3)
365	To Thee, great One in Three, the highest praises be (4)
366	while in essence only One, undivided God we claim thee (4)
369	long to see the blessed Three in the Almighty One (2)
370	invocation of the same ... Three in One ... One in Three (1,7)
372	the one eternal God ere aught that now appears (1)
374	but all their joys are one (1)
374	The whole creation joins in one to bless the sacred Name (4)
379	let creation sing before him ... exalt him with one voice (1)
379	God is Love ... enfolds us, all the world in one embrace (2)
382	Seven whole days, not one in seven, I will praise thee (3)
385	thou star-abiding one (2)
394, 395	your gospel claims one family with a billion names (4)
399	your voice in homage raise to him who makes all one (3)
400	praise the Spirit, Three in One (7)
405	the ripe fruits in the garden, he made them every one (3)
406, 407	no one is worthy thee to name (1)
406, 407	from whom no one alive can flee (7)

413	fall before the Mighty One (1)
419	till all thy living altars claim one holy light (4)
419	one heavenly flame (4)
421	You only are the Holy One (3)
430	hither bring in one consent heart ... voice ... instrument (1)
430	this huge wide orb we see shall one choir, one temple be (4)
437, 438	his holy Name -- The Lord, the Mighty One (2)
453	As Jacob with travel was weary one day (1)
477	Let every tongue confess with one accord (5)
477	with one accord in heaven and earth (5)
488	thou in me dwelling, and I one with thee (2)
489	as one with us he dwelt with us, and bore a human name (4)
492	sinless one, among the sinful (3)
492	till he see ... all things gathered into one (4)
498	see the very dying form of one who suffered there for me (2)
501, 502	that as one body we may sing (5)
503, 504	of both to be but One (7)
508	until with thee I will one will, to do or to endure (2)
517	One day within thy courts excels a thousand spent away (4)
518	binding all the Church in one (1)
518	God the One in Three adoring in glad hymns eternally (2)
519, 520	laud and honor to the Spirit, ever Three, and ever One (5)
525	The Church's one foundation is Jesus Christ her Lord (1)
525	Elect from every nation, yet one o'er all the earth (2)
525	her charter of salvation, one Lord, one faith, one birth (2)
525	one holy Name she blesses, partakes one holy food (2)
525	to one hope she presses, with every grace endued (2)
525	Yet she on earth hath union with God, the Three in One (5)
526	all the servants of our King in heaven and earth are one (1)
526	One family we dwell in him, one Church, above, beneath (2)
526	One army of the living God, to his command we bow (3)
527	One the light of God's own presence (2)
527	one the object of our journey (2)
527	one the faith which never tires (2)
527	one the earnest looking forward (2)
527	one the hope our God inspires (2)
527	One the strain the lips of thousands lift (3)
527	lift as from the heart of one (3)
527	one the conflict, one the peril (3)
527	one the march in God begun (3)
527	one the gladness of rejoicing on the far eternal shore (3)
527	the one almighty Father reigns in love for evermore (4)
529	but one great fellowship of love (1)
529	all Christly souls are one in him (3)
529	one in him throughout the whole wide earth (3)
537	with one acord (3)
538	let all be, below, above, one in joy, and light and love (2)
539	he who made all nations is not willing one soul ... fail (1)
539	one soul should fail to know his love and might (1)
542	One Lord, in one great Name unite us all who own thee (3)
547	There is one Body and one hope, one Spirit and one call (3)
547	one Lord, one Faith ... Baptism, one Father of us all (3)
562	we are not divided, all one body we (3)
562	one in hope and doctrine, one in charity (3)
569	God the All-righteous One, earth hath defied thee (3)

572	we would raise, O Christ, one song (1)
576, 577	Loving him, let each love Christ in one another (1)
576, 577	When we Christians gather, members of one Body (2)
576, 577	let there be in us no discord but one spirit (2)
580	give us guidance till our goals and yours are one (4)
581	as members of his Body joined we are in him made one (5)
593	where there is strife, may we make one (1)
606	Since the love of Christ has joined us in one body (1)
606	As we are all of one body (2)
611	born to work and die for every one (1)
614	the whole Church at last be one (3)
617	We would be one in hatred of all wrong (2)
617	one in the love of all things sweet and fair (2)
617	one with the joy that breaketh into song (2)
617	one with the grief that trembleth into prayer (2)
617	one in the power that makes thy children free (2)
618	To God the Father ... Son ... Spirit, Three in One (4)
620	ten thousand times would one be blest who might ... hear (3)
623	through whom, the Spirit, with them ever One (5)
633	one with him beyond all telling (4)
633	Word of life, with one Bread feed us (4)
647	I know not if the way is long, and no one else can say (1)
661	Yet let us pray for but one thing ... peace of God (4)
664	one word of thy supporting breath drives ... fears away (2)
665	Christ doth call one and all (5)
673	The first one ever, oh, ever to know (1-3)
673	first one ... to know of the birth of Jesus was the Maid (1)
673	first one ... to know of Messiah, Jesus (2)
673	first one ... the Samaritan woman who drew from the well (2)
678, 679	with you has come to dwell ... Holy One of Israel (2)
678, 679	in your very midst, the great and Holy One (2)
682	e'en death itself, and all for one who was thine enemy (3)
687, 688	lo, his doom is sure, one little word shall fell him (3)
692	thirsty one, stoop down and drink, and live (2)
693	without one plea, but that thy blood was shed for me (1)
700	love of the Holy Ghost, fill thou each needy one (4)

one's

629	dares to bind to one's own sense the oracles of heaven (2)

oneness

443	his royalty from David's tree, praised be his Oneness (1)
606	when we gather let no discord or enmity break our oneness (2)

ones

340, 341	our blessed ones adore you, seated at our Father's board (3)
443	to simple ones his word was given (4)
492	thence his banished ones to save (2)
493	ye voiceless ones, your loosened tongues employ (5)
525	O happy ones and holy (5)
556, 557	the wearied ones shall rest (6)
602	These are the ones we should serve (3)
602	these are the ones we should love (3)
618	Ye watchers and ye holy ones (1)
623	those endless Sabbaths the blessed ones see (1)

623	crown for the valiant, to weary ones rest (1)
673	first ones ... to know of the rising of Jesus (3)
673	first ones ... were Mary, Joanna, and Magdalene (3)

only

6, 7	Christ, the true, the only Light (1)
10	Only, O Lord, in thy dear love, fit us for perfect rest (6)
74	He only to the humble reveals the face of God (3)
83	only begotten Son of the Father (2)
112	but his mother only, in her maiden bliss, worshiped (3)
129, 130	first and last and only One (4)
136, 137	from the cloud, the Holy One bears record to the only Son (2)
143	from age to age, the only Lord (5)
165, 166	Faithful cross, above all other, one and only noble tree (4)
167	he only could unlock the gate of heaven and let us in (4)
173	God the Father's only Son in the tomb is lying (1)
175	Redeemer, Son of the Father supreme, only begotten of God (6)
179	of the Father's God-head true and only Son (4)
183	Christ, who only is sinless, reconcileth sinners (2)
216	Son of the Father supreme, only begotten of God (4)
232	for ... those whose witness is only known to you (2/11-1)
243	but only in his heart a flame (1-3)
243	only in my heart a flame and in my soul a dream (4)
245	faithful shepherd of the flock ... sheep-fold's only door (2)
252	Jesus, only Name that's given under all the mighty heaven (5)
252	pleading only this we flee, helpless, O our God, to thee (6)
268, 269	when he made the Virgin Mary mother of his only Son (1)
291	He only is the Maker of all things near and far (2)
293	They lived not only in ages past (3)
327, 328	Salvation's giver, Christ, the only Son (3)
337	we here spread forth to thee that only offering perfect (1)
337	only offering perfect in thine eyes (1)
337	only look on us as found in him (2)
355	You only are immortal (1)
358	Only Immortal One, Mighty Creator (2)
360, 361	Only begotten, Word of God eternal (1)
362	only thou art holy, there is none beside thee (3)
364	O God, we praise thee, and confess ... thou the only Lord (1)
366	while in essence only One, undivided God we claim thee (4)
399	Your heavenly Father praise, acclaim his only Son (3)
421	You only are the Holy One (3)
421	only you are God's true Son, who was before creation (3)
421	You, only, Christ, as Lord we own (3)
423	Immortal, invisible, God only wise (1)
423	help us to see 'tis only the splendor of light hideth thee (4)
425	He only is the mighty Lord. He only can destroy the foe (3)
425	He only is to be adored for he alone can strength bestow (3)
457	thou only canst inform the mind and purify the heart (2)
498	my sinful self my only shame, my glory all the cross (3)
530	how his only Son he gave (2)
532, 533	Thou only art holy, thou only supreme (1)
552, 553	only believe ... see that Christ is all in all to thee (4)
563	trust only Christ, thy Captain (2)
636, 637	I only design thy dross to consume and thy gold to refine (4)
642	Jesus, our only joy be thou, as thou our prize wilt be (5)

647	or where it ends, I only know (1)
659, 660	in peace that only thou canst give (4)
665	only good and only true (1)
675	only those who bear the cross may hope to wear ... crown (5)
683, 684	help me to tear it from thy throne and worship only thee (4)
698	I only know my need, as deep as life (1)
698	only you can teach me how to pray (1)
701	only where thou art is pleasure, thee alone I treasure (1)
703	only with thee we journey safely on (2)
707	Take my voice, and let me sing always, only, for my King (2)
707	Take myself, and I will be ever, only, all for thee (2)
708	do thou, Lord, our only Savior ... our bosoms fill (2)

onward

24	while earth rolls onward into light (2)
119	leading onward, beaming bright (1)
357	Lead them onward, upward, to the holy place (4)
527	onward goes the pilgrim band (1)
546	forget the steps already trod, and onward urge thy way (2)
562	Onward, Christian soldiers, marching as to war (1,R)
562	Onward, then, ye people, join our happy throng (5)
625	onward as ye go some joyful anthem sing (3)

open

56	open wide our heavenly home (5)
68	The marriage-feast is waiting, the gates wide open stand (2)
157	Open for me the gates of righeousness (1)
257	O Zion, open wide thy gates (1)
305, 306	then open thou our eyes, that we may see (4)
434	Nature with open volume stands to spread ... praise (1)
436	Redeemer come, I open wide my heart to thee (4)
440	open thou our ears and heart (3)
519, 520	thy gates ... they are open evermore (3)
536	Open your ears, O faithful people (1,4)
536	Open your ears and hear God's word (1,4)
536	Open your hearts, O royal priesthood (1,4)
585	Open are the gifts of God (2)
630	God has spoken: praise God for his open word (1-4)
630	God is speaking; praise God for his open word (5)
681	give us open eyes to see thee as thou art (5)
690	Open now the crystal fountain (2)

opened

74	For him let doors be opened, no hearts against him barred (1)
107	He hath opened heaven's door (2)
174	hast opened paradise, and in thee thy saints shall rise (3)
180	He is risen ... He hath opened heaven's gate (4)
188, 189	Christ has opened paradise (1)
237	joy that martyrs won their crown opened heaven's portal (1)
364	hadst overcome death's sting and opened heaven's door (7)
366	on the cross thy dying breath opened ... heaven (6)
366	opened wide the realm of heaven (6)
495	opened is the gate of heaven, reconciled are we with God (2)
711	knock, and the door shall be opened unto you (RC)

opening
310, 311   opening wide the gate of heaven to us below (1)
680   they fly, forgotten, as a dream dies at the opening day (5)

opens
405   Each little flower that opens (1)

oppose
561   strength to strength oppose (2)

oppress
489   Not to oppress, but summon all their truest life to find (6)

oppressed
27, 28   by sin oppressed (3)
429   saves the oppressed, and feeds the poor (2)
525   Though with a scornful wonder men see her sore oppressed (3)
624   beneath thy contemplation sink heart and voice oppressed (1)
641   with care and woe oppressed (2)
648   oppressed so hard they could not stand (1)

oppressing
433   the wicked oppressing now cease from distressing (1)

oppression
145   oppression put to flight (3)
613   oppression, lust, and crime shall flee thy face before (3)
616   He comes to break oppression, to set the captive free (1)

oracles
629   dares to bind to one's own sense the oracles of heaven (2)

orb
106   heaven's whole orb with alleluias rang (3)
430   this huge wide orb we see shall one choir, one temple be (4)

orbs
409   amid their radiant orbs be found (3)

ordain
355   For so did you ordain when you created me (1)

ordained
162   ordained those holy limbs to bear (3)
320   What he did, at supper seated, Christ ordained (3)
320   ordained to be repeated, his memorial ne'er to cease (3)
346   ordained by thee, the everlasting Son (3)
398   I sing the wisdom that ordained the sun to rule the day (1)

ordainest
569   King who ordainest thunder thy clarion (1)

ordaineth
390   granted in what he ordaineth (2)

ordaining
433 ordaining, maintaining his kingdom divine (2)

order
21, 22 you order time and change aright (1)
175 order our ways in thy peace (8)
216 order our ways in thy peace (6)
398 clouds arise, and tempests blow by order from thy throne (3)
431 So order too this life of mine, direct it all my days (4)
531 confusion, order in thy path (3)
680 Before the hills in order stood (3)
681 thine is the mighty plan, the steadfast order sure (1)

ordered
31, 32 ordered seasons in their round (4)
381 while thine ordered seasons run (1)
652, 653 let our ordered lives confess the beauty of thy peace (4)

orderest
56 who orderest all things mightily (2)

organ
390 join the great throng, psaltery, organ, and song (1)

organs
413 Trumpets and organs set in motion such sounds (2)
432 loud organs, his glory forth tell in deep tone (3)

Orient
128 We three kings of Orient are (1)

origin
506, 507 breath of God, life's origin (1)

original
409 their great Original proclaim (1)

Orion's
459 light-years frame the Pleiades and point Orion's sword (1)

orphans
460, 461 not as orphans are we left in sorrow now (2)

other
105 with true love and charity each other now embrace (4)
165, 166 Faithful cross, above all other, one and only noble tree (4)
167 There was no other good enough to pay the price of sin (4)
185, 186 faith lives upon no other (4)
252 Jesus, Name of wondrous love, Name all other names above (1)
305, 306 One with each other, Lord, for one in thee (4)
351 Thus may they abide in union with each other and the Lord (2)
360. 361 this is none other than the gate of heaven (4)
376 teach us how to love each other (3)
498 I ask no other sunshine than the sunshine of his face (3)
581 let us love each other well in Christian holiness (3)

634	I have none other help but thee (1)
662	when other helpers fail and comforts flee (1)
699	Other refuge have I none (2)

other's
| 581 | Forgive we now each other's faults ... our faults confess (3) |

others
3, 4	keep us from causing others pain (2)
140, 141	Wilt thou forgive that sin, by which I won others to sin (2)
400	forgiving others, take your part (5)
580	serving others, honoring you (4)
585	bound in setting others free (4)
664	There ... I find a settled rest while others go and come (3)

ought
10	all we ought to ask: room to deny ourselves (5)
554	'tis the gift to come down where we ought to be (1)
644	when I see thee as thou art, I'll praise thee as I ought (5)

ourselves
10	all we ought to ask: room to deny ourselves (5)
116	No more we'll count ourselves our own but his (5)
148	our self-wrought miseries have made us trust ourselves (2)
148	trust ourselves the more (2)
149	knowing ourselves baptized into your death (2)
554	when we find ourselves in the place just right (1)
584	lest, maddened by the lust for power ... ourselves destroy (4)
705	help us to give ourselves each day (3)

out
18	so bright it cancelled out the sun (4b)
51	praise him who called us out of sin and darkness (1)
76	To heal the sick stretch out thine hand (4)
78, 79	where misery cries out to thee, Son of the mother mild (4)
78, 79	cast out our sin and enter in, be born in us today (5)
99	when lo! above the earth rang out the angel chorus (2)
108	on this day of days tell out redemption's story (1)
127	out of thee the Lord from heaven came to rule his Israel (1)
170	acted out their grim charade to its appointed end (3)
173	pouring out his life that he might to life restore us (2)
175	pour out thy balm on our souls (8)
180	He is risen, he is risen! Tell it out with joyful voice (1)
193	the sun shone out with fairer light (1)
210	The day of resurrection, Earth tell it out abroad (1)
216	pour out thy balm on our souls (6)
235	as, in the prophet's vision from out the amber flame (2)
246	aching hearts in every land cry out (3)
246	cry out, "We cannot understand" (3)
268, 269	chosen people out of whom the Lord did come (2)
270	out of darkness brings our Day (1)
284	out from death's vast room, up from the grave, he leapt (6)
308, 309	O purest fountain, welling from out the Savior's side (2)
320	Full and clear sing out thy praising (4)
353	the perfect love that casts out fear (1)

413	let every instrument and voice peal out the praise (2)
413	peal out the praise of grace abounding (2)
437, 438	Tell out, my soul, the greatness of the Lord (1,4)
437, 438	Tell out, my soul, the greatness of his Name (2)
437, 438	Tell out, my soul, the greatness of his might (3)
437, 438	Tell out, my soul, the glories of his word (4)
452	that strong Light puts out the sun and all is ended (4)
460, 461	Jesus out of every nation hath redeemed us by his blood (1,5)
476	Can we by searching find out God or formulate his ways (1)
501, 502	life rises vibrant out of death (1)
506, 507	let your flame break out within us (5)
517	my very heart and flesh cry out, O living God, for thee (1)
534	God is working his purpose out as year succeeds to year (1)
534	God is working his purpose out ... time is drawing near (1)
539	pour out thy soul for them in prayer victorious (3)
542	cast out our pride and shame that hinder to enthrone thee (3)
556, 557	pour out the strains of joy and bliss (2)
574, 575	Search out our hearts and make us true (2)
574, 575	consume the ill, purge out the shame (4)
590	seek out the lonely and God's mercy share (2)
599	out from the gloomy past (2)
603, 604	his arms stretched out above through every culture (1)
618	Cry out, dominions, princedoms, powers (1)
618	cry out ... virtues, archangels, angels' choirs (1)
665	beauty springeth out of nought (3)
666	Out of the depths I call, to God I send my cry (1)
666	My longing eyes look out for thy enlivening ray (3)
668	guard thy going out and in, both now and evermore (4)
678, 679	tell out his exalted Name (2)
695, 696	we take it ... out of so good and so beloved a hand (3)
700	O love that casts out fear, O love that casts out sin (1)

outburst
208	let shout of holy joy outburst (2)

outcast
477	by thee the outcast and the poor were sought (2)

outlive
168, 169	Lord, let me never, never, outlive my love for thee (4)

outpass
516	yearning ...shall far outpass the power of human telling (3)

outpour
190	now your songs of joy outpour (3)
428	sun ... moon ... stars ... your endless praise outpour (2)

outpoured
327, 328	drink the holy Blood for you outpoured (1)
406, 407	to thee be ceaseless praise outpoured (1,8)
432	Thanksgiving and song to him be outpoured all ages along (4)
621, 622	There for ever and for ever alleluia is outpoured (2)
698	fulfillment of my life in love outpoured (3)

outpouring

633   your love outpouring (2)

outpours

585   spares not, keeps not, all outpours (3)

outshines

85, 86   one precious truth outshines the sun (4)

outside

167   There is a green hill far away, outside a city wall (1)

outward

152   abstinence in outward things with inward fasting (4)
329-331   faith, our outward sense befriending, makes ... clear (5)

over

1, 2   Father, we praise thee, now the night is over (1)
38, 39   watchful guardian over all (1)
42   Now the day is over, night is drawing nigh (1)
46   yet when life's day is over (3)
47   On this day the eternal Son over death his triumph won (2)
67   her warfare now is over (1)
73   when right shall triumph over wrong (4)
89, 90   when peace shall over all the earth its ... splendors (4)
99   Go tell it on the mountain, over the hills and everywhere (R)
109   right over the place where Jesus lay (4)
128   King for ever, ceasing never over us all to reign (2)
176, 177   Over the chaos of the empty waters hovered the Spirit (1)
180   Jesus' woes are over now (2)
194, 195   to him the throne over all the world is given (4)
201   who over death had victory won (2)
210   our Christ hath brought us over with hymns of victory (1)
268, 269   when the love of God the Father over sin the victory won (1)
360, 361   joy over sorrow (3)
390   over all things he gloriously reigneth (2)
416   for the love ... from our birth over and around us lies (1)
494   Crown him of lords the Lord, who over all doth reign (4)
522, 523   his love his people raises over self to reign as kings (4)
531   bid mercy triumph over wrath (3)
535   his kingdom is glorious, he rules over all (1)
598   O love that triumphs over loss (4)
599   We have come over a way that with tears has been watered (2)
614   O Christian women, Christian men, all the world over (2)
659, 660   in trust that triumphs over wrong (3)

overcame

236   Dying, through thee they overcame (3)
243   on his lips a sword wherewith he smote and overcame (1)
243   overcame the foemen of the Lord (1)

overcome

55   no night shall overcome it now (5)
347   Christ at length ... overcome all darkness with his light (3)
364   hadst overcome death's sting and opened heaven's door (7)

overflow
321   thy cup with love doth overflow (1)
636, 637   the rivers of woe shall not thee overflow (3)

overhead
187   Like the cloud that overhead ... Israel led (2)

overpast
142   Abide with us, that so, this life of suffering overpast (5)

overthrew
448, 449   for us the tempter overthrew (2)

overthrown
598   all those nations' pride, overthrown (2)
598   pride, overthrown, went down to dust beside thee (2)

owe
285   What thanks and praise to thee we owe ... for Luke (1)
288   all to thee, our God, we owe (1)
631   all the best we have we owe thee (1)
674   how small the debts men owe to us (3)

own
24   till all thy creatures own thy sway (4)
43   keep me, King of kings, beneath thine own almighty wings (1)
46   for joy of beauty not our own (2)
49   Then let us render him his own (3)
50   he calls the hours his own (1)
51   into his own light (1)
51   This is the Lord's day, day of God's own making (3)
51   his own life imparting, food everlasting (4)
57, 58   claim the kingdom for thine own (4)
60   you came, O Savior, to set free your own (2)
60   set free your own in glorious liberty (2)
66   By thine own eternal Spirit rule in all our hearts alone (4)
70   bringing God's own love and power (4)
76   restore earth's own true loveliness once more ((4)
102   through his own redeeming love (5)
115   come, peasant, king, to own him (3)
116   No more we'll count ourselves our own but his (5)
131, 132   cleanse his people from their own (3)
139   in his great endeavor to save us, his own blood was shed (2)
146, 147   Christ by his own example sealed (2)
146, 147   Remember, Lord ... in your own image were we made (4)
151   thus my hope is in the Lord and not in my own merit (3)
156   Father ... expects his own anointed Son (4)
158   By foes derided, by thine own rejected, O most afflicted (1)
170   your sorrow heal our own (1)
171   God's own sacrifice complete (3)
179   'tis thine own third morning! rise, O buried Lord! (5)
193   thine own redeemed for ever shield (4)
199, 200   but today amidst thine own thou didst stand (4)
210   may hear so calm and plain his own "All hail" (2)
215   mighty Lord, in thine ascension, we ... behold our own (3)

215	in thine ascension, we by faith behold our own (3)
220, 221	thou claim'st the kingdom as thine own (2)
225	Hark, for in myriad tongues Christ's own ... preach (3)
230	all in their own tongues did the Gospel understand (2)
232	Praise ... Lord's own brother, James of Jerusalem (2/10-23)
235	while each his own commission fulfills in every line (2)
247	charged ... his men of might, in his own sight (2)
253	our praise for his own pattern given (4)
277	sing of God's own Son most holy (1)
278	heavenly breath of God's own being (3)
284	while mortals sing with you their own Redeemer's praise (8)
286	these in God's own truth arrayed (2)
290	come to God's own temple, come (1)
290	All the world is God's own field (2)
292	repay thee of thine own (3)
300	Source of all our gifts and graces, Christ we own (2)
305, 306	thyself at thine own board make manifest (1)
305, 306	make manifest in thine own Sacrament of Bread and Wine (1)
313	Wilt thou own the gift I bring (4)
314	O memorial wondrous of the Lord's own death (3)
306	make manifest in thine own Sacrament of Bread and Wine (1)
324	he will give ... his own self for heavenly food (2)
329, 331	gives himself with his own hand (3)
337	in thine own service make us glad and free (4)
342	of God's own love his dearest token (1)
348	Lord, we have come at your own invitation (1)
349	give them life, your own to be (2)
359	each age for thine own solemn task prepares (1)
381	breathed thine own life-giving breath (2)
381	bright with thine own holiness (3)
419	we ask no luster of our own (3)
421	You, only, Christ, as Lord we own (3)
433	sing praises to his Name, he forgets not his own (1)
460, 461	King eternal, thee the Lord of lords we own (4)
472	by our own false hopes and aims are spent (1)
475	his own ... worship lowly, yield their spirits wholly (1)
476	makes birth and death his own (4)
478	Good Shepherd of your sheep, your own defending (2)
478	lead us then day by day in your own steps, we pray (2)
484, 485	prepares ... mansions for his own (1)
488	thou my great Father, thine own may I be (2)
489	He came as Savior to his own, the way of love he trod (5)
494	Hark, how the heavenly anthem drowns all music but its own (1)
494	takes and bears them for his own, that all in him may rest (2)
506, 507	Tell of how the ascended Jesus armed a people for his own (4)
516	visit it with thine own ardor glowing (1)
522, 523	formed thee for his own abode (1)
524	saved with his own precious blood (1)
525	with his own blood he bought her ... for her life he died (1)
527	One the light of God's own presence (2)
542	new life, new hope awakes, for all who own his sway (1)
542	One Lord, in one great Name unite us all who own thee (3)
543	ten thousand stars in nobler spheres his influence own (4)
546	his own hand presents the prize to thine aspiring eye (3)
561	arm of flesh will fail you, ye dare not trust your own (3)

562	we have Christ's own promise, and that cannot fail (4)
573	Bind us in thine own love for better seeing thy Word (5)
579	ocean deep its own appointed limits keep (1)
584	make their might our own (1)
586	Where the many toil together ... art thou among thine own (2)
587	who dost in love proclaim each family thine own (1)
592	which God doth touch and own cannot for less be told (4)
596	Crown, O God, thine own endeavor (3)
603, 604	may I in Christ be free to welcome and accept his own (4)
608	its own appointed limits keep (1)
629	dares to bind to one's own sense the oracles of heaven (2)
635	so do thine own part faithfully (2)
640	Traveler, ages are its own (2)
665	God unknown, he alone calls my heart to be his own (1)
668	his own he safely keeps (2)
669	in his own time grant thee the sun of joy at last (4)
677	God is his own interpreter, and he will make it plain (6)
687, 688	Did we in our own strength confide (2)
687, 688	the man of God's own choosing (2)
697	seal me for thine own (3)
707	take my heart, it is thine own (1)

owned

567	youth renewed and frenzy calmed owned thee, the Lord (2)

owns

128	incense owns a Deity nigh (3)

ox

92	ox and ass beside him from the cold would hide him (2)
107	ox and ass before him bow, and he is in the manger now (1)
115	mean estate where ox and ass are feeding (2)

oxen

102	with the oxen standing round (6)
110	the ass and oxen shared the roof with them (2)

page

285	O happy saint, his sacred page, so rich in ... truth (2)
630	word was written in the Bible's sacred page (3)
632	we praise thee for the radiance that ... scripture's page (1)

pageantry

9	purple pageantry of dawning and of dying days (1)

paid

162	in that same flesh our ransom paid (1)
278	saw the price of our redemption paid (2)
278	paid to set the sinner free (2)
281	He sat to watch o'er customs paid (1)
621, 622	hereafter these thy labors may with endless gifts be paid (5)

pain

3, 4	keep us from causing others pain (2)

18	help us to share your pain and grief (3a)
42	Comfort every sufferer watching late in pain (4)
150	strong with thee to suffer pain (2)
156	bow thy meek head to mortal pain (5)
159	With what pain and desolation (2)
164	Grant us with thee to suffer pain (4)
173	Who would not weep with heartfelt pain and sighing (1)
180	the passion that he bore -- sin and pain can vex no more (2)
184	He who bore all pain and loss comfortless upon the cross (3)
196, 197	Good Jesus Christ inside his pain looked down (2)
204	when our hearts are wintry, grieving, or in pain (4)
222	he takes upon his heart the cares, the pain, and shame (3)
231	they're free from pain and cares (2/12-28)
246	not yet was he to share our pain (2)
246	we share your pain and find your joy (5)
276	he drank thy cup of pain (4)
284	When hope was dim, and pain and grief beyond belief (4)
313	by the pain and death, I now claim ... love unfailing (3)
345	thy peace in life, the balm of every pain (4)
355	where sorrow and pain are no more (1)
358	Grief and pain ended, and sighing no longer (1,4)
400	All you that pain and sorrow bear (5)
441, 442	Bane and blessing, pain and pleasure ... sanctified (4)
450, 451	praise him whose way of pain ye trod (2)
472	who by this sign didst conquer grief and pain (5)
492	bore the pain, the cross, the grave (2)
519, 520	for Christ's dear Name ... pain and tribulation bore (3)
519, 520	in this world pain and tribulation bore (3)
521	O Vanquisher of pain (4)
542	the world has waited long, has travailed long in pain (3)
566	perfect day when pain and death shall cease (2)
574, 575	whate'er the pain and shame may be, bring us ... nearer (1)
582, 583	no night, no need, nor pain (1)
582, 583	wring gold from human pain (2)
609	make haste to heal these hearts of pain (4)
617	give or withhold, let pain or pleasure be (3)

painful
| 286 | painful conflict o'er, God has bid them weep no more (4) |

pains
167	We may not know, we cannot tell what pains he had to bear (2)
182	not ... untouched, unmoved by human pains (3)
207	pains which he endured ... our salvation have procured (3)
479	Glory be to Jesus, who in bitter pains poured for me (1)

paints
| 291 | he paints the wayside flower, he lights the evening star (2) |

palace
| 215 | riding on the clouds ... to his heavenly palace gate (1) |
| 519, 520 | therewith hath willed for ever ... palace ... be decked (4) |

pale
| 400 | pale silver moon that gently gleams (1) |

pales
190   All the glory of the morning pales before those wounds (2)

Palestine
182   No longer bound to distant years in Palestine (2)

palm
104   The palm shall strew its branches (2)

palms
154, 155   The people of the Hebrews with palms before thee went (3)
156   thy humble beast pursues his road with palms ... strowed (1)
156   with palms and scattered garments strowed (1)
275   holding palms of victory in their hands (1)
480   for joy they plucked the palms (3)

palsied
135   Manifest in making whole palsied limbs and fainting soul (3)
567   To thee they went, the blind ... deaf ... palsied ... lame (1)

pangs
113   meanwhile the pangs of my sorrow are soothed (1)
113   pangs of my sorrow are soothed and put to rest (1)
171   O the pangs his soul sustained (2)

panoply
548   take to arm you for the fight, the panoply of God (3)

Paraclete
500   the Father's promised Paraclete (2)

paradise
144   nearer draws the day of days when paradise shall bloom (4)
145   arise, arise, and make a paradise (5)
174   hast opened paradise, and in thee thy saints shall rise (3)
188, 189   Christ has opened paradise (1)
287   sweet is the calm of paradise the blest (6)
354   Into paradise may the angels lead you (1)
356   May choirs of angels lead you to Paradise on high (1)

pardon
33-35   that you may grant us pardon for offenses (4)
59   comes with pardon down from heaven (3)
70   Herald, sound the note of pardon (3)
151   Thou grantest pardon through thy love (2)
223, 224   grant us pardon, grant us peace (4)
674   How can your pardon reach and bless the unforgiving heart (2)
693   wilt receive, wilt welcome, pardon, cleanse, relieve (4)

pardoned
559   thus provided, pardoned, guided (3)

pardoning
152   grant unto us thy pardoning grace (2)

pardons
411   He pardons all thy sins, prolongs thy feeble breath (4)

parent
416   joy of human love, brother, sister, parent, child (4)

parent's
258   blessed was the parent's eye that watched (1)

parents
587   bless thou all parents, guarding well (1)
599   place for which our parents sighed (2)

part
112   If I were a wiseman, I would do my part (3)
213   so united in heart, let us nevermore part (4)
228   occupy its inmost part with your dazzling purity (3)
238, 239   glorious and victorious, bravely bore the martyr's part (2)
268, 269   let the Church ... part in her thanksgiving claim (3)
281   O wise exchange, with these to part (4)
337   grant us nevermore to part from thee (4)
352   Christ, grant that neither grief nor place ... may part (2)
352   nor life nor death may part those ... one in heart (2)
400   forgiving others, take your part (5)
402, 403   above all, the heart must bear the longest part (2)
487   such a love as none can part (3)
508   till all this earthly part of me glows (3)
526   part of the host have crossed the flood (3)
526   part are crossing now (3)
625   My soul, bear thou thy part, triumph in God above (4)
635   so do thine own part faithfully (2)
681   till truth from falsehood part ... find no rest (2)

partake
281   let them of Matthew's wealth partake (4)
305, 306   One body we, one Body who partake (3)
592   All may of thee partake, nothing can be so mean (2)
717   let mortal tongues awake, let all that breathe partake (3)

partaker
339   let me be a fit partaker of ... blessed food from heaven (2)
620   joy, and of the same partaker ever be (5)

partakes
525   one holy Name she blesses, partakes one holy food (2)

parted
215   he is parted from his friends (2)

partial
629   crude, partial, and confined (1)

parting
240, 241   Christ ... triumphed in his parting breath (3)

672	kindling to the perfect day that never shall be past (3)
680	O God, our help in ages past, our hope for years to come (1,5)
699	hide me, O my Savior ... till the storm of life is past (1)
718	Thy love divine hath led us in the past (2)

pastors

| 231 | Lord, make your pastors faithful (2/1-18) |

pastures

75	to pastures of peace he'll lead them (3)
624	the pastures of the blessed are decked in glorious sheen (2)
645, 646	where the verdant pastures grow (2)
663	In pastures green (1)
664	pastures fresh he makes me feed beside the living stream (1)
708	in thy pleasant pastures feed us (1)

path

31, 32	its gleaming path declares the wonders of your ... power (2)
31, 32	guide us on our path to you (5)
56	to us the path of knowledge show (2)
56	close the path to misery (5)
120	chose the path his Father willed (1)
179	tread the path of darkness, saving strength to show (5)
232	whose gospel words declare ... your path (2/9-21)
232	worldly gain forsaking, your path of life we share (2/9-21)
253	long cloud of witnesses show the same path to heaven (4)
255	God's light ... broke across the path (1)
388	dark is his path on the wings of the storm (2)
419	sheds on our path the glow of day (2)
472	showing to wandering souls the path of light (3)
480	Like him may we be found below in wisdom's path of peace (1)
490	Clear sun of righteousness, shine on my path (2)
516	clothe me round, the while my path illuming (2)
527	brightening all the path we tread (2)
531	confusion, order in thy path (3)
545	Behold a Witness nobler still who trod affliction's path (3)
552, 553	Christ is the path and Christ the prize (2)
556, 557	Yes, on through life's long path ... chanting as ye go (4)
599	treading our path through the blood of the slaughtered (2)
599	keep us forever in the path, we pray (3)
616	love, joy, hope, like flowers spring in his path to birth (3)
627	Lamp of our feet, whereby we trace our path (1)
632	teach thy wandering pilgrims by this their path to trace (3)
672	O guide us till our path is done (4)
703	however rough and steep the path may be (3)
709	Through each perplexing path of life (3)

paths

444	He guides the feet of pilgrims along the paths of peace (3)
509	lead us in those paths of life whereon the righteous go (2)
609	from paths where hide the lures of greed (2)
659, 660	in lowly paths of service free (1)
663	helps me take ... the paths of righteousness (2)
664	leads me ... in paths of truth and grace (1)

703	Lead us, O Father, in the paths of peace (1)
703	Lead us, O Father, in the paths of right (2)
718	thy word our law, thy paths our chosen way (2)

pathway

70	make a pathway through the desert (2)
70	pathway ... for the one who brings God near (2)
175	treading the pathway of death, life ... bestowest on all (4)
541	till the long shadows o'er our pathway lie (5)
636, 637	When through fiery trials thy pathway shall lie (4)
655	nor wander from the pathway if thou wilt be my guide (1)

patience

151	his help I wait with patience (3)
280	All his faith and prayer and patience (3)
411	He will not always chide; he will with patience wait (3)
490	When we have run with patience the race ... know the joy (3)
586	by thy patience ... courage ... taught us toil is good (1)
659, 660	Teach me thy patience (3)
666	My soul with patience waits for thee, the living Lord (2)

patient

170	O patient Lord (3)
260	for him ...was the patient life of faith and humble name (3)
293	saints of God, patient and brave and true (1)
329, 331	he closed with wondrous ending his most patient life (2)
337	most patient Savior, who canst love us still (4)
349	patient faith, the crown to win (2)

Patmos

| 231 | John, your loved disciple, exiled to Patmos' shore (2/12-27) |
| 661 | homeless, in Patmos died (3) |

Patriarch

| 275 | Patriarch, and holy prophet, who prepared the way (2) |

patriarchs

| 618 | ye patriarchs and prophets blest (3) |

patriarchs'

| 370 | the patriarchs' prayers, the prophets' scrolls (3) |

pattern

102	For he is our life-long pattern (4)
253	our praise for his own pattern given (4)
656	to dwell in lowliness with us, our pattern and our King (2)

Paul

18	At noontime Paul beheld your light (4b)
232	we praise you for Saint Paul (2/6-29)
256	Saint Paul was changed by God's free love (3)
273, 274	The words of Paul assure us of Christ's redeeming word ((3)
676	if you cannot pray like Paul (2)

Paul's
231   Lord, for Paul's conversion we bless your Name today (2/1-25)
256   with Paul's new vision, let us see (4)

pave
104   lie within the roadway To pave his kingdom come (2)

pavilioned
388   pavilioned in splendor, and girded with praise (1)

pay
11   joyful rise to pay thy morning sacrifice (1)
108   What tribute shall we pay to him who came in weakness (2)
158   Therefore, kind Jesus, since I cannot pay thee (5)
162   the price which none but he could pay (4)
167   There was no other good enough to pay the price of sin (4)
246   innocents the price must pay (2)
248, 249   To the Name of our salvation laud and honor let us pay (1)
307   Here our humblest homage pay we (2)
454   again in glory; let us then our homage pay (4)

peace
3, 4   that we may serve, and know his peace (3)
16, 17   Lamb of God restored our peace (2)
18   seek our victory in your peace (2a)
21, 22   pouring healing peace upon our soul (2)
31, 32   like moon and night, give loving peace (5)
33-35   for ever resting in the peace of Jesus (5)
40, 41   O Spirit, bond of peace and love (5)
43   with the world, myself, and thee, I ... at peace may be (2)
43   I, ere I sleep, at peace may be (2)
44, 45   rested bodies wake in peace (2)
49   he rose, the prince of life and peace (1)
56   be thyself our King of Peace (7)
61, 62   Midnight's peace their cry has broken (1)
65   His rule is peace and freedom ... justice, truth and love (2)
67   speak ye peace, thus saith our God (1)
67   Speak ye to Jerusalem of the peace that waits for them (1)
71, 72   glad hosannas, Prince of Peace, thy welcome ... proclaim (4)
75   to pastures of peace he'll lead them (3)
78, 79   praises sing to God the King, and peace to men on earth (2)
87   Peace on earth and mercy mild (1)
87   hail, the heaven-born Prince of Peace (3)
89, 90   Peace on the earth, good will to men (1)
89, 90   when peace shall over all the earth its ... splendors (4)
91   the power of Satan breaking, our peace eternal making (1)
92   born on earth to save us; peace and love he gave us (4)
94, 95   All glory be to God on high and on the earth be peace (6)
106   peace on the earth, and unto men good will (3)
108   with mercies infinite our Christ hath brought us peace (2)
111   Holy infant, so tender and mild, sleep in heavenly peace (1)
114   boy, who brings you beauty, peace, and joy (4)
125, 126   His name shall be the Prince of Peace for evermore adored (4)
125, 126   peace abound below (5)

399	O Dove of peace, on us descend (3)
401	triumphant o'er the world and sin, the Prince of Peace (3)
413	whose truth victorious establishes the world in peace (3)
416	peace on earth and joy in heaven (6)
421	peace on earth from heaven (1)
426	awoke the morn when the Prince of Peace was born (2)
429	sends the laboring conscience peace (3)
441, 442	lo, it glows with peace and joy (2)
441, 442	peace is there that knows no measure (4)
444	God shall fulfill his promise and bring his people peace (1)
444	He guides the feet of pilgrims along the paths of peace (3)
454	came with peace from realms on high (1)
478	the God of peace acclaim as Lord and Savior (3)
480	Like him may we be found below in wisdom's path of peace (1)
482	your peace in our hearts, Lord, at the end of the day (4)
489	grace and peace to bring (3)
493	'tis life and health and peace (3)
499	Lord God, you have set your servant free to go in peace (1)
499	go in peace as promised in your word (1)
501, 502	turn nations to the ways of peace (5)
503, 504	Keep far our foes, give peace at home (6)
513	with the peace beyond compare (3)
515	hear our supplication, blessed Spirit, God of peace (2)
519, 520	vision dear of peace and love (1)
521	increase ... in depth and height, her unity and peace (1)
521	steadfast faith our unity, their peace our heritage (3)
525	she waits the consummation of peace for evermore (4)
530	word of how the Spirit came bringing peace in Jesus' name (4)
539	Publish glad tidings: tidings of peace (R)
540	watchmen who never held their peace by day or night (1)
542	heal its ancient wrong, come, Prince of Peace, and reign (3)
547	to give the Spirit's unity, the very bond of peace (2)
555	holiness shall whisper the sweet amen of peace (2)
559	nothing can our peace destroy (3)
566	fill the earth with health and light and peace (2)
569	give to us peace in our time, O Lord (1-3)
569	thou wilt give peace in thy time, O Lord (4)
570, 571	all who cry for peace and justice (1)
570, 571	honor, peace, and love retreating (2)
570, 571	offering peace from Calvary's hill (4)
578	O God of love, O King of peace (1)
578	give peace, O God, give peace again (1-3)
581	be his the glory that we seek, be ours his holy peace (4)
586	thou, the peace that passeth knowledge (2)
587	every home ... may be the dwelling place of peace (3)
588, 589	let it yield a hundred-fold the fruits of peace and joy (3)
593	Lord, make us servants of your peace (1,5)
596	plead in silence for their peace (2)
597	O day of peace that dimly shines through all our hopes (1)
597	till by God's grace our warring world shall see ... peace (1)
597	Christ's promised reign of peace (1)
597	the hope of peace shall be fulfilled (2)
598	seek the kingdom of thy peace (3)
598	thy peace by which alone we choose thee (3)

600, 601	Bring to our world of strife thy sovereign word of peace (4)
606	our boundless source of joy and truth, of peace and love (3)
607	when hatred and division give way to love and peace (4)
608	give, for wild confusion, peace (3)
610	counsel, aid, and peace we give (4)
613	Where is thy reign of peace, and purity, and love (2)
615	when knowledge, hand in hand with peace (5)
616	before him on the mountains shall peace, the herald, go (3)
621, 622	vision whence true peace doth spring (1)
623	city of peace that brings joy evermore (2)
640	peace and truth its course portends (2)
640	Traveler, lo, the Prince of Peace ... Son of God is come (3)
649, 650	we seek the peace your love imparts (1)
652, 653	let our ordered lives confess the beauty of thy peace (4)
656	Lord, who left the heavens our life and peace to bring (2)
659, 660	in peace that only thou canst give (4)
661	before they ever knew the peace of God (2)
661	peace ... filled their hearts brimful and broke them, too (2)
661	The Peace of God, it is no peace (4)
661	no peace, but strife closed in the sod (4)
661	Yet let us pray for but one thing ... peace of God (4)
661	the marvelous peace of God (4)
674	our lives will spread your peace (4)
681	Thou hidden fount of love, of peace ... truth ... beauty (5)
700	Well-spring of heavenly peace, thou Living Water, come (2)
703	Lead us, O Father, in the paths of peace (1)
709	at our Father's loved abode our souls arrive in peace (4)
718	thy bounteous goodness nourish us in peace (3)
720	Blest with victory and peace (2)

peaceably
| 406, 407 | Happy, who peaceably endure (6) |

peaceful
89, 90	with peaceful wings unfurled (2)
121	as peaceful as a dove and yet as urgent as a flame (1)
282, 283	so that for the peaceful all things may prosper (2)
460, 461	Hark, the songs of peaceful Zion thunder (1,5)
509	the wings of peaceful love (4)
563	nor dream of peaceful rest (3)
661	Contented, peaceful fishermen (2)

peak
| 129, 130 | Christ upon the mountain peak stands alone in glory (1) |

peal
| 413 | let every instrument and voice peal out the praise (2) |
| 413 | peal out the praise of grace abounding (2) |

pearl
| 287 | through gates of pearl streams in the countless host (8) |
| 519, 520 | Bright thy gates of pearl are shining (3) |

pearls
| 61, 62 | Twelve great pearls, the city's portals (3) |

117, 118   gems of the mountain, and pearls of the ocean (3)

peasant
115   come, peasant, king, to own him (3)

peculiar
544   Let every creature rise and bring peculiar honors (5)
544   peculiar honors to our King (5)

peer
165, 166   None in foliage ... blossom ... fruit thy peer may be (4)

pelt
114   gifts of fox and beaver-pelt (3)

pen
591   From all that terror teaches ... lies of tongue and pen (2)
642   this nor tongue nor pen can show (4)

penitence
142   through these days of penitence ... thy Passion-tide (4)
144   Lord, grant that we in penitence may offer you our praise (3)
148   For this ... we come to you in penitence (4)
250   with joy and penitence sincere (1)
313   all my penitence I give thee (4)
568   stir up our leaders and peoples to penitence (1)

penitent
152   the penitent who keep this holy fast of Lent (1)

penitential
643   worship thee with trembling hope and penitential tears (4)

Pentecost
12, 13   clothed with power on Pentecost (3)
230   A mighty sound from heaven at Pentecost there came (1)
612   of thy gifts at Pentecost (1)

Pentecostal
223, 224   hail the Pentecostal morn (1)

penury
97   nought but need and penury; why thus cradled here (1)

people
48   This day, God's people meeting, his Holy Scripture hear (3)
51   We the Lord's people, heart and voice uniting (1)
51   This is the Lord's house, home of all his people (2)
51   break and give them to all his people (4)
66   Come ... long-expected Jesus, born to set thy people free (1)
66   Born thy people to deliver (3)
67   Comfort, comfort ye my people (1)
73   Thy people pray, come quickly, King of kings (5)
75   Proclaim to a desolate people the coming of their King (2)

76	whose advent doth thy people free (5)
85, 86	now hear the prayers your people pray (2)
108	in a manger lay to teach his people meekness (2)
120	Christ, the Son of God, had come to lead his ... people (2)
120	lead his scattered people home (2)
120	On you may all your people feed (6)
125, 126	people who in darkness walked have seen a glorious light (1)
131, 132	he, to whom no sin was known, might cleanse his people (3)
131, 132	cleanse his people from their own (3)
154, 155	The people of the Hebrews with palms before thee went (3)
184	Christ, today your people feed. Alleluia (R)
202	thy captive people are set free (4)
223, 224	Lord, to you your people bend (3)
226, 227	To thy people who adore and confess thee evermore (5)
230	Then come, all Christian people, keep festival today (3)
235	where with a holy people God dwells in Unity (3)
252	promise that it gave, "Jesus shall his people save" (3)
268, 269	Blessed were the chosen people (2)
268, 269	chosen people out of whom the Lord did come (2)
268, 269	let all faithful people sing the honor of her name (3)
268, 269	what Christ's mother sang in gladness ... people sing (3)
268, 269	let Christ's people sing the same (3)
290	Come, ye thankful people, come (1)
290	gather thou thy people in, free from sorrow ... from sin (4)
304	as his people in the world we'll live (5)
332	Here may thy faithful people know ... thy love (2)
336	light ... in thy people everywhere (2)
338	intercession ... for all thy people, living and departed (2)
347	to serve God's people every day and hour (4)
365	come, and thy people bless; come, give thy word success (2)
377, 378	All people that on earth do dwell, sing to the Lord (1)
390	Let the amen sound from his people again (4)
391	We are his people, we his care (3)
410	Praise him for his grace and favor to his people (2)
410	grace and favor to his people in distress (2)
412	Athlete and band, loud cheering people (5)
417, 418	whose blood set us free to be people of God (1)
417, 418	Sing with all the people of God (3)
421	God's good will unfailingly be to all people given (1)
425	came to set his people free (2)
428	people bless the Lord like righteous souls of yore (5)
443	his people saw him die at last, praised be his teaching (2)
444	God shall fulfill his promise and bring his people peace (1)
459	where his loving people meet to share the gift divine (2)
472	Save us, thy people, from consuming passion (1)
495	thy people are forgiven through the virtue of by blood (2)
499	the glory of your people, and their light (1)
501, 502	To fuller life your people bring (5)
506, 507	Tell of how the ascended Jesus armed a people for his own (4)
522, 523	his love his people raises over self to reign as kings (4)
527	light ... o'er his ransomed people shed (2)
531	Name of Jesus glorify till every people call him Lord (4)
532, 533	till earth's every people confess thee their God (2)
536	Open your ears, O faithful people (1,4)

people's

peoples

perceiving

perfect

233, 234	the perfect love of Christ they know (3)
248, 249	who its perfect wisdom reacheth ... joy possesseth (3)
302, 303	perfect it in thy love, unite it (2)
337	we here spread forth to thee that only offering perfect (1)
337	only offering perfect in thine eyes (1)
338	All-perfect Offering, sacrifice immortal (1)
353	the perfect love that casts out fear (1)
357	where thy saints made perfect gaze upon thy face (4)
362	perfect in power, in love, and purity (3)
416	each perfect gift of thine to the world so freely given (6)
435	filled it with the glory of that perfect rest (3)
492	till he see, renewed and perfect (4)
508	but live with thee the perfect life of thine eternity (4)
566	hasten, Lord, that perfect day (2)
566	perfect day when pain and death shall cease (2)
568	Holiest Trinity, perfect in unity (4)
610	upon the cross, forsaken, offered mercy's perfect deed (1)
615	day of perfect righteousness, the promised day of God (5)
617	from ... night profound into the glory of the perfect day (1)
657	glory in thy perfect love (2)
672	kindling to the perfect day that never shall be past (3)
704	Still let me prove thy perfect will (4)

perfume

128	Myrrh is mine; its bitter perfume ... gathering gloom (4)
128	perfume breathes a life of gathering gloom (4)
544	his Name like sweet perfume shall rise (2)

peril

447	Can persecution, nakedness, or peril, or the sword (2)
527	one the conflict, one the peril (3)
579	hear us when we cry to thee for those in peril on the sea (1)
579	protect them ... from every peril on the land (2)
579	keep them by thy watchful care from every peril in the air (3)
608	cry to thee for those in peril on the sea (1-3)

perils

10	new perils past, new sins forgiven (2)

period

386, 387	period, power, and enterprise commences, reigns and ends (1)

perish

18	ten thousand perish at our side (2c)
75	Like the flowers of the field they perish (2)
140, 141	fear ... I shall perish on the shore (3)
423	then wither and perish, but nought changeth thee (3)
562	Crowns and thrones may perish, kingdoms rise and wane (4)
598	in the night of hate and war we perish as we lose thee (3)

perjuries

228	bring to light our perjuries (4)

perpetual

503, 504	Enable with perpetual light ... our blinded sight (4)

518   in exultant jubilation pours perpetual melody (2)

perplexed
396, 397   keep us in his grace, and guide us when perplexed (2)

perplexity
641   through darkness and perplexity point ... heavenly way (3)

persecuted
560   Blessed ... who are persecuted for righteousness sake (8)

persecutes
560   Blessed are you when the world reviles ... persecutes (9)

persecution
447   Can persecution, nakedness, or peril, or the sword (2)

persecutor
231   praise for the glorious vision the persecutor saw (2/1-25)

persevere
337   crown thy gifts with strength to persevere (3)

persevering
559   yet unfearing, persevering, to thy passion thou didst go (2)

person
603, 604 he sees not labels but a face, a person, and a name (3)

Persons
360, 361 God in three Persons, Father everlasting (6)
362   God in three Persons, blessed Trinity (1,4)

pervadest
475   Thou pervadest all things (3)

Peter
18   In noonday vision Peter saw (4c)
231   We praise you, Lord, for Peter (2/1-18)
232   We praise you for Saint Peter (2/6-29)
242   Christ of Peter and of John ... Christ of Thomas too (1)
254   Oh, Peter was most blest with blessedness unpriced (2)
273, 274 the works of Peter show us how we may serve the Lord (3)
661   Peter ... hauled the teeming net, head-down was crucified (3)
676   If you cannot preach like Peter (2)

petitions
360, 361 with tender mercy hear our petitions (5)

petty
606   May all our petty jealousies and hatred cease (2)

Pharaoh's
199, 200 loosed from Pharaoh's bitter yoke (1)
202   free from Pharaoh's cruel tyranny (2)

Philip
231   We praise you, Lord, for Philip (2/5-1)

physician
232   For Luke, beloved physician, all praise (2/10-18)
357   heal them, Good Physician, with the balm of life (3)

pierce
6, 7   Pierce the gloom of sin and grief (3)
25, 26   the lamps are lit to pierce the night (2)
515   pierce the clouds of nature's night (1)
598   new thorns to pierce that steady brow (1)

pierced
57, 58   pierced, and nailed him to the tree (2)
159   pierced by anguish so amazing (4)
172   Were you there when they pierced him in the side (3)
174   washed us with the tide flowing from his pierced side (1)
206   My pierced side, O Thomas, see (4)
255   His presence pierced and blinded the zealot in his wrath (1)
278   of the sword that pierced her through (2)

pierces
55   its splendor pierces all our gloom (5)
314   faith, that comes by hearing, pierces through the veil (2)

piercing
159   in her heart the piercing sword (1)

Pilate
212   as Pilate gave them leave (4)

pilgrim
48   That light our hope sustaining, we walk the pilgrim way (4)
51   rest for the pilgrim, haven for the weary (2)
149   walking once more the pilgrim way of Lent (1)
236   strength of the pilgrim on the way (1)
343   bless thy chosen pilgrim flock with manna (1)
527   Singing songs of expectation ... goes the pilgrim band (1)
527   onward goes the pilgrim band (1)
564, 565   his first avowed intent to be a pilgrim (1)
564, 565   he will make good his right to be a pilgrim (2)
564, 565   I'll labor night and day to be a pilgrim (3)
690   pilgrim through this barren land (1)
692   in that light of life I'll walk till pilgrim days are done (3)

pilgrim's
517   happy they whose hearts are set upon the pilgrim's quest (2)
717   land where my fathers died, land of the pilgrim's pride (1)

pilgrims
181   You pilgrims on the road to Zion's city, sing (3)
308, 309   O Food to pilgrims given, O Bread of life from heaven (1)
360, 361   strangers and pilgrims, seeking homes eternal (4)

360, 361	strangers and pilgrims ... pass through its portals (4)
444	He guides the feet of pilgrims along the paths of peace (3)
556, 557	pilgrims find their Father's house, Jerusalem the blest (6)
632	teach thy wandering pilgrims by this their path to trace (3)
647	with them, the pilgrims of the faith (3)

pillar
627	pillar of fire, through watches dark (3)
690	let the fire and cloudy pillar lead me all my journey (2)

pillow
453	at night on a stone for a pillow he lay (1)

pining
596	Still the weary folk are pining (2)
596	pining for the hour that brings release (2)

pinions
375	beneath thy shadowing pinions (2)

pipes
412	Trumpet and pipes, loud clashing cymbals (3)

pity
74	pity the proud and haughty (2)
158	think on thy pity ... love unswerving, not my deserving (5)
164	through our pity and our shame love answers love's appeal (2)
168, 169	for this thy dying sorrow, thy pity without end (4)
468	wasn't that a pity and a shame, Lord, Lord (1-4)
566	From thee ... all pity, care, and love (1)
569	show forth thy pity on high where thou reignest (1)
590	seeking to gather all in love and pity (3)
633	Be our Word in pity spoken (3)

pitying
496, 497	deigned to cast a pitying eye upon his helpless creature (2)
545	for the joy before him set, and moved by pitying love (4)

place
65	His tidings of salvation proclaim in every place (3)
77	A maid in lowly human place became ... the chosen (3)
102	he leads his children on to the place where he is gone (5)
105	Now to the Lord sing praises, all you within this place (4)
106	till our first heavenly state again takes place (5)
109	right over the place where Jesus lay (4)
112	in the bleak midwinter a stable-place sufficed (2)
182	conquer every place and time (2)
217, 218	by a new way none ever trod Christ takes his place (1)
217, 218	Christ takes his place -- the throne of God (1)
230	filled the place of meeting with rushing wind and flame (1)
231	For one in place of Judas (2/2-24)
251	look down from heaven, thy dwelling place (1)
266	He met a maiden in that place (2)
286	Now in God's most holy place, blest they stand (5)

343	in strength of which we travel on to our abiding place (2)
352	Christ, grant that neither grief nor place ... may part (2)
357	Lead them onward, upward, to the holy place (4)
371	in earth's darkest place, let there be light (3)
422	thy truth and light our dwelling place for evermore (3)
430	in this chorus take your place (3)
469, 470	There is no place where earth's sorrows are more felt (2)
469, 470	no place ... sorrows are more felt than up in heaven (2)
469, 470	no place ... earth's failures have such kindly judgment (2)
483	highest place that heaven affords is his ... by right (2)
495	there thou dost our place prepare (3)
498	I take, O cross, thy shadow for my abiding place (3)
514	To thee, whose faithful love had place in ... grace (2)
516	for none can guess its grace, till Love create a place (3)
516	a place wherein the Holy Spirit makes a dwelling (3)
517	How lovely is thy dwelling-place, O Lord of hosts, to me (1)
554	when we find ourselves in the place just right (1)
580	heavens infinite in time and place (1)
587	our children bless, in every place (2)
587	every home ... may be the dwelling place of peace (3)
599	have not our wearied feet come to the place (2)
599	place for which our parents sighed (2)
614	place the same hope in this great Name (2)
620	they still rejoice in that most happy place (2)
629	notions of our day and place (1)
630	See its glory undiminished by the change of time or place (4)
644	my shield and hiding place (3)
657	till in heaven we take our place (3)
670	Lord, for ever at thy side let my place and portion be (1)
692	I found in him a resting place, and he has made me glad (1)

placed

31, 32	who in the high arched sky has placed the sun (1)
232	saw the risen Savior and placed his faith in him (2/10-23)

places

67	make the rougher places plain (3)
75	make straight all the crooked places (1)
145	who build the old waste places and in the darkness shine (4)
215	there we sit in heavenly places (3)
519, 520	in their places now compacted by the heavenly Architect (4)
599	Lest our feet stray from the places ... we met thee (3)
599	places our God, where we met thee (3)

plain

67	make the rougher places plain (3)
128	Born a King on Bethlehem's plain (2)
210	may hear so calm and plain his own "All hail" (2)
288	flocks that whiten all the plain (2)
388	it streams from the hills, it descends to the plain (4)
541	Who dares stand idle on the harvest plain (1)
579	O Christ, the Lord of hill and plain (2)
677	God is his own interpreter, and he will make it plain (6)

719   for purple mountain majesties above the fruited plain (1)

plains
89, 90   above its sad and lowly plains they bend on hovering wing (2)
100   while fields and floods, rocks, hills and plains repeat (2)
385   thy fingers spread the mountains and plains (1)

plaint
284   ye saw his agony, ye heard the plaint he cried (4)

plan
42   those who plan some evil from their sin restrain (4)
681   thine is the mighty plan, the steadfast order sure (1)
681   Where goodness comes to light we glimpse thy plan (4)
681   thy plan unfolding (4)

plane
482   strong hands were skilled at the plane and the lathe (2)

planets
409   all the planets in their turn (2)
412   Earth and all stars, loud rushing planets (1)
617   Eternal Ruler of the ceaseless round of circling planets (1)
617   planets singing on their way (1)

planned
80   The blessing which the Father planned (4)
452   faith achieves what reason planned (3)
702   thou knowest all that I have planned (1)

plant
398   not a plant or flower below but makes thy glories known (3)
512   plant holy fear in every heart (2)
588, 589   the rising plant destroy (3)

planted
244   the better Eden planted by our Lord most dear (2)
302, 303   Father, we thank thee who hast planted thy holy Name (1)
302, 303   planted thy holy Name within our hearts (1)

play
8   born of the one light Eden saw play (3)
570, 571   wasted work and wasted play (3)

plea
84   love for plea and gift and sign (3)
333   Now the kneeling Now the plea ... Father's arms in welcome (1)
693   without one plea, but that thy blood was shed for me (1)

plead
5   O Father, glorious evermore, we plead with thee (3)
5   we plead with thee for grace and power to conquer (3)
68   With hearts and hands uplifted, we plead, O Lord, to see (3)
231   to plead at God's right hand (2/12-26)

243	he had no friend to plead his cause (2)
315	draw us the nearer each to each, we plead (2)
460, 461	earth's Redeemer, plead for me (3)
596	homesteads and the woodlands plead in silence (2)
596	plead in silence for their peace (2)

pleading
115	for sinners here the silent Word is pleading (2)
240, 241	Christ, for cruel traitors pleading (3)
252	pleading only this we flee, helpless, O our God, to thee (6)
338	pleading before thee (2)
440	help us by thy Spirit's pleading (3)
495	There for sinners thou art pleading (3)
605	Will God your pleading hear, while crime and cruelty grow (2)

pleads
| 337 | having with us him that pleads above, we here present (1) |
| 447 | now pleads our cause at God's right hand (1) |

pleasant
| 405 | the cold wind in the winter, the pleasant summer sun (3) |
| 708 | in thy pleasant pastures feed us (1) |

pleased
| 87 | Pleased as man with us to dwell; Jesus, our Emmanuel (2) |

pleaseth
| 265 | To me be as it pleaseth God (3) |

pleasure
248, 249	Name of gladness, Name of pleasure (2)
302, 303	Thou, Lord, didst make all for thy pleasure (1)
435	'tis the Father's pleasure we should call him Lord (1)
441, 442	Bane and blessing, pain and pleasure ... sanctified (4)
559	pleasure that can never cloy (3)
574, 575	From love of pleasure, lust of gold ... wean us (2)
617	give or withhold, let pain or pleasure be (3)
621, 622	full of vigor ... of pleasure that shall last eternally (4)
665	pleasure leads us where we go (4)
686	I hope, by thy good pleasure, safely to arrive at home (2)
701	only where thou art is pleasure, thee alone I treasure (1)
701	thou art all my pleasure, Jesus, my desire (2)

pleasures
122, 123	our Savior in his fasting pleasures of the world forebore (3)
475	pride of life and sinful pleasures (2)
549, 550	still he calls, in cares and pleasures (4)

pledge
33-35	mirror of daybreak, pledge of resurrection (2)
340, 341	By this pledge, Lord, that you love us (2)
471	the measure and the pledge of love (5)

pledged
| 246 | till, pledged to build and not destroy (5) |

pledges
321   here its sacred pledges tastes (2)
327, 328   take the pledges of salvation here (5)

Pleiades
459   light-years frame the Pleiades and point Orion's sword (1)

plenitude
531   in all thy plenitude of grace (1)

plenteous
500   Plenteous of grace, come from on high (3)
666   plenteous source and spring (4)
699   Plenteous grace with thee is found (3)

plentiful
469, 470   plentiful redemption in the blood that has been shed (2)

plenty
288   All the plenty summer pours (2)
570, 571   In your day of wealth and plenty (3)

ploughshare
542   to ploughshare beat the sword, to pruning hook the spear (2)

plow
291   We plow the fields and scatter the good seed on the land (1)

plowing
424   For the plowing, sowing, reaping (1)

plucked
480   for joy they plucked the palms (3)

plunged
46   plunged us into strife (3)

poets
631   poets, prophets, scholars, saints, each a word from God (2)

point
406, 487   stars that ... soon will point the glittering heavens (3)
459   light-years frame the Pleiades and point Orion's sword (1)
641   through darkness and perplexity point ... heavenly way (3)
662   shine through the gloom, and point me to the skies (4)

points
316, 317   yet, passing, points to the glad feast above (3)
669   who points the clouds their way (1)

pole
409   spread the truth from pole to pole (2)

polished
519, 520   Many a blow and biting sculpture polished ... stones (4)

pomp
74	Not robed in royal splendor, in power and pomp comes he (1)
75	power and pomp of nations shall pass like a dream away (2)
97	Here no regal pomp we see (1)
156	In lowly pomp ride on to die (2,5)

ponder
173	Blest shall they be eternally who ponder in their weeping (3
324	ponder nothing earthly minded (1)
390	ponder anew what the Almighty can do (3)

pondering
257	pondering all things in her heart (4)

poor
71, 72	treasures of his grace to enrich the humble poor (3)
77	to shepherds poor the Lord Most High ... was revealed (4)
83	Child for us sinners poor and in the manger (5)
102	with the poor, the scorned, the lowly lived ... Savior (2)
102	Not in that poor lowly stable ... we shall see him (6)
103	The babe within a manger poor (2)
106	from his poor manger to his bitter cross (5)
109	certain poor shepherds in fields as they lay (1)
110	thus that manger poor became a throne (4)
112	What can I give him, poor as I am (4)
117, 118	dearer to God are the prayers of the poor (4)
226, 227	Come, protector of the poor (1)
247	this poor youngling for whom we sing ... lully lullay (1)
247	That woe is me, poor child for thee (3)
292	that we may feed the poor aright (3)
354	with Lazarus who once was poor may you have peace (2)
356	As angels gave poor Lazarus from all his ills release (3)
382	Small it is in this poor sort to enroll thee (3)
429	saves the oppressed, and feeds the poor (2)
468	It was poor little Jesus, yes, yes (1-4)
477	by thee the outcast and the poor were sought (2)
493	mournful broken hearts rejoice, the humble poor believe (4)
537	the poor, and them that mourn (1)
560	Blessed are the poor in spirit (1)
568	truly to care for the poor of the earth (2)
585	poor in making many rich (4)
594, 595	rich in things and poor in soul (3)
602	Neighbors are rich and poor (2)
616	to help the poor and needy, and bid the weak be strong (2)
629	We limit not the truth of God to our poor reach of mind (1)
643	thou hast stooped to ask of me the love of my poor heart (5)
693	poor, wretched, blind ... all I need, in thee to find (3)

poorest
74	clad as are the poorest, such his humility (1)

portal
199, 200	Neither might the gates of death ... tomb's dark portal (4)
237	joy that martyrs won their crown opened heaven's portal (1)

portals

61, 62	Twelve great pearls, the city's portals (3)
208	the bars from heaven's high portals fell (4)
215	portals high are lifted to receive their heavenly King (1)
360, 361	strangers and pilgrims ... pass through its portals (4)
436	Fling wide the portals of your heart (3)

portends

640	Traveler, blessedness and light ... portends (2)
640	peace and truth its course portends (2)

possess

193	do thou thyself our hearts possess (3)
351	possess, in sweet communion, joys ... earth cannot afford (2)
462	thou art he who shalt by right the nations all possess (3)

possessed

563	Satan's host is vanquished and heaven is all possessed (3)

possesseth

248, 249	who its perfect wisdom reacheth ... joy possesseth (3)
248, 249	heavenly joy possesseth here (3)

possessing

244	thy holy word possessing, Jesus may thy love adore (3)
344	let us each, thy love possessing, triumph (1)
559	yet possessing every blessing, if our God our Father be (1)

possession

506, 507	white-hot in your possession (5)
573	Lust of possession worketh desolations (4)

pounding

412	Engines and steel, loud pounding hammers (4)

pour

5	pour down thy radiance from above (2)
19, 20	pour forth into our hearts, we pray, the fullness (1)
63, 64	pour light upon us from above (2)
175	pour out thy balm on our souls (8)
216	pour out thy balm on our souls (6)
219	upon his Church his grace to pour (3)
226, 227	pour on us thy love divine (1)
232	Your wine and oil, O Savior, upon our spirits pour (2/10-18)
474	pour contempt on all my pride (1)
500	come, pour thy joys on humankind (1)
539	pour out thy soul for them in prayer victorious (3)
556, 557	pour out the strains of joy and bliss (2)
566	O pour them from above (1)
594, 595	on thy people pour thy power (1)

poured

52	first o'er the earth the light was poured (1)
152	with many a tear poured forth by all (1)
174	Where the Paschal blood is poured (2)

223, 224	morn when our ascended Lord ... his Spirit poured (1)
223, 224	on his Church his Spirit poured (1)
235	voice proclaimed salvation that poured upon the night (1)
295	praise the Holy Spirit poured forth upon the earth (3)
313	Let thy Blood in mercy poured (1)
327, 328	drink the holy Blood for you outpoured (1)
340, 341	for the wine which you have poured (1)
406, 407	to thee be ceaseless praise outpoured (1,8)
432	Thanksgiving and song to him be outpoured all ages along (4)
479	Glory be to Jesus, who in bitter pains poured for me (1)
479	poured for me the life-blood from his sacred veins (1)
621, 622	There for ever and for ever alleluia is outpoured (2)
698	fulfillment of my life in love outpoured (3)

pouring

21, 22	pouring healing peace upon our soul (2)
36	our wonted hymn out-pouring (2)
173	pouring out his life that he might to life restore us (2)
225	pouring on all human souls infinite riches of God (2)
333	Now the hearing ... power ... vessel brimmed for pouring (1)
633	your love outpouring (2)

pours

285	pours on the Church from age to age the healing unction (2)
288	All the plenty summer pours (2)
429	The Lord pours eyesight on the blind (3)
518	in exultant jubilation pours perpetual melody (2)
543	his all-resplendent grace he pours around thy head (2)
585	spares not, keeps not, all outpours (3)

poverty

| 568 | Blessed Lord Jesus, who camest in poverty (2) |

power

5	we plead with thee for grace and power to conquer (3)
10	restored to life and power and thought (1)
12, 13	the third hour your faithful band was clothed with power (3)
12, 13	clothed with power on Pentecost (3)
18	may we, too, trust your sovereign power (2b)
23	O Spirit, bringing power and health (4)
31, 32	its gleaming path declares the wonders of your ... power (2)
31, 32	wonders of your glorious power (2)
49	may feel his resurrection's power (2)
56	trust thy mighty power to save (4)
57, 58	Savior, take the power and glory (4)
70	bringing God's own love and power (4)
74	Not robed in royal splendor, in power and pomp comes he (1)
74	All power is his, all glory (3)
75	power and pomp of nations shall pass like a dream away (2)
91	the power of Satan breaking, our peace eternal making (1)
105	save us all from Satan's power when we were gone astray (1)
105	free all ... from Satan's power and might (3)
120	grant us the Holy Spirit's power to shield us (5)
124	leads them on with power benign to seek the Giver (3)
125, 126	His power increasing still shall spread (5)

135	manifest in power divine, changing water into wine (2)
138	All praise to you, O Lord, who by your mighty power (1)
148	grant us your power to make us strong (1)
156	then take, O God, thy power and reign (5)
161	That blood retains its living power (2)
161	the worst gain power to be good (5)
162	Still may thy power with us avail to save us sinners (5)
164	thy cross may bring us to thy joy and resurrection power (4)
168, 169	thy power is all expired ... quenched the light of light (2)
168, 169	My days are few, O fail not, with thine immortal power (5)
171	Go to dark Gethsemane, ye that feel the tempter's power (1)
174	From sin's power do thou set free soul's new-born (4)
175	Spirit of life and of power, now flow in us (7)
176, 177	seek through the power of the new creation (2)
181	Sing of his dying love, his resurrection power (2)
185, 186	stripped of power, no more he reigns (2)
216	Spirit of life and of power (5)
219	in power and might excelling (1)
222	shall come in all love's glorious power to rule (4)
226, 227	Cleanse us with thy healing power (4)
231	May we, in ... weakness, receive your power divine (2/4-25)
231, 232	ascribe all power and glory and praise to God alone (3)
240, 241	heaven-endowed with grace and power (2)
243	When Stephen, full of power and grace, went forth (1)
255	that we, in every hour ... will trust your hidden power (2)
292	all fostering power, all influence sweet breathe (2)
296	The Spirit's power shakes the Church of God (3)
299	You came in power; the Church was born (2)
302, 303	thine is the power, be thine the praise (1)
333	Now the hearing ... power ... vessel brimmed for pouring (1)
346	as far as lies within our mortal power (1)
347	richly from above his love supplies the grace and power (2)
347	the grace and power we seek (2)
347	rejoicing in the Holy Spirit's power (4)
349	come ... with your strengthening gift of power (2)
349	daily power to conquer sin (2)
350	in power to do and grace to bear (2)
359	fill them with power, their lips make eloquent (2)
362	perfect in power, in love, and purity (3)
363	thine is the quickening power that gives increase (4)
365	ne'er from us depart, Spirit of power (3)
370	by power of faith (2)
370	I bind unto myself the power of the great love (3)
370	I bind unto myself today the power of God (5)
370	the power of God to hold and lead (5)
373	Hosts on high, his power proclaim (2)
374	Jesus is worthy to receive honor and power divine (3)
375	What God hath wrought to show his power he ... sustaineth (3)
386, 387	period, power, and enterprise commences, reigns and ends (1)
388	O gratefully sing his power and his love (1)
388	Almighty, thy power hath founded of old (3)
391	His sovereign power without our aid formed us of clay (2)
391	he saved us from the power of death (2)
398	I sing the mighty power of God (1)
398	power of God that made the mountains rise (1)

401	we shall behold his face, we shall his power adore (2)
408	the God of all creation, the God of power (1)
408	What God's almighty power hath made ... mercy keepeth (2)
409	The unwearied sun from day to day ... power display (1)
409	does his Creator's power display (1)
414	age to age his power shall teach (2)
414	proclaim thy sovereign power (6)
417, 418	Power, riches, wisdom, and strength ... are his (2)
434	which ... best is writ ... power ... wisdom, or the love (3)
435	let his will enfold you in its light and power (5)
447	no power earth can afford will separate us (4)
450, 451	All hail the power of Jesus' Name (1)
455, 456	We read thy power to bless and save (4)
465, 466	eternal power, be my support (1)
489	He sent him not in wrath and power (3)
495	Worship, honor, power, and blessing thou art worthy (4)
496, 497	Incarnate God, put forth thy power (3)
501, 502	Your power the whole creation fills (4)
505	unless thy grace the power should give, none can believe (2)
506, 507	showing us God's wonders, is himself the power to gaze (2)
506, 507	by whose love and power, in Jesus God himself was seen (3)
513	with the power to love and witness (3)
514	for all thy grace and power benign (1)
514	To thee, whose faithful power doth heal (3)
515	come with unction and with power (2)
516	yearning ... shall far outpass the power of human telling (3)
531	give power and unction from above (2)
535	All glory and power, all wisdom and might (4)
548	strong in the Lord of hosts, and in his mighty power (2)
551	quickened by the Spirit's power (3)
560	Remember your servants, Lord, when you come in ... power (A)
560	when you come in your kingly power (A)
579	O Trinity of love and power (4)
580	probed the secrets of the atom, yielding unimagined power (3)
584	God, you have given us power to sound depths ... unknown (1)
584	lest, maddened by the lust for power ... ourselves destroy (4)
585	weak in giving power to be (4)
594, 595	on thy people pour thy power (1)
600, 601	O day of God, draw nigh in beauty and in power (1)
607	From search for wealth and power (2)
608	O Trinity of love and power (4)
617	one in the power that makes thy children free (2)
643	thine endless wisdom, boundless power, and aweful purity (3)
662	what but thy grace can foil the tempter's power (2)
665	But God's power, hour by hour, is my temple and my tower (2)
685	cleanse me from its guilt and power (1)
687, 688	his craft and power are great (1)
702	I feel thy power on every side (2)
702	my support thy power divine (4)
707	take my intellect ... use every power as thou ... choose (2)
720	may the heaven-rescued land praise the Power (2)
720	Power that hath made and preserved us a nation (2)
408	all who know his power proclaim aloud the wondrous story (3)

powerful

447	all powerful to save (1)
690	hold me with thy powerful hand (1)

powers

11	that all my powers, with all their might ... may unite (3)
11	all my powers ... in thy sole glory may unite (3)
82	powers, dominions bow before him (3)
174	hell's fierce powers beneath thee lie (1)
194, 195	life, nor death, nor powers of hell tear us (3)
208	The powers of death have done their worst (2)
324	powers of hell may vanish as the darkness clears away (3)
364	to thee the powers on high ... continually do cry (2)
369	all the heavenly powers conspire eternal praise to sing (4)
426	amidst eternal joy songs of praise their powers employ (6)
429	praise shall employ my nobler powers (1,4)
437, 438	Powers and dominions lay their glory by (3)
509	descend with all thy gracious powers (1,5)
510	with all thy quickening powers (1,4)
548	tread all the powers of darkness down (4)
573	there is no meekness in the powers of earth (4)
580	your children in your likeness, share inventive powers (1)
580	we ... share inventive powers with you (1)
598	must bring to doom the powers which crucified thee (2)
618	Cry out, dominions, princedoms, powers (1)
619	Ye powers who stand before the eternal Light (2)
629	make us all go on to know with nobler powers conferred (3)
687, 688	That word above all earthly powers ... abideth (4)
695, 696	By gracious powers so wonderfully sheltered (1)

practice

500	practice all that we believe (3)

praise

1, 2	Father, we praise thee, now the night is over (1)
3, 4	guard ... our ears from empty praise and lies (3)
3, 4	may praise and bless his holy Name (4)
3, 4	to God the Holy Ghost we raise our ... praise (5)
3, 4	our equal and unceasing praise (5)
5	all praise, eternal Son, to thee (5)
5	in equal and unending praise (5)
8	Praise for the singing, Praise for the morning (1)
8	Praise for them, springing fresh from the Word (1)
8	Praise for the sweetness of the wet garden (2)
8	Praise with elation (3)
8	praise every morning, God's recreation of the new day (3)
9	shout with their shout of praise (5)
11	Praise God, from whom all blessings flow (4)
11	praise him, all creatures here below (4)
11	praise him above, ye heavenly host (4)
11	praise Father, Son and Holy Ghost (4)
12, 13	Amid our customary round, we offer ... prayer and praise (1)
12, 13	we praise and bless you every hour (4)
16, 17	Now let us sing our praise to God (1)
18	we praise and bless you every hour (5)

23	we praise and bless you every hour (4)
24	thy praise shall sanctify our rest (1)
24	nor dies the strain of praise away (3)
25, 26	Praise Father, Son, and Spirit (2)
25, 26	Worthy are you of endless praise, O Son of God (3)
29, 30	To thee our morning song of praise (2)
29, 30	O grant us with thy saints on high to praise thee (2)
29, 30	praise thee through eternity (2)
29, 30	to God the Holy Ghost we raise our ... praise (3)
29, 30	our equal and unceasing praise (3)
33-35	joyfully chanting holy hymns to praise you (3)
36	To thee of right belong all praise of holy songs (3)
40, 41	to you be thanks and endless praise (5)
43	All praise to thee, my God this night (1)
43	Praise God, from whom all blessings flow (4)
43	praise him, all creatures here below (4)
43	praise him above, ye heavenly host (4)
43	praise Father, Son, and Holy Ghost (4)
44, 45	your praise and glory we shall sing (3)
47	On this day, the first of days, God ... we praise (1)
47	God the Father's Name we praise (1)
49	fill his courts with songs of praise (3)
50	praise surround the throne (1)
50	highest heavens in which he reigns shall give ... praise (5)
50	shall give him nobler praise (5)
51	praise him who called us out of sin and darkness (1)
52	All praise to God the Father be (4)
52	all praise, eternal Son, to thee (4)
55	All praise, O unbegotten God (6)
55	all praise to you, eternal Word (6)
55	all praise, life-giving Spirit, praise (6)
60	praise, honor, might, and glory be from age to age (6)
63, 64	praise, honor, might and glory be (5)
65	Lift high your praise resounding (2)
76	All praise, eternal Son, to thee (5)
77	angels in the sky sang praise above the silent field (4)
77	all praise to thee, O Virgin-born (5)
77	all praise, O Holy Ghost, to thee (5)
85, 86	let songs of praise your Name adorn (6)
92	lay their gifts before him, praise him and adore him (3)
96	See him in a manger laid whom the angels praise above (4)
97	Christ we praise with voices bold (3)
97	purer praise than ours on earth, angels' songs afford (3)
103	We praise you, Holy Trinity ... adoring you eternally (4)
106	eternal praise to heaven's almighty King (6)
108	Now yield we thanks and praise to Christ (1)
110	to praise the Father, Son, and Holy Ghost (4)
124	to ... Holy Ghost we raise our equal and unceasing praise (5)
129, 130	let us, if we dare to speak ... praise him (1)
129, 130	with the saints and angels praise him (1)
133	May all who seek to praise aright ... show ... your light (3)
135	Songs of thankfulness and praise ... to thee we raise (1)
135	praise ... Jesus, Lord, to thee we raise (1)
136, 137	the voice of prayer, the hymn of praise (4)
138	All praise to you, O Lord, who by your mighty power (1)

143	celebrate with songs of praise (1)
144	Lord, grant that we in penitence may offer you our praise (3)
152	fast of forty days may work our profit and thy praise (5)
154, 155	praise and prayers and anthems before thee we present (3)
154, 155	To thee before thy passion they sang ... hymns of praise (4)
164	let all praise be given thee who livest evermore (3)
165, 166	Praise and honor to the Father (6)
165, 166	praise and honor to the Son (6)
165, 166	praise and honor to the Spirit, ever Three and ever One (6)
174	At the Lamb's high feast we sing praise (1)
174	praise to our victorious King (1)
174	praise we him, whose love divine gives his sacred Blood (1)
174	Praise we Christ, whose blood was shed (2)
174	Hymns of glory, songs of praise, Father ... we raise (4)
174	risen Lord, all praise to thee with the Spirit ever be (4)
175	Praise to the Giver of good (8)
178	Alleluia, alleluia, Give praise to his Name (R)
178	Come, let us praise the living God (4)
179	hours and passing moments praise thee in their flight (3)
179	Vanquisher of darkness, bring their praise to thee (3)
181	praise the Savior's name (1)
181	Soon ... each raptured tongue his endless praise proclaim (4)
182	learns his joy, his justice, love, and praise (5)
191	sing to God a hymn of praise (1)
193	that we may give thee all our days ... praise (3)
193	the willing tribute of our praise (3)
193	All praise, O risen Lord, we give to thee (5)
193	to God the Father equal praise (5)
198	Thou hallowed chosen morn of praise (1)
199, 200	to whom we give laud and praise undying (2)
201	day ... whereon the faithful give God praise (1)
201	in praise of Christ, our risen Lord (4)
202	All praise be thine, O risen Lord (5)
202	all praise to God the Father be and Holy Ghost eternally (5)
203	in laud and jubilee and praise (5)
205	Sing songs of praise along his way (2)
205	Praise we in songs of victory that love (3)
207	Hymns of praise then let us sing (2)
207	praise ... unto Christ our heavenly King (2)
207	Sing we to our God above ... praise eternal as his love (4)
207	praise him, all ye heavenly host (4)
208	let hymns of praise his triumphs tell (4)
211	And all you living things make praise (3)
213	Now with singing and praise, let us spend all the days (2)
216	Praise to the Giver of good (6)
217, 218	all praise to you let earth accord (3)
220, 221	by thee redeemed thy praise we sing (1)
220, 221	O risen Christ, ascended Lord, all praise to thee (4)
225	Praise to the Spirit of Life (4)
225	all praise to the fount of our being (4)
230	to the blessed Three in One be honor, praise and merit (2)
231	praise, O Lord, for Andrew, the first to follow (2/11-30)
231	All praise, O Lord, for Thomas (2/12-21)
231	All praise, O Lord, for Stephen (2/12-26)

231	for his faithful record we praise you evermore (2/12-27)
231	praise for his mystic vision (2/12-27)
231	Praise for your infant martyrs (2/12-28)
231	We praise you, Lord, for Peter (2/1-18)
231	Praise for the light from heaven ... voice of awe (2/1-25)
231	praise for the glorious vision the persecutor saw (2/1-25)
231	All praise, O God, for Joseph (2/3-19)
231	For Mark, O Lord, we praise you (2/4-25)
231	We praise you, Lord, for Philip (2/5-1)
231	For Barnabas we praise you (2/6-11)
231	Then let us praise the Father and worship God the Son (3)
231	ascribe all power and glory and praise to God alone (3)
232	All praise for John the Baptist (2/6-24)
232	We praise you for Saint Peter (2/6-29)
232	we praise you for Saint Paul (2/6-29)
232	All praise for Mary Magdalene (2/7-22)
232	O Lord, for James, we praise you (2/7-25)
232	Praise for your blest apostle surnamed Bartholomew (2/8-24)
232	We praise you, Lord, for Matthew (2/9-21)
232	For Luke, beloved physician, all praise (2/10-18)
232	Praise ... Lord's own brother, James of Jerusalem (2/10-23)
232	Praise, Lord, for your apostles (2/10-28)
232	walking in their footsteps we give you praise anew (2/11-1)
232	Then let us praise the Father and worship God the Son (3)
232	ascribe all power and glory and praise to God alone (3)
233, 234	hymns of thankful love and praise (1)
237	God himself to joy and praise turns our human sadness (1)
238, 239	with meetest praise and sweetest, honor them for evermore (1)
245	Praise God for John, the evangelist (1)
245	We praise you that John's voice still lives (3)
246	songs of praise and joy (1)
253	Our glorious Leader claims our praise (4)
253	our praise for his own pattern given (4)
257	with speechless praise adored (4)
260	Come now, and praise the humble saint of David's house (1)
261, 262	To God eternal be all praise and glory (3)
263, 264	whose might they show, whose praise they tell (1)
263, 264	Lord Jesus, Virgin-born ... eternal praise and glory be (4)
267	Praise we the Lord this day, this day so long foretold (1)
268, 269	in his praise I lift my voice (4)
271, 272	with thanks and praise his light to hail (1)
271, 272	praise, honor, might, and glory ... age to age eternally (5)
276	For thy blest saints ... we praise thy Name, O Lord (1)
282, 283	help us to praise thee (5)
284	while mortals sing with you their own Redeemer's praise (8)
285	What thanks and praise to thee we owe ... for Luke (1)
288	Praise to God, immortal praise (1,3)
288	Praise to God ... for the love that crowns our days (1)
288	let thy praise our tongues employ (1)
288	Lord, for these our souls shall raise ... praise (2)
288	grateful vows and solemn praise (2)
288	singing thus through all our days praise to God (3)
289	with all who passed before us, we praise thy Name today (1)
289	days of old have dowered us with gifts beyond all praise (3)
290	fruit unto his praise to yield (2)

292	That we may praise thee all our days (3)
295	Sing praise to our Creator, O you of Adam's race (1)
295	praise the Holy Spirit poured forth upon the earth (3)
300	Glory, love, and praise, and honor for our food (1)
302	thine is the power, be thine the praise (1)
303	thine is the power, be thine the praise (2)
304	we see and praise him here (4)
304	we'll live and speak his praise (5)
310, 311	All praise and thanks to thee ascend for evermore (2)
319	You, Lord, we praise in songs of celebration (1)
320	Zion, praise thy Savior, singing hymns with exultation (1)
320	praise thy King and Shepherd true (1)
325	Let us praise God together on our knees (3)
326	From glory to glory advancing, we praise thee, O Lord (1)
329-331	honor, thanks, and praise addressing (6)
334	Praise the Lord, rise up rejoicing (1)
345	Savior, again to thy dear Name we raise ... praise (1)
345	with one accord our parting hymn of praise (1)
346	to whom be praise while endless ages run (3)
359	with thankful praise (3)
360, 361	thine be the glory, praise and adoration, now and forever (6)
362	All thy works shall praise thy Name (4)
362	praise thy Name in earth, and sky, and sea (4)
363	O Triune God, with heart and voice adoring, praise we (5)
363	praise we the goodness that doth crown our days (5)
364	O God, we praise thee, and confess ... thou the only Lord (1)
364	apostles glorious company ... thy constant praise recite (4)
365	help us to praise (1)
366	Holy God, we praise thy Name (1)
369	all the heavenly powers conspire eternal praise to sing (4)
370	praise to the Lord of my salvation (7)
372	Praise to the living God! All praised be his Name (1,4)
372	Lo, he is Lord of all. Creation speaks his praise (2)
373	Praise the Lord, ye heavens adore him (1)
373	praise him angels in the height (1)
373	Praise the Lord, for he hath spoken (1)
373	Praise the Lord, for he is glorious (2)
373	Praise the God of our salvation (2)
373	praise him, all ye stars of light (1)
375	Give praise and glory unto God ... Father of all blessing (1)
375	To God be praise and glory (1-3)
376	center of unbroken praise (2)
377, 378	him serve with mirth, his praise forth tell (1)
377, 378	O enter then his gates with praise (3)
377, 378	praise, laud, and bless his Name always (3)
377, 378	from men and ... angel host be praise and glory evermore (5)
380	From all that dwell below the skies let ... praise arise (1)
380	let the Creator's praise arise (1)
380	thy praise shall sound from shore to shore (2)
380	Praise God, from whom all blessings flow (3)
380	praise him, all creatures here below (3)
380	praise him above, ye heavenly host (3)
380	praise Father, Son, and Holy Ghost (3)
381	Alleluia, alleluia, Praise to thee who light dost send (1-3)
381	to ... Light of Light begotten, praise be sung eternally (4)

381	mortals, angels, now and ever praise the Holy Trinity (4)
382	Seven whole days, not one in seven, I will praise thee (3)
388	pavilioned in splendor, and girded with praise (1)
389	Let us, with a gladsome mind, praise the Lord (1,7)
390	Praise to the Lord (1-4)
390	O my soul, praise him for he is thy health and salvation (1)
391	fill thy courts with sounding praise (4)
393	Praise our great and gracious Lord (1)
394, 395	let sun and moon and stars and light ... praise (1)
394, 395	what lies hidden praise your might (1)
394, 395	until we praise you face to face (4)
396, 397	All praise and thanks to God the Father now be given (3)
399	Your heavenly Father praise, acclaim his only Son (3)
400	O praise him, O praise him, Alleluia, alleluia, alleluia (R)
400	you clouds that ride the heavens aloft, O praise him (2)
400	Fair rising morn, with praise rejoice (2)
400	O praise him, Alleluia (2,4,6,7,R)
400	praise God, and cast on him your care (5)
400	Praise God the Father, praise the Son (7)
400	praise the Spirit, Three in One (7)
401	The God of Abraham praise, who reigns enthroned above (1)
401	all might and majesty are thine, and endless praise (5)
402, 403	The heavens are not too high, his praise may thither fly (1)
404	you, God and King, are worthy of all praise (1)
404	praise we your glory while on you we wait (2)
406, 407	to thee be ceaseless praise outpoured (1,8)
408	Sing praise to God who reigns above (1)
408	to God all praise and glory (1-3)
408	Let all who name Christ's holy Name give God all praise (3)
408	give God all praise and glory (3)
410	Praise, my soul, the King of heaven (1)
410	Praise the everlasting King (1)
410	Praise him for his grace and favor to his people (2)
410	praise him still the same as ever (2)
410	Praise with us the God of grace (4)
412	I, too, will praise him with a new song (R)
413	let every instrument and voice peal out the praise (2)
413	peal out the praise of grace abounding (2)
413	find a voice to praise his Name (3)
414	still will I thy praise proclaim (1)
415	I'm lost in wonder, love, and praise (1)
415	eternity's too short to utter all thy praise (5)
416	this our hymn of grateful praise (R)
420	Let every instrument be tuned for praise (5)
421	we raise for your great glory thanks and praise (1)
423	almighty, victorious, thy great Name we praise (1)
425	All praise and thanks to him belong who came to ... free (2)
426	Songs of praise the angels sang (1)
426	Songs of praise awoke the morn (2)
426	songs of praise arose when he captive led captivity (2)
426	songs of praise shall crown that day (3)
426	songs of praise shall hail their birth (3)
426	psalms and hymns and songs of praise (4)
426	still in songs of praise rejoice (5)
426	songs of praise to sing above (5)

511	thee we praise with endless worship (1)
511	praise ... for thy fruits and gifts unpriced (1)
517	praise thee without rest (2)
517	temple rings with praise to thee (3)
524	her hymns of love and praise (3)
532, 533	How wondrous and great thy works, God of praise (1)
537	inspired with hope and praise, to Christ belong (4)
538	Let thy people praise thee, Lord (2)
543	pursue his praise (3)
562	Hell's foundations quiver at the shout of praise (2)
567	that whole and sick and weak and strong may praise thee (3)
567	praise thee evermore (3)
579	thus evermore shall rise to thee glad praise (4)
579	glad praise from space, air, land, and sea (4)
594, 595	free our hearts to faith and praise (2)
605	What does the Lord require for praise and offering (1)
608	thus evermore shall rise to thee glad hymns of praise (4)
608	hymns of praise from land and sea (4)
614	O friends upraise anthems of joy and holy praise (1)
614	praise for his brave saints of ancient days (1)
616	all nations shall adore him, his praise all people sing (4)
619	Sing alleluia forth in duteous praise (1)
623	while for thy grace, Lord ... voices of praise ... raise (3)
623	voices of praise thy blessed people eternally raise (3)
625	take what he gives and praise him still (3)
625	praise him still, through good or ill, who ever lives (3)
625	Let all thy days till life shall end ... praise (4)
625	days ... whate'er he send, be filled with praise (4)
628	live a life of praise (3)
630	God has spoken: praise God for his open word (1-4)
630	God is speaking; praise God for his open word (5)
631	Praise we God (3)
631	praise him for the Word made flesh (3)
632	we praise thee for the radiance that ... scripture's page (1)
644	accept the praise I bring (4)
644	when I see thee as thou art, I'll praise thee as I ought (5)
645, 646	Good Shepherd, may I sing thy praise (6)
645, 646	sing thy praise within thy house for ever (6)
652, 653	in deeper reverence, praise (1)
657	pray and praise thee without ceasing (2)
657	lost in wonder, love, and praise (3)
658	Hope still ... sing the praise of him who is thy God (3)
663	I may tell thy praise, and dwell for ever in thy home (5)
664	may thy house be mine abode and all my work be praise (3)
665	from earth to God eternal sacrifice of praise be done (5)
667	God the same abiding, his praise shall tune my voice (4)
671	we've no less days to sing God's praise (5)
678, 679	Praise the Lord, who has done great things (2)
681	hint at the glorious praise of thy eternal song (3)
682	in thy praise will sing solely because thou art my God (6)
686	Streams of mercy ... call for songs of loudest praise (1)
686	Praise the mount, O, fix me on it (1)
704	return in humble prayer and fervent praise (2)
707	let them flow in ceaseless praise (1)
718	glory, laud, and praise be ever thine (4)

720   may the heaven-rescued land praise the Power (2)

praised
336   Come with us, O King of glory, by angelic voices praised (3)
372   Praise to the living God! All praised be his Name (1,4)
406, 407   My Lord be praised by brother sun (2)
406, 407   My Lord be praised by sister moon and all the stars (3)
406, 407   be praised by brother fire (4)
406, 407   By mother earth my Lord be praised (5)
406, 407   My Lord be praised by those who prove ... their love (6)
406, 407   For death our sister, praised be (7)
427   may Jesus Christ be praised (1-5)
433   thy Name be ever praised! O Lord, make us free (3)
443   his royalty from David's tree, praised be his Oneness (1)
443   his people saw him die at last, praised be his teaching (2)
443   bade the fallen to come in, praised be his mercy (3)
443   his work done, went up to heaven, praised be his coming (4)
443   the King abased to honor all, praised be your glory (5)

praiseful
430   in such a praiseful tone we will sing what he hath done (5)

praises
37   Worthy are thou ... to receive our hallowed praises, Lord (3)
48   We sing to thee our praises, O Father, Spirit, Son (4)
48   Church her voice upraises to thee, blest Three in One (4)
61, 62   for ever let our praises ring (3)
78, 79   praises sing to God the King, and peace to men on earth (2)
82   angel hosts, his praises sing (3)
82   O Holy Ghost, to thee ... unwearied praises be (4)
104   In praises of the Child (4)
105   Now to the Lord sing praises, all you within this place (4)
106   praises of redeeming love they sang (3)
108   Let every house be bright; let praises never cease (2)
109   Then let us all with one accord sing praises (6)
109   sing praises to our heavenly Lord (6)
154, 155   Thou didst accept their praises (5)
182   Let streets and homes with praises ring (1)
183   Christians, to the Paschal victim offer your ... praises (1)
183   offer your thankful praises (1)
212   again rejoice and on his praises dwell (1)
213   his rapturous praises, repeat (5)
232   yet she her voice upraises God's glory to proclaim (2/8-15)
282, 283   hear our thankful praises (6)
294   faithfully now God's praises we sing (1)
294   thankfully now God's praises we sing (2)
294   joyfully now God's praises we sing (3)
300   Christ alone calls for all our praises (2)
339   there with joy thy praises render unto him (1)
365   To Thee, great One in Three, the highest praises be (4)
365   highest praises be, hence evermore (4)
390   All that hath life and breath come now with praises (4)
390   come now with praises before him (4)
402, 403   earth is not too low, his praises there may grow (1)
410   evermore his praises sing (1)

413	praises be his that never cease (3)
433	sing praises to his Name, he forgets not his own (1)
440	Hear the cry thy Church upraises (3)
440	hear, and bless our prayers and praises (3)
458	Sometimes they strew his way and his strong praises sing (3)
492	praises of your Savior let his house resound again (1)
495	highest praises, without ceasing ... give (4)
495	highest praises ... right it is for us to give (4)
522, 523	as priests, his solemn praises ... a thankoffering brings (4)
535	The praises of Jesus the angels proclaim (3)
544	praises throng to crown his head (2)
576, 577	be our bliss while endless ages sing your praises (3)
618	more glorious than the seraphim, lead their praises (2)
621, 622	glorious are the praises which of thee the prophets sing (1)
623	Low before him with our praises we fall (5)
625	God's praises sound (2)
665	high above all praises praising for ... Christ, his son (5)
690	songs of praises, I will ever give to thee (3)

praiseth
| 375 | host of heaven praiseth thee, O Lord of all dominions (2) |

praising
92	praising Christ, heaven's King (4)
94, 95	angels praising God, who thus addressed their joyful song (5)
97	for these mercies manifold join the hosts in praising (3)
128	prayer and praising, gladly raising (3)
154, 155	The company of angels is praising thee on high (2)
244	thee with all thy ransomed praising ever ... evermore (3)
286	praising loud their heavenly King (1)
320	Christ ... who surpasseth all thy praising (1)
320	Full and clear sing out thy praising (4)
366	cherubim and seraphim, in unceasing chorus praising (2)
376	praising thee, their sun above (1)
611	praising God by labor at his bench (3)
665	high above all praises praising for ... Christ, his son (5)

pray
10	new mercies ... around us hover while we pray (2)
10	help us ... every day, to live more nearly as we pray (6)
19, 20	pour forth into our hearts, we pray, the fullness (1)
27, 28	we pray you, Father, calm our fears (2)
33-35	Give heed, we pray you, to our supplication (4)
40, 41	We pray you, O most holy Lord, to be our guardian (2)
44, 45	we pray that in your constant clemency (1)
44, 45	we pray ... our guard and keeper you would be (1)
52	grace to pray (4)
60	we pray you hear us when we call (1)
60	Come in your holy might, we pray (5)
73	Thy people pray, come quickly, King of kings (5)
78, 79	Where children pure and happy pray to the blessed Child (4)
78, 79	O holy Child of Bethlehem, descend to us, we pray (5)
85, 86	now hear the prayers your people pray (2)
88	O renew us, Lord, we pray, with thy Spirit day by day (5)
101	love me I pray (3)

122, 123	Therefore in our hymns we pray thee (4)
142	for us didst fast and pray (1)
144	shine in our hearts, we pray (1)
146, 147	Therefore, we pray you, Lord, forgive (5)
158	I do adore thee, and will ever pray thee (5)
171	learn of Jesus Christ to pray (1)
173	with tears I pray thee, hear me (4)
223, 224	blessings of this sacred day grant us ... we pray (3)
223, 224	grant us, dearest Lord, we pray (3)
279	humbly pray that we may follow them in holiness (4)
280	number us, we pray, with them (4)
298	With one accord, O God, we pray, grant us the Holy Spirit (2)
307	here for faith's discernment pray we (2)
315	Thou, who at thy first Eucharist didst pray (1)
315	pray that all thy Church might be for ever one (1)
339	Jesus, Bread of life, I pray thee (3)
350	pray for these before thee now (1)
363	to thee all knees are bent, all voices pray (1)
363	pray we that thou wilt hear us (5)
371	hear us, we humbly pray (1)
433	pray that thou still our defender wilt be (3)
478	lead us then day by day in your own steps, we pray (2)
482	and give us, we pray (1-4)
506, 507	Pray we then, O Lord the Spirit, on our lives descend (5)
517	thou shalt surely bless ... who live the words they pray (4)
518	hear thy servants as they pray (3)
522, 523	manna which he gives them when they pray (3)
548	wrestle, and fight, and pray (4)
563	cease not to watch and pray (2)
563	O pray that faith and virtue may keep thee to the last (4)
599	keep us forever in the path, we pray (3)
606	Now we pray that with the blessed you grant us grace (3)
607	deliver every nation, eternal God, we pray (2)
613	We pray thee, Lord, arise, and come in thy great might (4)
615	Thy kingdom come, on bended knee the passing ages pray (1)
635	Sing, pray, and keep his ways unswerving (2)
647	for light and strength I pray (2)
654	Day by day, dear Lord, of thee three things I pray (1)
657	pray and praise thee without ceasing (2)
661	Yet let us pray for but one thing ... peace of God (4)
674	you taught us, Lord, to pray (1)
676	if you cannot pray like Paul (2)
691	Now hear me while I pray, take all my guilt away (1)
698	only you can teach me how to pray (1)
698	Come, pray in me the prayer I need this day (2)

prayed

143	Christ ... himself has fasted and has prayed (1)
448, 449	For us he prayed, for us he taught (3)
623	nor do things prayed for come short of the prayer (2)

prayer

1, 2	singing we offer prayer and meditation: thus we adore (1)
5	With prayer the Father we implore (3)
10	some softening gleam of love and prayer shall dawn (4)

12, 13	Amid our customary round, we offer ... prayer and praise (1)
23	At prayer time, near the Temple gate (2)
24	the voice of prayer is never silent (3)
29, 30	to thee our evening prayer we raise (2)
49	with solemn prayer approach the throne (3)
128	prayer and praising, gladly raising (3)
136, 137	for which in joyful strains we raise the voice of prayer (4)
136, 137	the voice of prayer, the hymn of praise (4)
143	full oft in fast and prayer with thee (4)
143	to thee be every prayer addressed (5)
145	Lent calls to prayer, to trust and dedication (1)
150	fasting with unceasing prayer (2)
152	Kind Maker of the world, O hear the fervent prayer (1)
243	on his lips a prayer that God ... spare (3)
248, 249	who in prayer this Name beseecheth ... comfort findeth (3)
275	have watched to prayer ... are there (2)
278	in prayer with Christ's apostles, waited on his ... word (3)
280	All his faith and prayer and patience (3)
286	in prayer full oft have striven (4)
336	through our work as through our prayer (2)
337	our prayer so languid, and our faith so dim (2)
365	our prayer attend (2)
427	God's holy house of prayer hath none that can compare (2)
436	adorned with prayer and love and joy (3)
454	again in answer to our earnest heartfelt prayer (2)
486	house of prayer, where we assembled in thy Name (3)
513	with the ceaseless voice of prayer (3)
537	with fervent prayer (2)
539	pour out thy soul for them in prayer victorious (3)
544	To him shall endless prayer be made (2)
558	faith and prayer shall win all nations unto thee (2)
561	put on the Gospel armor, and watching unto prayer (3)
616	to him shall prayer unceasing and daily vows ascend (4)
617	one with the grief that trembleth into prayer (2)
623	nor do things prayed for come short of the prayer (2)
638, 639	be conquered by my instant prayer (3)
669	God ever sends his blessing in answer to thy prayer (2)
698	Come, pray in me the prayer I need this day (2)
704	return in humble prayer and fervent praise (2)

prayers

16, 17	calls the faithful to their noon-day prayers (1)
85, 86	now hear the prayers your people pray (2)
117, 118	dearer to God are the prayers of the poor (4)
154, 155	praise and prayers and anthems before thee we present (3)
154, 155	accept the prayers we bring (5)
370	the patriarchs' prayers, the prophets' scrolls (3)
440	hear, and bless our prayers and praises (3)
509	Spirit divine, attend our prayers (1,5)
524	For her my tears shall fall, for her my prayers ascend (2)
597	through all our hopes and prayers and dreams (1)
709	Our vows, our prayers, we now present (2)
709	Such blessings ... our humble prayers implore (5)
716	For her our prayers shall rise to God, above the skies (2)

praying

preach

preached

preachest

precede

preceding

precepts

precious

preparation

prepare

69	prepare for joy in the winter night (2)
71, 72	let every heart prepare a throne, and every voice a song (1)
75	Prepare in the desert a highway, a highway for our God (1)
76	let each heart prepare a home (2)
100	let every heart prepare him room (1)
495	there thou dost our place prepare (3)
695, 696	salvation for which, O Lord, you taught us to prepare (2)
708	for our use thy folds prepare (1)

prepared

275	Patriarch, and holy prophet, who prepared the way (2)
275	prepared the way for Christ (2)
499	prepared by you for all the world to see (1)

prepares

359	each age for thine own solemn task prepares (1)
484, 485	now prepares in heavenly regions unfailing mansions (1)
484, 485	prepares ... mansions for his own (1)

preparing

| 198 | for heavenly joy preparing (2) |

presence

48	living presence greeting, through Bread and Wine made near (3)
109	offered there in his presence their gold (5)
149	moved by your love and toward your presence bent (1)
151	could we abide thy presence? (1)
222	he makes his glorious presence clear (2)
232	May we discern your presence (2/8-24)
242	O Savior, make thy presence known to all who doubt (5)
255	His presence pierced and blinded the zealot in his wrath (1)
261, 262	Christ in whose presence hosts of hell must tremble (2)
278	from on high ... glory of the Spirit's presence came (3)
278	blazing glory of the Spirit's presence (3)
290	there, forever purified, in thy presence to abide (4)
304	His presence, always near (4)
304	His presence ... is in such friendship better known (4)
324	cherubim ... veil their faces to the Presence (4)
326	O Lord, evermore to thy servants thy presence be nigh (2)
332	O God, unseen yet ever near, thy presence may we feel (1)
337	by this prevailing presence we appeal (3)
353	Bless those who in your presence wait (2)
360, 361	voices rise to thy presence (1)
436	here, Lord, abide! Let me thy inner presence feel (4)
445, 446	God's presence and his very self, and essence all divine (4)
482	whose voice is contentment, whose presence is balm (4)
488	waking or sleeping, thy presence my light (1)
527	One the light of God's own presence (2)
535	still he is nigh, his presence we have (2)
642	sweeter far thy face to see and in thy presence rest (1)
649, 650	glad, when your presence we discern (3)
656	Lord, we thy presence seek (4)
662	I need thy presence every passing hour (2)
664	thy presence is my stay (2)
702	wither from thy presence flee (3)

present

138	water reddening into wine proclaims the present Lord (2)
154, 155	praise and prayers and anthems before thee we present (3)
217, 218	You are a present joy, O Lord (2)
337	having with us him that pleads above, we here present (1)
357	now we hail thee present on thine altar throne (1)
360, 361	by thy past blessings, by thy present bounty, favor (5)
398	everywhere that I could be, thou, God, art present there (3)
576, 577	Christ, our God, be always present here among us (2)
599	sing a song full of the hope ... the present has brought (1)
600, 601	to match our present hour (1)
667	set free from present sorrow, we cheerfully can say (2)
709	Our vows, our prayers, we now present (2)
709	present before thy throne of grace (2)

presented

259	before thy Father's face may all presented be (4)

presents

359	through them thy Church presents ... true sacrifice (3)
546	his own hand presents the prize to thine aspiring eye (3)

preserve

21, 22	from passion's heat preserve our life (2)
247	O sisters, too, how may we do for to preserve this day (1)
352	Spirit of God, whom we adore: preserve, protect, defend (3)

preside

229	Unfailing Comfort, heavenly Guide ... preside (3)
229	still o'er thy holy Church preside (3)
512	o'er every thought and step preside (1)

presiding

232	presiding at the council that set the Gentiles free (2/10-23)

press

150	Then if Satan on us press, Jesus, Savior, hear our call (3)
237	press through toil and sorrow (3)
310, 311	our foes press on from every side (1)
381	glorious now, we press toward glory (3)
422	Help us to press on toward that mark (3)
545	Thither ... press we to God's right hand (5)
546	press with vigor on (1,4)

pressed

284	Ye thronged to Calvary and pressed with sad desire (5)
480	when mothers round him pressed (2)

presses

525	to one hope she presses, with every grace endued (2)

pretended

158	man to judge thee hath in hate pretended (1)

pretension

348   teach us to serve without pride or pretension (2)

prevail

254   the saints of God at last prevail (1)
373   sin and death shall not prevail (2)
409   Soon as the evening shades prevail (2)
445, 446   should strive and should prevail (3)
562   gates of hell can never 'gainst that Church prevail (4)
581   Where charity and love prevail there God is ever found (1)

prevaileth

360, 361   sin is forgiven, hope o'er fear prevaileth (3)

prevailing

238, 239   Faith prevailing, hope unfailing (2)
337   by this prevailing presence we appeal (3)
687, 688   our helper he amid the flood of mortal ills prevailing (1)

prey

162   to spoil the spoiler of his prey (4)

price

10   new treasures still, of countless price, God will provide (3)
162   the price which none but he could pay (4)
167   There was no other good enough to pay the price of sin (4)
246   innocents the price must pay (2)
278   saw the price of our redemption paid (2)
329, 331   the Blood, all price excelling (1)
685   in my hand no price I bring, simply to thy cross I cling (2)

priceless

252   Jesus, Name of priceless worth to the fallen of the earth (3)

pride

146, 147   grant repentance for our pride (3)
148   evils wrought by human pride recoil on unrepentant heads (3)
148   our foolish confidence, our pride of knowledge ... sin (4)
348   teach us to serve without pride or pretension (2)
371   rolling in fullest pride, through the world far and wide (4)
420   adoration leaves no room for pride (1)
474   pour contempt on all my pride (1)
475   pride of life and sinful pleasures (2)
498   content to let my pride go by, to know no gain nor loss (3)
542   cast out our pride and shame that hinder to enthrone thee (3)
568   judgment is thine, and condemneth our pride (1)
574, 575   for pride ambitious to succeed (3)
591   take not thy thunder from us, but take away our pride (1)
594, 595   bend our pride to thy control (3)
598   all those nations' pride, overthrown (2)
598   pride, overthrown, went down to dust beside thee (2)
598   our pride is dust, our vaunt is stilled (4)
607   from pride of race and nation and blindness to your way (2)
665   Mortal pride and earthly glory (2)
670   strip me of the robe of pride (1)

717   land where my fathers died, land of the pilgrim's pride (1)

priest
135   Prophet, Priest, and King supreme (2)
174   Christ the victim, Christ the priest (1)
219   Our great High Priest hath gone before (3)
257   a priest and victim, both in one (1)
293   one was a soldier, and one was a priest (2)
327, 328   himself the Victim, and himself the Priest (4)
460, 461   our great High Priest (4)
460, 461   thou on earth both Priest and Victim (4)
460, 461   Priest and Victim in the eucharistic feast (4)
591   Tie in a living tether the prince and priest and thrall (3)
644   O Prophet, Priest, and King (4)

priesthood
51   that he might anoint us a royal priesthood (1)
359   help them intercede with all the royal priesthood (3)
359   priesthood born of grace (3)
443   his priesthood from Melchizedek (1)
536   Open your hearts, O royal priesthood (1,4)

priests
286   These, like priests, have watched and waited (5)
359   Anoint them priests (3)
506, 507   who enlightened priests and prophets with the word (3)
522, 523   Jesus ... makes them kings and priests to God (4)
522, 523   as priests, his solemn praises ... a thankoffering brings (4)
528   Let your priests, for earth's true glory, daily lift (3)

primal
31, 32   you in the primal world once set the boundaries (4)

prince
49   he rose, the prince of life and peace (1)
71, 72   glad hosannas, Prince of Peace, thy welcome ... proclaim (4)
87   hail, the heaven-born Prince of Peace (3)
98   "A prince," he said, "in Jewry!" (3)
125, 126   His name shall be the Prince of Peace for evermore adored (4)
173   the glorious Prince of Life should in death be sleeping (3)
183   the Prince of life, who died, reigns immortal (3)
233, 234   these lay the prince of this world low (3)
315   by drawing all to thee, O Prince of Peace (2)
401   triumphant o'er the world and sin, the Prince of Peace (3)
426   awoke the morn when the Prince of Peace was born (2)
458   a murderer they save, the Prince of Life they slay (5)
474   cross where the young Prince of Glory died (1)
492   Prince of life, among the dead (3)
542   heal its ancient wrong, come, Prince of Peace, and reign (3)
591   Tie in a living tether the prince and priest and thrall (3)
624   the Prince is ever in them, the daylight is serene (2)
640   Traveler, lo, the Prince of Peace ... Son of God is come (3)
687, 688   the prince of darkness grim, we tremble not for him (3)

princedoms
618   Cry out, dominions, princedoms, powers (1)

princely
29, 30 O Unity of princely might (1)

princes
233, 234 The princes of the Church are they (2)

prints
214   See! he shows the prints of love (3)

prison
180   he has burst his three days' prison (1)
180   we are free from sin's dark prison (4)
192   Had Christ ... ne'er burst his three-day prison (R)
199, 200 Christ hath burst his prison (2)

prisoned
179   Loose the souls long prisoned, bound with Satan's chain (6)

prisoner
255   O Love that sought and held him a prisoner of his Lord (2)
429   grants the prisoner sweet release (3)

prisoners
71, 72 He comes, the prisoners to release (2)
444   On prisoners of darkness the sun begins to rise (3)
544   the prisoners leap to lose their chains (4)

private
528   Yet we hoard as private treasure all that you ... give (4)

prize
27, 28 strive to gain the heavenly prize (4)
145   love shall be the prize (5)
431   more rich than any prize (3)
524   Beyond my highest joy I prize her heavenly ways (3)
546   his own hand presents the prize to thine aspiring eye (3)
552, 553 Christ is the path and Christ the prize (2)
642   Jesus, our only joy be thou, as thou our prize wilt be (5)

probe
584   to probe earth's hidden mysteries (1)

probed
580   probed the secrets of the atom, yielding unimagined power (3)

proceed
165, 166 from that holy body broken blood and water forth proceed (3)

proceeding
128   westward leading, still proceeding (R)
440   Light of Light, from God proceeding (3)

procession
157   form a procession with branches (R)

proclaim
65   His tidings of salvation proclaim in every place (3)
71, 72   glad hosannas, Prince of Peace, thy welcome ... proclaim (4)
75   Proclaim to a desolate people the coming of their King (2)
78, 79   O morning stars, together proclaim the holy birth (2)
87   with the angelic host proclaim Christ is born (1)
93   who sang creation's story now proclaim Messiah's birth (1)
106   amazed, the wondrous story they proclaim (4)
106   employ our grateful voices to proclaim the joy (5)
121   sent you his kingdom to proclaim, his holy will to do (2)
181   Soon ... each raptured tongue his endless praise proclaim (4)
232   yet she her voice upraises God's glory to proclaim (2/8-15)
236   glory unceasing we proclaim (4)
243   on his eyes a light wherewith God's daybreak to proclaim (2)
245   your glory to proclaim whereby your Spirit give us life (3)
259   no shouts proclaim him nigh, no crowds his coming wait (1)
263, 264   God's new message did proclaim (2)
292   with the Father's Name ... Savior's love proclaim (3)
368   Holy Jesus, Lord of glory, whom angelic hosts proclaim (2)
368   dear Redeemer, in our hearts thy peace proclaim (2)
373   Hosts on high, his power proclaim (2)
393   all his mighty acts proclaim (1)
394, 395   proclaim your care (2)
409   their great Original proclaim (1)
411   His grace to thee proclaim (1)
414   still will I thy praise proclaim (1)
414   proclaim thy sovereign power (6)
473   Lift high the cross, the love of Christ proclaim (R)
484, 485   we confess, proclaim, adore thee (2)
493   My gracious Master and my God, assist me to proclaim (2)
535   Ye servants of God, your Master proclaim (1)
535   The praises of Jesus the angels proclaim (3)
539   Proclaim to every people, tongue and nation (2)
540   the circle of the earth shall then proclaim thy kingdom (3)
540   proclaim ... the glory of thy Name (3)
543   loud that grace proclaim, which makes thy darkness bright (3)
544   infant voices shall proclaim their early blessings (3)
587   who dost in love proclaim each family thine own (1)
614   with the same faith his word proclaim (2)
615   proclaim the day is near (3)
628   to live the faith which we proclaim (2)
678, 679   all his works his might proclaim (2)
408   all who know his power proclaim aloud the wondrous story (3)

proclaimed
133, 134   your Father's voice his Son proclaimed (2)
230   the ears of all who heard proclaimed salvation's wonder (1)
235   voice proclaimed salvation that poured upon the night (1)
240, 241   Living, they proclaimed salvation (2)

proclaimeth
127   gold the King of kings proclaimeth (4)

proclaiming
129, 130   God proclaiming in its thunder Jesus as his Son by name (3)

proclaims
138   water reddening into wine proclaims the present Lord (2)
162   each crimsoned bough proclaims the King of glory now (3)
457   the rending tomb proclaims thy conquering arm (3)

proclamation
244   peace on earth their proclamation (1)

procured
207   pains which he endured ... our salvation have procured (3)

profanation
591   from sale and profanation of honor, and the sword (2)

profess
116   His Name we will profess (4)
352   O God, to those who here profess their vows (1)

profit
152   fast of forty days may work our profit and thy praise (5)
476   our profit counts as loss (3)
483   profit and their joy to know the mystery of his love (5)
669   what profit doth it bring thee to pine in grief and care (2)

profound
420   as worship moved us to a more profound Alleluia (2)
617   from ... night profound into the glory of the perfect day (1)

prolong
316, 317   here let me feast, and feasting still prolong (1)
316, 317   prolong the brief, bright hour of fellowhip with thee (1)
717   let rocks their silence break, the sound prolong (3)

prolongs
411   He pardons all thy sins, prolongs thy feeble breath (4)

promise
74   Christ, who is the Promise, who has atonement made (2)
209   but in his promise we rejoice (2)
228   As your promise we believe (5)
252   promise that it gave, "Jesus shall his people save" (3)
267   promise shone with cheering ray on waiting saints of old (1)
268, 269   blessed ... land of promise fashioned for his ... home (2)
294   heirs of salvation, trusting his promise (1)
373   never shall his promise fail (2)
429   none shall find his promise vain (2)
437, 438   tender to me the promise of his word (1)
437, 438   Firm is his promise, and his mercy sure (4)
444   God shall fulfill his promise and bring his people peace (1)
460, 461   shall our hearts forget his promise (2)
486   in faith thy parting promise claim (3)
528   That the world may trust your promise (2)

562	we have Christ's own promise, and that cannot fail (4)
572	weary of all songs that sing promise, non-fulfilling (1)
580	May our dreams prove rich with promise (4)
640	what its signs of promise are (1)
666	hopes are on thy promise built, thy never-failing word (2)
670	my doubts I sorely feel, thy sure promise I believe (3)
693	because thy promise I believe (4)

promised

71, 72	the Savior promised long (1)
106	this day hath God fulfilled his promised word (2)
125, 126	To us the promised Child is born, to us the Son is given (3)
230	what Christ had promised now occurred (1)
230	until you reach the promised goal, a kingdom to inherit (3)
253	they reached the promised rest (3)
259	in his hands takes up the promised child (3)
267	virgin born of David's line shall bear the promised seed (2)
278	waited on his promised word (3)
298	that as is promised here we may eternal life inherit (2)
393	how he leads his chosen unto Canaan's promised land (1)
473	as thou hast promised, draw the world to thee (3)
499	go in peace as promised in your word (1)
500	the Father's promised Paraclete (2)
527	marching to the promised land (1)
597	Christ's promised reign of peace (1)
613	When comes the promised time that war shall be no more (3)
615	day of perfect righteousness, the promised day of God (5)
640	Traveler, yes, it brings the day, promised day of Israel (1)
641	take thy promised rest (2)
655	Jesus, I have promised to serve thee to the end (1,3)
655	O Jesus, thou hast promised to all who follow thee (3)
671	The Lord has promised good to me (3)

promises

| 626 | thy promises my hope; thy providence my guard (2) |

pronounced

| 398 | formed the creatures ... then pronounced them good (2) |

prophecy

69	Who hears, O God, the prophecy (1)
358	God-spoken prophecy, word at creation (3)
612	Prophecy will fade away, melting in the light of day (3)

prophet

124	True spake the prophet from afar who told the rise (2)
135	Prophet, Priest, and King supreme (2)
145	The prophet spoke (3)
161	to see a prophet crucified (3)
232	last and greatest prophet, he saw the dawning ray (2/6-24)
267	The prophet gave the sign for faithful folk to read (2)
271, 272	woman born shall never be a greater prophet than was he (4)
275	Patriarch, and holy prophet, who prepared the way (2)
444	the prophet of salvation, the harbinger of Day (2)
615	gird up your loins, ye prophet souls (3)

644   O Prophet, Priest, and King (4)

prophet's
235   as, in the prophet's vision from out the amber flame (2)
271, 272 greater than a prophet's name (4)
372   in prophet's word he spoke of old, he speaketh still (3)
605   Still down the ages ring the prophet's stern commands (3)

prophetic
116   He seals the sure prophetic word (1)
162   in true prophetic song of old (2)
271, 272 prophetic utterance told his actions great and manifold (2)

prophets
89, 90 by prophets seen of old (4)
129, 130 All the prophets and the Law shout through them (2)
129, 130 Law and prophets fade before him (4)
133, 134 Two prophets, who had faith to see (2)
232   Apostles, prophets, martyrs ... the noble throng (2/11-1)
359   God of the prophets, bless the prophets' heirs (1)
359   Anoint them prophets. Teach them thine intent (2)
364   prophets crowned with light (4)
366   prophets swell the loud refrain (3)
444   The prophets spoke of mercy, of freedom and release (1)
453   many prophets and martyrs have trod it before (3)
491   Prophets, shepherds, kings, advise (1)
491   so weak and lowly as unheeded prophets taught (2)
506, 507 who enlightened priests and prophets with the word (3)
618   ye patriarchs and prophets blest (3)
621, 622 glorious are the praises which of thee the prophets sing (1)
631   poets, prophets, scholars, saints, each a word from God (2)

prophets'
359   God of the prophets, bless the prophets' heirs (1)
370   the patriarchs' prayers, the prophets' scrolls (3)

prosper
282, 283 so that for the peaceful all things may prosper (2)
390   who doth prosper thy way and defend thee (3)

prospering
288   As thy prospering hand hath blessed, may we give (3)

prosperity
250   such a Lord to lead our way in hazard and prosperity (4)

prostrate
450, 451 Let angels prostrate fall (1)
643   by prostrate spirits day and night incessantly adored (2)
697   Before the cross of him who died, behold, I prostrate fall (2)

protect
40, 41 with your right hand you will protect those who believe (3)
110   to guard him, and protect his mother mild (3)
352   Spirit of God, whom we adore: preserve, protect, defend (3)

579	wherever, Lord, thy people go, protect them (2)
579	protect them by thy guarding hand (2)
579	protect them ... from every peril on the land (2)
579, 608	from rock and tempest, fire and foe, protect them (4)
579, 608	protect them wheresoe'er they go (4)
717	protect us by thy might, great God, our King (4)

protected

202	Protected in the Paschal night (2)
202	Protected ... from the destroying angel's might (2)

protecting

486	O Savior, with protecting care abide in this thy house (3)

protector

226, 227	Come, protector of the poor (1)
501, 502	protector in the midst of strife (2)

protects

631	for the Spirit which protects us (3)

proud

24	never, like earth's proud empires, pass away (4)
74	pity the proud and haughty (2)
304	each proud division ends (3)
437, 438	Proud hearts and stubborn wills are put to flight (3)
573	building proud towers which shall not reach to heaven (3)

proudly

580	Proudly rise our modern cities (2)
720	what so proudly we hailed at the twilight's last gleaming (1)

prove

10	love our wakening and uprising prove (1)
100	makes the nations prove the glories of his righteousness (4)
231	whose short-lived doubtings prove (2/12-21)
288	by deeds of kindly love for thy mercies grateful prove (3)
406, 407	My Lord be praised by those who prove ... their love (6)
406, 407	prove in free forgivingness their love (6)
414	all his works his goodness prove (5)
434	nor wit can guess, nor reason prove which of the letters (3)
552, 553	trust, and thy trusting soul shall prove Christ ... life (3)
580	May our dreams prove rich with promise (4)
693	of thy great love ... to prove (6)
693	love, the breadth, length, depth, and height to prove (6)
704	Still let me prove thy perfect will (4)

provide

10	new treasures still, of countless price, God will provide (3
10	God will provide for sacrifice (3)
290	God, our Maker, doth provide for our wants to be supplied (1)
308, 309	of thine abundance give us, and all we need provide (2)
348	intention ever to cherish the gifts you provide (2)
552, 553	his boundless mercy will provide (3)
709	give us each day our daily bread ... raiment fit provide (3)

provided

320	as of old the Lord provided (2)
559	thus provided, pardoned, guided (3)

providence

626	thy promises my hope; thy providence my guard (2)
677	behind a frowning providence he hides a smiling face (4)

provident

569	God the All-provident (4)

pruning

542	to ploughshare beat the sword, to pruning hook the spear (2)

psalm

404	each day we live our psalm to you we raise (1)
406, 407	repeat the psalm (3)
420	did not Jesus sing a psalm that night (4)
427	There to the eternal Word the eternal psalm is heard (3)

psalms

402, 403	Church with psalms must shout, no door can keep them out (2)
426	No, the Church delights to raise psalms and hymns (4)
426	psalms and hymns and songs of praise (4)
681	hymns thy people raise, the psalms and anthems strong (3)

psaltery

390	join the great throng, psaltery, organ, and song (1)

publish

535	publish abroad his wonderful Name (1)
539	Publish glad tidings: tidings of peace (R)

published

630	word is published in the tongues of every race (4)

publishes

409	publishes to every land the work of an almighty hand (1)

purchased

40, 41	whom you have purchased with your blood (4)

pure

18	all you made was pure and clean (4c)
78, 79	Where children pure and happy pray to the blessed Child (4)
105	this day is born a Savior of a pure virgin bright (3)
110	'Twas Mary, daughter pure of holy Anne (2)
111	Son of God, love's pure light radiant beams (3)
119	so may we with holy joy, pure and free from sin's alloy (3)
194, 195	alone to Jesus living, pure in heart may we abide (2)
210	Our hearts be pure from evil, that we may see aright (2)
231	lives as pure as theirs (2/12-28)
244	Come, pure hearts, in joyful measure sing (1)
267	Mary, the pure and lowly maid, the favored of the Lord (4)
277	Sing of Mary, pure and lowly, virgin mother undefiled (1)

290	grant, ... Lord, that we wholesome grain and pure may be (2)
337	the one true, pure, immortal sacrifice (1)
337	From tainting mischief keep them pure and clear (3)
400	Swift flowing water, pure and clear, make music (3)
416	offering up on every shore thy pure sacrifice of love (5)
440	by thy teachings pure and holy (1)
443	the Pure baptized, the Life who died (5)
467	to make salvation sure, guides us by his Spirit pure (3)
486	make our secret soul to be a temple pure and worthy thee (4)
508	until my heart is pure (2)
519, 520	all thy streets and all thy bulwarks of pure gold (2)
519, 520	of pure gold are fashioned (2)
530	Word of life, most pure and strong (5)
556, 557	Rejoice, ye pure in heart! Rejoice, give thanks and sing (1)
556, 557	on, ye pure in heart! Rejoice, give thanks and sing (7)
560	Blessed are the pure in heart, for they shall see God (6)
572	we ... join in singing that great music pure and strong (1)
574, 575	more pure, more true, more nobly wise (4)
621, 622	all is pure ... holy that within thy walls is stored (2)
638, 639	Pure Universal Love thou art (4)
641	make me pure within (1)
645, 646	what transport of delight from thy pure chalice floweth (5)
656	Blest are the pure in heart, for they shall see our God (1)
656	for his dwelling ... throne will choose the pure in heart (3)
656	give us a pure and lowly heart, a temple fit for thee (4)
657	pure, unbounded love thou art (1)
657	pure and spotless let us be (3)
691	may my love to thee pure, warm, and changeless be (2)
699	make and keep me pure within (3)

purer

97	purer praise than ours on earth, angels' songs afford (3)
133, 134	through purer lives show forth your light (3)
159	a purer love attaining, may with thee acceptance find (5)
383, 384	Jesus is fairer, Jesus is purer (2)
383, 384	Jesus shines purer than all the angels heaven can boast (3)
543	with his radiance fill those fairer purer skies (4)
652, 653	in purer lives thy service find (1)
683, 684	purer light ... mark the road that leads me to the Lamb (5)

purest

286	clad in robes of purest whiteness (2)
308, 309	O purest fountain, welling from out the Savior's side (2)
576, 577	Shine on us, O purest Light of all creation (3)
632	O make thy Church, dear Savior, a lamp of purest gold (3)

purge

290	from his field shall in that day all offenses purge away (3)
357	Every taint of evil, frailty and decay ... purge away (3)
357	good and gracious Savior, cleanse and purge away (3)
509	Come as the fire, and purge our hearts (3)
509	purge our hearts like sacrificial flame (3)
574, 575	consume the ill, purge out the shame (4)
596	with thy living fire of judgment purge this land (1)
596	purge this land of bitter things (1)

641   purge away my sin (1)

purged
185, 186   word of grace hath purged away the old and wicked leaven (4)
481   when he had purged our stains, he took his seat above (2)

purging
297   Descend, O Spirit, purging flame (1)

purified
290   there, forever purified, in thy presence to abide (4)

purify
457   thou only canst inform the mind and purify the heart (2)
574, 575   Let the fierce fires which burn and try ... purify (4)
574, 575   our inmost spirits purify (4)

purity
228   occupy its inmost part with your dazzling purity (3)
362   perfect in power, in love, and purity (3)
370   purity of virgin souls (3)
613   Where is thy reign of peace, and purity, and love (2)
643   thine endless wisdom, boundless power, and aweful purity (3)

purple
9   purple pageantry of dawning and of dying days (1)
161   its purple limbs a royal throne (4)
170   In mock acclaim ... they snatched a purple cloak (2)
180   breaking o'er the purple east (3)
448, 449   in purple robe arrayed (4)
719   for purple mountain majesties above the fruited plain (1)

purpose
477   Wherefore, by God's eternal purpose, thou ... exalted (4)
528   help us witness to your purpose with renewed integrity (1)
534   God is working his purpose out as year succeeds to year (1)
534   God is working his purpose out ... time is drawing near (1)
574, 575   for lives bereft of purpose high, forgive (3)
580   lost to purpose and to meaning (2)
580   children of creative purpose (4)
610   consecrating to your purpose every gift that you impart (1)
698   help me to see your purpose and your will (2)

pursue
284   The joyous notes pursue and louder anthems raise (8)
543   pursue his praise (3)
667   In holy contemplation we sweetly then pursue the theme (2)

pursues
156   thy humble beast pursues his road with palms ... strowed (1)

put
56   death's dark shadow put to flight (6)
85, 86   you put our human vesture on (3)
113   pangs of my sorrow are soothed and put to rest (1)

145	oppression put to flight (3)
168, 169	O sacred head, sore wounded, defiled and put to scorn (1)
179	mankind to deliver, manhood didst put on (4)
437, 438	Proud hearts and stubborn wills are put to flight (3)
457	who put their trust in thee nor death nor hell ... harm (3)
496, 497	Incarnate God, put forth thy power (3)
521	Put forth, O God, thy Spirit's might (1)
548	Soldiers of Christ, arise, and put your armor on (1)
561	put on the Gospel armor, and watching unto prayer (3)

puts

16, 17	it puts the noon-day sun in shade (3)
452	that strong Light puts out the sun and all is ended (4)
602	Loving puts us on our knees (4)

quail

168, 169	hold me that I quail not in death's most fearful hour (5)

quake

111	shepherds quake at the sight (2)
652, 653	speak through the earthquake, wind, and fire (5)

quarrel

576, 577	Banished now be anger, strife and every quarrel (2)

queen

198	fair Easter, queen of all the days (1)
199, 200	Now the queen of seasons, bright with the day of splendor (3)
293	one was a doctor, and one was a queen (1)

quelling

135	manifest in valiant fight, quelling all the devil's might (3)

quench

21, 22	Quench now on earth the flames of strife (2)
649, 650	our thirsting souls to quench and fill (2)

quenched

168, 169	thy power is all expired ... quenched the light of light (2)
692	my thirst was quenched, my soul revived (2)

quenching

245	thirst-quenching stream. All these I am, and more (2)

quest

253	his zeal inspired their quest (3)
517	happy they whose hearts are set upon the pilgrim's quest (2)
681	it is because thou art we're driven to the quest (2)

questions

231	To all who live with questions (2/12-21)
460, 461	he is near us, faith believes, nor questions how (2)

quick

204	quick from the dead my risen Lord is seen (3)

574, 575   give us a conscience quick to feel (1)

quicken
567   restore and quicken (3)

quickened
359   to human need their quickened hearts awake (2)
551   quickened by the Spirit's power (3)
610   light ... dawns upon our quickened sight (3)

quickening
148   speak to our souls the quickening word (5)
321   Drawn by thy quickening grace, O Lord (3)
350   Whatever comes to be their share of quickening joy (2)
350   share of quickening joy or burdening care (2)
363   thine is the quickening power that gives increase (4)
419   Sun of our life, thy quickening ray sheds ... the glow (2)
506, 507   Spirit, moving on the waters quickening worlds to life (1)
506, 507   quickening worlds to life within (1)
510   with all thy quickening powers (1,4)
511   quickening, strengthening and absolving (2)

quickly
73   Thy people pray, come quickly, King of kings (5)
208   The three sad days are quickly sped (3)
290   Even so, Lord, quickly come to thy final harvest-home (4)

quicksands
632   mid mists and rocks and quicksands still guides (2)

quiet
40, 41   bestow on us who rest in you ... a quiet night (2)
40, 41   the blessing of a quiet night (2)
370   Christ in quiet, Christ in danger (6)
600, 601   quiet of a steadfast faith, calm of a call obeyed (2)
640   hie thee to thy quiet home (3)
670   When I come before thy Word, quiet my anxiety (2)

quietly
475   so let me quietly in thy rays imbue me (3)

quietness
38, 39   rest in night's enfolding quietness (2)
652, 653   Drop thy still dews of quietness (4)

quit
145   Now quit your care and anxious fear and worry (1)

quite
36   Now, ere day fadeth quite, we see the evening light (2)

quiver
562   Hell's foundations quiver at the shout of praise (2)

rabbit
114   a ragged robe of rabbit skin enwrapped his beauty round (2)

race
50   comes, in God his Father's name, to save our sinful race (4)
54   Mighty God and Mary's son, eager now his race to run (2)
82   bore the Savior of our race (2)
85, 86   O Savior of our fallen race (1)
85, 86   how once, to save our fallen race (3)
88   he on Adam's fallen race sheds the fullness of his grace (3)
120   to heal and save a race undone (4)
146, 147   Your love, O Lord, our sinful race has not returned (3)
295   Sing praise to our Creator, O you of Adam's race (1)
368   every tongue and race combine (4)
379   every child of every race (2)
394, 395   your arms embrace all now despised for creed or race (3)
431   rising sun renews the race that measures all our days (2)
450, 451   heirs of Israel's chosen race, ye ransomed from the fall (4)
452   grace when Christ restores the fallen race (3)
467   ever watchful o'er our race (1)
490   When we have run with patience the race ... know the joy (3)
529   Join hands ... whate'er your race may be (2)
531   descend on our apostate race (1)
542   the Day-star clear and bright of every race and nation (1)
545   strive in the Christian race (2)
546   a heavenly race demands thy zeal (1,4)
552, 553   Run the straight race through God's good grace (2)
568   bind in thy love every nation and race (4)
580   since the childhood of our race (3)
581   Love can exclude no race or creed if honored be God's Name (6)
603, 604   Where generation, class, or race divide us to our shame (3)
607   O God of every nation, of every race and land (1)
607   from pride of race and nation and blindness to your way (2)
609   where sound the cries of race and clan (1)
625   Ye blessed souls at rest, who ran this earthly race (2)
630   word is published in the tongues of every race (4)
709   O God of Israel, be the God of this succeeding race (2)

races
542   In Christ all races meet, their ancient feuds forgetting (2)
573   Races and peoples, lo, we stand divided (2)

Rachel
231   O Rachel, cease your weeping (2/12-28)

racing
211   Then shout beneath the racing skies (2)

radiance
5   pour down thy radiance from above (2)
85, 86   bathes all the world in radiance bright (4)
193   His risen flesh with radiance glowed (2)
357   shed on them the radiance of thy heavenly light (4)
441, 442   from the cross the radiance streaming adds more luster (3)
543   with his radiance fill those fairer purer skies (4)

580   flung the suns in burning radiance through ... space (1)
632   we praise thee for the radiance that... scripture's page (1)

radiancy
6   Fill me, radiancy divine (3)
624   what radiancy of glory, what bliss beyond compare (1)

radiant
33- 35   you make the daytime radiant with the sunlight (1)
48   O day of radiant gladness, O day of joy and light (1)
55   Our faith reflects those radiant beams (5)
111   Son of God, love's pure light radiant beams (3)
111   radiant beams from thy holy face (3)
114   Come kneel before the radiant boy (4)
180   Come ... with glad smile and radiant brow (2)
214   Wide unfold the radiant scene (2)
409   amid their radiant orbs be found (3)
475   let thy radiant beauty light mine eyes to see my duty (3)
627   radiant cloud by day (3)

rage
246   Still rage the fires of hate today (3)
458   What makes this rage and spite (4)
608   calm amid its rage didst sleep (2)
687, 687   his rage we can endure (3)

ragged
114   a ragged robe of rabbit skin enwrapped his beauty round (2)

raging
247   Herod the King, in his raging charged he hath this day (2)
425   horse ... rider ... sword he cast into the raging sea (1)
608   hushed their raging at thy word (2)

raiment
133, 134   your raiment whiter than the snow (1)
232   who wear the spotless raiment (2/11-1)
709   give us each day our daily bread ... raiment fit provide (3)

rain
191   rain and dew and gleams of glory from ... thy face (4)
291   the breezes and the sunshine, and soft refreshing rain (1)
292   At temper fair with gentle air the sunshine and the rain (2)
388   sweetly distills in the dew and the rain (4)
412   Hail, wind, and rain, loud blowing snow-storms (2)
633   living rain from heaven descending (1)
667   to cheer it after rain (1)

rain's
8   Sweet the rain's new fall sunlit from heaven (2)

rains
228   With your soft, refreshing rains break our drought (4)
235   a house to stand unshaken by floods or winds or rains (3)

raise

3, 4	to God the Holy Ghost we raise our ... praise (5)
5	all glory to the Spirit raise (5)
29, 30	to thee our evening prayer we raise (2)
29, 30	to God the Holy Ghost we raise our ... praise (3)
49	our joyful hearts and voices raise (3)
50	Hosanna in the highest strains the Church ... can raise (5)
50	the highest strains the Church on earth can raise (5)
66	by thine all-sufficient merit raise us (4)
66	raise us to thy glorious throne (4)
87	born to raise us from the earth (3)
96	while we raise our hearts in love (4)
124	to ... Holy Ghost we raise our equal and unceasing praise (5)
136, 137	for which in joyful strains we raise the voice of prayer (4)
154, 155	to thee, now high exalted, our melody we raise (4)
179	all that now is fallen raise to life again (6)
190	Raise your weary eyelids, Mary (2)
191	alleluia! Hearts and voices heavenward raise (1)
193	God the Holy Ghost, we raise (5)
199, 200	Come, ye faithful, raise the strain of triumphant gladness (1)
203	to God your hears and voices raise (5)
210	hearing, may raise the victor strain (2)
214	raise our hearts to reach thy height (4)
232	from all unrighteous mammon, O raise our eyes anew (2/9-21)
232	raise the ceaseless song (2/11-1)
233, 234	with hearts of gladness raise due hymns (1)
237	Let us now our voices raise, wake the day with gladness (1)
245	Our thanks we raise that all John wrote bears witness (3)
284	The joyous notes pursue and louder anthems raise (8)
288	Lord, for these our souls shall raise ... praise (2)
290	raise the song of harvest-home (1)
290	raise the glorious harvest-home (4)
299	From living waters raise new saints (2)
335	And I will raise them up on the last day (R)
345	Savior, again to thy dear Name we raise ... praise (1)
358	Yet at the grave shall we raise up our glad song (3)
382	in my heart, though not in heaven, I can raise thee (3)
391	high as the heaven our voices raise (4)
399	your voice in homage raise to him who makes all one (3)
401	With heaven our songs we raise (5)
404	each day we live our psalm to you we raise (1)
415	Through all eternity, to thee a joyful song I'll raise (5)
416	Christ our God, to thee we raise this our hymn (R)
420	Let all rejoice who have a voice to raise (5)
426	No, the Church delights to raise psalms and hymns (4)
430	O come, our voices raise, sounding God Almighty praise (1,6)
444	a Savior comes among us to raise us up to heaven (2)
465, 466	Eternal life, raise me from death (2)
480	Hosanna our glad voices raise, hosanna to our King (3)
495	all your noblest anthems raise (4)
543	till sovereign love in worlds above the glory raise (3)
556, 557	Your clear hosannas raise, and alleluias loud (3)
562	Christians, lift your voices, loud your anthems raise (2)
572	we would raise, O Christ, one song (1)
618	raise the glad strain (1)

618	all saints triumphant raise the song (3)
619	ye citizens of heaven, O sweetly raise (1)
619	Then let the holy city raise the strain (3)
623	while for thy grace, Lord ... voices of praise ... raise (3)
623	voices of praise thy blessed people eternally raise (3)
681	hymns thy people raise, the psalms and anthems strong (3)

raised

122, 123	alleluia is the anthem ever raised by choirs on high (1)
136, 137	faithful hearts are raised on high by this ... mystery (4)
139	He taught, he healed, he raised the dead (2)
215	Thou hast raised our human nature ... to God's right hand (3)
278	raised high with saints and angels, in Jerusalem above (4)
296	We know that Christ is raised and dies no more (1)
336	in our hearts as in thy heaven ... anthems raised (3)
336	be enraptured anthems raised (3)
453	has raised up a ladder of mercy for me (R)
623	Now, in the meanwhile, with hearts raised on high (4)

raises

| 522, 523 | his love his people raises over self to reign as kings (4) |

raising

97	laud and honor raising (3)
128	prayer and praising, gladly raising (3)
244	unto thee our voices raising (3)
366	Hark, the loud celestial hymn angel choirs ... raising (2)
366	angel choirs above are raising (2)
393	raising hymns in glad accord (1)

ram

| 173 | The Paschal Lamb, like Isaac's ram (2) |

ramparts

| 720 | o'er the ramparts we watched (1) |

ran

| 625 | Ye blessed souls at rest, who ran this earthly race (2) |

rang

99	when lo! above the earth rang out the angel chorus (2)
106	heaven's whole orb with alleluias rang (3)
114	but as the hunter braves drew nigh, the angel-song rang (2)
114	angel-song rang loud and high (2)
426	heaven with alleluias rang when creation was begun (1)

rank

| 324 | Rank on rank the host of heaven spreads its vanguard (3) |
| 701 | e'en as though they were not rank and fortune's hire (2) |

ranks

| 435 | through all ranks of creatures, to the central height (3) |
| 473 | the hosts of God in conquering ranks combine (1) |

ransom
56	O come, O come, Emmanuel and ransom captive Israel (1,8)
161	the ransom of a world set free (4)
162	in that same flesh our ransom paid (1)

ransomed
38, 39	let him never lead astray those you have ransomed (3)
38. 39	those you have ransomed by your blood (3)
57, 58	cause of endless exultation to his ransomed worshipers (3)
119	bring our ransomed souls at last where they need no star (4)
202	in triumph went the ransomed (2)
231, 232	till all the ransomed number who stand before the throne (3)
244	thee with all thy ransomed praising ever ... evermore (3)
410	ransomed, healed, restored, forgiven (1)
450, 451	heirs of Israel's chosen race, ye ransomed from the fall (4)
492	rules and guides the world he ransomed (4)
494	for ransomed sinners slain (4)
527	light ... o'er his ransomed people shed (2)
539	let none whom he hath ransomed fail to greet him (4)
645, 646	my ransomed soul he leadeth (2)

ransoming
329, 331	shed for this world's ransoming (1)

ransoms
411	he healeth thine infirmities and ransoms thee from death (4)

Raphael
282, 283	Send from the heavens Raphael thine archangel (4)

rapture
57, 58	with what rapture gaze we on those glorious scars (3)
257	Anna welcomes Israel's hope, with holy rapture fired (3)
556, 557	true rapture, noblest mirth (2)
717	my heart with rapture thrills like that above (2)

raptured
181	Soon ... each raptured tongue his endless praise proclaim (4)

rapturous
213	his rapturous praises, repeat (5)

rare
119	offered gifts most rare at that manger rude and bare (3)
127	Eastern sages at his cradle make oblations rich and rare (3)
201	At early morn, with spices rare (2)
463, 464	you will see rare beasts and have unique adventures (1)

rattling
607	fear of rattling saber, from dread of war's increase (3)

ray
12, 13	O Spirit, love's life-giving ray (4)
14, 15	you, from the morn till evening's ray (1)
21, 22	you send the early morning ray (1)

27, 28	You joined the morn and evening ray (2)
29, 30	shed thou within our hearts thy ray (1)
180	not one darksome cloud is dimming ... morning ray (3)
180	dimming yonder glorious morning ray (3)
228	shed on us a shining ray (1)
232	last and greatest prophet, he saw the dawning ray (2/6-24)
267	promise shone with cheering ray on waiting saints of old (1)
370	glorious sun's life-giving ray (4)
371	where the Gospel day sheds not its glorious ray (1)
419	Sun of our life, thy quickening ray sheds ... the glow (2)
640	Watchman, does its beauteous ray ... hope foretell (1)
659, 660	in hope that sends a shining ray far down the ... way (4)
666	My longing eyes look out for thy enlivening ray (3)

rays

210	the Lord in rays eternal of resurrection light (2)
376	earth and heaven reflect thy rays (2)
475	so let me quietly in thy rays imbue me (3)
543	while rays divine stream all abroad (1)

reach

214	raise our hearts to reach thy height (4)
230	until you reach the promised goal, a kingdom to inherit (3)
273, 274	by hope of God united they reach to heaven above (1)
320	never canst thou reach his due (1)
369	soaring spirits upward rise to reach the burning throne (2)
414	Honor great our God befitteth, who his majesty can reach (2)
488	may I reach heaven's joys, bright heaven's Sun (3)
510	our souls, how heavily they go to reach eternal joys (2)
573	building proud towers which shall not reach to heaven (3)
629	We limit not the truth of God to our poor reach of mind (1)
674	How can your pardon reach and bless the unforgiving heart (2)
689	Thou didst reach forth thy hand and mine enfold (2)

reached

253	they reached the promised rest (3)
453	many millions have climbed it and reached Zion's hill (2)
647	some I love have reached the end (2)
672	till ... we have reached the shore (4)

reacheth

248, 249	who its perfect wisdom reacheth ... joy possesseth (3)

read

267	The prophet gave the sign for faithful folk to read (2)
415	But thou canst read it there (2)
455, 456	we read thee in the sky above (2)
455, 456	we read thee in the earth below (2)
455, 456	read thee ... in seas that swell and streams that flow (2)
455, 456	read thee best in him who came to bear for us the cross (3)
455, 456	We read thy power to bless and save (2)
455, 456	still more in resurrection light we read the fullness (4)
455, 456	in resurrection light we read the fullness of thy might (4)
627	guide and chart wherein we read of realms beyond the sky (2)
638, 639	look on thy hands, and read it there (2)

ready

16, 17	with fervent heart and ready mind (1)
228	make us ready to receive gifts from your unbounded store (5)
232	youthful and unready, she heard the angel's word (2/8-15)
411	his wrath is ever slow to rise and ready to abate (3)
546	forget the steps already trod, and onward urge thy way (2)
574, 575	a ready mind to understand the meaning of thy chastening (1)
582, 583	Already in the mind of God that city riseth fair (4)
615	And lo, already on the hills the flags of dawn appear (3)
671	I have already come (4)

real

409	What though no real voice nor sound ... be found (3)

realm

366	opened wide the realm of heaven (6)
474	Were the whole realm of nature mine (4)
540	break down the realm of Satan, death, and sin (3)

realms

93	Angels, from the realms of glory (1)
209	in realms of clearer light we may behold you as you are (4)
324	Light of Life descendeth from the realms of endless day (3)
359	forth may they go to tell all realms thy grace (5)
454	came with peace from realms on high (1)
494	now lives in realms of light (4)
519, 520	from celestial realms descending (2)
544	People and realms of every tongue dwell on his love (3)
580	known the ecstasy of winging through untraveled realms (3)
580	untraveled realms of space (3)
613	When shall all hatred cease, as in the realms above (2)
625	through the realms of light fly at your Lord's command (1)
627	guide and chart wherein we read of realms beyond the sky (2)

reap

289	They reap not where they labored (3)
289	we reap what they have sown (3)

reapers

125, 126	joyous as when the reapers bear their ... treasures home (2)

reaping

424	For the plowing, sowing, reaping (1)

rear

391	what lasting honors shall we rear ... to thy Name (3)

reason

293	there's not any reason ... why I shouldn't be one too (2)
293	not any reason -- no, not the least (2)
369	Our reason stretches all its wings (3)
369	Our reason ... climbs above the skies (3)
434	nor wit can guess, nor reason prove which of the letters (3)
452	faith achieves what reason planned (3)

reason's
409 In reason's ear they all rejoice (3)

rebellious
236 Turn our rebellious hearts (3)

rebirth
295 who sanctifies and guides us, made strong in our rebirth (3)

reborn
296 Reborn we share with him an Easter life (2)
593 Dying, we live, and are reborn (5)
593 reborn through death's dark night to endless day (5)

recall
304 in awe and wonder to recall his life laid down for me (1)
581 Let us recall that in our midst dwells God's begotten Son (5)

receive
37 Worthy are thou ... to receive our hallowed praises, Lord (3)
53 he will then receive thee, heal thee, and forgive thee (3)
78, 79 in this world of sin, where meek souls will receive him (3)
100 let earth receive her King (1)
144 through your saving sacrifice receive your gift of grace (3)
213 while his grace we receive from his bounty (2)
215 portals high are lifted to receive their heavenly King (1)
219 The heavens with joy receive their Lord (2)
228 make us ready to receive gifts from your unbounded store (5)
231 with "Lord, receive my spirit" (2/12-26)
231 May we, in ... weakness, receive your power divine (2/4-25)
279 followed thee, obeyed, adored, our grateful hymn receive (1)
339 through the gifts thou here dost give me ... receive me (3)
339 as thy guest in heaven receive me (3)
354 At your coming may the martyrs receive you (1)
374 Jesus is worthy to receive honor and power divine (3)
435 Humbled for a season, to receive a Name (2)
493 He speaks, and listening to his voice ... receive (4)
493 new life the dead receive (4)
495 Worship ... thou art worthy to receive (4)
500 make us eternal truth receive (3)
593 for in our giving we receive (4)
657 Come, almighty to deliver, let us all thy life receive (2)
670 What thy Spirit doth reveal, that may I in faith receive (3)
693 wilt receive, wilt welcome, pardon, cleanse, relieve (4)
699 O receive my soul at last (1)

received
278 blessed Mother who received the angel's word (1)
459, 460 And have the bright immensities received our risen Lord (1)
461 though the cloud from sight received him (2)
632 The Church from our dear Master received the word divine (2)
680 Before ... earth received her frame (3)

receives
70 God receives his wayward children (3)

305, 306   faith still receives the cup as from thy hand (2)

receiving
48   grace more grace receiving on this blest day of light (3)
334   By your Blood new life receiving (2)

recite
364   apostles glorious company ... thy constant praise recite (4)
388   Thy bountiful care, what tongue can recite (4)

reclaim
85, 86   his banished children to reclaim (5)
152   our weakened souls to health reclaim (3)

reclaimed
537   new-born souls, whose days, reclaimed from error's ways (4)

reclining
117, 118   angels adore him in slumber reclining (2)

recoil
148   evils wrought by human pride recoil on unrepentant heads (3)

recollections
238, 239   with affection's recollections greet we your return again (1)

recompense
63, 64   to recompense each hidden sin (3)

reconciled
87   God and sinners reconciled (1)
104   By whose descent among us The worlds are reconciled (4)
495   opened is the gate of heaven, reconciled are we with God (2)
674   then, reconciled to God and man (4)

reconciles
139   he cleanses, reconciles to God (3)

reconcileth
183   Christ, who only is sinless, reconcileth sinners (2)
183   Christ ... reconcileth sinners to the Father (2)

reconciling
531   preach the reconciling word (2)

record
49   with thanks his dying love record (3)
136, 137   from the cloud, the Holy One bears record to the only Son (2)
231   for his faithful record we praise you evermore (2/12-27)
531   far and nigh the triumphs of the cross record (4)
630   record of the revelation showing God to every age (3)

records
245   Your great I AM's Saint John records (2)

recreation

8   praise every morning, God's recreation of the new day (3)

red

187   Through the Red Sea brought at last (1)
199, 200 led them with unmoistened foot through the Red Sea waters (1)
202   the Red Sea past (1)
720   the rockets' red glare, the bombs bursting in air (1)

reddened

131, 132 when water reddened into wine (4)

reddening

138   water reddening into wine proclaims the present Lord (2)

redeem

60   redeem us for eternal day (5)
97   all creation to redeem I alone am able (2)
207   did once upon the cross ... suffer to redeem our loss (1)
207   sinners to redeem and save (2)
479   stream which from sin and sorrow doth the world redeem (3)
541   redeem the time, its hours too swiftly fly (4)
607   redeem the whole creation with your almighty hand (1)

redeemed

106   sing, redeemed, a glad triumphal song (6)
193   thine own redeemed for ever shield (4)
220, 221 by thee redeemed thy praise we sing (1)
256   redeemed for ever and restored (4)
454   in sounds of gladness, leading souls redeemed to heaven (3)
460, 461 Jesus out of every nation hath redeemed us by his blood (1,5)
486   thy flock, redeemed from sinful stain ... praise again (5)
537   redeemed at countless cost from dark despair (2)
630   life redeemed from death and sin (5)
705   a world redeemed by Christ-like love (2)

Redeemer

38, 39   Jesus, Redeemer of the world (1)
40, 41   O Christ, Redeemer of the world (5)
55   Redeemer of the nations come (1)
60   O Christ, Redeemer of us all (1)
82   Babe ... world's Redeemer first revealed his sacred face (2)
85, 86   O Christ, Redeemer virgin-born (6)
116   I come, the great Redeemer cries, to do thy will, O Lord (1)
117, 118 guide where our infant Redeemer is laid (1,5)
133, 134 Jesus, Redeemer of the earth (1)
154, 155 All glory, laud, and honor to thee, Redeemer, King (R)
159   Fount of love, Redeemer kind (5)
165, 166 Jesus Christ, the world's Redeemer ... reigns as King (1)
175   Redeemer, Son of the Father supreme, only begotten of God (6)
179   Maker and Redeemer, life and health of all (4)
216   enlighten our minds, thou Redeemer (4)
229   the deeds our great Redeemer wrought (2)
368   dear Redeemer, in our hearts thy peace proclaim (2)
388   Our Maker, Defender, Redeemer, and Friend (5)

436	Redeemer come, I open wide my heart to thee (4)
460, 461	earth's Redeemer, plead for me (3)
494	their God, Redeemer, King (4)
524	the Church our blest Redeemer saved (1)
568	Father, Redeemer, and Spirit of grace (4)

Redeemer's
163	on the Redeemer's thorn-crowned brow the wonders ... view (1)
171	your Redeemer's conflict see (1)
284	while mortals sing with you their own Redeemer's praise (8)
380	Let the Redeemer's Name be sung through every land (1)
493	O for a thousand tongues to sing my dear Redeemer's praise (1)
509	let our whole soul an offering be to our Redeemer's Name (3)
522, 523	Blest inhabitants of Zion, washed in the Redeemer's blood (4)

redeemeth
| 183 | A lamb the sheep redeemeth (2) |

redeeming
102	through his own redeeming love (5)
105	this holy tide of Christmas doth bring redeeming grace (4)
106	praises of redeeming love they sang (3)
111	with the dawn of redeeming grace (3)
167	we must love him too, and trust in his redeeming blood (5)
188, 189	Love's redeeming work is done (1)
190	those wounds redeeming (2)
273, 274	The words of Paul assure us of Christ's redeeming word (3)
344	triumph in redeeming grace (1)
371	come to bring on thy redeeming wing healing and sight (2)
394, 395	Redeeming God (3)
431	my rock, and my redeeming Lord, in all my words and ways (4)
498	the wonders of redeeming love and my unworthiness (2)
669	what loving wisdom chooseth, redeeming might will do (3)

redeems
| 444 | he visits and redeems us, he grants us liberty (1) |

redemption
68	see the day of earth's redemption, and ever be with thee (3)
278	saw the price of our redemption paid (2)
298	Through Christ's redemption we shall stand (1)
454	Jesus came for our redemption (1)
469, 470	plentiful redemption in the blood that has been shed (2)
492	thus he wrought the full redemption (3)
539	tidings of Jesus, redemption and release (R)
540	spread the glory of redemption (2)
666	source and spring from whence redemption ever flows (4)

redemption's
| 108 | on this day of days tell out redemption's story (1) |

redress
| 145 | who feed the hungry in their need, and wrongs redress (4) |
| 462 | this wicked earth redress (3) |

redressing
53   Once he came in blessing, all our ills redressing (1)

reecho
432   each jubilant chord reecho around (3)
619   let all your choirs reecho to the height (2)

reed
165, 166   vinegar, and spear, and reed (3)
170   A sceptered reed ... they thrust into your hand (3)

refine
226, 227   Every bitter tear refine (2)
445, 446   highest gift of grace should flesh and blood refine (4)
636, 637   I only design thy dross to consume and thy gold to refine (4)

reflect
245   words reflect, like eagles' wings, the glory of our Lord (1)
376   earth and heaven reflect thy rays (2)
543   In honor to his Name reflect that sacred light (3)

reflected
31, 32   moon with cool reflected glow will bring the silences (3)
231   reflected from your throne (1)
232   ever shine in splendor reflected from your throne (1)

reflects
55   Our faith reflects those radiant beams (5)
681   reflects the vast design by which thy house is built (4)

refrain
366   prophets swell the loud refrain (3)

refresh
38, 39   refresh us now with restful sleep (4)
245   O Word made flesh, your deeds and words refresh (3)
245   your deeds and words refresh our hearts like dew (3)
320   Lord, refresh us and defend us (5)
343   Shepherd of souls, refresh and bless thy chosen (1)
344   O refresh us, traveling through this wilderness (1)
718   Refresh thy people on their toilsome way (4)

refreshed
327, 328   with souls refreshed, we render thanks to God (2)

refreshing
138   those refreshing streams which you alone can give (3)
228   With your soft, refreshing rains break our drought (4)
291   the breezes and the sunshine, and soft refreshing rain (1)
658   longs my soul, O God, for thee and thy refreshing grace (1)
683, 684   Where is the soul-refreshing view of Jesus and his word (2)

refreshment
360, 361   light in our blindness, in our toil refreshment (3)

refuge
51	school for the faithful, refuge for the sinner (2)
76	our refuge, and our great reward (3)
318	Here is my robe, my refuge, and my peace (4)
393	God it is who grants us sure retreat and refuge nigh (2)
471	the sinner's refuge here below (5)
636, 637	to you that for refuge to Jesus have fled (1)
699	Other refuge have I none (2)

refuse
124	let not our slothful hearts refuse the guidance (4)
392	Let those refuse to sing that never knew our God (2)
598	shall we again refuse thee (3)
706	for my heart would still refuse you (2)

refused
104	God's blood upon the spear-head, God's love refused again (3)

regal
97	Here no regal pomp we see (1)

regenerated
176, 177	By the same Spirit we, regenerated (2)
176, 177	regenerated into the body of our risen Savior (2)

regions
358	rest with your saints in the regions of light (1,4)
453	here are regions of light, here are mansions of bliss (4)
484, 485	now prepares in heavenly regions unfailing mansions (1)

reign
16, 17	who, conquering death, reign gloriously with God (4)
38, 39	who, conquering death, reign gloriously with God (5)
57, 58	Alleluia, Christ the Lord returns to reign (1)
57, 58	Alleluia, Thou shalt reign, and thou alone (4)
63, 64	bid the saints their reign begin (3)
66	born to reign in us forever (3)
67	as befits his holy reign (3)
112	heaven and earth shall flee away when he comes to reign (2)
125, 126	his reign no end shall know (5)
128	King for ever, ceasing never over us all to reign (2)
156	then take, O God, thy power and reign (5)
170	To mock your reign ... they made a crown of thorns (1)
185, 186	the reign of death was ended (2)
194, 195	rest and reign with him in heaven (4)
216	day when the Christ ascends, high in the heavens to reign (R)
238, 239	Therefore, ye that reign in glory (3)
270	He that comes despised shall reign (2)
273, 274	who with the Holy Spirit, now reign, blest Three in One (4)
275	Now they reign in heavenly glory (4)
344	May we ever reign with thee in endless day (3)
366	infinite thy vast domain, everlasting is thy reign (1)
375	Through all his kingdom's wide domain ... justice reign (3)
375	his righteousness and justice reign (3)
379	Love for ever o'er the universe must reign (3)

435	with his Father's glory o'er the earth to reign (6)
448, 449	for us he went on high to reign (5)
472	thou art our Lord, Thou dost for ever reign (5)
483	they reign with him above (5)
484, 485	Thy reign extend world without end (2)
492	your songs exalt his reign (1)
494	Crown him of lords the Lord, who over all doth reign (4)
518	hereafter in thy glory evermore with thee to reign (4)
521	to serve thee is to reign (4)
522, 523	his love his people raises over self to reign as kings (4)
542	heal its ancient wrong, come, Prince of Peace, and reign (3)
544	Jesus shall reign where'er the sun (1)
561	they with the King of glory shall reign eternally (4)
582, 583	O holy city ... where Christ, the Lamb, doth reign (1)
585	throned in easy state to reign (6)
597	Christ's promised reign of peace (1)
607	dawns the morning glorious when truth and justice reign (4)
613	Where is thy reign of peace, and purity, and love (2)
616	Hail, in the time appointed, his reign on earth begun (1)

reigned

55	reigned once more from God's high throne (3)

reignest

292	thou reignest (1)
423	Thou reignest in glory, thou rulest in light (4)
569	show forth thy pity on high where thou reignest (1)

reigneth

339	high o'er all the heavens he reigneth (1)
390	over all things he gloriously reigneth (2)

reigning

161	They stumbled on a mystery: Messiah reigning from a tree (3)
162	for God is reigning from the tree (2)
278	beholds her Son and Savior reigning as the Lord of love (4)
278	looked upon her Son ... reigning from the awful tree (2)

reigns

50	highest heavens in which he reigns shall give ... praise (5)
100	Joy to the world! the Savior reigns (2)
165, 166	Jesus Christ, the world's Redeemer ... reigns as King (1)
165, 166	from that cross now reigns as King (1)
182	our Savior with the Father reigns (3)
183	the Prince of life, who died, reigns immortal (3)
185, 186	stripped of power, no more he reigns (2)
215	Jesus reigns, adored by angels (3)
222	he reigns invisible but near (2)
222	He reigns, but with a love that shares the troubles (3)
222	He reigns in heaven until the hour when he ... shall come (4)
386, 387	period, power, and enterprise commences, reigns and ends (1)
396, 397	the Son, and him who reigns with them in highest heaven (3)
401	The God of Abraham praise, who reigns enthroned above (1)
401	the God who reigns on high the great archangels sing (4)
401	glorious with his saints in light, for ever reigns (3)

408	Sing praise to God who reigns above (1)
481	The Lord the Savior reigns, the God of truth and love (2)
505	his dear Son, who reigns above (5)
527	the one almighty Father reigns in love for evermore (4)
544	Blessings abound wheree'er he reigns (4)
545	now he reigns above (4)

rejected

102	scorned, rejected, tears and smiles like us he knew (4)
157	the same stone which the builders rejected (R)
158	By foes derided, by thine own rejected, O most afflicted (1)

rejects

| 452 | Glorious the day when Christ fulfills what self rejects (4) |
| 452 | what self rejects yet feebly wills (4) |

rejoice

50	let heaven rejoice, let earth be glad (1)
56	Rejoice, rejoice, Emmanuel shall come to thee, O Israel (R)
68	Rejoice, rejoice, believers, and let your lights appear (1)
103	therefore rejoice Jerusalem (1)
107	Good Christian friends, rejoice (1-3)
107	rejoice with heart and soul and voice (1-3)
157	we will rejoice and be glad in it (R)
180	let the whole wide earth rejoice (1)
205	Good Christians all, rejoice and sing (1)
205	let all the earth rejoice and say (2)
209	but in his promise we rejoice (2)
212	rejoice in Christ (1)
212	again rejoice and on his praises dwell (1)
213	arise and rejoice in the day thou wast born (1)
222	Rejoice, the Lord of life ascends in triumph (1)
231	the lot fell to Matthias for whom we now rejoice (2/2-24)
250	rejoice, with thanks embrace another year of grace (1-3,5)
268, 269	in my Savior I rejoice (4)
373	sun and moon, rejoice before him (1)
376	call us to rejoice in thee (2)
377, 378	come ye before him and rejoice (1)
379	God is love, let earth rejoice (1)
392	Hosanna, hosanna! Rejoice, give thanks and sing (R)
400	Fair rising morn, with praise rejoice (2)
409	In reason's ear they all rejoice (3)
413	calling the whole world to rejoice (2)
420	Let all rejoice who have a voice to raise (5)
426	Saints below, with heart and voice ... rejoice (5)
426	still in songs of praise rejoice (5)
432	rejoice in his word, ye angels of light (1)
437, 438	in God my Savior shall my heart rejoice (1)
443	he for the righteous did rejoice (3)
481	Rejoice, the Lord is King, Your lord and King adore (1)
481	Rejoice, again I say rejoice (R)
481	Rejoice in glorious hope. Our Lord the Judge shall come (4)
493	mournful broken hearts rejoice, the humble poor believe (4)
496, 497	Rejoice, ye heavens; thou earth, reply (3)
556, 557	Rejoice, ye pure in heart! Rejoice, give thanks and sing (1)

556	Rejoice, rejoice, rejoice, give thanks, and sing (R)
556, 557	on, ye pure in heart! Rejoice, give thanks and sing (7)
557	Hosanna, hosanna, rejoice, give thanks, and sing (R)
560	Rejoice and be exceeding glad (9)
606	let us rejoice and be glad now and always (1)
620	they still rejoice in that most happy place (2)
626	Lord, be thy word my rule; in it may I rejoice (1)
667	while in him confiding, I cannot but rejoice (4)
678, 679	rejoice as you draw water from salvation's living spring (1)

rejoices

211	The whole bright world rejoices now (1)
396, 397	in whom his world rejoices (1)
496, 497	the host of heaven rejoices (1)

rejoicing

51	day for rejoicing (3)
181	rejoicing in the Lamb of God, to Christ the eternal King (3)
190	Lift your voice rejoicing, Mary (1)
332	go rejoicing on our way, renewed with strength divine (4)
334	Praise the Lord, rise up rejoicing (1)
347	rejoicing in the Holy Spirit's power (4)
454	to hearts rejoicing, bringing news of sins forgiven (3)
479	angel hosts, rejoicing, make their glad reply (4)
527	one the gladness of rejoicing on the far eternal shore (3)
599	Let our rejoicing rise high as the listening skies (1)
645, 646	home, rejoicing, brought me (3)
649, 650	stand rejoicing in your sight (1)

rekindle

| 352 | increase, rekindle, and restore their love (3) |

relate

| 404 | your mighty acts with joy and fear relate (2) |

relaxing

| 165, 166 | Thy relaxing sinews bend (5) |

release

3, 4	from selfishness our hearts release (3)
53	Come, then, O Lord Jesus, from our sins release us (4)
66	from our fears and sins release us (1)
71, 72	He comes, the prisoners to release (2)
319	in you finds release that we all might live in peace (1)
356	As angels gave poor Lazarus from all his ills release (3)
429	grants the prisoner sweet release (3)
444	The prophets spoke of mercy, of freedom and release (1)
495	Thou didst suffer to release us (1)
501, 502	From inner strife grant us release (5)
539	tidings of Jesus, redemption and release (R)
547	To us on earth he came to bring from sin and fear release (2)
587	by this release (3)
596	pining for the hour that brings release (2)
597	our hearts from envy find release (1)
598	From old unfaith our souls release (3)

607   Lord, strengthen all who labor that we may find release (3)

released
624   there from care released, the shout of them that triumph (3)
625   now, from sin released, behold the Savior's face (2)

relent
564, 565   There's no discouragement shall make him once relent (1)

reliance
162   O cross, our one reliance, hail (5)

relief
228   Source of strength and sure relief (2)

rely
429   How happy they whose hopes rely on Israel's God (2)
522, 523   Jesus, whom their souls rely on (4)

remain
213   Now created again that our lives may remain ... thine (3)
213   lives may remain, throughout time and eternity thine (3)
307   in its fullness undiminished shall for evermore remain (4)
562   but the Church of Jesus constant will remain (4)

remained
185, 186   the victory remained with life (2)

remainest
462   thou in thy everlasting seat remainest God alone (5)

remains
23   do what still remains (1)
185, 186   an empty form alone remains; his sting is lost for ever (2)
235   Four-square ... foundation the Church of Christ remains (3)

remember
85, 86   Remember, Lord of life and grace (3)
105   remember Christ our Savior was born on Christmas Day (1)
146, 147   Remember, Lord ... in your own image were we made (4)
453   remember, each step that by faith we pass o'er (3)
560   Remember your servants, Lord, when you come in ... power (A)
578   Remember, Lord, thy works of old (2)
578   remember not our sin's dark stain (2)
695, 696   we shall remember all the days we lived through (4)

remembered
346   Thy death remembered, feeding thus on thee (1)

rememberest
151   If thou rememberest every sin (1)

remembrance
342   Do this for me in my remembrance (1)

remotely
182   Not throned above, remotely high (3)

remotest
277   Church the strain re-echoes unto earth's remotest ends (3)
530   to earth's remotest bound all may heed the joyful sound (1)
538   thy saving health extend unto earth's remotest end (1)

remove
151   Our works could ne'er our guilt remove (2)
228   remove our stains; bind up all our injuries (4)
522, 523   all fear of want remove (2)
530   word of how the Savior's love ... burden doth remove (3)
530   earth's sore burden doth remove (3)
588, 589   Let not our selfishness and hate this holy seed remove (2)
616   the tide of time shall never his covenant remove (5)
638, 639   thy mercies never shall remove (4)

rend
145   or rend the soul, such grief is not Lent's goal (2)
243   rend the veils of night (2)

render
9   Not here for high and holy things we render thanks (1)
49   Then let us render him his own (3)
199, 200   with the royal feast of feasts, comes its joy to render (3)
300   Glory ... for our food now bestowed render we the Donor (1)
327, 328   with souls refreshed, we render thanks to God (2)
339   there with joy thy praises render unto him (1)
347   render to no one evil (3)
413   New songs of celebration render to him (1)
413   new songs ... render to him who has great wonders done (1)
423   all laud we would render (4)
472   we render back the love thy mercy gave us (4)
475   love and honor will I render (4)

rending
342   all veils thus rending, Emmanuel, our joy unending (3)
457   the rending tomb proclaims thy conquering arm (3)

renew
11   Lord, I my vows to thee renew (2)
44, 45   the fire of love in us renew (3)
88   O renew us, Lord, we pray, with thy Spirit day by day (5)
251   thy loving care renew (2)
256   Renew us with your love, O Lord (4)
353   every day their love renew (2)
366   Lord, renew our hearts within us (7)
501, 502   come to create, renew, inspire (1)
665   he doth still my trust renew (1)

renewed
48   We journey on, believing, renewed with heavenly might (3)
49   in perfect righteousness renewed (2)
232   to tread the way renewed (2/10-28)

332 go rejoicing on our way, renewed with strength divine (4)
348 vows are renewed, and our courage restored (3)
492 till he see, renewed and perfect (4)
528 help us witness to your purpose with renewed integrity (1)
567 youth renewed and frenzy calmed owned thee, the Lord (2)

renews
411 like the eagle he renews the vigor of thy youth (5)
431 rising sun renews the race that measures all our days (2)

renown
292 O Jesus, crowned with all renown (1)

rent
472 speak to our fearful hearts by conflict rent (1)
525 by schisms rent asunder, by heresies distressed (3)

repay
292 repay thee of thine own (3)

repeat
100 while fields and floods, rocks, hills and plains repeat (2)
100 repeat the sounding joy (2)
213 his rapturous praises, repeat (5)
406, 407 repeat the psalm (3)
544 earth repeat the loud amen (5)
704 my acts of faith and love repeat (4)

repeated
320 ordained to be repeated, his memorial ne'er to cease (3)
367 repeated each to each the alternate hymn (1)

repeating
631 each a word from God repeating (2)

repeats
409 nightly to the listening earth repeats the story (2)
409 repeats the story of her birth (2)

repel
40, 41 repel our dread, malicious foe (4)

repent
152 now we repent, and seek thy face (2)

repentance
67 calling us to new repentance (2)
146, 147 grant repentance for our pride (3)

repentant
231 so eager and so bold, thrice failing, yet repentant (2/1-18)

repenting
70 those repenting are forgiven (3)

replenish
68	See that your lamps are burning, replenish them with oil (2)
312	bodies by thy Body fed with thy new life replenish (3)

replied
382	alone, when they replied, thou didst hear me (2)
386, 387	at once, above, beneath, around, all nature ... replied (2)
386, 387	nature without voice or sound replied, O Lord, thou art (2)

replies
128	heaven sings alleluia: alleluia the earth replies (5)

reply
96	the mountains in reply echoing their brave delight (1)
145	reply, reply with love to love most high (1)
154, 155	we with all creation in chrous make reply (2)
374	Worthy the Lamb, our lips reply, for he was slain for us (2)
479	angel hosts, rejoicing, make their glad reply (4)
486	Hosanna Lord, thine angels cry ... thy saints reply (2)
496, 497	Rejoice, ye heavens; thou earth, reply (3)
666	Lord, hear my supplicating voice and graciously reply (1)

repose
42	Jesus, give the weary calm and sweet repose (2)
43	O may my soul on thee repose (3)
357	Think, O Lord, in mercy on the souls ... in death repose (2)
357	in faith gone from us, now in death repose (2)
522, 523	what can shake thy sure repose (1)
636, 637	The soul that to Jesus hath fled for repose (5)
701	Jesus, all my gladness, my repose in sadness (1)

reposeth
46	each flower and tree reposeth (1)

reproach
537	with us the work to share, with us reproach to dare (3)

reproving
255	O strong, reproving Word (2)

request
382	Thou hast granted my request, thou hast heard me (1)

require
605	What does the Lord require for praise and offering (1)

requited
339	be thy love with love requited (3)

rescue
445, 446	second Adam to the fight and to the rescue came (2)
686	to rescue me from danger, interposed his precious blood (2)

rescued
434	But in the grace that rescued man his ... glory shines (2)

720   may the heaven-rescued land praise the Power (2)

rescues
410   rescues us from all our foes (3)

residing
93   God with you is now residing (2)
232   presiding at the council that set the Gentiles free (2/10-23)

resignation
159   with ... grief and resignation Mary watched her dying son (2)
594, 595 Save us from weak resignation to the evils we deplore (4)

resigned
159   in death by all forsaken, till his spirit he resigned (3)

resisting
634   never resisting but to increase in faith more and more (1)

resound
492   praises of your Savior let his house resound again (1)
599   let it resound loud as the rolling sea (1)

resoundest
122, 123 Alleluia thou resoundest, true Jerusalem and free (2)

resounding
1, 2   thine is the glory, gleaming and resounding (3)
1, 2   glory, gleaming and resounding through all creation (3)
65   Lift high your praise resounding (2)
413   Joyfully, heartily resounding (2)
458   resounding all the day hosannas to their King (3)
619   with glad songs resounding wake again (3)

resource
501, 502 You are the seeker's sure resource (2)

resplendent
135   Manifest on mountain height, shining in resplendent light (4)
196, 197 Look there! the Christ, our Brother, comes resplendent (1,4)
196, 197 resplendent from the gallows tree (1,4)
543   his all-resplendent grace he pours around thy head (2)
621, 622 glorious and resplendent, fragile body, shalt thou be (4)

respond
618   Respond, ye souls in endless rest (3)

responsive
281   he rose, responsive to the call, and left his task (3)

rest
10   Only, O Lord, in thy dear love, fit us for perfect rest (6)
10   fit us for perfect rest above (6)
24   thy praise shall sanctify our rest (1)

33-35	strength for our weak hearts, rest for aching bodies (4)
38, 39	give to our wearied bodies rest (2)
38, 39	rest in night's enfolding quietness (2)
40, 41	bestow on us who rest in you ... a quiet night (2)
48	at length our rest attaining, our endless Sabbath day (4)
51	rest for the pilgrim, haven for the weary (2)
66	let us find our rest in thee (1)
74	He offers to the burdened the rest and grace they need (4)
102	We, like Mary, rest confounded (3)
105	God rest you merry, gentlemen, let nothing you dismay (1)
109	o'er Bethlehem it took its rest (4)
113	pangs of my sorrow are soothed and put to rest (1)
113	so rest in the arms of your mother who sings you a la ru (2)
115	What child is this, who, laid to rest, on Mary's lap (1)
139	let us not heed worldly lies nor rest upon our merit (3)
151	I rest upon his faithful word to them of contrite spirit (3)
173	O Jesus blest, my help and rest (4)
192	My flesh in hope shall rest, and for a season slumber (3)
194, 195	rest and reign with him in heaven (4)
228	in our labor inward rest (2)
231, 232	By all your saints still striving, for all ... at rest (1)
253	they reached the promised rest (3)
259	watched by her duteous love, in her fond arms at rest (2)
287	For all the saints, who from their labors rest (1)
287	soon, soon to faithful warriors cometh rest (6)
289	safe rest they in thy keeping (2)
305, 306	with all thy saints on earth and saints at rest (3)
321	Nor let thy spreading Gospel rest (4)
351	rest upon them from above (1)
355	Give rest, O Christ, to your servant with your saints (1)
357	there, the warfare ended, bid them rest in peace (2)
357	Rest eternal grant them, after weary fight (4)
358	Christ the Victorious, give to your servants rest (1,4)
358	rest with your saints in the regions of light (1,4)
376	ocean-depth of happy rest (3)
435	filled it with the glory of that perfect rest (3)
453	when we arrive at the haven of rest, we shall hear (4)
486	But chiefest, in our cleansed breast ... rest (4)
486	Eternal, bid thy Spirit rest (4)
494	takes and bears them for his own, that all in him may rest (2)
498	a home within the wilderness, a rest upon the way (1)
512	lead us to God, our final rest (4)
515	Rest upon this congregation ... fullness of thy grace (2)
517	praise thee without rest (2)
525	the great Church victorious shall be the Church at rest (4)
525	mystic sweet communion with those whose rest is won (5)
541	No time for rest, till glows the western sky (5)
544	the weary find eternal rest (4)
556, 557	the wearied ones shall rest (6)
563	nor dream of peaceful rest (3)
578	Where rest but on thy faithful word (3)
582, 583	O shame to us who rest content while lust and greed (2)
586	lead us to our Sabbath rest (3)
611	he will ease your load and give you rest (6)
616	O'er every foe victorious, he on his throne shall rest (5)

618	Respond, ye souls in endless rest (3)
619	Such song is rest and food and deep delight (6)
621, 622	there no night brings rest from labor (3)
623	crown for the valiant, to weary ones rest (1)
624	Jesus, in mercy bring us to that dear land of rest (4)
625	Ye blessed souls at rest, who ran this earthly race (2)
634	My heart is never set at rest till thy sweet word (1)
641	take thy promised rest (2)
642	sweeter far thy face to see and in thy presence rest (1)
644	'tis manna to the hungry soul, and to the weary, rest (2)
651	I rest me in the thought of rock and trees (1)
652, 653	O Sabbath rest by Galilee, O calm of hills above (3)
664	There ... I find a settled rest while others go and come (3)
670	let my heart find rest in thee (2)
681	till truth from falsehood part ...find no rest (2)
681	our hearts can find no rest (2)
683, 684	Return, O holy Dove, return, sweet messenger of rest (3)
692	Come unto me and rest (1)
702	Lord thou ... dost know where'er I rest, where'er I go (1)
703	Lead us, O Father, to the heavenly rest (3)

rested

| 44, 45 | rested bodies wake in peace (2) |

restful

| 38, 39 | refresh us now with restful sleep (4) |

resting

33-35	for ever resting in the peace of Jesus (5)
183	bright angels attesting, the shroud and napkin resting (6)
692	I found in him a resting place, and he has made me glad (1)

restless

44, 45	Save us from troubled, restless sleep (2)
537	the wayward and the lost, by restless passions tossed (2)
549, 550	tumult of our life's wild, restless sea (1)
567	crowded street, by restless couch ... Gennesaret's shore (2)
579, 608	whose arm hath bound the restless wave (1)
609	among these restless throngs abide (4)
649, 650	For you our restless spirits yearn (3)
658	Why restless, why cast down, my soul (3)

restore

76	shine forth, and let thy light restore (4)
76	restore earth's own true loveliness once more ((4)
144	restore us by your loving care to peace and joy within (2)
162	wealth that did the world restore (4)
162	as by the cross thou dost restore (6)
164	thou dost light and life restore (3)
173	pouring out his life that he might to life restore us (2)
352	increase, rekindle, and restore their love (3)
352	restore their love till life shall end (3)
370	Christ to comfort and restore me (6)
567	restore and quicken (3)
668	shall thy strength restore (4)

restored

10	restored to life and power and thought (1)
16, 17	Lamb of God restored our peace (2)
193	to their longing eyes restored (1)
202	endless life restored in thee (4)
202	from death to endless life restored (5)
205	the life restored (4)
212	O Solitude again command your host from heaven restored (5)
232	wholeness was restored by you, her faithful Master (2/7-22)
256	redeemed for ever and restored (4)
296	The universe restored and whole will sing (4)
340, 341	by your gift of peace restored (2)
348	vows are renewed, and our courage restored (3)
410	ransomed, healed, restored, forgiven (1)
432	For love in creation, for heaven restored (4)
569	earth by thy chastening yet shall ... be restored (4)
569	earth ... shall to freedom and truth be restored (4)
657	see thy great salvation perfectly restored in thee (3)

restores

452	grace when Christ restores the fallen race (3)
663	To wholeness he restores my soul (2)

restoring

187	souls restoring from the dead (2)
528	faith and hope and love restoring (5)
633	saving Word, the world restoring, speak to us (2)

restrain

3, 4	Our hearts and lips may he restrain (2)
42	those who plan some evil from their sin restrain (4)
578	the wrath of nations now restrain (1)

rests

24	and rests not now by day or night (2)
139	This is my dear beloved Son upon whom rests my favor (1)

resurrection

9	resurrection of the world (3)
33-35	mirror of daybreak, pledge of resurrection (2)
51	day of creation, day of resurrection (3)
164	thy cross may bring us to thy joy and resurrection power (4)
181	Sing of his dying love, his resurrection power (2)
183	the glory of Jesus' resurrection (5)
191	glorious life ... immortal, on his resurrection morn (2)
191	we with him to life eternal by his resurrection rise (2)
198	today the branches with the root in resurrection sharing (2)
199, 200	with true affection welcomes ... Jesus' resurrection (3)
199, 200	welcomes in unwearied strains Jesus' resurrection (3)
210	The day of resurrection, Earth tell it out abroad (1)
210	the Lord in rays eternal of resurrection light (2)
335	I am the resurrection, I am the life (4)
346	we here have known the resurrection hour (1)
455, 456	still more in resurrection light we read the fullness (4)
455, 456	in resurrection light we read the fullness of thy might (4)

resurrection's
49   may feel his resurrection's power (2)

retain
518   what they gain from thee, forever ... to retain (4)
518   with the blessed to retain (4)

retains
161   That blood retains its living power (2)

retreat
393   God it is who grants us sure retreat and refuge nigh (2)

retreating
570, 571 honor, peace, and love retreating (2)

retrieved
106   trace we the Babe, who hath retrieved our loss (5)

return
6, 7   joyless is the day's return till thy mercy's beams I see (2)
213   with singing to Zion return (1)
223, 224 Hail this joyful day's return (1)
238, 239 with affection's recollections greet we your return again (1)
355   formed of the earth, and to earth shall we return (1)
355   saying, "You are dust, and to dust you shall return" (1)
358   to the earth shall we all return (2)
358   You came from dust and to dust shall return (3)
435   Christians, this Lord Jesus shall return again (6)
463   great city that has expected your return for years (2)
464   a great city that has expected your return for years (2)
581   with heart and mind and strength now love him in return (2)
593   May we not look for love's return (4)
657   suddenly return, and never, nevermore thy temples leave (2)
683, 684 Return, O holy Dove, return, sweet messenger of rest (3)
704   trembling to its source return (2)
704   return in humble prayer and fervent praise (2)

returned
55   you returned to that same source (3)
146, 147 Your love, O Lord, our sinful race has not returned (3)
146, 147 your love ... not returned but falsified (3)
179   all fresh gifts returned with her returning King (2)

returning
10   New mercies, each returning day around us hover (2)
179   all fresh gifts returned with her returning King (2)
190   welcome with your smiles returning (1)
348   When, at your table, each time of returning (3)

returns
57, 58   Alleluia, Christ the Lord returns to reign (1)
170   road from which no one returns (1)
175   every good gift of the year now with its Master returns (1)
179   bring again our daylight: day returns with thee (6)

219   Lo, he returns ... to his eternal dwelling (1)
431   The dawn returns in splendor, the heavens burn and blaze (2)

reveal
55   reveal yourself in virgin birth (1)
353   reveal your will in all we do (3)
436   thy grace and love in me reveal (4)
452   whose life and death that love reveal which mortals need (1)
509   Come as the light, to us reveal our emptiness and woe (2)
670   What thy Spirit doth reveal, that may I in faith receive (3)

revealed
3, 4   to Christ, revealed in earthly night (5)
29, 30   to Christ revealed in earthly night (3)
77   to shepherds poor the Lord Most High ... was revealed (4)
82   Babe ... world's Redeemer first revealed his sacred face (2)
102   revealed to faithful eye (6)
124   to Christ, revealed in earthly night (5)
146, 147   The covenant, so long revealed to those of faith (2)
413   revealed to every nation his everlasting righteousness (1)
615   day by whose clear shining light all wrong ... revealed (4)
615   all wrong shall stand revealed (4)

Revealer
381   Holy Spirit, Light-Revealer, glory, glory be to thee (4)

revealeth
563   When morn his face revealeth thy dangers all are past (4)

revealing
18   grant us that same revealing light (4c)
610   till your love's revealing light ... dawns (3)

reveals
74   He only to the humble reveals the face of God (3)
674   In blazing light your cross reveals the truth (3)

revelation
320   today the new oblation of the new King's revelation (4)
598   we wait thy revelation (4)
630   record of the revelation showing God to every age (3)

revere
85, 86   earth and sea and sky revere the love of him (5)
248, 249   we, in love adoring, this most blessed Name revere (4)
329-331   this great Sacrament revere (5)
633   Word almighty, we revere you (1)

reverence
307   here in loving reverence bow (2)
652, 653   in deeper reverence, praise (1)

reverent
259   There Joseph at her side in reverent wonder stands (3)
363   to thee in reverent love our hearts are bowed (2)

reverently
109   full reverently upon their knee (5)

reviles
560   Blessed are you when the world reviles ... persecutes (9)

revive
299   revive in us baptismal grace (3)
308, 309   We faint with thirst; revive us (2)
613   revive our longing eyes, which languish for thy sight (4)

reward
53   One who thus endureth bright reward secureth (4)
76   our refuge, and our great reward (3)
151   if nought but just reward we win (1)
217, 218   you will be ever our reward (2)
220, 221   as thou wilt be our great reward (3)
226, 227   boundless mercy our reward (5)
243   no vengeance, no reward (4)
337   between our sins and their reward, we set the passion (2)
406, 407   with thee, Lord, their reward is sure (6)
424   In the just reward of labor (2)
560   for great is your reward in heaven (9)
626   thine arm my strong support; thyself my great reward (2)
682   with the hope of gaining aught, not seeking a reward (5)

rewarder
545   Jesus, the author, finisher, rewarder of our faith (3)

rich
127   Eastern sages at his cradle make oblations rich and rare (3)
285   O happy saint, his sacred page, so rich in ... truth (2)
285   so rich in words of truth and love (2)
288   autumn's rich o'erflowing stores (2)
431   more rich than any prize (3)
474   or thorns compose so rich a crown (3)
500   rich in thy sevenfold energy (3)
580   May our dreams prove rich with promise (4)
585   poor in making many rich (4)
594, 595   rich in things and poor in soul (3)
602   Neighbors are rich and poor (2)
691   May thy rich grace impart strength to my fainting heart (2)

richer
117, 118   richer by far is the heart's adoration (4)

riches
97   By this lowly birth of mine, sinner, riches ... thine (2)
225   pouring on all human souls infinite riches of God (2)
231   leaving earthly treasures, sought riches from above (2/6-11)
417, 418   Power, riches, wisdom, and strength ... are his (2)
693   sight, riches, healing of the mind ... in thee to find (3)

richest
474   my richest gain I count but loss (1)
515   bringing down the richest treasure we can wish (1)
515   richest treasure we can wish or God can send (1)

richly
347   richly from above his love supplies the grace and power (2)

richness
596   feed ... with the richness of thy word (3)

ride
104   This child through David's city Shall ride in triumph by (2)
156   Ride on! ride on in majesty! (1-5)
156   In lowly pomp ride on to die (2,5)
400   you clouds that ride the heavens aloft, O praise him (2)
496, 497   ride on, great Conqueror, till all know thy salvation (3)

rider
425   horse ... rider ... sword he cast into the raging sea (1)

riding
215   riding on the clouds ... to his heavenly palace gate (1)
370   his riding up the heavenly way (2)

rift
182   In every insult, rift, and war (4)

right
9   to serve right gloriously the God (6)
36   To thee of right belong all praise of holy songs (3)
40, 41   with your right hand you will protect those who believe (3)
70   warning us of right and wrong (1)
73   when right shall triumph over wrong (4)
75   he will right the wrong (3)
102   Christ ... set at God's right hand on high (6)
109   right over the place where Jesus lay (4)
145   to fight, to fight till every wrong's set right (3)
153   It is right to give him thanks and praise ever. Amen (2)
185, 186   but now at God's right hand he stands (1)
185, 186   sing to God right thankfully loud songs of alleluia (1)
215   Thou hast raised our human nature ... to God's right hand (3)
215   on the clouds to God's right hand (3)
231   to plead at God's right hand (2/12-26)
266   Said the maiden, "Verily, I am your servant right truly" (6)
293   they followed the right, for Jesus' sake (2)
293   followed the right ... whole of their good lives long (2)
300   God, who thus blessest us, right it is to bless thee (1)
347   hold fast the good, be urgent for the right (3)
364   thou didst ascend to God's right hand in glory evermore (7)
366   In the glory of that land ... set at God's right hand (6)
375   thy creative might that doeth all things well and right (2)
386, 387   from whose right arm, beneath whose eyes (1)
408   all is just and all is right (2)
421   as you sit at God's right hand ... mercy, Lord, upon us (2)

447	now pleads our cause at God's right hand (1)
462	thou art he who shalt by right the nations all possess (3)
477	yield the glory that of right was thine (1)
483	highest place that heaven affords is his ... by right (2)
495	highest praises ... right it is for us to give (4)
535	Then let us adore, and give him his right (4)
545	Thither ... press we to God's right hand (5)
552, 553	Christ is thy strength and Christ thy right (1)
554	when we find ourselves in the place just right (1)
554	till by turning, turning we come round right (1)
564, 565	he will make good his right to be a pilgrim (2)
568	lift up our lives to thy standard of right (3)
607	scorn of truth and right (2)
615	for the everlasting right the silent stars are strong (2)
687, 688	were not the right man on our side (2)
703	Lead us, O Father, in the paths of right (2)

righteous

157	he who is righteous may enter (R)
381	Thy strong word bespeaks us righteous (3)
413	Righteous, commanding, ever glorious (3)
428	people bless the Lord like righteous souls of yore (5)
443	he for the righteous did rejoice (3)
496, 497	O righteous branch, O Jesse's Rod (1)
509	lead us in those paths of life whereon the righteous go (2)
541	by feeblest agents may our God fulfill his righteous will (3)
569	God the All-righteous One, earth hath defied thee (3)
588, 589	let the dew of heaven descend and righteous fruits abound (1)
636, 637	upheld by my righteous, omnipotent hand (2)

righteousness

6, 7	Sun of Righteousness, arise (1)
49	in perfect righteousness renewed (2)
87	hail, the Sun of Righteousness (3)
100	makes the nations prove the glories of his righteousness (4)
116	Thus it becomes us to fulfill all righteousness, he said (2)
116	like him desirous to fulfill God's will in righteousness (4)
120	God's righteousness he thus fulfilled (1)
144	Lord Jesus, Sun of Righteousness, shine in our hearts (1)
145	For righteousness and peace will show their faces (4)
162	save ... from our sin, God's righteousness for all to win (5)
318	Mine is the sin, but thine the righteousness (4)
318	thy Blood, thy righteousness, O Lord, my God (4)
359	eloquent for righteousness that shall all evil break (2)
365	stablish thy righteousness, Savior and friend (2)
368	look upon the Mediator, clothe us with his righteousness (1)
375	his righteousness and justice reign (3)
401	There dwells the Lord, our King ... our Righteousness (3)
413	revealed to every nation his everlasting righteousness (1)
462	before him righteousness shall go, his royal harbinger (1)
490	Clear sun of righteousness, shine on my path (2)
560	Blessed ... who hunger and thirst after righteousness (4)
560	Blessed ... who are persecuted for righteousness sake (8)
615	day of perfect righteousness, the promised day of God (5)

61, 62	Rise up, and give us light (1)
67	let the valleys rise to meet him (2)
68	rise up, ye heirs of glory, the Bridegroom is at hand (2)
87	Joyful, all ye nations, rise (1)
88	God comes down that we may rise (4)
106	rise to adore the mystery of love (1)
124	True spake the prophet from afar who told the rise (2)
124	who told the rise of Jacob's star (2)
170	though empires rise and fall ... Kingdom shall not cease (3)
174	hast opened paradise, and in thee thy saints shall rise (3)
175	Rise from the grave now ... author of life and creation (4)
179	'tis thine own third morning! rise, O buried Lord! (5)
188, 189	Death in vain forbids him rise (1)
188, 189	made like him, like him we rise (3)
190	Let your alleluias rise (1-3)
191	we with him to life eternal by his resurrection rise (2)
211	To him who rose that we might rise (2)
214	Hail the day that sees him rise (1)
232	we, whate'er our station may rise and follow you (2/9-21)
253	Give us wings of faith to rise within the veil (1)
287	the saints triumphant rise in bright array (7)
316, 317	Too soon we rise; we go our several ways (2)
334	Praise the Lord, rise up rejoicing (1)
345	thy peace in death, the hope to rise again (4)
360, 361	hear now thy servants when their joyful voices rise (1)
360, 361	voices rise to thy presence (1)
362	Early in the morning our song shall rise to thee (1)
369	soaring spirits upward rise to reach the burning throne (2)
380	till suns shall rise and set no more (2)
398	power of God that made the mountains rise (1)
411	his wrath is ever slow to rise and ready to abate (3)
444	On prisoners of darkness the sun begins to rise (3)
458	at these themselves displease, and 'gainst him rise (4)
458	They rise, and needs will have my dear Lord made away (5)
462	Rise, God, judge thou the earth in might (3)
510	in vain we strive to rise (3)
543	There on his holy hill a brighter sun shall rise (4)
544	his Name like sweet perfume shall rise (2)
544	rise with every morning sacrifice (2)
544	Let every creature rise and bring peculiar honors (5)
547	Awake, O sleeper, rise from death (1)
551	rise up, ye saints of God (1,2,3)
561	let courage rise with danger (2)
562	Crowns and thrones may perish, kingdoms rise and wane (4)
566	to rise, like incense, each to thee (1)
566	rise, like incense ... in noble thought and deed (1)
574, 575	a new-born people may we rise (4)
579	thus evermore shall rise to thee glad praise (4)
580	Proudly rise our modern cities (2)
599	Let our rejoicing rise high as the listening skies (1)
608	thus evermore shall rise to thee glad hymns of praise (4)
652, 653	let us, like them, without a word, rise up and follow (2)
665	Evermore from his store new-born worlds rise and adore (3)
672	thy people long that thou, their Sun, wouldst rise (2)
685	rise to worlds unknown and behold thee on thy throne (3)

692	look unto me, your morn shall rise (3)
699	spring thou up within my heart, rise to all eternity (3)
716	For her our prayers shall rise to God, above the skies (2)

risen

61, 62	her star is risen, her light grows bright (2)
87	Risen with healing in his wings (3)
144	we shall be at one with you, Lord, risen from the tomb (4)
174	risen Lord, all praise to thee with the Spirit ever be (4)
176, 177	regenerated into the body of our risen Savior (2)
178	Alleluia, alleluia, Give thanks to the risen Lord (R)
178	Jesus has died and has risen (2)
180	He is risen, he is risen! Tell it out with joyful voice (1)
180	He is risen ... He hath opened heaven's gate (4)
180	risen to a holier state (4)
183	Christ indeed from death is risen (8)
184	Christ the Lord is risen again (1)
190	Christ has risen from the tomb (1)
191	Jesus ... now is risen from the dead (1)
191	Christ is risen (3,4)
191	we are risen! Shed upon us heavenly grace (4)
193	the apostles saw their risen Lord (1)
193	His risen flesh with radiance glowed (2)
193	Christ was risen from the grave (2)
193	All praise, O risen Lord, we give to thee (5)
199, 200	from three days' sleep in death as a sun hath risen (2)
201	For Christ is risen from the tomb (1)
201	The Lord is risen from the dead (3)
201	in praise of Christ, our risen Lord (4)
202	All praise be thine, O risen Lord (5)
204	Forth he came at Easter, like the risen grain (3)
204	quick from the dead my risen Lord is seen (3)
205	The Lord of life is risen today (2)
205	Your Name we bless, O risen Lord (4)
206	how they had seen the risen Lord, he doubted (3)
207	Jesus Christ is risen today ... our triumphant holy day (1)
208	all glory to our risen Head (3)
210	for Christ the Lord is risen, our joy that hath no end (3)
217, 218	O risen Christ, ascended Lord (3)
220, 221	O risen Christ, ascended Lord, all praise to thee (4)
232	her Lord, the risen Christ (2/7-22)
232	saw the risen Savior and placed his faith in him (2/10-23)
242	He saw thee risen (4)
278	Sing again the joys of Mary when she saw the risen Lord (3)
299	let new tongues hail the risen Lord (2)
305, 306	Come, risen Lord, and deign to be our guest (1)
307	Risen, ascended, glorified (5)
422	crucified and risen might of Christ, the incarnate Word (2)
459	And have the bright immensities received our risen Lord (1)
468	he's risen from darkness ... he's 'scended into glory (4)
570, 571	Risen Lord, shall yet the city be the city of despair (5)

rises

208	he rises glorious from the dead (3)
501, 502	O Holy Spirit, by whose breath life rises vibrant (1)

501, 502	life rises vibrant out of death (1)
667	it is the Lord who rises with healing in his wings (1)

riseth

204	Now the green blade riseth from the buried grain (1)
582, 583	Already in the mind of God that city riseth fair (4)

rising

73	O haste the rising of the morn (3)
125, 126	To hail thy rising, Sun of life, the ... nations come (2)
219	His rising, his ascension sing with grateful adoration (2)
284	all adored your rising Lord with joy unknown (6)
294	one with his rising, freed and forgiven (2)
325	when I fall on my knees, with my face to the rising sun (R)
400	Fair rising morn, with praise rejoice (2)
415	When all thy mercies, O my God, my rising soul surveys (1)
431	rising sun renews the race that measures all our days (2)
588, 589	the rising plant destroy (3)
590	O Jesus Christ, may grateful hymns be rising (1)
590	hymns be rising in every city for your love and care (1)
599	facing the rising sun of our new day begun (1)
630	Deeds and words and death and rising (2)
673	first ones ... to know of the rising of Jesus (3)
680	before the rising sun (4)

rite

329-331	for the newer rite is here (5)

rites

33-35	Therefore we come now evening rites to offer (3)
329, 331	its rites demand (3)

riven

286	whose hearts were riven, sore with woe and anguish tried (4)
308, 309	Grant when the veil is riven, we may behold, in heaven (3)
454	now the gate of death is riven (3)

river

120	in the river shared our stain (1)
192	since Jesus crossed the river (2)
275	now they drink, as from a river, holy bliss and infinite (4)
363	from thee have flowed, as from a mighty river, our faith (4)
370	his baptism in the Jordan river (2)
405	The purple-headed mountain, the river running by (2)
522, 523	Who can faint when such a river ever ... thirst assuage (2)

rivers

244	See the rivers four that gladden, with their streams (2)
413	Rivers and seas and torrents roaring, honor the Lord (3)
636, 637	the rivers of woe shall not thee overflow (3)
681	All beauty speaks of thee: the mountains and the rivers (3)

road

10	a road to bring us daily nearer God (5)

149	we walk the road, Lord Jesus, that you trod (2)
156	thy humble beast pursues his road with palms ... strowed (1)
170	set you with taunts along that road (1)
170	road from which no one returns (1)
181	You pilgrims on the road to Zion's city, sing (3)
512	holiness, the road that we must take to dwell with God (3)
599	Stony the road we trod, bitter the chastening rod (2)
647	I know not where the road will lead I follow day by day (1)
647	Through light and dark the road leads on (3)
683, 684	a light to shine upon the road that leads me to the Lamb (1)
683, 684	purer light ... mark the road that leads me to the Lamb (5)

roadway
| 104 | lie within the roadway To pave his kingdom come (2) |

roar
| 299 | rush of wind and roar of flame (1) |
| 428 | O storms and thunder's roar, O fields and forests bless (3) |

roaring
| 413 | Rivers and seas and torrents roaring, honor the Lord (3) |

rob
| 161 | He lived to rob death of its sting (1) |

robber
| 468 | nailed him to the cross, Lord ... hung him with a robber (3) |

robe
114	a ragged robe of rabbit skin enwrapped his beauty round (2)
170	though we merit blame you will your robe of mercy throw (2)
318	Here is my robe, my refuge, and my peace (4)
388	whose robe is the light, whose canopy space (2)
448, 449	in purple robe arrayed (4)
598	robe of sorrow round thee (1)
670	strip me of the robe of pride (1)

robed
57, 58	Every eye shall now behold him robed in dreadful majesty (2)
74	Not robed in royal splendor, in power and pomp comes he (1)
160	robed in mortal flesh is dying, crucified by sin for me (2)
240, 241	martyrs robed in white (1)
356	dwell the white-robed martyrs who now no more can die (1)
366	the white robed martyrs follow (3)
383, 384	woodlands robed in the blooming garb of spring (2)
460, 461	thou within the veil hast entered, robed in flesh (4)

robes
9	royal robes of autumn moors the golden gates of spring (2)
286	clad in robes of purest whiteness (2)
286	robes whose luster ne'er shall fade (2)
624	for ever and for ever are clad in robes of white (3)

robust

406, 407	jocund is he, robust and bright (4)

rock

287	Thou wast their rock, their fortress, and their might (2)
307	smitten Rock with streaming side (5)
343	manna in the wilderness, with water from the rock (1)
391	firm as a rock thy truth must stand (5)
399	To God with gladness sing, your Rock and Savior bless (1)
431	my rock, and my redeeming Lord, in all my words and ways (4)
498	the shadow of a mighty rock within a weary land (1)
522, 523	on the Rock of Ages founded (1)
579, 608	from rock and tempest, fire and foe, protect them (4)
635	Who trusts in God's unchanging love builds on a rock (1)
635	a rock which nought can move (1)
644	Dear Name, the rock on which I build (3)
651	I rest me in the thought of rock and trees (1)
685	Rock of ages, cleft for me, let me hide myself in thee (1,3)

rocks

100	while fields and floods, rocks, hills and plains repeat (2)
370	the deep salt sea, around the old eternal rocks (4)
632	mid mists and rocks and quicksands still guides (2)
717	I love thy rocks and rills, thy woods and templed hills (2)
717	let rocks their silence break, the sound prolong (3)

rod

379	when human hearts are breaking under sorrow's iron rod (2)
496, 497	O righteous branch, O Jesse's Rod (1)
574, 575	wean us and train us with thy rod (2)
613	Break with thine iron rod the tyrannies of sin (1)
645, 646	thy rod and staff my comfort still (4)

rode

284	When all arrayed in light the shining conqueror rode (7)
480	When Jesus into Zion rode, the children sang around (3)

roll

280	In the roll of your apostles stands the name Bartholemew (2)
372	his love shall be our strength and stay while ages roll (4)
409	confirm the tidings as they roll (2)
555	nor roll of stirring drums, but deeds of love and mercy (2)
699	while the nearer waters roll (1)

rolled

89, 90	beneath the heavenly hymn have rolled two thousand years (3)
284	Ye rolled the stone (6)

rolling

371	rolling in fullest pride, through the world far and wide (4)
391	when rolling years shall cease to move (5)
599	let it resound loud as the rolling sea (1)
680	Time, like an ever-rolling stream (5)

rolls
  24   while earth rolls onward into light (2)

Roman
  161   A Roman soldier drew a spear to mix his blood with water (2)

roof
  110   the ass and oxen shared the roof with them (2)

room
  10   all we ought to ask: room to deny ourselves (5)
  69   in great humility is hid all heaven in a little room (3)
  100   let every heart prepare him room (1)
  187   by his tomb Christ makes room (2)
  284   out from death's vast room, up from the grave, he leapt (6)
  305, 306   We meet, as in that upper room they met (2)
  420   adoration leaves no room for pride (1)
  592   who sweeps a room, as for thy laws, makes that ... fine (3)
  598   O aweful Love, which found no room in life (2)
  598   found no room in life where sin denied thee (2)

root
  198   today the branches with the root in resurrection sharing (2)
  588, 589   give it root in every heart to bring forth fruits of love (2)

rooted
  273, 274   Two stalwart trees both rooted in faith and holy love (1)
  323   Jesus, may we ever be grafted, rooted, built in thee (2)
  422   Rooted and grounded in thy love (2)

rose   (see also arose)
  48   day for our salvation Christ rose from depths of earth (2)
  49   he rose, the prince of life and peace (1)
  49   rose triumphant from the dead (1)
  50   Today he rose and left the dead, and Satan's empire fell (2)
  52   in might victorious rose again (2)
  81   Lo, how a Rose e'er blooming from tender stem hath sprung (1)
  81   Isaiah 'twas foretold it, the Rose I have in mind (2)
  120   and with you rose (6)
  139   death could hold him never. He rose and lives forever (2)
  198   Christ rose from death ... adore for ever ... evermore (1)
  203, 206   King of heaven ... o'er death and hell rose triumphing (1)
  211   To him who rose that we might rise (2)
  231, 232   You rose, our King victorious (1)
  231   he rose to meet your challenge (2/11-30)
  232   You rose ... that they might wear the crown (1)
  242   at once he rose to full belief's unclouded height (4)
  281   he rose, responsive to the call, and left his task (3)
  447   Christ who died but rose again triumphant from the grave (1)
  448, 449   For us he rose from death again (5)
  452   Glorious the day when Christ arose (2)
  494   rose victorious in the strife for those he came to save (3)
  494   his glories now we sing who died, and rose on high (3)

rough

161	With what strange light the rough trunk shone (4)
647	but rough or smooth, up hill or down (1)
703	however rough and steep the path may be (3)

rougher

67	make the rougher places plain (3)

round

10	The trivial round, the common task, will furnish all (5)
12, 13	Amid our customary round, we offer ... prayer and praise (1)
31, 32	ordered seasons in their round (4)
42	their white wings above me, watching round my bed (5)
102	with the oxen standing round (6)
110	the angels hovered round, and sang this song (3)
111	all is calm ... bright round yon virgin mother and child (1)
114	a ragged robe of rabbit skin enwrapped his beauty round (2)
114	The earliest moon of winter-time is not so round and fair (3
150	round us ... angels shine, such as ministered to thee (4)
210	round world keep high triumph, and all that is therein (3)
276	saw the glory round thy head, one of the chosen three (3)
280	live for ever round your throne (1)
284	O ye immortal throng of angels round the throne (1)
292	gathering round thy throne ... in the holy angel's sight (3)
367	Round the Lord in glory seated cherubim and seraphim (1)
374	angels round the throne (1)
388	and round it hath cast, like a mantle, the sea (3)
409	What though in solemn silence all move round (3)
409	all move round the dark terrestrial ball (3)
409	whilst all the stars that round her burn (2)
430	Let in praise of God, the sound run a never-ending round (4)
441, 442	all the light of sacred story gathers round its head (1,5)
441, 442	gathers round its head sublime (1,5)
480	when mothers round him pressed (2)
484, 485	His praise shall sound all nature round (1)
516	clothe me round, the while my path illuming (2)
519, 520	bridal glory round thee shed (2)
522, 523	Round each habitation hovering, see the cloud and fire (3)
542	whole round world complete, from sunrise to its setting (2)
543	the nations round thy form shall view (2)
543	while round his throne ten thousand stars (4)
554	till by turning, turning we come round right (1)
564, 565	Who so beset him round with dismal stories (2)
594, 595	Lo, the hosts of evil round us scorn thy Christ (2)
598	robe of sorrow round thee (1)
614	round him drew thousands of servants brave and true (1)
617	Eternal Ruler of the ceaseless round of circling planets (1)
651	round me rings the music of the spheres (1)

rouses

590	grant the glad surprising that your blest Spirit rouses (1)
590	Spirit rouses everywhere (1)

row

580	stately buildings row on row (2)

royal

9	royal robes of autumn moors the golden gates of spring (2)
51	that he might anoint us a royal priesthood (1)
74	Not robed in royal splendor, in power and pomp comes he (1)
102	Once in royal David's city stood a lowly cattle shed (1)
128	star with royal beauty bright (R)
135	branch of royal David's stem in thy birth at Bethlehem (1)
154, 155	Thou art the King of Israel, thou David's royal Son (1)
161	its purple limbs a royal throne (4)
161	its load a royal treasury (4)
162	The royal banners forward go (1)
199, 200	with the royal feast of feasts, comes its joy to render (3)
215	see the King in royal state (1)
281	that royal summons, "Follow me" (2)
318	here drink with thee the royal Wine of heaven (2)
359	help them intercede with all the royal priesthood (3)
450, 451	bring forth the royal diadem (1)
462	before him righteousness shall go, his royal harbinger (1)
483	a royal diadem adorns the mighty victor's brow (1)
536	Open your hearts, O royal priesthood (1,4)
561	lift high his royal banner, it must not suffer loss (1)
562	Christ, the royal Master, leads against the foe (1)
707	it shall be thy royal throne (1)

royalty

443	his royalty from David's tree, praised be his Oneness (1)

rude

119	offered gifts most rare at that manger rude and bare (3)
286	ne'er be touched by time's rude hand ((2)
566	our rude work deface no more the handiwork of God (2)
608	chaos dark and rude (3)

rule

65	He brings God's rule, O Zion, he comes from heaven above (2)
65	His rule is peace and freedom ... justice, truth and love (2)
65	Fling wide your gates, O Zion, your Savior's rule embrace (3)
66	By thine own eternal Spirit rule in all our hearts alone (4)
103	will rule the world for evermore (2)
127	out of thee the Lord from heaven came to rule his Israel (1)
162	so rule and guide us evermore (6)
222	shall come in all love's glorious power to rule (4)
222	to rule the world for which he died (4)
226, 227	rule us by thy judgment's line (4)
281	alike the symbol ... tool of foreign master's hated rule (1)
365	thou, who almighty art, now rule in every heart (3)
398	I sing the wisdom that ordained the sun to rule the day (1)
566	thy just rule shall fill the earth (2)
607	Christ shall rule victorious o'er all the world's domain (4)
613	Thy kingdom come, O God! Thy rule, O Christ, begin (1)
616	to take away transgression, and rule in equity (1)
617	rule in our hearts that we may ever be ... upheld (1)
626	Lord, be thy word my rule; in it may I rejoice (1)

ruler

175	Lord and the ruler of nature (2)
216	Lord and the ruler of nature (1)
261, 262	Ruler of all things, Lord of earth and heaven (2)
282, 283	maker of all things, ruler of all nations (1)
383, 384	Fairest Lord Jesus, Ruler of all nature (1)
436	the city blest where Christ the ruler is confessed (2)
488	still be my vision, O Ruler of all (3)
573	Father eternal, Ruler of creation (1)
617	Eternal Ruler of the ceaseless round of circling planets (1)
716	ruler of wind and wave (1)
718	be thou our ruler, guardian, guide, and stay (2)

rulers

573	led by no star, the rulers of the nations still fail (4)
573	rulers ... still fail to bring us to the blissful birth (4)
591	our earthly rulers falter, our people drift and die (1)
605	Rulers of earth, give ear. Should you not justice show (2)

rules

100	He rules the world with truth and grace (4)
327, 328	He that his saints in this world rules and shields (6)
481	His kingdom cannot fail, he rules o'er earth and heaven (3)
492	from his Father's throne the Son rules and guides (4)
492	rules and guides the world he ransomed (4)
535	his kingdom is glorious, he rules over all (1)

rulest

175	God the Creator ... who rulest the earth and the heavens (5)
216	God ... who rulest the earth and the heavens (2)
423	nor wanting, nor wasting, thou rulest in might (2)
423	Thou reignest in glory, thou rulest in light (4)
568	Father all loving, who rulest in majesty (1)

ruleth

535	God ruleth on high, almighty to save (2)

ruling

12, 13	O God, creation's ruling force (4)
18	O God, creation's ruling force (5)
23	O God, creation's ruling force (4)

run

11	Awake, my soul ... with the sun thy daily stage of duty run (1)
54	Mighty God and Mary's son, eager now his race to run (2)
59	with the everlasting Spirit while unending ages run (4)
140	Wilt thou forgive those sins through which I run (1)
140, 141	do run still, though still I do deplore (1)
141	Wilt thou forgive those sins through which I run (1)
165, 166	one in might and one in glory while eternal ages run (6)
217, 218	while endless ages run, with Father and with Spirit, One (3)
220, 221	let earth accord, who art, while endless ages run (4)
251	Another year its course has run (2)
257	all glory, Holy Ghost, to thee, while endless ages run (5)
321	till through the world thy truth has run (4)

329-331	while eternal ages run (6)
346	to whom be praise while endless ages run (3)
381	while thine ordered seasons run (1)
389	He the golden-tressed sun caused all day his course to run (4)
406, 407	sun who through the skies his course doth run (2)
430	Let in praise of God, the sound run a never-ending round (4)
458	He made the lame to run, he gave the blind their sight (4)
490	When we have run with patience the race ... know the joy (3)
519, 520	consubstantial, coeternal, while unending ages run (5)
544	where'er the sun doth his successive journeys run (1)
552, 553	Run the straight race through God's good grace (2)

running

| 405 | The purple-headed mountain, the river running by (2) |

runs

| 579 | traffic runs amain by mountain pass or valley low (2) |

rush

299	Spirit of God, unleashed on earth with rush of wind (1)
299	rush of wind and roar of flame (1)
513	like the vigor of the wind's rush (1)

rushing

228	Shake with rushing wind our will (4)
230	filled the place of meeting with rushing wind and flame (1)
400	Great rushing winds and breezes soft (2)
412	Earth and all stars, loud rushing planets (1)

rustles

| 9 | dawn that rustles through the trees (3) |

rustling

| 412 | Flowers and trees, loud rustling dry leaves (2) |

Sabbath

48	at length our rest attaining, our endless Sabbath day (4)
586	lead us to our Sabbath rest (3)
652 , 653	O Sabbath rest by Galilee, O calm of hills above (3)

Sabbaths

| 623 | those endless Sabbaths the blessed ones see (1) |

saber

| 607 | fear of rattling saber, from dread of war's increase (3) |

sackcloth

| 145 | To bow the head in sackcloth and in ashes (2) |

sacrament

305, 306	make manifest in thine own Sacrament of Bread and Wine (1)
315	through this blest sacrament of unity (1-2)
329-331	this great Sacrament revere (5)
586	Bread of heaven, art broken in the sacrament of life (2)

sacraments
315 So, Lord, at length when sacraments shall cease (3)

sacred
65 Greet One who comes in glory, foretold in sacred story (1)
82 Babe ... world's Redeemer first revealed his sacred face (2)
84 worship we our Jesus, but wherewith for sacred sign (2)
127 Sacred gifts of mystic meaning (4)
131, 132 Within the Jordan's sacred flood the ... Lamb ... stood (3)
168, 169 O sacred head, sore wounded, defiled and put to scorn (1)
174 praise we him, whose love divine gives his sacred Blood (1)
174 gives his sacred Blood for wine (1)
223, 224 blessings of this sacred day grant us ... we pray (3)
229 wonders of this sacred day (1)
284 Around his sacred tomb a willing watch ye kept (6)
285 O happy saint, his sacred page, so rich in ... truth (2)
321 here its sacred pledges tastes (2)
329, 331 wine his sacred Blood he maketh (4)
349 When the sacred vow is made (2)
365 thy sacred witness bear in this glad hour (3)
366 Lo, the apostolic train join, thy sacred Name to hallow (3)
368 touch our hearts with sacred fire (3)
374 The whole creation joins in one to bless the sacred Name (4)
391 Before the Lord's eternal throne ... bow with sacred joy (1)
391 ye nations bow with sacred joy (1)
401 we bow and bless the sacred Name for ever blest (1)
401 On Zion's sacred height his kingdom he maintains (3)
441, 442 all the light of sacred story gathers round its head (1,5)
473 till all the world adore his sacred Name (R)
479 poured for me the life-blood from his sacred veins (1)
500 come, and thy sacred unction bring to sanctify us (2)
505 make us to love thy sacred word (3)
510 kindle a flame of sacred love in ... cold hearts of ours (1)
543 In honor to his Name reflect that sacred light (3)
630 word was written in the Bible's sacred page (3)
704 kindle a flame of sacred love upon the altar of my heart (1)

sacrifice
10 God will provide for sacrifice (3)
11 joyful rise to pay thy morning sacrifice (1)
47 by love inflamed, arise unto thee a sacrifice (4)
97 willingly this yoke I take, and this sacrifice I make (2)
128 King and God and Sacrifice (5)
144 through your saving sacrifice receive your gift of grace (3)
156 sad and wondering eyes to see the approaching sacrifice (3)
164 Alone thou goest forth, O Lord, in sacrifice to die (1)
171 God's own sacrifice complete (3)
202 all sufficient Sacrifice, beneath thee hell defeated lies (4)
320 making thus our sacrifice of peace (3)
323 this blest cup of sacrifice (2)
337 the one true, pure, immortal sacrifice (1)
338 All-perfect Offering, sacrifice immortal (1)
359 through them thy Church presents ... true sacrifice (3)
359 in word and deed Christ's one true sacrifice (3)
416 offering up on every shore thy pure sacrifice of love (5)

474 all the vain things that charm me most, I sacrifice (2)
474 I sacrifice them to his blood (2)
544 rise with every morning sacrifice (2)
605 What sacrifice desire, or tribute bid you bring (1)
665 from earth to God eternal sacrifice of praise be done (5)
704 make the sacrifice complete (4)

sacrificed
421 for the world was sacrificed upon the cross to save us (2)

sacrificial
509 purge our hearts like sacrificial flame (3)
590 Grant us new courage, sacrificial, humble (2)

sad
56 bid thou our sad divisions cease (7)
80 who hears your sad and bitter cry (3)
89, 90 above its sad and lowly plains they bend on hovering wing (2)
122, 123 by Babylon's sad waters mourning exiles now are we (2)
156 sad and wondering eyes to see the approaching sacrifice (3)
180 Come, ye sad and fearful hearted (2)
208 The three sad days are quickly sped (3)
284 Ye thronged to Calvary and pressed with sad desire (5)
284 sad desire that aweful sight to see (5)
284 ye mourned the dead in sad surprise (5)
315 make thou our sad divisions soon to cease (2)
692 I came to Jesus as I was, so weary, worn, and sad (1)

sadness
48 O balm of care and sadness, most beautiful, most bright (1)
70 turning us from sin and sadness (1)
102 Thus he feels for all our sadness (4)
199, 200 God hath brought his Israel into joy from sadness (1)
237 God himself to joy and praise turns our human sadness (1)
300 He dispels our sin and sadness, life imparts (3)
339 leave the gloomy haunts of sadness (1)
376 Melt the clouds of sin and sadness (1)
478 Jesus, our mighty Lord, our strength in sadness (1)
515 Holy Ghost, dispel our sadness (1)
701 Jesus, all my gladness, my repose in sadness (1)
701 with me in earth's sadness, Jesus, all my gladness (3)

safe
56 make safe the way that leads on high (5)
75 bring them safe to his fold (3)
289 safe rest they in thy keeping (2)
480 Safe from the world's alluring harms (2)
522, 523 safe they feed upon the manna which he gives them (3)
526 bring us safe to heaven (5)
668 From evil he shall keep thee safe (4)
671 'tis grace that brought me safe thus far (4)
690 land me safe on Canaan's side (3)
699 safe into the haven guide (1)
700 so shall our way be safe, our feet no straying know (2)

safely

10	through sleep and darkness safely brought (1)
290	all is safely gathered in, ere the winter storms begin (1)
390	borne as on eagle-wings, safely his saints he sustaineth (2)
663	by streams serene, he safely doth me lead (1)
668	his own he safely keeps (2)
686	I hope, by thy good pleasure, safely to arrive at home (2)
703	only with thee we journey safely on (2)

safety

231	saved him from King Herod when safety there was none (2/3-19)

sages

50	Blest be the Lord who comes to us with messages of grace (4)
93	Sages, leave your contemplations (3)
124	eastern sages with amaze upon the wondrous token gaze (2)
127	Eastern sages at his cradle make oblations rich and rare (3)
131, 132	The eastern sages saw from far (2)
135	manifested by the star to the sages from afar (1)

said

94, 95	"Fear not" said he (2)
98	"A prince," he said, "in Jewry!" (3)
105	"Fear not then," said the angel, "Let nothing you affright" (3)
116	"Thus it becomes us to fulfill all righteousness," he said (2)
201	"Whom seek ye here?" the angel said
203	said, "My peace be on all here" (4)
206	said, "My peace be on all here" (2)
242	He loved thee well, and firmly said, "Come, let us go ..."(2)
266	said, "Hail Mary, full of grace." (2)
266	Said the angel, "Have no fear ..." (4)
266	Said the maiden, "Verily, I am your servant right truly" (6)
386, 387	"Tell them I AM," the Lord God said (2)
636, 637	What more can he say than to you he hath said (1)
673	Jesus, when he said, "I am he" (2)
675	"Take up your cross," the Savior said (1)

sailors

42	guard the sailors tossing on the deep, blue sea (3)

saint

110	Saint Joseph, too, was by to tend the child (3)
232	We praise you for Saint Peter (2/6-29)
232	we praise you for Saint Paul (2/6-29)
232	Saint Simon and Saint Jude (2/10-28)
245	Your great I AM's Saint John records (2)
254	For of your Church, Lord, you made known this saint (2)
254	this saint a true foundation-stone (2)
256	Saint Paul was changed by God's free love (3)
260	Come now, and praise the humble saint of David's house (1)
261, 262	to Saint Joseph gave supernal honor (3)
275	king, apostle, saint, confessor, martyr and evangelist (2)
280	for this faithful saint we offer ... our thanks to you (2)
285	Luke, thy saint, through whom we know so many ... words (1)
285	O happy saint, his sacred page, so rich in ... truth (2)

549, 550   as, of old, Saint Andrew heard it by the Galilean lake (2)

sainthood
273, 274   both triumph in their dying ... glorious sainthood gain (2)

saintly
275   saintly maiden, godly matron, widows who have watched (2)

saints
1, 2   bring us to heaven where thy saints united joy (2)
29, 30   O grant us with thy saints on high to praise thee (2)
50   today the saints his triumphs spread (2)
57, 58   thousand saints attending swell the triumph of his train (1)
61, 62   let saints and angels sing before you (3)
63, 64   bid the saints their reign begin (3)
63, 64   with thy saints for evermore behold thee (4)
73   let the endless bliss begin, by weary saints foretold (4)
93   Saints before the altar bending (4)
102   but in heaven, where his saints his throne surround (6)
122, 123   at the last to keep thine Easter with thy faithful saints (4)
122, 123   with thy faithful saints on high (4)
129, 130   with the saints and angels praise him (1)
174   hast opened paradise, and in thee thy saints shall rise (3)
212   Oh, with what gladness and surprise the saints ... greet (2)
212   saints their Savior greet (2)
219   by saints, by angel hosts adored (2)
231, 232   By all your saints still striving, for all ... at rest (1)
233, 234   Theirs is the steadfast faith of saints (3)
253   see the saints above, how great their joys (1)
254   the saints of God at last prevail (1)
260   where saints and angels throng (4)
267   promise shone with cheering ray on waiting saints of old (1)
276   For thy blest saints ... we praise thy Name, O Lord (1)
276   saints, a noble throng (1)
277   from all saints the song ascends (3)
278   raised high with saints and angels, in Jerusalem above (4)
279   For thy dear saints, O Lord, who strove in thee to live (1)
279   Thine earthly members fit to join thy saints above (3)
280   God of the saints (1)
280   many saints by earth forgotten live for ever (1)
282, 283   may the assembly of the saints in heaven ... help us (5)
287   For all the saints, who from their labors rest (1)
287   fight as the saints who nobly fought of old (3)
287   the saints triumphant rise in bright array (7)
293   I sing a song of the saints of God (1)
293   saints of God, patient and brave and true (1)
293   they were all of them saints of God (1)
293   the world is bright with the joyous saints (3)
293   saints who love to do Jesus' will (3)
293   for the saints of God are just folk like me (3)
299   With tongues of fire saints spread good news (1)
299   From living waters raise new saints (2)
305, 306   with all thy saints on earth and saints at rest (3)

315	one with thy saints in one unbroken peace (3)
315	one with thy saints in one unbounded love (3)
320	grant us, with thy saints, though lowest (6)
326	one heart ... song have the saints upon earth and above (2)
327, 328	He that his saints in this world rules and shields (6)
355	Give rest, O Christ, to your servant with your saints (1)
357	where thy saints made perfect gaze upon thy face (4)
358	rest with your saints in the regions of light (1,4)
362	All the saints adore thee (2)
364	dwell ... with all thy saints in joy surpassing thought (8)
366	Grant that with thy saints we may dwell (7)
373	God hath made his saints victorious (2)
390	borne as on eagle-wings, safely his saints he sustaineth (2)
401	glorious with his saints in light, for ever reigns (3)
414	thee shall all thy saints adore (6)
422	saints on earth and saints above we join in full accord (2)
426	Saints below, with heart and voice ... rejoice (5)
486	Hosanna Lord, thine angels cry ... thy saints reply (2)
493	saints below and saints above (6)
494	where saints with angels sing their songs (4)
525	yet saints their watch are keeping (3)
526	Let saints on earth in concert sing (1)
532, 533	How just, King of saints, and true are thy ways (1)
545	with the Savior and his saints (5)
551	rise up, ye saints of God (1,2,3)
556, 557	With all the angel choirs, with all the saints of earth (2)
562	Christians, we are treading where the saints have trod (3)
614	praise for his brave saints of ancient days (1)
618	all saints triumphant raise the song (3)
619	to saints forgiven, let them all unite (6)
620	Thy saints are crowned with glory great (2)
625	Ye saints, who toil below, adore your heavenly King (3)
631	poets, prophets, scholars, saints, each a word from God (2)
636, 637	How firm a foundation, ye saints of the Lord (1)
677	Ye fearful saints, fresh courage take (3)
680	thy saints have dwelt secure (2)

saith

9	that clear voice that saith (3)
67	speak ye peace, thus saith our God (1)

sake

281	who yield up all for Jesus' sake (4)
293	they followed the right, for Jesus' sake (2)
448, 449	God ... should take our mortal form for mortal's sake (1)
452	for the sake of those he grieves transcends the world (2)
458	O who am I that for my sake my Lord should ... die (1)
549, 550	leaving all for his dear sake (2)
560	Blessed ... who are persecuted for righteousness sake (8)
560	utters all manner of evil against you falsely for my sake (9)
592	with this tincture, "for thy sake," (2)
663	for his Name's sake (2)
664	for his mercy's sake (1)
682	not for the sake of winning heaven, nor any fear of hell (4)

sale
591   from sale and profanation of honor, and the sword (2)

Salem
519, 520 Blessed city, heavenly Salem (1)
621, 622 Light's abode, celestial Salem (1)

Salem's
230   In Salem's street was gathered a crowd from many a land (2)

salt
370   the deep salt sea, around the old eternal rocks (4)

salute
106   Christians awake, salute the happy morn (1)

salvation
1, 2   send us thy salvation (3)
16, 17   For at this hour to all the world ... salvation came (2)
16, 17   grace of true salvation came (2)
48   day for our salvation Christ rose from depths of earth (2)
50   bring salvation from thy throne (3)
57, 58   once for our salvation slain (1)
65   His tidings of salvation proclaim in every place (3)
68   look now for your salvation, the end of sin and toil (2)
69   Now comes the day of salvation (4)
69   O let salvation dawn (4)
76   For thou art our salvation, Lord (3)
85, 86   salvation comes from you alone (4)
99   God sent us salvation that blessed Christmas morn (3)
115   the King of kings salvation brings (3)
157   for you answered me and have become my salvation (R)
158   thy bitter passion, for my salvation (4)
159   Him she saw for our salvation mocked (3)
168, 169 with thee for my salvation upon the cross to die (3)
191   for the world's salvation bled (1)
207   pains which he endured ... our salvation have procured (3)
226, 227 Grant us thy salvation, Lord (5)
232   as once for our salvation your mother she became (2/8-15)
235   voice proclaimed salvation that poured upon the night (1)
240, 241 Living, they proclaimed salvation (2)
244   blessed tidings of salvation (1)
244   drink, and find salvation here (2)
248, 249 To the Name of our salvation laud and honor let us pay (1)
258   who brought forth the world's salvation (2)
261, 262 Jesus, source of salvation (1)
275   Captain of salvation, thee, their Savior and their King (3)
294   heirs of salvation, trusting his promise (1)
298   baptized shall see the Lord's salvation (1)
319   for this feast of our salvation (1)
321   may each soul salvation see (2)
327, 328 take the pledges of salvation here (5)
344   may the fruits of thy salvation ... abound (2)
363   O holy Jesus, Lord of our salvation (3)

368	In the song of thy salvation every tongue ... combine (4)
370	his death on cross for my salvation (1)
370	praise to the Lord of my salvation (7)
370	salvation is of Christ the Lord (7)
373	Praise the God of our salvation (2)
381	broke the light of thy salvation (2)
386, 387	him that brought salvation down by meekness, Mary's son (4)
390	O my soul, praise him for he is thy health and salvation (1)
408	the God of love, the God of our salvation (1)
413	He has made known his great salvation (1)
413	salvation which all his friends with joy confess (1)
421	who came for our salvation (3)
432	for grace of salvation, O praise ye the Lord (4)
444	the prophet of salvation, the harbinger of Day (2)
458	He came from his blest throne salvation to bestow (2)
467	to make salvation sure, guides us by his Spirit pure (3)
477	by thy death was God's salvation wrought (2)
478	you gave yourself to die for our salvation (1)
484, 485	his holy arm hath wrought salvation (1)
495	thou didst free salvation bring (1)
496, 497	Jesus, grant us ... to inherit thy salvation (2)
496, 497	ride on, great Conqueror, till all know thy salvation (3)
525	her charter of salvation, one Lord, one faith, one birth (2)
535	ascribing salvation to Jesus our King (2)
535	Salvation to God who sits on the throne (3)
542	Christ is the world's true Light ... captain of salvation (1)
543	tell all the earth thy joys, and boast salvation nigh (1)
594, 595	let the gift of thy salvation be our glory evermore (4)
598	to finish thy salvation (4)
633	crucified for our salvation (2)
657	visit us with thy salvation, enter every trembling heart (1)
657	see thy great salvation perfectly restored in thee (3)
667	theme of God's salvation, and find it ever new (2)
695, 696	O give our frightened souls the sure salvation (2)
695, 696	salvation for which, O Lord, you taught us to prepare (2)

salvation's

230	the ears of all who heard proclaimed salvation's wonder (1)
327, 328	Salvation's giver, Christ, the only Son (3)
522, 523	With salvation's walls surrounded, thou may'st smile (1)
678, 679	rejoice as you draw water from salvation's living spring (1)

same

18	grant us that same revealing light (4c)
55	you returned to that same source (3)
105	unto certain shepherds brought tidings of the same (2)
109	by the light of that same star three wise men came (3)
157	the same stone which the builders rejected (R)
159	Jesus, may her deep devotion stir in me the same emotion (5)
162	in that same flesh our ransom paid (1)
176, 177	By the same Spirit we, regenerated (2)
176, 177	By the same Spirit we are called to worship God (3)
253	long cloud of witnesses show the same path to heaven (4)
268, 269	let Christ's people sing the same (3)

370	invocation of the same ... Three in One ... One in Three (1,7)
372	who was, and is, and is to be, for ay the same (1,4)
379	find that self-same aching deep within the heart of God (2)
401	Who was, and is, the same, and evermore shall be (4)
410	praise him still the same as ever (2)
437, 438	his mercy sure, from age to age the same (2)
505	enlighten us by that same word (4)
581	our common life embraces all whose Father is the same (6)
614	Christ through all ages is the same (2)
614	place the same hope in this great Name (2)
614	with the same faith his word proclaim (2)
620	joy, and of the same partaker ever be (5)
667	God the same abiding, his praise shall tune my voice (4)
680	from everlasting thou art God, to endless years the same (3)
687, 688	Lord Sabaoth his Name, from age to age the same (2)

sanctified

| 441, 442 | Bane and blessing, pain and pleasure ... sanctified (4) |
| 441, 442 | by the cross are sanctified (4) |

Sanctifier

| 176, 177 | God our Creator, Savior, Sanctifier (3) |
| 368 | Holy Spirit, Sanctifier, come with unction from above (3) |

sanctifies

| 295 | who sanctifies and guides us, made strong in our rebirth (3) |

sanctify

24	thy praise shall sanctify our rest (1)
500	come, and thy sacred unction bring to sanctify us (2)
500	sanctify us while we sing (2)
514	enlighten, sanctify, and seal (3)
636, 637	and sanctify to thee thy deepest distress (3)

sanctifying

| 5 | Spirit's sanctifying beam upon our earthly senses stream (2) |

sanctity

| 191 | Alleluia! to the Spirit, fount of love and sanctity (5) |

sanctuary

| 475 | let my soul, like Mary, be thine earthly sanctuary (4) |

sang

77	angels in the sky sang praise above the silent field (4)
93	who sang creation's story now proclaim Messiah's birth (1)
106	praises of redeeming love they sang (3)
110	the angels hovered round, and sang this song (3)
154, 155	To thee before thy passion they sang ... hymns of praise (4)
268, 269	what Christ's mother sang in gladness ... people sing (3)
284	for such a birth ye sang aloud (2)
312	Lord, may the tongues which "Holy" sang keep free (2)
426	Songs of praise the angels sang (1)
480	When Jesus into Zion rode, the children sang around ((3)

sapphire
156   Father on his sapphire throne (4)

sat
203   sat and spake unto the three (3)
281   He sat to watch o'er customs paid (1)

Satan
91   the power of Satan breaking, our peace eternal making (1)
142   As thou with Satan didst contend and ... the victory win (2)
150   Then if Satan on us press, Jesus, Savior, hear our call (3)
215   he has vanquished sin and Satan (2)
284   when Satan fled the Savior's might (3)
540   break down the realm of Satan, death, and sin (3)

Satan's
50   Today he rose and left the dead, and Satan's empire fell (2)
56   free them from Satan's tyranny (4)
71, 72   in Satan's bondage held (2)
105   save us all from Satan's power when we were gone astray (1)
105   free all ... from Satan's power and might (3)
179   Loose the souls long prisoned, bound with Satan's chain (6)
270   Gabriel's message does away Satan's curse and ... sway (1)
562   At the sign of triumph Satan's host doth flee (2)
563   Satan's host is vanquished and heaven is all possessed (3)

satisfied
161   The crowd would have been satisfied to see ... crucified (3)
560   for they shall be satisfied (4)

Saul
255   Saul, the church's spoiler, came spreading fear and hate (1)
256   then Saul fell blinded to the ground (1)

save
44, 45   Save us from troubled, restless sleep (2)
49   Who died to save the world he made (1)
50   comes, in God his Father's name, to save our sinful race (4)
53   bore the cross to save us, hope and freedom gave us (1)
56   trust thy mighty power to save (4)
77   his fallen creatures all to save (2)
81   from sin and death now save us, and share our every load (3)
85, 86   how once, to save our fallen race (3)
92   born on earth to save us; him the Father gave us (1)
92   born on earth to save us; peace and love he gave us (4)
105   save us all from Satan's power when we were gone astray (1)
107   Jesus Christ was born to save (3)
107   Christ was born to save (3)
120   to heal and save a race undone (4)
139   in his great endeavor to save us, his own blood was shed (2)
162   Still may thy power with us avail to save us sinners (5)
162   save ... from our sin, God's righteousness for all to win (5)
167   where our dear Lord was crucified who died to save us all (1)
184   exalted now to save, wresting victory from the grave (3)

188, 189	Once he died our souls to save (2)
207	sinners to redeem and save (2)
252	promise that it gave, "Jesus shall his people save" (3)
256	It was the blessed Son come down to save him (2)
256	to save him from his fearful ways and free him (2)
302, 303	in mercy, save it from evil, guard it still (2)
313	Blessed Lord, thou cam'st to save me(2)
318	nor do I need another arm save thine to lean upon (3)
322	When Jesus died to save us, a word, an act he gave us (1)
421	for the world was sacrificed upon the cross to save us (2)
447	all powerful to save (1)
454	comes to save us from despair (2)
455, 456	We read thy power to bless and save (4)
455, 456	bless and save e'en in the darkness of the grave (4)
458	a murderer they save, the Prince of Life they slay (5)
472	Save us, thy people, from consuming passion (1)
472	by thy cross didst save us from death and dark despair (4)
472	save us ... from sin and guilt (4)
474	boast, save in the cross of Christ, my God (2)
488	all else be nought to me, save that thou art (1)
489	in love God sent his Son to save not to condemn mankind (6)
492	thence his banished ones to save (2)
494	rose victorious in the strife for those he came to save (3)
530	earth from sin and death to save (2)
535	God ruleth on high, almighty to save (2)
539	tell how he stooped to save his lost creation (2)
547	who died that he might save (4)
567	strong to heal and save (1)
579	Almighty Father, strong to save (1)
579	O Wind of heaven, by thy might save all (3)
579	save all who dare the eagle's flight (3)
591	bind all our lives together, smite us and save us all (3)
594, 595	Save us from weak resignation to the evils we deplore (4)
608	Eternal Father, strong to save (1)
610	use the love your Spirit kindles still to save (2)
610	save and make us whole (2)
669	God, in his great mercy, will save thee, hold thee fast (4)
685	thou must save and thou alone (2)
716	do thou our country save by thy great might (1)
716	to thee aloud we cry, God save the state (2)

saved

106	saved by his love, incessant we shall sing (6)
167	saved by his precious blood (3)
231	saved him from King Herod when safety there was none (2/3-19)
252	burst their fetters and are saved (5)
256	a sinner saved by Jesus' grace (2)
327, 328	Saved by that Body and that holy Blood (2)
391	when like wandering sheep we strayed, he saved us (2)
391	he saved us from the power of death (2)
425	he saved us from our enemy (2)
524	the Church our blest Redeemer saved (1)
524	saved with his own precious blood (1)
671	how sweet the sound that saved a wretch like me (1)

saves

429	saves the oppressed, and feeds the poor (2)
450, 451	hail him who saves you by his grace (4)
678, 679	Surely it is God who saves me (1)

saving

16, 17	by virtue of his saving cross (2)
54	Come, O Father's saving Son, who o'er sin the victory won (4)
144	through your saving sacrifice receive your gift of grace (3)
179	tread the path of darkness, saving strength to show (5)
248, 249	saving us from sin and hell (2)
296	We share by water in his saving death (2)
310, 311	O saving Victim (1)
538	thy saving health extend unto earth's remotest end (1)
539	make known to every heart his saving grace (4)
540	till all the world thy saving grace shall know (2)
573	his saving cross no nation yet will bear (2)
598	mocked thy saving kingship (1)
633	saving Word, the world restoring, speak to us (2)
678, 679	his saving help is near (1)

Savior

33-35	Christ, mighty Savior, Light of all creation (1)
33-35	in light or darkness worshiping our Savior (5)
33-35	worshiping our Savior now and for ever (5)
36	our Savior Jesus Christ, joyful in thine appearing (1)
54	Savior of the nations, come (1)
57, 58	Savior, take the power and glory (4)
60	you came, O Savior, to set free your own (2)
70	Christ, the Savior King, has come (R)
71, 72	Hark! the glad sound! the Savior comes (1)
71, 72	the Savior promised long (1)
80	he will himself your Savior be (3)
81	To show God's love aright, she bore to us a Savior (2)
82	bore the Savior of our race (2)
85, 86	O Savior of our fallen race (1)
94, 95	Savior who is Christ the Lord ... this shall be the sign (3)
97	stretching infant hands on high, Savior, long awaited (1)
100	Joy to the world! the Savior reigns (2)
102	with the poor, the scorned, the lowly lived ... Savior (2)
102	lived on earth our Savior holy (2)
105	remember Christ our Savior was born on Christmas Day (1)
105	this day is born a Savior of a pure virgin bright (3)
106	morn whereon the Savior of the world was born (1)
106	this day is born a Savior, Christ the Lord (2)
106	her Son, the Savior, in a manger laid (4)
111	Christ, the Savior, is born (2)
116	The Savior Jesus, well-beloved (4)
117, 118	Maker and Monarch and Savior of all (2)
122, 123	our Savior in his fasting pleasures of the world forebore (3)
139	for he is Christ the Savior (1)
150	Then if Satan on us press, Jesus, Savior, hear our call (3)
150	O keep us, Savior dear, ever constant by thy side (5)
165, 166	this the Savior freely willed (2)
176, 177	regenerated into the body of our risen Savior (2)

176, 177	God our Creator, Savior, Sanctifier (3)
178	joyfully sing to our Savior (4)
182	our Savior with the Father reigns (3)
191	Alleluia! to the Savior who has won the victory (5)
194, 195	glory to our Savior giving (2)
212	saints their Savior greet (2)
231	Like you, our suffering Savior ... he blessed (2/12-26)
231	O Christ, our Lord and Savior (2/6-11)
232	her Savior and her Lord (2/7-22)
232	Your wine and oil, O Savior, upon our spirits pour (2/10-18)
232	saw the risen Savior and placed his faith in him (2/10-23)
242	O Savior, make thy presence known to all who doubt (5)
266	by conception without compare the Savior ... bear. (4)
266	the Savior Jesus shall you bear (4)
268, 269	in my Savior I rejoice (4)
275	Captain of salvation, thee, their Savior and their King (3)
278	beholds her Son and Savior reigning as the Lord of love (4)
278	looked upon her Son and Savior (2)
282, 283	May the blest mother of our God and Savior ... help us (5)
284	join with our earth-bound song to make the Savior known (1)
305, 306	who art one Savior and one living Head (4)
320	Zion, praise thy Savior, singing hymns with exultation (1)
336	Come with us, O mighty Savior (2)
337	most patient Savior, who canst love us still (4)
338	intercession through him our Savior, Son of God incarnate (2)
343	Savior, abide with us, and spread thy table in our heart (3)
344	call us, Savior, from the world away (3)
345	Savior, again to thy dear Name we raise ... praise (1)
351	May the grace of Christ our Savior (1)
357	good and gracious Savior, cleanse and purge away (3)
365	stablish thy righteousness, Savior and friend (2)
366	Son of God, as Savior given (6)
366	Savior, who hast died to win us (7)
368	heavenly Father, through the Savior hear and bless (1)
399	To God with gladness sing, your Rock and Savior bless (1)
434	cross where Christ my Savior loved and died (4)
435	he is God the Savior, he is Christ the Lord (4)
436	the Savior of the world is here (1)
437, 438	in God my Savior shall my heart rejoice (1)
444	a Savior comes among us to raise us up to heaven (2)
444	O bless our God and Savior with songs that never cease (3)
465, 466	eternal Savior, come to me (2)
469, 470	there is mercy with the Savior (1)
478	the God of peace acclaim as Lord and Savior (3)
481	The Lord the Savior reigns, the God of truth and love (2)
486	To Christ, Creator Savior, King ... hosanna sing (1)
486	O Savior, with protecting care abide in this thy house (3)
489	He came as Savior to his own, the way of love he trod (5)
491	show me where my Savior lies (1)
492	praises of your Savior let his house resound again (1)
493	ye blind, behold, your Savior comes (5)
495	Hail, thou universal Savior, bearer of our sin and shame (1)
499	my eyes have seen the Savior, Christ the Lord (1)
524	Jesus, thou friend divine, our Savior and our King (4)
536	Israel comes to greet the Savior (3)

538	Shine upon us, Savior, shine (1)
538	Let the nations shout and sing glory to their Savior King (2)
545	with the Savior and his saints (5)
549, 550	By thy mercies, Savior, may we hear thy call (5)
559	Savior, breathe forgiveness o'er us (2)
576, 577	when we see your face, O Savior, in its glory (3)
632	O make thy Church, dear Savior, a lamp of purest gold (3)
642	the Savior of mankind (2)
675	Take up your cross, the Savior said (1)
689	it was not I that found, O Savior true (1)
691	Savior divine (1)
699	hide me, O my Savior ... till the storm of life is past (1)
708	Savior, like a shepherd lead us (1)
708	do thou, Lord, our only Savior ... our bosoms fill (2)

Savior's

65	Fling wide your gates, O Zion, your Savior's rule embrace (3)
99	chorus that hailed our Savior's birth (2)
106	Behold, I bring good tidings of a Savior's birth (2)
106	the earliest heralds of the Savior's name (4)
181	praise the Savior's name (1)
240, 241	they died in imitation of their Savior's final hour (2)
267	the incarnate Savior's birth (5)
284	when Satan fled the Savior's might (3)
285	Historian of the Savior's life (3)
286	they who have contended for their Savior's honor long (3)
292	with the Father's Name ... Savior's love proclaim (3)
308, 309	O purest fountain, welling from out the Savior's side (2)
368	fill them with the Savior's love (3)
368	Source of comfort, cheer us with the Savior's love (3)
458	My song is love unknown, my Savior's love to me (1)
467	bought us with the Savior's blood (3)
480	Should we forget our Savior's praise, the stones ... sing (3)
495	help to sing our Savior's merits (4)
510	come, shed abroad a Savior's love (4)
530	word of how the Savior's love ... burden doth remove (3)
625	now, from sin released, behold the Savior's face (2)

saw

8	born of the one light Eden saw play (3)
18	to us, like her who saw your need (4a)
18	In noonday vision Peter saw (4c)
92	Bethlehem saw his birth (2)
109	They looked up and saw a star shining in the east (2)
129, 130	Trembling at his feet we saw Moses and Elijah speaking (2)
131, 132	The eastern sages saw from far (2)
135	disciples filled with awe thy transfigured glory saw (4)
143	Alone and fasting Moses saw the loving God (2)
159	when she saw the crucifixion of the sole-begotten one (2)
159	Him she saw for our salvation mocked (3)
159	saw him then from judgment taken (3)
193	the apostles saw their risen Lord (1)
206	he saw the feet, the hands, the side (5)
231	who, martyred, saw you stand to help (2/12-26)
231	praise for the glorious vision the persecutor saw (2/1-25)

232	last and greatest prophet, he saw the dawning ray (2/6-24)
232	saw the kingdom come (2/6-29)
232	saw the risen Savior and placed his faith in him (2/10-23)
237	for by faith they saw the land decked in all its glory (2)
242	when thou didst thine appearance make, he saw and hailed (3)
242	saw and hailed his Lord Divine (3)
242	He saw thee risen (4)
246	But down the ages rings the cry of those who saw (2)
256	he saw the love of God ... beyond the law (3)
260	The Architect's high miracles he saw, and what was done (2)
276	saw the glory round thy head, one of the chosen three (3)
276	slain by Herod's flashing blade, he saw thy face again (4)
278	Sing again the joys of Mary when she saw the risen Lord (3)
278	saw the price of our redemption paid (2)
284	Ye saw the heaven-born child in human flesh arrayed (2)
284	ye saw his agony, ye heard the plaint he cried (4)
312	eyes which saw thy love be bright (2)
443	his people saw him die at last, praised be his teaching (2)
453	he saw in a vision a ladder so high (1)
683, 684	Where is the blessedness I knew when first I saw the Lord (2)

sawest

183	Speak, Mary, declaring what thou sawest, wayfaring (4)

say

3	he, in all we do or say, would keep us free from harm (1)
4	that he, in all we do or say, would keep us free (1)
11	all I design, or do, or say (3)
59	"Christ is nigh," it seems to say (1)
107	give ye heed to what we say: Jesus Christ is born today (1)
109	The first Nowell the angel did say was to ... shepherds (1)
179	"Welcome, happy morning!" age to age shall say (1,R)
184	take our sin and guilt away that with angels we may say (2)
205	let all the earth rejoice and say (2)
247	for thy parting nor say nor sing bye-bye, lully lullay (3)
265	Christian folk throughout the world will ever say (4)
315	grant us at every Eucharist to say ... "Thy will be done" (1)
458	What may I say? Heaven was his home (6)
481	Rejoice, again I say rejoice (R)
541	to each servant does the Master say, "Go work today" (1)
564, 565	Then fancies flee away; I'll fear not what men say (3)
636, 637	What more can he say than to you he hath said (1)
647	I know not if the way is long, and no one else can say (1)
667	set free from present sorrow, we cheerfully can say (2)
674	you alone can grant us grace to live the words we say (1)
676	say "He died for all" (2)
692	I heard the voice of Jesus say (1-3)
698	I know not how to ask or what to say (1)
720	O say can you see by the dawn's early light (1)
720	O say does that star-spangled banner yet wave (1)

saying

139	baptized by John, there came a voice from heaven saying (1)
355	saying, "You are dust, and to dust you shall return" (1)
549, 550	saying "Christian, follow me" (1)

549, 550   saying "Christian, love me more" (3)

scales
256   the scales fell from his eyes (3)

scan
476   Although his being is too bright for human eyes to scan (2)
677   Blind unbelief is sure to err and scan his work in vain (6)

scarcely
580   scarcely caring where they go (2)

scars
57, 58   with what rapture gaze we on those glorious scars (3)
193   those scars their solemn witness gave (2)

scatter
6   scatter all my unbelief (3)
291   We plow the fields and scatter the good seed on the land (1)

scattered
120   lead his scattered people home (2)
156   with palms and scattered garments strowed (1)
302   grain, once scattered on the hillsides (2)
303   As grain, once scattered on the hillsides (4)
334   Scattered flock, one shepherd sharing, lost and lonely (2)
614   scattered companies unite in service to the Lord of light (3)

scene
214   Wide unfold the radiant scene (2)

scenes
10   Old friends, old scenes, will lovelier be (4)

scepter
97   Scepter, crown, and sphere (1)
366   all on earth thy scepter claim (1)
460, 461   sing to Jesus, his the scepter, his the throne (1,5)
467   all is by his scepter swayed (2)

sceptered
170   A sceptered reed ... they thrust into your hand (3)

schemes
145   for schemes are vain and fretting brings no gain (1)
597   delivered from our selfish schemes (1)

schisms
525   by schisms rent asunder, by heresies distressed (3)

scholar's
585   scholar's truth, flight of swallows, autumn leaves (1)

scholars
631   poets, prophets, scholars, saints, each a word from God (2)

school
51   school for the faithful, refuge for the sinner (2)
293   You can meet them in school, or in lanes, or at sea (3)

science
566   From thee all skill and science flow (1)

score
140, 141   but wallowed in a score (2)

scorn
168, 169   O sacred head, sore wounded, defiled and put to scorn (1)
182   where color, scorn or wealth divide, he suffers still (4)
443   The dissolute he did not scorn (3)
452   born to wear the crown that Ceasars scorn (1)
591   the walls of gold entomb us, the swords of scorn divide (1)
594, 595   Lo, the hosts of evil round us scorn thy Christ (2)
607   scorn of truth and right (2)
701   Be it blame or scorn or shame, thou art with me (3)

scorned
102   with the poor, the scorned, the lowly lived ... Savior (2)
102   scorned, rejected, tears and smiles like us he knew (4)
281   a man of scorned and hardening trade (1)

scornful
525   Though with a scornful wonder men see her sore oppressed (3)

scourged
159   mocked with cruel acclamation, scourged and crowned (3)
448, 449   For us to wicked hands betrayed, scourged, mocked (4)

scripture
48   This day, God's people meeting, his Holy Scripture hear (3)

scripture's
632   we praise thee for the radiance that ... scripture's page (1)

scrolls
370   the patriarchs' prayers, the prophets' scrolls (3)
631   many diverse scrolls completing (2)

sculpture
519, 520   Many a blow and biting sculpture polished ... stones (4)

sea
9   the splendor of the sea (1)
42   guard the sailors tossing on the deep, blue sea (3)
85, 86   earth and sea and sky revere the love of him (5)
179   Brightness of the morning, sky and fields and sea (3)
187   Through the Red Sea brought at last (1)
187   In that cloud and in that sea ... baptized were we (3)

199, 200	led them with unmoistened foot through the Red Sea waters (1)
202	the Red Sea past (1)
263, 264	The Word whom earth and sea and sky adore (1)
275	chanting at the crystal sea ... alleluia, Lord, to thee (1)
276	not lingering by the sea (2)
293	You can meet them in school, or in lanes, or at sea (3)
362	casting down their golden crowns around the glassy sea (2)
362	praise thy Name in earth, and sky, and sea (4)
370	the deep salt sea, around the old eternal rocks (4)
372	deep writ upon the human heart, on sea and land (3)
375	mortals then, on land and sea ... exult (2)
376	flashing sea, chanting bird and flowing fountain (2)
388	and round it hath cast, like a mantle, the sea (3)
399	he made the sea and land, he brought the world to birth (2)
422	Not far beyond the sea, nor high above the heavens (1)
425	horse ... rider ... sword he cast into the raging sea (1)
428	earth and sea, O all that live in water or on shore (4)
460, 461	songs of all the sinless sweep across the crystal sea (3)
469, 470	There's a wideness in God's mercy like the ... sea (1)
469, 470	like the wideness of the sea (1)
534	filled ... as the waters cover the sea (1-4)
549, 550	tumult of our life's wild, restless sea (1)
559	lead us o'er the world's tempestuous sea (1)
579	hear us when we cry to thee for those in peril on the sea (1)
579	glad praise from space, air, land, and sea (4)
599	let it resound loud as the rolling sea (1)
608	cry to thee for those in peril on the sea (1-3)
608	hymns of praise from land and sea (4)
632	It is the chart and compass that o'er life's surging sea (2)
652, 653	simple trust like theirs who heard beside the Syrian sea (2)
677	plants his footsteps in the sea ... rides upon the storm (1)
681	line of lifted sea, where spreading moonlight quivers (3)
689	I walked and sank not on the storm-vexed sea (2)
719	crown thy good with brotherhood from sea to shining sea (1,3)

seal

199, 200	nor the watchers, nor the seal hold thee as a mortal (4)
473	Each new-born servant of the Crucified bears ... seal (2)
473	bears on the brow the seal of him who died (2)
514	enlighten, sanctify, and seal (3)
686	here's my heart, oh, take and seal it (3)
686	seal it for thy courts above (3)
697	seal me for thine own (3)
704	till death thy endless mercies seal (4)

sealed

128	sealed in the stone-cold tomb (4)
146, 147	Christ by his own example sealed (2)
212	His enemies had sealed the stone (4)
294	Baptized in water, sealed by the Spirit (1-3)

seals

116	He seals the sure prophetic word (1)

search
476	There God breaks in upon our search (4)
574, 575	Search out our hearts and make us true (2)
607	From search for wealth and power (2)

searching
476	Can we by searching find out God or formulate his ways (1)

seas
363	through seas dry-shod, through weary wastes bewildering (2)
385	deep seas obey thy voice (1)
398	spread the flowing seas abroad and built the lofty skies (1)
413	Rivers and seas and torrents roaring, honor the Lord (3)
429	made the sky and earth and seas with all their train (2)
455, 456	read thee ... in seas that swell and streams that flow (2)
651	of skies and seas, his hand the wonders wrought (1)
651	all earth and trees, all skies and seas (2)

season
69	Dark is the season, dark our hearts and shut to mystery (1)
192	My flesh in hope shall rest, and for a season slumber (3)
435	Humbled for a season, to receive a Name (2)
667	he grants the soul again a season of clear shining (1)
693	here for a season, then above (6)

seasons
31, 32	ordered seasons in their round (4)
198	of seasons, best, divinest (1)
199, 200	Now the queen of seasons, bright with the day of splendor (3)
381	while thine ordered seasons run (1)
428	O changing seasons bless the Lord (2)

seat
119	so may we with willing feet ever seek thy mercy seat (2)
462	thou in thy everlasting seat remainest God alone (5)
481	when he had purged our stains, he took his seat above (2)
643	how beautiful thy mercy seat in depths of burning light (1)

seated
94, 95	all seated on the ground (1)
320	What he did, at supper seated, Christ ordained (3)
340, 341	our blessed ones adore you, seated at our Father's board (3)
367	Round the Lord in glory seated cherubim and seraphim (1)
495	seated at the Father's side (3)

second
87	born to give us second birth (3)
176, 177	so from the empty tomb the Second Adam issued triumphant (1)
191	will all its full abundance at his second coming yield (3)
297	Forbid us not this second birth (2)
445, 446	When all was sin and shame, a second Adam ... came (2)
445, 446	second Adam to the fight and to the rescue came (2)

secret
14, 15	O God, creation's secret force (1)
486	make our secret soul to be a temple pure and worthy thee (4)
563	fear not the secret foe (2)
656	the secret of the Lord is theirs (1)
659, 660	tell me thy secret (1)

secrets
63, 64	the secrets of our hearts to try (3)
580	probed the secrets of the atom, yielding unimagined power (3)

secure
117, 118	vainly with gifts would his favor secure (4)
429	whose truth for ever stands secure (2)
600, 601	Bring justice to our land, that all may dwell secure (3)
663	secure in all alarms (4)
669	O trust the Lord then wholly, if thou wouldst be secure (2)
680	thy saints have dwelt secure (2)

secureth
53	One who thus endureth bright reward secureth (4)

see
3, 4	that we may see and serve his Son (2)
6, 7	joyless is the day's return till thy mercy's beams I see (2)
9	see how the giant sun soars up (5)
10	as more of heaven in each we see (4)
18	O turn us now to see your face (4b)
18	that we may see your world is good (4c)
36	Now, ere day fadeth quite, we see the evening light (2)
49	that all may see his love displayed (2)
54	grant that we its glories see (4)
57, 58	deeply wailing, shall the true Messiah see (2)
67	all flesh shall see the token (3)
68	See that your lamps are burning, replenish them with oil (2)
68	With hearts and hands uplifted, we plead, O Lord, to see (3)
68	see the day of earth's redemption, and ever be with thee (3)
69	to see the branch that begins to bloom (3)
78, 79	O little town of Bethlehem, how still we see thee lie (1)
82	that future years shall see (1)
83	See how the shepherds, summoned to his cradle (4)
87	Veiled in flesh the God-head see (2)
96	What great brightness did you see (2)
96	Come to Bethlehem and see him whose birth the angels sing (3)
96	See him in a manger laid whom the angels praise above (4)
97	Here no regal pomp we see (1)
98	but the very beasts could see that he all men surpasses (2)
102	And our eyes at last shall see him (5)
102	Not in that poor lowly stable ... we shall see him (6)
106	In Bethlehem the happy shepherds sought to see (4)
106	see the wonder God for us had wrought (4)
120	Above him see the heavenly Dove (3)
127	see them give, in deep devotion (3)

422	though our vision now is dark, to live by what we see (3)
422	when we see thee face to face (3)
423	help us to see 'tis only the splendor of light hideth thee (4)
427	Sing, suns and stars of space ... ye that see his face (5)
430	this huge wide orb we see shall one choir, one temple be (4)
463, 464	you will see rare beasts and have unique adventures (1)
465, 466	eternal brightness, help me see (2)
471	Inscribed upon the cross we see in shining letters (2)
471	we see in shining letters, God is love (2)
474	See, from his head, his hands, his feet (3)
475	let thy radiant beauty light mine eyes to see my duty (3)
490	I want to see the brightness of God (2)
492	till he see, renewed and perfect (4)
492	till he see ... all things gathered into one (4)
498	Upon the cross of Jesus mine eyes at times can see (2)
498	see the very dying form of one who suffered there for me (2)
499	prepared by you for all the world to see (1)
500	give us thyself, that we may see the Father and the Son (3)
510	See how we trifle here below, fond of these earthly toys (2)
522, 523	See, the streams of living waters (2)
522, 523	Round each habitation hovering, see the cloud and fire (3)
525	Though with a scornful wonder men see her sore oppressed (3)
536	Judah is glad to see his day (3)
539	through thy neglect, unfit to see his face (4)
552, 553	only believe ... see that Christ is all in all to thee (4)
560	Blessed are the pure in heart, for they shall see God (6)
562	forward into battle, see, his banners go (1)
567	to hands that work and eyes that see (3)
572	suffering all, that we may see triumph in surrender (3)
576, 577	when we see your face, O Savior, in its glory (3)
592	Teach me, my God and King, in all things thee to see (1)
597	till by God's grace our warring world shall see ... peace (1)
606	grace to see your exalted glory, O Christ our God (3)
609	yet long these multitudes to see the true compassion (3)
612	Faith and hope and love we see (4)
615	faithful souls have yearned to see ... that kingdom's day (1)
615	see on earth that kingdom's day (1)
620	Thy joys when shall I see (1)
620	they see God face to face (2)
620	Jerusalem, God grant that I may see thine endless joy (5)
623	those endless Sabbaths the blessed ones see (1)
630	See its glory undiminished by the change of time or place (4)
632	clouds and darkness ended, they see thee face to face (3)
633	Word that caused blind eyes to see (3)
638, 639	whom still I hold, but cannot see (1)
640	Traveler, o'er yon mountain's height see ... star (1)
640	see that glory-beaming star (1)
640	see, it bursts o'er all the earth (2)
641	when the flood is passed, I may the eternal brightness see (4)
642	sweeter far thy face to see and in thy presence rest (1)
644	when I see thee as thou art, I'll praise thee as I ought (5)
654	to see thee more clearly, love thee more dearly (1)
656	Blest are the pure in heart, for they shall see our God (1)

657	see thy great salvation perfectly restored in thee (3)
669	Thy lasting truth and mercy, O Father, see aright (3)
671	was blind but now I see (1)
673	blessed are they who see the Lord (3)
681	give us open eyes to see thee as thou art (5)
697	that I may see thy glorious face (3)
698	help me to see your purpose and your will (2)
720	O say can you see by the dawn's early light (1)

seed

267	virgin born of David's line shall bear the promised seed (2)
291	We plow the fields and scatter the good seed on the land (1)
329, 331	the seed of truth to sow (2)
534	till God gives life to the seed (4)
541	to sow the tares, to snatch the seed away (2)
588, 589	Almighty God, your word is cast like seed upon the ground (1)
588, 589	Let not our selfishness and hate this holy seed remove (2)

seeing

46	we, this marvel seeing, forget our selfish being (2)
69	blind-hearted seeing no light (2)
159	seeing Christ in torment languish (1)
573	Bind us in thine own love for better seeing thy Word (5)

seek

18	seek our victory in your peace (2a)
93	seek the great Desire of nations (3)
109	to seek for a king was their intent (3)
119	so may we with willing feet ever seek thy mercy seat (2)
124	leads them on with power benign to seek the Giver (3)
124	to seek the Giver of the sign (3)
124	grace impels us on to seek thy face (4)
133, 134	May all who seek to praise aright ... show ... your light (3)
152	now we repent, and seek thy face (2)
176, 177	seek through the power of the new creation (2)
176, 177	seek ... life everlasting (2)
201	"Whom seek ye here?" the angel said
203	the faithful women went their way to seek the tomb (2)
203	seek the tomb where Jesus lay (2)
209	seek where you are found (3)
232	seek, like him, your will (2/8-24)
255	In us you seek disciples to share your cross and crown (3)
336	Now we go to seek and serve thee (2)
342	For all we seek your grace sustaining (2)
347	the grace and power we seek (2)
440	let our hearts and souls be stirred now to seek and love (1)
440	to seek and love and fear thee (1)
457	who would the Father seek, must seek him, Lord, by thee (1)
463, 464	He is the Truth. Seek him in the Kingdom of Anxiety (2)
516	Come down, O love divine, seek thou this soul of mine (1)
552, 553	lift up thine eyes and seek his face (2)
570, 571	seek the Lord, who is your life (2)
581	be his the glory that we seek, be ours his holy peace (4)

590	seek out the lonely and God's mercy share (2)
593	may we not seek to be consoled, but to console (3)
593	but seek to love unselfishly (4)
598	seek the kingdom of thy peace (3)
614	seek again the Way disciples followed then (2)
642	how good to those who seek (3)
649, 650	we seek the peace your love imparts (1)
656	Lord, we thy presence seek (4)
681	though we who seek to find thee have tried (2)
687, 688	for still our ancient foe doth seek to work us woe (1)
689	afterward I knew he moved my soul to seek him, seeking me (1)
708	Early let us seek thy favor, early let us learn thy will (2)
711	Seek ye first the kingdom of God and its righteousness (RC)
711	seek, and he shall find (RC)

seeker's

501, 502	You are the seeker's sure resource (2)

seeking

334	seeking peace in every nation (3)
360, 361	strangers and pilgrims, seeking homes eternal (4)
448, 449	by words and signs and actions, thus still seeking ... us (3)
448, 449	seeking not himself but us (3)
590	seeking to gather all in love and pity (3)
623	seeking Jerusalem, dear native land (4)
682	with the hope of gaining aught, not seeking a reward (5)
689	afterward I knew he moved my soul to seek him, seeking me (1)

seem

243	the stones of earthly shame a jeweled crown may seem (4)
625	assist our song, for else the theme too high doth seem (1)
625	too high doth seem for mortal tongue (1)

seemed

102	child who seemed so helpless is our Lord in heaven above (5)

seemly

377, 378	for it is seemly so to do (3)

seems

59	"Christ is nigh," it seems to say (1)
640	for the morning seems to dawn (3)

seen

89, 90	by prophets seen of old (4)
93	ye have seen his natal star (3)
125, 126	people who in darkness walked have seen a glorious light (1)
127	seen in fleshly form on earth (2)
204	quick from the dead my risen Lord is seen (3)
206	how they had seen the risen Lord, he doubted (3)
206	How blest are they who have not seen (6)
210	let all things seen and unseen their notes together blend (3)

390	Hast thou not seen how all thou needest hath been granted (2)
499	my eyes have seen the Savior, Christ the Lord (1)
506, 507	by whose love and power, in Jesus God himself was seen (3)
506, 507	in Jesus God himself was seen and heard (3)
582, 583	O holy city, seen of John (1)

seers
81	Of Jesse's lineage coming as seers of old have sung (1)
265	thy Son shall be Emmanuel, by seers foretold (2)
386, 387	seers that stupendous truth believed (4)

sees
214	Hail the day that sees him rise (1)
257	The aged Simeon sees at last his Lord, so long desired (3)
603, 604	he sees not labels but a face, a person, and a name (3)
719	O beautiful for patriot dream that sees beyond the years (3)

seize
| 582, 583 | yea, bids us seize the whole of life and build its glory (4) |

seized
| 94, 95 | for mighty dread has seized their troubled mind (2) |
| 715 | a trembling fear seized all the guilty world around (RC) |

self
142	so teach us, gracious Lord, to die to self (3)
149	So daily dying to the way of self (2)
324	he will give ... his own self for heavenly food (2)
445, 446	God's presence and his very self, and essence all divine (4)
452	Glorious the day when Christ fulfills what self rejects (4)
452	what self rejects yet feebly wills (4)
498	my sinful self my only shame, my glory all the cross (3)
522, 523	his love his people raises over self to reign as kings (4)
587	who teachest us to find the love from self set free (3)
719	who more than self their country loved (2)
719	confirm thy soul in self control, thy liberty in law (2)

selfish
46	we, this marvel seeing, forget our selfish being (2)
251	help us here on earth to live from selfish passions free (4)
594, 595	shame our wanton, selfish gladness (3)
597	delivered from our selfish schemes (1)
609	above the noise of selfish strife (1)

selfishness
| 3, 4 | from selfishness our hearts release (3) |
| 588, 589 | Let not our selfishness and hate this holy seed remove (2) |

send
1, 2	send us thy salvation (3)
21, 22	you send the early morning ray (1)
157	Hosanna, Lord, hosanna. Lord, send us now success (R)
223, 224	unto us your Spirit send (3)

230	curse of Babel was undone when God did send the Spirit (2)
282, 283	Send thine archangel Michael to our succor (2)
282, 283	Send thine archangel Gabriel the mighty herald of heaven (3)
282, 283	Send from the heavens Raphael thine archangel (4)
320	eternal goodness send us in the land of life to see (5)
340, 341	in the world to which you send us, let your kingdom come (4)
381	Alleluia, alleluia, Praise to thee who light dost send (1-3)
489	in kindness, as a king might send his son, himself a king (3)
514	to thee, by Jesus Christ send down (4)
515	richest treasure we can wish or God can send (1)
539	Send heralds forth to bear the message glorious (3)
540	Send forth, O Lord, thy strong Evangel (3)
625	days ... whate'er he send, be filled with praise (4)
629	O Father, Son, and Spirit, send us increase from above (3)
666	Out of the depths I call, to God I send my cry (1)

sending

1, 2	banish our weakness, health and wholeness sending (2)
489	He sent him down as sending God, in flesh to us he came (4)

sends

291	sends the snow in winter, the warmth to swell the grain (1)
429	sends the laboring conscience peace (3)
633	Word that sends us from above God the Spirit (4)
659, 660	in hope that sends a shining ray far down the ... way (4)
669	God ever sends his blessing in answer to thy prayer (2)

sense

19, 20	Let mouth and tongue, mind, sense, and strength (2)
329-331	faith, our outward sense befriending, makes ... clear (5)
416	for the mystic harmony linking sense to sound and sight (3)
440	our knowledge, sense, and sight lie in deepest darkness (2)
585	gifts of love to mind and sense (2)
629	dares to bind to one's own sense the oracles of heaven (2)
652, 653	let sense be dumb, let flesh retire (5)
677	Judge not the Lord by feeble sense (4)

senses

5	Spirit's sanctifying beam upon our earthly senses stream (2)
329, 331	though the senses fail to see (4)
501, 502	Flood our dull senses with your light (4)

sent

48	this day our Lord victorious the Spirit sent from heaven (2)
85, 86	love of him who sent you here (5)
99	God sent us salvation that blessed Christmas morn (3)
114	God the Lord of all the earth sent angel-choirs instead (1)
121	sent you his kingdom to proclaim, his holy will to do (2)
266	he was sent from the Trinity, to Nazareth in Galilee (1)
291	All good gifts around us are sent from heaven above (R)
448, 449	for us he sent his Spirit here (5)
455, 456	sent by the Father from on high, our life to live (3)
489	He sent no angel of his host to bear this mighty word (2)
489	He sent him not in wrath and power (3)
489	He sent him down as sending God, in flesh to us he came (4)

| 489 | in love God sent his Son to save not to condemn mankind (6) |
| 579 | Spirit ... the Father sent to spread abroad the firmament (3) |

sentinel
| 587 | with constant love as sentinel (1) |

separate
447	What now can separate us from the love of Christ our Lord (2)
447	no power earth can afford will separate us (4)
447	separate us from the love of Jesus Christ our Lord (4)

sepulcher
| 127 | myrrh his sepulcher foreshows (4) |

seraph
94, 95	Thus spake the seraph (5)
324	At his feet the six-winged seraph (4)
367	With his seraph train before him (2)

seraph's
| 491 | Far beyond the seraph's thought (2) |

seraphim
112	cherubim and seraphim thronged the air (3)
212	O Dead arise! O Friendless stand by seraphim adored (5)
362	cherubim and seraphim falling down before thee (2)
364	both cherubim and seraphim (2)
366	cherubim and seraphim, in unceasing chorus praising (2)
367	Round the Lord in glory seated cherubim and seraphim (1)
370	the service of the seraphim (3)
496, 497	by highest seraphim adored (2)
618	more glorious than the seraphim, lead their praises (2)

seraphs
| 618 | bright seraphs, cherubim, and thrones (1) |

serene
624	the Prince is ever in them, the daylight is serene (2)
663	by streams serene, he safely doth me lead (1)
683, 684	calm and serene my frame (5)

serenely
| 31, 32 | evening stars serenely light the darkening sky (3) |
| 681 | stars serenely burn above this earth's confusion (1) |

servant
121	God called you his beloved Son ... his servant true (2)
266	Said the maiden, "Verily, I am your servant right truly" (6)
355	Give rest, O Christ, to your servant with your saints (1)
473	Each new-born servant of the Crucified bears ... seal (2)
477	who wast a servant that we might be free (3)
499	Lord God, you have set your servant free to go in peace (1)
541	to each servant does the Master say, "Go work today" (1)
572	Captain Christ, O lowly Lord, Servant King (2)
592	A servant with this clause makes drudgery divine (3)

| 641 | let me thy loving servant be (2) |
| 655 | that where thou art in glory there shall thy servant be (3) |

servant's

| 492 | stooped to wear the servant's vesture (2) |

servanthood

| 582, 583 | city ... whose laws are love, whose crown is servanthood (3) |

servants

208	from death's dread sting thy servants free (5)
231	we with all your servants may wear the crown of life (2/5-1)
255	in those least expected true servants you can find (3)
282, 283	grant of thy mercy ... us thy servants steps up to heaven (1)
289	Our Father, by whose servants our house was built of old (1)
326	O Lord, evermore to thy servants thy presence be nigh (2)
338	Wherefore, O Father, we thy humble servants here bring (1)
349	draw near to your servants gathered here (1)
358	Christ the Victorious, give to your servants rest (1,4)
360, 361	hear now thy servants when their joyful voices rise (1)
360, 361	here may thy servants, at the mystic banquet (2)
366	help thy servants, drawing near (7)
481	take his servants up to their eternal home (4)
518	with thy wonted lovingkindness hear thy servants (3)
518	hear thy servants as they pray (3)
518	Here vouchsafe to all thy servants what they ask of thee (4)
526	all the servants of our King in heaven and earth are one (1)
535	Ye servants of God, your Master proclaim (1)
541	Servants, well done (5)
560	Remember your servants, Lord, when you come in ... power (A)
593	Lord, make us servants of your peace (1,5)
607	with faith that none can alter, your servants undergird (3)
610	we, your servants, bring the worship not of voice alone (1)
610	that your servants, Lord, in freedom may your mercy know (4)
614	round him drew thousands of servants brave and true (1)

serve

3, 4	that we may see and serve his Son (2)
3, 4	that we may serve, and know his peace (3)
9	to serve right gloriously the God (6)
43	vigorous make to serve my God when I awake (3)
121	freely as Son of Man to serve and give your life for all (3)
231	not betray our calling but serve you to the end (2/2-24)
258	love thee most and serve thee best (2)
273, 274	the works of Peter show us how we may serve the Lord (3)
286	day and night they serve him still (5)
289	our Father, make us faithful to serve the coming days (3)
336	Now we go to seek and serve thee (2)
347	to serve God's people every day and hour (4)
348	teach us to serve without pride or pretension (2)
377, 378	him serve with mirth, his praise forth tell (1)
406, 407	serve in great humility (8)
521	to serve thee is to reign (4)
528	may we serve as you intend (5)
549, 550	serve and love thee best of all (5)

551	to serve the King of kings (1)
561	ye that are his now serve him against unnumbered foes (2)
570, 571	All who love and serve your city (1)
602	show us how to serve the neighbors we have from you (R)
602	These are the ones we should serve (3)
655	O Jesus, I have promised to serve thee to the end (1)
655	Jesus, I have promised to serve thee to the end (3)
657	serve thee as thy hosts above (2)
698	Come with the vision and the strength I need to serve (3)
698	serve my God and all humanity (3)
705	serve thy cause and share thy love with all humanity (3)

serves

| 529 | Who serves my Father as his child is surely kin to me (2) |

service

51	In the Lord's service bread and wine are offered (4)
121	likewise in God's service we may perfect freedom find (4)
255	give you final service in glory at your throne (3)
282, 283	in thy service, he may wisely guide us (4)
297	Enlist us in your service, Lord (2)
312	Strengthen for service, Lord, the hands (1)
326	ever fit us by service on earth for thy service on high (2)
337	in thine own service make us glad and free (4)
340, 341	In your service, Lord, defend us (4)
370	the service of the seraphim (3)
528	Lord, you call us to your service (2)
541	No arm so weak but may do service here (3)
610	Lord, whose love through humble service bore the weight (1)
610	Called by worship to your service (4)
614	scattered companies unite in service to the Lord of light (3)
652, 653	in purer lives thy service find (1)
659, 660	in lowly paths of service free (1)
697	life shall be thy service, Lord (4)

serving

347	serving Christ, our every gift employ (4)
580	serving others, honoring you (4)
594, 595	serving thee whom we adore (4)
602	serving as though we were slaves (4)
617	enough to know that we are serving thee (3)

set

9	So let the love of Jesus come and set thy soul ablaze (5)
10	If on our daily course our mind be set (3)
10	mind be set to hallow all we find (3)
31, 32	you in the primal world once set the boundaries (4)
38, 39	you set the bounds of night and day (2)
57, 58	those who set at nought and sold him (2)
60	you came, O Savior, to set free your own (2)
60	set free your own in glorious liberty (2)
66	Come ... long-expected Jesus, born to set thy people free (1)
80	from all sin will set you free (3)
102	Christ ... set at God's right hand on high (6)
145	to fight, to fight till every wrong's set right (3)

161	the ransom of a world set free (4)
170	set you with taunts along that road (1)
174	From sin's power do thou set free soul's new-born (4)
174	set free soul's new-born, O Lord, in thee (4)
202	thy captive people are set free (4)
232	presiding at the council that set the Gentiles free (2/10-23)
236	glory to Christ, who set us free (4)
259	Come to thy temples here, that we, from sin set free (4)
278	paid to set the sinner free (2)
320	Bread ... now in truth before thee set (2)
337	between our sins and their reward, we set the passion (2)
337	we set the passion of thy Son our Lord (2)
364	humbly thou cam'st to set us free (6)
366	from morn till set of sun ... the song goes on (3)
366	In the glory of that land ... set at God's right hand (6)
380	till suns shall rise and set no more (2)
385	thy hands have set the heavens with stars (1)
413	Trumpets and organs set in motion such sounds (2)
417, 418	whose blood set us free to be people of God (1)
425	came to set his people free (2)
436	make it a temple set apart from earthly use (3)
436	a temple set apart from earthly use for heaven's employ (3)
444	Blessed be the God of Israel, who comes to set us free (1)
490	God set the stars to give light to the world (1)
499	Lord God, you have set your servant free to go in peace (1)
500	from sin and sorrow set us free (1)
506, 507	till ... we, too, set the world alight (5)
517	happy they whose hearts are set upon the pilgrim's quest (2)
534	to set their captives free (3)
545	for the joy before him set, and moved by pitying love (4)
567	leper set apart and shunned, the sick with fevered frame (1)
587	who teachest us to find the love from self set free (3)
600, 601	set thy judgments in the earth (5)
613	arise, O Morning Star, arise, and never set (5)
616	He comes to break oppression, to set the captive free (1)
634	My heart is never set at rest till thy sweet word (1)
641	from harmful passions set me free (1)
667	set free from present sorrow, we cheerfully can say (2)
706	did not freely choose you till by grace you set me free (2)

sets

242	the truth that sets us free (5)
586	Every task, however simple, sets the soul ... free (3)
586	every task ... sets the soul that does it free (3)
706	Now my heart sets none above you (3)

setting

33-35	Now comes the day's end as the sun is setting (2)
511	setting captive sinners free (2)
541	a glad sound comes with the setting sun (5)
542	whole round world complete, from sunrise to its setting (2)
585	bound in setting others free (4)

seven

382	Seven whole days, not one in seven, I will praise thee (3)

sevenfold
225   sevenfold mystical offering (2)
500   rich in thy sevenfold energy (3)
503, 504   who dost thy sevenfold gifts impart (2)

sever
194, 195   our hearts know well nought from us his love shall sever (3)
701   nought that I may suffer ever shall from Jesus sever (2)

several
316, 317   Too soon we rise; we go our several ways (2)

severed
623   wish and fulfillment are not severed there (2)

severing
187   deep and wide flows the tide severing us from bondage past (1)
559   yet unfearing, persevering, to thy passion thou didst go (2)

shade
16, 17   it puts the noon-day sun in shade (3)
46   shade creeps o'er wild and wood (1)
226, 227   in our summer, cooling shade (2)
228   freshening breeze and cooling shade (2)
276   he knelt beneath the olive shade (4)
408   by morning glow or evening shade ... ne'er sleepeth (2)
522, 523   Thus deriving from their banner, light ... and shade (3)
522, 523   light by night and shade by day (3)
663   valley of death's shade (3)
668   thy shelter and thy shade (3)

shades
6, 7   Triumph o'er the shades of night (1)
144   dispel the gloom that shades our minds (1)
409   Soon as the evening shades prevail (2)
664   When I walk through the shades of death (2)

shadow
56   death's dark shadow put to flight (6)
267   like her whom heaven's Majesty came down to shadow o'er (3)
498   the shadow of a mighty rock within a weary land (1)
498   I take, O cross, thy shadow for my abiding place (3)
680   under the shadow of thy throne (2)
699   cover my defenseless head with the shadow of thy wing (2)

shadowed
40, 41   you drive away the shadowed night (1)
476   his meaning lights our shadowed world through Christ (2)
599   shadowed beneath thy hand may we for ever stand (3)
609   on shadowed thresholds dark with fears (2)

shadowing
375   beneath thy shadowing pinions (2)

shadows

18	all shadows of the morn and eve converged (3b)
42	shadows of the evening steal across the sky (1)
180	Death's long shadows have departed (2)
235	drove away the shadows, and filled the world with light (1)
314	who thy glory hidest 'neath these shadows mean (1)
329-331	types and shadows have their ending (5)
427	When evening shadows fall, this rings my curfew call (1)
541	till the long shadows o'er our pathway lie (5)
638, 639	the morning breaks, the shadows flee (4)
662	heaven's morning breaks, and earth's vain shadows flee (4)
703	involved in shadows of a darksome night (2)

shake

11	shake off dull sloth (1)
228	Shake with rushing wind our will (4)
522, 523	what can shake thy sure repose (1)
636, 637	that soul, though all hell shall endeavor to shake (5)

shakes

296	The Spirit's power shakes the Church of God (3)

shame

162	gone is thy shame (3)
164	through our pity and our shame love answers love's appeal (2)
170	mercy throw around our naked shame (2)
171	Shun not suffering, shame or loss (2)
222	he takes upon his heart the cares, the pain, and shame (3)
222	shame of human strife (3)
243	the stones of earthly shame a jeweled crown may seem (4)
345	guard thou the lips from sin, the hearts from shame (1)
445, 446	When all was sin and shame, a second Adam ... came (2)
455, 456	the cross of shame (3)
468	wasn't that a pity and a shame, Lord, Lord (1-4)
476	Our boastfulness is turned to shame (3)
483	To them the cross with all its shame ... grace is given (4)
483	though shame and death to him (6)
495	Hail, thou universal Savior, bearer of our sin and shame (1)
498	my sinful self my only shame, my glory all the cross (3)
542	cast out our pride and shame that hinder to enthrone thee (3)
545	He ... endured the cross, despised the shame (4)
574, 575	whate'er the pain and shame maybe, bring us ... nearer (1)
574, 575	consume the ill, purge out the shame (4)
582, 583	O shame to us who rest content while lust and greed (2)
594, 595	shame our wanton, selfish gladness (3)
603, 604	Where generation, class, or race divide us to our shame (3)
675	heed not the shame, and let your foolish heart be still (3)
701	Be it blame or scorn or shame, thou art with me (3)

shamed

161	The best are shamed before that wood (5)

shameful

448, 449	he bore the shameful cross and death (4)

shan't
554   to bow and to bend we shan't be ashamed (1)

share
18   help us to share your pain and grief (3a)
61, 62   that you the wedding feast may share (1)
70   Christ has come to share our life (4)
80   that in his kingdom bright and fair ... his glory share (4)
80   you may with us his glory share (4)
81   from sin and death now save us, and share our every load (3)
136, 137 O vision fair of glory that the Church may share (1)
150   Should not we thy sorrow share (2)
159   who ... would not share her sorrows deep (4)
161   grant, most blessed Trinity ... all may share the victory (5)
164   as we share this hour, thy cross may bring us to thy joy (4)
168, 169 In thy most bitter passion my heart to share doth cry (3)
202   The Lamb's high banquet called to share (1)
213   For the glory we were first created to share (3)
213   share both the nature and kingdom divine (3)
231   to share your peace above (2/12-28)
232   worldly gain forsaking, your path of life we share (2/9-21)
246   not yet was he to share our pain (2)
246   we share your pain and find your joy (5)
255   In us you seek disciples to share your cross and crown (3)
296   We share by water in his saving death (2)
296   Reborn we share with him an Easter life (2)
304   As Christ breaks bread and bids us share (3)
346   oh, count us worthy, Christ, thy joys to share (2)
350   Whatever comes to be their share of quickening joy (2)
350   share of quickening joy or burdening care (2)
363   summoning all to share thy new creation (3)
421   with the Spirit, you alone share in the Father's glory (3)
459   where his loving people meet to share the gift divine (2)
512   Lead us to heaven, that we may share the fullness of joy (4)
528   asking ... world around us share your children's liberty (3)
537   with us the work to share, with us reproach to dare (3)
541   Claim the high calling angels cannot share (4)
573   sharing not our griefs, no joy can share (2)
580   your children in your likeness, share inventive powers (1)
580   we ... share inventive powers with you (1)
590   seek out the lonely and God's mercy share (2)
610   your abundant life to share (3)
630   Word Incarnate heights and depths of life did share (2)
641   share thy joy at last (4)
652, 653 Jesus knelt to share with thee the silence of eternity (3)
705   serve thy cause and share thy love with all humanity (3)

shared
85, 86   O Son who shared the Father's might (1)
110   the ass and oxen shared the roof with them (2)
120   in the river shared our stain (1)

shares
77   our very flesh our Maker shares (2)

102	he shares in all our gladness (4)
222	He reigns, but with a love that shares the troubles (3)
232	the one who shares our woes (2/10-18)

sharing

18	sharing, know life's victory won (3a)
198	today the branches with the root in resurrection sharing (2)
334	Christ, your cross and passion sharing (1)
334	Scattered flock, one shepherd sharing, lost and lonely (2)
424	in the harvests we are sharing (2)
568	sharing a stable with beasts at thy birth (2)
573	sharing not our griefs, no joy can share (2)

sharp

448, 449	for us temptations sharp he knew (2)

sharpest

237	vain the tyrant's sharpest aim, vain each fierce endeavor (2)

shatter

145	To shatter every yoke (3)

sheathe

572	your dying bade us sheathe the foolish sword (2)

sheathes

174	death's dark angel sheathes his sword (2)

sheaves

288	yellow sheaves of ripened grain (2)

shed

29, 30	shed thou within our hearts thy ray (1)
67	For the glory of the Lord now o'er earth is shed abroad (3)
102	Once in royal David's city stood a lowly cattle shed (1)
120	now by the Holy spirit shed upon the Son's anointed head (3)
139	in his great endeavor to save us, his own blood was shed (2)
160	where the blood of Christ was shed (1,4)
174	Praise we Christ, whose blood was shed (2)
191	we are risen! Shed upon us heavenly grace (4)
228	shed on us a shining ray (1)
229	O shed thine influence from above (1,3)
284	E'en angel eyes slow tears did shed (5)
301	Wine of the soul, in mercy shed (1)
301	look on the tears by sinners shed (1)
329, 331	Blood ... which the Gentiles' Lord and King ... shed (1)
329, 331	shed for this world's ransoming (1)
357	shed on them the radiance of thy heavenly light (4)
469, 470	plentiful redemption in the blood that has been shed (2)
510	come, shed abroad a Savior's love (4)
518	thy fullest benediction shed within its walls alway (3)
519, 520	bridal glory round thee shed (2)
527	light ... o'er his ransomed people shed (2)

631	Light of knowledge ... shed on us thy deathless learning (3)
649, 650	shed o'er the world your holy light (4)
693	without one plea, but that thy blood was shed for me (1)
719	God shed his grace on thee (1,3)

shedding

| 631 | shedding light that none can measure (1) |

sheds

88	he on Adam's fallen race sheds the fullness of his grace (3)
371	where the Gospel day sheds not its glorious ray (1)
419	Sun of our life, thy quickening ray sheds ... the glow (2)
419	sheds on our path the glow of day (2)
459	an altar candle sheds its light as surely as a star (2)

sheen

| 624 | the pastures of the blessed are decked in glorious sheen (2) |

sheep

109	lay keeping their sheep on a cold winter's night (1)
158	Lo, the Good Shepherd for the sheep is offered (3)
183	A lamb the sheep redeemeth (2)
377, 378	for his sheep he doth us take (2)
391	when like wandering sheep we strayed, he saved us (2)
399	O God Most High, we are your sheep (2)
478	Good Shepherd of your sheep, your own defending (2)

shelter

102	his shelter was a stable, and his cradle was a stall (2)
563	Lord has been thy shelter, the Lord will be thy light (4)
668	thy shelter and thy shade (3)
680	our shelter from the stormy blast, and our eternal home (1)

shepherd

75	He shall feed his flock like a shepherd (3)
77	Lord Most High, the one great Shepherd (4)
112	If I were a shepherd, I would bring a lamb (4)
158	Lo, the Good Shepherd for the sheep is offered (3)
245	faithful shepherd of the flock ... sheep-fold's only door (2)
293	one was a shepherd on the green (1)
320	praise thy King and Shepherd true (1)
320	Very Bread, good Shepherd, tend us (5)
334	Scattered flock, one shepherd sharing, lost and lonely (2)
343	Shepherd of souls, refresh and bless thy chosen (1)
478	Good Shepherd of your sheep, your own defending (2)
644	O Jesus, Shepherd, Guardian, Friend (4)
645, 646	The King of love my shepherd is (1)
645, 646	Good Shepherd, may I sing thy praise (6)
663	The Lord my God my shepherd is (1)
664	My Shepherd will supply my need, Jehovah is his Name (1)
708	Savior, like a shepherd lead us (1)

shepherd's

| 399 | on us you keep your shepherd's eye (2) |

shepherds

77	to shepherds poor the Lord Most High ... was revealed (4)
83	See how the shepherds, summoned to his cradle (4)
91	O shepherds, greet that glorious sight (1)
93	Shepherds in the field abiding (2)
94, 95	While shepherds watched their flocks by night (1)
96	Shepherds, why this jubilee (2)
99	While shepherds kept their watching (1)
99	The shepherds feared and trembled (2)
105	unto certain shepherds brought tidings of the same (2)
106	Then to the watchful shepherds it was told (2)
106	In Bethlehem the happy shepherds sought to see (4)
106	Let us, like these good shepherds, then employ (5)
109	The first Nowell the angel did say was to ... shepherds (1)
109	certain poor shepherds in fields as they lay (1)
111	shepherds quake at the sight (2)
115	while shepherds watch are keeping (1)
115	This, this is Christ the King who shepherds guard (R)
115	whom shepherds guard and angels sing (R)
491	Prophets, shepherds, kings, advise (1)

shield

18	shield frail human eyes from all the woe you bore for us (3b)
59	may he with his mercy shield us (4)
120	grant us the Holy Spirit's power to shield us (5)
120	shield us in temptation's hour (5)
193	from every weapon death can wield ... shield (4)
193	thine own redeemed for ever shield (4)
243	he bore no shield before his face (1)
243	no shield I ask, no faithful friend (4)
316, 317	here with us -- our Shield and Sun (2)
370	his hand to guide, his shield to ward (5)
388	Our shield and defender, the Ancient of Days (1)
579	our people shield in danger's hour (4)
608	thy children shield in danger's hour (4)
617	thy trusty shield, thy sword of love divine (3)
644	my shield and hiding place (3)
671	he will my shield and portion be as long as life endures (3)
690	strong deliverer, be thou still my strength and shield (2)

shields

327, 328	He that his saints in this world rules and shields (6)
678, 679	For the Lord defends and shields me (1)

shine

31, 32	Like sun and day, shine in our hearts (5)
37	one by one the lamps of evening shine (2)
47	shine, blest Spirit in my heart (5)
52	O Lord, this day upon us shine (1)
76	shine forth, and let thy light restore (4)
104	And straw like gold shall shine (1)
140, 141	swear by thyself, that at my death thy Son shall shine (3)
140, 141	thy Son shall shine as he shines now, and heretofore (3)
144	Lord Jesus, Sun of Righteousness, shine in our hearts (1)

144	shine in our hearts, we pray (1)
145	who build the old waste places and in the darkness shine (4)
150	round us ... angels shine, such as ministered to thee (4)
226, 227	come within our hearts to shine (1)
231	that we might wear the crown and ever shine in splendor (1)
231	Come shine within our darkness (2/1-25)
232	ever shine in splendor reflected from your throne (1)
287	We feebly struggle, they in glory shine (4)
368	God the Lord ... let thy wondrous mercies shine (4)
368	God the Lord, through every nation ... shine (4)
389	The horned moon to shine by night (5)
409	for ever singing as they shine (3)
431	So shine the Lord's commandments to make the simple wise (3)
459	there heavenly splendors shine (2)
465, 466	Eternal light, shine in my heart (1)
475	let thy light shine through me (3)
477	that in our darkened hearts thy grace might shine (1)
490	Shine in my heart, Lord Jesus (R)
490	Clear sun of righteousness, shine on my path (2)
499	to shine on nations trapped in darkest night (1)
516	let thy glorious light shine ever on my sight (2)
534	glorious gospel of truth may shine throughout the world (3)
538	Shine upon us, Savior, shine (1)
543	Cheerful in God, arise and shine (1)
576, 577	Shine on us, O purest Light of all creation (3)
632	still that light is lifted o'er all the earth to shine (2)
662	shine through the gloom, and point me to the skies (4)
683, 684	a light to shine upon the road that leads me to the Lamb (1)

shined
| 157 | God is the Lord; he has shined upon us (R) |

shines
18	As now the sun shines down at noon (1)
25, 26	Now sunset comes, but light shines forth (2)
31, 32	for you the dazzling star shines forth (2)
55	Your cradle shines with glory's light (5)
59	shines upon the morning skies (2)
93	yonder shines the infant Light (2)
124	It shines to herald forth the King (1)
124	within them shines a clearer light (3)
140, 141	thy Son shall shine as he shines now, and heretofore (3)
162	the cross shines forth in mystic glow (1)
163	lo, a more heavenly lamp shines here (2)
246	Lord Jesus, through our night of loss shines ... the cross (4)
342	your love shines though your strength is waning (2)
383, 384	Jesus shines brighter (3)
383, 384	Jesus shines purer than all the angels heaven can boast (3)
388	It breathes in the air, it shines in the light (4)
398	moon shines full at his command and all the stars obey (1)
406, 407	shines in brilliant splendor (2)
434	But in the grace that rescued man his ... glory shines (2)
434	his brightest form of glory shines (2)
597	O day of peace that dimly shines through all our hopes (1)
632	a lantern to our footsteps, shines on from age to age (1)

shinest
198   best and greatest shinest (1)

shineth
78, 79   yet in thy dark streets shineth the everlasting Light (1)
582, 583   where the sun that shineth is God's grace for human good (3)
702   the darkness shineth as the light (5)

shining
6, 7   more and more thyself display, shining to the perfect day (3)
94, 95   forthwith appeared a shining throng of angels (5)
109   They looked up and saw a star shining in the east (2)
109   shining in the east beyond them far (2)
117, 118   Cold on his cradle the dewdrops are shining (2)
135   Manifest on mountain height, shining in resplendent light (4)
136, 137   With shining face and bright array (3)
228   shed on us a shining ray (1)
284   When all arrayed in light the shining conqueror rode (7)
400   stars nightly shining, find a voice (2)
409   spangled heavens, a shining frame (1)
471   Inscribed upon the cross we see in shining letters (2)
471   we see in shining letters, God is love (2)
519, 520   Bright thy gates of pearl are shining (3)
615   day by whose clear shining light all wrong ... revealed (4)
659, 660   in hope that sends a shining ray far down the ... way (4)
667   he grants the soul again a season of clear shining (1)
671   bright shining as the sun (5)
672   where thou, our everlasting Sun, art shining evermore (4)
718   in beauty all the starry band of shining worlds (1)
719   crown thy good with brotherhood from sea to shining sea (1,3)

shocks
370   the whirling wind's tempestuous shocks (4)

shod
363   through seas dry-shod, through weary wastes bewildering (2)

shone
25, 26   in you the Father's glory shone (1)
94, 95   the angel of the Lord came down, and glory shone around (1)
99   behold, throughout the heavens there shone a holy light (1)
110   The snow lay on the ground, the stars shone bright (1)
161   With what strange light the rough trunk shone (4)
193   the sun shone out with fairer light (1)
225   day ... Holy Ghost shone in the world with God's grace (R)
233, 234   In them the Father's glory shone (4)
242   How oft, O Lord, thy face hath shone on doubting souls (1)
255   God's light shone down from heaven (1)
256   A light from heaven shone around (1)
267   promise shone with cheering ray on waiting saints of old (1)

shoots
149   as through stony ground the green shoots break (3)

shop

582, 583	greed for gain in street and shop and tenement (2)
705	farm and market, shop and home (1)

shops

293	in church, or in trains, or in shops, or at tea (3)

shore

77	From east to west, from shore to shore (1)
140, 141	fear ... I shall perish on the shore (3)
231	John, your loved disciple, exiled to Patmos' shore (2/12-27)
380	thy praise shall sound from shore to shore (2)
416	offering up on every shore thy pure sacrifice of love (5)
428	earth and sea, O all that live in water or on shore (4)
526	greet the ever-living bands on the eternal shore (4)
527	one the gladness of rejoicing on the far eternal shore (3)
544	his kingdom stretch from shore to shore (1)
567	crowded street, by restless couch ... Gennesaret's shore (2)
623	Truly, "Jerusalem," name we that shore (2)
672	till ... we have reached the shore (4)

short

14, 15	Grant us, when this short life is past, the glorious ... (2)
38, 39	Lord, while we live for this short time (4)
382	e'en eternity's too short to extol thee (3)
415	eternity's too short to utter all thy praise (5)
623	nor do things prayed for come short of the prayer (2)
680	short as the watch that ends the night (4)

should

60	In sorrow that the ancient curse should doom to death (2)
102	confounded that a stable should display heaven's Word (3)
150	Should not we thy sorrow share (2)
162	how God the nations' King should be (2)
168, 169	should I fainting be (4)
173	the glorious Prince of Life should in death be sleeping (3)
212	he should their skill deceive (4)
243	in sweet forgiveness' name, should understand and spare (3)
267	Ask not how this should be, but worship and adore (3)
271, 272	that John should be that herald's name (2)
435	'tis the Father's pleasure we should call him Lord (1)
445, 446	should strive afresh against the foe (3)
445, 446	should strive and should prevail (3)
445, 446	highest gift of grace should flesh and blood refine (4)
448, 449	God, the Son of God, should take our mortal form (1)
448, 449	God ... should take our mortal form for mortal's sake (1)
458	O who am I that for my sake my Lord should ... die (1)
458	Lord should take frail flesh and die (1)
467	what are we that he should show so much love to us below (2)
469, 470	we should take him at his word (3)
474	Forbid it, Lord, that I should boast (2)
480	Should we forget our Savior's praise, the stones ... sing (3)
505	unless thy grace the power should give, none can believe (2))

539	one soul should fail to know his love and might (1)
602	These are the ones we should serve (3)
602	these are the ones we should love (3)
602	this is the way we should live with you (4)
605	Rulers of earth, give ear. Should you not justice show (2)
667	Though vine nor fig tree neither ... wonted fruit should (4)
667	though all the fields should wither (4)
682	Then why ... should I not love thee well (4)
685	Should my tears for ever flow (2)
685	should my zeal no languor know (2)
687, 688	though this world, with devils filled should threaten (3)

shouldn't

293	there's not any reason ... why I shouldn't be one too (2)

shout

9	shout with their shout of praise (5)
61, 62	shout of rampart-guards surrounds us (1)
129, 130	All the prophets and the Law shout through them (2)
129, 130	shout through them their joyful greeting (2)
208	let shout of holy joy outburst (2)
211	Then shout beneath the racing skies (2)
402, 403	Church with psalms must shout, no door can keep them out (2)
538	Let the nations shout and sing glory to their Savior King (2)
562	Hell's foundations quiver at the shout of praise (2)
624	there from care released, the shout of them that triumph (3)

shouting

412	O victory, loud shouting army (1)

shouts

259	no shouts proclaim him nigh, no crowds his coming wait (1)

show

56	to us the path of knowledge show (2)
81	To show God's love aright, she bore to us a Savior (2)
133, 134	more bright than day your face did show (1)
133, 134	May all who seek to praise aright ... show ... your light (3)
133, 134	through purer lives show forth your light (3)
145	For righteousness and peace will show their faces (4)
168, 169	show me, O Love most highest, the brightness of thy face (2)
179	tread the path of darkness, saving strength to show (5)
179	show thy face in brightness, bid the nations see (6)
206	my hands, my feet, I show to thee (4)
253	long cloud of witnesses show the same path to heaven (4)
263, 264	whose might they show, whose praise they tell (1)
273, 274	the works of Peter show us how we may serve the Lord (3)
375	What God hath wrought to show his power he ... sustaineth (3)
400	flowers and fruits that in you grow ... glory also show (4)
400	let them his glory also show (4)
462	truth ... like a flower shall bud and blossom show (2)
467	what are we that he should show so much love to us below (2)
490	show me the way to the Father (2)
491	show me where my Savior lies (1)

528	Lord, you show us love's true measure (4)
536	he will show the way (3)
538	God of mercy ... grace, show the brightness of thy face (1)
569	show forth thy pity on high where thou reignest (1)
580	Great Creator, still creating, show us what we yet may do (1)
590	Show us your Spirit, brooding o'er each city (3)
602	show us how to serve the neighbors we have from you (R)
605	Rulers of earth, give ear. Should you not justice show (2)
610	love in living deeds to show (4)
642	this nor tongue nor pen can show (4)

showed

| 193 | his wounded hands and feet he showed (2) |
| 631 | showed his glory (2) |

shower

515	as a gracious shower descend (1)
515	with thy grace our spirits shower (2)
607	trust in bombs that shower destruction through the night (2)

showers

| 616 | He shall come down like showers upon the fruitful earth (3) |

showest

| 320 | where the heavenly feast thou showest (6) |

showing

472	showing to wandering souls the path of light (3)
506, 507	showing us God's wonders, is himself the power to gaze (2)
522, 523	showing that the Lord is near (3)
630	record of the revelation showing God to every age (3)

shown

139	The Holy Spirit then was shown, a dove on him descending (2)
458	love to the loveless shown that they might lovely be (1)
501, 502	In you God's energy is shown (3)
532, 533	To nations of earth thy light shall be shown (2)

shows

136, 137	which Christ upon the mountain shows (1)
144	The universe your glory shows, blest Father, Spirit, Son (5)
214	See! he shows the prints of love (3)
232	whose Gospel shows the healer of the nations (2/10-18)
434	every labor of his hands shows something worthy of a God (1)
487	such a light as shows a feast (2)
585	he who shows us God helpless hangs upon the tree (5)

shrine

| 104 | A stall become a shrine (1) |

shrined

| 244 | in the holy Gospels shrined (1) |
| 314 | tranced as it beholds thee, shrined within the cloud (1) |

shrink
406, 407   nor shrink from tribulation (6)

shroud
183   bright angels attesting, the shroud and napkin resting (6)

shrouded
440   in deepest darkness shrouded (2)

shun
140, 141   Wilt thou forgive that sin which I did shun a year or two (2)
171   Shun not suffering, shame or loss (2)
364   nor Virgin womb didst shun (6)

shunned
567   leper set apart and shunned, the sick with fevered frame (1)

shut
69   Dark is the season, dark our hearts and shut to mystery (1)

sick
76   To heal the sick stretch out thine hand (4)
371   heal to the sick in mind, sight to the inly blind (2)
443   He did not disregard the sick (4)
528   Heal the sick and preach the word (1)
537   sin-sick and sorrow-worn, whom Christ doth heal (1)
567   leper set apart and shunned, the sick with fevered frame (1)
567   that whole and sick and weak and strong may praise thee (3)
610   As, O Lord, your deep compassion healed the sick (2)
610   healed the sick and freed the soul (2)
676   there is a balm in Gilead to heal the sin-sick soul (R)

sickness
360, 361   Here in our sickness healing grace aboundeth (3)

side
18   ten thousand perish at our side (2c)
101   stay by my side until morning is nigh (2)
150   O keep us, Savior dear, ever constant by thy side (5)
172   Were you there when they pierced him in the side (3)
174   washed us with the tide flowing from his pierced side (1)
206   My pierced side, O Thomas, see (4)
206   he saw the feet, the hands, the side (5)
209   We may not touch his hands and side (2)
243   no spokesman at his side (2)
259   There Joseph at her side in reverent wonder stands (3)
276   For James who left his father's side (2)
277   though he went forth from her side (2)
307   smitten Rock with streaming side (5)
308, 309   O purest fountain, welling from out the Savior's side (2)
310, 311   our foes press on from every side (1)
433   thou, Lord, wast at our side: all glory be thine (2)
434   his dear wounds and bleeding side (4)
495   seated at the Father's side (3)
609   O Master, from the mountain side (4)

655	I shall not fear the battle, if thou art by my side (1)
670	Lord, for ever at thy side let my place and portion be (1)
685	water and the blood from thy wounded side that flowed (1)
687, 688	were not the right man on our side (2)
690	land me safe on Canaan's side (3)
702	I feel thy power on every side (2)
717	from every mountain-side let freedom ring (1)

sigh

623	we for that country must yearn and must sigh (4)

sighed

599	place for which our parents sighed (2)

sighing

128	sorrowing, sighing, bleeding, dying (4)
173	Who would not weep with heartfelt pain and sighing (1)
355	neither sighing, but life everlasting (1)
358	Grief and pain ended, and sighing no longer (1,4)
616	give them songs for sighing … darkness turn to light (2)

sight

61, 62	No eye has known the sight, no ear heard such delight (3)
61, 62	the Bridegroom is in sight (1)
91	O shepherds, greet that glorious sight (1)
111	shepherds quake at the sight (2)
143	So Daniel trained his mystic sight (3)
168, 169	Thy beauty, long desired, hath vanished from our sight (2)
209	We walk by faith, and not by sight (1)
209	with full and endless sight (4)
214	Lord beyond our mortal sight (4)
247	charged … his men of might, in his own sight (2)
284	sad desire that aweful sight to see (5)
292	gathering round thy throne … in the holy angel's sight (3)
336	glory veiling so that we may bear the sight (2)
357	in the mystic symbols veiled from earthly sight (1)
371	come to bring on thy redeeming wing healing and sight (2)
371	heal to the sick in mind, sight to the inly blind (2)
416	for the mystic harmony linking sense to sound and sight (3)
423	thine angels adore thee, all veiling their sight (4)
440	our knowledge, sense, and sight lie in deepest darkness (2)
458	He made the lame to run, he gave the blind their sight (4)
459	The heaven that hides him from our sight (2)
460, 461	though the cloud from sight received him (2)
503, 504	Enable with perpetual light … our blinded sight (4)
503, 504	the dullness of our blinded sight (4)
506, 507	fire our hearts and clear our sight (5)
516	let thy glorious light shine ever on my sight (2)
567	thy touch … gave hearing, strength, and sight (2)
610	light … dawns upon our quickened sight (3)
613	revive our longing eyes, which languish for thy sight (4)
616	souls, condemned and dying were precious in his sight (2)
625	as in his sight with sweet delight ye do abound (2)
643	How wonderful, how beautiful, the sight of thee must be (3)
645, 646	Thou spread'st a table in my sight (5)

78, 79	Above thy deep and dreamless sleep the silent stars go by (1)
82	let no tongue on earth be silent (3)
99	o'er silent flocks by night (1)
111	Silent night, holy night (1-3)
115	for sinners here the silent Word is pleading (2)
257	But silent knelt the mother blest of the yet silent word (4)
289	changeful years unresting their silent course have sped (2)
423	Unresting, unhasting, and silent as light (2)
424	silent growth while we are sleeping (1)
580	through the silent fields of space (1)
599	God of our weary years, God of our silent tears (3)
615	for the everlasting right the silent stars are strong (2)

silently

78, 79	How silently, how silently, the wondrous gift is given (3)
602	silently washes their feet (1)

silver

9	silver glistering of all the million million stars (2)
400	pale silver moon that gently gleams (1)

Simeon

257	The aged Simeon sees at last his Lord, so long desired (3)
259	filled with holy joy, old Simeon (3)

Simon

232	Saint Simon and Saint Jude (2/10-28)

simple

431	So shine the Lord's commandments to make the simple wise (3)
443	to simple ones his word was given (4)
554	'Tis the gift to be simple, 'tis the gift to be free (1)
574, 575	for crafty trade and subtle snare to catch the simple (3)
574, 575	to catch the simple unaware (3)
586	Every task, however simple, sets the soul ... free (3)
627	simple, child-like hearts (5)
652, 653	simple trust like theirs who heard beside the Syrian sea (2)
661	such happy, simple fisher-folk before the Lord came down (1)

simplicity

554	When true simplicity is gained (1)

sin

3, 4	with conscience free from sin and blame (4)
6, 7	Pierce the gloom of sin and grief (3)
27, 28	by sin oppressed (3)
27, 28	to turn from sin and cease from wrong (4)
31, 32	Free us from bonds of blinding sin (5)
42	those who plan some evil from their sin restrain (4)
51	praise him who called us out of sin and darkness (1)
52	Jesus, may we lifted be from death of sin to life in thee (2)
54	Come, O Father's saving Son, who o'er sin the victory won (4)
63, 64	to recompense each hidden sin (3)
68	look now for your salvation, the end of sin and toil (2)

479	stream which from sin and sorrow doth the world redeem (3)
484, 485	o'er sin, and death, and hell victorious (2)
495	Hail, thou universal Savior, bearer of our sin and shame (1)
500	from sin and sorrow set us free (1)
530	earth from sin and death to save (2)
534	fight we the fight with sorrow and sin (3)
540	break down the realm of Satan, death, and sin (3)
545	freed from every weight of sin ... holy footsteps trace (2)
547	To us on earth he came to bring from sin and fear release (2)
596	the city's crowded clangor cries aloud for sin to cease (2)
598	found no room in life where sin denied thee (2)
613	Break with thine iron rod the tyrannies of sin (1)
625	now, from sin released, behold the Savior's face (2)
630	life redeemed from death and sin (5)
633	heal the world, by our sin broken (3)
638, 639	my misery or sin declare (2)
641	purge away my sin (1)
649, 650	chase the night of sin away (4)
685	let the water and the blood ... be of sin the double cure (2)
685	all for sin could not atone (2)
697	let every sin be crucified, and Christ be all in all (2)
699	grace to cleanse from every sin (3)
700	O love that casts out fear, O love that casts out sin (1)

sin's

85, 86	our constant star in sin's deep night (2)
119	so may we with holy joy, pure and free from sin's alloy (3)
174	From sin's power do thou set free soul's new-born (4)
180	we are free from sin's dark prison (4)
555	till sin's fierce war shall cease (2)
578	remember not our sin's dark stain (2)

Sinai's

56	who to thy tribes on Sinai's height in ancient times (3)

since

67	since the kingdom now is here (2)
158	Therefore, kind Jesus, since I cannot pay thee (5)
192	since Jesus crossed the river (2)
266	six months gone since Elizabeth conceived John (5)
292	since thou the earth hast trod (1)
363	with light and life since Eden's dawning day (1)
564, 565	Since, Lord, thou dost defend us with thy Spirit (3)
580	since the childhood of our race (3)
606	Since the love of Christ has joined us in one body (1)

sincere

250	with joy and penitence sincere (1)
327, 328	Approach ye then with faithful hearts sincere (5)

sincerity

174	with sincerity and love eat we manna from above (2)
606	so let us in sincerity love all people (1)

sinews

165, 166	Thy relaxing sinews bend (5)

sinful

50	comes, in God his Father's name, to save our sinful race (4)
146, 147	Your love, O Lord, our sinful race has not returned (3)
255	grace, by ways mysterious, our sinful wrath can bind (3)
286	following not the sinful throng (3)
362	though the sinful human eye thy glory may not see (3)
460, 461	here the sinful flee to thee from day to day (3)
475	pride of life and sinful pleasures (2)
486	thy flock, redeemed from sinful stain ... praise again (5)
492	sinless one, among the sinful (3)
498	my sinful self my only shame, my glory all the cross (3)

sing

9	stars, the silent song they sing (2)
16, 17	Now let us sing our praise to God (1)
44, 45	your praise and glory we shall sing (3)
48	sing, "Holy, holy, holy," to the great God Triune (1)
48	We sing to thee our praises, O Father, Spirit, Son (4)
61, 62	let saints and angels sing before you (3)
61, 62	therefore we sing to greet our King (3)
70	till once more we sing the song (1)
75	get thee up to the heights and sing (2)
77	let every heart awake and sing the holy child
78, 79	praises sing to God the King, and peace to men on earth (2)
80	gladly sing (1)
82	angel hosts, his praises sing (3)
83	Sing, choirs of angels, sing in exultation (3)
83	sing, all ye citizens of heaven above (3)
87	Hark! the herald angels sing glory to the new-born King (1,R)
88	Sing, O sing, this blessed morn, unto us a child is born (1)
88	O sing, this blessed morn, Jesus Christ today is born (R)
89, 90	The world in solemn stillness lay to hear the angels sing (1)
89, 90	ever o'er its Babel-sounds the blessed angels sing (2)
89, 90	hear the angels sing (3)
89, 90	world give back the song which now the angels sing (4)
92	song children sing to the Lord, Christ our King (1)
92	On this day angels sing (4)
96	Come to Bethlehem and see him whose birth the angels sing (3)
100	heaven and nature sing (1)
105	Now to the Lord sing praises, all you within this place (4)
106	Then may we hope, the angelic throngs among, to sing (6)
106	sing, redeemed, a glad triumphal song (6)
106	saved by his love, incessant we shall sing (6)
109	Then let us all with one accord sing praises (6)
109	sing praises to our heavenly Lord (6)
111	heavenly hosts sing alleluia (2)
115	whom shepherds guard and angels sing (R)
119	there for ever may we sing alleluias to our King (5)
122, 123	in the house of God abiding thus they sing eternally (1)
122, 123	alleluia, joyful mother, all thy children sing with thee (2)
165, 166	Sing, my tongue, the glorious battle (1)
165, 166	of the mighty conflict sing (1)

174	At the Lamb's high feast we sing praise (1)
175	all things created on earth sing to the glory of God (2)
178	joyfully sing to our Savior (4)
181	Awake and sing the song of Moses and the Lamb (1)
181	Sing of his dying love, his resurrection power (2)
181	sing how he interecedes above for ... whose sins he bore (2)
181	You pilgrims on the road to Zion's city, sing (3)
181	sing in sweeter notes the song of Moses and the Lamb (4)
182	Let Christians sing (1)
185, 186	sing to God right thankfully loud songs of alleluia (1)
191	sing to God a hymn of gladness (1)
191	sing to God a hymn of praise (1)
202	we now would sing to Jesus our triumphant King (1)
203, 206	O sons and daughters, let us sing (1)
205	Good Christians all, rejoice and sing (1)
205	Sing songs of praise along his way (2)
205	sing with hearts uplifted high (3)
205	sing today with one accord the life laid down (4)
205	we sing for life in us begun (5)
207	Hymns of praise then let us sing (2)
207	where the angels ever sing (3)
207	Sing we to our God above ... praise eternal as his love (4)
208	that we may live and sing to thee (5)
211	The birds do sing on every bough (1)
213	Hallelujah we sing, to our Father and King (5)
213	sing, all heaven, and fall at his feet (5)
215	Hark, the choirs of angel voices joyful alleluias sing (1)
216	all things created on earth sing to the glory of God (1)
217, 218	A hymn of glory let us sing (1)
219	His rising, his ascension sing with grateful adoration (2)
220, 221	by thee redeemed thy praise we sing (1)
231, 232	sing to God the Spirit, eternal Three in One (3)
232	We sing with joy of Mary (2/8-15)
233, 234	The eternal gifts of Christ the King ... we sing (1)
233, 234	the apostles' glorious deeds we sing (1)
235	Come sing, ye choirs exultant, those messengers of God (1)
244	Come, pure hearts, in joyful measure sing (1)
244	sing of those who spread the treasure in the holy Gospels (1)
247	this poor youngling for whom we sing ... lully lullay (1)
247	for thy parting nor say nor sing bye-bye, lully lullay (3)
248, 249	but with holy exultation we may sing aloud today (1)
248, 249	that hereafter, heavenward soaring, we may sing (4)
248, 249	we may sing with angels there (4)
255	We sing the glorious conquest before Damascus' gate (1)
268, 269	sing the wonders that were done (1)
268, 269	let all faithful people sing the honor of her name (3)
268, 269	what Christ's mother sang in gladness ... people sing (3)
268, 269	let Christ's people sing the same (3)
277	Sing of Mary, pure and lowly, virgin mother undefiled (1)
277	sing of God's own Son most holy (1)
277	Sing of Jesus, son of Mary, in the house at Nazareth (2)
278	Sing we of the blessed Mother (1)
278	sing we of the joys of Mary (1)
278	Sing again the joys of Mary when she saw the risen Lord (3)
278	Sing the chiefest joy of Mary (4)

439	sing and joyful be, and through eternity, I'll sing on (3)
458	Sometimes they strew his way and his strong praises sing (3)
458	Here might I stay and sing, no story so divine (7)
460, 461	sing to Jesus, his the scepter, his the throne (1,5)
467	Sing, my soul, his wondrous love (1)
467	Sing, my soul, adore his Name (4)
471	We sing the praise of him who died (1)
478	Glorious their life who sing, with glad thanksgiving (3)
480	Should we forget our Savior's praise, the stones ... sing (3)
480	the stones themselves would sing (3)
481	Mortals, give thanks and sing, and triumph evermore (1)
486	To Christ, Creator Savior, King ... hosanna sing (1)
486	let earth, let heaven, hosanna sing (1)
492	Sing, ye faithful, sing with gladness (1)
492	Sing how he came forth from heaven (2)
493	O for a thousand tongues to sing my dear Redeemer's praise (1)
494	awake, my soul, and sing of him who died for thee (1)
494	his glories now we sing who died, and rose on high (3)
494	where saints with angels sing their songs (4)
494	sing ... before him day and night (4)
495	help to sing our Savior's merits (4)
500	sanctify us while we sing (2)
501, 502	that as one body we may sing (5)
514	To thee, O Comforter divine ... sing we alleluia (1)
514	sing we alleluia, alleluia (1-4)
526	Let saints on earth in concert sing (1)
526	in concert sing with those whose work is done (1)
535	the great congregation his triumph shall sing (2)
537	Christ for the world we sing (1-4)
538	Let the nations shout and sing glory to their Savior King (2)
556, 557	Rejoice, ye pure in heart! Rejoice, give thanks and sing (1)
556, 557	Rejoice, rejoice, rejoice, give thanks, and sing (R)
556, 557	on, ye pure in heart! Rejoice, give thanks and sing (7)
562	this through countless ages we with angels sing (5)
572	weary of all songs that sing promise, non-fulfilling (1)
576, 577	be our bliss while endless ages sing your praises (3)
599	Lift every voice and sing till earth and heaven ring (1)
599	Sing a song full of the faith (1)
599	sing a song full of the hope ... the present has brought (1)
616	all nations shall adore him, his praise all people sing (4)
618	O friends, in gladness let us sing (4)
619	Sing alleluia forth in duteous praise (1)
619	Almighty Christ, to thee our voices sing (7)
621, 622	glorious are the praises which of thee the prophets sing (1)
623	we the sweet anthems of Zion shall sing (3)
625	onward as ye go some joyful anthem sing (3)
625	with a well-tuned heart sing thou the songs of love (4)
635	Sing, pray, and keep his ways unswerving (2)
642	No voice can sing, no heart can frame (2)
645, 646	Good Shepherd, may I sing thy praise (6)
645, 646	sing thy praise within thy house for ever (6)
658	Hope still ... sing the praise of him who is thy God (3)
671	we've no less days to sing God's praise (5)
678, 679	his mercies sing (1)
682	in thy praise will sing solely because thou art my God (6)

686	tune my heart to sing thy grace (1)
707	Take my voice, and let me sing always, only, for my King (2)
710	O sing the honor of his holy Name (RC)
717	of thee I sing (1)
717	to thee we sing (4)

singing

1, 2	singing we offer prayer and meditation: thus we adore (1)
8	Praise for the singing, Praise for the morning (1)
33-35	creation joining hearts and voices singing your glory (3)
61, 62	Zion hears the watchman singing (2)
96	singing sweetly through the night (1)
122, 123	alleluia in our singing, let us for a while give o'er (3)
122, 123	there to thee for ever singing alleluia joyfully (4)
213	with singing to Zion return (1)
213	Now with singing and praise, let us spend all the days (2)
275	joined in holy concert, singing to the Lord of all (2)
287	singing to Father, Son, and Holy Ghost, Alleluia (8)
288	singing thus through all our days praise to God (3)
320	Zion, praise thy Savior, singing hymns with exultation (1)
367	Holy, holy ... singing, Lord of hosts ... Lord Most High (2)
409	for ever singing as they shine (3)
527	Singing songs of expectation ... goes the pilgrim band (1)
572	we ... join in singing that great music pure and strong (1)
617	planets singing on their way (1)
678, 679	Zion, lift your voice in singing (2)

single

| 238, 239 | loving Christ with single heart (2) |
| 591 | lift up a living nation, a single sword to thee (3) |

sings

113	so rest in the arms of your mother who sings you a la ru (2)
128	heaven sings alleluia: alleluia the earth replies (5)
405	each little bird that sings (1)
431	through the silences of space ... soundless music sings (1)
620	Our Lady sings Magnificat with tune surpassing sweet (4)
651	to my listening ears all nature sings (1)
667	Sometimes a light surprises the Christian while he sings (1)

sink

| 624 | beneath thy contemplation sink heart and voice oppressed (1) |

sinking

| 37 | the sun is sinking now (2) |

sinless

120	The sinless one to Jordan came (1)
183	Christ, who only is sinless, reconcileth sinners (2)
460, 461	songs of all the sinless sweep across the crystal sea (3)
492	sinless one, among the sinful (3)

sinned

| 158 | the slave hath sinned, and the Son hath suffered (3) |

sinner

51	school for the faithful, refuge for the sinner (2)
76	bid the fallen sinner stand (4)
97	By this lowly birth of mine, sinner, riches ... thine (2)
256	a sinner saved by Jesus' grace (2)
278	paid to set the sinner free (2)
469, 470	welcome for the sinner, and more graces for the good (1)

sinner's

444	the dawning of forgiveness upon the sinner's eyes (3)
471	the sinner's hope let sin deride (1)
471	the sinner's refuge here below (5)
493	'tis music in the sinner's ears (3)

sinners

52	This day the Lord for sinners slain (2)
83	Child for us sinners poor and in the manger (5)
87	God and sinners reconciled (1)
115	for sinners here the silent Word is pleading (2)
162	Still may thy power with us avail to save us sinners (5)
183	Christ, who only is sinless, reconcileth sinners (2)
183	Christ ... reconcileth sinners to the Father (2)
207	sinners to redeem and save (2)
236	sinners who are burdened by the wrong we do (2)
301	look on the tears by sinners shed (1)
342	O Bread of life, for sinners broken (1)
435	Name from the lips of sinners, unto whom he came (2)
450, 451	Sinners, whose love can ne'er forget the wormwood (5)
460, 461	Intercessor, friend of sinners (3)
494	for ransomed sinners slain (4)
495	There for sinners thou art pleading (3)
496, 497	with praise, ye sinners, fill the sky (3)
511	setting captive sinners free (2)

sins

10	new perils past, new sins forgiven (2)
11	disperse my sins as morning dew (2)
53	from the sins that hurt us, would to Truth convert us (2)
53	Come, then, O Lord Jesus, from our sins release us (4)
66	from our fears and sins release us (1)
67	tell her that her sins I cover (1)
100	No more let sins and sorrows grow (3)
140	Wilt thou forgive those sins through which I run (1)
142	teach us with thee to mourn our sins (1)
151	I lay my sins before thee (1)
152	Spare us, O Lord, who now confess our sins (3)
152	confess our sins and all our wickedness (3)
141	Wilt thou forgive those sins through which I run (1)
164	Our sins, not thine, thou bearest, Lord (2)
181	sing how he intercedes above for ... whose sins he bore (2)
199, 200	all the winter of our sins, long and dark (2)
226, 227	to thy love our sins consign (4)
301	in whose death our sins are dead (1)
334	Sins forgiven, wrong forgiving, we go forth alert (3)
337	between our sins and their reward, we set the passion (2)

382	Thou my sins against me cried, thou didst clear me (2)
411	He pardons all thy sins, prolongs thy feeble breath (4)
454	to hearts rejoicing, bringing news of sins forgiven (3)
471	he bears our sins upon the tree (2)
495	all our sins on thee were laid (2)
568	sorrow for sins that for vengeance have cried (1)
574, 575	from sins which make the heart grow cold, wean us (2)
574, 575	For sins of heedless word and deed (3)
674	Forgive our sins as we forgive (1)
683, 684	I hate the sins that made thee mourn (3)

sins's

| 250 | For Jesus came to wage sins's war (2) |

sister

406, 407	My Lord be praised by sister moon and all the stars (3)
406, 407	By sister water be thou blessed (4)
406, 407	For death our sister, praised be (7)
416	joy of human love, brother, sister, parent, child (4)

sisters

| 247 | O sisters, too, how may we do for to preserve this day (1) |
| 389 | moon ... mid her spangled sisters bright (5) |

sit

67	comfort those who sit in darkness (1)
215	there we sit in heavenly places (3)
421	as you sit at God's right hand ... mercy, Lord, upon us (2)

sits

| 374 | Name of him that sits upon the throne (4) |
| 535 | Salvation to God who sits on the throne (3) |

sittest

| 363 | Ancient of Days, who sittest throned in glory (1) |

six

| 266 | There are yet but six months gone (5) |
| 266 | six months gone since Elizabeth conceived John (5) |

skies

6, 7	Christ, whose glory fills the skies (1)
49	our Lord who made both earth and skies (1)
59	shines upon the morning skies (2)
87	join the triumph of the skies (1)
88	lifted by him to the skies (4)
89, 90	Still through the cloven skies they come (2)
148	Creator of the earth and skies (1)
148	to the skies our monuments of folly soar (2)
188, 189	ours the cross, the grave, the skies (3)
211	Then shout beneath the racing skies (2)
213	Come away to the skies, my beloved (1)
214	glorious to his native skies (1)
369	Our reason ... climbs above the skies (3)
380	From all that dwell below the skies let ... praise arise (1)

398	spread the flowing seas abroad and built the lofty skies (1)
406, 407	sun who through the skies his course doth run (2)
416	For the beauty of the earth, for the beauty of the skies (1)
427	When morning gilds the skies, my heart, awaking, cries (1)
431	writes in fire across the skies God's majesty and praise (2)
543	with his radiance fill those fairer purer skies (4)
599	Let our rejoicing rise high as the listening skies (1)
651	of skies and seas, his hand the wonders wrought (1)
651	all earth and trees, all skies and seas (2)
662	shine through the gloom, and point me to the skies (4)
669	him whose faithful mercy the skies above declare (1)
716	For her our prayers shall rise to God, above the skies (2)
718	in splendor through the skies (1)
719	O beautiful for spacious skies, for amber waves of grain (1)

skill

212	he should their skill deceive (4)
566	From thee all skill and science flow (1)
611	grew in wisdom as he grew in skill (2)
677	Deep in unfathomable mines, with never-failing skill (2)

skilled

482	strong hands were skilled at the plane and the lathe (2)

skillful

611	Skillful craftsman, blessed carpenter (3)

skin

114	a ragged robe of rabbit skin enwrapped his beauty round (2)

sky

3, 4	Now that the daylight fills the sky, we lift our hearts (1)
9	The lark is in the sky (4)
12, 13	The golden sun lights up the sky (1)
18	On Golgatha the sky turned dark (3b)
31, 32	who in the high arched sky has placed the sun (1)
31, 32	evening stars serenely light the darkening sky (3)
42	shadows of the evening steal across the sky (1)
73	crowned with glory like the sun ... lights the morning sky (2)
77	angels in the sky sang praise above the silent field (4)
85, 86	earth and sea and sky revere the love of him (5)
101	The stars in the bright sky looked down where he lay (1)
101	I love thee, Lord Jesus! Look down from the sky (2)
104	A stable lamp is lighted Whose glow shall wake the sky (1)
104	The sky shall groan and darken (3)
156	the angel armies of the sky look down (3)
165, 166	earth, and stars, and sky, and ocean (3)
179	Brightness of the morning, sky and fields and sea (3)
182	His cross stands empty to the sky (1)
207	now above the sky he's King (3)
210	From death to life eternal, from earth unto the sky (1)
254	For ever be adored that Name in earth and sky (1)
263, 264	The Word whom earth and sea and sky adore (1)
362	praise thy Name in earth, and sky, and sea (4)
385	maker of earth and sky (1)

398	if I survey the ground I tread, or gaze upon the sky (2)
405	the sunset and the morning that brightens up the sky (2)
409	with all the blue ethereal sky (1)
429	made the sky and earth and seas with all their train (2)
453	its foot was on earth and its top in the sky (1)
455, 456	we read thee in the sky above (2)
496, 497	with praise, ye sinners, fill the sky (3)
541	No time for rest, till glows the western sky (5)
566	when ever-blue the sky shall gleam (2)
585	Morning glory, starlit sky, soaring music (1)
627	guide and chart wherein we read of realms beyond the sky (2)
632	O Truth, unchanged, unchanging, O Light of our dark sky (1)

slain

52	This day the Lord for sinners slain (2)
57, 58	once for our salvation slain (1)
163	sin is slain, and death brings life (3)
192	Had Christ, that once was slain (R)
202	Now Christ our Passover is slain (3)
204	In the grave they laid him, Love whom hate had slain (2)
213	to the Lamb that was slain, hallelujah again (5)
270	he that cannot die, be slain (2)
273, 274	One on a cross is martyred, one by the sword is slain (2)
276	slain by Herod's flashing blade, he saw thy face again (4)
293	one was slain by a fierce wild beast (2)
307	finished once for all when thou was slain (4)
374	Worthy the Lamb, our lips reply, for he was slain for us (2)
417, 418	Worthy is Christ, the Lamb who was slain (1)
417, 418	the Lamb who was slain has begun his reign. Alleluia (5)
494	for ransomed sinners slain (4)

slaughtered

599	treading our path through the blood of the slaughtered (2)

slave

77	form and fashion of a slave (2)
158	the slave hath sinned, and the Son hath suffered (3)
602	Master who acts as a slave to them (1)

slaves

602	serving as though we were slaves (4)

slay

247	all young children to slay (2)
458	a murderer they save, the Prince of Life they slay (5)

sleep

10	through sleep and darkness safely brought (1)
38, 39	refresh us now with restful sleep (4)
40, 41	be our guardian while we sleep (2)
40, 41	Although our eyes in sleep be closed (3)
43	I, ere I sleep, at peace may be (2)
43	with sweet sleep mine eyelids close (3)
43	sleep that shall me more vigorous make (3)
44, 45	Save us from troubled, restless sleep (2)

78, 79	Above thy deep and dreamless sleep the silent stars go by (1)
78, 79	gathered all above, while mortals sleep (2)
111	Holy infant, so tender and mild, sleep in heavenly peace (1)
113	Oh sleep now, holy baby, with your head against my breast (1)
199, 200	from three days' sleep in death as a sun hath risen (2)
541	while we in sleep our duty have forgot, he slumbered not (2)
591	from sleep and from damnation, deliver us, good Lord (2)
608	calm amid its rage didst sleep (2)

sleeper
547	Awake, O sleeper, rise from death (1)

sleepers
61, 62	"Sleepers, wake!" A voice astounds us (1)

sleepeth
408	by morning glow or evening shade ... ne'er sleepeth (2)
408	his watchful eye ne'er sleepeth (2)

sleeping
115	on Mary's lap is sleeping (1)
173	the glorious Prince of Life should in death be sleeping (3)
424	silent growth while we are sleeping (1)
482	be there at our sleeping (4)
488	waking or sleeping, thy presence my light (1)

sleepless
324	cherubim with sleepless eye (4)

sleeps
204	laid in the earth like grain that sleeps unseen (2)
668	watchful and untiring eye he slumbers not, nor sleeps (2)

sleepy
98	Cradled in a stall was he with sleepy cows and asses (2)

slept
443	The Watcher slept, the Great was small (5)

slighted
569	slighted thy word (2)

slope
196, 197	Jesus ... looked down Golgatha's stony slope (2)

sloth
11	shake off dull sloth (1)
59	Christ our sun, all sloth dispelling (2)

slothful
124	let not our slothful hearts refuse the guidance (4)

slow
284	E'en angel eyes slow tears did shed (5)
404	slow to anger, merciful and kind (3)

410	slow to chide and swift to bless (2)
411	his wrath is ever slow to rise and ready to abate (3)
414	Full of kindness and compassion, slow to anger (5)
462	The Lord will come and not be slow (1)
615	But the slow watches of the night not less to God belong (2)
659, 660	Help me the slow of heart to move (2)

slumber
33-35	Though bodies slumber, hearts shall keep their vigil (5)
117, 118	angels adore him in slumber reclining (2)
192	My flesh in hope shall rest, and for a season slumber (3)

slumbered
| 541 | while we in sleep our duty have forgot, he slumbered not (2) |

slumbering
| 258 | that watched thy slumbering infancy (1) |

small
382	Small it is in this poor sort to enroll thee (3)
405	all creatures great and small (R)
423	To all life thou givest, to both great and small (3)
443	The Watcher slept, the Great was small (5)
474	that were an offering far too small (4)
506, 507	God's will ... by a still small voice conveys (2)
597	nor shall the fierce devour the small (2)
607	your still small voice be heard (3)
652, 653	O still, small voice of calm (5)
674	how small the debts men owe to us (3)

smile
180	Come ... with glad smile and radiant brow (2)
522, 523	With salvation's walls surrounded, thou may'st smile (1)
522, 523	thou may'st smile at all thy foes (1)

smiles
| 102 | scorned, rejected, tears and smiles like us he knew (4) |
| 190 | welcome with your smiles returning (1) |

smite
| 591 | bind all our lives together, smite us and save us all (3) |

smitten
307	smitten Rock with streaming side (5)
386, 387	Moses while on earth in dread and smitten to the heart (2)
498	from my smitten heart with tears two wonders I confess (2)

smoldering
| 299 | fan our smoldering lives to flame (3) |

smote
| 243 | on his lips a sword wherewith he smote and overcame (1) |

snare
| 524 | thy hand from every snare and foe ... deliverance bring (4) |

574, 575   for crafty trade and subtle snare to catch the simple (3)

snatch
541   to sow the tares, to snatch the seed away (2)

snatched
170   In mock acclaim ... they snatched a purple cloak (2)

snow
110   The snow lay on the ground, the stars shone bright (1)
112   snow had fallen snow on snow (1)
133, 134   your raiment whiter than the snow (1)
265   his wings as drifted snow, his eyes as flame (1)
291   sends the snow in winter, the warmth to swell the grain (1)

soar
148   to the skies our monuments of folly soar (2)
188, 189   Soar we now where Christ has led (3)
519, 520   by virtue of his merits thither faithful souls do soar (3)

soaring
248, 249   that hereafter, heavenward soaring, we may sing (4)
369   soaring spirits upward rise to reach the burning throne (2)
423   thy justice like mountains high soaring above (2)
585   Morning glory, starlit sky, soaring music (1)

soars
9   see how the giant sun soars up (5)

society
528   May your care and mercy lead us to a just society (4)

sod
566   ever-green the sod (2)
661   no peace, but strife closed in the sod (4)

soft
9   velvet of soft summer nights (2)
228   With your soft, refreshing rains break our drought (4)
291   the breezes and the sunshine, and soft refreshing rain (1)
400   Great rushing winds and breezes soft (2)

softened
419   star of our hope, thy softened light cheers the ...night (2)

softening
10   some softening gleam of love and prayer shall dawn (4)

soiled
503, 504   Anoint and cheer our soiled face with ... thy grace (5)

solace
596   solace all its wide dominion with the healing of thy wings (1)

sold

57, 58	those who set at nought and sold him (2)

soldier

161	A Roman soldier drew a spear to mix his blood with water (2)
293	one was a soldier, and one was a priest (2)
563	Go forward, Christian soldier (1-4)

soldier's

170	your passion turned ... into a soldier's joke (2)

soldiers

246	The soldiers sought the child in vain (2)
287	O may thy soldiers, faithful, true, and bold (3)
548	Soldiers of Christ, arise, and put your armor on (1)
561	ye soldiers of the cross (1)
562	Onward, Christian soldiers, marching as to war (1,R)
562	on, then, Christian soldiers, on to victory (2)

sole

11	all my powers ... in thy sole glory may unite (3)

solely

440	drawn from earth to love thee solely (1)
682	in thy praise will sing solely because thou art my God (6)

solemn

49	with solemn prayer approach the throne (3)
59	Wakened by the solemn warning (2)
89, 90	The world in solemn stillness lay to hear the angels sing (1)
193	those scars their solemn witness gave (2)
288	grateful vows and solemn praise (2)
349	come in this most solemn hour (2)
359	each age for thine own solemn task prepares (1)
409	What though in solemn silence all move round (3)
522, 523	as priests, his solemn praises ... a thankoffering brings (4)
524	her sweet communion, solemn vows (3)

solitary

586	where the solitary labor, thou art there with them alone (2)

solitude

212	O Solitude again command your host from heaven restored (5)

some

10	some softening gleam of love and prayer shall dawn (4)
42	those who plan some evil from their sin restrain (4)
289	some are long forgotten (2)
625	onward as ye go some joyful anthem sing (3)
647	some I love have reached the end (2)
647	some with me may stay (2)
659, 660	move by some clear, winning word of love (2)
686	Teach me some melodious sonnet (1)

something
434   every labor of his hands shows something worthy of a God (1)

sometimes
172   Oh! Sometimes it causes me to tremble, tremble (1-4)
458   Sometimes they strew his way and his strong praises sing (3)
667   Sometimes a light surprises the Christian while he sings (1)
676   Sometimes I feel discouraged and think my work's in vain (1)

Son
1, 2   All holy Father, Son, and equal Spirit, Trinity blessed (3)
3, 4   that we may see and serve his Son (2)
5   all praise, eternal Son, to thee (5)
11   praise Father, Son and Holy Ghost (4)
19, 20   Now Holy Spirit, ever One with God the Father and the Son (1)
25, 26   blest are you, his holy Son (1)
25, 26   Praise Father, Son, and Spirit (2)
25, 26   Worthy are you of endless praise, O Son of God (3)
27, 28   with your Son, and Spirit bright (5)
36   thee, his incarnate Son, and Holy Spirit adoring (2)
36   O Son of God, Life-giver (3)
37   we hymn the eternal Father ... Son ... Holy Ghost divine (2)
37   O Son of God, be thou ... through all the world adored (3)
43   Forgive me, Lord, for thy dear Son (2)
43   praise Father, Son, and Holy Ghost (4)
47   On this day the eternal Son over death his triumph won (2)
48   We sing to thee our praises, O Father, Spirit, Son (4)
50   Hosanna to the anointed King, to David's holy Son (3)
52   all praise, eternal Son, to thee (4)
53   came in likeness lowly, Son of God most holy (1)
54   Virgin's Son, make here your home (1)
54   Mighty God and Mary's son, eager now his race to run (2)
54   Come, O Father's saving Son, who o'er sin the victory won (4)
56   mourns in lonely exile here until the Son of God appear (1,8)
59   Honor, glory, might, and blessing to the Father ... Son (4)
60   To God the Father ... Son, ... Spirit, Three in One (6)
61, 62   now come, most worthy Lord, God's Son, Incarnate Word (2)
63, 64   To God the Father ... Son ... Spirit, ever One (5)
76   All praise, eternal Son, to thee (5)
78, 79   where misery cries out to thee, Son of the mother mild (4)
80   This is the Christ, God's Son most high (3)
80   the Son holds in his infant hand (4)
83   only begotten Son of the Father (2)
85, 86   O Son who shared the Father's might (1)
85, 86   and came to us as Mary's son (3)
88   unto us a son is given (1)
97   wondrous charity of thy Son, our Lord (3)
98   Now may Mary's son, who came so long ago to love us (4)
105   how that in Bethlehem was born the Son of God by name (2)
106   tidings ... of God incarnate and the Virgin's Son (1)
106   found, with Joseph and the blessed maid, her Son (4)
106   her Son, the Savior, in a manger laid (4)
108   in holiness conceived, the Son of God was born (1)
110   for he whom Mary bore was God the Son (4)
110   to praise the Father, Son, and Holy Ghost (4)

111	Son of God, love's pure light radiant beams (3)
115	haste to bring him laud, the babe, the son of Mary (R)
116	This is my Son, my well-beloved in whom I take delight (3)
120	Christ, the Son of God, had come to lead his ... people (2)
121	God called you his beloved Son ... his servant true (2)
121	freely as Son of Man to serve and give your life for all (3)
125, 126	To us the promised Child is born, to us the Son is given (3)
129, 130	God proclaiming in its thunder Jesus as his Son by name (3)
129, 130	This is God's beloved Son (4)
133, 134	your Father's voice his Son proclaimed (2)
136, 137	from the cloud, the Holy One bears record to the only Son (2)
136, 137	O Father, with the eternal Son ... Holy Spirit, ever One (5)
139	This is my dear beloved Son upon whom rests my favor (1)
140, 141	swear by thyself, that at my death thy Son shall shine (3)
140, 141	thy Son shall shine as he shines now, and heretofore (3)
143	O Father, Son, and Spirit blest (5)
144	The universe your glory shows, blest Father, Spirit, Son (5)
154, 155	Thou art the King of Israel, thou David's royal Son (1)
156	Father ... expects his own anointed Son (4)
158	the slave hath sinned, and the Son hath suffered (3)
159	with ... grief and resignation Mary watched her dying son (2)
165, 165	praise and honor to the Son (6)
173	God the Father's only Son in the tomb is lying (1)
175	Redeemer, Son of the Father supreme, only begotten of God (6)
179	of the Father's God-head true and only Son (4)
201	all to anoint fair Mary's Son (2)
205	To God the Father ... Son ... Spirit, always One (5)
207, 211	Father, Son, and Holy Ghost (4)
216	Son of the Father supreme, only begotten of God (4)
230	by the triumph of the Son the curse of Babel was undone (2)
231	the guardian of your Son (2/3-19)
231, 232	Then let us praise the Father and worship God the Son (3)
233, 234	the Son himself exults in them (4)
244	drink, O Zion's son and daughters (2)
254	You are the Christ, O Lord, the Son of God most high (1)
256	It was the blessed Son come down to save him (2)
257	All glory to the Father be, all glory to the Son (5)
260	Virgin's spouse ... guardian of great David's greater Son (2)
260	before the Son (4)
263, 264	Hail, Mary, you shall bear a son (2)
265	thy Son shall be Emmanuel, by seers foretold (2)
266	to be the herald of God's Son (5)
268, 269	when he made the Virgin Mary mother of his only Son (1)
271, 272	To God the Father, God the Son ... Spirit, Three in One (5)
273, 274	All glory to the Father, all glory to the Son (4)
277	sing of God's own Son most holy (1)
277	Son most holy, who became her little child (1)
277	Sing of Jesus, son of Mary, in the house at Nazareth (2)
277	Glory be to God the Father ... Son ... the Spirit (3)
278	Mary at whose breast the child was fed who is Son of God (1)
278	Son of God eternal and the everlasting Bread (1)
278	beholds her Son and Savior reigning as the Lord of love (4)
278	looked upon her Son ... reigning from the awful tree (2)
278	looked upon her Son and Savior (2)
282, 283	Father Almighty, Son and Holy Spirit, God ever blessed (6)

629	O Father, Son, and Spirit, send us increase from above (3)
640	Traveler, lo, the Prince of Peace ... Son of God is come (3)
658	To Father, Son, and Holy Ghost, the God whom we adore (4)
665	high above all praises praising for ... Christ, his son (5)
665	gift of Christ, his son (5)
700	Love of the living God, of Father and of Son (4)
705	O thou who gavest us thyself in Jesus Christ thy Son (3)

Son's

| 120 | now by the Holy spirit shed upon the Son's anointed head (3) |
| 333 | Now the Spirit's visitation Now the Son's epiphany (1) |

song

9	stars, the silent song they sing (2)
29, 30	To thee our morning song of praise (2)
70	till once more we sing the song (1)
71, 72	let every heart prepare a throne, and every voice a song (1)
89, 90	that glorious song of old (1)
89, 90	world give back the song which now the angels sing (4)
92	On this day earth shall ring with the song (1)
92	song children sing to the Lord, Christ our King (1)
92	with their song earth shall ring (4)
94, 95	angels praising God, who thus addressed their joyful song (5)
106	sing, redeemed, a glad triumphal song (6)
110	the angels hovered round, and sang this song (3)
114	but as the hunter braves drew nigh, the angel-song rang (2)
114	angel-song rang loud and high (2)
114	O children of the forest free, the angel song is true (4)
122, 123	Alleluia, song of gladness, voice of joy that cannot die (1)
162	in true prophetic song of old (1)
181	Awake and sing the song of Moses and the Lamb (1)
181	sing in sweeter notes the song of Moses and the Lamb (4)
208	the song of triumph has begun (1)
210	Now let the heavens be joyful, let earth her song begin (3)
231	his witness in his gospel becomes victorious song (2/4-25)
232	raise the ceaseless song (2/11-1)
260	beside his spouse ... he joins the heavenly song (4)
266	When the maiden heard his song (3)
277	from all saints the song ascends (3)
284	join with our earth-bound song to make the Savior known (1)
287	steals on the ear the distant triumph song (5)
290	raise the song of harvest-home (1)
293	I sing a song of the saints of God (1)
316, 317	This is the hour of banquet and of song (1)
326	one heart ... song have the saints upon earth and above (2)
355	yet even at the grave we make our song: Alleluia (1)
358	Yet at the grave shall we raise up our glad song (3)
362	Early in the morning our song shall rise to thee (1)
366	from morn till set of sun ... the song goes on (3)
366	through the Church the song goes on (3)
368	In the song of thy salvation every tongue ... combine (4)
390	join the great throng, psaltery, organ, and song (1)
392	join in a song with sweet accord (1)
392	Then let our song abound and let our tears be dry (4)

songs

soothe

567   soothe and bless with thine almighty breath (3)

soothed

113   meanwhile the pangs of my sorrow are soothed (1)
113   pangs of my sorrow are soothed and put to rest (1)

soothes

644   It soothes our sorrows, heals our wounds (1)

soothing

33-35   soothing the weary (4)

sore

168, 169   O sacred head, sore wounded, defiled and put to scorn (1)
286   whose hearts were riven, sore with woe and anguish tried (4)
448, 449   for us he bore his holy fast and hungered sore (2)
525   Though with a scornful wonder men see her sore oppressed (3)
530   earth's sore burden doth remove (3)

sorrow

59   let us haste, with tears of sorrow (3)
60   In sorrow that the ancient curse should doom to death (2)
113   meanwhile the pangs of my sorrow are soothed (1)
113   pangs of my sorrow are soothed and put to rest (1)
150   Should not we thy sorrow share (2)
158   for me ... thy mortal sorrow, and thy life's oblation (4)
159   such a cup of sorrow drinking (4)
160   Cross of Jesus, cross of sorrow (1,4)
164   is this thy sorrow nought to us who pass unheeding by (1)
164   make us thy sorrow feel (2)
168, 169   what sorrow mars thy grandeur (1)
168, 169   for this thy dying sorrow, thy pity without end (4)
170   your sorrow heal our own (1)
173   O sorrow deep! Who would not weep (1)
179   speak his sorrow ended, hail his triumph now (2)
190   Ended now the night of sorrow (3)
192   This joyful Eastertide, away with sin and sorrow (1)
237   press through toil and sorrow (3)
290   wheat and tares together sown, unto joy or sorrow grown (2)
290   gather thou thy people in, free from sorrow ... from sin (4)
301   look on the heart by sorrow broken (1)
355   where sorrow and pain are no more (1)
360, 361   joy over sorrow (3)
400   All you that pain and sorrow bear (5)
460, 461   not as orphans are we left in sorrow now (2)
474   sorrow and love flow mingled down (3)
474   Did e'er such love and sorrow meet (3)
479   stream which from sin and sorrow doth the world redeem (3)
500   from sin and sorrow set us free (1)
527   through the night of doubt and sorrow (1)
534   fight we the fight with sorrow and sin (3)
568   sorrow for sins that for vengeance have cried (1)
570, 571   in your day of loss and sorrow (2)
598   robe of sorrow round thee (1)

| 667 | set free from present sorrow, we cheerfully can say (2) |
| 703 | through joy or sorrow, as thou deemest best (3) |

sorrow's

| 379 | when human hearts are breaking under sorrow's iron rod (2) |

sorrowing

| 128 | sorrowing, sighing, bleeding, dying (4) |

sorrows

100	No more let sins and sorrows grow (3)
159	who ... would not share her sorrows deep (4)
278	Sing we, too, of Mary's sorrows (2)
313	all that love of God could give Jesus by his sorrows gave (2)
469, 470	There is no place where earth's sorrows are more felt (2)
469, 470	no place ... sorrows are more felt than up in heaven (2)
469, 470	joy for all the members in the sorrows of the Head (2)
493	Name that ... bids our sorrows cease (3)
549, 550	In our joys and in our sorrows (4)
620	When shall my sorrows have an end (1)
644	It soothes our sorrows, heals our wounds (1)
691	bid darkness turn to day, wipe sorrows tears away (2)
703	doubts appall, and sorrows still increase (1)

sorrows'

| 67 | mourning 'neath their sorrows' load (1) |

sort

| 382 | Small it is in this poor sort to enroll thee (3) |

sought

106	In Bethlehem the happy shepherds sought to see (4)
131, 132	he who offers heavenly birth sought not the kingdoms (1)
131, 132	sought not the kingdoms of this earth (1)
231	the apostles sought God's choice (2/2-24)
231	leaving earthly treasures, sought riches from above (2/6-11)
246	The soldiers sought the child in vain (2)
255	O Love that sought and held him a prisoner of his Lord (2)
477	by thee the outcast and the poor were sought (2)
525	from heaven he came and sought her to be his holy bride (1)
645, 646	but yet in love he sought me (3)
686	Jesus sought me when a stranger (2)
689	I sought the Lord (1)

soul

6, 7	Visit then this soul of mine (3)
9	So let the love of Jesus come and set thy soul ablaze (5)
11	Awake, my soul ... with the sun thy daily stage of duty run (1)
21, 22	pouring healing peace upon our soul (2)
43	O may my soul on thee repose (3)
71, 72	the bleeding soul to cure (3)
107	rejoice with heart and soul and voice (1-3)
135	Manifest in making whole palsied limbs and fainting soul (3)
145	or rend the soul, such grief is not Lent's goal (2)
152	so that we in heart and soul may dwell with thee (4)

625	My soul, bear thou thy part, triumph in God above (4)
635	God never yet forsook in need the soul that trusted him (2)
635	soul that trusted him indeed (2)
636, 637	The soul that to Jesus hath fled for repose (5)
636, 637	that soul, though all hell shall endeavor to shake (5)
644	'tis manna to the hungry soul, and to the weary, rest (2)
645, 646	my ransomed soul he leadeth (2)
655	O speak, and make me listen, thou guardian of my soul (2)
656	their soul is Christ's abode (1)
656	he to the lowly soul will still himself impart (3)
658	longs my soul, O God, for thee and thy refreshing grace (1)
658	For thee ... the living God, my thirsty soul doth pine (2)
658	Why restless, why cast down, my soul (3)
663	To wholeness he restores my soul (2)
665	his desire our soul delighteth (4)
666	My soul with patience waits for thee, the living Lord (2)
667	he grants the soul again a season of clear shining (1)
668	sun by day nor moon by night need make thy soul afraid (3)
676	there is a balm in Gilead to heal the sinsick soul (R)
676	but then the Holy Spirit revives my soul again (1)
689	afterward I knew he moved my soul to seek him, seeking me (1)
689	for thou wert long beforehand with my soul (3)
692	my thirst was quenched, my soul revived (2)
699	Jesus, Lover of my soul, let me to thy bosom fly (1)
699	O receive my soul at last (1)
699	hangs my helpless soul on thee (2)
700	True sunlight of the soul, surround us as we go (2)
719	confirm thy soul in self control, thy liberty in law (2)

soul's

174	From sin's power do thou set free soul's new-born (4)
174	set free soul's new-born, O Lord, in thee (4)
226, 227	thou, the soul's most welcome guest (2)
245	the light, the living vine, your soul's true bread (2)
337	O do thine utmost for their soul's true weal (3)
383, 384	thou my soul's glory, joy, and crown (1)

souls

52	fill our souls with light divine (1)
78, 79	in this world of sin, where meek souls will receive him (3)
116	may such bonds for ever draw our souls to things above (5)
119	bring our ransomed souls at last where they need no star (4)
148	speak to our souls the quickening word (5)
152	our weakened souls to health reclaim (3)
175	pour out thy balm on our souls (8)
179	Loose the souls long prisoned, bound with Satan's chain (6)
185, 186	Christ alone our souls will feed (4)
187	souls restoring from the dead (2)
188, 189	Once he died our souls to save (2)
199, 200	'Tis the spring of souls today (2)
216	pour out thy balm on our souls (6)
225	pouring on all human souls infinite riches of God (2)
242	How oft, O Lord, thy face hath shone on doubting souls (1)
242	doubting souls whose wills were true (1)
242	flows to Christian souls (4)

281	it came, true Lord of souls, from thee (2)
288	Lord, for these our souls shall raise ... praise (2)
301	be thy feast to us the token that ... our souls are fed (1)
301	by thy grace our souls are fed (1)
323	ever may our souls be fed with this true and living Bread (1)
327, 328	with souls refreshed, we render thanks to God (2)
343	Shepherd of souls, refresh and bless thy chosen (1)
357	Think, O Lord, in mercy on the souls ... in death repose (2)
370	purity of virgin souls (3)
391	our souls and all our mortal frame (3)
428	people bless the Lord like righteous souls of yore (5)
440	let our hearts and souls be stirred now to seek and love (1)
454	in sounds of gladness, leading souls redeemed to heaven (3)
472	bringing to hungry souls the bread of life (2)
472	showing to wandering souls the path of light (3)
475	souls in silence fear him (1)
503, 504	Come, Holy Ghost, our souls inspire (1)
510	our souls, how heavily they go to reach eternal joys (2)
519, 520	by virtue of his merits thither faithful souls do soar (3)
522, 523	Jesus, whom their souls rely on (4)
529	all Christly souls are one in him (3)
531	souls without strength inspire with might (3)
537	new-born souls, whose days, reclaimed from error's ways (4)
582, 583	how its splendor challenges the souls that greatly dare (4)
598	From old unfaith our souls release (3)
615	faithful souls have yearned to see ... that kingdom's day (1)
615	gird up your loins, ye prophet souls (3)
616	souls, condemned and dying were precious in his sight (2)
618	Respond, ye souls in endless rest (3)
625	Ye blessed souls at rest, who ran this earthly race (2)
627	bread of our souls, whereon we feed (2)
628	that yearning souls may find the Christ (3)
629	enlarge, expand all living souls to comprehend your love (3)
649, 650	our thirsting souls to quench and fill (2)
652, 653	take from our souls the strain and stress (4)
674	Lord, cleanse the depths within our souls (4)
695, 696	O give our frightened souls the sure salvation (2)
709	at our Father's loved abode our souls arrive in peace (4)

sound

61, 62	as harps and cymbals swell the sound (3)
70	Herald, sound the note of judgment (1)
70	Herald, sound the note of gladness (2)
70	Herald, sound the note of pardon (3)
70	Herald, sound the note of triumph (4)
70	Sound the trumpet, Tell the message (R)
71, 72	Hark! the glad sound! the Savior comes (1)
230	A mighty sound from heaven at Pentecost there came (1)
275	Hark, the sound of holy voices, chanting (1)
284	struck your strings of sweetest sound (7)
344	Thanks we give and adoration for thy Gospel's joyful sound (2)
380	thy praise shall sound from shore to shore (2)
386, 387	nature without voice or sound replied, O Lord, thou art (2)
390	Let the amen sound from his people again (4)
409	What though no real voice nor sound ... be found (3)

416	for the mystic harmony linking sense to sound and sight (3)
420	a new dimension in the world of sound (2)
427	Let all the earth around ring joyous with the sound (4)
430	Sound the trumpet, touch the lute (2)
430	nor ... creature found that hath neither note nor sound (2)
430	Let in praise of God, the sound run a never-ending round (4)
432	All things that give sound (3)
484, 485	His praise shall sound all nature round (1)
486	both dead and living swell the sound (2)
486	shall swell the sound of praise again (5)
530	to earth's remotest bound all may heed the joyful sound (1)
531	whene'er the joyful sound is heard (2)
541	a glad sound comes with the setting sun (5)
584	God, you have given us power to sound depths ... unknown (1)
609	where sound the cries of race and clan (1)
625	God's praises sound (2)
642	nor can the memory find a sweeter sound than Jesus' Name (2)
671	how sweet the sound that saved a wretch like me (1)
717	let rocks their silence break, the sound prolong (3)

soundeth

549, 550	day by day his clear voice soundeth (1)

sounding

59	Hark, a thrilling voice is sounding (1)
100	repeat the sounding joy (2)
235	through whom the living Gospels came sounding all abroad (1)
390	sounding in glad adoration (1)
391	fill thy courts with sounding praise (4)
412	Knowledge and truth, loud sounding wisdom (6)
430	O come, our voices raise, sounding God Almighty praise (1,6)

soundless

431	through the silences of space ... soundless music sings (1)

sounds

89, 90	ever o'er its Babel-sounds the blessed angels sing (2)
413	Trumpets and organs set in motion such sounds (2)
413	such sounds as make the heavens ring (2)
434	speak his Name in sounds to mortal ears unknown (5)
454	in sounds of gladness, leading souls redeemed to heaven (3)
644	How sweet the Name of Jesus sounds in a believer's ear (1)

source

14, 15	yourself unmoved, all motion's source (1)
27, 28	O blest Creator, source of light (1)
55	you returned to that same source (3)
82	he is Alpha and Omega, he the source, the ending he (1)
226, 227	come, thou source of blessings sure (1)
228	Source of strength and sure relief (2)
261, 262	Jesus, source of salvation (1)
288	bounteous source of every joy (1)
288	source whence all our blessings flow (1)
300	Source of all our gifts and graces, Christ we own (2)
353	for all love finds its source in you (1)

368	source of mercy, love, and peace (1)
368	Source of comfort, cheer us with the Savior's love (3)
386, 387	We sing of God, the mighty source of all things (1)
478	the Father's conquering Word, true source of gladness (1)
500	O Source of uncreated light (2)
501, 502	of burning love the living source (2)
506, 507	source of breath to all things breathing (1)
506, 507	praise the Word, Source, and Truth, and Inspiration (6)
515	come, thou source of joy and gladness (1)
606	our boundless source of joy and truth, of peace and love (3)
666	plenteous source and spring (4)
666	source and spring from whence redemption ever flows (4)
704	trembling to its source return (2)
705	God the giver of all good, the source of bounteous yield (1)

South

529	in him no South or North (1)
529	in him meet South and North (3)

sovereign

18	may we, too, trust your sovereign power (2b)
365	thy sovereign majesty may we in glory see (4)
391	His sovereign power without our aid formed us of clay (2)
414	proclaim thy sovereign power (6)
436	So come, my Sovereign, enter in (5)
489	the sovereign God of heaven (1)
543	till sovereign love in worlds above the glory raise (3)
600, 601	Bring to our world of strife thy sovereign word of peace (4)
677	works his sovereign will (2)

sow

329, 331	the seed of truth to sow (2)
541	to sow the tares, to snatch the seed away (2)
593	where there is hate, may we sow love (1)
593	Where all is doubt, may we sow faith (2)
593	where all is gloom, may we sow hope (2)
593	where all is night, may we sow light (2)
593	where all is tears, may we sow joy (2)

sowed

23	we harvest what the morning sowed (1)

sowing

424	For the plowing, sowing, reaping (1)

sown

289	we reap what they have sown (3)
290	wheat and tares together sown, unto joy or sorrow grown (2)

space

250	what need we fear in earth or space in this new year (4)
251	O God, whom neither time nor space can limit (1)
251	neither time nor space can limit, hold, or bind (1)
388	whose robe is the light, whose canopy space (2)
394, 395	your fingers trace the bold designs of farthest space (1)

410	dwellers all in time and space (4)
427	Sing, suns and stars of space ... ye that see his face (5)
430	song shall over-climb all the bounds of space and time (6)
431	through the silences of space ... soundless music sings (1)
459	Lord of interstellar space and Conqueror of time (1)
579	glad praise from space, air, land, and sea (4)
580	flung the suns in burning radiance through ... space (1)
580	through the silent fields of space (1)
580	untraveled realms of space (3)

spacious

| 409 | The spacious firmament on high (1) |
| 719 | O beautiful for spacious skies, for amber waves of grain (1) |

spake

94, 95	Thus spake the seraph (5)
124	True spake the prophet from afar who told the rise (2)
203	sat and spake unto the three (3)
322	He was the Word that spake it (2)
426	when God spake and it was done (1)

spangled

389	moon ... mid her spangled sisters bright (5)
409	spangled heavens, a shining frame (1)
580	God, who stretched the spangled heavens (1)
720	O say does that star-spangled banner yet wave (1)
720	the star-spangled banner in triumph shall wave (2)

spare

152	Spare us, O Lord, who now confess our sins (3)
243	on his lips a prayer that God ... spare (3)
243	in sweet forgiveness' name, should understand and spare (3)

spared

| 382 | thou didst note my working breast, thou hast spared me (1) |

spares

| 410 | Father-like he tends and spares us (3) |
| 585 | spares not, keeps not, all outpours (3) |

speak

67	speak ye peace, thus saith our God (1)
67	Speak ye to Jerusalem of the peace that waits for them (1)
129, 130	let us, if we dare to speak ... praise him (1)
138	You speak, and it is done; obedient to your word (2)
148	speak to our souls the quickening word (5)
179	speak, his sorrow ended, hail his triumph now (2)
183	Speak, Mary, declaring what thou sawest, wayfaring (4)
240, 241	strive to think him, speak him, live him (4)
304	we'll live and speak his praise (5)
392	children of the heavenly King may speak their joys abroad (2)
414	speak of thy dread acts the story (3)
434	I would for ever speak his Name (5)
434	speak his Name in sounds to mortal ears unknown (5)
472	Christ of great compassion, speak to our fearful hearts (1)

472	speak to our fearful hearts by conflict rent (1)
501, 502	Teach us to speak, teach us to hear (3)
633	saving Word, the world restoring, speak to us (2)
633	speak and heal our mortal blindness (3)
638, 639	speak to my heart, in blessings speak (3)
638, 639	Speak, or thou never hence shalt move (3)
652, 653	speak through the earthquake, wind, and fire (5)
655	O speak to reassure me, to hasten or control (2)
655	O speak, and make me listen, thou guardian of my soul (2)
704	work, and speak, and think for thee (3)

speaketh
372	in prophet's word he spoke of old, he speaketh still (3)

speaking
129, 130	Trembling at his feet we saw Moses and Elijah speaking (2)
381	at thy speaking it was done (1)
630	God is speaking; praise God for his open word (5)
655	O let me hear thee speaking in accents clear and still (2)
694	God be in my mouth, and in my speaking (1)

speaks
116	The Father speaks from heaven's exalted height (3)
248, 249	'Tis the Name that whoso preachest speaks like music (3)
248, 249	speaks like music to the ear (3)
372	Lo, he is Lord of all. Creation speaks his praise (2)
476	he speaks to us in human terms to make his glory known (4)
493	He speaks, and listening to his voice ... receive (4)
506, 507	through your voice which speaks within us (6)
633	Word that speaks your Father's love (4)
681	All beauty speaks of thee: the mountains and the rivers (3)

spear
161	A Roman soldier drew a spear to mix his blood with water (2)
165, 166	vinegar, and spear, and reed (3)
542	to ploughshare beat the sword, to pruning hook the spear (2)
682	for us didst bear the nails and spear (2)

sped
119	As with joyful steps they sped to that lowly manger bed (2)
208	The three sad days are quickly sped (3)
289	changeful years unresting their silent course have sped (2)

speech
370	the word of God to give me speech (5)

speeches
591	from all the easy speeches that comfort cruel men (2)

speechless
257	with speechless praise adored (4)

speed
371	speed forth thy flight (3)
539	give of thy wealth to speed them on their way (3)

speedy
616   He comes with succor speedy to those who suffer wrong (2)

spend
9   to spend thyself nor count the cost (6)
213   Now with singing and praise, let us spend all the days (2)
458   my friend, indeed, who at my need his life did spend (2)
458   in whose sweet praise I all my days could gladly spend (7)

spent
18   athirst and spent, you asked for aid (4a)
81   amid the cold of winter, when half spent was the night (1)
81   when half spent was the night (1,2)
289   long spent their hopes and fears (2)
472   by our own false hopes and aims are spent (1)
517   One day within thy courts excels a thousand spent away (4)
585   God, whose arms of love aching, spent, the world sustain (6)

sphere
68   arise, thou Sun so longed for, above this darkened sphere (3)
97   Scepter, crown, and sphere (1)
419   center and soul of every sphere (1)

spheres
54   gracing his created spheres (3)
543   ten thousand stars in nobler spheres his influence own (4)
651   round me rings the music of the spheres (1)

spiced
370   his bursting from the spiced tomb (2)

spices
201   At early morn, with spices rare (2)

spilled
165, 166   where his precious blood is spilled (2)

Spirit
1, 2   All holy Father, Son, and equal Spirit, Trinity blessed (3)
5   all glory to the Spirit raise (5)
11   with thyself my spirit fill (2)
12, 13   Bestow your Spirit on us now (3)
12, 13   O Spirit, love's life-giving ray (4)
14, 15   whom with the Spirit we adore forever and forevermore (3)
16, 17   Creator of all things and with the Spirit, Comforter (4)
18   O Spirit bringing truth and love (5)
19, 20   Now Holy Spirit, ever One with God the Father and the Son (1)
19, 20   whom with the Spirit we adore forever and for evermore (3)
21, 22   Spirit we adore for ever and for evermore (3)
23   O Spirit, bringing power and health (4)
25, 26   Praise Father, Son, and Spirit (2)
27, 28   with your Son, and Spirit bright (5)
36   thee, his incarnate Son, and Holy Spirit adoring (2)
38, 39   with the Spirit, Comforter (5)
40, 41   O Spirit, bond of peace and love (5)

44, 45	whom with the Spirit we adore for ever and for evermore (4)
47	this day the Spirit came with his gifts of living flame (2)
47	shine, blest Spirit in my heart (5)
48	this day our Lord victorious the Spirit sent from heaven (2)
48	We sing to thee our praises, O Father, Spirit, Son (4)
51	day of the Spirit, sign of heaven's banquet (3)
52	This day the Holy Spirit came (3)
52	O Spirit, fill our hearts this day with grace to hear (4)
52	with the Spirit, we adore for ever and for evermore (4)
55	but from the Spirit of our God (2)
55	all praise, life-giving Spirit, praise (6)
59	with the everlasting Spirit while unending ages run (4)
60	To God the Father ... Son, ... Spirit, Three in One (6)
63, 64	To God the Father ... Son ... Spirit, ever One (5)
66	By thine own eternal Spirit rule in all our hearts alone (4)
76	whom with the Father we adore and Holy Spirit evermore (5)
85, 86	whom with the Father we adore and Holy Spirit evermore (6)
88	O renew us, Lord, we pray, with thy Spirit day by day (5)
120	now by the Holy spirit shed upon the Son's anointed head (3)
121	God's Spirit on you came (1)
121	Baptize us with your Spirit, Lord (4)
127	unto thee, with God the Father and the Spirit, glory be (5)
136, 137	O Father, with the eternal Son ... Holy Spirit, ever One (5)
139	The Holy Spirit then was shown, a dove on him descending (2)
139	trust in Christ who will baptize with water and the Spirit (3)
143	O Father, Son, and Spirit blest (5)
144	The universe your glory shows, blest Father, Spirit, Son (5)
151	I rest upon his faithful word to them of contrite spirit (3)
159	in death by all forsaken, till his spirit he resigned (3)
165, 166	praise and honor to the Spirit, ever Three and ever One (6)
174	risen Lord, all praise to thee with the Spirit ever be (4)
175	Spirit of life and of power, now flow in us (7)
176, 177	Over the chaos of the empty waters hovered the Spirit (1)
176, 177	By the same Spirit we, regenerated (2)
176, 177	By the same Spirit we are called to worship God (3)
182	His Spirit burns through this and every future age (5)
191	Alleluia! to the Spirit, fount of love and sanctity (5)
205	To God the Father ... Son ... Spirit, always One (5)
216	Spirit of life and of power (5)
217, 218	while endless ages run, with Father and with Spirit, One (3)
220	with Father and with Spirit, One (4)
221	with Father and with Spirit, One. Alleluia (4)
223, 224	morn when our ascended Lord ... his Spirit poured (1)
223, 224	on his Church his Spirit poured (1)
223, 224	on the twelve the Spirit came (2)
223, 224	unto us your Spirit send (3)
225	Praise to the Spirit of Life (4)
226, 227	Come, thou Holy Spirit bright (1)
228	Holy Spirit, font of light, focus of God's glory bright (1)
229	Spirit of mercy, truth, and love (1,3)
230	curse of Babel was undone when God did send the Spirit (2)
230	for God the Holy Spirit dwells with the Church alway (3)
230	whole in body, mind, and spirit (3)
231	with "Lord, receive my spirit" (2/12-26)
231, 232	sing to God the Spirit, eternal Three in One (3)

236	and to the Spirit, living flame (4)
245	your glory to proclaim whereby your Spirit give us life (3)
263, 264	blest in the work the Spirit wrought (3)
263, 264	whom with the Father we adore and Holy Spirit evermore (4)
271, 272	To God the Father, God the Son ... Spirit, Three in One (5)
273, 274	who with the Holy Spirit, now reign, blest Three in One (4)
277	Glory be to God the Father ... Son ... the Spirit (3)
282, 283	Father Almighty, Son and Holy Spirit, God ever blessed (6)
294	Baptized in water, sealed by the Spirit (1-3)
295	praise the Holy Spirit poured forth upon the earth (3)
297	Descend, O Spirit, purging flame (1)
298	With one accord, O God, we pray, grant us the Holy Spirit (2)
299	Spirit of God, unleashed on earth with rush of wind (1)
299	O Holy Spirit, come again (2)
314	grant my spirit ever by thy life may live (3)
326	thy Name with the Father and Spirit be ever adored (1)
334	alert and living in your Spirit, strong and free (3)
345	peace in each heart, thy Spirit from above (3)
346	blest by the Spirit, breath and flame of life (3)
347	in God's good Spirit daily to increase (1)
348	led by your Spirit, defender and guide (2)
349	Holy Spirit, Lord of love, who descended from above (1)
352	Spirit of God, whom we adore: preserve, protect, defend (3)
359	Anoint them with the Spirit of thy Son (4)
360, 361	Son coeternal, ever-blessed Spirit (6)
365	ne'er from us depart, Spirit of power (3)
366	Holy Father, holy Son, Holy Spirit, three we name thee (4)
368	Holy Spirit, Sanctifier, come with unction from above (3)
370	eternal Father, Spirit, Word (7)
371	Spirit of truth and love, life-giving, holy Dove (3)
372	His Spirit floweth free, high surging where it will (3)
381	Holy Spirit, Light-Revealer, glory, glory be to thee (4)
400	praise the Spirit, Three in One (7)
421	with the Spirit, you alone share in the Father's glory (3)
424	For the harvests of the Spirit (3)
434	Her noblest life my spirit draws from his dear wounds (4)
436	Holy Spirit guide us on until the glorious crown be won (5)
437, 438	Unnumbered blessings give my spirit voice (1)
440	till thy Spirit breaks our night with the beams of truth (2)
448, 449	for us he sent his Spirit here (5)
448, 449	Spirit here to guide, to strengthen, and to cheer (5)
465, 466	eternal Spirit, give me breath (2)
467	to make salvation sure, guides us by his Spirit pure (3)
471	holds the fainting spirit up (3)
471	It makes the coward spirit brave (4)
472	still let thy Spirit unto us be given (2)
475	Come, indwelling Spirit, with transfiguring splendor (4)
486	Eternal, bid thy Spirit rest (4)
500	Creator Spirit ... come visit every humble mind (1)
501, 502	O Holy Spirit, by whose breath life rises vibrant (1)
501, 502	and to the Spirit: God the Lord (6)
503, 504	Thou the anointing Spirit art (2)
503, 504	praise to thy eternal merit, Father, Son and Holy Spirit (9)
505	O Spirit of Life, O Spirit of God (1-4)
506, 507	Praise the Spirit in creation, breath of God (1)

506, 507	Spirit, moving on the waters quickening worlds to life (1)
506, 507	Praise the Spirit (1,2,3)
506, 507	Spirit, close companion of our inmost thoughts and ways (2)
506, 507	Pray we then, O Lord the Spirit, on our lives descend (5)
506, 507	Praise, O praise the Holy Spirit, praise the Father (6)
509	Spirit divine, attend our prayers (1,5)
509	O come, great Spirit, come (1,5)
510	Come, Holy Spirit, heavenly Dove (1,4)
511	Holy Spirit, ever living as the Church's very life (1)
511	Spirit, ever striving through her in a ceaseless strife (1)
511	Spirit, ever forming in the Church the mind of Christ (1)
511	Holy Spirit, ever working through the Church's ministry (2)
511	Holy Spirit, ever binding age to age and soul to soul (2)
512	Come, Gracious Spirit, heavenly Dove (1)
513	come, Holy Spirit, come (1-3)
515	hear our supplication, blessed Spirit, God of peace (2)
516	a place wherein the Holy Spirit makes a dwelling (3)
519, 520	laud and honor to the Spirit, ever Three, and ever One (5)
530	word of how the Spirit came bringing peace in Jesus' name (4)
531	O Spirit of the living God (1)
540	Awake, thou Spirit of the watchmen (1)
547	There is one Body and one hope, one Spirit and one call (3)
559	Spirit of our God, descending, fill our hearts (3)
560	Blessed are the poor in spirit (1)
563	he can with bread of heaven thy fainting spirit feed (1)
564, 565	Since, Lord, thou dost defend us with thy Spirit (3)
568	Come, Holy Spirit, create in us holiness (3)
568	Father, Redeemer, and Spirit of grace (4)
573	Spirit of life which moved ere form was made (1)
576, 577	let there be in us no discord but one spirit (2)
579	Spirit ... the Father sent to spread abroad the firmament (3)
587	O Spirit, who dost bind our hearts in unity (3)
590	grant the glad surprising that your blest Spirit rouses (1)
590	Spirit rouses everywhere (1)
590	Show us your Spirit, brooding o'er each city (3)
608	Most Holy Spirit, who didst brood upon the chaos (3)
610	use the love your Spirit kindles still to save (2)
612	Gracious Spirit, Holy Ghost (1)
618	To God the Father ... Son ... Spirit, Three in One (4)
623	through whom, the Spirit, with them ever One (5)
624	who art, with God the Father, and Spirit, ever blest (4)
629	O Father, Son, and Spirit, send us increase from above (3)
631	for the Spirit which protects us (3)
633	Word that sends us from above God the Spirit (4)
644	It makes the wounded spirit whole (2)
664	brings my wandering spirit back when I forsake his ways (1)
669	Hope on, then, broken spirit; hope on, be not afraid (4)
670	What thy Spirit doth reveal, that may I in faith receive (3)
675	let not its weight fill your weak spirit with alarm (2)
675	his strength shall bear your spirit up (2)
675	brace your spirit, and nerve your arm (2)
676	but then the Holy Spirit revives my soul again (1)
687, 688	the Spirit and the gifts are ours through him (4)
698	Eternal Spirit of thy living Christ (1)
701	my heart long paineth, ah, my spirit straineth (1)

Spirit's

5	Spirit's sanctifying beam upon our earthly senses stream (2)
120	grant us the Holy Spirit's power to shield us (5)
230	each Apostle spoke the word beneath the Spirit's thunder (1)
233, 234	in them the Spirit's will was done (4)
245	John ... who bore the Spirit's sword (1)
278	from on high ... glory of the Spirit's presence came (3)
278	blazing glory of the Spirit's presence (3)
279	learned from thy Holy Spirit's breath to suffer and to do (2)
292	with the Father's Name, and with the Holy Spirit's gifts (3)
296	The Spirit's power shakes the Church of God (3)
333	Now the Spirit's visitation Now the Son's epiphany (1)
347	rejoicing in the Holy Spirit's power (4)
351	Father's boundless love, with the Holy Spirit's favor (1)
440	help us by thy Spirit's pleading (3)
521	Put forth, O God, thy Spirit's might (1)
528	the Spirit's gifts empower us for the work of ministry (R)
547	to give the Spirit's unity, the very bond of peace (2)
551	quickened by the Spirit's power (3)
572	Trumpet with your Spirit's breath (2)
572	with your Spirit's breath through each height and hollow (2)
630	Word is answered by the Spirit's voice within (5)

spirits

143	our spirits strengthen with thy grace (4)
232	Your wine and oil, O Savior, upon our spirits pour (2/10-18)
369	soaring spirits upward rise to reach the burning throne (2)
475	his own ... worship lowly, yield their spirits wholly (1)
495	Help, ye bright angelic spirits (4)
515	with thy grace our spirits shower (2)
574, 575	our inmost spirits purify (4)
643	by prostrate spirits day and night incessantly adored (2)
649, 650	For you our restless spirits yearn (3)

spite

458	What makes this rage and spite (4)
558	living still in spite of dungeon, fire, and sword (1)

spitting

165, 166	He endures the nails, the spitting (3)

splendor

5	O splendor of God's glory bright (1)
9	the splendor of the sea (1)
16, 17	Then let us all with joy embrace the flaming splendor (3)
16, 17	splendor of such grace (3)
27, 28	you gave the day with splendor bright (1)
36	eternal splendor wearing; celestial, holy, blest (1)
46	Now all the heavenly splendor breaks forth (2)
55	its splendor pierces all our gloom (5)
60	but not in splendor bright (3)
74	Not robed in royal splendor, in power and pomp comes he (1)
81	dispel in glorious splendor the darkness everywhere (3)
168, 169	O countenance whose splendor the hosts of heaven adore (1)
199, 200	Now the queen of seasons, bright with the day of splendor (3)

231	that we might wear the crown and ever shine in splendor (1)
232	ever shine in splendor reflected from your throne (1)
232	light that grows in splendor until the perfect day (2/6-24)
296	The Father's splendor clothes the Son with life (3)
307	Lord, enthroned in heavenly splendor (1)
314	face to face thy splendor, I at last shall see (4)
339	come into the day-light's splendor (1)
366	Son of God enthroned in splendor (5)
388	pavilioned in splendor, and girded with praise (1)
406, 407	shines in brilliant splendor (2)
423	help us to see 'tis only the splendor of light hideth thee (4)
431	The dawn returns in splendor, the heavens burn and blaze (2)
475	Come, indwelling Spirit, with transfiguring splendor (4)
572	leaving all, that we may be partners in your splendor (3)
582, 583	how its splendor challenges the souls that greatly dare (4)
596	Judge eternal, throned in splendor (1)
665	splendor, light, and life attend him (3)
718	in splendor through the skies (1)

splendors

31, 32	brings the splendors of the dawn (1)
89, 90	when peace shall over all the earth its ... splendors (4)
89, 90	its ancient splendors fling (4)
459	there heavenly splendors shine (2)

spoil

| 162 | to spoil the spoiler of his prey (4) |

spoiled

| 215 | he by death has spoiled his foes (2) |
| 284 | Ye in the wilderness beheld the Tempter spoiled (3) |

spoiler

| 162 | to spoil the spoiler of his prey (4) |
| 255 | Saul, the church's spoiler came spreading fear and hate (1) |

spoke

106	He spoke ... straightway the celestial choir ... conspire (3)
131, 132	He spoke the word, and forth it flowed (4)
145	The prophet spoke (3)
209	him who spoke as none e'er spoke (1)
230	each Apostle spoke the word beneath the Spirit's thunder (1)
255	O Voice that spoke within him (2)
372	in prophet's word he spoke of old, he speaketh still (3)
444	The prophets spoke of mercy, of freedom and release (1)

spoken

8	black-bird has spoken like the first bird (1)
61, 62	their urgent summons clearly spoken (1)
301	by whom the words of life were spoken (1)
314	what the Truth hath spoken, that for truth I hold (2)
322	still that word is spoken, and still the bread is broken (1)
340, 341	for the words which you have spoken (1)
342	we hear the words so gently spoken (1)
358	God-spoken prophecy, word at creation (3)

373	Praise the Lord, for he hath spoken (1)
522, 523	Glorious things of thee are spoken, Zion city of our God (1)
536	God has spoken to his people, Hallelujah (R)
630	Word was spoken in the deed that made the earth (1)
630	God has spoken: praise God for his open word (1-4)
633	Be our Word in pity spoken (3)

spokesman
| 243 | no spokesman at his side (2) |

spot
| 640 | Watchman, will its beams alone gild the spot (2) |
| 640 | gild the spot that gave them birth (2) |

spotless
232	who wear the spotless raiment (2/11-1)
338	spotless oblation (1)
435	faithfully he bore it spotless to the last (2)
657	pure and spotless let us be (3)

spouse
260	Virgin's spouse ... guardian of great David's greater Son (2)
260	beside his spouse ... he joins the heavenly song (4)
261, 262	appointed spouse of the Virgin (1)

spread
42	Through the long night watches may thine angels spread (5)
50	today the saints his triumphs spread (2)
125, 126	His power increasing still shall spread (5)
178	Spread the good news o'er all the earth (2)
242	yet when thine Easter-news was spread (2)
244	sing of those who spread the treasure in the holy Gospels (1)
299	With tongues of fire saints spread good news (1)
316, 317	this is the heavenly table spread for me (1)
321	My God, thy table now is spread (1)
337	we here spread forth to thee that only offering perfect (1)
343	Savior, abide with us, and spread thy table in our heart (3)
379	God who spread the heavens above (1)
385	thy fingers spread the mountains and plains (1)
398	spread the flowing seas abroad and built the lofty skies (1)
409	spread the truth from pole to pole (2)
434	Nature with open volume stands to spread ... praise (1)
434	spread her Maker's praise abroad (1)
450, 451	go, spread your trophies at his feet (5)
493	spread through all the earth abroad the honors of thy Name (2)
509	Come as the dove, and spread thy wings (4)
515	breathe thy life and spread thy light (1)
530	spread, thou mighty word, spread the kingdom of the Lord (1)
530	word for which the nations long, spread abroad (5)
532, 533	thy truth and thy judgments shall spread all abroad (2)
540	spread the glory of redemption (2)
579	Spirit ... the Father sent to spread abroad the firmament (3)
663	Thou hast in grace my table spread (4)
664	Thy hand ... doth still my table spread (2)
674	our lives will spread your peace (4)

| 691 | griefs around me spread (3) |
| 709 | O spread thy sheltering wings around (4) |

spreading
255	Saul, the church's spoiler came spreading fear and hate (1)
321	Nor let thy spreading Gospel rest (4)
631	bringing freedom, spreading truth (1)
667	beneath the spreading heavens no creature but is fed (3)
681	line of lifted sea, where spreading moonlight quivers (3)

spreads
148	far and wide the wreckage of our hatred spreads (3)
324	Rank on rank the host of heaven spreads its vanguard (3)
324	spreads its vanguard on the way (3)

spring
5	O Light of Light, light's living spring (1)
6, 7	Day-spring from on high, be near (1)
9	royal robes of autumn moors the golden gates of spring (2)
47	creation's Lord and spring (1)
55	From human will you do not spring (2)
56	O come, Thou Day-spring from on high (6)
145	your health shall spring (5)
179	Earth her joy confesses, clothing her for spring (2)
199, 200	'Tis the spring of souls today (2)
300	sing Christ the Spring, never, never ceasing (2)
376	well-spring of the joy of living (3)
383, 384	woodlands robed in the blooming garb of spring (2)
393	'tis the Day-spring from on high (2)
616	love, joy, hope, like flowers spring in his path to birth (3)
621, 622	vision whence true peace doth spring (1)
658	thy health's eternal spring (3)
666	plenteous source and spring (4)
666	source and spring from whence redemption ever flows (4)
678, 679	rejoice as you draw water from salvation's living spring (1)
699	spring thou up within my heart, rise to all eternity (3)
700	Well-spring of heavenly peace, thou Living Water, come (2)
700	Spring up, and never cease (3)

springeth
| 204 | Love is come again like wheat that springeth green (R) |
| 665 | beauty springeth out of nought (3) |

springing
8	Praise for them, springing fresh from the Word (1)
61, 62	her heart with joyful hope is springing (2)
522, 523	living waters, springing from eternal love (2)

springs
11	guard my first springs of thought and will (2)
152	Give us the discipline that springs from abstinence (4)
196, 197	to fill the springs of living hope (2)
431	vault of heaven springs mute witness (1)
517	desert vale ... filled with springs (3)
672	turn our face to where the daylight springs (5)

springtime
149   glorious in springtime dress of leaf and flower (3)

sprung
8   sprung in completeness where his feet pass (2)
81   Lo, how a Rose e'er blooming from tender stem hath sprung (1)
192   My Love, the Crucified, hath sprung to life this morrow (1)
491   Worth from worth immortal sprung (3)

spun
140, 141   I have a sin of fear that when I've spun my last thread (3)

spurns
570, 571   drawing near a world that spurns him (4)

square
235   Four-square ... foundation the Church of Christ remains (3)
582, 583   within whose four-square walls shall come no night (1)

stable
97   For the world a love supreme brought me to this stable (2)
102   his shelter was a stable, and his cradle was a stall (2)
102   confounded that a stable should display heaven's Word (3)
102   Not in that poor lowly stable ... we shall see him (6)
104   A stable lamp is lighted Whose glow shall wake the sky (1)
112   stable ... sufficed the Lord God incarnate, Jesus Christ (2)
370   the stable earth (4)
568   sharing a stable with beasts at thy birth (2)

stablish
365   stablish thy righteousness, Savior and friend (2)

stablished
388   hath stablished it fast by a changeless decree (3)

stage
11   Awake, my soul ... with the sun thy daily stage of duty run (1)

stain
120   in the river shared our stain (1)
165, 166   by that blood from stain are freed (3)
202   the Lamb of God without a stain (3)
307   Cleansing us from every stain (4)
486   thy flock, redeemed from sinful stain ... praise again (5)
578   remember not our sin's dark stain (2)

stains
228   remove our stains; bind up all our injuries (4)
481   when he had purged our stains, he took his seat above (2)

stalks
18   By noon's bright light, destruction stalks (2c)

stall
98   Cradled in a stall was he with sleepy cows and asses (2)

102	his shelter was a stable, and his cradle was a stall (2)
104	A stall become a shrine (1)
110	She laid him in a stall at Bethlehem (2)
117, 118	low lies his head with the beasts of the stall (2)

stalwart

| 273, 274 | Two stalwart trees both rooted in faith and holy love (1) |

stamped

| 49 | stamped the day for ever his (1) |

stand

1, 2	active and watchful, stand we all before thee (1)
23	Now grant us undiminished strength to stand (1)
68	The marriage-feast is waiting, the gates wide open stand (2)
76	bid the fallen sinner stand (4)
168, 169	Ah, keep my heart thus moved to stand thy cross beneath (3)
199, 200	but today amidst thine own thou didst stand (4)
212	O Dead arise! O Friendless stand by seraphim adored (5)
215	there with thee in glory stand (3)
231	who, martyred, saw you stand to help (2/12-26)
231, 232	till all the ransomed number who stand before the throne (3)
235	a house to stand unshaken by floods or winds or rains (3)
237	where triumphant now they stand with the victor's story (2)
286	these before God's throne who stand (1)
286	Now in God's most holy place, blest they stand (5)
286	blest they stand before his face (5)
298	Through Christ's redemption we shall stand (1)
298	stand among the glorious heavenly band (1)
305, 306	thou at the table, blessing, yet dost stand (2)
324	and with fear and trembling stand (1)
359	stand at last with joy before thy face (5)
372	Established is his law, and changeless it shall stand (3)
391	firm as a rock thy truth must stand (5)
393	how the word we have heard firm and changeless ... stand (1)
393	changeless still shall stand (1)
421	we for judgment there must stand (2)
452	when doubters kneel and waverers stand (3)
476	earthly values stand beside the manger and the cross (3)
498	Beneath the cross of Jesus I fain would take my stand (1)
541	Who dares stand idle on the harvest plain (1)
545	there ... triumphantly to stand (5)
548	Stand then in his great might (3)
548	stand complete at last (5)
561	Stand up, stand up for Jesus (1-4)
561	stand in his strength alone (3)
573	Races and peoples, lo, we stand divided (2)
599	till now we stand at last (2)
599	shadowed beneath thy hand may we for ever stand (3)
615	all wrong shall stand revealed (4)
616	Name shall stand for ever, his changeless Name of Love (5)
619	Ye powers who stand before the eternal Light (2)
624	They stand, those halls of Zion, all jubilant with song (2)

636, 637	I'll strengthen thee, help thee, and cause thee to stand (2)
648	oppressed so hard they could not stand (1)
649, 650	stand rejoicing in your sight (1)
665	Love doth stand at his hand (4)
716	firm may she ever stand through storm and night (1)
720	O thus be it ever when free men shall stand (2)

standard
| 556, 557 | Still lift your standard high, still march in firm array (5) |
| 568 | lift up our lives to thy standard of right (3) |

standeth
| 569 | yet to eternity standeth thy word (3) |

stands
24	thy kingdom stands, and grows for ever (4)
75	he stands in the midst of nations (3)
78, 79	charity stands watching and faith holds wide the door (4)
129, 130	Christ upon the mountain peak stands alone in glory (1)
182	His cross stands empty to the sky (1)
185, 186	but now at God's right hand he stands (1)
259	There Joseph at her side in reverent wonder stands (3)
275	Multitude which none can number ... in glory stands (1)
280	In the roll of your apostles stands the name Bartholemew (2)
429	whose truth for ever stands secure (2)
434	Nature with open volume stands to spread ... praise (1)
459	there stands he with unhurrying feet (2)
620	David stands with harp in hand as master of the choir (3)

star
6, 7	Day-star, in my heart appear (1)
31, 32	for you the dazzling star shines forth (2)
40, 41	as Day-star you precede the dawn (1)
61, 62	her star is risen, her light grows bright (2)
84	star and angels gave the sign (1)
85, 86	our constant star in sin's deep night (2)
92	God's bright star, o'er his head (3)
93	ye have seen his natal star (3)
109	They looked up and saw a star shining in the east (2)
109	by the light of that same star three wise men came (3)
109	to follow the star wherever it went (3)
109	This star drew night to the northwest (4)
117, 118	star of the east, the horizon adorning (1,5)
119	As with gladness men of old did the guiding star behold (1)
119	bring our ransomed souls at last where they need no star (4)
119	no star to guide, where no clouds thy glory hide (4)
124	What star is this, with beams so bright (1)
124	who told the rise of Jacob's star (2)
124	The guiding star above is bright (3)
124	O Jesus, while the star of grace impels us on (4)
127	Fairer than the sun at morning was the star (2)
127	the star that told his birth (2)
128	following yonder star (1)
128	O star of wonder, star of night (R)
128	star with royal beauty bright (R)

394, 395	let sun and moon and stars and light ... praise (1)
398	moon shines full at his command and all the stars obey (1)
400	stars nightly shining, find a voice (2)
406, 407	My Lord be praised by sister moon and all the stars (3)
406, 407	stars that ... soon will point the glittering heavens (3)
409	whilst all the stars that round her burn (2)
412	Earth and all stars, loud rushing planets (1)
416	sun and moon, and stars of light (2)
427	Sing, suns and stars of space ... ye that see his face (5)
428	O sun and moon and stars of heaven (2)
428	sun ... moon ... stars ... your endless praise outpour (2)
431	The stars declare his glory (1)
490	God set the stars to give light to the world (1)
543	while round his throne ten thousand stars (4)
543	ten thousand stars in nobler spheres his influence own (4)
615	for the everlasting right the silent stars are strong (2)
681	whose stars serenely burn above this earth's confusion (1)
720	whose broad stripes and bright stars (1)

state

97	If a monarch, where thy state (1)
106	till our first heavenly state again takes place (5)
180	risen to a holier state (4)
215	see the King in royal state (1)
259	not with his angel host, not in his kingly state (1)
585	throned in easy state to reign (6)
716	to thee aloud we cry, God save the state (2)

stately

580	stately buildings row on row (2)

statesman's

631	statesman's, teacher's, hero's treasure (1)

station

232	we, whate'er our station may rise and follow you (2/9-21)

stay

101	stay by my side until morning is nigh (2)
101	I ask thee to stay close by me for ever (3)
109	there it did both stop and stay (4)
142	close by thee to stay (1)
370	his eye to watch, his might to stay (5)
372	his love be our strength and stay while ages roll (4)
458	Here might I stay and sing, no story so divine (7)
460, 461	Bread of Heaven, thou on earth our food, our stay (3)
564, 565	No foes shall stay his might, though he with giants fight (2)
612	love will ever with us stay (3)
627	our anchor and our stay (3)
638, 639	With thee all night I mean to stay (1)
647	some with me may stay (2)
649, 650	O Jesus, ever with us stay (4)
659, 660	teach me the wayward feet to stay (2)
662	Who, like thyself, my guide and stay can be (2)
664	thy presence is my stay (2)

| 669 | he will guide thy footsteps and be thy staff and stay (1) |
| 718 | be thou our ruler, guardian, guide, and stay (2) |

stead

| 202 | his flesh ... is freely offered in our stead (3) |
| 319 | You, Lord, in our stead to the grave descended (2) |

steadfast

121	Straightway and steadfast until death (2)
135	from there thou leddest them steadfast to Jerusalem (4)
231	a steadfast faith afford (2/12-21)
233, 234	Theirs is the steadfast faith of saints (3)
458	Yet steadfast he to suffering goes (5)
521	steadfast faith our unity, their peace our heritage (3)
600, 601	quiet of a steadfast faith, calm of a call obeyed (2)
634	steadfast faith grant me therefore (1)
681	thine is the mighty plan, the steadfast order sure (1)

steady

| 598 | new thorns to pierce that steady brow (1) |
| 599 | yet, with a steady beat (2) |

steal

| 42 | shadows of the evening steal across the sky (1) |

steals

| 287 | steals on the ear the distant triumph song (5) |

steeds

| 143 | to Elijah fasting, came the steeds and chariots of flame (2) |

steel

| 412 | Engines and steel, loud pounding hammers (4) |

stem

81	Lo, how a Rose e'er blooming from tender stem hath sprung (1)
135	branch of royal David's stem in thy birth at Bethlehem (1)
307	branch and flower of Jesse's stem (3)

step

422	For each new step of faith we take thou hast more truth (1)
453	remember, each step that by faith we pass o'er (3)
512	o'er every thought and step preside (1)

Stephen

231	All praise, O Lord, for Stephen (2/12-26)
243	When Stephen, full of power and grace, went forth (1)
243	When Stephen preached against the laws (2)
243	When Stephen, young and doomed to die, fell crushed (3)

stepping

| 527 | stepping fearless through the night (1) |

steps

| 106 | treading his steps, assisted by his grace (5) |

119	As with joyful steps they sped to that lowly manger bed (2)
282, 283	grant of thy mercy ... us thy servants steps up to heaven (1)
289	new comrades ever bringing in comrades' steps to tread (2)
478	lead us then day by day in your own steps, we pray (2)
546	forget the steps already trod, and onward urge thy way (2)

stern

| 605 | Still down the ages ring the prophet's stern commands (3) |

stilled

| 598 | our pride is dust, our vaunt is stilled (4) |

stillness

| 89, 90 | The world in solemn stillness lay to hear the angels sing (1) |

stills

| 375 | his comfort all my anguish stills (1) |
| 408 | every faithless murmur stills (1) |

sting

161	He lived to rob death of its sting (1)
185, 186	an empty form alone remains; his sting is lost for ever (2)
188, 189	where, O death, is now thy sting (2)
208	from death's dread sting thy servants free (5)
364	hadst overcome death's sting and opened heaven's door (7)
366	Thou didst take the sting from death (6)
662	Where is death's sting? where, grave, thy victory? (3)

stir

69	Who then shall stir in this darkness (2)
159	Jesus, may her deep devotion stir in me the same emotion (5)
568	stir up our leaders and peoples to penitence (1)
568	stir us to work for thy justice and charity (2)
568	stir every will to new ventures of faithfulness (3)
704	still stir up the gift in me (3)

stirred

232	whose heart with awe was stirred (2/8-15)
281	But grace within his heart had stirred (2)
440	let our hearts and souls be stirred now to seek and love (1)
629	let a new and better hope within our hearts be stirred (1)

stirring

| 555 | nor roll of stirring drums, but deeds of love and mercy (2) |
| 610 | stirring us to tireless striving (3) |

stone

104	And every stone shall cry (1-4)
112	earth stood hard as iron, water like a stone (1)
157	the same stone which the builders rejected (R)
212	His enemies had sealed the stone (4)
254	this saint a true foundation-stone (2)
284	Ye rolled the stone (6)
453	at night on a stone for a pillow he lay (1)
592	This is the famous stone that turneth all to gold (4)

598   till not a stone was left on stone (2)

stones
243   crushed beneath the stones (3)
243   the stones of earthly shame a jeweled crown may seem (4)
413   mountains and stones look up adoring (3)
480   Should we forget our Savior's praise, the stones ... sing (3)
480   the stones themselves would sing (3)
519, 520   living stones art builded in the height of heaven above (1)
519, 520   Many a blow and biting sculpture polished ... stones (4)
519, 520   Many a blow ... polished well those stones elect (4)

stony
149   as through stony ground the green shoots break (3)
196, 197   Jesus ... looked down Golgatha's stony slope (2)
599   Stony the road we trod, bitter the chastening rod (2)

stood
18   The sun stood still for Joshua (2a)
102   Once in royal David's city stood a lowly cattle shed (1)
112   earth stood hard as iron, water like a stone (1)
131, 132   Within the Jordan's sacred flood the ... Lamb ... stood (3)
131, 132   heavenly Lamb in meekness stood (3)
159   At the cross her vigil keeping stood the mournful mother (1)
276   he stood with thee beside the dead (3)
324   as of old on earth he stood (2)
377, 378   his truth at all times firmly stood (4)
453   has stood hundreds of years and is not yet decayed (2)
582, 583   city that hath stood too long a dream (3)
680   Before the hills in order stood (3)

stooped
492   stooped to wear the servant's vesture (2)
539   tell how he stooped to save his lost creation (2)
643   thou hast stooped to ask of me the love of my poor heart (5)

stop
109   there it did both stop and stay (4)

store
228   make us ready to receive gifts from your unbounded store (5)
290   but the fruitful ears to store in his garner evermore (3)
388   The earth, with its store of wonders untold (3)
549, 550   worship of the vain world's golden store (3)
665   Evermore from his store new-born worlds rise and adore (3)

stored
367   earth is with thy fullness stored (1,3)
621, 622   all is pure ... holy that within thy walls is stored (2)

stores
288   autumn's rich o'erflowing stores (2)
644   filled with boundless stores of grace (3)

stories

564, 565   Who so beset him round with dismal stories (2)

storm

388   dark is his path on the wings of the storm (2)
677   plants his footsteps in the sea ... rides upon the storm (1)
699   hide me, O my Savior ... till the storm of life is past (1)
716   firm may she ever stand through storm and night (1)

storms

290   all is safely gathered in, ere the winter storms begin (1)
412   Hail, wind, and rain, loud blowing snow-storms (2)
428   O storms and thunder's roar, O fields and forests bless (3)
655   above the storms of passion, the murmurs of self-will (2)

story

65   Greet One who comes in glory, foretold in sacred story (1)
93   who sang creation's story now proclaim Messiah's birth (1)
106   amazed, the wondrous story they proclaim (4)
108   on this day of days tell out redemption's story (1)
237   where triumphant now they stand with the victor's story (2)
363   thy love has blessed the wide world's wondrous story (1)
368   while we hear thy wondrous story (2)
409   nightly to the listening earth repeats the story (2)
409   repeats the story of her birth (2)
414   speak of thy dread acts the story (3)
432   tell ... sweet harp, the story of what he hath done (3)
441, 442   all the light of sacred story gathers round its head (1,5)
458   Here might I stay and sing, no story so divine (7)
594, 595   crown thine ancient Church's story (1)
631   till they came, who told the story of the Word (2)
408   all who know his power proclaim aloud the wondrous story (3)

straight

67   Make ye straight what long was crooked (3)
75, 76   make straight all the crooked places (1)
120   Straight to the wilderness he goes to wrestle (4)
552, 553   Run the straight race through God's good grace (2)

straightway

106   He spoke ... straightway the celestial choir ... conspire (3)
121   Straightway and steadfast until death (2)

strain

24   nor dies the strain of praise away (3)
199, 200   Come, ye faithful, raise the strain of triumphant gladness (1)
210   hearing, may raise the victor strain (2)
277   Church the strain re-echoes unto earth's remotest ends (3)
492   wake your noblest, sweetest strain (1)
527   One the strain the lips of thousands lift (3)
618   raise the glad strain (1)
619   Then let the holy city raise the strain (3)
652, 653   take from our souls the strain and stress (4)
659, 660   help me bear the strain of toil, the fret of care (1)

strains

50	Hosanna in the highest strains the Church ... can raise (5)
50	the highest strains the Church on earth can raise (5)
136, 137	for which in joyful strains we raise the voice of prayer (4)
199, 200	welcomes in unwearied strains Jesus' resurrection (3)
556, 557	pour out the strains of joy and bliss (2)

strand

623	through our long exile on Babylon's strand (4)

strange

161	With what strange light the rough trunk shone (4)
185, 186	It was a strange and dreadful strife (2)
458	but men made strange (2)

stranger

370	Christ in mouth of friend and stranger (6)
429	He helps the stranger in distress (3)
458	in death no friendly tomb but what a stranger gave (6)
491	Where is this stupendous stranger (1)
664	no more a stranger or a guest, but like a child at home (3)
686	Jesus sought me when a stranger (2)

strangers

304	and strangers now are friends (3)
360, 361	strangers and pilgrims, seeking homes eternal (4)
360, 361	strangers and pilgrims ... pass through its portals (4)

straw

104	And straw like gold shall shine (1)

stray

517	happy they who keep thy laws nor from thy precepts stray (4)
599	Lest our feet stray from the places ... we met thee (3)
627	when wont to stray (1)
647	I must not fear nor stray (3)
691	nor let me ever stray from thee aside (3)
697	that I from thee no more may stray (1)

strayed

391	when like wandering sheep we strayed, he saved us (2)
645, 646	Perverse and foolish oft I strayed (3)

stream

5	Spirit's sanctifying beam upon our earthly senses stream (2)
61, 62	through them we stream to join the immortals (3)
111	glories stream from heaven afar (2)
116	At Jordan's stream, behold (1)
135	Manifest at Jordan's stream (2)
139	Jesus went to Jordan's stream his Father's will obeying (1)
180	a brighter Easter beam on our longing eyes shall stream (4)
308, 309	O stream of love past telling (2)
479	Blest through endless ages be the precious stream (3)
479	stream which from sin and sorrow doth the world redeem (3)
526	though now divided by the ... narrow stream of death (2)

526	when the word is given bid Jordan's narrow stream divide (5)
543	while rays divine stream all abroad (1)
627	stream from the fount of heavenly grace (1)
664	pastures fresh he makes me feed beside the living stream (1)
680	Time, like an ever-rolling stream (5)
690	fountain, whence the healing stream doth flow (2)
692	I came to Jesus, and I drank of that life-giving stream (2)

streaming

307	smitten Rock with streaming side (5)
441, 442	from the cross the radiance streaming adds more luster (3)
720	o'er the ramparts we watched were so gallantly streaming (1)

streams

131, 132	in streams that nature ne'er bestowed (4)
138	in you always to live and drink of those ... streams (3)
138	those refreshing streams which you alone can give (3)
244	See the rivers four that gladden, with their streams (2)
287	through gates of pearl streams in the countless host (8)
332	the streams that through the desert flow (2)
388	it streams from the hills, it descends to the plain (4)
455, 456	read thee ... in seas that swell and streams that flow (2)
522, 523	See, the streams of living waters (2)
645, 646	Where streams of living water flow ... he leadeth (2)
658	As longs the deer for cooling streams (1)
663	by streams serene, he safely doth me lead (1)
686	Streams of mercy never ceasing (1)
686	Streams of mercy ... call for songs of loudest praise (1)
699	let the healing streams abound (3)

street

230	In Salem's street was gathered a crowd from many a land (2)
567	crowded street, by restless couch ... Gennesaret's shore (2)
582, 583	greed for gain in street and shop and tenement (2)
620	blessed martyrs' harmony doth ring in every street (4)

streets

78, 79	yet in thy dark streets shineth the everlasting Light (1)
182	Let streets and homes with praises ring (1)
519, 520	all thy streets and all thy bulwarks of pure gold (2)
580	windows ... stare on canyoned streets below (2)
609	O tread the city's streets again (4)

strength

12, 13	give us strength to do your will (3)
19, 20	Let mouth and tongue, mind, sense, and strength (2)
23	Now grant us undiminished strength to stand (1)
33-35	strength for our weak hearts, rest for aching bodies (4)
55	Oh, fill our weak and dying frame with godly strength (4)
55	strength which never fails (4)
61, 62	glorious in strength of grace, in truth victorious (2)
66	Israel's strength and consolation (2)
138	So, led from strength to strength, grant us ... to see (4)
142	O give us strength in thee to fight ... to conquer sin (2)
179	tread the path of darkness, saving strength to show (5)

190	the strength of death is broken (3)
228	Source of strength and sure relief (2)
236	strength of the pilgrim on the way (1)
254	though mortal strength may fail (1)
310, 311	thine aid supply, thy strength bestow (1)
318	my strength is in thy might, thy might alone (3)
323	day by day with strength supplied (1)
323	strength supplied through the life of him who died (1)
326	strength unto strength we go forward on Zion's highway (1)
332	go rejoicing on our way, renewed with strength divine (4)
337	crown thy gifts with strength to persevere (3)
342	your love shines though your strength is waning (2)
343	in strength of which we travel on to our abiding place (2)
347	go to the world in strength (3)
348	yours is the strength that sustains our vocatiion (1)
372	his love shall be our strength and stay while ages roll (4)
386, 387	the stupendous force on which all strength depends (1)
404	We love you with our heart and strength and mind (3)
417, 418	Power, riches, wisdom, and strength ... are his (2)
425	God is our strength, he is our song (2)
425	He only is to be adored for he alone can strength bestow (3)
478	Jesus, our mighty Lord, our strength in sadness (1)
480	grace and knowledge grow as years and strength increase (1)
482	strength in our hearts, Lord, at the noon of the day (2)
487	Come, my Light, my Feast, my Strength (2)
487	such a strength as makes his guest (2)
491	strength of infant weakness, if eternal is so young (3)
531	souls without strength inspire with might (3)
534	March we forth in the strength of God (3)
548	strong in the strength which God supplies (1)
548	who in the strength of Jesus trusts is more than conqueror (2)
548	with all his strength endued (3)
548	From strength to strength go on (4)
551	give heart and soul and mind and strength (1)
552, 553	Christ is thy strength and Christ thy right (1)
561	strength to strength oppose (2)
561	stand in his strength alone (3)
564, 565	do but themselves confound, his strength the more is (2)
567	thy touch ... gave hearing, strength, and sight (2)
581	with heart and mind and strength now love him in return (2)
582, 583	Give us, O God, the strength to build the city (3)
590	strong in your strength to venture and to dare (2)
631	Book of books, our people's strength (1)
635	he'll give thee strength whate'er betide thee (1)
647	for light and strength I pray (2)
668	shall thy strength restore (4)
675	his strength shall bear your spirit up (2)
675	in his strength, and calmly every danger brave (4)
681	inspire us from above with joy and strength for duty (5)
687, 688	Did we in our own strength confide (2)
690	strong deliverer, be thou still my strength and shield (2)
691	May thy rich grace impart strength to my fainting heart (2)
698	Come with the vision and the strength I need to serve (3)

strengthen

143	our spirits strengthen with thy grace (4)
312	Strengthen for service, Lord, the hands (1)
347	strengthen the faint, give courage to the weak (2)
448, 449	Spirit here to guide, to strengthen, and to cheer (5)
607	Lord, strengthen all who labor that we may find release (3)
636, 637	I'll strengthen thee, help thee, and cause thee to stand (2)

strengthened

617	guided and strengthened and upheld by thee (1)

strengthening

349	come ... with your strengthening gift of power (2)
511	quickening, strengthening and absolving (2)

stress

357	Here mid stress and conflict toils can never cease (2)
570, 571	all who bear its daily stress (1)
652, 653	take from our souls the strain and stress (4)

stretch

76	To heal the sick stretch out thine hand (4)
544	his kingdom stretch from shore to shore (1)
546	Awake, my soul, stretch every nerve (1)
546	Then wake, my soul, stretch every nerve (4)

stretched

580	God, who stretched the spangled heavens (1)
603, 604	his arms stretched out above through every culture (1)

stretches

369	Our reason stretches all its wings (3)

stretching

97	stretching infant hands on high, Savior, long awaited (1)

strew

104	The palm shall strew its branches (2)
458	Sometimes they strew his way and his strong praises sing (3)

strewn

289	for thine unfailing mercies far-strewn along our way (1)

strife

21, 22	Quench now on earth the flames of strife (2)
27, 28	Lest we, beset by doubt and strife forget (3)
46	plunged us into strife (3)
70	granting victory in our strife (4)
89, 90	Yet with the woes of sin and strife (3)
89, 90	O hush the noise and cease your strife (3)
156	Thy last and fiercest strife is nigh (4)
163	Here in o'erwhelming final strife (3)
168, 169	see in my last strife to me thine arms extended (5)
184	He who gave for us his life ...for us endured the strife (2)

185, 186	It was a strange and dreadful strife (2)
208	The strife is o'er, the battle done (1)
222	his strife with human hatred ends (1)
222	shame of human strife (3)
231	grant us grace to know you, the victor in the strife (2/5-1)
237	Who will venture on the strife (3)
280	all his toiling and his strife, all are veiled from us (3)
285	through weary years of toil and strife ... faithful (3)
287	when the strife is fierce, the warfare long (5)
345	peace to thy Church from error and from strife (3)
357	Often were they wounded in the deadly strife (3)
379	guides us through our earthly strife (3)
399	that strife may end and joy increase (3)
472	to heal earth's wounds and end her bitter strife (2)
487	such a truth as ends all strife (1)
494	rose victorious in the strife for those he came to save (3)
501, 502	protector in the midst of strife (2)
501, 502	From inner strife grant us release (5)
511	Spirit, ever striving through her in a ceaseless strife (1)
521	O Judge divine of human strife (4)
547	for us ... conquered in the strife (5)
558	we will love both friend and foe in all our strife (3)
561	the strife will not be long (4)
570, 571	in your day of helpless strife (2)
576, 577	Banished now be anger, strife and every quarrel (2)
581	Let strife among us be unknown (4)
586	thou ... dwellest in the daily strife (2)
593	where there is strife, may we make one (1)
600, 601	Bring to our world of strife thy sovereign word of peace (4)
609	above the noise of selfish strife (1)
661	no peace, but strife closed in the sod (4)
719	O beautiful for heroes proved in liberating strife (2)

string

| 430 | let no tongue nor string be mute (2) |

strings

| 284 | waved around your golden wings and struck your strings (7) |
| 284 | struck your strings of sweetest sound (7) |

stripes

| 208 | Lord! by the stripes which wounded thee (5) |
| 720 | whose broad stripes and bright stars (1) |

stripped

| 185, 186 | stripped of power, no more he reigns (2) |

strive

12, 13	strive to follow where you lead (2)
27, 28	strive to gain the heavenly prize (4)
240, 241	strive to think him, speak him, live him (4)
445, 446	should strive afresh against the foe (3)
445, 446	should strive and should prevail (3)
510	in vain we strive to rise (3)

| 545 | Let us, with zeal like theirs inspired, strive (2) |
| 545 | strive in the Christian race (2) |

striven

| 286 | in prayer full oft have striven (4) |
| 286 | striven with the God they glorified (4) |

striving

231, 232	By all your saints still striving, for all ... at rest (1)
282, 283	may he banish from us striving and hatred (2)
511	Spirit, ever striving through her in a ceaseless strife (1)
610	stirring us to tireless striving (3)
687, 688	our striving would be losing (2)

strong

27, 28	for you alone can make us strong (4)
75	the arm of the Lord is strong (3)
148	grant us your power to make us strong (1)
150	strong with thee to suffer pain (2)
185, 186	Christ Jesus lay in death's strong bands (1)
231	the weak by grace made strong (2/4-25)
231	as faithful branches grow strong in you, the Vine (2/4-25)
255	O strong, reproving Word (2)
266	she was filled with confusion strong (3)
270	Weakness shall the strong confound (3)
287	hearts are brave again, and arms are strong (5)
293	their love made them strong (2)
295	who sanctifies and guides us, made strong in our rebirth (3)
307	Thou alone, our strong defender (1)
334	alert and living in your Spirit, strong and free (3)
370	I bind unto myself today the strong Name of the Trinity (1)
370	bind unto myself the Name ... strong Name of the Trinity (7)
381	Thy strong word did cleave the darkness (1)
381	Thy strong word bespeaks us righteous (3)
406, 407	strong to lighten all the night (4)
435	Name him, Christians ... with love strong as death (4)
452	that strong Light puts out the sun and all is ended (4)
453	The ladder is long, it is strong and well made (2)
455, 456	O Love of God, how strong and true (1)
458	Sometimes they strew his way and his strong praises sing (3)
462	wonders great by thy strong hand are done (5)
482	strong hands were skilled at the plane and the lathe (2)
516	so the yearning strong, with which the soul will long (3)
530	Word of life, most pure and strong (5)
540	Send forth, O Lord, thy strong Evangel (3)
548	strong in the strength which God supplies (1)
548	strong in the Lord of hosts, and in his mighty power (2)
555	through days of preparation thy grace has made us strong (1)
567	Thine arm, O Lord, in days of old was strong to heal (1)
567	strong to heal and save (1)
567	that whole and sick and weak and strong may praise thee (3)
572	we ... join in singing that great music pure and strong (1)
579	Almighty Father, strong to save (1)
590	strong in your strength to venture and to dare (2)
608	Eternal Father, strong to save (1)

612	love than death itself more strong (2)
615	for the everlasting right the silent stars are strong (2)
616	to help the poor and needy, and bid the weak be strong (2)
618	Ye holy twelve, ye martyrs strong (3)
621, 622	full of health, and strong, and free (4)
626	thine arm my strong support; thyself my great reward (2)
651	though the wrong is great and strong (2)
659, 660	in work that keeps faith sweet and strong (3)
672	Our hopes are weak, our fears are strong (2)
681	hymns thy people raise, the psalms and anthems strong (3)
690	strong deliverer, be thou still my strength and shield (2)
718	be thy strong arm our ever sure defense (3)

stronger
| 359 | make each one stronger, nobler than the last (1) |

strove
| 279 | For thy dear saints, O Lord, who strove in thee to live (1) |
| 420 | when utmost evil strove against the Light (4) |

strowed
156	thy humble beast pursues his road with palms ... strowed (1)
156	with palms and scattered garments strowed (1)
480	strowed their garments on the ground (3)

struck
| 284 | waved around your golden wings and struck your strings (7) |
| 284 | struck your strings of sweetest sound (7) |

struggle
| 18 | so may we struggle faithfully (2a) |
| 287 | We feebly struggle, they in glory shine (4) |

stubborn
| 226, 227 | Bend the stubborn heart and will (4) |
| 437, 438 | Proud hearts and stubborn wills are put to flight (3) |

study
| 628 | study, that your laws may be inscribed upon our hearts (1) |

stumble
| 590 | to lift the fallen, guide the feet that stumble (2) |
| 703 | blindly we stumble when we walk alone (2) |

stumbled
| 12, 13 | you stumbled, Lord, beneath its weight (2) |
| 161 | They stumbled on a mystery: Messiah reigning from a tree (3) |

stupendous
183	Death and life have contended in that combat stupendous (3)
386, 387	the stupendous force on which all strength depends (1)
386, 387	seers that stupendous truth believed (4)
491	Where is this stupendous stranger (1)

subdue
5	with love all envy to subdue (4)
435	there let him subdue all that is not holy ... not true (5)
563	the Lord himself, thy Leader, shall all thy foes subdue (1)

subject
261, 262	to his earthly father freely was subject (2)

sublime
146, 147	the Lord of love, in love sublime (2)
160	O mysterious condescending! O abandonment sublime! (3)
441, 442	gathers round its head sublime (1,5)
459	suns his footsteps trace through corridors sublime (1)

subtle
574, 575	for crafty trade and subtle snare to catch the simple (3)

succeed
574, 575	for pride ambitious to succeed (3)

succeeds
534	God is working his purpose out as year succeeds to year (1)

success
157	Hosanna, Lord, hosanna. Lord, send us now success (R)
365	come, and thy people bless; come, give thy word success (2)

succession
179	Months in due succession, days of lengthening light (3)

successive
544	where'er the sun doth his successive journeys run (1)

succor
282, 283	Send thine archangel Michael to our succor (2)
616	He comes with succor speedy to those who suffer wrong (2)

such
16, 17	splendor of such grace (3)
54	Marvel ... that the Lord chose such a birth (1)
61, 62	No eye has known the sight, no ear heard such delight (3)
74	clad as are the poorest, such his humility (1)
76	a home where such a mighty guest may come (2)
115	Why lies he in such mean estate (2)
116	may such bonds for ever draw our souls to things above (5)
145	or rend the soul, such grief is not Lent's goal (2)
150	round us ... angels shine, such as ministered to thee (4)
159	such a cup of sorrow drinking (4)
232	equip us for such sufferings as glorify your Name (2/7-25)
250	such a Lord to lead our way in hazard and prosperity (4)
284	for such a birth ye sang aloud (2)
304	His presence ... is in such friendship better known (4)
320	who on earth such food bestowest (6)
413	Trumpets and organs set in motion such sounds (2)
413	such sounds as make the heavens ring (2)

430	in such a praiseful tone we will sing what he hath done (5)
453	Who would not want to climb such a ladder as this (4)
469, 470	no place ... earth's failures have such kindly judgment (2)
469, 470	such kindly judgment given (2)
474	Did e'er such love and sorrow meet (3)
487	such a way as gives us breath (1)
487	such a truth as ends all strife (1)
487	such a life as killeth death (1)
487	such a light as shows a feast (2)
487	such a feast as mends in length (2)
487	such a strength as makes his guest (2)
487	such a joy as none can move (3)
487	such a love as none can part (3)
487	such a heart as joys in love (3)
522, 523	Who can faint when such a river ever ... thirst assuage (2)
587	in all our hearts such love increase (3)
619	Such song is rest and food and deep delight (6)
661	such happy, simple fisher-folk before the Lord came down (1)
709	Such blessings from thy gracious hand (5)
709	Such blessings ... our humble prayers implore (5)

suddenly

93	suddenly the Lord, descending, in his temple shall appear (4)
225	he whom the Lord foretold suddenly, swiftly descends (1)
657	suddenly return, and never, nevermore thy temples leave (2)

suffer

150	strong with thee to suffer pain (2)
160	perfect Man on thee did suffer (1,4)
164	Grant us with thee to suffer pain (4)
207	did once upon the cross ... suffer to redeem our loss (1)
215	He who on the cross did suffer (2)
277	forth to preach, and heal, and suffer (2)
279	learned from thy Holy Spirit's breath to suffer and to do (2)
483	They suffer with their Lord below (5)
495	Thou didst suffer to release us (1)
544	all those who suffer want are blest (4)
561	lift high his royal banner, it must not suffer loss (1)
616	He comes with succor speedy to those who suffer wrong (2)
701	nought that I may suffer ever shall from Jesus sever (2)

suffered

55	You suffered death and harrowed hell (3)
89, 90	the world has suffered long (3)
158	the slave hath sinned, and the Son hath suffered (3)
167	but we believe it was for us he hung and suffered there (2)
275	Gladly, Lord, with thee they suffered (3)
498	see the very dying form of one who suffered there for me (2)

sufferer

42	Comfort every sufferer watching late in pain (4)
282, 283	health-bringer blessed, aiding every sufferer (4)

suffering

142	Abide with us, that so, this life of suffering overpast (5)

171	Shun not suffering, shame or loss (2)
190	on the cross a suffering victim (1)
231	Like you, our suffering Savior ... he blessed (2/12-26)
232	He drank the cup of suffering (2/7-25)
278	beneath the cross of Jesus ... weight of suffering knew (2)
458	Yet steadfast he to suffering goes (5)
545	They, once like us with suffering tried (1)
572	suffering all, that we may see triumph in surrender (3)
695, 696	bitter suffering, hard to understand (3)

sufferings
| 160 | Very God himself is bearing all the sufferings of time (3) |
| 232 | equip us for such sufferings as glorify your Name (2/7-25) |

suffers
182	where color, scorn or wealth divide, he suffers still (4)
182	he suffers still, yet loves the more (4)
182	suffers still, yet loves the more (4)
612	Love is kind, and suffers long (2)

sufficed
112	in the bleak midwinter a stable-place sufficed (2)
112	stable ... sufficed the Lord God incarnate, Jesus Christ (2)
232	On Easter morning early, a word from you sufficed (2/7-22)

sufficient
66	by thine all-sufficient merit raise us (4)
202	all sufficient Sacrifice, beneath thee hell defeated lies (4)
636, 637	my grace, all sufficient, shall be thy supply (4)
680	sufficient is thine arm alone, and our defense is sure (2)

suggest
| 11 | Direct, control, suggest, this day, all I design (3) |

sum
| 514 | of all his gifts the sum and crown (4) |

summer
9	velvet of soft summer nights (2)
226, 227	in our summer, cooling shade (2)
288	All the plenty summer pours (2)
405	the cold wind in the winter, the pleasant summer sun (3)

summon
489	Not to oppress, but summon all their truest life to find (6)
572	To the triumph of your cross summon all the living (3)
572	summon us to love by loss, gaining all by giving (3)

summoned
| 83 | See how the shepherds, summoned to his cradle (4) |

summoning
| 363 | summoning all to share thy new creation (3) |

sunrise
163   Sunset to sunrise changes now (1)
542   whole round world complete, from sunrise to its setting (2)

suns
380   till suns shall rise and set no more (2)
427   Sing, suns and stars of space ... ye that see his face (5)
459   Do flaming suns his footsteps trace (1)
459   suns his footsteps trace through corridors sublime (1)
580   flung the suns in burning radiance through ... space (1)
621, 622   endless noon-day ... from the Sun of suns is there (3)

sunset
25, 26   Now sunset comes, but light shines forth (2)
163   Sunset to sunrise changes now (1)
405   the sunset and the morning that brightens up the sky (2)

sunshine
185, 186   by his grace he doth impart eternal sunshine to the heart (3)
191   ripened by his glorious sunshine (3)
291   the breezes and the sunshine, and soft refreshing rain (1)
292   At temper fair with gentle air the sunshine and the rain (2)
383, 385   Fair is the sunshine, fairer still the moonlight (3)
498   I ask no other sunshine than the sunshine of his face (3)
662   Through cloud and sunshine, Lord, abide with me (2)

sup
343   Lord, sup with us in love divine, thy Body and thy Blood (4)

supernal
261, 262   to Saint Joseph gave supernal honor (3)
618   supernal anthems echoing (4)

supper
138   grant us, O Lord, to see the marriage supper of the Lamb (4)
320   What he did, at supper seated, Christ ordained (3)
329, 331   That last night at supper lying (3)

supplication
33-35   Give heed, we pray you, to our supplication (4)
238, 239   join to ours your supplication (3)
496, 497   hear, O hear our supplication (2)
515   hear our supplication, blessed Spirit, God of peace (2)

supplied
290   God, our Maker, doth provide for our wants to be supplied (1)
323   day by day with strength supplied (1)
323   strength supplied through the life of him who died (1)

supplies
323   Vine of heaven, thy Blood supplies this blest cup (2)
347   richly from above his love supplies the grace and power (2)
389   his full hand supplies their need (6)
548   strong in the strength which God supplies (1)
548   God supplies through his eternal Son (1)

supply

308, 309	We hunger; Lord, supply us (1)
310, 311	thine aid supply, thy strength bestow (1)
522, 523	well supply thy sons and daughters (2)
636, 637	my grace, all sufficient, shall be thy supply (4)
664	My Shepherd will supply my need, Jehovah is his Name (1)

supplying

329, 331	then, more precious food supplying, gives himself (3)

support

465, 466	eternal power, be my support (1)
626	thine arm my strong support; thyself my great reward (2)
699	still support and comfort me (2)
702	my support thy power divine (4)

supports

429	the Lord supports the fainting mind (3)

supreme

97	For the world a love supreme brought me to this stable (2)
135	Prophet, Priest, and King supreme (2)
175	Redeemer, Son of the Father supreme, only begotten of God (6)
216	Son of the Father supreme, only begotten of God (4)
414	King supreme shall they confess thee (6)
532, 533	Thou only art holy, thou only supreme (1)

sure

116	He seals the sure prophetic word (1)
226, 227	come, thou source of blessings sure (1)
228	Source of strength and sure relief (2)
377, 378	his mercy is forever sure (4)
389	for his mercies ay endure, ever faithful, ever sure (R)
393	God it is who grants us sure retreat and refuge nigh (2)
406, 407	with thee, Lord, their reward is sure (6)
437, 438	his mercy sure, from age to age the same (2)
437, 438	Firm is his promise, and his mercy sure (4)
445, 446	most sure in all his ways (1,5)
467	to make salvation sure, guides us by his Spirit pure (3)
501, 502	You are the seeker's sure resource (2)
518	Christ is made the sure foundation (1)
522, 523	what can shake thy sure repose (1)
524	Sure as thy truth shall last (5)
664	The sure provisions of my God attend me all my days (3)
669	bring to sure fulfillment thy counsel good and true (3)
670	my doubts I sorely feel, thy sure promise I believe (3)
677	Blind unbelief is sure to err and scan his work in vain (6)
680	sufficient is thine arm alone, and our defense is sure (2)
681	thine is the mighty plan, the steadfast order sure (1)
687, 688	lo, his doom is sure, one little word shall fell him (3)
695, 696	O give our frightened souls the sure salvation (2)
718	be thy strong arm our ever sure defense (3)

surely

390	surely his goodness and mercy shall ever attend thee (3)

459	an altar candle sheds its light as surely as a star (2)
517	thou shalt surely bless ... who live the words they pray (4)
529	Who serves my Father as his child is surely kin to me (2)
534	nearer draws the time, the time that shall surely be (1,4)
663	surely I can trust thy love for all the days to come (5)
678, 679	Surely it is God who saves me (1)

surest
452 the surest friend of all his foes (2)

surging
372 His Spirit floweth free, high surging where it will (3)
632 It is the chart and compass that o'er life's surging sea (2)

surnamed
232 Praise for your blest apostle surnamed Bartholomew (2/8-24)

surpasses
98 but the very beasts could see that he all men surpasses (2)

surpasseth
320 Christ ... who surpasseth all thy praising (1)

surpassing
364 dwell ... with all thy saints in joy surpassing thought (8)
414 works of love surpassing measure (4)
620 Our Lady sings Magnificat with tune surpassing sweet (4)

surprise
212 Oh, with what gladness and surprise the saints ... greet (2)
284 ye mourned the dead in sad surprise (5)

surprising
590 grant the glad surprising that your blest Spirit rouses (1)

surrender
366 but deliverence to bring thou all honors didst surrender (5)
413 awed by his love his foes surrender (1)
475 Help us to surrender earth's deceitful treasures (2)
572 suffering all, that we may see triumph in surrender (3)

surrendered
314 lo, to thee surrendered, my whole heart is bowed (1)

surround
50 praise surround the throne (1)
61, 62 as we with joy your throne surround (3)
102 but in heaven, where his saints his throne surround (6)
376 All thy works with joy surround thee (2)
392 thus surround the throne (1)
700 True sunlight of the soul, surround us as we go (2)

surrounded
168, 169 O kingly head, surrounded with mocking crown of thorn (1)
522, 523 With salvation's walls surrounded, thou may'st smile (1)

573   in wrath and fear, by jealousies surrounded (3)

surrounds
61, 62   shout of rampart-guards surrounds us (1)

survey
398   if I survey the ground I tread, or gaze upon the sky (2)
474   When I survey the wondrous cross where ... died (1)
546   A cloud of witnesses around hold thee in full survey (2)

surveys
415   When all thy mercies, O my God, my rising soul surveys (1)

suspend
165, 166   awhile the ancient rigor that thy birth bestowed, suspend (5)

sustain
112   Our God, heaven cannot hold him, nor earth sustain (2)
585   God, whose arms of love aching, spent, the world sustain (6)

sustained
171   O the pangs his soul sustained (2)
286   these, who well the fight sustained (3)
406, 407   Sustained by thee, through evry hour, she bringeth forth (5)

sustaineth
375   What God hath wrought to show his power he ... sustaineth (3)
375   What God hath wrought ... he evermore sustaineth (3)
390   borne as on eagle-wings, safely his saints he sustaineth (2)

sustaining
48   That light our hope sustaining, we walk the pilgrim way (4)
342   For all we seek your grace sustaining (2)
394, 395   Sustaining God (2)

sustains
348   yours is the strength that sustains our vocatiion (1)

swallows
517   Beside thine altars ... the swallows find a nest (2)
585   scholar's truth, flight of swallows, autumn leaves (1)

swathing
94, 95   all meanly wrapped in swathing bands (4)

sway
24   till all thy creatures own thy sway (4)
270   Gabriel's message does away Satan's curse and ... sway (1)
364   the world is with the glory filled of thy majestic sway (3)
406, 407   signifies thy boundless sway (2)
542   new life, new hope awakes, for all who own his sway (1)

swayed
467   all is by his scepter swayed (2)

swear
140, 141   swear by thyself, that at my death thy Son shall shine (3)

sweep
460, 461   songs of all the sinless sweep across the crystal sea (3)

sweeps
592   who sweeps a room, as for thy laws, makes that ... fine (3)

sweet
8   Sweet the rain's new fall sunlit from heaven (2)
42   Jesus, give the weary calm and sweet repose (2)
43   with sweet sleep mine eyelids close (3)
101   the little Lord Jesus laid down his sweet head (1)
115   Whom angels greet with anthems sweet (1)
154, 155   to whom the lips of children made sweet hosannas ring (R)
243   in sweet forgiveness' name, should understand and spare (3)
287   sweet is the calm of paradise the blest (6)
292   all fostering power, all influence sweet breathe (2)
321   let them thy sweet mercies know (1)
337   by this food, so awesome and so sweet, deliver us (4)
351   possess, in sweet communion, joys ... earth cannot afford (2)
352   enjoying your sweet grace (2)
366   fill the heavens with sweet accord (2)
370   the sweet "Well done" in judgment hour (3)
392   join in a song with sweet accord (1)
429   grants the prisoner sweet release (3)
431   more sweet than honey to the taste (3)
432   tell ... sweet harp, the story of what he hath done (3)
434   Oh, the sweet wonders of that cross (4)
458   Sweet injuries! (4)
458   in whose sweet praise I all my days could gladly spend (7)
480   Sweet were his words and kind his look (2)
524   her sweet communion, solemn vows (3)
525   mystic sweet communion with those whose rest is won (5)
544   his Name like sweet perfume shall rise (2)
555   holiness shall whisper the sweet amen of peace (2)
617   one in the love of all things sweet and fair (2)
620   Our Lady sings Magnificat with tune surpassing sweet (4)
623   we the sweet anthems of Zion shall sing (3)
624   Oh, sweet and blessed country, the home of God's elect (4)
624   Oh, sweet and blessed country that eager hearts expect (4)
625   as in his sight with sweet delight ye do abound (2)
634   My heart is never set at rest till thy sweet word (1)
634   till thy sweet word have comforted me (1)
644   How sweet the Name of Jesus sounds in a believer's ear (1)
659, 660   in work that keeps faith sweet and strong (3)
671   how sweet the sound that saved a wretch like me (1)
677   bud may have a bitter taste ... sweet will be the flower (5)
683, 684   Return, O holy Dove, return, sweet messenger of rest (3)
717   My country, 'tis of thee, sweet land of liberty (1)
717   ring from all the trees sweet freedom's song (3)

sweetens
471   sweetens every bitter cup (3)

sweeter

181	sing in sweeter notes the song of Moses and the Lamb (4)
642	sweeter far thy face to see and in thy presence rest (1)
642	nor can the memory find a sweeter sound than Jesus' Name (2)

sweetest

165, 166	sweetest wood and sweetest iron (4)
165, 166	sweetest weight is hung on thee (4)
238, 239	with meetest praise and sweetest, honor them for evermore (1)
248, 249	sweetest comfort findeth near (3)
284	struck your strings of sweetest sound (7)
492	wake your noblest, sweetest strain (1)
544	dwell on his love with sweetest song (3)

sweetly

96	singing sweetly through the night (1)
388	sweetly distills in the dew and the rain (4)
619	ye citizens of heaven, O sweetly raise (1)
667	In holy contemplation we sweetly then pursue the theme (2)

sweetness

8	Praise for the sweetness of the wet garden (2)
81	with sweetness fills the air (3)
248, 249	Name of sweetness, passing measure (2)
314	to my taste thy sweetness never failing give (3)
642	thought of thee with sweetness fills the breast (1)

swell

57, 58	thousand saints attending swell the triumph of his train (1)
61, 62	as harps and cymbals swell the sound (3)
212	let Easter music swell (1)
291	sends the snow in winter, the warmth to swell the grain (1)
366	prophets swell the loud refrain (3)
455, 456	read thee ... in seas that swell and streams that flow (2)
479	Lift ye then your voices, swell the mighty flood (5)
486	both dead and living swell the sound (2)
486	shall swell the sound of praise again (5)
717	Let music swell the breeze (3)

swift

129, 130	Swift the cloud of glory came (3)
400	Swift flowing water, pure and clear, make music (3)
410	slow to chide and swift to bless (2)
482	your hands swift to welcome, your arms to embrace (3)

swiftly

225	he whom the Lord foretold suddenly, swiftly descends (1)
250	Now greet the swiftly changing year with joy (1)
541	redeem the time, its hours too swiftly fly (4)

sword

159	in her heart the piercing sword (1)
174	death's dark angel sheathes his sword (2)
232	To cross and sword they yielded (2/6-29)
232	who fell to Herod's sword (2/7-25)

243	on his lips a sword wherewith he smote and overcame (1)
243	a knight without a sword (4)
245	John ... who bore the Spirit's sword (1)
273, 274	One on a cross is martyred, one by the sword is slain (2)
276	fell by fire and sword, or early died or flourished long (1)
278	of the sword that pierced her through (2)
359	theirs not a monarch's crown or tyrant's sword (4)
425	horse ... rider ... sword he cast into the raging sea (1)
447	Can persecution, nakedness, or peril, or the sword (2)
459	light-years frame the Pleiades and point Orion's sword (1)
542	to ploughshare beat the sword, to pruning hook the spear (2)
558	living still in spite of dungeon, fire, and sword (1)
569	the lightening thy sword (1)
572	your dying bade us sheathe the foolish sword (2)
591	from sale and profanation of honor, and the sword (2)
591	lift up a living nation, a single sword to thee (3)
596	cleave our darkness with thy sword (3)
617	thy trusty shield, thy sword of love divine (3)
665	sword and crown betray our trust (2)

swords

555	for not with swords loud clashing (2)
591	the walls of gold entomb us, the swords of scorn divide (1)
597	May swords of hate fall from our hands (1)

sworn

401	He by himself hath sworn: we on his oath depend (2)

symbol

180	symbol of our Easter feast (3)
281	alike the symbol ... tool of foreign master's hated rule (1)

symbols

257	let symbols disappear (1)
357	in the mystic symbols veiled from earthly sight (1)

table

305, 306	thou at the table, blessing, yet dost stand (2)
316, 317	this is the heavenly table spread for me (1)
319	Here at your table every life you nourish (1)
320	when the twelve, divinely guided, at the holy table met (2)
321	My God, thy table now is spread (1)
321	O let thy table honored be (2)
343	Savior, abide with us, and spread thy table in our heart (3)
348	When, at your table, each time of returning (3)
348	Here, at your table, confirm our intention (2)
645, 646	Thou spread'st a table in my sight (5)
663	Thou hast in grace my table spread (4)
664	Thy hand ... doth still my table spread (2)

taint

357	Every taint of evil, frailty and decay ... purge away (3)

tainting

337	From tainting mischief keep them pure and clear (3)

take

51	that Christ may take them, bless them, break and give (4)
55	take our flesh and grow as child in Mary's womb (2)
57, 58	Savior, take the power and glory (4)
97	willingly this yoke I take, and this sacrifice I make (2)
116	This is my Son, my well-beloved in whom I take delight (3)
156	then take, O God, thy power and reign (5)
184	take our sin and guilt away that with angels we may say (2)
214	take the King of glory in (2)
240, 241	Take from him what ye will give him (4)
242	His brethren's word he would not take (3)
276	when thou shalt come to take us up (5)
290	For the Lord our God shall come ... take his harvest home (3)
322	what that Word did make it, I do believe and take it (2)
327, 328	Draw nigh and take the Body of the Lord (1)
327, 328	take the pledges of salvation here (5)
360, 361	humbly adoring, take thy Body broken (2)
366	Thou didst take the sting from death (6)
377, 378	for his sheep he doth us take (2)
400	forgiving others, take your part (5)
422	For each new step of faith we take thou hast more truth (1)
430	in this chorus take your place (3)
448, 449	God, the Son of God, should take our mortal form (1)
448, 449	God ... should take our mortal form for mortal's sake (1)
458	Lord should take frail flesh and die (1)
469, 470	we should take him at his word (3)
472	take thou our lives, and use them as thou wilt (4)
481	take his servants up to their eternal home (4)
498	Beneath the cross of Jesus I fain would take my stand (1)
498	I take, O cross, thy shadow for my abiding place (3)
512	holiness, the road that we must take to dwell with God (3)
548	take to arm you for the fight, the panoply of God (3)
591	take not thy thunder from us, but take away our pride (1)
616	to take away transgression, and rule in equity (1)
619	ye victors, now take up the eternal song (4)
625	take what he gives and praise him still (3)
641	take thy promised rest (2)
652, 653	take from our souls the strain and stress (4)
657	till in heaven we take our place (3)
663	helps me take ... the paths of righteousness (2)
675	Take up your cross (1-5)
675	Take up your cross, the Savior said (1)
675	take up your cross with willing heart (1)
677	Ye fearful saints, fresh courage take (3)
686	here's my heart, oh, take and seal it (3)
691	Now hear me while I pray, take all my guilt away (1)
695, 696	we take it thankfully and without trembling (3)
695, 696	we take it ... out of so good and so beloved a hand (3)
699	freely let me take of thee (3)
702	If I the wings of morning take (4)
707	Take my life, and let it be consecrated, Lord, to thee (1)
707	take my moments and my days (1)
707	Take my hands ... let them move at the impulse of thy love (1)
707	take my heart, it is thine own (1)
707	Take my voice, and let me sing always, only, for my King (2)

707	take my intellect ... use every power as thou ... choose (2)
707	Take my will, and make it thine ... no longer mine (2)
707	Take myself, and I will be ever, only, all for thee (2)

taken

159	saw him then from judgment taken (3)
312	hands that holy things have taken (1)
336	in our life thy love divine ... flesh and blood has taken (1)

takes

106	till our first heavenly state again takes place (5)
217, 218	by a new way none ever trod Christ takes his place (1)
217, 218	Christ takes his place -- the throne of God (1)
222	he takes upon his heart the cares, the pain, and shame (3)
259	in his hands takes up the promised child (3)
277	our very brother, takes our nature by his birth (1)
296	as Christ's new body takes on flesh and blood (4)
367	earth takes up the angels'cry (2)
409	the moon takes up the wondrous tale (2)
471	The cross, it takes our guilt away (3)
471	it takes its terror from the grave (4)
494	takes and bears them for his own, that all in him may rest (2)
640	Traveler, darkness takes its flight (3)

taketh

| 329, 331 | Word made flesh, the bread he taketh (4) |

taking

| 320 | command for guidance taking, bread and wine we hallow (3) |

tale

| 409 | the moon takes up the wondrous tale (2) |

talk

| 414 | They shall talk of all thy glory (3) |

tares

290	wheat and tares together sown, unto joy or sorrow grown (2)
290	in the fire the tares to cast (3)
541	to sow the tares, to snatch the seed away (2)

tarries

| 551 | His kingdom tarries long (2) |

tarry

| 569 | falsehood and wrong shall not tarry beside thee (3) |
| 700 | tarry no more without, but come and dwell within (1) |

task

10	The trivial round, the common task, will furnish all (5)
281	he rose, responsive to the call, and left his task (3)
281	left his task, his gains, his all (3)
359	each age for thine own solemn task prepares (1)
424	world-wide task of caring for the hungry and despairing (2)
586	Every task, however simple, sets the soul ... free (3)

142	teach us with thee to mourn our sins (1)
142	so teach us, gracious Lord, to die to self (3)
148	Teach us to know and love you, Lord (5)
242	teach us in that Word alone to find the truth (5)
348	teach us to serve without pride or pretension (2)
359	Anoint them prophets. Teach them thine intent (2)
370	the wisdom of my God to teach (5)
376	teach us how to love each other (3)
414	age to age his power shall teach (2)
501, 502	Teach us to speak, teach us to hear (3)
503, 504	Teach us to know the Father, Son, and thee (7)
505	teach us to know the Father's love (4)
528	In my name baptize and teach (2)
574, 575	teach us to know our faults, O God (2)
592	Teach me, my God and King, in all things thee to see (1)
611	teach us how to do all work for God (7)
628	to teach the beauty of your ways (3)
632	teach thy wandering pilgrims by this their path to trace (3)
659, 660	teach me the wayward feet to stay (2)
659, 660	Teach me thy patience (3)
670	teach me thou alone art Lord (2)
686	Teach me some melodious sonnet (1)
698	only you can teach me how to pray (1)

teacher's

631	statesman's, teacher's, hero's treasure (1)

teaches

591	From all that terror teaches ... lies of tongue and pen (2)

teachest

587	who teachest us to find the love from self set free (3)

teaching

443	his people saw him die at last, praised be his teaching (2)
627	to its heavenly teaching turn, with ... childlike hearts (5)

teachings

440	by thy teachings pure and holy (1)

tear

152	with many a tear poured forth by all (1)
194, 195	life, nor death, nor powers of hell tear us (3)
194, 195	tear us from his keeping ever (3)
226, 227	Every bitter tear refine (2)
683, 684	help me to tear it from thy throne and worship only thee (4)
715	the falling tear in mercy flowed beyond all bound (RC)

tears

59	let us haste, with tears of sorrow (3)
102	scorned, rejected, tears and smiles like us he knew (4)
173	with tears I pray thee, hear me (4)
190	Whom your tears in death were mourning, welcome (1)
284	E'en angel eyes slow tears did shed (5)
301	look on the tears by sinners shed (1)

392	Then let our song abound and let our tears be dry (4)
498	from my smitten heart with tears two wonders I confess (2)
524	For her my tears shall fall, for her my prayers ascend (2)
582, 583	tears are wiped from eyes that shall not weep again (1)
593	where all is tears, may we sow joy (2)
599	We have come over a way that with tears has been watered (2)
599	God of our weary years, God of our silent tears (3)
609	we catch the vision of thy tears (2)
643	worship thee with trembling hope and penitential tears (4)
662	ills have no weight, and tears no bitterness (3)
685	Should my tears for ever flow (2)
691	bid darkness turn to day, wipe sorrows tears away (2)
719	thine alabaster cities gleam, undimmed by human tears (3)

tell

19, 20	God's mighty actions tell at length (2)
50	all his wonders tell (2)
67	tell her that her sins I cover (1)
70	tell the news that Christ is here (2)
70	Sound the trumpet, Tell the message (R)
78, 79	We hear the Christmas angels the great glad tidings tell (5)
99	Go tell it on the mountain, over the hills and everywhere (R)
99	go tell it on the mountain, that Jesus Christ is born (R)
108	on this day of days tell out redemption's story (1)
165, 166	tell the triumph of the victim (1)
167	We may not know, we cannot tell what pains he had to bear (2)
180	He is risen, he is risen! Tell it out with joyful voice (1)
208	let hymns of praise his triumphs tell (4)
210	The day of resurrection, Earth tell it out abroad (1)
248, 249	Name beyond what words can tell (2)
263, 264	whose might they show, whose praise they tell (1)
359	forth may they go to tell all realms thy grace (5)
375	his mighty wonders tell abroad (1)
377, 378	him serve with mirth, his praise forth tell (1)
386, 387	Tell them I AM, the Lord God said (2)
388	O tell of his might, O sing of his grace (2)
405	lips that we might tell how great is God Almighty (4)
414	thy deeds of wonder tell (2)
432	loud organs, his glory forth tell in deep tone (3)
432	tell ... sweet harp, the story of what he hath done (3)
437, 438	Tell out, my soul, the greatness of the Lord (1,4)
437, 438	Tell out, my soul, the greatness of his Name (2)
437, 438	Tell out, my soul, the greatness of his might (3)
437, 438	Tell out, my soul, the glories of his word (4)
506, 507	Tell of how the ascended Jesus armed a people for his own (4)
539	mission ... to tell to all the world that God is Light (1)
539	tell how he stooped to save his lost creation (2)
543	tell all the earth thy joys, and boast salvation nigh (1)
585	nails and crown of thorns tell of what God's love must be (5)
619	the hymns which tell the honor of your King (5)
633	loose our tongues to tell your kindness (3)
638, 639	I need not tell thee who I am (2)
638, 639	I ask thee, who art thou? Tell me thy name (2)
638, 639	tell me now (2)
638, 639	tell me if thy name is Love (3)

640	Watchman, tell us of the night (1-3)
648	tell old Pharoah to let my people go (R)
659, 660	tell me thy secret (1)
663	I may tell thy praise, and dwell for ever in thy home (5)
676	you can tell the love of Jesus (2)
678, 679	tell out his exalted Name (2)

telling

308, 309	O stream of love past telling (2)
404	telling the wonders which to you belong (2)
516	yearning ... shall far outpass the power of human telling (3)
633	one with him beyond all telling (4)

temper

| 292 | At temper fair with gentle air the sunshine and the rain (2) |

tempest

| 579, 608 | from rock and tempest, fire and foe, protect them (4) |
| 699 | while the tempest still is high (1) |

tempests

| 398 | clouds arise, and tempests blow by order from thy throne (3) |
| 716 | when the wild tempests rave (1) |

tempestuous

| 370 | the whirling wind's tempestuous shocks (4) |
| 559 | lead us o'er the world's tempestuous sea (1) |

temple

23	At prayer time, near the Temple gate (2)
93	suddenly the Lord, descending, in his temple shall appear (4)
259	Hail to the Lord who comes, comes to his temple gate (1)
290	come to God's own temple, come (1)
360, 361	This is the temple; here thy presence-chamber (2)
360, 361	Lord, we beseech thee, as we throng thy temple (5)
367	cherubim and seraphim filled his temple (1)
399	into his temple bring your songs of thankfulness (1)
430	this huge wide orb we see shall one choir, one temple be (4)
436	make it a temple set apart from earthly use (3)
436	a temple set apart from earthly use for heaven's employ (3)
486	make our secret soul to be a temple pure and worthy thee (4)
517	climb from height to height till Zion's temple rings (3)
517	temple rings with praise to thee (3)
518	To this temple, where we call thee, come, O Lord (3)
656	give us a pure and lowly heart, a temple fit for thee (4)
665	tower and temple fall to dust (2)
665	But God's power, hour by hour, is my temple and my tower (2)

temple's

| 443 | he taught within the temple's gates (2) |

temples

259	Come to thy temples here, that we, from sin set free (4)
282, 283	watching o'er the temples where thou art worshiped (3)
500	make thy temples worthy thee (1)

657   suddenly return, and never, nevermore thy temples leave (2)

temptation
146, 147   keep vigil with our heavenly Lord in his temptation (1)
146, 147   keep vigil ... in his temptation and his fast (1)

temptation's
5   conquer in temptation's hour (3)
120   shield us in temptation's hour (5)
435   crown him as your Captain in temptation's hour (5)

temptations
448, 449   for us temptations sharp he knew (2)

tempted
102   daily, when on earth he grew, he was tempted (4)
150   forty days and forty nights tempted, and yet undefiled (1)

tempter
284   Ye in the wilderness beheld the Tempter spoiled (3)
448, 449   for us the tempter overthrew (2)

tempter's
171   Go to dark Gethsemane, ye that feel the tempter's power (1)
662   what but thy grace can foil the tempter's power (2)

tempting
472   walk thou beside us lest the tempting byways lure us (3)

ten
18   ten thousand perish at our side (2c)
374   ten thousand thousand are their tongues (1)
391   earth, with her ten thousand tongues ... fill thy courts (4)
415   Ten thousand ... precious gifts my daily thanks employ (3)
543   while round his throne ten thousand stars (4)
543   ten thousand stars in nobler spheres his influence own (4)
620   ten thousand times would one be blest who might ... hear (3)
671   When we've been there ten thousand years (5)

tend
110   Saint Joseph, too, was by to tend the child (3)
219   may all within us upward tend to him who ever liveth (3)
320   Very Bread, good Shepherd, tend us (5)

tended
284   ye tended him (4)

tender
46   forth in starlight tender from myriad world's unknown (2)
81   Lo, how a Rose e'er blooming from tender stem hath sprung (1)
81   O Flower, whose fragrance tender ... fills the air (3)
101   Bless all the dear children in thy tender care (3)
111   Holy infant, so tender and mild, sleep in heavenly peace (1)
114   Within a lodge of broken bark the tender babe was found (2)
360, 361   with tender mercy hear our petitions (5)

388   thy mercies, how tender, how firm to the end (5)
437, 438   tender to me the promise of his word (1)
475   As the tender flowers eagerly unfold them (3)
708   much we need thy tender care (1)

tenderest
42   with thy tenderest blessing may our eyelids close (2)
643   fear ... with deepest, tenderest fears (4)

tends
410   Father-like he tends and spares us (3)

tenement
582, 583   greed for gain in street and shop and tenement (2)

tents
555   henceforth in fields of conquest thy tents ... our home (1)

terms
232   he welcomed them as kindred on equal terms to be (2/10-23)
476   he speaks to us in human terms to make his glory known (4)

terrestrial
409   all move round the dark terrestrial ball (3)
450, 451   Let every kindred, every tribe on this terrestrial ball (6)

terror
69   in joy and terror the Word is born (4)
471   it takes its terror from the grave (4)
527   chasing far the gloom and terror (2)
591   From all that terror teaches ... lies of tongue and pen (2)
640   doubt and terror are withdrawn (3)

terrors
194, 195   thy terrors now can no longer, death, appall us (1)
569   bid not thy wrath in its terrors awaken (2)

test
412   Classrooms and labs loud boiling test tubes (5)

tether
591   Tie in a living tether the prince and priest and thrall (3)

thank
24   We thank thee that thy Church, unsleeping (2)
157   You are my God, and I will thank you (R)
168, 169   mourn thee, well beloved, yet thank thee for thy death (3)
168, 169   What language ... borrow to thank thee, dearest friend (4)
291   then thank the Lord, O thank the Lord for all his love (R)
291   We thank thee ... O Father, for all things bright and good (3)
302, 303   Father, we thank thee who hast planted thy holy Name (1)
381   for created light we thank thee (1)
396, 397   Now thank we all our God with heart and hands and voices (1)
428   O all ye works of God, now come to thank him and adore (1)
631   Thank we those who toiled in thought (2)

678, 679   in the day of your deliverance thank the Lord (1)

thankful
183   offer your thankful praises (1)
233, 234   hymns of thankful love and praise (1)
282, 283   hear our thankful praises (6)
290   Come,ye thankful people, come (1)
291   but chiefly thou desirest our humble thankful hearts (3)
300   Thankful for our every blessing, let us sing (2)
359   with thankful praise (3)
391   We'll crowd thy gates with thankful songs (4)

thankfully
185, 186   sing to God right thankfully loud songs of alleluia (1)
294   thankfully now God's praises we sing (2)
695, 696   we take it thankfully and without trembling (3)

thankfulness
135   Songs of thankfulness and praise ... to thee we raise (1)
399   into his temple bring your songs of thankfulness (1)

thankoffering
522, 523   as priests, his solemn praises ... a thankoffering brings (4)

thanks
9   Not here for high and holy things we render thanks (1)
40, 41   to you be thanks and endless praise (5)
46   let us, as night is falling ... give thanks to him (1)
49   with thanks his dying love record (3)
108   Now yield we thanks and praise to Christ (1)
153   Let us give thanks to the Lord our God (2)
153   It is right to give him thanks and praise ever. Amen (2)
157   I will enter them; I will offer thanks to the Lord (1)
157   I will give thanks to you (R)
157   Give thanks to the Lord, for he is good (R)
178   Alleluia, alleluia, Give thanks to the risen Lord (R)
213   We with thanks do approve the design of that love (4)
245   Our thanks we raise that all John wrote bears witness (3)
250   rejoice, with thanks embrace another year of grace (1-3,5)
271, 272   with thanks and praise his light to hail (1)
280   for this faithful saint we offer ... our thanks to you (2)
280   year by year our thanks to you (2)
285   What thanks and praise to thee we owe ... for Luke (1)
310, 311   All praise and thanks to thee ascend for evermore (2)
327, 328   with souls refreshed, we render thanks to God (2)
329-331   honor, thanks, and praise addressing (6)
334   worship, thanks, devotion voicing (1)
340, 341   now we give you thanks, O Lord (1)
344   Thanks we give and adoration for thy Gospel's joyful sound (2)
392   Hosanna, hosanna! Rejoice, give thanks and sing (R)
396, 397   All praise and thanks to God the Father now be given (3)
401   The whole triumphant host give thanks to God on high (5)
406, 407   Let creatures all give thanks to thee (8)
415   Ten thousand ... precious gifts my daily thanks employ (3)
421   we raise for your great glory thanks and praise (1)

424 thanks be to God (1,3)
425 All praise and thanks to him belong who came to ... free (2)
481 Mortals, give thanks and sing, and triumph evermore (1)
535 thanks never ceasing and infinite love (4)
556, 557 Rejoice, ye pure in heart! Rejoice, give thanks and sing (1)
556, 557 Rejoice, rejoice, rejoice, give thanks, and sing (R)
556, 557 on, ye pure in heart! Rejoice, give thanks and sing (7)
630 Thanks to God (1-5)
687, 688 no thanks to them, abideth (4)

thanksgiving
82 hymn and chant and high thanksgiving (4)
268, 269 let the Church ... part in her thanksgiving claim (3)
320 Let the Bread ... be our theme of thanksgiving (2)
326 Thanksgiving and glory and worship ... blessing and love (2)
469, 470 life would be thanksgiving for the goodness of the Lord (3)
478 Glorious their life who sing, with glad thanksgiving (3)

theme
320 Let the Bread, life giving, living, be our theme (2)
320 Let the Bread ... be our theme of thanksgiving (2)
439 while millions join the theme, I will sing (2)
467 Let his glory be thy theme (4)
471 the angel's theme in heaven above (5)
483 his people's hope ... wealth, their everlasting theme (6)
625 assist our song, for else the theme too high doth seem (1)
667 In holy contemplation we sweetly then pursue the theme (2)
667 theme of God's salvation, and find it ever new (2)

themselves
151 For none may boast themselves of aught (2)
458 at these themselves displease, and 'gainst him rise (4)
480 the stones themselves would sing (3)
564, 565 do but themselves confound, his strength the more is (2)

thence
458 that he his foes from thence might free (5)
492 thence his banished ones to save (2)

therefore
33-35 Therefore we come now evening rites to offer (3)
36 thee, therefore, O Most High, the world doth glorify (3)
61, 62 therefore we sing to greet our King (3)
103 therefore rejoice Jerusalem (1)
122, 123 Therefore in our hymns we pray thee (4)
146, 147 Therefore, we pray you, Lord, forgive (5)
158 Therefore, kind Jesus, since I cannot pay thee (5)
185, 186 therefore let us joyful be (1)
238, 239 Therefore, ye that reign in glory (3)
329-331 Therefore we, before him bending (5)
612 therefore, give us love (2-3)
634 steadfast faith grant me therefore (1)

therein
210 round world keep high triumph, and all that is therein (3)

therewith
519, 520   therewith hath willed for ever ... palace ... be decked (4)

thick
569   through the thick darkness thy kingdom is hastening (4)
573   through the thick darkness covering every nation (1)
613   wherever near or far thick darkness broodeth yet (5)
672   thick darkness blinds our eyes (2)

things
1,2   Monarch of all things, fit us for thy mansions (2)
9   Not here for high and holy things we render thanks (1)
9   but for the common things of earth (1)
16, 17   Creator of all things and with the Spirit, Comforter (4)
27, 28   you brought all things to glorious birth (1)
38, 39   God, Creator of all things (5)
44, 45   To you before the close of day, Creator of all things (1)
56   who orderest all things mightily (2)
60   all things on earth with one accord ... call you Lord (4)
74   All things are in his hand, all ages and all peoples (3)
82   of the things that are, that have been and that future (1)
116   may such bonds for ever draw our souls to things above (5)
119   when earthly things are past (4)
143   Christ, through whom all things were made (1)
152   abstinence in outward things with inward fasting (4)
175   all things created on earth sing to the glory of God (2)
210   let all things seen and unseen their notes together blend (3)
211   And all you living things make praise (3)
216   all things created on earth sing to the glory of God (1)
257   pondering all things in her heart (4)
261, 262   Ruler of all things, Lord of earth and heaven (2)
282, 283   maker of all things, ruler of all nations (1)
282, 283   so that for the peaceful all things may prosper (2)
291   He only is the Maker of all things near and far (2)
291   We thank thee ... O Father, for all things bright and good (3)
312   hands that holy things have taken (1)
318   here would I touch and handle things unseen (1)
320   thou, who all things canst and knowest (6)
365   Father whose love unknown all things created own (1)
375   thy creative might that doeth all things well and right (2)
386, 387   We sing of God, the mighty source of all things (1)
389   All things living he doth feed (6)
390   over all things he gloriously reigneth (2)
396, 397   who wondrous things hath done (1)
400   Let all things their creator bless (7)
405   All things bright and beautiful (R)
405   all things wise and wonderful ... Lord God made them all (R)
405   God Almighty, who has made all things well (5)
412   He has done marvelous things (R)
413   all things that live in earth and ocean make music (2)
431   mute witness of the Master's hand in all created things (1)
432   All things that give sound (3)
474   all the vain things that charm me most, I sacrifice (2)
475   Thou pervadest all things (3)
492   till he see ... all things gathered into one (4)

506, 507	source of breath to all things breathing (1)
522, 523	Glorious things of thee are spoken, Zion city of our God (1)
545	forgetting things behind (5)
548	having all things done, and all your conflicts past (5)
551	have done with lesser things (1)
592	Teach me, my God and King, in all things thee to see (1)
594, 595	rich in things and poor in soul (3)
596	purge this land of bitter things (1)
617	one in the love of all things sweet and fair (2)
623	nor do things prayed for come short of the prayer (2)
634	hold by thy word evermore, above all things (1)
654	Day by day, dear Lord, of thee three things I pray (1)
678, 679	Praise the Lord, who has done great things (2)
711	all these things shall be added unto you (RC)

think
158	think on thy pity ... love unswerving, not my deserving (5)
240, 241	strive to think him, speak him, live him (4)
357	Think, O Lord, in mercy on the souls ... in death repose (2)
641	Lord Jesus, think on me (1-4)
675	follow Christ, nor think till death to lay it down (5)
676	Sometimes I feel discouraged and think my work's in vain (1)
704	work, and speak, and think for thee (3)

thinking
159	Who, on Christ's dear mother thinking (4)
204	thinking that never he would wake again (2)
694	God be in my heart, and in my thinking (1)

thinks
612	love is meek, and thinks no wrong (2)

third
12, 13	At the third hour you took your cross (2)
12, 13	the third hour your faithful band was clothed with power (3)
179	'tis thine own third morning! rise, O buried Lord! (5)

thirst
142	As thou didst hunger bear and thirst (3)
308, 309	We faint with thirst; revive us (2)
335	they who believe in me shall not thirst (1)
458	for his death they thirst and cry (3)
522, 523	Who can faint when such a river ever ... thirst assuage (2)
560	Blessed ... who hunger and thirst after righteousness (4)
692	my thirst was quenched, my soul revived (2)
706	for your grace alone I thirst (3)

thirsting
327, 328	gives living waters to the thirsting soul (7)
649, 650	our thirsting souls to quench and fill (2)

thirsty
517	thirsty soul desires and longs within thy courts to be (1)
658	For thee ... the living God, my thirsty soul doth pine (2)
692	thirsty one, stoop down and drink, and live (2)

thirty
165, 166   Thirty years among us dwelling (2)

thither
83   we too will thither bend our joyful footsteps (4)
321   be all thy children thither led (1)
356   at your coming thither may you be brought by them (2)
402, 403   The heavens are not too high, his praise may thither fly (1)
519, 520   by virtue of his merits thither faithful souls do soar (3)
545   Thither ... press we to God's right hand (5)

Thomas
206   When Thomas first the tidings heard (3)
206   My pierced side, O Thomas, see (4)
206   No longer Thomas then denied (5)
231   All praise, O Lord, for Thomas (2/12-21)
242   Christ of Peter and of John ... Christ of Thomas too (1)

thorn
168, 169   O kingly head, surrounded with mocking crown of thorn (1)

thorns
100   nor thorns infest the ground (3)
159   crowned with thorns entwined (3)
170   To mock your reign ... they made a crown of thorns (1)
170   that thorns would flower upon your brow (1)
313   By the thorns that crowned thy brow (3)
474   or thorns compose so rich a crown (3)
483   The head that once was crowned with thorns (1)
483   once ... with thorns, is crowned with glory now (1)
585   nails and crown of thorns tell of what God's love must be (5)
598   mocked ... by thorns with which they crowned thee (1)
598   still our wrongs may weave thee now new thorns (1)
598   new thorns to pierce that steady brow (1)

thought
10   restored to life and power and thought (1)
11   guard my first springs of thought and will (2)
47   let my every thought be thine (3)
77   in ways beyond all thought (3)
226, 227   word and deed and thought twisted from thy true design (3)
364   dwell ... with all thy saints in joy surpassing thought (8)
372   first, the last, beyond all thought his timeless years (1)
414   works of mercy passing thought (4)
429   praise ... while life and thought and being last (1,4)
448, 449   how passing thought and fantasy, that God (1)
455, 456   beyond all knowledge and all thought (1)
477   Thou cam'st to us in lowliness of thought (2)
488   thou my best thought, by day or by night (1)
491   Far beyond the seraph's thought (2)
512   o'er every thought and step preside (1)
566   rise, like incense ... in noble thought and deed (1)
631   Thank we those who toiled in thought (2)
642   Jesus, the very thought of thee (1)
642   thought of thee with sweetness fills the breast (1)

644	cold my warmest thought (5)
651	I rest me in the thought of rock and trees (1)
665	deep his wisdom passing thought (3)
697	every thought and work and word, to thee be ever given (4)

thoughts

10	new thoughts of God, new hopes of heaven (2)
251	let all our thoughts and all our ways be goverened (3)
416	for all gentle thoughts and mild (4)
506, 507	Spirit, close companion of our inmost thoughts and ways (2)
628	our thoughts and words and deeds may glorify your Name (2)
681	tried with thoughts uncouth, in feeble words to bind thee (2)

thousand

18	ten thousand perish at our side (2c)
57, 58	thousand saints attending swell the triumph of his train (1)
89, 90	beneath the heavenly hymn have rolled two thousand years (3)
89, 90	two thousand years of wrong (3)
374	ten thousand thousand are their tongues (1)
391	earth, with her ten thousand tongues ... fill thy courts (4)
415	Ten thousand ... precious gifts my daily thanks employ (3)
493	O for a thousand tongues to sing my dear Redeemer's praise (1)
517	One day within thy courts excels a thousand spent away (4)
543	while round his throne ten thousand stars (4)
543	ten thousand stars in nobler spheres his influence own (4)
620	ten thousand times would one be blest who might ... hear (3)
671	When we've been there ten thousand years (5)
680	A thousand ages in thy sight are like an evening gone (4)

thousands

293	there are hundreds of thousands still (3)
527	One the strain the lips of thousands lift (3)
614	round him drew thousands of servants brave and true (1)

thrall

| 591 | Tie in a living tether the prince and priest and thrall (3) |

thread

| 140, 141 | I have a sin of fear that when I've spun my last thread (3) |

threatening

| 27, 28 | But now the threatening darkness nears (2) |

threats

| 607 | hate and fear divide us and bitter threats are hurled (1) |

three

47	God, the blessed Three in One dwell within my heart alone (6)
48	Church her voice upraises to thee, blest Three in One (4)
60	To God the Father ... Son, ... Spirit, Three in One (6)
92	Wise Men three to him led, kneel they low by his bed (3)
109	by the light of that same star three wise men came (3)
109	three wise men came from country far (3)
109	Then entered in those wise men three (5)
128	We three kings of Orient are (1)

144	we shall acclaim your majesty, eternal Three in One (5)
162	To thee, eternal Three in One (6)
165, 166	praise and honor to the Spirit, ever Three and ever One (6)
180	he has burst his three days' prison (1)
199, 200	from three days' sleep in death as a sun hath risen (2)
201	the women three assembled there (2)
203	sat and spake unto the three (3)
204	he that for three days in the grave had lain (3)
208	The three sad days are quickly sped (3)
222	for in the midst of two or three (2)
230	to the blessed Three in One be honor, praise and merit (2)
231, 232	sing to God the Spirit, eternal Three in One (3)
271, 272	To God the Father, God the Son ... Spirit, Three in One (5)
273, 274	who with the Holy Spirit, now reign, blest Three in One (4)
276	saw the glory round thy head, one of the chosen three (3)
277	glory to the Three in One (3)
296	Baptized we live with God the Three in One (3)
310, 311	blest One in Three (2)
360, 361	God in three Persons, Father everlasting (6)
362	God in three Persons, blessed Trinity (1,4)
365	To Thee, great One in Three, the highest praises be (4)
366	Holy Father, holy Son, Holy Spirit, three we name thee (4)
369	long to see the blessed Three in the Almighty One (2)
370	invocation of the same ... Three in One ... One in Three (1,7)
371	Holy and blessed Three, glorious Trinity (4)
400	praise the Spirit, Three in One (7)
518	God the One in Three adoring in glad hymns eternally (2)
519, 520	laud and honor to the Spirit, ever Three, and ever One (5)
525	Yet she on earth hath union with God, the Three in One (5)
612	but the greatest of the three, and the best, is love (4)
618	To God the Father ... Son ... Spirit, Three in One (4)
654	Day by day, dear Lord, of thee three things I pray (1)

thresholds

609	on shadowed thresholds dark with fears (2)

thrice

231	so eager and so bold, thrice failing, yet repentant (2/1-18)
231	thrice charged to feed your fold (2/1-18)
500	thrice holy Fount, thrice holy Fire (2)

thrilling

59	Hark, a thrilling voice is sounding (1)

throne

24	thy throne shall never ... pass away (4)
49	with solemn prayer approach the throne (3)
50	praise surround the throne (1)
50	bring salvation from thy throne (3)
54	then the heavenly throne ascends (3)
55	reigned once more from God's high throne (3)
57, 58	high on thine eternal throne (4)
61, 62	as we with joy your throne surround (3)
66	raise us to thy glorious throne (4)

71, 72	let every heart prepare a throne, and every voice a song (1)
85, 86	For from the Father's throne you came (5)
102	but in heaven, where his saints his throne surround (6)
110	thus that manger poor became a throne (4)
125, 126	justice shall guard his throne above (5)
131, 132	King Herod trembled for his throne (1)
156	Father on his sapphire throne (4)
161	its purple limbs a royal throne (4)
194, 195	to him the throne over all the world is given (4)
215	Man with God is on the throne (3)
217, 218	Christ takes his place -- the throne of God (1)
220, 221	Ascending to the Father's throne (2)
231, 232	ever shine in splendor reflected from your throne (1)
231, 232	till all the ransomed number who stand before the throne (3)
255	give you final service in glory at your throne (3)
259	but, borne upon the throne of Mary's gentle breast (2)
280	live for ever round your throne (1)
284	O ye immortal throng of angels round the throne (1)
284	ye hailed his wondrous flight up to the throne of God (7)
286	these before God's throne who stand (1)
292	gathering round thy throne ... in the holy angel's sight (3)
357	now we hail thee present on thine altar throne (1)
365	build in our hearts thy throne, Ancient of Days (1)
369	soaring spirits upward rise to reach the burning throne (2)
374	angels round the throne (1)
374	Name of him that sits upon the throne (4)
391	Before the Lord's eternal throne ... bow with sacred joy (1)
392	thus surround the throne (1)
398	clouds arise, and tempests blow by order from thy throne (3)
408	Cast each false idol from its throne (3)
414	day by day thy throne addressing (1)
419	before thy ever-blazing throne we ask no luster (3)
434	worship at his Father's throne (5)
435	to the throne of Godhead, to the Father's breast (3)
458	He came from his blest throne salvation to bestow (2)
460, 461	sing to Jesus, his the scepter, his the throne (1,5)
460, 461	born of Mary, earth thy footstool, heaven thy throne (4)
467	from yon bright throne above ... extends his grace (1)
480	When Jesus left his Father's throne (1)
484, 485	exalt him on his Father's throne (1)
492	from his Father's throne the Son rules and guides (4)
494	Crown him with many crowns, the Lamb upon his throne (1)
505	thou comest forth from God's great throne (1)
532, 533	their worship and vows shall come to thy throne (2)
535	Salvation to God who sits on the throne (3)
543	while round his throne ten thousand stars (4)
574, 575	Before thy throne, O God, we kneel (1)
616	O'er every foe victorious, he on his throne shall rest (5)
624	There is the throne of David (3)
656	for his dwelling ... throne will choose the pure in heart (3)
680	under the shadow of thy throne (2)
683, 684	help me to tear it from thy throne and worship only thee (4)
685	rise to worlds unknown and behold thee on thy throne (3)
697	worship near thy throne (3)

707   it shall be thy royal throne (1)
709   present before thy throne of grace (2)
718   our grateful songs before thy throne arise (1)

throned

38, 39   Word of the Father throned on high (1)
160   throned in light ere worlds could be (2)
182   Not throned above, remotely high (3)
363   Ancient of Days, who sittest throned in glory (1)
419   Lord of all being, throned afar (1)
478   your Name we glorify, O Jesus, throned on high (1)
517   in glory throned, Lord God, great King of kings (3)
542   when Christ is throned as Lord all ... forsake their fear (2)
585   throned in easy state to reign (6)
596   Judge eternal, throned in splendor (1)
615   when justice shall be throned in might (4)
633   Word eternal, throned on high (2)

thrones

494   Crown him with many crowns, as thrones before him fall (5)
562   Crowns and thrones may perish, kingdoms rise and wane (4)
618   bright seraphs, cherubim, and thrones (1)

throng

94, 95   forthwith appeared a shining throng of angels (5)
103   Come, join the angel throng in songs of joy (R)
232   Apostles, prophets, martyrs ... the noble throng (2/11-1)
260   where saints and angels throng (4)
276   saints, a noble throng (1)
284   O ye immortal throng of angels round the throne (1)
286   following not the sinful throng (3)
360, 361   Lord, we beseech thee, as we throng thy temple (5)
390   join the great throng, psaltery, organ, and song (1)
430   amid the mortal throng, be you masters of the song (3)
544   praises throng to crown his head (2)
562   Onward, then, ye people, join our happy throng (5)
619   Ye who have fought and joined the starry throng (4)
624   bright with many an angel, and all the martyr throng (2)

thronged

112   cherubim and seraphim thronged the air (3)
284   Ye thronged to Calvary and pressed with sad desire (5)

throngs

106   Then may we hope, the angelic throngs among, to sing (6)
609   among these restless throngs abide (4)

throughout

85, 86   throughout the world this holy day (2)
99   behold, throughout the heavens there shone a holy light (1)
142   Lord, who throughout these forty days for us didst fast (1)
213   lives may remain, throughout time and eternity thine (3)
217, 218   new hymns throughout the world shall ring (1)
243   went forth throughout the land (1)

265	Christian folk throughout the world will ever say (4)
345	Grant us thy peace throughout our earthly life (3)
529	fellowship of love throughout the whole wide earth (1)
529	one in him throughout the whole wide earth (3)
534	glorious gospel of truth may shine throughout the world (3)
540	Throughout the world their cry is ringing still (1)
578	make wars throughout the world to cease (1)

throw

170	though we merit blame you will your robe of mercy throw (2)
170	mercy throw around our naked shame (2)

thrust

170	A sceptered reed ... they thrust into your hand (3)

thunder

129, 130	God proclaiming in its thunder Jesus as his Son by name (3)
230	each Apostle spoke the word beneath the Spirit's thunder (1)
460, 461	Hark, the songs of peaceful Zion thunder (1,5)
460, 461	thunder like a mighty flood (1,5)
569	King who ordainest thunder thy clarion (1)
591	take not thy thunder from us, but take away our pride (1)

thunder's

428	O storms and thunder's roar, O fields and forests bless (3)

thunderclouds

388	His chariots of wrath the deep thunderclouds form (2)

tide

105	this holy tide of Christmas doth bring redeeming grace (4)
142	through these days of penitence ... thy Passion-tide (4)
174	washed us with the tide flowing from his pierced side (1)
187	deep and wide flows the tide severing us from bondage past (1)
371	wisdom, love, might; boundless to ocean's tide (4)
498	from the burning of the noon-tide heat (1)
534	vainly we hope for the harvest-tide till God gives life (4)
616	the tide of time shall never his covenant remove (5)

tidings

65	His tidings of salvation proclaim in every place (3)
75	O Zion, that bringest good tidings (2)
76	awake and hearken, for he brings glad tidings (1)
76	glad tidings of the King of kings (1)
78, 79	We hear the Christmas angels the great glad tidings tell (5)
80	Glad tidings of great joy I bring to all the world (1)
89, 90	warring human-kind hears not the tidings which they bring (3)
94, 95	Glad tidings of great joy I bring to you and all mankind (2)
96	What glad tidings did you hear (2)
105	O tidings of comfort and joy (R)
105	unto certain shepherds brought tidings of the same (2)
106	with them the joyful tidings first begun (1)
106	tidings ... of God incarnate and the Virgin's Son (1)
106	Behold, I bring good tidings of a Savior's birth (2)
206	When Thomas first the tidings heard (3)

time's

286   ne'er be touched by time's rude hand ((2)

timeless

372   first, the last, beyond all thought his timeless years (1)

600, 601   come with thy timeless judgment now (1)

timely

281   there needed but the timely word (2)

292   kindly earth with timely birth may yield her fruits again (2)

times

37   Worthy art thou at all times (3)

56   who to thy tribes on Sinai's height in ancient times (3)

377, 378   his truth at all times firmly stood (4)

498   Upon the cross of Jesus mine eyes at times can see (2)

620   ten thousand times would one be blest who might ... hear (3)

tincture

592   with this tincture, "for thy sake," (2)

tireless

610   stirring us to tireless striving (3)

tires

527   one the faith which never tires (2)

today

19, 20   fullness of your grace today (1)

50   Today he rose and left the dead, and Satan's empire fell (2)

50   today the saints his triumphs spread (2)

63, 64   as we hear thy truth today (2)

78, 79   cast out our sin and enter in, be born in us today (5)

85, 86   Today, as year by year its light bathes all the world (4)

88   O sing, this blessed morn, Jesus Christ today is born (R)

107   give ye heed to what we say: Jesus Christ is born today (1)

107   Christ is born today (1)

114   the holy child of earth and heaven is born today for you (4)

136, 137   Christ deigns to manifest today what glory shall be (3)

179   hell today is vanquished, heaven is won today (1)

184   Christ, today your people feed. Alleluia (R)

198   today the branches with the root in resurrection sharing (2)

199   'Tis the spring of souls today (2)

199, 200   but today amidst thine own thou didst stand (4)

205   The Lord of life is risen today (2)

205   sing today with one accord the life laid down (4)

207   Jesus Christ is risen today ... our triumphant holy day (1)

228   come and touch our hearts today (1)

230   Then come, all Christian people, keep festival today (3)

231   Lord, for Paul's conversion we bless your Name today (2/1-25)

246   Still rage the fires of hate today (3)

248, 249   but with holy exultation we may sing aloud today (1)

289   with all who passed before us, we praise thy Name today (1)

320   hymns ... in thy heart and soul today (4)

| 524 | till toils and cares shall end (2) |
| 671 | Through many dangers, toils, and snares (4) |

token

67	all flesh shall see the token (3)
67	token that the word is never broken (3)
84	Love shall be our token; love be yours and love be mine (3)
124	eastern sages with amaze upon the wondrous token gaze (2)
301	be thy feast to us the token that ... our souls are fed (1)
313	be to me ... Lord, of thy boundless love the token (1)
342	of God's own love his dearest token (1)

tokens

| 57, 58 | dear tokens of his passion still his dazzling body bears (3) |

told

106	Then to the watchful shepherds it was told (2)
124	True spake the prophet from afar who told the rise (2)
124	who told the rise of Jacob's star (2)
127	the star that told his birth (2)
162	Fulfilled is all that David told (2)
252	Jesus, Name decreed of old, to the maiden mother told (2)
271, 272	prophetic utterance told his actions great and manifold (2)
314	I believe whate'er the Son of God hath told (2)
578	the wonders that thy people told (2)
592	which God doth touch and own cannot for less be told (4)
631	till they came, who told the story of the Word (2)
648	The Lord told Moses what to do (2)

tomb

128	sealed in the stone-cold tomb (4)
144	we shall be at one with you, Lord, risen from the tomb (4)
172	Were you there when they laid him in the tomb (4)
173	God the Father's only Son in the tomb is lying (1)
176, 177	so from the empty tomb the Second Adam issued triumphant (1)
183	The tomb of Christ, who is living (5)
187	by his tomb Christ makes room (2)
190	Christ has risen from the tomb (1)
201	For Christ is risen from the tomb (1)
201	the tomb is empty: enter in (3)
203	the faithful women went their way to seek the tomb (2)
203	seek the tomb where Jesus lay (2)
284	Around his sacred tomb a willing watch ye kept (6)
294	dead in the tomb with Christ our King (2)
321	Bread that lives beyond the tomb (3)
370	his bursting from the spiced tomb (2)
457	the rending tomb proclaims thy conquering arm (3)
458	in death no friendly tomb but what a stranger gave (6)
458	Heaven was his home, but mine the tomb wherein he lay (6)
591	the walls of gold entomb us, the swords of scorn divide (1)
701	Want and gloom, cross, death and tomb (2)

tomb's

| 199, 200 | Neither might the gates of death ... tomb's dark portal (4) |

tone

430	in such a praiseful tone we will sing what he hath done (5)
432	loud organs, his glory forth tell in deep tone (3)

tongue

19, 20	Let mouth and tongue, mind, sense, and strength (2)
82	let no tongue on earth be silent (3)
165, 166	Sing, my tongue, the glorious battle (1)
181	wake every heart and every tongue (1)
181	Soon ... each raptured tongue his endless praise proclaim (4)
229	In every clime, by every tongue, be God's ... glory sung (2)
329, 331	Now, my tongue, the mystery ... sing (1)
368	In the song of thy salvation every tongue ... combine (4)
368	evry tongue and race combine (4)
380	sung ... by every tongue (1)
388	Thy bountiful care, what tongue can recite (4)
420	witness to the truth in every tongue (3)
430	let no tongue nor string be mute (2)
435	every tongue confess him King of glory now (1)
477	Let every tongue confess with one accord (5)
484, 485	hymns on every tongue abound (1)
501, 502	yours is the tongue and yours the ear (3)
539	Proclaim to every people, tongue and nation (2)
544	People and realms of every tongue dwell on his love (3)
591	From all that terror teaches ... lies of tongue and pen (2)
625	too high doth seem for mortal tongue (1)
642	this nor tongue nor pen can show (4)

tongues

52	with fiery tongues of cloven flame (3)
223, 224	Like to cloven tongues of flame on the twelve ... came (2)
223, 224	tongues, that earth may hear their call (2)
225	Hark, for in myriad tongues Christ's own ... preach (3)
230	all in their own tongues did the Gospel understand (2)
288	let thy praise our tongues employ (1)
299	With tongues of fire saints spread good news (1)
299	let new tongues hail the risen Lord (2)
312	Lord, may the tongues which "Holy" sang keep free (2)
374	ten thousand thousand are their tongues (1)
391	earth, with her ten thousand tongues ... fill thy courts (4)
493	O for a thousand tongues to sing my dear Redeemer's praise (1)
493	ye voiceless ones, your loosened tongues employ (5)
510	hosannas languish on our tongues and our devotion dies (3)
531	Give tongues of fire and hearts of love to preach (2)
573	Envious of heart, blind-eyed, with tongues confounded (3)
629	the nations, tongues and climes and all the ages given (2)
630	word is published in the tongues of every race (4)
633	loose our tongues to tell your kindness (3)
686	sung by flaming tongues above (1)
717	let mortal tongues awake, let all that breathe partake (3)

tonight

78, 79	hopes and fears of all the years are met in thee tonight (1)

took
12, 13	At the third hour you took your cross (2)
109	o'er Bethlehem it took its rest (4)
322	he took the bread and brake it (2)
371	chaos and darkness ... took their flight (1)
480	infants in his arms he took and on his bosom blessed (2)
481	when he had purged our stains, he took his seat above (2)
689	'twas not so much that I on thee took hold (2)

tool
281	alike the symbol ... tool of foreign master's hated rule (1)

top
453	its foot was on earth and its top in the sky (1)

torment
53	not in torment hold us, but in love enfold us (2)
159	seeing Christ in torment languish (1)
231	to help in time of torment (2/12-26)
237	Never flinched they from the flame ... the torment never (2)

tormenting
521	hatred and tormenting fear pass with the passing night (2)

torn
607	in love and mercy guide us and heal our strife-torn world (1)

torrents
413	Rivers and seas and torrents roaring, honor the Lord (3)

tossed
537	the wayward and the lost, by restless passions tossed (2)
693	though tossed about with many a conflict, many a doubt (2)

tossing
42	guard the sailors tossing on the deep, blue sea (3)
627	when waves would whelm our tossing bark (3)

touch
89, 90	to touch their harps of gold (1)
204	thy touch can call us back to life again (4)
209	We may not touch his hands and side (2)
228	come and touch our hearts today (1)
242	but craved to touch those hands of thine (3)
314	Taste and touch and vision to discern thee fail (2)
318	here would I touch and handle things unseen (1)
337	deliver us from every touch of ill (4)
368	touch our hearts with sacred fire (3)
430	Sound the trumpet, touch the lute (2)
567	lo, thy touch brought life and health (2)
567	thy touch ... gave hearing, strength, and sight (2)
590	healing those who touch your garment's hem (3)
592	which God doth touch and own cannot for less be told (4)
633	touch our hearts and bring to birth faith and hope (1)

touched

| 286 | ne'er be touched by time's rude hand ((2) |
| 394, 395 | let every life be touched by grace (4) |

toward

60	When this old world drew on toward night you came (3)
149	moved by your love and toward your presence bent (1)
381	glorious now, we press toward glory (3)
422	Help us to press on toward that mark (3)

towering

| 441, 442 | towering o'er the wrecks of time (1,5) |

towers

| 573 | building proud towers which shall not reach to heaven (3) |

town

| 78, 79 | O little town of Bethlehem, how still we see thee lie (1) |
| 94, 95 | To you, in David's town, this day is born of David's line (3) |

toys

| 510 | See how we trifle here below, fond of these earthly toys (2) |

trace

106	trace we the Babe, who hath retrieved our loss (5)
394, 395	your fingers trace the bold designs of farthest space (1)
459	Do flaming suns his footsteps trace (1)
459	suns his footsteps trace through corridors sublime (1)
545	freed from every weight of sin ... holy footsteps trace (2)
627	Lamp of our feet, whereby we trace our path (1)
632	teach thy wandering pilgrims by this their path to trace (3)

trade

231	He taught the trade of builder (2/3-19)
281	a man of scorned and hardening trade (1)
574, 575	for crafty trade and subtle snare to catch the simple (3)

traffic

| 579 | traffic runs amain by mountain pass or valley low (2) |

train

57, 58	thousand saints attending swell the triumph of his train (1)
366	Lo, the apostolic train join, thy sacred Name to hallow (3)
367	With his seraph train before him (2)
386, 387	glorious the comet's train (3)
429	made the sky and earth and seas with all their train (2)
574, 575	wean us and train us with thy rod (2)

trained

| 143 | So Daniel trained his mystic sight (3) |

trains

| 293 | in church, or in trains, or in shops, or at tea (3) |

traitors
240, 241   Christ, for cruel traitors pleading (3)

tranced
314   tranced as it beholds thee, shrined within the cloud (1)

transcends
452   for the sake of those he grieves transcends the world (2)
452   transcends the world he never leaves (2)

transfigured
135   disciples filled with awe thy transfigured glory saw (4)

transfiguring
475   Come, indwelling Spirit, with transfiguring splendor (4)

transgression
616   to take away transgression, and rule in equity (1)

transmitteth
414   Age to age his works transmitteth (2)

transported
415   transported with the view, I'm lost in wonder (1)

trapped
499   to shine on nations trapped in darkest night (1)

travailed
542   the world has waited long, has travailed long in pain (3)

travel
343   in strength of which we travel on to our abiding place (2)
453   As Jacob with travel was weary one day (1)
536   From east and west the peoples travel (3)

traveler
638, 639   Come, O thou Traveler unknown (1)
640   Traveler, o'er yon mountain's height see ... star (1)
640   Traveler, yes, it brings the day, promised day of Israel (1)
640   Traveler, ages are its own (2)
640   Treveler, blessedness and light ... portends (2)
640   Traveler, darkness takes its flight (3)
640   Traveler, lo, the Prince of Peace ... Son of God is come (3)

traveler's
627   brook by the traveler's way (1)

traveling
344   O refresh us, traveling through this wilderness (1)

traverse
128   bearing gifts we traverse afar (1)

treacherous

563 heed not the treacherous voices that lure thy soul astray (2)

tread

179 tread the path of darkness, saving strength to show (5)
232 to tread the way renewed (2/10-28)
289 new comrades ever bringing in comrades' steps to tread (2)
312 feet that tread thy hallowed courts (3)
398 if I survey the ground I tread, or gaze upon the sky (2)
494 who tread where he hath trod, crown him the Son of man (2)
527 brightening all the path we tread (2)
548 tread all the powers of darkness down (4)
551 Tread where his feet have trod (3)
559 thou didst tread this earth before us (2)
609 O tread the city's streets again (4)
690 When I tread the verge of Jordan (3)
691 While life's dark maze I tread (3)

treading

106 treading his steps, assisted by his grace (5)
175 treading the pathway of death, life ... bestowest on all (4)
562 Christians, we are treading where the saints have trod (3)
599 treading our path through the blood of the slaughtered (2)

treason

158 Alas, my treason, Jesus, hath undone thee (2)

treasure

244 sing of those who spread the treasure in the holy Gospels (1)
248, 249 Jesus is the Name we treasure (2)
339 from this banquet let me measure, Lord ... its treasure (3)
339 how vast and deep its treasure (3)
414 Nor shall fail from memory's treasure works ... wrought (4)
515 bringing down the richest treasure we can wish (1)
515 richest treasure we can wish or God can send (1)
528 Yet we hoard as private treasure all that you ... give (4)
585 memory's treasure, grace of youth (1)
631 statesman's, teacher's, hero's treasure (1)
686 Here I find my greatest treasure (2)
701 only where thou art is pleasure, thee alone I treasure (1)
701 Hence with earthly treasure (2)

treasures

10 new treasures still, of countless price, God will provide (3)
71, 72 treasures of his grace to enrich the humble poor (3)
119 all our costliest treasures bring (3)
125, 126 joyous as when the reapers bear their ... treasures home (2)
125, 126 their harvest treasures home (2)
231 leaving earthly treasures, sought riches from above (2/6-11)
281 lay up treasures in the heart (4)
475 Help us to surrender earth's deceitful treasures (2)
677 he treasures up his bright designs (2)

treasury

161 its load a royal treasury (4)

tressed
389   He the golden-tressed sun caused all day his course to run (4)

trials
447   troubles that are ours to bear are trials we cannot flee (3)
563   His love fortells thy trials (1)
636, 637   When through fiery trials thy pathway shall lie (4)

tribe
298   heavenly band of every tribe and nation (1)
450, 451   Let every kindred, every tribe on this terrestrial ball (6)

tribes
56   who to thy tribes on Sinai's height in ancient times (3)
125, 126   him shall the tribes of earth obey (3)
156   Hark, all the tribes hosanana cry (1)

tribulation
406, 407   nor shrink from tribulation (6)
433   Let thy congregation escape tribulation (3)
519, 520   for Christ's dear Name ... pain and tribulation bore (3)
519, 520   in this world pain and tribulation bore (3)
525   Mid toil and tribulation, and tumult of her war (4)
701   Joy from tribulation, hope from desolation (3)

tribute
108   What tribute shall we pay to him who came in weakness (2)
165, 166   to his cross thy tribute bring (1)
193   the willing tribute of our praise (3)
410   to his feet thy tribute bring (1)
605   What sacrifice desire, or tribute bid you bring (1)

tried
243   by those laws was tried (2)
286   whose hearts were riven, sore with woe and anguish tried (4)
545   They, once like us with suffering tried (1)
630   his the fires that tried her worth (1)
681   though we who seek to find thee have tried (2)
681   tried with thoughts uncouth, in feeble words to bind thee (2)

trifle
510   See how we trifle here below, fond of these earthly toys (2)

Trinity
1, 2   All holy Father, Son, and equal Spirit, Trinity blessed (3)
27, 28   Trinity whom we adore be with us now and evermore (5)
29, 30   O Trinity of blessed light (1)
103   We praise you, Holy Trinity ... adoring you eternally (4)
122, 123   grant us, blessed Trinity ... to keep thine Easter (4)
152   Grant, O thou blessed Trinity ... O unchanging Unity (5)
161   grant, most blessed Trinity ... all may share the victory (5)
196, 197   offer us the worlds of light that live inside the Trinity (3)
266   he was sent from the Trinity, to Nazareth in Galilee (1)
275   beatific vision of the blessed Trinity (4)
315   more blessed ... to be one with the Trinity in Unity (3)

triple

triumph

| 659, 660 | in trust that triumphs over wrong (3) |

Triune
48	sing, "Holy, holy, holy," to the great God Triune (1)
55	all glory to our God Triune (6)
139	Triune God is thus made known in Christ as love unending (2)
191	alleluia! to the Triune Majesty (5)
363	O Triune God, with heart and voice adoring, praise we (5)
396, 397	eternal, Triune God, whom earth and heaven adore (3)

trivial
| 10 | The trivial round, the common task, will furnish all (5) |

trod
75	a call from the ways untrod (1)
131, 132	by light their way to Light they trod (2)
149	we walk the road, Lord Jesus, that you trod (2)
209	nor follow where he trod (2)
217, 218	by a new way none ever trod Christ takes his place (1)
253	They marked the footsteps that he trod (3)
292	since thou the earth hast trod (1)
400	for Christ our Lord that way has trod (6)
450, 451	praise him whose way of pain ye trod (2)
453	many prophets and martyrs have trod it before (3)
489	He came as Savior to his own, the way of love he trod (5)
494	who tread where he hath trod, crown him the Son of man (2)
531	where'er the foot of man hath trod (1)
534	From utmost east to utmost west, wherever foot hath trod (2)
545	Behold a Witness nobler still who trod affliction's path (3)
546	forget the steps already trod, and onward urge thy way (2)
551	Tread where his feet have trod (3)
562	Christians, we are treading where the saints have trod (3)
599	Stony the road we trod, bitter the chastening rod (2)
609	and follow where thy feet have trod (5)
627	without thee how could earth be trod (4)
672	whose feet this earth's dark valley trod (1)

troops
| 246 | King Herod's troops would soon appear (1) |

trophies
| 450, 451 | go, spread your trophies at his feet (5) |

troubled
44, 45	Save us from troubled, restless sleep (2)
94, 95	for mighty dread has seized their troubled mind (2)
600, 601	Bring to our troubled minds, uncertain and afraid (2)
644	calms the troubled breast (2)

troubles
222	He reigns, but with a love that shares the troubles (3)
222	troubles of our earthly life (3)
447	troubles that are ours to bear are trials we cannot flee (3)
623	There, where no troubles distaction can bring (3)
636, 637	for I will be with thee, thy troubles to bless (3)

true

5	O thou true Sun of heavenly love (2)
6, 7	Christ, the true, the only Light (1)
16, 17	grace of true salvation came (2)
57, 58	deeply wailing, shall the true Messiah see (2)
67	let your hearts be true and humble (3)
76	restore earth's own true loveliness once more ((4)
81	true man, yet very God (3)
105	with true love and charity each other now embrace (4)
114	O children of the forest free, the angel song is true (4)
121	God called you his beloved Son ... his servant true (2)
122, 123	Alleluia thou resoundest, true Jerusalem and free (2)
124	True spake the prophet from afar who told the rise (2)
162	in true prophetic song of old (2)
179	Him their true Creator, all his works adore (1)
179	of the Father's God-head true and only Son (4)
179	come then, true and faithful, now fulfill thy word (5)
185, 185	let us feast this holy day on the true bread of heaven (4)
198	whom as true God and our hymns adore for ... evermore (2)
199, 200	with true affection welcomes ... Jesus' resurrection (3)
202	his flesh, the true unleavened bread (3)
226, 227	word and deed and thought twisted from thy true design (3)
231	witnessed to his brother, "This is Messiah true" (2/11-30)
231	the depth of your true love (2/12-21)
231	May we like true apostles your holy Church defend (2/2-24)
231	your true consolation may through the world extend (2/6-11)
232	our true Elijah, making a highway for the Lord (2/6-24)
232	know not his achievements but know that he was true (2/8-24)
232	with true balm of Gilead anoint us evermore (2/10-18)
233, 234	true lights that lighten every land (2)
236	crown of the true of every land (1)
242	doubting souls whose wills were true (1)
245	the light, the living vine, your soul's true bread (2)
254	this saint a true foundation-stone (2)
255	in those least expected true servants you can find (3)
281	it came, true Lord of souls, from thee (2)
287	thou, in the darkness drear, the one true Light (2)
287	O may thy soldiers, faithful, true, and bold (3)
293	saints of God, patient and brave and true (1)
307	Jesus true and living Bread (1)
310, 311	life ... in our true native land with thee (2)
320	praise thy King and Shepherd true (1)
323	ever may our souls be fed with this true and living Bread (1)
329, 331	faith alone the true heart waketh to behold the mystery (4)
337	the one true, pure, immortal sacrifice (1)
337	O do thine utmost for their soul's true weal (3)
353	you consecrate all that is lovely, good, and true (2)
356	God's true Jerusalem (2)
359	through them thy Church presents ... true sacrifice (3)
359	in word and deed Christ's one true sacrifice (3)
421	only you are God's true Son, who was before creation (3)
423	in all life thou livest, the true life of all (3)
435	there let him subdue all that is not holy ... not true (5)
455, 456	O Love of God, how strong and true (1)
457	thy word alone true wisdom can impart (2)

475	life's true way decreeing (2)
478	the Father's conquering Word, true source of gladness (1)
478	true hymns to Christ the King in all their living (3)
488	Be thou my wisdom, and thou my true word (2)
528	Let your priests, for earth's true glory, daily lift (3)
528	Lord, you show us love's true measure (4)
532, 533	How just, King of saints, and true are thy ways (1)
542	Christ is the world's true Light ... captain of salvation (1)
554	When true simplicity is gained (1)
556, 557	true rapture, noblest mirth (2)
558	holy faith! We will be true to thee till death (R)
563	beneath his banner true (1)
574, 575	Search out our hearts and make us true (2)
574, 575	more pure, more true, more nobly wise (4)
576, 577	God is love ... where true love is, God himself is there (R)
597	all creatures find their true accord (2)
599	true to our God, true to our native land (3)
606	Where true charity and love dwell, God himself is there (A)
609	yet long these multitudes to see the true compassion (3)
609	the true compassion of thy face (3)
614	round him drew thousands of servants brave and true (1)
621, 622	vision whence true peace doth spring (1)
627	true manna from on high (2)
632	to bear before the nations thy true light as of old (3)
635	thou yet shall find it true for thee (2)
649, 650	the fount of life and our true light (1)
665	only good and only true (1)
669	bring to sure fulfillment thy counsel good and true (3)
689	it was not I that found, O Savior true (1)
700	True sunlight of the soul, surround us as we go (2)
703	lead us through Christ, the true and living Way (1)
705	Church of Christ is calling us to make the dream come true (2)
718	thy true religion in our hearts increase (3)

truest
489	Not to oppress, but summon all their truest life to find (6)

trump
192	trump from east to west shall make the dead in number (3)

truly
74	By those who truly listen his voice is truly heard (2)
108	who truly have believed that on this blessed morn (1)
266	Said the maiden, "Verily, I am your servant right truly" (6)
568	truly to care for the poor of the earth (2)
623	Truly, "Jerusalem," name we that shore (2)

trumpet
70	Sound the trumpet, Tell the message (R)
386, 387	glorious the trumpet and alarm (3)
412	Trumpet and pipes, loud clashing cymbals (3)
430	Sound the trumpet, touch the lute (2)
561	the trumpet call obey (2)
572	Trumpet with your Spirit's breath (2)

trumpeting
572   Weary of all trumpeting, weary of all killing (1)

trumpets
413   Trumpets and organs set in motion such sounds (2)

trunk
161   With what strange light the rough trunk shone (4)

trust
18   may we, too, trust your sovereign power (2b)
40, 41   those who believe and trust in you (3)
53   but wilt trust him boldly nor dost love him coldly (3)
56   trust thy mighty power to save (4)
105   free all those who trust in him ... (3)
139   trust in Christ who will baptize with water and the Spirit (3)
145   Lent calls to prayer, to trust and dedication (1)
148   our self-wrought miseries have made us trust ourselves (2)
148   trust ourselves the more (2)
151   he is merciful and just, here is my comfort and my trust (3)
167   we must love him too, and trust in his redeeming blood (5)
212   nor will they trust their ears and eyes (2)
255   that we, in every hour ... will trust your hidden power (2)
388   in thee do we trust, nor find thee to fail (5)
457   who put their trust in thee nor death nor hell ... harm (3)
467   trust his love for all to come (4)
482   whose trust, ever child-like, no cares could destroy (1)
528   That the world may trust your promise (2)
552, 553   trust, and thy trusting soul shall prove Christ ... life (3)
561   arm of flesh will fail you, ye dare not trust your own (3)
563   trust only Christ, thy Captain (2)
578   Whom shall we trust but thee, O Lord (3)
607   trust in bombs that shower destruction through the night (2)
635   If thou but trust in God to guide thee (1)
635   trust his word, though undeserving (2)
651   He trust us with his world, to keep it clean and fair (2)
652, 653   simple trust like theirs who heard beside the Syrian sea (2)
659, 660   in trust that triumphs over wrong (3)
663   surely I can trust thy love for all the days to come (5)
665   he doth still my trust renew (1)
665   sword and crown betray our trust (2)
666   Let Israel trust in God, no bounds his mercy knows (4)
669   O trust the Lord then wholly, if thou wouldst be secure (2)
670   Israel, now and evermore in the Lord Almighty trust (4)
677   trust him for his grace (4)
699   All my trust on thee is stayed (2)
705   With gratitude and humble trust we bring our best to thee (3)
720   this be our motto, "In God is our trust" (2)

trusted
435   ever to be worshiped, trusted, and adored (4)
635   God never yet forsook in need the soul that trusted him (2)
635   soul that trusted him indeed (2)

420	through centuries of wrong, borne witness to the truth (3)
420	witness to the truth in every tongue (3)
422	For each new step of faith we take thou hast more truth (1)
422	more truth and light to break forth from thy Holy Word (1)
422	thy truth and light our dwelling place for evermore (3)
429	whose truth for ever stands secure (2)
440	till thy Spirit breaks our night with the beams of truth (2)
440	beams of truth unclouded (2)
457	Thou art the Truth (2)
457	Thou art the Way, the Truth, the Life (4)
457	grant us that way to know, that truth to keep (4)
462	Truth from the earth (2)
462	truth ... like a flower shall bud and blossom show (2)
481	The Lord the Savior reigns, the God of truth and love (2)
487	Come, my Way, my Truth, my Life (1)
487	such a truth as ends all strife (1)
489	his holy and immortal truth to all on earth hath given (1)
500	make us eternal truth receive (3)
506, 507	his the truth behind the wisdoms (3)
506, 507	praise the Word, Source, and Truth, and Inspiration (6)
512	The light of truth to us display (2)
524	Sure as thy truth shall last (5)
532, 533	thy truth and thy judgments shall spread all abroad (2)
534	glorious gospel of truth may shine throughout the world (3)
551	Lord, bring the day of truth and love (2)
558	through the truth that comes from God (2)
569	earth ... shall to freedom and truth be restored (4)
585	scholar's truth, flight of swallows, autumn leaves (1)
597	guide us to justice, truth, and love (1)
606	our boundless source of joy and truth, of peace and love (3)
607	scorn of truth and right (2)
607	dawns the morning glorious when truth and justice reign (4)
617	free to follow truth, and thus to follow thee (2)
629	We limit not the truth of God to our poor reach of mind (1)
629	the Lord has yet more light and truth (1-3)
629	more light and truth to break forth from his word (1-3)
631	bringing freedom, spreading truth (1)
632	O Truth, unchanged, unchanging, O Light of our dark sky (1)
633	Word of truth, to all truth lead us (4)
640	peace and truth its course portends (2)
647	The way is truth, the way is love (2)
664	leads me ... in paths of truth and grace (1)
669	Thy lasting truth and mercy, O Father, see aright (3)
674	In blazing light your cross reveals the truth (3)
674	the truth we dimly knew (3)
681	Thou art thyself the truth (2)
681	till truth from falsehood part ... find no rest (2)
681	Thou hidden fount of love, of peace ... truth ... beauty (5)
687, 688	for God hath willed his truth to triumph through us (3)
687, 688	the body they may kill, God's truth abideth still (4)

truths

424	for the truths that still confound us (3)
628	to learn the truths your word imparts (1)

try
63, 64   the secrets of our hearts to try (3)
167   try his works to do (5)
574, 575   Let the fierce fires which burn and try ... purify (4)

tubes
412   Classrooms and labs loud boiling test tubes (5)

tumult
525   Mid toil and tribulation, and tumult of her war (4)
549, 550   Jesus calls us o'er the tumult (1)
549, 550   tumult of our life's wild, restless sea (1)
608   bid its angry tumult cease (3)

tumults
573   by wars and tumults love is mocked, derided (2)

tune
48   this day the high and lowly, through ages joined in tune (1)
510   In vain we tune our formal songs (3)
543   O Zion, tune thy voice, and raise thy hands on high (1)
620   Our Lady sings Magnificat with tune surpassing sweet (4)
667   God the same abiding, his praise shall tune my voice (4)
686   tune my heart to sing thy grace (1)

tuned
420   Let every instrument be tuned for praise (5)
625   with a well-tuned heart sing thou the songs of love (4)

tuneful
432   in tuneful accord (2)

turn
3, 4   night in turn is drawing on (4)
5   to make ill fortune turn to fair (4)
18   O turn us now to see your face (4b)
27, 28   to turn from sin and cease from wrong (4)
146, 147   author of mercy, turn your face (3)
148   turn our darkness into day (5)
171   turn not from his griefs away (1)
236   Turn our rebellious hearts (3)
237   turn from fear, and heed the call to a glorious morrow (3)
398   thy wonders are displayed where'er I turn my eye (2)
409   all the planets in their turn (2)
443   nor turn from those who were in sin (3)
501, 502   turn nations to the ways of peace (5)
516   O let it freely burn, till earthly passions turn to dust (2)
516   turn to dust and ashes in its heat consuming (2)
554   to turn, turn, will be our delight
616   give them songs for sighing ... darkness turn to light (2)
627   to its heavenly teaching turn, with ... childlike hearts (5)
672   turn our face to where the daylight springs (5)
681   Our God, to whom we turn when weary with illusion (1)
691   bid darkness turn to day, wipe sorrows tears away (2)

turned

18	On Golgatha the sky turned dark (3b)
170	your passion turned ... into a soldier's joke (2)
296	our despair he turned to blazing joy (1)
476	Our boastfulness is turned to shame (3)
506, 507	hundred men and women turned the known world upside down (4)
542	freedom her bondage breaks, and night is turned to day (1)
549, 550	turned from home and toil and kindred (2)

turneth

592	This is the famous stone that turneth all to gold (4)

turning

70	turning us from sin and sadness (1)
554	till by turning, turning we come round right (1)

turns

237	God himself to joy and praise turns our human sadness (1)

twelve

61, 62	Twelve great pearls, the city's portals (3)
223, 224	Like to cloven tongues of flame on the twelve ... came (2)
223, 224	on the twelve the Spirit came (2)
320	when the twelve, divinely guided, at the holy table met (2)
329, 331	mid the twelve, his chosen band (3)
618	Ye holy twelve, ye martyrs strong (3)

twinkling

383, 384	all the twinkling, starry host (3)

twisted

226, 227	word and deed and thought twisted from thy true design (3)

two

89, 90	beneath the heavenly hymn have rolled two thousand years (3)
89, 90	two thousand years of wrong (3)
133, 134	Two prophets, who had faith to see (2)
140, 141	Wilt thou forgive that sin which I did shun a year or two (2)
222	for in the midst of two or three (2)
232	O God, your two apostles won life through martyrdom (2/6-29)
257	two young doves, her humble offerings (2)
273, 274	Two stalwart trees both rooted in faith and holy love (1)
498	from my smitten heart with tears two wonders I confess (2)

type

136, 137	O wondrous type (1)

types

329-331	types and shadows have their ending (5)

tyrannies

613	Break with thine iron rod the tyrannies of sin (1)

tyranny

56	free them from Satan's tyranny (4)

uncertain
501, 502   confirm our weak, uncertain wills (4)
600, 601   Bring to our troubled minds, uncertain and afraid (2)

unchanged
632   O Truth, unchanged, unchanging, O Light of our dark sky (1)

unchanging
152   Grant, O thou blessed Trinity ... O unchanging Unity (5)
632   O Truth, unchanged, unchanging, O Light of our dark sky (1)
635   Who trusts in God's unchanging love builds on a rock (1)
686   mount of God's unchanging love (1)

unclouded
214   there thy face unclouded see (4)
242   at once he rose to full belief's unclouded height (4)
440   beams of truth unclouded (2)

uncomprehended
455, 456   uncomprehended and unbought (1)

unconquerable
614   Let Love's unconquerable might ... unite (3)

uncreated
500   O Source of uncreated light (2)

unction
285   pours on the Church from age to age the healing unction (2)
285   healing unction from above (2)
368   Holy Spirit, Sanctifier, come with unction from above (3)
500   come, and thy sacred unction bring to sanctify us (2)
503, 504   Thy blessed unction from above is comfort, life and fire (3)
515   Author of the new creation, come with unction (2)
515   come with unction and with power (2)
531   give power and unction from above (2)
645, 646   thy unction grace bestoweth (5)

undefiled
54   Wondrous birth ... wondrous child of the Virgin undefiled (2)
150   forty days and forty nights tempted, and yet undefiled (1)
277   Sing of Mary, pure and lowly, virgin mother undefiled (1)
587   with heart still undefiled, thou didst to manhood come (2)

under
252   Jesus, only Name that's given under all the mighty heaven (5)
379   when human hearts are breaking under sorrow's iron rod (2)
680   under the shadow of thy throne (2)

undergird
607   with faith that none can alter, your servants undergird (3)

undergo
179   Thou, of life the author, death didst undergo (5)

understand
230   all in their own tongues did the Gospel understand (2)
243   in sweet forgiveness' name, should understand and spare (3)
246   cry out, "We cannot understand" (3)
574, 575   a ready mind to understand the meaning of thy chastening (1)
593   but look for hearts to understand (3)
695, 696   bitter suffering, hard to understand (3)

understanding
584   give understanding to the mind (3)
593   nor look to understanding hearts (3)
694   God be in my head, and in my understanding (1)

undeserving
635   trust his word, though undeserving (2)

undeterred
236   hear us as now we celebrate faith undeterred (2)
236   faith undeterred by cruel hate (2)

undiminished
23   Now grant us undiminished strength to stand (1)
307   in its fullness undiminished shall for evermore remain (4)
630   See its glory undiminished by the change of time or place (4)

undimmed
9   of faith and hope and love undimmed (3)
719   thine alabaster cities gleam, undimmed by human tears (3)

undivided
366   while in essence only One, undivided God we claim thee (4)

undone
120   to heal and save a race undone (4)
158   Alas, my treason, Jesus, hath undone thee (2)
230   by the triumph of the Son the curse of Babel was undone (2)
230   curse of Babel was undone when God did send the Spirit (2)

undreamed
580   We have ventured worlds undreamed of (3)

undying
9   undying still through death (3)
199, 200   to whom we give laud and praise undying (2)
704   burn with ever bright, undying blaze (2)

unending
5   in equal and unending praise (5)
59   with the everlasting Spirit while unending ages run (4)
139   Triune God is thus made known in Christ as love unending (2)
142   an Easter of unending joy we may attain at last (5)
342   all veils thus rending, Emmanuel, our joy unending (3)
478   in love your children keep to life unending (2)
511   binding ... in a fellowship unending (2)
519, 520   consubstantial, coeternal, while unending ages run (5)

621, 622   for unending, for unbroken is the feast-day of the Lord (2)
633   love unending (1)

unexplored
629   The ocean unexplored (2)

unfailing
229   Unfailing Comfort, heavenly Guide ... preside (3)
238, 239   Faith prevailing, hope unfailing (2)
289   for thine unfailing mercies far-strewn along our way (1)
313   by the pain and death, I now claim ... love unfailing (3)
313   I now claim, O Christ, thy love unfailing (3)
379   with unfailing grasp God holds us (2)
484, 485   now prepares in heavenly regions unfailing mansions (1)

unfailingly
421   God's good will unfailingly be to all people given (1)

unfaith
598   From old unfaith our souls release (3)

unfearing
559   yet unfearing, persevering, to thy passion thou didst go (2)

unfeeling
580   yet their windows, blank, unfeeling, stare (2)

unfit
539   through thy neglect, unfit to see his face (4)

unfold
214   Wide unfold the radiant scene (2)
231   his words to us unfold (2/12-27)
270   so, behold, all the gates of heaven unfold (R)
376   hearts unfold like flowers before thee (1)
400   Dear mother earth, you day by day unfold your blessings (4)
400   unfold your blessings on our way (4)
475   As the tender flowers eagerly unfold them (3)

unforgiven
573   nation by nation still goes unforgiven (3)

unfurled
89, 90   with peaceful wings unfurled (2)
245   Your brightness, O eternal Word, Apostle John unfurled (1)
534   with the banner of Christ unfurled that the light (3)

unhasting
423   Unresting, unhasting, and silent as light (2)

unheard
528   Lest ... the Gospel go unheard (1)

unheeded
491   so weak and lowly as unheeded prophets taught (2)

unheeding
164   is this thy sorrow nought to us who pass unheeding by (1)

unhonored
480   like us, unhonored and unknown, he came to dwell on earth (1)

unhurrying
459   there stands he with unhurrying feet (2)

unimagined
580   probed the secrets of the atom, yielding unimagined power (3)

union
351   Thus may they abide in union with each other and the Lord (2)
525   Yet she on earth hath union with God, the Three in One (5)

unique
463, 464 you will see rare beasts and have unique adventures (1)

unite
11   that all my powers, with all their might ... may unite (3)
11   all my powers ... in thy sole glory may unite (3)
302, 303 perfect it in thy love, unite it (2)
367   thus unite we to adore him (2)
501, 502 in mutual love our hearts unite (4)
542   One Lord, in one great Name unite us all who own thee (3)
614   Let Love's unconquerable might ... unite (3)
614   scattered companies unite in service to the Lord of light (3)
619   to saints forgiven, let them all unite (6)

united
1, 2   bring us to heaven where thy saints united joy (2)
213   so united in heart, let us nevermore part (4)
253   with united breath, ascribe their conquest to the Lamb (2)
273, 274 by hope of God united they reach to heaven above (1)
305, 306 one Church united in communion blest (3)

uniting
51   We the Lord's people, heart and voice uniting (1)

unity
29, 30 O Unity of princely might (1)
146, 147 may with you for ever live in love and unity and peace (5)
152   Grant, O thou blessed Trinity ... O unchanging Unity (5)
235   where with a holy people God dwells in Unity (3)
315   through this blest sacrament of unity (1-2)
315   more blessed ... to be one with the Trinity in Unity (3)
319   Thus may we ever be yours in peace and unity (2)
521   increase ... in depth and height, her unity and peace (1)
521   steadfast faith our unity, their peace our heritage (3)
547   to give the Spirit's unity, the very bond of peace (2)
568   Holiest Trinity, perfect in unity (4)
587   O Spirit, who dost bind our hearts in unity (3)

universal
495   Hail, thou universal Savior, bearer of our sin and shame (1)
638, 639   Pure Universal Love thou art (4)

universe
60   doom to death a universe (2)
144   The universe your glory shows, blest Father, Spirit, Son (5)
296   The universe restored and whole will sing (4)
379   Love for ever o'er the universe must reign (3)
629   That universe, how much unknown (2)

unknown
36   Father of might unknown (2)
46   forth in starlight tender from myriad world's unknown (2)
106   in hymns of joy, unknown before (3)
284   all adored your rising Lord with joy unknown (6)
289   our harvest may be garnered by ages yet unknown (3)
365   Father whose love unknown all things created own (1)
434   speak his Name in sounds to mortal ears unknown (5)
458   My song is love unknown, my Savior's love to me (1)
480   like us, unhonored and unknown, he came to dwell on earth (1)
581   Let strife among us be unknown (4)
584   God, you have given us power to sound depths ... unknown (1)
584   depths hitherto unknown (1)
621, 622   for unknown are toil and care (3)
629   That universe, how much unknown (2)
638, 639   Come, O thou Traveler unknown (1)
665   God unknown, he alone calls my heart to be his own (1)
667   let the unknown tomorrow bring with it what it may (2)
685   rise to worlds unknown and behold thee on thy throne (3)
693   thy love unknown has broken every barrier down (5)

unleashed
299   Spirit of God, unleashed on earth with rush of wind (1)

unleavened
202   his flesh, the true unleavened bread (3)

unless
335   No one can come to me unless the Father draw them (1)
335   Unless you eat of the Flesh of the Son of Man (3)
335   Unless you ... drink of his Blood (3)
335   Unless ... you shall not have life within you (3)
505   unless thy grace the power should give, none can believe (2)
534   All we can do is nothing worth unless God blesses the deed (4)

unlikeness
463, 464   He is the Way. Follow him through the Land of Unlikeness (1)

unlock
167   he only could unlock the gate of heaven and let us in (4)

unmasked
284   unmasked in every dress, in every combat foiled (3)

unmeasured
630   Here we drink of joy unmeasured (5)
702   unfathomed depth, unmeasured height (2)

unmoistened
199, 200   led them with unmoistened foot through the Red Sea waters (1)

unmoved
14, 15   yourself unmoved, all motion's source (1)
182   not ... untouched, unmoved by human pains (3)

unnoticed
580   the lonely drift unnoticed in the city's ebb and flow (2)

unnumbered
437, 438   Unnumbered blessings give my spirit voice (1)
561   ye that are his now serve him against unnumbered foes (2)

unprepared
406, 407   Woe to the unprepared (7)

unpriced
254   Oh, Peter was most blest with blessedness unpriced (2)
511   praise ... for thy fruits and gifts unpriced (1)

unready
232   youthful and unready, she heard the angel's word (2/8-15)

unrelenting
18   held by your unrelenting grace (2c)

unrepentant
148   evils wrought by human pride recoil on unrepentant heads (3)

unresting
289   changeful years unresting their silent course have sped (2)
423   Unresting, unhasting, and silent as light (2)

unrighteous
232   from all unrighteous mammon, O raise our eyes anew (2/9-21)

unsearchable
404   great and unsearchable in all your ways (1)

unseen
204   laid in the earth like grain that sleeps unseen (2)
210   let all things seen and unseen their notes together blend (3)
314   Humbly I adore thee, Verity unseen (1)
318   here would I touch and handle things unseen (1)
332   O God, unseen yet ever near, thy presence may we feel (1)

unselfishly
593   but seek to love unselfishly (4)

unshaken
235   a house to stand unshaken by floods or winds or rains (3)

unsleeping
24   We thank thee that thy Church, unsleeping (2)

unswerving
158   think on thy pity ... love unswerving, not my deserving (5)
635   Sing, pray, and keep his ways unswerving (2)

untold
388   The earth, with its store of wonders untold (3)
394, 395   your hands uphold earth's mysteries known or yet untold (2)

untouched
182   not ... untouched, unmoved by human pains (3)

untraveled
580   known the ecstasy of winging through untraveled realms (3)
580   untraveled realms of space (3)

untrod
75   a call from the ways untrod (1)

unwearied
82   O Holy Ghost, to thee ... unwearied praises be (4)
199, 200   welcomes in unwearied strains Jesus' resurrection (3)
409   The unwearied sun from day to day ... power display (1)

unworthiness
498   the wonders of redeeming love and my unworthiness (2)

unyielding
238, 239   by contempt of every anguish, by unyielding battle done (2)

upborne
401   we shall, on eagle-wings upborne, to heaven ascend (2)

upheld
617   rule in our hearts that we may ever be ... upheld (1)
617   guided and strengthened and upheld by thee (1)
636, 637   upheld by my righteous, omnipotent hand (2)

uphold
394, 395   your hands uphold earth's mysteries known or yet untold (2)

upholds
411   clothes thee with his love, upholds thee with his truth (5)

uplifted
68   With hearts and hands uplifted, we plead, O Lord, to see (3)
205   sing with hearts uplifted high (3)
333   Now the silence Now the peace ... empty hands uplifted (1)

upper
305, 306   We meet, as in that upper room they met (2)

upraise
614   O friends upraise anthems of joy and holy praise (1)

upraised
406, 407   governed by thee she hath upraised what ... is needful (5)

upraises
48   Church her voice upraises to thee, blest Three in One (4)
232   yet she her voice upraises God's glory to proclaim (2/8-15)
440   Hear the cry thy Church upraises (3)

upraising
320   Honor Christ, thy voice upraising (1)
320   gracious hymns of joy upraising in thy heart and soul (4)

uprising
10   love our wakening and uprising prove (1)
120   Uprising from the waters there (2)

upside
506, 507   hundred men and women turned the known world upside down (4)

upward
219   may all within us upward tend to him who ever liveth (3)
357   Lead them onward, upward, to the holy place (4)
369   soaring spirits upward rise to reach the burning throne (2)
556, 557   while answering echoes upward float (3)
556, 557   echoes upward float like wreaths of incense cloud (3)

urge
546   forget the steps already trod, and onward urge thy way (2)

urgent
61, 62   their urgent summons clearly spoken (1)
121   as peaceful as a dove and yet as urgent as a flame (1)
347   hold fast the good, be urgent for the right (3)

use
124   the guidance of thy light to use (4)
436   make it a temple set apart from earthly use (3)
436   a temple set apart from earthly use for heaven's employ (3)
472   take thou our lives, and use them as thou wilt (4)
610   use the love your Spirit kindles still to save (2)
707   take my intellect ... use every power as thou ... choose (2)
708   for our use thy folds prepare (1)

useful
406, 407   water ... most humble, useful, precious, chaste (4)

usher
91   Break forth, O beauteous light, and usher in the morning (1)

utmost
| | |
337 O do thine utmost for their soul's true weal (3)
382 Wherefore with my utmost art, I will sing thee (2)
420 when utmost evil strove against the Light (4)
534 From utmost east to utmost west, wherever foot hath trod (2)

utter
409 utter forth a glorious voice (3)
415 eternity's too short to utter all thy praise (5)

utterance
271, 272 prophetic utterance told his actions great and manifold (2)

utters
560 utters all manner of evil against you falsely for my sake (9)

vain
145 for schemes are vain and fretting brings no gain (1)
188, 189 Death in vain forbids him rise (1)
192 our faith had been in vain (R)
232 Lord, curb our vain impatience for glory ... fame (2/7-25)
237 vain the tyrant's sharpest aim, vain each fierce endeavor (2)
246 The soldiers sought the child in vain (2)
429 none shall find his promise vain (2)
474 all the vain things that charm me most, I sacrifice (2)
510 In vain we tune our formal songs (3)
510 in vain we strive to rise (3)
549, 550 Jesus calls us from the worship of the vain world's (3)
549, 550 worship of the vain world's golden store (3)
578 None ever called on thee in vain (3)
582, 583 Christ hath died in vain (2)
662 heaven's morning breaks, and earth's vain shadows flee (4)
676 Sometimes I feel discouraged and think my work's in vain (1)
677 Blind unbelief is sure to err and scan his work in vain (6)

vainly
117, 118 Vainly we offer each ample oblation (4)
117, 118 vainly with gifts would his favor secure (4)
534 vainly we hope for the harvest-tide till God gives life (4)

vale
376 field and forest, vale and mountain, blooming meadow (2)
416 hill and vale, and tree and flower (2)
517 They who go through the desert vale will find it filled (3)
517 desert vale ... filled with springs (3)
645, 646 In death's dark vale I fear no ill (4)

valiant
135 manifest in valiant fight, quelling all the devil's might (3)
561 To valiant hearts triumphant a crown of life shall be (4)
564, 565 He who would valiant be 'gainst all disaster (1)
623 crown for the valiant, to weary ones rest (1)

valley
65 Let every hill and valley a level way appear (1)

554 'twill be in the valley of love and delight (1)
579 traffic runs amain by mountain pass or valley low (2)
616 righteousness in fountains from hill to valley flow (3)
663 Yea, even when I must pass through the valley (3)
663 valley of death's shade (3)
672 whose feet this earth's dark valley trod (1)

valleys
67 let the valleys rise to meet him (2)
75 valleys shall be exalted, the lofty hills brought low (1)

values
476 earthiy values stand beside the manger and the cross (3)

vanguard
324 Rank on rank the host of heaven spreads its vanguard (3)
324 spreads its vanguard on the way (3)

vanish
324 powers of hell may vanish as the darkness clears away (3)

vanished
168, 169 Thy beauty, long desired, hath vanished from our sight (2)

vanquished
179 hell today is vanquished, heaven is won today (1)
215 he has vanquished sin and Satan (2)
561 till every foe is vanquished and Christ is Lord indeed (1)
563 Satan's host is vanquished and heaven is all possessed (3)

Vanquisher
179 Vanquisher of darkness, bring their praise to thee (3)
521 O Vanquisher of pain (4)

vapor
621, 622 cloud nor passing vapor dims the brightness of the air (3)

varied
501, 502 to us your varied gifts make known (3)

vast
284 out from death's vast room, up from the grave, he leapt (6)
339 how vast and deep its treasure (3)
366 infinite thy vast domain, everlasting is thy reign (1)
369 dwells amidst the dazzling light of vast eternity (1)
391 vast as eternity thy love (5)
414 vast in love, God is good to all creation (5)
681 reflects the vast design by which thy house is built (4)

vault
201 the vault with alleluias ring (4)
431 vault of heaven springs mute witness (1)

vaunt
598 our pride is dust, our vaunt is stilled (4)

veil

253	Give us wings of faith to rise within the veil (1)
307	Though the lowliest form doth veil thee as of old (3)
308, 309	Grant when the veil is riven, we may behold, in heaven (3)
314	faith, that comes by hearing, pierces through the veil (2)
324	cherubim ... veil their faces to the Presence (4)
460, 461	thou within the veil hast entered, robed in flesh (4)

veiled

87	Veiled in flesh the God-head see (2)
280	all his toiling and his strife, all are veiled from us (3)
280	veiled ... but written in the Lamb's great book of life (3)
357	in the mystic symbols veiled from earthly sight (1)

veiling

336	thou art God, thy glory veiling
336	glory veiling so that we may bear the sight (2)
423	thine angels adore thee, all veiling their sight (4)

veils

243	rend the veils of night (2)
342	all veils thus rending, Emmanuel, our joy unending (3)

veins

479	poured for me the life-blood from his sacred veins (1)

velvet

9	velvet of soft summer nights (2)

vengeance

243	no vengeance, no reward (4)
568	sorrow for sins that for vengeance have cried (1)

vengeful

243	no curse nor vengeful cry for those who broke his bones (3)

Venite

110	Venite adoremus Dominum (1,3,R)

venture

237	Who will venture on the strife (3)
590	strong in your strength to venture and to dare (2)

ventured

580	We have ventured worlds undreamed of (3)

ventures

568	stir every will to new ventures of faithfulness (3)
585	ventures all, its all expends (3)

verily

266	Said the maiden, "Verily, I am your servant right truly" (6)

Verity

314	Humbly I adore thee, Verity unseen (1)

very
77	our very flesh our Maker shares (2)
81	true man, yet very God (3)
85, 86	O Jesus, very Light of Light (2)
98	but the very beasts could see that he all men surpasses (2)
160	Very God himself is bearing all the sufferings of time (3)
277	our very brother, takes our nature by his birth (1)
320	Very Bread, good Shepherd, tend us (5)
422	very high thy voice, O God, is heard (1)
445, 446	God's presence and his very self, and essence all divine (4)
491	incarnate, and a native of the very world he made (4)
496, 497	whole creation's Head and Lord ... assumed our very nature (2)
498	see the very dying form of one who suffered there for me (2)
511	Holy Spirit, ever living as the Church's very life (1)
517	my very heart and flesh cry out, O living God, for thee (1)
547	to give the Spirit's unity, the very bond of peace (2)
642	Jesus, the very thought of thee (1)
672	O very God of very God, and very Light of Light (1)
678, 679	in your very midst, the great and Holy One (2)

vessel
77	chosen vessel of his grace (3)
333	Now the hearing ... power ... vessel brimmed for pouring (1)

vesture
85, 86	you put our human vesture on (3)
324	Lord of lords in human vesture (2)
492	stooped to wear the servant's vesture (2)

vex
180	the passion that he bore -- sin and pain can vex no more (2)

vibrant
501, 502	O Holy Spirit, by whose breath life rises vibrant (1)
501, 502	life rises vibrant out of death (1)

victim
165, 166	tell the triumph of the victim (1)
174	Christ the victim, Christ the priest (1)
174	Paschal victim, Paschal bread (2)
174	Mighty victim from on high (3)
183	Christians, to the Paschal victim offer your ... praises (1)
190	on the cross a suffering victim (1)
191	He, who on the cross a victim (1)
257	a priest and victim, both in one (1)
310, 311	O saving Victim (1)
327, 328	himself the Victim, and himself the Priest (4)
460, 461	thou on earth both Priest and Victim (4)
460, 461	Priest and Victim in the eucharistic feast (4)

victor
150	Victor in the wilderness, grant we may not faint nor fall (3)
183	have mercy, victor King, ever reigning. Amen. Alleluia (8)
190	now as victor he is come (1)
210	hearing, may raise the victor strain (2)

| 231 | grant us grace to know you, the victor in the strife (2/5-1) |
| 233, 234 | in heaven's hall a victor band (2) |

victor's
237	where triumphant now they stand with the victor's story (2)
287	win, with them, the victor's crown of gold (3)
483	a royal diadem adorns the mighty victor's brow (1)
561	this day the noise of battle, the next the victor's song (4)

victories
| 617 | we ask no victories that are not thine (3) |

victorious
48	this day our Lord victorious the Spirit sent from heaven (2)
52	in might victorious rose again (2)
61, 62	glorious in strength of grace, in truth victorious (2)
174	praise to our victorious King (1)
231, 232	You rose, our King victorious (1)
231	his witness in his gospel becomes victorious song (2/4-25)
238, 239	glorious and victorious, bravely bore the martyr's part (2)
240, 241	they, like Christ, in death victorious (1)
358	Christ the Victorious, give to your servants rest (1,4)
373	God hath made his saints victorious (2)
413	whose truth victorious establishes the world in peace (3)
423	almighty, victorious, thy great Name we praise (1)
435	brought it back victorious, when from death he passed (2)
472	O Christ, o'er death victorious (5)
484, 485	o'er sin, and death, and hell victorious (2)
494	rose victorious in the strife for those he came to save (3)
525	the great Church victorious shall be the Church at rest (4)
535	the Name all-victorious of Jesus extol (1)
539	pour out thy soul for them in prayer victorious (3)
607	Christ shall rule victorious o'er all the world's domain (4)
616	O'er every foe victorious, he on his throne shall rest (5)

victors
| 238, 239 | victors at the last, they triumph (2) |
| 619 | ye victors, now take up the eternal song (4) |

victory
18	seek our victory in your peace (2a)
18	sharing, know life's victory won (3a)
54	Come, O Father's saving Son, who o'er sin the victory won (4)
56	give them victory o'er the grave (4)
70	granting victory in our strife (4)
82	honor, glory and dominion, and eternal victory (4)
142	As thou with Satan didst contend and ... the victory win (2)
161	grant, most blessed Trinity ... all may share the victory (5)
163	the Lord of life hath victory (3)
180	Christ has won the victory (1)
184	exalted now to save, wresting victory from the grave (3)
185, 186	the victory remained with life (2)
188, 189	where thy victory, O grave (2)
191	Alleluia! to the Savior who has won the victory (5)
201	who over death had victory won (2)

205	Praise we in songs of victory that love (3)
208	the victory of life is won (1)
210	our Christ hath brought us over with hymns of victory (1)
220, 221	grace has won the victory (1)
236	thus win a like victory in us (3)
253	We ask them whence their victory came (2)
268, 269	when the love of God the Father over sin the victory won (1)
275	holding palms of victory in their hands (1)
299	With burning words of victory won inspire our hearts (3)
327, 328	by his dear cross and blood the victory won (3)
334	by this Eucharist declaring yours the final victory (1)
363	thou, Lord, by death hast won life's victory (3)
412	O victory, loud shouting army (1)
417, 418	This is the feast of victory for our God. Alleluia (R)
447	yet he who loved us from the first ensures our victory (3)
460, 461	his the triumph, his the victory alone (1,5)
473	praise to the Crucified for victory (4)
488	High King of heaven, when victory is won (3)
561	from victory unto victory his army shall he lead (1)
562	on, then, Christian soldiers, on to victory (2)
563	wear in endless glory the crown of victory (3)
599	let us march on, till victory is won (1)
662	Where is death's sting? where, grave, thy victory? (3)
675	leads you to victory o'er the grave (4)
720	Blest with victory and peace (2)

view

94, 95	to human view displayed (4)
163	on the Redeemer's thorn-crowned brow the wonders ... view (1)
163	the wonders of that dawn we view (1)
171	view the Lord of life arraigned (2)
279	They all in life and death, with thee their Lord in view (2)
284	his beauteous face in heaven ye view (1)
415	transported with the view, I'm lost in wonder (1)
540	look down on us and view how white the fields (2)
543	the nations round thy form shall view (2)
683, 684	Where is the soul-refreshing view of Jesus and his word (2)

vigil

33-35	Though bodies slumber, hearts shall keep their vigil (5)
40, 41	let hearts in constant vigil watch (3)
146, 147	Now let us all with one accord ... keep vigil (1)
146, 147	keep vigil with our heavenly Lord in his temptation (1)
146, 147	keep vigil ... in his temptation and his fast (1)
159	At the cross her vigil keeping stood the mournful mother (1)

vigor

12, 13	sun ... imparting vigor to the day (1)
411	like the eagle he renews the vigor of thy youth (5)
513	like the vigor of the wind's rush (1)
546	press with vigor on (1,4)
621, 622	full of vigor ... of pleasure that shall last eternally (4)

vigorous

| 43 | sleep that shall me more vigorous make (3) |

43   vigorous make to serve my God when I awake (3)

vine
231   as faithful branches grow strong in you, the Vine (2/4-25)
245   the light, the living vine, your soul's true bread (2)
323   Vine of heaven, thy Blood supplies this blest cup (2)
513   to the branches of the Vine (2)
667   Though vine nor fig tree neither ... wonted fruit should (4)

vine's
198   Come, let us taste the vine's new fruit (2)

vinegar
165, 166 vinegar, and spear, and reed (3)

virgin
54   Wondrous birth ... wondrous child of the Virgin undefiled (2)
55   reveal yourself in virgin birth (1)
80   Mary, chosen virgin mild (2)
81   with Mary we behold it, the Virgin Mother kind (2)
82   Virgin, full of grace, by the Holy Ghost conceiving (2)
105   this day is born a Savior of a pure virgin bright (3)
111   all is calm ... bright round yon virgin mother and child (1)
257   lowly Virgin brings her new-born babe (2)
261, 262 appointed spouse of the Virgin (1)
267   virgin born of David's line shall bear the promised seed (2)
268, 269 when he made the Virgin Mary mother of his only Son (1)
277   Sing of Mary, pure and lowly, virgin mother undefiled (1)
364   nor Virgin womb didst shun (6)
366   wast of a virgin born humbly on that blessed morn (5)
370   purity of virgin souls (3)

Virgin's
54   Virgin's Son, make here your home (1)
83   lo! he abhors not the Virgin's womb (2)
87   offspring of the Virgin's womb (2)
106   tidings ... of God incarnate and the Virgin's Son (1)
260   Virgin's spouse ... guardian of great David's greater Son (2)

virtue
16, 17   by virtue of his saving cross (2)
495   thy people are forgiven through the virtue of by blood (2)
519, 520 by virtue of his merits thither faithful souls do soar (3)
563   O pray that faith and virtue may keep thee to the last (4)

virtues
370   bind unto myself today the virtues of the starlit heaven (4)
618   cry out ... virtues, archangels, angels' choirs (1)

virtuous
558   by kindly deeds and virtuous life (3)

visibly
37   in whom his truth and grace are visibly expressed (1)

59	Hark, a thrilling voice is sounding (1)
61, 62	"Sleepers, wake!" A voice astounds us (1)
67	Hark, the voice of one that crieth in the desert (2)
71, 72	let every heart prepare a throne, and every voice a song (1)
74	By those who truly listen his voice is truly heard (2)
75	There's a voice in the wilderness crying (1)
82	every voice in concert ring (3)
106	who heard the angelic herald's voice (2)
107	rejoice with heart and soul and voice (1-3)
116	Hark, a glad voice (3)
120	the Father's voice did then declare (2)
122, 123	Alleluia, song of gladness, voice of joy that cannot die (1)
133, 134	your Father's voice his Son proclaimed (2)
136, 137	for which in joyful strains we raise the voice of prayer (4)
136, 137	the voice of prayer, the hymn of praise (4)
139	baptized by John, there came a voice from heaven saying (1)
180	He is risen, he is risen! Tell it out with joyful voice (1)
190	Lift your voice rejoicing, Mary (1)
212	Awake, arise, lift up your voice (1)
231	Praise for the light from heaven ... voice of awe (2/1-25)
232	yet she her voice upraises God's glory to proclaim (2/8-15)
235	voice proclaimed salvation that poured upon the night (1)
245	We praise you that John's voice still lives (3)
255	O Voice that spoke within him (2)
256	in that light a voice was heard (1)
268, 269	in his praise I lift my voice (4)
281	Enough ... to hear thy voice, to meet thine eye (3)
320	Honor Christ, thy voice upraising (1)
324	as with ceaseless voice they cry, "Alleluia" (4)
334	one voice hearing, ears attentive to your word (2)
345	Then, when thy voice shall bid our conflict cease (4)
363	O Triune God, with heart and voice adoring, praise we (5)
373	worlds his mighty voice obeyed (1)
377, 378	sing to the Lord with cheerful voice (1)
379	let creation sing before him ... exalt him with one voice (1)
385	deep seas obey thy voice (1)
386, 387	nature without voice or sound replied, O Lord, thou art (2)
399	your voice in homage raise to him who makes all one (3)
400	stars nightly shining, find a voice (2)
409	What though no real voice nor sound ... be found (3)
409	utter forth a glorious voice (3)
413	let every instrument and voice peal out the praise (2)
413	find a voice to praise his Name (3)
420	Let all rejoice who have a voice to raise (5)
422	very high thy voice, O God, is heard (1)
426	Saints below, with heart and voice ... rejoice (5)
429	when my voice is lost in death praise shall employ (1,4)
430	hither bring in one consent heart ... voice ... instrument (1)
437, 438	Unnumbered blessings give my spirit voice (1)
481	Lift up your heart, lift up your voice (R)
482	whose voice is contentment, whose presence is balm (4)
484, 485	with voice and minstrelsy extol his majesty: Alleluia (1)
493	He speaks, and listening to his voice ... receive (4)

506, 507	God's will ... by a still small voice conveys (2)
506, 507	through your voice which speaks within us (6)
513	with the ceaseless voice of prayer (3)
534	by... mouth of many messengers goes forth the voice of God (2)
543	O Zion, tune thy voice, and raise thy hands on high (1)
546	God's all-animating voice that calls thee from on high (3)
549, 550	day by day his clear voice soundeth (1)
599	Lift every voice and sing till earth and heaven ring (1)
607	your still small voice be heard (3)
608	O Christ, whose voice the waters heard (2)
609	we hear thy voice, O Son of Man (1)
610	we, your servants, bring the worship not of voice alone (1)
610	not of voice alone, but heart (1)
624	beneath thy contemplation sink heart and voice oppressed (1)
630	His the voice that called a nation (1)
630	Word is answered by the Spirit's voice within (5)
642	No voice can sing, no heart can frame (2)
652, 653	O still, small voice of calm (5)
666	Lord, hear my supplicating voice and graciously reply (1)
667	God the same abiding, his praise shall tune my voice (4)
678, 679	Zion, lift your voice in singing (2)
692	I heard the voice of Jesus say (1-3)
707	Take my voice, and let me sing always, only, for my King (2)

voiceless

| 430 | nor a voiceless creature found (2) |
| 493 | ye voiceless ones, your loosened tongues employ (5) |

voices

33-35	creation joining hearts and voices singing your glory (3)
49	our joyful hearts and voices raise (3)
65	their voices will adore him (3)
97	Christ we praise with voices bold (3)
104	The stars shall bend their voices (1,4)
106	employ our grateful voices to proclaim the joy (5)
191	alleluia! Hearts and voices heavenward raise (1)
203	to God your hears and voices raise (5)
215	Hark, the choirs of angel voices joyful alleluias sing (1)
237	Let us now our voices raise, wake the day with gladness (1)
244	unto thee our voices raising (3)
275	Hark, the sound of holy voices, chanting (1)
336	Come with us, O King of glory, by angelic voices praised (3)
360, 361	hear now thy servants when their joyful voices rise (1)
360, 361	voices rise to thy presence (1)
363	to thee all knees are bent, all voices pray (1)
391	high as the heaven our voices raise (4)
396, 397	Now thank we all our God with heart and hands and voices (1)
400	All creatures of our God and King, lift up your voices (1)
430	O come, our voices raise, sounding God Almighty praise (1,6)
479	Lift ye then your voices, swell the mighty flood (5)
480	Hosanna our glad voices raise, hosanna to our King (3)
496, 497	We, too, will lift our voices (1)
544	infant voices shall proclaim their early blessings (3)

562   Christians, lift your voices, loud your anthems raise (2)
562   blend with ours your voices in the triumph song (5)
563   heed not the treacherous voices that lure thy soul astray (2)
619   Almighty Christ, to thee our voices sing (7)
623   while for thy grace, Lord ... voices of praise ... raise (3)
623   voices of praise thy blessed people eternally raise (3)

voicing
334   worship, thanks, devotion voicing (1)

volume
250   the volume of a whole year's needs (3)
434   Nature with open volume stands to spread ... praise (1)

vouchsafe
136, 137   vouchsafe to bring us by thy grace to see thy glory (5)
518   Here vouchsafe to all thy servants what they ask of thee (4)

vow
349   When the sacred vow is made (2)
350   that closely knit in holy vow, they may in thee be one (1)

vows
11   Lord, I my vows to thee renew (2)
288   grateful vows and solemn praise (2)
348   vows are renewed, and our courage restored (3)
352   O God, to those who here profess their vows (1)
352   their vows of life-long love (1)
524   her sweet communion, solemn vows (3)
532, 533   their worship and vows shall come to thy throne (2)
616   to him shall prayer unceasing and daily vows ascend (4)
709   Our vows, our prayers, we now present (2)

wafts
479   Oft as earth exulting wafts its praise on high (4)

wage
250   For Jesus came to wage sins's war (2)

wailing
57, 58   deeply wailing, shall the true Messiah see (2)

wait
97   Where thy court on thee to wait (1)
151   his help I wait with patience (3)
259   no shouts proclaim him nigh, no crowds his coming wait (1)
259   O Light of all the earth, thy children wait for thee (4)
353   Bless those who in your presence wait (2)
404   praise we your glory while on you we wait (2)
411   He will not always chide; he will with patience wait (3)
598   we wait thy revelation (4)
625   Ye holy angels bright, who wait at God's right hand (1)
665   joy doth wait on his command (4)
672   We wait in faith (5)
716   on him we wait (2)

waited

159	there she waited in her anguish (1)
278	in prayer with Christ's apostles, waited on his ... word (3)
278	waited on his promised word (3)
286	These, like priests, have watched and waited (5)
542	the world has waited long, has travailed long in pain (3)

waiting

68	The marriage-feast is waiting, the gates wide open stand (2)
267	promise shone with cheering ray on waiting saints of old (1)
340, 341	may the Church still waiting for you keep love's tie (3)
349	gifts of blessing to bestow on your waiting Church below (1)
400	most gentle death, waiting to hush our final breath (6)
570, 571	the Lord is waiting still (4)
695, 696	confidently waiting come what may (1)

waits

67	Speak ye to Jerusalem of the peace that waits for them (1)
214	There the glorious triumph waits (2)
436	behold the King of glory waits (1)
525	she waits the consummation of peace for evermore (4)
666	My soul with patience waits for thee, the living Lord (2)

wake

44, 45	rested bodies wake in peace (2)
61, 62	"Sleepers, wake!" A voice astounds us (1)
104	A stable lamp is lighted Whose glow shall wake the sky (1)
149	so in the Father's glory shall we wake (3)
181	wake every heart and every tongue (1)
192	trump from east to west shall wake the dead in number (3)
204	thinking that never he would wake again (2)
237	Let us now our voices raise, wake the day with gladness (1)
492	wake your noblest, sweetest strain (1)
546	Then wake, my soul, stretch every nerve (4)
593	to wake at last in heaven's light (5)
619	with glad songs resounding wake again (3)

waken

312	let ears that now have heard thy songs ... never waken (1)
312	to clamor never waken (1)

wakened

59	Wakened by the solemn warning (2)

wakening

10	love our wakening and uprising prove (1)

wakes

61, 62	she wakes and hurries through the night (2)
78, 79	dark night wakes, the glory breaks (4)

waketh

329, 331	faith alone the true heart waketh to behold the mystery (4)

waking
38, 39	that waking we may watch with you (4)
482	be there at our waking (1)
488	waking or sleeping, thy presence my light (1)

walk
23	Apostles made a lame man walk (2)
23	now give us grace to walk your way (2)
48	That light our hope sustaining, we walk the pilgrim way (4)
149	we walk the road, Lord Jesus, that you trod (2)
209	We walk by faith, and not by sight (1)
275	now they walk in golden light (4)
472	walk thou beside us lest the tempting byways lure us (3)
490	I want to walk as a child of the light (1)
547	Then walk in love as Christ has loved (4)
605	Do justly, love mercy, walk humbly with your God (1-3)
605	Then justly, in mercy we'll humbly walk with God (4)
615	knowledge ... shall walk the earth abroad (5)
647	I walk the King's highway (1-3)
647	through the years of life, to God I walk (2)
647	when I shall know why in this life I walk (3)
659, 660	O Master, let me walk with thee (1)
664	When I walk through the shades of death (2)
683, 684	O for a closer walk with God, a calm and heavenly frame (1)
683, 684	So shall my walk be close with God (5)
689	I find, I walk, I love (3)
692	in that light of life I'll walk till pilgrim days are done (3)
703	blindly we stumble when we walk alone (2)

walked
125, 126	people who in darkness walked have seen a glorious light (1)
689	I walked and sank not on the storm-vexed sea (2)

walkedst
608	who walkedst on the foaming deep (2)

walking
149	walking once more the pilgrim way of Lent (1)
232	walking in their footsteps we give you praise anew (2/11-1)

wall
167	There is a green hill far away, outside a city wall (1)

wallowed
140, 141	but wallowed in a score (2)

walls
518	thy fullest benediction shed within its walls alway (3)
522, 523	With salvation's walls surrounded, thou may'st smile (1)
540	contending from the walls of Zion against the foe (1)
582, 583	within whose four-square walls shall come no night (1)
591	the walls of gold entomb us, the swords of scorn divide (1)
621, 622	all is pure ... holy that within thy walls is stored (2)

wander

610	Still your children wander homeless (2)
655	nor wander from the pathway if thou wilt be my guide (1)
686	prone to wander, Lord, I feel it (3)

wandering

144	Give guidance to our wandering ways (2)
391	when like wandering sheep we strayed, he saved us (2)
472	showing to wandering souls the path of light (3)
632	teach thy wandering pilgrims by this their path to trace (3)
664	brings my wandering spirit back when I forsake his ways (1)
686	wandering from the fold of God (2)
686	Let thy goodness ... bind my wandering heart to thee (3)
709	our wandering footsteps guide (3)

wanderings

146, 147	so when our wanderings here shall cease (5)
223, 224	till our earthly wanderings cease (4)
640	Watchman, let thy wanderings cease (3)
709	till all our wanderings cease (4)

wane

544	till moons shall wax and wane no more (1)
562	Crowns and thrones may perish, kingdoms rise and wane (4)

waneth

375	his mercy never waneth (3)

waning

342	your love shines though your strength is waning (2)

want

453	Who would not want to climb such a ladder as this (4)
490	I want to walk as a child of the light (1)
490	I want to follow Jesus (1)
490	I want to see the brightness of God (2)
490	I want to look at Jesus (2)
490	I want to be with Jesus (3)
522, 523	all fear of want remove (2)
544	all those who suffer want are blest (4)
663	how could I want or need (1)
701	Want and gloom, cross, death and tomb (2)

wanting

423	nor wanting, nor wasting, thou rulest in might (2)
561	when duty calls, or danger, be never wanting there (3)

wanton

594, 595	shame our wanton, selfish gladness (3)

wants

290	God, our Maker, doth provide for our wants to be supplied (1)

war

182	In every insult, rift, and war (4)

250	For Jesus came to wage sins's war (2)
525	Mid toil and tribulation, and tumult of her war (4)
555	till sin's fierce war shall cease (2)
562	Onward, Christian soldiers, marching as to war (1,R)
598	in the night of hate and war we perish as we lose thee (3)
600, 601	war may haunt the earth no more and desolation cease (4)
607	Keep bright in us the vision of days when war shall cease (4)
613	When comes the promised time that war shall be no more (3)

war's

607	fear of rattling saber, from dread of war's increase (3)
718	From war's alarms, from deadly pestilence (3)
720	between their loved homes and the war's desolation (2)

ward

| 340, 341 | in our hearts keep watch and ward (4) |
| 370 | his hand to guide, his shield to ward (5) |

warfare

67	her warfare now is over (1)
287	when the strife is fierce, the warfare long (5)
357	there, the warfare ended, bid them rest in peace (2)

warm

6, 7	glad my eyes, and warm my heart (2)
226, 227	melt the frozen, warm the chill (4)
505	that charity may warm each heart (3)
691	may my love to thee pure, warm, and changeless be (2)

warms

| 185, 186 | Christ ... the sun that warms and lights us (3) |

warmth

291	sends the snow in winter, the warmth to swell the grain (1)
400	fire ... you give to us both warmth and light (3)
415	how shall words with equal warmth the gratitude declare (2)
419	whose light is truth, whose warmth is love (3)

warning

59	Wakened by the solemn warning (2)
67	Oh, that warning cry obey (2)
70	warning us of right and wrong (1)
246	Then warning came of danger near (1)

warring

89, 90	warring human-kind hears not the tidings which they bring (3)
594, 595	Cure thy children's warring madness (3)
597	till by God's grace our warring world shall see ... peace (1)

warriors

| 287 | soon, soon to faithful warriors cometh rest (6) |
| 556, 557 | as warriors through the darkness toil (5) |

wars

| 573 | by wars and tumults love is mocked, derided (2) |

578   make wars throughout the world to cease (1)

washed
174   washed us with the tide flowing from his pierced side (1)
522, 523   Blest inhabitants of Zion, washed in the Redeemer's blood (4)

washes
602   silently washes their feet (1)

wasn't
468   wasn't that a pity and a shame, Lord, Lord (1-4)

waste
76   without thy grace we waste away like flowers (3)
145   who build the old waste places and in the darkness shine (4)

wasted
570, 571   wasted work and wasted play (3)

wastes
363   through seas dry-shod, through weary wastes bewildering (2)

wasting
423   nor wanting, nor wasting, thou rulest in might (2)

watch
24   through all the world her watch is keeping (2)
38, 39   that waking we may watch with you (4)
40, 41   let hearts in constant vigil watch (3)
68   up, watch in expectation, at midnight comes the cry (1)
78, 79   angels keep their watch of wondering love (2)
115   while shepherds watch are keeping (1)
171   watch with him one bitter hour (1)
281   He sat to watch o'er customs paid (1)
284   Around his sacred tomb a willing watch ye kept (6)
302, 303   Watch o'er thy Church, O Lord (2)
340, 341   in our hearts keep watch and ward (4)
370   his eye to watch, his might to stay (5)
525   yet saints their watch are keeping (3)
563   cease not to watch and pray (2)
666   more duly than the morning watch to spy the dawning day (3)
680   short as the watch that ends the night (4)

watched
94, 95   While shepherds watched their flocks by night (1)
159   with ... grief and resignation Mary watched her dying son (2)
258   blessed was the parent's eye that watched (1)
258   that watched thy slumbering infancy (1)
259   watched by her duteous love, in her fond arms at rest (2)
275   saintly maiden, godly matron, widows who have watched (2)
275   have watched to prayer ... are there (2)
286   These, like priests, have watched and waited (5)
720   o'er the ramparts we watched were so gallantly streaming (1)

watcher

443   The Watcher slept, the Great was small (5)

watchers

199, 200   nor the watchers, nor the seal hold thee as a mortal (4)
618   Ye watchers and ye holy ones (1)

watches

42   Through the long night watches may thine angels spread (5)
375   he watches o'er us every hour (3)
419   cheers the long watches of the night (2)
615   But the slow watches of the night not less to God belong (2)
627   pillar of fire, through watches dark (3)

watchful

1, 2   active and watchful, stand we all before thee (1)
38, 39   watchful guardian over all (1)
106   Then to the watchful shepherds it was told (2)
408   his watchful eye ne'er sleepeth (2)
467   ever watchful o'er our race (1)
480   beneath his watchful eye (2)
579   keep them by thy watchful care from every peril in the air (3)
668   watchful and untiring eye he slumbers not, nor sleeps (2)
716   thou who art ever nigh, guarding with watchful eye (2)

watching

42   Comfort every sufferer watching late in pain (4)
42   their white wings above me, watching round my bed (5)
78, 79   charity stands watching and faith holds wide the door (4)
93   watching o'er your flocks by night (2)
93   watching long in hope and fear (4)
99   While shepherds kept their watching (1)
282, 283   watching o'er the temples where thou art worshiped (3)
541   The enemy is watching night and day (2)
561   put on the Gospel armor, and watching unto prayer (3)
563   far more o'er thee are watching than human eyes can know (2)

watchman

61, 62   Zion hears the watchman singing (2)
640   Watchman, tell us of the night (1-3)
640   Watchman, does its beauteous ray ... hope foretell (1)
640   Watchman, will its beams alone gild the spot (2)
640   Watchman, let thy wanderings cease (3)

watchmen

540   Awake, thou Spirit of the watchmen (1)
540   watchmen who never held their peace by day or night (1)

water

18   your living water give to drink (4a)
112   earth stood hard as iron, water like a stone (1)
131, 132   Oh, what a miracle divine, when water ... into wine (4)
131, 132   when water reddened into wine (4)
135   manifest in power divine, changing water into wine (2)
138   water reddening into wine proclaims the present Lord (2)

139	He came by water and by blood to heal our lost condition (3)
139	trust in Christ who will baptize with water and the Spirit (3)
161	A Roman soldier drew a spear to mix his blood with water (2)
161	mix his blood with water clear (2)
161	the water cleanses to this hour (2)
165, 166	from that holy body broken blood and water forth proceed (3)
294	Baptized in water, sealed by the Spirit (1-3)
296	We share by water in his saving death (2)
343	manna in the wilderness, with water from the rock (1)
400	Swift flowing water, pure and clear, make music (3)
406, 407	By sister water be thou blessed (4)
406, 407	water ... most humble, useful, precious, chaste (4)
428	earth and sea, O all that live in water or on shore (4)
525	she is his new creation by water and the word (1)
609	The cup of water given for thee (3)
645, 646	Where streams of living water flow ... he leadeth (2)
678, 679	rejoice as you draw water from salvation's living spring (1)
685	let the water and the blood ... be of sin the double cure (2)
685	water and the blood from thy wounded side that flowed (1)
692	Behold, I freely give the living water (2)
700	Well-spring of heavenly peace, thou Living Water, come (2)

water's

394, 395	let water's fragile blend with air, enabling life (2)

watered

291	but it is fed and watered by God's almighty hand (1)
599	We have come over a way that with tears has been watered (2)

waters

120	Uprising from the waters there (2)
122, 123	by Babylon's sad waters mourning exiles now are we (2)
176, 177	Over the chaos of the empty waters hovered the Spirit (1)
199, 200	led them with unmoistened foot through the Red Sea waters (1)
244	Christ the fountain, these the waters (2)
299	From living waters raise new saints (2)
327, 328	gives living waters to the thirsting soul (7)
385	Lo, at thy word the waters were formed (1)
506, 507	Spirit, moving on the waters quickening worlds to life (1)
522, 523	See, the streams of living waters (2)
522, 523	living waters, springing from eternal love (2)
534	filled ... as the waters cover the sea (1-4)
608	O Christ, whose voice the waters heard (2)
636, 637	When through the deep waters I call thee to go (3)
699	while the nearer waters roll (1)

waters'

371	Move on the waters' face bearing the gifts of grace (3)

wave

174	Israel's hosts triumphant go through the wave (2)
174	through the wave that drowns the foe (2)
191	golden ears of harvest will their heads before him wave (3)
556, 557	Your glorious banner wave on high (1,7)
579, 608	whose arm hath bound the restless wave (1)

716	ruler of wind and wave (1)
720	O say does that star-spangled banner yet wave (1)
720	the star-spangled banner in triumph shall wave (2)

waved

| 284 | waved around your golden wings and struck your strings (7) |

waver

| 139 | till God's will is fully done he will not bend or waver (1) |
| 231 | hold them when they waver with your almighty arm (2/1-18) |

waverers

| 452 | when doubters kneel and waverers stand (3) |

waves

291	the winds and waves obey him, by him the birds are fed (2)
541	while all around us waves the golden grain (1)
627	when waves would whelm our tossing bark (3)
719	O beautiful for spacious skies, for amber waves of grain (1)

wax

| 544 | till moons shall wax and wane no more (1) |

way

23	now give us grace to walk your way (2)
29, 30	the fiery sun now goes his way (1)
48	That light our hope sustaining, we walk the pilgrim way (4)
56	make safe the way that leads on high (5)
65	Prepare the way, O Zion, your Christ is drawing near (1)
65	Let every hill and valley a level way appear (1)
67	Now prepare for God a way (2)
76	make straight the way for God within (2)
119	Holy Jesus, every day keep us in the narrow way (4)
131, 132	by light their way to Light they trod (2)
145	your way through life adorning (5)
148	humbly follow in your way (5)
149	walking once more the pilgrim way of Lent (1)
149	So daily dying to the way of self (2)
149	so daily living to your way of love (2)
203	the faithful women went their way to seek the tomb (2)
205	Sing songs of praise along his way (2)
217, 218	by a new way none ever trod Christ takes his place (1)
231	guide us in the Way (2/1-25)
232	to tread the way renewed (2/10-28)
236	strength of the pilgrim on the way (1)
245	I am the way, the truth, the life (2)
250	such a Lord to lead our way in hazard and prosperity (4)
275	Patriarch, and holy prophet, who prepared the way (2)
275	prepared the way for Christ (2)
287	the King of glory passes on his way (7)
289	for thine unfailing mercies far-strewn along our way (1)
324	spreads its vanguard on the way (3)
332	go rejoicing on our way, renewed with strength divine (4)
345	Grant us thy peace upon our homeward way (2)
349	you have led them on their way (1)

370	his riding up the heavenly way (2)
390	who doth prosper thy way and defend thee (3)
393	guides his Israel on their way … darkness into light (2)
396, 397	who from our mother's arms hath blessed us on our way (1)
396, 397	blessed us on our way with countless gifts of love (1)
400	unfold your blessings on our way (4)
400	for Christ our Lord that way has trod (6)
441, 442	light and love upon my way (3)
444	Before him goes his herald, forerunner in the way (2)
450, 451	praise him whose way of pain ye trod (2)
457	Thou art the Way (1)
457	Thou art the Way, the Truth, the Life (4)
457	grant us that way to know, that truth to keep (4)
458	Sometimes they strew his way and his strong praises sing (3)
473	Led on their way by this triumphant sign (1)
475	life's true way decreeing (2)
478	You are yourself the Way (2)
487	Come, my Way, my Truth, my Life (1)
487	such a way as gives us breath (1)
489	He came as Savior to his own, the way of love he trod (5)
490	show me the way to the Father (2)
498	a home within the wilderness, a rest upon the way (1)
512	make us know and choose thy way (2)
512	Lead us to Christ, the living way (3)
536	who would learn the way of wisdom … hear God's word (2)
536	he will show the way (3)
539	give of thy wealth to speed them on their way (3)
546	forget the steps already trod, and onward urge thy way (2)
552, 553	life with its way before us lies (2)
599	We have come over a way that with tears has been watered (2)
599	thou who hast brought us thus far on the way (3)
602	this is the way we should live with you (4)
607	from pride of race and nation and blindness to your way (2)
607	when hatred and division give way to love and peace (4)
614	seek again the Way disciples followed then (2)
617	planets singing on their way (1)
627	brook by the traveler's way (1)
641	through darkness and perplexity point … heavenly way (3)
644	my Lord, my Life, my Way, my End (4)
647	I know not if the way is long, and no one else can say (1)
647	The way is truth, the way is love (2)
648	Go down, Moses, way down in Egypt's land (R)
659, 660	guide them in the homeward way (2)
659, 660	in hope that sends a shining ray far down the … way (4)
659, 660	the future's broadening way (4)
669	who points the clouds their way (1)
677	God moves in a mysterious way his wonders to perform (1)
700	so shall our way be safe, our feet no straying know (2)
703	lead us through Christ, the true and living Way (1)
718	thy word our law, thy paths our chosen way (2)
718	Refresh thy people on their toilsome way (4)

wayfaring

| 183 | Speak, Mary, declaring what thou sawest, wayfaring (4) |

ways

18	let us cling always to your love (2c)
56	teach us in her ways to go (2)
75	a call from the ways untrod (1)
77	in ways beyond all thought (3)
144	Give guidance to our wandering ways (2)
175	order our ways in thy peace (8)
211	He guideth you on all your ways (3)
216	order our ways in thy peace (6)
251	let all our thoughts and all our ways be goverened (3)
255	grace, by ways mysterious, our sinful wrath can bind (3)
256	to save him from his fearful ways and free him (2)
304	Together met, together bound, we'll go our different ways (5)
316, 317	Too soon we rise; we go our several ways (2)
404	great and unsearchable in all your ways (1)
431	my rock, and my redeeming Lord, in all my words and ways (4)
445, 446	most sure in all his ways (1,5)
476	Can we by searching find out God or formulate his ways (1)
501, 502	turn nations to the ways of peace (5)
506, 507	Spirit, close companion of our inmost thoughts and ways (2)
524	Beyond my highest joy I prize her heavenly ways (3)
532, 533	How just, King of saints, and true are thy ways (1)
537	new-born souls, whose days, reclaimed from error's ways (4)
569	earth hath forsaken thy ways all holy (2)
594, 595	assail his ways (2)
609	Where cross the crowded ways of life (1)
628	to teach the beauty of your ways (3)
635	hope in him through all thy ways (1)
635	Sing, pray, and keep his ways unswerving (2)
652, 653	Dear Lord and Father of mankind forgive our foolish ways (1)
658	longs the deer ... in parched and barren ways (1)
664	brings my wandering spirit back when I forsake his ways (1)
670	him, in all his ways, adore, wise ... wonderful ... just (4)
702	all my ways are in thy hand (1)

wayside
291	he paints the wayside flower, he lights the evening star (2)

wayward
70	God receives his wayward children (3)
537	the wayward and the lost, by restless passions tossed (2)
659, 660	teach me the wayward feet to stay (2)

weak
33-35	strength for our weak hearts, rest for aching bodies (4)
55	Oh, fill our weak and dying frame with godly strength (4)
231	the weak by grace made strong (2/4-25)
347	strengthen the faint, give courage to the weak (2)
491	so weak and lowly as unheeded prophets taught (2)
501, 502	confirm our weak, uncertain wills (4)
541	No arm so weak but may do service here (3)
567	that whole and sick and weak and strong may praise thee (3)
585	weak in giving power to be (4)
594, 595	Save us from weak resignation to the evils we deplore (4)
616	to help the poor and needy, and bid the weak be strong (2)

638, 639	I am weak but confident in self-despair (3)
644	Weak is the effort of my heart (5)
672	Our hopes are weak, our fears are strong (2)
675	let not its weight fill your weak spirit with alarm (2)
690	I am weak, but thou art mighty (1)

weakened
| 152 | our weakened souls to health reclaim (3) |

weakness
1, 2	banish our weakness, health and wholeness sending (2)
108	What tribute shall we pay to him who came in weakness (2)
231	May we, in ... weakness, receive your power divine (2/4-25)
270	Weakness shall the strong confound (3)
491	strength of infant weakness, if eternal is so young (3)
540	make haste to help us in our weakness (3)
559	all our weakness thou dost know (2)

weal
| 337 | O do thine utmost for their soul's true weal (3) |

wealth
162	Blest tree, whose chosen branches bore the wealth (4)
162	wealth that did the world restore (4)
182	where color, scorn or wealth divide, he suffers still (4)
281	let them of Matthew's wealth partake (4)
292	Thine is the health and thine the wealth (1)
292	thine the wealth that in our halls abound (1)
483	his people's hope ... wealth, their everlasting theme (6)
539	give of thy wealth to speed them on their way (3)
570, 571	In your day of wealth and plenty (3)
607	From search for wealth and power (2)
705	the wealth of this good land (1)

wean
574, 575	From love of pleasure, lust of gold ... wean us (2)
574, 575	from sins which make the heart grow cold, wean us (2)
574, 575	wean us and train us with thy rod (2)

weapon
| 193 | from every weapon death can wield ... shield (4) |
| 243 | no weapon in his hand (1) |

wear
231	that we might wear the crown and ever shine in splendor (1)
231	we with all your servants may wear the crown of life (2/5-1)
232	You rose ... that they might wear the crown (1)
232	who wear the spotless raiment (2/11-1)
452	Glorious the day when Christ was born to wear the crown (1)
452	born to wear the crown that Ceasars scorn (1)
484, 485	the crown ere-long to wear: Alleluia (2)
492	stooped to wear the servant's vesture (2)
563	wear in endless glory the crown of victory (3)
675	only those who bear the cross may hope to wear ... crown (5)

wearied
38, 39   give to our wearied bodies rest (2)
556, 557 the wearied ones shall rest (6)
599   have not our wearied feet come to the place (2)

weariness
318   all my weariness upon thee lean (1)
692   in your weariness lay down your head upon my breast (1)

wearing
36   eternal splendor wearing; celestial, holy, blest (1)
286   Each a golden crown is wearing (1)

wears
77   Behold, the world's creator wears the form and fashion (2)

weary
33-35   soothing the weary (4)
42   Jesus, give the weary calm and sweet repose (2)
51   rest for the pilgrim, haven for the weary (2)
73   let the endless bliss begin, by weary saints foretold (4)
89, 90   still ... heavenly music floats o'er all the weary world (2)
190   Raise your weary eyelids, Mary (2)
277   toil and labor cannot weary love enduring unto death (2)
285   through weary years of toil and strife ... faithful (3)
357   Rest eternal grant them, after weary fight (4)
363   through seas dry-shod, through weary wastes bewildering (2)
453   As Jacob with travel was weary one day (1)
498   the shadow of a mighty rock within a weary land (1)
544   the weary find eternal rest (4)
572   Weary of all trumpeting, weary of all killing (1)
572   weary of all songs that sing promise, non-fulfilling (1)
596   Still the weary folk are pining (2)
599   God of our weary years, God of our silent tears (3)
623   crown for the valiant, to weary ones rest (1)
644   'tis manna to the hungry soul, and to the weary, rest (2)
681   Our God, to whom we turn when weary with illusion (1)
692   I came to Jesus as I was, so weary, worn, and sad (1)

weathers
406, 407 Let wind and air and cloud and calm and weathers all (3)

weave
598   still our wrongs may weave thee now new thorns (1)

wedding
61, 62   that you the wedding feast may share (1)
135   at Cana, wedding guest, in thy God-head manifest (2)
333   Now the wedding Now the songs ... heart forgiven leaping (1)
443   He joined with guests at wedding feast (2)

weep
159   Who, on Christ's dear mother gazing ... would not weep (4)

173	O sorrow deep! Who would not weep (1)
173	Who would not weep with heartfelt pain and sighing (1)
286	painful conflict o'er, God has bid them weep no more (4)
582, 583	tears are wiped from eyes that shall not weep again (1)

weeping
159	mother weeping, where he hung, the dying Lord (1)
173	Blest shall they be eternally who ponder in their weeping (3)
231	O Rachel, cease your weeping (2/12-28)
525	soon the night of weeping shall be the morn of song (3)

weight
12, 13	you stumbled, Lord, beneath its weight (2)
165, 166	sweetest weight is hung on thee (4)
278	beneath the cross of Jesus ... weight of suffering knew (2)
545	freed from every weight of sin ... holy footsteps trace (2)
610	Lord, whose love through humble service bore the weight (1)
610	the weight of human need (1)
662	ills have no weight, and tears no bitterness (3)
675	let not its weight fill your weak spirit with alarm (2)

welcome
51	all find a welcome (2)
71, 72	glad hosannas, Prince of Peace, thy welcome ... proclaim (4)
179	"Welcome, happy morning!" age to age shall say (1,R)
190	Whom your tears in death were mourning, welcome (1)
190	welcome with your smiles returning (1)
226, 227	thou, the soul's most welcome guest (2)
333	Now the keeling Now the plea ... Father's arms in welcome (1)
354	May the choirs of angels welcome you (2)
356	so may they give you welcome to everlasting peace (3)
469, 470	welcome for the sinner, and more graces for the good (1)
482	your hands swift to welcome, your arms to embrace (3)
603, 604	may I in Christ be free to welcome and accept his own (4)
693	wilt receive, wilt welcome, pardon, cleanse, relieve (4)

welcomed
| 232 | he welcomed them as kindred on equal terms to be (2/10-23) |

welcomes
199, 200	with true affection welcomes ... Jesus' resurrection (3)
199, 200	welcomes in unwearied strains Jesus' resurrection (3)
257	Anna welcomes Israel's hope, with holy rapture fired (3)

well
18	At noon you came to Jacob's well (4a)
168, 169	mourn thee, well beloved, yet thank thee for thy death (3)
194, 195	our hearts know well nought from us his love shall sever (3)
242	He loved thee well, and firmly said, "Come, let us go" (2)
248, 249	ear and heart delighting well (2)
286	these, who well the fight sustained (3)
321	furnished well with joyful guests (2)
370	the sweet "Well done" in judgment hour (3)

375	thy creative might that doeth all things well and right (2)
405	God Almighty, who has made all things well (5)
410	well our feeble frame he knows (3)
453	The ladder is long, it is strong and well made (2)
519, 520	Many a blow ... polished well those stones elect (4)
522, 523	well supply thy sons and daughters (2)
541	Servants, well done (5)
580	each endeavor well begun (4)
581	let us love each other well in Christian holiness (3)
587	bless thou all parents, guarding well (1)
673	first one ... the Samaritan woman who drew from the well (2)
682	Then why ... should I not love thee well (4)
706	knowing well, that if I love you, you ... loved me first (3)

welling

308, 309	O purest fountain, welling from out the Savior's side (2)

went

109	to follow the star wherever it went (3)
139	Jesus went to Jordan's stream his Father's will obeying (1)
154, 155	The people of the Hebrews with palms before thee went (3)
202	in triumph went the ransomed (2)
203	the faithful women went their way to seek the tomb (2)
243	When Stephen, full of power and grace, went forth (1)
243	went forth throughout the land (1)
277	though he went forth from her side (2)
443	his work done, went up to heaven, praised be his coming (4)
448, 449	for us he went on high to reign (5)
526	by faith we join our hands with those that went before (4)
567	To thee they went, the blind ... deaf ... palsied ... lame (1)
598	pride, overthrown, went down to dust beside thee (2)

wept

590	as you once wept above Jerusalem (3)
715	When Jesus wept (RC)

west

77	From east to west, from shore to shore (1)
192	trump from east to west shall wake the dead in number (3)
287	The golden evening brightens in the west (6)
529	In Christ there is no East or West (1)
529	In Christ now meet both East and West (3)
534	From utmost east to utmost west, wherever foot hath trod (2)
536	From east and west the peoples travel (3)
603, 604	Still east and west his love extends (2)

western

541	No time for rest, till glows the western sky (5)

westward

128	westward leading, still proceeding (R)

wet

8	Praise for the sweetness of the wet garden (2)

9   the fields are wet with diamond dew (4)

whate'er
5   to guide whate'er we nobly do (4)
151   grace hath wrought whate'er in them is worthy (2)
232   we, whate'er our station may rise and follow you (2/9-21)
314   I believe whate'er the Son of God hath told (2)
529   Join hands ... whate'er your race may be (2)
574, 575   whate'er the pain and shame may be, bring us ... nearer (1)
625   days ... whate'er he send, be filled with praise (4)
635   he'll give thee strength whate'er betide thee (1)
683, 684   The dearest idol I have known, whate'er that idol be (4)

whatever
350   Whatever comes to be their share of quickening joy (2)
488   Heart of my heart, whatever befall (3)

wheat
204   wheat that in dark earth many days has lain (1)
204   Love is come again like wheat that springeth green (R)
290   wheat and tares together sown, unto joy or sorrow grown (2)

whelm
627   when waves would whelm our tossing bark (3)

whence
253   We ask them whence their victory came (2)
286   Whence comes all this glorious band (2)
288   source whence all our blessings flow (1)
339   Fount, whence all my being floweth (2)
621, 622   vision whence true peace doth spring (1)
666   source and spring from whence redemption ever flows (4)
668   from whence shall come my aid (1)
690   fountain, whence the healing stream doth flow (2)

whene'er
531   whene'er the joyful sound is heard (2)
558   O how our hearts beat high with joy whene'er we hear (1)
558   whene'er we hear that glorious word (1)

where'er
398   thy wonders are displayed where'er I turn my eye (2)
531   where'er the foot of man hath trod (1)
544   Jesus shall reign where'er the sun (1)
544   where'er the sun doth his successive journeys run (1)
555   gladness breaks like morning where'er thy face appears (3)
649, 650   where'er our changing lot is cast (3)
702   Lord thou ... dost know where'er I rest, where'er I go (1)

whereby
245   your glory to proclaim whereby your Spirit give us life (3)
252   whereby those to sin enslaved, burst their fetters (5)
627   Lamp of our feet, whereby we trace our path (1)

wheree'er
544   Blessings abound wheree'er he reigns (4)

wherefore
338   Wherefore, O Father, we thy humble servants here bring (1)
382   Wherefore with my utmost art, I will sing thee (2)
477   Wherefore, by God's eternal purpose, thou ... exalted (4)

wherein
458   Heaven was his home, but mine the tomb wherein he lay (6)
516   a place wherein the Holy Spirit makes a dwelling (3)
627   guide and chart wherein we read of realms beyond the sky (2)

whereon
106   morn whereon the Savior of the world was born (1)
175   day whereon Christ arose, breaking the kingdom of death (R)
201   day ... whereon the faithful give God praise (1)
509   lead us in those paths of life whereon the righteous go (2)
627   bread of our souls, whereon we feed (2)

wheresoe'er
579, 608   protect them wheresoe'er they go (4)

wherever
109   to follow the star wherever it went (3)
534   From utmost east to utmost west, wherever foot hath trod (2)
579   wherever, Lord, thy people go, protect them (2)
613   wherever near or far thick darkness broodeth yet (5)

wherewith
84   worship we our Jesus, but wherewith for sacred sign (2)
243   on his lips a sword wherewith he smote and overcame (1)
243   on his eyes a light wherewith God's daybreak to proclaim (2)
572   music ... wherewith heaven is ringing (1)

whirling
370   the whirling wind's tempestuous shocks (4)

whisper
555   holiness shall whisper the sweet amen of peace (2)
638, 639   I hear thy whisper in my heart (4)

white
42   their white wings above me, watching round my bed (5)
202   arrayed in garments white and fair (1)
203   An angel clad in white they see (3)
240, 241   martyrs robed in white (1)
275   clothed in white apparel (1)
366   the white robed martyrs follow (3)
540   look down on us and view how white the fields (2)
599   where the white gleam of our bright star is cast (2)
602   neighbors are black and white (2)
624   for ever and for ever are clad in robes of white (3)

whiten
288   flocks that whiten all the plain (2)

whiteness
286   clad in robes of purest whiteness (2)
370   the whiteness of the moon at even (4)

whiter
133, 134   your raiment whiter than the snow (1)

whole
 21, 22   while you keep our body whole (2)
 38, 39   The whole creation's architect (2)
106   heaven's whole orb with alleluias rang (3)
135   Manifest in making whole palsied limbs and fainting soul (3)
180   let the whole wide earth rejoice (1)
211   The whole bright world rejoices now (1)
230   his grace within shall make you whole (3)
230   whole in body, mind, and spirit (3)
250   His love abundant far exceeds ... a whole year's needs (3)
250   the volume of a whole year's needs (3)
293   followed the right ... whole of their good lives long (2)
296   The universe restored and whole will sing (4)
314   lo, to thee surrendered, my whole heart is bowed (1)
327, 328   with heavenly bread he makes the hungry whole (7)
374   The whole creation joins in one to bless the sacred Name (4)
382   Seven whole days, not one in seven, I will praise thee (3)
401   The whole triumphant host give thanks to God on high (5)
411   bless his holy Name, whose grace hath made thee whole (6)
413   calling the whole world to rejoice (2)
420   it is as though the whole creation cried (1)
427   God's whole creation o'er both now and evermore (5)
434   Here his whole Name appears complete (3)
474   Were the whole realm of nature mine (4)
496, 497   whole creation's Head and Lord ... assumed our very nature (2)
501, 502   Your power the whole creation fills (4)
509   let our whole soul an offering be to our Redeemer's Name (3)
529   fellowship of love throughout the whole wide earth (1)
529   one in him throughout the whole wide earth (3)
542   whole round world complete, from sunrise to its setting (2)
567   that whole and sick and weak and strong may praise thee (3)
568   flood the whole Church with thy glorious light (3)
582, 583   yea, bids us seize the whole of life and build its glory (4)
607   redeem the whole creation with your almighty hand (1)
610   save and make us whole (2)
614   the whole Church at last be one (3)
644   It makes the wounded spirit whole (2)
676   There is a balm in Gilead to make the wounded whole (R)
689   the whole of love is but my answer, Lord, to thee (3)
695, 696   our whole life shall then be yours alone (4)

wholeness
 1, 2   banish our weakness, health and wholeness sending (2)
232   wholeness was restored by you, her faithful Master (2/7-22)
663   To wholeness he restores my soul (2)

wholesome

290   grant, ... Lord, that we wholesome grain and pure may be (2)

wholly

475   his own ... worship lowly, yield their spirits wholly (1)
508   till I am wholly thine (3)
669   O trust the Lord then wholly, if thou wouldst be secure (2)
691   O let me from this day be wholly thine (1)

whoso

248, 249   'Tis the Name that whoso preachest speaks like music (3)

why

96   Shepherds, why this jubilee (2)
96   why these songs of happy cheer (2)
97   nought but need and penury; why thus cradled here (1)
115   Why lies he in such mean estate (2)
293   there's not any reason ... why I shouldn't be one too (2)
377, 378   For why? the Lord our God is good (4)
458   Why, what hath my Lord done (4)
647   when I shall know why in this life I walk (3)
658   Why restless, why cast down, my soul (3)
682   Then why ... should I not love thee well (4)

wicked

185, 186   word of grace hath purged away the old and wicked leaven (4)
433   the wicked oppressing now cease from distressing (1)
448, 449   For us to wicked hands betrayed, scourged, mocked (4)
462   this wicked earth redress (3)

wickedness

145   of wickedness the grievous bands to loosen (3)
152   confess our sins and all our wickedness (3)

wide

56   open wide our heavenly home (5)
65   Fling wide your gates, O Zion, your Savior's rule embrace (3)
68   The marriage-feast is waiting, the gates wide open stand (2)
78, 79   charity stands watching and faith holds wide the door (4)
148   far and wide the wreckage of our hatred spreads (3)
180   let the whole wide earth rejoice (1)
187   deep and wide flows the tide severing us from bondage past (1)
214   Wide unfold the radiant scene (2)
257   O Zion, open wide thy gates (1)
287   From earth's wide bounds, from ocean's farthest coast (8)
310, 311   opening wide the gate of heaven to us below (1)
363   thy love has blessed the wide world's wondrous story (1)
366   opened wide the realm of heaven (6)
371   rolling in fullest pride, through the world far and wide (4)
375   Through all his kingdom's wide domain ... justice reign (3)
391   Wide as the world is thy command (5)
424   world-wide task of caring for the hungry and despairing (2)
430   this huge wide orb we see shall one choir, one temple be (4)
436   Fling wide the portals of your heart (3)
436   Redeemer come, I open wide my heart to thee (4)

529	fellowship of love throughout the whole wide earth (1)
529	one in him throughout the whole wide earth (3)
596	solace all its wide dominion with the healing of thy wings (1)

widely

410	Widely yet his mercy flows (3)

wideness

469, 470	There's a wideness in God's mercy like the ... sea (1)
469, 470	like the wideness of the sea (1)

widowed

429	the widowed and the fatherless (3)

widows

275	saintly maiden, godly matron, widows who have watched (2)

wield

193	from every weapon death can wield ... shield (4)

wife

353	join every husband, every wife in mutual love (3)

wild

46	shade creeps o'er wild and wood (1)
150	Forty days and forty nights thou wast fasting in the wild (1)
293	one was slain by a fierce wild beast (2)
413	honor the Lord with wild acclaim (3)
549, 550	tumult of our life's wild, restless sea (1)
608	give, for wild confusion, peace (3)
716	when the wild tempests rave (1)

wilderness

75	There's a voice in the wilderness crying (1)
120	Straight to the wilderness he goes to wrestle (4)
150	Victor in the wilderness, grant we may not faint nor fall (3)
284	Ye in the wilderness beheld the Tempter spoiled (3)
343	manna in the wilderness, with water from the rock (1)
344	O refresh us, traveling through this wilderness (1)
443	yet in the wilderness did fast (2)
498	a home within the wilderness, a rest upon the way (1)

will (noun)

11	guard my first springs of thought and will (2)
12, 13	give us strength to do your will (3)
23	do your will (3)
89, 90	Peace on the earth, good will to men (1)
94, 95	good will henceforth from heaven to men (6)
94, 95	good will ... begin and never cease (6)
106	peace on the earth, and unto men good will (3)
116	I come, the great Redeemer cries, to do thy will, O Lord (1)
116	like him desirous to fulfill God's will in righteousness (4)
121	sent you his kingdom to proclaim, his holy will to do (2)
135	manifest in gracious will, ever bringing good from ill (3)
139	Jesus went to Jordan's stream his Father's will obeying (1)

139	till God's will is fully done he will not bend or waver (1)
226, 227	Bend the stubborn heart and will (4)
228	Shake with rushing wind our will (4)
232	seek, like him, your will (2/8-24)
233, 234	in them the Spirit's will was done (4)
251	be governed by thy will (3)
286	offering up to Christ their will (5)
293	saints who love to do Jesus' will (3)
296	The universe restored and whole will sing (4)
302, 303	cleansed and conformed unto thy will (2)
315	grant us at every Eucharist to say ... "Thy will be done" (1)
353	reveal your will in all we do (3)
372	everywhere above, below, his will obeys (2)
406, 407	blest be they who do thy will and follow thy commandments (7)
421	God's good will unfailingly be to all people given (1)
424	God's will be done (2)
433	he chastens and hastens his will to make known (1)
435	let his will enfold you in its light and power (5)
489	he came to win us by good will, for force is not of God (5)
506, 507	God's will ... by a still small voice conveys (2)
508	until with thee I will one will, to do or to endure (2)
530	word of how the Father's will made the world (2)
540	bringing peoples to thy holy will (1)
541	by feeblest agents may our God fulfill his righteous will (3)
568	stir every will to new ventures of faithfulness (3)
573	thy kingdom come, O Lord, thy will be done (R)
605	Let Christ endue our will with grace to fortify (4)
610	hope and health, good will and comfort ... give (4)
614	so shall God's will on earth be done (3)
626	thy glory be my aim, thy holy will my choice (1)
627	word of the ever-living God, will of his glorious Son (4)
655	above the storms of passion, the murmurs of self-will (2)
677	works his sovereign will (2)
698	help me to see your purpose and your will (2)
704	Still let me prove thy perfect will (4)
707	Take my will, and make it thine ... no longer mine (2)
708	Early let us seek thy favor, early let us learn thy will (2)

willed

120	chose the path his Father willed (1)
165, 165	this the Savior freely willed (2)
519, 520	therewith hath willed for ever ... palace ... be decked (4)
687, 688	for God hath willed his truth to triumph through us (3)

willing

119	so may we with willing feet ever seek thy mercy seat (2)
193	the willing tribute of our praise (3)
284	Around his sacred tomb a willing watch ye kept (6)
539	he who made all nations is not willing one soul ... fail (1)
675	take up your cross with willing heart (1)

willingly

| 97 | willingly this yoke I take, and this sacrifice I make (2) |

wills

242	doubting souls whose wills were true (1)
437, 438	Proud hearts and stubborn wills are put to flight (3)
452	what self rejects yet feebly wills (4)
501, 502	confirm our weak, uncertain wills (4)

win

53	Still he comes within us, still his voice would win us (2)
120	go forth with you a world to win (5)
142	As thou with Satan didst contend and ... the victory win (2)
151	if nought but just reward we win (1)
162	save ... from our sin, God's righteousness for all to win (5)
206	for they eternal life shall win (6)
236	thus win a like victory in us (3)
237	Christians, up and win it (3)
287	win, with them, the victor's crown of gold (3)
349	patient faith, the crown to win (2)
366	Savior, who hast died to win us (7)
370	Christ before me, Christ beside me, Christ to win me (6)
440	thou alone to God canst win us (2)
457	that life to win, whose joys eternal flow (4)
489	he came to win us by good will, for force is not of God (5)
540	by many messengers, all hearts to win (3)
548	win the well-fought day (4)
558	faith and prayer shall win all nations unto thee (2)
687, 688	he must win the battle (2)
701	they who love God win (3)

wind

112	In the bleak midwinter, frosty wind made moan (1)
228	Shake with rushing wind our will (4)
230	filled the place of meeting with rushing wind and flame (1)
278	manifest in wind and flame (3)
299	Spirit of God, unleashed on earth with rush of wind (1)
299	rush of wind and roar of flame (1)
405	the cold wind in the winter, the pleasant summer sun (3)
406, 407	Let wind and air and cloud and calm and weathers all (3)
412	Hail, wind, and rain, loud blowing snow-storms (2)
506, 507	dark and furthest corners by the wind of heaven blown (4)
579	O Wind of heaven, by thy might save all (3)
652, 653	speak through the earthquake, wind, and fire (5)
716	ruler of wind and wave (1)

wind's

370	the whirling wind's tempestuous shocks (4)
513	like the vigor of the wind's rush (1)

windows

580	yet their windows, blank, unfeeling, stare (2)
580	windows ... stare on canyoned streets below (2)

winds

235	a house to stand unshaken by floods or winds or rains (3)
291	the winds and waves obey him, by him the birds are fed (2)
292	let frost and heat, and winds and dews be given (2)

400	Great rushing winds and breezes soft (2)
669	who gives the winds their courses (1)

wine

48	living presence greeting, through Bread and Wine made near (3)
51	In the Lord's service bread and wine are offered (4)
131, 132	Oh, what a miracle divine, when water ... into wine (4)
131, 132	when water reddened into wine (4)
135	manifest in power divine, changing water into wine (2)
138	water reddening into wine proclaims the present Lord (2)
174	give his sacred Blood for wine (1)
232	Your wine and oil, O Savior, upon our spirits pour (2/10-18)
301	Wine of the soul, in mercy shed (1)
305, 306	make manifest in thine own Sacrament of Bread and Wine (1)
308, 309	hidden in forms of bread and wine (3)
316, 317	the Bread and Wine consumed (2)
318	here drink with thee the royal Wine of heaven (2)
320	command for guidance taking, bread and wine we hallow (3)
325	Let us drink wine together on our knees (2)
329, 331	wine his sacred Blood he maketh (4)
340, 341	for the wine which you have poured (1)
343	living bread, that heavenly wine, be our immortal food (4)
599	our hearts drunk with the wine of the world (3)

wing

89, 90	above its sad and lowly plains they bend on hovering wing (2)
93	wing your flight o'er all the earth (1)
201	So let our songs to heaven wing (4)
371	come to bring on thy redeeming wing healing and sight (2)
699	cover my defenseless head with the shadow of thy wing (2)

winged

324	At his feet the six-winged seraph (4)

winging

580	known the ecstasy of winging through untraveled realms (3)

wings

42	their white wings above me, watching round my bed (5)
43	keep me, King of kings, beneath thine own almighty wings (1)
87	Risen with healing in his wings (3)
89, 90	with peaceful wings unfurled (2)
245	words reflect, like eagles' wings, the glory of our Lord (1)
253	Give us wings of faith to rise within the veil (1)
265	his wings as drifted snow, his eyes as flame (1)
284	waved around your golden wings and struck your strings (7)
369	Our reason stretches all its wings (3)
388	dark is his path on the wings of the storm (2)
390	borne as on eagle-wings, safely his saints he sustaineth (2)
401	we shall, on eagle-wings upborne, to heaven ascend (2)
405	he made their tiny wings (1)
509	Come as the dove, and spread thy wings (4)
509	the wings of peaceful love (4)
596	solace all its wide dominion with the healing of thy wings (1)
667	it is the Lord who rises with healing in his wings (1)

672   with healing in thy wings (5)
702   If I the wings of morning take (4)
709   O spread thy sheltering wings around (4)

winning
433   so from the beginning the fight we were winning (2)
659, 660   move by some clear, winning word of love (2)
682   not for the sake of winning heaven, nor any fear of hell (4)

winter
69   prepare for joy in the winter night (2)
81   amid the cold of winter, when half spent was the night (1)
175   from the death of the winter arising (1)
199, 200   all the winter of our sins, long and dark (2)
290   all is safely gathered in, ere the winter storms begin (1)
291   sends the snow in winter, the warmth to swell the grain (1)
405   the cold wind in the winter, the pleasant summer sun (3)

winter's
109   lay keeping their sheep on a cold winter's night (1)
109   cold winter's night that was so deep (1)

wintry
204   when our hearts are wintry, grieving, or in pain (4)

wiped
582, 583   tears are wiped from eyes that shall not weep again (1)

wisdom
56   O come, thou Wisdom from on high (2)
248, 249   who its perfect wisdom reacheth ... joy possesseth (3)
370   the wisdom of my God to teach (5)
371   wisdom, love, might; boundless to ocean's tide (4)
398   I sing the wisdom that ordained the sun to rule the day (1)
412   Knowledge and truth, loud sounding wisdom (6)
417, 418   Power, riches, wisdom, and strength ... are his (2)
434   which ... best is writ ... power ... wisdom, or the love (3)
445, 446   O loving wisdom of our God (2)
457   thy word alone true wisdom can impart (2)
465, 466   eternal wisdom, make me wise (1)
484, 485   wisdom and might to thee belong (2)
488   Be thou my wisdom, and thou my true word (2)
535   All glory and power, all wisdom and might (4)
536   And his words are words of wisdom (R)
536   who would learn the way of wisdom ... hear God's word (2)
584   that as to knowledge we attain we may in wisdom grow (2)
594, 595   Grant us wisdom, grant us courage (1-4)
611   grew in wisdom as he grew in skill (2)
627   Lord, grant us all aright to learn the wisdom it imparts (5)
631   wisdom comes to those who know thee (1)
631   inspired those whose wisdom still directs us (3)
632   O Christ, the Word Incarnate, O Wisdom from on high (1)
643   thine endless wisdom, boundless power, and aweful purity (3)
665   deep his wisdom passing thought (3)
669   what loving wisdom chooseth, redeeming might will do (3)

wisdom's

480	Like him may we be found below in wisdom's path of peace (1)
567	give wisdom's heavenly lore (3)
584	Let wisdom's godly fear dispel the fears ... hate impart (3)

wisdoms

506, 507	his the truth behind the wisdoms (3)
506, 507	wisdoms which as yet know not the Lord (3)

wise

61, 62	The time has come, O maidens wise (1)
92	Wise Men three to him led, kneel they low by his bed (3)
109	by the light of that same star three wise men came (3)
109	three wise men came from country far (3)
109	Then entered in those wise men three (5)
148	grant us your truth to make us wise (1)
281	O wise exchange, with these to part (4)
405	all things wise and wonderful ... Lord God made them all (R)
423	Immortal, invisible, God only wise (1)
431	So shine the Lord's commandments to make the simple wise (3)
465, 466	eternal wisdom, make me wise (1)
574, 575	more pure, more true, more nobly wise (4)
670	him, in all his ways, adore, wise ... wonderful ... just (4)

wisely

282, 283	in thy service, he may wisely guide us (4)

wiseman

112	If I were a wiseman, I would do my part (3)

wisest

445, 446	O wisest love, that flesh and blood, which ... did fail (3)

wish

515	bringing down the richest treasure we can wish (1)
515	richest treasure we can wish or God can send (1)
623	wish and fulfillment are not severed there (2)

wit

434	nor wit can guess, nor reason prove which of the letters (3)

withdrawn

640	doubt and terror are withdrawn (3)

wither

76	flowers that wither and decay (3)
423	then wither and perish, but nought changeth thee (3)
667	though all the fields should wither (4)
702	wither from thy presence flee (3)

withhold

617	give or withhold, let pain or pleasure be (3)

withholds

163	E'en though the sun withholds its light (2)

within

29, 30	shed thou within our hearts thy ray (1)
47	God, the blessed Three in One dwell within my heart alone (6)
53	Still he comes within us, still his voice would win us (2)
76	make straight the way for God within (2)
103	The babe within a manger poor (2)
104	lie within the roadway To pave his kingdom come (2)
105	Now to the Lord sing praises, all you within this place (4)
114	Within a lodge of broken bark the tender babe was found (2)
124	within them shines a clearer light (3)
131, 132	Within the Jordan's sacred flood the ... Lamb ... stood (3)
144	restore us by your loving care to peace and joy within (2)
175	guard us from harm without, cleanse from the evil within (5)
216	guard us from harm without, cleanse us from evil within (3)
219	may all within us upward tend to him who ever liveth (3)
226, 227	come within our hearts to shine (1)
230	his grace within shall make you whole (3)
231	Come shine within our darkness (2/1-25)
253	Give us wings of faith to rise within the veil (1)
255	O Voice that spoke within him (2)
260	now within the Father's grace (4)
281	But grace within his heart had stirred (2)
297	sign us as Christ's, within, without (1)
302, 303	planted thy holy Name within our hearts (1)
314	tranced as it beholds thee, shrined within the cloud (1)
335	Unless ... you shall not have life within you (3)
346	as far as lies within our mortal power (1)
366	Lord, renew our hearts within us (7)
370	Christ be with me, Christ within me, Christ behind me (6)
379	find that self-same aching deep within the heart of God (2)
408	Within the kingdom of his might, Lo, all is just (2)
411	all that is within me join to bless his holy Name (1)
415	gratitude ... that glows within my fervent heart (2)
431	a law of love within our hearts (3)
440	thou must work all good within us (2)
443	he taught within the temple's gates (2)
460, 461	thou within the veil hast entered, robed in flesh (4)
475	God is here within us (1)
475	Come, abide within me (4)
492	passed within the gates of darkness (2)
498	the shadow of a mighty rock within a weary land (1)
498	a home within the wilderness, a rest upon the way (1)
506, 507	quickening worlds to life within (1)
506, 507	let your flame break out within us (5)
506, 507	through your voice which speaks within us (6)
516	O Comforter, draw near, within my heart appear (1)
517	thirsty soul desires and longs within thy courts to be (1)
517	One day within thy courts excels a thousand spent away (4)
518	thy fullest benediction shed within its walls alway (3)
582, 583	within whose four-square walls shall come no night (1)
587	O Christ, thyself a child within an earthly home (2)
621, 622	all is pure ... holy that within thy walls is stored (2)
629	let a new and better hope within our hearts be stirred (1)
630	Word is answered by the Spirit's voice within (5)
641	make me pure within (1)

645, 646	sing thy praise within thy house for ever (6)
674	Lord, cleanse the depths within our souls (4)
681	May thy fresh light arise within each clouded heart (5)
693	fightings and fears within, without (2)
699	make and keep me pure within (3)
699	spring thou up within my heart, rise to all eternity (3)
700	tarry no more without, but come and dwell within (1)

without

1, 2	joy without ending (2)
76	without thy grace we waste away like flowers (3)
168, 169	for this thy dying sorrow, thy pity without end (4)
175	guard us from harm without, cleanse from the evil within (5)
202	the Lamb of God without a stain (3)
216	guard us from harm without, cleanse us from evil within (3)
243	a knight without a sword (4)
266	by conception without compare the Savior ... bear (4)
297	sign us as Christ's, within, without (1)
348	teach us to serve without pride or pretension (2)
377, 378	without our aid he did us make (2)
381	Alleluia, alleluia, Alleluia without end (1-3)
386, 387	nature without voice or sound replied, O Lord, thou art (2)
391	His sovereign power without our aid formed us of clay (2)
406, 407	blessings without measure (1,8)
484, 485	Thy reign extend world without end (2)
495	highest praises, without ceasing ... give (4)
517	praise thee without rest (2)
531	souls without strength inspire with might (3)
606	for ever and for evermore, world without end (3)
616	his kingdom still increasing, a kingdom without end (4)
627	without thee how could earth be trod (4)
652, 653	let us, like them, without a word, rise up and follow (2)
657	pray and praise thee without ceasing (2)
693	without one plea, but that thy blood was shed for me (1)
693	fightings and fears within, without (2)
695, 696	we take it thankfully and without trembling (3)
700	tarry no more without, but come and dwell within (1)
703	without thy guiding hand we go astray (1)

witness

97	Better witness to thy worth (3)
193	those scars their solemn witness gave (2)
231	his witness in his gospel becomes victorious song (2/4-25)
232	for ... those whose witness is only known to you (2/11-1)
235	In one harmonious witness the chosen four combine (2)
245	Our thanks we raise that all John wrote bears witness (3)
245	witness, Lord, to you (3)
271, 272	John, still unborn, yet gave aright his witness (3)
271, 272	his witness to the coming light (3)
271, 272	Christ, the Sun of all the earth fulfilled that witness (3)
271, 272	Christ ... fulfilled that witness at his birth (3)
365	thy sacred witness bear in this glad hour (3)
420	through centuries of wrong, borne witness to the truth (3)
420	witness to the truth in every tongue (3)
431	vault of heaven springs mute witness (1)

431	mute witness of the Master's hand in all created things (1)
513	with the power to love and witness (3)
528	help us witness to your purpose with renewed integrity (1)
545	Behold a Witness nobler still who trod affliction's path (3)

witnessed
231	witnessed to his brother, "This is Messiah true" (2/11-30)

witnesses
253	long cloud of witnesses show the same path to heaven (4)
545	Lo, what a cloud of witnesses encompass us around (1)
546	A cloud of witnesses around hold thee in full survey (2)

woe
18	shield frail human eyes from all the woe you bore for us (3b)
151	From deepest woe I cry to thee (1)
159	Deep the woe of her affliction (2)
247	That woe is me, poor child for thee (3)
252	when the cup of human woe first he tasted here below (4)
286	whose hearts were riven, sore with woe and anguish tried (4)
406, 407	Woe to the unprepared (7)
471	The balm of life, the cure of woe (5)
509	Come as the light, to us reveal our emptiness and woe (2)
556, 557	youth to age, by night and day, in gladness and in woe (4)
559	thou didst feel its keenest woe (2)
636, 637	the rivers of woe shall not thee overflow (3)
641	with care and woe oppressed (2)
687, 688	for still our ancient foe doth seek to work us woe (1)

woeful
383, 304	who makes the woeful heart to sing (2)

woes
89, 90	Yet with the woes of sin and strife (3)
180	Jesus' woes are over now (2)
232	the one who shares our woes (2/10-18)
441, 442	When the woes of life o'ertake me (2)

wolf
597	Then shall the wolf dwell with the lamb (2)

woman
159	born of woman (4)
271, 272	woman born shall never be a greater prophet than was he (4)
673	first one ... the Samaritan woman who drew from the well (2)

womb
55	take our flesh and grow as child in Mary's womb (2)
83	lo! he abhors not the Virgin's womb (2)
87	offspring of the Virgin's womb (2)
258	blessed was the womb that bore thee (1,2)
268, 269	more blessed far the mother ... who bore him in her womb (2)
364	nor Virgin womb didst shun (6)

women

201	the women three assembled there (2)
203	the faithful women went their way to seek the tomb (2)
238, 239	Blessed feasts of blessed martyrs, holy women, holy men (1)
428	O men and women, bless the Lord (4)
506, 507	hundred men and women turned the known world upside down (4)
614	O Christian women, Christian men, all the world over (2)

won

18	sharing, know life's victory won (3a)
47	On this day the eternal Son over death his triumph won (2)
54	Come, O Father's saving Son, who o'er sin the victory won (4)
140, 141	Wilt thou forgive that sin, by which I won others to sin (2)
179	hell today is vanquished, heaven is won today (1)
180	Christ has won the victory (1)
188, 189	fought the fight, the battle won (1)
191	Alleluia! to the Savior who has won the victory (5)
201	who over death had victory won (2)
208	the victory of life is won (1)
220, 221	grace has won the victory (1)
232	O God, your two apostles won life through martyrdom (2/6-29)
237	joy that martyrs won their crown opened heaven's portal (1)
227	fill our lives which Christ has won (3)
268, 269	when the love of God the Father over sin the victory won (1)
299	With burning words of victory won inspire our hearts (3)
327, 328	by his dear cross and blood the victory won (3)
359	theirs by the love of Christ a kingdom won (4)
363	thou, Lord, by death hast won life's victory (3)
420	Then let us sing, for whom he won the fight (4)
436	Holy Spirit guide us on until the glorious crown be won (5)
488	High King of heaven, when victory is won (3)
525	mystic sweet communion with those whose rest is won (5)
599	let us march on, till victory is won (1)
627	or heaven itself be won (4)

wonder

106	see the wonder God for us had wrought (4)
128	O star of wonder, star of night (R)
129, 130	Nations cry aloud in wonder (3)
220, 221	angels wonder when they see how changed is our humanity (2)
230	the ears of all who heard proclaimed salvation's wonder (1)
246	the wonder of your cross (4)
259	There Joseph at her side in reverent wonder stands (3)
304	in awe and wonder to recall his life laid down for me (1)
414	thy deeds of wonder tell (3)
415	transported with the view, I'm lost in wonder (1)
415	I'm lost in wonder, love, and praise (1)
435	name with awe and wonder and with bated breath (4)
525	Though with a scornful wonder men see her sore oppressed (3)
657	lost in wonder, love, and praise (3)

wonderful

125, 126	the Wonderful, the Counsellor, the mighty God and Lord (4)
225	Christ and his wonderful works (3)
405	all things wise and wonderful ... Lord God made them all (R)

445, 446   in all his words most wonderful (1,5)
535   publish abroad his wonderful Name (1)
643   My God, how wonderful thou art (1)
643   How wonderful, how beautiful, the sight of thee must be (3)
670   him, in all his ways, adore, wise ... wonderful ... just (4)

wonderfully
469, 470   the heart of the Eternal is most wonderfully kind (3)
695, 696   By gracious powers so wonderfully sheltered (1)

wondering
78, 79   angels keep their watch of wondering love (2)
114   wondering hunters heard the hymn (1)
156   sad and wondering eyes to see the approaching sacrifice (3)

wonderously
77   For this how wonderously he wrought (3)

wonders
31, 32   its gleaming path declares the wonders of your ... power (2)
31, 32   wonders of your glorious power (2)
50   all his wonders tell (2)
100   wonders of his love (4)
163   on the Redeemer's thorn-crowned brow the wonders ... view (1)
163   the wonders of that dawn we view (1)
229   still from age to age convey the wonders of this ... day (1)
229   wonders of this sacred day (1)
238, 239   wonders, worthy of the Name they bore (1)
268, 269   sing the wonders that were done (1)
375   his mighty wonders tell abroad (1)
388   The earth, with its store of wonders untold (3)
398   Lord, how thy wonders are displayed (2)
398   thy wonders are displayed where'er I turn my eye (2)
401   sing the wonders of his grace for evermore (2)
404   telling the wonders which to you belong (2)
413   new songs ... render to him who has great wonders done (1)
424   For the wonders that astound us (3)
434   Oh, the sweet wonders of that cross (4)
462   wonders great by thy strong hand are done (5)
498   from my smitten heart with tears two wonders I confess (2)
498   the wonders of redeeming love and my unworthiness (2)
506, 507   showing us God's wonders, is himself the power to gaze (2)
578   the wonders that thy people told (2)
651   of skies and seas, his hand the wonders wrought (1)
677   God moves in a mysterious way his wonders to perform (1)

wondrous
54   Wondrous birth ... wondrous child of the Virgin undefiled (2)
55   a wondrous birth, befitting God (1)
78, 79   How silently, how silently, the wondrous gift is given (3)
97   Father, glory be to thee for the wondrous charity (3)
97   wondrous charity of thy Son, our Lord (3)
106   amazed, the wondrous story they proclaim (4)
124   eastern sages with amaze upon the wondrous token gaze (2)
136, 137   O wondrous type (1)

252	Jesus, Name of wondrous love, Name all other names above (1)
252	Jesus, Name of wondrous love (6)
267	through whom that wondrous mercy came (5)
284	On earth ye knew his wondrous grace (1)
284	ye hailed his wondrous flight up to the throne of God (7)
314	O memorial wondrous of the Lord's own death (3)
329, 331	he closed with wondrous ending his most patient life (2)
339	whose grace unbounded hath this wondrous banquet founded (1)
363	thy love has blessed the wide world's wondrous story (1)
368	while we hear thy wondrous story (2)
368	God the Lord ... let thy wondrous mercies shine (4)
369	How wondrous great, how glorious bright ... our Creator (1)
396, 397	who wondrous things hath done (1)
409	the moon takes up the wondrous tale (2)
439	What wondrous love is this, O my soul, O my soul (1)
455, 456	O wide-embracing, wondrous Love (2)
467	Sing, my soul, his wondrous love (1)
474	When I survey the wondrous cross where ... died (1)
494	crown him the King, to whom is given the wondrous name (5)
494	the wondrous name of Love (5)
532, 533	How wondrous and great thy works, God of praise (1)
702	wondrous knowledge, awful might (2)
408	all who know his power proclaim aloud the wondrous story (3)

wont

627	when wont to stray (1)

wonted

36	our wonted hymn out-pouring (2)
518	with thy wonted lovingkindness hear thy servants (3)
667	Though vine nor fig tree neither ... wonted fruit should (4)

wood

46	shade creeps o'er wild and wood (1)
161	The best are shamed before that wood (5)
165, 166	sweetest wood and sweetest iron (4)

woodlands

383, 384	Fair are the meadows, fairer still the woodlands (2)
383, 384	woodlands robed in the blooming garb of spring (2)
596	homesteads and the woodlands plead in silence (2)

word

8	Praise for them, springing fresh from the Word (1)
38, 39	Word of the Father throned on high (1)
49	with meekness hear the gospel word (3)
52	This day at thy creating word (1)
54	Thus on earth the Word appears (3)
55	O Word of God, come (2)
55	all praise to you, eternal Word (6)
61, 62	now come, most worthy Lord, God's Son, Incarnate Word (2)
63, 64	O heavenly Word, eternal Light (1)
67	token that the word is never broken (3)
69	in joy and terror the Word is born (4)
75	but the word of our God endureth (3)

370	the word of God to give me speech (5)
370	eternal Father, Spirit, Word (7)
371	Thou, whose almighty word chaos and darkness heard (1)
372	in prophet's word he spoke of old, he speaketh still (3)
380	truth eternal is thy word (2)
381	Thy strong word did cleave the darkness (1)
381	Thy strong word bespeaks us righteous (3)
385	Lo, at thy word the waters were formed (1)
393	how the word we have heard firm and changeless ... stand (1)
398	he formed the creatures with his Word (2)
422	more truth and light to break forth from thy Holy Word (1)
422	crucified and risen might of Christ, the incarnate Word (2)
427	There to the eternal Word the eternal psalm is heard (3)
432	rejoice in his word, ye angels of light (1)
435	who from the beginning was the mighty Word (1)
437, 438	tender to me the promise of his word (1)
437, 438	Tell out, my soul, the glories of his word (4)
440	Blessed Jesus, at thy word we are gathered all to hear (1)
443	to simple ones his word was given (4)
457	thy word alone true wisdom can impart (2)
465, 466	invited by your holy word (3)
469, 470	we should take him at his word (3)
478	the Father's conquering Word, true source of gladness (1)
486	Hosanna to the living Lord ... to the incarnate Word (1)
488	Be thou my wisdom, and thou my true word (2)
489	He sent no angel of his host to bear this mighty word (2)
494	once on earth the incarnate Word (4)
499	go in peace as promised in your word (1)
501, 502	Praise to the Father, Christ, his Word (6)
505	make us to love thy sacred word (1)
505	enlighten us by that same word (4)
506, 507	who enlightened priests and prophets with the word (3)
506, 507	praise the Word, Source, and Truth, and Inspiration (6)
522, 523	he whose word cannot be broken formed thee (1)
525	she is his new creation by water and the word (1)
526	when the word is given bid Jordan's narrow stream divide (5)
528	Heal the sick and preach the word (1)
530	spread, thou mighty word, spread the kingdom of the Lord (1)
530	word of how the Father's will made the world (2)
530	word of how the Savior's love ... burden doth remove (3)
530	word of how the Spirit came bringing peace in Jesus' name (4)
530	Word of life, most pure and strong (5)
530	word for which the nations long, spread abroad (5)
531	preach the reconciling word (2)
536	Open your ears and hear God's word (1,4)
536	who would learn the way of wisdom ... hear God's word (2)
558	whene'er we hear that glorious word (1)
569	slighted thy word (2)
569	yet to eternity standeth thy word (3)
570, 571	call to mind the word of Jesus (3)
573	Bind us in thine own love for better seeing thy Word (5)
573	thy Word made flesh, and in a manger laid (5)
574, 575	For sins of heedless word and deed (3)
578	Where rest but on thy faithful word (3)
588, 589	Almighty God, your word is cast like seed upon the ground (1)

596	feed ... with the richness of thy word (3)
600, 601	Bring to our world of strife thy sovereign word of peace (4)
608	hushed their raging at thy word (2)
614	with the same faith his word proclaim (2)
617	our inspiration be thy constant word (3)
618	Thou bearer of the eternal Word (2)
626	Lord, be thy word my rule; in it may I rejoice (1)
627	word of the ever-living God, will of his glorious Son (4)
628	to learn the truths your word imparts (1)
629	more light and truth to break forth from his word (1-3)
630	Word was spoken in the deed that made the earth (1)
630	God has spoken: praise God for his open word (1-4)
630	Word Incarnate heights and depths of life did share (2)
630	word was written in the Bible's sacred page (3)
630	word is published in the tongues of every race (4)
630	Word is answered by the Spirit's voice within (5)
630	God is speaking; praise God for his open word (5)
631	poets, prophets, scholars, saints, each a word from God (2)
631	each a word from God repeating (2)
631	till they came, who told the story of the Word (2)
631	praise him for the Word made flesh (3)
632	O Christ, the Word Incarnate, O Wisdom from on high (1)
632	The Church from our dear Master received the word divine (2)
633	Word of God, come down on earth (1)
633	Word almighty, we revere you (1)
633	Word made flesh, we long to hear you (1)
633	Word eternal, throned on high (2)
633	Word that brought to life creation (2)
633	Word that came from heaven to die (2)
633	saving Word, the world restoring, speak to us (2)
633	Word that caused blind eyes to see (3)
633	Be our Word in pity spoken (3)
633	Word that speaks your Father's love (4)
633	Word that sends us from above God the Spirit (4)
633	Word of truth, to all truth lead us (4)
633	Word of life, with one Bread feed us (4)
634	My heart is never set at rest till thy sweet word (1)
634	till thy sweet word have comforted me (1)
634	hold by thy word evermore, above all things (1)
635	trust his word, though undeserving (2)
636, 637	is laid for your faith in his excellent word (1)
652, 653	let us, like them, without a word, rise up and follow (2)
659, 660	move by some clear, winning word of love (2)
664	one word of thy supporting breath drives ... fears away (2)
666	hopes are on thy promise built, thy never-failing word (2)
670	When I come before thy Word, quiet my anxiety (2)
671	his word my hope secures (3)
683, 684	Where is the soul-refreshing view of Jesus and his word (2)
687, 688	lo, his doom is sure, one little word shall fell him (3)
687, 688	That word above all earthly powers ... abideth (4)
697	every thought and work and word, to thee be ever given (4)
718	thy word our law, thy paths our chosen way (2)

words

59	with words of love draw near (4)

148	to whom the words of life belong (1)
209	no gracious words we hear from him (1)
231	his words to us unfold (2/12-27)
232	whose gospel words declare ... your path (2/9-21)
245	words reflect, like eagles' wings, the glory of our Lord (1)
245	O Word made flesh, your deeds and words refresh (3)
245	your deeds and words refresh our hearts like dew (3)
248, 249	Name beyond what words can tell (2)
273, 274	The words of Paul assure us of Christ's redeeming word (3)
285	Luke, thy saint, through whom we know so many ... words (1)
285	through whom we know so many gracious words of thine (1)
285	so rich in words of truth and love (2)
299	With burning words of victory won inspire our hearts (3)
301	by whom the words of life were spoken (1)
340, 341	for the words which you have spoken (1)
342	we hear the words so gently spoken (1)
415	how shall words with equal warmth the gratitude declare (2)
431	my rock, and my redeeming Lord, in all my words and ways (4)
445, 446	in all his words most wonderful (1,5)
448, 449	by words and signs and actions, thus still seeking ... us (3)
453	hear the glad words, "Come to me all the blest" (4)
476	can ... words contain his praise (1)
480	Sweet were his words and kind his look (2)
517	thou shalt surely bless ... who live the words they pray (4)
528	Lord, you bless with words assuring (5)
536	And his words are words of wisdom (R)
628	our thoughts and words and deeds may glorify your Name (2)
630	Deeds and words and death and rising (2)
674	you alone can grant us grace to live the words we say (1)
681	tried with thoughts uncouth, in feeble words to bind thee (2)
702	My words from thee I cannot hide (2)

work

9	Awake, awake to love and work (4)
148	in us the work of grace begin (4)
152	fast of forty days may work our profit and thy praise (5)
188, 189	Love's redeeming work is done (1)
263, 264	blest in the work the Spirit wrought (3)
278	joy of Mary when on earth her work was done (4)
336	through our work as through our prayer (2)
409	publishes to every land the work of an almighty hand (1)
440	thou must work all good within us (2)
443	his work done, went up to heaven, praised be his coming (4)
492	till the appointed work be done (4)
526	in concert sing with those whose work is done (1)
528	the Spirit's gifts empower us for the work of ministry (R)
537	with us the work to share, with us reproach to dare (3)
541	to each servant does the Master say, "Go work today" (1)
566	our rude work deface no more the handiwork of God (2)
567	to hands that work and eyes that see (3)
568	stir us to work for thy justice and charity (2)
570, 571	wasted work and wasted play (3)
570, 571	I must work while it is day (3)
586	Jesus ... divine Companion, help us all to work our best (3)
611	born to work and die for every one (1)

611	teach us how to do all work for God (7)
659, 660	in work that keeps faith sweet and strong (3)
664	may thy house be mine abode and all my work be praise (3)
669	his work must thou consider for thy work to endure (2)
677	Blind unbelief is sure to err and scan his work in vain (6)
687, 688	for still our ancient foe doth seek to work us woe (1)
697	every thought and work and word, to thee be ever given (4)
704	Jesus, confirm my heart's desire to work ... for thee (3)
704	work, and speak, and think for thee (3)
705	until life's work is done (3)

worker

605	To merchant, worker, king he brings God's high demands (3)
611	Christ the worker, born in Bethlehem (1)
611	Christ the worker, Love alive for us (7)

workers

412	Limestone and beams, loud building workers (4)
586	by thy lowly human birth ... come to join the workers (1)
586	workers, burden bearers of the earth (1)

worketh

573	Lust of possession worketh desolations (4)

working

382	thou didst note my working breast, thou hast spared me (1)
511	Holy Spirit, ever working through the Church's ministry (2)
534	God is working his purpose out as year succeeds to year (1)
534	God is working his purpose out ... time is drawing near (1)

works

59	Cast away the works of darkness, O ye children of the day (1)
75	like grass our works decay (2)
151	Our works could ne'er our guilt remove (2)
167	try his works to do (5)
179	Him their true Creator, all his works adore (1)
225	Christ and his wonderful works (3)
273, 274	the works of Peter show us how we may serve the Lord (3)
362	All thy works shall praise thy Name (4)
376	All thy works with joy surround thee (2)
385	Many and great, O God, are thy works (1)
414	Age to age his works transmitteth (2)
414	Nor shall fail from memory's treasure works ... wrought (4)
414	works by love and mercy wrought (4)
414	works of love surpassing measure (4)
414	works of mercy passing thought (4)
414	all his works his goodness prove (5)
414	All thy works, O Lord, shall bless thee (6)
415	day and night divide thy works no more (4)
428	O all ye works of God, now come to thank him and adore (1)
448, 449	for us his daily works he wrought (3)
521	works of darkness disappear before thy conquering light (2)
532, 533	How wondrous and great thy works, God of praise (1)
578	Remember, Lord, thy works of old (2)
677	works his sovereign will (2)

858 / works

678, 679   all his works his might proclaim (2)

world
9   resurrection of the world (3)
16, 17   For at this hour to all the world ... salvation came (2)
18   that we may see your world is good (4c)
19, 20   hearts of all the world inspire (2)
24   through all the world her watch is keeping (2)
31, 32   you in the primal world once set the boundaries (4)
36   thee, therefore, O Most High, the world doth glorify (3)
37   O Son of God, be thou ... through all the world adored (3)
38, 39   Jesus, Redeemer of the world (1)
40, 41   O Christ, Redeemer of the world (5)
43   with the world, myself, and thee, I ... at peace may be (2)
47   did the world from darkness bring (1)
49   Who died to save the world he made (1)
59   the world is wrapped in fear (4)
60   When this old world drew on toward night you came (3)
63, 64   born for blessing to a world forlorn (1)
78, 79   in this world of sin, where meek souls will receive him (3)
80   Glad tidings of great joy I bring to all the world (1)
85, 86   before the world knew day or night (1)
85, 86   throughout the world this holy day (2)
85, 86   Today, as year by year its light bathes all the world (4)
85, 86   bathes all the world in radiance bright (4)
89, 90   The world in solemn stillness lay to hear the angels sing (1)
89, 90   still ... heavenly music floats o'er all the weary world (2)
89, 90   the world has suffered long (3)
89, 90   world give back the song which now the angels sing (4)
97   For the world a love supreme brought me to this stable (2)
98   came he to a world forlorn, the Lord of every nation (1,5)
100   Joy to the world! the Lord is come (1)
100   Joy to the world! the Savior reigns (2)
100   He rules the world with truth and grace (4)
103   will rule the world for evermore (2)
106   morn whereon the Savior of the world was born (1)
110   that brought into this world the God made man (2)
120   go forth with you a world to win (5)
122, 123   our Savior in his fasting pleasures of the world forebore (3)
127   to the world its God announcing (2)
152   Kind Maker of the world, O hear the fervent prayer (1)
161   the ransom of a world set free (4)
162   wealth that did the world restore (4)
163   for God doth make his world anew (1)
175   Jesus the health of the world, enlighten our minds (6)
184   Now through all the world it rings (1)
194, 195   to him the throne over all the world is given (4)
205   To all the world glad news we bring (1)
210   round world keep high triumph, and all that is therein (3)
211   The whole bright world rejoices now (1)
216   Jesus the health of the world (4)
217, 217   new hymns throughout the world shall ring (1)
222   to rule the world for which he died (4)
225   day ... Holy Ghost shone in the world with God's grace (R)
231   your true consolation may through the world extend (2/6-11)

233, 234	these lay the prince of this world low (3)
235	drove away the shadows, and filled the world with light (1)
245	fullness of your grace and truth for us and all the world (1)
265	Christian folk throughout the world will ever say (4)
287	Who thee by faith before the world confessed (1)
290	All the world is God's own field (2)
293	the world is bright with the joyous saints (3)
301	Bread of the world, in mercy broken (1)
304	as his people in the world we'll live (5)
321	till through the world thy truth has run (4)
327, 328	He that his saints in this world rules and shields (6)
335	my Flesh for the life of the world (2)
335	the Son of God who has come into the world (5)
340, 341	in the world to which you send us, let your kingdom come (4)
344	call us, Savior, from the world away (3)
347	go to the world in peace (1)
347	go to the world in love (2)
347	go to the world in strength (3)
347	go to the world in joy (4)
348	So, in the world where each duty assigned us (4)
364	the world is with the glory filled of thy majestic sway (3)
371	rolling in fullest pride, through the world far and wide (4)
379	God is Love ... enfolds us, all the world in one embrace (2)
389	He with all-commanding might filled the new-made world (3)
389	filled the new-made world with light (3)
391	Wide as the world is thy command (5)
396, 397	in whom his world rejoices (1)
396, 397	free us from all ills in this world and the next (2)
399	he made the sea and land, he brought the world to birth (2)
401	triumphant o'er the world and sin, the Prince of Peace (3)
402, 403	Let all the world in every corner sing, my God and King (R)
413	calling the whole world to rejoice (2)
413	whose truth victorious establishes the world in peace (3)
416	each perfect gift of thine to the world so freely given (6)
420	a new dimension in the world of sound (2)
421	for the world was sacrificed upon the cross to save us (2)
436	the Savior of the world is here (1)
452	for the sake of those he grieves transcends the world (2)
452	transcends the world he never leaves (2)
463, 464	He is the Life. Love him in the World of the Flesh (3)
471	for this we count the world but loss (1)
472	Hope of the world (1-5)
473	till all the world adore his sacred Name (R)
473	as thou hast promised, draw the world to thee (3)
476	his meaning lights our shadowed world through Christ (2)
479	stream which from sin and sorrow doth the world redeem (3)
484, 485	Thy reign extend world without end (2)
490	God set the stars to give light to the world (1)
491	incarnate, and a native of the very world he made (4)
492	rules and guides the world he ransomed (4)
499	prepared by you for all the world to see (1)
506, 507	hundred men and women turned the known world upside down (4)
506, 507	till ... we, too, set the world alight (5)
509	make a lost world thy home (5)
519, 520	in this world pain and tribulation bore (3)

528	That the world may trust your promise (2)
528	asking ... world around us share your children's liberty (3)
530	word of how the Father's will made the world (2)
530	made the world and keeps it still (2)
530	how forever, in its need ... the world is freed (3)
530	through his death the world is freed (3)
530	until from night all the world awakes to light (5)
534	glorious gospel of truth may shine throughout the world (3)
537	Christ for the world we sing (1-4)
537	The world to Christ we bring (1-4)
539	mission ... to tell to all the world that God is Light (1)
540	Throughout the world their cry is ringing still (1)
540	till all the world thy saving grace shall know (2)
542	whole round world complete, from sunrise to its setting (2)
542	the world has waited long, has travailed long in pain (3)
560	Blessed are you when the world reviles ... persecutes (9)
570, 571	drawing near a world that spurns him (4)
573	if we love not the world which thou hast made (5)
578	make wars throughout the world to cease (1)
585	God, whose arms of love aching, spent, the world sustain (6)
597	till by God's grace our warring world shall see ... peace (1)
599	our hearts drunk with the wine of the world (3)
600, 601	Bring to our world of strife thy sovereign word of peace (4)
606	for ever and for evermore, world without end (3)
607	in love and mercy guide us and heal our strife-torn world (1)
609	till all the world shall learn thy love (5)
614	O Christian women, Christian men, all the world over (2)
633	saving Word, the world restoring, speak to us (2)
633	heal the world, by our sin broken (3)
649, 650	shed o'er the world your holy light (4)
651	This is my Father's world (1,2)
651	He trust us with his world, to keep it clean and fair (2)
681	the world began, endures, and shall endure (1)
682	for that thou didst all the world upon the cross embrace (2)
687, 688	though this world, with devils filled should threaten (3)
687, 688	though this world ... threaten to undo us (3)
695, 696	Yet when again in this new world you give us the joy (4)
705	A world in need now summons us to labor, love and give (2)
705	a world redeemed by Christ-like love (2)
706	else this world had still enthralled me (1)
715	a trembling fear seized all the guilty world around (RC)

world's

46	forth in starlight tender from myriad world's unknown (2)
77	Behold, the world's creator wears the form and fashion (2)
82	Babe ... world's Redeemer first revealed his sacred face (2)
102	the world's creator, cradled there on Christmas Day (3)
165, 166	Jesus Christ, the world's Redeemer ... reigns as King (1)
191	for the world's salvation bled (1)
258	who brought forth the world's salvation (2)
329, 331	shed for this world's ransoming (1)
363	thy love has blessed the wide world's wondrous story (1)
480	Safe from the world's alluring harms (2)
500	by whose aid the world's foundations first were laid (1)
542	Christ is the world's true Light ... captain of salvation (1)

549, 550	Jesus calls us from the worship of the vain world's (3)
549, 550	worship of the vain world's golden store (3)
559	lead us o'er the world's tempestuous sea (1)
588, 589	Let not the world's deceitful cares ... destroy (3)
607	Christ shall rule victorious o'er all the world's domain (4)
692	I am this dark world's light (3)

worldly

139	let us not heed worldly lies nor rest upon our merit (3)
150	from worldly joys abstain (2)
232	worldly gain forsaking, your path of life we share (2/9-21)

worlds

9	worlds awake to cry their blessings on the Lord of life (4)
9	God who gave all worlds that are, and all that are to be (6)
82	Of the Father's love begotten, ere the worlds began to be (1)
104	By whose descent among us The worlds are reconciled (4)
160	throned in light ere worlds could be (2)
196, 197	offer us the worlds of light that live inside the Trinity (3)
373	worlds his mighty voice obeyed (1)
392	we're marching through Emmanuel's ground to fairer worlds (4)
392	fairer worlds on high (4)
489	The great Creator of the worlds (1)
489	him through whom the worlds were made (2)
494	Crown him the Son of God before the worlds began (2)
494	Crown him the Lord of heaven, enthroned in worlds above (5)
506, 507	Spirit, moving on the waters quickening worlds to life (1)
506, 507	quickening worlds to life within (1)
543	till sovereign love in worlds above the glory raise (3)
580	We have ventured worlds undreamed of (3)
665	Evermore from his store new-born worlds rise and adore (3)
685	rise to worlds unknown and behold thee on thy throne (3)
718	in beauty all the starry band of shining worlds (1)

wormwood

171	O the wormwood and the gall (2)
450, 451	Sinners, whose love can ne'er forget the wormwood (5)
450, 451	ne'er forget the wormwood and the gall (5)

worn

| 537 | sin-sick and sorrow-worn, whom Christ doth heal (1) |
| 692 | I came to Jesus as I was, so weary, worn, and sad (1) |

worry

| 145 | Now quit your care and anxious fear and worry (1) |

worship

31, 32	beckons us to worship you (2)
84	Worship we the Godhead, love incarnate, love divine (2)
84	worship we our Jesus, but wherewith for sacred sign (2)
93	come and worship, worship Christ, the new-born King (R)
128	worship him, God Most High (3)
176, 177	By the same Spirit we are called to worship God (3)
231, 232	Then let us praise the Father and worship God the Son (3)
267	Ask not how this should be, but worship and adore (3)

307	heaven and earth with loud hosanna worship thee (5)
307	worship thee, the Lamb who died (5)
307	We in worship join with them (3)
326	Thanksgiving and glory and worship ... blessing and love (2)
334	worship, thanks, devotion voicing (1)
368	meet and worship in thy Name (2)
388	O worship the King, all glorious above (1)
400	worship him in humbleness (7)
401	eternal Father, great I AM, we worship thee (4)
420	as worship moved us to a more profound Alleluia (2)
421	We bless, we worship you ... O God, Almighty Father (1)
432	worship before him, in brightness arrayed (1)
434	worship at his Father's throne (5)
475	his own ... worship lowly, yield their spirits wholly (1)
495	Worship, honor, power, and blessing thou art worthy (4)
495	Worship ... thou art worthy to receive (4)
511	thee we praise with endless worship (1)
511	thee we worship and extol (2)
532, 533	their worship and vows shall come to thy throne (2)
535	fall down on their faces, and worship the Lamb (3)
549, 550	Jesus calls us from the worship of the vain world's (3)
549, 550	worship of the vain world's golden store (3)
590	inspire our worship (1)
610	we, your servants, bring the worship not of voice alone (1)
610	As we worship, grant us vision (3)
610	Called by worship to your service (4)
643	worship thee with trembling hope and penitential tears (4)
683, 684	help me to tear it from thy throne and worship only thee (4)
697	worship near thy throne (3)

worshiped
112	but his mother only, in her maiden bliss, worshiped (3)
112	worshiped the beloved with a kiss (3)
127	Jesus, whom the Gentiles worshiped at thy glad epiphany (5)
282, 283	watching o'er the temples where thou art worshiped (3)
435	ever to be worshiped, trusted, and adored (4)

worshipers
| 57, 58 | cause of endless exultation to his ransomed worshipers (3) |

worshiping
| 33-35 | in light or darkness worshiping our Savior (5) |
| 33-35 | worshiping our Savior now and for ever (5) |

worst
| 161 | the worst gain power to be good (5) |
| 208 | The powers of death have done their worst (2) |

worth
97	Better witness to thy worth (3)
228	All that gives to us our worth (3)
252	Jesus, Name of priceless worth to the fallen of the earth (3)
297	grant unto us the greater worth (2)
491	Worth from worth immortal sprung (3)
534	All we can do is nothing worth unless God blesses the deed (4)

630   his the fires that tried her worth (1)

worthy

25, 26	Worthy are you of endless praise, O Son of God (3)
37	Worthy art thou at all times (3)
37	Worthy are thou ... to receive our hallowed praises, Lord (3)
61, 62	now come, most worthy Lord, God's Son, Incarnate Word (2)
151	grace hath wrought whate'er in them is worthy (2)
238, 239	Worthy deeds they wrought (1)
238, 239	wonders, worthy of the Name they bore (1)
238, 239	by his grace we may be worthy of eternal bliss at last (3)
346	oh, count us worthy, Christ, thy joys to share (2)
374	Worthy the Lamb that died, they cry, to be exalted thus (2)
374	Worthy the Lamb, our lips reply, for he was slain for us (2)
374	Jesus is worthy to receive honor and power divine (3)
404	you, God and King, are worthy of all praise (1)
406, 407	no one is worthy thee to name (1)
417, 418	Worthy is Christ, the Lamb who was slain (1)
434	every labor of his hands shows something worthy of a God (1)
486	make our secret soul to be a temple pure and worthy thee (4)
495	Worship, honor, power, and blessing thou art worthy (4)
495	Worship ... thou art worthy to receive (4)
500	make thy temples worthy thee (1)

would

3	he, in all we do or say, would keep us free from harm (1)
3	that he ... would keep us free from harm this day (1)
4	that he, in all we do or say, would keep us free (1)
18	he knew you, Lord, would answer him (2b)
44, 45	we pray ... our guard and keeper you would be (1)
53	Still he comes within us, still his voice would win us (2)
53	from the sins that hurt us, would to Truth convert us (2)
74	he would have us bear it so he can make us free (4)
83	we would embrace thee, with love and awe (5)
83	who would not love thee, loving us so dearly (5)
92	ox and ass beside him from the cold would hide him (2)
112	If I were a shepherd, I would bring a lamb (4)
112	If I were a wiseman, I would do my part (3)
117, 118	vainly with gifts would his favor secure (4)
122, 123	Alleluia though we cherish and would chant for evermore (3)
159	Who, on Christ's dear mother gazing ... would not weep (4)
159	who ... would not share her sorrows deep (4)
161	The crowd would have been satisfied to see ... crucified (3)
170	that thorns would flower upon your brow (1)
173	O sorrow deep! Who would not weep (1)
173	Who would not weep with heartfelt pain and sighing (1)
202	we now would sing to Jesus our triumphant King (1)
204	thinking that never he would wake again (2)
242	His brethren's word he would not take (3)
246	King Herod's troops would soon appear (1)
318	here would I touch and handle things unseen (1)
318	Here would I feed upon the Bread of God (2)
318	here would I lay aside each earthly load (2)
343	would not live by bread alone, but by thy word of grace (2)
423	all laud we would render (4)

434	I would for ever speak his Name (5)
453	Who would not want to climb such a ladder as this (4)
457	who would the Father seek, must seek him, Lord, by thee (1)
458	none the longed-for Christ would know (2)
469, 470	life would be thanksgiving for the goodness of the Lord (3)
472	we would be faithful to thy gospel glorious (4)
480	the stones themselves would sing (3)
498	Beneath the cross of Jesus I fain would take my stand (1)
536	who would learn the way of wisdom ... hear God's word (2)
549, 550	from each idol that would keep us (3)
564, 565	He who would valiant be 'gainst all disaster (1)
572	we would raise, O Christ, one song (1)
617	We would be one in hatred of all wrong (2)
620	ten thousand times would one be blest who might ... hear (3)
627	when waves would whelm our tossing bark (3)
657	Thee we would be alway blessing (2)
675	if you would my disciple be (1)
687, 688	our striving would be losing (2)
706	for my heart would still refuse you (2)

wouldst

508	do what thou wouldst do (1)
669	O trust the Lord then wholly, if thou wouldst be secure (2)
672	thy people long that thou, their Sun, wouldst rise (2)

wound

270	by the hands, in grave clothes wound (3)
313	by the spear-wound and the nailing (3)

wounded

168, 169	O sacred head, sore wounded, defiled and put to scorn (1)
193	his wounded hands and feet he showed (2)
208	Lord! by the stripes which wounded thee (5)
357	Often were they wounded in the deadly strife (3)
598	O wounded hands of Jesus, build in us thy new creation (4)
644	It makes the wounded spirit whole (2)
676	There is a balm in Gilead to make the wounded whole (R)
685	water and the blood from thy wounded side that flowed (1)

wounds

190	see the wounds for you he bore (2)
190	All the glory of the morning pales before those wounds (2)
190	those wounds redeeming (2)
323	Lord, thy wounds our healing give (2)
434	Her noblest life my spirit draws from his dear wounds (4)
434	his dear wounds and bleeding side (4)
472	to heal earth's wounds and end her bitter strife (2)
644	It soothes our sorrows, heals our wounds (1)

wrapped

59	the world is wrapped in fear (4)
94, 95	all meanly wrapped in swathing bands (4)
114	a ragged robe of rabbit skin enwrapped his beauty round (2)

wrath
255   His presence pierced and blinded the zealot in his wrath (1)
255   grace, by ways mysterious, our sinful wrath can bind (3)
388   His chariots of wrath the deep thunderclouds form (2)
411   his wrath is ever slow to rise and ready to abate (3)
489   He sent him not in wrath and power (3)
531   bid mercy triumph over wrath (3)
569   bid not thy wrath in its terrors awaken (2)
573   in wrath and fear, by jealousies surrounded (3)
578   the wrath of nations now restrain (1)

wreaths
435   for all wreaths of empire meet upon his brow (6)
556, 557   echoes upward float like wreaths of incense cloud (3)

wreckage
148   far and wide the wreckage of our hatred spreads (3)

wrecks
441, 442   towering o'er the wrecks of time (1,5)

wresting
184   exalted now to save, wresting victory from the grave (3)

wrestle
120   Straight to the wilderness he goes to wrestle (4)
120   wrestle with his people's foes (4)
548   wrestle, and fight, and pray (4)
638, 639   wrestle till the break of day (1)

wrestling
286   wrestling on till life was ended (3)

wretchedness
609   In haunts of wretchedness and need (2)

wring
582, 583   wring gold from human pain (2)

wrings
494   who every grief hath known that wrings the human breast (2)

writ
372   deep writ upon the human heart, on sea and land (3)
434   which ... best is writ ... power ... wisdom, or the love (3)

write
248, 249   holy Jesus, thee imploring so to write it in us here (4)

writes
431   writes in fire across the skies God's majesty and praise (2)

written
280   veiled ... but written in the Lamb's great book of life (3)
630   word was written in the Bible's sacred page (3)

wrong

27, 28	to turn from sin and cease from wrong (4)
63, 64	all wrong desires may burn away (2)
70	warning us of right and wrong (1)
73	when right shall triumph over wrong (4)
75	he will right the wrong (3)
89, 90	two thousand years of wrong (3)
236	sinners who are burdened by the wrong we do (2)
266	feared that she had done a wrong (3)
334	Sins forgiven, wrong forgiving, we go forth alert (3)
420	through centuries of wrong, borne witness to the truth (3)
542	heal its ancient wrong, come, Prince of Peace, and reign (3)
551	end the night of wrong (2)
569	falsehood and wrong shall not tarry beside thee (3)
612	love is meek, and thinks no wrong (2)
615	day by whose clear shining light all wrong ... revealed (4)
615	all wrong shall stand revealed (4)
616	He comes with succor speedy to those who suffer wrong (2)
617	We would be one in hatred of all wrong (2)
651	let us not forget that though the wrong is great (2)
651	though the wrong is great and strong (2)
659, 660	in trust that triumphs over wrong (3)

wrong's

145	to fight, to fight till every wrong's set right (3)

wrongs

5	to give us grace our wrongs to bear (4)
145	who feed the hungry in their need, and wrongs redress (4)
598	still our wrongs may weave thee now new thorns (1)
674	broods on wrongs and will not let old bitterness depart (2)

wrote

245	Our thanks we raise that all John wrote bears witness (3)

wrought

77	For this how wonderously he wrought (3)
106	see the wonder God for us had wrought (4)
148	our self-wrought miseries have made us trust ourselves (2)
148	evils wrought by human pride recoil on unrepentant heads (3)
151	grace hath wrought whate'er in them is worthy (2)
229	the deeds our great Redeemer wrought (2)
238, 239	Worthy deeds they wrought (1)
263, 264	blest in the work the Spirit wrought (3)
375	What God hath wrought to show his power he ... sustaineth (3)
375	what God hath wrought ... he evermore sustaineth (3)
414	Nor shall fail from memory's treasure works ... wrought (4)
414	works by love and mercy wrought (4)
448, 449	for us his daily works he wrought (3)
477	by thy death was God's salvation wrought (2)
484, 485	his holy arm hath wrought salvation (1)
492	thus he wrought the full redemption (3)
651	of skies and seas, his hand the wonders wrought (1)

yawning

208	He closed the yawning gates of hell (4)

yea

57, 58	Yea, amen, let all adore thee (4)
83	Yea, Lord, we greet thee, born this happy morning (6)
142	yea, evermore, in life and death, Jesus, with us abide (4)
151	yea, e'en the best life faileth (2)
359	Anoint them kings. Yea, kingly kings, O Lord (4)
582, 583	yea, bids us seize the whole of life and build its glory (4)
663	Yea, even when I must pass through the valley (3)
693	now to be thine, yea, thine alone (5)

year

85, 86	Today, as year by year its light bathes all the world (4)
140, 141	Wilt thou forgive that sin which I did shun a year or two (2)
175	every good gift of the year now with its Master returns (1)
250	Now greet the swiftly changing year with joy (1)
250	rejoice, with thanks embrace another year of grace (1-3,5)
250	what need we fear in earth or space in this new year (4)
250	in this new year of grace (4)
251	Another year its course has run (2)
280	year by year our thanks to you (2)
534	God is working his purpose out as year succeeds to year (1)

year's

250	His love abundant far exceeds ... a whole year's needs (3)
250	the volume of a whole year's needs (3)

yearn

623	we for that country must yearn and must sigh (4)
649, 650	For you our restless spirits yearn (3)

yearned

615	faithful souls have yearned to see ... that kingdom's day (1)

yearning

516	so the yearning strong, with which the soul will long (3)
516	yearning ... shall far outpass the power of human telling (3)
628	that yearning souls may find the Christ (3)

years

9	sun ... great lord of years and days (5)
78, 79	hopes and fears of all the years are met in thee tonight (1)
82	that future years shall see (1)
89, 90	beneath the heavenly hymn have rolled two thousand years (3)
89, 90	two thousand years of wrong (3)
89, 90	with the everlasting years shall come the time foretold (4)
165, 166	Thirty years among us dwelling (2)
182	No longer bound to distant years in Palestine (2)
285	through weary years of toil and strife ... faithful (3)
289	changeful years unresting their silent course have sped (2)
289	who changest not with years (2)
292	thine the beauty ... joy with which the years are crowned (1)
372	first, the last, beyond all thought his timeless years (1)

391	when rolling years shall cease to move (5)
453	has stood hundreds of years and is not yet decayed (2)
459	light-years frame the Pleiades and point Orion's sword (1)
463, 464	great city that has expected your return for years (2)
480	like him in grace and knowledge grow as years (1)
480	grace and knowledge grow as years and strength increase (1)
599	God of our weary years, God of our silent tears (3)
643	How dread are thine eternal years, O everlasting Lord (2)
647	through the years of life, to God I walk (2)
671	When we've been there ten thousand years (5)
680	O God, our help in ages past, our hope for years to come (1,5)
680	from everlasting thou art God, to endless years the same (3)
680	Time ... bears all our years away (5)
719	O beautiful for patriot dream that sees beyond the years (3)

yellow

| 288 | yellow sheaves of ripened grain (2) |

yes

183	Yes, Christ my hope is arisen (7)
335	Yes, Lord, we believe that you are the Christ (5)
468	It was poor little Jesus, yes, yes (1-4)
556, 557	Yes, on through life's long path ... chanting as ye go (4)
640	Traveler, yes, it brings the day, promised day of Israel (1)

yet

46	yet when life's day is over (3)
66	born a child, and yet a king (3)
78, 79	yet in thy dark streets shineth the everlasting Light (1)
81	true man, yet very God (3)
89, 90	Yet with the woes of sin and strife (3)
102	yet this child, our Lord and brother, brought us love (3)
104	Yet he shall be forsaken, and yielded up to die (3)
112	yet what I can I give him give my heart (4)
121	as peaceful as a dove and yet as urgent as a flame (1)
149	far off yet here -- the goal of all desire (1)
150	forty days and forty nights tempted, and yet undefiled (1)
168, 169	mourn thee, well beloved, yet thank thee for thy death (3)
182	he suffers still, yet loves the more (4)
182	suffers still, yet loves the more (4)
206	yet whose faith has constant been (6)
231	made flesh, yet God and Lord (2/12-21)
231	so eager and so bold, thrice failing, yet repentant (2/1-18)
232	yet she her voice upraises God's glory to proclaim (2/8-15)
242	yet when thine Easter-news was spread (2)
246	not yet was he to share our pain (2)
257	But silent knelt the mother blest of the yet silent word (4)
266	There are yet but six months gone (5)
271, 272	John, still unborn, yet gave aright his witness (3)
287	yet all are one in thee, for all are thine (4)
287	But lo, there breaks a yet more glorious day (7)
289	our harvest may be garnered by ages yet unknown (3)
305, 306	thou at the table, blessing, yet dost stand (2)
305, 306	"This is my Body", so thou givest yet (2)
316, 317	yet all our days thou still art here with us (2)

316, 317	yet, passing, points to the glad feast above (3)
324	King of kings, yet born of Mary (2)
332	O God, unseen yet ever near, thy presence may we feel (1)
339	yet to dwell with thee he deigneth (1)
355	yet even at the grave we make our song: Alleluia (1)
358	Yet at the grave shall we raise up our glad song (3)
394, 395	your hands uphold earth's mysteries known or yet untold (2)
410	Widely yet his mercy flows (3)
419	yet to each loving heart how near (1)
443	yet in the wilderness did fast (2)
447	yet he who loved us from the first ensures our victory (3)
452	what self rejects yet feebly wills (4)
453	has stood hundreds of years and is not yet decayed (2)
455, 456	eternal and yet ever new (1)
458	Yet steadfast he to suffering goes (5)
492	Now on high, yet ever with us (4)
496, 497	Jesus, Holy, holy, yet most lowly draw thou near us (1)
506, 507	wisdoms which as yet know not the Lord (3)
525	Elect from every nation, yet one o'er all the earth (2)
525	yet saints their watch are keeping (3)
525	Yet she on earth hath union with God, the Three in One (5)
528	Yet we hoard as private treasure all that you ... give (4)
559	yet possessing every blessing, if our God our Father be (1)
559	yet unfearing, persevering, to thy passion thou didst go (2)
569	yet to eternity standeth thy word (3)
569	earth by thy chastening yet shall ... be restored (4)
570, 571	Risen Lord, shall yet the city be the city of despair (5)
573	his saving cross no nation yet will bear (2)
580	Great Creator, still creating, show us what we yet may do (1)
580	yet their windows, blank, unfeeling, stare (2)
584	yet greater far this gift, O God, bestow (2)
599	yet, with a steady beat (2)
609	yet long these multitudes to see the true compassion (3)
613	wherever near or far thick darkness broodeth yet (5)
629	the Lord has yet more light and truth (1-3)
635	thou yet shall find it true for thee (2)
635	God never yet forsook in need the soul that trusted him (2)
640	higher yet that star ascends (2)
643	Yet I may love thee too, O Lord, almighty as thou art (5)
645, 646	but yet in love he sought me (3)
651	God is our Father yet (2)
661	Yet let us pray for but one thing ... peace of God (4)
682	nor yet for fear that loving not I might for ever die (1)
695, 696	Yet is this heart by its old foe tormented (2)
695, 696	Yet when again in this new world you give us the joy (4)
720	O say does that star-spangled banner yet wave (1)

yield

71, 72	gates of brass before him burst, the iron fetters yield (2)
108	Now yield we thanks and praise to Christ (1)
117, 118	Shall we then yield him, in costly devotion, odors (3)
191	will all its full abundance at his second coming yield (3)
222	as sin and death their conquests yield (1)
281	who yield up all for Jesus' sake (4)
290	fruit unto his praise to yield (2)

292	kindly earth with timely birth may yield her fruits again (2)
475	his own ... worship lowly, yield their spirits wholly (1)
477	All praise to thee, for thou, O King divine, didst yield (1)
477	yield the glory that of right was thine (1)
524	brightest glories earth can yield (5)
588, 589	let it yield a hundred-fold the fruits of peace and joy (3)
638, 639	Yield to me now (3)
705	God the giver of all good, the source of bounteous yield (1)

yielded
| 104 | Yet he shall be forsaken, and yielded up to die (3) |
| 232 | To cross and sword they yielded (2/6-29) |

yielding
| 580 | probed the secrets of the atom, yielding unimagined power (3) |

yields
| 233, 234 | the hope that never yields or faints (3) |
| 327, 328 | to all believers life eternal yields (6) |

yoke
74	Gentle is he and humble, And light his yoke shall be (4)
97	willingly this yoke I take, and this sacrifice I make (2)
145	To shatter every yoke (3)
199, 200	loosed from Pharaoh's bitter yoke (1)
611	Yoke maker, fashioned by his hands (4)

yokes
| 611 | easy yokes that made the labor less (4) |

yon
111	all is calm ... bright round yon virgin mother and child (1)
467	from yon bright throne above ... extends his grace (1)
640	Traveler, o'er yon mountain's height see ... star (1)

yonder
93	yonder shines the infant Light (2)
128	following yonder star (1)
180	dimming yonder glorious morning ray (3)

yore
| 428 | people bless the Lord like righteous souls of yore (5) |
| 567 | now, O Lord, be near to bless, almighty as of yore (2) |

young
231	young James the faithful, who heard and followed you (2/5-1)
243	When Stephen, young and doomed to die, fell crushed (3)
247	all young children to slay (2)
257	two young doves, her humble offerings (2)
474	cross where the young Prince of Glory died (1)
491	strength of infant weakness, if eternal is so young (3)
541	to young and old the Gospel gladness bear (4)
661	Young John who trimmed the flapping sail ... died (3)

youngling
247   this poor youngling for whom we sing ... lully lullay (1)

yourself
14, 15   yourself unmoved, all motion's source (1)
55   reveal yourself in virgin birth (1)
348   bind us, Lord, to yourself, in obedience and joy (4)
478   you gave yourself to die for our salvation (1)
478   You are yourself the Way (2)

youth
411   like the eagle he renews the vigor of thy youth (5)
556, 557   youth to age, by night and day, in gladness and in woe (4)
567   youth renewed and frenzy calmed owned thee, the Lord (2)
585   memory's treasure, grace of youth (1)
610   go to the child, the youth, the aged (4)

youthful
232   youthful and unready, she heard the angel's word (2/8-15)

zeal
232   May we with zeal as earnest (2/10-28)
253   his zeal inspired their quest (3)
537   with loving zeal (1)
545   Let us, with zeal like theirs inspired, strive (2)
546   a heavenly race demands thy zeal (1,4)
585   gives with zeal, with eager hands (3)
685   should my zeal no languor know (2)
691   my zeal inspire (2)

zealot
255   His presence pierced and blinded the zealot in his wrath (1)

zenith
16 , 17   each day the sun at zenith calls the faithful (1)

Zion
61, 62   Zion hears the watchman singing (2)
65   Prepare the way, O Zion, your Christ is drawing near (1)
65   He brings God's rule, O Zion, he comes from heaven above (2)
65   Fling wide your gates, O Zion, your Savior's rule embrace (3)
75   O Zion, that bringest good tidings (2)
213   with singing to Zion return (1)
257   O Zion, open wide thy gates (1)
320   Zion, praise thy Savior, singing hymns with exultation (1)
460, 461   Hark, the songs of peaceful Zion thunder (1,5)
480   When Jesus into Zion rode, the children sang around ((3)
522, 523   Glorious things of thee are spoken, Zion city of our God (1)
522, 523   Blest inhabitants of Zion, washed in the Redeemer's blood (4)
524   to Zion shall be given the brightest glories (5)
539   O Zion, haste, thy mission high fulfilling (1)
539   He comes again, O Zion, ere thou meet him (4)
540   contending from the walls of Zion against the foe (1)
543   O Zion, tune thy voice, and raise thy hands on high (1)
623   we the sweet anthems of Zion shall sing (3)

Zion's

NUMERICAL INDEX OF FIRST LINES

MORNING

1	Father, we praise thee, now the night is over
2	Father, we praise thee, now the night is over
3	Now that the daylight fills the sky
4	Now that the daylight fills the sky
5	O splendor of God's glory bright
6	Christ, whose glory fills the skies
7	Christ, whose glory fills the skies
8	Morning has broken like the first morning
9	Not here for high and holy things we render thanks to thee
10	New every morning is the love our wakening and uprising prove
11	Awake, my soul, and with the sun thy daily stage of duty run

NOONDAY

12	The golden sun lights up the sky
13	The golden sun lights up the sky
14	O God, creation's secret force
15	O God, creation's secret force
16	Now let us sing our praise to God with fervent heart
17	Now let us sing our praise to God with fervent heart
18	As now the sun shines down at noon
19	Now Holy Spirit, ever One with God the Father and the Son
20	Now Holy Spirit, ever One with God the Father and the Son
21	O God of truth, O Lord of might
22	O God of truth, O Lord of might
23	The fleeting day is nearly gone

EVENING

24	The day thou gavest, Lord, is ended
25	O gracious Light, Lord Jesus Christ
26	O gracious Light, Lord Jesus Christ
27	O blest Creator, source of light
28	O blest Creator, source of light
29	O Trinity of blessed light, O Unity of princely might
30	O Trinity of blessed light, O Unity of princely might
31	Most Holy God, the Lord of heaven
32	Most Holy God, the Lord of heaven
33	Christ, mighty Savior, Light of all creation
34	Christ, mighty Savior, Light of all creation
35	Christ, mighty Savior, Light of all creation
36	O gladsome Light, O grace of God the Father's face
37	O brightness of the immortal Father's face

COMPLINE

38	Jesus, Redeemer of the world
39	Jesus, Redeemer of the world
40	O Christ, you are both light and day
41	O Christ, you are both light and day
42	Now the day is over, night is drawing nigh

EPIPHANY

LENT

LITURGY OF THE PALMS

HOLY WEEK

EASTER

CONFIRMATION

MARRIAGE

BURIAL

ORDINATION

CONSECRATION OF A CHURCH

THE HOLY TRINITY

JESUS CHRIST OUR LORD

THE HOLY SPIRIT

THE CHURCH

THE CHURCH'S MISSION

CHRISTIAN VOCATION AND PILGRIMAGE

563 Go forward, Christian soldier, beneath his banner true
564 He who would valiant be 'gainst all disaster
565 He who would valiant be 'gainst all disaster

CHRISTIAN RESPONSIBILITY

566 From thee all skill and science flow, all pity, care, and love
567 Thine arm, O Lord, in days of old was strong to heal and save
568 Father all loving, who rulest in majesty
569 God the Omnipotent! King, who ordainest thunder thy clarion
570 All who love and serve your city
571 All who love and serve your city
572 Weary of all trumpeting, weary of all killing
573 Father eternal, Ruler of creation
574 Before thy throne, O God, we kneel
575 Before thy throne, O God, we kneel
576 Here in Christ we gather, love of Christ our calling
577 Here in Christ we gather, love of Christ our calling
578 O God of love, O King of peace
579 Almighty Father, strong to save
580 God, who stretched the spangled heavens infinite in time
581 Where charity and love prevail there God is ever found
582 O holy city, seen of John, where Christ, the Lamb, doth reign
583 O holy city, seen of John, where Christ, the Lamb, doth reign
584 God, you have given us power to sound depths hitherto unknown
585 Morning glory, starlit sky, soaring music, scholar's truth
586 Jesus, thou divine Companion, by thy lowly human birth
587 Our Father, by whose Name all fatherhood is known
588 Almighty God, your word is cast like seed upon the ground
589 Almighty God, your word is cast like seed upon the ground
590 O Jesus Christ, may grateful hymns be rising in every city
591 O God of earth and altar, bow down and hear our cry
592 Teach me, my God and King, in all things thee to see
593 Lord, make us servants of your peace
594 God of grace and God of glory, on thy people pour thy power
595 God of grace and God of glory, on thy people pour thy power
596 Judge eternal, throned in splendor, Lord of lords
597 O day of peace that dimly shines through all our hopes and prayers
598 Lord Christ, when first thou cam'st to earth
599 Lift every voice and sing till earth and heaven ring
600 O day of God, draw nigh in beauty and in power
601 O day of God, draw nigh in beauty and in power
602 Kneels at the feet of his friends
   (R: Jesu, Jesu, fill us with your love)
603 When Christ was lifted from the earth
604 When Christ was lifted from the earth
605 What does the Lord require for praise and offering
606 Since the love of Christ has joined us in one body
   (A: Where true charity and love dwell, God himself is there)
607 O God of every nation, of every race and land
608 Eternal Father, strong to save
609 Where cross the crowded ways of life
610 Lord, whose love through humble service bore the weight
611 Christ the worker, Christ the worker, born in Bethlehem
612 Gracious Spirit, Holy Ghost, taught by thee we covet most

THE KINGDOM OF GOD

THE CHURCH TRIUMPHANT

HOLY SCRIPTURE

THE CHRISTIAN LIFE

ROUNDS AND CANONS

NATIONAL SONGS